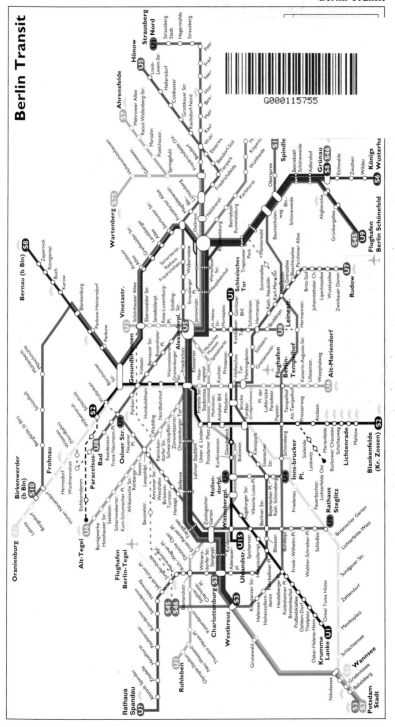

G000115755

Munich Transit

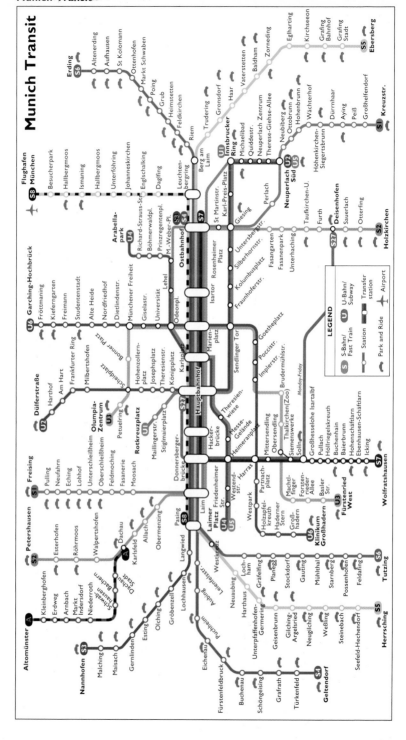

Hamburg Transit

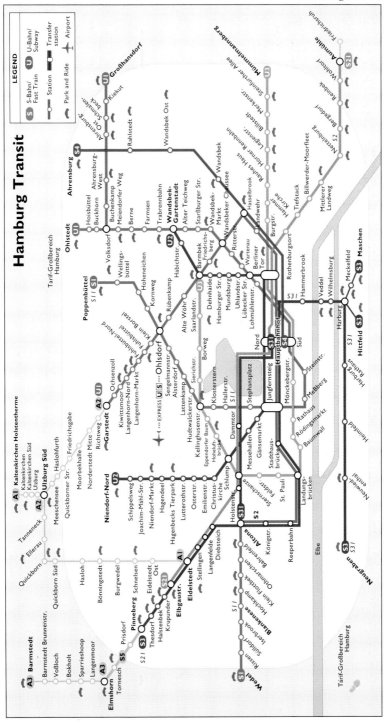

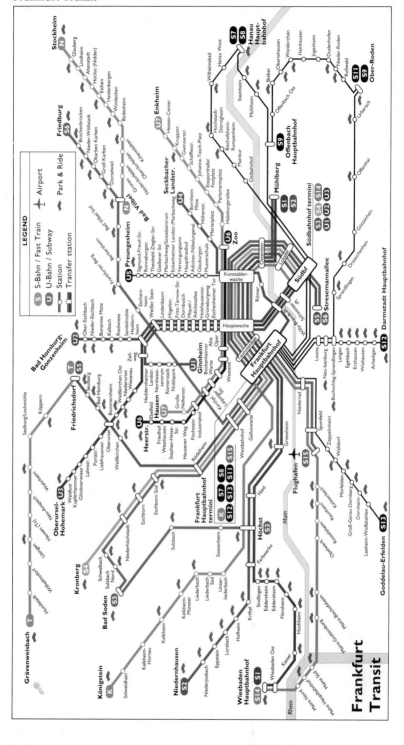

LET'S GO:
Germany

"Its yearly revision by a new crop of Harvard students makes it as valuable as ever." —*The New York Times*

"Value-packed, unbeatable, accurate, and comprehensive." —*The Los Angeles Times*

"A world-wise traveling companion—always ready with friendly advice and helpful hints, all sprinkled with a bit of wit." —*The Philadelphia Inquirer*

"Lighthearted and sophisticated, informative and fun to read. [Let's Go] helps the novice traveler navigate like a knowledgeable old hand." —*Atlanta Journal-Constitution*

"All the essential information you need, from making a phone call to exchanging money to contacting your embassy. [Let's Go] provides maps to help you find your way from every train station to a full range of youth hostels and hotels." —*Minneapolis Star Tribune*

"Unbeatable: good sight-seeing advice; up-to-date info on restaurants, hotels, and inns; a commitment to money-saving travel; and a wry style that brightens nearly every page." —*The Washington Post*

▪ Let's Go researchers have to make it on their own.

"The writers seem to have experienced every rooster-packed bus and lunar-surfaced mattress about which they write." —*The New York Times*

"Retains the spirit of the student-written publication it is: candid, opinionated, resourceful, amusing info for the traveler of limited means but broad curiosity." —*Mademoiselle*

▪ No other guidebook is as comprehensive.

"Whether you're touring the United States, Europe, Southeast Asia, or Central America, a Let's Go guide will clue you in to the cheapest, yet safe, hotels and hostels, food and transportation. Going beyond the call of duty, the guides reveal a country's latest news, cultural hints, and off-beat information that any tourist is likely to miss." —*Tulsa World*

▪ Let's Go is completely revised each year.

"Up-to-date travel tips for touring four continents on skimpy budgets." —*Time*

"Inimitable.... Let's Go's 24 guides are updated yearly (as opposed to the general guidebook standard of every two to three years), and in a marvelously spunky way." —*The New York Times*

Let's Go Publications

Let's Go: Alaska & The Pacific Northwest
Let's Go: Britain & Ireland
Let's Go: California
Let's Go: Central America
Let's Go: Eastern Europe
Let's Go: Ecuador & The Galápagos Islands
Let's Go: Europe
Let's Go: France
Let's Go: Germany
Let's Go: Greece & Turkey
Let's Go: India & Nepal
Let's Go: Ireland
Let's Go: Israel & Egypt
Let's Go: Italy
Let's Go: London
Let's Go: Mexico
Let's Go: New York City
Let's Go: Paris
Let's Go: Rome
Let's Go: Southeast Asia
Let's Go: Spain & Portugal
Let's Go: Switzerland & Austria
Let's Go: USA
Let's Go: Washington, D.C.

Let's Go **Map Guide:** Boston
Let's Go **Map Guide:** London
Let's Go **Map Guide:** New York City
Let's Go **Map Guide:** Paris
Let's Go **Map Guide:** San Francisco
Let's Go **Map Guide:** Washington, D.C.

LET'S GO

The Budget Guide to

Germany

1997

Eugene D. Mazo
Editor

Catherine E. Winiarski
Associate Editor

Macmillan

HELPING LET'S GO

If you want to share your discoveries, suggestions, or corrections, please drop us a line. We read every piece of correspondence, whether a postcard, a 10-page e-mail, or a coconut. All suggestions are passed along to our researcher-writers. Please note that mail received after May 1997 may be too late for the 1998 book, but will be retained for the following edition. **Address mail to:**

> **Let's Go: Germany**
> **67 Mt. Auburn Street**
> **Cambridge, MA 02138**
> **USA**

Visit Let's Go at **http://www.letsgo.com,** or send e-mail to:

> **Fanmail@letsgo.com**
> **Subject: "Let's Go: Germany"**

In addition to the invaluable travel advice our readers share with us, many are kind enough to offer their services as researchers or editors. Unfortunately, the charter of Let's Go, Inc. enables us to employ only currently enrolled Harvard-Radcliffe students.

Published in Great Britain 1997 by Macmillan, an imprint of Macmillan General Books, 25 Eccleston Place, London SW1W 9NF and Basingstoke.

Maps by David Lindroth copyright © 1997, 1996, 1995, 1994, 1993, 1992, 1991, 1990, 1989, 1988 by St. Martin's Press, Inc.

Map revisions pp. xii-xiii, xiv-xv, 85, 100-101, 131, 153, 167, 189, 206-207, 297, 369, 396-397, 391, 435, 501, 277 by Let's Go, Inc.

Published in the United States of America by St. Martin's Press, Inc.

ISBN: 0 333 68675 6

First edition
10 9 8 7 6 5 4 3 2 1

Let's Go: Germany is written by Let's Go Publications, 67 Mt. Auburn Street, Cambridge, MA 02138, USA.

Let's Go® and the thumb logo are trademarks of Let's Go, Inc. Printed in the USA on recycled paper with biodegradable soy ink.

About Let's Go

THIRTY-SIX YEARS OF WISDOM

Back in 1960, a few students at Harvard University banded together to produce a 20-page pamphlet offering a collection of tips on budget travel in Europe. This modest, mimeographed packet, offered as an extra to passengers on student charter flights to Europe, met with instant popularity. The following year, students traveling to Europe researched the first, full-fledged edition of *Let's Go: Europe*, a pocket-sized book featuring honest, irreverent writing and a decidedly youthful outlook on the world. Throughout the 60s, our guides reflected the times; the 1969 guide to America led off by inviting travelers to "dig the scene" at San Francisco's Haight-Ashbury. During the 70s and 80s, we gradually added regional guides and expanded coverage into the Middle East and Central America. With the addition of our in-depth city guides, handy map guides, and extensive coverage of Asia, the 90s are also proving to be a time of explosive growth for Let's Go, and there's certainly no end in sight. The first editions of *Let's Go: India & Nepal* and *Let's Go: Ecuador & The Galápagos Islands* hit the shelves this year, and research for next year's series has already begun.

We've seen a lot in 37 years. *Let's Go: Europe* is now the world's bestselling international guide, translated into seven languages. And our new guides bring Let's Go's total number of titles, with their spirit of adventure and their reputation for honesty, accuracy, and editorial integrity, to 30. But some things never change: our guides are still researched, written, and produced entirely by students who know first-hand how to see the world on the cheap.

HOW WE DO IT

Each guide is completely revised and thoroughly updated every year by a well-traveled set of 200 students. Every winter, we recruit over 120 researchers and 60 editors to write the books anew. After several months of training, Researcher-Writers hit the road for seven weeks of exploration, from Anchorage to Ankara, Estonia to El Salvador, Iceland to Indonesia. Hired for their rare combination of budget travel sense, writing ability, stamina, and courage, these adventurous travelers know that train strikes, stolen luggage, food poisoning, and marriage proposals are all part of a day's work. Back at our offices, editors work from spring to fall, massaging copy written on Himalayan bus rides into witty yet informative prose. A student staff of typesetters, cartographers, publicists, and managers keeps our lively team together. In September, the collected efforts of the summer are delivered to our printer, who turns them into books in record time, so that you have the most up-to-date information available for *your* vacation. And even as you read this, work on next year's editions is well underway.

WHY WE DO IT

At Let's Go, our goal is to give you a great vacation. We don't think of budget travel as the last recourse of the destitute; we believe that it's the only way to travel. Living cheaply and simply brings you closer to the people and places you've been saving up to visit. Our books will ease your anxieties and answer your questions about the basics—so you can get off the beaten track and explore. Once you learn the ropes, we encourage you to put Let's Go away now and then to strike out on your own. As any seasoned traveler will tell you, the best discoveries are often those you make yourself. When you find something worth sharing, drop us a line. We're Let's Go Publications, 67 Mt. Auburn St., Cambridge, MA 02138, USA (e-mail: fanmail@letsgo.com).

HAPPY TRAVELS!

Stuck for cash? Don't panic. With Western Union, money is transferred to you in minutes. It's easy. All you've got to do is ask someone at home to give Western Union a call on US 1 800 3256000. Minutes later you can collect the cash.

Contents

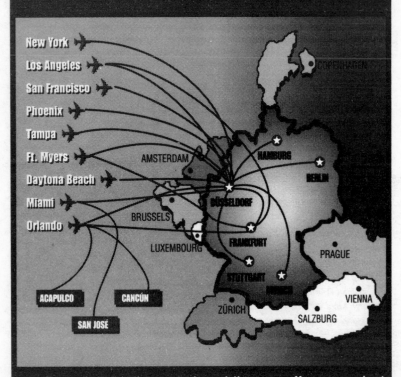

Maps

Color Maps

Acknowledgments

This work would have been nothing without the encouragement of some special individuals. Mentors Jim Shenton, Mark von Hagen, and Wallace Gray inspired in me a love of knowledge. Richard Korb taught my brilliant introductory German class. Alex Travelli made me scholar. Suellen Newman taught me to reach for the stars. Kitty delivered my funk. David Snelbecker payed for many lunches. Friends in Copenhagen, Edinburgh, and Istanbul were gracious hosts. Benjamin Cramer, Janet Kilian, Rajen Parekh, Kate Blumenreich, and many others shared with me the most memorable four years of my life. Roar, Lion, Roar! Dear friends Steven Pestka, Eve and Amelia Kaplan, Alexis Charnée, and their parents, always believed in me. Amelia, especially, was my little sister in a big, big way. There are no words great enough to express love and thanks to my family: Felix, Kisa, Papa, Mama, Babushka, and, of course, Philip, who will blaze many of his own trails in the not-too-distant future. This book, and the energy and inspiration behind it, is dedicated to two courageous women, Vlada Mazo and Sophie Lando, who in 1979 brought a little five-year-old boy from Moscow to America. What they accomplished is greater than they could ever imagine.—**EDM**

My congratulations to my dear editor, Gene Mazo, for never sinking to my blood pressure level. My thanks go to the cast of the Cold Room Jamboree (Anne, Dan, Megan, Jeremy, Ali, David): "compelling ... provocative ... the sequel will suck." A spoonful each of special editorial lovin' to Ali, Anne, Andrew, Siham, and DF. To Alex Travelli, for *savoir-faire* without *machismo*. You're a dish, nay, an entrée. To DF, DA or MIA? To Alan Wissenberg, who was our *deus ex machina*. To Mom and Dad, and that mountain of want ads. To all the family: Eileen, Kaz, Mike, Rhonda, Nicholas, Andreas, Matt, Caitlin, Tim, Anne, Steve, Liz, Lauren. To Grace, Ellen, Amy, and the night of 10,000 revelations; Kelly, Hanna, Jenny, and very powerful witches. Hey, guppy, drop me a line. To BMK and the number that wasn't (Portuguese Man o' War #?). To the Lampoon, for showing me the other path to the water. A special sacrifice for the elves that influence our lives in so many unseen and terrible ways. A round for Great Literature, indeed the cognac of the human vintage. To all *bon-bons, bonhommes,* and *homines seriosi.* And one final libation for the Buried Life...

—**CEW**

Editor	Eugene David Mazo
Associate Editor	Catherine E. Winiarski
Managing Editor	Alexander H. Travelli
Publishing Director	Michelle C. Sullivan
Production Manager	Daniel O. Williams
Associate Production Manager	Michael S. Campbell
Cartography Manager	Amanda K. Bean
Editorial Manager	John R. Brooks
Editorial Manager	Allison Crapo
Financial Manager	Stephen P. Janiak
Personnel Manager	Alexander H. Travelli
Publicity Manager	SoRelle B. Braun
Associate Publicity Manager	David Fagundes
Associate Publicity Manager	Elisabeth Mayer
Assistant Cartographer	Jonathan D. Kibera
Assistant Cartographer	Mark C. Staloff
Office Coordinator	Jennifer L. Schuberth
Director of Advertising and Sales	Amit Tiwari
Senior Sales Executives	Andrew T. Rourke
	Nicholas A. Valtz, Charles E. Varner
General Manager	Richard Olken
Assistant General Manager	Anne E. Chisholm

Researcher-Writers

Ruth Halikman   *Schleswig-Holstein, Meck.-Vorpommern, Berlin*

City-slicker Ruth first made us wise to the wiles of Hamburg. She then gave us a peek at the northern pleasure islands and made us feel Baltic sea breezes. And when Ruth decided that she had had enough *Matjes* for a lifetime, she got down to some *serious* business. Using her journalistic skills to write veritable exposés about the cities of the East, Ruth uncovered the treasures buried in deep post-socialist soil. Yet the decaying *Altstädte* of the GDR and majestic cliffs of Rügen Island could only hold Ruth's attention for so long—it was the urban buzz of Berlin she was really after. When you find yourself roaming the corridors of the Pergamon or Dahlem in search of lost treasures, think of Ruth, our *Kulturmeister*. She thanks Tatjana Suchy in Berlin.

Kimble Poon   *Lower Saxony, North Rhine-Westphalia, Hesse*

Kimble arrived in Germany just fine. His backpack didn't. But that didn't stop fearless Kimble, who knew there was a job to be done. Washing his lone set of clothes each night, Kimble sped through his itinerary each day. Backpack or no backpack, he kept his eyes on the prize. "Boss," yelled Kimble one day, "I got my pack—now it's slowin' me down." Armed with more wit than Jay Leno, more style than the Fonz, and certainly more energy than the Energizer Bunny, Kimble kept going and going. A rest break for Kimble? Hell no! After entertaining German *Schulkinder* and taking part in small-scale search-and-rescue operations, he sped back to hometown Atlanta for the Olympics. For his charm, enthusiasm, and dedication, Kimble gets thumbs up!

Lisa K. Pinsley   *Frankfurt, Hesse, Bavaria*

Pinch hitter Lisa hit a grand slam. How were we to know she would be such a pro? While spending the summer unearthing Bavaria's kitsch and *Gemütlichkeit* (and showing us the three-ring *and* sideshow attractions of concrete Frankfurt, too), Lisa managed to impress many on her romantic journey. Munich, however, will always remember Lisa best. Charming everyone she met (including the enemy from Cali), she got us backstage passes to all of the best scenes of the summer. With amazing writer know-how, Lisa concocted the spiciest cultural morsels we have to offer, while impressing tourist officials, hostel owners, and even the bike man. Lisa, you'll never have to put your shoes out with us. She thanks two British blokes and Berkeley Ben.

Caitlin A. Roxby   *Rhineland-Palatinate, Saarland, Baden-Württemberg*

Some researchers let their itineraries wear their pants. But not Caitlin. Moving to her own vigorous beat, *she* wore the pants, or rather, hiking shorts, all over scenic southern Germany. It was a crazy summer, and Caitlin certainly met her share of cuckoos—not to mention cuckoo-clocks—along the way. In the sloping hills of the Black Forest, Caitlin found more *Eis*-salons than we knew existed, went on more hikes than we asked, watched more movies than we ever heard of, and still found the time to buy new shoes. Indeed, Caitlin found the natural wonders of Germany to her liking. But we knew she would before she even set off. You can take the girl out of Maine, as they say, but you just can't take Maine out of the girl.

Alexander Z. Speier   *Sachsen-Anhalt, Thuringia, Saxony, Berlin*

When you're partying away in the East's hottest techno clubs, take a moment to think of Alex. After all, if it wasn't for this man, you'd never even be here. For an entire summer, Alex slept by day, partied by night. For a man of lesser character, such a lifestyle might have been overwhelming. For Alex, it was just part of the job. After staring into the face of madness in the Harz and witnessing the creep of capitalism in Leipzig and Dresden, Alex got downright salacious in Berlin—where he visited all of the dives that burn it at both ends. His copy was laced with a succulent crop of impressions, his satirical eye popping every pretension and delighting us page after blessed page. In the words of Montgomery Burns, Alex was "eeexceeeellent!"

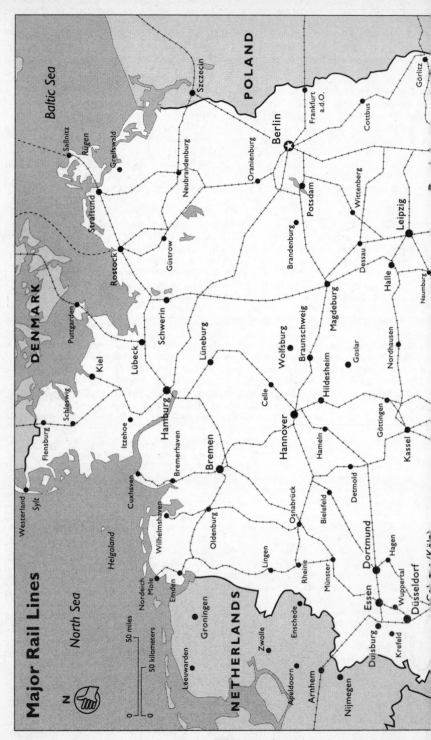

Major Rail Lines

N

North Sea

Baltic Sea

DENMARK

POLAND

NETHERLANDS

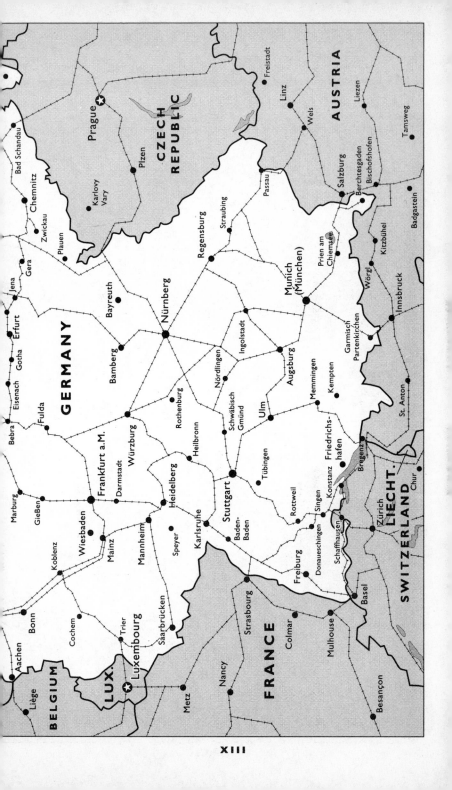

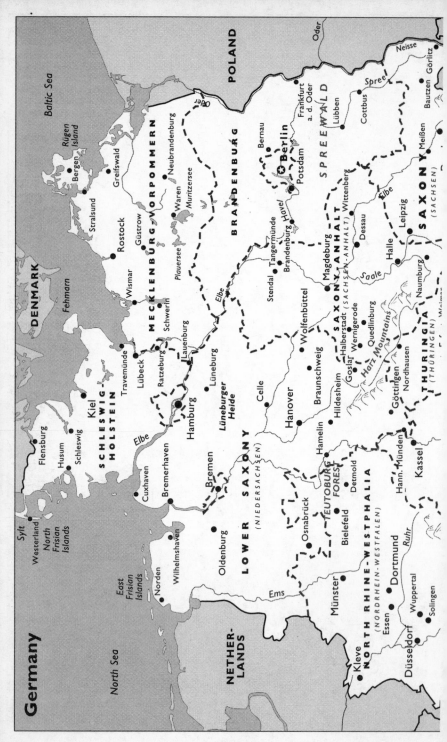

Germany

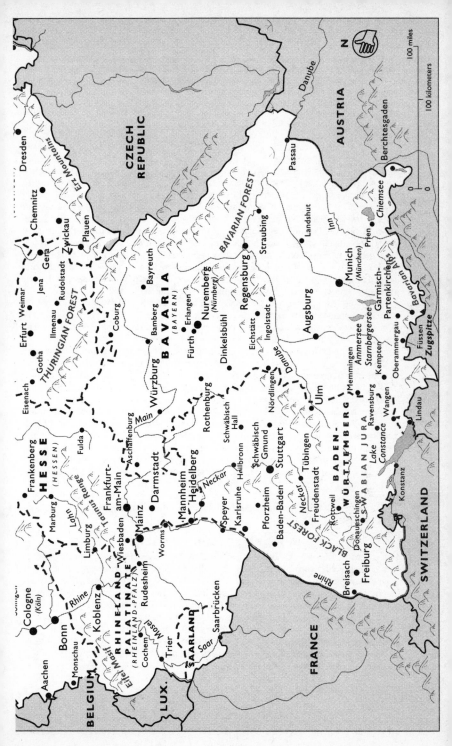

How to Use This Book

This book is for those who love to travel—or rather, for those who love to travel and also have a sense of humor. All summer long we worked our tails off to bring you the best-researched and most exciting guide to Germany on the market. Now it's time for you to go out and test whether or not the fruit of our labor is a success.

We have split up the book into four parts. The first, called the **Essentials** section, should be read *before* you leave for your trip. It lists important addresses of embassies and consulates, provides an assorted list of budget travel agencies, discusses health and safety concerns, and demystifies obscure bureaucracy. We'll show you how to buy a Eurailpass, keep yourself healthy, and even get lost in cyberspace. Take particular care to read categories like **Planning Your Trip** and **Traveling in Germany,** which provide helpful addresses, publications, and travel tips to get you started. The **Once There** section includes crucial information you'll need once you've arrived. Sub-categories **Getting Around, Accommodations,** and **Keeping in Touch** will not only help you orient yourself in your new surroundings, but they'll also explain how to best reach your next exciting destination, review how to buy a hostel membership, and guide you through German customs and etiquette. We offer special tips for students, seniors, women, gay and lesbian travelers, and others.

Following Essentials comes **Germany: An Introduction,** which fills you in on German history, politics, art, architecture, film, and literature. We'll tell you about literary luminaries Goethe and Schiller and philosophical giants Hegel and Marx, as well as about kaisers like the Wilhelms and crazies like Ludwig II of Bavaria. We'll also include cultural information about topics as diverse as beer gardens and *Lederhosen.*

Once you've passed this section, you'll enter the real meat of the book, the part where our five researchers—*Sauerkraut*-lovin' Ruth Halikman, *gemütlichkeit*-adoring Lisa Pinsley, *froh*-go-lucky Kimble Poon, *Burg*-climbing Caitlin Roxby, and *"nichts ist verboten"* Alex Speier—poured their hearts and souls out into covering modern-day Deutschland. The coverage is divided into 13 sections, each divided primarily along the lines of Germany's *Länder* (Federal States). **Orientation and Practical Information** directs you to resources, facilities, and transport connections, while **Food** and **Accommodations** list specific establishments in order of *value;* the one listed first may not be the cheapest, but it should give you the most for your *Mark.* We cover **Sights, Entertainment,** and **Nightlife** in every city with a heartbeat, and in some cases, in cities with two heartbeats. Finally, check out the **Appendices** for instructions on using the German telephone system, for pronounciation guidelines, useful phrases, and more at-your-fingertips reference information.

Okay, now dig in!

A NOTE TO OUR READERS

The information for this book is gathered by *Let's Go*'s researchers during the late spring and summer months. Each listing is derived from the assigned researcher's opinion based upon his or her visit at a particular time. The opinions are expressed in a candid and forthright manner. Other travelers might disagree. Those traveling at a different time may have different experiences since prices, dates, hours, and conditions are always subject to change. You are urged to check beforehand to avoid inconvenience and surprises. Travel always involves a certain degree of risk, especially in low-cost areas. When traveling, especially on a budget, always take particular care to ensure your safety.

ESSENTIALS

PLANNING YOUR TRIP

A fun and inexpensive trip to Germany requires preparation. For better or for worse, there is a big industry designed to help travelers tackle it. The many organizations listed below, especially national tourist offices, will send you daunting mounds of literature. Dive in and plan a trip tailored to your specific interests. You can design an historical, hiking, even a beer tour of Germany. The possibilities are endless, but resist the urge to see everything, because a madcap schedule will only detract from your enjoyment. If you try to see Berlin, Munich, and Cologne in a week, you'll come away with only vague memories of train stations and youth hostels. Similarly, choose your traveling companions carefully; traveling with a group of friends may effectively insulate you from genuine intimacy with local culture. On the other hand, they will share food and lodging costs, provide extra safety in numbers, and often serve as an invaluable sources of energy and comfort. Along your journey, you are certain to meet many fascinating folks; a lone traveler is never truly alone. Make sure to use the information provided by *Let's Go* and other sources to assemble your "support system," both in terms of what you bring and the arrangements you make; it's been said that all you really need are time and money, but on a budget voyage you don't want to waste either due to lack of planning.

■ When To Go

In July and August, airfares, temperatures, and tempers rise right along with the number of tourists. In winter months, some hostels hibernate and museum hours may be abbreviated. The cloudy, temperate months of May, June, and September are perhaps your best bet. But bear in mind that many school field trips to historic sites take place in June, and that youth hostels may be inundated with schoolchildren. Winter sports gear up in November and continue through April; high season for skiing hits in mid-December to mid-January and February to March. Germans head to vacation spots en masse with the onset of school vacations; airports and train stations become jammed and the traffic on the Autobahn can be measured in meters per hour. The staggering of vacation periods among the federal states has alleviated the crunch a tad, but you should still avoid trekking across Germany the day after school lets out, or risk being buried by throngs. See the **Appendix** for further holiday and weather information.

■ Useful Information

GOVERNMENT INFORMATION OFFICES

These official German outposts in your native country can be a great help in planning your trip; have them send you information and brochures before you leave. The **German National Tourist Offices** distribute useful publications such as *Travel Tips, Camping in Germany,* and *Youth Hostels.*

U.S.: New York, 122 East 42nd St., Chanin Building, 52nd Floor, New York, NY 10168-0072 (tel. (212) 661-7200; fax 661-7174); **Los Angeles,** 11766 Wilshire Blvd., Suite 750, Los Angeles, CA 90025 (tel. (310) 575-9799; fax 575-1565). The **German Information Center,** 950 Third Ave., New York, NY 10022 (tel. (212) 888-9840; fax (212) 752-6691; e-mail gic1@ix.netcom.com), will send you a useful, updated guide of basic historical and cultural information about Germany. Also publishes *This Week in Germany,* a free newspaper for Americans.

Canada: 175 Bloor St. East, North Tower, Suite 604, Toronto, Ont. M4W 3R8 (tel. (416) 968-1570; fax 968-1986).

U.K.: Nightingale House, 65 Curzon St., London W1Y 7PE (tel. (0171) 495 39 90; fax 495 61 29).

Australia: Lufthansa House, 9th floor, 143 Macquarie St., Sydney 2000 (tel. (012) 367 38 90; fax 367 38 95).

South Africa: 22 Girton Road, Parktown, Johannesburg 2000 (tel. (011) 643 16 15; fax 484 27 50).

TRAVEL ORGANIZATIONS

Council on International Educational Exchange (Council), 205 East 42nd St., New York, NY 10017-5706 (tel. (888) COUNCIL (268-6245); fax (212) 822-2699; e-mail info@ciee.org; http://www.ciee.org). A private, nonprofit organization, Council administers work, volunteer, and academic programs around the world. They also offer identity cards, including the ISIC and the GO25, and a range of publications, including the magazine *Student Travels* (free). Call or write for more information.

Federation of International Youth Travel Organizations (FIYTO), Bredgade 25H, DK-1260 Copenhagen K, Denmark (tel. (45) 33 33 96 00; fax 33 93 96 76; e-mail mailbox@fiyto.org), is an international organization promoting educational, cultural and social travel for young people. Member organizations include language schools, educational travel companies, national tourist boards, and accommodation centers for youth and students. FIYTO sponsors the GO25 Card.

International Student Travel Confederation, Herengracht 479, 1017 BS Amsterdam, The Netherlands (tel. (31) 20 421 2800; fax 20 421 2810; http://www.istc.org; e-mail istcinfo@istc.org). The ISTC is a nonprofit confederation of student travel organizations whose focus is to develop, promote, and facilitate travel among young people and students. Member organizations include International Student Rail Association (ISRA), Student Air Travel Association (SATA), and the International Association for Educational and Work Exchange Programs.

USEFUL PUBLICATIONS

The publications we list here should be useful in preparation for your trip. If you're interested in books on culture or history, see Further Reading (p. 71).

Council on International Educational Exchange (CIEE), 205 East 42nd St., New York, NY 10017-5706 (888-COUNCIL; fax (212)-822-2699; http://www.ciee.org), publishes *Student Travels* (free) and *Travel and Adventure Abroad.* Call or write for further information. See Useful Organizations above.

Atlantik-Brücke, Adenauerallee 131, 53113 Bonn (tel. (0228) 21 41 60; fax 21 46 59). Devoted to promoting mutual understanding (hence "Atlantic Bridge"), it publishes *These Strange German Ways*—a must for any American planning on living in Germany—as well as *Meet United Germany, German Holidays and Folk Customs,* and *Speaking Out: Jewish Voices from United Germany.*

Forsyth Travel Library, P.O. Box 480800, Kansas City, MO 64148 (tel. (800) 367-7984; fax (816) 942-6969; http://www.forsyth.com). A mail-order service that stocks a wide range of city, area, and country maps, as well as guides for rail and ferry travel in Europe; sells rail tickets and passes, and offers reservation services. Sells the *Thomas Cook European Timetable* for trains (see p. 37). Call or write for a free catalogue, or visit their web site.

Hunter Publishing, 300 Raritan Center Parkway, Edison, NJ 08818 (tel. (908) 225-1900; fax 417-0482). Has an extensive catalog of travel books, guides, language learning tapes, and quality maps, among them a *Charming Small Hotel Guide* for Germany (US$13).

Transitions Abroad, 18 Hulst Rd., P.O. Box 1300, Amherst, MA 01004-1300 (tel. (413) 256-3414; fax 256-0375; e-mail trabroad@aol.com). Invaluable magazine lists publications and resources for overseas study, work, and volunteering. Publishes *The Alternative Travel Directory,* a comprehensive guide to living, learning, and working overseas (US$20; postage US$4).

INTERNET RESOURCES

Along with everything else in the 90s, budget travel is moving rapidly into the information age. And with the growing user-friendliness of personal computers and internet technology, much of this information can be yours with the click of a mouse.

There are a number of ways to access the **Internet.** Most popular are commerical internet providers, such as **America Online** (tel. (800) 827-6394) and **CompuServe** (tel. (800) 433-0389). Many employers and schools also offer gateways to often at no cost (unlike the corporate gateways above). The most useful to 'net-surfing budget travelers are the World Wide Web and Usenet newsgroups.

The World Wide Web

Increasingly the Internet forum of choice, the **World Wide Web** provides its users with graphics and sound, as well as textual information. The introduction of **search engines** (services that search for web pages under specific subjects) has aided the search process some. **Lycos** (http://a2z.lycos.com) and **Infoseek** (http://guide.infoseek.com) are the two of the most popular. **Yahoo!** is a slightly more organized search engine; check out its travel links at http://www.yahoo.com/Recreation/Travel. However, it is often better to know a good site, and start "surfing" through links from one web page to another. So we at *Let's Go* have come up with some of our favorite travel sites. A search tool for Germany is the suffix web.de.

City.Net (http://www.city.net) is a very impressive collection of regional- or city-specific web pages. Use (http://www.leo.org/demap) to connect to Germany.

German Information Office, in New York has great links to other sites pertaining to Germany. Try (germany-info.org/sites/travel.htm) and be on your way.

Exploring Germany (http://www.commed.de/germany) is designed for young travelers. Covers the attractions of all 16 federal states with illustrations.

Frau Richardson's Pictorial Homepage (http://ibis.ups.edu) gives introductions to a number of major German cities, outstanding photography at no extra charge.

The Student and Budget Travel Guide (http://asa.ugl.lib.umich.edu/chdocs/travel/travel-guide.html) is just what it sounds like.

Foreign Language for Travelers (http://www.travelang.com) can help you brush up on your Thai, Swahili, Uzbek, Tajik, and, yes, German.

Usenet Newsgroups

Another popular source of information are **newsgroups,** which are forums for discussion of specific topics. One user "posts" a written question or thought, which other users read and respond to in kind. There are a number of useful newsgroups for the traveler. **Usenet,** the name for the family of newsgroups, can be accessed easily from most Internet gateways. In UNIX systems, a good newsreader is "tin" (just type "tin" at the prompt). Commercial providers also offer access to Usenet.

There are a number of different hierarchies for newsgroups. The "soc" hierarchy deals primary with issues related to society and culture. The "rec" (recreation) hierarchy is especially good for travelers, with newsgroups such as **rec.travel.air** or **rec.travel.europe.** The "alt" (alternative) hierarchy houses a number of different types of discussion, such as **alt.current-events.balkans.** Finally, "Clari-net" posts AP news wires for many different topics, such as **clari.world.europe.germany.** Commercial providers often have their own version of Usenet, limited to the members of the provider, which have similar information.

■ Documents and Formalities

Be sure to file all applications at least one month in advance of your planned departure date. U.S. citizens in particular should plan ahead; an unusually high number of U.S. passports were due to expire in 1996, creating longer delays in processing.

When you travel, always carry on your person two or more forms of identification, including at least one photo ID. A passport combined with a driver's license or birth certificate usually serves as adequate proof of your identity and citizenship. Many establishments require several IDs before cashing traveler's checks. Also, carry extra passport-size photos that you can attach to the sundry IDs or railpasses you will eventually acquire. For an extended stay, register your passport with the nearest consulate. U.S. citizens seeking information about documents, formalities and travel abroad should request the booklet *Your Trip Abroad* (US$1.25) from the **Superintendent of Documents,** U.S. Government Printing Office, P.O. Box 371954, Pittsburgh, PA 15250-7954 (tel. (202) 512-1800; fax 512-2250).

GERMAN EMBASSIES AND CONSULATES

The German embassy or consulate in your home country can supply you with legal information concerning your trip, arrange for visas, and direct you to a wealth of other information about tourism, education, and employment in Germany.

U.S.: Embassy: 4645 Reservoir Rd. NW, Washington, DC 20007-1998 (tel. (202) 298-8140; fax 298-4249; http://www.germany-info.org). **Consulates: New York,** 460 Park Ave., New York, NY 10022 (tel. (212) 308-8700; fax 308-3422); **Los Angeles,** 6222 Wilshire Blvd., Suite 500, Los Angeles, CA 90048 (tel. (213) 930-2703; fax 930-2805); other consulates in Atlanta, Boston, Chicago, Detroit, Houston, San Francisco, and Seattle.

Canada: Embassy: 1 Waverly St., Ottawa, Ont. K2P OT8 (tel. (613) 232-1101; fax 594-9330); **Consulates:** 1250 bd. René-Lévesque Ouest, Suite 4315, Montréal, Que. H3B 4X1 (tel. (514) 931-2277; fax 931-7239); other consulates in Toronto and Vancouver.

United Kingdom: Embassy: 23 Belgrave Sq., London SW1X 8PZ (tel. (0171) 235 5033 or 824 1300; fax 235 0609).**Consulates: Manchester,** Westminster House, 11 Portlant St., Manchester M60 1HY (tel. (0161) 237 5255; fax 237 5244); **Edinburgh,** 16 Eglinton Crescent, Edinburgh EH12 5DG, Scotland (tel. (0131) 337 2323; fax 346 1578).

Ireland: Embassy: 31 Trimleston Ave., Booterstown, Blackrock, Co. Dublin (tel. (01) 269 30 11 or 269 31 23; fax 269 39 46).

Australia: Embassy: 119 Empire Circuit, Yarralumla, A.C.T. 2600 (tel. (616) 270 1911; fax 270 1951); **Consulates:** 480 Punt Rd., South Yarra, Vic. 3141 (tel. (03) 98 28 68 88; fax 98 20 24 14); another consulate in Wollahra, N.S.W.

New Zealand: Embassy: 90-92 Hobson St., Thorndon, Wellington (tel. (644) 473 6063; fax 473 6069).

South Africa: Embassy: 180 Blackwood St., Arcadia, Pretoria 0083 (tel. (2712) 344 3854 59; fax 343 9401).**Consulate: Johannesburg,** 16 Kapteijnstreet, P.O.B. 45 51, Johannesburg 2000 (tel. (011) 725 1519; fax 725 4475); **Cape Town,** 825 St. Martini Gardens, Queen Victoria St., Cape Town 8001 (tel. (021) 24 24 10; fax 24 94 03).

PASSPORTS

Before you leave, photocopy the page of your passport that contains your photograph and identifying information, especially your passport number and any visa stamps. Carry this photocopy in a safe place apart from your passport, and leave another copy at home. These measures will help prove your citizenship if you lose the original document. Consulates also recommend you carry an expired passport or an official copy of your birth certificate in a part of your baggage separate from other documents. You can request a duplicate birth certificate from the Bureau of Vital Records and Statistics in your state or province of birth.

If you do lose your passport, it may take weeks to process a replacement. In addition, any visas stamped in your old passport will be irretrievably lost. If this happens, immediately notify the nearest embassy or consulate of your home government. To expedite the replacement of your passport, you will need to know all information previously recorded and show proof of citizenship. In an emergency, ask for temporary traveling papers that will permit you to reenter your home country.

United States United States Citizens may apply for a passport, valid for 10 years (five years if under 18) at any federal or state **courthouse** or **post office** authorized to accept passport applications, or at a **U.S. Passport Agency,** located in Boston, Chicago, Honolulu, Houston, Los Angeles, Miami, New Orleans, New York, Philadelphia, San Francisco, Seattle, Stamford, or Washington DC. Refer to the "U.S. Government, State Department" section of the telephone directory, or call your local post office for addresses. Parents must apply in person for children under age 13. You must apply in person if this is your first passport, if you're under age 18, or if your current passport is more than 12 years old or was issued before your 18th birthday. You must submit the following: 1) proof of U.S. citizenship; 2) identification bearing your signature and either your photograph or physical description; and 3) two identical, passport-size (2in. by 2in.) photographs with a white or off-white background taken within the last six months. It will cost US$65 (under 18 US$40). You can **renew** your passport by mail or in person for US$55. Processing takes two to four weeks. Passport agencies offer **rush service** for a surcharge of US$30 if you have proof that you're departing within ten working days. Abroad, a U.S. embassy or consulate can usually issue a new passport. If your passport is lost or stolen in the U.S., report it in writing to Passport Services, U.S. Department of State, 111 19th St., NW, Washington DC, 20522-1705 or to a passport agency. For more info, contact the U.S. Passport Information's **24-hour recorded message** (tel. (202) 647-0518).

Canada Application forms in English and French are available at all **passport offices, post offices,** and most **travel agencies.** Citizens may apply in person at any one of 28 regional Passport Offices across Canada. Canadian citizens residing abroad should contact the nearest Canadian embassy or consulate. Along with the application form, a citizen must provide: 1) citizenship documentation; 2) two identical passport photos taken within the last year; 3) any previous Canadian passport; and 4) a CDN$60 fee to Passport Office, Ottawa, Ont. K1A OG3. The application and one of the photographs must be signed by an eligible guarantor. All above information is outlined on the application form. Processing takes approximately five business days for in-person applications and three weeks for mailed ones. A passport is valid for five years and is not renewable. If it is lost abroad, Canadians must be able to prove citizenship with another document. For additional info, call (800) 567-6868 (24hr.; from Canada only) or call the Passport Office at (819) 994-3500. In Metro Toronto, call (416) 973-3251. Montréalers should dial (514) 283-2152. Refer to the booklet *Bon Voyage, But ...* for further help and a list of Canadian embassies and consulates abroad. It is available free of charge from any passport office.

United Kingdom British citizens, British Dependent Territories citizens, British Nationals (overseas), and British Overseas citizens may apply for a **full passport,** which is valid for 10 years (five years if under 16). Apply in person or by mail to a passport office, located in London, Liverpool, Newport, Peterborough, Glasgow, or Belfast. The fee is UK£18. Children under 16 may be included on a parent's passport. Processing by mail usually takes four to six weeks. The London office offers same-day, walk-in rush service; arrive early.

Ireland Citizens can apply for a passport by mail to either the Department of Foreign Affairs, Passport Office, Setanta Centre, Molesworth St., Dublin 2 (tel. (01) 671 16 33), or the Passport Office, 1A South Mail, Cork (tel. (021) 627 25 25). Obtain an application at a local Garda station or request one from a passport office. The new Passport Express Service offers a two-week turn-around and is available through post offices for an extra IR£3. Passports cost IR£45 and are valid for 10 years. Citizens under 18 or over 65 can request a three-year passport that costs IR£10.

Australia Citizens must apply for a passport in person at a post office, a passport office, or an Australian diplomatic mission overseas. An appointment may be necessary. Passport offices are located in Adelaide, Brisbane, Canberra City, Darwin,

Hobart, Melbourne, Newcastle, Perth, and Sydney. A parent may file an application for a child who is under 18 and unmarried. Application fees are adjusted frequently. For more info, call toll-free (in Australia) 13 12 32.

New Zealand Application forms for passports are available in New Zealand from travel agents and Department of Internal Affairs Link Centres, and overseas from New Zealand embassies, high commissions, and consulates. Completed applications may be lodged at Link Centres and at overseas posts, or forwarded to the Passport Office, PO Box 10-526, Wellington, New Zealand. Processing time is 10 working days from receipt of a correctly completed application. An urgent passport service is also available. The application fee for an adult passport is NZ$80 in New Zealand, and NZ$130 overseas for applications lodged under the standard service.

South Africa Citizens can apply for a passport at any Home Affairs Office. Two photos, either a birth certificate or an identity book, and a SAR80 fee must accompany a completed application. South African passports remain valid for 10 years. For further information, contact the nearest Department of Home Affairs Office.

ENTRANCE REQUIREMENTS AND VISAS

U.S., Canadian, Australian, British, Irish, and **New Zealand citizens** do not need to obtain a visa ahead of time to enter Germany. These citizens need to carry only a valid passport in order to remain for up to three months. **South African citizens** require a visa. Contact the nearest German Consulate General for more information.

If your travels extend beyond Germany, remember that some other countries in Europe require a visa. Carry proof of your **financial independence,** such as a visa to the next country on your itinerary, a return air ticket, enough money to cover the cost of your living expenses, etc.

If you wish to stay longer, apply for a visa at the German embassy or consulate in your home country well before your departure. You may also apply for an extended-stay visa at a local aliens' authority after entry. You must obtain a work permit before seeking temporary employment in Germany, presuming you have already obtained a residence permit from a local immigration office (see Work and Volunteer, p. 19). You should apply for these permits at least 8 weeks in advance.

For more information, send for *Foreign Entry Requirements* (US$0.50) from the **Consumer Information Center,** Pueblo, CO 81009 (tel. (719) 948-3334), or contact the **Center for International Business and Travel (CIBT),** 25 West 43rd St. #1420, New York, NY 10036 (tel. (800) 925-2428 or (212) 575-2811). This organization secures visas for travel to and from all countries.

CUSTOMS: ENTERING GERMANY

Don't mention the war!

—Basil Fawlty (John Cleese)

Unless you plan to import a BMW or a barnyard beast, you will probably pass right over the customs barrier with minimal ado. The many rules and regulations of customs and duties hardly constitute significant cause for concern to the budget traveler. Germany prohibits or restricts the importation of firearms, explosives, ammunition, fireworks, controlled substances, many plants and animals, lottery tickets, and obscene literature or films. To prevent problems with transporting **prescription drugs,** ensure that the bottles are clearly marked, and carry a copy of your prescription to show customs officials. When dealing with customs officers, do your utmost to be polite and look responsible; whether or not they give you a difficult time is ultimately a personal decision on their part, unfortunately (or fortunately).

Citizens of European Union (EU) countries can bring up to 300 **cigarettes** into Germany; travelers from outside the EU can bring 200. Germany allows 1.5 Liters of **alcoholic beverages** above 44 proof for EU members, 1 Liter for travelers from outside the EU. No one under age 17 is entitled to these allowances. There are no regulations on the import or export of currency. **Gifts** and commodities for personal use are allowed into Germany with the following regulations: the total value of goods imported from the EU cannot exceed DM780, while goods from outside the EU cannot exceed DM115. You can obtain more details from the German Consulate General in your own country. Generally, a budget traveler need not worry about these regulations; you'll want to bring only the bare necessities (see Packing, p. 26).

CUSTOMS: GOING HOME

For large purchases, you may be eligible for a refund of **VAT** (Germany's 15% Value-Added tax). Acquire a Tax Free Shopping Check at the time of purchase and consult German customs when leaving the country (and before checking the goods). You may also obtain a stamp on your VAT refund form at a German embassy or consulate in your home country—you must present the items, sales slips, and your passport. Upon returning home, you must declare all articles you acquired abroad and pay a duty on the value of those articles that exceed the allowance established by your country's customs service. Goods and gifts purchased at duty-free shops abroad are not exempt from duty or sales tax at your point of return; you must declare these items. "Duty-free" means that you need not pay a tax in the country of purchase.

YOUTH, STUDENT, & TEACHER IDENTIFICATION

In the world of budget travel, youth has its privileges. Two main forms of student and youth identification are accepted worldwide. The **International Student Identity Card (ISIC)** is the most widely accepted form of student identification. Flashing this card can procure you discounts for many services throughout Germany. Present the card wherever you go, and ask about discounts even when none are advertised. It also provides accident insurance of up to US$3000 with no daily limit. In addition, cardholders have access to a toll-free Traveler's Assistance hotline whose multilingual staff can provide help in medical, legal, and financial emergencies overseas.

Many student travel offices issue ISICs. When you apply for the card, request a copy of the *International Student Identity Card Handbook,* which lists some of the available discounts. The card is valid from September to December of the following year. The fee is US$18. Applicants must be at least 12 years old and degree-seeking students of a secondary or post-secondary school. The US$19 **International Teacher Identity Card (ITIC)** offers similar but limited discounts, as well as medical insurance coverage. For more info on these handy cards consult the organization's new web site (http:\\www.istc.org).

Federation of International Youth Travel Organizations (FIYTO) issues a discount card to travelers who are under 26 but not students. Known as the **GO25 Card,** this one-year card offers many of the same benefits as the ISIC, and most organizations that sell the ISIC also sell the GO25 Card. A brochure that lists discounts is free when you purchase the card. To apply, you will need a passport, valid driver's license, or copy of a birth certificate, and a passport-sized photo with your name printed on the back. The fee is US$16, CDN$15, or UK£5. For information, contact Council in the U.S. or FIYTO in Denmark.

INTERNATIONAL DRIVER'S PERMIT

If you plan to drive a car while abroad, you may want an **International Driving Permit (IDP),** though Germany does allow travelers to drive with a valid American or Canadian license for one year, with certain stipulations (see By Car, p. 39). A valid driver's license from your home country must always accompany the IDP. It may be a good idea to get one anyway, in case you're in a situation where the police may not read or speak English.

Your IDP must be issued in your own country. U.S. license holders can obtain an IDP (US$10), valid for one year, at any **American Automobile Association (AAA)** office or by writing to the main office, AAA Florida, Travel Agency Services Depart-

ment, 1000 AAA Drive (mail stop 28), Heathrow, FL 32746-5080 (tel. (407) 444-4245; fax 444-4247). For further information, contact a local AAA office. Canadian license holders can obtain an IDP (CDN$10) through any **Canadian Automobile Association (CAA)** branch office in Canada, or by writing to CAA Central Ontario, 60 Commerce Valley Drive East, Thornhill, Ontario L3T 7P9 (tel. (416) 221-4300).

Most credit cards cover standard insurance. If you rent, lease, or borrow a car, you will need a **green card,** or **International Insurance Certificate,** to prove that you have liability insurance, which is required by law in Germany. Obtain it through the car rental agency; most of them include coverage in their prices. If you lease a car, you can obtain a green card from the dealer. Some travel agents offer the card, and it may be available at the border. Verify whether your auto insurance applies abroad; even if it does, you will still need a green card to certify this to foreign officials. Rental agencies may require you to purchase theft insurance; ask your agency.

■ Money Matters

US$1 = 1.48 Deutschmark (DM)	**1DM= US$0.68**
CDN$1 = 1.07DM	**1DM = CDN$0.93**
AUS$1 = 1.14DM	**1DM = AUS$0.88**
IR£ = 2.38DM	**1DM = IR£0.42**
NZ$1 = 1.01DM	**1DM = NZ$0.99**
SAR1 = 0.33DM	**1DM = SAR3.05**
UK£1 = 2.29DM	**1DM = UK£0.44**

The *Deutsche Mark* or *Deutschmark* (abbreviated DM, occasionally M) is the primary unit of currency in Germany. It is one of the most stable and respected currencies in the world; indeed, in most hard currency markets in Eastern Europe, "hard currency" means U.S. Dollars and DM exclusively. One DM equals 100 *Pfennig* (Pf). Coins come in 1, 2, 5, 10, and 50Pf, and DM1, 2, and 5 amounts. Bills come in DM5, 10, 20, 50, 100, 200, 500, and 1000 denominations. Though some (especially Americans) may think of minted metal disks as inconsequential pieces of aluminum, remember that a DM5 coin can easily buy you a meal at a supermarket. Also keep in mind that fewer **credit card** and **ATM** opportunities exist in Germany than in many Western countries; locals tend to carry large wads of hard cash in their pockets. All this means is that you should *not* rely on your plastic; carry **traveler's checks.** A new barrage of bills was unleashed recently upon the people of Germany. The old bills are *no longer valid currency,* although banks will exchange them for new bills. Accept only new bills (they have an embedded silver stripe). *Deutschmark*s and foreign currency may be freely exported and imported. Old East German currency lost all but sentimental value in July 1990.

If you stay in hostels and prepare your own food, expect to spend anywhere from US$20-80 per person per day in Germany. Transportation will increase these figures. Don't sacrifice your health or safety for a cheaper tab. If you plan to travel for more than a couple of days, you will need to keep handy a larger amount of cash than usual. You can cash personal checks at AmEx offices worldwide (if you are a member) but few places otherwise, no matter how many forms of I.D. you present.

CURRENCY AND EXCHANGE

It is more expensive to buy foreign currency than to buy domestic. In other words, *Deutschmark*s are less expensive in Deutschland than in the U.S. However, converting some money before you go will allow you to zip through the airport while others languish in exchange lines and prevents the problem of finding yourself stuck with no money after banking hours or on Sundays and holidays. It's a good idea to bring enough foreign currency to last for the first 24-72 hours of a trip. Banks generally have the best rates, but this is by no means a hard and fast rule; sometimes tourist offices or exchange kiosks have the best rates. A good rule of thumb is to go only to banks or *bureaux de change* which have only a 5% margin between their buy and sell prices. Anything more, and they are making too much profit.

Since you lose money with every transaction, convert in large sums, but don't convert more than you need, because it may be difficult to change it back to your home currency, or to a new one. One percent is a decent commission rate in Germany, although it can go as high as 10% for small amounts. If you are using traveler's checks or bills, be sure to carry some in small denominations (US$50 or less), especially for times when you are forced to exchange money at disadvantageous rates.

TRAVELER'S CHECKS

Traveler's checks are one of the safest and least troublesome means of carrying funds in Germany. Several agencies and many banks sell them, usually for face value plus a 1% commission. (Members of the American Automobile Association can get American Express checks commission-free through AAA). American Express and Visa are the most widely recognized. There will probably be at least one place in every town where you can exchange traveler's checks for local currency.

You should expect a fair amount of red tape and delay in the event of theft or loss of traveler's checks. To expedite the refund process, keep your check receipts separate from your checks and store them in a safe place or with a traveling companion; record check numbers when you cash them and leave a list of check numbers with someone at home; and ask for a list of refund centers when you buy your checks. American Express and Bank of America have over 40,000 centers worldwide. Be sure never to countersign your checks until you're prepared to cash them and be sure to bring your passport with you when you plan to use the checks.

It may not be to your advantage to purchase traveler's checks in *Deutschmarks* because they are not readily accepted as cash in Germany. Most travelers carry traveler's checks in American dollars or British pounds sterling and then exchange them for marks once in Germany.

American Express: Call (800) 221-7282 in the U.S. and Canada; in the U.K. (0800) 52 13 13; in New Zealand (0800) 44 10 68; in Australia (008) 25 19 02). Elsewhere, call U.S. collect (801) 964-6665. American Express traveler's checks are available in 11 currencies, including *Deutschmarks*. They are the most widely recognized worldwide and the easiest to replace if lost or stolen. American Express offices cash their checks commission-free, although they often offer slightly worse rates than banks. Request American Express booklet listing travel offices and stolen check hotlines for each European country.

Citicorp: Call (800) 645-6556 in the U.S. and Canada; in the U.K. (0181) 297 4781; from elsewhere call U.S. collect (813) 623-1709. Sells both Citicorp and Citicorp Visa traveler's checks in US$ and 7 other currencies, including DM. Commission is 1-2% on check purchases. Checkholders are automatically enrolled for 45 days in the Travel Assist Program (hotline (800) 250-4377 or collect (202) 296-8728) which provides travellers with English-speaking doctor, lawyer, and interpreter referrals as well as check refund assistance and general travel information.

Thomas Cook MasterCard: Call (800) 223-9920 in the U.S. and Canada; elsewhere call U.S. collect (609) 987-7300; from the U.K. call (0800) 622 101 free or (1733) 502 995 collect or (44 1733 318 950) collect. Offers checks in 13 currencies. Commission 1-2% for purchases. If you cash your checks at a Thomas Cook Office they will not charge you commission (whereas most banks will).

Visa: Call (800) 227-6811 in the U.S.; in the U.K. (0800) 895 492; from anywhere else in the world call (01733) 318 949, which is a pay call, but you can reverse the charges. Call any of the above numbers, if you give them your zip code, they will tell you where the closest office to you is to purchase their traveler's checks. Any kind of Visa traveler's checks can be reported lost at the Visa number.

CREDIT CARDS

Credit cards are not always useful to the budget traveler in Germany—many establishments will not accept them, and those enticing, pricier establishments accept them all too willingly. However, they can prove extremely valuable in an emergency. Many German banks will allow ATM withdrawals from their machines with a credit card. Visa and Mastercard are the most commonly accepted, followed by American Express and Diners Club.

There are some nifty things that one can do with credit cards abroad. Major credit cards instantly extract cash advances from associated banks and teller machines throughout Germany in *Marks*. This can be a bargain because credit card companies get the wholesale exchange rate, which is generally 5% better than the retail rate used by banks and even better than that used by other currency exchange establishments. **American Express** cards also work in some ATMs. All such machines require a **Personal Identification Number (PIN)**, which credit cards in the United States do not usually carry. You must ask American Express, MasterCard, or Visa to assign you one before you leave. Keep in mind that MasterCard and Visa have different names elsewhere ("EuroCard" or "Access" for MasterCard and "Carte Bleue" or "Barclaycard" for Visa). Credit cards are also invaluable in an emergency—an unexpected hospital bill or ticket home or the loss of traveler's checks—which may leave you temporarily without other resources. Some credit cards offer an array of other services, from insurance to emergency assistance.

American Express (tel. (800) CASH-NOW (528-4800)) has a hefty annual fee (US$55) but offers a number of services. AmEx cardholders can cash personal checks at AmEx offices abroad. U.S. Assist, a 24-hr. hotline offering medical and legal assistance in emergencies, is also available (tel. (800) 554-2639 in U.S. and Canada; from abroad call U.S. collect (301) 214-8228). Cardholders can also take advantage of the American Express Travel Service; benefits include assistance in changing airline, hotel, and car rental reservations, sending mailgrams and international cables, and holding your mail at one of the more than 1700 AmEx offices around the world.

MasterCard (tel. (800) 999-0454) and **Visa** (tel. (800) 336-8472) are issued in cooperation with individual banks and some other organizations.

CASH CARDS

Automatic Teller Machines (ATMs) offer 24-hour service in banks, groceries, gas stations, and even telephone booths. Most banks in larger European cities are connected to an international money network. Happily, the ATM machines get the same wholesale exchange rate as credit cards. Despite these perks, there is often a limit on the amount of money you can withdraw per day, and computer network failures are not uncommon. Be sure to memorize your PIN code in numeral form, since machines abroad often don't have letters on the keys. Also, if your PIN is longer than four digits, be sure to ask your bank whether the first four digits will work, or whether you need a new number. The two international money networks you should know about are **Cirrus** (U.S. tel. (800) 4-CIRRUS (424-7787)) and **PLUS** (U.S. tel. (800) 843-7587)). Cirrus now has international cash machines in 80 countries and territories. It charges US$1-2 to withdraw non-domestically depending on your bank. PLUS is not quite as extensive, only covering 51 countries.

MONEY FROM HOME

One of the easiest ways to get money from home is to bring an **American Express** card. AmEx allows card holders to draw cash from their checking accounts at any of its major offices and many of its representatives' offices. AmEx also offers **Express Cash,** with over 100,000 ATMs located in airports, hotels, banks, office complexes, and shopping areas around the world. Card holders may withdraw up to US$1000 in a seven-day period. There is a 2% transaction fee for each cash withdrawal with a US$2.50 minimum. To enroll in Express Cash, Cardmembers may call 1-800-CASH NOW (227-4669). Outside the U.S. call collect (904) 565-7875.

Money can also be wired abroad through international money transfer services operated by **Western Union** (tel. (800) 325-6000). In the U.S., call Western Union any time at (800) CALL-CASH (225-5227) to cable money with your Visa or MasterCard

WITH OUR RAIL PASSES YOU'LL HAVE UP TO 70% MORE MONEY TO WASTE.

With savings of up to 70% off the price of point to point tickets, you'll be laughing all the way to the souvenir stand. Rail passes are available for travel throughout Europe or the country of your choice and we'll even help you fly there. So all you'll have to do is leave some extra room in your suitcase. To learn more call **1-800-4-EURAIL** (1-800-438-7245). *Rail Europe*

within the domestic United States. Credit card transfers do not work; you must send cash. The rates for sending cash are generally $10 cheaper than with a credit card.

In emergencies, U.S. citizens can have money sent via the State Department's **Overseas Citizens Service, American Citizens Services,** Consular Affairs, Public Affairs Staff, Room 4831, U.S. Department of State, Washington, DC 20520 (tel. (202) 647-5225, at night and on Sundays and holidays (202) 647-4000); fax 647-3000; or http://travel.state.gov. For a fee of US$15, the State Department will forward money within hours to the nearest consular office, which will then disburse it. The office serves only Americans abroad in the direst of straits.

TIPPING AND BARGAINING

Germans generally round up to the nearest *Mark* when tipping. However, tipping is not practiced as liberally as it is in the United States—most Germans only tip in restaurants and beer halls, or when they are the beneficiary of a service, such as a taxi ride. It is sometimes customary to tip as much as 5-10% in fancier restaurants, especially if the service is particularly excellent. As a rule, Germans never bargain. Prices are posted next to their products in all stores and are not negotiable.

■ Safety and Security

SAFETY

Violent crime is less common in Germany than in most countries, but it exists, especially in big cities like Frankfurt and Hamburg. Neo-Nazi skinheads in the large cities of eastern Germany have been known to attack foreigners, especially non-whites.

Tourists are particularly vulnerable to crime for two reasons: they often carry large amounts of cash and they are not as street savvy as locals. Respecting local customs (in many cases, this means dressing more conservatively) can often placate would-be hecklers. Walking directly into a shop to check your map beats checking it on a street. Muggings are more often impromptu than planned. An obviously bewildered bodybuilder is more likely to be harassed than a stern and confident 98-pound weakling. When exploring a new city, extra vigilance may be wise. When you get to a place where you'll be spending some time, find out about unsafe areas. Both men and women may want to carry a small **whistles** to scare off attackers or attract attention. The number to contact the police in Germany is generally **110.**

If you are using a **car,** learn local driving signals. Be sure to park your vehicle in a garage or well-traveled area. Wearing a seatbelt is law in many areas. Children under 40lb. should ride only in a specially-designed carseat, which can be obtained for a small fee at most car rental agencies. **Sleeping in your car** is one of the most dangerous ways to get your rest. Sleeping out in the open can be even more dangerous.

Let's Go does not recommend **hitchhiking** (see By Thumb, p. 41).

A good self-defense course will give you more concrete ways to react to different types of aggression, but it might cost you more money than your trip. **Model Mugging,** a national organization with offices in several major cities, teaches a very effective course on self-defense. Contact Lynn S. Auerbach on the East Coast (tel. (617) 232-7900); Alice Tibits in the Midwest (tel. (612) 645-6189); and Cori Couture on the West Coast (tel. (415) 592-7300). Course prices vary from US$400-500. Community colleges frequently offer self-defense courses at more affordable prices.

To order publications from the **United States Department of State,** including the pamphlet *A Safe Trip Abroad,* write them at Superintendent of Documents, U.S. Government Printing Office, Washington, DC 20402, or call (202) 783-3238.

SECURITY

Among the more colorful aspects of large German cities are the **con artists.** Con artists and hustlers often work in groups, and children, unfortunately, are among the most effective at the game. Be aware of certain classics: sob stories that require money or mustard spilled onto your shoulder distracting you for enough time to snatch your bag. Do not respond or make eye contact, walk quickly away, and keep a solid grip on your belongings.

Don't put money in a wallet in your back pocket. Never count your money in public and carry as little as possible. As far as packs are concerned, buy some small combination padlocks which slip through the two zippers, securing the pack shut. A **money belt** is the best way to carry cash. A **neck pouch** is equally safe, although far less accessible. Refrain from pulling out your neck pouch in public. Do avoid keeping anything precious in a fanny-pack (even if it's worn on your stomach): your valuables will be highly visible and easy to steal. If you must say your calling-card number, do so very quietly and make sure no one is looking over your shoulder. Making **photocopies** of important documents will allow you to recover them in case they are lost or filched. Keep some money separate from the rest to use in an emergency or in case of theft. Label every piece of luggage.

Be particularly watchful of your belongings on **buses,** don't check baggage on trains, especially if you're switching lines, and don't trust anyone to "watch you bag for a second." **Trains** are notoriously easy spots for thieving. Professionals wait for tourists to fall asleep and then carry off everything they can. When traveling in pairs, sleep in alternating shifts; when alone, use good judgment in selecting a train compartment. Keep important documents and other valuables on your person and try to sleep on top bunks with your luggage stored above you (if not in bed with you).

Let's Go lists locker availability in hostels and train stations. Lockers are useful if don't want to lug everything with you, but don't store valuables in them. Never leave your belongings unattended; even the most demure-looking hostel (convents included) may be a den of thieves. If you feel unsafe, look for places with either a curfew or a night attendant. Keep valuables on your person at all times. If you take a **car** on your travels, try not to leave valuable possessions in it.

More complete information on safety while traveling may be found in *Americans Traveling Abroad: What You Should Know Before You Go,* available at *Barnes and Noble* booksellers across the country.

DRUGS

In 1991, 1271 of the 3050 Americans who ended up in foreign jails were brought up on drug charges. Remember that you are subject to the laws of the country that you are traveling in, not to those of your home country. Cocaine and narcotics are illegal in Germany, and the penalties for possession range from severe to horrific. It is not uncommon for a dealer to increase profits by first selling drugs to tourists and then turning them in to authorities for a reward. Even reputedly liberal cities like Frankfurt take a dim view of strung-out tourists. The drinking age in Germany is 16, though it is skimpily enforced. However, you should avoid public drunkenness; it is one of the easiest ways to simultaneously jeopardize your safety and earn the disdain of locals. The maximum permissible blood alcohol level while driving in Germany is 0.08%, lower than in the United States. The worst thing you can possibly do is to carry drugs across an international border; not only could you end up in prison, you could be blessed with a "Drug Trafficker" stamp on your passport for the rest of your life. If arrested, call your country's consulate. Embassies may not be willing to help those arrested on drug charges. Make sure you get a statement and prescription from your doctor if you'll be carrying insulin, syringes, or any narcotic medications. Refuse to carry even an apparent nun's excess luggage onto a plane; you're more likely to wind up in jail for possession of drugs than in heaven.

■ Health

Common sense is the simplest prescription for good health. To minimize the effects of jet lag, "reset" your body's clock by adopting the time of your destination upon arrival. Most travelers feel acclimatized to a new time zone after two or three days.

BEFORE YOU GO

In your passport, write the names of any people you wish to be contacted in case of a medical emergency, and also list any allergies or medical conditions you would want doctors to be aware of. If you wear glasses or contact lenses, carry an extra prescription and a pair of glasses. Allergy sufferers should find out if their conditions are likely to be aggravated in the regions they plan to visit, and obtain a full supply of any necessary medication before the trip, since matching a prescription to a foreign equivalent is not always easy, safe, or possible.

If you are concerned about being able to access medical support while traveling, contact one of these two services: **Global Emergency Medical Services (GEMS)** provides 24-hour international medical assistance and support coordinated through registered nurses who have on-line access to your medical information, your primary physician, and a worldwide network of screened, credentialed English-speaking doctors and hospitals. For more information call (800) 860-1111, fax (770) 475-0058, or write: 2001 Westside Drive, Suite 120, Alpharetta, GA 30201. The **International Association for Medical Assistance to Travelers (IAMAT)** offers a directory of English-speaking doctors around the world who treat members for a set fee schedule, and detailed charts on immunization requirements. Membership is free. Contact chapters in the **U.S.,** 417 Center St., Lewiston, NY 14092 (tel. (716) 754-4883; fax (519) 836-3412; e-mail iamat@sentex.net; http://www.sentex.net/iamat), **Canada,** 40 Regal Road, Guelph, Ontario, N1K 1B5 (tel. (519) 836-0102) or 1287 St. Clair Avenue West, Toronto, M6E 1B8 (tel. (416) 652-0137; fax (519) 836-3412), or **New Zealand,** P.O. Box 5049, Christchurch 5.

HOT AND COLD

Common sense goes a long way. Always drink enough liquids to keep your urine clear. Alcoholic beverages are dehydrating, as are coffee, strong tea, and caffeinated sodas. If you'll be sweating a lot, be sure to eat enough salty food to prevent electrolyte depletion, which causes severe headaches. Less debilitating, but still dangerous, is **sunburn.** If you're prone to sunburn, bring sunscreen with you.

Extreme cold, which you might well encounter on a summer day in the Alps, is just as dangerous as heat—overexposure to cold brings the risk of **hypothermia.** To avoid hypothermia, keep dry and stay out of the wind. In wet weather, wool and most synthetics will keep you warm but most other fabric, especially cotton, will make you colder. Dress in layers, and watch for frostbite when the temperature is below freezing. Travelers in **high altitudes** should allow their body two days to adjust to the lower atmospheric oxygen levels before engaging in any strenuous activity. This particularly applies to those setting out on alpine hikes. Extra fluids are imperative during and after physical exertion, especially at altitude. One alcoholic beverage may have the same effect as three at a lower altitude. Always consider that German brews may have higher alcohol content than many American beers.

SPECIFIC MEDICAL CONCERNS

Travelers with chronic medical conditions should consult with their physicians before leaving. Always go prepared with any medication you may need while away as well as a copy of the prescription and/or a statement from your doctor, especially if you will be bringing insulin, syringes, or narcotics. Be aware that matching prescriptions with foreign equivalents may be difficult. To get a prescription filled in Germany you must go to an *Apotheke;* a *Drogerie* sells only toilet articles. Most German cities have a rotating pharmacy schedule to ensure that services are available 24 hours per day. Check the Practical Information section for each particular city for the location of the major pharmacy, which will post the 24-hour rotation schedule.

The World At a Discount

Save 20% to 50% on Airfare (major carriers)

Save 10% to 50% on Museums & Theaters

Save 10% on AT&T Calls to the U.S.

Save up to 40% on Train Passes

Save 15% on Greyhound Travel

Worldwide Discounts in more than 90 countries

Save 10% to 30% on Accommodations

The International Student Identity Card
Your Passport to Discounts & Benefits

With the ISIC, you'll receive discounts on airfare, hotels, transportation, computer services, foreign currency exchange, phone calls, major attractions, and more. You'll also receive basic accident and sickness insurance coverage when traveling outside the U.S. and access to a 24-hour, toll-free Help Line. Call now to locate the issuing office nearest you (over 555 across the U.S.) at:

Free 40-page handbook with each card!

1-888-COUNCIL (toll-free)

For an application and complete discount list, you can also visit us at http://www.ciee.org/

Council

CIEE: Council on International Educational Exchange

BIRTH CONTROL

Reliable contraceptive devices may be difficult to find while traveling. Women on the pill should bring enough to allow for possible loss or extended stays and should bring a prescription, since forms of the pill vary a good deal. If you use a diaphragm, be sure that you have enough contraceptive jelly on hand. Condoms *(Kondom)* are widely available in Germany.

If you are overseas and want an **abortion,** contact the **United States abortion hotline** (tel. (800) 772-9100; open Mon.-Fri. 9:30am-12:30pm, 1:30-5:30pm), 1436 U St. NW, Washington, DC 20009. The hotline can direct you to organizations which provide information on the availability of and techniques for abortion in other countries. Or contact your embassy to receive a list of ob/gyn doctors. For general information on contraception, condoms, and abortion, contact the **International Planned Parenthood Federation,** European Regional Office, Regent's College Inner Circle, Regent's Park, London NW1 4NS (tel. (0171) 486 0741; fax 487 7950). For info on **abortion laws in Germany,** see Women Travelers, p. 21.

AIDS, HIV, STDS

The easiest mode of HIV transmission is through direct blood-to-blood contact with an HIV-positive person; *never* share intravenous drug, tattooing, or other needles. The most common mode of transmission is sexual intercourse. Since it isn't always easy to buy condoms when traveling, take a supply with you before you depart for your trip. **Bavaria** requires foreigners seeking a residency permit for more than six months to be HIV-negative, and they do not accept the results of tests taken abroad.

Sexually transmitted diseases (STDs) such as gonorrhea, chlamydia, genital warts, syphilis, and herpes are a lot easier to catch than HIV, and can be just as deadly. It's a wise idea to actually *look* at your partner's genitals before you have sex. If anything looks amiss, that should be a warning. When having sex, condoms may protect you from certain STDs, but oral contact can lead to transmission.

■ Insurance

Beware of buying unnecessary travel coverage—your regular policies may well extend to many travel-related accidents. **Medical insurance** (especially university policies) often cover costs incurred abroad; check with your provider. **Medicare's** foreign travel coverage is valid only in Canada and Mexico. Canadians are protected by their home province's health insurance plan for up to 90 days after leaving the country; check with the provincial Ministry of Health or Health Plan Headquarters for details. Australia has Reciprocal Health Care Agreements (RHCAs) with several countries; when traveling in these nations, Australians are entitled to many of the services that they would receive at home. The Commonwealth Department of Human Services and Health can provide more information. Your **homeowners' insurance** (or your family's coverage) often covers theft during travel up to US$500.

ISIC and **ITIC** provide US$3000 worth of accident and illness insurance and US$100 per day for up to 60 days of hospitalization. They also offer up to US$1000 for accidental death or dismemberment, up to US$25,000 if injured due to an airline, and up to $25,000 for emergency evacuation due to an illness. The cards also give access to a toll-free Traveler's Assistance hotline (in the US and Canada tel.(800) 626-2427; elsewhere call collect to the US (tel. (713) 267-2525)) whose multilingual staff can provide help in emergencies overseas. **Council** offers the inexpensive Trip-Safe plan with options covering medical treatment and hospitalization, accidents, baggage loss, and even charter flights missed due to illness; **STA** offers a more expensive, more comprehensive plan. **American Express** cardholders receive automatic car rental insurance (does not cover collisions) and travel accident insurance on flights purchased with the card. (Customer Service tel. (800) 528-4800.)

ESSENTIALS

Globalcare Travel Insurance, 220 Broadway Lynnfield, MA 01940 (tel. (800) 821-2488; fax (617) 592-7720); e-mail global@nebc.mv.com; (http://nebc.mv.com/globalcare). Complete medical, legal, emergency, and travel-related services.

Travel Assistance International, by Worldwide Assistance Services, Inc., 1133 15th St. NW, Suite 400, Washington, DC 20005-2710 (tel. (800) 821-2828 or (202) 828-5894; fax (202) 828-5896; e-mail wassist@aol.com). TAI provides its members with a 24-hr. free hotline for travel emergencies and referrals.

Travel Guard International, 1145 Clark St., Stevens Point, WI 54481 (tel. (800) 826-1300 or (715) 345-0505; fax (715) 345-0525). Comprehensive insurance programs starting at US$44. Programs cover trip cancellation and interruption, bankruptcy and financial default, lost luggage, medical coverage abroad, emergency assistance, accidental death. 24-hr. hotline.

■ Alternatives to Tourism

STUDY

Foreign study programs vary tremendously in expense, academic quality, living conditions, degree of contact with local students, and exposure to the local culture and language. Most American undergraduates enroll in programs sponsored by U.S. universities, and many colleges give academic information about study abroad programs. Take advantage of their counselors and libraries. Ask for the names of recent participants in the programs, and impose on them. The Internet has a study abroad website at **www.studyabroad.com/liteimage.html.** If you have extensive language skills, consider direct enrollment; German universities are far cheaper than those in North America.

ABI (Aktion Bildungsinformation e.V.), Alte Poststr. 5, 53111 Bonn-Bad Godesberg, has published various leaflets with information on travel for the purpose of studying a language, e.g. *Learning a Foreign Language in Germany.*

American Field Service (AFS), 220 E. 42nd St., 3rd floor, New York, NY 10017 (tel. (800) 237-4636 or AFS-INF0, 876-2376; fax (212) 949-9379; http://www.afs.org/usa). AFS offers summer, semester, and year-long homestay international exchange programs for high school students and graduating high school seniors and short-term service projects for adults. Financial aid available.

Council sponsors over 40 study abroad programs throughout the world. Contact them for more information (see Travel Organizations, p. 2).

Deutscher Akademischer Austauschdienst (DAAD), 950 3rd Ave., New York NY 10022 (tel. (212) 758 3223); in Germany, Kennedyallee 50, 53175 Bonn-Bad Godesberg. Information on language instruction and exchanges. The place to contact if you want to enroll in a German university; distributes application forms and the valuable *Academic Study in the Federal Republic of Germany.*

Eurocentres, 101 N. Union St. #300, Alexandria, VA 22314 (tel. (800) 648-4809; fax (703) 684-1495); http://www.clark.net/pub/eurocent/home.htn) or Eurocentres, Head Office, Seestrasse 247, CH-8038 Zurich, Switzerland (tel. (01) 485 50 40; fax 481 61 24). Coordinates language programs and homestays for college students and adults in Germany (Cologne, Weimar). Programs cost about US$500-5000 and last from 2 weeks to 3 months. Some financial aid is available.

Goethe Institute runs numerous language programs in Germany and abroad. For information on these and on their many cultural offerings, contact your local Goethe Institute (American branches in New York, Washington, DC, Boston, Atlanta, San Francisco, Los Angeles, and Seattle) or write to Goethe House New York, 1014 Fifth Ave., New York, NY 10028 (tel. (212) 439-8700; fax 439-8705; http://www.goethe.de/uk/ney/enindex.htm).

Peterson's Guides, P. O. Box 2123, Princeton, NJ 08543-2123 (tel. (800) 338-3282; fax (609) 243-9150; http://www.petersons.com). Their comprehensive *Study Abroad* annual guide lists programs in countries all over the world and provides essential information on the study abroad experience in general. Purchase a copy at your local bookstore (US$27) or call their toll-free number.

WORK AND VOLUNTEER

There is no better way to submerge yourself in a foreign culture than to become part of its economy. But unless you have connections, it will rarely be glamorous and may not even pay for your ticket over. Getting permission to work in Germany is a challenge. If you hold EU citizenship, you may work in Germany without special permission, though you must register with local police to take up residence. The organizations and publications listed below can help point you toward employment abroad; you should speak with former clients before paying any registration fees.

With unemployment on the rise even before reunification, Germany's days as a mecca for unskilled foreign workers are over. The German government maintains a series of federally run employment offices, the **Bundesanstalt für Arbeit,** throughout the country. Foreign applications are directed to the central office at Feuerbachstr. 42-6, 60325 Frankfurt am Main. The office tends to treat EU citizens with specific skills more favorably than those from other countries. The youth division is a bit more welcoming for foreign students ages 18-30 seeking summer employment; jobs frequently involve manual labor. If you don't know anyone in Germany, don't have the flexibility to perform casual labor, and are a full-time student at a U.S. university, then consider applying for a **temporary student work visa** through the **Council on International Educational Exchange (Council).** For US$160, Council can procure temporary work permits for American university students in Germany and several other countries. Officially, you can hold a job in European countries only with a **work permit.** Your prospective employer must obtain this document, usually by demonstrating that you have skills that locals lack.

The best tips on jobs for foreigners often come from other travelers, so be alert and inquisitive. Some follow the grape harvest in the fall—mostly in France, but also in Germany's Mosel Valley. Menial jobs can be found anywhere in Europe; ski resorts leave much of the gruntwork to foreigners. Ask at pubs, cafés, restaurants, and hotels. Be sure to be aware of your rights as an employee; should a crafty national try to refuse payment at the end of the season, it'll help if you have a written confirmation of your agreement. Youth hostels often provide room and board to travelers willing to stay a while and help run the place. Consider a job **teaching English.** Post a sign in markets or learning centers stating that you are a native speaker, and scan the classifieds of local newspapers. It may be your only option in eastern Germany. Organizations in the U.S. will place you in a (low-paying) teaching job; professional positions are harder to get. Most European schools require at least a bachelor's degree and training in teaching English as a foreign language.

Addison-Wesley, Jacob Way, Reading, MA 01867 (tel. (800) 822-6339). Published *International Jobs: Where They Are, How to Get Them* in 1993-1994 (US$16).
Council (see Travel Organizations, above) offers 2- to 4-week environmental or community service projects in over 30 countries around the globe through its Voluntary Services Department (US$250-750 placement fee). Participants must be at least 18 years old.
Office of Overseas Schools, A/OS Room 245, SA-29, Dept. of State, Washington, DC 20522-2902 (tel. (703) 875-7800). Teaching jobs abroad.
Transitions Abroad Publishing, Inc., 18 Hulst Rd., P.O. Box 1300, Amherst, MA 01004-1300 (tel. (800) 293-0373; fax (413) 256-0373; e-mail trabroad@aol.com). Publishes a bimonthly magazine listing all kinds of opportunities and printed resources for those seeking to study, work, or travel abroad. They also publish *The Alternative Travel Directory,* a truly exhaustive encyclopedia for the "active international traveler." For subscriptions (U.S. US$20 for 6 issues, Canada US$26, other countries US$38), contact them at Dept. TRA, Box 3000, Denville, NJ 07834.
Surrey Books, 230 E. Ohio St., Chicago, IL 60611(tel. (800) 326-4430; fax (312) 751-7330) publishes *How to Get a Job in Europe: The Insider's Guide.*
Vacation Work Publications, 9 Park End St., Oxford OX1 1HJ (tel. (01865) 24 19 78; fax 79 08 85). Publishes a wide variety of excellent guides and directories with

job listings and information for the working traveler. Opportunities for summer or full-time work in countries all over the world. Write for a catalogue.

World Trade Academy Press, Suite 509, 50 E. 42nd St. New York, NY 10017-5480 (tel. (212) 752-0329). Publishes *The Directory of American Firms Operating in Foreign Countries* (1996) for US$200 and *The Directory of Foreign Firms Operating in the United States* (1995) for US$150. These may be found in bookstores or libraries.

Teaching English abroad is thus a common and practical choice (see Work and Volunteer, p. 19). In addition, the following *au pair* agencies can help you find work as a nanny in Germany.

InterExchange, 161 Sixth Avenue, New York, NY 10013 (tel. (212) 924-0446; fax 924-0575). Provides information in pamphlet form on international work programs and *au pair* positions in Germany and many other European countries.

Childcare International, Ltd., Trafalgar House, Grenville Place, London NW7 3SA (tel. (01819) 59 36 11 or 06 31 16; fax 06 34 61; e-mail office@child-int.demon.co.uk; http://www.ipi.co.uk/childint). Member of the International *Au Pair* Association. UK£60 application fee. The organization prefers a long placement but does arrange summer work.

Volunteer jobs are readily available almost everywhere. You may receive room and board in exchange for your labor, and the work can be fascinating. In Germany, opportunities include community and work camp projects. Keep in mind: the organizations that arrange placement sometimes charge high application fees in addition to the work camps' charges for room and board. You can sometimes avoid this extra fee by contacting the individual work camps directly. Listings in Vacation Work's *International Directory of Voluntary Work* (UK£9; see above) can be helpful.

Council publishes *Volunteer! The Comprehensive Guide to Voluntary Service in the U.S. and Abroad* (US$13 plus US$1.50 postage). Available from Council Travel offices and Council's Voluntary Services Dept., 205 E. 42nd St., New York, NY 10017 (tel. (888) COUNCIL (268-6245); fax (212) 822-2699; http://www.ciee.org). Department also offers 2-4 week environmental or community service projects in over 30 countries around the globe. Participants must be at least 18 years of age. US$195 placement fee.

Service Civil International Voluntary Service (SCI-VS), 5474 Walnut Level Rd., Crozet, VA 22932 (tel. (804) 823-1826; fax 823-5027; e-mail sciivsusa@igc.apc.org). Arranges placement in work camps in Europe (ages 18 and over). Registration fees US$50-250, depending on the camp location.

Volunteers for Peace, 43 Tiffany Rd., Belmont, VT 05730 (tel. (802) 259-2759; fax 259-2922; e-mail vfp@vermontel.com; http://www.vfp.org). A non-profit organization that arranges for speedy placement in over 800 work camps in 60 countries. Many camps last for 2-3 weeks and are comprised of 10-15 people.

Willing Workers on Organic Farms (WWOOF) distributes a list of names of organic farmers who offer room and board in exchange for help on the farm. Include an international postal reply coupon with the request. Contact: WWOOF, Postfach 615, CH-9001 St. Gallen, Switzerland (e-mail fairtours@gn.apc.org). Wwith a wwittle wwillingness, wwone can wwork wwonders.

LONGER STAYS

Those planning to remain in Germany for an extended period of time should contact the local **Mitwohnzentrale,** an accommodation-finding office, in the city where they plan to be. Located throughout Germany, *Mitwohnzentralen* match apartments with apartment seekers. The stay can be anywhere from a few days to as long as a couple of months, depending on the availablity of apartments and the price you are willing to pay. Look under the Practical Information listing for each individual city to find the address and phone number of each individual *Mitwohnzentrale.*

■ Specific Concerns

WOMEN TRAVELERS

Women exploring on their own inevitably face additional safety concerns. Always trust your instincts: if you'd feel better somewhere else, move on. Always carry extra money for a phone call, bus, or taxi. Consider staying in hostels which offer single rooms that lock from the inside or in religious organizations that offer rooms for women only. Stick to centrally-located accommodations and avoid late-night treks or metro rides. Hitching is never safe for lone women. You must be over 18 to purchase and use various pocket-sized containers of mace (DM12-18), available in many knife and scissor stores. Yes, knife and scissor stores. Look as if you know where you're going and consider approaching women or couples for directions if you're lost. In general, dress conservatively, especially in rural areas.

If you spend time in cities, you may be harassed no matter how you're dressed. Your best answer to verbal harassment is no answer at all (a reaction is what the harasser wants). Wearing a conspicuous wedding band may deter such behavior. Carry a whistle or an airhorn on your keychain, and don't hesitate to use it in an emergency. *Let's Go* lists emergency numbers (including rape crisis lines) in the Practical Information listings of most cities. Memorize the emergency numbers in Germany (police: 110, ambulance: 115). If need be, turn to an older woman for help in an uncomfortable situation; her stern rebukes will usually be enough to embarrass the most persistent jerks. Unlike in some parts of southern Europe, catcalls and whistling are not acceptable behavior in Germany; you can feel comfortable rebuking your harasser. Loudly saying *"Laß mich in Ruhe!"* ("Leave me alone!"; pronounced LAHSS MEEKH EEN ROOH-eh) should suffice. German standards of public behavior are fairly reserved, and you can often rebuff a harasser by calling the attention of passersby to his behavior.

For general information, contact the **National Organization for Women (NOW)**, which boasts branches across the country that can refer women travelers to rape crisis centers and counseling services, and provide lists of feminist events. Main offices include 22 W. 21st St., 7th Fl., **New York,** NY 10010 (tel. (212) 260-4422); 1000 16th St. NW, 7th Fl., **Washington, DC** 20004 (tel. (202) 331-0066); and 3543 18th St., **San Francisco,** CA 94110 (tel. (415) 861-8960).

Directory of Women's Media is available from the National Council for Research on Women, 530 Broadway, 10th Floor, New York, NY 10012 (tel. (212) 274-0730; fax 274-0821). The publication lists women's publishers, bookstores, theaters, and news organizations (mail orders, US$30).

A Journey of One's Own, by Thalia Zepatos (Eighth Mountain Press US$17). The latest thing on the market, interesting and full of good advice, plus a specific and manageable bibliography of books and resources.

Women Travel: Adventures, Advice & Experience by Miranda Davies and Natania Jansz (Penguin, US$13). Info on specific foreign countries plus a decent bibliography and resource index. And the sequel, *More Women Travel,* is $15.

Women Going Places, a women's travel and resource guide emphasizing women-owned enterprises. Geared towards lesbians, but offers advice appropriate for all women. US$14 from Inland Book Company, 1436 W. Randolph St. Chicago, IL 60607 (tel. (800) 243-0138) or order from a local bookstore.

Abortion is a complicated legal issue in Germany. It is only available within the first trimester, and not on demand; a woman must indicate a reason, and only certain reasons are accepted. In practice, the restrictions simply necessitate a search for a willing doctor. In 1995, new legislation considerably eased legal barriers to abortion in most of the country. Still, if you find yourself with an unwanted pregnancy in Germany and choose to seek an abortion, be aware of the bureaucracy involved, which is stricter in certain states (notably Bavaria) than in others (notably the northwestern *Länder*). The German word for abortion is *Abtreibung;* the word for abortion rights is *Abtreibungsrecht.* The "morning after" pill is available in Germany, but the *Abtreibungspille* (RU486; the French "abortion pill") is not.

OLDER TRAVELERS

Senior citizens are eligible for a wide range of discounts on transportation, museums, movies, theaters, concerts, restaurants, and accommodations. If you don't see a senior citizen price listed, ask and you may be delightfully surprised.

AARP (American Association of Retired Persons), 601 E St., NW, Washington, D.C. 20049 (202-434-2277). Members 50 and over receive benefits and services including the AARP Motoring Plan from AMOCO (800-334-3300), and discounts on lodging, car rental, and sight-seeing. Annual fee US$8 per couple; lifetime membership US$75.

Elderhostel, 75 Federal St., 3rd Fl., Boston, MA 02110-1941 (tel. (617) 426-7788; fax 426-8351; http://www.elderhostel.org). For those 55 or over (spouse of any age). Programs at colleges, universities, and other learning centers in over 50 countries on varied subjects lasting 1-4 weeks.

National Council of Senior Citizens, 1331 F St. NW, Washington, D.C. 20004 (202-347-8800). Memberships are US$12 a year, US$30 for three years, or US$150 for a lifetime. Individual or couple can receive hotel and auto rental discounts, a senior citizen newspaper, use of a discount travel agency, supplemental Medicare insurance (if you're over 65), and a mail-order prescription drug service.

BISEXUAL, GAY, AND LESBIAN TRAVELERS

Germany is fairly tolerant of homosexuality. The German word for gay is *Schwul,* for lesbian *Lesben. Let's Go* provides information on local bisexual, gay, and lesbian culture in Practical Information listings and Entertainment sections of city descriptions. In general, the larger the city and the farther north you travel, the more tolerant the attitudes towards bisexual, gay, and lesbian travelers. The major centers of gay life are Berlin, Hamburg, Frankfurt and Munich; there is also a scene in Cologne. Women should look for *Frauencafés* and *Frauenkneipen*. It should be stressed though, that while such cafés are for women only, they are *not* for lesbians only. The local *Frauenbuchladen* (women's bookstore) is a good resource.

Are You Two … Together? A Gay and Lesbian Travel Guide to Europe. A travel guide with anecdotes and tips for gays and lesbians traveling in Europe. Includes overviews of regional laws relating to gays and lesbians, lists of gay/lesbian organizations, and establishments catering to, friendly to, or indifferent to gays and lesbians. Available in bookstores. Random House, US$18.

Bruno Gmünder, Postfach 11 07 29, 10837 Berlin (tel. 030 615-92-03; fax 030 615 90 08). Publishes travel guides to Berlin, Stuttgart, Hamburg, Munich, Cologne, Düsseldorf, and Frankfurt for gay men in German/English editions. Also publishes the **Spartacus International Gay Guides,** which list bars, restaurants, hotels, and bookstores around the world catering to gays, as well as gay hotlines and homosexuality laws for each country.

Ferrari Guides, PO Box 37887, Phoenix, AZ 85069 (tel. (602) 863-2408; fax 439-3952; e-mail ferrari@q-net.com). Gay and lesbian travel guides: *Ferrari Guides' Gay Travel A to Z* (US$16), *Ferrari Guides' Men's Travel in Your Pocket* (US$14), *Ferrari Guides' Women's Travel in Your Pocket* (US$14), *Ferrari Guides' Inn Places* (US$16). Available in bookstores or by mail order.

Gay Europe (Perigee Books, US$14). A gay guide providing a quick look at gay life in countries throughout Europe, including restaurants, clubs, and beaches. Intros to each country cover laws and gay-friendliness. Available in bookstores.

Giovanni's Room, 345 S. 12th St., Philadelphia, PA 19107 (tel. (215) 923-2960; fax 923-0813; e-mail gilphilp@netaxs.com). A feminist, lesbian, and gay bookstore with mail-order service which carries many of the publications listed here.

International Gay Travel Association, Box 4974, Key West, FL 33041 (tel. (800) 448-8550; fax (305) 296-6633; e-mail IGTA@aol.com; http://www.rainbow-mall.com/igta). An organization of over 1100 companies serving gay and lesbian travelers worldwide. Call for lists of travel agents, accommodations, and events.

DISABLED TRAVELERS

By and large, Germany is one of the more accessible countries for travelers with disabilities (*Behinderte* or *Schwerbehinderte*). Germany's excellent public transportation systems make most places easily accessible for both older travelers and for travelers with disabilities *(Behinderte);* many public transport systems are wheelchair-accessible. The international **wheelchair** icon or a large letter "B" indicates access. Major cities have audible crossing signals for the blind. Trains have a few seats or an integrated compartment reserved for passengers with disabilities. Almost all EuroCity (EC) trains in and out of Germany have wheelchair facilities. Many platforms can be hard to reach; alternative ones sometimes exist. For more information, contact **Rail Europe** in the U.S. at (800) 4-EUROPE (438-7245). Germany requires a health certificate, issued by a licensed veterinarian in a period 12 months to 3 months prior to entry, for all dogs and cats being brought into the country, including guide dogs. A notarized German translation of this certificate is also necessary.

American Foundation for the Blind, 11 Penn Plaza, New York, NY 10011 (tel. (212) 502-7600), open Mon.-Fri. 8:30am-4:30pm. Provides information and services for the visually impaired. For a catalogue of products, contact Lighthouse Y, 10011(tel. (800) 829-0500).

Graphic Language Press, P.O. Box 270, Cardiff by the Sea, CA 92007 (tel. (619) 944-9594). Publishers of *Wheelchair Through Europe* (US$13). Comprehensive advice for the wheelchair-bound traveler. Specifics on wheelchair-related resources and accessible sites in various cities throughout Europe.

Mobility International, USA (MIUSA), P.O. Box 10767, Eugene, OR 97440 (tel. (503) 343-1284 voice and TDD; fax 343-6812). International Headquarters in Brussels, rue de Manchester 25 Brussles, Belgium, B-1070 (tel. (322) 410 6297; fax 410 6874). Contacts in 30 countries. Information on travel programs, international work camps, accommodations, access guides, and organized tours for those with physical disabilities. Membership US$25 per year, newsletter US$15.

The following organizations arrange tours or trips for disabled travelers:

Directions Unlimited, 720 N. Bedford Rd., Bedford Hills, NY 10507 (tel. (800) 533-5343 or (914) 241-1700; fax (914) 241-0243). Specializes in arranging individual and group vacations, tours, and cruises for the physically disabled.

Flying Wheels Travel Service, 143 W. Bridge St., Owatonne, MN 55060 (tel. (800) 535-6790; fax 451-1685). Arranges trips abroad for groups and individuals in wheelchairs or with other sorts of limited mobility.

The Guided Tour Inc., Elkins Park House, Suite 114B, 7900 Old York Road, Elkins Park, PA 19027-2339 (tel. (800) 783-5841 or (215) 782-1370; fax (215) 635-2637). Organizes travel programs for persons with developmental and physical challenges and those requiring renal dialysis. Call, fax, or write for a free brochure.

KOSHER AND VEGETARIAN TRAVELERS

For historic and political reasons, few Jews choose to live in Germany; the kosher offerings are correspondingly small. *Let's Go* makes every attempt to identify kosher restaurants in Germany, which lie mostly in large urban areas. Your own synagogue or college Hillel should have access to lists of Jewish institutions across the nation. If you are strict in your observance, consider preparing your own food on the road.

Although Germany is unapologetically carnivorous, vegetarian restaurants have proliferated along with the blooming "alternative scene" in larger cities. *Let's Go* makes an effort to identify restaurants that offer vegetarian choices. Dairy products

are excellent, and fish is widely available on the North Sea coast and in lakeside towns. Tourist offices often publish lists of kosher and vegetarian restaurants.

The European Vegetarian Guide to Restaurants and Hotels (US$13.95, plus $1.75 shipping) is available from the Vegetarian Times Bookshelf (orders only, tel. (800) 435-9610).

Jewish Chronicle Publications, 25 Furnival St., London EC4A IJT (tel. (0171) 405 92 52; fax 831 51 88). Publishes the *Jewish Travel Guide* (US$12, postage US$1.75). Available in the U.S. from Sepher-Hermon Press, 1265 46th St., Brooklyn, NY 11219 (tel. (718) 972-9010). In the U.K., order from Jewish Chronicle Publications, 25 Furnival St., London EC4A. Lists synagogues, kosher restaurants and institutions in over 80 countries.

North American Vegetarian Society, P.O. Box 72, Dolgeville, NY 13329 (tel.(518) 568-7970). Membership to the Society is US$20; family membership is US$26 and members receive a 10% discount on all publications—ask about them.

MINORITY TRAVELERS

Germany has a significant minority population composed mainly of ethnic Turks. In addition, there are refugees from Eastern and Southern Europe and, facing increasing hostility, a number of Romany-Sinti people (also known as Gypsies). Eastern Germany also has a number of Vietnamese residents. All the same, conspicuously non-German foreigners may stand out.

> In certain regions, tourists of color or members of certain religious groups may feel threatened by local residents. Neo-Nazi skinheads in the large cities of former East Germany, as well as in western Germany, have been known to attack foreigners, especially non-whites. In these areas, common sense will serve you best. Either historical or newly developed discrimination against established minority residents may surface against travelers who are members of those minority groups. *Let's Go* researchers are instructed not to include within our guides establishments which are known to discriminate.

RELIGIOUS TRAVELERS

It is impossible to discuss religion in present-day Germany without hearing the many voices of past and present: the voices of Holocaust survivors, the voices of young neo-Nazis, the voices of the courageous East German pastors who led the peaceful resistance against the communists, and the voice of the modern Basic Law which states that "freedom of faith and conscience as well as freedom of religious or other belief shall be inviolable. The undisturbed practice of religion shall be guaranteed" (paragraph 4). Despite having had until recently Europe's most liberal immigration policies for asylum-seekers, Germany remains an overwhelmingly Christian nation and some of these policies have been rescinded in the recent anti-foreigner climate. The total Jewish population in Germany today is approximately 40-50,000. The largest Jewish congregations are in Berlin and Frankfurt am Main, which together are home to over 10,000 Jews. Aside from these two major Jewish community centers there are few **kosher** restaurants in Germany. An influx of foreign workers has brought along with it a strong Islamic population; today, almost two million Muslims, mostly from Turkey, live in the Federal Republic of Germany. For information, contact any of the following organizations.

Protestant: Kirchenamt der Evangelischen Kirche in Deutschland, Herrenhäuser-Str. 12, 30419 Hanover (tel. (0511) 279 60; fax 279 67 07; e-mail ekd@ekd.de).

Catholic: Katholisches Auslandssekretariat der Deutschen Bischofskonferenz Tourismus und Urlauberselsorge, Kaiser-Friedrich-Str. 9 53113 Bonn (tel. (0228) 91 14 30; fax 22 07 22; http://kath.de)

Muslim: Islamische Gemeinschaft. **Munich:** Bergmannstr. 13, (tel. (400) 502 55 25). **Berlin:** Einemstr. 8 D-10787 Berlin-Schöneberg (tel./fax (030) 262 54 69).

Jewish: There are Jewish community centers in each of the following cities. **Berlin:** Fasanenstr. 79-80 (tel. (030) 884 20 30); **Bonn:** Tempelstr. 2-4 (tel. (0228) 21 35 60); **Cologne:** Roonstr. 50 (tel. (0221) 23 56 26 or 23 56 27); **Düsseldorf:** Zietenstr. 50 (tel. (0211) 48 03 13); **Frankfurt:** Altkönigstr. 27 (tel. (069) 72 38 03) and Westendstraße 43, 60325 (tel. (069) 74 07 21 5; **München:** Reichenbachstraße 27, 80469 (tel. (089) 20 24 00 0).

TRAVELERS WITH CHILDREN

Youth hostel organizations often offer special family memberships. Call ahead to hotels and hostels to make sure they are child-friendly. If you rent a car, make sure the rental company provides a car seat for younger children. Virtually all museums and tourist attractions have a children's rate. Be sure that your child carries some sort of ID in case of an emergency or he or she gets lost. Arrange a reunion spot in case of separation when sight-seeing. Some of the following publications offer tips for adults traveling with children.

Backpacking with Babies and Small Children (US$10). Published by Wilderness Press, 2440 Bancroft Way, Berkeley, CA 94704 (tel. (800) 443-7227 or (510) 843-8080; fax 548-1355).

Take Your Kids to Europe by Cynthia W. Harriman (US$14). A budget travel guide geared towards families. Published by Mason-Grant Publications, P.O. Box 6547, Portsmouth, NH 03802 (tel. (603) 436-1608; fax 427-0015; e-mail charriman@masongrant.com).

Travel with Children by Maureen Wheeler (US$11.95, postage US$1.50). Published by Lonely Planet Publications, Embarcadero West, 155 Filbert St., #251, Oakland, CA 94607 (tel. (800) 275-8555 or (510) 893-8555; fax 893-8563; e-mail info@lonelyplanet.com; http://www.lonelyplanet.com). Also P.O. Box 617, Hawthorn, Victoria 3122, Australia.

■ Packing

If you want to get away from it all, don't take it all with you.

The more you know, the less you need, so plan your packing according to the type of travel (multi-city backpacking tour, week-long stay in one place, etc.) and the high and low temperatures in the area you will be visiting. If you don't pack lightly, your back and wallet will suffer. The larger your pack, the more cumbersome it is to store safely. Before you leave, pack your bag, strap it on, and imagine yourself schlepping around Berlin or the Bavarian Alps. A good general rule is to lay out only what you absolutely need, then take half the clothes and twice the money. Remember to pack valuables and necessities in your carry-on luggage.

LUGGAGE

Backpack: If you plan to cover most of your itinerary by foot, the unbeatable baggage is a sturdy backpack. Many packs are designed specifically for travelers, while others are for hikers. Get a pack with a strong, padded hip belt to transfer weight from your shoulders to your hips. When carried correctly, a pack's weight should rest entirely on your hips. Avoid excessively low-end prices—you get what you pay for. Quality packs cost US$150 to US$420.

Suitcase/trunk/other large or heavy luggage: Fine if you plan to live in 1 or 2 cities and explore from there, but a bad idea if you're going to be moving around a lot—trust us. Make sure it has wheels and consider how much it weighs. Soft-sided luggage should have a PVC frame, a strong lining to resist bad weather and rough handling, and its should be seams triple-stitched for durability.

Daypack, rucksack, or courier bag: Bringing a smaller bag in addition to your pack or suitcase allows you to leave your big bag in the hotel while you go sight-seeing. More importantly, it can be used as an airplane carry-on.

Moneybelt or neck pouch: Guard your money, passport, railpass, and other important articles in either one of these, and keep it with you *at all times*. Money belts and neck pouches are available at any good camping store. For more information on protecting you and your valuables, see Safety and Security, p. 13.

CLOTHING AND FOOTWEAR

Clothing: Packing lightly does not mean dressing badly. Aim for versatility and comfort, and avoid fabrics that wrinkle easily. Because you will probably be wearing the same thing several times, remember that solid colors mix best. Men should bring khakis and the essential white button-up shirt. Women should bring a simple, solid-color dress. Black is ideal because it is always in fashion. Always bring a jacket or wool sweater. As the original Easy Rider Peter Fonda said, "Pack less than you'd ever imagine … there are always laundromats."

Walking shoes: Not a place to cut corners. Well-cushioned **sneakers** are good for walking, though you may want to consider a good water-proofed pair of **hiking boots.** A double pair of socks will cushion feet, keep them dry, and help prevent blisters. Bring a pair of flip-flops for protection against the foliage and fungi that inhabit some hostel showers. Make sure you break in your shoes before you leave.

Rain gear: Essential. A waterproof jacket and a backpack cover will take care of you and your stuff at a moment's notice. Gore-Tex® is a miracle fabric that's both waterproof and breathable; it's all but mandatory if you plan on hiking. Avoid cotton.

MISCELLANEOUS

Only Noah had a complete list. However, you will find the following items valuable: umbrella; sealable plastic bags (for damp clothes, soap, food, shampoo and other spillables); alarm clock; sun hat; moleskin (for blisters); needle and thread; safety pins; sunglasses; a personal stereo with headphones; pocketknife; plastic water bottle; string (makeshift clothesline and lashing material); towel; padlock; whistle; rubber bands; toilet paper; flashlight; cold-water soap; earplugs; insect repellant; electrical tape (for patching tears); clothespins; maps and phrasebooks; tweezers; garbage bags; sunscreen; vitamins. Some items not always readily available or affordable on the road are deodorant, razors, condoms, and tampons. It is always a good idea to bring along a **first-aid kit.** And don't forget your travel guide!

Sleepsacks: If planning to stay in **youth hostels,** make the requisite sleepsack yourself (instead of paying the linen charge). Fold a full-size sheet in half the long way, then sew it closed along the open long side and one of the short sides.

Washing clothes: *Let's Go* attempts to provide information on laundromats in the Practical Information listings for each city, but sometimes it may be in your best interest to just use a sink. Bring a small bar or tube of detergent soap, a rubber squash ball to stop up the sink, and a travel clothesline.

Electric current: In most European countries, electricity is 220 volts AC, enough to fry any 110V North American appliance. Hardware stores have adapters (which changes the shape of the plug) and a converter (which changes the voltage).

Film is expensive just about everywhere, so bring lots of film from home. If you're not a serious photographer, you might want to consider bringing a **disposable camera.** Whatever kind of camera you use, be aware that, despite disclaimers, airport security X-rays *can* fog film, so either buy a lead-lined pouch or ask the security to inspect it by hand. Always pack it in your carry-on luggage.

GETTING THERE

■ Budget Travel Agencies

Students and people under 26 ("youth") with proper ID qualify for enticing reduced airfares. These are usually available from student travel agencies (see Budget Travel

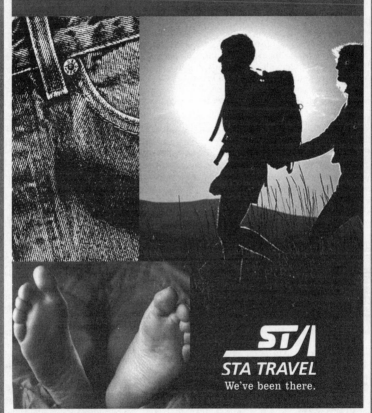

Agencies, p. 27). These agencies negotiate special reduced-rate bulk purchases with the airlines, then resell them to the youth market; in 1996, peak season round-trip rates from the East Coast of North America to even the offbeat corners of Europe rarely topped US$800 and off-season fares or fares were considerably lower. Round-trip fares from Australia or New Zealand through STA cost around US$1400. Return-date change fees also tend to be low (around US$25 per segment). Most flights are on major airlines, though in peak season some agencies may sell seats on less reliable chartered aircraft. Student agencies can also help non-students and people over 26, but probably won't be able to get the same low fares.

Council Travel (http://www.ciee.org/cts/ctshome.htm), the travel division of Council, is a full-service travel agency specializing in youth and budget travel. They offer railpasses, discount airfares, hosteling cards, guidebooks, budget tours, travel gear, and student (ISIC), youth (GO25), and teacher (ITIC) identity cards. U.S. offices include: Emory Village, 1561 N. Decatur Rd., **Atlanta,** GA 30307 (tel. (404) 377-9997); 2000 Guadalupe, **Austin,** TX 78705 (tel. (512) 472-4931); 273 Newbury St., **Boston,** MA 02116 (tel. (617) 266-1926); 1138 13th St., **Boulder,** CO 80302 (tel. (303) 447-8101); 1153 N. Dearborn, **Chicago,** IL 60610 (tel. (312) 951-0585); 10904 Lindbrook Dr., **Los Angeles,** CA 90024 (tel. (310) 208-3551); 1501 University Ave. SE, **Minneapolis,** MN 55414 (tel. (612) 379-2323); 205 E. 42nd St., **New York,** NY 10017 (tel. (212) 822-2700); 953 Garnet Ave., **San Diego,** CA 92109 (tel. (619) 270-6401); 530 Bush St., **San Francisco,** CA 94108 (tel. (415) 421-3473); 4311½ University Way, **Seattle,** WA 98105 (tel. (206) 632-2448); 3300 M St. NW, **Washington, D.C.** 20007 (tel. (202) 337-6464). **For U.S. cities not listed,** call 800-2-COUNCIL (226-8624). Also 28A Poland St. (Oxford Circus), **London,** W1V 3DB (tel. (0171) 437 7767).

STA Travel, 6560 Scottsdale Rd. #F100, Scottsdale, AZ 85253 (tel. (800) 777-0112 nationwide; fax (602) 922-0793). A student and youth travel organization with over 100 offices worldwide offering discount airfares for young travelers, railpasses, accommodations, tours, insurance, and ISICs. 16 offices in the U.S. including: 297 Newbury Street, **Boston,** MA 02115 (tel. (617) 266-6014); 429 S. Dearborn St., **Chicago,** IL 60605 (tel. (312) 786-9050); 7202 Melrose Ave., **Los Angeles,** CA 90046 (tel. (213) 934-8722); 10 Downing St., Ste. G, **New York,** NY 10003 (tel. (212) 627-3111); 4341 University Way NE, **Seattle,** WA 98105 (tel. (206) 633-5000); 2401 Pennsylvania Ave., **Washington, DC** 20037 (tel. (202) 887-0912); 51 Grant Ave., **San Francisco,** CA 94108 (tel. (415) 391-8407), **Miami,** FL 33133 (tel. (305) 461-3444). In the U.K., 6 Wrights Ln., **London** W8 6TA (tel. (0171) 938 47 11 for North American travel). In New Zealand, 10 High St., **Auckland** (tel. (09) 309 97 23). In Australia, 222 Faraday St., **Melbourne** VIC 3050 (tel. (03) 349 69 11).

Let's Go Travel, Harvard Student Agencies, 67 Mt. Auburn St., Cambridge, MA 02138 (tel. (800) 5-LETS GO (553-8746) or (617) 495-9649). Railpasses, HI-AYH memberships, ISICs, ITICs, FIYTO cards, guidebooks, maps, bargain flights, and a complete line of budget travel gear. All items available by mail; catalog featured in this book.

Campus Travel, 52 Grosvenor Gardens, London SW1W 0AG (http://www.campus-travel.co.uk.) 41 branches in the U.K. Student and youth fares on plane, train, boat, and bus travel. Flexible airline tickets. Discount and ID cards for youths, travel insurance for students and those under 35, and maps and guides. Puts out travel suggestion booklets. Telephone booking service: in Europe call (0171) 730 3402; in North America call (0171) 730 2101; worldwide call (0171) 730 8111; in Manchester call (0161) 273 1721; in Scotland (0131) 668 3303. For more information, visit their web site (http://www.campustravel.co.uk).

Eurolines, 52 Grosvenor Gardens Victoria, London SW1W 0AU (main office tel. (01582) 404 511, in London (0171) 730 8235). Specializes in coach travel all over Europe. Open April-Oct. Mon.-Sat. 8am-8pm; June 18-Sept. 10 Sun. 10am-4pm; all other times Mon.-Sat. 8-6.

Travel CUTS (Canadian Universities Travel Services Limited): 187 College St., Toronto, Ont. M5T 1P7 (tel. (416) 979-2406; fax 979-8167; e-mail mail@travelcuts). Canada's national student travel bureau and equivalent of Council, with 40 offices across Canada. Also in the U.K., 295-A Regent St., **London** W1R 7YA (tel. (0171) 637 3161). Discounted domestic and international airfares open to all; special student fares to all destinations with valid ISIC. Issues ISIC, FIYTO, GO25, and HI hostel cards, as well as railpasses. Offers free *Student Traveler* magazine, as well as information on the Student Work Abroad Program (SWAP).

Usit Youth and Student Travel, 19-21 Aston Quay, O'Connell Bridge, Dublin 2 (tel. (01) 602 1200; fax 671 2408). In the USA: New York Student Center, 895 Amsterdam Ave., New York, NY, 10025 (tel. (212) 663 5435). Additional offices in Cork, Galway, Limerick, Waterford, Maynooth, Coleraine, Derry, Athlone, Jordanstown, Belfast, and Greece. Specializes in youth and student travel. Offers low cost tickets and flexible travel arrangements all over the world. Supplies ISIC and FIYTO-GO25 cards.

Wasteels, 7041 Grand National Drive #207, Orlando, FL 32819 (tel. (407) 351-2537; in **London** (0171) 834 7066). A huge chain in Europe, with 200 locations. Information in English can be requested from the London office (tel. 4471-834-7066; fax (4471-630-7628). Sells the Wasteels BIJ tickets, which are discounted (30-45% off regular fare) 2nd-class international train tickets with unlimited stopovers (must be under 26 on the first day of travel); sold only in Europe.

■ By Plane

The first challenge to the budget traveler is getting there. The **airline industry** attempts to squeeze every dollar from customers. Call every toll-free number and don't be afraid to ask about discounts. Have several knowledgeable **travel agents** guide you; better yet, have an agent who specializes in the region(s) you will be travelling to guide you. **TravelHUB** (http://www.travelhub.com) will help you search for travel agencies on the web. Also try the **Air Traveler's Handbook** (http://www.cis.ohio-state.edu/hypertext/faq/usenet/travel/air/handbook/top.html).

Most airfares peak between mid-June and early September. Midweek (Mon.-Thurs. morning) round-trip flights run about US$40-50 cheaper than on weekends. Traveling from hubs such as New York, Atlanta, Dallas, Chicago, Los Angeles, San Francisco, Vancouver, Toronto, Sydney, Melbourne, Brisbane, Auckland, or Wellington to Frankfurt will win a more competitive fare than from smaller cities. Flying to London is usually the cheapest way across the Atlantic, though special fares to other cities such as Amsterdam, Luxembourg, or Brussels, which are conveniently close to Germany, can be even lower. Traveling with an "open return" ticket can be pricier than fixing a return date and paying to change it.

COMMERCIAL AIRLINES

The commercial airlines' lowest regular offer is the **APEX** (Advance Purchase Excursion Fare); specials advertised in newspapers may be cheaper, but have more restrictions and fewer available seats. APEX fares provide you with confirmed reservations and allow "open-jaw" tickets (landing in and returning from different cities). Generally, reservations must be made seven to 21 days in advance. Book APEX fares early during the peak season; by May you will have a hard time getting the departure date you want. The national airline of Germany—**Deutsche Lufthansa** (tel. (800) 645-3880 in the U.S.; (416) 368-4777 in Canada)—serves the most cities, but fares tend to be high.

Look into flights to less-popular destinations or on smaller carriers. **Icelandair** (tel. (800) 223-5500) has last-minute offers and a stand-by fare from New York to Luxembourg, convenient to Cologne and the Rhineland (April-June 15 and Sept.-Oct. US$398; June 15-Aug. US$598). Reservations must be made within three days of departure. Even if you pay an airline's lowest published fare, you may waste hundreds of dollars. But before shopping around, it is a good idea to find out the average commercial price in order to measure just how great a "bargain" you are getting.

TICKET CONSOLIDATORS

Ticket consolidators resell unsold tickets on commercial and charter airlines at unpublished fares. Consolidator flights are the best deals if you are traveling: on short notice; on a high-priced trip; to an offbeat destination; or in the peak season, when published fares are jacked way up. Unlike tickets bought through an airline, you won't be able to use your tickets on another flight if you miss yours, and you will have to go back to the consolidator to get a refund. These tickets are often for coach seats on connecting (not direct) flights on airlines, and frequent-flyer miles may not be credited.

Consolidators come in three varieties: wholesale only, who sell only to travel agencies; specialty agencies (both wholesale and retail); and **"bucket shops"** or discount retail agencies. As a private consumer, you can deal directly only with the latter, but you have access to a larger market if you use a travel agent, who can also get tickets from wholesale consolidators. Look for bucket shops' tiny ads in weekend papers (in the U.S., the *Sunday New York Times* Travel Section is best). In London, the Air Travel Advisory Bureau (tel. (0171) 636 5000) provides a list of consolidators. Be a smart and careful shopper. Among the many reputable and trustworthy companies are, unfortunately, some shady wheeler-dealers. Ask to receive your tickets as quickly as possible and get the company's policy in writing: insist on a **receipt** that gives full details about the tickets, refunds, and restrictions. Ask also about accommodations and car rental discounts; some consolidators have fingers in many pies.

For destinations worldwide, try **Airfare Busters,** with offices in Washington, D.C. (tel. (800) 776-0481, Boca Raton, FL (tel. (800) 881-3273), and Houston, TX (tel. (232-8783). For a processing fee, **Travel Avenue,** Chicago, IL (tel. (800) 333-3335) will search for the lowest international airfare available and even give you a rebate on fares over US$300; also try **Rebel,** Valencia, CA (tel. (800) 227-3235) or Orlando, FL (tel. (800) 732-3588; or **Discount Travel International,** New York, NY (tel. (212) 362-3636; fax 362-3236).

Kelly Monaghan's *Consolidators: Air Travel's Bargain Basement* (US$7 plus US$2 shipping) from the Intrepid Traveler, P.O. Box 438, New York, NY 10034 (e-mail intreptrav@aol.com), is an source for information and lists of consolidators by location. Cyber-resources include **World Wide** (http://www.tmn.com/wwwanderer/WWWa) and Edward Hasbrouck's incredibly informative **Airline ticket consolidators and bucket shops** (http://www.gnn.com/gnn/wic/wics/trav.97.html).

STAND-BY FLIGHTS

Airhitch, 2641 Broadway, Third Floor, New York, NY 10025 (tel. (800) 326-2009 or (212) 864-2000) and Los Angeles, CA (tel. (310) 726-5000), will add a certain thrill to the prospects of when you will leave and where exactly you will end up. Complete flexibility on both sides of the Atlantic is necessary; flights cost US$169 each way when departing from the Northeast, US$269 from the West Coast or Northwest, and US$229 from the Southeast and Midwest. The snag is that you buy not a ticket, but the promise that you will get to a destination near where you're intending to go within a window of time (usually 5 days) from a location in a region you've specified. You call in before your date-range to hear all of your flight options for the next seven days and your probability of boarding. You then decide which flights you want to try to make and present a voucher at the airport which grants you the right to board a flight on a space-available basis. This procedure must be followed again for the return trip. Be aware that you may only receive a refund if all available flights which departed within your date and destination-range were full. There are several offices in Europe, so you can wait to register for your return; the main one is in Paris (tel. (1) 47 00 16 30). **Air-Tech, Ltd.,** 584 Broadway #1007, New York, NY 10012 (tel. (212) 219-7000; fax 219-0066) offers a very similar service. Their Travel Window is one to four days; rates to and from Europe (continually updated; call and verify) are: Northeast US$169; West Coast US$249; Midwest/Southeast US$199. Be sure to read all the fine print in your agreements with either company.

CHARTER FLIGHTS

The theory behind a **charter** is that a tour operator contracts with an airline (usually one specializing in charters) to fly extra loads of passengers to peak-season destinations. Charter flights fly less frequently than major airlines and have more restrictions, particularly on refunds. They are also almost always fully booked, and schedules and itineraries may change or be cancelled at the last moment (as late as 48 hr. before the trip, and without a full refund); you'll be much better off purchasing a ticket on a regularly scheduled airline. As always, pay with a credit card.

Try **Interworld** (tel. (305) 443-4929); **Travac** (tel. (800) 872-8800); or **Rebel,** Valencia, CA (tel. (800) 227-3235) or Orlando, FL (tel. (800) 732-3588).

Eleventh-hour **discount clubs** and **fare brokers** offer members savings on European travel, including charter flights and tour packages. Research your options carefully. **Last Minute Travel Club,** 1249 Boylston St., Boston, MA 02215 (tel. (800) 527-8646 or (617) 267-9800), and **Discount Travel International** New York, NY (tel. (212) 362-3636; fax 362-3236) are among the few travel clubs that don't charge a membership fee. Others include **Moment's Notice** New York, NY (tel. (718) 234-6295; fax (718) 234 6450); US$25 annual fee) and **Travelers Advantage**, Stamford, CT, (tel. (800) 835-8747; US$49 annual fee); and **Travel Avenue** (tel. (800) 333-3335). Study these organizations' contracts closely; you don't want to end up with an unwanted overnight layover.

COURIER FLIGHTS

Those who travel light should consider flying to Europe as a **courier.** The company hiring you will use your checked luggage space for freight; you're only allowed to bring carry-ons. You are responsible for the safe delivery of the baggage claim slips to the representative waiting for you when you arrive. Restrictions to watch for: you must be over 18, have a valid passport, and procure your own visa; most flights are round-trip only with short fixed-length stays (usually one week); only single tickets are issued; and most flights are from New York. Round-trip fares to Western Europe from the U.S. range from US$250-400 (during the off-season) to US$400-550 (during the summer). **NOW Voyager,** 74 Varick St. #307, New York, NY 10013 (tel. (212) 431-1616), acts as an agent for many courier flights worldwide primarily from New York. They offer special deals to Frankfurt for as little as US$200 round-trip plus a US$50 registration fee. Other agents to try are **Halbart Express,** 147-05 176th St., Jamaica, NY 11434 (tel. (718) 656-5000), **Courier Travel Service,** 530 Central Avenue, Cedarhurst, NY 11516 (tel. (516) 763-6898), and **Discount Travel International** (tel. (212) 362-3636).

You can also go directly through courier companies in New York, or check your bookstore or library for handbooks such as *Air Courier Bargains* (US$15 plus US$3.50 shipping from the Intrepid Traveler, P.O. Box 438, New York, NY 10034). *The Courier Air Travel Handbook* (US$10 plus US$3.50 shipping) explains how to travel as an air courier and contains names, phone numbers, and contact points of courier companies. It can be ordered directly from Bookmasters, Inc., P.O. Box 2039, Mansfield, OH 44905 (tel. (800) 507-2665).

■ By Train

European trains retain the charm and romance their North American counterparts lost long ago, but don't forget you're in the modern world. Bring food and a water bottle you can fill at your hostel and take with you on train trips; the on-board café can be pricey, and train water undrinkable. Trains are not theft-proof; lock your compartment door if you can, and keep your valuables on your person at all times.

Many train stations have different counters for domestic and international tickets, seat reservations, and info—check before lining up. On major lines, reservations are always advisable, and often required, even with a railpass; make them at least a few hours in advance at the train station (US$3-10). Also, while use of many of Europe's high speed or quality trains (such as EuroCity, InterCity, Sweden's X2000, or France's TGV) is included in the price of a railpass, a supplement is required to ride certain other trains, such as Spain's AVE and Italy's ETR (usually around US$10). You can sometimes pay for this supplement on board, but that costs a bit more.

A sleeping berth in a couchette car is an affordable luxury (about US$20; reserve at the station at least several days in advance). Very few countries give students or young people direct discounts on regular domestic rail tickets, but many will sell a student or youth card valid for 20-50% off all fares for an entire year.

■ By Ferry

Travel by boat is a bewitching alternative much favored by Europeans but overlooked by most foreigners. Most European ferries are comfortable and well-equipped. You should check in at least two hours early for a prime spot and allow plenty of time for late trains and getting to the port. Fares jump sharply in July and August. Ask for discounts; ISIC holders can often get student fares, and Eurail passholders get many reductions and free trips (check the brochure that comes with your railpass). You'll occasionally have to pay a small port tax (under US$10).

Ferries in the **North Sea** and **Baltic Sea** are universally reliable and go everywhere. Ferries run from Rostock, Kiel, Lübeck, Hamburg, and Rügen Island to Scandinavia, Russia, and England. Those content with deck passage rarely need to book ahead. The best American source for info on British and Scandinavian ferries and visa-free cruises to Russia is **EuroCruises,** 303 W. 13th St., New York, NY 10014 (tel. (800) 688-3876 or (212) 691-2099). **Riverboats** acquaint you with many towns that trains can only wink at. For more details, see By Boat, p. 40.

ONCE THERE

■ Tourist Offices

Every German town of any touristic importance whatsoever is served by a local tourist office. These go by a bewildering variety of names—*Verkehrsamt, Fremdenverkehrsbüro, Verkehrsverein, Fremdenverkehrsverein, Tourist-Information, Gemeindeamt,* and (in spa towns) *Kurverwaltung* or *Kurverein.* To simplify things, all are marked by a standard thick lowercase "i" sign. Tourist offices are usually located in the town square or by the main train station—sometimes both. Exploit these offices for city maps (often free), cycling routes and rental options, information on sights and museums, and lists of accommodations. Many offices will track down a vacant room for you and make a reservation, sometimes for free, otherwise for DM2--5. The major caveat is that, while western German tourist personnel can be relied upon to speak fluent English, the situation is quite otherwise in the eastern half of the country. Here, most schoolchildren were made to learn Russian instead of English, and non-German speakers may occasionally encounter difficulties. *Let's Go* lists tourist offices in the Practical Information sections.

■ Embassies and Consulates

If you're seriously ill or in trouble, your embassy can provide a list of doctors or pertinent legal advice, and can also contact your relatives. In *extreme* cases, they can offer emergency financial assistance. Embassies are located in Bonn; consulates can be found in other major cities. For the addresses of consulates not listed here, check the Practical Information sections of individual cities.

United States: Embassy *(Botschaft der Vereinigte Staaten von Amerika):* **Bonn,** Deichmanns Aue 29, 53179 (tel. (0228) 339 20 53; fax 339 26 63). **Consulates: Berlin,** Clayallee 170, 14169 (tel. (030) 832 49 87; consulate section tel. (030) 819 74 54). **Frankfurt Am Main,** Siesmayerstr. 21, 60323 (tel. (069) 753 50); **Leipzig,** Wilhelm-Seyfferth-Str. 4, 04107 (tel. (0341) 211 78 66). **Hamburg,** Alsterufer 27, 20354 (tel. (040) 41 17 13 51). **Munich,** Königinstr 5, 80539 (tel. (089) 29 06 50). **Stuttgart,** Urbanstr. 7, 70182 (tel. (0711) 21 00 80).
Canada: Embassy *(Botschaft von Kanada):* **Bonn,** Friedrich-Wilhelm-Str. 18, 53133 (tel. (0228) 96 80; fax 968 39 04). **Consulates: Berlin,** Friedrichstr. 95, 10117 (tel. (030) 261 11 61); **Düsseldorf,** Yorckstr. 19, 40476 (tel. (0211) 944 80). **Hamburg,** ABC-Str. 45, 20354 (tel. (040) 35 55 62 90; fax 35 55 62 94). **Munich,** Tal 29, 80331 (tel. (089) 29 06 50).
U.K.: Embassy *(Botschaft des Vereinigten Königreichs):* **Berlin,** Unter Den Linden 32-34 10117 (tel. (030) 20 18 40). **Consulates: Düsseldorf,** Yorckstr. 19, 40476 (tel. (0211) 944 80). **Frankfurt Am Main,** Generalkonsulat, Bockenheimer Landstr. 42, 60323 (tel. (069) 170 00 20). **Hamburg,** Harvestehuferweg 8a, 20148 (tel. (040) 448 03 20). **Hanover,** Berliner Allee 5, 30175 (tel. (0511) 388 38 08). **Munich,** Bürkheinstr. 10, 4th flr. (tel. (089) 21 10 90). **Stuttgart,** Breite-Str. 2, 70173 (tel. (0711) 16 26 90). The **Bonn** embassy has no consular services.
Australia: Embassy *(Australische Botschaft):* **Bonn,** Godesberger Allee 105-107, 53175 (tel. (0228) 810 30; fax 37 62 68). **Consulates: Berlin,** Uhlandstr. 181-3 (tel. (030) 880 08 80). **Frankfurt am Main,** Gutleutstr. 85, 60329 (tel. (069) 273 90 90).
Ireland: Embassy *(Botschaft von Irland):* **Bonn,** Godesberger Allee 119, 53175 (tel. (0228) 37 69 37 or 37 69 39). **Consulates: Berlin,** Ernst-Reuter-Platz 10, 10587 (tel. (030) 34 80 08 22). **Munich,** Mauerkircherstr. 1a, 81679 (tel. (089) 98 57 23 or 98 57 23 25).
New Zealand: Embassy *(Botschaft von Neuseeland):* **Bonn,** Bundeskanzlerplatz 2-10, 53113 (tel. (0228) 22 80 70; fax 22 16 87).

South Africa: Consulats: Berlin, Douglasstr. 9, 14171 (tel./fax (030) 82 50 11). **Munich:** Sendlinger-Tor-Platz 5, 80366 (tel. (089) 231 16 30).

■ Getting Around

BY PLANE

More than 100 international airlines serve Germany, but flying across the country is generally expensive and unnecessary. Nearly all airlines cater to business travelers and set prices accordingly. If you are 24 or under, special fares on most European airlines requiring ticket purchase either the day before or the day of departure are an exception to this rule. These are often cheaper than the corresponding regular train fare, though not always as cheap as student rail tickets or railpasses. The headquarters for **Lufthansa German Airlines,** the national carrier (tel. (0221) 82 60), are at Deutsche Lufthansa AG, Von-Gablenz-Str. 2-6, 50679 Cologne. Its air hub is located in Frankfurt am Main; from there, all its destinations can be reached in an average of 50 minutes. *Let's Go* lists airports and flight information telephone numbers in the Practical Information sections of major cities. Usually, S-Bahn or buses run between the airport and the nearest city's main train station.

BY TRAIN

"The trains run on time." It's a cliché, almost a joke, and not infallibly true. At the same time, it points out an important truth about getting around in Germany—if the trains aren't perfect, they do go almost everywhere a traveler would want to go, with the exception of some very rural areas. In fact, the train system's obligation to run line to inaccessible areas, even at a loss, is written into Germany's Basic Law. The **Deutsche Bahn** sprung from the integration of the western **Deutsche Bundesbahn (DB)** and old eastern **Deutsche Reichsbahn (DR).** Integration is still taking place; many connections are as yet incomplete. Moving from west to east, there are significant differences in quality and service. One problem is connections; on an indirect route, allow about twice as much time as you would in the west. Averaging over 120kph including stops and connecting some 7000 locations, the DB network is probably Europe's best, and also one of its most expensive.

Commuter trains, marked "City-Bahn" (CB) or "Nahverkehrszug" (N), are fairly slow. "S-Bahn" trains are commuter rail lines that run from a city's center out to its suburbs; they are frequently integrated with the local subway or streetcar system. "D" and "E" (Eilzug) trains are slightly faster and "FD" trains are faster still. "InterRegio" (IR) trains, between neighboring cities, are speedy and comfortable. "IC" (InterCity) trains zoom along between major cities every hour. You must purchase a supplementary "IC Zuschlag" to ride an "IC" or "EC" train (DM6 when bought in the station, DM8 on the train). Even the IC yields to the futuristic-looking InterCity Express (ICE) trains, which approach the luxury and speed of an airplane: they run at speeds up to 174mph. For these, railpass users usually do not pay a *Zuschlag,* unless the train requires a mandatory seat reservation fee.

Most German cities have a main train station; in German, *der Hauptbahnhof.* (This is the point referred to when *Let's Go* gives directions "from the station.") In train stations, yellow signs indicate departures *(Abfahrt),* white signs indicate arrivals *(Ankunft).* The number next to *"Gleis"* is the track number.

The railway system of Germany is perhaps the best in Europe. Second-class travel is pleasant, and compartments (seating six) are excellent places to meet friendly folks of all ages and nationalities. Many train stations have different counters for domestic tickets, international tickets, seat reservations, and information; check before lining up. On major lines, reservations are always advisable even if you have a railpass; make them at least a few hours in advance at the train station.

Railpasses Ideally conceived, a railpass allows you to jump on any train in Europe, go wherever you want whenever you want, and change your plans at will. The handbook that comes with your railpass tells includes a timetable for major routes, a map, and details on ferry discounts. You still must stand in line to pay for seat reservations, supplements, and couchette reservations, as well as to have your pass validated when you first use it. However, railpasses don't always pay off. Find a travel agent with a copy of the **Eurail tariff manual** to weigh the wisdom of purchasing them. Add up the second-class fares for your planned routes and deduct 5% for comparison. If you're under age 26, the BIJ tickets are probably a viable option (see Rail Tickets, p. 39).

Eurailpass, P.O. Box 10383, Stamford, CT 06904, remains the best option in European rail passes for non-EU travelers. Eurailpasses are valid in most of continental Europe. Eurailpasses and Europasses are designed by the EU itself, and are only purchasable by non-Europeans from non-European distributors. The first-class **Eurailpass** rarely pays off; it is offered for 15 days (US$522), 21 days (US$678), one month (US$838), two months (US$1148), or three months (US$1468). If you are traveling in a group, you might prefer the **Eurail Saverpass,** which allows unlimited first-class travel for 15 days (US$452), 21 days (US$578), or one month (US$712) per person in groups of two or more (3 or more April-Sept.). Travelers under age 26 on their first day of travel can buy a **Eurail Youthpass,** good for 15 days (US$418), one month (US$598), or two months (US$798) of second-class travel. It's hard to get your money's worth from a one-month pass; the two-month pass is more economical. **Eurail Flexipasses** allow limited first-class travel within a two-month period (10 days US$616, 15 days US$812). **Youth Flexipasses,** for those under 26 who wish to travel second-class, are available for US$438 or US$588, respectively. Missing as of 1996 is the former 5-day Flexipass option.

The **Europass** allows travelers to combine the most popular European countries in one travel plan. Europass offers rail travel through a number of countries determined by the number of travel days selected. For instance, a five- to seven-day trip allows you unlimited travel in three of the participating countries, an eight- to 10-day trip allows you four and an 11- to 15-day trip allows unlimited travel in all five countries. If you take one of the first two options, the three or four countries you visit must be adjacent to each other. First class prices begin at US$316 (US$237 for two adults traveling together at all times) and the second class youth version (which starts with 5-10 travel days in 4 countries) at US$210. All passes are valid for two months and come with options for increasing the number of days of travel (for an additional fee). The Europass introduces planning complications that are not present with a simple Eurailpass; you must plan your routes so that they only make use of countries that you've "purchased." You can also add other associate countries for a nominal fee. Europasses are not appropriate if you like to take lots of side trips and day trips from big destinations. Also, if you are tempted to add lots of extra rail days and lots of associate countries, you should consider the cheaper Eurailpass.

You'll almost certainly find it easiest to buy a Eurailpass before you arrive in Europe; contact Council Travel, Travel CUTS, or Let's Go Travel, or any of many other travel agents (see p. 27). If you're stuck in Europe and unable to find someone to sell you a Eurailpass, make a transatlantic call to an American railpass agent, who should be able to send a pass by express mail. Eurailpasses are not refundable once validated; you can get a replacement for a lost pass only if you have purchased insurance on it under the Pass Protection Plan (US$10) offered by railpass agents. All Eurailpasses can be purchased from a travel agent or from **Rail Europe, Inc.,** 226-230 Westchester Ave., White Plains, NY 10604 in the U.S. (tel. (800) 438-7245; fax (800) 432-1329; and in Canada (800) 361-7245); fax (905) 602-4198; http://www.raileurope.com), which publishes the free *Europe on Track.*

For EU citizens who cannot get Eurail passes, there are **InterRail** passes, for which six months' residence in Europe makes you eligible. The Under 26 InterRail Card allows either 15 days or 1 month of unlimited travel within 1, 2, 3, or all of the 7 zones into which InterRail divides Europe; the cost is determined by the number of zones the pass is to cover. Prices begin at UK£185. The Over 26 InterRail Card offers unlimited 2nd-class travel in 19 countries in Europe for 15 days or 1 month for UK£215 and £275, respectively. Tickets are available from travel agents.

Youth and Student Fares For travelers under 26 on their first day of travel, **BIJ** tickets (Billets Internationals de Jeunesse, sold under the names **Wasteels, Eurotrain,** and **Route 26**) are a great alternative to railpasses. Available for international trips within Europe and for travel within France as well as most ferry services, they knock 25-40% off regular second-class fares. Tickets are all good for 60 days after purchase and allow a number of stopovers along the normal direct route of the train journey. Issued for a specific international route between two points, they must be used in the direction and order of the designated route without side- or back-tracking. You must buy BIJ tickets in Europe. They are available from European travel agents, at Wasteels or Eurotrain offices (usually in or near train stations), or directly at the ticket counter in some nations. Contact Wasteels in London's Victoria Station, adjacent to Platform 2 (tel. (0171) 834 70 66; fax 630 76 28).

German Railpasses Non-Germans can purchase the tourist-oriented **German Railpass** in their home countries. The pass allows 5, 10, or 15 days of rail travel within a one-month period on all DB trains (for info on types of trains, see p. 35). The first-class version costs US$260 for five days, US$410 for 10 days, and US$530 for 15 days in a month. The second-class version costs US$178 for five days, US$286 for 10 days, and US$386 for 15. There is also a **German Rail Youth Pass** version, available to non-Germans age 12-25, which comes only in a second-class version. It costs US$138 for five days, US$188 for 10, and US$238 for 15.

There are also several "internal" national railpasses, which can *only* be purchased once you've arrived. For anyone under age 27, a decent deal is the **Tramper-Ticket,** which allows you to pick 10 days of unlimited second-class rail travel in a month on all DB trains (including the ICE), the railroad-run buses *(Bahnbusse),* and the local S-Bahns in cities, all for DM349. The pass is only available between June 15 and October 15. Note that the Tramper-Ticket is a *new* pass from Deutsche Bahn.

The **BahnCard** is a very good option for those planning to make extensive use of German trains. It is valid for one year, and gets you a 50% discount on all rail tickets, DB and DR alike, including the ICE. A second-class BahnCard is a great deal for young travelers: students under 27 and anyone under 23 can get one for DM110; first-class cards are DM220. Seniors over 60 can get BahnCards at the same discounts. (Normal rates are DM220 second-class; DM440 first-class.) Crazier still: starting in 1995, BahnCards have been used as **credit cards** for many sorts of purchases in Germany. See a DB brochure for details. Passes are only available at major train stations throughout Germany, and all require a small photo. You may contact **Deutsche Bundesbahn** in Germany at Rhabanusstr. 3 55118 Mainz; in the US at 9501 W. Devon Ave. Rosemont, IL 60018-4832 (tel. (800) 782-2424; fax (800) 282-7474); or in Canada at 904 The East Mall Etobicoke, Ontario M9B 6K2 (tel. (416) 695-1211; fax 695-4700).

Useful Resources The ultimate reference for planning rail trips is the **Thomas Cook European Timetable** (US$28; US$39 includes a map of Europe highlighting all train and ferry routes; postage US$4.50). This timetable, updated regularly, covers all major and most minor train routes in Europe. In the U.S., order it from Forsyth Travel Library (see Useful Publications, p. 2). Available in most bookstores or from **Houghton Mifflin Co.,** 222 Berkeley St., Boston, MA 02116 (tel. (617) 351-5974; fax 351-1113) is the annual **Eurail Guide to Train Travel in the New Europe** (US$15), giving timetables, instructions, and prices for international train trips, daytrips, and excursions in Europe. The annual railpass special edition of Rick Steves' free **Europe Through the Back Door** travel newsletter and catalog, 120 Fourth Ave. N., P.O. Box 2009, Edmonds, WA 98020 (tel. (206) 771-8303; fax 771-0833; e-mail ricksteves@aol.com; http://www.halcyon.com) provides a comprehensive comparative

analysis of European railpasses with national or regional passes and point-to-point tickets sold in Europe.

BY BUS

Germany does have a few regions inaccessible by train, and some bus lines fill the gap. Bus service between cities and to small, outlying towns usually run from the *Zentral Omnibus Bahnhof (ZOB),* which is often near the main train station. Buses are usually slightly more expensive than the train for comparable distances. Check the bulletin boards in university buildings or the classified pages of local magazines for occasional deals. Railpasses are not valid on any buses other than those (relatively few) run by the national rail company (DB). Most lines are run either by regional or local public transit authorities, or by private companies.

BY CAR

Cars offer great speed and freedom, access to the countryside, and an escape from the town-to-town mentality of trains. Unfortunately, they also insulate you from the *esprit de corps* that European rail travelers enjoy. Although a single traveler won't save by renting a car, four usually will. If you can't decide between train and car travel, you may benefit from a combination of the two; Rail Europe and other railpass vendors offer economical rail-and-drive packages for both individual countries and all of Europe. Travel agents may have other rail-and-drive packages, including the German Rail's **Rail 'n' Drive Pass.**

Americans and Canadians may drive for one year in Germany with a valid national or international license (see International Driver's Permit, p. 7). The national license must be officially translated by a German diplomatic office, an international motor vehicle office in the country where the license was issued, or a German automobile club (see ADAC below). If you are planning to stay in Germany for more than one year, you must obtain a German driver's license, available upon presentation of your national license. Vehicle liability insurance is required by law in Germany. Foreign motorists must present the green international insurance card or purchase temporary insurance at the point of entry.

You can **rent** a car from a U.S.-based firm with its own European offices, from a European-based company with local representatives, or from a tour operator. Expect to pay US$125-500 a week, plus tax (5-25%), for a teensy car. Rates are lower in Germany than elsewhere in Europe. Ask your airline about special packages; you may get a week of free rental. Try **Auto Europe,** 39 Commercial St., Portland, ME (tel. (800) 223-5555); **Avis Rent a Car** (tel. (800) 331-1084); **Bon Voyage By Car** (tel. (800) 272-3299; in Canada (800) 253-3876); **Budget Rent a Car** (tel. (800) 472-3325); **Europe by Car,** One Rockefeller Plaza, New York, NY 10020 (tel. (800) 223-1516 or (212) 581-3040; fax (212) 246-1458); **Europcar,** 145 Avenue Malekoff, 75016 Paris (tel. (800) 227-3876; (800) 227-7368 in Canada; (1) 45 00 08 06 in France); and **Hertz Rent a Car** (tel. (800) 654-3001).

If you're brave and know what you're doing, **buying** a used car or van in Europe and selling it just before you leave can provide the cheapest wheels on the Continent for longer trips. David Shore and Patty Campbell's **Europe by Van and Motorhome** (US$14; postage US$2, overseas US$6) guides you through the entire process of renting, leasing, buying, and selling vehicles on the Continent. Write to Shore/Campbell Publications, 1842 Santa Margarita Dr., Fallbrook, CA 92028 (tel./fax (800) 659-5222 or (619) 723-6184). **How to Buy and Sell a Used Car in Europe** (US$6, postage US$1; from Gil Friedman, 1735 J Street, Arcata, CA 95521, tel. (707) 822-5001) contains practical info on wrangling for a used car in Europe. Before setting off, be sure you know the laws of the countries in which you'll be driving. The **Association for Safe International Road Travel (ASIRT)** can provide more information about conditions in specific countries. They are located at 5413 West Cedar Lane, Suite 103C, Bethesda, MD 20814 (tel. (301) 983-5252; fax 983-3663).

Yes, Virginia, there really is no speed limit on the *Autobahn*. Germans drive *fast;* before venturing on the road, be *very* familiar with traffic rules and especially signs and symbols. Germans drive on the right side of the road. It is dreadfully **illegal to pass on the right,** *even on superhighways.* When not otherwise indicated, the speed limit in Western Germany is 100kph (62mph) for passenger cars, 50kph (31 mph) in cities and towns. The recommended speed on the *Autobahn* is 130kph (81 mph), but if you drive that slowly in the left lane, cars will loom in your rear-view mirror with lights flashing. Passenger cars with trailers are limited to 80kph (50 mph). In Eastern Germany, the speed limit for cars on the highway is 100kph in rural areas, 80kph in urban ones. Drivers might want to know that dotting the *Autobahn* along its 10,000 toll-free kilometers are 169 restaurants and 268 service stations open 24 hours per day.

German law requires that both front and back seat passengers wear **seat belts;** motorcycle drivers and riders must wear **helmets** if traveling over 24kph. Children under 12 may not sit in the front seat unless special seats have been installed. Studded snow tires are also *verboten.* The maximum permissible **blood alcohol** content is 0.08%, lower than the limit in the United States, and even lower amounts are illegal if you're involved in a violation—basically, if you even *think* of alcohol, you're probably over the limit. Other rules and regulations apply; for more information, contact **Allgemeiner Deutscher Automobil Club e.v. (ADAC)** by mail at: Redaktion ADAC Motorwelt, 81360 München, or visit the office once in Germany at Am Westpark 8, Munich-Sendling (tel. (089) 767 60; emergency tel. (089) 22 22 22; fax 76 76 25 00). Or contact **Automobil Club von Deutschland (AvD),** Lyoner-Str. 16, 60528 Frankfurt-Neiderrad (tel. (069) 66 03 60, emergency (069) 660 66 00). ADAC maintains **Straßenwachthilfe** units which patrol the roads and assist disabled vehicles. ADAC will provide **road assistance** free of charge if the damage can be repaired within half an hour; if not, you'll pay repair and towing fees. Orange emergency telephones indicated by blue *Notruf* (emergency call) signs summon the free service. A critically important word is **Stau,** meaning "traffic jam"—Germany has plenty. Tune into local radio stations for traffic reports.

BY BOAT

River boat and motor boat services abound on many inland waters in Germany. In addition to connecting towns within Germany, many passenger and car ferries make connections to offshore islands (the Frisian Islands, for example) in the North and Baltic Seas. On the Danube, Elbe, Main, Mosel, Neckar, Rhine, Oder, Saale, and Weser rivers you can hop a ferry and enjoy seeing Germany from a new perspective. The Mosel, Rhine and Danube steamers have been overrun by tourists; less commercial-looking lines can be more alluring. *Let's Go* details schedules in many towns. Be sure to ask about discounts if you're holding any kind of railpass or ISIC. The German Rail Youth Pass qualifies you for this special bonus: free travel on the KD River Day Steamer on the Rhine, Main, and Mosel between selected major cities.

BY BICYCLE

Today, biking is one of the key elements of the classic budget Eurovoyage. Everyone else in the youth hostel is doing it, and with the proliferation of mountain bikes, you can do some serious natural sight-seeing. Be aware that touring involves pedaling both yourself and whatever you store in the panniers (bags which strap to your bike). For info about touring routes, consult national tourist offices or any of the numerous books available. **The Mountaineers Books,** 1001 S.W. Klickitat Way #201, Seattle, WA 98134 (tel. (800) 553-4453 or (206) 223-6303; fax 223-6306) offers several nation-specific tour books (Germany included), as well as **Europe By Bike,** by Karen and Terry Whitehill (US$15; shipping US$3), a great source of specific area tours in 11 countries. **Cycling Europe: Budget Bike Touring in the Old World,** by N. Slavinski (US$13), may be a good addition to your library.

If you are nervous about striking out on your own, **CBT Bicycle Tours** offers one-to seven-week tours, priced around $90 per day, including all lodging, breakfasts, one-third of all dinners, complete van support, airport transfers, and extensive route notes and maps each day. Tours run May through August, with departures every seven to 10 days. In 1997, CBT will visit Germany among other European countries. Contact CBT Bicycle Tours, 415 W. Fullerton Pkwy., #1003, Chicago, IL 60614 (tel. (800) 736-BIKE (2453) or (312) 404-1710; fax (312) 404-1833).

Germany makes biking easy with its wealth of trails and bike tours, including some organized through hostels and through the rail system. In urban areas, a bicycle can be one of the most efficient ways to get around. German cities and towns usually have designated bike lanes, sometimes in the street, and sometimes laid out in the sidewalk itself. Pedestrians should look out for tell-tale bike icons or changes in pavement color; it may look like those bikers are on the sidewalk, but they move fast, have right-of-way, and with all the conviction of self-righteous biking zeal, expect you to be the one to get out of the way—quickly.

A sturdy if unexciting one-speed model will cost US$8-12 per day; be prepared to lay down a sizable deposit. Some youth hostels rent bicycles for low prices. Bike rentals are also available at approximately 250 train stations throughout the country where German Rail's Fahrrad am Bahnhof ("Bikes at the Station") program has rentals at DM6-10 per day. Usually bikes can be rented from one station and returned at another with a deposit of some kind; ask for details at the station. For information about bike routes, regulations, and maps, contact Allgemeiner Deutscher Fahrrad-Club, Postfach 10 77 47, 28077 Bremen. The ADFC is the biggest bicycle club for commuters and touring cyclists and an invaluable source of information and support. Ask for the Fahrradtourismus Info-übersicht pamphlet (in German) by sending a self-addressed envelope along with one IRC (international reply coupon). A bike tour guidebook, including extensive maps, is available from Deutsches Jugendherbergswerk (DJH); see its address under Accommodations: Hostels, p. 43.

BY THUMB

> *Let's Go* strongly urges you to consider seriously the risks before you choose to hitch. We do not recommend hitching as a safe means of transportation, and none of the information presented here is intended to do so.

No one should hitch without careful consideration of the risks involved. Not everyone can be an airplane pilot, but almost any bozo can drive a car. Hitching means risking theft, assault, sexual harassment, and unsafe driving. In spite of this, there are advantages to hitching. Favorable hitching experiences allow you to meet local people and get where you're going. The choice, however, remains yours.

Depending on the circumstances and the norms of the country, men and women traveling in groups and men traveling alone might consider hitching (called "autostop" in much of Europe) beyond the range of bus or train routes. If you are a woman traveling alone, never hitch; it's just too dangerous. A man and a woman are a safer combination, two men will have a harder time, and three will go nowhere.

Finally, success will depend on what one looks like. Successful hitchers travel light and stack their belongings in a compact but visible cluster. Most Europeans signal with an open hand, rather than a thumb; many write their destination on a sign in large, bold letters and draw a smiley-face under it. Drivers prefer hitchers who are neat and wholesome. No one stops for anyone wearing sunglasses. Safety-minded hitchers avoid getting in the back of a two-door car, and never let go of their backpacks. Hitchhiking at night can be particularly dangerous; experienced hitchers stand in well-lit places, and expect drivers to be leery of nocturnal thumbers (or open-handers). They will not get into a car that they can't get out of again in a hurry. If they ever feel threatened, they insist on being let off, regardless of where they are.

It is illegal to hitch on the *Autobahnen* (expressways). Hitchers must stand in front of the *"Autobahn"* signs at on-ramps, or at **Raststätten** (rest stops) and **Tankstellen** (gas stations). *Autobahn* hitchers will need a good map to navigate the tangled interchanges in the Rhine-Ruhr area, and should pay attention to license plates; B=Berlin, M=Munich, F=Frankfurt, HH=Hamburg. There's also plentiful hitching on the heavily traveled *Bundesstraßen,* scenic secondary roads marked by signs with a yellow diamond. **Mitfahrzentralen** (ride-share centers) pair drivers with riders, with a fee to agency (about US$20) and driver (per km). Some belong to nation-wide chains (**CityNetz Mitfahrzentrale** have computerized listings); others are local store-front operations. *Let's Go* lists *Mitfahrzentralen* under the Practical Information sections each city; check the white and yellow pages under *"Mitfahrzentrale."*

BY FOOT

Germany's grandest scenery can often be seen only by foot. *Let's Go* describes many daytrips for those who want to hoof it, but native inhabitants (Europeans are fervent, almost obsessive hikers), hostel proprietors, and fellow travelers are the best source of tips. Many European countries have hiking and mountaineering organizations; alpine clubs provide inexpensive, simple accommodations in splendid settings. **Walking Europe from Top to Bottom** by S. Margolis and G. Harmon details one of Europe's most popular trails (US$11); check your local bookstore for others.

BY PUBLIC TRANSPORTATION

Urban public transit is excellent in the west and fairly good in the east. You'll see four types in German cities: **Straßenbahn** (streetcars), **S-Bahn** (commuter rail), **U-Bahn** (subways), and regular **buses.** Eurailpass holders get free passage *only* on the S-Bahn, which, in large cities, doesn't usually go everywhere one needs to go. Berlin, Cologne, Düsseldorf, Frankfurt, Hamburg, Munich, and Stuttgart have U-Bahn systems; Hanover has partially underground streetcar lines. Consider purchasing a day card *(Tageskarte, Tagesnetzkarte)* or multiple-ride ticket (*Mehrfahrkarte* or *Sammelkarte*), which usually pay for themselves by the third ride. German subways and commuter rails (and many streetcar and bus systems) operate on an "honor system." The usual procedure is to buy your ticket from a kiosk or an automat and then **validate** it by inserting the indicated edge into a little upright box marked with an **"E"** *(Entwerten).* The ticket is then "clicked" and marked with the time at which you validated it. On subways, you must do this *before* getting in the car or, if the box is inside the car, *as soon as* you enter and before the subway begins to move. Once the doors are sealed and the train gets underway, plainclothes inspectors may appear and thrust an orange badge in your face that says *"Kontrolle."* (The adjectival description of this experience is "being controlled.") If you cannot produce a valid ticket that has been properly cancelled, you will be subject to large fines (DM60 is typical) and immense humiliation. The inspectors don't take excuses and they don't take American Express; if you can't pay up on the spot, a police officer will meet you at the next stop to take you to jail. English-speaking backpackers have a very bad reputation for *Schwarzfahren* ("black riding," or riding without a ticket), so don't expect any sympathy. If you try the "I didn't understand, I don't speak German," excuse, the inspector will brusquely point out the explanatory signs in English. "I thought my Eurailpass was valid," never works, either. Don't assume that everyone else is riding illegally because you don't see them canceling tickets; when the inspector appears, you'll discover that they're all carrying monthly passes.

■ Accommodations

Let's Go is not an exhaustive guide to budget accommodations—but we try, we really do try. Most local tourist offices distribute extensive listings free of charge and will also reserve a room for a small fee. National Tourist Offices and travel agencies will supply more complete lists of campsites and hotels.

HOTELS AND ROOMS

The cheapest hotel-style accommodations are places with *Gasthof, Gästehaus,* or *Hotel-Garni* in the name. Breakfast *(Frühstück),* almost always included, consists of rolls, butter, jam, coffee or tea, and some sausage and cheese slices. Rooms in private homes *(Privatzimmer)* or guest houses are widely available and are less expensive than hotels or *Pensionen,* though most require a minimum stay of two or more nights. Bookings are usually handled by local tourist offices, either for free or for a DM2-5 fee; in less urban areas, look for signs saying *Zimmer frei* (room available), and just knock. Finding affordable hotel rooms, or any at all, in the New Federal States of the east is generally a challenge. During the week most are booked solid, as the available pool was not ready to meet the new tide of tourists and Westerners working on reconstructing the former GDR.

Hotels are quite expensive in Germany: rock bottom for singles is US$17-20, for doubles US$22-24, and the price is never subject to haggling. Inexpensive European hotels might come as a rude shock to pampered North American travelers. A bathroom of your own is a rarity and costs extra when provided. Hot showers may also cost extra. *Pension* (guesthouse) owners run smaller establishments and will often direct you to points of interest in the town and countryside. Unmarried couples will generally have no trouble getting a room together, although couples under 21 may occasionally encounter resistance. If you wish to make reservations (at hotels or hostels), you can ensure a prompt reply by enclosing two International Postal Reply Coupons (available at any post office). Indicate your night of arrival and the number of nights you plan to stay. The hotel will send you a confirmation and may request payment for the first night. Not all hotels accept reservations, and few accept checks in U.S. currency. The **Deutscher Hotel-und Gaststättenverband e.V.** (German Hotel Association or DEHOGA) is located at Kronprinzenstr. 46, Postfach 20 04 55, 53173 Bonn (tel. (0228) 82 00 80; fax 820 08 46).

The best bet in the east is often a **private room** *(Privatzimmer)* in a home. Costs generally run DM25-35 per person, less than for comparable *Privatzimmer* in the west. This option works best if you have a rudimentary knowledge of German, since room owners prefer to lay down a few household rules before handing over the keys for the night. Simply appraise the local tourist office of your language abilities (if any) when you ask for a room reference. Travelers over 26 who would otherwise pay senior prices at youth hostels will find these rooms well within budget range.

HOSTELS

In 1908, a German named Richard Schirmann, believing that life in industrial cities was harmful to the physical and moral development of youth, built in Altena the world's first **youth hostel**—a budget dormitory that would bring travel within the means of poor youth. Germany has been a leader in hosteling ever since, and Schirmann is something of a mythic figure. Construction of hostels *(Jugendherbergen)* in Germany exploded as neo-Romantic folk groups fled the cities for the rejuvenation of the wilds. The Nazis found hostels especially useful as a resource for Hitler Youth wilderness trips.

Hostels are the hubs of the backpacker subculture that overtakes Europe every summer, providing innumerable opportunities to meet travelers from all over the world. Hostel prices are extraordinarily low—US$9-16 a night for shared rooms. Only camping is cheaper. Meals are frequently available, though they are rarely delicious. For those who wish to cook for themselves, many hostels have fully equipped kitchen facilities. Some hostels are set in strikingly beautiful castles, others in rundown barracks far from the town center. The most common disadvantage is an early curfew—fine if you're climbing a mountain the next morning, but a distinct cramp in your style if you plan to rage in Berlin, Munich, or Cologne. Hostels generally feature dorm-style accommodations with large rooms and bunk beds; some allow families and couples to have private rooms. Some have kitchens and utensils for your use, storage areas, laundry facilities, and even bike, moped, or other rentals. Often there's also little privacy, rooms are usually segregated by sex, and you may run into more screaming pre-teen tour groups than you care to remember. Finally, there is often a lockout from morning to mid-afternoon. Sheet sleeping sacks are required at many of these hostels. Sleeping bags are usually prohibited (for sanitary reasons), but most hostels provide free blankets. You can make your own sheet sack by folding a sheet and sewing it shut on two sides, or order one (about US$14) from Let's Go Travel or AYH (see Budget Travel Organizations, p. 27).

A **one-year membership** permits you to stay at youth hostels all over Germany at unbeatable prices. Despite the name, you need not be a youth. Most guests are ages 17 to 26, but hostels are rapidly becoming a resource for all ages (except in Bavaria; see below); travelers over 26 pay only a bit more. Many German hostels are open to families. It's best to procure a membership card before you leave home; some hostels do not sell them on the spot. Membership cards are available from some travel agencies and from Hostelling International affiliates:

HI is the largest such organization. Its 5000 official youth hostels worldwide will normally display the new HI logo (a blue triangle) alongside the symbol of one of the 70 national hostel associations. The guide *Hostelling International, Vol. 1: Europe and the Mediterranean* (US$14 including postage and handling; available from any hostel association) lists up-to-date information on HI hostels in English, French, German, and Spanish. HI has recently instituted an **International Booking Network.** To reserve space in high season, obtain an International Booking Voucher from any national hostel association and send it to a participating hostel (4-8 weeks in advance, US$2 in local currency). If your plans are firm, pre-booking is wise. Other organizations such as American Association of Independent Hostels, Backpackers Resorts International, Budget Backpackers Hostels, or Federation of International Youth Hostels may be worth considering. Lastly, if you have Internet access, check out the **Internet Guide to Hostelling** (http://hostels.com). Reservations for HI hostels may be made via the International Booking Network (IBN), a computerized system which allows you to book to and from HI hostels (more than 300 centers worldwide) months in advance for a nominal fee.

Hosteling Membership

Hostelling International-American Youth Hostels (HI-AYH), 733 15th St. NW, Suite 840, Washington, DC 20005 (tel. (202) 783-6161; fax 783-6171; http://www.taponline.com/tap/travel/hostels/pages/hosthp.html). HI-AYH maintains 34 offices. 12-month HI memberships: adults US$25; under 18 US$10; over 54 US$15; and US$35 for family cards. Reservations may be made by letter, phone, fax, or through IBN.

Hostelling International-Canada (HI-C), 400-205 Catherine St., Ottawa, Ontario K2P 1C3, Canada (tel. (613) 237-7884; fax 237-7868). Canada-wide membership/customer service line (800) 663-5777. Membership fees: 1yr., under 18 CDN$12; 1yr., over 18 CDN$25; 2yr., over 18 CDN$35; lifetime CDN$175.

Youth Hostels Association of England and Wales (YHA), Trevelyan House, 8 St. Stephen's Hill, St. Albans, Hertfordshire AL1 2DY, England (tel. (01727) 855 215; fax 844 126). Enrollment fees are: UK£9.30; under 18 UK£3.20; UK£18.60 for both parents with children under 18 enrolled free; UK£9.30 for one parent with children under 18 enrolled free; UK£125.00 for lifetime membership.

An Óige (Irish Youth Hostel Association), 61 Mountjoy St., Dublin 7 (tel. (01) 830 4555; fax 830 5808; http://www.touchtel.ie). One-year membership is IR£7.50, under 18 IR£4, family IR£7.50 for each adult with children under 16 free.

Youth Hostels Association of Northern Ireland (YHANI), 22 Donegall Rd., Belfast BT12 5JN, Northern Ireland (tel. (01232) 315 435; fax 439 699). Annual memberships UK£7, under 18 UK£3, family UK£14 for up to 6 children.

Scottish Youth Hostels Association (SYHA), 7 Glebe Crescent, Stirling FK8 2JA (tel. (01786) 45 11 81; fax 45 01 98). Membership UK£6, under 18 UK£2.50.

Australian Youth Hostels Association (AYHA), Level 3, 10 Mallett St., Camperdown NSW 2050 (tel. (02) 565 1699; fax 565 1325; e-mail YHA@zeta.org.au). AUS$42, renewal AUS$26; under 18 AUS$12.

Youth Hostels Association of New Zealand (YHANZ), P.O. Box 436, 173 Glouces-
ter St., Christchurch 1 (tel. (643) 379 9970; fax 365 4476; e-mail hostel.opera-
tions@yha.org.nz; http://yha.org.nz/yha). Annual membership fee NZ$24.
Hostel Association of South Africa, P.O. Box 4402, Cape Town 8000 (tel. (21)
419 1853; fax 216937). Between SAR25-1100 a night, with 14 IBN-linked (and 36
total) hostels in South Africa. Membership SAR45; Students SAR30; group SAR120;
family SAR90; lifetime SAR225.

Hosteling in Germany is overseen by **Deutsches Jugendherbergswerk (DJH)** (tel.
(05231) 740 10; fax 74 01 67). The DJH has, in recent years, initiated a growing number of *Jugendgästehäuser* (youth guest-houses), the more adult face of the HI system.
These are generally more expensive, have more facilities, and attract slightly older
guests. All German hostels are rated according to a six-category scale. The most basic
fall in category I, the modern *Jugendgästehäuser* in category VI. Prices correspond
roughly to these categories. The nightly charge builds from the odd category I hostel
in eastern Germany asking DM14 per night, to the demand for DM32 for a bed in a
four-person room from a brand-new *Jugendgästehaus*. However, because the prices
are set locally rather than nationally, this system is not uniform; a category III hostel
might be less expensive than a category II spot elsewhere. The DJH has absorbed
hundreds of hostels in Eastern Germany with remarkable efficiency—although somewhere in the process of unification, prices leapt upwards. Many of the better eastern
hostels have been converted into costly hotels, or closed outright while bureaucrats
try to decipher ownership, since new laws allow the original owners of property
nationalized by the GDR to re-claim their assets. Still, Germany currently has about
600 hostels—more than any other nation on Earth—and the state hostel associations
comprise the well-maintained infrastructure of a youth culture that has no equal anywhere.

DJH publishes *Deutsches Jugendherbergsverzeichnis* (DM6), a guide to all feder-
ated German hostels, available at German bookstores and major train station newsstands; or write to DJH-Hauptverband, Postfach 1455, 32704 Detmold, Germany.

> HI hostels in Bavaria do not accept guests over the age of 26.

ALTERNATIVE ACCOMMODATIONS

Ask at tourist offices in university/college towns whether student dormitories are
available to travelers when school is not in session. When they are, the rent is a nominal fee, usually comparable to youth hostel prices. You usually won't have to share a
room with strangers or endure stringent curfew and eviction regulations. Most rooms
are reserved for students looking for apartments. **Discount Travel International,** 114
Forest Ave. #203, Narberth, PA 19072 (tel. (215) 668-7184) is worth a glimpse if
you're not into the alternatives. For those addicted to Hiltons and Hyatts beyond their
means, the US$45 annual membership provides discounts on unsold hotel rooms.
Mitwohnzentralen in most German cities match people who want to lease apartments from a few days to a couple of months. A number of host networks will help
you find accommodations with families throughout Europe. See also Willing Workers
on Organic Farms in Work and Volunteer (p. 21).

CAMPING AND THE OUTDOORS

There are something like 2600 campsites in Germany, most accessible by public
transportation, and about 400 of which are open in the winter. If you're prepared to
go rustic, camping is the best option. Often however, they resemble battlegrounds,
with weary travelers and screaming children stacked next to each other. The money
and time expended in getting to the site may eat away at your budget and patience.
Campgrounds in the countryside are more attractive, but considerably less convenient if you have no car. Showers, bathrooms, and a restaurant or store are common.
Prices range US$1-10 per person with additional charge for tents and vehicles.

Blue signs with a black tent on a white background indicate official sites. **Deutscher Camping-Club e.v. (DCC),** Mandlstr. 28, 80802 München (tel. (089) 33 40 21), and **Allgemeiner Deutscher Automobil-Club (ADAC)** (see Getting Around: By Car, p. 39) have specific info on campgrounds, and the National Tourist Office distributes a free map, *Camping in Germany,* with a full list of campgrounds.

A variety of publishing companies offer hiking guidebooks to meet the educational needs of novice or expert:

Family Campers and RVers/National Campers and Hikers Association, Inc., 4804 Transit Rd., Bldg. #2, Depew, NY 14043 (tel./fax (716) 668-6242). This all-volunteer conservation group publishes *Camping Today,* which comes with the US$20 membership fee. For US$30, you can also get the International Camping Carnet, which is required by some European campgrounds, but can usually be bought on the spot.

The Mountaineers Books, 1001 SW Klickitat Way, Ste. 201, Seattle, WA 98134 (tel. (800) 553-4453 or (206) 223-6303; fax 223-6306; http://mbooks@mountaineers.org). Many titles on hiking (the *100 Hikes* series), biking, mountaineering, natural history, and conservation.

Wilderness Press, 2440 Bancroft Way, Berkeley, CA 94704-1676 (tel. (800) 443-7227 or (510) 843-8080; fax 548-1355). Publishes over 100 hiking guides and maps for the western U.S. including *Backpacking Basics* (US$11, including post age), and *Backpacking with Babies and Small Children* (US$11).

REI, P.O. Box 1700, Sumner, WA 98352-0001 (tel. (800) 426-4840), publishes *Europa Camping and Caravanning* (US$20), an annually updated catalog of European campsites. Few of their books are offered via mail-order, so check their retail stores.

At the core of your necessary equipment is the **sleeping bag.** Most of the better sleeping bags are rated according to the lowest outdoor temperature at which they will still keep you warm. If you're using a sleeping bag for serious camping, you should also have either a foam **pad** or an air mattress. Just as with selecting a mate, your major considerations in selecting a **tent** should be shape and size. The best tents are free-standing, with their own frames and suspension systems; they set up quickly and require no staking. Low-profile dome tents are the best all-around. Good two-person tents start at about $135; $200 for a four-person. You can, however, often find last year's version for half the price. If you intend to do a lot of hiking, you should have a **frame backpack.** External-frame packs are more comfortable for long hikes over even terrain. Buy a backpack with an internal frame, however, if you'll be hiking on difficult trails that require a lot of bending and maneuvering. Sturdy backpacks cost anywhere from US$125-400. Other necessities include: **battery-operated lantern,** plastic **groundcloth** for the floor of your tent, **nylon tarp** for general purposes, **"stuff sack"** or plastic bag to keep your sleeping bag dry; rain gear; synthetic tops, socks, and underwear; a canteen or water bottle; a camp stove; waterproof matches; Swiss Army knife; insect repellent. The following outfits can provide you with advice and a wide selection of camping paraphenalia:

Campmor, P.O. Box 700, Saddle River, NJ 07458-0700 (tel. (800) 526-4784; http://www.campmor.com). Has a wide selection of name brand equipment at low prices. One-year guarantee for unused or defective merchandise.

L.L. Bean, Casco St., Freeport, ME 04033-0001 (U.S. and Canada tel. (800) 221-4221, international, tel. (207) 865-3111; U.S. fax (207) 797-8867, Canada and international (207) 878-2104). Equipment and preppy outdoor clothing favored by northeastern Americans; high-quality and chock-full of information.

Sierra Design, 1255 Powell St., Emeryville, CA 94608 (tel. (510) 450-9555; fax 654-0705) has a wide array (all seasons and types) of especially small and lightweight tent models.

■ Sports

Germany enjoys a long tradition of sports and outdoor recreation and outstanding facilities to boot. The *Vereine* (club) culture, encompassing most sports, as well as hiking and crafts, produces almost religious fervor and devotion among many of its members. Nearly every city and town in Germany—especially resort towns—have swimming pools and spas. The North and Baltic Sea coasts, as well as the Frisian Islands (see p. 360) and Rügen (see p. 537), offer attractive beaches in the warm months. In winter, the German Alps, Harz Mountains, Black Forest, and Bavarian Forest are host to all sorts of snow sports, including skiing, ski-jumping, tobogganing, skating, hockey, and bobsledding. Garmisch-Partenkirchen, in the Bavarian Alps (see p. 230), sports high-caliber winter Olympics facilities. The following organizations can provide valuable information:

German Sports Association, Haus des Sportes Otto-Fleck Schneise 12 60528 Frankfurt a. Main (tel. (069) 670 00; fax 67 49 06).

German Hiking and Climbing Association, Reichsstr. 4 66111 Saarbrücken (tel. (0681) 39 00 70; fax 390 46 50). Local chapters maintain over 82,000 miles of marked hiking trails. This organization provides information about trails, shelters, and huts.

German Alpine Association, Von-Kahr-Str. 2-4 80997 München (tel. (089) 14 00 30; fax 140 03 11). The association maintains over 9000mi. of trails in the Alps and 252 huts open to all mountaineers. They also offer courses, treks, and guided expeditions.

German Sailing Association, Grundgenstr. 18 22309 Hamburg (tel. (040) 632 00 90; fax 63 20 09 28). The association can provide you with a list of more than 180 schools operating on the North and Baltic sea coasts.

German Aero Club, Rudolf-Braas-Str. 20, 63150 Heusenstamm (tel. (06104) 699 60; fax 69 96 11). This parent organization serves over 50 flying schools and 1000 gliding clubs throughout Germany.

German Fishing Association, Siemensstrasse 11-13, 63071 Offenbach (tel. (069) 670 00; fax 67 49 06). Fishers must obtain a license *(Fischereischein)* from local or municipal authorities for a small fee and a second permit *(Fischereierlaubnisschein)* from the leaseholder or owner of the fishing waters. In Germany, there is no free fish! Local species include carp, pike, perch, rockfish, eel, bream, roach, river and sea trout, char, and grayling.

German Golf Association, Friedrichstrasse 12 65185 Wiesbaden (tel. (06121) 99 02 00; fax 990 20 40). Foreign visitors are always welcome! Step up to the tee for about DM30 Mon.-Fri. and DM30-60 on weekends.

■ Keeping in Touch

MAIL

Germany's postal code system is similar to the one in the United States; codes are based on geographic zones and most cities are divided into many postal code zones. Large companies and industries even have their own postal codes. The codes are all five digits long and should be prefaced with the German name of the town. While we will, for example, refer to Cologne by its English name in our text, the German spelling, "Köln," should be used in its mailing address. Ditto for Munich, which is "München," Brunswick (which is "Braunschweig"), and a few others.

SENDING MAIL TO GERMANY

Mail can be sent to Germany through **Poste Restante** (the international phrase for General Delivery; *Postlagernde Briefe* in German) to any city or town; it's well worth using and much more reliable than you might think. Mark the envelope "HOLD" ("BITTE HALTEN" in German) and address it, for example, "Philip <u>MAZO</u>, *Postlagernde Briefe*, Köln, Germany." The last name should be capitalized and underlined. The mail will go to a special desk in the central post office, unless you specify a post office by street address or postal code. As a rule, it is best to use the largest post office in the area; sometimes, mail will be sent there regardless of what you write on the envelope. When possible, it is usually safer and quicker to send mail express or registered.

When picking up your mail, bring your passport or other ID. If the clerks insist that there is nothing for you, have them check under your first name as well. In a few countries you may have to pay a minimal fee per item received. Let's Go lists post offices in the Practical Information section for each city and most towns.

American Express offices throughout the world will act as a mail service for cardholders if you contact them in advance. Under this free **"Client Letter Service,"** they will hold mail for 30 days, forward upon request, and accept telegrams. Just like *Poste Restante*, the last name of the person to whom the mail is addressed should be capitalized and underlined. *Let's Go* lists AmEx office locations for most large cities. A complete list is available free from AmEx (tel. (800) 528-4800) in the booklet *Traveler's Companion*.

Airmail between North America and Germany takes 7 to 10 days. Allow at least two weeks for Australia and New Zealand. Postcards and letters cost 50¢ and 60¢ respectively. It is *vital* to distinguish your airmail from surface mail by labeling it "air mail" in the appropriate language (in German, *"Mit Luftpost"*).

SENDING MAIL FROM GERMANY

Surface mail is by far the cheapest and slowest way to send mail. It takes one to three months to cross the Atlantic, appropriate for sending large quantities of items you won't need to see for a while. It is vital, therefore, to distinguish your airmail from surface mail by explicitly labeling "airmail" in the appropriate language. When ordering books and materials from abroad, always include one or two **International Reply Coupons (IRCs)**—a way of providing the postage to cover delivery. IRCs should be available from your local post office (US$1.05).

Aerogrammes, printed sheets that fold into envelopes and travel via airmail, are available at post offices. It helps to mark "airmail" in the appropriate language if possible (*Mit Luftpost* in German), though *Par Avion* is universally understood. Most post offices will charge exorbitant fees or simply refuse to send Aerogrammes with enclosures. Airmail between Europe and the U.S. averages one to two weeks. Allow *at least* two weeks for Australia, New Zealand, and most of Africa. Much depends on the national post office involved.

Mail moves significantly faster within Western Germany than within the East, and crossovers are even slower. Still, you can generally get a piece of regular mail from one city in Germany to another overnight. **Postcards** within Germany cost DM0.80, to any international destination DM2. **Letters** (up to 20g) cost DM1 within Germany, DM3 (airmail) beyond. Despite postal unity, it's still slower to mail letters from eastern Germany. **Mailboxes** are distinguished by their bright yellow color.

TELEPHONES

The German telephone system is operated by the postal system (although it is scheduled to be privatized in 1997), so you can always be sure of finding a **public phone** in a post office.

EMERGENCY

Police: tel. 110. **Fire:** tel. 112. **Ambulance:** tel. 115.

Collect calls are not possible from public phones. If you spend a week or more in Germany, invest in a **Telefonkarte** (telephone card), the most sensible way to make calls from public phones. The cards come in DM3, DM6, and, more commonly, DM12, DM20, and DM50 denominations. The two German phone systems merged in

1993, although the availability of private phone lines is still a problem in the east (many businesses get by with mobile phones). Still, except in some very small towns, you should have no trouble finding a public card phone. Without a card, you must insert 20-30Pf, and then feed the meter while talking. The earpiece will usually emit a beep to alert you to add more money.

To **call Germany,** first dial the international access code (in the US, 011), then the **country code** (49), then the city code minus the first zero, then the telephone number. For information on international calls (including calling card calls) from Germany, for basic information on how to make phone calls from cities within Germany, or for more country code information, see our Appendices, p. 545.

LOCAL CALLS

Local calls should be made with a *Telefonkarte* (telephone card). This is by *far* the best option available; cards are sold in all post offices. Use them. See Keeping in Touch, p. 47. Another option is to feed **coins** to the phone. In the booth, pick up the receiver, deposit coins (even if your call is toll-free) and dial. **Local calls** cost 30pf. Phones accept 10pf, DM1, and DM5 coins, but not DM2 or 50pf. A digital display indicates how much money is left. If you only use 10pf coins, the excess will be returned at the end of the call. You can also pay by **credit card,** although they are not generally accepted. In larger cities and at many post offices, there are some machines that take Mastercard, Visa, American Express, or Carte Blanche. Insert your card and talk away.

INTER-CITY CALLS

Inter-city calls entail dialing the city telephone code (including the first zero that appears in the code) and the number. Do not be confused by the fact that there is no standard length for telephone numbers. The smaller the city, the more digits in the telephone code *(Vorwahl)*, while the telephone number *(Rufnummer)* varies in length. In **eastern Germany,** the phone system is chaotic, fluctuating, and still lacking. Fortunately, the system is being integrated into the West's. Listings operators dispense information about any German city. The **national information number** is 011 88. For information within the EU, call 00 11 88.

INTERNATIONAL CALLS

You can place **international calls** from most telephones. To call direct from the U.S., dial the universal international access code (011) followed by the country code, the city code, and the local number. Country codes and city codes may sometimes be listed with a zero in front (e.g., 049), but when using 011 (or whatever your international access code happens to be), drop successive zeros (e.g., 011 49).

English-speaking operators are often available for both local and international assistance. Operators in most countries will place **collect calls** for you. It's cheaper to find a pay phone and deposit just enough money to be able to say "Call me" and give your number. In Germany, pay phones marked with a bell allow you to receive calls. The number of the pay phone is printed conspicuously on it.

A **calling card** is another, cheaper alternative; your local long-distance phone company will have a number for you to dial while traveling (either toll-free or charged as a local call) to connect instantly to an operator in your home country. The calls (plus a small surcharge) are then billed either collect or to a calling card. For more information, call **AT&T** about its **AT&T Direct** service (tel. (800) 331-1140 ext. 740, from abroad (412) 553-7458 ext. 840), **Sprint** (tel. (800) 877-4646), or **MCI WorldPhone** and **World Reach** (tel. (800) 996-7535). For similar services for countries outside the U.S., contact your local phone company. In Canada, contact Bell Canada **Canada Direct** (tel. (800) 565 4708); in the U.K., British Telecom **BT Direct** (tel. (800) 34 51 44); in Ireland, Telecom Éireann **Ireland Direct** (tel. (800) 250 250); in Australia, Telstra **Australia Direct** (tel. 13 22 00); in New Zealand, **Telecom New Zealand** (tel. 123); and in South Africa, **Telkom South Africa** (tel. 09 03).

Remember **time differences** when you call. Germany is on Western European Time, six hours ahead of U.S. Eastern Standard Time. To make a direct international call from Germany, you must use the **international access code:** 00.

OTHER COMMUNICATION

Domestic and international **telegrams** offer an option slower than phone but faster than post. Fill out a form at any post or telephone office; cables to North America arrive in one or two days. Telegrams can be quite expensive, so you may wish to consider **faxes,** for more immediate, personal, and cheaper communication.

Between May 2 and *Octoberfest,* **EurAide,** P.O. Box 2375, Naperville, IL 60567 (tel. (708) 420-2343; fax 420-2369), offers **Overseas Access,** a service useful to travelers without a set itinerary. The cost is US$15 per week or US$40 per month plus a US$15 registration fee. To reach you, people call, fax, or use the Internet to leave a message; you receive it by calling Munich, which is cheaper than calling overseas. You may leave messages for callers to pick up by phone. For an additional US$20 per month, EurAide will forward mail sent to Munich to any addresses you specify.

If you're spending a year abroad and want to keep in touch with friends or colleagues in a research institution, **electronic mail (e-mail)** is an attractive option. Befriend college students as you go and ask if you can use their e-mail accounts or look for bureaus that offer access to e-mail. Search through http://www.easy-net.co.uk/pages/cafe/ccafe.htm to find a list of cybercafés around the world from which you can drink a cup of joe and e-mail him too. Another possibility is **America Online,** 8615 Westwood Center Drive, Vienna, VA 22070 (tel. (800) 827-6364), which offers "GLOBALnet," making it possible for American net-junkies to access the Internet and e-mail through their home accounts while traveling in 70 countries.

▓ Let's Go Picks

After a summer of wandering and wishing, we at *Let's Go Germany* have come up with our very own list of the best of the best. We tracked celestial movements, consulted our in-house research team, and flew in experts from abroad. You've been dreaming this moment would come. So now, without further ado, the winners are …

Best Museums: If you haven't had a chance to see the **Dahlem** (see p. 417) and **Pergamon** (see p. 422) in Berlin, you might as well not have come. The Dahlem has more Rembrandts than you could shake a stick at, while the Pergamon features some pretty groovy relics from the ancient world—our only question is, how'd they get 'em through the door? Close seconds are the **Museum für Moderne Kunst** in Frankfurt (see p. 302), which features the best of Claes Oldenberg, Roy Lichtenstein, and Jasper Johns, and, for the Mr. Wizard in all of us, the **Deutsches Museum** of science and technology in Munich (see p.220).

Best Art Show: *documenta x* will hit Kassel like a meteor in the summer of 1997 (see p. 318). Art critics from all over the world are going to be there, and Christo might show up as well; that is, if he ever comes out of post-*Reichstag*-wrapping-withdrawal. Dieter from Sprockets is certain to be on hand, rocketed into vertigo and nausea by the sordid beauty of it all. Appearing once every five years, this show is so avant-garde, it's already being written up in lower case letters. Beat that, e.e. cummings.

Best Beaches: When one of our of researchers sent us a naughty postcard from the North Frisian island of **Sylt,** we were so excited we almost quit our jobs to move there (see p. 388). Unfortunately, the powers that were said no way. But while we were breathing hot and heavy (from typing in batches of research, of course), we thought we'd at least do you a favor by letting you in on the secret: *"FKK" (Freie Körper Kultur)* means nude beach—don't take our word for it, go strip for yourself.

Best Castles: Anything built by Bavaria's **Mad King Ludwig** is well worth a healthy gawking. **Neuschwanstein** and **Hohenschwangau** make Disney look like *Bauhaus* (see p. 237). After all, it was none other than old Walt who *copied* Ludwig for his Sleeping Beauty's Castle. Let's all give some credit where credit is due.

Best Travel Services: Alan Wissenberg's **EurAide** office in the Munich *Hauptbahnhof* is a godsend (see p. 209). Wissenberg, an American emigré, knows anything and everything there is to know about travel in Germany. In addition, his office and its staff are kind, courteous, and professional. They'll answer your questions and send you off on your way smiling. We're not sure why they do it, but they do.

Best Hostels: Jugendherberge Koblenz used to be a fortress (see p. 127). Now you can sleep in it and pretend you're defending the Rhine from would-be Mosel attackers. Make sure you reserve ahead, though, or you'll be disappointed. Other travelers know about this place too, and they're willing to fight to the death for a spot. The *Jugendherberge* in **Füssen** is blessed by a lovely location and a lovely staff (see p. 235). Guess not everyone needs a castle to live like a king (or, in our case, queen).

Best Laundromat: Groove Station, in Dresden (see p. 454). Come for the nifty self-serve wash 'n' dry. Stay to see in-house tattoo-ings and body-piercings. Dance into it.

Best Spas: Baden-Baden may seem the exclusive playground of the rich and famous, but you'll thank yourself for making a small investment and de-vestment at the **Friedrichsbad** or the **Caracalla-Thermen** (see p. 180). Lounge in the aqua-salons of these marble palaces or get parched, steamed, soaked, scrubbed, doused, and pummelled by professionals. Thousands of dead (but happy) Romans couldn't all be wrong.

GERMANY (DEUTSCHLAND)

It seems appropriate that as the world reinvents itself, Germany is once again at the center of it all. Called a "metaphor of our times," Germany's modern experience encapsulates all the promises and betrayals of life in the twentieth century and exposes the fracture line of Western civilization itself. It has proved the most volatile political crucible of recent times, passing through six political systems in 70 years. Events in Germany precipitated the end of the "long 19th century" in 1914 and the end of the "short 20th century" in 1990, when Germany inaugurated the end of the Cold War through its own reunification. All the while, the "German Question" has been formulated and re-formulated. Is there a distinct "German character" that has informed such a peculiar historical path? Is that path indeed "peculiar" at all? There are, to be sure, certain German characteristics—industriousness, efficiency, and a mystifying refusal to cross the street against the light—but the generation of Germans who came of age after the war have, in many ways, striven to defy the negative stereotype of the humorless, heel-clicking German authoritarian. The broad social and political range of the nation certainly defies easy categorization.

Despite its long history of reactionary governments, Germany has always been a wellspring of revolutionaries and innovators—for better and for worse. One of the first heroes of German history, **Charlemagne** (Karl der Große) was the first to unify post-Roman Europe under enlightened rule. A small-town German monk, **Martin Luther,** stands as one of the most influential figures in Western history as the author of the revolutionary Protestant Reformation. **Johann Sebastian Bach** and **Ludwig van Beethoven** turned the world of music upside down. Socialist pioneers **Karl Marx** and **Friedrich Engels** equipped the revolutionary groundswell of 19th-century Europe with an ideology and a project whose power has been re-channeled but never defused. **Adolf Hitler,** one of the most loathsome figures in history, organized in his country the capacity to perform deeds—the seizure of power, the conquest of Europe, the **Holocaust**—that simply defy explanation. This last image, of course, indelibly colors all subsequent German history. Germans must grapple with the wrenching fact that the cradle of **Johann Wolfgang von Goethe** and **Immanuel Kant** also nurtured **Auschwitz** and **Treblinka.** Condemned to shoulder the crimes of the Third Reich, Germany is also blessed with an incomparable cultural tradition. No major European artistic movement of the last 500 years is entirely without debt to Germans, and quite a few would be unthinkable without German influence.

Not that you'll hear all of this from the Germans themselves, who these days are busy typecasting each other as lazy *Ossis* and materialistic *Wessis* as they try to reconcile their recently divergent pasts. The Wall had barely come down when West Berlin dilettantes started cracking jokes about putting it back up. The "Wall in the Mind" *(die Mauer im Kopf)* may continue to separate Germans for at least a generation. Yet as the Germans are turning inward, their global position is becoming increasingly significant. In the wake of Europe's most recent wave of revolution, a newly reunited Germany's pivotal position between East and West is even more important than it was during the Cold War. Finally, as a nation forced to face the moral bankruptcy of its nationalism, Germany brings an unique perspective and motivation to recent nationalist conflicts and the project of an integrated Europe.

It's worth remembering all of this in your travels. The historical and cultural legacies that Germany has offered posterity over centuries of war and division represent a healthy chunk of Western civilization's collective past. But lest you forget all of this history during the course of your itinerary, stop for a moment to remember the words of philosopher George Santayana: "Those who cannot remember the past are doomed to repeat it." They will remind you that the exploits of Germany's exemplars offer insight into the present, and, perhaps, even a glimpse into the future.

■ History

The Germans make everything difficult, both for themselves and everyone else.

—Goethe

All history involves conflict, but in Germany it is especially contested ground. Witness the *Historikerstreit* (Historians' Dispute) of the early 1980s, when a disagreement among historians as how to best locate the Third Reich in the context of European history erupted into a highly public brawl which divided politicians and excited the tabloid press. Even the starting point of German history is debatable. Ancestors of *homo sapiens* lived in Germany 50,000 years ago; the first remains to be identified as those of **Neanderthal Man** were dug up near Düsseldorf in 1856. At the opposite extreme, the first ruler of an entity identified as "Germany" was Henry of Saxony, in the early 10th century. Nominally speaking, "German" history began in 90BC when the Roman author Posidonius first gave that appellation to the peoples that had migrated around 1000BC from Southern Scandinavia, Denmark, and Schleswig to territories contained in modern Belgium, the Netherlands, Germany, Poland, Switzerland, and Austria. That's where we pick up the story.

THE ROMAN ERA: HAIR-BUTTERERS AND THINGS

In early German society, individuals of common ancestry lived communally in a clan, the basic social unit. All men able to fight were expected to do so to protect the clan's honor. Personal loyalty (and the occasional bounty) bound warriors to their leaders. Regular **Things** (general assemblies), usually held outdoors in the absence of primitive convention centers, convened to discuss their leader's proposals. Clans supported themselves by farming land on the outskirts of their villages.

That "ß" Thing,
Plus A Few Necessary German Words

In your travels, it is useful to pick up a number of words for common tourist attractions and services, even if you speak no German. To this end, *Let's Go: Germany* uses a limited number of foreign words in the text without translation. But to read some of them, and many of the titles and phrases in the book, you need to be let in on the mysterious secret of the **"ß"**, a special consonant which Germans call an "ess-tsett." **It is pronounced exactly like a double "S"** in English; hence, *Straße*, the German word for street, is pronounced "SHTRAH-ssuh." Meißen, a small town in Saxony, is pronounced "MIGH-ssen."

With that aside, here is a list of the most essential German tourist terms that you will see used (all over the place) in this text:

das Schloß (say "SHLOSS", remember?) = **castle**
die Altstadt (AHLT-shtaht) = **old city,** the historic section of town
das Rathaus (RAHT-hauss) = **town hall,** often located in the *Altstadt*
der Dom (DOME) = **cathedral**
die Kirche (KEER-hkuh) = **church**
die Kneipe (k'NIGH-puh) = a **bar** for students or young people
der Hauptbahnhof (HAUWPT-bahn-hohf) = a town/city's **main train station**
die Pension (PAHN-tzee-OHN) = small, cheap, often family-run **hotel**
das Privatzimmer (pree-VAHT-tsim-mer) = a **private room,** in a home
die Jugendherberge (YOO-gent-hair-BARE-guh) = **youth hostel**
die Mensa (MEN-zah) = **cafeteria** (often at a university)

The expanding **Roman Republic** waged war against the German clans for centuries; by 58BC the Rhine was its northeast frontier. However, a particularly celebrated thumping at the hands of **Arminius** (Hermann), leader of the Cherusci tribe, in the Teutoburg Forest in 9AD, put an end to Roman expansion. In his chronicle *Germania*, the Roman author **Tacitus** memorably vilified the wild, dairy-loving Germans as "barbarians who buttered their hair." Beginning in 90AD the now-Roman Empire built a string of fortifications between the Rhine and the Danube, but these were broken in the 3rd century and Germanic tribes began to migrate into the Empire, sanctioned as **foederati** (allies): the Romans hired the tribes to protect the outlying regions of the empire against other tribes. Not all clans cooperated, however. Driven by an envy of Roman luxuries, the non-*foederati* clans accelerated their attacks while *foederati* reneged on their treaties and established their own sovereign monarchies on Roman territory. Eventually, German tribes laid siege to Rome itself; Visigoths pillaged the city in 410, Vandals seized it in 455, and **Odoacer,** leader of the Ostrogoths, deposed Emperor Romulus Augustus in 476, the date at which the empire in the west is generally considered to have come to an end. But despite the decline in Roman authority, the Germanic tribes preserved many imperial administrative apparatuses and institutions.

While other German tribes were busy knocking off the ancient equivalents of liquor stores and gas stations, the **Franks** got serious and spent their time expanding their rule in the Rhine Valley. Through a series of victories over other clans, **Clovis** consolidated the power of the Franks over the northwestern territories of modern France. After converting to **Christianity** late in the 5th century, Clovis employed church institutions to help govern his burgeoning kingdom. Since Clovis issued religious laws and appointed bishops, he essentially controlled the ecclesiastical administration (this entanglement of king and church would be a major sticking point in later centuries). According to custom, Clovis's heirs split the kingdom after his death. They soon added Provence, Burgundy, and Bavaria to their domains.

THE AGE OF CHARLEMAGNE

In the process of trying to unify and expand the territories under their control, the Merovingian royal family turned over administration of the kingdom to **major-domos** (mayors of the palace), who served as the head of the royal household and as one of the king's chief retainers. The **Carolingian** family dominated the post for generations. One of them, **Charles Martel** ("The Hammer") was responsible for stopping a wholesale invasion of Western Europe by the Muslim Saracens in 732 from in Spain. The power of the *major-domos* began to visibly eclipse that of the king; in 751, the son of Charles, **Pepin the Short,** became the titular as well as effective ruler of the Franks in a bloodless coup. Pope Zachary—whose power was considerably less than that of future Popes—blessed his rule, reaffirming the king's religious role and establishing papal approval as a basis and necessity of kingship.

The Carolingian empire reached its height under the rule of Pepin's son **Charlemagne** ("Charles the Great"), whom Germans know as **Karl der Große.** By medieval or modern standards, Charlemagne was an extremely busy man; he subdued Saxony, the Papal States, and Bavaria. At the same time, Christian missionaries extended his influence among the Slavs (setting the stage for centuries of conflict). Pope Leo III attempted to reconstitute the lost Roman empire of the west, as well as increase his own influence, by crowning Charlemagne the **Holy Roman Emperor** on Christmas Day 800 (although whether he did so only at Charlemagne's request is a matter of historical debate), and the Byzantine emperor recognized Chuck as his equal in the **Treaty of Aachen.** Charlemagne's rule was relatively enlightened; his administrative wisdom and love of learning were reflected in a variety of legacies. He restructured the Carolingian administration by creating *missi dominici* (royal messengers) who oversaw secular and sacred local officials; under his stewardship monasteries became centers of learning and preservers of classical traditions; and commerce within Europe and with the Arab and Byzantine worlds was revived.

However, this Dark Age "renaissance" did not endure. Several factors were at fault: a new wave of **invasions** from Vikings to the north, Magyars (Hungarians) to the east, and Arabs to the south; the lack of a sufficient infrastructure to support such a vast empire, encompassing virtually all of Christian Europe; and the end of a long lucky streak in which only one male Carolingian had emerged in every generation to rule. After the death of Charlemagne's son, **Louis the Pious,** the 843 **Treaty of Verdun** split the empire into three kingdoms. Civil wars ensued, further dismembering the Frankish lands. Vassals asserted their independence from their lords; those that remained loyal demanded greater power. Out of the hundreds of new semi-sovereign principalities emerged a few strong duchies, namely Swabia, Saxony, Bavaria, and Franconia, formed as a defense against the invasions the center had proven incapable of stopping. **Otto I** defeated the Slavs and pushed the Franks' borders as far east as the Oder River. Otto secured the tacit support of the other lords and made a difficult trek to Rome through hostile territory; he was crowned Holy Roman Emperor in 962, invigorating a title which had been in disrepute for over a century. But other powerful kingdoms retained an influence on "German" affairs; within the boundaries of the old/new empire were Burgundy, northwestern Italy, and Bohemia in the modern Czech Republic.

THE ROOTS OF DIVISION

The relationship between the church and the empire deteriorated in the following centuries. **Pope Gregory VII** excommunicated **Henry IV** twice in fights over the appointment of bishops during the **Investiture Conflict;** ironically both had been proponents of church reform. In the 1122 **Concordat of Worms,** Henry's son **Henry V** conceded his Italian claims to the Pope and agreed to exert no influence over the elections of bishops other than to attend the ceremonies. Because of the conflict, Henry V lost the church's administrative support and its powerful backing. Territorial lords rose up and challenged him, further reducing his imperial authority.

Late in the 12th century, emperor **Frederick Barbarossa** united the houses of Guelph and Hohenstaufen and feudalized and federalized the Holy Roman Empire. He created a new class of **imperial princes** below the emperor and above the other nobles, winning the support of strong territorial lords for his plans by promoting them to these positions. His designs were undermined by his own grandson, **Frederick II.** In exchange for support from princes and the Pope for his Italian military expeditions, Frederick ceded significant legal, administrative, and judicial authority to them, further fragmenting German lands. Squabbles between the princes after Frederick's death in 1250 left the empire without clear leadership. Despite (or perhaps because of) these renewed conflicts and rivalries, the centuries that followed were later to be known as an age of chivalry, and were marked by the construction of cathedrals and the growth of towns.

A compromise between warring factions, the **Golden Bull of 1356,** declared that electors from seven major territories—three archbishops and four secular leaders—would approve the selection of each emperor. Aspirants to the throne bribed the electors with territorial and political concessions, further diluting the power of the emperor. Vassals performed little if any military service and provided even less financial assistance; an emperor's own troops, tax base, and land determined his real strength. The electors made a financial killing every time an emperor died. Under these daunting conditions members of the well-heeled **House of Habsburg** maneuvered their way to the top, occupying the throne for the next five centuries (except for one brief interregnum) with the support of their Austrian domains. Meanwhile, settlers left their homes in western Germany and moved to eastern Germany, Bohemia, and Austria; the phrase describing this movement, *Drang nach Osten* (drive to the East), was resurrected by the Nazis centuries later. In 1358 several German merchant towns organized the **Hanseatic League,** designed to help its members protect their trading interests. Emperor Maximilian I was the first Holy Roman Emperor to receive papal permission to be crowned without going to Rome to have the Pope perform the ceremony. As time passed, Italy and the other outlying areas of the empire slipped out of its control entirely.

THE REFORMATION AND THE THIRTY YEARS WAR

On Halloween Day 1517, **Martin Luther,** a monk and professor of Biblical studies at Wittenberg University in Saxony, posted his **Ninety-Five Theses** on the door of the city's castle church. The reverberations of the **Protestant Reformation** he unleashed are still felt today. Luther attacked the Roman Catholic Church for the extravagance of the papal court in Rome and its practice of selling **indulgences**—essentially gift certificates for the soul which promised to shorten the owner's stay in purgatory. Luther insisted that salvation came only through God's grace, not through good works. The stern, indefatigable Luther revolutionized everything he touched; one of the greatest salvos of his war against Catholicism was a **new translation of the Bible,** a document whose publication single-handedly crystallized the patchwork of German dialects into a standard, literary High German language.

Luther's crusade found immediate support for his views with Frederick the Wise, Elector of Saxony, who had not permitted the sale of papal indulgences. Other princes soon adopted Lutheranism, captivated by hopes of being able to stem the flow of money to Rome and to seize church assets without going to Hell for it. Armed conflicts soon erupted. The disturbances quickly became more than just religious conflicts; the serfs rebelled during the **Peasants' Wars** in 1524-1526. The chaos was too much for Luther, who called upon the princes to crush the bands of peasants. But Lutheranism continued to spread throughout Europe. The Habsburg Emperor **Charles V**—the most powerful monarch since Charlemagne—declared his intention to uproot the subversive doctrine and destroy those who professed it. However, in the 1555 **Peace of Augsburg,** Charles was compelled to suspend the **Counter-Reformation** and concede to individual princes the right to determine the religion practiced in their territory, a system that led to a number of absurd overnight conversions and further divided and paralyzed the empire.

Charles's successors did not keep the bargain. When Ferdinand of Styria tried to impose Catholicism on Bohemia, Protestants rebelled, leading to the "uplifting" **Defenestration of Prague.** Soon Sweden joined the conflict on behalf of the Protestants. Catholics were on the verge of turning the tide when France, suspicious of Habsburg Austria, put religious affiliation aside and intervened on behalf of Sweden. The **Thirty Years War** (1618-48) was a catastrophe for Germany. Half the population of the Holy Roman Empire was wiped out, towns were laid to waste, and famine stalked the population. The **Peace of Westphalia,** which ended the war, granted 300 princes the right to participate as electors of the emperor. The Habsburg retained the right to interfere in intra-state squabbles, but the imperial administration had once and for all effectively been dismantled. Moreover, the principle of local rulers determining the religion of their subjects remained in place. The Holy Roman Empire had never had a centralized system of law, language, or loyalties. Although it lingered on for another 150 years, it was now effectively a dead institution, and its demise left Germany greatly divided.

THE RISE OF BRANDENBURG-PRUSSIA

The war indirectly benefited the leaders of **Brandenburg-Prussia.** Elector Frederick William of the **House of Hohenzollern** concluded a peace agreement with Sweden that did not estrange him from the Habsburgs. He enlisted the support of the landed nobility, the **Junkers,** by making them officers in the army. His son, Frederick II—known as **Frederick the Great**—further consolidated the heartland of the rising Prussian state. Frederick is revered in German history as an enlightened ruler, notable for his administrative and military skill as well as his patronage of the arts. He was also reputed to be gay, which did not sit well with his father. When Maria Theresa became the empress of the Habsburg domains in 1740, Frederick seized the opportunity to snatch the prosperous province of **Silesia.** By the end of the Seven Years War in 1763, Prussia was recognized as one of Europe's **great powers.** Frederick II and his nephew then joined forces with Russia (and at times Austria) to **divide up Poland** and physically link Brandenburg and Prussia for the first time.

These skirmishes paled in comparison to the havoc wreaked by France in the wake of the French Revolution. **Napoleon** conquered and disbanded the Holy Roman Empire, fusing hundreds of territories into the **Confederation of the Rhine** in 1806. But despite the incorporation of hundreds of thousands of German soldiers, Napoleon's armies bogged down in Russia, and a general rebellion known as the **Wars of Liberation,** culminating in the 1813 Battle of Leipzig, ejected Napoleon from German territory. The **Congress of Vienna** in 1815 in part restored the pre-war German state system by creating the Austrian-led 39-member **German Confederation,** although no attempt was made to restore most of the princelings. The congress awarded Prussia portions of Rhineland-Westphalia, Germany's future industrial heartland and a beachhead for Prussia in the west. In 1834, Prussia sponsored the **Zollverein,** a customs union that linked most German territories—except Austria—in a free trade zone.

In 1848, revolution broke out again in France, and the discontent spread rapidly to other parts of Europe. The German Confederation agreed to let an elected assembly decide the future of the confederation. This **National Assembly** met in Frankfurt, drafted a liberal constitution, and invited King Frederick William IV of Prussia to serve as emperor. In a victory of absolutism over democracy, he spurned the offer, saying that he would not accept a crown created by the rabble. The assembly disbanded, and the ensuing revolt in Frankfurt was crushed by the Prussian army. This dashing of democratic hopes was to resound throughout the years to come.

BISMARCK AND THE SECOND REICH

In 1862, Prussian King William I appointed a worldly Junker aristocrat named **Otto von Bismarck** as Chancellor. History's greatest practitioner of *Realpolitik,* Bismarck's career was marked by a remarkably complex series of alliances and compromises that were more than once dissolved in favor of more violent tactics—*"Blut und Eisen"* (Blood and Iron), Bismarck liked to point out, were all that mattered in the long run. Like his fellow Junker conservatives, Bismarck despised liberals and parliamentarians; unlike them, he strongly believed in the cause of German unity, and was prepared to go to war to achieve it. This he did often and well. In 1864, he fought Denmark and seized control of Schleswig and Holstein. The fallout from this dispute led to conflict with Austria, which Prussia quashed in 1866 at **Sadowa** (Königgrätz). Viewing Austria as a future ally, Bismarck did not impose a humiliating peace. Instead, he made it clear that Prussia would now dominate German affairs; Austria should mind its own affairs in the east. In 1867, the German Confederation was disbanded and replaced it with the Prussian-dominated **North German Confederation.** Bismarck realized that France would never willingly acquiesce to a fully united Germany under Prussian domination. Through a series of trivial diplomatic slights he lured France into a misguided declaration of war in 1870; the technologically superior Prussian army and its allies swept through France and trounced the French army at **Sedan,** capturing Emperor Napoleon III. Parisians declared a republic and vowed to carry on the fight. Bismarck gleefully besieged Paris and had William crowned **Emperor of the German Reich** *(Kaiser)* in the Hall of Mirrors at the nearby Palace of Versailles. Even today, idealized murals depicting this militaristic scene can be found in numerous German castles and museums.

With France thus disposed of, Bismarck was free to **unify Germany** on his own terms; the remaining independent German states were unable to resist him. He presented German liberals with an offer they couldn't refuse: unification in exchange for an authoritarian monarchy. The nationalist wing of the liberals split off to become the National Liberal Party, a coalition which supported Bismarck. Not that parliamentary majorities meant much in the Second Reich; the chancellor was responsible to the emperor, not parliament. Military power remained the exclusive realm of the monarch. Prussia, the dominant state in the empire, also retained an anti-democratic **three-class voting system** which preserved the political supremacy of the Junkers despite their clear minority. British Prime Minister William Gladstone suggested that "Bismarck made Germany great, but the Germans small."

THE CONSERVATIVE EMPIRE

By the 1870s, reformist sentiment was gaining ground in Germany. Led by a burgeoning trade union movement and the newly founded **Social Democratic Party** (*Sozialdemokratische Partei Deutschlands*—SPD), working-class radicalism began to pose a serious threat to the old, reactionary order. In one of the world's great instances of political Machiavellianism, Bismarck engaged in a long series of initiatives that alternatively revolved around reforms and repression (known as the **Kulturkampf**). Bismarck pioneered **social welfare programs** for the working class such as unemployment insurance, but harshly repressed trade unions and the Social Democrats with the **Anti-Socialist Laws** of 1878. He established a strong legacy of paternalism in the Chancellorship through his attempts to de-fang the proletariat and make it dependent upon a "benevolent" authoritarian regime. His 1879 **Alliance of Iron and Rye** brought together the two leading conservative forces in society: the industrialists and the agrarian aristocrats. Traditionally, *Junker* farmers had been free-traders, while the industrialists were protectionists. But the aristocrats' stance changed when a revolution in shipping technology suddenly made American wheat so competitive on the European market that it threatened to drive them out of business. Bismarck was so successful that in 1890 the new Kaiser William II judged him superfluous, and the Iron Chancellor was dismissed.

The so-called **conservative empire** garnered popular support by fomenting an aggressive nationalism and colonialist sentiment. **Naval leagues** formed to agitate for a German navy that could compete with Britain in the race for overseas colonies. Naval construction, however, represented only a tiny fraction of the breakneck **industrialization** that Germany underwent in the last decades of the 19th century. In the space of less than 40 years, one of the most backward nations in Europe developed the most advanced industrial base on the continent—yet it retained a medieval political system completely incompatible with modern liberal ideals. Many historians have thus dubbed Germany the "belated nation" *(die verspätete Nation)*.

Such rapid progress produced tremendous social friction. The numbers of the proletariat exploded, but protectionist tariffs kept food absurdly expensive. Germany accelerated its pattern of foreign adventurism in part to quell unrest at home—a policy derisively known as **"Flucht nach vorn"** (flight to the front). Disputes over colonial issues left Germany isolated diplomatically in Europe, and tension between Germany and its neighbors mounted. Meanwhile, the democratic opposition had begun to become a unified challenge to the authoritarian regime. For the Kaiser and the anachronistic elites which supported him, it was increasingly clear that dramatic action might be required to preserve their positions. Unfortunately, this served to encourage German militarism and militaristic treaties.

WORLD WAR I

On the eve of World War I, Europe was entangled in a complex system of alliances in which minor disputes could easily escalate into a full-blown continental war. The situation was further destabilized by the prevailing thinking among the German General Staff. The **Schlieffen Plan** was a design to win a war on two fronts: a lightning thrust through Belgium would deliver a knock-out blow to France, whereupon Germany could turn to the east and defeat the Czar before he could mobilize his backward army. As Russia's rail network was modernized, the generals saw their window of opportunity closing; they were strongly inclined to mobilize at the first sign of a crisis. That crisis broke out in 1914, when a Serbian nationalist assassinated the Habsburg heir to the Austrian throne, **Archduke Franz-Ferdinand**, in Sarajevo.

Germany could have persuaded Austria to exercise restraint but did not. Austria, which wanted a small and quick war, marched on Serbia. Russia, posing as the champion of its brother Slavs, announced mobilization. Almost the entire Reichstag, including the Social Democratic delegates (who despised the Russian Czar), voted to mobilize for war. The decision received popular support from the young generation of German men who, as yet untried in combat, were eager to test themselves on the battlefield. After Russia ignored an ultimatum to rescind the mobilization, Germany entered the war on the side of Austria, prompting France to mobilize. Germany then declared war on France and demanded that Belgium allow its army to cross its frontier. Belgium refused. Britain, which was treaty-bound to defend Belgian neutrality, declared war on Germany. Germany quickly advanced through Belgium and northern France, and suddenly virtually all of Europe was at war.

After advancing within 50km of Paris, the German offensive stalled at the **Battle of the Marne.** Four years of agonizing **trench warfare** followed. The slaughter was staggering, magnified by the introduction of new weapons such as tanks, airplanes, flame-throwers, and poison gas. In an ironic inversion of the Schlieffen Plan, Germany prevailed first on the Russian front, where General **Paul von Hindenburg** crushed the Czar's army at **Tannenberg.** After the Bolsheviks took control of the Russian government and concluded the **Treaty of Brest-Litovsk** in 1918, Germany was free to concentrate its energies on France. But Germany's policy of **unrestricted submarine warfare** on all ships entering European waters had provoked the United States into entering the war on the side of the Triple Entente. After the imperial navy was checked by England in the **Battle of Jutland,** Germany was rapidly choked by a **naval blockade.** That, coupled with the industrial capacity and vast fresh armies of the U.S., gave the Entente the margin of victory.

THE WEIMAR REPUBLIC

In late 1918, with the German army on the brink of collapse, riots and mutinies broke out on the home front. On November 9, 1918, Social Democratic leader **Philipp Scheidemann** declared a republic in Berlin. **Friedrich Ebert** became its first president. The Kaiser and his flunkies fled to the Netherlands. Ignoring the advice of American President Woodrow Wilson, France insisted on a harsh peace in the **Treaty of Versailles,** which imposed staggering reparations payments and a clause ascribing the blame for the war to Germany. The new republican government had little choice but to accept the treaty, as the continuing Allied blockade was starving the country. Even before a constitution was drawn up in the city of Weimar, the republic was stuck with the stigma of the humiliating treaty; because the war had never reached German soil and the Kaiser's propaganda had promised a smashing victory right up to the end, Germans were psychologically unprepared for defeat. The **legend of the stab-in-the-back** (*Dolchstoßlegende*) found a willing audience.

The newly formed **Communist Party** (*Kommunistische Partei Deutschlands*—KPD) led a revolt in Berlin that found some support. The Republic crushed the revolution by appealing to bands of right-wing army veterans called **Freikorps.** In a fit of reactionary fervor, the **Freikorps,** led by **Wolfgang Kapp,** then turned against the government. Ironically, the left helped save the day. Workers staunchly supported the new republic; they responded with a general strike, and a force of 50-80,000 was organized against the coup in the Ruhr industrial area. The republic emerged bruised but intact. Its leaders met to draw up a constitution in the city of **Weimar,** chosen for its historical legacy as the birthplace of the German Enlightenment; it now gave its name to a period of intense cultural activity but economic and political uncertainty. For at look at the artistic side, see Culture (page 69).

Outstanding war debts and the burden of reparations produced the staggering **hyperinflation** of 1922-23, during which time the German *Reichsmark* sunk from four to 4.2 trillion to the U.S. dollar. Eventually, the Republic achieved a degree of stability with help from the American **Dawes Plan,** and an age of relative calm and remarkable artistic activity ensued. But the seeds of authoritarianism never became sterile. The old, reactionary order still clung to power in many segments of society: the army, police, big business, civil service, and the judiciary. When an Austrian corporal named **Adolf Hitler** was arrested for treason after his abortive 1923 **Beer Hall Putsch,** he was not deported on the grounds that he "believed he was German" and was sentenced to the minimum term of five years, of which he served only 10 months. During his time in jail, Hitler wrote a book—*Mein Kampf*—and decided that his party, the National Socialist German Workers Party *(Nationalsozialistische Deutsche Arbeiterspartei*—NSDAP), also known as the **Nazis,** would have to seize power by constitutional means. Two aspects of the Weimar constitution, intended to establish a perfectly representative and functional democracy, in fact expedited this process. **Pure proportional representation** encouraged a spectrum of political parties and discouraged stable governments. The infamous **Article 48** gave the chancellor the power to rule by decree for short periods of time during crises (sociologist Max Weber had drafted the article, believing that occasional charismatic dictatorship was an antidote to periodic parliamentary and bureaucratic stagnation).

The Nazi party expanded its highly efficient, blindly obedient bureaucracy and nearly quadrupled its membership to 108,000 by 1929. Even so, it was still a fringe party in 1928, receiving only 2.5% of the vote. But when the **Great Depression** struck in 1929, 25% of the population was unemployed within months. Membership in the NSDAP exploded to more than a million by 1930—the **SA** *(Sturmabteilung),* its paramilitary arm, grew as large as the German army. The slogan "Germany, awake!" was a call to root out Jewish, Bolshevist, and other supposed "foreign influences" that had allegedly poisoned Germany's national spirit and led it into disgrace. Hitler's own powerful oratory and the brilliant propaganda apparatus of Josef Goebbels amplified the message. Hitler failed in a presidential bid against the nearly senile war-hero Hindenburg in 1932, but the parliamentary elections that same year made the Nazis the largest party (winning 37% of the vote and seats) in the *Reichstag.* After various political maneuvers, President Hindenburg reluctantly appointed Hitler as the Chancellor of a coalition government on January 30, 1933.

THE THIRD REICH

The conservatives who backed the Hitler government had always been hostile to the republic, and naively believed they could control Hitler and establish an authoritarian regime ruled by the traditional elites. When Hitler's government was formed in January 1933, the Nazis controlled only two cabinet ministries and one minister-without-portfolio. But during the next two months, Hitler persuaded Hindenburg to dissolve the *Reichstag* and call new elections; this gave him the chance to invoke Article 48, and gained him seven weeks to **rule by decree.** During this time, he curtailed freedom of the press, authorized the SA and SS as auxiliary police, and brutalized opponents. A week before the elections, the mysterious **Reichstag fire** gave Hitler an occasion to declare a state of emergency and begin rounding up Communists, Socialists, and other political opponents, many of whom were relocated to newly built **concentration camps.** In the elections of March 5, 1933, the Nazis fell well short of a majority. Nonetheless, they arrested and browbeat enough opposing legislators to pass an **Enabling Act** making Hitler the **legal dictator** of Germany—authorized to ban all opposition and rule by decree indefinitely. In a policy known as **Gleichschaltung** (roughly, "coordination") the Nazis established party control over the country—not just the government, but universities, professional associations, and even local chess clubs. Press, radio, books, and every imaginable aspect of public life was "Nazified," that is, strictly regulated by the state.

One of the government's first acts was to institute a **boycott of Jewish businesses** and to expel Jews from professions and the civil service. In 1935, the first of the anti-Semitic **Racial Purity Laws** deprived Jews of German citizenship and prohibited intercourse between "Aryan" and Jew. After a respite during the 1936 Berlin Olympics, the program resumed in earnest in 1938 with **Kristallnacht** (Night of Broken Glass). On November 9, Nazis destroyed thousands of Jewish businesses, burned synagogues, killed scores of Jews, and sent at least 20,000 to concentration camps.

For those fortunate enough not to be Jews, Gypsies, Communists, Social Democrats, artists, free-thinkers, disabled, gay, or concerned about any of them, the early years of the Third Reich were in many ways a marked improvement over the Weimar era. A massive program of industrialization restored full employment. The destruction of Jewish businesses meant less competition for shopkeepers and professionals. Hitler abrogated the Versailles Treaty, thus freeing Germany from reparations payments and allowing it to re-arm. Although the *Autobahn* highway project was planned during the republic—as were other improvements for which the Nazis claimed credit—Hitler pushed it in earnest, recognizing its military implications. Residents of the Saarland, which had been under French occupation since the war, overwhelmingly voted to join the Third Reich. When Hitler boldly **re-militarized the Rhineland,** thousands cheered him in the streets. Next, Hitler stared down Mussolini and the West to annex Austria. Then he demanded territorial concessions from Czechoslovakia, home to thousands of ethnic Germans. British Prime Minister Neville Chamberlain assured Hitler in the notorious 1938 **Munich Agreement** that Britain would not interfere (Czechoslovakia was not consulted). After annexing part of Czechoslovakia and establishing a puppet government in the rest, Hitler's appetite for territory was only whetted, not sated. One of the fundamental tenets of Nazi ideology was the necessity of acquiring **Lebensraum** (living space) from the "subhuman" Slavs in the East; many historians suggest that Hitler had planned from the very beginning to go to war to get it. Hitler's uncompromising "Guns *and* Butter" policies in the 30s proved tremendously expensive, necessitating the eventual plunder of foreign economies.

WORLD WAR II

On September 1, 1939, German tanks rolled into Poland. Britain and France, which were bound by treaty to defend Poland, immediately declared war on Germany but did not attack. Although Poland possessed what was then the sixth-largest army in the world, Germany's new tactic of mechanized **Blitzkrieg** (literally, lightning war) quickly crushed it. Because Germany's vulnerability to blockade and lack of immediate access to strategic materials put it at a disadvantage in a protracted war, Hitler innovated the use of rapidly thrusting columns of armor and aircraft to destroy enemy armies quickly. In a month, Poland was vanquished, and Hitler and Stalin divided it under the terms of a secret agreement. The French and English remained hunkered down behind the Maginot Line. On April 9, 1940, Hitler relieved the tedium by rolling over Denmark and Norway. A month later, the *Blitzkrieg* roared through the Ardennes Forest of Luxembourg and quickly overwhelmed Belgium, the Netherlands, and France. Only a heroic but desperate sea-lift at Dunkirk saved the British army from total destruction. However, the Nazis failed to bomb London into submission in the aerial struggle of the **Battle of Britain.** Preparations for a cross-channel invasion were shelved and Hitler turned his attentions to his most despised enemy, Russia. The German **invasion of the USSR** in June 1941 ended the Hitler-Stalin pact. Despite the Red Army's overwhelming manpower, the invasion came close to success due to the pathetic state of the Soviet officer corps after Stalin's purges. At the peak of his conquests in late 1941, Hitler held an empire stretching from the Arctic Circle to the Sahara Desert, from the Pyrénées to the Urals.

The Soviets suffered extremely high casualties, but the *Blitzkrieg* faltered in the Russian winter and Hitler sacrificed thousands of German soldiers in his adamant refusal to retreat. The titanic and bloody battle of **Stalingrad** was the critical turning point in the East. Hitler committed a second fateful error when he declared war on the United States after his Japanese allies bombed Pearl Harbor. His attempt to bail out his ally Mussolini in North Africa led to the Nazi's first battlefield defeats, and soon Germany was retreating on all fronts. The Allied landings in Normandy on **D-Day** (June 6, 1944) preceded an arduous, bloody advance across Western Europe. An **assassination attempt** against Hitler led by Klaus von Stauffenberg and a circle of aristocrats failed in July 1944, ensuring that the war would continue until the bitter end. The Third Reich's final offensive, the **Battle of the Bulge,** failed in December 1944. In March 1945, the Allies crossed the Rhine. The Red Army in the east overcame bitter resistance to take Berlin in April 1945. With Red Army troops overhead, Hitler married Eva Braun just prior to killing himself in his bunker. The Third Reich, which Hitler had boasted would endure for 1000 years, had lasted only 12.

THE HOLOCAUST

Hitler's twisted racist ideology regarded history as a series of catastrophic confrontations between racial groups. The German *Volk,* he believed, had to triumph or perish forever. He made no secret of his desire to exterminate all Jews, who, associated with internationalism, pacifism, and democracy, represented the very antithesis of Hitler's fanatic nationalism, militarism, and the sacred myth of the *"Führer."* The Nazis' **"Final Solution to the Jewish problem"** can be seen as the extension of the persecution, deprivation, and deportation to which Jews had been subjected since the first days of the Third Reich. Another precedent was the gassing of the handicapped in the 30s. Nevertheless, the mass gassing of Jews in specially constructed **extermination camps** began only in 1942, although **SS Sonderkommando** (special commands) which followed the *Wehrmacht* through Russia had earlier staged mass executions. Seven full-fledged extermination camps, **Auschwitz, Buchenwald, Chelmno, Treblinka, Majdanek, Sobibor,** and **Belzec,** plus dozens of nominal "labor" camps such as **Bergen-Belsen, Dachau,** and **Sachsenhausen** were operating before war's end. Some six million Jews, two-thirds of Europe's Jewish population, representing every Nazi-occupied country but mostly from Poland and the Soviet Union, were gassed, shot, starved, worked to death, or killed by exposure. All together, more than 4950 cities and towns saw their Jewish populations destroyed. Five million other victims—Soviet prisoners of war, Slavs, Gypsies, homosexuals, the mentally retarded, and political opponents of the regime—also died in Nazi camps. What occurred during the years of Nazi tyranny reaches beyond the scope of tragedy to a horror so great that it is, for most, inconceivable.

How much did the average German know about the Holocaust? No one can say for sure, but it is certain that the vicious persecution and small-scale murder of Jews in pre-war Germany and the "resettlement" of Jews in the east were abundantly clear for all to see. However, the Nazis were careful to keep the grisly details of gas chambers and crematoria out of reach, even among the top party leadership. By the time the Holocaust got underway in 1942, the Nazi terror machine was in high gear, and Germany was suffering catastrophic losses on the Eastern front. Germans suffering the privations of the war were not likely to focus their attention on the fate of Jewish neighbors who had disappeared years before—or so many Germans claim. The reality is that many Germans who now express horror at the genocide were willing to tolerate—or even approve of—the Nazis' earlier, less deadly expressions of anti-Semitism. Very few were as daring as industrialist Oskar Schindler or the Scholl siblings, who led the "White Rose" student resistance movement.

Today, while Holocaust survivors and their families still grapple with questions of faith and loss, scores of scholarly works confront "revisionist" theories that claim the Holocaust never happened. As the living memory of the Holocaust slowly fades, the aging remains of concentration camps become the most crucial, tangible testimony available to any audience willing to see and listen. Robert Musil wrote that "there is nothing in this world as invisible as a monument," and just as a monument can lose its power to shock by becoming all-too-familiar to the passer-by, so can the very existence of "museums" and guided tours seem to trivialize what occurred at them. The very fact that concentration camps are noted as points of interest in many travel guides (including this one), must be recognized as somewhat troubling in itself. If you choose to visit one, keep in mind that while some treat these grounds as "just another stop" on a list of things to see, coming in ignorance and leaving unaffected, many visitors come with a knowledge of the camp's past or perhaps a personal memory of a loved one who perished within its walls. Make an effort not to treat them and the grounds with disrespect. In addition, know that the exhibits here do not tell the whole story; no single medium can embrace such a narrative. Read up before you come. Better yet, a discussion with a survivor will inevitably shed more light on the dark history of these camps than any exhibit ever will.

OCCUPATION AND DIVISION

Germans call their defeat in the Second World War **Nullpunkt**—"Point Zero"—the moment at which everything began again. Unlike in World War I, Germany's battlefield defeat was total and indisputable. The Allies occupied and partitioned the country: the east under the Soviets, the west under the British and Americans, and Berlin under joint control. The economy was in shambles. Virtually every city had been bombed into ruin. More than five million German soldiers and civilians had been killed in the war, and millions more remained in POW camps. All German territory east of the Oder and Neisse Rivers—a quarter of the nation's land area—was confiscated and placed under Soviet and Polish "administration," while the coal-rich Saarland was placed under French control. Ten to twelve million ethnic Germans were expelled from Poland and Sudeten Czechoslovakia; more than two million perished during the exodus. Every institution and existing source of authority was discredited by involvement with the Nazi regime. As the horrible details of the Nazi genocidal project became public, "German" became synonymous with "barbaric."

The Allied program for the **Occupation**—demilitarization, democratization, and de-Nazification—proceeded apace, but growing animosity between the Soviets and the Western allies made joint control of Germany increasingly difficult. De-Nazification proceeded in quite disparate ways in East and West, paving the way for total division in 1949. Blaming bourgeois capitalism for the Nazi nightmare, the Soviets purged all former elites, leaving the common people exempt from any responsibility; the Allies prosecuted Nazis individually, yet often so inadequately that many retained their posts. In 1947, the Western Allies merged their occupation zones into a single economic unit known as **Bizonia** (later Trizonia, after a French occupation zone was carved out of the British and American zones). The Western Allies began to rebuild their zone along the lines of a market economy with the aid of huge cash infusions from the **Marshall Plan.** The Soviets, who had suffered immeasurably more in the war than the U.S. or Britain, had neither the desire nor the spare cash to help the east rebuild—they plundered it instead, as the Potsdam agreement allowed them. The Soviet Union carted away everything that wasn't fixed in concrete and a lot of things (such as factories and railroads) that were. The Western Allies ceased their contribution to this "giant sucking sound" in 1948 and then effectively severed the East's economy from the West's by introducing a new currency to Bizonia, the **Deutschmark.** Though the imposition of the new Marks seemed draconian at the time, most historians agree that it was the single greatest cause of the eventual stabilization of Western Germany. "On June 21, 1948, goods reappeared in the stores," wrote one economist, "and money resumed its normal function; the spirit of the country changed overnight. The gray, hungry, dead-looking figures wandering about the streets came to life as, pocketing their DM40, they went out on a first spending spree." The dispute over currency reform was the proximate cause of the **Berlin Blockade** (see Berlin: History, page 392) and the ultimate **division of Germany** in 1949.

THE FEDERAL REPUBLIC

The Federal Republic of Germany (*Bundesrepublik Deutschland*) was established as a provisional government of western Germany on May 24, 1949. A **Basic Law** (*Grundgesetz*), drawn up by German academics and politicians under the direction of the Western Allies, safeguarded individual rights and established a system of Federal States. The word "constitution" was deliberately avoided to emphasize the provisional character of the government. Although similar in many ways to the Weimar Constitution, the Basic Law had significant departures: it made the Chancellor responsible to Parliament, banned anti-democratic parties, renounced militarism, emasculated the presidency, and established a more stable parliamentary system. One of the most visionary paragraphs of the Basic Law was the one which established a Right of Asylum, guaranteeing refuge to any person fleeing persecution. Ratification of the Basic Law, however, did not restore German sovereignty; the Allies retained supreme power over the country, including the right to veto legislation.

As the only party entirely untainted by the Third Reich, the **Social Democratic Party (SPD)** seemed poised to dominate post-war German politics. Under the leadership of **Kurt Schumacher,** a fierce anti-communist and anti-fascist maimed in a concentration camp, the SPD ran under the slogan "Only one party stood against every war, every dictator." Another new party, the **Free Democratic Party** (*Freidemokratische Partei*—FDP), assembled bourgeois liberals and professionals together with a disconcertingly high number of former Nazis. Although the FDP remained small and was often disparaged as the *"fast drei Prozent"* (almost 3%) party, it acquired power as a coalition partner. The Communists did notably poorly in the West, a reflection of public anger at the ruthless domination of the Eastern Zone. Remarkably, Germany's historically fragmented conservatives and centrists managed to unite around a new party, the **Christian Democratic Union** (*Christliche Demokratische Union*—CDU); with former Cologne Mayor **Konrad Adenauer** at the helm, the CDU won a small plurality of *Bundestag* seats.

Adenauer, who was an astonishing 73 years old when he assumed office, was perhaps the Federal Republic's greatest Chancellor. His unflaggingly pursued goals were the integration of Germany into a unified Europe and, at the same time, the return of German national self-determination. He achieved both of these aims, first in 1951 with West Germany's entrance into the European Coal and Steel Community, the precursor of the modern European Union (EU), and then in 1955 when the Western Allies recognized the West German government's sovereignty. The idealistic Adenauer also helped to restore the self-esteem and purpose of his defeated people, without rekindling the nationalistic fervor of the past.

By the mid-1950s, Germany's post-war **Economic Miracle** (*Wirtschaftswunder*) was in full swing, and the CDU's dominance of German politics seemed unshakable. Adenauer left the development of the so-called social-market economy to Economics Minister Ludwig Erhard, while the powerful chancellor concerned himself with integrating Germany into Western Europe and winning back sovereignty from the Allies. Rebuilding progressed rapidly, and Germany's industrial production increased sixfold between 1949 and 1966, with a heavy emphasis on manufacturing for export. Germany achieved full employment by the late 1950s and soon began recruiting thousands of foreign guest workers **(Gastarbeiter).** Despite the opposition of the SPD, which feared that alignment with the West would solidify the division of the country, Adenauer's Germany aligned itself with NATO (North Atlantic Treaty Organization) in a common defense bloc.

The SPD, whose fortunes seemed so promising in 1945, had found itself relegated to the electoral wilderness for more than two decades. The party's Marxist rhetoric, at odds with its reformist practice, prevented it from expanding beyond its loyal working-class base. In 1961, its Bad Godesberg Program jettisoned Marx and located the roots of social democracy in Christian ethics and the Western humanism. The SPD found a dynamic young leader in **Willy Brandt,** the charismatic former Berlin mayor who had worked in the anti-Nazi resistance. The electorate, anxious for a new era of energetic reform, responded positively. Germany's first post-war recession in 1967 badly hurt the CDU and the 1969 *Bundestag* elections catapulted the SPD into power.

With Brandt as chancellor, the **Social-Liberal Coalition** of the SDP and FDP enacted a number of overdue **domestic reforms** in education, governmental administration, social security, and industrial relations. Its most dramatic policy innovation, however, was in the sphere of **foreign relations.** Under the old **Hallstein Doctrine,** the Federal Republic had refused to recognize the German Democratic Republic, to the point of severing relations with any country that recognized the GDR. This effectively meant that West Germany was entirely cut off from the entire Eastern Bloc. Under Brandt's **Ostpolitik** (Eastern Policy), the Federal Republic actively sought to improve relations with East Germany, the Soviet Union, and other eastern Bloc nations—a policy symbolized by the famous image of a tearful Brandt dropping to his knees in front of a Polish war memorial. Brandt and FDP Foreign Minister **Walter Scheel** concluded several important treaties, including a pledge to respect the 1945 German-Polish border and an agreement establishing **normal relations** with the GDR. For this, Brandt was awarded the Nobel Peace Prize. By 1973, West Germany had normalized relations with every Communist nation except for Albania.

The late 1960s and early 70s also saw the emergence of a radical **youth rebellion,** aimed against the American war in Vietnam and the stifling intellectual conformity of 1950s West Germany. Although most of this protest took the same peaceful form as American campus demonstrations, radical groups such as the **Baader-Meinhof** gang and their more violent offshoot, the **Red Army Faction (RAF),** launched a wave of violent terrorist attacks, which in the 1970s claimed the lives of several prominent officials. The government responded with an extremely controversial set of **emergency laws** that placed restrictions on civil liberties and banned communists from employment in the civil service (which includes all teaching positions).

After Brandt resigned in the wake of a 1974 spy scandal, his articulate and highly respected economics minister, **Helmut Schmidt,** assumed the chancellorship. West Germany under Schmidt racked up an economic record that was the envy of the industrialized world. Nevertheless, persistent structural problems in heavy industry contributed to **mounting unemployment** and dissatisfaction with the SPD in the late 1970s. Fortunately for the government, the CDU shot itself in the foot by nominating the disagreeable, arch-conservative "Uncrowned King of Bavaria" **Franz-Josef Strauss** as its candidate for chancellor in 1980. But in 1982, the FDP and the CDU formed a government under **Helmut Kohl** after FDP leader **Hans-Dietrich Genscher** abruptly abandoned the Social-Liberal coalition.

Kohl's government pursued a policy of welfare state retrenchment, tight monetary policy, and military cooperation with the U.S. Around the same time, a new political force emerged in Germany: the **Green Party** *(die Grünen),* which fought for disarmament and environmentalism, won a surprisingly large following by rejecting the traditional coalition politics of the Left. The Greens were divided between the unstructured idealism of the *fundis* and the pragmatism of the *realos*, which ended their meteoric rise. In 1984, Richard von Weizsäcker of the CDU was elected to the largely symbolic post of Federal President, from which he urged Germans to shoulder fully their moral responsibility for the Third Reich—an implicit rebuke of politicians like Kohl who spoke of "the grace of late birth."

THE GERMAN DEMOCRATIC REPUBLIC

When the Red Army occupied Eastern Germany, a cadre of German Communists who had spent the war in exile in Moscow came close on their heels. Even before the surrender was signed, these party functionaries had begun setting up an apparatus to run the Soviet occupation zone. The first party licensed to operate in the Soviet Sector was the communist KPD under **Wilhelm Pieck** and **Walter Ulbricht,** but versions of the Western parties were established shortly afterwards. At first, the German Communists pledged to establish a parliamentary democracy and a distinctively "German path to socialism." However, their dependence on Moscow became apparent. The Social Democrats were forced to join them in a common working-class anti-fascist front, the **Socialist Unity Party** *(Sozialistische Einheitspartei Deutschlands—* SED).

In Berlin, the one area where the SPD was permitted to operate freely, it soundly defeated the SED at the ballot box. The Soviets responded by not holding any more freely contested elections; future elections required voters to approve or reject a "unity list" of candidates that ensured the dominance of the SED. On October 7, 1949, a People's Congress selected by such methods declared the establishment of the **German Democratic Republic** *(Deutsche Demokratische Republik),* with the national capital in Berlin. Although the first constitution of the GDR guaranteed civil liberties and payed elaborate lip service to parliamentary democracy, these were but empty words. Real power lay in the hands of the SED's *Politburo* and the party's general secretary, Walter Ulbricht. Although the SPD was nominally an equal partner in the SED, some 200,000 SPD members were purged for the crime of *Sozialdemokrat-ismus.* Many died in labor camps.

After the death of Stalin, political conditions relaxed a bit in the GDR, though the nationalization of industry proceeded without hesitation. Impossibly high work goals, sharpened by the drainage of workers to the West, led to a **workers' revolt** across the GDR on June 17, 1953, which was ruthlessly crushed with the aid of Soviet tanks (see Berlin: History, page 392). The insurrection marked the end of the mildly reformist, post-Stalinist **New Course.** In response to the Federal Republic's rehabilitation in the West, the GDR was recognized by the Soviet Union in 1954 and became a party to the **Warsaw Pact** in 1955.

In 1961, the GDR decided to remedy the exodus of skilled young workers to the Federal Republic; although borders to the West had been sealed off, escape through Berlin remained a possibility. On the night of August 12-13, the first, rudimentary barriers of the **Berlin Wall** were laid (see History, p. 392). The regime called it an "anti-fascist protective wall," but Berliners knew which way the guns were pointed. Stanching the flow of refugees gave Ulbricht room to launch his hard-line **New Economic System** and to establish the GDR's **second constitution** in 1968. This document jettisoned most constitutional rights, already ignored in practice, and abandoned all pretense of parliamentary democracy. In 1968, units of the People's Army assisted in the Soviet suppression of Czechoslovakia's Prague Spring.

Ulbricht's iron grip on power was broken in 1971 when he ran afoul of his Soviet patrons. His replacement, **Erich Honecker,** was a party functionary even more doctrinaire and colorless than his predecessor. He returned East Germany to unquestioning subservience to the Soviet Union and eliminated all reformist experiments. By 1973 the boastful watchword of the regime was **"real existing socialism."** A **third constitution** adopted in 1974 reflected the new thinking. Relations with the West improved remarkably during the era of Willy Brandt's **Ostpolitik,** and many Westerners were permitted to visit relatives in the GDR for the first time. But meanwhile, the hated secret police, the **Stasi,** maintained a network of hundreds of thousands of agents and paid informants that strove to monitor every citizen. Still, despite the scars of the war and the inefficiency of central planning, by the late 1970s East Germans enjoyed the highest standard of living in the Eastern Bloc.

With the ascension of the *glasnost*-minded **Mikhail Gorbachev** to the leadership of the Soviet Union in 1985, reform began to spread throughout the Eastern Bloc— except the GDR, which adhered to a rigid, Brezhnev-style orthodoxy. In May 1989, Hungary began dismantling the barbed-wire border with Austria, giving some 55,000 East Germans a route to the West. By October, Czechoslovakia was tolerating a flood of GDR citizens into the West German embassy; thousands were permitted to emigrate. On October 6, while on a state visit to celebrate the GDR's 40th birthday, Gorbachev publicly reprimanded Honecker and announced that the Soviet Union would not interfere in the GDR's domestic affairs. Clandestine dissident groups (supported and protected by the Lutheran church) such as **New Forum** began to operate more freely, and massive **anti-government demonstrations** broke out in the streets of Leipzig, Dresden, Berlin, and other cities, demanding free elections, freedom of the press, and freedom to travel. Faced with the rising pressure of the citizenry, Honecker soon resigned. His successor, **Egon Krenz** (whose name bears an uncanny similarity to the word for "border") promised reforms. Meanwhile, tens of thousands of GDR citizens—largely young professionals—continued to flee via Czechoslovakia, which had completely opened its border with West Germany. The entire GDR Politburo resigned on November 8, and a day later, a spokesperson for the Central Committee announced the **opening of all borders to the West,** including the Berlin Wall.

REUNIFICATION

The opening of the Wall did not immediately herald the demise of the GDR or the Communist regime. It was more than a week afterwards that Prime Minister **Hans Modrow** pledged to hold free elections. The constitution was re-written to remove references to the leading role of the SED, but the party remained in power and the

Stasi continued to operate, despite pressure. Throughout December, popular demonstrations continued unabated. Honecker was whisked away to the Soviet Union and the SED renamed itself the **Party of Democratic Socialism (PDS).** The year 1990 began with another ecstatic celebration on top of the Berlin Wall, but the apparent community belied a furious political struggle going on in both Germanies. In the East, opposition parties took shape and assumed positions in the existing government as the West's political parties frantically scrambled to assert their influence; eventually, all of them linked up with like-minded parties in the GDR in preparation for **elections** in March. The SPD was crippled in the elections by its expressed reluctance about the prospect of reunification, which inhibited it from making allies in the East. Buoyed by Kohl's success at getting Moscow to assent to unification, the CDU-backed **Alliance for Germany** emerged the winner. A broad coalition government of non-Communist parties authorized **economic and social union** with the Federal Republic. On **D-Mark Day** (as July 2 was known in the English press), GDR citizens exchanged their worthless Ostmarks for mighty D-Marks. The wartime Allies agreed to permit the **complete political reunification** of Germany; the last obstacle, the Soviet Union's insistence that a united Germany remain outside NATO, was overcome when Kohl traded promises of substantial economic aid and a pledge not to station NATO troops in the East for Gorbachev's approval of unification.

Despite catch-phrases such as *Wiedervereinigung* (reunification), East and West Germany did not unify on an equal basis to create a new nation-state. Rather, East Germany was absorbed into the Federal Republic, accepting the institutions and structures of the West. The Basic Law, embodied in its paragraph 146, was intended to be a provisional constitution until eventual unification. However, under the Basic Law's paragraph 23, any territory had the power to accede, or simply declare themselves ready to be annexed by, the Federal Republic. This was a faster route to unity, and after a great deal of debate, it was the one Germany took. On **October 3, 1990,** the Allies forfeited their occupation rights, the GDR ceased to exist, and Germany became one united, sovereign nation for the first time in 45 years, to the accompaniment of fireworks and pealing bells. Germans now distinguish between East and West with the labels **"New Federal States"** and **"Old Federal States."**

GERMANY TODAY

Immediately following the quick pace of events in 1989-90, nationalistic euphoria blurred the true state of matters for Germans on both sides of the wall. Rapidly the problems became blatantly apparent. The inefficient industries and institutions in the East led to massive unemployment and the Federal Republic's worst-ever recession. Many westerners have resented the inflation and taxes brought on by the cost of rebuilding the new federal states; Easterners have had to give up the generous social benefits Communism had afforded them. A rightward-moving political climate in the west pulled the east with it, restricting social programs not only in welfare but also in areas such as abortion (see page 68).

Recently, the anger has spread to an intense distrust of **foreigners,** especially immigrants from Eastern Europe and the *Gastarbeiter*s (see page 64), some of whom have been living in Germany for decades. German law does not automatically grant citizenship to children born in Germany; parentage is considered the paramount factor. This has become more and more of a troubling point as the children of immigrants grow up in Germany, speak only German, know no other home, but are defined as life-long outsiders. Violent attacks on foreigners, sometimes resulting in murder, have become more frequent throughout Germany. In 1992, particularly wide-scale assaults resulting in multiple deaths were launched against immigrants in Mölln and Rostock; in June 1993, an arson attack on the home of a Turkish family in the western town of Solingen claimed several lives, including those of a number of young children. Violence has continued despite various attempts at crackdowns. Although the general reaction in Germany has been outrage, there have been statements of "understanding" for the attackers' motives, including an implicit one from the government itself: soon after Solingen, Germany's liberal **Asylum Law** was repealed. Nazi graffiti is most apparent in the new federal states, although neo-Nazis are also active, if not as visible, in the west.

After the dramatic fall of the Berlin Wall in 1989, Kohl and his CDU seemed insurmountable. Carrying their momentum into the first all-German elections, the CDU scored a stunning victory. After then, however, Kohl's popularity plummeted to the point where on one occasion eastern voters pelted him with rotten fruit during a visit and his party failed to carry his own state in *Land* elections. But the CDU bounced back; in 1994 it accomplished a hat trick of victories in the elections for President (**Roman Herzog** being the victorious CDU candidate), the European Parliament, and finally the German Parliament. But Kohl's majority is narrow, and dependent on the increasingly-marginalized liberal FDP. The SPD now views itself as a government-in-waiting, perhaps with the support of the Greens, who have themselves done poorly in recent elections but remain a viable third force.

Abortion laws have changed abruptly a number of times in the years since Reunification. Paragraph 218 of the Basic Law vaguely refers to a "right to life." Prior to reunification, abortion was technically legal in Germany, but not available on demand. Germany worked according to an "indication" model—a woman must show that the reason she is seeking an abortion is acceptable to the state. These include medical (woman's life is in danger) and legal (the pregnancy is a result of rape). There is one loose category, a "social indication," meaning that the pregnancy would unacceptably disrupt the woman's life. The problem was that whether or not a woman met this standard was determined on a state-by-state basis. In the GDR, abortion was a means of birth control, fully available on demand. In 1992, the unified Bundestag voted to do away with the indications model, but still mandated counseling and a lengthy process of bureaucratic maneuvering. Bavaria promptly sued the federal government in the Constitutional Court. In May 1993, the court decided against liberalization, and actually set limits which were stricter for *everyone* than they were before reunification. In 1994, a bill that would have further restricted abortion was rejected by the upper house of Germany's parliament; in 1995, limited liberalizing legislation was approved. The conflict continues.

Europe, or more specifically the new Germany's place in it, is currently the big political question. The burden of the past makes everyone nervous about German intervention into European foreign policy, not least the Germans themselves. The last initiative, an attempt to bring about the diplomatic recognition of the splinter states of the former Yugoslavia, ended in disaster; Germany has been content to stick to the sidelines since. The dominant feeling right now, promulgated by Kohl's CDU coalition, is that Germany should stay out of foreign policy, acting instead as a large, benign economic machine at the heart of the European Union. But Germany is not Switzerland; such a neutral stance may not always be possible for the most populous and economically powerful nation in Europe. There are thinkers on the political Left, with some support in the Greens and the PDS, who would like to see the unified Germany take on the mission of embodying a "third way," a corrective to the excesses of both Eastern socialism and Western capitalism.

It is hard to end an essay on German history, because it is a narrative which reaches in many directions across time. There are always bursts of change which seem to have no precedent. There are moments when one seems to be hearing the same story again, to hear the same turns of phrase deployed in different settings, the same insistence and the same denial. It is easy to be caught and lost in what Bertolt Brecht called "this Babylonian confusion of words," the narrative of Germany.

FURTHER READING

Gordon A. Craig's *Germany 1866-1945* provides a definitive history of those years. A more general picture of the character of modern Germany can be found in Craig's excellent *The Germans*, an accessible but never simplistic book. For an in-depth look at post-war German history, pick up Henry Ashby Turner's *The Two Germanies Since 1945*, or Peter J. Katzenstein's *Policy and Politics in Western Germany*. Ralf Dahrendorf's *Society and Democracy in Germany* is a great treatment of "the German Question." Also, read anything that novelist Günter Grass has written on Reunification. He criticizes the rapidity of the process and the forgetfulness and abandonment of the historic lessons Germany might have learned in the years since the war. Grass has emerged as a powerful moral voice in contemporary Germany, one worthy of attention. His novels are also excellent (see Literature, p. 71).

■ Culture

Germany, the Germans like to say, is the land of *"Dichter und Denker"*—poets and philosophers. Poet Bertolt Brecht, with inspired cynicism, claimed that a truer epithet was land of the *"Richter und Henker"*—the judge and the hangman. But Brecht's own literary life helped to belie his statement. What is striking about Germany are the ways in which a peculiarly German sense of the role culture plays in everyday life intersects with the "peculiarities" of German history. German nationalists of the past have opposed the concept of pithy, muscular German "culture" to supposedly lighter, superficial Anglo-French "civilization." Germany's cultural legacy is indeed rich, richer than that of almost any nation in Europe. This inheritance extends to the visual arts, architecture, music, literature, philosophy, and film.

VISUAL ART

Art in Germany extends back to Celtic and Roman artifacts and tribal folk decorations. With the rise of Christianity, the artistic impulse in medieval Germany focused on religious themes. Distinctively German painting flourished in the Renaissance. The **School of the Danube,** a group of South German painters, advanced the idea of the **Cologne School** still farther into the secular world, giving the landscape or architectural environment primary importance over human subjects. **Lucas Cranach** was particularly taken with the idea of combining the beauty of nature with the sublimity of divine subjects. Cranach produced paintings like a man possessed; there's barely a town or city in east-central Germany that doesn't boast a sizable Cranach collection. **Hans Holbein the Younger** is renowned for his portraits, executed at both the German and English courts; his *Henry VIII* is an eerie, detached portrait of the noble with the standard *memento mori.* **Matthias Grünewald** clung to medieval forms for his haunting, highly symbolic religious works. His medium of choice was the altar dip- or triptych. **Albrecht Dürer,** one of Germany's most renowned Renaissance artists, worked in painting, drafting, and woodcuts; his work in all three is dark in psychological atmosphere and masterful in line. In the fateful year 1500, on a featureless black background, Dürer painted one of the era's great images—Europe's first self-portrait. After the Thirty Years War virtually halted construction and laid Germany to waste, the **Baroque** era invigorated Renaissance architecture with bold, flamboyant decoration. The outstanding figure of this period was **Tilman Riemenschneider,** a wood-carver who produced statuary for churches and palaces.

The cool simplicity of **Neoclassicism** softened into **Romanticism,** harking back to German national idioms and to local Gothic and Romanesque architectural styles. The Wars of Liberation (as Germans call the Napoleonic Wars) infused paintings with highly **national themes** of German landscape and legend, some frolicsome and pastoral, others mystical and serious. The intriguing master of the latter type was **Caspar David Friedrich,** with his brilliant, haunting landscapes obsessed with man's solitude and insignificance. Many of his works capture dramatic, uninhabitable landscapes such as icy oceans and wind-blown cemeteries. If you squint your eyes, you can see the world the way **Max Liebermann** did—he began as a master Impressionist (viz. *Munich Beer Garden*) and from there went on to lead the Berlin faction of the **Secession movement** in the 1890s: in two words, decadence and eroticism. This trend became **Jugendstil** (literally, "youth-style"), which rose to popularity in Berlin, Vienna, Prague, and Budapest in the early 20th century.

The years of the **Weimar Republic** saw an extraordinary proliferation of artistic genius. The Symbolist tendencies of *Jugendstil* intensified into the larger **Expression-**

ist movement, with a deliberately anti-naturalist aesthetic that distorted objects and colors in order to identify them with an abstract idea or interior state of mind. A series of city-based groups created consortia of Expressionist effort. **Die Brücke** (The Bridge), including Ernst Ludwig Kirschner, was the earliest of these, founded at Dresden in 1905 with the explicit aim of heightening the intensity of expression in art. The **Blaue Reiter** (Blue Rider) group was founded in Munich in 1909 by the Russian emigré **Wassily Kandinsky** and named after one of his paintings. Kandinsky's epoch-making contribution was a series of works called *Improvisations* painted in 1910-11, which are considered to be the first totally **non-representational paintings** in Western civilization. The *Blaue Reiter* also included **Franz Marc** and **Paul Klee. Max Beckmann** left a large body of Expressionist works (although he shunned the label) focused on the anxieties of a dehumanized culture. The smaller German **Realist** movement devoted itself to bleak, critical works such as **Käthe Kollwitz's** posters for social reform. **Ernst Barlach** combined realism with religious themes, inflaming Nazi censors, who banned his work.

The rise of Nazism drove most Weimar artists into exile. They were either the "wrong" race or religion, or their works were branded "decadent and subversive" and banished from view, after the Nazis displayed it in a huge exhibition to showcase its "degeneracy." In contrast to the complex and eclectic variety of banned art, wartime art was limited by Nazi ideology. Visual arts in Nazi Germany were dominated by themes of **Blut und Boden** (Blood and Soil), depicting the mythical union of *völkisch* blood and German soil through idealized images of workers, farmers, and soldiers. A reject from the Vienna School of Art, Hitler favored sterile, bombastic idealism, including nude representations of members of the "master race."

Postwar artistic effort has not spawned any unified movement. Much postwar art from West Germany incorporated intense performative strategies meant to challenge the relation between art and politics. Some of the old Expressionist masters were still alive and working in the 50s and 60s, but the fragmentation of "postmodern" culture has splintered newer artists into a host of different styles that borrow and reshape the idioms and icons of German culture. The Düsseldorf **Zero Group** produced abstractions during the first decades after the war. A neo-Expressionist group called the **Junge Wilde** (Young Savages) surfaced in Berlin in the late 70s, using vivid colors and strong movement. **Josef Beuys** was a charismatic, controversial figure who created deliberately low-brow juxtapositions, such as felt and lard.

Art in the GDR had a more nuanced history than the western stereotype of a socialist cultural desert would imply. After an initial flirtation with liberal tolerance, the ruling SED "Stalinized" the arts. The regime-sponsored orthodox style was known as **Socialist Realism,** exemplified by paintings such as **Lea Grundig's** *Coal and Steel for Peace* and **Otto Nagel's** *Jungpioniere* (Young Pioneers). The painters **Hans Grundig, Rudolf Bergander,** and **Eva Schulze-Knabe** and the sculptor **Fritz Cremer** (who designed the Buchenwald Memorial) were also leading figures in the movement. Ambiguity had no place in Socialist Realism: the GDR and the SED were glorified, and "bourgeois influence" was repressed. East German artists managed a remarkable amount of innovation and experimentation despite the repression.

ARCHITECTURE AND DESIGN

In the medieval period, violent, highly stylized images and masterworks of carving and glasswork ornamented the quiet, somber lines of the cathedrals. The **Romanesque** period followed, spanning the years 1000 to 1300, with a style of architecture that emerged in direct imitation of antique ruins. Outstanding Romanesque cathedrals can be found at Speyer, Trier, and Mainz. The **Gothic** style gradually replaced the Romanesque from 1300 to 1500. The 14th century was a transitional period that spawned the **Cologne Cathedral.** Stained glass filled the windows of Gothic cathedrals with ever more elaborate patterns of divine light.

The Lutheran reforms of the 1550s put a damper on the unrestrained extravagance of cathedrals. Although the **Renaissance** saw a modicum of church-building, efforts were mostly channelled into such secular buildings as the **Augsburg Rathaus** (town hall) and **Heidelberg Castle.** Early Baroque shows itself in the **Rathaus** in Leipzig and that in Bremen, as well as the **Würzburg Residenz.** Baroque developed quickly into the extravagant ornamentation of **Rococo;** Munich's **Amalienburg Palace** and **Residenztheater** are typical of the hyper-ornate flamboyance of that movement. The French Revolution snuffed out the courtliness that fueled Baroque and Rococo, replacing them with ideals of "noble simplicity" *(Einfachheit)*. These ideals spawned a Greek revival of clean lined classical forms, visible in the cluster of historic Prussian buildings along **Unter Den Linden** in central Berlin.

Wertheim's Department Store in Berlin and the **Exhibition** buildings at Darmstadt are two architectural manifestations of *Jugendstil,* the early 20th-century movement of decorative, stylized design (discussed in detail in Visual Art section, above). **Erich Mendelsohn** later brought the Expressionist aesthetic to architecture, creating curvaceous structures like the **Einstein Tower** at Potsdam, a structure Einstein himself approved with a single word: "Organic." The ideas behind **Neue Sächlichkeit** (New Objectivity) revolutionized design. **Peter Behrens** pioneered these ideas; he designed objects to suit the efficient new materials of industry, concentrating on unornamented geometric harmonies. **Walter Gropius** designed several sensational buildings with clean forms, flat roofs, and broad windows, all made possible by new concrete-and-steel construction techniques.

In 1919 Gropius founded the **Bauhaus,** a ground-breaking school of design that combined theoretical training in the new principles of efficiency with exposure to the realities of mass production. "Form follows function" was its oft-quoted principle of construction. The school moved to **Dessau** in 1925, where Gropius designed the school's new facility, which became the symbol of the modern style. While Bauhaus's sleek, austere lines informed some of the most brilliant designs of the century, the school must also bear some of the responsibility for the later abuse of its principles: the soulless, box-like skyscrapers of cities like Frankfurt and New York would not have been possible without its example.

Hitler disapproved of the new buildings; he named a design school reject, **Albert Speer,** as his minister of architecture, and commissioned buildings of a ponderous Neoclassical style, intended to last the "Thousand-Year Reich." Many were intended for public rallies, such as the **Congress Hall** and **Stadium** at Nuremberg.

The architecture in the GDR was decidedly un-*Bauhaus:* a pseudo-Classical, sterile, Stalinist style. The overblown buildings lining the then-**Karl-Marx-Allee** in Eastern Berlin represent the apogee, such as it is, of **Socialist Realist** architecture. The East's most noted architect, **Hermann Henselmann,** was a former *Bauhaus* member who apparently forgot everything he had learned. As Chief of Architecture for the development projects in Berlin from 1953 to 1959, he designed several of the sterile edifices on **Alexanderplatz** in Berlin and conceived the plan for the television tower. The hideous "Sharp Tooth" building at the heart of the former **Karl Marx Universität** in Leipzig bears his mark as well.

LITERATURE

The history of German literature can be traced back to pre-Christian times, to the earliest records of specifically Germanic gods. They were the subjects of the tales told before the advent of writing, heroic tales of warriors like the legendary **Dietrich** (based on Theodric the Great) and the **Walküre** (battlemaidens). In the 10th-11th centuries, villagers flocked to hear **Spielmänner,** itinerant poet-entertainers, recite tall tales of the exotic or marvelous. At court, nobles amused themselves with chivalric romances (11th-13th centuries). The 12th century master of this form, **Gottfried von Strassburg,** concerned himself more with aesthetics than jousting in his take on the *Tristan(ne)* legend. **Wolfram von Eschenbach's** *Parzival* is the seminal story of a noble boy brought up away from his birthright who regains it and rides of in search of the Holy Grail. Clerics in monasteries transcribed these and earlier tales.

By the 13th century heroic lyrics had developed into full-fledged **epics.** The most famous and popular of these is the **Nibelungenlied,** the story of Prince Siegfried, his wooing of the valkyrie Brunhilde, his murder, and the subsequent downfall of the

Burgundians. Shorter lyric forms gave rise to the wandering **Minnesänger,** the greatest of whom was **Walther von der Vogelweide;** his songs embroiled him with both women and politics. Lyric of this era could range from humorous legend to courtly subjects, with an emphasis on originality and form as it became an art instead of a form of record-keeping. Although the literature of the following **Reformation** consisted primarily of propagandist prose tracts, one event brought the German language to great heights of expression and away from Latin influences: the landmark High German **translation of the Bible** by Martin Luther. Through the 17th century, however, Germany followed trends originating elsewhere in Europe.

A self-consciously German canon emerged in the 18th century. The dramatist **Gotthold Ephraim Lessing** produced a series of plays that diverged sharply from contemporary French-influenced drama. Lessing broke the ground for the overtly critical and emotional works to come in the series of sub-movements around the turn of the 19th century. The writers of the well-known **Sturm und Drang** (Storm and Stress) movement ventured further into the depths of human emotion. The works of this era emphasize the primacy of individual conscience, intuition, and emotion over reason. **Johann Wolfgang von Goethe** was the first major success of this movement, and remains a monumental figure in German literature as a whole. His hugely popular *Die Leiden des jungen Werthers* (The Sorrows of Young Werther) spawned a wave of sentimental *Weltschmerz.* This and other early works virtually ignored the principle of dramatic simplicity. Instead they were powerful, psychological works with vigorous, complex characters and an unrestrained natural form that had been fostered by the teaching of the elder figure of the *Sturm und Drang,* **Johann Gottfried Herder.** Herder's insistence on originality of image and on a distinctly national style characterized his literary criticism. **Friedrich von Schiller** also catapulted to continental fame. By the 1790s the *Sturm und Drang* had begun to metamorphose into a quieter movement balancing feeling and reason, a tendency that gave the period its **Classical** label. Schiller and Goethe composed masterworks in this mature, innovative period just before the full flowering of **Romanticism.** At Weimar, Goethe completed *Faust* and *Wilhelm Meister,* which became the favorite of the later Romantics. As the 18th century ceded place to the 19th, a great and difficult young poet named **Friedrich Hölderlin** composed sonorous, strangely modern hymns about the disappearance of the Greek gods and the spiritual textures of Germany's hills and rivers. Hölderlin was the college roommate of the philosophers Hegel and Schelling; his life was touched with tragedy because of his contemporaries' failure to understand his work and of his gradual descent into permanent madness after 1800. At the same time, the **Brothers Grimm** assembled their famous collections of fairy tales, providing a foundation for German philology. **Heinrich Wilhelm von Kleist** wove pessimistic tales; the best known is *Die Marquise von O.*

Many writers, even during the height of Romanticism, were members of the politicized, anti-mystical, anti-Goethe **Young Germany** school banned as subversive by the *Bundesrat* in 1835. **Heinrich Heine** professed allegiance to this Young German movement. His *Wintermärchen* considers the stultifying climate engendered by political repression. Heine has been called the greatest master of German prose; he was also a Jew, and it is hard to say which irritated the patriotic *Bürger*s more: his beautifully ironic criticism of German society or his Jewishness. **Georg Büchner** was Heine's counterpart in drama; his *Woyzeck* introduced the first lower-class tragic hero in German literature. Finally, toward the end of the century, the volatile philosopher **Friedrich Nietzsche** took his place among the greatest of German writers. In his poetic, apocalyptic discourse *Also Sprach Zarathustra (Thus Spoke Zarathustra),* Nietzsche darkly declared that "God is dead" and tried to create a counter-ideal to what he saw as a mediocre, enervating Christianity.

The turn of the century saw a progression into the **Naturalistic** mode, inspired by the work of Zola. In Germany, the movement was based on finding beauty and value in the objects and patterns of everyday life. **Gerhart Hauptmann** was the foremost author of Naturalist drama. Naturalism was opposed by the **Symbolist** movement in the 20th-century years before the war. **Stefan George** utterly rejected Naturalism in favor of fleeting, sonorous image-poems, and gathered around him a passionate circle of like-minded, well-dressed artists.

The truly brilliant works of these years were written by Rilke, Hesse, and Mann. **Rainer Maria Rilke** composed supple rhymes and haunting images that captured fragments of experience. His uncanny poems express the difficulty of finding spirituality in the modern era. **Hermann Hesse** had a similar interest; his *Steppenwolf* considers the plight of modernity and the breakdown of bourgeois identity. **Thomas Mann** carried Symbolism to its purest form with *Der Zauberberg* (The Magic Mountain) and *Doktor Faustus*, two allegorical recountings of Germany's fateful history. Mann's brother **Heinrich,** also a novelist, wrote passionate novels including *Der Untertan* (The Subject), an attack on the subservience of the Germans.

The **Weimar era** marked an intense and magnificent outpouring of artistic expression, producing more masterpieces in less time than any other period in German history. Germany's version of the Parisian "Lost Generation" articulated its disillusionment in the **Neue Sachlichkeit** (New Objectivity) movement. The most famous was **Erich Maria Remarque,** who wrote *Im Westen nichts Neues* (All Quiet on the Western Front), a blunt, uncompromising account of the horror of war. Inspired by the ferment of Viennese Art Nouveau and nonrepresentational art, **Expressionism** picked up the torch of Symbolism after World War I. **Alfred Döblin's** novel *Berlin Alexanderplatz* traces shifts in consciousness in the metropolis. **Bertolt Brecht's** dramas and poems present humankind in all its grotesque absurdity, and sought to awake the consciousness of his audience. His *Dreigroßchenoper* (Three-Penny Opera) was set to music by Kurt Weill. The years of the Third Reich yielded little of artistic note; the official attitude toward literature was summed up by Nazi propaganda minister **Goebbels,** who once sneered, "Whenever I hear the word 'culture,' I reach for my gun." Some 2500 authors went into exile, and others underwent "internal emigration" and ceased to write. Many of Brecht's plays were written while he was in wartime exile.

The experience of war, defeat, and genocide inspired greater social conscience in many Germans. Many authors of the **Social Realist** movement convened formally in 1947 to reform German writing. The resulting coalition, known as **Gruppe 47,** maintained heavy influence on German literature well into the 70s. A major issue for these postwar German authors was how to reclaim their language after its corruption under fascist rule. *Gruppe 47*'s ranks include most of the largest names in contemporary German literature. **Heinrich Böll,** one of the founding members, won the Nobel Prize for Literature in 1972. **Günter Grass** wrote a stunning series of novels relating to recent German history, including *Der Blechtrommel* (The Tin Drum). **Peter Handke** is an on-the-road modern writer; his *Der kurze Brief zum langen Abschied*

Günter Grass: Of Cats, Mice and Tin Drums

Considered Germany's most celebrated contemporary writer, Günter Grass was born in Danzig in 1927. In the immediate post-war period, he quickly became the most famous member of the lively and critical literary *Gruppe 47*. His brilliant works, *Cat and Mouse, Dog Years,* and *The Tin Drum* were each uncompromising attempts to come to terms with the horrors of the Nazi experience. With dwarves, toads, and flounders serving as his central characters and an incredible eye for detail, Grass' eccentric and humorous literary style launched his career and catapulted him to fame. Grass has never flinched from his opinion that the writer as intellectual must be actively engaged with the political landscape and democratic process. Not surprisingly, he became an active supporter of the Social Democratic Party in the 1960s. In later years, Grass has applied his versatile, often satirically perverse, literary talents through poetry, essays, plays and drawings. Since 1989, he has consistently professed a strong, and increasingly isolated, criticism of German unification. With Auschwitz, Grass argues, Germany lost for all time the right to reunify. This radical view is contained in his most recent work *Two States—One Nation?*

is set entirely in America. A new school of drama developed through playwrights like **Rolf Hochhuth** *(Die Soldaten)* and **Peter Weiss** *(Marat/Sade)*.

The state of letters in the **GDR** followed the same pattern of waxing and waning government control that affected the visual arts (see page 69). Many expatriate writers, particularly those with Marxist leanings from before the war, returned to the East with great hopes. Brecht made his home in the GDR after the war. But the communist leadership was not interested in eliciting free artistic expression. The combination of personal danger and the burden of censorship led many immensely talented writers to leave, including **Ernst Bloch, Uwe Johnson, Sarah Kirsch,** and **Heiner Kipphardt.** Disillusionment drove many others to emigrate. In the 1970s and 80s, some East German writers were able to publish in the West, though not at home, and took that option as a middle ground. **Christa Wolf,** one of the most prominent German women writers, voluntarily remained in the GDR. Another prominent dissident author was **Stefan Heym.** Radical-left GDR playwright **Heiner Müller** shocked audiences throughout the 70s with the disgusted protagonists and stripped-down scenarios of Beckett-esque plays such as *Hamletmachine.* Since reunification, there has been a period of artistic anxiety and occasional malaise; in the new Federal States (the former GDR) many authors are caught up in controversies over co-workers who may have worked with the *Stasi.* Others, both East and West, have found that just thinking about the future of their country and what it means to be a German today, consumes their emotional and creative energies.

PHILOSOPHY

Karl Marx griped a lot about his fellow Germans' passion for philosophy; he saw their frenzied intellectual activity as the natural reaction of a servile people that lacked the capacity for real political action. "The philosophers have only interpreted the world in various ways," he wrote; "the point is to change it." To which one can imagine a German philosophy professor's response: "That, Herr Marx, is an interesting philosophical interpretation."

The Germans like to name their streets after philosophers; nearly every town has a *Kantstraße* or a *Schopenhauerstraße*, though *Marxstraßen* have waned significantly in popularity of late. When you reflect that this is the land that gave birth to Protestantism, Marxism, Transcendental Idealism, modern logic, and quantum mechanics, it makes sense; off-the-wall theories have always been tied up with life in Germany. A brief list of German thinkers would include:

Luther Leibniz Kant Fichte Schelling Hegel Feuerbach Marx Schopenhauer Nietzsche von Hartmann Fischer Husserl Cassirer Paulsen Simmel Weber Frege Benjamin Bloch Carnap Horkheimer Adorno Marcuse Mannheim Löwenthal Heidegger Löwith Jaspers Arendt Habermas

(Memorize them. There will be a test at the end of the book.)

FILM

The newborn medium of film was used brilliantly by directors in the **Weimar era.** Simply put, these early German films, along with a few American silents, form the basis of all serious study of film today. *Das Kabinett des Dr. Caligari (The Cabinet of Dr. Caligari),* an early horror film, plays out a melodrama of autonomy and control against brilliantly expressive sets of painted shadows and tilted walls. **Fritz Lang** produced a remarkable succession of classic films, including *M., Dr. Mabuse der Spieler,* and *Metropolis,* a dark and brutal vision of the techno-fascist city of the future. **Ernst Lubitsch, F. W. Murnau,** and **Josef von Sternberg** rounded out the field in the 1920s with their silent classics. Meanwhile, **Carl Zuckmayer** extended the tradition into sound with his satiric and pathetic *Der blaue Engel* (The Blue Angel), based on Heinrich Mann's novel *Professor Unrath*—it starred the immortal Marlene Dietrich as a cabaret singer.

Understanding Hitler's prediction that "without motor-cars, sound films, and wireless, (there can be) no victory for National Socialism," propaganda minister **Joseph**

Goebbels became a masterful manipulator. Most **Nazi film** fell into two categories: political propaganda and escapism. *Der Ewige Jude* (The Eternal Jew) and *Jud Süss* glorified anti-Semitism. The uncanny, masterful propaganda films of **Leni Riefenstahl,** including *Triumph des Willens* (Triumph of the Will), which depicted a Nuremberg Party Rally, and *Olympiad,* found a wide audience.

Film has been perhaps the most vigorous artistic medium in **post-war** Germany. The late 60s and the 70s saw the greatest flood of cinematic excellence. The renaissance began in 1962 with the Oberhausen Manifesto, a declaration by independent filmmakers demanding artistic freedom and enough production technology to create competitive feature films; within a few years, the government was granting subsidies to a constellation of young talents. **Rainer Werner Fassbinder** made fatalistic films about individuals corrupted or defeated by society, including a mammoth screen production of Alfred Döblin's mammoth novel *Berlin Alexanderplatz.* Fassbinder's film *Die Ehe der Maria Braun* (The Marriage of Maria Braun) and **Volker Schlöndorf's** *Der Blechtrommel* (The Tin Drum, based on the novel by Günter Grass) were the films that brought the new German wave to the wider, international audience. **Werner Herzog's** *Nosferatu,* a characteristically fantastic, bizarre vampire film starring the demented Klaus Kinski, won the 1976 Critic's Prize at the Cannes Film Festival. **Margarethe von Trotta** focused mainly on women and politics, notably in her film *Die bleierne Zeit* (The Leaden Time). **Wolfgang Petersen** directed the epic *Das Boot* (The Boat), one of the most successful German feature projects to date. **Wim Wenders's** restless, romantic quest films, particularly his "road films" like *Paris, Texas,* express his fascination with America. Also in 1984, **Edgar Reitz,** a director of the 60s generation, created the 15-hour epic *Heimat* (Home). The film was a reaction against what Reitz considered the cheap and shallow treatment of German war guilt in the American TV mini-series *Holocaust;* his film captured the full range of detail and experience involved, from the depths of war to the epiphanies of love, following a German family from 1919 to 1982.

East German film was subject to more constraints than other artistic media, owing to the difficulty of producing films without large-scale financial backing which only the state could provide. Just after the war, directors in the Soviet Zone produced several internationally acclaimed films, among them **Wolfgang Staudte's** *Die Mörder sind unter uns (The Murderers are Among Us),* about a Nazi war criminal who evades detection and goes on to lead the good life; **Kurt Maetzig's** *Ehe im Schatten (Marriage in the Shadows),* and **Erich Engel's** *Affaire Blum (The Blum Affair).* After the establishment of the GDR, the ministry of culture operated its own studios, the German Film Corporation (DEFA). **Slatan Dudow** produced the first of DEFA's films, *Unser tägliches Brot (Our Daily Bread),* a paean to the nationalization of industry, and went on to make one of the best East German films, *Stärker als die Nacht (Stronger than the Night),* which tells the story of a Communist couple persecuted by the Nazis. After a brief post-Stalinist thaw, few East German films departed from the standard format of socialist heroism or love stories. **Egon Günther's** *Lots Weib* (Lot's Wife), an explicitly feminist exploration of marital breakdown and divorce, was one notable exception. The next year, 1966, saw three major films, Maetzig's *Das Kaninchen bin ich (The Rabbit is Me),* **Frank Vogel's** *Denk bloß nicht, ich heule (Just Don't Think I'm Crying),* and **Frank Beyer's** *Spur der Steine (Track of Stones).* Beyer later made the critically acclaimed *Jakob der Lügner (Jacob the Liar),* which was nominated for an Oscar. Another promising director stifled by the GDR, **Konrad Wolf,** produced such films as *Ich war neunzehn (I was Nineteen), Goya,* and *Sonnensucher (Sun Seekers),* the last of which was not permitted to be released until 14 years after its completion. The GDR also devoted a healthy portion of its filmmaking resources to the **documentary** genre. A handful managed to critique the prevailing political situation, although the majority of directors, such as Andrew and Annelie Thorndike, Walter Heynowski, and Gerhard Scheumann concocted predictable and unremarkable films glorifying the Soviet Union and the SED and denouncing the Federal Republic and the United States.

MUSIC

Documented German music goes back to the medieval songs of the **Minnesänger,** the German troubadours, whose tradition of sung poetry passed gradually to the **Meistersänger,** commoners who had passed through five ranks from apprentice to *Meister* (Master). Singers remained in local guilds; their instrumental counterparts were the **town-pipers,** whose own guilds were the forerunners of modern orchestras. Lutheran hymns applied new polyphonic techniques to folk song forms. The 16th century saw both the *cantata* and the passion, a work thematizing a saint's transcendence. **Michael Praetorius** and **Johann Pachelbel** (best known for his *Canon*) worked in these modes. **Georg Friedrich Händel's** passion *Messiah* is now familiar Christmas music throughout the Western world.

Johann Sebastian Bach was the stand-out in a long line of musically successful Bachs. He began his career as an instrumentalist at various courts and churches, composing music for the organ, clavichord, and harpsichord, often accompanied by strings. Bach's keyboard works construct worlds whose meticulous symmetries and regularities reflect a careful spiritual order. In mid-career he produced more secular works; the *Brandenburg Concerti* are famous for their exploration of the happy tensions between solo instruments and chamber orchestra. After moving to Leipzig in 1723, he returned to the somber Lutheran sound; his *St. Matthew Passion* used Biblical texts with the arias and choruses. Explorations of orchestral forms moved farther in the next generation of composers. The Austrians Franz Josef Haydn, Wolfgang Amadeus Mozart, and their contemporaries attempted in their music to reject the institutionalized religious feeling of their predecessors and replace it with personal emotion, in keeping with the Romantic ideology in the literature of the era.

The 19th century was an era of German musical hegemony. **Ludwig van Beethoven's** symphonies and piano sonatas bridged Classicism and Romanticism. His monumental *Ninth Symphony* and late string quartets were written in the 1820s. Influenced by Romantic literature, including lyric poetry and songs, **Robert Schumann** and **Franz Schubert** composed settings for the poetry of Goethe, Byron, Scott, and Heinrich Heine. The ethereal work of **Felix Mendelssohn-Bartholdy** is well-represented by his overture to *A Midsummer Night's Dream.* The immigrants **Franz Liszt** and **Frederic Chopin** pushed piano music and the now-mature symphony form into still farther reaches of unorthodox harmony and arrangement.

The second generation of Romantic composers included **Johannes Brahms,** a protégé of Schumann's, whose talent for variation begat many popular German *Lieder* (songs). **Richard Wagner** embodied both the artistic strengths and ideological weaknesses of late 19th-century Romanticism. He composed many of the world's best-known operas—*Tannhäuser, Die Meistersinger, Der Ring des Nibelungen*—in an attempt to revolutionize the form with topics chosen specially for musical suitability, simple characters, and a mythic plot filled with divinity and the supernatural. He envisioned a stream of "endless melody" distinguishing itself through changes in mood or key, or through the reappearance of a *Leitmotif.* Wagner's plots are highly nationalistic in their simplicity and celebration of Germanic legend and were easily exploited by German-Aryan supremacists. Wagner himself wrote a nasty, anti-Semitic tract called *Jewishness in Music.* Eventually, Wagner's once-disciple Nietzsche began to write brilliantly satiric tracts about the composer's pomposity: he described Wagner's swirling music as a "narcotic" and a "sickness." The center of musical genius shifted to **Vienna** in the late 19th and early 20th centuries as Romanticism over-ripened into decadence.

The unstable economy of the Weimar Republic and the anti-Romantic backlash encouraged smaller, cheaper musical forms such as jazz. A new movement of *Gebrauchsmusik* (utilitarian music) engendered music for amateur players and film scores. **Arnold Schönberg**'s disciples, **Anton Webern** and **Alban Berg** mastered the possibilities of 12-tone composition. Berg's opera *Wozzeck* described squalor and tragedy through a progression of forms. **Paul Hindemith** headed a group of Neoclassicists influenced by the Neue Sachlichkeit (New Objectivity) and the emphasis on craftsmanship introduced by the *Werkbund* and *Bauhaus.* They embraced the older, variational forms (such as the sonata) most suited to the abstract aesthetic of the time. **Carl Orff,** Hitler's favorite composer, is most noted for his eclectic *Carmina Burana,* a resurrection of bawdy 13th-century lyrics with a bombastic score. The work was later reinterpreted as a well-loved ballet, though Orff's legacy is tainted by his work under the Third Reich. Lighter music-hall works were popular until World War II, breeding satiric operettas and songs of the political avant-garde. **Kurt Weill's** partnership with Bertolt Brecht produced such masterpieces of the genre as *Die Dreigroßchenoper* (Three-Penny Opera).

Contemporary German pop music is generally dreadful, but this has not always been the case. The 1960s produced the influential "Kraut Rock" movement, with groups like **Neu, Can,** and the **Silver Apples** pairing fragmented electronic sounds and biting guitar riffs. The electronic motif came into its own in the 1970s with **Kraftwerk** (Power Plant), a group of Düsseldorf engineering students who single-handedly invented techno-pop, designing their own equipment from the ground up. They began robotically, with compositions like the 1975 international hit "Autobahn," then gradually shifted to the disco-inflected. Theatrical, glam-rock **Nina Hagen** screamed from the 70s to 80s. **Einstürzende Neubauten** (Collapsing Buildings) combine noise-collage with punk rock. The **Scorpions** have been churning out garden-variety heavy metal for more than two decades. On a sour note, we've heard that **David Hasselhoff** has a brilliant singing career in Germany.

■ Food and Drink

German cuisine gets bad press. Though it is neither as sophisticated as French cooking nor as sultry as Italian or Hungarian food, *Deutsche Küche* has a robust, earthy charm of its own. While vegetarians will have a rough time outside of the major cities, meat-and-potatoes lovers will find the food in Germany hearty and satisfying. And if the local food is not to your taste, Germany's larger cities offer a wide variety of good ethnic restaurants. Be careful when ordering from a German menu if you don't speak the language; ingredients such as eel *(Aal),* blood sausage *(Blutwurst),* and brains *(Gehirn)* are not uncommon, and may represent an acquired taste. Don't let this deter you from taking risks—brains are probably a lot tastier than you think.

The typical German **breakfast** (*Frühstück,* literally "early piece") is coffee or tea with rolls *(Brötchen),* butter, marmalade, slices of bread, cold sausage *(Wurst),* and cheese *(Käse).* **Lunch** *(Mittagsessen)* is usually the main meal of the day, consisting of soup, broiled sausage or roasted meat, potatoes or dumplings, and a salad or some vegetables. **Supper** *(Abendessen* or *Abendbrot)* is a re-enactment of breakfast, only beer replaces coffee and the selection of meat and cheese is wider. **Dessert** after meals isn't common, but many Germans indulge in a daily ritual of **Kaffee und Kuchen** (coffee and cakes), a snack analogous to English "tea-time," at 3-4pm.

Bread *(Brot)* is the staff of life in Germany; the country's bakeries produce loaves of astonishing quality and variety. *Vollkornbrot* is whole-wheat (which has a completely different meaning in Germany) and *Roggenbrot* is rye bread. *Schwarzbrot* (black bread) is a dense, dark loaf that's slightly acidic and most delicious when it's fresh. Go to a bakery *(Bäckerei)* and point to whatever looks good. Generally they sell you the whole loaf; for half, ask for *ein Halbes.* Those traveling on the cheap can ward off hunger for a few dozen *Pfennigs* by entering a bakery and requesting *zwei Brötchen,* a pair of fresh, warm rolls to take out.

Beer and wine (see below) are the meal-time **beverages.** Fruit juice *(Saft),* plain or mixed with sparkling water *(gespritzt),* is an alternative. Germans rarely drink water; if they do, it's carbonated mineral water. If you ask for *Wasser* in a restaurant, you get mineral water (which costs). This is one aspect of the national taste that often produces culture shock, especially in Americans who are used to slugging thirst-quenchers in quantity. For tap water, ask for *Leitungswasser,* and be prepared for funny looks. You may have better luck asking for bottled *Evian* by name; it's sometimes carried by cafés in big cities.

Unpretentious **restaurants** (that's most of them) expect you to seat yourself. If there are no tables free, feel free to ask someone for permission to take a free seat (ask *"Darf ich Platz nehmen?"*, pronounced "DAHRF eekh PLAHTS nay-men"). In traditional restaurants, address waiters "Herr Ober," and waitresses (but no one else) as "Fräulein." In a hip *Kneipe* (bar), just say *hallo*. When you're finished, pay at the table. Ask the server *Zahlen, bitte* ("TSAH-len, BIT-tuh": "check, please"). Taxes *(Mehrwertsteuer)* and service are usually included in the price, but it is customary to leave a little something extra, usually by rounding up the bill by a mark or two.

Eating in restaurants at every meal will quickly drain your budget. One strategy is to stick to the daily *prix-fixé* option, called the *Tagesmenu*. A cheaper option is to buy food in grocery stores, which *Let's Go* lists in major cities. German university students eat at cafeterias called **Mensa**. Most *Mensen* require an ISIC (or charge higher prices for non-students), and some are open only to local students, though travelers often evade this requirement by casually strolling in as if they belonged. In smaller towns, the best budget option is to stop by a bakery *(Bäckerei)* for bread and garnish it with sausage purchased from a butcher *(Fleischerei or Metzgerei)*.

Besides bread, the staples of the German diet are *Wurst* (sausage, in myriad varieties), *Schweinefleisch* (pork), *Rindfleisch* (beef), *Kalbsfleisch* (veal), *Kartoffeln* (potatoes), and *Eier* (eggs). Dairy products, including *Käse* (cheese) and *Butter*—but especially *Schlagsahne* (whipped cream)—are favorites. Some travel guides recommend a portable cholesterol test kit, but the typical budget traveler might be young enough to survive unaided. To sample the various **local specialties** as you travel around Germany is to appreciate the diversity of the German tradition. Everyone knows *Wiener Schnitzel* (a breaded veal cutlet) and *Sauerkraut* (pickled cabbage), but there's much more to German cuisine. In **Bavaria**, *Knödel* (potato and flour dumplings, sometimes filled with meat) are ubiquitous. *Leberknödel* are filled with liver. *Weißwurst* is also a Bavarian specialty; it is a sausage made with milk. It spoils so quickly that it has to be eaten the day it's made. **Thuringia** and Northern Bavaria are famed for their succulent grilled *Bratwurst*, the classic, garlicky, roasting sausage eaten with potatoes or bought from a street vendor clasped in a roll. The preferred vehicles for starch in **Baden** and **Swabia** are *Spätzle* (noodles) and *Maultaschen* (pasta pockets). German *Pfannkuchen* (pancakes) are much heavier and bigger than the flapjacks back home, and are served with toppings. *Kaiserschmarren* is chopped-up pancake with powdered sugar. **Hessians** do amazing things with potatoes, like smothering them in delectable *grüne Soße* (green sauce).

BEER

> *Where does the German begin? Where does it end? May a German smoke? The majority says no ... But a German may drink beer, indeed as a true son of Germanias he should drink beer ...*
>
> —Heinrich Heine

Germans have brewed frothy malt beverages since the 8th century BC, and they've been consuming and exporting them in prodigious quantities ever since. The province of Bavaria alone, in fact, contains about one-fifth of all the breweries in the world. And the Germans drink more than 140 liters of beer per person per year—the most of any people on Earth. According to legend, the German king Gambrinus invented the modern beer recipe when he threw some hops into the fermenting malt. Brewers still honor him. During the Middle Ages, monastic orders refined the art of brewing, imbibing to stave off starvation during long fasts. It wasn't long before the monks' lucrative trade caught the eye of secular lords, who established the first court breweries (Hofbräuereien). The variety of beers in Germany boggles the mind. Most beer is Vollbier, containing about 4% alcohol. Export (5%) is also popular, and stout, tasty Bockbier (6.25%) is brewed in the spring. Doppelbock (double bock) is an eye-popping concoction understandably reserved for special occasions. Ordering "ein Helles" will get you a standard light-colored beer, while "Dunkles" can look like anything from Coca-Cola to molasses.

Though generalizations are difficult, the average German beer is maltier and more "bread-like" than Czech, Dutch, or American beers. (An affectionate German slang term for beer is *flüßiges Brot,* "liquid bread.") Among the exceptions is *Pils,* or Pilsner, which is most popular in the north. Its characteristic clarity and bitter taste come from the addition of extra hops. From the south, especially Bavaria, comes *Weißbier,* a smooth, refreshing brew. Despite the name, *Weißbier* is not white, but a rich brown. (The name is a corruption of *Weizenbier,* meaning wheat beer.) The term *Weizenbier* now generally refers to a darker wheat beer, while *Hefe-Weizen* is wheat beer with a layer of yeast in the bottom. *Faßbier* simply means beer from a barrel. Sampling local brews numbers among the finest of Germany's pleasures. In Cologne, one drinks smooth *Kölsch,* an extraordinarily refined, light-colored beer; a Düsseldorf specialty is *Altbier,* a darker top-fermented beer. Berliners are partial to *Berliner Weiße,* a mixture of beer and lime-flavored syrup (or *Berliner Rote* with raspberry syrup). On hot summer days, lightweight drinkers prefer *Radler,* a Bavarian mix containing half beer and half lemon-lime soda. *Diesel* is a mixture of *Bier* and cola that will get your engine started.

The variety of places to drink beer is almost as staggering as the variety of brews. The traditional *Biergarten* consists of outdoor tables under chestnut trees. The broad leaves of the trees originally kept beer barrels cool in the days before refrigeration, until one enterprising brewer figured out that they could do the same thing for beer drinkers. The *Bierkeller* is an indoor version of the *Biergarten,* where local breweries dispense their product. During the summer, breweries sponsor carnivals with rides and beer under a tent. To order *"Ein Bier,"* hold up your thumb, not your index finger. Raise your glass to a *"Prost,"* and drink. (For more on Beer Halls (in Munich), see Beer, Beer Halls and Beer Gardens, p. 223.) Another option for beer drinking is the *Gaststätte,* a simple, local restaurant. It's considered bad form to order only drinks at a *Gaststätte* during mealtimes, but any other time, friends can linger at a table for hours over beers. Many *Gaststätten* have a *Stammtisch* (regulars' table), marked by a flag, where interlopers should not sit. The same group of friends may meet at the *Stammtisch* every week for decades, doing nothing but drinking, playing cards, and shooting the breeze; keep in mind that your visa has an expiration date. *Kneipen* are small bars where young people gather.

WINE AND SPIRITS

Though overshadowed by Germany's more famous export beverage, German wines win over connoisseurs and casual drinkers alike. Virtually all German wines are white, though they vary widely in character. Generally, German wines are sweeter and fresher-tasting than French wines, though not as gutsy as Mediterranean wines. Because Germany is the northernmost of the wine-producing countries, the quality of a vineyard's produce can vary considerably with the climate from year to year.

The cheapest wines are classified as *Tafelwein* (table wine), while the good stuff (which is still pretty affordable) is *Qualitätswein* (quality wine). *Qualitätswein mit*

Das Reinheitsgebot: Germany's Beer Purity Law

One of the most despised characters in medieval Germany was the shoddy brewer who tried to cut costs by substituting lesser grains for the noble cereal at the heart of beer—barley. In 1516, Duke William IV of Bavaria decreed that beer could contain only pure water, barley, and hops. William's Purity Law *(Reinheitsgebot)* has endured to this day, with minor alterations to permit the cultivation of Bavaria's trademark wheat-based beers. The law even applies to imports—none of the filler-laden products of the major American breweries (Samuel Adams is an exception) can be imported into Germany. But with the arrival of the European Union, the law was challenged by other European countries, who saw it as an unfair trade barrier. Now the "impure" foreign beers are being admitted to the market, but to the joy of drinkers worldwide, the German breweries have all reaffirmed their full commitment to the *Reinheitsgebot.*

Prädikat (quality wine with distinction) designates a wine derived from a particular varietal grape. The *Prädikat* wines are further subdivided according to the ripeness of the grapes when harvested; from driest to sweetest, they are *Kabinett, Spätlese, Auslese, Beerenauslese,* or *Trockenbeerenauslese.* The grapes that produce the *Trockenbeerenauslese* are left on the vine until they have shriveled up into raisins and begun to rot—no kidding. The label *Qualitätswein bestimmter Anbaugebiete*, or *Q. b. A.*, designates quality wine from a specific cultivation region.

The major concentrations of viniculture lie along the Rhine and Mosel valleys, along the Main River in Franconia, and in Baden. Rhine wines are bottled in brown glass, all others in green. Of the dozens of varieties, the most famous are *Riesling, Müller-Thurgau,* and *Traminer* (source of *Gewürztraminer*). But don't miss the equally delicious wines made from the *Lemberger, Spätburgunder,* and *Trollinger* varieties. In wine-producing towns, thirsty travelers can stop by a *Weinstube* to sample the local produce. In Hessen, the beverage of choice is *Äppelwoi* or *Äpfelwein* (apple wine), a hard cider similar in potency to beer. After a meal, many Germans aid their digestion by throwing back a shot of *Schnapps,* distilled from fruits. *Kirschwasser,* a cherry liqueur from the Black Forest, is the best known and probably the easiest to stomach, but adventurous sorts can experiment with *Zwetschgenwasser* (made from plums, also known as *Schliwowitz*), *Aprikosenlikör* (from apricots), and *Himbeergeist* (from raspberries). Each year, unsuspecting tourists are seduced into buying little green bottles of *Jägermeister,* an herb liqueur slightly more palatable than raw eggs flavored with soap.

■ Media

British dailies, such as the *Times, Financial Times,* and *Guardian* are widely available at train stations and kiosks in major cities. The *International Herald Tribune* and the European edition of the *Wall Street Journal* (DM3) are the most common U.S. papers. American and British armed forces maintain English-language radio stations. German-speakers can keep track of things with the informative, Hamburg-based weekly *Der Spiegel,* one of the world's leading news magazines. *Die Zeit* is a witty, left-leaning weekly journal of opinion. The *Frankfurter Allgemeine Zeitung* is a stodgy, leading newspaper comparable to the *New York Times.* Munich's *Süddeutsche Zeitung* is Germany's best daily paper, though the racy, trashy, semi-rag *Bild Zeitung* is far more popular. For perspective on *Bild,* read Heinrich Böll's *Lost Honor of Katerina Blum,* an open attack on the tabloid and its distinctive style. Coming at you from Berlin are the properly liberal *Berliner Tagesspiegel* and the iconoclastic, left leaning *Tageszeitung (TAZ).*

■ Social Life

> —You do not seem to know how rude you are.
> —When you're polite in German, you are lying.
> —Mephisto and Baccalaureus, in Goethe's *Faust, Part II*

An afternoon of relaxation at a park in Berlin or a café in any college town (cafés are made for people-watching) will teach you more about Germany than one spent in a museum. Many Germans know Americans and Britons only through contact with NATO soldiers, who haven't always made the best impression. A special note to U.S. citizens: anti-Americanism is still a powerful sentiment among many young Germans, but this doesn't necessarily mean they don't like Americans; it just means that they are concerned about what they perceive as the American government's failure to exercise moral leadership in the world. If you are sensitive to this concern, you will find that most Germans have a passionate interest in the U.S.

Take the time to actually meet people. A photo of Walter and Gisela Schmidt who put you up for the night in Laßunsgehendorf will contain more memories than a postcard of the Brandenburg Gate. Europeans in general are sincerely interested in other lands and cultures, but have a very strong sense of their own cultural history; if you insult or belittle it, you'll only seem ignorant (and rude). Above all, don't automatically equate "our way" with "better." Unless you're very homesick, try to avoid McDonald's in favor of the local *Biergarten.*

The byzantine rules surrounding German etiquette make Emily Post look like a gas station attendant. Of course, it varies dramatically depending on who you're trying to impress, but it's generally true that the Germans are much more formal than Americans and Australians, and incredibly big on punctuality (especially to meals).

Among the older generations, be careful not to use the informal *"du"* (you) or a first name without being invited to do so. *"Du"* is appropriate when addressing fellow students and friends at a youth hostel, or when addressing children. In all other circumstances, use the formal *"Sie"* for "you," as in the question *"Sprechen Sie Englisch?"* Only waitresses in traditional restaurants are addressed as *"Fräulein"*; address all other women as *Frau* (followed by a name). Remember that most Europeans know no English; ask humbly (you're the one who should speak their language) *"Sprechen Sie Englisch?"* (SPREH-shen zee AYN-glish?) before launching into a question. Better yet, try to learn a little German and don't be afraid to try it out. The language is intimately related to English, and you can learn the pronunciation system and some useful phrases in about 15 minutes (see Language, p. 546). In any case, learn at least two phrases: please (*bitte*; BIT-tuh) and thank you (*danke;* DAHNK-uh). At the table, Germans eat with the fork in the left hand and the knife in the right. While eating, it is polite to keep the tines of your fork pointing down at all times. An invitation to a German home is a major courtesy; you should bring along flowers for the hostess. As anywhere, write a thank-you note.

Everything you've heard about the Germans' compulsive abidance of law is true. The first time you see a German standing at an intersection in the pouring rain, with no cars in sight, waiting for the "Walk" signal, you'll know what we mean. Jaywalking is only one of the petty offenses that will mark you as a foreigner (and subject you to fines); littering is another. The younger generation takes matters a bit less seriously. Although **police** are polite and businesslike, they aren't to be messed with. If you fail to treat officers with proper respect (for instance, addressing them with the familiar *"du"* rather than the formal *"Sie"*), they can slap you with on-the-spot fines (see Insults for Sale, p. 236). Few officers speak more than a bit of English. The **drinking age** is 16 and skimpily enforced; driving under the influence, however, is treated as a severe offense.

North Rhine-Westphalia (Nordrhein-Westfalen)

In 1946, the victorious Allies attempted to speed Germany's recovery by merging the traditionally distinct regions of Westphalia, Lippe, and the Rhineland to unify the economic nucleus of post-war Germany and speed the nation's recovery. The resulting *Land,* North Rhine-Westphalia *(Nordrhein-Westfalen)* meets no typical German stereotype, a fact which has unfairly tarnished its image. True, the avant-garde multiculturalism of Berlin, the *Lederhosen* and beer halls of Bavaria, and the unspoiled natural beauty of the Black Forest are all far from here, but it is this region's dense concentration of highways, rail lines, and people that connects and unites these diverse elements. With its 17 million inhabitants and the mighty Ruhr Valley, North Rhine-Westphalia is the most heavily populated and most economically powerful area in Germany. But industry has brought strife to the region in the past: the industrial boom of the late 19th century sparked social democracy, trade unionism, and revolutionary communism—the popular moniker "Red Ruhr" didn't refer to the color of the water. Despite downturns in heavy industry and persistently high unemployment, the great industrial wealth of the region continues to support a multitude of cultural offerings for the citizens and visitors of its lively towns and beautiful river valleys. And while the region's industrial squalor may have inspired the philosophy of Karl Marx and Friedrich Engels, the natural beauty of the Teutoburg and Eifel and the cultural and intellectual energy of Cologne and Düsseldorf have spurred the muses of writers from Heine to Böll.

▓ Cologne (Köln)

Founded as a Roman colony (*Colonia,* hence *Köln*) in 48 AD, almost everything in Cologne had its beginnings with the the Romans. Petrarch called Cologne his "city of dreams" back when the rest of Germany was just a wilderness. The city's prime location at the intersection of several international trade routes ushered in a Golden Age during the Middle Ages and the Renaissance. Cologne also began supporting an unsurpassed intellectual tradition beginning in 1389, when it opportunistically recruited professors fleeing from the plague in Heidelberg to teach at the first municipally founded German university.

This period also witnessed the first phase of construction of Cologne's majestic and legendary *Dom;* designed to surpass every other church in the world in magnificence, the Gothic structure took an amazing 632 years to build. During World War II, the *Dom* was struck by at least 14 bombs. Amazingly, it survived and has since become the nation's most powerful symbol of rebirth. The rest of the city, however, did not escape the war's wrath. On May 31, 1942, Cologne was the target of the Allies' first experimental 1000-bomber air raid, which by 1945 left 90% of the city center in ruins. But in the post-war period, Cologne began a miraculous recovery. Today, as the largest city in North Rhine-Westphalia and the most important commercially, it is a prosperous, modern city with a grip on the past and a burgeoning fine arts capital with a penchant for bibulous celebrations, like the annual *Karneval.*

Modern Cologne is also the city of Nobel Prize-winning novelist Heinrich Böll, who set *The Lost Honor of Katharina Blum* and the scandalous *Clown* here. The novels concern the venom of press slander and the violation of civil liberties, both topics appropriate to a city which serves as Germany's media capital. Cologne is still the base of many national media and TV networks, just as it was during the days of Karl Marx, who began his revolutionary career here in 1848 as the editor of a local newspaper. Though Cologne's citizens conduct their own communications in the impenetrable "Kölsch" dialect, show them you know what it's all about by ordering a

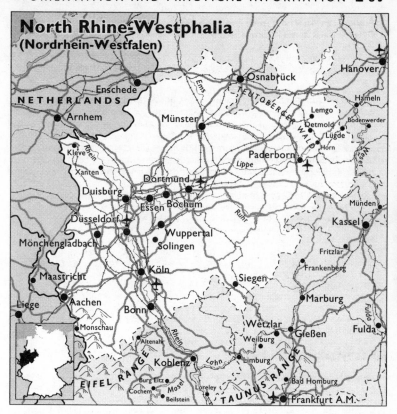

North Rhine-Westphalia
(Nordrhein-Westfalen)

locally brewed *Kölsch* beer. This elegant drink can bring to visitors' taste buds the kind of experience that the heavenly *Dom* delivers to their eyes.

ORIENTATION AND PRACTICAL INFORMATION

Eight bridges carry Cologne, just north of Bonn, across the Rhine. Germany's fourth-largest city, Cologne is a half-hour from Düsseldorf by frequent trains, 2½ hours from Frankfurt, and linked by direct lines to Munich, Hamburg, and Berlin.

Dom Hotel, across from the *Dom* to the southwest, is the place to buy the **Köln Bonbon,** a packet of vouchers for free goods. The vouchers entitle the holder to a great print of the 1531 town panorama woodcut, several of the brochures that aren't free at the tourist office, discounts on various Rhine cruises, reduced admission to area attractions, and a three-day pass valid for free entry into all of the city's museums (Bonbon DM15; with voucher for 2-hour discounted **city bus tour** DM26).

Tourist Office: Verkehrsamt, Unter Fettenhennen 19 (tel. 221 33 45; fax 221 33 20; http://www.koeln.org.verkehrsamt), across from the main entrance to the cathedral. Will provide you with a free city map (you must pay for most other brochures), book you a room (for a DM5 fee), and try to sell you a poster. Ask about English **tours** of the city and cathedral. Be kind to the helpful multilingual staff—they're overworked and underpaid. Like us. Be sure to pick up the *Monatsvorschau* (DM2), a booklet with essential info and a complete monthly schedule of events. Open May-Oct. Mon.-Sat. 8am-10:30pm, Sun. 9am-10:30pm; Nov.-April Mon.-Sat. 8am-9pm, Sun. 9:30am-7pm.

Budget Travel: STA Travel, Zülpicherstr. 178 (tel. 44 20 11).

Currency Exchange: There's an office at the **train station** (open daily 7am-9pm), but the service charges are lower at the post office. No charge on AmEx traveler's checks at American Express (see below).

American Express: Burgmauerstr. 14 (tel. 925 90 10), near the *Dom.* **ATM.** Cardmembers' mail held free for 4 weeks. Open Mon.-Fri. 9am-5:30pm, Sat. 9am-noon.

Telephones: In the station outside the post office.

Flights: Flights depart from **Köln-Bonn Flughafen** for 50 destinations non-stop; a shuttle to Berlin leaves 24 times per day. Call (02203) 40 40 01 for more information. Bus #170 leaves stop #4 of the *Hauptbahnhof* at 5:40, 6, and 6:30am, and then every 15min. 7am-8pm, and every 30min. 8-11pm; it stops at Köln-Deutz 5min. later, then proceeding to the airport (15min.; DM8.20, children DM4.50).

Public Transportation: Any **VRS** (Verkehrsverbund Rhein-Seig) office will have a plan of the S- and U-Bahn lines throughout the Cologne-Bonn area, as well as maps of city bus and streetcar lines. One is downstairs in the train station near the U-Bahn. Major convergence points include the *Hauptbahnhof,* Köln-Deutz, Appellhofplatz, and Barbarossaplatz. Tickets are priced by distance. 1-ride tickets DM2-13.20. 4-ride tickets DM7.60-30. Day cards DM10.50-33; the DM10.50 card will get you anywhere in Cologne.

Ferries: Köln-Düsseldorfer (tel. 258 30 11; fax 208 82 38) sails to 40 Rhine landings between Cologne and Mainz, including the cliffs and waterfalls at Königswinter (round-trip DM39). Connections to Mosel River ferries. Seniors half-price on Mon. and Fri. Students and children ages 4-12 half-price. Most trips (excluding the super-cool hydrofoils) are free with Eurail and many German rail passes.

Gondola: Rheinseilbahn, Europe's only river-crossing **gondola lift,** spans the Rhine north of the city; it runs between the zoo on the west bank and the Rheinpark on the east. DM6.50, children DM3.50; round-trip DM9.50, children DM5. Times change daily (call 76 20 06 for more information).

Taxi: Funkzentrale (tel. 28 82). History is funk.

Car Rental: Avis, Clemensstr. 29 (tel. 23 43 33); **Hertz,** Bismarckstr. 19-21 (tel. 51 50 84).

Bike Rental: Kölner Fahrradverleihservice, Sedanstr. 27 (tel. 72 36 27). From the station, walk along the shore towards Deutzer Bridge. Go right at the spiral staircase. DM4 per hr. DM20 per day. Open Mon.-Sat. 8am-8pm, Sun. 11am-8pm.

Mitfahrzentrale: Citynetz Mitfahrzentrale, at Maximinstr. 2 (tel. 194 40), to the left of the train station, lists rides. Open Mon.-Fri. 9am-6pm, Sat. 9am-2pm.

Hitchhiking: *Let's Go* does not recommend hitchhiking as a safe mode of transportation. For all destinations, hitchers say to take bus #132 to the last stop.

Bookstore: Mayerische Buchhandlungs, Hohestr. 68-82 (tel. 257 57 85), has a fine paperback selection. Open Mon.-Wed. and Fri. 9:30am-6:30pm, Thurs. 9:30am-8:30pm, Sat. 9:30am-4pm.

Cultural Centers: Amerika Haus, Apostelnkloster 13-15 (tel. 20 90 10; fax 24 45 43), by St. Aposteln church, is a valuable resource for English cultural activities. A full English-language **library** is open Tues.-Fri. 1-6pm. The **British Council** (tel. 20 64 40), around the corner at Hahnenstr. 6 on Neumarkt, serves much the same purpose with a British accent and a better Monty Python collection. Library open Mon.-Wed. and Fri. 1-5pm, Thurs. 1-7pm (closed for 6 weeks in July and Aug.).

Laundry: Öko-Express, at Neue Weyerstr. 1, is ökey-dökey. Wash DM6. Dry DM1 per 10min. Soap included. Open Mon.-Sat. 6am-11pm. Also available at Zülpicher Wall 2 (same times and prices) and at the **Köln-Deutz** hostel.

Women's Resources: The municipal **Frauenamt,** Markmansgasse 7 (tel. 221 64 82), fields questions on cultural opportunities and services. Open Mon.-Thurs. 8:30am-1pm and 2-4pm, Fri. 8:30am-12:30pm, but it's best to call for an appointment. **Women's crisis hotline:** tel. 420 16 20.

Pharmacy: Dom Apotheke, Komodienstr. 5 (tel. 257 67 54), near the station. Their *Pharmacie-Internationale* advises in English, and has a list of other afterhours pharmacies posted outside. Open Mon.-Fri. 8am-6:30pm, Sat. 8:30am-2pm.

Emergency: Police: tel. 110.

Post Office: Main office at An den Dominikanern, 50668 Köln. From the *Dom* exits of the train station, head down Dompropst Ketzerstr. (left of the big pink church);

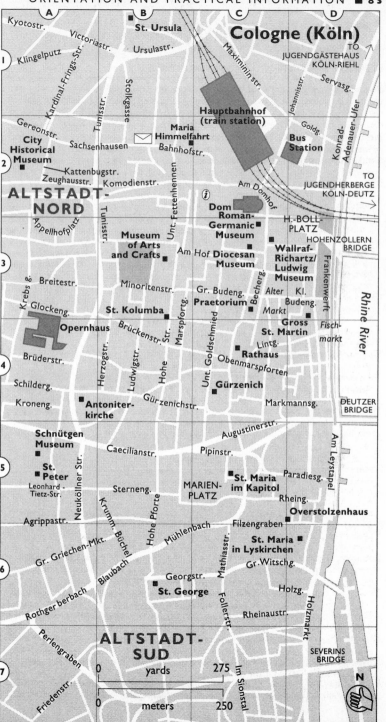

Cologne (Köln)

Kyotostr.

Klingelputz

Victoriastr.

Kardinal-Frings-Str.

St. Ursula

Ursulastr.

Stolkgasse

Maximinin str.

TO
JUGENDGÄSTEHAUS
KÖLN-RIEHL

Johannisstr.

Servasg.

Gereonstr.

Tunisstr.

Sachsenhausen

**Maria
Himmelfahrt**

Bahnhofstr.

**Hauptbahnhof
(train station)**

Goldg.

Konrad-Adenauer-Ufer

**City
Historical
Museum**

Kattenbugstr.

Zeughausstr.

Komodienstr.

**Bus
Station**

TO
JUGENDHERBERGE
KÖLN-DEUTZ

**ALTSTADT-
NORD**

Appellhofplatz

Tunisstr.

Unt. Fettenhennen

Am Domhof

(i)

Dom

**Roman-
Germanic
Museum**

**H.-BOLL-
PLATZ**

HOHENZOLLERN
BRIDGE

Breitestr.

Krebs g.

Glockeng.

**Museum
of Arts
and Crafts**

Am Hof

**Diocesan
Museum**

**Wallraf-
Richartz/
Ludwig
Museum**

Frankenwerft

Rhine River

Minoritenstr.

Gr. Budeng.

Becherg.

Alter

Kl.
Budeng.

Praetorium

St. Kolumba

Marspforg.

Markt

**Gross
St. Martin**

Fisch-
markt

Opernhaus

Brückenstr.

Herzogstr.

Ludwigstr.

Hohe Str.

Unt. Goldschmied

Lintg.

Rathaus

Obenmarspforten

Fischmarkt

Brüderstr.

Schilderg.

Kroneng.

Gürzenichstr.

Gürzenich

Markmannsg.

DEUTZER
BRIDGE

**Antoniter-
kirche**

**Schnütgen
Museum**

Caecilianstr.

Augustinerstr.

Pipinstr.

Am Leystapel

**St.
Peter**

Leonhard -
Tietz-Str.

Neuköllner Str.

Sterneng.

**MARIEN-
PLATZ**

**St. Maria
im Kapitol**

Paradiesg.

Rheing.

Overstolzenhaus

Agrippastr.

Krumm. Büchel

Hohe Pforte

Mühlenbach

Filzengraben

**St. Maria
in Lyskirchen**

Gr. Griechen-Mkt.

Blaubach

Mathiasstr.

Gr. Witschg.

Holzg.

Holzmarkt

Rothger berbach

St. George

Georgstr.

Follerstr.

Rheinaustr.

Perlengraben

**ALTSTADT-
SÜD**

Friedenstr.

Im Sionstal

SEVERINS
BRIDGE

0 ___ yards ___ 275

0 ___ meters ___ 250

N

it becomes An den Dominikaneren. Open Mon.-Fri. 8am-6pm, Sat. 8am-6pm, Sun. 8am-1pm. Limited service Mon.-Fri. 6-8pm, Sat. 1-6pm, Sun. 11am-6pm. **Telephone Code:** 0221.

ACCOMMODATIONS AND CAMPING

The brisk convention and tour business in Cologne has produced a wealth of rooms; the trick is pinning one down. Hotels fill up (and prices set sail) in the spring and fall when trade winds blow conventioneers this way. Summer, in turn, is high season for Cologne's two hostels, both of which are brimming to the beams from June to September. The main hotel haven, on the less interesting side of the *Bahnhof*, centers around Brandenburger Str. The **Mitwohnzentrale,** An der Bottmühle 16 (tel. 32 70 84), is an alternative matching service for longer stays (open Mon.-Thurs. 8:30am-1pm and 2-4pm, Fri. 8:30am-12:30pm). Scrounging for a last-minute room during *Karneval* (Feb. 6-11, 1997) is futile. If all else fails, schlepp down to Bonn.

Jugendherberge Köln-Deutz (HI), Siegesstr. 5a (tel. 81 47 11; fax 88 44 25), just over the Hohenzollern Bridge. From the main exit of the train station, walk down Neuhöfferstr., the first street to the left of the mirrored building, and take the first right; the hostel is tucked behind the courtyard with big trees (2min.). Or take S-Bahn #6, 11, or 12 to "Köln-Deutz" (1 stop). Cramped rooms and wimpy showers, but an unbeatable location, with two pinball machines and free laundry (soap DM1). House buffets DM8. The 374 beds fill quickly and the staff is overworked, to say the least. Best check-in is 6-9am. Later is riskier, but reception open again 12:30pm-12:30am. Curfew 12:30am. DM27, over 26 DM31.50. Sheets included.

Jugendgästehaus Köln-Riehl (HI), An der Schanz 14 (tel. 76 70 81; fax 76 15 55), on the Rhine north of the zoo. Take U-Bahn #16 or 18 (direction: Ebertplatz/Mülheim) to "Boltensternstr.," or walk along the Rhine on Konrad-Adenauer-Uferstr. until it becomes Niederländer-Ufer and finally An der Schanz (40min.). Huge common areas with plush sofas and lockers big enough to hide in. Reception open 24hr. No curfew. DM32.50. Breakfasts and sheets included. The **Köln-Treff Café** sells beer, baguettes, and fries. Open daily 8pm-12:30am.

Hotel Im Kupferkessel, Probsteigasse 6 (tel. 13 53 38; fax 12 51 21). From the train station bear right; follow the street as it changes from Dompropost-Ketzer-Str. to An den Dominikern to Unter Sachsenhausen to Gereonstr. and on to become Christophstr. Now turn right on Probsteigasse. Newly renovated building with sharplooking rooms. Reception open daily 7am-9pm, or call. Singles DM48, with shower, phone, toilet, and TV DM78. Doubles with all the goodies DM110. Breakfast included. AmEx, Diners, MC, and Visa.

Hotel Heinzelmännchen, Köln-Riehl, Hohe Pforte 5-7 (tel. 21 12 17; fax 21 57 12). Take bus #132 (direction: der Frankenstr.) to "Waidmarkt," or walk all the way down the Hohe-Str. shopping zone until it becomes Hohe Pforte. Bright hallways and firm mattresses. Reception open until 10:30pm. Singles DM58, with shower and toilet DM65. Doubles DM95, with shower and toilet DM105. Triples DM125. Breakfast included. Discounts for stays of 3 days or longer.

Hotel Hubertus Hof, Mühlenbach 30 (tel. 21 73 86; fax 21 55 89). Follow above directions to Hohe Pforte, then turn left onto Mühlenbach. Monster-size rooms and fuzzy carpets to tickle your feet. Reception open 7am-9pm. Singles DM60. Doubles DM80. Showers and toilets off the hall. Breakfast included.

Das kleine Stapelhäuschen, Fischmarkt 1-3 (tel. 257 78 62; fax 257 42 32). 3 nifty houses with a great view of the Rhine. Classic oak furniture and color-coordinated sheets. For huge medieval oaken mill wheels suspended above your bed, ask for the *historisches Turmzimmer* (DM220). Singles DM70-80, with shower DM102, with shower and toilet DM110. Doubles DM105, with shower DM165, with shower and toilet DM185. Breakfast buffet included. AmEx, Eurocard, and Visa.

Hotel Berg, Brandenburger Str. 6 (tel. 12 11 24; fax 139 00 11). Bear left onto Johannisstr. from the back exit of the train station and take the third left onto Brandenburger Str. A standout for its well-kept rooms, and down-home breakfast room. Reception open 24hr. Singles DM55, with shower DM90. Doubles DM90, with showers DM160. Breakfast included. AmEx, Diners, MC, and Visa.

Hotel Brandenburger Hof, Brandenburger Str. 2-4 (tel. 12 28 89; fax 13 53 04). Small, tidy rooms and tiny outdoor *Biergarten.* Reception open 24hr. Singles DM65, with shower and toilet DM85. Doubles DM85, with shower and toilet DM120. 3- and 4-bed rooms available (DM120 and DM140). Breakfast included.

Camping: Campingplatz Poll, at Weidenweg on the Rhine (tel. 83 19 66), southeast of the *Altstadt.* From the station take U-Bahn #16 to "Marienburg" and cross the Roddenkirchener Bridge. Reception open 8am-noon and 3-10pm (later in the summer). DM4 per tent. DM6 per person. DM4 per car. DM6 per mobile home.

FOOD

Small cafés packed by students and cheap restaurants offering quick meals line **Zülpicherstr.** all the way to the university complex. Take U-Bahn #12, 14, 16, or 18 to "Neumarkt," then U-Bahn #7 or 9 to "Zülpicherplatz" to get there. Mid-priced restaurants with a fine selection of ethnic cuisine are concentrated around the perimeter of the *Altstadt,* particularly from Hohenzollernring to Hohenstaufenring. For glitzy cafés, the city's wealthy patrons head to **Neumarkt.** Don't pass through Köln without sampling the city's eponymous and extraordinarily smooth **Kölsch beer,** served in little glasses (0.2L). Local brews of the delightful stuff include *Sion, Küppers, Früh,* and the devout *Dom.* Cologne offers hungry visitors the *Rievekoochen* (dialect for "potato pancakes"), a slab of fried potato dunked in *Apfulmuß* (apple sauce). The most interesting area for inexpensive eats is in the Turkish district on Weidengasse. An open-air **Markt** on Wilhelmsplatz takes over the northern Nippes neighborhood to offer farm-fresh joys (open Mon.-Sat. 7-11:30am).

Café Rendezvous, Heinsberg 11a (tel. 23 34 98), at the corner of Heinsberg and Zülpicherstr. As Marilyn Monroe and Clark Gable look blissfully on, let pizzas and pastas have a close encounter with your stomach (all under DM10). Breakfast spreads served all day. Open Sun.-Thurs. 8am-1am, Fri.-Sat. 8am-3am.

Crimson Café, Zülpicherstr. 25 (tel. 240 50 37), offers combo meals of pizza, salad, and noodles (DM9) before 6pm, with a bit of *veritas* in every bite. Nighttime crowd is a wild pack of lushes, red in the face from the impressive menu of drinks. Live soul and jazz every Fri. Open 11am-1pm.

Mini-Mensa, Zülpicherstr. 58 (tel. 42 81 22). Not quite as cheap as the real *Mensa* (now closed), but longer hours and 6 combo meals for DM5.90 make this a good place to stuff yourself. Open Mon.-Fri. 11am-10:30pm, Sat.-Sun. noon-12:30am.

Café Waschsalon, Friesenstr. 80 (tel. 13 33 78), is filled with washers; turn on the spin cycle in your head with their fine assortment of drinks. Breakfast (DM6.50 and up) served until 4pm. No dryers—let the balmy breezes dry you instead. Open Mon.-Thurs. 8am-1am, Fri. 8am-3am, Sat. 10am-3am, Sun. 10am-1am.

SIGHTS

The Dom

When sightseeing in Cologne, it's impossible to save the best for last. Most train stations offer only an assortment of drunks, beggars, and transients, but visitors exiting Cologne's *Bahnhof* are immediately treated to the beauty, power, and sorrow that emanate from the colossal **Dom,** Germany's greatest cathedral. Dedicated to St. Peter and St. Mary and visually overwhelming in intricacy and scale, the edifice took six centuries to build, finally reaching completion in 1880. For 500 years, the giant wooden crane, now kept inside, was as much Cologne's trademark as the two massive towers. Inside, the stunning array of stained glass—enough to cover the floor twice—casts a fragile display of colored light over the interior. Moving toward the front, the section to the right of the center altar bears the **Dombild triptych,** a masterful painting and gilded altarpiece from the 15th-century Cologne School of Painting; the enormous sculpture shining brilliantly even in the dim light is the **Shrine of the Magi,** a reliquary of the Three Kings in blinding gold, brought to Cologne in 1164. The Three Kings are the town's holy patrons; they stand behind the altar in a magnificent 1531 woodcut of the town by Anton Woensam, and their three crowns grace

NORTH RHINE-WESTPHALIA

Cologne's official heraldic shield. Tapestries of Rubens' *Triumph of the Eucharist* line the central nave. While in the *Dom,* look for the 976 **Gero Crucifix,** the oldest intact sculpture of **Christus patiens** (depicting Christ during crucifixion with closed eyes) in the world. (Cathedral open daily 6am-7pm. English tours (for info call 52 19 77) Sun.-Fri. 2pm, Sat. 10:30am. DM6, children DM4. Free organ concerts mid-June-Sept. Tues. 8pm.)

Five hundred and nine steps and 15 minutes are all it takes to top the **Südturm** (south tower), and peer down at the river below. Catch your breath at the *Glocken-stube* (400 steps up), a chamber for the tower's nine bells. Four of the *Glocken* date from the Middle Ages, but the 19th-century upstart known affectionately as **Der große Peter** (at 24 tons, the world's heaviest swinging bell) rings loudest. Hailed as "Germany's bell on the Rhine," it bears an engraved call for national unity (tower open May-Sept. 9am-6pm; March-April and Oct. 9am-5pm; Nov.-Feb. 9am-4pm; admission DM3, students DM1.50). The **Domschatzkammer** in a corner of the cathedral holds the requisite clerical artwork and reliquaries: thorn, cross, and nail bits as well as pieces of 18 saints (open April-Oct. Mon.-Sat. 9am-5pm, Sun 1-4pm; Nov.-March Mon.-Sat. 9am-4pm, Sun. 1-4pm; admission DM3, under 18 and students DM1.50). Find more ecclesiastical favors in the **Diözesan Museum,** at Roncalliplatz 2, just outside the south portal in the red building (open Fri.-Wed. 10am-5pm; free).

The allure of the cathedral illuminated from dusk 'til midnight is irresistible, and draws natives and tourists alike to the expansive **Domvorplatz** plaza for a daily carnival of relaxation, art, and activism. Since time and acid rain have corroded much of the cathedral's original detail, every piece is gradually being reproduced and replaced with new, treated stone. To help speed up this tedious task, you can play the "*Dom* lottery" at posts around the plaza and save a statue's fingernail (DM1-2).

Central City

In the shadow of the cathedral, the **Hohenzollern Brücke** crosses the Rhine. The majestic bridge empties out onto a promenade guarded by equestrian statues of the imperial family. A monumental flight of stairs leads to the **Heinrich Böll Cultural Center** (see Museums, p. 90), a piece of modern architecture that actually complements the *Dom.* Farther on, the squares and crooked streets of the old **Fischmarkt** district open onto paths along the Rhine; the café patios give way to a wide expanse of grass along the river, perfect for a picnic serenaded by musicians.

The **Rathaus** (Town Hall) was partially bombed to the ground, but has been reconstructed in its original style (or styles). The Gothic **tower** stands guard over Baroque cherubs flying around an ornate 1570 Renaissance arcade called the *loggia,* the only section to survive the war. The tower is adorned with a mind-boggling array of historical figures; Marx and Rubens loom above rows of popes and emperors. On the *Rathaus* façade, a **Glockenspiel** gleefully chimes daily at noon and 5pm (open Mon.-Thurs. 7:30am-4:45pm, Fri. 7:30am-2pm; tours Wed. at 3pm). Classical historians and *Ben Hur* fans will be more impressed by the **Römisches Praetorium und Kanal,** the excavated ruins of the former Roman military headquarters from the province of Niedergermania (Lower Germany). To get there from the *Rathaus* porch, take a right down to the swarm of hotels and then a left onto Kleinen Budengasse. Looking like an abandoned set from a gladiator movie, the museum displays the remains of various Roman gods and a befuddling array of rocks left by the city's early inhabitants (open Tues.-Fri. 10am-4pm, Sat.-Sun. 11am-4pm; admission DM3, students DM1.50). The glass pyramid visible to your left as you exit the *Rathaus* shelters the **Mikwe,** a 12th-century Jewish ritual bath that burrows 15m down to groundwater. Legend has it that bathers could not wear anything to experience the life-giving water, but all you need is a passport to get the key from the *Rathaus* (open Mon.-Thurs. 8am-4pm, Fri.-Sat. 8am-2pm; free).

Goethe, the original 18th-century gigolo, noted "how grateful the women are for the fragrance of Eau de Cologne." This magic water, once prescribed as a drinkable curative, made the town (or the oft-mimicked export) a household name. Be sure your tourist bottle says *"Echt kölnisch Wasser"* (real Cologne water) if you're after the authentic article; or look for the world-renowned "4711" label. Its name comes from the Mühlens family house, where Eau de Cologne has been produced since 1792, and which was labeled **House #4711** by the Napoleonic system that abolished street names. It has now been converted into a perfect boutique, with a small fountain constantly dispensing the famous scented water. Visit regularly, and you'll never need to shower again. The house is on Glockengasse, at the intersection with Tunisstr.; from Hohestr., turn right on Brückenstr., which becomes Glockengasse. The **Glockenspiel** on the house chimes on the hour daily from 9am to 10pm with old German songs (#4711 open Mon.-Fri. 9am-6:30pm, Sat. 9am-2pm).

The **Rheinseilbahn** (gondola; see p. 84) touts a terminus near Köln-Riehl's **zoo** (open daily 9am-6pm; in winter 9am-5pm), **aquarium** (open daily 9:30am-6pm), and **botanical garden** (open daily 8am-dusk). Take U-Bahn #16 or 18 to "Zoo/Flora." The combined entrance for the zoo and aquarium for adults is DM15, for students DM8.50, and for children DM7.50. Sorry Lassie, you can't come. Köln-Bayenthal, south of the city center, hosts the **Historische Braustätte der Küppers-Kölsch-Brauerei,** Alteburgerstr. 157, the brewery where the refined *Küppers* beer is still made as it has been for 100 years (only open Sat. 11am-4pm; bus #132: "Bonntor").

Churches

Cologne's success in building awe-inspiring churches began hundreds of years before the idea for the *Dom* was even conceived. The Romanesque period of the 10th to mid-13th century saw the construction of 12 churches roughly in the shape of a semicircle around the *Altstadt,* using the holy bones of the saints to protect the city. Beautiful even in inevitable comparison to the *Dom,* Cologne's 12 churches attest to the sacred glory and tremendous wealth of what was, at the time, the most important city north of the Alps. The city's piety even received poetic embodiment in a Samuel Taylor Coleridge poem: "In Köln, a town of monks and bones/ And pavements fanged with murderous stones/ And rags, and hags, and hideous wenches/ I counted two-and-seventy stenches…"

One of the first medieval structures to use the unique decagon layout, **St. Gereon** (tel. 13 49 22), houses a very interesting floor mosaic of David hacking off the head of Goliath. The 10 ribbed arches in the dome create the third largest church vault in the world (open Mon.-Fri. 10am-6pm, Sat. 10am-12:30pm and 1:30-6pm, Sun. 2-4pm). Along with the majestic *Dom,* **Groß St. Martin** defines the legendary Rhine panorama of Cologne. After being totally destroyed in World War II, the church was completely restored in 1963. Crypts downstairs house an esoteric collection of stones and diagrams (church and crypt open Mon.-Fri. 10:15am-6pm, Sat. 10am-6pm, Sun. 2-4pm; crypt admission DM1, stud(ent)s and children DM0.50). Visitors to the **St. Maria im Kapitol** are treated to amazingly ornate carved wooden panels detailing the life of Christ (open daily 8am-6pm). On the portal behind **St. Cäecilian** (tel. 221 23 10) stands "Death"—no, not the work of drunken vandals but the masterpiece of a professional sprayer (open Tues.-Fri. 10am-4pm, Sat.-Sun. 11am-4pm).

The **St. Ursula** church, north of the *Dom,* commemorates Ursula's desperate struggle for celibacy despite her betrothal. She and 11 virgins under her tutelage were mistaken for Roman legionnaires and burnt at sea. The Latin record of the tale indicated "11M," meaning 11 martyrs, but was later misconstrued as 11 *thousand* virgins. (Sort of like Yale.) The walls of the inside **Goldene Kammer** are lined with over 700 human skulls and innumerable reliquaries. (Church and Goldene Kammer open Mon. and Thurs.-Sat. 9am-noon and 3-5pm, Wed. 9:30am-noon and 3-5pm. Admission to chamber DM2, children DM1.)

Though not as well-known as those of the Romanesque period, churches of various styles and times can be found throughout Köln. **St. Peter's** church, a tiny construction just south of St. Cäecilien (entrance on Leonard-Tietzstr.), provides a rare opportunity to see a masterwork in its original position: Rubens' **The Crucifixion of St. Peter** hangs above the main altar, and its beauty fills the small church completely (open Tues.-Sun. 11am-6pm). Behind the *Rathaus,* inside the now overgrown ruins of the bombed **Alt St. Alban** church, life-sized parents mourn the children of war in a statue by Käthe Kollwitz.

MUSEUMS

Köln's religious and economic significance to Europe throughout history has stocked this rich city's museums with a vast and impressive array of holdings. The main museums are free with the **Köln Bonbon** (see Practical Information, p. 83). Many smaller, more specialized "museums" stretch the definition of the word to its limit; look around before you plunk down your DM2, or you might end up with nothing more than a peek in someone's junk drawer.

Near the Cathedral

Römische-Germanisches Museum, Roncalliplatz 4 (tel. 221 44 38), was built over the ruins of a Roman villa. The displays include the world-famous Dionysus Mosaic, the 2-story tomb of Publicus, an intimidating 6-breasted sphinx, and a few very naughty candle-holders. Admission DM7, students and children DM4. Call to arrange a tour. Open Tues.-Fri. 10am-4pm. Sat.-Sun. 11am-4pm.

Heinrich-Böll-Platz, Bischofsgartenstr. 1, behind the Römische-Germanisches Museum (tel. 221 48 02). This unusual building, designed to maximize the natural lighting, houses 3 complementary collections. The **Wallraf-Richartz Museum** (tel. 221 23 72) features crackly masterpieces of the 13th to 19th centuries, right up to Renoir and Manet. The **Museum Ludwig** (tel. 221 23 70) then travels from Impressionism through Picasso, Dalí, and Roy Lichtenstein, to art where the glue and paint have yet to dry. The **Agfa Foto-Historama** (tel. 221 24 11) chronicles chemical art of the last 150 years, including rotating displays of works by Man Ray and others. Comprehensive admission DM13, students DM7. A dazzling array of tours. Free with the *Bonbon.* All open Tues.-Fri. 10am-6pm, Sat.-Sun. 11am-6pm.

Museum für Andgewandte Kunst (Museum of Applied Art), An der Rechtschule (tel. 221 67 14), west of the *Dom* across Wallrafplatz. A giant arts and crafts fair spanning 7 centuries with a fabulous 20th-century design display but no tie-dye stand. Lots of English captions. Tours Tues. at 6:30pm, Sun. at 11:30am. Admission DM8, students and children DM4. Free with *Bonbon.* Open Tues.-Fri. 11am-5pm, Sat.-Sun. noon-5pm.

Elsewhere in Cologne

Das Mmmuseum (Imhoff-Stollwerk Museum), Rheinauhafen 1a, near the Severins bridge (tel. 931 88 80). Better than Willy Wonka's Chocolate Factory. Salivate at every step of chocolate production from the rainforests to the gold fountain that spurts streams of silky, heavenly, creamy… As you view the provocative photos, resist the urge to slobber uncontrollably on yourself. Free petite samples. Exhibits in German. Tours (DM3) Sat. at 2 and 4pm, Sun. at 11:30am, 2, and 4pm; Admission DM10, students, seniors, children DM5. Open Mon.-Fri. 10am-6pm (last entry 5pm), Sat.-Sun. 11am-7pm (last entry 6pm).

EL-DE-Haus, Am Appellhofplatz 23/25 (tel. 43 40). From the side of the Stadtmuseum opposite the entrance, follow the angel's wing, which points down Appellhofplatz. A moving indictment of war in the basement of the Gestapo's former headquarters. 1200 wall inscriptions by political prisoners. Tours first Sat. of each month at 2pm. Open Tues.-Fri. 10am-4pm, Sat.-Sun. 11am-4pm. Free.

Kölnisches Stadtmuseum, Zeughausstr.1-3 (tel. 221 23 98). Take the U-Bahn to "Appellhofplatz/Zeughaus." Within the 16th-century armory, aerial photos and 3-D maps show Cologne's itinerary from Roman ruins to post-war rubble and back again. Tours Sat. at 2:30pm and Sun. at 11:15am. Admission DM6, students and children DM3. Free with the *Bonbon.* Open Tues.-Sun. 10am-4pm.

Käthe Kollwitz Museum, Neumarkt 18-24 (tel. 227 23 63), in the Neumarkt-Passage. Take U-Bahn #9, 12, 14, 16, or 18 to "Neumarkt." The world's largest collection of sketches, sculptures and prints by the brilliant artist and activist. Kollwitz's images chronicle the sadness of early 20th-century Berlin in stark black-and-white. Tours Sun. at 11am. Admission DM5, students and children DM2. Open Tues.-Wed. and Fri.-Sun. 10am-5pm, Thurs. 10am-8pm.

Beatles Museum, Heinsbergstr. 13 (tel. 21 25 98), off Zülpicherstr. Take U-Bahn #12, 16, or 18 to "Barbarossaplatz." Crammed with Fab Four memorabilia. With new 60s-style café, it's bigger, but bigger than Jesus? Not in Cologne (see Sights: The *Dom*, p. 87*)*. With admission (DM5) you get coffee and a souvenir sack. Open Sept.-July Wed.-Fri. 10am-2pm and 3-7pm. Sat. 10am-3pm.

Schnütgen Museum, Cäcilienstr. 29 (tel. 221 36 20), in the St. Cecilia Church. Take the U-Bahn to "Neumarkt." Ecclesiastical art from the Middle Ages to the Baroque, notably tapestry and priestly fashion displays. Tours Sun. at 11am, Wed. at 2:30pm. Admission DM5, students DM2.50. Free with the *Bonbon*. Open Tues.-Fri. 10am-4pm, Sat.-Sun. 11am-4pm.

ENTERTAINMENT

Cologne explodes in celebration during **Karneval,** a week-long pre-Lenten festival. Celebrated in the hedonistic spirit of the city's Roman past, *Karneval* is made up of fifty major and minor neighborhood processions in the weeks before Ash Wednesday. **Weiberfastnacht,** on the Thursday before Ash Wednesday (Feb. 6 in 1997), is the first major to-do; the mayor mounts the platform at *Alter Markt* and abdicates leadership of the city to a trio of fools. For the rest of the day, the city's *Weiber* (an archaic and not too politically correct term for women) are given rule of the roost. In the afternoon, the first of the big parades begins at Severinstor. The weekend builds up to the out-of-control, dancing-in-the-streets parade on **Rosenmontag,** the last Monday before Lent (Feb. 10 in 1997). Everyone's in costume and gets and gives a couple dozen *Bützchen (Kölsch* dialect for a kiss on a stranger's cheek). Arrive early, get a map of the route, and don't stand anywhere near the station or cathedral—you'll be pulverized by the lollapaloozian crowds. While most revelers nurse their hangovers on Shrove Tuesday, pubs and restaurants set fire to the straw scarecrows hanging out of their windows. For more information on the festival and tickets to events, inquire at the **Festkomitee des Kölner Karnevals,** Antwerpener Str. 55 (tel. 57 40 00). Also pick up the *Köln, Karneval* booklet at the tourist office.

Cologne's traditional entertainment offers some competition, with over 30 theaters including the **Oper der Stadt Köln** (*Abendkasse* (evening box office) tel. 221 82 48) and the **Kölner Schauspielhaus** (*Abendkasse* tel. 221 82 52), near Schildergasse on Offenbachplatz. For more info on Cologne's theaters, check the *Monatsvorschau*. The **Cinemanthek** (tel. 257 59 21) entrance is on the ground floor of the three-museum building in Heinrich-Böll-Platz; current movies show almost daily, with most films in the original English. Pick up a schedule at the information kiosk inside for movie times. "V.O." *(Originalfassung)* denotes an original version, "OmdT" is an original with German subtitles, and "DF" *(deutsche Fassung)* means they've (unspeakably) dubbed it in German (check the *Monatvorscham* for film info). The 200-seat **Philharmonic Hall** (tel. 28 01) is located in the basement of the same building; check the tourist office for info. The brand new 3000-seat **Cinedom** (tel. 95 19 51 95 98), with 13 screens, is part of the **Media Park.** A converted train station, it opened its doors in 1992. From April to October, catch the **craft market** the last weekend of every month in the *Altstadt,* around Groß St. Martin church.

NIGHTLIFE

Celebrating life with lavish festivities has long been a tradition in Cologne. Roman mosaics dating back to 3AD record the wild excesses of the city's early residents. But instead of grape-feeding and fig-wearing, modern life in Cologne now focuses on house music and a more sophisticated bump-and-grind. Remember that even though Cologne does everything, including nightlife, on a large scale, the closer you venture to the Rhine and the *Dom,* the more that scale applies directly to your wallet. The nightly jazz at **Papa Joe's Jazzlokal,** Buttermarkt 37 (tel. 21 79 50), near Fischmarkt and the Rhine, is as good as jazz gets in these parts, although Coltrane fans should beware: German "jazz" is ultra-traditional, bordering on ragtime (open Mon.-Sat. 7pm-2am, Sun. 3:30pm-1am; jazz from 8:30pm). For diehards, "Four o'clock Jazz" starts every Sunday at 3:30pm and goes for eight hours. **Papa Joe's Biersalon,** Alter Markt

50-52 (tel. 258 21 32), is a simple piano saloon with pistol-pointing lottery machines (open Sun.-Thurs. 11am-1am, Fri.-Sat. 11am-2am).

For fun of a less hokey sort, students congregate in the **Quartier Lateng,** a.k.a. the *Bermuda Dreieck* (triangle). The area is bounded by Zülpicherstr., Zülpicher Platz, Roonstr. and Luxemburgstr. The center of gay nightlife runs up **Matthiasstr.** to Mühlenbach, Hohe Pforte, Marienplatz, and up to Heumarkt in the area by the Deutzer Brücke. Radiating westward from Friesenplatz, the **Belgisches Viertel** is spiced with slightly more sophisticated and expensive bars and cafés.

The worshippers of Dionysus boozed themselves into stupors here, and the tradition of getting plastered is still highly respected in Cologne. Here at the various *Brauhäuser,* where the original *Kölsch* is brewed and served in-house, the *Köbes* will bring one glass after another until you fall under the table, unless you place your coaster over your glass. Saying *"Ich bin nicht zum Spaß hier"* ("I'm not here to fool around") informs the *Köbes* of your serious intentions; just watch that the lines on your coaster correspond to the number of beers you actually drank—it's said they might count on the fact that you won't be able to count.

Museum, Zülpicherplatz 9 (tel. 23 20 98). No temple of science is complete without a 2-story **dinosaur** looking out over blood alcohol experiments. RRRRAWR! Popular Köln University field trip. Open Sun.-Thurs. 6pm-1am, Fri.-Sat. 6pm-3am.

Café Magnus, Zülpicherstr. 48 (tel. 24 16 69). Brimming with students jamming to party music from the good ol' U.S. of A. Open daily 9am-3am.

Päffgen Brauhaus, Friesenstr. 64-66 (tel. 13 54 61). A local favorite since 1883. Legendary *Kölsch* is brewed on the premises and consumed in big cave-like halls or in the *Biergarten* (0.2L shot DM2.20). Follow *Brauhaus* rules as enumerated above. Open 10am-midnight. Kitchen open 11am-11pm.

42 D.P. ("Don't Panik"), Hohenstaufenring 25-27 (tel. 24 79 71). Popular, smoky, and very *noir*. All flavors of techno. For novices who can't distinguish between goth and ambient, "The Basics of Techno" is offered Wed. (cover DM10). Cover on other nights varies, often DM15 Fri.-Sat. Open Wed.-Sun. 11pm-4:30am.

Altstadt Päffgen, Heumarkt 62 (tel. 257 77 65), is the same thing. Less authentic, but also less crowded during key drinking hours. Open Tues.-Sun. noon-midnight.

Tingle Tangel, Maastrichterstr. 6-8 (tel. 25 26 01). Red velvet ex-brothel draws in the sexy and freaky for roaring good times; gets going around 1am. Belly-dancing or poetry performances (3 per week) from Aug.-Nov. No cover most weeknights, but Fri. and Sat. cost DM10, whether it's just for the café or a transvestite diva singing TV's greatest theme songs. Open Tues.-Sun. 11pm-5am.

Luxor, Luxemburgstr. 40 (tel. 21 95 03). The club's small, intimate stage draws some great up-and-coming American and European bands, which provide relatively cheap, high-quality concerts. Open daily 8pm-3am.

Gloria, Apostelnstr. 11 (tel. 25 44 33). Crowded and popular gay and lesbian café offers theater, film, and dancing in a converted porn theater. Call for a schedule. Cover averages DM10. Café open Sun.-Thurs. 9am-1am, Fri.-Sat. 9am-3am.

Broadway, Ehrenstr. 11 (tel. 25 52 14). The hip joint for local artists and painters. To fit in, wear a black coat and a red scarf. Open daily 10am-1am.

Filmdose, Zülpicherstr. 39 (tel. 23 96 43). "Film Can." Café-bar with a creative performance space. Theater starts one hour after opening time, followed by a carnival-like *Discothek.* Cover DM5. Call ahead for scheduling. No shows during the thick of the soccer season. Open Tues.-Thurs. 7pm-3am, Fri.-Sat. 6:30pm-3am.

Star-Treff, Alte Wallgasse at the corner of Ehrenstr. (tel. 25 50 63). Not quite the hangout for the crew of the *Enterprise,* the pink building contains a transvestite cabaret and some serious freaks. DM35 buys you a ticket (call ahead) to a night you'll never forget. Showtimes Wed., Thurs., and Sun. 7:30pm, Fri.-Sat. 7pm and 10:10pm. Call to drag out more information.

Café Störchen, Ursula Kloster 4-6 (tel. 13 17 12), in the shadow of the St. Ursula church. Sink into a swank couch, beer in hand (DM1.80), and dish out a schoolin' to some suckas at Monopoly. Open Mon.-Fri. 11am-1am, Sun. 10am-1am.

■ Aachen

Aachen jives day and night in four different languages, exuding a youthful internationalism that belies its great age. Charlemagne first brought the city to life in the 8th century, when he made it the capital of his Frankish empire. Students at the universities and travelers from around the world come to Aachen with quite different ambitions but infuse a similar vitality. This is not to say that Aachen has forgotten its history. From the 14th-century stone *Rathaus* to the smaller bronze statue, the *Marktplatz* overflows with living monuments, each with its own story to tell.

ORIENTATION AND PRACTICAL INFORMATION

At the crossroads between Germany, Belgium, and the Netherlands, Aachen is also a departure point for trains to France (Aachen-Paris Twen-Tickets fare: DM62.10) and Britain (Aachen-London Twen-Tickets fare: DM76.50). Cologne is less than 1 hr. away by train, and many make the 15-minute bike ride to Holland to buy cheese.

Tourist Office: Aachen's central tourist office, **Atrium Elisenbrunnen,** on Friedrich-Wilhelm Platz (tel. 180 29 60; fax 180 29 31), dispenses literature and finds rooms (starting at DM35) for DM3. From the train station, cross the street and head up Bahnhofstr., turn left into Theaterstr., which becomes Theaterplatz, and then right onto Kapuzinergraben, which becomes Friedrich-Wilhelm Platz; the atrium is on your left. Check here for city **tours,** like the DM2 guided stroll through the *Dom.* Open Mon.-Fri. 9am-6:30pm, Sat. 9am-1pm.

Currency Exchange: At the post office in the train station. Open Mon.-Fri. 9am-6pm, Sat. 9am-1pm, Sun. 10am-noon.

Public Transportation: Tickets are priced by distance with one-way trips running DM2.30-9.30. *24-Stunden* tickets provide a full day of unlimited travel for DM8-20, but the DM8 kind gets you anywhere in Aachen. For those under 21, a weekend pass for all buses can be purchased on Saturdays for DM5. Some hotels also offer a DM7 *Hotelgastkarte* good for 2 days of unlimited travel. Call for details.

Bike Rental: Park & Bike, Parkhaus Wirichsbongardstr. 47 (tel. 312 43). Go up the street directly across from the tourist office; it's in the blue parking garage. Prices start at DM8 per 3 hours, DM20 per day. Open 24hr.

Mitfahrzentrale: Roesmonder Str. 4 (tel. 194 40). Matches riders and drivers. After hours, call 15 20 17. Open Mon.-Thurs. 10am-6pm, Fri. 9am-7pm, Sat. 10am-4pm.

Bookstore: Mayersche Buchhandlung, at Ursulinerstr. 17-19 (tel. 477 70), at the corner of Buchkremerstr. *Cliff's Notes,* children's books, and much more. Open Mon.-Wed. and Fri. 9:30am-6:30pm, Thurs. 9:30am-8:30pm, Sat. 9:30am-2pm.

Laundromat: Waschcenter, Heinrichsallee 30. Wash DM6 (soap included). Dry DM1 per 15min. Open Mon.-Sat. 6am-11pm; last call at 10pm.

Emergency: Police: tel. 110.

Post Office: The *Hauptpostamt,* Kapuzinergraben, is to the left of the station. Walk down Lagerhausstr., right down Franzstr., and then right on Kapuzinergraben. Open Mon.-Fri. 9am-6pm, Sat. 9am-1pm. The **postal code** is 52064.

Telephone Code: 0241.

ACCOMMODATIONS AND CAMPING

Aachen has too much history for a town of its size, and the oodles of visitors push the lodging prices up; it helps to call ahead. The **Mitwohnzentrale,** at Süsterfeldstr. 24 (tel. 87 53 46), will set you up with lodging for longer stays. To get there, take bus #7 (direction: Siedlung Schönau) or 33 (direction: Vaals) to "Westbahnhof" (open Mon.-Fri. 9am-1pm and 3-6pm).

Jugendherberge (HI), Maria-Theresia-Allee 260 (tel. 711 01; fax 70 82 19). Two buses go to the hostel leaving from the "Finanzamt" bus stop. To get to this departure point from the station, walk left on Lagerhausstr. until it intersects Karmeliterstr. and Mozartstr.; the bus stop will be on the other side of the street. Take bus #2 (direction: Preusswald) to "Ronheide" or bus #12 (direction: Diepenbendem) to

NORTH RHINE-WESTPHALIA

"Colynshof." Cooped-up like chickens in old rooms, you'll enjoy the company of interesting travelers and the good cheer of the staff. E-I-E-I-O. Reception open until 10pm. Curfew 11:30pm. DM22, over 26 DM26.50.

Hotel Dura, Lagerhausstr. 5 (tel. 40 31 35), is left down Lagerhausstr., 1 block from the station. Rooms vary in style but are spacious and clean. Singles DM60, with shower and toilet DM75. Doubles DM90, with shower and toilet DM110.

ETAP-Hotel, Strangenhäuschen 15 (tel. 91 19 29; fax 15 53 04). From the *Bushof* take bus #51 to "Strangenhäuschen." Though remote, this discount hotel chain is an unbeatable bargain. Fri.-Sun.: all rooms (doubles and singles with showers) only DM60. All other times: singles with shower DM60, doubles with shower DM70. Reception open 6:30-10am and 5-11pm.

Hotel Marx, Hubertusstr. 33-35 (tel. 375 41; fax 267 05). Just a hop, skip, and jump from the station. Hop left on Lagerhausstr. which becomes Boxgraben, skip right on Stephanstr., and jump left on Hubertusstr. Nice-looking furniture and cool comforter designs. Singles DM60, with shower and toilet DM85. Doubles DM100, with shower and toilet DM140. Breakfast included.

Hotel Cortis, Krefelder-Str. 52 (tel. 15 60 11; fax 15 60 12). From the central bus station *(Bushof)*, take bus #51 to "Rolandstr." Continue down Paßstr., then turn left on Krefeldstr. Farther out, but bright and comfortable with access to a multitude of umbrellas. Reception open 24hr. Singles DM57, with shower DM67. Doubles DM89, with shower DM114. Breakfast included.

FOOD

The hungry mouths of the book- and beer-laden are fed by a dense concentration of student restaurants and pubs that line **Pontstraße** from the edge of the pedestrian zone to the medieval Pont Tor. But beware—this region is also the prowling ground of the *Bahkauv*, a fearsome mythical blend of dog, puma, and dragon, which inexplicably derives its name from *"Bachkalb"* (stream calf) and pounces on the throats of drunken revelers, inducing head-splitting hangovers. The *Bahkauv's* bronze incarnation is on Buchkremerstr. near the open-air cafés of the *Markt*. According to legend, this ferocious creature attacks only males, thus preventing their offensive advances on the female population; but recent student questionnaires suggest that the *Bahkauv* has now become an equal-opportunity employer. Equally unique is the remarkable Aachen *Printen*, a spicy gingerbread biscuit, a refinement of an old Belgian recipe. It's now a world-famous snack with an annual production of 4500 tons—try it at any bakery. East of the **Katschhof** between the *Dom* and *Rathaus,* a morning **market** vends its vegetables on Tuesdays and Thursdays.

Van Den Daele, Büchel 18 (tel. 357 24), just off the *Markt*. The finest selection of baked goods in Aachen's oldest house. Built in 1655, this *Printen* factory was made famous by artist/baker Leo van den Daele. Besides the hard gluger bread tack, the house specialty is *Reisfladden* (rice pudding)—DM3.80 gets you one momma of a slice. Open Mon.-Fri. 9am-6:30pm, Sat. 9am-6pm, Sun. noon-6pm.

Café Seminar, Templergraben 46 (tel. 379 97), directly across from the university, offers a hearty combo breakfast menu for DM4.50. All entrees under DM10. Party Harty Marty. Open daily 7:30am-11pm.

Katakomben Studentenzentrum, Pontstr. 74-76 (tel. 470 01 41), encloses **Café Chico Mendes,** a co-op café of the Catholic College. DM6 or DM9 for the larger portion. Half-off a very long list of drinks during Happy Hour (Sun. 8:30-9:30pm). Open Mon.-Fri. 4:30pm-1am, Sat. 6pm-1am.

Egmont, Pontstr. 1 (tel. 40 60 44). Just off the *Rathaus*. Droves of Aacheners come here to eat and drink under the watchful eye of Charlemagne. The bar is popular come nightfall. Open daily 9am-1am.

Mensa, in the green-trimmed building on Pontwall (tel. 80 37 92), near the Pont Tor. Meals DM2.80-3.60. Guest meals DM5.80-6.90. Open Mon.-Thurs. 11:30am-2:15pm, Fri. 11:30am-2:15pm.

SIGHTS

In 765, the Frankish King Pepin the Short took a dip in the hot springs north of Aachen's present city center. When his son, **Charlemagne,** assumed power, the family's former vacation spot became the capital of the rapidly expanding kingdom, and later of the Holy Roman Empire. The emperor's presence still dominates the city and local legends claim that in WWII, a bomb aimed at the cathedral was deflected by a statue of Charlemagne. The 8th-century dome at its center tops three tiers of marble arches that separate the gilded roof from the mosaic floor. Built in a neo-Byzantine style, the octagonal structure joins Western religious practice with the forms of the Eastern Orthodox church. Charlemagne's throne is a simple chair of marble slabs. Stained glass rings the 15th-century Gothic choir, and beneath the chancel lie the bones of the big guy himself. Their place is marked by the gold-and-gem *Karlschreine* with a blinking doll-sized effigy. (Cathedral open daily 7am-7pm. Individual tours Mon. at 11am and noon; Tues.-Fri. 11am, noon, 2:30, and 3:30pm; Sat.-Sun. 12:30, 2:30, and 3:30pm. DM3. For group tours or English-speaking guides, call 47 70 91 27. The gateway to the throne and shrine open for tours only.)

Old Charlie cuts more of a figure in the **Schatzkammer,** around the corner to the right from the *Dom* exit, tucked into the Klostergasse. The most famous likeness of the emperor, a solid gold bust *(die Karlsbüste)* shines in this exceptionally rich treasury. Not bad-looking. Among the other golden tidbits of Chuck, you'll find Christ's supposed belt and scourge rope as well as the Imperial Crown Jewels. Groupies shouldn't miss Charlemagne's wall-size "Missionary Man" tour map. (Open Mon. 10am-1pm, Tues.-Wed. and Fri.-Sun. 10am-6:30pm, Thurs. 10am-9pm. Last entrance 30min. before closing. Admission DM3, students, seniors, and children DM1.50.)

The 14th-century stone **Rathaus** (tel. 432 73 10), built on the ruins of Charlemagne's palace, looms over the wide *Marktplatz* beside the cathedral. Seventeeth-century citizens with a decorative obsession added Baroque flourishes to the façade. On the northern face stand 50 statues of former German sovereigns, 31 of whom were crowned in Aachen (open daily 10am-1pm and 2-5pm; admission DM3, students and children DM1.50). A copy of the famed **Charlemagne statue** draws a pic-

---

Pulling the Wool Over the Devil's Eyes

Aacheners have always had a reputation for being clever; they carry the distinction of having tricked the **Devil** not once, but twice. The first incident occurred just before the opening of the *Dom*. Knowing that the city's construction funds were depleted, the **Prince of Darkness** posed as a wealthy businessman and offered an unlimited supply of cash to the city in exchange for the soul of the first living being to enter the church, knowing full well that a bishop traditionally leads the procession in the consecration ceremony. The Aacheners accepted but cleverly let a wolf into the *Dom* just ahead of the bishop. **Satan** pounced on the wolf, ripping out the poor canine's soul. Furious at this fraud, he slammed the door shut, but left his thumb in the way and got it severed off. The wolf, its soul (represented by a pineapple), the devil's thumb, and the rage-induced crack in the door—unambiguous proof of the legend—are all to be found at the *Dom*.

It wasn't long before **Mesphistopheles,** incensed by his initial failure, came back for revenge. Shouldering an enormous bag of sand, he walked from his little hellhole to the Maas River with the intention of burying the accursed city. But instead of arriving in central Aachen, poor **Lucifer,** never the geography bee of his class, managed to get lost a few kilometers northwest of the city center. Doing his best to hide the 5000-ton bag of sand, he sweetly asked a village girl for directions, but she, the ever-clever Aachener, told him he was nowhere near Aachen, but thousands of miles away. Disappointed and developing a backache, the disgusted **Beelzebub** slammed down his sack of sand and stormed off to wherever guys like him live. The resulting Lons Mountains and a bronze monument to the young heroine celebrate this crowning moment in Aachen's history.

nicking, multi-colored-hair crowd to the fountain on the square; the real thing is inside the *Rathaus* along with copies of the Imperial Crown Jewels. The **Puppenbrunnen,** a fountain whose lovable characters represent Aachen's clever townspeople, is at the intersection of Krämerstr. and Hofstr.

MUSEUMS

Although the range of museums in Aachen is limited, the streets, especially in the *Altstadt,* shelter numerous little galleries worth browsing. The area to the left of the station, centered around Langerhausstr., is filled with antique stores.

Ludwig Forum für Internationale Kunst, Jülicherstr. 97-109 (tel. 180 70). Look for the large clown in drag. The *Forum* scorns the title "museum"; it's more of a works-in-progress arena. The converted *Bauhaus* umbrella factory provides the setting for all the modern musts, from Andy Warhol to Barbara Kruger. The *Forum* opened in 1991 with enough space to invest in a stunning, hot-off-the-press Eastern European collection. Admission DM6, students DM3. Free tour Wed. at 8pm. Open Tues. and Thurs. 10am-5pm, Wed. and Fri. 10am-8pm, Sat.-Sun. 11am-5pm. Last entrance 30min. before closing.

Internationales Zeitungsmuseum, Pontstr. 13 (tel. 432 45 08), just up from the *Markt.* "What's black and white and re(a)d all over?" This museum houses over 120,000 different international newspapers, including press from the revolutions of 1848, World War I, World War II, and the day Hitler died. Free. Open Tues.-Fri. 9:30am-1pm and 2:30-5pm, Sat. 9:30am-1pm. Last entry 30min. before closing.

Couven Museum, Hühnermarkt 17 (tel. 432 44 21), near the *Rathaus.* Restored house of wealthy Aachen pharmacist beautifully re-creates upper-crust life in the 18th century. Admission DM2, students DM1. Open Tues.-Wed. and Fri.-Sun. 10am-5pm, Thurs. 10am-1pm.

ENTERTAINMENT AND NIGHTLIFE

Aachen has a lively theater scene, beginning with the **Stadttheater,** on Theaterplatz (tel. 478 42 44), in the central city (box office open Mon.-Sat. 9am-1pm, 5-7pm, and 30min. before performances). A small strip of newer, unconventional theaters line Gasbornstr., spearheaded by the **Aachener Kultur und Theater Initiative,** at Gasborn 9-11 (tel. 274 58). For those who would rather be horsing around, Aachen annually hosts the **World Equestrian Festival,** to be held in June 1997. Contact the tourist office for info.

At night, the streets come alive as swarms of students hit the cafés and pubs for a study break with the *Bahkauv.* **Klenkes Magazine** (DM3.50) offers readers a few hundred ways to have fun with movies and music listings galore. **Stonewall TAC** has a thorough listing of gay and lesbian events.

Tangente, Pontstr. 141 (tel. 224 67). Catch the hip crowd and snag a delicious shake (DM3.70) while you're at it. But beware: **B**ahkauv **A**lert **R**ating very high, prime stalking ground. Open Sun.-Thurs. 9:30am-1:30am, Fri.-Sat. 9:30am-2:30am.

Domkeller, Hof 1 (tel. 342 65). Standing at the Puppenbrunnen and facing away from the *Dom,* bear right and cross the small square. A silly array of fish and groovy jazz music magically attracts all types: Bahn workers, businesspeople, and, of course, you. B.A.R.: low. Open Sun.-Thurs. 9:30am-1am, Fri.-Sat. 9:30am-3am.

Gaststätte Söller, Lindenplatz 19 (tel. 237 82). Located west of the *Rathaus* off Jacobstr., it is a bit far from the traditional hunting grounds. Wooden interior colorfully graffitied. Perhaps the only place in Germany that serves Irish beer without obnoxious, drunken Americans. Drink, dance, sing, cry—it is but once we live. B.A.R.: medium. Open Mon.-Thurs. 7pm-1am., Fri.-Sat. 7pm-3am.

Café Kittel, 39 Pontstr. (tel. 365 60). Like scales on a fish, posters smother the walls with announcements for live music, parties, and special events. Enjoy bowls of coffee on the outdoor patio, in the greenhouse, or amid concert posters. Vegetable quiches DM4.50. Daily menu DM5-10. Take it down with the house specialty, milk coffee (DM4.80). B.A.R.: low. Coffee makes the *Bahkauv* nervy and anxious. Open Mon.-Thurs. 10am-2am, Fri.-Sat. 10am-3am, Sun. 11am-2am.

▓ Eifel Massif

These wooded hills rise just north of the Mosel Valley and stretch to Aachen in the north and Belgium and Luxembourg in the west. On the Belgian side of the border, the Eifel becomes the Ardennes, remembered as the site of the Battle of the Bulge. While tourism is still the main industry, visitors to the Eifel Massif tend to be less obtrusive, blending quietly into the countryside in their hiking knickers and thick socks. It's undeniably more peaceful and relaxed than the Black Forest. Transportation, however, is difficult: nearly all the local rail lines are no longer open, and the bus lines are tryingly slow. The most heavily traveled—and accessible—part of the Eifel is the **Ahrtal** (Ahr Valley), south of Bonn, most scenic around the tiny town of **Altenahr.** The **Hohe Eifel** (High Eifel) in the center of the Massif is notable for its crater lakes and odd rock formations that now-dormant volcanoes produced as recently as 10,000 years ago. The **Nordeifel** (North Eifel) is home to the Seven Lakes—all artificial, but nonetheless popular venues for fishing and water sports. The Eifel is famous for its *Schinken* (ham), a specialty left over from the Roman occupation. The popularity of the pig is rivaled by that of the *Ahrtalwein,* fruit of the valley's vineyards. Infinitely more kosher, vegetarian, and drinkable than the ham, it is also much more pleasant to see produced.

MONSCHAU

The tiny town of Monschau is unique in North Rhine-Westphalia for its unusually strong French character. A flood of Huguenots fleeing Catholic persecution settled in this region, plying their traditional skills to stimulate a thriving cloth industry. In 1794, Napoleon captured the town, kicking off 12 years of occupation. After some international horse-trading, Monschau again became part of Germany. Nevertheless, many residents still have French names, and the local cuisine offers many treats from Germany's friendly neighbor to the west. However, Monschau still *looks* distinctly North Rhine-Westphalian. In a narrow, secluded valley cut by the swift-flowing Ruhr about 30km south of Aachen, the town is a visual compendium of gray slate roofs, cobblestones, and brickwork. The surrounding rolling hills are filled with hiking trails. In the city proper, the Ahr winds around tall, stone houses with small, flowered balconies, and the streets are lined with lovely cafés and terraces.

Egomaniacs who find this serene beauty boring can indulge their monarchical fantasies at the **Burg,** ruins of a massive castle perched above the town. A steep set of stairs leads to the castle from the center of town; imagine yourself as ruler of all you survey. Midway up, the 1649 **Alte Katherine Pfarrkirche** sits pretty in gray with its shingled onion-turret. Alongside mounds of ecclesiastical booty stolen by Napoleon and traded to Monschau's cloth makers, the peasants pray to escape your iron fist. It works, temporarily, as you are diverted by the **Glashütte** (glassworks museum), at Burgaustr. 15 (tel. 32 16), which has demonstrations every hour on the half-hour between 10:30am and 4:30pm (open daily 10am-6pm; admission DM3, students and children DM2). As you descend from your royal perch, kick aside peasants and notice how the **Rotes Haus** (red house), at Laufenstr. 10 (tel. 50 71), provides a striking break in the color scheme. Built by a local cloth merchant in 1760, the building now contains a museum of period pieces. (Tours Easter-Nov. Tues.-Sun. at 10, 11am, and 2, 3, and 4pm; admission DM4, students and children DM2.) Across the bridge in the **Evangelische Pfarrkirche** chapel, your minions seek divine salvation.

Close your ears to the peasants' pitiful cries, and follow your nose to the other end of town where the authentic 19th-century **Senfmühle** (mustard mill), Laufenstr. 18 (tel. 22 45), awaits your royal highness; Monschau is famous for its mustard (open for demonstrations March-Oct. Wed. at 11am and 2pm; admission DM4, students and children DM2). As you greedily sample the shop's twelve varieties, the townspeople escape on the hourly bus #166 to Aachen (DM5.50 one way), arriving safely at the

Aachen *Bushof.* Dejected, you climb back up to the **tourist office,** Stadtstr. 1 (tel. 33 00; fax 45 34), across from the steps leading to the *Burg* (open Mon.-Fri. 9am-noon and 1-4pm, Sat. 11am-3pm, Sun. 11am-2pm; Oct.-Easter Mon.-Fri. 9am-noon and 1-4pm). To curry your royal favor, they will book rooms (starting at DM25) for a DM5 fee and give you maps. You opt instead for the **Jugendherberge Monschen (HI),** Auf dem Schloß 4 (tel. 23 14; fax 43 91), which is teeming with rebellious school children who shriek at you in German, French, and Flemish. (Should you wish to stay and engage them in battle, pay DM21, over 26 DM25. Sheets DM6. Breakfast is included, but cauldrons of scalding oil to pour over the battlements and onto the treacherous young villains are not. Reception open 8:30-9am, 12:30-1pm, 6:30-7pm. Curfew 10pm.) To seek a safer haven, head to the larger, more modern **Jugendherberge "Monschau-Hargard" (HI),** Hargarasgasse 5 (tel. 21 80; fax 45 27), just outside of town. Take bus #166 (direction: Hargard) from in front of the post office in the direction of Aachen to the "Hargard" stop, backtrack 100m, and follow the sign. (Reception open until 9pm. Curfew 10pm. DM21.50, over 26 DM26. Breakfast included. Sheets DM6.) **Hotel-Café Flosdorff,** am Markt 7 (tel. 23 03), is also on the main square next to the river. The rooms are brighter-colored versions of the picturesque town. (Singles DM30. Doubles DM65.) To satisfy the royal appetite without emptying the royal treasury, feast on personal pizzas (DM4-8) at **Tavola,** Stadtstr. 42 (tel. 72 17 63; open daily 10am-9pm). The **telephone code** is 02472, but you (plural) already knew that.

ALTENAHR

People come to this region of Germany to hike—everything else is incidental. While one might not go so far as to say "the hills are alive," they are very beautiful. In addition to its gorgeous location on the **Ahr,** Altenahr boasts **Burg Ahr,** a castle built by Count Theodrich von Ahr around 1100; the village developed afterwards through the demand for a handy supply of working peasants. After a nine-month siege, the castle fell to French troops in 1690, and was wrecked in 1714 after it proved to be a stronghold for bandits. Today it is refreshingly free of bandits, evidenced by the lack of souvenir stands waiting at the end of the 15-minute walk from the train station. Heading right along Brückenstr., the trail begins across from the *Rathaus.* To get there, brave the **Sommer-Rodelbahn** (tel. 23 21). It's like a luge, but without the cold, snow, and embarrassingly tight suits. Cables haul your mini-sled to the summit and then send you down a 500-m steel track. A brake is provided for yellowbellies. At DM3.50 per ride, DM5 for two (cheaper the more you ride and the larger your group), it's quite possibly Germany's cheapest thrill. The 4-km hike from Altenahr (follow *Autobahn* 357 towards Bonn) doesn't seem to dissuade crowds. Sundays are especially thronged (open April-Oct. daily 10am-7pm; Nov.-March Sat.-Sun. 10am-5pm). Lazy and well-heeled thrill seekers can take a cab from the station (DM2.50 per person; 4 person minimum) directly to the *Sommer-Rodelbahn.*

Information on hikes, lodgings, and train tickets is available at the **tourist office,** Altenburger 1a (tel. 84 48; fax 35 16), located in the station (open Mon.-Fri. 9am-noon and 2-5pm, Sat. 9am-noon; Nov.-April Mon.-Fri. 10am-noon and 3-5pm). The 24-km *Rottweinwanderweg* begins here; follow the red grapes for a comprehensive tour of the valley. The **SeilBahn** (tel. 83 83), left from the train station (8min.), will haul your butt up the hill to one of the hiking routes (DM3.50, children DM2) or bring you up and back down (DM6, children DM3). The **Jugendherberge Altenahr,** Langfigtal 8 (tel. 18 80), is in a nature reserve 20 minutes from town by foot. From the station, cross the bridge and turn right on Brückenstr., which becomes Tunnelstr. Don't go through the tunnel; walk along the river, cross the next bridge, and follow the promenade through the woods. (Reception officially open Mon.-Sat. 8-9pm and Sun. 8:30-9pm, but there are always people around; call ahead. Curfew 10pm. DM19, over 26 DM24. Breakfast included. Sheets DM5.) Bad-Neuenahr-Ahrweiler's **Jugendherberge,** St. Piusstr. 7 (tel. (02641) 349 24), is large and brand-spankin' new. Get off the train at "Ahrweiler" and follow the *Jugendgästehaus* signs. (DM22.50, over 26 DM25. Doubles DM34.50, over 26 DM40. Breakfast and sheets included. In-house bar.) The town is a good base for area hiking. To see how the other half lives, head towards Bad Neuenahr along the river for 3km. On the Ahr, a lone **campground** (tel. 85 03) offers its bosom to your tired sole. Head right as you face the tracks, follow them on the footpath, and take a left when you reach Altenburgerstr. The campground is on your right across the river. (Reception open 8am-10pm. Adults DM6, children DM5. Tents DM10.) The **telephone code** is 02643.

Most of Altenahr seems to have been built to stuff tourists with wine and traditional food. To not break the DM10 barrier without using a plastic *Imbiß* fork, visit **Im Weinhäuschen,** Brückenstr. 27 (tel. 31 15). This down-home restaurant has specials (under DM10) and potato pancakes and apple sauce (DM6.50). At night, the bar is popular with locals (open daily 11am-midnight). To sample the fruit of the Ahr, try the *Weinprobe* (local wine tasting) at **Mayschloß-Altenahr,** on Tunnelstr (tel. 936 00). Probe each delicate *Ahrtal* vintage, inhale the aromatic flavor, or just chug 'em (open Mon.-Sat. 8am-noon and 1-6pm, Sun. 10am-6pm).

■ Düsseldorf

As Germany's mod-ish fashion and advertising center, multinational corporation base, and capital of the densely populated province of North Rhine-Westphalia, Düsseldorf runneth over with German patricians and wanna-be aristocrats. Founded in the 13th century, the city has endured a series of terrific pummelings during its relatively long history. After suffering calamitous destruction during the Thirty Years War, the War of Spanish Succession, and the Second World War, Düsseldorf has rebounded each time with an indefatigable resilience that translates into fierce pride among the city's residents. Set on the majestic Rhine, Germany's *"Hautstadt"* (a pun on *Hauptstadt,* "capital," and *haute couture)* is a stately, modern metropolis. Residents have a maxim that Düsseldorf is not on the Rhine, but the **Königsallee** (the central promenade, a.k.a. "the Kö"), a kilometer-long fashion runway that sweeps down either side of the old town moat. At night, propriety (and sobriety) are cast aside as Düsseldorfers flock to the 500 pubs of the *Altstadt,* trading in their monacles and Rolexes for a pair of beer goggles and a damn good time.

ORIENTATION AND PRACTICAL INFORMATION

Tourist Office: Main office, Konrad-Adenauer Platz (tel.17 20 20; fax 35 04 04). Walk up and to the right from the station and look for the towering Immermanhof building. Their free monthly *Düsseldorf Monatsprogram* is packed with information. Open for ticket sales (12% fee) and general services Mon.-Fri. 8:30am-6pm, Sat. 9am-12:30pm; open for hotel reservations (DM5) Mon.-Sat. 8am-8pm, Sun. 4-10pm. The **branch office,** Heinrich Heine Allee 24 (tel. 899 23 46), specializes in cultural listings. Open Mon.-Fri. 9am-5pm.

Budget Travel: Council Travel, Graf Adolf Str. 64, 40212 Düsseldorf (tel. 36 30 30). Open Mon.-Fri. 9am-1pm, Sat. 10am-1pm.

Consulates: Canada and **United Kingdom,** Yorckstr. 19 (tel. 944 80). Open Mon-Fri. 8am-noon.

Currency Exchange: Deutsche Verkehrs Credit Bank, in the *Hauptbahnhof* or at the airport. Open Mon.-Sat. 7am-9pm, Sun. 8am-9pm. Better rates on traveler's checks with no service charge are available at AmEx (see below).

American Express: Neusserstr. 111 (tel. 90 13 50). Mail held up to 4 weeks for card members. All financial services rendered. Open Mon.-Fri. 9am-5:30pm, Sat. 8:30am-noon.

Telephones: At main post office, and at the *Hauptbahnhof.*

Flights: Frequent S-Bahns and a Lufthansa shuttle travel from the station to the international **Flughafen Düsseldorf.** Call 421 22 23 for flight information. Open 5am-12:30am.

Trains: All trains arrive at **Düsseldorf Hauptbahnhof** (tel. 194 19).

Public Transportation: The *Rheinbahn* includes subways, streetcars, buses, and the S-Bahn. **Single tickets** cost DM1.90-11.70, depending on distance traveled. The *Tagesticket* (DM9.50; higher prices for longer distances) is the best value

Düsseldorf

N

Kaiser-Friedrich-Ring

Leo-strasse

Fischer-str.

Stadthalle

Kunstmuseum

Hofgarten-ufer

Scheiben Str.

Landesmuseum Volk und-Wirtschaft

Theater an der Luegallee

Ⓤ

Lueg-allee

Ring

Oberkasseler Brücke

Ⓤ

Tonhalle

Schloss-ufer

Kunstakademie

Salier-str.

Kreuzherrenkirche

Ratinger Str.

Rhine

Kunstsammlung Nordrhein-Westfalen

St. Lambertus Kirche

Mahn- und Gedenkstätte

Städtische Kunsthalle

Düsseldorfer Str.

Kaiser-Wilhelm-Ring

Burgplatz

St. Andreas

Heine-Allee

Jugendgästehaus

Neanderkirche

Kunstverein für die Rheinland Westfalen

Ⓤ

Rathaus

Berger Kirche

Junges Theater

Hejens-Museum

Graben-str.

Benrather Str.

St. Maximilian Kirche

Rathaus-ufer

Rheinkniebrücke

Berger Allee

Post str.

Heinrich-Heine-Institut

Marionettentheater

Kasernen-str.

Rhine

Harold-strasse

Landtag

Rheinturm

Ständehaus

0		1/2 mile
0	1/2 kilometer	

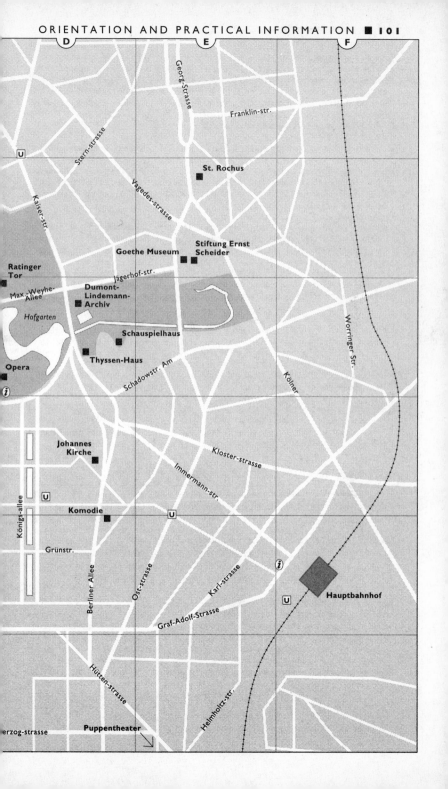

around—groups of up to 5 people and one dog can travel 24hr. on any line. Tickets are sold mostly by vending machine; pick up the *Fahrausweis* brochure in the tourist office (see above) for step-by-step instructions. Düsseldorf's S-Bahn is integrated into the mammoth regional **VRR** *(Verkehrsverbund Rhein-Ruhr)* system, which connects Bochum, Dortmund, Duisburg, Essen, Hagen, Krefeld, Mönchengladbach, Mühlheim, Oberhausen, Recklinghausen, Solingen, and Wuppertal. **Schedule Information:** tel. 582 28.

Taxi: tel. 333 33.

Car Rental: Hertz, Immermannstr. 65 (tel. 35 70 25). Open Mon.-Fri. 7am-6pm, Sat. 8am-noon.

Bike Rental: Zweirad Egert, Ackerstr. 143 (tel. 66 21 34). Take S-Bahn #6 (direction: Essen) to "Wehrbahn" and walk 10min. Call ahead to check availability. Bikes DM17.25 per day, DM40.75 per week. DM50 deposit and ID required. Open Mon.-Fri. 9:30am-6:30pm, Sat. 9am-2pm.

Mitfahrzentrale: Konrad-Adenauer Platz 13 (tel. 37 60 81), to the left as you exit the station, and upstairs over a tiny travel office. Open Mon.-Fri. 9am-6:30pm, Sat.-Sun. 11am-3pm. **City-Netz Mitfahrzentrale,** Kruppstr. 102 (tel. 194 44), is a more professional chain with slightly higher prices. Open Mon.-Fri. 9am-7pm, Sat. 9am-4pm, Sun. 11am-3pm.

Bookstore: Stern-Verlag, Friedrichstr. 24-26 (tel. 388 10). A huge selection of English paperbacks. Open Mon.-Fri. 9am-6:30pm, Sat. 9am-2pm.

Women's Agency: Any questions or concerns regarding women's issues can be directed to the **Frauenbüro,** Mühlenstr. 29, 2nd floor (tel. 899 36 03), at the municipal office. Walk-ins Mon.-Thurs. 8am-4pm, Fri. 8am-1:30pm.

Laundromat: Wasch Center, Friedrichstr. 92, down the street from the Kirchplatz S-Bahn. Wash DM6. Dry DM1 per 15min. Soap included. Open daily 6am-11pm. Also available at **Jugendherberge Düsseldorf** (wash DM9; free soap and drying) and **Jugendherberge Duisburg-Wedau** (wash and dry DM2.50 each).

Pharmacy: In the *Hauptbahnhof.* Closed pharmacies post lists of nearby open ones. **Emergency pharmacy:** tel. 115 00. **Emergency Doctor:** tel. 192 92.

Emergency: Police: tel. 110. **Ambulance** and **Fire:** tel. 112.

Post Office: Hauptpostamt, Konrad-Adenauer-Platz, 40210 Düsseldorf, to right of the tourist office, a stone's throw away. Open Mon.-Fri. 8am-6pm, Sat. 9am-2pm, Sun. noon-1pm. Limited service Mon.-Fri. 6pm-8pm, Sun. 10am-2pm. **Branch office** in *Hauptbahnhof* open Mon.-Fri. 8am-6pm, Sat.-Sun. 2pm-midnight.

Telephone Code: 0211.

ACCOMMODATIONS AND CAMPING

The old saying goes, "piss-poor planning leads to piss-poor performance," but in Düsseldorf, it can be slightly modified to "piss-poor planning leaves one piss poor." **Call ahead.** Düsseldorf is a convention city where corporate crowds make rooms scarce and costly; it's not unusual for hotels to double their prices during a convention. If you're considering a budget hotel stay, call the tourist office for trade fair *(Messe)* dates and show up during a lull. Most spots go for at least DM40 per person even in the off-season. Check around the train station or consider the hostels in Duisberg, Mönchengladbach, Neuss, or Ratingen (all within 30min. by S-Bahn).

Jugendgästehaus Düsseldorf (HI), Düsseldorfer Str. 1 (tel. 55 73 10; fax 57 25 13), is conveniently located in the Oberkassel part of town, just over the Rheinkniebrücke bridge from the *Altstadt.* Take U-Bahn #70, 74, 75, 76, or 77 to "Luegplatz," then walk 500m down Kaiser-Wilhelm-Ring. Unbeatable location with private lockers and cool key cards. Reception open 7am-1am. Curfew 1am, but doors opened at 2, 3, 4, 5, and 6am—such martinets. DM31.50. Laundry available.

Jugendherberge Duisburg-Wedau, Kalkweg 148E (tel. (0203) 72 41 64; fax 72 08 34). Take S-Bahn #1 or 21 to Duisburg *Hauptbahnhof,* then bus #934 to "Jugendherberge." Düsseldorf is accessible by frequent trains and buses. Old but clean rooms and those mysterious flushing toilets (no hands, mom!). Reception open 8:30-9am, 12:30-1pm, and 6:30-7pm. Open mid.-Jan.-mid-Dec. Closed one weekend of every month. Laundry available. DM20.50, over 26 DM25.

CVJM-Hotel, Graf-Adolf-Str. 102 (tel. 17 28 50; fax 361 31 60), down the street to the left of the train station. The *Christliche Verein Junger Männer* (German YMCA) offers affordable solace. The pious will enjoy the Biblical literature, but couples and 70s disco-pop sextets alike will relish the spotless, spacious rooms. You can do whatever you feel. Rooms have hot water and inspirational messages on the walls; showers are in the hall. Reception open 24hr. Singles DM62. Doubles DM101. Noisier streetside rooms DM57 and DM95. Breakfast DM8.

Hotel Diana, Jahnstr. 31 (tel. 37 50 71; fax 36 49 43), 5 blocks from the station. Head left down Graf-Adolf-Str., turn left on Hüttenstr., and then make a quick jog to the right onto Jahnstr. Small but comfortable and clean rooms with phone and TV. Reception open 8am-7pm. Singles DM55. Doubles DM85, with shower and toilet DM125. Breakfast included. All major credit cards accepted.

Hotel Manhattan, Graf-Adolf-Str. 39 (tel. 37 02 44; fax 37 02 47), straight up from the station. The mirror-plated lobby (with a touch of neon) shines of 1970s dance fever, but the clean, desk-equipped rooms are surprisingly un-metropolitan in their charm. Singles DM68-95. Doubles DM100-140, all depending on ritziness of furnishings and whether it's convention time. Breakfast buffet included. Reception open 24hr. Credit cards accepted. Call far in advance, if possible.

Hotel Amsterdam, Stresemannstr. 20 (tel. 84 05 89; fax 840 50), between Oststr. and Berliner Allee. From the station, start up Graf-Adolf-Str. and turn right at Stresemannplatz. Blue Baroque-style rooms, princess-style furniture. Reception open daily 7am-midnight. Four walls and a bed DM50, with shower, TV, and breakfast DM90. Doubles start at DM120. Credit cards accepted. Call ahead.

Hotel Bristol, Aderstr. 8 (tel. 37 07 50; fax 37 37 54), 1 block south of Graf-Adolf-Str. at the bottom tip of the Königsallee. A well-appointed, friendly place to retire after a stroll on the Kö. Call ahead. Singles with TV DM60, with shower DM120, with shower, toilet, and TV DM130. Breakfast included. Credit cards accepted.

Camping: Kleiner Torfbruch (tel. 899 20 38). Take the S-Bahn to "Düsseldorf Gereshiem," then change to bus #735 (direction: Stamesberg) to "Seeweg." DM6 per person. Tent DM9.

FOOD

For a cheap meal, the conglomeration of dives in the **Altstadt** can't be beat. Endless rows of pizzerias, *Döner Kebabs,* and Chinese diners reach from Heinrich Heine Allee to the banks of the Rhein. The **Markt** on Karlsplatz offers shoppers lots of foreign fruits and a local favorite, *Sauerbraten* (pickled beef). For *trés chic* cafés that provide the beautiful people with abundant atmosphere and high prices, hit the **Kö.**

Heine Geburtshaus, Bolkerstr. 53 (tel. 13 32 00). Pop off a lid and drain a beer where the great poet himself popped out. Read a selection from Heine's brilliantly satirical *Winterreise* (A Winter's Tale) while you wait to be served. Enough pictures on the walls to make a comic flip book. Open daily noon-midnight.

China New World Restaurant, Oststr. 120 (tel. 36 23 86), has an unbeatable lunch menu. Get an entree, soup, fried roll, dessert, and specialty *Flammenwein* for a price phatter than Confucius (DM12-15). Open daily 11:30am-midnight.

Galerie Burghof, Burgallee 1-3 (tel. 40 14 23), in Kaiserwerth next to Frederick's Rhine ruins. Take U-Bahn #79 to "Klemensplatz." Like IHOP putting on the ritz. Specializes in matrimony between beer and pancakes (DM9.50). A packed *Biergarten* jammed in every nook and cranny. Open daily 11am-1am, but pancakes only come out Mon.-Fri. 6pm-10:45pm, Sat. 2-10:45pm, Sun 2-11pm.

Arlecchino, Andreasstr. 3 (tel. 32 43 50), a block north and parallel to Bolkerstr. One cannot live by beer alone, but their hearty one-topping personal pizza (DM4) will have you fed and back on your barstool in no time. Open daily 10am-1am.

Marché, at Königsallee 60 (tel. 32 06 81), in the Kö-Galerie mall. The only way to dine on the Kö and keep your savings intact. Red stripes and funny hats. Entrees start at DM6. Open daily 7:30am-11pm (café-bar only), 8am-11pm otherwise.

Uerige, Bergerstr. 1 (tel. 86 69 90). Some hormone in the air attracts all the cool Germans over 25 out into the streets here. Try house specialties of *Blutwurst* (blood sausage) for DM3.10 and *Mainzer* (Mainz cheese) for DM3.75. Open daily 10am-midnight. Kitchen open Mon.-Fri. 6-9pm, Sat. 11am-4pm.

SIGHTS

The glitzy **Kö** located just outside the *Altstadt* embodies the vitality and glamour of Düsseldorf. No bargains here, but the Kö sports the best of everything; you, too, can window-shop at Armani or ogle the Lotus parked outside. To get there, head down Graf-Adolf-Str. from the station (10min.). Properly called the Königsallee (the vowel sound in Kö is halfway between "oh" and "uh"), the *belle époque* expanse was laid out over a century ago. Stone bridges span the little river that runs down the middle to trickle at the toes of a decadent statue of the sea god Triton. Three shopping guides for the Kö are printed by the tourist office. Midway up is the awesome **Kö-Galerie**—in Nietzschean terms, an *Übermall* (with *über*-prices). Items *start* at US$100 here, and even the mannequins have attitude. At the upper end of the Kö, the **Hofgarten** park is an oasis of green and culture inside urban Düsseldorf. **Schloß Jägerhof**, at the western end, houses the **Goethe Museum** behind its pink façade and white iron gates. The Hofgarten meets the Rhine at the **Ehrenhof**, a plaza of museums (see below). The **Deutsches Oper am Rhein** (opera house) is here, as well as the Neoclassical Napoleonic gate-house called **Ratinger Tor.**

Düsseldorf has had mixed luck with its cultural heroes. Famed composer **Robert Schumann** was so miserable here that he tried to drown his sorrows by jumping off a town bridge. Beloved poet **Heinrich Heine** is a more popular son. His birthplace and homestead are marked by plaques, and every third restaurant and fast-food stand on his Bolkerstr. block bears his name. **The Heinrich Heine Institut,** Bilkerstr. 12-14 (tel. 899 55 71), is the official shrine with a collection of manuscripts and a discomfiting death mask (open Tues.-Fri. and Sun. 11am-5pm, Sat. 1-5pm; admission DM4, students DM2). Further up the *Altstadt*, the **Burgplatz** used to be the site of a glorious castle, but tired citizens have saved only a single tower. The castle was built in 1324, burnt in 1490, rebuilt in 1559, razed in 1794, rebuilt in 1851, and flattened in 1872, at which point the townsfolk gave up—only the tower was reconstructed in 1900, and *that* was bombed to rubble in World War II. The pessimistic citizens waited until 1984 to rebuild the tower. Tread carefully. The **Radschlager**, the legendary Düsseldorf "somersaulting boys," top a fountain on Burgplatz, and grace every city manhole cover. In summer, you might even catch the real thing.

North on the Rhine but still in Düsseldorf dwell the **ruins** of Emperor Frederick's palace in the tiny town of **Kaiserwerth.** Built in 1184, the palace was destroyed in 1702 in the War of Spanish Succession, but the gloomy *Kaiserpfalz* frame remains. Take U-Bahn #79 to "Klemensplatz," then follow Kaiserwerther Markt to the Rhine, and walk left another 150m (open daily 8am-12:30pm; free). Just in case you're curious, the **confusing tower** with the blinking lights visible from the Rhine at night is actually a clock called the *Rheinturm*. From bottom to top, the dots represent 1 second, 10 seconds, 1 minute, 10 minutes, 1 hour, and 10 hours.

MUSEUMS

This is a city of museums. Most cluster around the Hofgarten. Internationally important holdings abound in the string of museums along Grabbeplatz and Ehrenhof.

Grabbeplatz

Kunstsammlung Nordrhein-Westfalen, Grabbeplatz 5 (tel. 838 10), is the black-reflecting-glass thing west of the Hofgarten. Take U-Bahn #70, 75, 76, 78, or 79 to "Heinrich-Heine-Allee" and walk north 2 blocks, or take bus #725 to "Grabbeplatz." A surpassingly good modern art museum. Skylights lavish sunshine on the exhibits—Matisse, Picasso, Surrealists, and Expressionists. The collection of sly works by hometown boy Paul Klee is one of the most extensive in the world. Tours Sun. at 11am and Wed. at 3:30pm. Admission DM5, students DM3. Special exhibits DM10, students DM6. Open Tues.-Sun. 10am-6pm.

Städtische Kunsthalle, Grabbeplatz 4 (tel. 889 62 40), across the square from the Kunstsammlung Nordrhein-Westfalen. Quality visiting exhibits of every shape and size, with a specialty in the bizarre. Admission depends entirely on the exhibit; usually DM10, students and buckaroos DM7. Open Tues.-Sun. 11am-6pm.

Ehrenhof—Hofgarten

Kunstmuseum Düsseldorf, Ehrenhof 5 (tel. 889 24 60 or 892 90 46), surrounding the fountain. A spectacular collection of sculpture, painting, weaving, and crafts spanning 2 stories and 11 centuries. Don't miss the stunning glassware or the 80,000 prints and Baroque and Renaissance drawings. Admission DM8, students and kiddies DM4. Open Tues.-Sun. 11am-6pm. The **Kunstpalast** is an extension of the Kunstmuseum across the fountain at Ehrenhof 5, devoted entirely to rotating contemporary collections.

Landesmuseum Volk und Wirtschaft, Ehrenhof 2 (tel. 492 11 08), dissects every nugget of the area's development, with a side order of social history. Admission DM2, students DM1. Open Mon.-Tues. and Thurs.-Fri. 9am-5pm, Wed. 9am-8pm, Sun. 10am-6pm.

Dumont-Lindemann Archiv, Jägerhofstr. 1 (tel. 899 46 60), sits at the end of a tree-lined promenade off the *Hofgarten*, in the chief gardener's old house. This tiny **Theater Museum** lovingly offers costumes, puppets, marionettes, playbills, and paper stages celebrating the art of local thespians. Admission DM4, students and youngsters DM2. Open Tues.-Fri. Sun. 11am-5pm., Sat. 1-5pm.

Goethe Museum, Jakobistr. 2 (tel. 899 62 62), in Schloß Jägerhof, at the east end of the garden. Take streetcar #707 or bus #752 to "Schloß Jägerhof." The museum makes up for its lack of hometown advantage with the extent of its collection—30,000 souvenirs of the poet and his friends. Everything in the mini-palace is furnished as Goethe would have wished it: to evoke his character. Admission DM4, students and children DM2. Open Tues.-Fri. and Sun. 11am-5pm, Sat. 1-5pm. Library open Tues.-Fri. 10am-noon and 2-4pm.

Elsewhere in Düsseldorf

Film Museum/Hetjens Museum, Schulstr. 4 (tel. 899 42 00), south of the *Schloß-turm* on Rheinuferstr. Hetjens provides a comprehensive history of ceramics, while the film museum showcases 4 floors of costumes, photos, and even clips of classics (alas, all dubbed in German). Admission to each DM6, students and children DM3. Both open Tues. and Thurs-Sun. 11am-5pm, Wed. 11am-9pm.

Stadtmuseum, at Berger Allee 2 (tel. 899 61 70), by the Rheinkniebrücke. The new building clashes with its turn-of-the-century surroundings, but the exhibits summarize Düsseldorf's lavish consumer history perfectly. Admission DM5, students DM2.50. Open Tues. and Thurs.-Sun. 11-5pm, Wed. 11am-9pm.

Mahn-und Gedenkstätte, Mühlenstr. 29 (tel. 899 62 06). Stark museum and document collection commemorating those who suffered under the Third Reich. Free. Open Tues.-Fri. and Sun. 11am-6pm, Sat. 1-5pm.

Düsseldorf Schiffahrt-Museum, in the tower in the Burgplatz (tel. 899 41 95). Recreates 3000 years of the town's nautical glory in model boats and paintings. Admission DM3, students DM1.50. Open Wed. and Sat. 2-6pm, Sun. 11am-6pm.

Neanderthal Museum, Thekhauser Quall (tel. (02104) 311 49), in the suburb of Erkrath. Take S-Bahn #8 to "Hochdahl," then bus #741 to "Neandertal." Ooga! A museum where low-brows, thick-skulls, and knuckle-draggers can feel comfortable. Exhibits on the history and significance of our 60,000-year-old ancestors. Admission DM2, students DM1. Open Tues.-Sat. 10am-5pm, Sun. 11am-6pm.

ENTERTAINMENT AND NIGHTLIFE

Folklore holds that Düsseldorf's 500 pubs make up *"die längste Theke der Welt"* (the longest bar in the world). **Bolkerstr.** is jam-packed nightly with street performers of the musical and beer-olympic varieties. *Prinz* magazine (DM4.50) is Düsseldorf's fashion cop and scene detective; it's often given out free at the youth hostel. The free cultural guides *Coolibri* and *Biograph* are less complete but more than you'll ever need to keep it (your thang, that is) shakin' all night long. **Das Kommödchen** ("The Little Commode"; tel. 32 94 43) is a tiny, extraordinarily popular theater behind the Kunsthalle at Grabbeplatz (box office open Mon.-Sat. 1-8pm, Sun. 3-8pm; must call at least 2 days ahead). Ballet and opera tickets are best bought (without service charge) at the **Opernhaus** (tel. 890 82 11), on Heinrich Heine Allee (box office open Mon.-Fri. 11am-6:30pm, Sat. 11am-1pm, and 1hr. before performances). Tickets can be purchased by phone (Mon.-Fri. 9am-5pm). **Black Box,** Schulstr. 4 (tel. 899 24 90), off Rathaus-Ufer along the Rhine, serves the art-film aficionado with unadulterated foreign flicks (admission DM8, students DM6).

Brauerei Schumacher, Bolkerstr. 44 (tel. 32 60 07), is Düsseldorf's oldest house brewery. It gets packed with a fresh crowd every night. Open Mon.-Thurs., Sun. 10am-midnight, Fri.-Sat. 10am-1am.

Tor 3, Ronsdorferstr. 143 (tel. 733 64 97). Take U-Bahn #75 to "Ronsdorferstr." Facing away from downtown turn right onto Ronsdorferstr. Prepare alternate transport home from this factory-turned-disco for the fashion elite—the S-Bahn stops running far too early. Cover DM15. Open Fri.-Sat. 10pm-5am.

Stahlwerk, Ronsdorfer 134., just across the street from Tor 3. Bizarre combination of trippy multi-floor dance hall and old-fashioned beer patio. Filled with fresh-faced Düsseldorfers. An average night draws 1500 of the city's coolest and most bizarre. Cover DM10. Opens Fri.-Sat. and last Sun. of every month at 10pm.

ZAKK (Zentrum für Aktion, Kultur, und Kommunikation), Fichtenstr. 40 (tel. 973 00 10). Take Strassenbahn #706 to "Fichtenstr," bus #732 to "Oberbilker Markt," or U-Bahn #75 to "Kettwigerstr." Lets loose every weekend with themes like 80s, jazz, and disco. The American music will have you hooting like blowfish. Disco, concerts, readings, and *merengue.* Cover DM8. Open Wed. and Fri.-Sat. at 8pm.

Rheinterasse, Hofgartenufer 7 (tel. 49 40 43). Take U-Bahn #70 or 74-77 to "Tonhalle." It's 200m downstream on the left. Gargantuan *Biergarten* which fabulously fills its 1000-person capacity. A heterogenous crowd—Hell's Angels, silky boys, and assorted lushes of all ages. Open Mon.-Sat. 5-11pm, Sun. 11am-11pm.

Brauerei zum Uel, Rattinger 16, in the *Altstadt.* Papered with listings for musical happenings. Drink up that *Schlösser Alt* (DM2.30 for 0.2L). On good nights the crowds of students block traffic on Rattingstr. Open Sun.-Tues. and Thurs. 10am-1am, Wed. and Fri. and Sat. 10am-3am.

Engelchen, Kurzestr. 11 (tel. 32 73 56). Raphael's cute cherubs get red in the face with alterna-trendies. Open Mon.-Fri. 9am-1am, Sat. 10am-3am, Sun. 10am-3am.

McLaughlin's Irish Pub, Kurzestr. 11, loads up on live bands and Americans loading up. Don't even try to speak German here—practice your brogue instead. Open Sun.-Thurs. 11am-1am, Fri.-Sat. 11am-3am.

■ Near Düsseldorf

MÖNCHENGLADBACH

Eighteen km west of Düsseldorf, past Lülu the cow grazing in her fields and Farmer Braun drinking his *Alt,* is the city of Mönchengladbach, a wonderfully refreshing respite from the industrial scenery of the *Ruhrgebiet.* Standing out prominently against the skyline is the **Abteiberg,** the hill Archbishop Gero chose as the site of a Benedictine monastery in 974. A thousand years later, the French kicked the sonorously chanting monks out, and since then, the deserted building has served as the **Rathaus.** Next door towers the 11th-century **Münster** whose ecclesiastical treasures include a portable altar and a bust of St. Vitus, the city's guardian. (Church open Mon.-Sat. 8am-6pm, Sun. noon-6pm. Museum inside open Tues.-Sat. 2-6pm, Sun. noon-6pm.) Around the corner, the mirrored **Städtisches Museum Abteiberg,** Abteistr. 27 (tel. 25 26 37), just beyond the *Rathaus,* houses a hip collection of 20th-century art including pieces by Andy Warhol, Roy Lichtenstein, and George Segal (open Tues.-Sun. 10am-6pm; admission DM5, students and children DM2.50). Also at the top of the Abteiberg is the **Alter Markt,** an old cobblestone square now studded by small diners and craft shops. Gaze down at the residential district, a dense blanket of pastel-decorated houses with oodles of flowers spilling out the windows. To reach the *Alter Markt,* turn left out of the train station and head up Hindenburgstr. past the snazzy new stores or take bus #13 or 23 up the hill.

Just outside of town stands the majestic **Schloß Rheydt** (tel. 201 01). From the station, take bus #6 to "Bonnenbroich" and then bus #16 to "Sparkasse" (30-min. ride, but worth it). This Renaissance castle swims in a lily-padded pond surrounded by winding hiking paths and besieged by the castle's famous peacocks. Inside, a museum displays 15th- to 17th-century artifacts, including a special exhibit on card games (open Tues.-Sat. 2-8pm, Sun. 11am-8pm; admission DM5, tykes DM2.50).

The **tourist office,** Bismarckstr. 23-27 (tel. 220 01; fax 27 42 22), to the left of the station, will help find a room (DM45 and up) for no fee (open Mon.-Fri. 9:30am-6pm, Sat. 9:30am-12:30pm). Mönchengladbach's **Jugendherberge Hardter Wald,** Brahmstr. 156 (tel. (02461) 55 95 12; fax 55 64 64), lies at the boundary of a wheat field and a forest. From the station, take bus #13 or 23 to "Hardtmarkt" (20min.), walk straight ahead and make a left at the *Jugendherberge* sign onto Brahmstr. (20min.). Newly renovated, the hostel boasts sparkling rooms; unfortunately, it's in the middle of nowhere. Nightlife offers little else than playing with the two resident chickens. (Reception open noon-10pm. DM21.50, over 26 DM26. Sheets DM6. Breakfast included.) Think of the *Alter Markt* as a giant feeding trough. **Grafici and König,** Alter Markt 23 (tel. 18 04 44), serves up good psychedlic brew. Frequent live music (open Sun.-Thurs. 9am-1am, Fri.-Sat. 9am-3am). The **telephone code** is 02161.

FAIRY-TALE CASTLES

Once upon a time up a tree-lined path, **Schloß Benrath** (pink-and-white like all good little castles; tel. 899 72 71) gazed into the looking-glass pool of its flowering gardens. *"Ach,"* it muttered, *"Ich bin* getting so tired of 1-hr. tours Tues.-Fri. every 30min. 11am-4pm, Sat.-Sun. every 30min. 10am-4pm (castle open Tues.- Fri. 10am-5pm; admission DM7, children DM3.5). *All die* touris*ten* mob go *Schloß*ing by S-Bahn #6 (direction: Köln) to 'Benrath,' *und ich bin* sick and *müde."* So Schloß Benrath grabbed a *Bananensaft* from the secret staff refrigerator, and set off by ferry to its friend **Schloß Friedestrom,** to find some peace.

Schloß Friedestrom lived very close, in the misty town of **Zons.** The **Zonser Personenschiffahrt** (tel. (02133) 421 49) floats there from Benrath. (May-Sept. only, Mon.-Sat. at 10:15am and every hour 11:30am-6:30pm; one-way DM3, under 12 DM2.50; round-trip DM5, under 12 DM4.) So our little castle took the once-upon-a time to see its friend. Gleeful in anticipation, the little *Schlößchen* sipped its banana juice and grinned into the wind.

"Ach, nein! Was ist denn happened here?" the *Schlößchen* shrieked in horror! Schloß B had followed the signs from the deck perfectly—but no Schloß Friedestrom. An old rampart, two towers, *"aber alles ist* ruins! Oh, this *ist Schrecklich,"* sobbed little Schloß B. "Why *ist* my friend *kaputt?"* A passing donkey noticed the quaking edifice, and, chewing on a *Pusteblume,* tried to comfort him. "You know, my *hee-haw hee*-friends at the *Schweinebrunnen* can make you merry-*haw* again." Seeing no change in Schloß B's stony expression, the donkey continued, "Don't worry, your friend is still happy. People come to watch Brothers Grimm fairy-tales staged as plays here-*haw* June-Sept. at the **Freilichtbühne Zons.** *Du* too can call (02133) 422 74 for open-air show information. Tickets cost DM8, under 14 DM6."

"So *dieser neue Look* is just because my friend has become an artist! *Ach, ja,* then I think I will support my *Schlößlein* palaroonie. I will *nicht* be sad*lich.* Wise donkey, will you *komm mit* me?" Comforted, Schloß Benrath and the peaceful donkey trotted along to the **tourist office,** behind the *Juddeturm* tower in the central square (tel. (02133) 37 72), to seek out more information (open Mon., Wed., Fri. 8:30am-noon, Tues. 8am-noon and 2:15-4pm, Thurs. 8:30am-noon and 2:15-5pm). *Und wenn sie nicht gestorben sind, dann leben sie noch Heute.*

■ Ruhr Region (Ruhrgebiet)

Düsseldorf owes most of its modern prosperity to the industry of the Ruhr Valley. Ever since huge coal deposits were discovered here in the 19th century, the Ruhr has been the heart of Germany's industrial machine. It was the German pioneers working in the factories and mills that dot the area who wrote the book on processing steel and laid the foundation for modern manufacturing. During World War II, the Allies bombed many of these towns to rubble, in an attempt to cripple the Nazi war machine. During the massive reconstruction that ensued, city planners added huge parks and gardens to brighten the region's image; though the myth of dreary smokestacks and depressing factories persists, visitors will be surprised by the cultural and natural gifts the Ruhr has to offer. An integrated S-Bahn, streetcar, bus, and U-Bahn system run by the Verkehrsverbund Rhein-Ruhr (VRR) links many of the cities in the sprawling conglomeration, making the Ruhr region the densest concentration of rail lines anywhere in the world.

ESSEN

Essen is in many ways like a reformed school bully. Once an untouchable, belching enough soot and ash to outsmoke Newcastle, England, Essen has since worked to change its image and clean up its air. The city's new look includes sleek building design, and its new attitude promotes unbridled creativity. But Essen still flexes its impressive industrial muscle; though its notorious smokestacks have been replaced by "lighter" factories, the city remains the cornerstone of the industrial Ruhr Valley.

Infamous 19th-century arms and railroad mogul **Alfred Krupp** perfected steel-casting in industrial Essen. **Villa Hügel**, the Krupp family home for decades (tel. 48 37), was given to the city in the 1950s in order to brighten the company's image, which was tarnished by affiliation with the Nazis. While exhibits and concerts showcase the villa's magnificent mahogany halls, the house itself reflects Krupp's gaudy arrogance. To get there, take S-Bahn #6 to "Essen-Hügel." (Grounds open daily 8am-8pm. Villa open Tues.-Sun. 10am-6pm. Special exhibits open Mon. and Wed.-Sun. 10am-7pm, Tues. 10am-9pm. Admission DM1.50.) The *Glockenspiel* on Kettwiger Str., in the city-center above the **Dietter clock store**, chimes and dances every hour from 9am to 8pm, in sync with Essen's humorous church bells. Essen's **Münster,** nearby on Burgplatz, is an ancient, cloistered string of flowering courtyards and hexagonal crypts. The 1000-year-old doll-like *Goldene Madonna* stands beside the nave (open daily 7:30am-6:30pm). Although Nazis eviscerated Essen's **Alte Synagoge** (tel. 452 80) in 1938, it stands today as the largest synagogue north of the Alps. Inside, slides, pictures, and objects from the Third Reich era make up the *Dokumentationsforum*, a monument to the Jews of Essen. Take the U-Bahn to "Porscheplatz" and follow the signs to the Schützenbahn; as you head south on the Schützenbahn, the synagogue is on your left (open Tues.-Sun. 10am-6pm; free.)

The **Deutsches Plakat Museum** (German Poster Museum), on the third floor of the shopping mall at the intersection of Rathenaustr. and Am Glockenspiel, features everything from the unusual (a one-eyed nude) to the downright bizarre (two pig heads eating a human head). Exhibits rotate every two months (open Tues.-Sun. noon-8pm; admission DM2, students and children free). The **Design Zentrum Nordrhein Westfalen,** Hindenburgstr. 25-27 (tel. 82 02 10), will fascinate design freaks for hours. Check out futuristic TVs and stereos from the 80s. To get there, take U-Bahn #17 or 18 to "Bismarckplatz" (open Tues.-Fri. 10am-6pm, Sat. 10am-2pm; free). **Museum Folkwang,** in the *Museumszentrum* at Goethestr. 41 (tel. 884 53 00), drops all the big names in modern art, while the Folkwang's **Fotographische Sammlung,** in the same complex, takes on camerawork from the early days. Take streetcar #101, 107, or 127 or U-Bahn #11 to "Rüttenscheider Stern." Follow signs to the Museumszentrum and continue (north) on Rüttenscheiderstr., then turn left on Kuhrstr., and right onto Goethestr. (Both open Tues.-Wed., Fri.-Sun. 10am-6pm, Thurs. 10am-

9pm. *Fotographische Sammlung* closed during summer holidays. Combined admission DM5, students and children DM3.)

The **tourist office,** located in the *Rathaus* (tel. 881 31 06), has lots of maps and other goodies but doesn't make hotel reservations. To get there, take the U-Bahn to "Porscheplatz" (open Mon.-Tues. 7:30am-4pm, Wed. 7:30am-3:30pm, Thurs. 7:30am-6pm, Fri. 7:30am-3pm). Essen's **U-Bahn** and **streetcar** lines cost DM2.90 per ride. Essen's **Mitfahrzentrale,** Freiheit 4 (tel. 194 40), pairs riders with drivers (open daily 9am-7pm). The **Jugendherberge (HI),** Pastoratsberg 2 (tel. 49 11 63; fax 49 25 05), home to the 8th-century **Abteikirche** and the **Luciuskirche,** the oldest parish churches north of the Alps, sits in a park in the Werden district. Take S-Bahn #6 to "Bahnhof Werden," then bus #190 to "Jugendherberge." If you feel like playing Alpine mountain climber, cross the bridge, take the second right onto Bungerstr., and follow Kemensborn uphill as it winds all over the map to a sharp right at Pastoratsberg. The *Jugendherberge*'s grounds contain a grass basketball court. (Reception open 7am-11:30pm. Curfew 11:30pm. DM21.50, over 26 DM26. Breakfast and sheets included.) The basic, comfortable **Hotel Kessing,** Hachestr. 30 (tel. 23 99 88; fax 23 02 89), is close to the train station; turn left on Hachestr. (Singles DM59, with shower and toilet DM85. Doubles DM118, with bath DM138. Breakfast included.) Camp at **"Stadt-Camping" Essen-Werden,** Im Löwental 67 (tel. 49 29 78), on the west bank of the Ruhr. Take the S-Bahn to "Essen-Werden" and continue south along the river. (Reception open daily 9am-1pm and 3-9:45pm. DM15 per tent, DM7.50 per adult, DM5 per child.) The **telephone code** is 0201.

The maze of stairs and escalators at **Porscheplatz,** near the *Rathaus,* is Cheap Food Central. Take the U-Bahn to "Porscheplatz." The university **Mensa** (tel. 18 31) is in the green-rimmed building at the university. Take the U-Bahn to "Universität," and follow the signs to the building (open Mon.-Fri. 7:30-3:30pm, Sat. 7:30-2:30pm). Just across the street from the *Mensa,* **Beaulongerie,** on Segerothstr. (tel. 32 62 12), offers huge (30cm), freshly baked baguettes (DM4.50) with a variety of fillings and sauces (open Mon.-Thurs. 11am-11pm, Fri.-Sat. 11am-1pm). Soak up the city ambience and marvel at sculptures crawling out of the walls at **Platz,** Salzmarkt 1 (tel. 22 67 76), near Kennedyplatz, where they offer daily specials (from DM7) and jazz on Tuesday nights (open Sun.-Thurs. 11am-1am, Fri.-Sat. 11am-3am).

DORTMUND

Take Milwaukee out of Wisconsin, put it in Germany, and you've got Dortmund. With the exception of its American soul-twin, Dortmund annually produces more beer than any other city in the world: 1000L for each of its 600,000 citizens (you do the math). The best known of Dortmund's sudsy brood is the ubiquitous *Dortmunder Union* beer. As part of Germany's industrial backbone, Dortmund was a tempting target for Allied bombers, and 93% of the city center was leveled in World War II. Today, the city is still largely industrial. But there is more to this town than brewing and drunken bowling—Dortmund's cultural assets are adding up as fast as its bar bills. The city follows its soccer team, **BVB09,** with a passion: walk down any street, and when you hear gnashing of teeth, the BVB has just given up a rare goal.

Museum am Ostwall, Ostwall 7 (tel. 502 32 47), was built in 1947 over the ruins of the *Altstadt* in order to make room for modern art, especially the kind suppressed by the Third Reich. The plastic-fruit-and-wooden-grass exhibit make the museum's Picasso look downright conventional. The German Expressionist canvases assembled here compose a definitive collection of the *Blaue Reiter* and *die Brücke* schools (open Tues.-Sun. 10am-5pm; admission DM4, seniors, students, and children DM1). The spiralling **Museum für Kunst und Kulturgeschichte,** Hansastr. 3 (tel. 502 55 22), two minutes from the station, is full of period rooms, decorative pieces, and daring special exhibits (open Tues.-Sun. 10am-6pm; admission DM4, seniors, students, and wee-ones DM1). The Lennies and Squiggies of the world, who may be intimidated by all of this high culture, will be more comfortable in the **Brauerei-Museum,** Märkische Str. 81 (tel. 541 32 89), located in the Kronen Beer Works, southeast of the city center. It's four floors of German art in the form of kegs, steins, and 5000 years of brewing history. Take U-Bahn #41, 45, or 47 to "Markgrafenstr." and walk along Landgrafenstr. in the direction of the tower (open Tues.-Sun. 10am-5pm; free, but no samples). The **Adlerturm,** at Kleppingstr. and Südwall, near the *Rathaus,* is the last remaining section of the old city walls (open Tues.-Sun. 10am-5pm; admission DM2; seniors, students, and children DM1). The tower has been bisected to show the layers of foundation. In the center of the city, amidst the shops and restaurants, the **St.-Reinoldi-Kirche,** on Am Markt, captures the medieval skyline (open Mon.-Fri. 10am-12:30pm and 2-6pm, Sat. 10am-1pm).

Dortmund is on the eastern edge of the tangle of cities in the Ruhr River area. The S-Bahn (#1 and 21) connects it to Essen and Düsseldorf. The **tourist office,** König-swall 20 (tel. 14 03 41; fax 16 35 93), across from the station, will book rooms for a DM3 fee (open Mon.-Fri. 9am-6pm, Sat. 9am-1pm, Sun. 10am-noon). **ADFC,** Haus-mannstr. 22 (tel. 13 66 85), **rents bikes** for DM9 per day (open Wed.-Mon. 10am-6pm). The **post office,** 44137 Dortmund (tel. 98 40), is located outside the north entrance of the *Hauptbahnhof* (open Mon.-Fri. 8am-6pm, Sat. 8am-1pm, Sun. 10am-11am). Send letters and cash traveler's checks, then feast your eyes on the statue outside, depicting two hands with legs fighting. The **telephone code** is 0231.

Hotel prices in Dortmund are high (singles start at DM50), and there is no hostel or campground, but hostelers can easily jump the train to nearby Essen (see p. 108). Close to the station, **Hotel-Garni Carlton,** Lütge-Brückstr. 5-7 (tel. 52 80 30; fax 52 50 20), has big, comfy rooms. Head left on Königswall as you exit the station, take a right on Gnadenort and then another right on Lütge-Brückstr. (Reception open Mon.-Fri. 7am-4am, Sat. 7am-2pm and 6:30pm-4am, Sun. 6:30pm-4am. Singles DM50, with shower and toilet DM65. Doubles DM90, with shower and toilet DM110. Breakfast included.) After satisfying your curiosity about beer mechanics at the Brauerei Museum, go for some interactive experience at **Hövels Hausbrauerei** (tel. 14 10 44), whose light brew is a town favorite (open daily 11am-1am; kitchen open 11am-12:30am). Explore the student life at **Dortmund University.** Take the S-Bahn (toward Essen) to "Universität." The **Dürchblick** café and bar, located at Vogelpothsweg 74, in the *Unicenter,* is always crowded (open daily 8am-midnight).

WUPPERTAL

Schwebebahn is a word that sticks to Wuppertal like a fly on horse dung. Indeed, the significance of this world-renowned suspension railway to the city (which pays its electricity bill) is paramount; the *Schwebebahn,* which was likened to a "flying milli-pede" when its tracks were laid down, was the glue that, in 1929, cemented together the several mill towns that now form Wuppertal, and it remains the number-one tour-ist attraction today. As you ride this orange-and-green roller-coaster railway, you'll float over the crowded pedestrian zone and see the many church steeples scattered throughout the modern buildings; then you'll skim along the Wupper River, lined with green trees and bushes on one side and pastel-colored warehouses on the other. Any local will gleefully tell you about Tuffi, the circus elephant who, on a promo-tional ride on the *Schwebebahn,* shocked everyone by jumping out of his train into the river below. Think the storyteller's nose just got a little longer? There are actual pictures of the baby elephant landing in the water, but of course the reporters were too stunned to snap up the epic voyage itself.

A statue of stone proletarians sits in front of the gray-slate **Engels-Haus,** Engelsstr. 10, where Marx's co-author and pamphleteer Friedrich Engels grew up. The guest book here is filled with all sorts of multilingual devotions. The **Museum für Frühin-dustrialisierung** (early industrialization), in an old textile mill to the rear of the house, explains some of Fred's political ire, documenting inhumane work conditions. Guides operate the old machinery, explaining every whirr. (Open Tues.-Sun. 10am-1pm and 3-5pm. The relentless process of commodification characteristic of indus-trial capitalism has enslaved even this museum—admission DM3. Ring the doorbell to enter.) This **Historisches Zentrum** (tel. 563 64 98), a house and a mill, is easily acces-sible from the Schwebebahn "Adlerbrücke" stop, the Wuppertal-Barmen train station (go down Flügelstr. and right past the Opera), and the #610 bus. **Friedrichstraße,** lined with bars, pubs, and cafés, ends at the copper tower of the Elberfeld *Rathaus* and a huge, flamboyant fountain of Neptune. Follow the sea-king's imperious gaze through Kirstenplatz as it curves to Poststr. 11 at intersection with Schwanenstr., where a *Glockenspiel* chimes (Mon.-Sat. at 10am, noon, 4, and 6pm; Sun. at noon, 4, and 6pm). Inside this same building, the **Wuppertaler Uhrenmuseum** (tel. 49 39 90) keeps on slipping into the future (open Mon.-Fri. 4-6pm, Sat. 10am-1pm; admission DM5, children under 12 DM2). To get there, continue down Poststr. and turn right onto Turmhof. **The Von der Heydt-Museum,** Turmhof 8 (tel. 563 22 23), houses an impressive array of works that will surely trigger memories of old English books and intro art classes (open Tues.-Wed., Fri.-Sun. 10am-7pm, Thurs. 10am-9pm; admission DM6, students and buckaroos DM4).

You can get a hotel reservation (rooms DM35 and up) at the **tourist office,** in the Döppersberg Pavillon (tel. 563 21 80; fax 563 80 52), at the foot of the "Hauptbahnhof" *Schwebebahn* stop. Take the tunnel from the station to the pedestrian zone, and turn right upon exiting (open Mon.-Fri. 9am-6pm, Sat. 9am-1pm). Wuppertal's **Jugendherberge (HI),** Obere Lichtenplatzerstr. 70 (tel. 55 23 72; fax 55 73 54), is in a park in Barmen, south of the city center. From the Barmen station, take bus #640 to "Jugendherberge" or walk right on Winklerstr., turn right on Fischertal, walk up the hill, and make a right on Amalienstr. Turn left on the path opposite Fischerstr. —the hostel is up the dirt path on the right. The six-bed rooms have sinks and new wood furnishings. (Reception open until 10pm. Curfew 11:30pm. DM21.50, over 26 DM26. Members only. Breakfast included. Sheets DM6.) From the *Hauptbahnhof,* go past the end of Poststr. and continue on Friedrichstr. past countless cafés to get to **Café-Kneipe Agathe,** Albrechtstr. 5 (tel. 44 61 45). This *crêpe* club of sorts (meals DM8-15) is a popular hangout, with event schedules lining the walls (entrees DM8-17.50; open Sun.-Thurs. 5pm-1am, Fri.-Sat. 5pm-3am). Those seeking mass quantities without the atmosphere should veer off Friedrichstr. at the sign for **Akzenta.** Here, in the province's largest grocery store, you can rub shoulders with the *bourgeoisie* that would have made Engels cry (open Mon.-Wed. 9am-6:30pm, Thurs. 9am-8:30pm, Fri. 8am-8:30pm, Sat. 8am-2pm). The **telephone code** is 0202.

SOLINGEN

Prized throughout the world for quality of the highest caliber, cutlery from Solingen has been a tradition for six centuries. Craftsmen from this tiny Ruhr city began making simple blades around 1300, but a period of almost continuous warfare and the aristocratic craving for status symbols gave rise to an extremely lucrative sword trade, with Solingen products setting the standards. Though the harsh 1919 Treaty of Versailles barred the production of bladed weapons, the Solingen tradition has persisted to this day—look for the city's name or the ubiquitous "Zwilling" emblem (two stock figures walking like Egyptians) on a pair of scissors near you. In June 1993, however, Germans came to think of Solingen in a very different light when the home of a Turkish family was set ablaze; two women and three small children died in the attack. The arsonists are believed to have been neo-Nazi extremists, as a swastika was found scratched in the children's sandbox. Since then, however, no violence has recurred in Solingen, and you should not be discouraged from visiting.

An industrial center in the midst of a rolling, green countryside, this town is like any other of the Ruhrgebiet. The word *Kotten,* defined as a small rural dwelling anywhere else in Germany, takes on unique meaning here. Since the end of the 14th century, it has referred to a mill operated by water power. The **Kotten at Balkhausen** (tel. 452 36), just outside of Solingen, has been preserved as a monument to the labor of early knife-grinders. From the Solingen station take bus #681 to "Hästen" (the last stop), then a left on Balkhauser Weg—it's 400m down the road. Learn how to grind (but not bump) for free (open Tues.- Sun. 10am-5pm, or by appointment). The **Klingenmuseum,** Klosterhof 4 (tel. 598 22), is also a monument to cutlery, emphasis on weapons. Exhibits include baguette-sized pocketknives and exotic African swords— very big and bad. Take bus #683 to "Täppken," follow the signs. Look for the 20-ft.-

high pair of silver scissors rooted in the courtyard (open Tues.-Thurs., Sat.-Sun. 10am-5pm, Fri. 2-5pm; admission DM5, students and children DM2.50).

The **tourist office,** in the *Rathaus* on Cronenbergerstr., Room 24 (tel. 290 23 33; fax 290 24 79), happily offers information on the town and the surrounding area (open Mon.-Tues. and Thurs. 7:30am-5pm, Wed. 7:30am-4pm, Fri. 7:30am-1pm). The **Jugendherberge Solingen-Gräfrath,** Flockertsholzerweg 10 (tel. 59 11 98; fax 59 41 79), labels its rooms with cute pictures of animals. Take bus #695 (direction: Abtei-weg) to "Eugen-Maurer-Heim," then walk up the hill, and turn right onto the street labeled with the f-word. Inside, the 2-, 4-, 6-, and 8-bed rooms are extremely clean. (Reception open until 10pm. Curfew midnight. DM22, over 26 DM25. Sheets DM6.) For accommodations closer to the scenic Burg an der Wupper, consider the **Hotel-Landhaus Ainz,** Burger Landstraße 249 (tel. 440 00; fax 479 14). Take bus #683 (direction: Burg) to "Jagenberg" and get off right at the door. Rooms are big and straight out of the Wolfman's showcase. (Reception open Sun.-Thurs. 5-10pm. Singles DM45, with shower and toilet DM65. Doubles DM80, with shower and toilet DM110.) An impressive array of cheap cafés and grocery stores line **Konrad-Ade-nauer-Str.** between Kronprinzstr. and Kölnerstr. The **telephone code** is 0212.

BURG AN DER WUPPER

In a setting straight out of a Grimms' fairy tale, the Burg an der Wupper perches majestically 110m above the softly flowing waters of the Wupper. The castle, erected in the 12th century by **Count Englebert II of Berg,** Archbishop of Cologne and Regent of the Holy Roman Empire of the German Nation, is surrounded by a lush forest in a valley untouched by time. The little town that lies below touts half-timbered houses with blossoming *Blümchen* billowing out of the windows. Wander the cobblestone streets along the river and pick a little bakery to sample the local specialty: *Bretzeln* (pretzels). To reach the **castle,** walk up the gently sloping paths through the forest or ride the **Seilbahn Burg** to experience the bizarre feeling of riding a chair lift without skis (open daily 10am-6pm; one way DM3, children DM1.50; round-trip DM4.50, children DM2.50). From Solingen, take bus #683 to "Burg Brücke" and then walk back 50m. As you approach the peak, the ivy-covered *Schloß* turrets will appear. Look back for a full view of the lush Wupper Valley. The castle is now a museum detailing every aspect of castle life from the cool defensive arrow slits in the battlements to the medieval privies (open Tues.-Sun. 10am-6pm, Mon. 1-6pm; Nov.-Feb. Tues.-Sun. 11am-5pm; admission DM6, students DM4.50, children DM2). Scents of a more pleasant nature waft from **Café-Restaurant Burghof,** Wermelskirchener Str. 2 (tel. 410 24), behind the castle. As you sit in the 17th-century half-timbered house on a tapestry chair, gaze over the rolling hills and savor a waffle (DM3.70) made from a secret *Burg* recipe (open Tues.-Sun. 8:30am-7pm). To reach the **Jugendherberge Burg an der Wupper,** An der Jugenherberge 11 (tel. 410 25; fax 494 49), walk to the bus stop behind the castle and take bus #266 up the hill to "Jugendherberge." Or for a little Alpine intensity breathing exercise, trudge up the hill, turn left on Jorgensfeld, make another left on Graf-Adolf-Str., and follow the curve around (10min. from the castle). (Reception open 2-6pm. Curfew 10pm. DM20.50, over 26 DM24.50. Sheets DM6.) The **telephone code** is 0212.

■ Teutoburg Forest (Teutoburger Wald)

Between the Ems and the Lippe rivers sit the rolling hills and towering trees of the Teutoburg Forest. It was here that Teutonic chief Hermann (or Arminius, in Latin) lured Roman general Quintilius Varus into a trap in 9AD, killing him and his three legions—20,000 men—in a victory so devastating that no one came to bury the dead for six years. The event left an indelible stamp on Emperor Augustus, who never again tried to conquer the land east of the Rhine, forever halting the spread of Roman influence on this region.

Ideally, the Teutoburt Forest should be biked or hiked, with short stops in the towns scattered through the woods. Only a few existing establishments offer bicycles, although public transportation in the region is excellent. Numerous buses run frequently, and trains connect Bielefeld, Detmold, and Attenbeken.

DETMOLD

Towering over the dense forest, the striking **Hermannsdenkmal** commemorates the Teutonic chief Arminius (Hermann), proclaiming him liberator of the German people. Over-eager nationalists erected Hermann's monolithic likeness on an old encampment in 1875, and Kaiser William I came to cut the ribbon. Complete with winged helmet, the statue wields a 7-m sword with the disconcerting inscription, "German unity is my power, my power is Germany's might." The memorial also serves as a source of Germanic historical confusion: research continually relocates the battle to other Teutoburg hills. The only truth agreed upon is that the colossus does *not* mark the spot of the battle. Climb up the pedestal or mingle just below Big H's humongous toes (open daily 9am-6:30pm; Nov.-Feb. 9:30am-4pm; admission DM2, children DM0.70). If the timing's right, you can catch a film at the small theater next door (1 per hr. from 9am-5pm; Nov.-Feb. 1 per hr. 10am-3pm). The hike is extremely beautiful, but rather steep for the inexperienced hiker. For a pleasant non-exhausting exercise, take bus #703 (direction: Sternschanze) to "Friedenstal," and trek to the top (35min.). Or just take bus #792 all the way to the top (perspiration-free bus leaves the train station May-Sept. daily at 10:30am at 2:30pm).

No less impressive and far more exhilarating is the **Adlerwarte** (Eagle's Watch; tel. 471 71), featuring over 80 birds of prey. Time your arrival with Bus #701 from Detmold (direction: Weidmüller) to "Adlerwarte" to catch a free flight exhibition. The falcons strafe the crowd, passing inches above startled faces and causing children and adults to shriek. (Park open March-Oct. 8:30am-6pm; displays at 11am, 3, and 4:30pm; Nov.-Feb. park open 9am-5pm; flights at 11am, 2:30pm, and 3:30pm. Admission DM6, students DM4.50, children DM2.50—it's worth every *Pfennig*.)

In the *Altstadt,* cannons still arm the courtyard of the **Fürstliches Residenzschloß** (tel. 225 07), a Renaissance castle in the town's central park. Its **Rotersaal** (Red Hall) remains red and decadent. Just down the hall are the **Jagdwaffen** (Hunting Weapons), an array of 400-year-old hunting equipment. (Tours April-Oct. daily on the hr. 10am-5pm; Nov.-Mar. at 10, 11am, 2, 3, and 4pm. Written English translations available. Admission DM6, children DM3, group members DM4.50.)

Detmold's unbeatable location makes it an ideal base for exploring the Teutoberger Wald. The staff at the **tourist office,** Rathaus am Markt (tel. 97 73 28; fax 97 74 47) supplies you with everything you need. From the station, head left on Bahnhofstr., turn right on Paulinenstr., then left on Bruchstr. into the pedestrian zone, and walk another five minutes to the *Rathaus.* Facing the red building, the tourist office should be on your right. The city brochure is excellent, with a map thorough enough for hikes to the *Denkmal* and surrounding area. For in-depth info for exploration by bike, pick up the "Lipperland" map (DM14.80). Rooms in town start at DM30, but the tourist office doesn't make reservations (open Mon.-Thurs. 9am-noon and 1-5pm, Fri. 9am-4pm, Sat. 9am-noon; Nov.-March Mon.-Thurs. 9am-noon and 1-5pm, Fri. 9am-noon). **City tours** of the *Altstadt* take off from the main entrance of the *Residenz-Schloß* (April-Oct. Sat. at 10am, Sun. at 11am; DM4, students DM2). To make the best use of the outstanding **bus** connections, swing by the **SVD** office, Langestr. 70 (tel. 97 77 44), at the "Rosental" bus stop and pick up little cards for each bus line (open Mon.-Fri. 9am-6pm, Sat. 9am-1pm). From the tourist office walk north on Lange Str. and then on to Richthofenstr. 14, where **Fahrradbüro Detmold** (tel. 97 74 01; fax 30 02 01) rents out old **bikes**. (DM6 per day, DM30 per week. Passport or ID and DM50 deposit required. Open Tues. and Thurs. 5-7pm, Sat. 10am–1pm). It might a good idea to pick up a bike in neighboring Lemgo or Horn and bring it here on the bus. The **telephone code** is 05231.

In addition to the regular pack of wild school children, the **Jugendherberge "Schanze" (HI),** Schirrmannstr. 49 (tel. 247 39, fax 289 27), features its own set of resident farm animals. From Bussteig 3 at the train station, take Bus #704 (direction: Hiddesen) to "Auf den Klippen," and walk 10 minutes down the trail. By foot from the station, walk up Hermannstr., continue onto Fürstengartenstr., turn right on Freiligrathstr. (which becomes Bandelstr.), and then left on Bülowstr. Take a shortcut by turning right up Schützentwete and then right onto Schützenberg (35min.). (Reception open until 10pm. Curfew 10pm, but guests are provided with keys. DM19.30, over 26 DM23.30. Breakfast included. Lunch DM7.40. Dinner DM6.40.)

LEMGO

From the Detmold *Hauptbahnhof,* hike, bike, or take bus #790 or #791 along the 12km trail to Lemgo, where the Weser Renaissance lives again. Those wondering what a Weser Renaissance is and why it should choose to happen here could do no better than to visit the aptly-named **Weserrenaissance Museum** (tel. 945 00) right inside **Schloß Brake** (central castle; open Tues.-Sun. 10am-6pm; admission DM4, students DM2, children under 6 free). Follow the signs as you enter the city, or ride #790 to "Schloß Brake." The current castle was built under Graf Simon VI zur Lippe from 1584 to 1592; his chambers and other period rooms are on display in the seven-story castle tower. If you find a revival of the classical fine arts less interesting than, say, burning people alive, then head down to the **Hexenbürgermeisterhaus Lemgo,** Breitestr. 19 (tel. 21 32 76), a collection of historical odds and ends focusing on the **witch-trial** era. Get off at the "Waisenhausplatz" bus stop and walk (5min.) up Breitestr. (open Tues.-Sun. 10am-12:30pm and 1:30-5pm; admission DM1.50, students DM1). Nearby, the 800-year-old **St. Nicolai Kirche** dominates the marketplace with twin towers. For more info or room-finding assistance (rooms start at DM35 per person), contact the **tourist office,** at Papenstr. 7 (tel. 21 33 47; fax 21 34 92; open March-Oct. Mon.-Fri. 10am-5pm, Sat. 10am-1pm; Nov.-Feb. Mon-Thurs. 10am-5pm, Fri. 10am-2pm). City tours leave every Saturday at 11am (April-Oct.) from the main portal of the Nicolaikirche (DM4, students DM2). Papenstr. branches off to the right of Breitestr. as you head away from the train station. Accommodations can also be found at the **Campgrounds,** Regenstorstr. 106 (tel. 148 58). From Breitestr., turn right onto Orpingstr.; when Orpingstr. becomes Regenturstr., the camp is to the left 100m ahead (DM6, children DM4). The **telephone code** is 05261.

HORN AND LÜGDE

Twelve hilly kilometers away from Detmold (1 stop before Detmold on the train from Alterbeker), in the southern Teutoburger Wald, Horn is home to the **Externsteine** ("Extern Stones"), the Rhineland's answer to Stonehenge. Who shaped these limestone monoliths? Was it pagans using the roofless chapel at its peak to worship the stars? Or Colonel Mustard in the grotto with the lead pipe? The only consensus is that this is an impressive group of rocks: breathtaking during the day and spooky at sunset (open April-Oct. daily 9am-6pm; admission DM1.50, students DM0.70; tours by appointment). To get there from the *Rathaus,* walk left on Mittelstr., then bear right on Externsteinestr. and follow the signs (25min. from *Rathaus*).

To learn more about the *Externsteine,* visit the **Horn Burgmuseum** in the imposing **Burg Horn,** Burgstr. 13 (tel. 20 12 00), following the signs from the *Rathaus* (open Nov.-April Tues.-Wed. 2-4pm, Thurs. 2-5:30pm, Fri. 10am-noon; admission DM1.50, students DM1). Info on rooms and sites is available at the **tourist office,** Rathausplatz 2 (tel. 20 12 62), in the monumentally ugly building next to the big yellow town hall (open Mon.-Wed. and Fri. 9am-noon, Thurs. 9am-noon and 3-5:30pm). From the Horn-Bad Meinberg train station, catch Bus #782 (direction: Detmold) to "Mittelstr." and backtrack five minutes. Or walk out the station door 20m and turn left. This short road becomes Kampstr.; follow it until it dead-ends into Mittelstr. and take a right (20min.).The **telephone code** is 05234. To reach the **Jugendherberge (HI),** Jahnstr. 36 (tel. 25 34; fax 691 99), follow the above instructions to the *Rathaus* and trek up Mittelstr., bearing left onto Paderbornerstr., then turn right onto the second "Jahnstr." sign. By bus from the train station, take the #782 to "Mittelstr." and continue in the same direction on foot, following the above. If you're coming from Detmold, take Bus #356 (direction: Paderborn/Bus/Hauptbahnhof) to "Jahnstr." *Herbergsvater* Herr Lenzing wakes you with a singsong on the intercom. (Reception open daily 5-10pm. Curfew 10pm. DM19.30, over 26 DM 23.30. Breakfast included. Full pension DM33.40, over 26 DM 37.40. Sheets DM6.)

The first night of Easter is the best time to visit the hamlet of **Lügde**. After a pagan feast, flaming giant **Catherine wheels** *(Osterräder)* tumble downhill. The rest of the time, Lügde reverts to being a nice little Christian town with a 13th-century church and ivy-covered towers. The Lügde **tourist office,** Forderestr. 81 (tel. 780 29), at the end of the main street, offers brochures (open Mon.-Fri. 10am-noon). Lügde is on the **train** line from Hanover to Alterbeker. The **telephone city code** is 05281.

■ Münster

Münster takes its name from the church founded here by one of Charlemagne's evangelists in 805. Since then, with a checkered history of fiery schism, fanatical heresy, and swift and terrible retribution, Münster has seen full well the passion, if not the virtue, of religious fervor. As the capital of the old Kingdom of Westphalia, Münster presided over the 1648 Peace which brought the Thirty Years War to an end, defining the borders of scores of German mini-states for hundreds of years. But the Münster of today offers much more than towering cathedrals and historic checkpoints: the 55,000 students of the **Wilhelmsuniversität**—the second largest university in Germany—know how to put those 9th-century reveling monks to shame.

ORIENTATION AND PRACTICAL INFORMATION

Münster is located at the confluence of the lower channels of the Ems River, in the midst of the Münsterland plain. Frequent trains running from Düsseldorf and Cologne to the southwest, and from Bremen to the northeast, stop in Münster.

Tourist Office: Klemenstr. 10 (tel. 492 27 10; fax 492 77 43). Cross Bahnhofstr. and head left, taking a sharp right onto Windthorstr., and veer right onto Stubengasse; the office is on your left as Stubengasse crosses Klemenstr. and becomes H.-Bruning-Str. The office books rooms for free (starting at DM50 per person), and offers tours and theater tickets. Open Mon.-Fri. 9am-6pm, Sat. 9am-1pm.

Flights: Flughafen Münster-Osnabrück, located to the northeast of the city, has flights daily to Berlin, Frankfurt, Munich, and Zürich, Sun.-Fri. to London, and Mon.-Fri. to Paris and to Amsterdam. Bus #S50 shuttles between the train station and the airport (board to the right of the station); the schedule is posted in the station. For **flight information,** call (02571) 94 15 50.

Car Rental: Hertz, Hammerstr. 186 (tel. 773 78). ID required. Open Mon.-Fri. 7:30am-7pm, Sat. 7:30am-2pm, Sun. 9:30-11:30am.

Bike Rental: Münster's train station has the second-largest train-station bike rental service (tel. 69 13 20) in Germany, with 300 bikes up for grabs. DM7, non-DB customers DM11. You can reserve your wheels by phone. Open daily 7am-10pm.

Boat Rental: Soverschmidt Yachtschule Aasee (tel. 803 03) offers rentals (sailboats DM15, row and paddleboats DM13) and basic lessons. To get there, take bus #4 to "Golden Brücke." Open daily 9am-6pm.

Mitfahrzentrale: AStA runs a ride-share office, Schloßplatz 1 (tel. 405 05). Open Mon.-Fri. 8:30am-4pm.

Laundromat: Wasch Center, Moltekestr. 5-7. Wash DM6. Open Mon.-Fri. 6am-11pm. Another branch, at Wolbeckerstr. 81, has the same prices and hours. To get there, take bus #11, 320, 330, 311, or 313 to "Sophienstr."

Emergency: Police: tel. 110.

Post Office: Berliner Str. 37, 48001 Münster. Located directly to the left of the train station. Open Mon.-Fri. 8am-6pm, Sat. 8am-5pm

Telephone Code: 0251.

ACCOMMODATIONS AND CAMPING

Some travelers hit up **students** for a place to sleep, because this little town is not cheap. The brand new *Jugendgästehaus* is no steal, and hotels fill up quickly; be sure to call ahead. In a pinch, there's a hostel in **Nottuln** (25km out of town), a 50-minute bus ride away (tel. (02502) 78 78; fax 96 19). Take bus #560/561 to "Rodeplatz," then follow the signs. (Reception open until 10pm. DM19.30, over 26 DM23.30. Breakfast included. Sheets DM6.)

Jugendgästehaus Aasee, Bismarckallee 31 (tel. 53 24 70; fax 52 12 71). Take bus #10 and 34 to "Hoppendamm." Orwellian vision of our hosteling future: huge brick and mirror-glass compound with **security cameras** and strict key policy. Still, it keeps you comfortable, with a toilet and bath in each room. 4-bed room DM35.50 per person, 2-bed room DM43 per person; less if you stay 5 days or more. Reception open 7am-1am. Curfew 1am. Breakfast buffet. Sheets included.

Haus vom Guten Hirten, Mauritz-Lindenweg 61 (tel. 33 78 70; fax 37 45 44), to the right of the train station. Go right onto Wolbeckerstr., left onto Hohenzollern-Ring, right onto Manfred-von-Richthofen-Str., and then left on Maurits-Lindenweg. Or take bus #14 to "Stadion," then turn left onto Maurits-Lindenweg. Its a considerable distance from both the station and the *Altstadt,* but spacious, immaculate rooms and a relaxing TV make it worth the extra effort. Reception open 6am-9pm. Singles DM50. Doubles DM90. Triples DM129. Breakfast included.

Hotel Bockhorn, Bremerstr. 24 (tel. 655 10), a 5-min. walk from the train. Go left out of the train station, turn left on Hamburgerstr. (made of asphalt), and then right on Bremerstr. Tidy rooms and powerful showers compensate for the dim hallways. Singles DM55. Doubles DM110. Full-service breakfast included.

Hotel zur Krone, Hammerstr. 67 (tel. 738 68). Go left on Bahnhofstr., right on Hafenstr, and left on Junkerstr. and follow as it turns into Bernhard Str. and emerges on Hammerstr.; take a left here. Or take bus #2, 9, 341, 342, 343, or 511 to "Josefskirche." Reasonable prices and a restaurant downstairs, but only 5 rooms. Singles DM58. Doubles DM100. Breakfast included. Call ahead.

Camping: Campingplatz Münster, auf der Laer 7 (tel. 31 19 82). Take bus #320 to "Wersewinkel." Reception open daily 8am-1pm and 3-6pm. DM4 per person. Tents DM4. Showers DM0.50.

FOOD

On Wednesdays and Saturdays, a farmer's **market** takes over the plaza in front of the *Dom,* vending fresh fruit, fresh meat, and fresh clothes (open 7am-2pm). The entire **Kuhviertel** (old student quarter) is lined with late-night *Kneipen* and inexpensive eateries.

Diesel, Harsewinkelgasse 1-4 (tel. 57 96), by the intersection of Windhorststr., Stubengasse, and Loerstr.; just look for the 2.5m pedestal surmounted by 0.5m cherries. Gobble down daily specials (DM5-11) next to fuel pumps amid fumes of cheap alcohol. Pool, darts, an extensive magazine collection, and enough complimentary food to feed a rhino. Kitchen open 7pm-11pm. Bar open 11am-1am.

Cavete Akademische Bieranstalt, Kreuzstr. 38 (tel. 457 00). Founded *by* students *for* students in 1959, with dark carnivalesque decor and delicious homemade spinach noodles in a variety of sauces (DM8-10). Open daily 7pm-1am, kitchen open until 12:30am.

Pizzeria Piccolo, Frauenstr. 26 (tel. 589 40). Enjoy pizza, pasta (DM7-13) and plants amid rose-colored lighting. About as Italian as it gets north of the Alps. Open daily 11:30am-3pm and 5:30pm-midnight.

Pulcinella, Kreuzstr. 28 (tel. 466 40). Fresh salad buffet and daily veggie specials (DM6.50-11.50). Meat can be added for carnivores. Open daily 11am-midnight.

SIGHTS

When Goethe's carriage turned onto the tree-lined **Promenade** encircling the Münster *Altstadt,* he would slow it and smell the seasonal flowers and fruits. It's an inexpensive literary habit worth imitating. To get there, continue through the Baroque façade of the **Schloß,** now the administrative center of **Wilhelmsuniversität,** into the Botanical Gardens (open Mar.-Oct. daily 8am-7pm, Nov.-Feb. daily 8am-4pm).

In the center of the *Altstadt,* on Domplatz, is the **St.-Paulus-Dom,** the largest cathedral in Westphalia. The *Dom* was nearly destroyed in World War II but has since been beautifully restored. A stone from the similarly bombed Cathedral of Coventry stands in the entranceway, carrying a wish for mutual forgiveness between Britain and Germany. From his pulpit in the cathedral, Bishop Clemens von Galen delivered a courageous sermon against the Nazi program of **euthanasia** for so-called "incurables." After the sermon was distributed widely, pressure from the church prompted a rare partial retreat by Hitler. The speech can be read in the **Domkammer** (open Tues.-Sat. 10am-noon and 2-6pm, Sun. 2-6pm; admission DM1). Inside, a barefooted statue of St. Christopher points its massive toes to the 16th-century **astronomical clock,** which recreates the movements of the planets and plays a merry *Glockenspiel* tune (Mon.-Sat. noon, Sun. 12:30pm; *Dom* open Mon.-Sat. 6am-6pm, Sun. 6:30am-7:30pm).

The seamy underbelly of the city's religious fervor is evidenced by the three cages hanging above the clock face of **Marktkirche St. Lamberti,** just off the Prinzipalmarkt. In the 16th century, rebel Anabaptists took over the town, led by the self-styled Prophet Jan van Leiden. He had 16 wives, and killed all who refused to surrender their property to his "New Zion" in Münster. After a bloodbath of episcopal reconquest, van Leiden and his two cohorts were executed, their bodies then hung in cages on the steeple. The authorities finally cleaned the cages out but left them hanging as a "reminder." Also suspended here is Germany's only free-hanging organ. Free concerts are given every long Saturday at noon. Next door to the church is the **Friedenssaal** (Hall of Peace), which kept one unknown woodcarver very busy for a very long time. The treaty that ended the Thirty Years War was sworn here. Among the many elaborate carvings are a mysterious withered human hand and the Golden Cock, a ceremonial carafe used to honor distinguished visitors. (Open Mon.-Fri. 9am-5pm, Sat. 9am-4pm, Sun. 10am-1pm. Admission DM1.50, children DM0.80.) Pick up a guide in English from the front desk; call 83 25 80 for group rates.

MUSEUMS

Other items of historical interest can be found in Münster's many museums. A **Railway Museum,** a **Carnival Museum,** and a **Museum of Organs** (unrelated to the Leprosy Museum), are located far off in the suburbs. Ask for info at the tourist office.

Landesmuseum für Kunst und Kultur, Domplatz 10 (tel. 59 07 01). Contains modern sculptures and ancient paintings, arranged on 3 floors around a central atrium. Exciting special exhibits planned include Paul Signac (Dec. 1996-Feb. 1997), August Project Sculpture (June-Sept. 1997), and Macke (late 1997). Admission DM5, students and children DM2. Free on Fri. Open Tues.-Sun. 10am-6pm.

Mühlenhof-Freilichtmuseum, Sentruperstr. 223 (tel. 820 74), is a completely restored industrial village with a bonus *Don Quixote*-style windmill, which sells pointy wooden shoes for DM20. Admission DM5, students and seniors DM3, children DM2.50. Open April-Oct. daily 10am-5pm; Nov.-March daily 11am-4pm.

Museum of Leprosy, Kinderhaus 15 (tel. 285 10), to the northwest of the *Altstadt,* is a little far away, but you should definitely drop by. The exhibits, including playful little leper-puppets, are strictly hands-off. Open Sun. 3-5pm. Free. Call for an appointment on other days.

Museum für Lackkunst, Windthorstr. 26 (tel. 41 85 10), just off the Promenade. The banana painted on the door leads to the world's only exhibition of all things **lacquered,** with videos and explanations of how to try this safely at home. Batteries not included; some assembly may be required. Revolving modern exhibits in the basement. Admission DM3, students and children DM1.50. Free on Tues. Open Tues. noon-8pm, Wed.-Sun. noon-6pm.

NORTH RHINE-WESTPHALIA

NIGHTLIFE

The best way to find out about night life is to check the posters on street walls and bus shelters. *Kneipen* line the streets across from the *Schloß* in the student quarter and discos abound farther southwest between the train station and the harbor. **Ultimo** provides semi-weekly print coverage of night-life and art openings in Münster and the surrounding area (free at the AStA and Diesel; DM3 at newsstands).

Blechtrommel, Hansaring 26 (tel. 442 10), features live music and a menu that changes weekly. The name refers to the famous post-war Günter Grass novel, "The Tin Drum." Foosball tournaments on Mon. and darts on Sat. Pizzas DM11-17.50, small pizzas DM8-12. Open daily 6pm-1am. Kitchen open 7-11:30pm.

Café Malik, Frauenstr. 14 (tel. 442 10). Fabulous zebra-striped bohemian coffee-house where a foil-wrapped chocolate and a large selection of international newspapers accompany each cup (DM2.20). Chat with the crowd or write home on the complimentary (and bizarre) postcards. Russian chocolate DM5.90 (with rum, of course). Open daily 9am-1am.

Cuba-Kneipe, Achtermannstr. 10-12 (tel. 58 217). Sip rum drinks to reggae and gear up for the Cuba-*fête* every 1st, 3rd, and 4th Sat. of the month. Young, hip crowd comes 11pm-3am. Otherwise open Mon.-Fri. 5pm-1am, Sat-Sun. 6pm-1am.

Gaststätte Pinkus Müller, Kreuzstr. 7 (tel. 451 51). About as hip as an elbow, but one of Germany's acutest joys is drinking beer in the house where it's brewed; the *Pinkus Alt* (DM3) here is a fine beer, with a fine name. Peruse the genealogy of the Müllers, including Carl "Pinkus" Müller himself, as you steel yourself for the Münster nightlife. Open Mon.-Sat. 11:30am-2pm and 5pm-midnight.

■ Lower Rhine

XANTEN

If all the cities of the lower Rhine Valley were to become people, Xanten would be an aging grampa while everyone else would still be zygotes. The only German town beginning with "X" and the only one flattened by Canadians in World War II, Xanten is one of the oldest settlements in Germany. In 105 AD, the Roman Emperor Trajan made Xanten a colony and stationed his legions here. More than 10,000 *veni-vidi-vici*-playing Romans lived here until it was abandoned in the 4th century. To the *Vergnügen* of modern historians, no one bothered to rebuild the city. The ground plan was left intact, and since 1977 the reconstructed site, creatively named the **Archäologischer Park** (tel. 29 99), has offered visitors a rare glimpse of the living past; the sheer enormity of the structures testifies to the skill of the Roman architects and to the size of the park's budget (open March-Nov. daily 9am-6pm; Dec.-Feb. daily 10am-4pm; admission DM7, students DM4, children DM2.50).

During the Middle Ages, Xanten flourished again, this time as a satellite to Cologne. To build the fortifications, the townspeople cleverly carted the walls of the Roman ruins down the street. Aptly named, the **Klever Tor,** in the southwest corner of the town, represents this era in the city's history, as do the buildings surrounding the cobblestone square in the **Markt,** in the center town. Towering above is the 12th-century **Dom St. Viktor** (tel. 017 131), built on the grave site of an early Christian martyr (open Mon.-Sat. 10am-6pm, Sun. 12:30pm-6pm; closed Jan.-Feb. noon-2pm). Beside the *Dom* is the **Regionalmuseum,** Kurfürstenstr. 7-9 (tel. 372 98), which exhibits the artifacts recovered from the Archäologischer Park, including those funny Roman helmets (open May-Sept. Tues.-Fri. 9am-5pm, Sat.-Sun. 11am-6pm; Oct.-April Tues.-Fri. 10am-5pm, Sat.-Sun. 11am-6pm; admission DM3, students and children DM1.50).

Xanten is 40 minutes from Kleve on an hourly bus (DM5). To reach the town from the train station, walk up Bahnhofstr. to the *Markt*. The **tourist office,** at the far end of the square (tel. 372 38), is located in the *Rathaus*. There is no hostel in Xanten and *Pensionen* start at DM30, but the friendly staff at the tourist office will book rooms in local hotels (starting at DM60) for a 12% fee (open Mon.-Sat. 10am-4:30pm, Sat.-Sun. 10am-4pm). If the office is closed, have fun with the computer outside. **Rent bikes** from **Reineke,** Marsstr. 19 (tel. 14 74), just off the *Markt,* for DM12 per day or DM8 after 3pm. The **telephone code** is 02821.

KLEVE

The town of **Kleve** ("Cleves" in English), is famed for its daughter, **Anne of Cleves,** the local princess whom Henry VIII *didn't* make the happiest woman in the world. Henry's third wife had just died, so he sent Hans Holbein out to bring back paintings of eligible princesses. Henry chose Anne, but when she arrived in England, he decided he'd been misled. Henry insulted her looks until she left and banished Holbein from court. Even so, Kleve retains a link to England, with red British mailboxes and telephones throughout the city. Anne's relatives are buried in the **St. Maria Himmelfahrt** church. The main ecclesiastical treasures are assembled in **Haus Köekkoek,** Kavarinerstr. 33 (tel. 843 02). From the *Bahnhof,* cross the bus stops heading left and follow Herzogstr. as it becomes Großestr., then turn right onto Kavarinerstr. The museum boasts illuminated manuscripts and Dutch Renaissance statuary (open Tues.-Sun. 10am-1pm and 2-5pm; admission free).

Kleve hugs the hill that the 11th-century **Schwanenburg** (Swan's Castle) perches upon. Legend tells of Princess Elsa: the Knight of the Swan won her love, but the condition of marriage was that she could never inquire as to his identity. When curiosity got the better of Elsa, a large swan came to lead her knightly true love away; the legend is cast in bronze in the city-center. The entire valley can be seen from the top of the castle's long-necked tower (open daily 11am-5pm; Nov.-March Sat.-Sun. 11am-5pm; admission DM2, students DM1, children DM0.50). Close to the hostel, the **Reichswald nature preserve** is ideal for hiking or just relaxing.

Kleve is accessible by **rail** from Krefeld or by a convenient hourly **bus** from Xanten (40min.). The town is also right on the Dutch border, and buses run regularly to museum-rich **Arnheim** (see *Let's Go: Europe*). The **tourist office,** on Kavariner-Str. in room 217 of the *Rathaus* (tel. 842 67; fax 237 59), gives out city maps, gossip about Anne and Henry, and a list of available rooms (starting at DM25) in the city (open Mon. and Wed. 8:30am-12:45pm and 2-5pm, Tues. and Thurs. 8:30am-12:45pm and 2-3:30pm, Fri. 8:30am-12:45pm). The **Sport & Reise Animation** (tel. 201 10) rents **bikes** with reservations only (DM10 per day, DM2.50 more if it's a weekend). The main hosteling option around here is the **Jugendherberge Kleve (HI),** St. Annaberg 2 (tel. 236 71; fax 247 78), in the west end of town—the next stopover is in the Netherlands. From the station, take bus #57 (direction: Richtung Haus Ida) to "Annabergstr.," then walk up the hill. After 6:30pm, you've gotta hike it. Follow Großestr. as it becomes Hagschestr. and veer right onto Steichban. When this ends, pick up the trail on Römer-Str. and follow Römer as it becomes Merowinger, then turn right onto Königsallee and trudge uphill to the hostel (30min.). (Reception open daily 4:30-4:45pm, 7:15-7:30pm, and 9:45-10pm. Curfew 10pm. DM20.50, over 26 DM24.50. Sheets DM6.). The **telephone code** is 02821.

▓ Bonn

Derisively called the *"Hauptdorf"* (capital village) by Germans, Bonn has been the whipping boy of Germany for 50 years, simply because it's not Berlin. Founded by the Romans, Bonn was a non-entity for most of its 2000-year history and made it big by chance. Konrad Adenauer, the Federal Republic's first chancellor, owned a house in the suburbs; the ever-considerate occupying powers made Bonn the "provisional capital" for the Western Occupation Zone, and eventually the *Hauptstadt* (capital) of the fledgling Republic. The summer of 1991 brought headlines of "Chaos in Bonn" as Berlin fought for the right to reclaim the seat of government in a political catfight that cleaved every party from the CDU to the Greens. By the narrowest of margins, Berlin won; the *Bundestag* will pack up and move within a decade or so. Easy come, easy go. Bonners have taken the loss well. Perhaps grateful to be out of the limelight, the sparkling streets of the *Altstadt* bustle with notable energy; you'd never guess that more than half of these people are civil servants. Berliners joke that Bonn is "half the size of a Chicago cemetery and twice as dead." But the fact remains that Bonn is free of big city pretension—no small feat for a capital. With its cultural spread of museums, respected university, and sunny civic disposition, Bonn remains a worthy destination, even without the political clout.

PRACTICAL INFORMATION

Tourist Office: Münsterstr. 20 (tel. 77 34 66; fax 69 03 68), tucked in a passageway at the edge of the pedestrian zone. Take the "Stadtmitte" exit from the station, walk 60m up Poststr. to Münsterstr., and turn left; the office is to the right. The staff will make same-day hotel reservations for a DM3-5 fee. They give out more info than you could shake a stick at. Inquire about the many tours, from the *"Heißluftballon"* (hot air balloon) to the "Political Bonn" tour (same thing, minus balloon). Open Mon.-Fri. 9am-6:30pm, Sat. 9am-5pm, Sun. 9:30am-12:30pm.

Consulates: If there's one thing Bonn's got, it's consulates. The 4-page alphabetical list (at the tourist office) runs from *Ägypten* (Egypt) to *Zypern* (Cyprus). **U.S.,** Deichmann Aue. 29 (tel. 339 20 53; fax 339 26 63). Take U-Bahn #16 or 63 to "Rhineallee," then bus #613 to "Deichman Aue." Open Mon.-Fri. 8:30-11:30am. **Canada,** Godesberger Allee 119 (tel. 81 00 60; fax 37 65 25). Open Mon.-Fri. 8am-noon, 1-4pm. **Ireland,** Godesberger Allee 119, 53175 (tel. 37 69 37 or 37 69 39). Open 9am-1pm, 2-5:30pm. **Australia,** Godesberger Allee 105 (tel. 810 30; fax 37 62 68). Take U-Bahn #16 or 63 to "Max-Löbne." Open Mon.-Fri. 9am-noon. **New Zealand,** Bundeskanzlerplatz 2-10 (tel. 22 80 70; fax 22 16 87). U-Bahn #16 or 63 to "Heussallee." Open 9am-1pm, 2-5:30pm. **U.K.** citizens should go to the consulate in Düsseldorf. **South African** citizens head to the mission in Berlin.

Flights: International departures from the **Köln-Bonn Flughafen.** Bus #670 shuttles between the *Hauptbahnhof* and the airport every 20min. 5am-10pm (DM7.70, children DM3.90).

Public Transportation: Bonn is linked to Cologne and other riverside cities by the massive **VRR** (Verkehrsverbund Rhein-Sieg) S-Bahn, U-Bahn, and Bundesbahn network. Areas are divided into **Tarifzonen;** the farther you go, the more you pay. Single tickets (DM1.90-12), 4-ride tickets (DM6-12.60), and day tickets (DM10) are available at *automaten* and designated vending stations. Stop by the **Vorverkaufsstelle VRS,** under the *Hauptbahnhof,* for network maps and more ticket information. Open Mon.-Wed. and Fri. 7am-7:35pm, Thurs. 7am-8:30pm, Sat. 8am-4pm. With the *Minigruppenkarte* (DM9 per day), 5 people can ride Mon.-Fri. after 9am, and all day on weekends. The *Bonncard* (DM12) offers the same transportation for one person, plus free entry to the city's museums.

Taxi: Funkzentrale (tel. 55 55 55). The funk is unbearable, and I want it to go on forever.

Car Rental: Hertz, Avis, InterRent Europcar, and **Sixt-Budget** all have offices at the airport.

Bike Rental: Kurscheid, Römerstr. 4 (tel. 63 14 33), charges DM16 per day and offers a DM20 per weekend special. Cars rented here as well. ID required for both. Open Mon.-Sat. 7am-7pm, Sun. 9am-1pm and 3-7pm.

Mitfahrzentrale: Herwarthstr. 11 (tel. 69 30 30), pairs drivers with riders. Open Mon.-Fri. 10am-6:30pm, Sat. 10am-2pm, Sun. for phone calls only 11am-2pm.

Bookstore: The mammoth **Bouvier,** Am Hof 28 (tel. 729 01 64), across from the University *Schloß,* has a wide range of foreign books on the top floor. There's even a complete shelf for Shakespeare. **Concert tickets** sold. Open Mon.-Fri. 9am-6:30pm, Sat. 9am-2pm.

Gay and Lesbian Center: Schwul & Lesben Zentrum (tel. 63 00 39) is located in a Mobil Autoöle parking lot. For counseling call 194 46; gay assault hotline 192 28. From bus stop "Kunsthalle," cross the street and go towards the Kunst Forum. At Cafe "Z," Mon. is gay night, Tues. is lesbian night, while Wed. and Thurs. are mixed. Open Mon.-Tues. and Thurs. 8pm-midnight, Wed. 9pm-midnight.

NORTH RHINE-WESTPHALIA

Laundromat: Wasch Center, on the corner of Breite-Str. and Kölnstr. Wash DM7. Dry DM1 per 10min. Soap included. Open Mon.-Sat. 7am-11pm.

Women's Resources: The **Frauenberatungstelle,** in an alley off of Kölnstr. (tel. 65 95 00), near Wilhelmplatz, will answer questions, provide help, and direct women to other agencies Mon. and Thurs. 5-7:30pm, Wed. and Fri. 10am-noon.

Rape Crisis Line: tel. 63 55 24.

Emergency: Police: tel. 110 or 151.

Post Office: Münsterplatz 17, 53111 Bonn. Walk down Poststr. from the station. Open Mon.-Fri. 8am-6pm, Sat. 8am-1pm, Sun. 11am-noon. For limited services, like changing money in small amounts, open Mon.-Wed. and Fri. 7am-7:30pm, Thurs. 7am-8:30pm, Sat. 7am-4pm, Sun. 10am-1pm.

Telephone Code: 0228.

ACCOMMODATIONS AND CAMPING

National capitals attract transients, and Bonn has responded with a fine stock of hotels to take them in. Most hotel prices are suited to politicians supported by a large tax base. With two *Jugendgästehäuser* but no *Jugendherberge,* even hosteling gets financially taxing in Bonn.

Jugendgästehaus Bonn-Venusberg (HI), Haager Weg 42 (tel. 28 99 70; fax 289 97 14), is far from the center of town. Take bus #621 (direction: Ippendorf Altenheim) to "Jugendherberge" (18min.). Numerous modern touches make it a first-rate place. The hostel's "Bistro Come Together" serves up a smooth *Kölsch* beer (0.2L for DM1.60) nightly 8pm-12:30am. Reception open 9am-1am. Curfew 1am. DM34.50. Breakfast and sheets included. Laundry DM7.50. Wheelchair access.

Jugendgästehaus Bonn-Bad Godesburg (HI), Horionstr. 60 (tel. 31 75 16; fax 31 45 37). From the main train station take U-Bahn #16 or 63 to "Rhein Allee" or the DB train to "Bonn-Bad Godesberg Bahnhof," and then bus #615 (direction: Stadt-wald/Evangelische Krankenhaus) to "Venner-Str."; look for the sign on the opposite side of the street. Neat, modern rooms. Reception open 8am-5pm and 8pm-1am. Curfew 1am. DM31.50 per person. Breakfast and sheets included.

Hotel Bergmann, Kasernenstr. 13 (tel. 63 38 91). From the train station, follow Poststr., turn left at Münsterplatz onto Vivatgasse. Bear right on Kasernenstr.; after 10min. the hotel will appear on your left. Cozy, elegant rooms. Bathrooms on the hall are *very* pink. Reception open 24hr. Singles DM60, doubles DM95.

Hotel Virneburg, Sandkaule 3a (tel. 63 63 66). Take U-Bahn #62, 64, or 66 to "Ber-tha-von-Suttner-Platz" or walk up Poststr. and bear right on Acherstr. at the north end of Münsterplatz. Turn left on Rathausgasse and left again onto Belderberg, which runs into Sandkaule. The hallways are peppered with statuettes. Rooms are cheap and convenient. Singles DM50, with shower DM55-65. Doubles DM70, with shower DM90. Breakfast included.

Hotel Haus Hofgarten, Fritz Tillman Str. 7 (tel. 22 34 82; fax 21 39 02). From the station, turn right onto Maximillianstr., continue on Kaiserstr., and then turn left on Fritz Tillman Str. Just like your granny's house. Everyone gets 96 channels of cable TV. Singles DM50-135. Doubles DM110-175. Breakfast included. Call ahead.

Hotel Mozart, Mozartstr. 1 (tel. 65 90 71; fax 65 90 75). From the south exit of the station, turn right onto Herwarthstr., left on Bachstr., then right on Mozartstr. It's around the corner from Beethovenplatz. Matches unbeatable convenience with first class rooms in a pleasant, quiet area. Singles DM75, with shower and toilet DM135. Doubles DM110, with shower and toilet DM195.

Camping: Campingplatz Genienaue, Im Frankenkeller 49 (tel. 34 49 49). Take U-Bahn #16 or 63 to "Rhein Allee," then change for bus #613 (direction: Giselherstr.) to "Gunterstr." Turn left on Guntherstr. for 120m and right on Frankenkeller for 300m until you reach the site. Rhine-side camping in the Mehlem suburb. Tents DM5.50-9. Family fun deal: Mom and Dad DM9 apiece, little Junior DM5, and ol' Sparky only DM1. Woof! Reception 9am-noon and 3-10pm.

FOOD

The market on **Münsterplatz** is the sight of Bonn's most torrid negotiations; it's teeming with haggling vendors and determined customers, all trying to get the best meat, fruit, and vegetables at the lowest prices. Come at the end of the day, when voices rise and prices fall (Mon.-Sat. 8am-6pm). Further from the *Altstadt* along Max und Dorothenstr., ethnic restaurants sustain high quality and low prices.

University Mensa, Nassestr. 11, is a 15-min. walk from the train station along Kaiserstr. In Bonn's glory days it swung with cosmopolitan flair. Reagan would sip *Dom Perignon* out of Maggie Thatcher's stilleto heels, and Helmut Kohl would lead the crowd in a round of bawdy German drinking songs. Now, it's just another *Mensa.* Cheap, edible meals DM1.80-4.50. DM1 extra for non-students. Lunch served Mon.-Thurs. 11:30am-2:15pm, Fri. 11:30am-2pm, Sat. noon-1:45pm. Dinner served Mon.-Fri. 5:30-8pm. Open late-Aug.-mid-July.

Rosa Lu, Vorgebirgsstr. 80 (tel. 63 77 30). From Berliner Platz, follow Maxstr. until it becomes Vorgebirgsstr. Bus stop: "Maxstr." Rotating lunch menu features an Indian platter (DM8.90-13.50) and large salads (DM10). Warm, cavernous feel. Open Mon.-Thurs. 11:30am-1am, Fri.-Sat. 4pm-1am, Sun. 10am-1am.

Pizzeria la Piccola, Bonngasse 4 (tel. 63 78 16), only a few steps from the *Beethovenhaus* and *Marktplatz.* The insidious scent curls out and drags in the unsuspecting. Pizzas a-plenty and large salads (DM10). Ubiquitous dark wood decor enlivened by hilarious waiters. Open daily 11am-1am. Visa, MC, Diners.

Cassius Garten, Maximilianstr. 28d, at the edge of the *Altstadt,* facing the station, with a back entrance in the court of the tourist office. A futuristic veggie bar where zealous disciples of health consume salads, noodles, and bread in a stark white glossed atrium. My God, Jim, that was our own planet! 50 kinds of salad, 30 teas and juices, and a whole-grain bake shop. Pay DM2.48 per 100g and seat yourself at a booth. Open Mon.-Fri. 8am-8pm, Thurs. 8am-9pm, Sat. 11:30am-3:30pm.

SIGHTS

Bonn's old town center winds into a lively pedestrian zone puddled with historic niches. First-time parents can indulge their fantasies at the **Beethoven Geburtshaus** (Bonn's biggest draw after the *Bundestag*), Bonngasse 20 (tel. 63 51 88), where busts and portraits, manuscripts, mementos, and musical instruments add spice to the collection; they even have the trumpets Beethoven stuck in his ears to improve his hearing. Take U-Bahn #62, 64, or 66 to "Bertha von Suttner Platz" or follow the signs through the pedestrian zone. (Open Mon.-Sat. 10am-5pm, Sun. 10am-1pm; Oct.-March Mon.-Sat. 10am-4pm, Sun. 10am-1pm. Admission DM5, students DM1.50. Call ahead for English tours.) The symphonic ghost haunts Bonn annually during the **Beethoven Festival.** The first fête, organized by Franz Liszt in 1845, was a riot, with Liszt brawling with French nationalist Berlioz while King Ludwig's mistress Lola Montez spontaneously table-danced. Despite upset plates and scandalized Bonners, the festival was in town to stay. Call the tourist office for information.

Farther down Bonngasse is the **Namen-Jesu Kirche.** The church appears to be suffering from an identity crisis, combining Romantic, Gothic, and Baroque elements. The primarily Gothic façade plays second fiddle to the astounding pink swirling marble Baroque altar, complete with gilded starbursts. The market takes place in the shadow of the voluptuous pink **Rathaus**—reminiscent of an overdone birthday cake—which presides over the *Marktplatz;* in the similarly colorful 1960s, de Gaulle, Kennedy, and Elizabeth II visited together for a photo-op. Though it is, indeed, a sight to behold, one might be better off beholding the **Münster basilika.** The cathedral holds its own with three stories of arches-within-arches that finally yield a gorgeous gold-leaf mosaic; a 12th-century cloister laced with crossways and latticed passages branches off to one side. Keep an eye out for the incongruous blue-red Expressionist windows. To get there, take Remigiusstr. towards the station. (Cloister open daily 9:30am-5:30pm. *Münster* never sleeps.)

The castles, palaces, and museums that lend the area its cultural wealth lie just outside the city center. Forty thousand students study within the **Kurfürstliches Schloß,** the huge 18th-century palace now serving as the center of Bonn's Friedrich-Wilhelms Universität. The *Schloß* is the gateway to the refreshing **Hofgarten** and **Stadtgarten,** forever filled with students and punks. To uncover Bonn's "other" palace, stroll down the Poppelsdorfer Allee promenade to the 18th-century **Poppelsdorfer Schloß.** This eclectic castle touts a French façade and an Italian courtyard, plus beautifully manicured **Botanical Gardens.** (Gardens open Mon.-Fri. 9am-6pm, Sun. 9am-1pm; Oct.-April Mon.-Fri. 9am-4pm. Greenhouses open Mon.-Fri. 10:30am-noon and 2-4pm; Oct.-March Mon.-Fri. 10:30am-noon and 2-4pm. Free.)

No visit to Bonn is complete without the obligatory governmental romp. The vaguely *Bauhaus* **Bundestag,** Bundeshaus, Eingang V (tel. 16 21 52), has earned the coveted title of "Least Prepossessing Parliament Building" in the whole world. Take U-Bahn #16, 63, or 66 to "Heussallee/Bundeshaus" or bus #610 from the main station to "Bundeshaus." Don't think you can just stroll in and table a motion or exercise the ol' pocket veto; to get in, you must take a less-than-enthralling tour which begins on the hour at Hermann-Ehlers-Str. 29, opposite the Hochhaus. (Tours Mon.-Fri. 9am-4pm, Sat.-Sun. 10am-4pm; Jan.-mid-March Mon.-Fri. 9am-4pm. Bring your passport.) For those hungry for more big functional buildings, the **Bundeshaus** (Germany's Parliament) is visible on Görresstr. from the bank of the Rhine. Notice how the postwar architectural mandate to turn this small city into a world-class capital has produced goofy results. A wacky example is the old **Post Ministry,** at Zweite Fahrgasse, on the river. The Rhine-side face sports the interpretive relief *Tier-Symbole der Fünf Kontinente* (Animal Symbols of the 5 Continents), with a megalithic eagle (America), bull (Europe), elephant (Africa), kangaroo (Australia), and a big friendly wildcat for Asia. An elaborate joke, you think? No, this is what happens when you give people money and tell them to go build a national capital.

As you walk down Adenauerallee, south of the city center, you'll pass the **Villa Hammerschmidt,** home of the German chancellor, and **Palais Schaumburg,** home of the German president. One of Germany and Bonn's most prominent figures is still the late ex-Chancellor **Konrad Adenauer,** the man whose leadership made West Germany into a stable, respectable nation. The **Denkmal** (monument) erected in Adenauer's honor is less than majestic, however. Nicknamed *"der Alte"* (the old guy), the postwar chancellor was Bonn's guiding light, but the 3-m hollow-cheeked bust at Adenauerallee 135-141 looks like a skull lifted from a pirate flag; see it for yourself. Engraved into his cranium are allegorical figures—various animals, a pair of bound hands, and two French cathedrals. This is how Bonners commemorate their *heroes,* mind you. Don't get on their bad side.

MUSEUMS

If the parliamentary side of Bonn sight-seeing leaves something to be desired, the museums certainly do not; as Bonn has enjoyed nearly 50 years of generous federal funding, much of the public wealth was channeled into the expansion of the town's museums. The **"Museum Mile"** begins at the **Museum Alexander Koenig.** To get there, take U-Bahn #16, 63, or 66. A **Bonncard** (DM12), available from the tourist office, will provide public transportation and free admission to eight museums.

Museum Mile

Kunstmuseum Bonn, Friedrich-Ebert Allee (tel. 77 62 60). Take U-Bahn #16, 63, or 66 to "Heussallee." A superb selection of Expressionist and modern German art transplanted from the old city museum. Enough Max Ernst to teach you the importance of being Ernst. Admission DM5, students DM3. Open Tues.-Sun. 10am-6pm.

Kunst-und Ausstellungshalle der BRD (tel. 917 12 00), takes you to utopia. Take U-Bahn #16, 63, or 66 to "Heussallee." The art here is so new, you can smell the glue. The 16 columns flanking the *Ausstellungshalle* represent the 16 *Bundesländer* of united Germany. Admission DM8, students DM4. Open Tues.-Sun. 10am-7pm.

Museum Alexander Koenig, south of the city (tel. 912 22 11). Take U-Bahn #16, 63, or 66 to "Museum Koenig." If taxidermy has a Louvre, this is it. People who dislike animals will take pleasure in the stuffed, sterilized, glass-encased exhibits. Snakes and lizards do crawl around in the basement. Admission DM4, students DM2. Open Tues.-Fri. 9am-5pm, Sat. 9am-12:30pm, Sun. 9:30am-5pm.

Haus der Geschichte, 1 block from the Kunstmuseum Bonn (tel. 916 50). A brand new, futuristic museum dedicated to critical and "interactive" German history. Beautiful exhibits with strong Western (German) bias are highlighted by some antique VWs and a black enclosure with the scrolling names of Holocaust victims. Free. Open Tues.-Sun. 9am-7pm.

Frauenmuseum has vast white galeries containing interactive, modern art pieces by women (tel. 69 13 44). Take U-Bahn #61 to "Rosental/Herrstr." The 2nd floor covers medieval women. Thought-provoking pieces include an occasional piece on the grassy roof and a Yoko Ono room. Open Tues.-Sat. 2-8pm, Sun. 11am-5pm.

Elsewhere in Bonn

Bundeskanzler-Adenauer-Haus, Konrad Adenauer Str. 8c. Take S-Bahn #66 to "Bad Honnef." Herr Adenauer, then mayor of Cologne, retired here in 1937 after being driven from office by local Nazis. The exhibits tell the story of his personal and political survival. Open Tues.-Sun. 10am-4:30pm. Last entry 4pm.

Akademisches Kunstmuseum, on the far side of the *Hofgarten* (tel. 73 77 38). Lazy sculpture fans can forget about going abroad to see the masterpieces, because they're all here, in the largest collection of plaster casts in Germany. Exhibits include Venus de Milo, the Colossus of Samos, and Laocöon. Better than the real thing. Admission DM1, students free. Open Sun.-Wed. and Fri. 10am-1pm, Thurs. 10am-1pm and 4-6pm.

NIGHTLIFE

Bonn has far too many discos to be as boring as its reputation might suggest. Though 70% of Bonn's citizens are civil servants, the town still hops—thanks largely to the students, journalists, and foreign visitors who, despite only making up only 30% of the population, comprise the majority of the town's party animals. Of Bonn's several cultural monthly glossies, **Schnüss** is a must for the who, what, when, and where, more complete than the free *Bonner Gästeführer* and *Szene Bonn.*

Brauhaus Bönnsch, Sterntorbrücke 4 (tel. 65 06 10), pours its own highly civilized *Bönnsch,* the smooth-as-butter illegitimate son of Cologne's *Kölsch* (DM2.30 for 0.2L). For DM5 you can buy their beer glasses—contoured to your hand for easy imbibing. They serve *Bönnsche Flammkuchen* made from a 250-year-old Alsatian recipe (DM10-17). Open Mon.-Thurs. and Sun. 11am-1am, Fri.-Sat. 11am-3am.

Rochehouen, next door to *Brauhaus Bönnsch,* is billed as *"Bonns Nacht Rock Cafe."* Alleviate yourself from the staid atmosphere next door. Open Tues.-Sun. 9pm-5am.

The Jazz Galerie, Oxfordstr. 24 (tel. 63 93 24), becomes a concert hub nearly every night. Cover for concerts DM10-20, for discos DM5. On concert nights opens at 8pm, while the action starts up around 9:15pm. Open 9pm-3am.

Sharon, Oxfordstr. 20-21, is a soul discotheque for those who haven't quite had enough. "What's missin' we got it" is their slogan. If the only thing missin' are strobe lights and a disco ball, then that's good advertising. 21 and over only. Clean clothes required. Cover DM10. Soul and funk Fri.-Sat. 10pm-5am.

Maxim and Kleopatra Discotheque, Maxstr. 18-20 (tel. 65 77 98), is *the* budget traveler's option. Get a load of DJ Ben. Cover DM5. House, soul, funk, and dance groove on Fri. Soul, reggae, hip hop, and house on Sat. Open Fri.-Sat. 10pm-5am.

The Pantheon, Bundeskanzlerplatz (tel. 21 25 21). Even though it's dangerously close to the *Bundeshaus,* the clientele of this popular disco tends to be younger, hipper, and more attractive than your average politician. Open Mon.-Sat. 8pm-3am. Cover DM10.

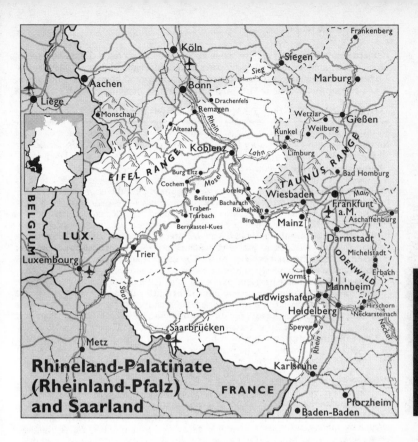

Rhineland-Palatinate (Rheinland-Pfalz)

A trip to the Rhineland-Palatinate to see the castles and wine towns along the Rhine is an obligatory tourist tromp—but with good reason. The region is a visual feast: the Mosel River curls downstream to the Rhine Gorge, a softer shore of castle-backed hills. Trier is a millennia-old collage of sights, while the medieval towns of Worms and Speyer bow down around glorious cathedrals. Politically potent since the days when its electors were the king-makers of the Holy Roman Empire, the Rhineland-Palatinate is now the home of the Federal Republic's chubby leader, Chancellor Helmut Kohl.

■ Koblenz

The etymology of "Koblenz," a corruption of the Latin word for "confluence," illuminates Koblenz's strategic importance. Over the past 2000 years, Rome, the Franks, France, Prussia, and Germany have all fought to control this beautiful city where the Rhein and Mosel converge. Though wars of conquest have died down in recent years, the frenetic activity has not. Trains rattle along both sides of the Rhein, as barges, ringed by flirtatious speedboats, plough through the water. For tourists, the rivers may be shining paths of history and legend, but they are also the conduits of modern German industry. Before reunification, the city served as the Bundesrepublik's largest munitions dump, but the pyrotechnics that light up the sky today are decorative, not destructive, as celebratory sparks illuminate Koblenz during the annual **Rhein in Flammen** (Rhine in Flames) fireworks festival, held in August.

ORIENTATION AND PRACTICAL INFORMATION

Koblenz's *Altstadt* merges with the Rhein and the Mosel, and is connected to the more southerly *Hauptbahnhof* by Löhrstr. To the east, the Pfaffendorfer Brücke (bridge) spans the Rhine, while the Europabrücke and the Balduinbrücke carry the town north across the Mosel.

Tourist Offices: The **main office,** across the street from the train station (tel. 313 04; fax 129 38 00), provides boat schedules and city maps with hotel, restaurant, and pub listings, as well as a simpler walking map. They'll find you a room for a DM2 fee (using the same list they can give you for free). Open May-June 15 Mon.-Fri. 8:30am-6pm, Sat. 11:30am-6pm; June 16-Oct. 15. Mon.-Sat. 8:30am-8:15pm, Sun. 2-7pm; Oct.16-April Mon.-Fri. 8:30am-5pm. The **Konrad-Adenauer-Ufer** branch, next to the docks (tel. 129 16 30), has the same service but with simpler hours and a river view. Open June-Sept. Tues.-Sun. noon-6:25pm. A walking tour leaves from this office June-Oct. Sat. at 2:30pm. Call ahead to arrange for groups or foreign language tours. **Rheinland-Pfalz information office,** Lohrstr. 103-105 (tel. 915 20 40), on the 3rd floor of an office building (or 4th floor, for our American readers) has enough glossy brochures to outrage a *Grüne.* Open Mon.-Tues. and Thurs. 8am-5pm, Wed. and Fri. 8am-3:30pm.

Public Transportation: The only option for public transit in Koblenz—ride the magic bus. 10 main lines bustle you around the city and into the 'burbs for DM1.80-4 per ride. Children's discount 50%. Day pass DM8. Tickets available from the driver. The **Hauptbahnhof, Zentralplatz,** and **Böhr Center** are the bus hubs.

Taxi: Funk Taxi (tel. 330 55). Funk is its own reward. Or go for the subtle elegance of **Bani's Funkmietwagen** (tel. 126 00), a fleet of white Mercedes-Benzes.

Bike Rental: Biking the Rhine and Mosel is more satisfying (and wet) than going it by boat or train. See the tourist office pamphlet *Rund ums Rad.* **Radschlag Fahrrad,** the cheapest, most personable option, has a selection that ranges from one-gear cycles (DM7 per day) to mountain bikes (DM18 per day), tandems, and the *Rikscha,* a 3-wheeled Laff Mobile (DM35 per day). Passport and DM30, DM50, or DM100 deposit, respectively, required. Open April-Jan. 10 Mon.-Fri. 8:30am-noon and 2-6pm, Sat. 9am-1pm; otherwise by appointment. If they fail you, **Fahrrad Franz,** Hohenfelderstr. 7 (tel. 184 78), has full service and air for your tires (open Mon.-Wed. and Fri. 9:30am-6:30pm, Thurs. 9:30am-8pm, Sat. 9am-2pm). **Vélo,** on Konrad-Adenauer-Ufer 1 (tel. 151 02), and **Campingplatz Rhein Mosel** will also outfit you (DM10-13 per day).

Bookstore: Reuffel, Löhrstr. 92 (tel. 30 30 70), has a fine selection of English paperbacks. Novels DM22. Open Mon.-Wed. and Fri. 9am-6:30pm, Thurs. 9am-8:30pm, Sat. 9am-2pm.

Laundromat: Wash that stink right out of your clothes at **Wasch Center,** on the corner of Rizzastr. and Löhrstr. Wash DM6, soap included. Dry DM2 per 15min. Open Mon-Sat. 6am-midnight, last call 11pm.

Pharmacy: Bahnhofs-Apotheke, directly across Bahnhofplatz as you exit the station, posts a list on the door of other pharmacies providing emergency service. Open Mon.-Fri. 8:30am-6:30pm, Sat. 9am-1pm,

Emergency: Police: tel. 110. **Ambulance:** tel. 192 22.

Post Office: Hauptpostamt, to the right of the train station exit, **exchanges currency,** cashes traveler's checks, and has plenty of telephone booths. Open Mon.-Fri. 8am-6pm, Sat. 8am-noon. Limited services rendered Mon.-Fri. 7-8am and 6-8pm, Sat. 7-8am and noon-4pm, Sun. 10am-1pm. **Postal Code:** 56068.

Telephone Code: 0261.

ACCOMMODATIONS AND CAMPING

Koblenz's *Judendherberge* is blessed by one of the most scenic locations of any hostel in Germany—even folks who can afford to stay elsewhere want to sleep here. The hostel surmounts the city, with all of Koblenz laid out below. The difficult trek deters practically no one, so call a day or two ahead. If the hostel is full, they'll send you straight back down the hill with your heavy pack. Some of the hotels nearer to the station offer inexpensive rooms, but they also go quickly—always call ahead.

Jugendherberge Koblenz (HI), in the castle (tel. 737 37; fax 70 27 07). Mailing address: Festung Ehrenbreitstein, 56077 Koblenz. Housing both a youth hostel and a museum, the *Festung* is a worthy destination for any visitor. Unfortunately, until very recently, it was also a crucial **military installation;** "easy access" was the furthest thing from its designers' minds. Fortunately, *Let's Go*'s crack intelligence squad has found breaches in the fortress's defenses for soldiers of every rank and budget. To storm the fortress, five options are available: **Generals:** Take bus #7 or 8 from the main station to Ehrenbreitstein *Bahnhof* (DM3). From here the *Sesselbahn* (chairlift) will carry your shiny stars and fat purse to the fortress. This is by far the least grueling option, if you can spare the cash (Mon.-Oct. daily 9am-5:50pm; DM8 round-trip, DM5 one way). Alternatively, take your staff car up Bergstr. to the lot. **Privates** (basically anyone with a big pack and DM3): Ride the bus with the generals, then continue north and take the main footpath on your right, a sloping 15-min. walk. **Frogmen:** From the *Altstadt*, a ferry will carry you across (Mon.-Fri. 7am-6:55pm, Sat.-Sun. 8:30am-6:55pm; DM1.50; boats leave when they are full). **Ninjas:** Sneak aboard the #9 bus and ride to "Neudorf/Bergstr." (DM2.80). Creep up Bergstr. to infiltrate the fortress from the rear. The steep hike levels out, no problem for a lightly-encumbered shadow warrior like you. Follow the signs. Even though you've (hopefully) called ahead, the hostel won't know you're rooming until it's too late. **Cabin Boy:** Blew your last *Deutschmark* in port, eh worm? Walk past the information office onto Markenbilchenweg, turn left onto Mainzer Str. then right on Rizzastr.; cross the Pfaffendorfer Brücke and bear left on Brückenstr. Keep to your left until you find the pedestrian path along the right side of the river, and when the path veers right for the second time, cross under the train tracks to take Hofstr. north until the footpath appears on the right (1hr.). Now buy yourself a beer—after the 1-hr. hike, you've earned it, sailor. Hostel reception hours are sporadic, so call ahead. Location is incredible, but the 4- to 10-bed rooms are standard issue. No lockers. Curfew 11:30pm. DM21, over 26 DM25. Sheets DM5. Breakfast included.

Hotel Jan-van-Werth, Van-Werth-Str. 9 (tel. 365 00; fax 365 06). This classy family-run establishment is the best value in Koblenz. From the station, walk through Bahnhofsplatz to Emil-Schuller-Str. up on your left. At the end take a left onto Hohenzollernstr. and walk left (5min.) onto Van-Werth-Str. Reception open daily 6:30am-10pm. Singles DM35, with shower and toilet DM63. Doubles DM85, with shower and toilet DM100-120. Gummi-bears on every pillow. Breakfast included.

Hotel Garni Weinand, Weißernonnengasse 4-6 (tel. 324 92), has unpretentious, comfortable rooms. Walk left from the *Hauptbahnhof* on Löhrstr., left on Altengrabenstr., and cross the street onto Weißergasse; Weißernonnergasse is the first street on the left. The shower stall is in the middle of the hall, but there are sinks in the rooms. Singles DM32. Doubles DM64. Breakfast included.

Zur Kaul, Heffensteinstr. 64 (tel. 752 56; fax 768 72), is a bit shoddy, but friendly and a bargain. Take a right up Humboldtstr.; the second left is Helfensteinstr. The bus stop is "Kaputzinerplatz." Single DM30. Doubles DM60.

Camping: Campingplatz Rhein-Mosel, Am Neuendorfer Eck. (tel. 827 19), across the Mosel from the Deutsches Eck. A ferry journeys across the river during the day (DM0.60). Reception open daily 7am-1pm and 2-10pm. DM5.50 per person, DM4.50-6 per tent. Open April-Oct. 15.

FOOD AND NIGHTLIFE

Restaurant-Café Dubrovnik, Obere Löhrstr. 91 (tel. 129 50), is a 10-min. walk to the left of the train station on Löhrstr. Decor is very elegant and very *Miami Vice.*

Daily specials (noon-3pm) are a steal (DM10-18 for soup and entree); evening dining is pricier, but quality is consistently good. Open daily 9am-midnight.

Salat Garten, where Casinostr. becomes Gymnasiumstr. in the *Altstadt.* The arteries (and taste buds) cry out for the vegetarian wonders that crop up here. Good salad bar. Self-service keeps prices low (daily specials DM8). Open Mon.-Wed. and Fri. 11am-7pm, Thurs. 11am-9pm, Sat. 11am-3pm.

Altes Brauhaus, Braugasse 4 (tel. 15 10 01). Wide selection of hearty, traditional German dishes for around DM12. Home brew between meals. Open Mon.-Sat. 10:30am-10pm. Kitchen open 11:30am-2:30pm and 5:30-10pm.

Tatort, Münzplatz 15 (tel. 42 19), occasionally turns Münzplatz into a ground for local bands. Otherwise it's a popular rock 'n' roll bar. Open daily 4pm-late.

No Name, Burgstr. 10, premiers dance parties (including house and soul) Tues.-Thurs. 7pm-1am. Non-alcoholic drinks DM1, alcoholic DM2.

SIGHTS AND ENTERTAINMENT

The focal point of Koblenz is the **Deutsches Eck** (German Corner). A peninsula at the confluence of the Rhine and Mosel, it purportedly witnessed the birth of the German nation when the Teutonic Order of Knights settled here in 1216. The tremendous, somewhat creepy **Mahnmal der Deutschen Einheit** (Monument to German Unity) stands on the right, commemorating a rather different sort of union. Erected in 1897, it stands in tribute to Kaiser William I for forcibly reconciling the internal conflicts of the German Empire (though the Kaiser actually played second fiddle to the political mastermind Chancellor Bismarck). The 14m-high equestrian statue of the Kaiser which once topped the monument was toppled in 1945. In a move that raised questions about German aesthetic sensibilities, not to mention resurgent nationalism, the statue was replaced by a duplicate on September 2, 1993.

Vibrant beauty of a less fervent sort can be found in Koblenz's many churches; most were miraculously restored after WWII. The **Florinskirche** towers shine with bursts of vibrant color (open daily 11am-5pm; free). The curvaceous **Herz-Jesu-Kirche,** on the corner of Moselring and Löhrstr., has free organ music the first Wednesday of every month at 5:45pm. In the north end of the city's pedestrian zone is the **Liebfrauenkirche,** built on the ruins of a hall from the fourth century. Its oval Baroque towers, emerald and sapphire stained glass, and intricate ceiling latticework are stunning; the choir windows document the role of women in the *Heilsgeschichte* (Passion and Salvation of Christ). The **Florinskirche** inside can be traced back to the 12th century. It was used by Napoleon as a military depot, but beautifully preserved windows and frescoes endure from the 13th century. Also part of the Liebfrauenkirche is the **St.-Kastor-Kirche,** rebuilt after World War II and stylistically refined to eliminate eleven centuries of ornamental accumulations. The **Jesuitenkirche,** on the *Marktplatz,* is a strange symbiosis of a modern interior and a masterful *Rheinisch* façade from the early 17th century. The cool darkness of the interior is interrupted only by light that streams in through the blazing rosette window (open daily 7am-6pm). Behind the *Mahnmal,* in the beautiful, unassuming **Blumenhof** (flower garden), lurks more blatant national braggadocio, though this time not on the Germans' part. Napoleon erected the **fountain** to commemorate his "certain impending victory" in the Russian campaign. The Russians, after routing the French army, added the mocking inscription "seen and approved."

All of this ground-level viewing got you down? The best way to see Koblenz is from above, by proudly straddling the battlements of **Festung Ehrenbreitstein,** a fortress that in Prussian days was the largest in Europe; it was used by the Prussians to accommodate the French troops stationed in Koblenz. (For more on reaching the fortress, see Jugendherberge Koblenz, p. 127.) In the valley below the fortress, at Wambachstr. 204, just off Hofstr., there's a typically German example of cultural obsession: a **museum** (tel. 129 25 02) in the house where **Beethoven's mother** was born (open April 15-Oct. 14. Thurs.-Sat. 11am-4pm, Sun. noon-4pm; call for appointments in the winter; free). All but the most ardent Ludwig aficionados will be disappointed by the few letters on display.

Both the **Kurfürstliches Schloß,** next to the Rhein Bridge, and the **Alte Burg,** next to the Baldwin Bridge, are castles now used for administrative purposes; they are best seen as you walk along the docks outside. Another sight best seen from afar is the **Schängelbrunnen,** a statue of a boy, standing defiantly near the *Rathaus,* who spews water on passers-by and drives kids into frenzied glee. **Theater** information and tickets are available at the *Rathaus* box office (tel. 129 28 40). Inquire about student discounts (open Tues.-Fri. 11am-1pm and 2-4pm, Sat. 11am-1pm).

MUSEUMS

Museum Ludwig im Deutschherrenhaus, Danziger Freiheit 1 (tel. 30 40 40), is right behind the *Mahnmal.* The bias is toward contemporary French artists, but expect anything and everything from the revolving collection, including Picasso and Christo, the *Reichstag* Wrapper himself. Admission DM5, students DM3. Open Tues.-Wed. and Fri.-Sat. 11am-5pm, Thurs. 11am-8pm, Sun. 11am-6pm.

Mittelrheinisches Museum, next to the Florinskirche, contains four floors filled with a little bit of everything, from 16th-century sculpture to 19th-century painting. And they've got Klimt, too. Good special exhibits. Admission DM5, students DM3. Open Tues. and Thurs.-Sat. 11am-5pm, Wed. 11am-8pm, Sun. 11am-6am.

Landesmuseum Koblenz, Hohe Ostfront, in Festung Ehrenbreitstein (tel. 970 30). A dangerous combination of cannons, wine, tobacco, and autos document the region's industrial past. Not as exciting as it could be (no live ammo or tasty samples), but free. Open mid-March-mid-Nov. daily 9am-12:30pm and 1-5pm.

Mittelrheinisches Postmuseum, Friedrich-Ebert-Ring 14-20 (tel. 128 20 60), in the Oberpostdirektion building. Enter on Friedrichstr. The evolution of stamps, mailboxes, and telephones from the days when mailmen carried swords. Also documents the unholy alliance between the German post and telephone systems. Admission free. Open through rain, hail, sleet, and snow Mon.-Thurs. 10am-4pm.

Rhein Museum Koblenz, Charlottenstr. 53a (tel. 70 34 50). Take bus #9 or 10 to "Charlottenstr." A private museum devoted to all things *Rheinisch,* including old boats, engines, fish, and even an old captain's seat. Four floors of marine history. A good double-header with Beethoven's mother's house. Admission DM4, children DM3. Open daily 10am-5pm.

■ The Rhine Gorge

> At present, the sun and moon alone cast their light upon these old buildings famed in story and gnawed by time, whose walls are falling stone by stone into the Rhine, and whose history is fast fading into oblivion. O noble tower! O poor, paralyzed giants! A steamboat packed with travelers now spews its smoke in your faces!
>
> —Victor Hugo

Though the Rhine River runs all the way from Switzerland to the North Sea, the Rhine of the imagination exists only in the 80km of the Gorge that stretch north of Mainz to Bonn. As the river rolls out to the sea, treacherous whirlpools and craggy shores surround the castles of aristocrats. This is the Rhine of sailors' nightmares, poets' dreams, and the rhetorical storms of nationalism. From the famed Lorelei Cliffs, legendary sirens lured passing sailors to their deaths on the sharp rocks below. Heinrich Heine immortalized the spot with his 1823 poem *"Die Lorelei,"* but he can hardly take sole credit for the literary resonances felt all along this river. The renown of Rhine wines from the hillside vineyards have inspired many a lesser illusion. Two different train lines (one on each bank) traverse this fabled stretch, but the line on the west bank that runs between Koblenz and Mainz sticks closer to the water and provides superior views. If you're willing to put up with lots of tourists, the best way to see the sights is probably by **boat.** The **Köln-Düsseldorfer (KD) Line** makes the complete Mainz-Koblenz cruise three times per day during the summer, while more frequent excursions travel along shorter stretches of the river (see Cologne: Practical Information, p. 83).

RÜDESHEIM

From the other side of the Rhein, Rüdesheim is a romantic's dream come true. The terraced vineyards stretch steeply up from the river, while a checkerboard of green lifts the heart. Across the river, however, the cruel goddess of commercialism has found a home; Rüdesheim's location in the heart of the Rheingau wine-producing region has made the town a formidable tourist magnet, and you can now almost set your watches by the hordes of tour buses that pour into the valley when they roll out the first barrels at 9am. The picturesque 12th-century **Brömserburg Fortress,** Rheinstr. 2, like the rest of Rüdesheim, has succumbed to Bacchanalian excess: it's now a **wine museum** (tel. 23 48) just five minutes from the train station along Rheinstr. The fortress boasts all important styles of architecture, from the Middle Ages through the Renaissance, Baroque, Rococo, Empire, Biedermeyer, *Jugendstil,* and Art Deco periods. (Open mid-March to mid-Nov. daily 9am-6pm. Last admission 5:15pm. Admission DM5, students and children DM3. Tour with wine tasting and souvenir glass DM8; tour with 4 tastings and same glass DM12. Call ahead.) Servings are available along the nearby **Drosselgasse,** a tiny alley lined solely with souvenir shops. Up Drosselgasse to the left, you'll find signs for **Siegfrieds Mechanisches Musikkabinett,** Oberstr. 29 (tel. 492 17; fax 45 87), the first German museum for automatic musical instruments and one of the largest collections of music boxes and player pianos in the world; short performances of the displayed instruments are available. (Open mid-March-mid-Nov. 10am-10pm. Obligatory tours leave every 15min.; English tours available. Admission DM8, students DM4.) The **Mittelalterliches Foltermuseum** (medieval torture museum), Grabenstr. 13 (tel. 475 10), is devoted to devices prisoners endured for salvation of their souls. Eighty instruments, as well as paintings, drawings, and etchings are on display (open May-Sept. daily 10am-6pm; Oct.-April Sat.-Sun. 10am-6pm; admission DM6, children DM3).

The **Niederwalddenkmal,** a 38-m tall monument crowned by the unnervingly nationalistic figure of *Germania* wielding a 1400-kg sword, looms high above the town. Erected to commemorate the establishment of the ill-fated Second Reich in 1871, the central frieze features winged emblems of war and peace flanking legions of 19th century aristocrats pledging their loyalty to the Kaiser. For the heavy of foot and purse, the bronze piece of allegorical extremism is best reached by the **chairlift** *(Seilbahn)* from the top of Christofelstr. that carries 1200 people every hour (open mid-March to mid-Nov. daily 9:30am-5pm; DM5.50, children, large dogs, and luggage DM3; round-trip DM8). To reach the chairlift, take the left directly before the tourist office (10min.). By foot, take Oberstr. from the station to the footpath leading uphill.

The **tourist office** *(Verkehrsamt),* Rheinstr. 16 (tel. 29 62; fax 34 85), is located right along the river. It offers walking-tour pamphlets and a room-finding service (10% fee; cheapest rooms DM40-50). It also exchanges money, cashes traveler's checks (no commission), and houses the **AmEx office** (open Mon.-Fri. 8:30am-6:30pm, Sat. 1:30-5:30pm, Sun. 2-6pm; Nov.-April Mon.-Fri. 8:30am-6:30pm). The **post office,** on Rheinstr., between the train station and the tourist office, also exchanges money (open Mon.-Fri. 8:30-11:30am and 2:30-5pm, Sat. 8:30-11:30am). The **telephone code** is 06722.

The **Jugendherberge (HI),** am Kreuzberg (tel. 27 11; fax 609 13 14), is in the vineyards high above the town, but the 25-min. walk through flowers, vines, and silence is worth the climb. Call ahead—they're often booked solid. From the train station, walk down Rheinstr. and make a left on any street that catches your fancy, up to and including Löhrstr. At Oberstr., turn right and bear left at the fork onto Germaniastr.; follow it to Kuhweg and the "Jugendherberge" signs. (Reception open 8-9am, 1-2pm, and 5-11:30pm. Curfew 11:30pm. DM21, over 26 DM25.60. Members only. Breakfast included. Sheets DM6.) **Campingplatz am Rhein** (tel. 25 28) has prime riverside real estate for those with portable roofs. From the train station, walk past town while hugging the Rhine, past the **Asbachbad** (swimming pool) and you'll run into the campsite. (Reception open 8am-10pm; DM6.40 per person, children DM4.20, tents DM6.10-8.20. Open May-Sept.)

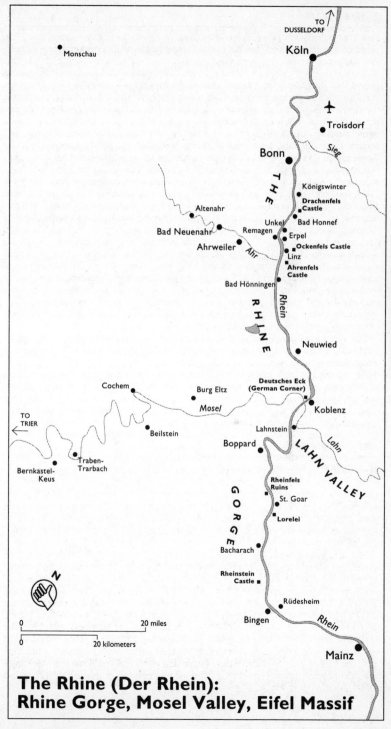

The Rhine (Der Rhein):
Rhine Gorge, Mosel Valley, Eifel Massif

BINGEN

On an island near the village of Bingen, downstream from Rüdesheim, the **Mäuseturm** (Mouse Tower) leans over the winding Rhine. According to legend, Archbishop (and arch-villain) **Hatto II** of Mainz was challenged by starving peasants who demanded the food he was hoarding in a famine. He proceeded to lock them up in a barn and set it on fire. Hearing their shrieks of pain, the sadistic Hatto cackled, "listen to my mice squeaking." Suddenly, a horde of mice rushed out of the barn, chased him into the tower, and ate him alive. Unfortunately, the tower can be visited only twice a year on a tour announced in the local newspaper. The town's main daytime attraction, **Burg Klopp** (tel. 149 86), is five minutes from the **tourist office** through maze-like streets (follow red mice signs). Besides the castle café, affordable only for royalty, Burg Klopp features the **Heimatmuseum,** displaying third-century Roman milestones and a view from the top of its tower (open April-Oct. Tues.-Sun. 9am-noon, 2-5pm; admission DM1, students and children DM0.50).

The **tourist office,** Rheinkaistr. 21 (tel. 18 42 05; fax 162 75), finds rooms for a DM3 fee (singles start at DM31) and offers a wealth of information on the 20km of hiking and biking trails that encircle the town. From the *Hauptbahnhof,* stick as close as possible to the tracks as they head east to Rheinkaistr. or get off at the Bingen station and head towards town for five minutes (open Mon.-Fri. 9am-6pm, Sat. 9am-1pm; Dec.-March Mon.-Fri. 9am-4pm). Bingen offers the best access to the Rhein Gorge, with two **train** stations, good connections to Frankfurt and Koblenz, and docks from which several brands of **ferries** depart; ferries go to Rüdesheim every 40 minutes (one way DM1.60, round-trip DM2.80; bikes, dogs, and strollers DM0.80). The ubiquitous **Kölner-Düsseldorfer** ferry sails to Koblenz (DM64.20) and Bacharach (DM21.40). For a **taxi,** call 356 49. The **Rettungsdienst** (ambulance) can be reached by dialing 427 47. The **telephone code** is 06721.

To get to the **Jugendherberge Bingen-Bingerbrück,** Herterstr. 51 (tel. 321 63; fax 340 12), follow the signs from the *Hauptbahnhof* across the bridge and bear left (15min.). The hostel boasts a great view of the shore. (Curfew 10pm. DM19, over 26 DM26.60. With 3 meals DM29.60. Breakfast included. Sheets DM5.) Everything pales in comparison to **Pallazzo,** Bingen's renowned **mega-disco.** The club's pulsating lasers and music attract hostelers all along the Gorge. The strategy is to leave at curfew, dance 'til five, and return to the hostel for breakfast. The disco is right on the river—you can't miss it (open Thurs.-Sun. at 8pm).

BACHARACH

If you speak a little German and know your Roman mythology, the name says it all: Altar to Bacchus. Natives and barbarians prostrate themselves to the god of **wine** and revelry in the town's numerous **Weinkeller** (wine cellars) and **Weinstuben** (wine pubs); see the tourist office (below) for detailed listings. View the source of the precious liquid from the **Wernerkapelle,** a red sandstone chapel that took 140 years to build (1294-1434) but only a few hours to destroy in the War of Palatine Succession in 1689; it's a short climb up the steps of the Gothic **Peterskirche.**

The **tourist office,** Overstr. 1 (tel. 12 97; fax 31 55), in the *Rathaus,* a 3-minute walk up to the right from the station, provides maps of hiking trails (open Mon.-Fri. 10am-noon and 3-5:15pm, Sat. 10am-1pm). A further 15-minute walk uphill from the Wernerkapelle ends at **Jugendherberge Stahleck (HI)** (tel.12 66; fax 26 84), a gorgeous 12th-century castle that hosts 35,000 overnight visitors every year and boasts a fabulous view of the Rhine Gorge. They are usually fully booked by 6pm, but the manager rarely turns guests away once they make the steep ascent. Sometimes he puts guests on the floor of the Knight's Hall, where moonlight filters silently through stained-glass windows onto sleeping faces. (Curfew 10pm. DM21, over 26 DM26. Breakfast included. Sheets DM5. Dinner DM9.) For those growing weary of too many uphill treks, **Haus Dettmar,** on Overstr. 8., is clean and right in town. (Singles DM30. Doubles DM50.) Ten minutes south of town is **Campingplatz Bacharach** (tel. 17 52), where you can camp for DM7 per person, DM5 per tent. The price is right at the uniquely named **Cafe Restaurant,** on Overstr. 40, where a three-course meal can be had for DM5-17. The **telephone city code** is 06743.

LORELEI CLIFFS AND CASTLES

"Art is a temptation, a seduction, a *Lorelei*," wrote H.L. Mencken. The mythic distortion of the Rhine peaks along the **Cliffs of the Lorelei.** This section of the river, with its switchbacks and boulders, was so difficult to navigate that a sailors' song developed about a siren *(Lorelei)* who seduced sailors with her intoxicating song, disastrously distracting them. Heinrich Heine's lyric *"Lorelei"* is so much of a part of German cultural history that, even when works by Heine (a converted Jew) were banned under the Third Reich, the poem was still published, attributed to "Anonymous." Jürgen Werner penned a brilliant parody of Heine's poem, entitled *"Die Lorelei 1973,"* protesting the pollution of the Rhine by the German chemical industry. These cliffs are remarkably similar to those just up and downstream, but the view almost lives up to the romance. Climb the marked path that begins 10 minutes south of the village of **St. Goarshausen,** on the east bank of the Rhine.

Directly above St. Goarshausen the fierce **Burg Katz** (Castle Cat) eternally stalks its prey, the smaller **Burg Maus** (Castle Mouse). Fortunately, the mouse hides away upstream in the Wellmich district of Goarshausen. About an hour by foot from the station, the smaller castle keeps eternally vigilant with daily hour-long displays of **Raubvogeldressur,** featuring eagles, falcons and other scary carnivorous birds, circling and sometimes landing on tourists' shoulders (11am, 2:30, and 4:30pm).

Two minutes away from the Lorelei cliffs the **Tuner-und-Jugendheim Loreley** (tel. 26 19; fax 81 89), a hostel, lures travelers in with friendly ditties of hip hostelers, only to drown them in crashing waves of school children. It boasts a picnic area, sports facilities, and an open-air stage nearby. (Curfew 10pm. DM18.50, over 26 DM20. Breakfast included.) Across the river, **St. Goar** boasts a standard **Jugendherberge (HI),** at Bismarckberg 17 (tel. (06741) 388; fax 28 69), 10 minutes from the train station. Hop on the car ferry (DM1.50) to get there. (Reception open 5-6pm, 7-8pm, and at 10pm. Curfew 10pm. DM19, over 26 DM24.40. Breakfast included. Sheets DM6.) Turn left and hug the Rhein to reach the **Campingplatz Loreleystadt** (tel. (06771) 25 92; fax (02137) 49 98), an eight-minute walk from the *Bahnhof.* (DM7, children DM4, dogs DM3). The **telephone code** is 06771.

REMAGEN

After Koblenz, the castles stop appearing around every corner, and the landscape mellows. Just upstream from the confluence of the Rhine and Ahr Rivers is Remagen. In March 1945, Nazi engineers were busy demolishing historic bridges across the Rhein to slow the Allied advance, when the Americans, who were preparing to ford the Rhine, unexpectedly found the bridge at Remagen intact. Under heavy fire, a company of American troops crossed the bridge—even though it was laden with explosives—and held off a German counterattack until the crossing could be secured. The event inspired Ken Hechler's popular novel *The Bridge at Remagen.* The numerous futile attempts by the Germans to destroy the bridge resulted in the court-martial and, later, the execution of four soldiers, who were charged with treason, even though the "Miracle at Remagen" was more likely the result of technological failure. The German and American governments have acknowledged the site's significance with monuments. They were not as generous with their funds; Remagen Mayor Hans Kuerten had to sell souvenir-sized chunks of the now-demolished bridge to fund the **Friedensmuseum** (Museum of Peace) that inhabits the restored bridge tower (tel. 218 63). Poems, letters, pictures, and artifacts inhabit the many rooms and tell the bridge's history (open March 7-Oct. daily; admission DM2.50, students DM1). Despite Kuerten's efforts, the grim blackened bridge ruins prove a much more potent warning against war. To reach the museum, take any street down to the Rhine, turn right on the promenade, and keep going. To get to the *Marktplatz* from the train station, follow Drususstr. and turn right onto Bachstr.

RHINELAND-PALATINATE

A few houses down from the tourist office lies the small **Römisches Museum** (Roman Museum), at Kirchstr. 9. Tickets are copies of the worthless currency printed during the hyperinflation of 1921. Excavations underneath the 16th-century chapel revealed Roman columns that are now publicly admired (open March-Oct. Wed.-Sun. 3-5pm; admission DM2, students DM1, children under 14 free). Heading west towards the Apollinariskirche, admire the quiet old **St. Peter and Paul** church and nearby 12th-century Romanesque gate. The jewel of Remagen remains the gorgeous mountainside **Apollinariskirche,** whose distinctive Gothic spires can be seen both from the Rhine and the town center. Nearly every interior surface is covered with shining Nazarean frescos; hike uphill on Bergstr. and visit the serene crypt.

The **tourist office,** right on the *Marktplatz* at Kirchstr. 6 (tel. 20 10), hands out maps and books rooms (starting at DM30) for a 10% fee (open Mon.-Thurs. 8:30am-noon and 2-4pm, Fri. 8:30am-noon). To reach the **Campingplatz Goldene Meile** (tel. 222 22) head east (right as you face the Rhine) on Marktstr. As it becomes Alte Str. and Goethestr., turn left at the sign (15min.; reception open daily 7:30am-noon and 2-6pm; DM7.50 per person, children 6-18 DM6.50; DM6-13 per tent.) If you're feeling sweaty, head to the swimming pool/aspiring water park, **Allwetterbad Remagen,** up the road toward Goethestr. The **telephone code** is 02642.

NONNENWERTH AND DRACHENFELS

At the northernmost end of the Rhine Gorge, between Bad Honnef and Königswinter, the Rhein Gorge is so richly seasoned with legend and beauty it's difficult to believe it's only minutes away from the blandest national capital in the world. The ivy-covered archway, high above the Rhein directly west of Bad Honnef, is all that remains of the **Rolandsbogen** castle, perhaps Europe's greatest monument to sexual frustration. Legendary hero Roland returned from the battle at Roncevalles to find that his wife, upon the (greatly exaggerated) news of his death, had taken a vow of chastity and retreated to the convent on **Nonnenwerth Island.** He channeled his sexual energy into building the **Rolandsbogen,** so he could catch occasional glimpses of her. Today, too late for Roland but convenient for modern convent peepers, ferries, departing from Königswinter, run from the east to west banks, and from the west bank to the island (1½hr.). Call (0228) 63 63 68 for more info.

The cultured tourist making his way past all the gummi dragons here might be inclined to sniff haughtily. But the origins (and the view) of the **Castle Drachenfels** are nothing to snuffle at. "The castled crag of Drachenfels frowns o'er the wide and winding Rhine," penned Lord Byron in "Childe Harold's Pilgrimage." In the *Nibelungenlied,* Siegfried slew a *Drachen* (dragon) here and bathed in its blood, which would have made him invincible if a leaf on his back hadn't left a vulnerable spot. Imbibing enough of the local *Drachenblut* (dragon blood) wine, cultivated on the mountain where the dragon lived, produces a similar feeling of invincibility; *Let's Go* does not recommend picking fights with any dragons in this condition, or in any condition. The ruins and the incredible view can be reached by U-Bahn #66 from Bonn and from **Königswinter.** Simply follow Drachensfelsstr. It's officially a 45-minute walk, but Siegfried wannabes can hustle up in under 25 minutes. The less heroic can take the **Drachenfelsbahn,** Drachenfelsstr. 53 (tel. (02223) 920 90), a railway leading to the top (DM10 up, DM9 down, DM12 round-trip; children ages 4-13 DM5, DM6, and DM7, respectively; dogs DM1). There are also donkey and carriage rides to the top. The **Nibelungshalle,** where the dragon once munched on tasty young virgins, is now a **reptile zoo** and **museum** (tel. (02223) 24150) relating the saga, complete with a 13m mock dragon. The museum demands no virgins, but the price is clear nonetheless (admission DM5, children DM4; open May 15-Nov. 15 daily 10am-7pm). Between the ruin and the museum, **Schloß Drachenburg** (tel. 261 55) reveals its ornate, exquisitely maintained 19th-century interior by way of hourly tours (April-Oct. Tues.-Sun. 11am-6pm; admission DM3, rug-rats DM2).

The Königswinter **tourist office** is at Drachenfelsstraße 11 (open Mon.-Wed. 11am-1:30pm and 2:30-5pm, Thurs.-Fri. 10am-1:30pm and 2:30-6pm, Sat. 11am-1:30pm and 2:30-5pm). Bad Honnef's **Jugendherberge,** Selhoferstr. 106 (tel. (02224) 713 00; fax

792 26), provides a convenient base to explore the mythical surroundings. From the train station, head up and left, and follow the "Stadtmitte" signs onto Menzenberger-str.; when this ends, go left on Linzerstr., and Selhoferstr. will be the first (unmarked) right. (Reception open 9-11am and 6-10pm. Curfew 11:30pm. DM21.50, over 26 DM26. Breakfast included. Sheets DM6.)

■ Mainz

Mainz may have become big and modern as the capital of the Rhineland-Palatinate, but the monumental dome and maze of narrow streets in the *Altstadt* are still the center of the city. Mainz combines modernity and antiquity as successfully as any German city, as concrete and cobblestone mesh seamlessly to carry people of every stamp through the vibrant city proper. Mainzers are known to be more friendly than their bureaucratic neighbors (we won't name names). To make the maze of Mainz maneuverable, streets running parallel to the Rhine sport blue nameplates, while streets running perpendicular to the river bear red ones. At the heart of Mainz lies the colossal sandstone **Martinsdom,** the resting place of the archbishops of Mainz, whose extravagant tombs line the walls (open Mon.-Fri. 9am-6:30pm, Sat. 9am-4pm, Sun. 12:45-3pm and 4-5pm; Oct.-March Mon.-Fri. 9am-5pm, Sat. 9am-4pm, Sun. 12:45-3pm; free). The adjacent **Dom Museum** houses artifacts dating from the beginning of the Holy Roman Empire. (Open Mon.-Wed. and Fri. 10am-4pm, Thurs. 10am-5pm, Sat. 10am-2pm. Free. Special exhibits DM4, students and tots DM1.)

Behind the *Dom,* the *Altstadt* stretches for a few blocks in and around Augustiner-str. On a hill several blocks to the south, in the opposite direction from the river, stands the Gothic **Stephanskirche,** notable for its stunning set of stained-glass windows created by the Russian artist-in-exile **Marc Chagall** in the eight years prior to his death in 1984. On a sunny day, the window bathes the church in an eerie blue light (open daily 10am-noon and 2-5pm). Favorite son Johannes Gutenberg, the father of movable type, is immortalized at the **Gutenberg Museum,** Liebfrauenplatz 5 (tel. 12 26 44), along with his most important creations. The museum contains woodcuts, lithographs, a variety of early printing presses, and some of the first printed books in the world, including several **Gutenberg Bibles.** (Open Tues.-Sat. 10am-6pm, Sun. 10am-1pm. Admission DM5, students and children DM2.50, free on Sun.). Near the museum, the **Experimental Print Shop,** at Fischtorstr. 2 (tel. 12 26 86), lets visitors try their luck at Gutenberg's craft by setting and printing their own designs (open Mon.-Fri. 10am-5pm; free, but call ahead). North of the Gutenberg Museum, on Rhein-straße, is the **Brückenturm-Galerie der Stadt Mainz**—a haven for contemporary art (open Tues.-Fri. 11am-6pm, Sat.-Sun. 11am-2pm).

North of the *Marktplatz* along Schurterstraße from the *Dom,* right on Christoph-straße, lies the **Pfarrkirche St. Cristoph,** a thought-provoking illustration of several centuries of history. The site of Gutenberg's baptism, the church was seriously damaged in World War II; the former tower is still used for services, but the main body is a ruin supported by concrete pillars, which seem to sprout from the bed of greenery within. Along the river near the Theodor-Heuss-Brücke rests the **Kurfürstliches Schloß,** former palace of the archbishopric and home to the **Römisch-Germanisches Museum's** smallish collection of Roman-era miscellany (open Tues.-Sun. 10am-6pm; free). A more comprehensive collection of art and archeology, including a Judaica division and enormous Roman arches, awaits in the **Landesmuseum,** up the street at Große Bleiche 49-51 (open Tues. 10am-8pm, Wed.-Sun. 10am-5pm; free).

The **tourist office,** Bahnhofstr. 15 (tel. 28 62 10; fax 286 21 55), down the street opposite the train station, has sightseeing maps and reserves rooms for DM5, but singles start at DM50 and blast into the stratosphere (open Mon.-Fri. 9am-6pm, Sat. 9am-1pm). The **Köln-Düsseldorfer Ferries** (tel. 22 45 11; fax 23 69 39) dock in Mainz and depart from the docks across from the ultramodern *Rathaus.* Purchase tickets to dance, theater, and concerts (DM12-25) at the **Mainzer Kammerspiele,** Emmerich-Joseph-Str. 13 (tel. 22 50 02; fax 22 50 04), off Schillerplatz (open Tues.-Fri. noon-

6pm). The **post office,** 55116 Mainz, is down Bahnhofstr. from the station (open Mon.-Tues. 8am-6pm, Sat. 8am-noon). The **telephone code** is 06131.

Mainz's **Jugendgästehaus (HI),** Otto-Brunfels-Schneise 4 (tel. 853 32; fax 824 22), is in Weisenau at the far right corner of the *Volkspark.* Take bus #1 to "Jugendherberge" or 22 to "Viktorstift." The hostel is large and well-maintained but can be noisy. (Reception open 5-10pm. Lockout midnight-6:30am. DM21, over 26 DM26.20. Doubles DM48.40, over 26 DM53.20. *Gästehaus* rooms with showers and toilets DM25.20, double DM34.50. Breakfast included. Sheets DM5.) **Hotel Stadt Coblenz,** Rheinstr. 49 (tel. 22 76 02), has inexpensive, finely furnished rooms near the city center. Take bus #13, 17, or 19 to "Rheingoldhalle."(Singles DM60-65. Doubles DM90, with shower and toilet DM140. Triples DM150. Breakfast included.)

Near the *Dom,* **Ristorante am Brand,** Mailandgasse 3 (tel. 23 61), serves some wicked linguini (DM5-8; open daily 11:30am-2:30pm and 5:30pm-midnight). At the *Uni,* **Taverne Academica** caters to the University crowd, serving cheap food and drinks. Take the bus to "Universität" and make a left (open Mon.-Fri. 11am-midnight, Sat. 11:30am-3pm and 6-11pm). **KUZ** *(Kulturzentrum),* Dagobertstr. 20b (tel. 28 68 60), mixes cultural events and hip crowds, hosting such dance gigs as "Perfect Beat Party" (open Wed. 9pm-3am and Fri. 9pm-4am; Sept.-June also Sat. 9pm-4am). After the city holiday of *Johannistag* in late June, Mainz celebrates **Johannisnacht**—three days of old-fashioned revelry dedicated to Gutenberg himself. Movable type and Bacchanalian revelry do not easily combine, but Mainz manages it in high style.

■ Worms

Once frequented by such Middle Age heavyweights as Charlemagne and Frederick Barbarossa, not much of historical importance has happened in Worms (VUHRMS) since 1521, when Emperor Charles V summoned the Imperial *Diet,* or council, to the city. The "Diet of Worms" sent Martin Luther into exile for refusing to renounce his heretical doctrines, thereby igniting centuries of Catholic-Protestant enmity in Germany. Over the next 300 years, the pious citizens of Worms set to work constructing churches, seven of which lie within a stone's throw of one another in and around the *Altstadt.* Worms is also remembered as the site of the Huns' crushing of the Burgundians in 436 in the battle that inspired the blood-and-guts saga of the *Nibelungenlied.*

Practical Information, and Accommodations The **tourist office,** Neumarkt 14 (tel. 250 45), is across the street from the Dom St. Peter, to the east (open Mon.-Fri. 9am-noon and 2-5pm, Sat. 9am-noon; Nov.-March Mon.-Fri. 9am-noon and 2-5pm). Guided walking **tours** (in German) meet at the south portal of the *Dom* Saturdays at 10am (2hr.; DM2, students DM1). To walk to the **Jugendgästehaus (HI),** Dechaneigasse 1 (tel. 257 80; fax 273 94), follow Bahnhofstr. from the main train station to Andreasstr. and proceed to the south side of the *Dom.* Or take bus #1 to "Domplatz." This large, rarely full, and very comfy hostel has bright two-, four-, and six-bed rooms, each with bath and shower and a majestic staircase. (DM25.50, over 26 DM30. Strict curfew 11:30pm.) **Weinhaus Weis,** Färbergasse 19 (tel. 235 00), has relaxed management and spacious rooms. (Reception generally opens whenever you call them. Singles DM45. Doubles DM75. Breakfast and showers included.) The **telephone code** is 06421.

Food and Entertainment The Worms University **Mensa** is your ticket to cheap food (open March-July and Oct.-Jan. Mon.-Fri. 11:45am-1:45pm). Travelers technically need an ID, but they often get by with language ability or good bluffing. To reach the campus, turn right as you come out of the station, go right across the bridge, walk down Friedrich-Ebert-Str., and turn left on Erenburgerstr. It's a block and a half up on your right, past the U.S. Army barracks. Lots of posters about current entertainment here. In the basement of the building opposite the *Mensa* is the **Taberna,** a groovy little *Studenten Kneipe* (student bar) with a purportedly authentic Kandinsky and a **disco** on Thursday nights. (Disco open 9pm-1am or 3am depending on the crowd. Any student ID will suffice. Taberna open Mon.-Thurs. 3pm-1am.) "Funk" is the watchword at **Ohne Gleich,** Kriemhildenstr. 11 (tel. 231 01), down the street to the right of the train station. This café will make you feel like you've stepped into a Magritte painting. (Banana juice DM3.80. Open Mon.-Thurs. 9am-1am, Fri.-Sat. 9am-2am, Sun. 10am-1am.) The farmer's produce **Markt** radiates at the *Marktplatz* on Monday, Thursday, and Saturday mornings. The Worms open-air **jazz festival** takes place every year in the beginning of July. The **Backfischfest** brings a party of 70,000 people to Worms for nine days beginning the last weekend in August. A **Christmas market** also comes to town the first week of December.

Sights At the north end of the Altstadt is the **Heylshofgarten,** marking the site where Luther appeared before the Diet and stunned its stodgy membership by declaring, "Here I stand, I can do no other" (open 9am-dusk). Inside the garden, the **Kunsthaus Heylshof** is an out-of-the-way-of-package-tours art museum housing a small collection of late Gothic and Renaissance art including Peter Paul Rubens' *Madonna with Child.* (Open Tues.-Sun. 10am-5pm; Oct.-April Tues.-Sat. 2-4pm, Sun. 10am-noon and 2-4pm. Admission DM3, students DM2.) On the edge of the pedestrian zone are the **Lutherplatz,** where students congregate, and the **Lutherdenkmal** (Luther Memorial); both are larger-than-life statues erected in 1868 to commemorate Luther's courageous stand.

   Chief amongst Worms' architectural treasures is the **Dom St. Peter,** a magnificent Romanesque cathedral with a spooky crypt. Let your vampire fantasies run wild, or stand and face the hounds of hell. According to the *Nibelungenlied,* Siegfried's wife Kriemhilde had a spat with her sister-in-law Brunhilde in the square in front of the *Dom.* (Open daily 8am-6pm. Free, but a usurious DM0.50 donation, students DM0.20, is requested.) Worms' other six churches pale in comparison with the majesty of the *Dom;* only the late-Gothic **Liebfrauenkirche,** Liebfrauenring 21 (tel. 442 67), several blocks to the north of the *Altstadt* off Mainzer Str., is noteworthy (open 9am-6pm, Nov.-March 9am-5pm). The vineyards surrounding the church produce the cloying, sweetly lingering *Liebfraumilch* (known in its export variety as "Blue Nun"). Across from the *Dom,* to the south and behind the youth hostel, is the tiny 1200-year-old **Magnuskirche,** the oldest Protestant church in Germany and starting point for the Reformation in Worms (open March-Nov. 10am-6pm).

   The 900-year-old **Heiliger Sand** (Holy Sand), the oldest Jewish cemetery in Europe, is the resting place for rabbis, martyrs, and leaders. The cemetery can be entered through a gate on Willy-Brandt-Ring, just south of Andreasstr. and the main train station. On the opposite end of the *Altstadt,* the area around the **Judengasse** stands as a witness to the thousand-year legacy of Worms' Jewish community, which thrived during the Middle Ages but was wiped out in the Holocaust. Just off Judengasse is the **synagogue** that houses the *yeshiva* of the famous Talmudic commentator Rabbi Shlomo Ben-Yitzhak, better known as Rashi (open May-Oct. daily 10am-noon and 2-5pm; Nov.-April 10am-noon and 2-4pm). Behind the synagogue is the **Judisches Museum** (tel. 85 33 45 and 85 33 70) in the *Raschi-Haus.* A modest collection traces the history of Worms' Jewish community (open Tues.-Sun. 10am-noon and 2-5pm; admission DM3, students DM1.50, free first Sun. of the month).

■ Mannheim

For nearly eight and a half centuries before receiving its town charter, Mannheim was content being a simple fishing village. In 1606, however, history took a step forward when the town became a military outpost at the confluence of the Rhine and Neckar Rivers. In 1720 Mannheim became the capital of the Rhineland-Palatinate when Elector Karl Philipp moved his court to the city. A mere 57 years later the court packed up and marched off to Munich when Elector Karl Theodor decided he didn't like either the Rhein or the Neckar. *Auf Wiedersehen, baby.* In spite of the desertion, the grand buildings which the nobility left behind make this city well-worth a visit. The regimented street plan which the Palatinate Electors designed for Mannheim survives to this day as one of the earliest and most creative examples of urban planning. As a result, Mannheim's street maps look like no other city's in Germany. Frequent trains from Frankfurt and Heidelberg make a jaunt quick and easy.

Orientation Mannheim sits on a peninsula partitioned by the **Kaiserringstraße** (directly in front of the *Hauptbahnhof*); to the west lies the **Innenstadt** ("inner city"), and to the east lies the rest of the city. The *Innenstadt* is divided into a grid of 144 blocks along a central axis, the **Kurpfalzerstraße,** which runs from the center of the *Residenzschloß* northward to the *Kurpfalzerbrücke* (bridge) on the Neckar River. Each block is designated by a letter and a number. Streets to the west of Kurpfalzerstr. are designated by the letters **A** through **K** (running from south to north) while streets to the east are similarly lettered **L** through **U**. The blocks on the central axis are numbered 1; the number of the block increases as you move away from Kurpfalzerstr. The giant grid is bounded by Bismarckstr. to the south, Parkring to the west, Luisenring to the north, and Friedrichsring and Kaiserring to the east. East of Kaiserringstr., streets assume regular names; perhaps the Palatinate electors discovered a more poetic side, or saw that they were running out of letters. Mannheim is only 20 minutes from Heidelberg by train, and 1½ hours from Frankfurt and Stuttgart. This Orientation section was brought to you by the letters **E** and **C**.

Practical Information The **tourist office,** Willy-Brandt-Platz 3 (tel. 10 10 11), a block down directly in front of the main train station, distributes maps (still handy), information on accommodations, and tickets to upcoming events and also serves as a **Mitfahrzentrale** (open Mon.-Fri. 8am-6pm, Sat. 9am-noon). Free 24-hr. **bike rental** for a DM5 deposit is available at ten train stations in the east of town. The *Tag & Nacht* brochure includes a map of the stations. A **laundromat** is on block G7 on the Luisenring side. (Wash DM6. Soap included. Dry DM1. Open daily 6am-11pm, last entry 10pm.) The **post office** is one block east of the main station, easily within sight. *Postlagernde mail* is at counters 10 and 11 (open Mon.-Fri. 8am-6pm).The **telephone code** is 0621.

Accommodations Mannheim's **Jugendherberge (HI),** Rheinpromenade 21 (tel. 82 27 18), is a 10-minute walk from the train station; it serves a marvellous breakfast and is just steps from the vast expanse of park by the Rhine. Walk through the underground passage (towards Gleis 10) and exit at the back of the train station, then take a right, follow Joseph-Kellnerstr., cross the tracks, continue down the street with the park on your right for about a block, and enter at the first official entrance, by the mailbox. (Reception open daily 8:30-9:30am, 1-2pm, 5-6pm, and 7:30-10pm. Curfew 11:30pm. Members only. DM19, over 26 DM24. Breakfast included. Sheets DM5.50.) The next best value is the spotless and conveniently located **Pension Arabella,** block M2, #12 (tel. 230 50), two blocks north of the *Schloß*. (Singles DM40. Doubles DM80. Triples DM100. Breakfast DM5.) **Goldene Gans,** Tattersallstr. 19 (tel. 10 52 77; fax 422 02 60), two blocks northwest of the train station, has its entrance around the corner. Friendly and efficient service in pleasant rooms is marred only by traffic noise, audible in street-side suites. (Reception open Mon.-Sat. 6am-midnight, Sun. 7am-1pm. Phones and sinks in rooms. Hall showers. Singles from DM55. Doubles from DM93. Breakfast included.)

Food and Nightlife The cheapest meals in town are at the government-subsidized **Studentenwerk Mannheim Mensa** (open Mon.-Fri. 11:30am-2pm) and the slightly more expensive adjacent **cafeteria** (open Mon.-Thurs. 8:30am-4pm, Fri. 8:30am-3:45pm). The *Mensa* is located behind the *Residenzschloß* in the southwest corner. An old piano, theater posters, and antique bicycles and clocks fill up **Harlekin,** Kaiserring 40 (tel. 10 33 54), on the corner of Moltkestr. It boasts an extensive menu with most meals under DM13 (open Mon.-Fri. 9am-1am, Sun. 5pm-1am; closed Sat.). **Rick's Café,** N5, #2 (tel. 10 69 58), serves simple meals on an ivy-enclosed terrace, but its specialty is nightlife, with a cover-free **disco**; Wednesday is soul/rap/funk night. (Café open Mon.-Thurs. 9am-1am, Fri.-Sat. 9am-5am, Sun. 10am-1am. Disco open Wed.-Sat. 11pm-3am.) *Ach was muß man oft von bösen Restaurants hören oder lesen!* For relief, eat at **Max and Moritz**, S4, #17-22 (tel. 273 48). *Schnuptiwup!* Salads, soups, and generous entrees are quickly served with a smile for DM10-18. Frequent foreign theme weeks, and cocktail parties (cocktails DM7.50) every Friday and Sat. The decor is a jolly yellow, but those two devilish Katzenjammer Kids are nowhere to be found (open Mon.-Thurs. 10am-1am, Fri.-Sat. 10am-3am, Sun. 10am-midnight; kitchen closes 1hr. before closing time). Butchers, bakers, and grocers gather at the **market** in the square at the intersection of Kurpfalzstr. and Kirchstr. at the center of the city grid (open Tues., Thurs. and Sat. 7am-2:30pm).

Sights To reach the city's emblematic masterpiece, the **Wasserturm** (water tower) and surrounding gardens of **Friedrichsplatz,** walk 10 minutes north from the train station on Kaiserring. Restored true to its original glory in 1956, the elegant sandstone tower topped by a statue of Amphitrite lives up to its billing as "the most beautiful water tower in the world." One block south of the manicured foliage and crystalline fountains of Friedrichsplatz is the **Kunsthalle,** on Friedrichsplatz, a museum surveying art from the mid-19th century to modern times (open Tues.-Wed. and Fri.-Sun. 10am-5pm, Thurs. noon-8pm; admission DM4, students DM2).

Along with a bizarre street-naming scheme, the Palatinate left the giant **Residenzschloß.** The largest palace of the Baroque period, it now houses the **Universität Mannheim.** In the oddly gaudy **Schloßkirche** (tel. 292 28 90), the sleek coffer of the crypt holds Karl Phillip's third wife, Violante von Thurn und Taxis. Even odder, a Masonic symbol (and a post horn) decorates the altar (open Tues.-Sun. 10am-noon and 3-5pm, Nov.-March Sat.-Sun. 10am-noon and 3-5pm; free). The **Reiß Museum** consists of three buildings located around C5, northwest of the *Schloß,* which contain exhibits on archeology and ethnology and natural science (open Tues.-Wed. and Fri.-Sun. 10am-5pm, Thurs. noon-5pm; admission DM4, students DM2, free on Thurs.; special exhibitions have separate entrance fee). Between the museum and the *Schloß* at block A4 stands the **Jesuit Church,** built as a symbol of the Palatinate court's reconversion to Catholicism. The poet Friedrich Hölderlin called it "the most splendid building I have encountered during my travels." This is perhaps poetically licentious, but the church is fantastic (open daily 8am-noon and 2-6:30pm).

On the other side of the *Innenstadt,* several blocks to the northeast of the *Wasserturm,* sprouts the 100-acre **Luisenpark** (tel. 41 00 50; fax 410 05 55). The greenhouses, flower gardens, aviary, zoo, water sports, mini-golf, and frequent afternoon concerts offer something for everyone (open daily 9am-twilight; admission DM4.50, students DM3.50). South of *Luisenpark,* due east of *Friedrichsplatz* on the *Augustanlage,* lies the terrific **Landesmuseum der Technik und Arbeit** (State Museum of Technology and Labor), Museumstr. 1 (tel. 292 47 50; fax 292 47 54).Take the bus to "Friedensplatz," and when Augustonlage branches, take the left branch. In its six stories, connected by tunnels and ramps, the museum covers "250 years of technical and social change and industrialization in Southwest Germany," and offers hands-on exhibits and large, creaky, rusty things. A working waterwheel, printing presses, and BMWs galore (open Tues. and Thurs.-Fri. 9:15am-5pm, Wed. 9:15am-8pm, Sat.-Sun. 10am-5pm; admission DM4, students DM2, families DM6). The Landesmuseum's largest exhibit is floating in the Neckar River—the paddle steamer **Mainz** which sank in 1956. It has since been retrieved from the Rhine's watery depths and now features an exhibit on the history of navigation.

■ Speyer

Speyer's political star rose and fell early. During the reign of the mighty Salian emperors in the 11th century, the town served as a principal meeting place for the Imperial Diets. As the emperors' power waned, Speyer slipped in significance until ultimately the entire city was burned to the ground during the Palatinate War of Succession. By the time the two World Wars rolled around, Speyer didn't merit destruction; its gracefully ramshackle **Altstadt** and several glorious churches, until recently well off the beaten path of mass tourism, were spared from the bombings.

Since its construction in the 12th century, the **Kaiserdom** (Imperial Cathedral) has been the symbol of Speyer. The immense Romanesque cathedral is noted for its main portals flanked by seven statues on each side, recounting the tale of Christ's crucifixion. The crypt under the east end coddles the remains of eight Holy Roman Emperors and their wives (open daily 9am-7pm; Nov.-March daily 9am-5pm; services at 7, 9, 10:30am and 6pm on Sun. and holidays). Just south of the *Dom*, the newly renovated **Historisches Museum der Pfalz,** Domplatz D (tel. 132 50), offers a comprehensive presentation on Palatinate history. The collection includes beautiful and well-preserved artifacts from the 1st to 16th centuries, one of the ostensible highlights being the **oldest bottle of wine in the world**—a slimy leftover from some wild Roman blowout in the 3rd century (open Tues.-Sun. 10am-6pm, Wed. 10am-8pm; DM8, students and children DM5, more for visiting exhibitions). A left down Große Pfaffengasse and a right down the Judengasse alley lead to the **Judenbad.** This Jewish ritual bathhouse (*mikwe*) dates from the 12th century (open April-Oct. Mon.-Fri. 10am-noon and 2-5pm; Sat.-Sun. 10am-5pm; admission DM1.50).

Speyer's main thoroughfare of Maximilianstr. spreads eastward from the *Dom,* culminating in the medieval **Altpörtel.** This former city gateway can be scaled for DM1.50 (open April-Oct. Mon.-Fri. 10am-noon and 2-4pm, Sat.-Sun. 10am-5pm). From the *Altpörtel,* a southward jaunt on Gilgenstr. leads to the **Church of St. Joseph** and its sister across the street, the **Gedächtniskirche.** The latter sends even jaded hearts soaring (open Mon.-Sat. 10am-noon and 2-6pm, Sun. 2-6pm). For those seeking something slightly more up-to-the-minute, the **Technik-Museum-Speyer,** Geibstraße 2 (tel. 788 44 or 670 80; fax 788 11 or 67 08 20), possesses 30,000 cubic meters of trains, planes, and automobiles, as well as an IMAX theater (program hotline tel. 67 08 50) and the "Adventure-simulator." To get there, take the city shuttle to the youth hostel stop. (Museum open daily 9am-6pm. Admission DM12, children DM7. IMAX DM10, children DM7. Combination ticket DM19, children DM10.)

Speyer is easily reached by rail from Mannheim (30-50min.) and Heidelberg. Also, bus #7007 from Heidelberg (1½hr.) deposits passengers at the steps of the cathedral. The ultra-helpful **tourist office,** Maximilianstr. 11 (tel. 143 92), two blocks ahead of the cathedral's main entrance, distributes maps and lists of *Pensionen.* To get there from the train station, take the city shuttle to Maximilianstr. (open Mon.-Fri. 9am-5pm, Sat. 10am-noon). **Tours** of the city depart from in front of the tourist office (April-Oct. Sat.-Sun. at 11am; DM5). The **shuttle bus** runs the length of the city every 10min. (1-day ticket DM1). The **post office** is on Postplatz, next to the Altpörtal. It **exchanges money** and cashes traveler's checks; the **postal code** is 67346 (open Mon.-Fri. 7:30am-6pm, Sat. 7:30-noon). The **telephone code** is 06232.

Speyer's **Jugendherberge (HI),** Geibstr. 5 (tel. 753 80), is rarely overcrowded. The hostel sits about 300m southeast of town next to the municipal swimming pool; the city shuttle stops just outside its gate. Single travelers are put in six- or eighteen-bed rooms. (Reception open 5-7pm and 9:30-10pm. Lockout 9-11am. Curfew 10pm. Members only. DM16.70, over 26 DM21.70.) Affordable housing is not common in Speyer. **Pension Grüne Au,** Grüner Winkel 28 (tel. 721 96, fax 721 96), has comfortable rooms with gleaming sinks. From Maximilianstr., go left in Salzgasse, continue to St. Georggasse, left through Fisch Markt, and right onto Grüner Winkel. (Singles DM50. Doubles DM70.) The side streets of Korngasse and Große Himmelsgasse, just north of Maximilianstr., shelter excellent small restaurants. The **Gaststätte "Zum Goldenen Hirsch,"** Maximilianstr. 90a (tel. 726 94), offers German and regional specialities (DM9.50-16.50; open Thurs.-Tues. 11am-midnight).

On the second weekend in July (Friday to Tuesday) Speyer celebrates its **Bretzelfest** (pretzel festival). The festivities involve all sorts of music, parades, and special events. During the second weekend of August, the **Kaisertafel Speyer** takes place—tables are set up along the streets and visitors are herded along and stuffed full of regional specialties. (To *Let's Go*'s knowledge, they are not then roasted.) Start your engines for the **car race** which takes over the Airbus airport in mid-April.

■ Trier

Older than any other German town, vastly older than Germany itself, Trier has weathered two millennia in the western end of Germany's Mosel Valley and stubbornly refuses to act its age. Founded by the Romans during the reign of Augustus, Trier reached the height of its prominence in the early 4th century as the capital of the western Roman Empire and the residence of Constantine. Each epoch has left its mark, making Trier a patchwork quilt of uncommon design and grace. The vitality of its visitors and students blend harmoniously with the dignity and beauty of its magnificent Roman ruins and well-preserved *Altstadt*. The birthplace and boyhood home of Karl Marx, Trier is one of the few places in the united Germany unwilling to give up its "Karl-Marx-Straße." Quiet yet energetic, old but new—Trier constantly re-invents itself, each day showing its unwillingness to relinquish its hold on the pulse of life.

ORIENTATION AND PRACTICAL INFORMATION

Trier lies less than 50km from the Luxembourg border on the Mosel River. Most of the sights sit in or around the compact *Altstadt*. The gate to the *Altstadt*, **Porta Nigra,** is a 10-minute walk from the train station down Theodor-Heuss-Allee or Christophstr. Though almost everything is within walking distance, the bus system will carry you any old place for DM2.40.

Tourist Office: Tourist-Information, in the shadow of the *Porta Nigra* (tel. 97 80 80; fax 447 59), offers **tours** in English daily at 2pm (DM9). Open Jan.-Feb. Mon.-Fri. 9am-5pm, Sat. 9am-1pm; March Mon.-Sat. 9am-6pm, Sun. 9am-3:30pm; April-Nov. 15 Mon.-Sat. 9am-6:30pm, Sun. 9am-3:30pm; Nov. 16-Dec. Mon.-Sat. 9am-6pm, Sun. 9am-1pm. Whew! During these constantly fluctuating hours, the staff hands out free maps and books rooms for free (5% deposit required). Pick up a **Trier Card,** which offers admission to 7 museums and reduced rates on tours and theater performances (among other things) over a 3-day period (single DM17, family (2 adults, 3 children) DM32). A **Trier Card Plus** also includes free public transportation (single DM25, family DM44).

Wine Information: Konstantinplatz 11 (tel. 736 90), near the Basilika. Staff and computers help you make decisions about **wine tasting** in the Mosel region (and in the amply-stocked office). Dry wine? Fruity wine? Wine with bold, ambitious flavor and ethereal after-taste? Open Mon.-Fri. 11am-1pm and 1:30-6:30pm, Thurs. 11am-1pm and 1:30-8pm, Sat. 10am-1pm and 1:30-4pm, Sun. 1-5pm.

Telephones: Inside and outside the post office by the train station.

Trains: Frequent trains to Koblenz (1½hr.), rosy Luxembourg (10 per day; 45min.; day excursion DM12.80), and Saarbrücken (1½hr.).

Ferries: Personen-Schiffahrt (tel. 263 17) sails the Mosel to Bernkastel-Kues from beside Kaiser-Wilhelm Brücke. May-Oct. daily at 9:15am. Round-trip DM44, tots under 13 DM22.

Taxi: Taxi-Funk (tel. 330 30). The proof is in the funk.

Bikes: Lasso yourself a two-wheeled filly at the station (tel. 200 25 18). DM10 per day with railpass or ticket. Bike rental open Mon.-Fri. 7am-7pm. Yippi-kay-yay!

Mitfahrzentrale: Mi(e)twohn- und Mitfahrzentrale, Kaiserstr. 13 (tel. 474 47; fax 492 32). The double whammy: rides and room rental hooked up in one office. Open Mon.-Tues. 10am-1pm, Wed.-Fri. 10am-1pm, 4:30-7pm, Sat. 10am-1pm.

Bookstore: Akademische Buchhandlung, Fleischstr. 62 (tel. 97 99 01). Open Mon.-Fri. 9am-6:30pm, Sat. 9am-2pm.

Laundry: Wasch Center, Brückenstr. 19-21, down the street from Karl Marx's house. Contemplate your relationship to the means of production as you wash (DM7) according to your abilities, dry (DM3 per 25min.) according to your needs. Although there will be a need for proletarian leaders, there's no need to bring your own soap; it's included. Open Mon.-Sat. 8am-10pm.

Post Office: Most convenient is the branch office on Bahnhofplatz, 45292 Trier, to the right of the train station. Open Mon.-Fri. 8am-6pm, Sat. 8am-noon. Limited services open Mon.-Fri. 7-8am and 6-8pm, Sat. 7am-2pm, Sun. 10am-noon.

Telephone Code: 0651.

ACCOMMODATIONS AND CAMPING

Jugendgästehaus (HI), An der Jugendherberge 4 (tel. 292 92; fax 240 80). Take bus #2 or 8 (direction: Trierweilerweg or Pfalzel/Quint) to "Moselbrücke," and walk 10min. downstream on the path along the river embankment. Or take the 30-min. walk from the station. Follow Theodor-Heuss-Allee as it becomes Nordallee, forks right onto Lindenstr., and ends at the bank of Mosel. Extensive array of ping-pong tables and vending machines, and funky music at the reception desk. Reception open 3-11:30pm. Lockout 9:30am-1pm. Loose midnight curfew. Quads with toilet and shower DM25.50. Breakfast included. Sheets included.

Jugendhotel Kolpinhaus/Hotel Kolpinhaus, Dietrichstr. 42 (tel. 97 52 50; fax 975 25 40), is conveniently located 1 block off the *Hauptmarkt*. Has a more urban, bohemian feel than the hostel. Reception open 8am-11pm. Singles DM34. Doubles DM68. Four-bed dorms DM25 per person. Key available for late returns. Breakfast included. Call as far ahead as possible.

Hotel Haus Runne, Engelstr. 35 (tel. 289 22). Follow Theodor-Heuss-Allee from the train station and turn right on Engelstr. after the *Porta Nigra*. Interior looks like it was designed by Carol Brady. Large rooms with shower, toilet, and TV. Singles DM45. Doubles DM85. Quads DM160. Breakfast included.

Hotel Handelshof, Lorenz-Kellner-Str. 1 (tel. 739 33). From *Porta Nigra* follow Simeonstr., then Fleischstr., then Brückenstr., and after Karl-Marx-Str. turn left. Stately Old-World quarters presided over by the owner and his German shepherd. Hall showers and toilets. Mounted antlers. Singles DM40. Doubles DM80.

Camping: Trier City Campingplatz, Luxemburgerstr. 81 (tel. 869 21). From Hauptmarkt, follow Fleischstr. to Bruckenstr. to Karl-Marx-Str. to the Römerbrücke. Cross the bridge, head left on Luxemburgerstr., and then left at camping sign. If you end up in Luxembourg, you've gone too far. Reception open daily 9-11am and 6-10pm in Gortätle Kranich, up from the river. DM7 per person. DM3 children 4-12yrs. Under 4 free. DM2 per dog.

FOOD

Astarix, Karl-Marx-Str. 11 (tel. 722 39), in a passageway next to Miss Marple's. If you get to the dreadfully tasteful sex shops, you've gone too far. Many students happily munching on cheap food. *Tortellini* DM6.90. Gorgonzola-tomato garlic toast DM5.90. Open Mon.-Thurs. 11am-1am, Fri.-Sat. 11am-2am, Sun. 6pm-1am.

Warsberger Hof, in the Kolpinhaus Hotel, Dietrichstr. 42 (tel. 97 52 50). Walk from *Porta Nigra* to the *Hauptmarkt* and turn right. Lunch specials and vegetarian fare for DM12.50. Evening menus available in English. Open daily 11am-midnight; kitchen closes at 11:30pm. Visa, MC, EuroCard, Diners.

Zum Domstein, Am Hauptmarkt 5 (tel. 744 90), across from the cathedral's main entrance. An excellent wine-tasting opportunity (*Weinprobe;* DM7-12). When you see two *Dom*s, you've had enough. Open daily 9am-midnight.

Bierakademie, Bahnhofstr. 28 (tel. 729 22), half a block down from the train station. Around the world in 100 beers. For those who foolishly insist that man cannot live by beer alone, simple combinations of meat, cheese and bread are available for under DM10. Open Mon.-Fri. 10am-1am, Sat. 6pm-2am.

SIGHTS AND ENTERTAINMENT

Trier is fraught with reminders of its Roman past, the most impressive of which is the **Porta Nigra** (Black Gate). Built in the 2nd century, the massive stone gate gained its name from the centuries of grime that have turned its originally light yellow sandstone face into uneven shades of gray. The gate once served as the strongest line of defense against attacks on the city. (Open daily Jan.-Palm Sunday and Oct.-Nov. 9am-5pm, Palm Sunday-Sept. 9am-6pm, Dec. 10am-4pm. Admission DM4, students DM2, children DM1.50. **One-day ticket** for admission to all Roman monuments DM9, DM4.50, and DM4 each season, respectively.) Inside the courtyard, the **Simeonstift** is an 11th century monastery that now holds the **Städtisches Museum** (tel. 718 24 40;

open April-Oct. Tues.-Fri. 9am-5pm, Sat.-Sun. 9am-3pm; Nov.-March Tues.-Fri. 9am-5pm, Sat.-Sun. 9am-1pm; admission DM3, students DM1.50).

The **Hauptmarkt** in the center of Trier is packed with stalls that sell fruit, flowers, and ice cream; it's nearly always crowded. The remarkably large pedestrian shopping district is also lined with a variety of architecturally diverse buildings. The most interesting of the lot is the colorful Gothic **Dreikönigshaus** (House of the Three Magi). A medieval merchant's home, the structure implies a great deal about the antagonistic relationship the original owner had with the rest of the town. The front door is located on the second story above street level, accessible only by a ladder that could be pulled up into the house when it was under siege by angry *Lumpenproletariat*. Growing up in such a neighborhood, it's no surprise that young Karl Marx was inspired to write his theory of class conflict. The **Karl-Marx-Haus,** where young Karl first walked, talked, and dreamed of labor alienation, still stands at Brückenstr. 10 (tel. 430 11), and is a must-see for indefatigable Marxists. Busts and copies of the Manifesto abound. (Open April-Oct. Mon. 1-6pm, Tues.-Sun. 10am-6pm; Nov.-March Mon. 3-6pm, Tues.-Sun. 10am-1pm and 3-6pm. Admission DM3, students DM2. Naturally, a group discount of DM1.) For the next leg of *Let's Go*'s "Fathers of Communism" Tour, see **Wuppertal** (birthplace of Friedrich Engels), p. 110. On Nagelstr., right around the corner from the Karl-Marx-Haus, placate your inner child at the **Spielzeug Museum** (toy museum) with two centuries of dolls, teddy bears, and automata. (Open Apr.-Oct. daily 11am-5pm, Nov.-March Tues.-Sun. noon-4pm. Admission DM7.50, children ages 10-18 DM4, under 10 DM3.)

From the *Marktplatz,* through the passage between two houses, lurks **Markt und Bürgerkirche St. Gangolf.** Begun in 964, it was rebuilt and restyled over the centuries. A left turn onto Sternstr. from the produce stands of the *Hauptmarkt* brings you to the 11th-century **Dom,** whose interior design is as impressive as any in Germany; its many nooks and crannies contain the tombs of archbishops from as recently as the 1980s. Enshrined at the eastern end of the cathedral is what is reputed to be the **Tunica Christi** (Holy Robe of Christ). Tradition tells that this relic was brought from Jerusalem to Trier around 300AD by St. Helena, mother of Emperor Constantine. It was last shown to the public in 1959 (open daily 6am-6pm; Nov.-March 6am-5:30pm; free). Also in the *Dom,* the **Schatzkammer** touts a treasury of religious artifacts (open Apr.-Oct. Mon.-Sat. 10am-5pm; Nov.-March Mon.-Sat. 10am-noon and 2-4pm; admission DM2, students and children DM1). Adjacent to the *Dom* is the magnificent Gothic **Liebfrauenkirche.** Its stained glass windows turn the interior of the cathedral a dark red and puddle the floor with color.

From here, Liebfrauenstr. leads to the **Konstantin Basilika,** originally the location of Emperor Constantine's throne room. Lavishly decorated in its 4th-century prime, this one-room monstrosity is now about as exciting to look at as an airplane hangar (open Mon.-Sat. 9am-6pm, Sun. 11am-6pm; free). Next door is the bubble-gum pink **Kurfürstliches Palais,** a former residence of the archbishop-electors of Trier that today houses municipal government offices. It overlooks the well-kept **Palastgarten** (palace garden) where the statues have abnormally elongated toes. Along the eastern edge of the garden lies the **Landesmuseum,** Ostallee 44, an impressive collection of Roman stonework, sculpture, and mosaics, as well as a few other random relics, including a 2700-year-old Egyptian casket complete with mummy (open Tues.-Fri. 9:30am-5pm, Sat.-Sun. 10:30am-5pm; admission DM5, students, seniors and children DM3). Nearby at the southeast end of the park are the **Kaiserthermen,** the ruins of the Roman baths where Constantine once scrubbed, with long dark underground passages that are easy to get lost in (same hours and admission as *Porta Nigra*). It's a 5-minute walk uphill from here along Olewigerstr. to the remains of the 2nd-century **Amphitheater.** Had the Rolling Stones toured in 169AD, this 20,000-seat venue (one of the largest in the Roman Empire) certainly would have been on the itinerary. Instead, it hosted a spectacle far more gruesome and pathetic than even aged rock stars belting out the oldies: the agents booked the acts that demonstrated the most spectacular and gruesome ways of inflicting pain (and death) on humans and animals (open daily April.-Sept. 9am-5:30pm, Oct.-March 9am-4:30pm; admission DM4, students DM2, children DM1.50). If you're simply not impressed, ride the **Kabinen Schwebelbahn** (gondola; tel. 14 72 30) across the Mosel to the Stadtwald and admire the forest primeval, the murmuring pines, and the hemlocks (open Mon.-Fri. 9am-6pm, Sat.-Sun. 9am-7pm; round-trip DM7, kids DM4; one way DM4.50 and DM3, respectively).

Several annual festivals each merit a visit. **Altstadtfest,** during the fourth weekend in June, brings live music and lots of wine and beer to the streets. The second weekend in July welcomes the **Moselfest,** with fireworks over the water on Saturday night. The first August weekend witnesses the arrival of the **Weinfest,** kicked off with fireworks on Friday.

NIGHTLIFE

Pubs, clubs and *Kneipen* of all flavors fan out from the *Hauptmarkt,* with an exceptionally dense collection at the northwesternly *Pferdemarkt.*

Blaues Blut, Pferdemarkt (tel. 412 53). Mellow blue lighting and tiles on the table make you feel like you're drinking on the floor of a swimming pool. Instead of getting an eyeful of chlorine, you can gawk at the beautiful, hip crowd and enjoy the funky music. Open Mon.-Thurs. 9am-1am, Fri.-Sat. 9am-2am, Sun. 10am-1am.

Exhaus, Zurmainer Str. 114 (tel. 251 91). Huge, graffiti-adorned complex that houses a *Biergarten.* A bewildering array of dance parties, as well as Trier's best concert venue. Hours and cover vary. Check posters or call for info.

Palais Walderdorff, across from the *Dom* (tel. 410 62). By day, a mellow café; by night a disco with creative and beautifully advertised themes. Open Mon.-Fri. 10am-6:30pm, Sat. 11am-3pm. Party times vary, but posters are everywhere.

Irish Pub, Jakobstr. 10 (tel. 495 39). No self-respecting city could carry on without music, beer, and real, live Irish people. No cover. Open daily 11am-1am.

■ Mosel Valley (Moseltal)

As if trying to avoid its inevitable surrender to the Rhine at Koblenz, the Mosel slowly meanders past the sun-drenched hills, pretty towns, and ancient castles of the softly cut Mosel Valley. The slopes aren't quite as steep as the Rhine's narrow gorge, but the countless, less-touristed vineyards of the gentle hillsides have been pressing quality vintages since the Romans first cultivated them around the time of Christ. The only local complaints heard about the region is that the summers are too dry (the least of worries for a visitor) and the winters too wet. Periodically, the mellow Mosel goes berserk, flooding and making the valley Venetian for a few days. In December 1993, many of the towns were buried under 2m of water. The headwaters of the Mosel flow from the Vosges Mountains of France, following a northeasterly course that winds over 200km of German territory from Trier to Koblenz.

The best way to view the valley's scenery is by boat, bus, or bicycle; the train line between Koblenz and Trier strays frequently from the course of the river, cutting through the unremarkable countryside. Although passenger **boats** no longer make

---

Karl Marx Streets

Immediately after reunification, there was a rush to change the names of streets in eastern Germany which commemorated Communist heroes of the GDR. But now a backlash to the revisionist movement is gaining strength. In many western cities, left-wing parties like the SPD and the Greens are agitating to preserve street names honoring 20th-century socialist and communist reformers like Ernst Thälmann and Rosa Luxemburg, who lost their lives for their ideals. In Berlin, the question of street-name reform was a hot issue in the 1996 local elections. Nuremberg is scheduled to vote on whether to designate a square in its central city as *Rosa-Luxemburg-Platz.* But in Trier, where it all began, **Karl-Marx-Straße** is there to stay.

the complete Koblenz-Trier run, several companies run daily trips along shorter stretches through the summer; local tourist offices can provide details. Some train stations will rent you a rugged three-speed **bike** for DM11 per day (bring or buy a ticket or railpass, otherwise rental prices double).

COCHEM

The town of Cochem seems to survive solely to produce wine and coddle tourists. The majestic and elaborately painted turrets of the **Reichsburg** castle (tel. 262 55) perch high on a vineyard-carpeted hill up above the town. Originally built in the 11th century, the castle was destroyed in 1689 (like much of the Palatinate) by French troops under Louis XIV. In 1868, it was rebuilt by a wealthy Berlin merchant in neo-Gothic style. The view from the castle grounds alone warrants the 15-minute uphill climb along Schloßstr. from the *Marktplatz*. Unfortunately, a peek into the castle's opulent interior can only be taken today as part of a guided tour. (Open March 15-Oct. daily 9am-5pm. Frequent 40min. tours; written English translations available. Admission DM6, students DM5, children DM3.) The tiny lane to the **Peterskapelle** (left as you walk down from the castle), built in plague year 1422, is enclosed by high walls and the ubiquitous trellises.

The path runs all the way back to town, passing through the Martinstor, the squat remains of the **Stadtmauer** (town wall) that was built in 1322. The castle is not the only vantage point in town. For a tremendous view of the area, the **Sesselbahn** (chairlift; tel. 226) runs to the **Pinnerkreuz,** on Endenstr., a lone cross standing on a high peak (lift runs June-Oct. daily 9:30am-7pm; Nov.-May daily 10am-6pm; one-way DM6.90, round-trip DM8.90; DM3.20 and DM4.50 for tykes, respectively). Cochem overlooks a bend in the river one-third of the way between Koblenz and Trier; it is well connected to both by rail. Down the street from the train station, at the foot of the Mosel Bridge, **Endertplatz** hosts open-air markets. The **tourist office,** on Endertplatz 1 (tel. 39 71 or 39 72; fax 84 10), right next to the bridge, makes same-day room reservations for free and doles out brochures like mad. From the train station, go to the river and turn right (open May-Nov.15 Mon.-Fri. 10am-1pm and 2-5pm, Sat. 10am-3pm). For bikes, **Fahhrad-Shop Kreutz,** Ravenestr. 7 (tel. 911 31), across from the tourist office, leases an array of two-wheeled chrome beauties (DM14 per day, DM70 per week; open Mon.-Fri. 9:30am-6pm, Sat. 9:30am-1pm, Sun. 10:30am-noon and 5:30-6:30pm). The post office is at the corner of Ravenestr. and Josefstr., one block from Endenplatz. They cash travelers checks and exchange money (open Mon.-Fri. 8am-noon and 2-5pm, Sat. 8am-noon). The **telephone code** is 02671.

Cochem's friendly but unadorned **Jugendherberge (HI),** Klottener-Str. 9 (tel. 86 33; fax 85 68), is 10 to 15 minutes from the station on the opposite shore. Cross the Nordbrücke (to the left as you exit the station); the youth hostel is next to the bridge on the right. (Reception open noon-1pm and 5-10pm. Late arrivals ring bell. Curfew 10pm. DM19.50, over 26 DM24.50. Breakfast included. Sheets DM5. Call a day or two ahead.) The cheaper accommodations tend to be across the river in Cochem-Cond. **Haus Dohler,** on Volwigerstr. (tel./fax 76 96), is small but friendly. Cross the Moselbrücke and take the last right by the church. (Singles DM30-35. Doubles DM30-40.) The two camping options are equidistant from the *Hauptbahnhof,* but **Camping Schausten-Reif,** Endertstr. 124 (tel. 75 28), provides superior *Sesselbahn* access. From the station, take a right to the Mosel Bridge; instead of crossing the river, take the road into the hills in the opposite direction. (Reception open 5pm-midnight. DM7 per person. DM9-12 per tent. Open Easter-Oct.) On the other side of the river, camp at **Campingplatz am Freizeitzentrum,** on Stadionstr. (tel. 44 09), just below the youth hostel. (Reception open daily 8am-9pm. DM6 per person, DM5-9 per tent. Easter-Oct. 4min. warm shower DM1.50. Washing machine and dryer DM2.) Right next door is the gigantic **Moselbad,** a complex of pools, saunas, jacuzzis and waterslides. (Open Mon. 2pm-10pm, Tues.-Fri. 11am-10pm, Sat.-Sun. 10am-7pm. All-day ticket to everything DM16, ages 12-17 DM6, ages 6-11 DM6, under 5 free. Outdoor heated pool only DM5, DM3, DM3, and free, respectively.) Indulge in food at the cheesy, good-hearted **Weinhexenkeller** (wine witches' cellar), on Hafenstr., across the

Moselbrücke. Local legend says that the guests who imbibe too much wine in the cellar fall under a witch's enchantment. Modern science says they only become drunk. Either way, you'll have a perfect excuse to go nuts when the live music kicks in at 7pm (open daily noon-1am).

The **Mosel-Wein-Woche** begins a week and a half after Pentecostal Monday and features some of the Mosel's finest vintages (DM1-2 per 100ml taste). During the last weekend in August, the **Weinfest** takes place, culminating in a dramatic Saturday night fireworks display. During the wine harvest in September and October visitors can often find work (ranging from a few days to a few weeks) if they can do the back-breaking labor of a wine harvesting. For information contact the tourist office or **Weingut Winzerhof** (tel. 72 97) at least four weeks in advance.

BEILSTEIN

Ten km upstream from Cochem lies **Beilstein,** a tiny hamlet with half-timbered houses and crooked cobblestone streets. With 162 residents, Beilstein takes pride in being the smallest official town in Germany (it received town rights in 1319). Spared in World War II, Beilstein's untarnished beauty has made it the idyllic backdrop of several movies and political summits. Adenauer and DeGaspari met here during the negotiations that created the European Economic Community (now the European Union). Beilstein's natural charm draws a tourist crowd that exponentially increases its population, and there has been the expected exponential rise in the number of hotels and restaurants. Fortunately, the delicious Mosel wine flows freely, mellowing the crowds and dampening the touristy vibrations.

Burg Metternich is the resident castle; the French sacked it in 1689, but the view is still spectacular (open April-Oct. daily 9am-7pm; admission DM2, students DM1.50, children DM0.50). Also worth a look is the Baroque **Karmelitenkirche,** with its intricately carved wooden altar and the famous **Schwarze Madonna von Beilstein** (black Madonna), a 16th-century Montserrat sculpture left behind by Spanish troops reintroducing Catholicism to the region. A private bus line (railpasses not valid) makes 5 trips per day between Cochem and Beilstein (20min.), stopping at the train station and on *Endertplatz.* Lay down your sleepy head at the comfortable **Pension Erna Burg,** Moselstr. 2 (tel. 14 24), next to the highway along the river. (DM32 per person per night. Breakfast included.) The boats of **Personenschiffahrt Kolb** (tel. 15 15) can also float you there (4 per day May-Oct.; 1hr.; round- trip DM19; railpasses not valid). The **telephone city code** is 02673. In **Senheim,** 4km away, the **Weinmuseum Schlagkamp-Desoye** covers every aspect of wine-making and drinking since the Romans. (Open Feb.-Dec. Mon.-Sat. 9:30am-4am. Admission DM4. Includes a glass of lip-smacking Riesling.)

BERNKASTEL-KUES

Yet another finalist in *Let's Go*'s Beautiful Double-Dorfs of the Mosel River Valley Pageant is Bernkastel-Kues. Its gorgeous setting and picturesque streets make it the gem of the valley whose glitter attracts tourists galore. The Bernkastel **Marktplatz,** located one block from the bridge, is a 400-year-old half-timbered *tour de force.* Around the corner, the narrow, steep-roofed edifice of the **Spitzhäuschen** leans to one side; it looks like it came straight out of a children's cartoon. A scenic but grueling 20-minute climb along a vine-laden path leads to the ruins of **Burg Landshut** above the town and valley. A summer home for the archbishops of Trier until it was gutted by fire in 1693, the ruins have since been rudely usurped by an outdoor café-restaurant. The gorgeous view remains the same (and DM1 augments it by allowing you to climb the tower). Back in town, walk north from the *Marktplatz* onto Graacherstr. to reach the **Graacher Tor,** the only preserved gate from the city wall of 1300. During the upheavals of 1848, revolutionaries from Trier met here. Today their meeting hall houses the **Heimat Museum** (tel. 72 60), covering local history and culture (significantly more interesting for German speakers); open Easter-Oct. Thurs.-Sun. 3-5pm; admission DM2, students DM1).

Across the river sits the poor relative of Kues; there are a few stately 19th-century mansions along the river and the **Cusanusstift** next to the bridge. Also known as the **St.-Nikolaus-Hospital,** this home for the aged and destitute was founded in the 15th century by a local humanitarian and includes an elaborately decorated chapel. The number of boarders is kept at a constant 33 in honor of the life expectancy of itinerant messianic Nazarene carpenters. Next door, the **Moselweinmuseum,** at Cusanusstr. 1, pays tribute to the tools of the wine-making trade (open April 16-Oct. daily 10am-5pm; Nov.-April 14 daily 2-5pm; admission DM2.50, students DM1.50).

By some freak of nature (or provincial engineering) the road connecting Traben-Trarbach and Bernkastel-Kues curls around the Mosel for some 24km, yet a footpath short cut separating the two towns makes a bee-line right through the vineyards in just 7km. The path is too steep to trek while toting a heavy backpack, but it's otherwise an easy and gorgeous hike. Rail service no longer connects Bernkastel-Kues to the outside world; instead, a private **bus** runs to Trier (DM12.20) and Traben-Trarbach (every 2hr.; DM7.30). Passenger boats also make the trip (May-Oct. daily; round-trip from Trier DM45, from Traben-Trarbach DM21). The **tourist office,** Am Gestade 5 (tel. 40 23; fax 79 53), across the street from the main bus stop in Bernkastel, will find rooms for a DM3 fee. (Open May-Oct. Mon.-Fri. 8:30am-12:30pm and 1-5pm, Sat. 9:30am-noon and 2-5pm; Nov.-April. Mon.-Tues. 8:30am-12:30pm and 1-5pm, Fri. 8:30am-12:30pm and 1-3:30pm.) The **telephone code** is 06531.

Bernkastel's **Jugendherberge,** Jugendherbergsstr. 1 (tel. 23 95; fax 15 29), shares the advantages and disadvantages of its neighbor **Burg Landshut** (this is not to imply that the hostel is in ruins): a scenic location but a traumatic 30-minute trek up on a hill to get there. Just follow the signs. The only other options are to get a room in town. (Reception open 7:30-9am, noon-1pm and 5-7pm. Curfew 10pm. DM19.50, over 26 DM24.50. Breakfast included. Sheets DM5.) Snuggle in at **Campingplatz Kueser Werth,** Am Hafen 2 (tel. 82 00), on the Kues side of the river. From the bridge, turn left and follow the road along the river for 1.5km. (Reception open 8am-noon and 3-7pm. DM6 per person, DM5 per tent. Open April.-Oct.) **Kapuzinerstübchen,** Römerstr. 35 (tel. 23 53), serves traditional German meals without traditional tourist trap prices. Soups DM2.50, entrees DM8-17 (open Tues.-Sat. 11:30am-2pm and 5:45-8:45pm). Thousands arrive into town for Bernkastel-Kues's **Weinfest,** held the first weekend in September (Sept. 3-6 in 1997). **Traben-Trarbach,** another double *Dorf* downstream from Bernkastel-Kues, offers the Ruine Grevensburg and winefests on the second and last weekends of July.

▒ Saarbrücken

Tossed between France and Germany like a ping-pong ball, the Saarland is a bruised victim of European politics. Until quite recently, Saarbrücken also had little cause to tout its location. Only a few kilometers from Metz, the town was the frontline for centuries of conflict. Aside from the occasional nationalistic jibe (in 1995 Saarbrücken's museum exhibited a vast collection of German caricatures of Napoleon), the enmity has lately subsided. Saarbrücken has become a haven for punks, art students, and the occasional tourist. The border location now gives Saarbrücken an international and cosmopolitan flair that it belies its small size.

Orientation and Practical Information The **tourist office,** Am Hauptbahnhof 4 (tel. 365 15; fax 905 33 00), lies to the left of the train station. They run a room-finding service (DM3) and provide free brochures and maps (open Mon.-Fri. 9am-6pm, Sat. 9am-3pm). The handy **Saarbrücken Card** provides transportation, free entrance to several museums and the zoo, and discounts on theater tickets. **Der Fahrradladen,** Nauuriserstr. 19 (tel. 370 98), rents bikes. **Mitfahrzentral,** Rosenstr. 32, near the Alte Sammlung, will hook you up with a chauffeur (open Mon-Fri. 10am-6pm, Sat. 10am-2pm, Sun. noon-3pm). Impress your mother by doing your **laundry** at Eisenbahnstr. 8. (Wash DM6, soap included. Dry DM1 per 10min. Open Mon.-Sat. 7am-10pm.) The **post office,** 66111 Saarbrücken, is to the right of the station (open

Mon.-Fri. 8am-6pm, Sat. 8am-1pm; limited services Mon.-Fri. 7am-7:30pm, Sat. 7am-3pm, Sun. 11am-2pm). The **telephone code** is 0681.

Accommodations and Camping Saarbrücken is not the tourist capital of the universe, but its hostels do brisk business. The **Jugendherberge,** Meerwiesertalweg 31 (tel. 330 40), is a 25-minute walk from the station; head downhill and left, at the intersection veer left onto Ursulinenstr., head left at the mammoth supermarket, and cross the parking lot. The eastern exit flows to Meerwiesertalweg. Or take bus #19 from the station to "Prinzenweiher" and backtrack to the hostel. The light flickers on magically as you walk down the hall. Wicked modern. Also, private toilets and showers! (Reception open 4-5:30pm and 7:30-11pm. Curfew 11:30pm. Quads DM25.70, over 26 DM30.70. Doubles DM32.40, over 26 DM36.40. Breakfast and sheets included.) **Gästehaus Weller,** Neugrabenweg 8 (tel. 37 19 03; fax 37 55 65), offers huge rooms with amazing color co-ordination. Go down Ursulinenstr, right on Mozartstr., carry on to Schumannstr., left on Fichtestr., and cross the bridge to Neugrabenweg. (Reception open daily 7am-10pm. Singles with bath, toilet, phone, and cable TV DM49-69. Doubles DM69-98. Call ahead.) **Hotel Atlantic,** Ursulinenstr. 59 (tel. 310 18; fax 37 45 03), is a 5-minute walk along Ursulinenstr. One of those lovely "chocolate-on-the-big-white-fluffy-comforter" places. (Reception open 24hr. Singles DM86 and up. Doubles DM96 and up. Breakfast included. AmEx, MC, Diners accepted.) **Hotel Schlosskrug,** Schmollerstr. 14 (tel. 354 48; fax 37 50 22), at the corner with Bruchwiesenstr., is 10-15 minutes from the station, in a quiet location near the hippest part of town. Go left onto Ursulinenstr., right on Richard-Wagner Str., and right on Schmollerstr. (Singles with shower DM55, with shower and toilet DM65. Doubles with shower DM100, with shower and toilet DM120. Triples with shower and toilet DM170.) **Campingplatz Saarbrücken,** Am Spicherer Berg (tel. 517 80), is far from the station. How far? Far. Take bus #42 to "Spicherer Weg," cross Untertürkheimstr., and head right uphill on Spicherer Weg. (Reception open daily 7am-1pm and 3-10pm. DM7 per person. DM8 per tent. Open April-Sept.)

Food The streets around **St. Johannis Markt** are brimming with bistros, beer gardens, and ethnic restaurants. Walk down Reichstr. and turn left on Bahnhofstr. **Schmokeloch,** on Kappenstr. (tel. 333 97), serves pizza and pasta for DM8.50-10.80 (open Mon.-Fri. noon-3:30pm and 6pm-1am, Sat. noon-1am, Sun. 6pm-1am). Come nightfall, students fill *Kneipen* in the **Chinesenviertel** between Rotenbergstr., Richard-Wagnerstr., Dudweilerstr., and Großherzog Friedrichstr. Traditional German food (DM7-13) can be had at **Spaten am Alten Brunnen,** on Türkenstr., right before the church (open Mon.-Fri. noon-1am, Sun. 5pm-1am). **Blue Moon,** on the corner of Schmollerstr. and Martin-Luther-Str. (tel. 317 80), serves up entrees for DM9-14 and such extranea as Crêpes Elvis (open Mon.-Fri. 10am-midnight; dinner starts at 6pm). **Hela,** at the end of Ursulinenstr., is a super-cali-fraga-listic-super-market-drugstore-hair-salon-rolled-into-one (open Mon.-Fri. 8:30am-6:30pm, Sat. 8:30-2pm).

Sights and Entertainment The dozens of post-war matchbox buildings around the train station swirl together into a blurring mundanity—but several structures around the St. Johanner's Markt are much easier on the eye. Since the details on the bronze doors of the **Basilika St. Johann** have faded since its 1754 construction, it's difficult to tell whether the engraved figures are writhing in hell-fire or heavenly ecstasy. But the doors (and pink-and-white interior of the church) are beautiful (opens Mon., Wed., and Fri. at 8:30am; Tues., Thurs., and Sun. 9:30am-evening mass; Sat. 9am-evening mass). To get there, head south from the market on Saarstr. and go right on Schillerstr. The massive mustard **Staatstheater,** on the right, rears its ugly head; it was presented to Hitler after the Saarland was re-integrated into Germany in 1935. Further down, the **Saarland Museum,** Bismarckstr. 11-19 (tel. 996 40), showcases works by Picasso, Matisse, and Beckmann. Medieval Madonnas from Lorraine are in the **Alte Sammlung,** Karlstr. 1, across the street. (Both museums open Tues.-

Sun. 10am-6pm, Wed. noon-8pm. Joint admission DM3, students and children DM1.50; for special exhibits DM8 and DM4, respectively.)

The **Saarbrücker Schloß** (tel. 50 62 47), on the other side of the Saar river, has morphed many times since the 9th century and now has tall sparkling glass columns on either side of its entrance. (Tours in German given Wed.-Sun. at 4:30pm and Sun. at 11am. Free.) Its plaza (the *Schloßplatz*) is officially the **Platz des unsichtbaren Mahnmals** (Place of the Invisible Reminder) and home to one of the most interesting monuments you'll never see. In 1990, students at a nearby art school, under cover of darkness, dug up 2196 stones in the plaza and carved the names of former Jewish cemeteries on their undersides. Three museums surround *Schloßplatz*. To the south, adjacent to the *Schloß*, the **Historisches Museum** (tel. 50 65 49) includes cars, chairs from the 70s, and a disturbing collection of war propaganda (open Tues.-Sun. 10am-6pm; free; special exhibits DM4, students DM2). To the north, the **Museum für Vor- und Frühgeschichte** (pre- and early history), at Schloßplatz 16 (tel. 584 96 34), has finds that include a Celtic countess's grave and jewelry from the 4th century BC. (Open Tues.-Sat. 9am-5pm, Wed. noon-8pm. Sun. 10am-6pm. Free. Special exhibits DM5.) The 1498 **Rathaus** west of the *Schloß* hosts the wacky **Abenteuer-museum** (tel. 517 47), which displays loot from the travels of the original globetrotter (take that, Sweet Lou Dunbar), Heinz Rox Schulz (open Tues.-Wed. 9am-1pm, Thurs.-Fri. 3-7pm; admission DM3, children DM2). The **Ludwigskirche** is only a five-minute walk down Schloßstr. and to the right. Although the church is still a gem, after World War II only two of its four galleries were rebuilt, giving it an unusual rectangular hall. The decor, with its bright white interior, is a radical departure from the usual gothic gloom. Watch for its high-powered concert series. Saarbrücken is the proud birthplace of renounced filmmaker Max Ophüls, and the town honors him annually with the **Max Ophüls Preis** film festival in late January. The *Kakadu* is Saarbrücken's free culture calendar. Ask for it by name (heh-heh!) at the tourist office.

Baden-Württemberg

Two powerful German stereotypes—the brooding romantic of the Brothers Grimm and the modern *homo economicus* exemplified by Daimler-Benz—battle it out in Baden-Württemberg. Pretzels, cuckoo clocks, and cars were all invented here, and the region is as diverse as its homegrown products. Baden, Württemberg-Hohenzollern, and Württemberg-Baden—three distinct states—were integrated at the founding of the Federal Republic in 1951 in a shotgun wedding masterminded by the Allies. Baden-Württemberg was meant to act as a conservative counterweight to socialist-leaning North Rhine-Westphalia. Although the merger was legitimated by a referendum, the Badeners and the Swabians (*never* "Württembergers") proudly proclaim their distinct identities. Rural custom and tradition live on in the lush hinterlands of the Black Forest and the Swabian Jura, while the modern capital city of Stuttgart celebrates the latter-day ascendancy of the German industrial machine. The province also hosts the ritzy millionaires' resort of Baden-Baden, the lovely vacation getaways of Lake Constance, as well as the exuberant, historic university towns of Freiburg, Tübingen, and Heidelberg.

■ Heidelberg

Many German cities claim to be rich in tradition, but few have retained that tradition with as much sheer style as Heidelberg. From the crumbling walls of the once-majestic *Schloß* to the historic gabled buildings and romantic, hodge-podge cobblestone streets of the *Altstadt*, Heidelberg has retained the spirit that once lured numerous writers, poets and artists—including Mark Twain, Goethe, Friedrich Hölderlin, Victor Hugo, and Robert Schumann—to this woodsy idyll. Today, during the high season, roughly 32,000 tourists *per day* (many of them English-speaking) also answer the call. The home of Germany's oldest university (founded in 1386) and a short hike down the road from one of the largest U.S. Army posts in Europe, Heidelberg gladly accommodates all kinds. The vast number of local cafés, bars, and restaurants make for a robust and diverse entertainment scene. Alas, this inclusiveness has its price: the city is crowded even in the most "off" of seasons. In late July and August, the students disappear and the tourist season begins with an inescapable vengeance. It's best to visit during spring or late fall, while school is in session; otherwise you might never meet the German Katja Henkelmann of your dreams.

ORIENTATION AND PRACTICAL INFORMATION

Heidelberg is built on both sides of the Neckar River, about 20km east of the river's convergence with the Rhine. To get to the *Altstadt* from the train station, take almost any bus or streetcar going into the city. From Bismarckplatz, take bus #33 (direction: Köpfel) to "Bergbahn" or bus #11 (direction: Karlstor) to "Universitätsplatz." The heavily touristed **Hauptstraße,** known as the longest shopping street in Germany, runs straight down the middle of the *Altstadt;* beginning at Bismarckplatz, it runs through the *Marktplatz* and the Kornmarkt and ends at the **Karlstor.**

Tourist Office: Directly in front of the station (tel. 277 35; fax 167 318). Pick up a copy of the mags *Meier* (DM2) or *Fritz* (free) to figure out what's up in town. Rooms reserved (7% down payment) and maps sold (DM1). You may want to call lodgings yourself, as the tourist office steers guests toward more expensive places. Open Mon.-Sat. 9am-7pm, Sun. 10am-6pm; Jan.-Feb. Mon.-Sat. 9am-7pm.

Currency Exchange: If banks and the post office are closed, try the *Hauptbahnhof*, where the exchange office stays open later. On holidays, one can change cash at the *Sparkassen* on Universitätsplatz and Bismarckplatz.

American Express: Brückenkopfstr. 1-2 (tel. 450 50; fax 41 03 33), at the north end of the Theodor-Heuss Brücke (Bridge). They hold mail for card members and own-

ers of AmEx traveler's checks. All banking services provided. Open Mon.-Fri. 9:30am-5:30pm, Sat. 10am-1pm.

Telephones: At the post office and the main train station.

Trains: Frequent trains run from Stuttgart (45min.) and Frankfurt (1hr.); Mannheim is less than 10min. away. Other trains run regularly to towns in the Neckar Valley.

Public Transportation: To get in, out, and around Heidelberg, buy a **24-hr. pass** that's good on all streetcars and buses (DM8.50). Passes are available at the tourist office or at the HSB Kiosk, loacted halfway across the street on Gneisenaustr., the street that runs by the side entrance to the train station. Or, more simply, buy a pass on any bus or streetcar. Single-ride tickets DM3.

Ferries: Rhein-Neckar-Fahrgastschiffahrt, down at the southern bank in front of the *Kongresshaus,* runs Neckar cruises. A popular destination is **Neckarsteinach** (May-Sept. 7 per day 9:30am-5:30pm; 1¼hr.; round-trip DM16.50). **Rent** Paddleboats and **rowboats** on the north shore of the Neckar by the Theodor-Heuss

Brücke at **Bootverleih Simon.** DM9 per half-hr., DM15 per hr. for a 3-person boat. DM11 per ½hr., DM18 per hr. for a 4-person boat. Open daily 10am-sundown.

Taxi: tel. 30 20 30. Weeee got the funk.

Bike Rental: Per Bike, Bergheimerstr. 125 (tel. 16 11 48; fax 16 11 09), has city, mountain, and children's bikes. DM15 per half-day. DM25 per day, DM20 per additional day. DM55 Fri.-Mon. weekend special. DM120 per week. DM50 deposit or ID required. Open Mon.-Fri. 9am-5pm; April-Oct. also open Sat. 9am-noon.

Hitchhiking: *Let's Go* does not recommend hitchhiking as a safe mode of transportation. Hitchers walk to the western end of Bergheimerstr. for all directions.

Mitfahrzentrale: Bergheimerstr. 125 (tel. 246 46 or 194 44; fax 14 59 59), matches riders and drivers in an orderly fashion. Paris DM51, Köln DM28, Hamburg DM54, Freiburg DM24. Open Mon.-Fri. 9am-5pm, and Apr.-Oct. Sat. 9am-noon.

Bookstores: Between the Lines, Plöck 93 (tel. 16 58 66), will let you trade in your old books, but also has new and used books, all in English, at very reasonable prices. Open Mon.-Wed. and Fri. 10am-6:30pm, Thurs. 10am-8:30pm, Sat. 10am-2pm. **Old Bridge Books,** Kaiserstr. 94 (tel. 121 26; fax 106 68), is a friendly new and used bookstore. Manager John C. McQueen is chairman of the American organization Democrats Abroad, and occasionally arranges local publicity ops for aspiring U.S. politicos. Ring the bell. Open Mon.-Fri. 11am-1:30pm and 3:30-6:30pm, Sat. 10am-2pm.

Laundromat: Wasch Salon SB, Post Str. 49, next to Kurfürst Hotel. Wash DM7. Dry DM1 per 20min. Beware: the machine does not give change; you could be forced to dry your clothes for hours. Open Mon.-Sat. 7am-11pm, Sun. 9am-8pm.

Women's Resources: Information tel. 33 30 88. **Frauennotruf** (women's emergency hotline; tel. 18 36 43). **Buchhandlung Himmelheber,** Theaterstr. 16 (tel. 222 01; fax 230 52), stocks books by, for, and about women, and also hosts readings. Open Mon.-Wed. and Fri. 9am-6:30pm, Thurs. 9am-8pm, Sat 9am-2pm.

AIDS Hilfe: tel. 194 11.

Emergency: tel. 110. **Police:** Rohrbacherstr. 11 (tel. 52 00).

Post Office: *Hauptpostamt,* Belfortstr., 69115 Heidelberg, diagonally to the right across from the front of the station. Held mail can be picked up at counters 15-17. Open Mon.-Fri. 8am-6pm, Sat. 8am-1pm. Limited services Mon.-Fri. 6-8pm.

Telephone Code: 06221.

ACCOMMODATIONS AND CAMPING

Finding a place to sleep in Heidelberg is a task not unlike spinning straw into gold, and the bill could demand your first-born. During the summer, save yourself a major headache by arriving early in the day or—better yet—calling ahead. Possible options for those with a little ingenuity and a railpass are the countless little towns and villages scattered around Heidelberg. There are **Jugendherbergen** in: Neckargmünd, 10 minutes from Heidelberg; Reilscheim, 18 minutes; Mauer, 20 minutes; Hirschhorn, 20 minutes; Eberbach, 25 minutes; and Zwingberg, 35 minutes. All these Neckar Valley towns lie along the Heidelberg-Heilbronn railroad; train service is reliable and regular between them. Best of all, a single room in a **private home** in these outlying areas can cost only a fraction of an impersonal place in one of Heidelberg's hotels.

Jugendherberge (HI), Tiergartenstr. 5 (tel. 41 20 66). From Bismarckplatz or the train station, take bus #33 (direction: Zoo-Sportzentrum) to "Jugendherberge" (first stop after Zoo). "The Jugendherberge is full today" sign on the tourist office door is practically permanent. Calling ahead rarely works. Become one of the lucky to stay in this teeming hostel by faxing your reservation. Crowded and noisy. Reception open until 11:30pm. Lockout 9am-1pm. Curfew 11:30pm (negotiable). Members only. DM19.50, over 26 DM24.50. Sheets DM5.50. Partial wheelchair access. Its small **disco** can be fun (open nightly).

Jeske Hotel, Mittelbadgasse 2 (tel. 237 33). From the train station, take bus #33 (direction: Köpfel) or #11 (direction: Karlstor) to "Bergbahn," then take a right (don't go back up the hill). Mittelbachgasse is the first right after Oberbadgasse. Erika Jeste runs a tight ship, drawing a whole subculture of (mostly English-speaking) students to her quiet overnighter in the heart of Heidelberg. Eugene Mazo

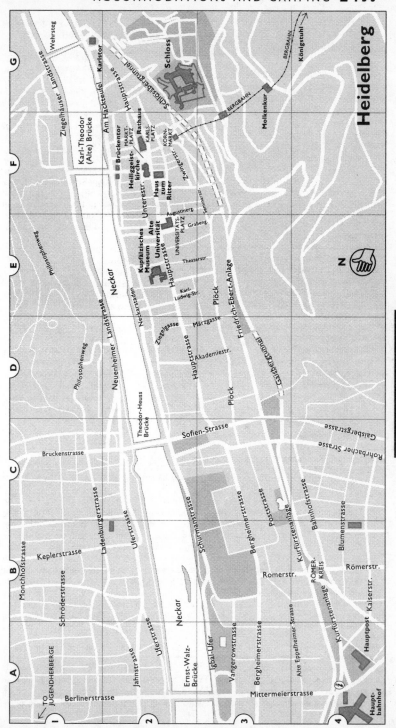

Heidelberg

Schloss

Königstuhl

BERGBAHN

Wehrsteg

Karlstor

Ziegelhäuser Landstrasse

Hauptstrasse

Am Hackteufel

BERGBAHN

Molkenkur

Schlossbergtunnel

Karl-Theodor
(Alte) Brücke

Brückentor

MARKT-
PLATZ

Rathaus

KARLS-
PLATZ

KORN-
MARKT

Heiliggeist-
kirche

Unterestr.

Haus
zum
Ritter

Zwingerstr.

Seminarstr.

Augustinerg.

Grabeng.

Kupfälzisches
Museum

Alte
Universität

UNIVERSITÄTS-
PLATZ

Philosophenweg

Neckar

Hauptstrasse

Theaterstr.

N

Karl-
Ludwig-Str.

Plöck

Neckarstaden

Neuenheimer Landstrasse

Ziegelgasse

Marzgasse

Friedrich-Ebert-Anlage

Philosophenweg

Hauptstrasse

Akademiestr.

Plöck

Gaisbergtunnel

Theodor-Heuss
Brücke

Sofien-Strasse

Gaisbergstrasse

Bruckenstrasse

Rohrbacher Strasse

Ladenburgerstrasse

Uferstrasse

Schurmanstrasse

Berghelmerstrasse

Poststrasse

Bahnhofstrasse

Blumenstrasse

Keplerstrasse

Romerstr.

Kurfurstenanlage

Römerstr.

Monchhofstrasse

Schroderstrasse

Neckar

Romerstr.

ROMER-
KREIS

Kurfurstenanlage

Hauptpost

Kaiserstr.

Jahnstrasse

Uferstrasse

Ernst-Walz-
Brücke

Iqbal-Ufer

Vangerowstrasse

Berghelmerstrasse

Alte Eppelheimer Strasse

Hauptbahnhof

TO
JUGENDHERBERGE

Berlinerstrasse

Mittermeierstrasse

A B C D E F G

I 2 3 4

even stayed here once. 2- to 5-bed rooms DM24 per person. Showers DM2. But you can't beat the prime location or the price. No breakfast. Open Feb. to mid-Nov. Other times call ahead.

Hotel-Pension Elite, Bunsenstr. 15 (tel. 257 33). From Bismarckplatz, follow Rohr-bacher Str. away from the river and turn right onto Bunsenstr.; the *Pension* is on the left. Truly nice rooms with elegant high ceilings and pastoral views. One narrow single DM75. Doubles DM95. DM15 per extra person. Toilette, shower, and TV in each room. Breakfast included. Reservations by mail and phone.

Hotel Garni Ballmann, Rohrbacker Sr. 28 (tel. 242 87 or 253 20; fax 18 20 35), has handsome rooms and a fuschia breakfast area. Reception open 24hr. Singles DM70-90. Doubles DM90-110. Triples DM120-150.

Camping: Haide (tel. (06223) 21 11), between Ziegelhausen and Kleingemünd. Take bus #35 to "Orthopedisches Klinik," then cross the river. DM7 per person. DM6 per tent. DM2 per car. Cabins DM14-16 (depending on number of people). If this side of the river doesn't float your boat, head to **Camping Heidelberg-Schlierbach,** located on the other bank (tel. 80 25 06), near the Orthopedic Clinic. Take Bus #35 (direction: Neckargmünd) to "Im Grund." DM7 per person. DM6 per tent. DM3 per car.

FOOD

Eating out tends to be depressingly expensive in Heidelberg; most of the restaurants on and around Hauptstr. are exorbitantly priced. However, just outside this central area are historic student pubs that offer better values. Fill up a picnic basket at **Handelshof,** Kurfürsten-Anlage 60, 200m in front of the train station, on the right (open Mon.-Wed. and Fri. 8am-6:30pm, Thurs. 8am-8:30pm, Sat. 8am-2pm).

Mensa, in the *Marstall,* on Marstallstr. Take bus #35 to "Marstallstr." or from the Alte Brücke take a left along the river; it's the huge stone installation on the left. State-subsidized cafeteria turns into a café in the afternoon. Cheap food, beer, and cheesecake. If you've forgotten your student ID, ask one of the students hanging out on the green in front to buy you *Mensa Marks* (each DM3; sold in fives). Open Mon.-Fri. 11:30am-2pm, Sat. 11:30am-1:30pm. During vacations, it alternates with the *Mensa* on Universitätsplatz. There's also a popular café right next door serving coffee, snacks, and beer (DM2.70-3). Board games. A student crossroads for after-dusk doings. Open Mon.-Fri. 9am-midnight, Sat. noon-1am.

Gastätte Essighaus, Plöck 97 (tel. 224 96), has tasty food and service that's quite quick by German standards. Specials include soup, salad, and entrees (DM10). Open daily 11:30am-12:30am, Wed. 5:30am-12:30pm.

Café Trotzkopf, Bergheimerstr. 71 (tel. 252 34), is a classy little café with *Biergarten* that offers warm, inexpensive food, and stained glass windows. *Chili con carne* DM9.80. Open daily 11am-1am.

Wirtshaus Zum Spreisel, Neckarstaden 66 (tel. 235 43), in Hotel Holländischer Hof, next to Goldener Hecht. Though individual meals are not cheap (DM15-40), the portions are so huge and the food so good that it's worth splitting a dish. The menu is a weighty leather tome, a dish per page. It may teem with tourists, but it hasn't lost its true German flavor. Open Mon.-Fri. 4:30pm-midnight, Sat.-Sun. 11:30am-midnight.

Presto, Kornmarkt 9 (tel. 270 91). A stand-up café with imaginative small crêpes (DM3-5.50), spiffy little sandwiches (DM3.50-4.50), and coffee (DM2.50-3.20). Open daily 9am-6:30pm.

Vater Rhein, Untere Neckarstr. 20-22 (tel. 213 71), near the Stadthalle. Where the dancing queens go after the dance. *Goulash* DM6. Pizza DM11.50. *Pilsner* DM4. Open daily 8pm-3am.

SIGHTS

American author Mark Twain's description of Heidelberg is the highlight of his 19th-century travelogue *A Tramp Abroad.* Twain recorded, with rare respect, his impressions of this university town's beauty. In the ensuing years, Heidelberg has lost none of the stateliness captured so well in Twain's description; its streets still bustle with an energy that would do a much younger city proud. Presiding over all the majestic elegence are the ramparts of the **Heidelberger Schloß** (tel. 53 84 14 or 538 40), the jewel in the crown of an already striking city. Its construction began early in the 13th century and lasted over 400 years. The conglomeration of styles ranges from Gothic to High Renaissance. Thrice destroyed, first by war (1622 and 1693) and later by nature (lightning in 1764), the castle's regal state of disrepair is best viewed from the *Philosophenweg* high above the northern bank of the Neckar. From the castle's broad terraces, the red roofs of the town act as the anchor to the far-reaching hills rolling in the distance; the castle's spacious gardens are striking in their measured symmetry. On the first Saturday in June and August and the second Saturday in July, fireworks illuminate the surrounding sky in the **Schloßbeleuchtung.** The *Schloß* is easily accessible by foot or by **Bergbahn** (cable car), which runs from the Bergbahn/ *Rathaus* bus stop to the castle (round-trip DM4.50) and farther up to Königstuhl (every 10min. 9am-8:25pm; DM7; departures from the Kornmarkt parking lot next to the bus stop). To get to the stop, take bus #11 to "Köpfel" or #33 to "Karlstor." The obligatory tour includes a visit to the **Faß,** one of the world's largest wine barrels. Local lore tells of a court jester and guardian of the *Faß* who drank nearly 18 bottles per day and finally perished after "accidentally" drinking a glass of water. (Castle and *Faß* open daily 8am-5pm. Tours in English and German 11am-3pm. Admission to both DM4, children DM2. Admission to castle DM2, students and children DM1.) The **Apothekenmuseum,** also in the castle (tel. 16 57 80), features a 17th-century pharmacy and alchemist's laboratory. They stopped dealing drugs here in 1693 (open daily April-Oct. 10am-5pm; Nov.-March Mon.-Fri. 10am-5pm, Sat.- Sun. 11am-5pm; admission DM3, students DM1.50).

The *Altstadt* centers on the **Marktplatz,** a cobbled square where **Hercules' Fountain** stands, and where, in the 15th century, accused witches and heretics were burned at the stake; now a legion of plastic chairs spreads across the cobbles while a **market** (Wed. and Sat.) purveys fruit. The two oldest structures in Heidelberg border the *Marktplatz.* The 14th-century **Heiliggeistkirche** is the largest Gothic church in the Palatinate and contains the tomb of Ruprecht I as well as an ancient library. Across from the church's southern face, the ornate façade of the swanky **Hotel zum Ritter,** built by a wealthy Huguenot refugee, dates from the 16th century. The stately **Rathaus** overlooks the entire spectacle from the far end of the square.

Walking west from the *Marktplatz* down Hauptstr. yields views of trendy shops and cafés, and history hiding behind them; five blocks down, the **Universitätsplatz,** centered about a stone-lion fountain, is the former headquarters of the **Alte Universität** (Old University). In the aristocratic tradition, students were exempt from prosecution by civil authorities; instead, the crimes of their misspent youth were tried and punished by the university faculty. Between 1778 and 1914, naughty students were jailed in the **Studentenkarzer** (tel. 54 23 34; enter via Augustinergasse behind the old university). Covered with graffiti, the wall tells of a group of honest students who were unjustly imprisoned for returning a loose cobblestone to its rightful owner— through a window (open Tues.-Sat. 10am-noon and 2-5pm; Nov.-March Tues.-Fri. 10am-noon and 2-5pm, Sat. 10am-1pm, Sun. 10am-1pm; admission DM1.50, students and children DM1). The **Kurpfälzisches Museum,** Hauptstr. 97 (tel. 58 34 02 or 58 34 00), is crammed with artifacts such as the jawbone of an unfortunate *homo Heidelbergensis,* a.k.a. "Heidelberg man," one of the oldest humans yet discovered. Elsewhere stand well-preserved works of art by Dürer, and a spectacular Gothic altarpiece by 15th-century sculptor Tilman Riemenschneider (open Tues. and Thurs.-Sun. 10am-5pm, Wed. 10am-9pm; admission DM5, students DM3, children free; free on Sun.). Between Hauptstr. and the river stands the new **Friedrich-Ebert Gedenkstätte,** Pfaffengasse 18 (tel. 910 70), the birthplace of Germany's first president, Friedrich Ebert. The exhibit recalls the rise of Ebert from saddle-maker to Social Democrat agitator to President of the ill-fated Weimar Republic (open Tues.-Wed. and Fri.-Sun. 10am-6pm, Thurs. 10am-8pm; absolutely free).

No trip to Heidelberg would be complete without a visit to the northern bank of the Neckar, opposite the *Altstadt.* Walk across the modern **Karl-Theodor-Brücke;** on the south side of the bridge stands a statue of the plump Prince-Elector himself, which he commissioned as a symbol of his modesty. On the left side of the bridge stretches a perfect picnic park. From the far end of the bridge, clamber up the **Schlangenweg,** a winding stone path, to the **Philosophenweg** (Philosophers' Path). The climb is worthwhile day or night: the path rewards with an excellent view of Heidelberg. G. W. F. Hegel, Max Weber, Karl Jaspers, and the editors of this book— among other intellectual luminaries—indulged in contemplative walks here.

Atop the **Heiligenberg,** the mountain traversed by the *Philosophenweg,* lie ruins of the 9th-century **St. Michael Basilika,** the 13th-century **St. Stephen Kloster,** and an **amphitheater** built under Hitler in 1934 on the site of an ancient Celtic gathering place. The ascent of this mountain is best tackled near the **Tiefburg,** a moated castle in neighboring Handschuhsheim, reached by Straßenbahn #1 or 3.

Heidelberg is home to a number of merry festivals. The **Faschings Parade (Carnival)** struts through the city on Shrove Tuesday, the day before Ash Wednesday. The two-week **Spring Festival** begins at the end of May. In the third weekend in June after-hours revelers in Heidelberg head to the town of Handschuhsheim, across the Neckar, for the Saturday, Sunday and Monday of the **Handschuhsheim Fest.** For five weeks from late July to late August, **Schloßfestspiele Heidelberg** features a series of concerts and plays (call 58 35 21 for information and tickets). On the third Saturday of September (Sept. 21 in 1997), the **Heidelberger Herbst** takes over town with a fair, stalls, and a fleamarket. The **Christmas market** runs from Nov. 29 to Dec. 22.

NIGHTLIFE

The true nightlife of Heidelberg lies along **Hauptstraße,** which, sadly, closes down a little after midnight. Still, if you search, you can find places open later in the little alleyways that scurry off the main drag; in particular, Untere Str. is alive until 1-2am. The most popular nighttime activity, drinking beer, can be enjoyed in the ever-crowded **historic student taverns,** the two best-known of which are **Roter Ochsen** and **Zum Sepp'l.** Much of Heidelberg's young nightlife also centers around the **Marktplatz,** which houses **Max Bar** and **Reichsapfel.** West of the Marktplatz, Heidelberg also boasts a number of nighttime spots reaching to Neuenheim, across the Neckar. The **Karlstorbahnhof,** right below the *Schloß,* hosts a never-ending series of dances and live performances—look for posters everywhere or call 97 89 14 for information. To get there, take bus #11 or 33 to "Karlstor."

Roter Ochsen, Hauptstr. 217 (tel. 209 77). A popular student hangout since 1703. Bismarck and Mark Twain used to get plastered here; so can you for DM4.50-25. It was most likely a conversation in these hallowed halls that inspired Twain's caustically funny essay, "The Awful German Language." Meals DM12-31. Open Mon.-Sat. 11:30-2pm and 5pm-midnight, Nov.-March Mon.-Sat. 5pm-midnight.

Zum Sepp'l, Hauptstr. 213 (tel. 230 85). Next door to Roter Ochsen with a similarly loud crowd that's been partying since 1634. Meals DM8-25. Beer DM4.80. Open daily 10am-midnight.

Max Bar, Marktplatz 5 (tel. 244 19), is hailed as Heidelberg's best pub. On a warm summer evening you'd be hard-pressed to find a more idyllic spot than this. Happy and eclectic young German crowds spill out onto the *Marktplatz.* Sit back and relax with a tall *Hefeweizen* (DM5 for 0.5L). Open daily 8pm-1am.

Reichsapfel, Unterestr. 35 (tel. 279 50), is a popular bar with locals. *Pils* DM4.60, and plenty of it. Open daily 6pm-1am.

Cave 54, Krämergasse 2 (tel. 278 40), jumps with 70s retro disco. Beer DM5-5.50. Live jazz on Sundays at 9:30pm. Cover DM5. Open 9:30pm-3am.

Mata Hari, located conveniently right off the Marktplatz, on the corner of Oberbadgasse (towards the Bergbahn bus stop). Bills itself as "The Gay Bar." Relaxed atmosphere. Open 10pm-3am.

Little Heaven, Fahrtgasse 18 (tel. 226 61). Where techno is God and house is perfectly divine. The smoke can get pretty ethereal too. Friday is officially gay night, though unofficially every night is. Open Wed.-Mon. 9pm-3am.

Schwimmbad Musik Club, Tiergartenstr. 13 (tel. 47 02 01), across the river. Conveniently located up the street from the hostel, it's the city's main catwalk for underground bands. Funky cats like Bim Skala Bim, the Goats, and Giant Sand all played here recently. Mainstream music on Fri. and Sat. nights. Open Wed.-Thurs. 8pm-2am, Fri.-Sat. 8pm-4am.

Neckar Valley (Neckartal)

A scenic stretch of narrow, thickly-wooded ridges embraces the Neckar River as it meanders from Heilbronn to Heidelberg. This is the Neckar Valley *(Neckartal),* much of which has been incorporated into the German Castle Road *(Burgenstraße)* that travels all the way to Nuremberg in the heart of Bavaria. The hills hugging the river are studded with castles built in the Middle Ages to protect merchant vessels from pirates. Still largely unspoiled by tourism, the valley is an excellent daytrip from Heidelberg, and its charms can be absorbed by land or water. Two train lines connect Heidelberg and Heilbronn regularly, with stops in the many smaller towns along both sides of the valley. One of the best ways to explore the valley is by biking along the well-maintained 85-km route.

Bike rentals are available at the **train station** in Neckargmünd, 12 minutes by train from Heidelberg (DM13 per day, DM9 with a train ticket). In town, **Rudi's Radladen,** Mühlgasse 2 (tel. (06223) 712 95), rents bikes for DM14 per day, DM55 per week (mountain bikes DM27 per day, DM75 per week). In Hirschhorn (see page 157), **Josef Riedel,** Hainbrunnerstr. 6 (tel. (06272) 20 17), has 'em for DM5 per half- day, DM10 per day. Finally, there's the **train station** in Eberbach (tel. (06271) 22 20), 30 minutes from Heidelberg. Also check **Per Bike** in Heidelberg (see page 150). The **Rhein-Neckar Fahrgastschiffahrt** runs **boat tours** from Easter through late October between Heidelberg (departing from in front of the *Stadthalle)* and Neckarsteinach (daily; round-trip DM16.50) as well as between Heidelberg and Hirschhorn (Tues., Thurs., and Sun.; DM22.50 round-trip). For information and departure times, call (06221) 201 81 or (06229) 526.

NECKARSTEINACH

At the north end of the valley, 14km upstream from Heidelberg, lies Neckarsteinach, notable for its four medieval **castles** all within 3km of one another along the north bank of the river. They were built by the same ruling clan, the Steinachs, during the 12th and 13th centuries. The two westernmost castles stand in ruins, while the two to the east are well-maintained and privately occupied. All can be reached by foot via the **Burgenweg** (castle path)—a journey of 30 minutes to several hours, depending on the strength of your legs and the weight of your backpack. Tourists may visit all but the first castle on the path. From the train station, turn right on Bahnhofstr. until you reach Hauptstr., turn left and follow the bend in the road to the Pizzeria Castello; the *Schloßsteige* begins at the brick path leading upward to the right and connects to the Bungenweg, whose trees are studded with identifying plaques (open March-Oct. Mon.-Sat. 9am-8pm). Neckarsteinach's **tourist office** *(Verkehrsamt),* Hauptstr. 7 (tel. 920 00), inside the *Rathaus,* is one block down from Bahnhofstr. in the same direction as the *Schloßsteige.* The office lists hotels, *Pensionen,* and private homes offering inexpensive rooms (open Mon.-Wed. 8am-noon and 1:30-3:30pm, Thurs. 8am-noon and 2-5pm, Fri. 8am-noon). The **postal code** is 69239. The **telephone code** is 06229. Fireworks streak over town on the last Saturday in July during the **Vierburgenbeleuchtung** (four-castle lighting). Rhein-Neckar-Fahrgastschiffahrt organizes trips for the fiery festivities (p. 151).

HIRSCHHORN AND BURG GUTTENBERG

Just south of Neckarsteinach sits Hirschhorn am Neckar, ruled for centuries by the Knights of Hirschhorn. In 1200, the knights built their castle on Stockelberg Mountain, cruelly displacing a happy herd of reindeer from their favorite grazing spot. History repeated itself many hundreds of years later, when an enterprising young capitalist bought the knights out; the mountain is now a pricey hotel/restaurant complex. Nevertheless, the surrounding countryside is excellent for hiking, and the former **castle of the knights of Hirschhorn** is still worth a peek. By foot, follow the gray brick of Schloßstr. upward from the *Bürgerhaus* intersection (15min.). Unless you are in a car, do not follow the road signs. The castle's terraces offer a fine panorama, and an even better one can be had at the top of the tower for a mere DM0.30. Stone stairs curl from the castle down into the *Altstadt;* along the way, they pass the 15th-century **Karmeliter Klosterkirche,** with a Gothic interior and graceful carved altar. Some days, the monks' chanting echoes softly through the church.

Detailed maps of the local trails are available at the **tourist office,** Alleeweg 2 (tel. 17 42 or 20 81), which books rooms for free. From the train station, turn left on Neckarsteinacherstr. and follow it to the intersection as it curves around the hotel; the office is across the street to the right, inside the **Haus des Gastes** that also houses an **art and natural history museum,** with an interesting collection of 17th- and 18th-century wooden statues, weaponry and a truly terrifying diorama that crams over 100 native fauna into a space the size of a king-size bed. (Office open Mon.-Fri. 8am-noon and 2-5pm; also April-Oct. Sat. 9am-noon. Museum open Tues. and Thurs.-Sat. 2-4pm, Sun. 10am-noon and 2-4pm; admission DM1, kids DM0.50.) The **post office,** down Alleeweg, is to the left of the tourist office (open Mon.-Fri. 8:30am-noon and 2-5pm, Sat. 8:30-noon). The **telephone code** is 06272. For overnight accommodations, check the hotels and *Pensionen* along Hauptstr and the board outside the tourist office. **Haus La Belle,** Hauptstr. 36, has cushy rooms (with shower, toilet, and TV) starting at DM30 per person. Camp between April and mid-October at **Odenwald Camping** (tel. 809 or 36 58), 1km outside of town in the direction of the castle; follow signs from the tourist office (DM7 per person).

Thirty km south of Hirschhorn along the German Castle Road *(Burgenstraße)* is **Burg Guttenberg.** The castle has gracefully and miraculously survived the sackings, sieges, bombings, and general plunder that laid waste to its less sturdy comrades along the Castle Road. More distinctive is the aviary for **birds of prey,** maintained by prominent ornithologist Claus Fentzloff. Twice per day (at 11am and 3pm; March and Nov. at 3pm only), Fentzloff sends eagles and vultures flying inches above the heads of the crowds, plucking poor little chickens out of the sky, while he launches into lengthy scientific diatribes. (Museum open March-Oct. daily 9:30am-5pm. Aviary open 9am-6pm. Admission for aviary and bird show DM10, for castle and aviary DM13.) To reach Burg Guttenberg by rail, get off at Gundelsheim (along the Heidelburg-Heilbronn run), cross the big bridge past the camping site, and walk 2km, following the signs along the road (15min.).

BAD WIMPFEN

Just downstream from Heilbronn, along an alternative rail route on the road to Heidelberg, is the village of Bad Wimpfen, one of the best-kept secrets in Southwest Germany. Though this seems to be just one more innocuous village set against the sweeping backdrop of fields, the town opens unexpectedly into four gnarled bumpy streets and rough-worked, half-timbered houses, built on the ruins of a Roman imperial castle on a ridge high above the Neckar.

From the recently renovated train station, the immaculately preserved *Altstadt* is a 10-minute walk. Go straight ahead and follow Karl-Ulrich-Str. as it bends right. Or, if your calves need toning, take the steep hiking trail, to the right of the station. Up we go. Laid out along the southern side of the old castle walls, easily accessible points on the ancient battlements offer incredible views of the valley and surrounding countryside. Along the castle ruins between the *Marktplatz* and the train station are the **Blauer Turm** and the **Steinhaus.** The former offers another view of the town and its environs to those willing to climb the 169 steps. The tower's dramatic 1984 decapitation by lightning is documented on the way up the stairs. Next door, the sandstone *Steinhaus* contains a museum of artifacts left behind by the Romans (both open Tues.-Sun. 10am-noon and 2-4:30pm, Nov.-April Mon.-Fri. 10am-noon; admission

DM2, students DM1). The **Kulturamt,** Hauptstr. 45 (tel. 531 51), distributes information on cultural events in town. A miniature **Puppenmuseum** (doll museum) is located on Salzgasse 6. Bears and toys for the *Kind* in all of us. From the Kulturamt, take 50 steps, say "Mother, may I?" and turn immediately right around the corner; it's on the right (open Tues.-Thurs. and Sat.-Sun. 2:30-4:30pm; admission DM3, students DM1.50). Bad Wimpfen also has claim to the world's only **Pig Museum,** Kronengäßchen 2 (tel. 66 89), detailing the history of swine (considered a good luck symbol in Germany) with collector's items and lucky charms. It's got everything but the squeal. (Open daily 10am-5pm. Admission DM4.99, students DM2.49, children less than 1m tall DM0.99—a lucky *pfennig* on each ticket.)

The **tourist office** is in the train station (tel. 972 00; fax 97 20 20). They do not find rooms, but they will allow you to leave your luggage while you explore the town (open Mon.-Fri. 10am-1pm and 2-5pm, Sat.-Sun. 10am-noon and 2-4pm). Two doors down from the *Steinhaus* crouches Bad Wimpfen's **Jugendherberge (HI),** Burgviertel 21 (tel. 70 69), in a pair of half-timbered houses directly in front of the castle ruins. Call ahead; the hostel is popular with German tourists in the know, and space is always scarce. (Reception open 5-6pm and 9:30-10pm or by arrangement. Lockout 9am-noon. Curfew 10pm. DM19, over 26 DM24. Dinner DM8. Full board DM30. Family rooms available. Breakfast included. Closed mid-Nov. to early-March.) **Hotel Garni Neckarblick,** Erich-Salier-Str. 48 (tel. 70 02; fax 85 48), offers affordable luxury with a capital "L," very hospitable management, and a stunning view of the valley. From the *Marktplatz,* follow Mathildenbadstr. from the pedestrian zone out to the street, then hang a right. Proceed for 15 minutes along Erich-Salier-Str. as it curves around the hillside (past the park); the hotel is on the right. All rooms include color TVs and telephones; free **bike rental** is available to guests. (Singles DM45, with shower and TV DM66. Doubles DM78, with shower and TV DM108. Triples with TV DM115. Call ahead or fax reservations.) The **telephone code** is 07063.

For traditional German fare, try **d'Wimpfener Dobel,** Hauptstr. 61 (tel. 82 12), where *Maultaschen* (Swabian pasta pockets) are the house specialty (DM9-13). Their salad bar (DM5) is a rare source of green fiber in the Neckar Valley (open Mon.-Sat. 10am-midnight, Sun. 10am-10pm). **Grocery stores** are located on the other side of the *Altstadt.*

■ Heilbronn

In a land of beer-drinkers, Heilbronn is famous as a center for wine production. After Heilbronn was nearly destroyed in World War II on account of its industrial potential, most of its historic sights were replaced by rows of identical apartment buildings. The few treasures that remain lie within a block or two of one another in the area surrounding the *Marktplatz.* Heilbronn is the central train station in the Neckar valley region. The city is ringed by parks and has a motley collection of festivals.

The 16th-century ornamental clock perched on the **Rathaus** façade displays the days of the week, the month, date, and position of the moon and sun, as well as the corresponding zodiacal sign. It tells the time, too. **St. Kilians Kirche** looms across from the *Rathaus;* it is regarded as the first significant Renaissance building north of the Alps. Climb the tower at your own risk (DM1; open daily March-Oct. 9:30am-5pm, Nov.-Feb. 9:30am-4pm). Fifty meters from the church down Kirch-Grummestr. is the **Deutschordensmünster** (minster of the Teutonic Knights), reputedly the oldest building in town (c. 1240). The adjacent **Deutschhof** building, Deutschhofstr. 6 (tel. 56 22 95 or 56 31 44; fax 56 31 94) houses the **town museum** (open Tues. and Thurs. 10am-7pm, Wed. and Fri.-Sun. 10am-5pm).

Trains depart for Stuttgart and Heidelberg every hour (May-Oct.; DM13-25). A **bus ticket** in Heilbronn costs DM2.20, but a day pass *(Tageskarte)* costs a mere DM4. The helpful but hurried **tourist office** (tel. 56 22 70) is in the corner of the square to the right of the *Rathaus.* From the the train station, follow Bahnhofstr. (which turns into Kaiserstr. across the river) straight ahead for 500m across the bridge to the *Marktplatz* (open Mon.-Wed. and Fri. 9am-5:30pm, Thurs. 9am-6pm, Sat. 9am-noon).

BADEN-WÜRTTEMBERG

Round-trip **river cruises** to Bad Wimpfen and Gundelsheim (and other places) depart twice per day from below the bridge near the *Marktplatz* (DM12 and 14). For information, call 854 30 or consult the tourist office. **Rent bikes** at the main train station (tel. 614 449); you can return them to other stations. The **telephone code** is 07131.

Heilbronn's **Jugendherberge,** Schirrmannstr. 9 (tel. 17 29 61), lies east of town. Take bus #1 (direction: Trappensee) to "Trappensee," continue uphill 200m, and take a hard left where you see the street sign. (Lockout 9-11am. Severe 10pm curfew, but you can leave a DM50 deposit to get yourself a key. Members only. DM19.50, over 26 DM24.50. Sheets DM5.50. Laundry DM8 per load.) **Camping** on Breitenauer See (tel. (07130) 85 58; fax 36 22) is open all year. (DM8 per person. DM6 per tent. DM3 per dog—it's not worth the disguise to save money.) For inexpensive Italian food, check out **La Spaghetteria,** Weinsbergerstr. 90 (tel. 17 47 34), across the street from the "Karlstor." stop of bus #1. They've got buxom bowls of spaghetti that invite Pavlovian reaction for DM6.50 (open daily noon-2pm and 6pm-midnight). The *Marktplatz* hosts a year-round open-air **market** on Tuesdays, Thursdays, and Saturdays (7am-1pm).

For nine days in mid-September, **Heilbronner Herbst** transforms the *Marktplatz* into a *Weindorf* (wine village) where hundreds of vintages are quaffed by the glass (DM1) or liter (DM9) to the wheezing accompaniment of accordions. The **Pferdemarkt** (horse market) dates from the early 18th century; 3km of streets close down to make way for horse traders and their snorting wares.

▨ Schwäbisch Hall

A former capital of the region's salt trade, Schwäbisch Hall takes its name from the archaic word for salt, *Hall.* Back when the salt business was booming, Schwäbisch Hall blossomed. The town was virtually ignored during the wars of the next few centuries, however, and the only bomb that fell in the *Altstadt* during World War II destroyed the decrepit *Rathaus,* which was promptly rebuilt to greater grandeur than ever. Today, those in the know wander about the wonderfully intact, steeply sloping *Altstadt* and marvel at the medieval architecture. Though tourism is certainly present, for now Schwäbish Hall still belongs to its inhabitants.

Orientation and Practical Information Schwäbisch Hall has two **train** stations. The *Hauptbahnhof* is close to town, but the larger and more important station is in **Schwäbisch Hall-Hessental,** which lies on the main rail line to Stuttgart. If you're coming from the south, you'll probably end up arriving here. Although you will be 3km away from the salty pleasures of the *Altstadt,* do not panic—bus #1 frequently connects the Hessental station to Schwäbisch Hall proper (DM2; every 10-20min.). Schwäbisch Hall's **tourist office,** Am Markt 9 (tel. 75 12 46; fax 75 13 75), next to St. Michael's, has maps and finds rooms for free (open April-Oct. Mon.-Fri. 10am-3pm, Sat. 9am-3pm; Nov.-March Mon.-Fri. 9am-5pm).To **rent a bike,** useful in navigating this very steep city, try the **Radstation,** at Langestr. 40 (tel. 87 72), where you can get a two-wheeler for DM15 per day (open Mon.-Fri. 10am-6pm). The **Mitfahrzentrale** is at Lange Str. 28 (tel. 848 40). The **post office,** Hafenmarkt 2, 74523 Schwäbisch Hall, hides behind the *Rathaus* (open Mon.-Fri. 8:30am-noon and 2:30-5:30pm, Sat. 8:30am-noon). The **telephone code** is 0791.

Accommodations and Food Schwäbisch Hall's **Jugendherberge (HI),** Langenfelder Weg 5 (tel. 410 50), is past the *Marktplatz* on the Galgenberg ("Gallows Mountain"). Follow Crailsheimer Str. up to take a left onto Langenfelderstr. A legion of couches decks the halls of an an unbeatably clean hostel. (Reception at desk open 4:30-7pm, in the kitchen until curfew at 10pm. DM19.50, over 26 DM24.50. Members only. Sheets DM6. Breakfast included.) **Gästehaus "Sölch,"** Hauffstr. 14 (tel. 518 07; fax 544 04), is located in a residential neighborhood. From the *Bahnhof,* take a right and walk until you reach an intersection. Hike the railed walkway up over the hill to a tiled plateau and then take a left up the stairs on the hill. Keep on going straight at the top of the stairs. The path will curve around to a road. Here take a left, then right onto Hauffstr. Or take bus #1 to "Mörikeplatz," then cross the street and head up Nox-Eythstr. (Singles with shower, toilet, and TV DM65. Doubles DM105. Breakfast included.) **Gasthof Dreikönig,** Neuestr. 25 (tel. 74 73; fax 87 12), offers large, simply furnished rooms with creaky floors. Yes, it does look like a restaurant—just barge right in. (Singles DM45. Doubles DM88, with shower DM98.) There is a **Campingplatz** (tel. 29 84) at Steinbacher See. Take bus #4 to "Steinbach/Mitte," then backtrack slightly and follow the signs. (DM7 per person, under 18 DM5; DM9 per tent. DM1 per shower. Open April to mid-Oct.) **Taverne bei Vangele,** Bahnhofstr. 15, serves a bewildering array of Grecian specialities with a sizable vegetarian section (entrees DM8.50-15; open Thurs.-Tues. 5pm-midnight, Wed. 11:30am-2pm). **Ilge,** Im Weiler 2 (tel. 716 84) is a postcard-perfect setting in which to drink a delectable yogurt shake (DM4-5.20; open daily 11am-1am).

Sights To reach the marvelously preserved *Altstadt* from the train station, cross Bahnhofstr. and head down the stone steps and footpath toward the river. Turn left on Mauerstr. and cross the wooden footbridges that connect the islands in the Kocher. Finally, follow the winding cobblestone streets to the **Marktplatz.** Use the church tower as a beacon. From the Hessental train station, take bus #1 and get off at "Spitalbach Ost," the last stop (DM2; 20min.). During summer evenings, the *Marktplatz* becomes the stage for the renowned *Freilichtspiele* (see page 161). The restrained Baroque *Rathaus* confronts the **Kirche St. Michael,** which perches precariously atop a treacherously steep set of stone stairs. The church's high altar is a Dutch-influenced series of painted panels; one of the paving stones behind the altar has been removed to reveal a medieval **ossuary.** (Webster's: "*n.* 1. a depository (vault, room, urn) for the bones of the dead.") Although the top floor of the tower is closed due to a recent suicide jump, you can still sneak a peek through the small windows near the top to see a perfect rug of red-tiled roofs sloping down into the valley. (Open Mon. 2-5pm, Tues.-Sat. 9am-noon and 2-5pm, Sun. 11am-noon and 2-5pm; mid-Nov.-April Tues.-Sat. 11am-noon and 2-3pm, Sun. 11am-noon.)

A Gothic spire tops the 16th-century square **fountain** that stands to one side of the market square. A number of 15th- and 16th-century *Fachwerk* edifices occupy narrow Obere Herrngasse, which leads off the *Marktplatz.* The old **Keckenburg** harbors the eight-story Romanesque **Keckenturm** and **Hällisch-Fränkisches Museum,** on Keckenhof, one street lower. The museum houses a distinguished set of wood carvings and a smashing Baroque room (Open Tues. and Thurs.-Sun. 10am-5pm, Wed. 10am-8pm. Tours Sun. at 11am and Wed. at 6:30pm. Free, but DM45 for group tours.) The **Henkersbrücke** (Hangman's Bridge), down Neuestr. from the Marktplatz, delivers a view of Schwäbisch Hall's waterfront—including a covered bridge and ducks. A few blocks farther into the lower city is the **Henkersturm** (Hangman's Tower—sense a trend here?), with a disappointingly less than grisly appearance. In the northern part of the *Altstadt,* the old street **Gelbinger Gasse** is the town's most beautiful section. For a relaxing walk along the river, the gardens of the **Ackeranlage** back the tremendous architectural vista with tall, shady trees.

Above town, on an adjacent hill, the **Comburg**—monastery, castle, and now an institute for teacher training—dates to the 11th century. The fully preserved wall provides peep holes for views of the valley, and the 18th-century Baroque truffle of a church, marble-gold flavor, satiates any craving for Bavaria. Take bus #4 to "Steinbach/Mitte," cross the street, and head left around and right up Bildersteige. The **Hohenloher Freilandmuseum** (open-air museum) in Museumsdorf Wackershofen (tel. 840 61) is a collection of 50 farm houses and their inhabitants (animal, vegetable, mineral) from four centuries. Experience authentic sounds, shapes, and smells and watch *Schnapps* being made. Touch a cow. (Open daily April-Oct. 10am-5:30pm, in summer 9am-6pm. Admission DM7, students DM5.)

Entertainment On summer evenings between mid-June and mid-August the **Freilichtspiele,** a series of old and modern plays running from Shakespeare to Brecht, are performed on the steps of the Kirche St. Michael. For schedules and tickets (DM20-45, with DM6-10 student discounts; some concerts run only DM7-10), contact **Freilichtspiele Schwäbisch Hall,** Am Markt 8 (tel. 75 13 11; open Mon.-Fri. 9am-noon, 2-5pm; during Freilichtspiele open Mon.-Fri. 9am-noon and 3-8:30pm, Sun. 3-8:30pm). When rehearsals occur on the steps (quite frequently), you can watch the directors do their thing for free. On the Saturday, Sunday, and Monday of Pentecost (May 26-28 in 1997) and again on the following Monday, Schwäbisch Hall celebrates the **Brunnenfest** (fountain festival), during which locals don 16th-century salt-boilers' costumes to dance a traditional jig. During **Sommernachtsfest** in the last weekend of August, 30,000 little candles light patterns along the Akeranlage. Live music and fireworks brighten these summer nights.

■ Swabian Jura (Schwäbische Alb)

The limestone plateaus, sharp ridges, and pine-forested valleys stretching from Tübingen in the north to Lake Constance in the south are collectively known as the Swabian Jura, a region often considered an ugly cousin of the adjacent Black Forest. But the periphery is colored by the brush of the exotic, and by a bit of the uncanny. Its rough-hewn landscape is scenic yet stubborn, with a harsh climate that often vents its wrath on travelers. The powerful medieval dynasties that held the area in their sway found the Swabian peaks perfect sites for fortification, as they command panoramic views of the surrounding valleys. Big-time families like the Hohenstaufens filled the region with castles and abbeys. The **Swabian Jura Road** *(Schwäbische Albstraße)* bisects the plateau, intersecting the Romantic Road at Nördlingen. A web of trails serves hikers; maps are available at regional tourist offices in major towns. These towns have a tranquil aura that is ideal for rest and rejuvenation; nightlife doesn't have much of a place in the Jura. Train service to many points is roundabout and often incomplete, but bus routes pick up the slack.

SCHWÄBISCH GMÜND

Baroque **Schwäbisch Gmünd,** located on the northern cusp of the range, provides the best base for excursions into the region. The town itself has been a center for metalworking—particularly silversmithing—since the 18th century. Beautifully wrought jewelry and ornaments can be found in many shops in the town center. The blossoming of this industry in the 18th century resulted in a building boom that left the town with a market square surrounded by Baroque plaster façades and *Fachwerk* buildings dating from the 15th and 16th centuries. An American military base once inhabited Schwäbisch Gmünd's Mutlangen suburb. Here protests erupted in the early 80s over the stationing of U.S. Pershing missiles in Germany, drawing the likes of brilliant writer and political activist Günter Grass to the town. However, the GIs left after the fall of eastern Germany, and the former barracks have now transformed into a campus for the **University of Maryland.** (Tuition DM9000. Room and board DM4100. Application fee DM100. Possible majors range from International Management to German Basket Weaving.)

The roof of the 14th-century **Heiligkreuzmünster** (Holy Cross Cathedral), on Münsterplatz, is a truncated, box-like architectural freak with no towers—the roof was too weak to support any. The Gothic interior is filled with statues, most dating from the 15th and 16th centuries. The **Silberwaren- und Bijouteriemuseum** (Silver and Jewelry Museum), across from the tourist office (tel. 389 10), features real, live silversmiths tooling silver in the traditional style. Exhibits cover the history of the silver trade, Silver Age, and silver arts (open Wed. and Sat. 2-5pm, Sun. 10am-noon and 2-5pm; admission DM5, students DM2). The 16th-century **Kornhaus,** an old grain storage building right off the square and two blocks behind the *Rathaus,* at the *Marktplatz,* now houses a **tourist office** (tel. 60 34 55; fax 60 34 59). They book rooms for free, but charge for hiking maps (open Mon.-Fri. 9am-5:30pm, Sat. 9am-noon). The post office is across from the train station (open Mon.-Fri. 8am-noon and 2:30-5:30pm). The telephone code is 07171.

Schwäbisch Gmünd's Jugendherberge (HI), Taubentalstr. 46/1 (tel. 22 60), is located on the edge of an idyllically forested region criss-crossed by footpaths, only 10 minutes from the train station. Turn left and pass underneath the railroad tracks. Follow the road, then veer left onto Taubentalstr. and keep on truckin' up the hill. At the end of the street, before you reach the recreational park parking lot, turn right up the hill toward that big cream-colored building in the sky with the letters "DJH" on it. (Reception open 5-8pm. Curfew 10pm. DM19, over 26 DM23.50. Sheets DM5.50. Breakfast included.) Call in advance, since Gmünd is a popular destination for high school end-of-year field trips. Gasthof Weißer Ochsen, Parlerstr. 47 (tel. 28 12), has discreet singles (DM35) and one double (DM62). Another accommodation option is the hostel in Hohenstaufen (see below). Gasthaus "Zum Lamm," Rinderbachgasse 19 (tel 26 61), has a nondescript daily menu (DM8.50-14.50) of Swabian specialties. (Open Tues.-Sat. 10am-2pm and from 6pm until the crowds go to bed, Sun. 11am-2pm, Mon. from 5pm until the nondescript daily menu of Swabian specialties goes to bed.) An open-air market fills the Münsterplatz every Wednesday and Saturday (7am-noon).

THE KAISERBERGE

Just south of Schwäbisch Gmünd lie the three conical peaks, Hohenstaufen, Hohenrechberg, and Stuifen, which make up the Kaiserberge. This curtain of mountains marks the beginning of the Swabian Jura. Hohenstaufen was named after the castle that once graced its summit, built by the Hohenstaufens, one of Germany's great medieval dynastic families. The castle is gone, but the view of the other two Kaiserberge peaks and of the Swabian Jura in the distance is spectacular. To reach Hohenstaufen, take bus #12 from Schwäbisch Gmünd to either Straßdorf or the village of Hohenstaufen (bus #13 on Sun. and holidays only). The trail to the top takes about 30 minutes. Or, take the bus to the Hohenstaufen *("Juhe")* stop and put yourself right in the middle of hill action around Jugendherberge Hohenstaufen, Schottengasse 45 (tel. (07165) 438; fax 14 18), which has six- and eight-bed rooms on a gently sloping plain. (DM18.50, over 26 DM23.50. Sheets DM5.50. Call ahead.)

Hohenrechberg, to the east, has a mysterious castle ruin and a Baroque Wallfahrtskirche (pilgrimage church). The old castle wall now functions as the foundation for a footpath. To reach Hohenrechberg, take the bus from Schwäbisch Gmünd to the village of Rechberg. It's about a 1-hour climb from there. Stuifen, also close to Rechberg, can also be hiked, though there are no flashy ruins and the view is nowhere near as compelling as it is from the other peaks. The tourist office in Schwäbisch Gmünd has a number of hiking maps with routes. All buses to the Kaiserberge from Schwäbisch Gmünd run from the train station.

HAIGERLOCH AND HECHINGEN

Haigerloch exemplifies both the rural charm and the isolation that mark much of the Swabian Jura. Omnibus #10 connects Haigerloch to the rest of the world only a few times per day, via Horb to the northwest (20min.; DM5.30), and Hechingen (40min.; DM6.20) to the east. The easiest place to catch the bus from either town is at the train station (next to the phone booth in Hechingen and at Steig 6 in Horb; make sure it's obvious that you're waiting or the bus will speed by). Centered around an S-shaped bend in the Eyach River, Haigerloch's layout has evolved into a confusing tangle. It is divided into an *Unterstadt* (lower city) on the valley floor and an *Oberstadt* (upper city) along the crescent-shaped southern ridge. Fortunately, the the town's sights are exceedingly well-marked.

The local Schloß is set on the northern ridge above the *Unterstadt*. Wide stairs head upwards from the central *Marktplatz*. The *Schloß* has been turned into a big art gallery exhibiting contemporary works by German artists. The poorer of these artists work in the modern studio complex on top of the hill; the museum-studio development is all for the purpose of artistic patronage. Check with the tourist office (see below) for a schedule of jazz and classical concerts sponsored by the castle. Halfway to the top of the hill, the **Schloßkirche** (open daily 9am-6pm) is a sumptuous Baroque church. Its walls drip with gold ornamentation and flamboyantly-colored biblical and historical scenes. At the zenith, the *Schloß* terrace proffers an awesome view; an even better one, looking out over the Haigerloch *Schloßbrau* factory and into the valley below, can be had by following the path marked **Kapf,** a 3-minute walk from the main courtyard. Back in the valley below, an old beer cellar underneath the *Schloßkirche* houses the tiny **Atomkeller Museum** ("atomic cellar"; tel. 18 00). Near the end of World War II, German physicists like Heisenberg and von Weizsäcker struggled unsuccessfully to generate a self-sustaining nuclear chain reaction. Today, their reactor can be seen much as it was when American troops marched in, in April 1945. The museum itself is a single cold room with bare rock walls and water dripping from the ceiling (open May-Sept. daily 10am-noon and 2-5pm; March-April and Oct.-Nov. Sat.-Sun. 10am-noon and 2-5pm; admission DM2). Not to be outdone, the back wall of the **Evangelische Kirche** sports an imitation of da Vinci's *The Last Supper*. As the church's only decoration, it certainly deserves a look. To reach this Christian mural from the *Marktplatz,* walk over the Noyaler Bridge to Hechinger Str. and make a sharp right 100m later onto Oberstadtstr. The church is 200m up the hill. The building further up the hill from the Evangelishe Kirche (visible from the *Schloß*) is the **Römerturm.** If your thirst for views still has not been quenched, you can climb up (open April-Oct. Sat.-Sun. 10am-6pm).

Buses drop passengers off at several different points in Haigerloch; the most common are the *Marktplatz* in the *Unterstadt* and the *Schulzentrum* on the outskirts of the *Oberstadt.* From anywhere else, just head into town—it's not far. The **tourist office,** Oberstadtstr. 11 (tel. 697 26 or 697 27), inside the *Rathaus,* has maps, information, and a little exhibit on the guy who plagiarized *The Last Supper* (open Mon.-Fri. 9am-noon, Mon.-Wed. 2-5pm, Thurs. 2-6:30pm). To reach the tourist office from the *Marktplatz,* cross the bridge, walk two blocks to Oberstadtstr., then turn right. From the *Schulzentrum,* follow Oberstadtstr.'s curvaceous descent for 10-15 minutes. Watch out for the "S" on bus schedules; it indicates buses that don't run on school holidays. Overnight visitors should head to **Krone,** Oberstadtstr. 47 (tel. 95 44 44; fax 954 40), between the *Römerturm* and St. Anna, which has handsome rooms with white fluffy pillows, all with TV and telephone. (Singles with shower DM45-60. Doubles DM75-95. Breakfast included. AmEx, Visa, and MC accepted). The **telephone code** is 07474.

In trying to get to or from Haigerloch, you will probably end up in **Hechingen,** a town that's virtually free of tourists. In the distance, often ringed by mist, **Burg Hohenzollern** rises majestically above a carpet of trees. The castle is the ancestral home of the Hohenzollern family, which ruled a unified Germany from 1871 to 1918 under Kaisers William I and II. The current edifice (most of it built during the first half of the 19th century) is a tremendous conglomeration of spiraling towers and imposing battlements that makes Snow White's castle pout with envy. It seems impossible even to associate it with the modern world—yet it was inhabited through the first half of the 20th century. An incredible panoramic view extends to the Swiss Alps on clear days. Admission to the castle includes a 45-min. tour in which everyone is required to wear enormous slippers to protect the floors (open daily 9am-5:30pm; mid-Oct.-mid-March 9am-4:30pm; admission DM7, students DM3). Unfortunately, no public transportation connects Hechingen to the castle. Taking a **taxi** will cost an outrageous DM24 for a round-trip, but get a personal estimate from your cabby before setting off. Some penny-pinching travelers hitch the distance. And there is always the good old one-foot-in-front-of-the-other. It's about an hour and a half from the train station through beautiful country. From the *Rathaus* (see below) walk down Heiligkreuzstr, take a left at the Heilig-Kreuz Frischof (cemetery), go under the railroad bridge, and take the first right towards the woods. There are a myriad of trails through the woods to the castle. Basically, if you keep heading up, you'll get there. This can all be greatly facilitated by the map distributed at the the **tourist office**

(Städtisches Verkehrsamt), Marktplatz 1 (tel. 18 51 14; fax 18 51 44), in the *Rathaus*. From the train station, go straight into the city and keep walking up. The *Rathaus* is adorned with a golden ball (open Mon.-Wed. and Fri. 7:50am-12:30pm, Thurs. 7:50am-12:30pm and 2-6pm).

■ Stuttgart

Surrounded by green hills, criss-crossed by leafy parks, and laced by a vineyard that stretches to the *Hauptbahnhof*, Stuttgart boasts one of the most verdant settings of any major German city. The city itself, however, is more prosperous and functional than beautiful. The burden of history does not weigh on Stuttgart as it does on so many other German cities: the city center is a glassy, modern vision whose huge, rotating Mercedes-Benz symbol reflects the blithe prosperity of one of the richest communities in Europe. On the other hand, the Swabian metropolis's wealth pays off nicely in top-notch museums, world-class galleries, wide parks, and a lively theater scene. As a *Land* capital, Stuttgart is solidly ensconced in both industry and bureaucracy, yet still finds time to entertain the throngs on its busy streets. Founded 1000 years ago as a stud farm *(Stutgarten)*, Stuttgart now remembers its equine past only through the horse on its coat of arms. Today, Porsche, Daimler-Benz, and a host of other corporate thoroughbreds live out their corporate lives here.

ORIENTATION AND PRACTICAL INFORMATION

At the heart of Stuttgart lies an enormous pedestrian zone where shops and restaurants stretch as far as the eye can see. **Königstr.** and **Lautenschlagerstr.** are the main pedestrian thoroughfares; from the train station, both are accessible through the underground **Arnulf-Klett-Passage.** To the left lies the tranquil swath of green called the *Schloßgarten,* to the right the thriving business sector. Stuttgart sells itself as a compact city, and in comparison to many American sprawlers, it is. But sooner or later you will have to ride a train or U-Bahn.

Tourist Office: I-Punkt, Königstr. 1 (tel. 222 82 40), directly in front of the escalator down into the Klett-Passage. Professional staff books rooms for free, sells excellent maps (DM1), distributes bus and train schedules, and speaks lovely English. Their *Monatsspiegel* (in German only; DM3.20) lists museum hours, cultural events, and musical performances, and includes a guide to restaurants and nightlife. Open May-Oct. Mon.-Fri. 9:30am-8:30pm, Sat. 9:30am-6pm, Sun. and public holidays 11am-6pm; Nov.-April same hours but Sun. and holidays only 1-6pm. **Tips 'n' Trips,** Hohe Str. 9 (tel. 226 80 01; fax 223 70 87), has a number of informative pamphlets for all facets of the Stuttgart experience (in English as well as German) and tons of information on travel and youth-oriented matters. Open Mon. and Fri. 10am-6pm, Tues. and Wed. noon-7pm, Thurs. noon-8pm.

Consulates: U.S., Urbanstr. 7 (tel. 21 00 80; fax 210 08 20). **U.K.,** Breite-Str. 2 (tel. 16 26 90).

American Express: Lautenschlagerstr. 3 (tel. 187 50; fax 187 51 32), 1 block south of the station. Holds mail and cashes traveler's checks. Open Mon.-Fri. 9:30-5:30pm, Sat. 9:30am-12:30pm.

Telephones: Plenty at both post offices and in the Arnulf-Klett-Passage above the U-Bahn entrances.

Flights: Flughaven Stuttgart has flights to every major city in Germany and to other countries (tel. 948 33 88 or 948 27 90 for schedule info). Take S-Bahn #2 or 3 to the city (30min.; DM4.30 one way).

Trains: tel. 194 19 for 24-hr. schedule information. A public transportation office (tel. 79 30 24) can be found at the station and at the airport, 1 floor downstairs from arrivals. Open Mon.-Fri. 7am-1pm and 1:30-6:40pm, Sat. 8:30am-2pm. The transportation hub of southwestern Germany, Stuttgart has direct rail links to most major German cities. Trains roll east to Munich 30 times per day.

Public Transportation: Information office, Arnulf-Klett-Passage (tel. 250 53 03), next to the escalator up to Königstr. Look for the *"Kundenberatung"* sign. Bus, streetcar, U-Bahn, and S-Bahn maps and schedules, along with needed map-and-schedule deciphering. Open Mon.-Fri. 9am-6pm, Sat. 9am-noon. A **single-ride ticket** runs DM2.70-8.70. 4-ride *Mehrfahrkarten* range DM9.80-32.60; they save you 10% off the single ride rates. *Tageskarten*—valid for trains and buses (except night buses)—are DM16.50; these handy passes also entitle you to free transport of up to 2 kids and a dog. A *Kurzestreck* pass (DM1.70) lets you travel short distances. Railpasses are valid *only* on the S-Bahn. **Nachtbus** (night bus) stops are marked with a purple-and-yellow sign. The tourist office has a free schedule.

Ferries: Neckar-Personen-Schiffahrt (tel. 54 10 73 or 541 07; fax 54 50 80). Boats cruise from **Bad Cannstatt** (across the river) to little towns along the Neckar (1-2 per day). Round-trip DM8.80-46. They're good for alternative transportation. Many older folks take the boats to dance polka and recall the good old days; bring your accordian. Harbor **tours** Sun.-Fri. 9am and 11am (2hr.; DM14).

Car Rental: Europcar (tel. 223 71 36; fax 223 88 05), **Hertz** (tel. 226 29 21; fax 226 27 10), **Avis** (tel. 223 72 58), and **Sixt/Budget** (tel. 223 78 22) share an office at the *Hauptbahnhof* next to track 16. Open Mon.-Fri. 8am-6pm, Sat. 8am-noon.

Bike Rental: Rent a Bike (tel. 209 90, 48 10 10, or 262 23 54). DM8 per hr., DM18 per 6hrs., DM25 per day, DM65 per weekend (Fri.-Sun.), DM100 per week.

Mitfahrzentrale: Stuttgart has 2 **Eurostop** offices: Stuttgart West, Lerchenstr. 65 (tel. 636 80 36), and Hauptstätterstr. 154 (tel. 60 36 06).

Luggage Storage: Lockers in the train station DM2; large lockers DM4.

Lost and Found: Fundbüro der Stadtverwaltung, Eberhardstr. 61f (tel. 216 20 16). Open Mon.-Wed. 8am-1pm, Thurs. 8:30am-3:30pm, Fri. 8:30am-12:30pm. **Fundbüro der Deutschen Bundesbahn,** Wolframstr. 19 (tel. 20 92 or 24 68). Open Mon.-Thurs. 8am-noon and 1-3:30pm, Fri. 8am-noon and 1-2:30pm.

Bookstore: Buchhaus Wittwer, Königstr. 30 (tel. 250 70), right off the *Schloßplatz*, has the largest selection. Check the sale bin outside where perfectly good books have been inexplicably, but happily, knocked down to bargain prices. Open Mon.-Wed. and Fri. 9am-6:30pm, Thurs. 9am-8:30pm, Sat. 9am-2pm.

Gay Information Line: Rosa Telefon (tel. 194 46). Fri. 7-9pm or leave a message.

Laundromat: SB Wasch Salon, Kienbachstr. 16 (tel. 52 30 08). Take S-Bahn #13 (direction: Giebel-Hedelfingen) to "Kienbachstr." DM8 to wash and dry for 10min. DM2 per 10 additional minutes of drying. Open daily 8am-10pm.

Rape Crisis Hotline: (tel. 29 64 32). Call Mon.-Fri. 9-11am and 6-8pm.

24-Hour Pharmacy: For a rotating pharmacy schedule, buy *Amtsblatt* for DM1.20 from the tourist office, or have a look at the copy posted at the *Rathaus*. **Internationale,** Königstr. 70 (tel. 22 47 80), is a centrally-located pharmacy. Open Mon.-Wed. and Fri. 8:30am-6:30pm, Thurs. 8:30am-8:30pm, Sat. 8:30am-2pm.

Hospital: Bürgerhospital, Tunzhoferstr. 14-16 (tel. 253 00).

Emergency: tel. 110. **Police:** Hahnemannstr. 1 (tel. 899 01).

Post Office: At the *Hauptbahnhof*, 70001 Stuttgart (tel. 226 03 30). Open Mon.-Fri. 8am-6pm, Sat. 8am-1pm, Sun. 11am-noon. *Postlagernde Briefe* at windows 3-4. To mail packages, use the post office at Bolzstr. 3, 18750 Stuttgart (tel. 225 43 31); does not hold mail. Open Mon.-Fri. 9am-6pm, Sat. 9am-1pm, Sun. 11am-noon.

Telephone Code: 0711.

ACCOMMODATIONS AND CAMPING

Most of Stuttgart's budget beds are located on the two ridges surrounding the downtown area and are easily accessible by streetcar. Accommodations around the pedestrian zone and train station cater to customers used to paying top *Mark* for creature comforts. Make "call ahead" your mantra. Contact Tips 'n' Trips for information on cheap overnighting in Stuttgart. If you have a railpass (or even if you don't), the *Jugendherbergen* in Esslingen and Ludwigsburg are good alternatives.

Jugendgästehaus Stuttgart, Richard-Wagner-Str. 2 (tel. 24 11 32). Take Straßenbahn #15 (direction: Heumaden) to "Bubenbad." Continue in direction of the U-Bahn on the right side of street and veer right immediately; the place is on the right. *Right.* Excellent dorm-hostel situated in a quiet residential neighborhood offers spotless rooms with a great view. Enjoy excellent facilities and a helpful,

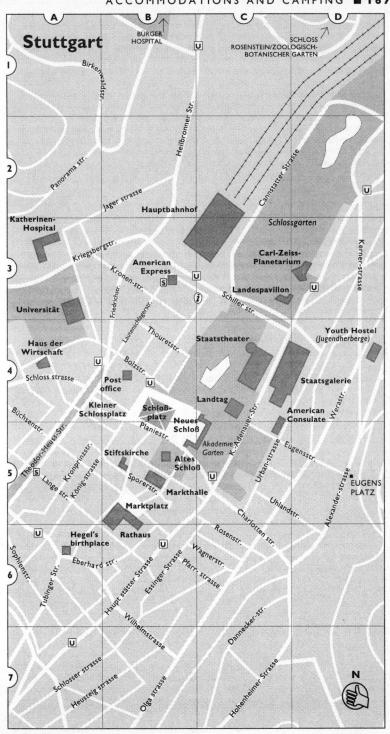

Stuttgart

A **B** **C** **D**

BÜRGER
HOSPITAL

SCHLOSS
ROSENSTEIN/ZOOLOGISCH-
BOTANISCHER GARTEN

1

Birkenwaldstr.

Heilbronner Str.

2

Panorama str.

Cannstatter Strasse

Jager strasse

Kerner-strasse

Hauptbahnhof

Schlossgarten

**Katherinen-
Hospital**

Kriegsbergstr.

**Carl-Zeiss-
Planetarium**

3

Kronen-str.

**American
Express**

Friedrichstr.

Landespavillon

Schiller str.

Universität

Laurenichbgerstr.

Thouretstr.

Youth Hostel
(Jugendherberge)

**Haus der
Wirtschaft**

Bolzstr.

Staatstheater

4

Schloss strasse

**Post
office**

Staatsgalerie

Büchsenstr.

**Kleiner
Schlossplatz**

**Schloß-
platz**

Landtag

**American
Consulate**

Werastr.

Theodor-Heuss-Str.

**Neues
Schloß**

Planiestr.

K.-Adenauer-Str.

Urban-strasse

Eugensstr.

Stiftskirche

Akademie
Garten

5

Lange str.

Kronprinzstr.

König-strasse

**Altes
Schloß**

Sporerstr.

**EUGENS
PLATZ**

Alexander-strasse

Markthalle

Uhlandstr.

Marktplatz

**Hegel's
birthplace**

Rathaus

Charlotten str.

Rosenstr.

6

Sophienstr.

Tubinger Str.

Eberhard str.

Hauptstätter Strasse

Essinger Strasse

Pfarr-
strasse

Wagnerstr.

Wilhelmstrasse

Dannecker-str.

7

Schlosser strasse

Heusteig strasse

Olga strasse

Hohenheimer Strasse

N

friendly staff. Reception open Mon.-Fri. 9am-8pm, Sat.-Sun. 11am-8pm. No curfew. Singles DM35, with bath DM45. Doubles DM60, with bath DM70. Triples DM90, with bath DM105. DM5 extra per person for single-night stays. Breakfast, showers, and lockers included. Dinner served at 6pm (DM7). Key deposit DM20.

Jugendherberge Stuttgart (HI), Haußmannstr. 27 (tel. 24 15 83; fax 236 10 41). Take U-Bahn #15 (direction: Heumaden) to "Eugensplatz" and go over the hill, bearing left down Kernerstr. Or walk left from the station on Schillerstr. and up, up, up the hill (follow stairs). Walk through the *Schloßgarten* along Schillerstr. (where you'll find a sidewalk). Entrance on Kernerstr. Despite the 220 beds, the rooms are often maddeningly full. Reception open 7-8:45am and noon-11pm. Lockout 9am-noon. Curfew 11pm (the next chance to get in is 6am). DM20, over 26 DM25. Sheets DM5.50. When super-full, a mattress on the floor goes for DM15. Breakfast included. Lunch served at noon (DM8), dinner at 6pm (DM8), both optional. Show up by noon and beg for a bed, even if they say there are none left.

Haus Berg, Karl-Schurz-Str. 16A (tel. 26 18 75; fax 286 46 39). Take U-Bahn #14 to "Mineralbäder," then bear left across the parking lot and climb the hill. Friendly staff and neat rooms in a quiet neighborhood. Reception open 24hr. Singles DM55, with shower DM66, with bath DM69. Doubles DM85, with shower DM98. Discounts for longer stays and breakfast skippers. Call ahead if arriving after 10pm.

Pension Märklin, Friedrichstr. 39 (tel. 29 13 15). Convenient, period. Take a right from the station and turn left on Friedrichstr. Singles DM45. Doubles DM80-90. You get what you pay for: no breakfast, but you can avail yourself of the showers and the bathtub. No lockouts, no rules—get your keys and kick back.

Tramper Point Stuttgart, Wiener Str. 317 (tel. 817 74 76; fax 237 28 10). Take U-Bahn #6 (direction: Giebel) to the "Sportpark Feuerbach," then go left. It's the mural-covered wood structure on the right. Funkiest alternative accommodations in town: shack up here on one of 25 cots in a crescent-shaped room, or an *Isomatte* in case of overflow. Reception open 5-11pm. 3-day max. stay. Ages 16-27 only. DM10 per night. Wool blanket DM1.50, or bring your own sleeping bag. Showers included. Breakfast DM4. Open late-June to early-Sept.

Camping: Campingplatz Stuttgart, Mercedesstr. 40 (tel. 55 66 96; fax 48 69 47), Cannstatter Wesen, on the river in Bad Cannstatt. Take streetcar #1 or U-Bahn #2 (direction: Obere Ziegelei or Fellbach). Reception open summer 7am-noon and 2-10pm; winter 7am-noon and 2-8pm. DM6 per tent. DM6 per person. DM4 per car. DM3.50 per child. DM4 per pet. DM2.50 per shower.

FOOD

Due to a sizable contingent of *Gastarbeiter* (guest workers), Stuttgart's restaurant scene is heartily spiced with Greek, Turkish, African, and Asian eateries as well as an astounding variety of snack bars. But the cuisine of the *Schwaben* region is itself one of the most successful forms of German food. *Spätzle* (thick noodles) and *Maultaschen* (pasta pockets filled with meat and spinach) are especially prevalent. Ask at Tips 'n' Trips for a pamphlet (in German or English) of inexpensive eateries and pubs (see Orientation and Practical Information, p. 165). On Königstr. a pretzel or *Laugenstange,* smothered in butter with optional ham, is Swabian bliss available at little wooden stands. The *Wochenmarkt* is on Marktplatz and Schillerplatz (Thurs. and Sat. 8am-3pm). For groceries, try the basement of **Kaufhof,** two blocks in front of the train station (open Mon.-Wed. and Fri. 9am-6:30pm, Thurs. 9am-8:30pm., Sat. 8:30am-2pm). **Restaurant Marché,** on Konigstr. 16, is a self-service chain restaurant with Papa Bear-sized bowls o' vegetables from which you construct your dream salad (meals under DM10). Take the U-Bahn to "Hauptbahnhof" (open daily 8am-11pm).

University Mensa, Holzgartenstr. 11. From the *Bahnhof,* take Kriegsbergstr. to Holzgartenstr., turn left, and go down the right side of the street over the underpass; it's on the right. A plain but functional place where quantity compensates for quality (meals DM4-5). Open during school (mid-April to late-July and mid-Oct.-mid.- Feb.) Mon.-Fri. 11:15am-2pm.; the rest of the year Mon.-Fri. 11:15am-1:30pm.

Iden, Eberhardstr. 1 (tel. 23 59 89). Take the U-Bahn to "Stadtmitte." Cheap, good vegetarian fare served cafeteria-style. 50 kinds of salad (DM2.50 per 100g), noodles, and potatoes. *Let's Go* recommends: *Eat your vegetables!* Open Mon.-Wed. and Fri. 11am-8pm, Thurs. 11am-9pm, Sat. 10am-4pm.

Taverna Litfass bei Ali, Eberhardstr. 37 (tel. 24 30 31). Take the U-Bahn to "Stadtmitte," then descend on the left side of the street below the rotating sign. Masses of Stuttgarters head here for delicious and relatively inexpensive Turkish and Swabian food (DM10-15) in an atmosphere half-way between a *Biergarten* and a sultan's harem. Drinks DM3-7. Keeps on serving into the wee hours. Live bands Fri. and Sat. after midnight (sorry, hostelers). Open daily 11:30am-5am.

Academie der Schönsten Künste, Charlottenstr. 5 (tel. 24 24 36). Take the U-Bahn to "Charlottenplatz." High ceilings, art-covered walls, a garden out back, and fewer seats than there should be at such a cool place. Breakfast served all day (DM2.50-12). Open Mon.-Fri. 7am-midnight, Sat.-Sun. 9am-3pm.

Weinhaus Stetter, Rosenstr. 32 (tel. 24 01 63). Take U-Bahn to "Charlottenplatz," walk down Esslingerstr. and take a left onto Rosenstr. Offers intriguing Swabian specialties (DM7-9), all to be washed down with an incredible wine selection (DM5-7). Open Mon.-Fri. 3-11pm, Sat.-Sun. 10am-2pm.

SIGHTS

Stuttgart is not exactly big on historic wonders. The **Schloßgarten,** Stuttgart's main municipal park, runs from the train station southward to the *Neues Schloß* and northeast to the Neckar; it's crammed with fountains and beautifully-tended flower gardens. The north end of the *Schloßgarten* contains the expansive **Rosensteinpark,** which also holds the **Wilhelma** (tel. 540 20), Stuttgart's famous zoo and botanical garden (open May-Aug. daily 8:15am-6pm; April and Sept. daily 8:15am-5:30pm; March and Oct. daily 8:15am-5pm; Nov.-Feb. 8:15am-4pm; admission DM11, students DM5). The *Schloßgarten* runs all the way to the **Schloßplatz,** off Königstr., upon which reposes the elegent, Baroque **Neues Schloß,** now home to a company of stodgy bureaucrats. The 16th-century **Altes Schloß** (across the street on Schillerplatz) is Stuttgart's only other architecturally notable sight. To interface with the *Weltgeist* (world-spirit), head to **Hegel's birthplace**—just a few doors down from a busy porn shop, at Eberhardstr. 53, a few blocks down Konrad-Adenauer-Str. (tel. 216 67 33). The house provides a thorough, if somewhat inscrutable, exegesis of the philosopher's life through letters, manuscripts, and notes (open Tues. and Fri. 10am-5:30pm, Wed. and Mon. 10am-5:30pm, Thurs. 10am-6:30; free).

MUSEUMS

Stuttgart's lack of beautiful old buildings is more than compensated for by an array of outstanding museums. The **Staatsgalerie Stuttgart** (tel. 212 40 50 or 212 40 28; fax 212 40 68), across from the *Schloßgarten* on Konrad-Adenauer-Str., is simply marvelous. The museum is composed of two parts: the collection of paintings in the *Staatsgalerie* spans from the Middle Ages to the 19th century; the **new wing** contains an essential collection of moderns including Picasso, Kandinsky, Beckmann, and Dalí. A controversial stroke of postmodern architecture, the new wing was designed by English architect James Stirling (open Wed. and Fri.-Sun. 10am-5pm, Tues. and Thurs. 10am-8pm; admission DM5, students DM3). Across from the *Schloß,* the **Württembergischer Kunstverein,** Schloßplatz 2 (tel. 22 33 70; fax 29 36 17), completes the circuit with artistic endeavor that's hot off the press—every year, eight to 10 exhibits document the art of our time (open Tues. and Thurs.-Sun. 11am-6pm, Wed. 11am-8pm; free, but DM8 for special exhibits, students DM6).

The **Württembergisches Landesmuseum** (tel. 279 34 00) in the *Altes Schloß* has a vast and absorbing collection detailing the history of the Württemberg region. From skulls and crown jewels to ornate medieval altarpieces and chains from the 17th to 20th centuries, this museum caters to all tastes. (Open Tues. 10am-1pm, Wed.-Sun. 10am-5pm. Admission DM5, students DM3. Wheelchair accessible).

The **Mercedes-Benz Museum** (tel. 172 25 78) resides in the actual workshop where Herr Daimler, automobile innovator extraordinaire, built the first generation of Mercedes-Benzes (his daughter was named Benz). Take bus #56 to "Stadion" or S-

Bahn #1 to "Gottlieb-Daimler-Stadion." The exhibit covers the history of the automobile from its invention to the strange, James Bond-worthy experimental models now on the drawing board (open Tues.-Sun. 9am-5pm; free). Not to be outdone, Dr. Ferdinand Porsche's **Porsche-Museum,** Porschestr. 42 (tel. 827 53 84; fax 827 51 11), tells much the same story, only with curvier cars. Take bus #52 or 99 to "Porsche" or S-Bahn #6 (direction: Weil der Stadt) to "Neuwirtshaus" (open Mon.-Fri. 9am-noon and 1-4pm; free). Unless you are a serious car freak, going to *both* of these museums will probably be a clunker; choose your make and stick with it.

The **Schwäbisches Brauereimuseum Stuttgart,** Robert-Koch-Str. 12 (tel. 737 02 01), features state-of-the-art technology of a different flavor. It's a teetotaler's nightmare: the "history of beer" exhibit culminates in a look at current brewing processes. To get there, take U-Bahn #1, 3, 6, or 14 to "Möhringer Landstr." or S-Bahn #1-3 to "Vaihingen." Sorry, no free samples—otherwise we'd put it on the back cover. (Open Tues.-Sun. 10:30am-5:30pm. Last tour at 4pm. Free.) **Haus der Wirtschaft,** Willi-Bleicher-Str. 19 (tel. 12 32 65 50 or 123 25 76), joins the plethora of museums devoted to German technological genius. Take U-Bahn #4 to "Berlinerplatz." The exhibits on automobile technology require an engineering degree to understand, but anyone can appreciate the design exhibit, featuring such inspired mundanities as the Bic lighter. It's zen for consumers (open Tues.-Sun. 11am-6pm; free). Analogous in appeal is the **Deutsches Spielkarten-Museum,** Schönbuchstr. 32 (tel 160 03 35). Take U-Bahn #5 to "Leinfelden." The most comprehensive of its kind in Europe, this playing-card museum displays Indian, Chinese, and European cards (open Tues.-Fri. 2-5pm, Sun. 10am-1pm).

ENTERTAINMENT

Stargazers, feast your eyes at the **Karl-Zeiss-Planetarium,** Willi-Brandt-Str. 25. (tel. 162 92 15; fax 216 39 12). Take U-Bahn #1, 4, 9, or 14 or streetcar #2 to "Staatsgalerie" or simply walk from the south exit of the main train station down into the *Schloßgarten* for about 200m. For DM8 (students DM5) you can attend one of the shows inside the big cupola with plenty of cool visual effects—stars falling, comets shooting around. (Shows Tues. at 10am and 3pm, Wed. at 8pm, Fri. at 10am, 3, and 8pm, Sat.-Sun. at 2, 4, and 6pm.) During nice weather, would-be astronomers can peer through the telescope at the canopy of heavens (Mon. and Wed.-Sat. at 8pm).

The **Staatstheater,** just across the plaza from the *Neues Schloß,* is Stuttgart's most famous theater, with opera, ballet, plays, and concerts by the dozen (24hr. ticket information tel. 197 03; box office tel. 22 17 95; telephone lines open Mon.-Fri. 9am-1pm and 2-5pm; box office open Mon.-Fri. 10am-6pm, Sat. 9am-1pm; DM16-90; student discounts available). There are 25 other local theaters, and tickets for them are usually much cheaper (DM10-25, students DM5-15). The tourist office provides schedules and sells tickets, which can also be purchased at the **Kartenhäusle,** Kleiner Schloßplatz (tel. 29 55 83; open Mon.-Fri. 9am-6pm, Sat. 9am-1pm; telephone lines open 9am-noon and 2-5pm). Also check out a *Lift* brochure from the tourist office. To find out about nightlife, get the Tips 'n' Trips (see Orientation and Practical Information, p. 165). fliers titled *Discos* or *Kneipen,* which list exhaustively in German and English what there is to do. For listings and updates on after dark doings, check out *Prinz* (DM5), available at newsstands. Be assured, Dionysus never sleeps in this city. The area along Königstr. and Calverstr. is alive in the early evenings with lazy conversations (and beers) spilling out of the numerous cafés onto sidewalk tables.

Corso Kino, Hauptstr. 6 (tel. 73 49 16), shows primarily original versions of movies with frequent special festivals and revivals. Make sure you're not paying to see a Japanese movie with German subtitles. *"O.m.U."* means the movie is original with subtitles; *"O.V."* means it's the original version. Take U-Bahn #1 to "Schillerplatz" or S-Bahn to "Vaihingen Bahnhof." Schedules in English available at the tourist office.

Palast der Republik, Friedrichstr. 27 (tel. 22 64 88). An island in the middle of a toiling sea of stylish young citizens, this joint gets hopping on weekends. Necessary vocab: *"Haben Sie Feuer?"* (Do you have a light?) Beer DM4. Come back the next morning for *crêpes* (DM4-6). Open daily 10am-3am.

Eiscafé Santin, Buchsenstr. 8, serves towering confections in tall glasses that are miracles of design and execution (DM6-12). Open Tues.-Sun. 10am-midnight.

Café Stella, Hauptstätter Str. 57 (tel. 640 25 83). Laid-back café with good food and great crowds. On Mondays catch the latest local jazz personalities playing. Open Mon.-Fri. 8pm-1am, Sat. 10pm-2am, Sun. 10pm-1am.

Café Merlin, Augustenstr. 72 (tel. 61 85 41), serves freshly ground coffee to live music and cabaret. The small garden is the best place to wear your black beret. Open Tues. 5pm-midnight, Wed.-Sat. 10am-midnight, Sun. 10am-6pm.

Kings Club, Calverstr. 21 (tel. 22 45 58). One of Stuttgart's premiere gay discos. Lots of Erasure fans and lots of energy. Open Wed.-Sun. 10pm-6am.

Laura's, Lautenschlagerstr. 20 (tel. 29 01 60). A women's disco with a bouncer who will keep it that way. Flirtier than Kings. Open daily 10pm-5am.

When you've had your fill, cleanse your system at one of Stuttgart's **mineral baths.** The spectacular facilities of **Mineralbad Leuze,** Am Leuzebad 2-6 (tel. 28 32 24 or 28 32 27), and **Mineral Bad Cannstatt,** Sulzerrainstr. 2 (tel. 216 92 40), have to be seen to be believed. Water spurts out of comical fixtures on the rolling hills, accompanied by jets of steam. (Swimming pool open Mon.-Fri. 6am-8pm, Sat. 6am-7pm, Sun. 6am-1pm. DM9.50 for 2hr., students DM8. Mineral baths at Leuze open Mon.-Fri. 8am-7:30pm, Sat. 8am-6:30pm, Sun. 8am-12:30pm. DM 10, students DM8. Sauna DM6. Massage DM29. Underwater massage DM42. Cannstatt open Mon.-Fri. 8am-9:30pm, Sat. 8am-9pm, Sun. 9am-5pm.) To get to Leuze, take U-Bahn #1 or 14 or streetcar #2 to "Mineralbäder" or S-Bahn #1-3 to "Bad Cannstatt." To get to Cannstatt, take street-car #2 to "Kursaal" or S-Bahn #1-3 to "Bad Cannstatt."

■ Near Stuttgart

ESSLINGEN AM NECKAR

Bounded by steep, terraced vineyards on one side and the Neckar River on the other, Esslingen nurtures an *Altstadt* surrounded by the remnants of the original town fortifications. Medieval Esslingen thrived as a stopover on the commercial route between Flanders and Venice. Though it has a population of over 100,000 and lies within Stuttgart's hegemonic industrial sprawl, Esslingen is a cozy town that defiantly celebrates with many festivals, including the fearsome **Zwiebelfest** (Onion Festival) with its own eye-wateringly delicious mascot—the **Esslingen Zwiebel.**

To reach the *Altstadt* from the train station, walk down Berlinerstr. over the bridge and to the right. The blazing mauve Renaissance façade of the **Altes Rathaus** looks out over one corner of the square. The **Glockenspiel** sitting atop it has a repertoire of more than 200 songs, including "Yankee Doodle." The asymmetrical towers of the **Stadtkirche St. Dionys,** connected by a small footbridge, guard the other corner of the *Marktplatz.* The church holds a gorgeous 15th-century rood screen and *pietà* (open daily 8am-6pm; enter through door 4). Up on the hill rises the Gothic stone spire of the **Liebfrauenkirche,** which contains luminous 14th-century stained glass (open daily 8am-7pm; enter through front door). Farther up the ridge, among the vineyards, stands the **Burg.** The squat, round, half-timbered tower at the right of the Burg, appropriately named **Dicker Turm** (fat tower), has a restaurant that can make you squat and round, too. A romantic view of the town with the Swabian Jura as backdrop can be accompanied here in the evening by chirping crickets and sounds of giggling couples. Find another *Let's Go* user and smooch away. Footpaths criss-cross the *Weinberge,* and maps identifying the grape-type for each section of the vineyard are available free at the tourist office. Every first Saturday of the month (April-Dec.), there is a **Flöhmarkt** in Blauerplatz where practically everything from vacuum hoses to *Lederhösen* is sold (call 37 15 47 for info).

Esslingen is on the **train** line between Stuttgart and Ulm, and can also be reached by S-Bahn #1 from Stuttgart (every 15-20min.; 20min.; DM4.30; railpasses valid). The

tourist office, in the *Neues Rathaus* (tel. 35 12 24 41), provides maps and books rooms for free (open Mon.-Fri. 8am-12:30pm and 1:30-5pm, Thurs. until 6pm, Sat. 11am-4pm). Esslingen's clean **Jugendherberge (HI),** Neuffenstr. 65 (tel. 38 18 48), is in the Zollberg section of town, about a 30-minute walk behind the train station. Take bus #118-120 to "Zollbergstr." (2-3 per hr.), then cross the street and follow the signs (10min.); overflow from Stuttgart's hostel is usually sent here. (Reception open 3:30-7:30pm and 8:30-9:30pm. Curfew 10pm, but for DM20 you can land yourself a key. DM19.50, over 26 DM23.20. Members only. Breakfast included. Sheets DM5.50.) **Gasthof Falken,** Bahnhofstr. 4 (tel. 35 72 88), has good clean rooms. Go right from the station until Bahnhofstr. (Singles DM30. Doubles DM50. No breakfast.) **Postal code:** 73728. The **telephone code** is 0711.

Esslingen's cup runneth over with *Weinstuben* serving the local wine. **Gastätte Burgeck,** Strohstr. 32, (tel. 35 37 26), past the *Rathaus* from the square, serves great daily specials at DM10-16 (open Wed.-Mon. 11am-midnight). A mosey down Herrgasse takes one past numerous notable eating and potable drinking establishments. **Weinkeller Einhorn,** Heugasse 17 (tel 35 35 90), serves Swabian specialties (DM8.50-16.50) and cool wine (DM5.80-6.80) from a 700-year-old cellar. Open daily 5pm-midnight. A **market** fills the square with fruit and vegetable stalls (Wed. and Sat. 7-11am). Esslingen is a young town, and youth must have its fun. **Cafe Mayer,** Unterer Metzgerbach 18/1 (tel. 35 69 60), sports stylish people in stylish chairs. (Beer DM3.10-4.50. Open Mon. 10am-6pm, Tues.-Fri. and Sun. 10am-midnight, Sat. 10am-1am.) **Krokodil,** Rossmarkt 9 (tel. 35 66 23), universally known as "Krok," is a popular bar (open Mon.-Sat. 11am-1am, Sun. 2pm-1am).

LUDWIGSBURG

Ludwigsburg popped out of the blue in the early 18th century at the behest of Duke Eberhard of Ludwig. His modest idea: to erect a residential castle in the Duchy's new capital bearing his own name. Unfortunately, Ludwig died before his playground was realized and although his successors finished decorating the castle, they preferred to live in Stuttgart. Even without the aristocratic element, Ludwigsburg lived on to become a lively Baroque city with a lovely little trio of palaces.

The opulent Baroque **Residenzschloß** is worth seeing, even if you find yourself lost among German office fieldtrips. (Open mid-March-mid-Oct. daily 9am-noon and 1-5pm; Nov.-Feb. Mon.-Fri. 10:30am-3pm. Tours in English daily at 1:30pm. The 75-min. guided journey is the only way to see Ludwig's 3-m long bed (he was big: 2m 10cm tall) and the rest of the lavish gold, marble, and velvet interior. The palace is situated in an expansive 30-hectare garden that earned Ludwig's complex the tourist brochure epithet **Blühendes Barock,** "Blooming Baroque" (open mid-March-mid-Dec. daily 7:30am-8:30pm; admission DM8, students DM3.50). In addition to various summer festivals held here, a perennial **Märchen Garten** recreates scenes of major fairy tales in a large park of more wild vegetation. Join 100 kids yelling, *"Rapunzel, Rapunzel, laß deinen Zopf herunter"* (admission DM11, students DM4.50). The **Favoritschloß** is an excellent destination for a stroll or picnic (open mid-March-mid-Oct. daily 9am-noon and 1-5pm; mid-Oct.-mid-March 10am-noon and 1:30-4pm). This smaller Baroque gem was built as a hunting lodge and big-time party venue for Duke Carl Engler. If you are a genuinely dedicated castle fiend, continue for 30 minutes up the alley through the **Favoriten Park** and marvel at the third of the Ludwig palaces—the Rococo **Montrepos** (tel. 225 50). Unfortunately, the castle is now a luxury hotel and closed to visitors, but you can vent your frustrations by renting a **boat** and rowing on the peaceful lake (open April-Sept.).

To reach Ludwigsburg, take Stuttgart S-Bahn #4 or 5 towards Marbach or Bietigheim (20min.; DM4.30). Another option is to take a **boat** run by Neckar-Personen-Schiffart (see Stuttgart: Practical Information, page 165). The **tourist office,** located at Wilhelmstr. 10 (tel. 91 02 52), provides plenty of information and books rooms for free (open Mon. 9am-noon and 2-5pm, Tues.-Fri. 8:30am-noon and 2-5pm, Sat. 9am-noon). The most convenient **post office,** at Myliusstr. 16 (tel. 91 55 21), is opposite the train station (open Mon.-Fri. 8:30am-6pm, Sat.-Sun. 8:30am-noon). The only cheap place in town is the **Jugendherberge Ludwigsburg (HI),** Gemsenbergstr. 21 (tel. 515 64; fax 594 40) Bus S: "Schlößlesfeld." Near the river, through the woods, over the hills, find the princess, in an idyllic forest setting. (Reception open 9am-1pm and 5-7pm. Curfew 10pm. DM19.80, over 26 DM24. Breakfast included. Lunch DM8, dinner DM8.) The **telephone code** is 07141.

There are several restaurants on or near the Holzmarkt. **Corfu,** Holymarkt Str 2, serves daily specials in the Greek idiom, including the *Gigante*—a giant bean salad (DM5) and a half-dozen vegetarian entrees (DM8.50-11.50; open daily 11:30am-2:30pm and 5pm-midnight). Grocery stores and bakeries run rampant along Myluis-str. and Arsenalstr.

MARBACH

Friedrich Schiller was born in Marbach, a fact that is difficult to ignore; from drug-stores to hair salons, the name of the Jena professor and prolific poet is ubiquitous. The **Schiller Geburthaus,** Niklastorstr. 31 (tel. 175 67), is where Schiller was born in 1759 (open daily 9am-5pm, except Dec. 25-Dec. 26; admission DM3, students DM1.50). To get there, follow the signs from the right corner of the railroad station. A live cat resting on a chair on the first floor and a golden pair of Schiller's pants are somewhat more absorbing than the displays of his birth certificates and cutlery. Still, unless you are a die-hard Schiller devotee, it'll probably be more exciting to visit the **Schiller-National Museum,** Schillerhöhe 8-10 (tel. 60 61), by following the clear signs from the train station (open daily 9am-5pm, except Christmas and New Year's Day; admission DM4, students DM2). The museum offers not only a detailed account of Schiller's life and work, but also teaches something about his Swabian contempo-raries. The audio-visual room at the end of the first-floor plays the authentic voices of Heine, Mann, and Brecht, who sings *"Mackie Messer,"* his wicked German song known to English-speakers as "Mack the Knife." The **Rathaus** has big racks of mate-rial, including walking tours and hotel and restaurant maps. The **telephone city code** is 07144. For **food,** head to Marktstr., where most of the restaurants in Marbach are located. To reach Marbach from Stuttgart, take S-Bahn #4 until they kick you off at the very end. Ouch!

WEIL DER STADT

In the 13th century, Weil der Stadt may have dwarfed its studly neighbor, but now it provides a relaxing break from Stuttgart's energy. The town is as old as Stuttgart is new. "Weil" is derived from the Latin "villa." Settled originally by Celts and Romans, Weil der Stadt was once the house of a goldsmith's guild and fraternity. Now the gold is exchanged rather than worked; the scene here is dominated by a constellation of tranquil shoppers who orbit in and out of fine-looking stores. But heavens, that's no wonder, since the town gave birth to the quasi-mystical, monkish astronomer **Johannes Kepler,** the man who first imagined the orbits of the planets as ellipses (which, in fact, they are), rather than perfect circles. The fact that you can still visit the great man's house keeps Weil der Stadt on the map (and in our guidebook). For non-physics types, there are mechanical models explaining Kepler's "revolutionary" astronomical discoveries. Leaving the museum into the *Marktplatz,* you'll encounter a bust of Kepler with a *serious* look on his face; on the base are the names of all of the physical sciences. To reach the *Marktplatz* from the train station, go right down Bahn-hofstr., turn left to Poststr., and follow it as it becomes Scheergasse. (Open Tues.-Fri. 10am-noon and 2-4pm, Sat. 11am-noon and 2-4pm; Oct.-May Sun. 10am-noon on the 1st and 3rd Sun. of every month. Admission DM1.)

Right on the *Marktplatz* is the **Stadt Museum** (open Sat.-Sun. 2-3pm; admission DM2). Just around the corner from Kepler's house is the **Church of St. Peter and Paul.** The original late Gothic hall-type church was destroyed in the town fire of 1648 and rebuilt in Baroque splendor. The interior is opulent swirled marble and gold. A stone ciborium dating from the Swabian Renaissance rises high along one wall. For something funky, continue down Stuttgartstr. to the **Museum der Narrenzunft.** The only thing more bizarre than this strange exhibition of carnival clowns and jesters is the fact that it's only open on the first Sun. of every month. But hardcore clown fans may make an appointment through the *Rathaus* (tel. 52 11 40).

Weil der Stadt is situated 28km from Stuttgart. To get there, take Stuttgart S-Bahn #6 to "Weil der Stadt" (30min.; DM7.60). The **tourist office** (tel. 52 11 40) is in the *Rathaus* (open Mon.-Tues. 9am-noon, Thurs. 9am-noon and 5-6:30pm). The **police** station is located at Poststr. 5 (tel. 527 70). The **post office**, 71263 Weil der Stadt (tel. 528 60), is at Paul-Reusch-Str. 7 (open Mon.-Fri. 9am-noon and 3-5:30pm, Sat. 9am-noon). The **telephone code** is 07033.

■ Tübingen

Tübingen rises like a nymph out of the conjunction of the willow-lined Neckar River and the edge of the Black Forest, gracefully retaining the aloofness of its intellectual origins. With nearly half the city's residents affiliated with the 500-year-old university, there is no doubt that Tübingen is venerably academic. In fact, literary giant Hermann Hesse launched his book-dealing career here. But things have not always been so peaceful in the forests of academe. The university has been a source of unpredictability, from the Middle Ages to the student uprisings of the late 60s and beyond; students have boycotted classes to protest everything from the educational system and the Nazi past of many politicians to American involvement in the Vietnam War. The *Altstadt*, a snail-shell sheltering a lively student life both by day and night, has successfully avoided the fate of over-touristed Heidelberg.

ORIENTATION AND PRACTICAL INFORMATION

Thirty km south of Stuttgart, Tübingen stands guard over the Neckar River, on the edge of the Black Forest. Easily reachable by rail, it is one of the larger cities in the black forest; it is connected by bus and train to many small towns in the Swabian Jura and the Black Forest.

Tourist office: Verkehrsverein, on Neckarbrücke (tel. 913 60; fax 350 70). From the front of the train station, turn right and walk to Karlstr., turn left and walk to the river. The office will book rooms in hotels or **private rooms** (DM25-60) for a DM5 fee, sells maps (DM1-5), and also acts as a box office. Open Mon.-Fri. 9am-6:30pm, Sat. 9am-2pm. Another branch at Haaggasse 1, just off the *Marktplatz*, provides same services. Open Mon.-Fri. 9am-6pm, Sat. 9am-5pm, Sun. 2-5pm.

Tours: Contact Sabine Göbel at the tourist office for one of the numerous **topic tours. City tours** (DM5) leave from the *Martkplatz* tourist office April-Oct. Wed. at 10am, Sat.-Sun. at 2:30pm. Just show up.

Telephones: At the post office and the train station.

Trains: Service to and from Stuttgart every 15-30min.

Boat Rental: Bootsverleih Märkle, on the river under the tourist office (tel. 31 52 29). Boats for 1-6 people DM3.50-4 per person per hr. Open mid-April-mid.-Oct. daily 11am-8pm.

Bike Rental: Julius Trautwein, Karlstr. 2 (tel. 329 30), a block from the tourist office. **RADlager,** Lazarettgasse 19-21 (tel. 55 16 51), in the *Altstadt*. DM18 per day; less for each additional day. Open Mon.-Tues. and Thurs.-Fri. 9:30am-1pm and 2-6pm, Wed. 2-6pm, Sat. 9:30am-1pm. Or at the **Rappernberghalde campsite** (tel. 431 45). DM16 per day. Members only.

Mitfahrzentrale: Münzgasse 6 (tel. 267 89 or 50 81). Rides to Munich DM9 (plus DM15 for gas). Open Mon.-Fri. 10am-1pm and 2:30-5:30pm, Sat.-Sun. 11am-1pm. Call 1-2 days in advance.

Mitwohnzentrale: Wilhelmstr. 2/3 (tel. 55 10 20; fax 55 10 70). For stays of 1 month or longer. Open Mon.-Tues. and Fri. 10am-noon, Wed. 10am-noon and 3-5pm, Thurs. 10am-noon and 4-6pm. Also check the bulletin boards in the *Mensa*.

Bookstores: The venerable, 400-year-old **Osiandersche Buchhandlung,** Wilhelmstr. 12 (tel. 920 16; fax 92 01 92), carries a wide literature selection. Open Mon.-Fri. 9am-6:30pm, Thurs. until 8pm, Sat. 9am-1:45pm. **Bücherkabine Antiquariat,**

Froschgasse 10 (tel. 237 35), houses used books in precious stacks that threaten to overwhelm the friendly proprietor. Open Mon.-Fri. 10am-6:30pm.

Laundromat: City Wascheservice, at the corner of Rupperstr. and Herrenbergerstr. (tel. 843 66). Student clientele. DM7 for 7kg. Open Mon.-Sat. 8am-9pm.

Cultural Center: German-American Institute, Karlstr. 3 (tel. 340 71).

Women's Resources: Women's café *(Frauencafé)*, Poststr. 3. Open Mon.-Fri. 8pm-midnight. **Women's bookstore** *(Frauenbuchladen)*, Bursagasse 2 (tel. 265 90 or 511 29—also the number for women's information). Open Mon.-Fri. 10am-6:30pm, Sat. 10am-1pm.

Rape Hotline: Frauenhaus (tel. 666 04).

Emergency: tel. 110. **Fire:** tel. 112.

Post Office: Europaplatz 2, 72072 Tübingen, 100m right of the train station. Open Mon.-Fri. 9am-6pm, Sat. 9am-noon.

Telephone Code: 07071.

ACCOMMODATIONS AND CAMPING

Most of the lodgings in the city are not priced to please; however, rooms rented out by **private families** are listed at the tourist office and are usually economical. In any case, call ahead, especially in the summer.

Jugendherberge (HI), Gartenstr. 22/2 (tel. 230 02; fax 250 61), is just a 12-min. walk from the station. Cross the bridge past the tourist office and make a right. Or take bus #11 from the station (DM2.50) to "Jugendherberge." Smallish rooms, but friendly staff and a huge bowl of yogurt for breakfast. Reception open 7:30-9am, noon-1pm, 5-8pm, and 10-10:15pm. Lockout 9am-5pm. Curfew midnight. Members only but you can join the club when you check in. DM19.50, over 26 DM25. Lockers in the basement (DM5 deposit). Breakfast included. Wheelchair access.

Hotel am Schloß, Burgsteige 18 (tel. 929 40; fax 92 94 10), on the hill leading to the *Schloß*. Great location and newly renovated rooms. The sign above the bench outside is exaggerated Schwäbisch dialect for "here sit those who always sit here" *(dohoggeddiadiaimmerdohogged)*. Singles DM50, with shower DM65, with bath DM99-130. Doubles with bath DM124-148. All rooms with cable TV and telephone. Heck, you can even send a fax. Breakfast included.

Hotel Kürner, Weizsäckerstr. 1 (tel. 227 35; fax 279 20), offers friendly management, fun 70s decor, and a restaurant downstairs, all 20min. from the *Altstadt*. Follow Wilhelmstr. past the university and go right on Weizsäckerstr. Or take bus #2, 3, 5, or 7 to "Brechtbau." Singles DM45. Doubles DM95. Breakfast included.

Camping: Rappernberghalde, on the river (tel. 431 45). Go upstream from the old town or left from the station, cross the river at the Alleenbrücke, and turn left (20-25min.). Follow the blue camping signs. Reception open daily 8am-12:30pm and 2:30-10pm. DM8.80 per person. DM5.80 per tent. Open April-mid-Oct.

FOOD

With pungent herbs and the smell of fresh bread hovering above, Tübingen's students keep a number of superb restaurants busy. Most of the inexpensive eating establishments cluster around the Metzergasse/Am Lutznauer Tor area. To buy your own bread and Nutella, go to **Pfannkuch,** Karlstr. 3, which lies next to the tourist office on the Neckarbrücke (open Mon.-Fri. 8:30am-6:30pm, Sat. 8am-1pm). The *Altstadt* bristles with grocery stores and bakeries. More upscale and distinctive is **Kelter,** an old warehouse that hides an unexpected assortment of food stands where yuppies pretend they're roughing it (open Mon.-Fri. 9am-6:30pm, Sat. 9am-1pm).

Marquardtei, Herrenbergstr. 34 (tel. 433 86). Take bus #8 or 9 to "Rappstr." Run by a gang of enterprising students; serves whole-wheat pizza and a vast selection of fine vegetarian and meat dishes to a mostly Red and Green clientele. Entrees DM9.50-14.30. Open Mon.-Fri. 11:30am-12:30am, Sat.-Sun. 10am-12:30am.

Mensa, on Wilhelmstr. between Gmelinstr. and Keplerstr. (on the left with teal trimming). Offers generic fare at low prices for the severely budget-conscious. Tübingen Univ. ID theoretically required, but the powers-that-be rarely check. Dish o' the day DM3.70. Stew *du jour* DM1.90. Open late-Aug.-late-July Mon.-Thurs. 11:30am-2pm and 6-8:15pm, Fri. noon-2pm, Sat. 11:45pm-1:15pm. Equally cheap is the ID-less **cafeteria** downstairs with cold food and sandwiches. Open Mon.-Thurs. 8am-8pm, Fri. 8am-6:30pm.

Trattoria Etna da Claudio, Metzgergasse 35 (tel. 55 03 65), offers authentic Italian at simply *bene* prices: big pizzas (DM5-6), sandwiches (DM4.50-7.50), pasta (DM5-8). Take out, or stand. Absolutely saliva-inducing. Open daily 11am-11pm.

Da Pino, Mühlstr 20 (tel. 551 086), is an eatery along the same lines, only smaller. Crust 'n' cheese in all shapes and sizes, and all eminently delicious. Pizzas DM6.50-9.50. Take out or stand at the counter. Open daily 11am-1am.

Die Wurstküche, Am Lustnauer Tor 8 (tel. 927 50). Dishes up regional specialties in a gorgeous dining room, with plenty of high *Schwäbisch* camp and friendly service. Entrees DM9-25. Vegetarian dishes DM13-15. Open daily 11am-midnight.

SIGHTS

Winding alleys and gabled houses surround the the 15th-century **Stiftskirche,** the focal point of the old city. In the chancel lie the tombs of 14 members of the House of Württemberg. Life-size stone sculptures of the deceased top the tombs: men in their finest suits of armor. From an entryway to the left of the chancel, the rickety stairs of the church tower lead to a view of red-tiled roofs and the surrounding green countryside. (Church open daily 9am-5pm. Chancel and tower open April-July and Oct. Fri.-Sun. 10:30am-5pm, Aug.-Sept. daily 10:30am-5pm. Admission to the chancel and tower DM2, students DM1.) On the square is **Buchhandlung Heckenhauer Antiquariat,** at Holzmarkt 5, where Hermann Hesse worked from 1895 until 1899. It's still selling rare books. Just down street from Kirchgasse is yet another opportunity for a free market economy; any day of the week, a mind-boggling array of vendors sets up shop beneath the incredibly ornate façade of the *Rathaus.*

Speaking of world culture, dwelling just down the road from the Stiftskirche on Kronenstr. is the **Tübingen Evangelischer Stift;** built as an Augustinian monastery in 1260, it has served as a seminary since 1547, and achieved great intellectual prominence for a brief period in the early 19th century. It boasts among its alumni such academic luminaries as Kepler, Hölderlin, Hegel, Schelling, and Mörike. Down Bursagasse from the Evangelischer Stift is the **Bursa,** an enormous re-shuttered pink building which once served as a dorm and philosophy lecture hall. Here, *Stift* roommates Hegel and Schelling, would sit through boring theology lectures, then retreat to their room for conversation and a bottle of Rhine wine. Unfortunately, the historic interest of these buildings rather outweights their visual splendor.

On top of the hill that rudely isolates the university from most of the city stands the **Schloß Hohentübingen,** a castle with a rough stone balcony overlooking the old town and valley beyond. The upper floors of the castle are occupied by various institutes, while the spooky basements are closed to protect the huge bat family which currently inhabits it. From the *Rathaus* (not the *Bathaus*), follow the signs marked *"Schloß"* leading up to the right in order to reach the castle. Along the river, the tree-lined path of the **Platanenallee**—which runs the length of a man-made island on the Neckar—makes for a pleasant walk with a view of the *Altstadt.* On the northern river bank is the **Hölderlinturm,** a tower where the great 18th- and 19th-century poet Friedrich Hölderlin, Hegel and Schelling's other roommate at the *Stift,* lived out the final 36 years of his life in a state of clinical insanity. The tower now contains a museum dedicated to his life. (Open Tues.-Fri. 10am-noon and 3-5pm, Sat.-Sun. 2-5pm. Tours Sat.-Sun. 5pm. Admission DM3, students DM2.) Hardcore Hölderlinists may want to contact the **Hölderlin-Gesellschaft,** Bursagasse 6 (tel. 220 40), a society/support group dedicated to helping those addicted to the poet's life and work. For auto enthusiasts, an exhibition of real and toy cars will entertain at the **Auto-und Spielzeugmuseum Boxenstop** (Automobile and Toy Museum), Brunnenstr. 18. (tel. 929 00; fax 92 90 99). Cute, cute, cute (open Wed. and Fri.-Sun. 10am-noon and 2-5pm; Nov.-March Sun. 10am-noon and 2-5pm; admission DM3.50).

Someone back home *really* misses you. Please call.

With **AT&T Direct**℠ Service it's easy to call back to the States from virtually anywhere your travels take you. Just dial the **AT&T Direct** Access Number for the country *you are in* from the chart below. You'll have English-language voice prompts or an AT&T Operator to guide your call. And our clearest,* fastest connections** will help you reach whoever it is that misses you most back home.

AUSTRIA● 022-903-011	GREECE● 00-800-1311	NETHERLANDS● ...06-022-9111
BELGIUM● 0-800-100-10	INDIA✖ 000-117	RUSSIA●▲♪ (Moscow) .755-5042
CZECH REP▲ 00-42-000-101	IRELAND 1-800-550-000	SPAIN◇ 900-99-00-11
DENMARK.................8001-0010	ISRAEL.................177-100-2727	SWEDEN...............020-795-611
FRANCE................0 800 99 0011	ITALY● 172-1011	SWITZERLAND● ..0-800-550011
GERMANY.................0130-0010	MEXICO▽ 95-800-462-4240	U.K▲ 0800-89-0011

*Non-operator assisted calls to the U.S. only. **Based on customer preference testing. ●Public phones require coin or card deposit. Public phones require local coin payment through call duration. From this country, AT&T Direct calls terminate to designated countries only. ▲May not be available from every phone/pay phone. ✖Not available from public phones. When calling from public phones, use phones marked "Ladatel." ♪Additional charges apply when calling outside of Moscow.

Can't find the Access Number for the country you're calling from? Just ask any operator for AT&T Direct Service.

Greetings from LET'S GO

With pen and notebook in hand, a change of clothes in our backpack, and the tightest of budgets, we've spent our summer roaming the globe in search of travel bargains.

We've put the best of our research into the book that you're now holding. Our intrepid researcher-writers went on the road for months of exploration, from Anchorage to Angkor, Estonia to Ecuador, Iceland to India. Editors worked from spring to fall, massaging copy into witty and informative prose. A brand-new edition of each guide hits the shelves every fall, just months after it is researched, so you know you're getting the most reliable, up-to-date, and comprehensive information available.

We try to make this book an indispensable companion, but sometimes the best discoveries are the ones you make on your own. If you've got something to share, please drop us a line. We're Let's Go Publications, 67 Mount Auburn Street, Cambridge, MA 02138 USA (e-mail: fanmail@letsgo.com). Good luck and happy travels!

Someone back home *really* misses you.
Please call.

With **AT&T Direct**^{SM} Service it's easy to call back to the States from virtually anywhere your travels take you. Just dial the **AT&T Direct** Access Number for the country *you are in* from the chart below. You'll have English-language voice prompts or an AT&T Operator to guide your call. And our clearest,* fastest connections** will help you reach whoever it is that misses you most back home.

AUSTRIA● 022-903-011	GREECE● 00-800-1311	NETHERLANDS● ...06-022-9111
BELGIUM● 0-800-100-10	INDIA✖ 000-117	RUSSIA ●,▲,▶ (Moscow).755-5042
CZECH REP▲ 00-42-000-101	IRELAND 1-800-550-000	SPAIN 900-99-00-11
DENMARK.................8001-0010	ISRAEL.................177-100-2727	SWEDEN................020-795-611
FRANCE...............0 800 99 0011	ITALY● 172-1011	SWITZERLAND● ..0-800-550011
GERMANY.................0130-0010	MEXICO 95-800-462-4240	U.K▲ 0800-89-0011

*Non-operator assisted calls to the U.S. only. **Based on customer preference testing. ●Public phones require coin or card deposit. Public phones require local coin payment through call duration. From this country, AT&T Direct calls terminate to designated countries only. ▲May not be available from every phone/pay phone. ✖ Not available from public phones. When calling from public phones, use phones marked "Ladatel." ▶Additional charges apply when calling outside of Moscow.

Can't find the Access Number for the country you're calling from? Just ask any operator for AT&T Direct Service.

Greetings from LET'S GO

With pen and notebook in hand, a change of clothes in our backpack, and the tightest of budgets, we've spent our summer roaming the globe in search of travel bargains.

We've put the best of our research into the book that you're now holding. Our intrepid researcher-writers went on the road for months of exploration, from Anchorage to Angkor, Estonia to Ecuador, Iceland to India. Editors worked from spring to fall, massaging copy into witty and informative prose. A brand-new edition of each guide hits the shelves every fall, just months after it is researched, so you know you're getting the most reliable, up-to-date, and comprehensive information available.

We try to make this book an indispensable companion, but sometimes the best discoveries are the ones you make on your own. If you've got something to share, please drop us a line. We're Let's Go Publications, 67 Mount Auburn Street, Cambridge, MA 02138 USA (e-mail: fanmail@letsgo.com). Good luck and happy travels!

ENTERTAINMENT AND NIGHTLIFE

Tübingen's nightlife is laid-back and easy-going. It mostly revolves around cafés that begin serving quiet cups of coffee at 10am and remain open well into the night, serving beer to groups of students. The *Altstadt* is paved with excellent pubs and cafés. **Sudhaus,** Hechinger Str. 203 (tel. 746 96), is a "Socio-cultural Center" which screens wacky art films and hosts dance parties and live acts. Schedules are available at the tourist office and are also plastered all over town. **Jazzkeller,** Haaggasse 15/2 (tel. 55 09 06; fax 221 63), goes from jazz to funk to salsa (often live) and back again. Tübingen also has two major theaters: the small progressive **Zimmertheater,** Bursagasse 16 (tel. 927 30), and the larger, more conservative **Landestheater,** Eberhardstr. 8 (tel. 931 31 49). Tickets and schedules are available at the tourist office and at the box office at Eberhardstr. 6 (open Tues.-Fri. 3:30-7pm, Sat. 10am-1pm).

Tangente-Night, Holzmarkt (tel. 230 07), by the Stiftskirche steps. A premier Tübingen student hangout for beer and company at night or a book and cappuccino in the morning (0.3L *Pils* DM3.50; coffee DM3). Most fun Sept.-April Thurs.-Sun., when a DJ spins house, acid jazz, and techno. Sun. is cocktail night and once a week there's live music, a cabaret, or a theme party. Open daily 10am-3am.

Marktschenke, Am Markt 11 (tel. 220 35). Happy students spill out onto Tübingen's largest square. Cartoons on the wall will keep you amused. *Hefe-Weizen* (wheat beer) DM4.90 for 0.5L. Coffee DM3.30. Open daily 9am-1am.

Zum Pfauen, Kornhausstr. 1 (tel. 230 95). Students chatter away in this bar's dark wood and maroon velour interior. Classy black and white French photography and a plethora of German newspapers lend style and substance, respectively. Drinks and small eats (DM5-9). Open Mon.-Sat. 10:30am-1am, Sun. noon-1am.

Neckarmüller, Gartenstr. 4, (tel. 278 48), is close to the youth hostel. Young and old alike drink and schmooze at picnic tables under big shady trees by the banks of the river. The only way to get closer to the Neckar is to rent your own boat. They serve their own brew: light or dark, DM3.30 for 0.25L. In case you want to send some to Uncle Jack, a 5L oaken cask is DM45. Open daily 10am-1am.

Ammerschlag, Ammergasse 13 (tel. 515 91). Narrow, noisy bar on a beautiful little street, brimming with hipsters. Blues and jazz on Sun. night; Caribbean or American theme party on Thurs. night. Open Mon.-Sat. 10:30am-1am, Sun. 3pm-1am.

■ Karlsruhe

By European standards, Karlsruhe was born yesterday. In 1715, local nobleman Margrave Karl Wilhelm built a castle retreat here for himself and his mistresses (hence the name, meaning "Karl's Rest"). He then designed a planned city, radiating out from the castle in the shape of a fan, to accompany his castle. It has been an architectural sensation ever since. Throughout the 19th century, Karlsruhe was a center for art and science; today the city attracts attention as a cultural hub, especially for its many excellent museums. Karlsruhe is also the home of Germany's two highest courts, the Federal Supreme Court and the Federal Constitutional Court. Don't be quick to judge it. Over the years, Karlsruhe has earned various nicknames and titles, but the one the citizens are proudest of is "Sun City"—with more than 1700 sunny hours per year, Karlsruhe is one of the sunniest cities in Germany.

Orientation and Practical Information From the station, the town center is a 25-minute walk away from the train tracks on Ettlinger Str. and Karl-Friedrich-Str., or you may take any of the streetcar lines to "Marktplatz" or "Europaplatz." The **tourist office,** Bahnhofplatz 6 (tel. 355 30), located across the street from the train station, finds rooms for free. They have lots of events information and give out the **Karlsruhe Extra,** an updated city bulletin (in English) with good maps (open Mon.-Fri. 9am-6pm, Sat. 9am-1pm). The **S-Bahn** costs DM3 per ride within the city, DM8 for a 24-hour ticket. If you are staying in the city for at least one night, you are entitled to a 35% discount on your train ticket; call the tourist office to make arrangements.

Braunsche Universitäts Buchhandlung, Kaiserstr. 120 (tel. 232 96), has a small but top-notch selection of English-language books. For a **taxi,** call 94 41 44. **Laundry** can be done at **s'Waschbrett,** Werderstr. 7 (tel. 37 79 87; open Mon.-Tues. and Thurs.-Fri. 8:30am-12:30pm and 2:30pm-7pm, Wed. 8:30am-12:30pm, Sat. 8:30am-noon). For an **ambulance,** call 192 22. The main **post office,** 76133 Karlsruhe, sprawls at Europaplatz. *Postlagernde Briefe* (Poste Restante) reception is at booths 21-24. The **telephone code** is 0721.

Accommodations There are a number of reasonably priced options in Karlsruhe. Prices tend to be lowest in the outlying areas; ask the tourist office for a comprehensive hotel map. Karlsruhe's **Jugendherberge (HI),** Moltkestr. 24 (tel. 282 48), is conveniently located near the *Schloß* and university, although it's far from the train station. Take S-Bahn #1, 3, or 11 to "Europaplatz," then follow Karlstr. until it ends. Turn left onto Seminarstr. and turn left again on Moltkestr.; it's behind #20. (Reception open briefly at 5, 7, and 9:30pm. Quiet 4- and 6-bed rooms. Curfew 11:30pm. Members only. DM19.50, over 26 DM24.50. Breakfast included.) **Kolpinghaus,** Karlstr. 115 (tel. 314 34), is near the station; from the *Bahnhof,* turn left onto Ebertstr. and right onto Karlstr. This place has 142 beds, and an entire floor is just for students. Plain rooms but surprisingly spacious doubles. (Singles DM54.50. Doubles DM105. Breakfast included.) Camping is available at **Türmbergblick,** Tiengerer Str. 40 (tel. 440 60), in the nearby village of Durlach. Take S-Bahn #3 to "Durlacher Tor," then change to S-Bahn #1 or 2 to "Durlach." (Reception open daily 8am-1pm and 3-9pm. DM8.80 per person. Children DM6.40. DM11.60 per tent.)

Food and Nightlife Karlsruhe is home to a very large *Fachhochschule* (trade school) that's brimming with students. To get to the school's *Mensa,* go up Karlstr. from Europaplatz, continue up Seminarstr., and turn left into the bleak blue-gray school complex (open Mon.-Thurs. 8:30am-4pm, Fri. 8:30am-2pm). For reasonably priced traditional German fare, try **Goldenes Kreuz,** Karlstr. 21a (tel. 220 54), where entrées go for DM10-20 (open daily 11am-midnight). Around the corner on Ludwigplatz is the hangout **Krokodil,** Waldstr. 63 (tel. 273 31), a restaurant and café offering salad buffets for DM7 (open daily 8am-1am). On a lazy afternoon, **Eiscafé Period,** Kaiserstr 33, offers up traditional ice cream (DM1.50-12) and rad interior design (open Mon.-Fri. 9am-6:30pm, Thurs. 9am-8:30pm, Sat. 9am-2pm). The **main market** caters to Durlach campers (open Mon.-Sat. 7:30am-12:30pm). Many cafés on Ludwigsplatz stay open until 1am, and the tourist office has a list of all local pubs, discos, and live music venues. **Harmonie,** Kaiserstr. 57 (tel. 37 42 09), is a hip pub that serves cheap eats (sausages or pasta DM9; beer DM3.50-5) and features live music (open daily 10am-1am).

Sights The best of Karlsruhe's sights is the easiest to find; all roads (literally) lead to the classical yellow *Schloß* at the end of the rainbow. The *Schloßgarten,* with its impeccably kept swathes of green and inviting benches, stretches out behind the castle for nearly ½km. The *Schloß* houses the **Landesmuseum** (State Museum; tel. 926 65 14 or 926 65 42; fax 926 65 37 or 926 65 49), a collection of antiques dominated by the third floor's *Türkenbeute* (Turkish Booty). This dazzling display of Turkish artifacts was brought back by a local count from his campaigns in the late 17th century. Other exhibits recount the history and fashion of head scarves. A climbable tower affords an aerial view of Karlsruhe (open Tues. and Thurs.-Sun. 10am-5pm, Wed. 10am-8pm; admission DM5, students DM3). The same entry fee allows you admission to the **Museum beim Markt,** Karl-Friedrich-Str. 6 (tel. 926 64 94), dedicated to design and illustration since the turn of the century (open Tues. and Thurs.-Sun. 10am-5pm, Wed. 1:30-8pm). Around the corner are the **Kunsthalle,** Hans-Thomas-Str. 2, and **Kunsthalle Orangerie,** Hans-Thomas-Str. 6, two top-notch art museums (tel. 926 33 55; fax 26 67 88). The Kunsthalle is adorned with European masterpieces from the 15th to 19th centuries—don't miss Grünewald's *Crucifixion*—while the Orangerie contains a smaller collection of modern art (both open Tues.-Fri. 10am-5pm, Sat.-Sun.

10am-6pm; admission DM5, students DM3). The **Kunstverein,** Waldstr. 3, exhibits a yet smaller but more modern collection (open Tues.-Sun. 10am-1pm and 2-6pm, Wed. 7-9pm; admission DM4, students DM2).

   The *Marktplatz,* designed by architect and city planner Friedrich Weinbrenner, is bordered on the west by the rose-colored **Rathaus** and on the east by the imposing columns of the **Stadtkirche;** the red sandstone pyramid in the center of the *Marktplatz* is the symbol of the city and Karl's final resting place.

   Occupying the upper floors of a former mansion, the **Prinz Max Palais** museum, Karlstr. 10 (tel. 133 44 01 or 133 42 30), has loaned exhibitions and a local history display that includes the purported first bicycle in the world and bathrooms coolly lit by black lights. Check with the tourist office for current exhibits. To reach the museum from the Orangerie, take Stephanienstr. to Karlstr. (open Tues., Thurs.-Sun. 10am-5pm, Wed. 11am-8pm; admission DM5, students DM3.50). In the basement of the same building, **Das Kino** (tel. 250 41) screens off-beat films on Friday and Saturday nights. Enter through the garden on Akademiestr. (DM8). The quirkiest of Karlsruhe's museums is indubitably the **Oberrheinisches Dichtermuseum** (Upper Rhine Poets' Museum), Röntgenstr. 6 (tel. 84 38 18), dedicated to lyrical legends such as von Scheffel, Hebel, and Flake. Flake? (Open Tues.-Sun. 10am-6pm, Sun. 2-6pm; admission DM5, students DM3.) More accessible is Karlsruhe's **Zoo,** in the *Stadtgarten* across the street from the train station. The overpasses afford free glimpses of peacocks and goats. Elephant feeding is at 4:30pm (open daily 8am-6:30pm; admission DM5, students DM4).

   The visually unremarkable **Bundesverfassungsgericht** (Federal Constitutional Court) stands next to the *Schloß.* Take a moment to consider this edifice; it embodies Germany's strongest legal safeguard against the return of totalitarian rule. Near Friedrichsplatz, the **Bundesgerichtshof** (Federal Supreme Court) has a security apparatus that makes its counterpart five blocks to the north look open-armed by comparison. Germany's most sensational postwar criminal trials were held here, including those of the infamous Baader-Meinhof terrorist gang. If you have a good imagination, then these buildings will have a mystique born of betrayal and humanity gone bad. Otherwise, they're just ugly buildings.

   Every year in mid-February, Karlsruhe hosts the **Händel-Festspiele,** a 10-day series of concerts of Händel's works. The appetizing **Brigande-Feschd** takes place in early May and brings with it a huge display of dishes from local specialty restaurants. As with all German festivals, the local breweries play an essential role in the reveling—*"Prosit!"* Unifest (known as *Das Fest*) is a 10-day orgy of live music, food stands, and free-roaming students clutching tumblers of beer that takes place at the end of Günther-Klatz-Anlage and is the biggest free, open-air concert in Germany.

■ Baden-Baden

You don't have to be fabulously wealthy to have a good time in Baden-Baden—but it sure helps. In its 19th-century heyday, Baden-Baden's guest list read like a *Who's Who* of European aristocracy. Although its status has since fallen, this spa town on the northern fringes of the Black Forest remains primarily a playground for the well-to-do; minor royalty, *Wirtschaftswunderkinder,* and the like gather here year-round to bathe in the mineral spas and drop fat sums of money in the elegant casino. But even if you haven't quite edged your way into the Fortune 500, all is not lost. The area around the Oosbach is especially lush and green and filled with fountains that trumpet the origins of Baden-Baden's wealth. The pedestrian area offers unparalleled window shopping. It's all so very lovely that it feels a bit too good to be true.

Orientation and Practical Information Baden-Baden's **train station** is inconveniently located 7km from town. If you're not up for the 90-minute walk along the park path, take bus #1 (direction: Lichtental/Oberbeuren) to "Augustaplatz" (one-way DM3; 24-hr. pass DM8). The **tourist office,** Augustaplatz 8 (tel. 275 20; fax 27 52 02), in a small kiosk, offers maps and a hotel list (open Mon.-Sat. 9am-8pm, Sun.

10am-8pm). **TaxiFunk** (tel. 621 12 or 538 88) provides taxi service. I am the anti-funk. The **post office** on Leopoldplatz, 76486 Baden-Baden (open Mon.-Fri. 8am-6pm, Sat. 8am-noon, Sun. 10:30 am-11:30am) has **telephones** and **exchanges money**, as do the casino and the spas. The **telephone code** is 07221.

Accommodations and Food The cheapest bed in town is at the modern, five-floor **Jugendherberge (HI),** Hardbergstr. 34 (tel. 522 23; fax 600 12), halfway between the station and the town center. Take bus #1 to "Grosse-Dollen-Str." and follow the signs uphill. The hostel has family apartments. The strange paucity of showers is perhaps explained by the overabundance of bathing facilities in town. (Reception open 5-6pm and briefly at 8 and 10pm. Curfew 11:30pm. Members only. DM20.30, over 26 DM25.30. Wheelchair-accessible. Call ahead.) The large public **swimming pool** next to the hostel has a curvy slide and is the cheapest way to take to the waters in Baden-Baden (open 10am-8pm; admission DM4.50, students DM3; after 5pm DM3, students DM2; hot shower DM1, deck chair DM4.50). Rooms in the center of the town are appropriately ritzy and expensive, with a couple of exceptions. **Hotel am Markt,** Marktpl. 18 (tel. 227 47 or 227 43; fax 39 18 87), is next to the *Friedrichsbad* and the Stiftskirche. Family manged for decades and smack in the middle of the pedestrian zone, it has lovely views of the city and a restaurant downstairs for guests. (Reception open 7am-10pm. Singles DM54-60, with shower DM85-95. Doubles DM95-105, with shower DM135-145. Breakfast included. Dinners DM8-15. Restaurant open 6-9pm.) The unassuming **Hotel Löhr,** Adlerstr. 2 (tel. 313 70 or 262 04; fax 383 08), has its reception 1½ blocks away at **Café Löhr,** Lichtentaler Str. 19, across the street from the "Augustaplatz" bus stop. The rooms are spotless but small. (Singles DM30-60. Doubles 70-120.)

Most restaurant prices in Baden-Baden aren't compatible with budget travel, but **daily specials** often run for under DM12. Another option is to fill up a picnic basket at the grocery stores **Plus,** on Albrecht-Durer-Str. next to the *Altes Bahnhof;* **Pfankuch,** at Augustaplatz; or **Pennymarkt,** at the Grosse-Dollenstr. bus stop. **Sino's Restaurant,** Gernsbacherstr. 18 (tel. 223 64), is one of the few affordable eateries in town, offering an eclectic menu with a Turkish accent. (Vegetarian dishes DM7.80-10.50. Open daily 9:30am-1pm.) While **nightlife** in Baden-Baden is designed for the rich, reasonably priced cafés along the pedestrian zone stay open at least until midnight. If you're in search of young, rich, marriageable Europeans, look no further than **Griffin's,** located in the basement of the *Kurhaus* under the casino. Beer is DM6 for 0.3L, if you know what we mean; *water* is DM7.50, for Lord's sake. (Admission a similarly steep DM10. Open 9pm-3am.)

Sights and Spas Baden-Baden's history as a resort goes back nearly two millennia, to the time when the Romans built the first **thermal baths** here, the remains of which are located in the parking garage underneath the Friedrichsbad (open Mon.-Fri. and Sun. 10am-noon and 1:30-4pm; admission DM2.50). The **Friedrichsbad,** Römerplatz 1 (tel. 27 59 20), is a beautiful 19th-century bathing palace where visitors are parched, steamed, soaked, scrubbed, doused, and pummelled by trained professionals for three hours. It's a marvelous experience, especially because not a stitch of clothing is permitted. (Open Mon.-Sat. 9am-10pm. Last entry 7:30pm. Baths are co-ed Tues. and Fri. 4-10pm, Sun. noon-10pm, and all day Wed. and Sat. DM36, with soap and brush massage DM48, with cream massage DM46, with both DM56. DM6 discount with hotel coupon. Credit cards accepted, of course.) The Friedrichsbad is the more traditional; its atmosphere of soothing silence re-creates the Baden-Baden of old. More modest or budget-minded cure-seekers should try next door at the also astounding **Caracalla-Thermen,** Römerplatz 11 (tel. 27 59 40), which is cheaper and more public, and allows bathing suits (open daily 8am-10pm; DM18 for 2hr., DM24 for 3hr.; with a youth hostel coupon DM14.40 and DM20, respectively). Whichever bath you choose, the experience will be unforgettable.

When they're not busy pruning themselves at the baths, Baden-Baden's affluent guests head to the oldest **casino** in Germany; the opulent decor, modeled after the palace at Versailles, can be viewed via daily guided tours. (Open April-Sept. daily 10am-noon; Oct.-March 9:30am-noon. Last tour leaves at 11:30am. Admission DM4.) Just walk across the river from Leopoldplatz. Attendance during gaming hours (Sun.-Thurs. 2pm-2am, Fri.-Sat. 2pm-3am) costs DM5 with a laundry list of restrictions: you must be 21 (or the spouse of someone who is) and wear appropriate dress (coat and tie for men; dress or suit for women). Technically, students are not allowed. Minimum bet is DM5, maximum bet DM20,000 (yeah, we were disappointed, too). If you live in Baden-Baden and want to bet, you need a note from the mayor. There are slot machines in a separate wing (open Sun.-Thurs. 2-11pm, Fri.-Sat. 2pm-midnight). Next to the casino is the massive Neoclassical **Trinkhalle** (Pump Room), which contains a gallery of paintings immortalizing area folk tales and flaunts a gold-plated fountain. The *Heilwasser* (healing water) is warm and slightly saline, and tastes like it's good for you (open daily 10am-6pm; free). A few blocks in the opposite direction down the paths of the **Lichtentaler Allee** is the **Kunsthalle,** which houses visiting exhibits of modern art (open Tues. and Thurs.-Sun. 11am-6pm, Wed. 11am-8pm; admission varies with exhibit but usually DM5, students DM2).

The **Black Forest Highway** begins in Baden-Baden. For a view of rolling green hills, mount the 68m **Merkur** peak east of town. Take bus #4 or 5 from Leopoldsplatz to "Merkurwald," then tackle the steep railway to the top (combined round-trip DM10). On the hill above the baths and the pedestrian zone, accessible by a steep set of stairs, sits the ivy-covered **Neues Schloß,** occupied by a museum of the town's history. (Open Tues.-Sun. 10am-12:30pm and 2-5pm. Tours Mon.-Fri. 3pm. Admission DM2, students DM1.) Baden-Baden lies at your feet from the neighboring garden. The view from the 12th-century **Altes Schloß** (tel. 269 48), however, extends all the way to France. The castle is a good walk behind the *Neues Schloß,* but bus #15 makes two loops on Sundays and holidays at 1:15pm and 4:15pm between Augustaplatz and the *Schloß* (open Tues.-Sun. 10am-10pm; free).

■ Freiburg Im Breisgau

Freiburg may be the "metropolis" of the Black Forest, but it has not succumbed to any of the hectic rhythms of city life. The relaxed university town emerges from the lush countryside with grace, managing to be active and relaxed at the same time. Indeed, it is astonishing how quickly the city melts away into the tiny suburbs of the surrounding landscapes. Historically and culturally, Freiburg is as much Austrian and French as it is German. Ruled by the Habsburg empire for much of its 800-year existence and frequently usurped by the French, Freiburg only became part of the German Grand Duchy of Baden in the 19th century. Some say the influence of the two peoples helps to make the Freiburgers more genial and humor-loving than "typical" dour Germans. This liminal quality may have helped to cause a disaster in May 1940, when a squadron of *Luftwaffe* pilots accidentally bombed Freiburg, mistaking it for a French border town. Today's *Altstadt* sees streetcars glide along cobbled streets as university students, artists, French accordionists, and Mongolian throat-singers mingle among the buildings and trees.

ORIENTATION AND PRACTICAL INFORMATION

Freiburg lies on the track between Karlsruhe (2hrs.) and Basel, Switzerland (1hr.), and is connected to both by frequent trains. Local trains and buses leave regularly for scattered Black Forest towns. Freiburg is also a natural point of departure for excursions into the **Massif.** Most of the city's sights and restaurants are within easy walking distance of one another in the *Altstadt,* a 15-minute walk straight ahead from the main train station.

Tourist Office: Rotteckring 14 (tel. 388 18 80; fax 370 03), 2 blocks down Eisenbahnstr. from the station. Helpful multi-lingual staff. Finds rooms for free, sells tickets to area events, and has free maps, but prefers to sell the comprehensive *Freiburg Official Guide* (in German or English) for DM6. Also has plenty of Black

Forest info. Open June-Sept. Mon.-Fri. 9:30am-5pm, Sat. 9:30am-6pm, Sun. 10am-noon; Oct.-May Mon.-Fri. 9:30am-6pm, Sat. 9:30am-2pm, Sun. 10am-noon.

Currency Exchange: At the main train station. Open Mon.-Sat. 9:15am-12:30pm and 1:15-6:15pm, Sun. 9am-1pm. Slightly better rates available at the post office.

Telephones: In front of the post office.

Public Transportation: Single fares on Freiburg's many bus and streetcar lines are DM3; 1-day adult ticket DM6.50, 2 adults DM9. If staying for a week, the deal gets better at DM18, students DM16. Unfortunately, to buy these, you need to traipse to **PlusPunkt,** Salzstr. 3, in the *Altstadt,* which serves your every transportation need and even sells t-shirts. Open Mon.-Fri. 8am-7pm, Sat. 8am-2pm.

Taxis: tel. 444 44. We want the funk.

Mitfahrzentrale: Belfortstr. 55 (tel. 194 44), south of the station, just off Schnewlingstr. You're going to vacation in Germany without riding on the Autobahn? No, no. Get a chauffeur. Open Mon.-Fri. 9am-7pm, Sat. 9am-1pm, Sun. 10am-1pm.

Hitchhiking: *Let's Go* does not recommend hitchhiking as a safe means of transportation. Hitchers say that public transportation can get you to the necessary starting spots. **North:** S-Bahn #5 (direction: Zähringen) to "Reutebachgasse;" those who hitch usually walk back some 50m. **West:** S-Bahn #1 to "Padua-Allee," then bus #31 or 32 to "Hauptstraße." **East:** S-Bahn #1 (direction: Littenweiler) to "Lassberg-str.," then bus #18 (direction: Langwatten) to "Strombad."

Bookstore: Walthari, Bertoldstr. 28 (tel. 387 70). A fairly large but pricey collection of English-language paperbacks. Carries guides to the Black Forest region. Open Mon.-Fri. 9am-6:30pm, Sat. 9am-2pm.

Laundromat: Café Fleck, Predigerstr. 3 (tel. 268 29). Laundro-café—get a sandwich at the adjacent bar. Wash including soap DM7. Dry DM1 per 10min. Laundromat open Mon.-Fri. 7am-1am. Café open Mon.-Fri. 7am-6:30pm, Sat. 8am-2pm.

Rape Crisis Hotline: tel. 333 39.

Gay Hotline: Rosa Hilfe, tel. 251 61.

Emergency: Police and **Ambulance:** tel. 110. **Fire:** tel. 112.

Post Office: Eisenbahnstr. 60, 79098 Freiburg, 1 block straight ahead from the train station. Open Mon.-Fri. 8:30am-6:30pm, Sat. 8:30am-2pm.

Telephone Code: 0761

ACCOMMODATIONS AND CAMPING

Most of Freiburg's hotels and *Pensionen* are expensive and are often located outside of the city center. The tourist office books cheaper rooms (DM25-45 for singles; DM45-80 for doubles) in private homes, but a stay of at least three nights is usually required. Unfortunately, Freiburg's youth hostel is large, impersonal, and distant from the *Altstadt.* If your accommodation is far away, purchasing the 24-hr. ticket for buses and streetcars will ultimately save money (p. 182).

Jugendherberge (HI), Kartäuserstr. 151 (tel. 676 56; fax 603 67). Take S-Bahn #1 (direction: Littenweiler) to "Römerhof," cross the tracks and backtrack 20m, then walk down Fritz-Geiges-Str., cross the stream, and follow the footpath to the right. Modern, crowded institutional accommodations in an arboreal setting. Unfortunately, the rampant school groups often displace individuals. Reception open 7am-11:30pm. Curfew 11:30pm. Members only. DM20.30, over 26 DM24.70. More expensive *Gästehaus* DM37. Sheets included.

Haus Lydia Kalchtaler, Peterhof 11 (tel. 671 19). S-Bahn #1 (direction: Littenweiler) to "Lassbergstr.," then bus #17 to "Kleintalstr." Turn around and follow Peterhof up and to the left to the large wooden farmhouse with the water trough in front. Operated by the tireless and loquacious Lydia Kalchtaler, this is a rest from institutional living at an unbeatable price. Best of all, you can lay off the trail mix for a few days because there's a kitchen—make yourself a good home-cooked meal. DM20 with showers. Some rooms DM15. Laundry DM5.

Hotel Zum Löwen, Breisgauer Str. 62 (tel. 846 61; fax 840 23), up the street from *Gasthaus* Hirschen. Friendly management and sunny, spacious rooms. Pretend you're in California with the marble floors and white stucco walls—it sure don't

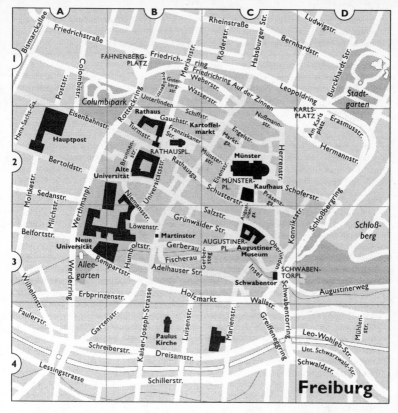

Freiburg

feel like budget travel. Singles DM45, with shower DM50. Doubles DM80, with shower DM100-130. Some rooms have TVs.

Gasthaus Hirschen, Breisgauer Str. 47 (tel. 821 18). Take S-Bahn #1 to "Padua-Allee," continue 30m along the tracks, and walk down Breisgauerstr. for 5min. Be careful: this *Gasthaus* is on the other side of town from the hotel of the same name; also, it isn't the same as Hirschengarten-Hotel, which is on top of it. Old house in a quiet farm neighborhood with rooms as cozy as the exterior would lead you to believe. Spotless pink tile bathroom. Reception open Fri.-Wed. Singles DM40, with shower DM56. Doubles DM70, with shower DM90. Triples DM110.

Hotel Schemmer, Eschholzstr. 63 (tel. 27 24 24; fax 220 10). From the train station, take the overpass that crosses the tracks, then go past the church and turn left. Friendly management and a central location. The sun shines in—it's as nice as pie. Some rooms look out on the garden, some on the street. Singles DM55, with shower DM65. Doubles DM85, with shower DM95. Breakfast included.

Pension Gisela, Am Vogelbach 27 (tel. 811 52; fax 811 52). Take bus #10 (direction Padua-Allee) to "Hofackerstr.," then double back 2 blocks and turn left, walk 250m, and turn left again. The tacky *Schwarzwald* theme mural on the outside wall should not deter you; it conceals large, comfy rooms. Quiet residential neighborhood. Breakfast included. Singles DM45. Doubles DM85-90.

Camping: Mosle Park, Waldseestr. 77 (tel. 729 38; fax 775 78). Take S-Bahn #1 to "Hasemannstr.," then a 15-min. walk, as follows: backtrack to Jahnstr. and then turn left. Follow Jahnstr. until it ends, then go left on Hammerschmiedstr. Follow that, cross the train tracks, then turn right on Littenweilerstr. Beautiful forested location, ideally situated for hiking. Reception open 8am-noon. DM8 per person. DM5 per child. DM4 per tent. Laundry facilities available: wash and dry DM13.

Hirzberg, Kartauserstr. 99 (tel. 350 54), on the other side of the Dreisam River, is cheaper and friendlier, but less idyllic. Take S-Bahn #1 to "Stadthalle," then cross the street via the underpass and walk straight (north) on Hirzbergstr. Cross river at Bertoldtsteg, walk across stream, then go 30m to the left. Near a quiet residential area. Bikes DM12 per day. DM7 per person. DM5 per child. DM5-7 per tent.

FOOD

In the early 15th century, the humanist Dietrich von Nieheim noted admiringly that "the supply of victuals is good and readily available" in Freiburg. With more than 23,000 university students to feed, Freiburg's budget eateries carry on the fine tradition. During the daytime, the **Freiburger Markthalle** next to the Martinstor is home to food stands serving ethnic specialties for under DM12 (open Mon.-Fri. 9am-6:30pm, Sat. 9am-2pm). At the open-air **market** on Münsterplatz, you can find everything from fresh radishes to crafts (open Mon.-Sat. 7am-1pm; Oct.-May 7:30am-1pm).

Mensa: Two university *Mensen*—the blue-trimmed building on **Rempartstr.** in the *Altstadt* (serves only lunch) and **Hebelstr.** on the main campus north of the city center (lunch and dinner). It's true you need a Freiburg student ID to buy *Menukarten* (5 for DM16.50; gets you a hot meal) and *Eintopfkarten* (5 for DM10.50; gets you a bowl of stew or fries), but local students are willing to help out. One flavor fits all. Location on Rempartstr. open Mon.-Fri. 11:30am-2pm, Sat. 11:30am-1:30pm. Hebelstr. location open Mon.-Fri. 11am-2pm and 5:30-7:30pm.

Salat Stube, Löwenstr. 1 (tel. 351 55), near the Martinstor. A health-food haven with an array of imaginatively smart salads. Watch out for those playful lettuce leafs (DM2.09 per 100g load). Even the desserts (DM4-5) are smart (IQ 150). Open Mon.-Fri. 11am-8pm, Sat. 11am-4pm, first Sat. of the month 11am-6pm.

Milano, Schusterstr. 7 (tel. 337 35), with its salmon-leather interior and prime location, looks fancier than its cost. Pizza (DM7-18), and pasta (DM7.50-15.50). Friendly service. Open daily 11am-midnight.

Hausbrauerei Feierling, Gerberaue 46 (tel. 266 78). Two enormous copper vats form the centerpiece and the service takes its time. Across the way, the *Biergarten* sports thick-shade chestnut trees. Excellent beer (*Inselhof* DM5.20 for 0.5L) and good food (DM4.80-14.50). Open Sun.-Fri. 11am-midnight, Sat. 1pm-midnight. Kitchen open noon-2pm and 6-10pm.

Papalapub, Moltkestr. 30. Near the *Stadttheater*. Certainly a place to be for the ever-funky students of Freiburg. Beer (of course), rock 'n' roll on the radio, and the rise and fall of conversation accompanies the excellent pastas and pizzas (DM6-10). Open Mon.-Sat. noon-1am and Sun 10am-1am.

Brennessel, Eschholzstr. 17 (tel. 281 187). A plucky student tavern that fills the student gullet without emptying the student wallet. Spaghetti (DM3.50) *Pfannkuchen* (DM5). Open daily 6pm-1am; kitchen open until midnight.

SIGHTS

Despite being mobbed with tourists, the Freiburg **Münster** and its 116-m spire remain a sight to be seen, even for the jaded backpacker. With various sections constructed between the 13th and 16th centuries, the chapel's interior is a wealth of architectural and artistic achievement. Many of the stained-glass windows represent different medieval guilds which financed the cathedral's construction, and the sculptures on the interior west porch depict a collection of various Biblical characters. You can climb the 329 steps of the tower to see all 27 tons of bells swing into motion and catch a 360-degree view of the city. There, it's impossible not to marvel at the delicate, lattice-like stonework framing the view that made philosopher Wilhelm von Humboldt say: "one cannot conceive of a more beautiful view than the blue heavens peeking through the thousand openings of this cupola." Gazing up from near the south entrance, you can see one of the gargoyles mooning the city. (Cathedral open daily 9am-7pm. Tower open Mon.-Sat. 9:30am-5pm, Sun. 1-5pm; Nov.-April Tues.-Sat. 9:30am-5pm. Admission DM1.50, students DM1.)

What buildings the errant *Luftwaffe* bombers didn't hit, the Allies decisively finished off one night in 1944, when most of the old city was obliterated. Since then, the citizens of Freiburg have painstakingly recreated the city's architecture and public spaces. On the south side of Münsterplatz sits the pink-tinted **Kaufhaus,** a merchants' hall dating from the 1500s. Two medieval gates—the **Schwabentor** and the **Martinstor**—still stand within blocks of one another in the southeast corner of the *Altstadt.* Sadly, the latter gate has been indelibly profaned by a McDonald's sign.

From the Schwabentor, you can take the pedestrian overpass across the heavily trafficked Schloßbergring and climb the glorified hill known as the **Schloßberg** (castle mountain) for a superb view of the city. Tucked away in the blocks between the *Münster* and the tourist office are the **Rathaus,** an amalgam of older buildings from whose tower chimes plays daily at noon, and the oddly named **Haus zum Walfisch** (House of the Whale), where Erasmus of Rotterdam lived in exile from Basel for two years following the Reformation. This gold-trimmed wonder is actually a careful recreation of the original, which was destroyed during World War II.

Freiburg's museum circuit is neither too large nor too small. The **Augustiner Museum,** Am Augustinerpl., Salzstr. 32 (tel. 201 25 31), housed in a former monastery, two blocks south of the *Münster,* has a large collection of primarily medieval artifacts. Many original works of stained glass and statuary from the *Münster* are housed here along with other religious art, and there is a section devoted to folk art from the Black Forest (open Tues.-Sun. 10am-5pm; admission DM4, students DM2). Farther south is the **Museum für Neuekunst** (Museum of Modern Art), Marienstr. 10a (tel. 201 25 83), which displays the works of 20th-century German artists inside a clean-lined modern building. Eat cake and discuss art in the café—or just eat cake (DM3.50-5; open Tues.-Sun. 10am-5pm; free). Around the corner from the tourist office is the **Zunfthaus der Narren** (Carnival Fools' Guildhall), Turmstr. 14 (tel. 226 11); the second floor showcases a colorful assortment of Carnival costumes (open Sat. 10am-2pm or by arrangement). **Museum für Völkerkunde,** Gerberau 32 (tel. 201 25 66), presents many interesting artifacts, with an excellent depiction of the past and present of non-European cultures (open Tues.-Sun. 10am-5pm; free). Conveniently located at the same-name stop of streetcar #1, **Brauerei Ganter,** Schwarzwaldstr. 43 (tel. 218 51 81), conducts tours tracking the production process of the malt beverage. The grand finale of the one-hour tour consists of a portion of *Fleisch-Käse,* bread, potato salad, and **lots of beer** atop one of the factory buildings. The view of the factory, the food finale, and the beer bash are all free (hint, hint). Call the above phone number ahead of time to get in on the group tours; generally on Tuesdays and Thursdays at 1:30pm. Unique to Freiburg is a system of narrow streams—known as **Bächle**—that run through the city. During medieval times, these swift-flowing gutters were used to water cattle and protect against fires, and served as open-air sewers. Today they are the bane of any tourist studying his map *too* hard. But there are compensations for sodden footwear; legend has it that any visitor whose feet are wetted by them will one day marry a resident of Freiburg.

ENTERTAINMENT AND NIGHTLIFE

Freiburg proclaims itself to be a city of wine and music. True to its word, it is awash with *Weinstuben* and clubs. For the current events in town, pick up a free copy of *Freiburg Aktuell* at the tourist office. **Freiburger Weinfest** is a two-day festival held during the last weekend of June. The annual three-week **Zeltmusikfestival** (Tent Music Festival), held in late June to early July, brings big-name classical, rock, and jazz performers to two circus tents pitched at the city's edge. Tickets (DM15-40) sell surprisingly fast. Take S-Bahn #5 to "Bisserstr." and catch the free shuttle bus to the site. **Freiburger Weintage** (Wine Days) is a 10-day festival held on Münsterplatz in late June and early July where you can stagger around from sample to sample of some 300 different vintages (DM3-6 per glass). In addition, the **Narrenfest** (Fools' Festival) is held the weekend before Ash Wednesday, and the **Weihnachtsmarkt** (Christmas Market) runs from late November until just a few days before Christmas.

Freiburg's nightlife keeps pace with the city's students; afternoon cafés stretch into pubs and discos at night. The streets around the university (Niemenstr., Löwenstr., Humboldtstr., and the accompanying alleyways) form the hub of a student scene that doesn't shut down until morning. To find out about popular hangouts, get a free copy of Freiburg's *Nachtleben* at the tourist office. Nightlife also revolves around the Martinstor, where pubs and clubs keep things hopping until the morning hours. **Jazzhaus,** Schnewlingstr. 1 (tel. 349 73; fax 47 31 14), features live performances almost every night (open Mon.-Tues., Thurs., and Sun. 8pm-1am, Wed. 8pm-2am, Fri.-Sat. 8pm-3am; *Büro* open Mon.-Fri. 6-8pm).

zum Schlappen, Löwenstr. 2, near Martinstor (tel. 334 94). Serious beer drinkers head here. For DM15 you can flex your mettle by polishing off the 2L **Stiefel,** a fearsome vessel known to English-speakers as "The Boot." Lots of posters, rather on the alternative side. Pizza DM6-8.50. Pasta DM6-11. Open Mon.-Thurs. noon-1am, Fri.-Sat. noon-2pm, Sun. 3pm-1am.

Dampfross, Löwenstr. 7 (tel. 259 39). Tiny student bar, with dark wood and American movie posters. *Pils* DM3.50 for 0.3L. Steak DM7.50-10 . The most popular dish is *Pommes mit Kräutercreme* (fries with herb cream; DM6). Divine. Connected through the back door to the café **Savo,** Löwenstr. 3-5 (same tel.), which plays stylish and mod to *Dampfross's* earthy and traditional. Drinks and food a bit more upscale. More room, too. Both open daily 10:30am-1am.

Uni-Cafe, Niemensstr. 7 (tel. 259 39). A strange mixture of hipsters conversing about Kierkegaard over cappuccino and families with energetic children spilling out into the shady square. Open Mon.-Wed. 8am-midnight, Thurs.-Fri. 8am-1am, Sat. 9am-1am, Sun. 10:30am-midnight.

Cafe Atlantik, Schwabentorring 7 (tel. 330 33). Spacious pub that stays in the groove with 70s music. *Echt grell.* Packed in the winter, when the *Biergärten* close. Cheap spaghetti DM6.50-8.50. Guinness on tap. Open daily until 1am.

Agar, Löwenstr. 8 (tel. 38 06 50), next to Martintor. Get down with Flower Power and the 80s. Tuesday and Wednesday are student nights—free with student ID. Lots of Attitude. See or be seen, pick up or be picked up. Open Sun.-Thurs. 10pm-2:30am, Fri.-Sat. 10pm-4am; last entry 1hr. before closing.

Greiffenegg-Schlößle, Schloßbergring 3 (tel. 327 28). Drink, eat, and look down over Freiburg from a terrace above the city. Faaabulous view. Far more relaxed than a disco. Beer (DM5-7). Gorgeous view. Seats 800 and fills up when the weather cooperates. Great view. Half-price salad buffet, happy hour on weekdays 11am-1pm. Open April-Oct. Tues.-Sun.11am-midnight. And how 'bout that view!

■ Near Freiburg: Breisach

Breisach lies 30km west of Freiburg. Walk over the bridge to sunbathe in France (10min.) or stay in Germany and stroll along the narrow cobbled streets, comparing prices in wine stores in this former frontier post of a wine-producing region. Perched high above the town is Breisach's main sightseeing attraction, the 12th-century cathedral of **St. Stephan.** The massive but unassuming façade hides 15th-century frescoes and an writhing, twisting altar, the work of the mysterious 16th-century artist designated only as **Master H.L.** The view from the top of the hill carries well into France. Across the *Altstadt* stand the remains of the town's fortifications, the well-preserved 13th-century **Kapftor** and 17th-century **Rheintor.** Connoisseurs should register for a tour of the largest wine cellar in Germany, **Badischer Winzerkeller** (tel. 90 00; fax 90 02 32; 3-7 samples DM5-9.50.) It's a 1km walk east of town. Go right from the train station on Bahnhofstr. and keep truckin' on Im Gelbstein. Closer by is the **Graflich von Kageneck'sche Wein & Sektkellerei,** Kupfertorstr. 35 (tel. 90 11 37; fax 90 11 99), specializing in sparkling wine *(Sekt).* Buy yourself a crate (closed Sun.; call the tourist office for tour times).

Near Breisach is the **Kaiserstuhl,** a volcanic area to the northwest. A hiker's paradise, it boasts flora and fauna normally found only much farther to the south. **Trains and buses** run regularly from Breisach's *Hauptbahnhof* to the towns of Ihringen and Wasenweiler, on the edge of the Kaiserstuhl. A rather infrequent private museum

train travels amongst the hills—call the Breisach tourist office for schedules and fares.
The **tourist office,** Marktplatz 9 (tel. 832 27; fax 807 18), finds rooms for a DM1 fee
and offers maps and hiking and biking information, as well as guides to the nearby
French towns of Colmar and Neuf-Breisach. From the train station, turn left onto Bahnhofstr. and continue going; keep the fountain with the huge moving ball on your left
and go down Rheinstr. into the *Marktplatz* (office open Mon.-Fri. 9am-12:30pm and
2-5pm, Sat. 9:30pm-noon; **market** open Sat. 8am-noon). **Rent bikes** at **Firma Bueb-
Schweizer,** Neutorstr. 31 (tel. 36 01), on the main pedestrian thoroughfare (open
Mon.-Fri. 8am-12:30pm and 2:30-6:30pm), or at **Zweirad Sütterlin,** Im Gelbstein 19
(tel. 63 99). Turn right from the train station and continue down Bahnhofstr. as it
becomes Im Gelbstein; take a left into the dead end (open Mon.-Fri. 8am-noon and 1-
6:30pm, Wed. 8am-1pm only, Sat. 8:30am-1pm). The **post office** is one block right of
the train station (open Mon.-Fri. 8am-noon and 2:30-5:30pm, Sat. 8:30am-noon). The
telephone code is 07667.

Breisach's modern and luxurious **Jugendherberge,** Rheinuferstr. 12 (tel. 766 65;
fax 18 47), is often booked to the rafters. From the train station, take a left and then
left again at the intersection. After 20m, take the path leading under the main road.
Cross the bridge to turn right, then walk along the river. A hostel sign is on the left,
facing away from you; turn left when you see it. (20min. Reception open 5-10pm.
Curfew 11:30pm. Members only. DM20.30, over 26 DM25. Meals DM8.50. Sheets
DM5.50.) For a bite of German-meets-French cuisine, try **Daisy's,** Rheinstr. 18 (tel. 86
82; open Mon.-Sat. 11am-10pm, Sun. 4-10pm).

■ Black Forest (Schwarzwald)

The Black Forest (*Schwarzwald*) looms large in the German cultural consciousness.
Fairy tales, storybooks, and Romantic lyrical poetry all owe their inspiration to the
deep, tangled expanse of evergreens where Hänsel and Gretel were left to their own
devices. Stretching west of the Rhine from Karlsruhe to Basel, the forest owes its
name to the eerie darkness that prevails under the canopy of vegetation. Today, a
generation's worth of acid rain has thinned this natural cover by at least half. Tradition and custom still play a leading role here—the area remained remarkably isolated
from the rest of Germany and the world until early in this century. Farmhouses sporting trademark straw roofs appear around every other turn in the road, as do venerable farmers sporting rural garb. The cuckoo clock originated here, and the tourist
shops, which penetrated the towns in the area soon after indoor plumbing, all proffer
local renditions of the classic timepiece. Hiking is a favorite pastime; trails are well-
marked throughout the forest and are used in winter for cross-country skiing. There
are downhill slopes at Feldberg and near Schwarzwälderhochstr.

The main entry points to the Black Forest are Freiburg, at its center; Baden-Baden
to the northwest; Stuttgart to the east; and Basel, Switzerland to the southwest. Public
transportation is sparse in this rugged region. Rail lines run along the perimeter from

BADEN-WÜRTTEMBERG

"Brennenestle"—German for Poison Nettles

Hikers in Germany are exceedingly lucky. There are no poisonous snakes and
few dangerous animals (unless, of course, you count cows). But there is, however, another pernicious hazard. Instead **Brennenestle** abounds, growing rampant throughout the woods and domestic pathways. The swath of green leaves
look innocent to the untrained eye—just like a happy little weed. However,
when they graze on an ankle or an arm, the leaves immediately cause an
unpleasent pain and itch that can develop into a rash. Although it isn't as
unpleasant as poison ivy, *Brennenestle* isn't a terrific amount of fun either. During World War II, the people of Germany were encouraged to collect the plant,
whose fibers used to further the war effort by being made into rope or cloth.
After the war the plant was allowed to lapse back into its status as a minor pest.

Baden-Baden to Freiburg and east from Freiburg to Donaueschingen and Stuttgart, but many of the inner regions are accessible only by infrequent bus service. Travelers making daytrips should check their return connections carefully in advance to avoid getting stranded overnight. Many bus lines are privately owned, rendering railpasses invalid. The most scenic route through the Black Forest is the stretch from northern Waldkirch to southeastern Hinterzarten, where the vistas extend to the Alps in the south and the Rhine Valley in the west.

■ High Black Forest (Hochschwarzwald)

High, rounded mountain tops and a thick carpet of trees maintain the centuries-old isolation of the remote villages of the High Black Forest *(Hochschwarzwald)*. Hospitable and traditional residents will confound you with their dialect and impress you with their generosity. The best source of general information about the area is probably the **Freiburg tourist office,** Rotteckring 14 (tel. (0761) 368 90 90; fax 37 00 37). The tourist offices of all the local towns will provide maps and information.

The best skiers in Germany come from the Black Forest and the best skiing in the Black Forest is on **Feldberg,** at 1493m the Schwarzwald's highest mountain (although by Alpine standards it's little more than a big hill). The ski lift runs in summer and winter (round-trip DM5). At 1234m above sea level, Feldberg's **Jugendherberge Hebelhof (HI),** Passhöhe 14 (tel. (07676) 221; fax 12 32), may be the highest in Germany. Take the Titisee-Schluchsee train to Feldberg-Bärental, then the bus to Hebelhof stop. (Reception open 8am-10pm. Curfew 10:45pm. Members only. DM18.50, over 26 DM23.50. Add DM2.10 *Kurtaxe.* Reserve in advance for winter.) For tourist information about Feldberg and 16 other ski lifts in the area, call the **tourist office** (tel. (07655) 80 19) or fax 'em at 801 43; for a **ski report,** call (07676) 12 14.

TITISEE AND SCHLUCHSEE

On hot summer days in Baden-Württemberg, Titisee is mobbed by Germans: the very young, very old, the leather-clad, and everyone in between, all seeking to soak up a little sun. Hourly trains connect Freiburg to Titisee; along the way, the train ride through the **Höllental** (Hell's Valley) is scenic now and then, but most of the time is spent in tunnels. Titisee itself is an attractive lake set against a backdrop of dark pine-forested ridges. The lake and its surroundings manage to assert their charms, and few other areas combine such natural beauty with so many modern conveniences.

The **tourist office,** Strandbadstr. 4 (tel. 980 40; fax 98 04 40), is in the *Kurhaus;* to reach the building, turn right in front of the train station, walk to the first intersection, and turn right at the entrances to the pedestrian zone. Look for a brown modern building and flags dotting the lawn in front. The office books rooms for a suggested DM3 fee, **rents bikes** (DM15 per day), and arranges horse and carriage rides. Also available are maps (DM1-15) of the 130km of hiking trails surrounding the lake (open Mon.-Fri. 8am-6pm; May-Oct., also Sat. 10am-noon and 3-5pm, also Sun. 10am-noon). Rent **paddleboats** from vendors along Seestr. (DM11-15 per hour). Guided boat tours of the lake depart from the same area courtesy of **Bootsverleih Winterhalder** (tel. 82 14; 25 min., DM5). The **telephone code** is 07651.

Titisee's **Jugendherberge Veltishof (HI),** Bruderhalde 27 (tel. (07652) 238; fax 756), is inconveniently located at the far end of the lake. From the train station, take Südbaden bus #7300 (every 1-3hr., DM3) to "Feuerwehrheim." By foot, it's a 30-minute walk along the main road from the *Kurhaus.* At DM8.50, the hostel serves the cheapest meal in town. (Reception open 5-6pm and 7:30-8pm. Curfew 10pm. Members only. DM19.30, over 26 DM23.70. Sheets DM5.50. DM1.90 resort tax.) **Campingplatz Weiherhof** (tel. (07652) 228 or 14 78) is on the water near the hostel and has laundry facilities. (DM8 per person, DM6.50 per tent. Free showers. Open mid-May-mid Oct.). The grocery store **Edeka,** Jägerstr. 5, is down from the tourist office (open Mon.-Tues. and Thurs.-Fri. 8am-12:30pm and 2:30-6pm, Wed. 8am-12:30pm, Sat. 8am-12:30pm). One of Titisee's special bonuses is a heated **Freibad,** down

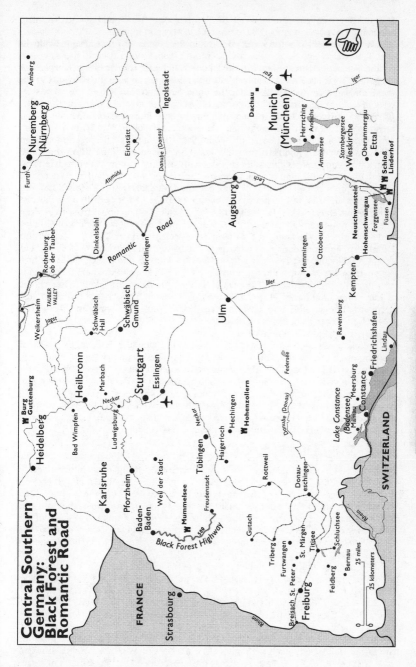

Strandbadstr. from the *Kurhaus* (tel. 82 72; open daily 9am-7pm, last entry 6:30pm; admission DM4.50, students DM2.20; open late May-mid-Sept.).

If the tourist density is too great, go south to the comparably picturesque **Schluch-see**. Two **trains** per hour make the 30-minute jaunt from Titisee to the towns of Schluchsee and Seebrugg, both on the lake. Schluchsee's **tourist office** (*Kurverwaltung;* tel. 77 32; fax 77 59) is a block into the pedestrian zone in the *Kurhaus.* From the *Bahnhof,* turn right, walk under the underpass, and turn left up the brick sidewalk of Kirchsteige. Sitting on the corner of Fischbacherstr. and Lindenstr., the office provides sightseeing (DM0.50) and hiking maps and finds accommodations (open July-mid-Sept. Mon.-Fri. 8am-6pm, Sat. 10am-noon and 4-6pm, Sun. 10am-noon; mid-Sept.-June Mon.-Fri. 8am-noon and 2-6pm, Sat. 10am-noon). The **Jugendherberge Schluchsee-Wolfsgrund (HI)** (tel. 329; fax 92 37), is ideally situated on the shore with a stunning lake-view; from the station, with your back to the water, turn left and follow the path parallel to the tracks across the bridge to Wolfsgrund 28. (Reception closed 2-5pm. Curfew 11pm. DM19.80, over 26 DM24.20. Dinner DM8.50. Laundry DM7.) Pick up a list of inexpensive *Pensionen* (DM24-30 per person) at the tourist office. **Haus Bergfrieden,** Dresselbacher Str. 23 (tel. 309), is uphill from the village center. Its tidy rooms are a steal at DM25-28 per person, breakfast included. Doubles and a few singles. **Camping at Campingplatz Wolfsgrund** (tel. 77 39). Walk left up Bahnhofstr. and continue onto Freiburgerstr., talk a left on Sägackerweg, follow it out past Am Waldrain, and then take another left. Stock up on groceries close to the hostel at **Schmidt's Markt,** Im Rappennest 2 (tel. 15 54). **Boat rental** near the hostel is considerably cheaper than in Titisee (DM10 per hour., DM6 per 30min.). **Rent bikes** at the train station or at **Pension Süßen Winkel Faulen,** Fürsterstr. 4 (tel. 206), just across the bridge (DM10 per day; open daily 8am-7pm). Rent **windsurfboards** from **Surfschule Ernst Pohl** in Aha-Schluchtsee (tel. (07656) 366) for DM15 per hour, DM60 per day (open 10am-5pm).

Three kilometers down the lake at the end of the train line, **Seebrugg** consists of nothing but a train station, a beach, and the **Jugendherberge Schluchsee-Seebrugg (HI),** at Seebrugg 9 (tel. 494). Then again, what more could you possibly want? It's a five-minute walk along the footpath from the train station (Reception open at noon, 5, 6:30, and 9:45pm. Curfew 10pm. Members only. DM17.50, over 26 DM22.50.) Wear your speedos at the **Spaßbad Aqua Schluchtsee** (tel. 77 38). Go right from the train station up to the big sign (open daily 9am-7pm; last entry at 6:30pm; admission DM5.50, students DM3.50). The **telephone code** is 07656.

ST. PETER AND ST. MÄRGEN

Although St. Peter and St. Märgen are only 15km from Freiburg, they are worlds away from the bustling cobble-stone city. Sunk deep into the valley between great green hills, the villages are a haven from the sweaty Eurailpass-clutching hordes. Bus #7216 runs regularly from Freiburg to St. Märgen via St. Peter; you can catch the bus from the Freiburg train station ("column" 4 at the *Bahnhof* bus stop) or 50m up Schwarzwald Str. (the busy street on the way to the youth hostel). Or take line #7295 to St. Peter through the scenic wine-growing valley of Glottertal; catch it at "column" 2 at the bus stop. (Both buses DM5; rail passes valid).

St. Peter's, designed by architect Peter Thumb, juts high in the curative air, where a halo of green farmland breaks through the dark crust of pine. Its *Klosterkirche* is aflutter with Baroque angels (tel. (07660) 910 10; tours Sun.-Wed.11:30am, Tues. 11am, Thurs. 2:30pm; admission DM5). To get to the **tourist office** (*Kurverwaltung),* Kosterhof tel. 91 02 24; fax 91 02 44), get off the bus at Zähringer Eck and walk up the street for 100m; the office is on your right, under the arch leading to the *Klosterkirche.* The tourist office has a list of affordable overnight accommodations starting at DM20 per person per night (but it does not book rooms) as well as maps. The **post office,** 79271 St. Peter, is across the street (open Mon.-Fri. 8am-noon and 2-5pm; June-Oct. Sat. 11am-1pm). The city **telephone code** is 07660. Many paths begin at the tourist office and abbey; they are well-marked with colored triangles, circles, and diamonds. A relatively easy, but very scenic 8-km path (follow the blue diamonds) takes you over to St. Märgen.

Known as a **Wanderparadies** (hiking paradise), St. Märgen sports a great number of amateurish one- to four-hour trails and provides a good base for longer hiking trips. 100m from the St. Märgen "Post" bus stop is the **tourist office** (*Kurverwaltung*), located in the *Rathaus* (tel. (07669) 91 18 17; fax 91 18 40; open July-Sept. Mon.-Fri. 8am-noon and 2-5pm, Sat. 10am-noon; open Nov.-Dec. 15 Mon.-Fri. 8am-noon; closed Sat. mid-Dec.-June and Oct.). Good hiking and biking maps are available (DM4-5) and they find rooms for free. Upstairs is the inevitable **clock museum,** tracing St. Märgen's role in the Black Forest clock-industry with more than 100 endearing locally-produced clocks from the 17th to 19th centuries crammed into two rooms. The **Folklore Museum's** piety peaks in the exhibit of a crucified-Christ-in-a-bottle by controversial artist Andreas *(Piss Christ)* Serrano. All of these sights dwell in the former Augustinian monastery (watch the doorways—they're short, to encourage the resident monks to stay hunched in humility), whose focal point is the two-tower Baroque church on the right. Unless you have extremely good timing, however, you'll probably miss these wonders. (Clock museum open on Thursday at 4:30pm. Folklore Museum open Friday at 4:30pm. Admission DM2 with a group. Call for arrangments.) The annual **Schwarzwälder Fohlenbrennen,** the annual branding of the young foals, takes place in mid-August.

■ Central Black Forest

DONAUESCHINGEN

At the tender but prodigious age of 10, while traveling from his native Vienna to Paris, Wolfgang Amadeus Mozart stopped in Donaueschingen and played three concerts in the castle. Since that time a variety of other famous personalities have passed through Donaueschingen; most, like Mozart, were on their way somewhere else. Located on the Baar Plateau between the Black Forest and the Swabian Jura, Donaueschingen is an ideal starting point for forays into the Black Forest or to the **Wutach Schlucht** (Wutach Gorge) 15km to the south.

The town's renown comes from its status as the "source" of the 2840km Danube River *(Donau),* the second-longest in Europe and the only major European river to flow west to east. Donaueschingen's claim has little geological validity (the headwaters of the Brigach and Breg Rivers that converge here more likely sources), but the town built a monument to the Danube anyway. The **Donauquelle** (Source of the Danube) is a shallow, rock-bottomed basin encased by mossy 19th-century stonework in the garden of the **Fürstenberg Schloß,** conveniently located next to the obligatory 20th-century Fürstenberg Souvenir Booth. The *Schloß* itself is a rarity. Its tapestries are its ostensible claim to fame, but even the tour guide perks up at the bathroom, a marble cave with a massage-shower (no, you don't get to try it). However, you may have to wait two to three hours for the obligatory tour. (Garden always open. Tours Easter-Sept. Wed.-Mon. 9am-noon and 2-5pm. Admission DM5, students DM4.) In the block behind the *Schloß* is the **Fürstenberg Sammlungen,** Karlsplatz 7, a museum displaying the collections of former princes of Fürstenberg. The collection's strong late Gothic holdings include works by masters such as Hans Holbein the Elder, and Cranach the Elder. (Open Dec.-Oct. Tues.-Sun. 9am-noon and 1:15-5pm. Admission DM5, students DM4.) The museum, the *Schloß,* and the adjacent puddle are all within a 10-minute walk of the train station; take a right in front of the station and walk one block to turn left at Josefstr., then cross the bridge and walk a few hundred meters more. On the way, you'll pass the **Johanniskirche** just above and behind the *Donauquelle;* the church's tame exterior conceals Baroque innards and a fairly intricate gold-and-marble altar. The town is blanketed morning, noon, and night with the velvet aromas of malt and hops emanating from the **Fürstliche Fürstenberger Brauerei,** between Haldenstr. and Poststr. (tel. 862 49). Single tourists can accompany larger groups on tours, which culminate in **free beer samples.** (Open Mon.-Fri.

Call for daily tour schedule.) For you bike fiends: running alongside the river, one end of the **Danube bicycle trail** connects Donaueschingen to Vienna. Take Josefstr. from the station, then turn right onto Parkanlage; cross a bridge to the left and follow the path to where the official trail begins.

To reach the **tourist office,** at Karlstr. 58 (tel. 85 72 21; fax 85 72 28), veer right up the hill past the *Schloß* and turn left at Karlstr. They find and book rooms for no fee (open June-Aug. Mon.-Fri. 8am-noon and 1:15-5pm, Sat. 9am-noon; Sept.-May Mon.-Fri. 8am-noon and 2-5pm). Information about Donaueschingen's annual **Internationales Dressur-, Spring-, und Fahrturnier,** a four-day tournament in September of show, jumping, and racing horses, and the October **Musiktage,** a modern music festival, is available at the tourist office. The **post office,** on Bahnhofstr., 78166 Donaueschingen, is across the street and to left of the train station (open Mon.-Fri. 8am-noon and 2:15pm-5:15pm, Sat. 8:30am-noon). The **telephone code** is 0771.

Alas, the illustrious **Southern-Cross Hostel** with body-piercing staff is no more. However, **Hotel Bären** Josefstr. 7-9 (tel. 25 18), offers rooms for DM25 if you can prove (with *Let's Go,* which of course you'd be using) you were looking for the Southern-Cross Hostel. You'll be snug as a bug in a rug in the small rooms (optional breakfast DM10). Go *au naturel* at **Reidsee Camping** (tel. 55 11; fax 151 38), about 8km east of town (DM8 per person and per tent). Donaueschingen is well-supplied with restaurants, and although the price of *Wienerschnitzel* can jump into the DM25 range, most have specials running DM10-14. Simply walk up Josephstr. towards the *Schloß* and let yourself be lured. Failing that, fill your tummy at **Tengelmann,** a grocery store 40m down Karlstr. beyond the tourist office (open Mon.-Fri. 8am-6:30pm, Sat. 7am-1pm)

■ Northern Black Forest (Nördlicher Schwarzwald)

The dark, meandering valleys of the Northern Black Forest, replete with an extensive network of trails, make for wonderful hiking. The area is easily accessible from the north; direct trains make the two-hour trip from Karlsruhe to Freudenstadt hourly, and the final 45-minute stretch is a panaroma of arching forested hills. The tourist office *(Kerverwaltung)* in Baden-Baden (tel. (07221) 27 52 00) is only marginally helpful. Far better is the office *(Kerverwaltung)* in Freudenstadt, at Promenadeplatz 1 (tel. (07441) 86 40; fax 851 76), which bulges with hiking maps (DM5) and provides information on excursions of every sort. (Bus excursion DM16. Bike tour (30km) mid-May-mid-Sept. Wed. at 1:30pm. Register by calling (07441) 86 47 32. Tourist office open Mon.-Fri. 10am-6pm, Sat. 10am-1pm.) From the *Hauptbahnhof* follow Bahnhofstr. to Turnhallestr. and make a left. The tourist office is at the end of the street, on the left near the *Kurhaus.* From the Stadt Bahnhof, follow Martin-Luther-Str. as it turns into Loßburgerstr to the Kurhaus plaza; it's on the corner to the left. The **Kurhaus,** Promenadeplatz 2 (tel. (07441) 86 40), across from the tourist office in the main square, rents **bikes** and books rooms when the tourist office is closed. (Bikes DM10 per ½day, DM7 per day, DM65 per week. Mountain bikes DM28 per day, DM125 per week.) The plethora of local travel agencies runs **buses** to most destinations in the region. Try **Reisebüro Klump,** Stuttgartstr. 9 (tel. (07442) 20 81; open Mon.-Fri. 9:30-11:45am and 3-6pm, Sat. 10am-noon). The **tourist office** is probably the highlight of **Freudenstadt** ("Town of Joy")—the town is impeccably maintained and little else. It does, however, have **Panorama Bad,** Ludwig-Jahn-Str. (tel. (07441) 89 06 20), a fancy swimming pool complex, with several pools and waterslides. From the youth hostel (see below) follow Ludwig-Jahn-Str. up and to the right (DM2.50 for 2½hr., students DM2; open Mon.-Fri. 9am-10pm, Sat.-Sun. 9am-8pm). The cheapest bed in town is the Freudenstadt **Jugendherberge (HI),** Eugen-Nägele-Str. 69 (tel. 77 20; fax 857 88). To reach it from the *Stadtbahnhof,* hang a left and follow the train tracks to a set of steps (10min.), then pass under the bridge and turn right at Gottlieb-Daimler Str. (Reception open 5-6:30pm and 9-9:45pm. Curfew 10pm. Members only. DM19.50, over 26 DM24. Sheets DM5.50. Sleep-sack DM3. Laundry DM5.) Another overnight option in Freudenstadt is **Hotel Adler,** Forststr. 17

(tel. 26 88), which has handsome rooms and accepts credit cards. (Singles DM42, with balcony DM44. Doubles DM55, with balcony DM57. Lunch DM10. Dinner DM8.) Buy groceries at **Pfannkuch,** across from the *Stadtbahnhof.*

■ The Black Forest Highway

The **Schwarzwaldhochstraße** (SHVARTS-vald HOHKH-shtrahs-suh; Black Forest Highway) stretches 65km from Freudenstadt in the south to Baden-Baden in the north. It contains some of Germany's most gorgeous scenery, as well as parts of the two *Bundesstraßen* (federal highways) B28 and B500. Even more arresting, however, is the accompanying footpath **(Westweg)** that spans the spine of the mountains overlooking the Rhine Valley and the Vosges Mountains of France. Along the Westweg, 17km northwest of Freudenstadt and 2km from the crossroads at Alexanderschanze, stands one of Germany's most comfortable youth hostels, the **Jugendherberge Zuflucht (HI)** (tel. (07804) 611; fax 13 23). A large, converted hotel built in the style of a Black Forest farmhouse, the hostel lets lodgers bask in spotless, carpeted six-bed dorm rooms; it also rents ski equipment and bikes. Bus #12 leaves from the *Hauptbahnhof Freizeitverkehr* and connects the hostel to Freudenstadt twice daily at 11:07am and 5:07pm. (No lockout. Curfew 10pm or by prior arrangement. Members only. DM19.80, over 26 DM24. Sheets DM5.50.) From the nearby settlement of **Ruhestein,** the Westweg leads over **Seiblesecke** and the **Mummelsee** to **Unterstmatt,** traversing the **Hornisgrinde** (1164m), the highest peak in the region. Unbeknownst to the busloads of tourists who are unwittingly dumped here, the Mummelsee is tiny and has little to recommend it save the possibilities inherent in a lovely little lake. Buy your *Walliser Brot* here (DM7.20 for 1kg). Bus #7106 departs daily from Augustplatz in Baden-Baden at 9:03am and 1:43pm (50min.; DM6.60) and returns to Baden-Baden at 10:25am and 4:40pm. There are better ways to spend your time, however. Down the hill after a rigorous hike rests the **Wildsee,** a more attractive lake inaccessible to automobiles and Europabuses.

■ Rottweil

Known in Roman times by the name *Alae Flaviae* (Flavius' Altar), Rottweil bears the distinction of being the oldest city in Baden-Württemberg. A free and independent city under the Holy Roman Empire, Rottweil's contributions to the world's wellbeing have included both flameless gunpowder (the unfortunate brainchild of one Herr Duttenhofer) and certain disagreeable and pernicious canines. The town, it can be said, specializes in the explosive and the overstated. But truly explosive is Rottweil's famous, traditional **Fastnet** celebration, which draws gawkers from all over Germany to watch 4000 *Rottweil Narren* (fools) storm through town in wooden masks and mega-expensive costumes in a festive attempt to expel winter (the next outbreak is in February 1997). The **Frohleichnam** ceremony, which in other cities is a modest festive occasion with greenery and brass bands, is transformed into a public spectacle in Rottweil. The still strong local guilds wind their way with their best clothes and lanterns to the Protestant part of town; however, every year, the procession finds the Protestants "coincidentally" cleaning their homes, in order to raise dust and trash to sully the Catholics' clothes. The festival will take place on June 7 in 1997 (Corpus Christi).

Rottweil's fanatic adherence to old traditions is not limited to celebrations. The town is a living architecture museum; the contrasting colors, meticulously crafted oriel windows, and historic murals gracing the façades transform nearly every building into a work of art. The less humble structures on Hauptstr. yield another impressive array of structures. At the hill's summit looms the 13th-century **Schwarzes Tor** (Black Gate). In this town of venerable buildings, the *Tor* is especially ancient; built in 1289, it was enlarged in 1571 and 1650. Halfway up Hauptstr., across from the **Altes Rathaus,** is the **Stadtmuseum,** Hauptstr. 20 (tel. 49 42 56). Its possessions include a 15th-century treaty between Rottweil and nine Swiss cantons—still valid to this day—and a collection of wooden masks from the *Fastnet* celebrations (open Tues.-Sat. 10am-noon and 2-5pm, Sun. 10am-noon; free).

To scale the ancient **Hochturm** and view the landscape, pick up the key from the tourist office or nearby **Café Schädle** in exchange for an ID as collateral. Behind the *Altes Rathaus,* the Gothic **Heilig-Kreuz-Münster** (Cathedral of the Holy Cross) will impress the inquisitor with its larger-than-life size crucifix. One block down from the *Münster,* the seemingly innocuous pink exterior of the **Evangelische Predigerkirche** conceals an enormous Baroque interior. Next to the Predigerkirche, the newly constructed **Dominikanermuseum** collection, on Kriegsdamm (tel. 78 62), includes a wide variety of religiously inspired sculptures and a large exhibit documenting Rottweil's Roman past, the highlight being a 2nd-century mosaic comprised of 570,000 tiles (open Tues.-Sun. 10am-1pm and 2-5pm; admission DM3).

Lying on the Stuttgart-Zürich rail line, Rottweil is easily accessible by train; the train station itself is a 15-minute uphill walk from the city center. Turn right upon leaving the station and head upward. When you reach the 12th-century bridge, take another right to cross it. Hauptstr., the cross-street at the second block on your left, leads right to the center of town. Halfway up the hill, 50m into Rathausgasse, is the **tourist office,** Hauptstr. 23 (tel. 49 42 80 or 49 42 81; fax 49 43 55); they offer maps, an English guide to the city, and *Freizeit Spiegel*—a free publication for young people—and book rooms for no fee (open Mon.-Fri. 9am-12:30pm and 2-5pm; May-Oct. also open Sat. 10am-noon). Free 90-minute **city tours** are also available every Saturday at 2:30pm from the tourist office and culminate, if the group is in a sudsy mood, in a round of pub drinking (May-Oct. only). **Alfred Kaiser,** Balinger Str. 9 (tel. 89 19) will cater to all your **bike rental** desires. The **post office** is on Königstr. 12 (open Mon.-Fri. 8am-noon, 2:30pm-6pm, Sat. 8am-noon). The **telephone code** is 0741.

Because everyone wants to visit Rottweil, inexpensive accommodations are often booked solid. Call early and often. To find the **Jugendherberge (HI),** Lorenzgasse 8 (tel. 76 64), walk left on Lorenzgasse (while walking downhill on Hauptstr.), go right at the ivy-covered building, and left at the *Jugendherberge* sign. Many of the rooms in this half-timbered house face out onto the terrifically steep plunge to the Neckar. (Reception open 5-10:30pm. Curfew 10:30pm. Members only. DM19, over 26 DM24.) The *Pension* **Goldenes Rad,** Hauptstr. 38 (tel. 74 12), is often booked solid several weeks in advance. (Reception open Thurs.-Tues. 11:30am-3pm and 5pm-on. Singles DM40. Doubles DM72.) **Gasthof Löwen,** Hauptstr. 66 (tel. 76 40), is just down the street. (Singles DM45, with shower DM50. Doubles DM80-90.) The "shower boxes" inside the rooms actually work, despite looking like portable public bathrooms. For traditional regional cooking, head to **Zum Goldenen Becher,** Hochbrücktorstr. 17, a hearty family restaurant where meals run DM12-30 (open Tues.-Sun.11am-midnight). At **Rotuvilla,** Hauptstr. 63 (tel. 416 95), feast on wood-oven pizza in many incarnations (DM6-16) in a half-timbered dining room (open Wed.-Mon. 11:30am-2pm and 5pm-midnight).

■ Lake Constance (Bodensee)

The third-largest lake in Europe, the Bodensee forms a graceful three-cornered border at the conjunction of Austria, Switzerland, and Germany. Ancient castles, manicured islands, and endless opportunities to tan to a melanomic crisp draw residents of all three countries all summer long. The 54 billion cubic meters of water are entirely drinkable and the lake is peppered with pocket-sized castles and expensive manor houses. Constance is the principal city on the lake, but ferries and roads lead from its gates to a ring of striking waterfront towns.

Ships depart about once per hour from behind the Constance train station to all the ports on the Bodensee. Consider the **cruise ship** that stops at Meersburg, Mainau, Unteruldigen, and Überlingen (June to late-Sept. daily, round-trip DM19). For more information and schedules, contact the **Weiße Bodenseeflotte** counter (tel. (07531) 28 13 98), in the harbor behind the train station.

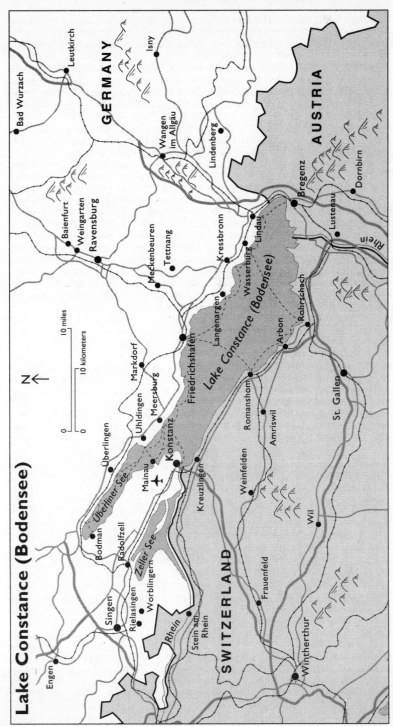

Lake Constance (Bodensee)

CONSTANCE (KONSTANZ)

Spanning the Rhine's exit from the Bodensee, the elegant university city of Constance may be the largest German city never struck by a bomb; part of the city actually extends into neighboring Switzerland, and the Allies were leery of accidentally striking neutral territory. This, and the fact that Constance (Konstanz, "kohn-SHTANTS" in German) belonged to Austria until 1805, give the place an open, international character. The narrow streets wind around beautifully painted Baroque and Renaissance façades in the central part of town, while along the river promenades, gabled and turreted 19th-century houses gleam with a confident gentility.

Orientation and Practical Information The **tourist office,** Bahnhofs-platz 13 (tel. 13 30 30; fax 13 30 60), in the arcade to the right of the train station (tel. 90 03 76; fax 90 03 64), provides an excellent walking map and lots of information about the area. They find rooms for a DM5 fee for a three night minimum stay in a private homes (open May-Oct. Mon.-Fri. 9am-6:30pm and Sat. 9am-1pm; Nov.-April Mon.-Fri. 9am-noon and 1-2-pm). **Buses** in Constance cost DM2.20 per ride, DM5.50 for a three-ride ticket, and DM6.50 for a one-day ticket for two adults and five children. The *Gästekarte,* available at any accommodation in the city, including the youth hostel, costs DM1.50 per night and gives you bus fare within Constance and free or discounted admission to some sights. The friendly **Mitfahrzentrale,** Münz-gasse 22 (tel. 214 44; fax 166 60), can help find you a ride (open Mon. 2-6pm, Tues.-Fri. 9:30am-12:30pm and 2-5pm, Sat. 10am-2pm). The posh **English Bookshop,** Münzgasse 10 (tel. 150 63; fax 150 66), has wide selection of books (open Mon.-Fri. 9am-6:30pm, Sat. 9am-2pm). The **telephone code** is 07531.

Tickets for the **Weiße Flotte** (the fleet that patrols Lake Constance) are on sale in the building behind the train station (open Sun.-Fri. 7:40am-6:10pm, Sat. 7:40am-8:15pm). Otherwise, buy your tickets on the ship. The tourist office offers a two-day pass (DM34) including transportation on buses, the ferry, the Weiße Flotte ship line to Meersburg and Mainau and back, as well as a city tour and admission to Mainau (see page 197). **Giess Personenschiffahrt** runs private boats hourly from behind the train station to **Freizeitbad Jakob** and **Freibad Horn** (45min. round-trip; June-Aug. daily 10:50am-5:50pm; May and Sept. Sun. only; DM7, children half-price). **Paddle-boats and rowboats** can be rented at Am Gondelhafen (tel. 218 81) for DM14-16 per hour (April-Oct. 10am-dusk). **Rent bikes** from **Velotours,** Mainaustr. 34 (tel. 982 80), for DM20 per day, DM100 per week; open March-Oct. daily 9am-5:30pm).

Accommodations Hosteling doesn't get any better than the pretty darn marvellous **Jugendherberge Kreuzlingen (HI),** Promenadenstr. 7 (tel. (071) 688 26 63; fax 688 47 61; remember to use the Swiss access code, 0041), which rests in an old manor on the water south of the border in Kreuzlingen, **Switzerland** (but is actually closer than the other hostel to beautiful downtown Constance). The hostel is located in a luxurious manor house (we're talking cushy leather furniture in a wood panelled library), with a multilingual staff practically breaking their collective necks to serve you. The best way there is by foot (20min.); leaving the *Bahnhof,* turn left, cross the metal bridge over the tracks, turn right, and go through the parking lot to the check-point "Klein Venedig." Keep walking along Seestr., through the gate, past the billy goats, right through the Seeburg castle parking lot, and take a right up the hill to the building with a Swiss flag on top. (Reception open 8-9am and 5-9pm. First night SFr21.20 (about DM26.50—they also accept *Deutschmarks*), subsequent nights SFr18.70 (DM23.40). Curfew 11pm. Breakfast and sheets included. Rents bikes for SFr12.50. Open March-Nov.)

Jugendherberge "Otto-Moericke-Turm" (HI), Zur Allmannshöhe 18 (tel. 322 60), has cramped rooms in a former German water tower next to a graveyard (for the other segment of *Those Wacky German Water Towers,* see Mannheim, p. 137.) There's a terrific view of the lake from bathrooms, which have poor drainage. Take bus #4 from the "Markstätte" stop (just around the corner from the post office in front of the station) to "Jugendherberge." (Reception open 4:30-5:30pm, 7-7:10pm, and 9:45-9:55pm. Curfew 10pm. Lockout 9am-4pm. DM19.50, over 26 DM24.50. Breakfast included. Sheets DM5.50. Open March-Oct. Call ahead.) **Jugendwohnheim Don Bosco,** Salesianerweg 5 (tel. 662 52; fax 606 88), is an excellent, quieter alternative to the hostels. From the station, take bus #1 to "Salzberg." Go back 25m and take the path on the left that becomes Brandesstr.; at the intersection, take Händelstr. until it reaches the alley, turn left, walk 150m, and look for the big yellow building on your left. Choose from 39 channels (MTV Europe, of course) in the comfortable dayroom. (Doubles DM30 per person. Bigger rooms DM25 per person. For young'uns (under 18), curfew 10pm.) **Campingplatz Konstanz-Bruderhofer,** Fohrenbühlweg 50 (tel. 313 88 or 313 92), offers a cheaper alternative. To get there, take bus #1 to "Staad." The campground is along the water. Call ahead, as it also fills up fast. (DM6.50 per person. DM5.50-8.50 per tent.)

Food The **University Mensa** dishes out Constance's cheapest food. Lunches, including dessert and a view of the lake, cost DM3-4 (DM1 discount with student ID). Take bus #9 from the station to the "Universität" (open Mon.-Fri. 8am-6pm; Aug. open Mon.-Fri. 11am-2pm). Also with a view is the **Volkshochschule Mensa.** You need an international student ID to get a card to put money on; ask the attendant. The hassle is worth it—meals cost DM4.40 (open Mon.-Fri. 8:30am-4pm). Stroll through the area around Rheingasse: it is the oldest part of Constance, and now the center of its vibrant alternative scene, with health-food stores, left-wing graffiti, and student cafés. There is a **Tengelmann grocery store** at the corner Münzgasse and Brotlaube (open Mon.-Fri. 8:30am-6:30pm, Sat. 8am-2pm). **Sedir,** Hofhaldestr. 11 (tel. 293 52), serves bowls of delectable vegetarian noodles for DM9.50. The photographs on the wall take you to Turkey, the music to America, circa 1970 (open Mon.-Fri. 11:30am-2pm and 6pm-midnight, Sat.-Sun. 6pm-midnight).

Sights Constance's **Münster,** built over the course of 600 years, has a soaring Gothic spire and 17th-century vaulting. (Open mid-April-mid-Oct. Mon.-Fri. 9am-5pm, Sat. 10am-5pm, Sun. 1-5pm. Free. Tower open Mon.-Sat. 10am-6pm, Sun. 1-6pm. Admission DM2, students DM1.) The elaborate frescoes on the **Rathaus** depict Constance history. Wander down **Seestraße,** near the yacht harbor on the lake, or or down **Rheinsteig** along the Rhine, two picturesque waterside promenades. The tree-filled **Stadtgarten,** next to Konstanz's main harbor, provides peace and an unbroken view of the Bodensee. The building that houses the **Rosgarten Museum Konstanz,** Rosgartenstr. 3-5 (tel. 90 02 46; fax 90 06 08), is the most exciting thing about this museum of history and culture. Built in 1324, its low ceilings, creaky floors, and carved wood panelling whisk you back centuries (open Tues.-Thurs. 10am-5pm, Fri.-Sun. 10am-4pm; admission DM3, students DM1.50). To get there, go up Markstr. from the station and then left on Rosgartenstr.

Constance boasts a number of **public beaches;** all are free and open from May to September. **Strandbad Horn** (tel. 635 50; bus #5), the largest and most crowded, sports a section for nude sunbathing modestly enclosed by peek-proof hedges. In inclement weather, head next door to **Freizeitbad Jakob,** Wilhelm-von-Scholz-Weg 2 (tel. 611 63), an ultra-modern indoor-outdoor pool complex with thermal baths and sun lamps. Walk 30 minutes along the waterfront from the train station, or take bus #5 to "Freizeitbad Jakob" (open daily 9am-9pm; admission DM8, students DM5). **Strandbad Konstanz-Litzelstetten** and **Strandbad Konstanz-Wallhausen** can both be reached via bus #4. The twenty-something set frolics on the beach at the university. Take bus #4 to "Egg" and walk past the *Sporthalle* and playing fields, or take a 10-minute walk down through the fields from the youth hostel.

MAINAU

The lush and exquisitely manicured garden covering the island of Mainau is the result of the horticultural prowess of generations of Baden princes and the Swedish royal family. An arboretum, greenhouses, and **huge animals made of flowers** surround the

Baroque palace built by the Knights of the Teutonic Order, who lived here from the 13th-18th centuries. Now thousands of happy little tourists scamper across the foot bridge from Constance to pose with the blooming elephants and ooh at the 30 different varieties of butterflies fluttering about the tropical-climate greenhouse. To reach the bridge from the Constance *Hauptbahnhof,* take bus #1 to "Staad." Or take a romantic boat trip from behind the train station (DM1 one way, DM13 round-trip). The busiest time on the island is during its official opening hours. (Open 7am-7pm; admission DM16, students DM8, seniors DM11, children DM5. Mid-Oct. to mid-March 9am-5pm; admission DM5, children free.) For more information call (07531) 30 30; fax 30 32 48.

FRIEDRICHSHAFEN

A former construction base for zeppelins, Friedrichshafen was almost entirely leveled by Allied bombing in 1944. The current town was rebuilt with relaxing, wide promenades and tree-lined boulevards. The **Graf-Zeppelin-Museum,** Hafenbahnhof, Seestr. 2 (tel. 380 10), details the history of the flying dirigibles and their inventor. The fleet of nine scale models is led by the 7.5m model of the "Hindenburg" Zeppelin—a replica of the unfortunate original, which went up in flames in New Jersey in 1936. (Open Tues.-Wed. and Fri.-Sun. 10am-5pm, Thurs. 10am-8pm. Admission DM8, students DM4). **Schulmuseum Friedrichshafen,** Friedrichstr. 14 (tel. 326 22), documents school life in Germany over the last five centuries and includes hordes of schoolchildren from this century. Don't miss the "punishment" exhibit, or the report cards of Bertolt Brecht and Karl Marx, whose teacher once commented, "In history and geography, Karl is a bit lost" (open daily 10am-5pm, mid-Nov.-mid-March Tues.-Sun. 2-5pm; free). The 17th-century **Schloßkirche,** on Friedrichstr., to the right of the station, was practically burned to the ground in 1944; it was restored to its former glory, complete with stucco ceiling and Baroque altar, in 1950. The high altar and the pulpit, however, are made of fake marble (open Sun.-Thurs. 9am-6pm, Fri. 10am-6pm). The beach is at the **Strandbad,** Königsweg 11 (tel. 280 78; open mid-May to mid-Sept. daily 9am-8pm; admission DM2).

Ask which hotels rent bikes at the **tourist office,** Bahnhofplatz 2 (tel. 300 10; fax 725 88), across the square to the left of the train station. From the harbor, follow Seestr. to the left and cross the park at the Zeppelin monument. The office provides free town maps, has an extensive library of biking routes, and reserves rooms for free (DM30-60; open Mon.-Thurs. 8am-noon and 2-5pm, Fri. 8am-1pm). The town has unusually good tourist orientation signs pointing to almost everything noteworthy from the *Bahnhof.* Friedrichshafen is connected by frequent **buses and boats** to Lindau and Meersburg and by frequent **trains** to Lindau and Ravensburg. There is a **boat** from Constance (90min.; DM10.80). **Rent bikes** at the train station (*Fahrkartenausgabe* counter; DM13 per day, DM9 with railpass). The **telephone code** is 07541.

Friedrichshafen's **Jugendherberge "Graf Zeppelin" (HI),** Lindauer Str. 3 (tel. 724 04; fax 749 86), is clean, renovated, and 50m from the water's edge. Call ahead; this place fills up just like the rest, especially in summer. Take the bus towards Lindau from the train station, or walk right down Seestr. (15min.) from the harbor. (Reception open 5-10pm. Non-negotiable 10pm curfew. DM19.50, over 26 DM24.50. Breakfast included. Sheets DM5.50.) Most food in town is overpriced. The **Naturkost am Buchhornplatz,** Buchhornplatz 1 (tel. 243 35), serves up homecooked vegetarian food in warm brown light and also offers a brisk take-out business (spinach pizza DM4.50). A supermarket, **Norma,** has a branch on Friedrichstr. (open Mon.-Fri. 8:30am-6:30pm, Sat. 8am-1pm).

MEERSBURG

Meersburg hugs the steep hillside directly across the lake from Constance. This glorious medieval town is graced by the **Altes Schloß,** Germany's oldest inhabited castle. Begun in the 7th century, the huge, medieval edifice now houses a pile of armor and an extensive collection of deer antlers. (Open March-Oct. daily 9am-6pm; Nov.-Feb.

10am-6pm. Admission DM8, students DM7, children DM5. Groups receive DM1 per person discount.) In the 18th century, a prince bishop declared the *Altes Schloß* unfit to house his regal self—so he commissioned the sherbet pink **Neues Schloß** to be built by architect Balthasar Neumann. The town's art collection and the **Dornier museum,** with models of Dornier airplanes, are housed there (open April-Oct. daily 10am-1pm and 2-6pm; admission DM4, students and children DM3). Meersburg's quirky **Zeppelin Museum,** Schloßplatz 8 (tel. 79 09), 20m below the old castle, presents a pressure gauge for the internal gas cells used by DELAG airships from 1890 to 1914, as well as anything else remotely connected with Zeppelins, including commemorative porcelain and a 30-minute video on the history and development of the flying cigars (open April-Oct. daily 9am-6pm; admission DM3.50). Beyond the new castle along the **Uferpromenade,** catch a mind-boggling view of the Bodensee against a backdrop of the Alps. Climb the steep **Steigstraße** left from the harbor past the crowded half-timbered houses.

The **tourist office** *(Kur- und Verkehrverwaltung),* Kirschstr. 4 (tel. 43 11 10; fax 43 11 20), at the top of the climb, provides token maps finds rooms (open Mon.-Fri. 9am-noon and 2-5pm, Sat. 10am-2pm; Nov.-April Mon.-Fri. 8am-noon and 2-5pm). Meersburg is half an hour from Constance by **boat** (DM4.40). It has no train station but uses the one in Uhldingen-Mühlhofen; Friedrichsafen is 25 minutes away. **Haus Mayer Bartsch,** Stettener 39 (tel. 60 50), has balcony rooms with TVs. From the Marktplatz, go up Obertorstr. through the gate, then head straight and bear right onto Stetterstr. (Singles DM45, with bath DM60. Doubles DM85, with bath DM135.) For tasty and honestly-priced pizza and spaghetti (DM9-16.50, slices DM3), **Da Nico,** Unterstadtstr. 41 (tel. 64 48), across the street from the harbor, offers organic Italian food (open daily 11:30am-11pm). The **telephone code** is 07532.

LINDAU IM BODENSEE

Connected to the lake shore by a narrow causeway, the romantic medieval city of **Lindau im Bodensee** looks out across the Bodensee, where the aquamarine water seems more like the Mediterranean than a lake at the foot of the Black Forest. Though most of the Bodensee borders Baden-Württemberg, Lindau is technically part of Bavaria. The central part of town around **Maximilianstraße** features captivating, half-timbered houses. The view of the Alps is almost the same as the one you see on good chocolates. The **Städtische Kunstsammelung** (town art museum) is located in **Cavazzen-Haus,** an ornate Baroque mansion (open April-Oct. Tues.-Sun. 10am-noon and 2-5pm; admission DM4, students DM1). The harbor is framed by a rather imposing 19th-century **Bavarian Lion** and the **New Lighthouse,** the latter offering an illuminating overview of the neighborhood (open daily 10am-7pm; admission DM2, students DM1). The **Rathaus,** halfway along Maximilianstr., is a fruity blend of frescoes. A walk down the less touristed equivalent of Maximilianstr.—In der Grube (In the Pit)—will lead you to **Diebstahl Turm** (robbery tower). Covered with ivy and newly renovated, the color-speckled tin-roofed turret looks more like Rapunzel's tower than a former prison. For those over 21 and in possession of a coat and tie or a formal dress, the **casino** on the island (one of four in Bavaria) is an entertaining option. The bet ceiling is DM12,000 (open 3pm-2am; admission DM5 and a passport—please daaarling, no jeans).

The **tourist office,** Am Hauptbahnhof (tel. 26 00 30; fax 26 00 26), across from the station, finds rooms for a DM5 fee (open mid-June-mid-Sept. Mon.-Fri. 9am-1pm and 2-7pm; mid-Sept.-mid.-June 9am-1pm and 2-6pm; Jan-March 9am-1pm and 2-5pm). **Tours** leave from the tourist office at 10am (Tues. and Fri. in German, Mon. in English; DM5, students DM3). **Ferries** link Lindau with Constance, stopping at Meersburg, Mainau, and Friedrichshafen (5-7 per day, 3hrs., one-way DM18). The **train** takes two hours (one-way DM13). Crazy kids can rent **boats** 50m to the left of the casino, right next to the bridge (tel. 55 14; open mid.-March-mid.-Sept. 9am-9pm; paddleboats DM12-15 per hr. for up to 5 people; power boat DM45). One-hour excursions (tel. 781 94) on a small boat leave from the dock behind the casino at 11:30am, 1, 2:30, and 6pm (DM12, children DM6). **Rent bikes** at the train station (tel.

212 61) for DM15 (DM1 discount for ticket holders; open Mon.-Fri. 9am-noon and 2:30-6pm, Sat. 9:30am-noon).The **post office,** 88101 Lindau im Bodensee (tel. 277 70), is 50m right from the train station. The **telephone code** is 08382.

The **Jugendherberge,** Herbergsweg 11 (tel. 58 13), is not on the island. Get off at the Reutin station, cut left on Bregenzerstr., and go right onto Herbergsweg. Or, from the Seebrücke, bear right up Bregenzenstr and go left onto Herbergsweg to the new hostel with 250 beds (DM25). You could eat off the floor in the fine rooms at **Gästehaus Holdereggen,** Näherweg 4 (tel. 65 74). Follow the railroad tracks across the causeway to the mainland (after the bridge, the path continues to the left of the tracks); turn right onto Holdereggengasse and left onto Jungfernburgstr. Näherweg is on the left. (20min.). (Singles DM30-35. Doubles DM32 per bed. DM3 extra per person for one-night stays. Showers DM2.) Camp at the **Campingplatz Lindau-Zech,** Frauenhoferstr. 20 (tel. 722 36), 3km south of the island on the mainland. It's within spitting range of the Austrian border and a beach. Take bus #1 or 2 from the station to "Anheggerstr.," then transfer to bus #3 (direction: Zech). (DM9 per person, DM4 per tent. Showers included. Cars DM3.50. Open April-mid-Oct.)

Lindau has three beaches (all open daily 10:30am-7:30pm). **Römerbad** is the smallest and most familial, located left of the harbor on the island (admission DM3, students DM1.50). To reach the quieter **Lindenhofbad** take bus #1 or 2 to "Anheggerstr." and transfer to bus #4 to "Alwind" (admission DM3.50, students DM2). Lindau's biggest beach is **Eichwald,** about a 30-minute walk away to the right facing the harbor along Uferweg. Alternatively, take bus #1 or 2 to "Anheggerstr.," then bus #3 to "Karmelbuckel" (admission DM4.50, students DM3). Sit down for Greek at **Taverna Pita Gyros,** Paradies Platz 16 (tel. 237 02), which offers big platters (DM6-15) on the sidewalk or inside (open daily 10am-9pm). There is a **Plus** grocery store in the basement of the department store at the conjunction of In der Grub and Cramergasse (open Mon.-Fri. 8:30am-6:30pm and Sat. 8am-1pm).

RAVENSBURG

Ravensburg is a white-stucco, red-tile gem nicknamed the "town of towers." The tallest of these is the so-called **Mehlsack** (flour sack), built by the citizens of Ravensburg to keep tabs on the constable of the **Veitsburg,** the castle that once stood farther up the bluff. Ravensburg itself had been a free city since the Middle Ages, but the higher castle remained in the hands of the former lords of the town as the truce between them grew uneasy (the castle is long gone; a restaurant stands in its place). Reach the Mehlsack up the hill via the steps from Marktstr. close to the fountain. To get the tower key, call 80 63 69 or 245 04 (Mehlsack open every third Sunday March-Oct. (except July) 10am-noon; free). During the last week of school, Ravensburg's pupils and teachers act out their enmity with the hill lords in the humorous **Rutenfest.** Check out the oddly-named **Humpis-Haus,** at the corner of Rossbachstr. and Burgstr. A half-timbered residence dating from the 15th century, it was the home of Ravensburg's richest medieval family, the Humpis.

The vibrant 15th-century windows came as a surprise in the simple, clean lines of the Gothic **Evangelische Stadtkirche** (Protestant town church), on Seestr., just below the Veitsburg. One block farther is the long **Marienplatz,** the central market square, lined with historic buildings and sidewalk restaurants. Here you'll find the late Gothic **Rathaus** and the charming, colorful Renaissance **Lederhaus,** the former quarters of the leather workers' guild. At the other end of the Marienplatz, the **Liebfrauenkirche** (Church of Our Lady) is a small, graceful Gothic church from the late 14th century that was completely renovated in the 1960s. Ensconced within is a copy of the noteworthy 15th-century sculpture, *Virgin of Ravensburg,* which the citizens of Ravensburg carried in a solemn procession during the war to ward off Allied bombing raids. The proliferation of old buildings attests to the statue's effectiveness. It worked, apparently: no bombs ever fell on the town.

Ravensburg is easily reached by **train** from Ulm (1hr.; DM20) and from Friedrichshafen (30min.; DM5), and makes a good base for trips to Lake Constance (DM5.40-13.20). The **tourist office** *(Verkehrsamt),* Kirchstr. 16 (tel. 823 24 or 823 26; fax 824

66), is in the Weingartner Hof building. From the train station, walk straight down Bahnhofstr., which becomes Eisenbahnstr., and take a left on Marienplatz. Then walk toward Herrenstr. to the side of the church; the office is on your right. The staff finds rooms for free (open Mon. 8am-12:30pm, Tues.-Fri. 8am-12:30pm and 2-5:30pm, Sat. 9am-noon). **Rent bikes** (DM13, DM9 with a railpass or ticket) at the train station. The main **post office** is at Eisenbahnstr. 44, 88212 Ravensburg (open Mon.-Fri. 8am-noon and 2-6pm, Sat. 8am-noon, Sun. 10-11am). The **telephone code** is 0751.

A friendly **Jugendherberge (HI),** Veitsburgstr. 1 (tel. 253 63; fax 137 69), in the *Veitsburg,* offers a breathtaking view of the valley with spotless rooms and a cheerful staff. The quickest way up from the *Bahnhof* is to take the steep stairway to the Mehlsack and follow it up to the Veitsburg area. (Reception open 5-7pm. Curfew 10pm. Lockout 9:30am-11:30am. DM19.50, over 26 DM24.50. Breakfast included. Sheets DM5.50. Open April-Oct. Call ahead.)

■ Near Ravensburg: Wangen in Allgäu

Every Wednesday since 1330, there has been an open-air **market** in Wangen's market square. Before that, it was on Fridays. Brightly painted buildings along the town square preserve this sleepy resort town's medieval flavor. The stately, frescoed 1608 **Frauentor** (Our Lady's Gate), also called the **Ravensburger Tor,** is the symbol of the town. The astonishingly pretty Herrenstraße, lined with muraled houses dating from the late 16th century, leads from the *Frauentor* to the **Rathaus,** whose architecture runs the gamut from Romanesque to Baroque. Since the 15th century, Wangen has sported delightfully refreshing **public fountains**—there are a total of 11. Recent additions include **the Donkey Fountain** on Spitalstr., whose four groups of figures display Aesopic anecdotes. **Der Wahrheitssucher** (The Seeker after Truth) depicts a man desperately trying to decipher a Magic Square, placed on a pile of books that include such heavy authors as Humboldt, Plato, Socrates, Sappho, Goethe, and that guy who wrote the Bible (of the Budget Traveler).

Well-to-do tuberculosis victims once visited Wangen to take a *Luftkur* (fresh air cure) in the pristine mountain atmosphere; take a deep breath and you'll understand why. Excellent **hiking** and **cycling** possibilities are a major attraction of Wangen—more than 350km of marked trails meander through the encircling forest and fields. The **tourist office** (*Gästeamt*) in the *Rathaus* (tel. 742 11; fax 741 11) offers hiking and cycling maps, simple city maps, and brochures on the area. They also find rooms for free and **rent bikes** to visitors staying in town up to three days (DM6 per day; open Mon.-Fri. 9am-noon and 2-5pm, Sat. 10am-noon). If closed, purchase an information packet for DM1 from the machine 30m to the right of the office. From the right side of the station, go straight on Bahnhofstr. until it ends, then go left through the orange *Martinstor,* and the office will be on the opposite side of the building. **Freibad Stephanshöfe** (tel. 12 25) has half a dozen pools, a twisting slide, and a 5-m high diving board; it's a short bus ride north of town. A free **tour** of the town departs every Tuesday and Thursday (in winter Thurs. only) at 3:30pm in front of the tourist office. Wangen im Allgäu is an 80-minute **bus** ride from Ravensburg (RAB line 7545; possible transfer in Tettnang; DM8) and has **trains** to most towns on Lake Constance. (DM7 to Lindau; 30min.). The **telephone code** is 07522.

▓ Ulm

Perhaps best known as the birthplace of Albert Einstein (though he lived here only a year), Ulm was also home to another, less rigorously scientific dreamer, the ill-fated **"Tailor of Ulm."** Albrecht Ludwig Berblinger, tailor by day, inventor by night, nearly drowned in 1811 while trying to fly across the Danube with his "kite-wings" in one of the earliest serious attempts at human flight. Citizens of Ulm apparently didn't appreciate his ingenuity, and poor miserable Berblinger was banished irrevocably from intelligent society for the remaining 16 years of his life. The tailor's destination, Neu Ulm, was originally part of Ulm, until Napoleon designated the Danube the border

between Bavaria and Württemberg, splitting the 800-year-old city. Despite the carto-
graphical nitpicking, Ulm remains Bavarian to its core.

Orientation and Practical Information The **tourist office,** Münsterplatz
50 (tel. 161 28 30; fax 161 16 41), can be found by walking toward the *Münster;* it's
the voluptuous white building next to the tall spire. They sell maps (DM0.50), the
brochure *Gästemagazin* (DM2), and a do-it-yourself cardboard *Münster* (cathedral)
sculpture kit (DM55). They also find rooms for free (open Mon.-Fri. 9am-6pm, Sat.
9am-12:30pm). The automat outside vends a list of accommodations (DM1). **Rent
bikes** for DM15 per day from **Ralf Reich,** Frauenstr. 34 (tel. 211 79). Satisfy your phar-
maceutical fancies at the **Bahnhof Apotheke,** Bahnhofstr. 16 (tel. 600 74), or check
the posted list there to find out which pharmacies in town are open after hours (open
Mon.-Fri. 8am-6:30pm, Sat. 8am-2pm). The **post office,** Bahnhofplatz 2, 89073 Ulm, is
to the left of the station. The **telephone code** is 0731.

Accommodations and Food Ulm's **Jugendherberge "Geschwister Scholl"
(HI),** Grimmelfinger Weg 45 (tel. 38 44 55; fax 38 45 11), is near the edge of town.
Take any bus from the train station to "Ehinger Tor," and there change to bus #4 or 9
(direction: Schulzentrum). Walk through the underpass just up the road, and continue all the way around the left side of the athletic complex, between the tennis
courts and the soccer field to the road, where you should see the *Jugendherberge*
sign. The hostel is named in memory of a brother and sister, students at the University
of Munich, who were executed in 1943 for conspiring against Hitler (see The Holocaust, p. 62). (Reception open 4:30-7pm and 7:45-8pm. Lockout 9-10am. Curfew
10pm, but on Wed. and Sat.-Sun. the doors open again from 11:15-11:30pm for night-
crawlers. DM20.30, over 26 DM25.30. Breakfast included. Sheets DM5.50.) **Münster-
Hotel,** Münsterplatz 14 (tel. 641 62), is located (surprise!) to the left of the Münster.
No showers in the hall. (Singles DM45, with shower DM65. Doubles with shower
DM90, with shower and toilet DM110.) Across the river in Neu Ulm, **Gasthof Rose,**
Kasernstr. 42a (tel. 778 03), has lovely rooms in a quiet district. (Singles DM40. Dou-
bles DM70, with shower DM80. Breakfast included. Pets allowed.)

Ulm's restaurants reflect the culinary influences of both Swabia and Bavaria. For
cheap and greasy *Imbiß* fare, wander around Bahnhofstr. and Hirschstr. on the way
to the *Münster.* Across from the *Rathaus,* the **Erstes Ulmer Weizenbierhaus,** Kro-
nengasse 12 (tel. 624 96), pours more than 20 varieties of *Weizenbier* and serves up
a number of decent dishes for DM5.50-12.80 (open daily 4pm-3am). Next to the Ulm
Museum, **Restaurant Marché,** on Neuestr., offers a dazzling and very tasty buffet of
fresh salads, pasta, and fish. Daily specials DM6-12. Local brews from the tap DM2.90
(open daily 8am-10pm). **Gaststätte Franziskaner,** Neuestr. 56 (tel. 680 13), housed
in an old water mill, serves platters from both Bavaria and Swabia (entrees DM14-28,
beer DM4-5; open daily 10am-midnight). A **farmer's market** springs up on *Münsterplatz* on Wednesday and Saturday mornings.

Sights At 161m (538ft), the steeple topping the **Ulm Münster** is the tallest in the
world. Next to the front portal of the cathedral is *The Man of Sorrows,* a famous representation of Christ by 15th-century sculptor Hans Multscher. Inside the Gothic
walls, extravagantly carved choir stalls (by Jörg Syrlin the Elder) contain a community
of busts: the lowliest tier depicts Greek and Roman philosophers. Climb the 768 dizzying corkscrew steps of the spire on a clear day to see the Alps. (Open daily 9am-
6:45pm. Church interior free. Free organ concerts Mon.-Fri. 11am-noon. Spire admission DM3.50, children DM2.50.) Toward the river along Neuestr., the **Rathaus,** built
in 1370, is decorated with brilliantly colored murals and an elaborate astronomical
clock, both from 1540. The old **Fishermen's Quarter** *(Fischerviertel),* down Kronen-
gasse from the *Rathaus,* has classical half-timbered houses, narrow cobblestone
streets, and canal-spanning footbridges. The **Schiefes Haus** (Crooked House), on
Schwörhausgasse, leans cutely. Further askew are the psychedelic shingles of the
14th-century **Metzgerturm** (Butcher's Tower) and the **Schiefer Turm** (Crooked

Tower), which leans out precariously over the Danube. The remnants of the city wall run along the river here, and the bank is now a grassy park.

On the other side of the *Rathaus* in a former *Patrizierhaus* is the **Ulmer Museum,** Marktplatz 9 (tel. 161 43 00), with a historical exegesis of the region from prehistory to the present. (Open Tues.-Sun. 11am-5pm, Thurs. 11am-8pm. Admission DM5, students DM3. Free on Fri. Special exhibits DM7, students, children, and seniors DM5.) The **Deutsches Brotmuseum** (German Bread Museum), Salzstadelgasse 10, documents 6000 years of breadmaking and waxes philosophical about "the *Leitmotiv* of Man and Bread." Understand—*really, really* understand, that is—the symbolism, history, and meaning of the *Brez'n* (pretzel) in German life and times. (Open Tues. and Thurs.-Sun. 10am-5pm, Wed. 10am-8:30pm. Admission DM5, students DM3.50). A simple monument marking **Albert Einstein's birthplace**, donated to Ulm by India, stands in front of the station. He only lived here a year, and the house has long since given way to a glass-and-chrome savings-and-loan establishment. Every year on the penultimate Monday of July, the mayor of Ulm takes the stand at the **Schwörhaus** (Oath House) to carry on a centuries-old tradition by swearing allegiance to the town's 1397 constitution. The whole affair is accompanied by excessive drinking—that is, merrymaking.

Bavaria (Bayern)

Bavaria is the Germany of Teutonic myth, Wagnerian opera, and—yes—fairy tales. From Bavarian Forest villages and the Baroque cities along the Danube to the turreted castles perched high in the Alps, this region is often the only part of Germany that tourists tread. Indeed, when most foreigners conjure up images of Germany, they are imagining Bavaria, land of beer halls, oom-pah bands, and *Lederhosen*. This is in part a relic of Germany's 45-year division, which shifted Western perceptions southward and prevented avant-garde Berlin from acting as a counterweight to straitlaced Munich. The region's independent residents have always been Bavarians first and Germans second. It took wars with France and Austria to pull the Kingdom of Bavaria into Bismarck's orbit, and local authorities still insist upon using the *Land's* proper name: the Free State of Bavaria. In a plebiscite, Bavaria was the only state to refuse to ratify the Federal Republic's Basic Law, and the ruling Christian Democratic Union still abides by a long-standing agreement not to compete in Bavarian elections (instead, a related party, the Christian Social Union, represents the Right). Though mostly rural, Catholic, and conservative (save for Munich), this largest of Germany's federal states nurtures flourishing commerce and industry, including such renowned companies as the Bayerische Motor Werke (BMW).

> **Reminder:** HI-affiliated hostels in Bavaria do not admit guests over age 26.

■ Munich (München)

Munich is Germany's Second City. The capital and cultural center of Bavaria, it is a sprawling, relatively liberal metropolis in the midst of solidly conservative southern Germany. In a way, the two cities of Munich and Berlin represent the two irreconcilable poles of the German character: southern Munich is unified, merry, sensual, and decidedly Western in feel; while northern Berlin is fragmented, wry, and cerebral, reflecting a spirit that hovers somewhere between East and West.

Munich shines unabashedly with Western German postwar economic glory. World-class museums, handsome parks and architecture, a rambunctious arts scene, and an urbane population collude to create a city of astonishing vitality. An ebullient mixture of sophistication and earthy Bavarian *Gemütlichkeit* keeps the city awake at (almost) all hours. The *Münchener* party zealously during *Fasching* (Feb. 15-20 in 1997), Germany's equivalent of Mardi Gras, and during the legendary *Oktoberfest* (Sept. 20-Oct. 5 in 1997). Before reunification, Munich was the shadow capital of West Germany; now that the Wall has fallen, its popularity has been eclipsed by the cutting-edge energy of Berlin and eastern cities like Prague and Budapest. Munich was once the beginning and end of the line; now many tourists view it as a stopover. Can the lure of beer and beautiful churches attract enough visitors as the travel industry spirals into the 21st century? Go to Munich and find out for yourself.

HISTORY

The stately monuments and public buildings that survived World War II testify to the imperial aspirations of the **House of Wittelsbach,** the dynasty that ruled Bavaria from the 12th to the early 20th century as dukes, prince-electors, and later kings. Though the *Münchener* are loath to admit it, their city was actually founded by a (shudder) northerner. Heinrich der Löwe (Henry the Lion) built a bridge across the Isar in 1158 to consolidate his hold on the Austrian salt trade. Even after the Wittelsbachs moved their court to Munich in the late 13th century, several other cities like Landshut and Straubing remained rivals for Bavarian supremacy. But the dynasty's ruthless acquisition of territory and privileges translated into wealth and grandeur for Munich. The Reformation was mercilessly suppressed in Wittelsbach lands. When Protestant King

Bavaria (Bayern)

Gustavus Adolphus of Sweden occupied Munich in the Thirty Years War, the city barely managed to save itself by paying ransom in blood: several prominent heads rolled. Periodic war, revolt and intrigue, however, failed to shake Wittelsbach rule through the 18th century; Frederick the Great kept Munich from falling under Austrian control. Napoleon's romp across Europe included a brief occupation of Munich, which then sided with the French against the Holy Roman Empire. When Napoleon dissolved the anachronistic empire, Bavaria was rewarded with the status of Kingdom, with Munich as its capital.

The Kingdom period is remembered as the **Bavarian Golden Age,** when enlightened (although still absolutist) rulers rationalized state administration, promoted commerce, and patronized the arts. Its most famous king, Ludwig II, spent little time in Munich, preferring his extravagant castles. In 1871, after Bismarck's successful wars solidified Prussian dominance of Germany, Ludwig presided over the absorption of Bavaria into the greater *Reich* (a process lubricated by Prussia's generous subsidization of Ludwig's wild building schemes). Bavaria was now a kingdom in name only. Munich, however, remained a cultural power rivalling hated Berlin (a city that the *Münchener*—the citizens are not called Munchkins—regarded as a glorified garrison town). Franz Wedekind, Paul Klee, Franz Marc, and others stimulated the artistic and intellectual scene of Munich at the turn of the century.

The Golden Age came to an abrupt end with Germany's defeat in World War I. Amidst the post-Versailles chaos, Munich briefly reigned as the capital of an independent Bavarian Soviet Republic until the revolutionaries were brutally suppressed by right-wing *Freikorps*. Weimar Munich was something of an incubator for reactionary and anti-Semitic movements. Adolf Hitler found the city such a fertile recruiting

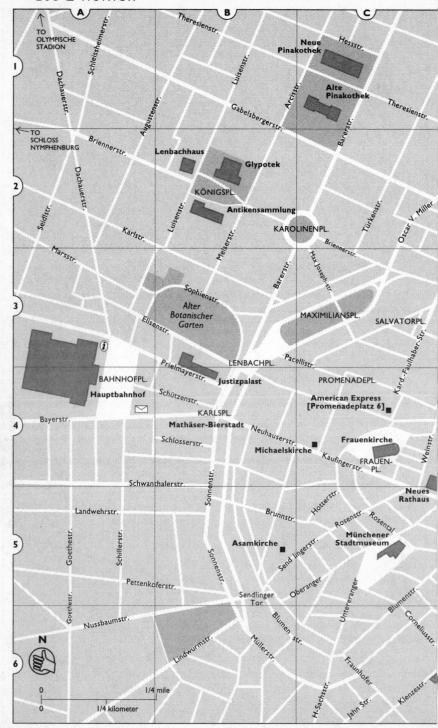

A   B   C

↑
TO
OLYMPISCHE
STADION

Theresienstr.

Schleissheimerstr.

**Neue
Pinakothek**

Hessstr.

Luisenstr.

Dachauerstr.

Augustenstr.

Arcisstr.

**Alte
Pinakothek**

Theresienstr.

1

←
TO
SCHLOSS
NYMPHENBURG

Briennerstr.

Gabelsbergerstr.

Barerstr.

Lenbachhaus

Glypotek

Dachauerstr.

Seidlstr.

Karlstr.

KÖNIGSPL.

Luisenstr.

Meiserstr.

Antikensammlung

KAROLINENPL.

Türkenstr.

Oscar V. Miller

2

Marsstr.

Briennerstr.

Sophienstr.

Barerstr.

Max Joseph-str.

*Alter
Botanischer
Garten*

MAXIMILIANSPL.

SALVATORPL.

Elisenstr.

Pacellistr.

Kard.-Faulhaber-Str.

3

ⓘ

Prielmayerstr.

LENBACHPL.

BAHNHOFPL.

Justizpalast

PROMENADEPL.

Hauptbahnhof

Schützenstr.

**American Express
[Promenadeplatz 6]** ■

✉

KARLSPL.

Bayerstr.

Mathäser-Bierstadt

Neuhauserstr.

Frauenkirche

Weinstr.

Schlosserstr.

Michaelskirche ■

Kaufingerstr.

**FRAUEN-
PL.**

4

Schwanthalerstr.

Sonnenstr.

Hotterstr.

**Neues
Rathaus**

Landwehrstr.

Brunnstr.

Rosenstr.

Rosental

Goethestr.

Schillerstr.

Asamkirche ■

Send lingerstr.

**Münchener
Stadtmuseum**

Untereranger

Blumenstr.

Corneliusstr.

5

Pettenkoferstr.

Sendlinger
Tor

Oberanger

Goethestr.

Nussbaumstr.

Lindwurmstr.

Müllerstr.

Blumen str.

Fraunhofer

H-Sachsstr.

Jahn Str.

Klenzestr.

N
☝

6

0   1/4 mile
0   1/4 kilometer

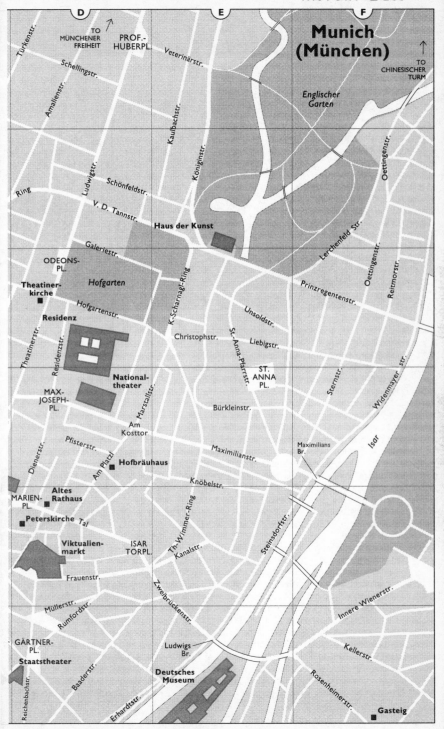

Munich (München)

TO MÜNCHENER FREIHEIT

PROF.-HUBERPL.

TO CHINESISCHER TURM

Türkenstr.

Schellingstr.

Amalienstr.

Veterinärstr.

Englischer Garten

Ring

Ludwigstr.

Schönfeldstr.

Kaulbachstr.

Königinstr.

Oettingenstr.

V. D. Tannstr.

Galeriestr.

Haus der Kunst

Lerchenfeld str.

Oettingenstr.

Reitmorstr.

ODEONS-PL.

Hofgarten

K.-Scharnagl-Ring

Prinzregentenstr.

Theatiner-kirche

Hofgartenstr.

Residenz

Theatinerstr.

Residenzstr.

Christophstr.

St.-Anna-Pfarrstr.

Unsoldstr.

Liebigstr.

Sternstr.

National-theater

ST. ANNA PL.

Widenmayer str.

MAX-JOSEPH-PL.

Marstallstr.

Bürkleinstr.

Isar

Am Kosttor

Pfisterstr.

Maximilianstr.

Maximilians Br.

Dienerstr.

Am Platzl

Hofbräuhaus

Knöbelstr.

MARIEN-PL.

Altes Rathaus

Peterskirche

Tal

Th.-Wimmer-Ring

Steinsdorfstr.

Viktualien-markt

ISAR TORPL.

Kanalstr.

Frauenstr.

Zweibrückenstr.

Innere Wienerstr.

Müllerstr.

Rumfordstr.

GÄRTNER-PL.

Staatstheater

Reichenbachstr.

Baderstr.

Ludwigs Br.

Deutsches Museum

Erhardtstr.

Kellerstr.

Rosenheimerstr.

Gasteig

ground for the new National Socialist German Workers Party (Nazis) that he later called Munich **"the capital of our movement."** In 1923, Hitler attempted to overthrow the municipal government and lead a march on Berlin to topple the Weimar Republic. His **Beer Hall Putsch** was quickly quashed and its leaders arrested, but Germany had not seen the end of the Austrian corporal. Munich is haunted by a number of other associations with the Third Reich: Neville Chamberlain's attempted appeasement of Hitler over the Sudetenland is remembered as the **"Munich Agreement,"** and one of the Nazis' first concentration camps was constructed just outside the city at Dachau (see Near Munich: Dachau, p. 228).

Despite Munich's fortuitous location deep inside the German air defenses, Allied bombing did a particularly thorough job of destroying the city; the post-war building boom was so intense that many salvageable old buildings were demolished anyway. The only substantial portion of Munich that looks the same as before the War is the area around the Marienplatz. When Munich hosted the 1972 Olympics, it was hoped that the Games would restore the city's tattered image at last. But a tragic attack by the Palestinian terrorist group *Black September* led to the death of 11 Israeli athletes in a police shoot-out and dashed Munich's hopes.

More recently, a potentially momentous upheaval was defused, at least for the time being, when 20,000 enraged citizens took to the streets in protest of a recent court ruling, concerning—what else?—beer. The issue at hand in this first-time "Bavarian Beer Garden Revolution" was the **Waldwirtschaft beer garden,** which can accommodate 2000 customers but only has 100 parking places. Numerous neighborhood complaints had finally led to a draconian court decision mandating a 9:30pm closing time for the beer garden. Though *Waldwirdschaft* agreed to build a sound-dampening wall and to tone down the music, the case is being appealed. For the moment, the revolutionaries have left the barricades and returned to their beer *Steins,* but Bavaria's oldest and most cherished tradition still remains in dispute.

ORIENTATION AND PRACTICAL INFORMATION

Munich sits on the banks of the Isar river in the middle of south-central Bavaria. From here, Mad King Ludwig's castles, the Bavarian Alps, and the weekend paradises of the Lake Region are but a hop, skip, and train ride away.

A map of Munich's center looks like a skewed circle quartered by one horizontal and one vertical line. The circle is the main traffic **Ring,** which changes its name several times as it encircles the city center. Within it lies the lion's share of Munich's sights. The east-west and north-south thoroughfares, in turn, cross at Munich's epicenter, the **Marienplatz** (home to the **Neues Rathaus**) and meet the traffic ring at **Karlsplatz** (called **Stachus** by locals) in the west, **Isartorplatz** in the east, **Odeonsplatz** in the north, and **Sendlinger Tor** in the south. The **Hauptbahnhof** (main train station) is just beyond Karlsplatz outside the Ring in the west. In the east beyond the Isartor, the **Isar River** flows by the city center, south to north. To get to Marienplatz from the train station, go straight on Schützenstr. to the yellow buildings of Karlsplatz. Then continue straight through Karlstor to Neuhauser Str., which becomes Kaufingerstr. before it reaches Marienplatz (15-20min.). Or take S-Bahn #1-8 two stops from the main train station *(Hauptbahnhof)* to "Marienplatz."

Beyond the Isartor, in the middle of the Isar river, sits the long, slender **Museumsinsel** (Museum Island), weighted down by the massive **Deutsches Museum.** Back at Odeonsplatz, the giant **Residenz** palace sprawls over a hefty piece of downtown land. Odeonsplatz is also the starting point for the long, wide **Ludwigstraße,** stretching north to the university district. The road was built by King Ludwig to connect Munich to his university, which was then in the middle of a rural cow pasture. **Leopoldstraße,** the continuation of Ludwigstraße, reaches farther toward **Schwabing.** This district, also known as "Schwabylon," is student country; it lies to the left of the maddeningly mobbed Leopoldstr. Here Türkenstr., Amalienstr., Schellingstr., and Barerstr. meander through the funk. To the east of Schwabing sprawls the **Englischer Garten;** to the west is the **Olympiazentrum,** a hyper-modern complex constructed

BAVARIA (BAYERN)

for the 1972 games, surrounded by the verdant **Olympiapark.** Further west sits the posh **Nymphenburg,** built around the eponymous **Nymphenburg Palace.** Southwest of Marienplatz, **Sendlingerstraße** leads past shops and the Baroque **Asamkirche** to the Sendlinger Tor. From there, Lindwurmstr. proceeds to Goetheplatz, from which Mozartstr. leads to **Theresienwiese,** site of the *Oktoberfest.*

There are several publications to help you find your way around Munich. The most comprehensive one (in English) is the monthly **Munich Found** (DM4), available at the "Internationale Presse" booth in the center of the train station, across from track 24, at the Anglia English Bookshop (p. 212), and elsewhere. The tourist office distributes the encyclopedic **Monatsprogramm** (DM2.50). The bi-weekly **In München** (free) gives a more intensive insider's look at the Munich scene in German. **Prinz** (DM5) is the hip and hefty monthly with endless tips on shopping, art, music, film, concerts, and food. EurAide's free publication **Inside Track** provides updated information in English on train connections as well as a few basic tips on getting started in Munich; it's available at EurAide (see below) or at the train-ticket *Reisezentrum* in the main hall of the station.

Tourist Offices:
  Main office: The Munich **Fremdenverkehrsamt** (tel. 23 33 02 56 or 23 33 02 57) is located on the front (east) side of the station, next to ABR Travel on Bahnhofplatz. The staff speaks English, but don't expect cheerfulness. Up to a 20min. wait in the summer. EurAide (below) is more helpful and provides better and faster service. The office books rooms for a DM5 per room fee (plus DM3-9 deposit), sells accommodations lists (DM0.50), and gives out excellent city maps (free). You can also buy bilingual maps (DM7.80). The English/German young people's guide *München Infopool* (DM1) lists beer gardens, *Mensas,* cinemas, and more. Call for recorded information in English on museums and galleries (tel. 23 91 62) or sights and castles (tel. 23 91 72). Open Mon.-Sat. 9am-9pm, Sun. 11am-7pm. **Branch office:** At the new ultra-modern **Flughafen Munich** airport (tel. 97 59 28 15), in the *Zentralgebäude.* Provides general information, but no room bookings. Open Mon.-Sat. 8:30am-10pm, Sun. 1-9pm.
  EurAide in English: (tel. 59 38 89; fax 550 39 65), along Track 11 (room 3) of the *Hauptbahnhof,* near the Bayerstr. exit. This is the magic mushroom of *Wunderland*—delve into the intricacies of Munich with one (sound) byte from EurAide's Mad Hatter, Alan R. Wissenberg; a solace for frazzled English-speaking tourists, he's a nearly omniscient American who can point you (free of charge) in the right direction (particularly on train connections), and make room reservations (for a DM6 fee). *Inside Track* available (free), Thomas Cook Timetables sold (DM37), and Eurail passes validated. EurAide also offers an outing to the Royal Castles *(Königsschlösser)* called the "Two Castle Tour" (see Tours, below), as well as Wissenberg-guided excursions to Dachau. Discounts on Panorama Tours with ISIC or railpass. Open May daily 7:30-11:30am and 1-4:30pm; June-early-Oct. daily 7:30-11:30am and 1-6pm.

Tours:
  Mike's Bike Tours: St. Bonifatiusstr. 2 (tel. 651 42 75; e-mail 101372.2014@compuserve.com.). Visit a pond-side *biergarten,* ponder the "Eunuch of Munich," skinny dip in the *Englischer Garten*—and see the sights of the city. The eponymous Mike, a 28-year-old emigré, is a man of extraordinary tenacity; try to resist the temptation to send a postcard to *Let's Go* telling us how much you enjoyed the tour. We believe you. Mike and his loyal disciples herd small groups of English-speaking bikers through Munich's cycling paths. Skinny-dipping not required. Ardent (and oblivious) enthusiasm, however, is a must. Tours leave (rain or shine) from the *Altes Rathaus* (by the Spielzeugmuseum) daily at 11:30am and 4pm. DM28 including bike rental. Reservations recommended.
  Panorama Tours: Arnulfstr. 8 (tel. 59 15 04; fax 59 81 60 for day excursions; tel. 120 44 18 for city excursions), offers staid bilingual **bus** tours that leave from across the street from the station's main entrance, in front of the Kaufhaus Hertie store on Bahnhofplatz. 1-hr. tour in an open-topped double-decker bus leaves

May-Oct. daily at 10am and 2:30pm. DM15, children DM8. 2½-hr. tour leaves daily at 10am and 2:30pm; on Tues.-Sun. the 2:30pm tour visits the Peterskirche or the Nymphenburg Palace. DM27, children DM14. They offer 6 other trips leaving from the Neptune Fountain, on Elisenstr. Tickets are sold on the bus, in some hotels, or in advance. Hotel pick-up available. 10% off day excursions with Eurailpass. Open Mon.-Fri. 7:30am-6pm, Sat.-Sun. 7:30-10am.

Two Castle Tour: For those who want to enter the world of Mad King Ludwig II, two options await: **Panorama Tours** offers a 10½-hr. bus excursion (in English) to Schloß Linderhof leaving Apr.-Oct. daily at 8:30am; Nov.-March Tues., Thurs., and Sat.-Sun. at 8:30am. DM75, with Eurailpass, Europass, InterRail, or German Railpass DM59; admission to the *Schloß* not included. Book in advance. **EurAide** leads an English-speaking half-bus, half-train *Schloß*-schlepp that also includes an extra stop at the Rococo *Wieskirche*. Meet June-July Wed. at 7:30am by track 11 in front of EurAide. DM70; with Eurailpass, InterRail, or flexipass DM55; price of admission not included, but EurAide will get you a DM1 discount. Or drop by EurAide for train and public bus schedules and see the castles on your own (see Hypertravel to the Castles, p. 238).

Budget Travel: Council Travel, Adalbertstr. 32, 80799 München (tel. 39 50 22; fax 39 70 04), near the university, distributes ISICs. Open Mon.-Fri. 9:30am-1pm and 2-6pm. **abr Reisebüro** (tel. 12 04 46), is located in the train station, and at 16 other locations city-wide. Open Mon.-Fri. 9am-6pm and Sat. 9am-noon.

Consulates: U.S., Königinstr. 5 (tel. 288 80). Take bus #53. Open Mon.-Fri. 8-11am. **Canada,** Tal 29 (tel. 219 95 70). Take the S-Bahn to "Isartor." Open Mon.-Thurs. 9am-noon and 2-5pm, Fri. 9am-noon and 2-2:30pm. **U.K.,** Bürkleinstr. 10 (tel. 21 10 90), fourth floor. Take U-Bahn #4 or 5 to "Lehel." Consular section open Mon.-Fri. 8:45-11:30am and 1-3:15pm. **Ireland,** Mauerkircherstr. 1a (tel. 985 72 35). Take streetcar #20 or bus #54 or 87. Open Mon.-Thurs. 9am-noon and 2-4pm, Fri. 9am-noon. **South Africa,** Sendlinger-Tor-Platz 5 (tel. 231 16 30). Take U-Bahn #1-3 or 6 to "Sendlinger Tor." Open Mon.-Fri. 9am-noon. **Australians** should go to the consulate in Frankfurt (tel. (069) 273 90 90), see p. 296. **New Zealanders** head to the consulate in Bonn (tel. (0228) 22 80 70), see p. 120.

Currency Exchange: The cheapest way to change money is to head to American Express; otherwise pick up a copy of EurAide's free publication *Inside Track* and take it to Deutsche Verkehrs-Bank (DVB). Two locations: in front of the main entrance to the main station on Bahnhofplatz (open daily 6am-11pm); and around the corner from EurAide at track 11 (open Mon.-Sat. 7:30am-7pm). Those with *Inside Track* get a 50% discount on commission if cashing US$50 or more in U.S. traveler's checks. Otherwise, pay regular DVB traveler's check commissions: DM5 for transactions of DM100 or less; 10% or DM7.50 —whichever fee is higher— for transactions above DM100 (for American Express checks), DM10 for other brands. All cash transactions DM3. Western Union services available. Credit card-operated phone and fax.

American Express: Promenadeplatz 6 (tel. 29 09 00; fax 29 09 01 18; 24hr. hotline (0130) 85 31 00), in the Hotel Bayerischer Hof. Holds mail, cashes traveler's checks, no *kiquebaque*. Open Mon.-Fri. 9am-5:30pm, Sat. 9:30am-12:30pm.

Telephones: International phone booths are located on various tracks and elsewhere in the train station. Make credit card and collect calls from the post office, on the second level of the train station, or across the street.

Flights: Flughafen München is accessible from the train station by S-Bahn #8, which runs daily every 20min., 3:22am-12:42am (DM13.20 or 8 stripes on the *Streifenkarte* 10-stripe ticket (DM13); Eurail, InterRail and German railpasses valid). Alternatively, Lufthansa offers a shuttle bus between the *Hauptbahnhof* and the airport (45min.), with a pickup at the U-Bahn stop "Nordfriedhof" in Schwabing. Buses leave from Arnulfstr., on the northern side of the train station, every 20min. 6:50am-7:50pm. Buses return from Terminal A *(Zentralbereich)* and Terminal D every 20min. 7:55am-8:55pm (one way DM15, round-trip DM25). For more info call Panorama Tours at 59 15 04. For flight info, call 97 52 13 13.

Trains: The transportation hub of southern Germany, Munich has connections to all major cities in Germany and throughout Europe, several times per day. To: Frankfurt (1 per hr.; 4hr.); Berlin (1-2 per hr. until 5:43pm; 8½hr.); Cologne (2 per hour;

5hr.); Hamburg (18 per day; 6hr.); Prague (4 per day; 7hr.); Zürich (6 per day; 4-5hr.); Vienna (1 per hr.; 4-5hr.); Paris (3 direct per day at 7:45am, 1:45pm, and 9pm; 10hr.); Amsterdam (17 per day; 9hr.); Füssen (7 direct and 13 via Buchloe per day; 2hr.). Call for **schedules and fare information** (tel. 194 19; open 6am-11pm) and **reservations** (in German only, tel. 13 08 23 33) Mon.-Fri. 8am-6pm, Sat.-Sun. 8am-3pm. **EurAide** (see Tourist Offices, p. 209), in the station, provides free train information in English. Otherwise, the best source is a **destination booklet** *(Städteverbindungen)* available at the counters in the *Reisezentrum.* These list all the possible connections between Munich and scores of other cities. Station open daily 4:30am-1:30am. Use entrance on Arnulfstr. to reach trains. **Reisezentrum** information counters open daily 6am-10:30pm. Reservation desk open 7am-9pm. Visa, MC, EuroCard, AmEx, and Diners accepted.

Public Transportation: Munich's public transport system **(MVV)** runs 5am-12:30am on weekdays and 5am-1:30am on weekends. A very select number of lines run through the night (once per hr.); double check the posted schedules. Eurail, InterRail, and German railpasses are valid on any S-Bahn (commuter rail) but *not* on the U-Bahn (subway), *Straßenbahn* (streetcars), or buses. Single ride tickets *(Einzelfahrkarten)* within the *Innenraum* (city center) cost DM3.30. *Kurzstrecke* (short trip) tickets cost DM1.70 and can be used for 2 stops on the U-Bahn or S-Bahn, or for 4 stops on a street car or bus. A *Streifenkarte* (10-strip ticket) costs DM13 and can be used by more than 1 person. Cancel 2 strips per person for a normal ride, or 1 strip per person for a *Kurzstrecke.* Single-day tickets *(Single-Tages-Karte;* DM8) give 1 person unlimited travel in the *Innenraum* until 6am the next day. A *Partner-Tages-Karte* (DM12) can be used by 2 adults, 3 children under 18, and a dog. Buy an *Innenraum* 1-week pass (DM34) from the MVV office in the *Hauptbahnhof.* Children under 15 pay reduced fares, and children under 4 ride free. Buy tickets at the blue *"MVV-Fahrausweise"* vending machines and be sure to stamp your ticket in the boxes marked with an "E" *before you go to the platform.* If you plan to jump the fare or don't validate correctly, bring along an extra DM60 for the fine. **Transit maps** can be picked up in the tourist office or EurAide, and at MVV counters near the subway entrance in the train station. The U-Bahn is safe, clean, and punctual; most trains run every 5min. during the day. *"Zurückbleiben"* means "stand back."

Taxi: Taxi-Zentrale (tel. 216 11 or 194 10) has large **stands** in front of the train station and every 5-10 blocks in the central city. Women can request a female driver. DM1 for each piece of luggage. Train station to airport costs about DM100.

Car Rental: Flach's Leihwagen, Landsberger Str. 289 (tel. 56 60 56), rents cars (DM60-112 per day) with no mileage charges. Open Mon.-Fri. 8am-8pm, Sat. 9am-noon. **Swing,** Schellingstr. 139 (tel. 523 20 05), has rents starting at DM45 per day. **Europcar/National** (tel. (0180) 52 21 22), **Sixt Budget** (tel. (0180) 525 25 25), **Hertz** (tel. 550 22 56), and **Avis** (tel. 550 12 12) all have offices in the *Mietwagenzentrum,* upstairs in the main train station.

Bike Rental: Radius Touristik, squats in the rear of the *Hauptbahnhof* (tel. 59 61 13; fax 59 47 14), behind the lockers opposite tracks 30-31. Chat it up with Patrick Holder, the gregarious English owner. 100 bikes in stock. DM10 for 2hr. DM25 for 10am-6pm. DM30 for 24hr. DM45 for 48hr. DM95 per week. Mountain bikes 50% more. DM100 deposit required for 3-6 speed bikes, DM200 for mountain bikes; passport or a credit card also acceptable. Students and Eurailpass holders receive a 10% discount. Open daily May-early-Oct. 10am-6pm. **Aktiv-Rad,** Hans-Sachs-Str. 7 (tel. 26 65 06), rents 'em out at DM18 per day. Take U-Bahn #1 or 2 to "Frauenhoferstr." (open Mon.-Fri. 9am-1pm and 2-6:30pm, Sat. 9am-1pm).

Hitchhiking: *Let's Go* does not recommend hitchhiking as a safe mode of transportation. Those looking to share rides scan the bulletin boards in the **Mensa,** on Leopoldstr. 13. Otherwise, hitchers try *Autobahn* on-ramps; *those who stand behind the blue sign with the white auto may be fined.* Hitchers who've gotta get to *Autobahn* A8/E52 (direction: Salzburg-Vienna-Italy) take U-Bahn #1 or 2 to "Karl-Preis-Platz." For A8/E52 in the opposite direction (direction: Stuttgart/France), they take U-Bahn #1 to "Rotkreuzplatz," then streetcar #12 to "Amalienburgstr.;" *or* S-Bahn #2 to "Obermenzing." Some are said to take bus #73 or 75 to "Blutenburg." Thumbers who want to get to the *Autobahn* A9/E45 interchange north to Berlin take U-Bahn #6 to "Studentenstadt" and walk 500m to the Frankfurter Ring. For *Autobahn* A96/E54 to Lake Constance and Switzerland, intrepid souls take U-Bahn #4 or 5 to "Heimeranplatz," then bus #33 to "Siegenburger Str." For Garmisch-Partenkirchen, hitchers head for the *Autobahn* A95/E533 south by taking U-Bahn #6 to "Westpark," then bus #33 to "Luise-Kesselbach-Platz."

Mitfahrzentrale: McShare Treffpunkt Zentrale, Klenzestr. 57b and Lämmerstr. 4 (tel. 194 40), near the train station matches McDrivers and McRiders (DM40 to Frankfurt, DM52 to Berlin, DM34 to Heidelberg, DM2 for additional insurance). Open Mon.-Sat. 8am-8pm. **Känguruh,** Amalienstr. 87 (tel. 194 44), is in the Amalienpassage near the university (Frankfurt DM40: DM25 for driver, DM15 for service). Open Mon.-Fri. 8:30am-7pm, Sat. 9am-3pm, Sun. 10am-7pm. **Frauenmitfahrzentrale,** Klenzestr. 57b (tel. 201 65 10), is for women only. Take U-Bahn #1 or 2 to "Fraunhoferstr.," then walk up Fraunhoferstr. away from the river, and turn right. Open Mon.-Fri. 8am-8pm.

Luggage Storage: At the **train station** (tel. 13 08 50 47) and **airport** (tel. 97 52 13 75). There's a staffed storage room *(Gepäckaufbewahrung)* in main hall of train station. Open Mon.-Fri. 7:10am-6:50pm, Sat.-Sun. 9:25am-6:50pm. DM4 per piece per calendar day. Lockers opposite tracks 16, 24, and 30 cost DM2-4 per 24hr.

Lost and Found: Fundstelle der Stadtverwaltung, Arnulfstr. 31 (tel. 12 40 80). Take the S-Bahn to "Hackerbrücke." Open Mon. and Wed.-Fri. 8:30am-noon, Tues. 8:30am-noon and 2-5:30pm. For items lost on trains, **Fundstelle der DB,** Bahnhofplatz 2 (tel. 13 08 66 64), across from track 24 on the 2nd floor in the main train station, can help. Open daily 6:30am-11:30pm. For items lost on S-Bahn or local trains, go to **Fundstelle im Ostbahnhof** (tel. 12 88 44 09). Open Mon.-Fri. 8am-5:30pm, Sat. 8am-11:45pm. For the airport, call 97 52 13 70.

Mitwohnzentrale: An der Uni, in tunnel passage of U-Bahn #3 or 6 stop "Universität" (tel. 28 10 88), has apartments available for 1 month or more. Open Mon.-Fri. 10am-1pm and 2:30-6pm, Sat. 11am-1pm. **City Mitwohnzentrale,** Klenzestr. 57b (tel. 194 40; fax 201 63 11), or Lämmerstr. 4 (tel. 194 22), has apartments and houses (furnished or not) for 4 days-eternity throughout Germany.

Bookstores: Anglia English Bookshop, Schellingstr. 3 (tel. 28 36 42), offers reams of English-language books in a a gloriously chaotic atmosphere. Take U-Bahn #3 or 6 to "Universität." Open Mon.-Fri. 9am-6:30pm, Sat. 10am-2pm. **Words' Worth,** at Schellingstr. 21a (tel. 280 91 41), a bit farther down, carries obscure English novels as well as a full range of literature from the greats. Lovely postcards and a picturesque backyard. Open Mon.-Wed. and Fri. 9am-6:30pm, Thurs. 9am-8:30pm, Sat. 10am-2pm. **Lillemor's Frauenbuchladen,** Arcisstr. 57 (tel. 272 12 05; fax 272 09 98), is a women's bookstore and center for women's events. Open Mon.-Fri. 10am-6:30pm, Sat. 10am-2pm.

Photocopies: University territory is cheapest. Try **Copyshop Zentrale,** Adalbertstr. 43. 7pf per copy. Open Mon.-Fri. 8:30am-9pm, Sat. 10am-2pm.

Libraries: Many of Munich's city libraries have a hefty English section. Anyone with ID can get a library card. **Bayerische Staatsbibliothek,** Ludwigstr. 16 (tel. 28 63 80; fax 28 63 82 93), one of the largest libraries in Germany, has endless magazines and newspapers. Open Mon.-Fri. 9am-7:30pm, Sat. 9am-4:30pm. **Universitätsbibliothek der Universität,** Geschwister-Scholl-Platz 1 (tel. 21 80 24 28). Open Mon.-Thurs. 9am-8pm, Fri. 9am-4pm; open Aug.-Nov. Mon.-Thurs. 9am-7pm, Fri. 9am-noon.

Cultural Centers: Amerika Haus, Karolinenplatz 3 (tel. 552 53 70; fax 55 35 78), is the cultural extension of the consulate. Take U-Bahn #2 to "Königsplatz." They have cultural resources and advice for Americans wishing to teach, a library for reading and research, and language courses. Open Mon.-Fri. 10am-1pm and 2-4:30pm. **British Council,** Rosenheimer Str. 116b, Haus 93 (tel. 290 08 60). **Deutsch-Kanadische-Gesellschaft,** Hildeboldstr. 5 (tel. 307 33 45). **Munich Scottish Association,** Keferstr. 246 (tel. 39 12 53).

Women's Centers: Kofra *(Kommunikationszentrum für Frauen),* Baaderstr. 30 (tel. 201 04 50). Job advice, a research job library, *Kaffeetrinken,* tons of magazines, lesbian politics, and books. Open Mon.-Fri. 4-10pm. **Frauentreffpunkt Neuperlach,** Oskar-Maria-Graf-Ring 20-22 (tel. 670 64 63), is an environmentally-conscious women's café/shop. Open Tues. and Thurs.-Fri. 10am-1pm, Wed. 10am-

1pm and 3-6pm. **Lesbentraum LeTra,** Dreimühlenstr. 23 (tel. 725 42 72). Information for lesbians. Open Thurs. 1:30-4pm; telephones open Thurs. 7-10pm.

Ticket Agencies: Advance tickets for concerts in the Olympiapark and soccer games are available at the **Kaufhof** department store either on Marienplatz, 3rd floor (tel. 260 32 49) or at Karlsplatz, ground floor (tel. 512 52 48). Both open Mon.-Wed. and Fri. 11am-6:30pm, Thurs. 11am-8:30pm, Sat. 9am-2pm. To order tickets by phone call **München Ticket** (tel. 54 81 81 81; fax 54 81 81 54). **Hertie Schwabing,** Leopoldstr. 82, 4th floor (tel. 33 66 59), sells tickets for smaller rock, pop, and theater events. Open Mon.-Fri. 9am-6:30pm, Sat. 9am-2pm.

Laundromat: The **Wäscherei,** Paul-Heyse-Str. 21, is close to the station. Exit at Paul-Heyse-Str. 21. Open daily 6am-10pm. **Münz Waschsalon,** Amalienstr. 61, is near the university. Wash DM6. Dry DM1. Soap DM1. Open Mon.-Fri. 8am-6:30pm, Sat. 8am-1pm. Another **Wäscherei** is at Landshüter Allee 77. Take U-Bahn #1 to "Rotkreuzplatz." Wash DM6. Dry DM0.50 per 15min. Open 24hr. *Bring your own change for all laundromats.*

Swimming Pools: Pool season is May-mid-Sept. Choose among 16 local dives. **Michaelibad,** Heinrich-Wieland-Str. 24 (tel. 40 76 91), is a huge pool complex with slides and 5 swimming areas. Take U-Bahn #2 or 5 to "Michaelibad." Open Mon. 10am-6pm, Tues.-Sun. 7am-9pm. **Müllerisches Volksbad,** Rosenheimer Str. 1 (tel. 23 61 34 29), has Art Nouveau indoor pools and Irish-Roman steam baths. Take S-Bahn #1-8 to "Isartor." Open Mon. 10am-5pm, Tues. and Thurs. 8am-7:30pm, Wed. 6:45am-7:30pm, Fri. 8am-8:45pm, Sat. 8am-5:30pm, Sun. 9am-6pm. **Dantebad,** Dante Str. 6 (tel. 15 28 74), in Neuhausen, is excellent and less crowded. Take streetcar #20 or 21 to "Baldurstr." Open daily 8am-7:30pm.

Weather Conditions: *(Wettervorhersage)* tel. 11 64.

Rape Crisis: Frauennotruf München, Güllstr. 3 (tel. 76 37 37).

AIDS Hotline: Call 520 73 87 or 520 74 12 (Mon.-Thurs. 8am-3pm, Fri. 8am-noon). Or 194 11 (Mon.-Sat. 7-10pm).

Poison Control: tel. 192 40.

Pharmacy: Bahnhof Apotheke, Bahnhofplatz 2 (tel. 59 41 19 or 59 81 19), on the corner outside the station. Open Mon.-Fri. 8am-6:30pm, Sat. 8am-2pm. The hours of all other pharmacies posted in the window. 24-hr. service rotates among the city's pharmacies—call 59 44 75 for recorded information (German only). The tourist office and EurAide also have free monthly schedules.

Medical Assistance: Klinikum Rechts d. Isar, clinic across the river on Ismaningerstr. Take U-Bahn #4 or 5 to "Max-Weber-Platz." STD and AIDS tests are free and anonymous at the **Gesundheitshaus,** Dachauer Str. 90 (tel. 520 71). Open Mon.-Thurs. 8-11am and 1-2pm, Fri. 8-11am. U.S. and British consulates carry a list of English-speaking doctors.

Emergency: Police: tel. 110. **Ambulance:** tel. 192 22. **Emergency medical service:** tel. 55 77 55. **Fire:** tel. 112.

Post Office: Post/Telegrafenamt, Bahnhofplatz 1, 80335 München (tel. 545 40), is directly opposite the main train station. *Poste restante* and money exchange at windows #8-10. Open Mon.-Fri. 7am-10pm, Sat.-Sun. 8am-10pm. To send packages and insured letters, go to the **branch office,** at Arnulfstr. 32. Go out of the train station and turn left onto Arnulfstr.; the post office will be on your right. Open Mon.-Fri. 8am-6pm, Sat. 8am-noon. **Postamt 31,** up the escalator in the train station (tel. 552 26 20), sells stamps, phone cards, and takes letters. Open Mon.-Fri. 8am-7pm, Sat. 8am-2pm. EurAide offers a "message-forwarding service."

Telephone Code: 089.

ACCOMMODATIONS AND CAMPING

Munich's accommodations usually fall into one of three categories: seedy, expensive, or booked solid. During times like *Oktoberfest,* there is one category. During summer, the best strategy is to start calling before noon or to book a few weeks in advance, especially for longer stays. Most singles (without private bath) range DM55 to 85, doubles DM80 to 120. If you're planning an extended stay in Munich, call the *Mitwohnzentrale* (see p. 212) or try bargaining with a *Pension* owner. Remember:

Bavarian HI hostels do not accept guests over age 26. At several of Munich's hostels you can check in all day, but try to start your search well before 5pm.

Sleeping in the *Englischer Garten* is unsafe and illegal; the police often patrol. Subway stops are similarly patrolled. Many wandering backpackers arrive too late to find lodging and end up cluttered in the main train station; this is extremely unsafe. If you sleep in the *Hauptbahnhof*'s *Warteraum* (waiting room), you'll awake to the thrashing of the railway police scurrying you away. A few options for the roomless do exist: the Augsburg youth hostel is 30 to 45 minutes away by train (2-3 per hr. until 11pm; DM10), but be mindful of the 1am curfew. Or, you can throw your luggage into a locker and party until 5am, and come back to re-evaluate the hotel lists afterwards. For railpass holders, a final option is to catch the 11:17pm train to Heidelberg, and, upon arriving at 3:12am, then catch the 3:20am train back to Munich. Arrive in Munich at 7:13am, and start looking for a real room immediately. Be sure to *double check* an up-to-date train schedule before attempting this stunt.

Hostels and Camping

Jugendlager Kapuzinerhölzl ("The Tent"), In den Kirschen 30 (tel. 141 43 00; fax 51 41 06 18). Take streetcar #17 from the *Hauptbahnhof* to "Botanischer Garten, Franz-Schrank-Str.," go straight on Franz-Schrank-Str., turn left at "In den Kirschen." The Tent is on the right. The last streetcar leaves around 1:30am. *Don't ride without a ticket*—inspections are especially rigorous. Sleep with 400 fellow "campers" under a big circus top tent. DM13 gets you a foam pad, blankets, bathrooms, a shower (not necessarily warm), a rudimentary breakfast, and enthusiastic management. Actual "beds" DM17. Spontaneous merrymaking around a bonfire at nightfall. 3-4-day max. stay. Reception open 5pm-9am. No lockers—use the ones at the station. Under 24 only (under 27 if there's room). No reservations. Open late June-early-Sept. Bike rental DM10 per day (Mon.-Sat. 8-10am), free city tours (Wed. at 9am), volleyball, ping-pong, and yes—a beer garden.

4 you münchen (ökologisches Jugendgästehaus), Hirtenstr. 18 (tel. 55 21 660; fax 55 21 66 66), is 200m from the *Hauptbahnhof*. Exit at Arnulfstr., go left, quickly turn right onto Pfefferstr., then hang a louie (that's a left) onto Hirtenstr. Beautiful ecological youth hostel awash in light beech wood, large windows, and granola good cheer. The place is 2 good 2 be true. Restaurant/bar, hang-out areas, a playroom for families—everything's *au natural*. Singles DM50. Doubles DM35 per person. 4-, 6-, or 8-bed rooms DM25. 10-bed rooms DM20. Sheets DM4, but you can bring your own sleeping bag. Cold breakfast DM6. Hot breakfast DM12. They have an adjoining hotel. Single with shower DM110. Doubles with shower DM130. Breakfast included. Handicapped accessible. Reserve be4 you arrive—unless you have good 4tune, acquiring an ecological bed will be a 4midable task.

Jugendherberge (HI), Wendl-Dietrich-Str. 20. (tel. 13 11 56). Take U-Bahn #1 to "Rotkreuzplatz." Cross Rotkreuzplatz and head right; then head down Wendl-Dietrich-Str. and make a right on Winthirplatz. The entrance is ahead on the right. Though it's 3 U-Bahn stops from the *Hauptbahnhof* and 5 stops from *Marienplatz*, this is the most "central" of the HI hostels. Management has just installed new safes in the reception area—*use them*, and keep keys on your person at *all* times. Check-in starts at 10:30am, but the lines form before 9am. Reception open 10am-1am. Under 27 only. Big dorm (37 beds) for men only DM21.50. 4-to-6-bed rooms for all else DM24. Mandatory DM20 key deposit. DM50 deposit for the use of safes. Breakfast and sheets included.

Jugendherberge Pullach Burg Schwaneck (HI), Burgweg 4-6 (tel. 793 06 43; fax 793 79 22), in a castle outside the city center. Take S-Bahn #7 (direction: Wolfratshausen) to "Pullach" (20min.), and follow the signs that begin on Margarethenstr. (15min.). Unmajestic but entirely adequate. Romantic surroundings swarm with schoolchildren. 4-to-8-bed rooms. Reception open 5-11pm. Curfew 11:30pm. Under 27 only. DM20 plus DM5.50 for sheets. Buy a shower token (DM1) early to beat the crowds. Breakfast included.

Jugendgästehaus München (HI), Miesingstr. 4 (tel. 723 65 50; fax 724 25 67). Take U-Bahn #1 or 2 to "Sendlinger Tor," then U-Bahn #3 (direction: Fürstenrieder West) to "Thalkirchen" (Zoo). From Thalkirchner Platz, follow Frauenbergstr. and go immediately left on Miesingstr; then follow the street as it curves left. Crowded and distant, but the rooms are immaculate. Reception open 7am-1am. Rooms available after 2pm. Curfew 1am. Under 27 only. 8-to-15-bed rooms DM26. Singles DM34. Doubles DM30 per person. Triples or quads DM28 per person. Sheets and breakfast included. No phone reservations in July.

CVJM (YMCA) Jugendgästehaus, Landwehrstr. 13, 80336 München (tel. 552 14 10; fax 550 42 82; e-mail muenchen@cvjm.org). Take the Bayerstr. exit from the station, head straight down Goethestr. or Schillerstr., take 2nd left onto Landwehrstr.; it's on the right. Central location with clean, no-frills rooms and showers off the hall. Reception open 8am-12:30am. Curfew 12:30am. Singles DM48. Doubles DM41 per person. Triples DM38 per person. Co-ed rooms only for married couples. Over 27 add 15% surcharge. Breakfast included. Reservations by mail, phone, and fax, or e-mail must arrive before 4pm. Nifty 50s-decorated restaurant offers dinner (DM6-10), soups, and salads 6:30-10pm. Restaurant open mid-Sept.-July. Closed during Easter and Dec.20-Jan. 7.

Jugendhotel Marienberge, Goethestr. 9, 80336 München (tel. 55 58 05), less than a block south of the train station. Rather rough neighborhood but in a secure building staffed by roly-poly nuns. The rooms in this Catholic hostel are comfortable and spotless. Kitchen and laundry facilities. Wash DM2, dry DM2. *Open only to women under 26.* Reception open 8am-midnight. Curfew midnight, before you turn into a pumpkin. Singles DM35. Doubles DM60. Triples DM90. Giant 7-bed rooms DM25 per person. Showers and breakfast included.

Kolpinghaus St. Theresia, Hanebergstr. 8, 80637 München (tel. 12 60 50; fax 12 605 212). Take U-Bahn #1 to "Rotkreuzplatz," then walk down Leonrodstr.; turn left at Platz der Freiheit onto Landshüter Allee., walk 4 blocks, turn left (20min.). Simple, tidy rooms and communal showers. Reception open 8am-3pm. Singles DM48. Doubles DM84. 4-to-8-bed rooms DM32 per person. Breakfast included.

Haus International, Elisabethstr. 87, 80797 München (tel. 12 00 60; fax 12 00 62 51). Take U-Bahn #2 (direction: Dülferstr.) to "Hohenzollernplatz," then streetcar #12 or bus #33 to "Barbarastr." It's the 5-story yellow building behind the BP gas station. Interior reminiscent of dorm life except that everything is delightfully clean. Free indoor pool, small beer garden, TV room, and newly-renovated disco. Reception open 24hr. Singles DM53, with shower and toilet DM83. Doubles DM100, with shower DM140. Triples DM45 per person, quads DM41, quints DM39.50. Reservations recommended in May-July and Sept. In summer you may be required to reserve with half-pension (add DM14 per person).

Camping: All three Munich campgrounds are open from mid-March to the end of October. **Campingplatz Thalkirchen,** Zentralländstr. 49, 81379 München (tel. 723 17 07; fax 724 31 77), is in the Isar River Valley Conservation Area. Take U-Bahn #1 or 2 to "Sendlinger Tor," then U-Bahn #3 to "Thalkirchen," and then change to bus #57 (20min.). Large grounds are well-run but crowded. Good hiking, and cycling paths. Laundry facilities, TV lounge, billiards, and a cheap restaurant (meals DM3-8). Curfew 11pm. DM7.80 per person. Under 14 DM2.50. Small tent DM5.50. Tent for 2 or more DM7. Motorcycle DM4. Car DM9. Trailer DM19. Showers DM2. **Obermenzing,** Lochhausener Str. 59, 81247 München (tel. 811 22 35). Take S-Bahn #3-6 or 8 to "Passing," then bus #76 to "Lochhausener Str." (10 stops). Head up the street (5min.); it's on the left. DM7 per person. Ages 2-14 DM4. Tent DM7.50. Car DM5. Trailer DM12. Showers DM2. Dishwashing DM3. **Langwieder See,** Eschenrieder Str. 119, 81249 München (tel. 864 15 66; fax 863 23 42), located near a nice lake, is hard to reach without a car. Go right off the Augsburg *Autobahn* A8, and exit at Lochhausen/Eschenried. The nearest train station is München-Lochhausen, but it's a 2-km schlepp towards Eschenried.

Hotels and Pensionen

Reputedly a city of 80,000 guest beds, Munich's dirt-cheapest overnight options crouch on back streets and are marked by aging and discreet *Pension* or *Gästhaus* signs. A slightly larger and cleaner establishment will run you at least DM55 to 65 for a single or DM80 to 100 for a double, but don't show up (especially during *Oktoberfest*) and expect affordable housing; always call ahead. Some establishments actually refuse service to English-speaking backpackers (their owners have cleaned up too many puddles of collegiate beer). The tourist office charges DM0.50 for a hotel list and DM5 to find lodgings. The friendlier EurAide staff (at the train station) will gladly walk you through the art of calling Munich's lodging establishments; for DM6, they'll even call for you. Don't be lured by seemingly low prices; factor in the possible extra costs of public transportation, shower fees, and one-night surcharges.

Near the Hauptbahnhof:

Hotel Kurpfalz, Schwanthalerstr. 121, 80339 München (tel. 540 98 60, fax 54 09 88 11, e-mail hotel-kurpfalz@munich-online.de). Take the Bayerstr. exit from the station, turn right, walk 5-6 blocks down Bayerstr., take a left onto Holzapfelstr., and make a right onto Schwanthalerstr. Or take tram #18 or 19 to "Holzapfelstr." (3 stops) and walk from there. The hotel's slick Sevdas Brothers add a dash of Bavaria to their proficiency in Americana. Cable TV, phones, showers, and hardwood furniture embellish each and every impeccable room. ESPN-pumped American sports bar. Reception open 24hr. Singles DM55-59. Doubles DM80-90. Room service. All-you-can-eat breakfast buffet included. Free Internet access. Overnight laundry service DM6 per load. Major credit cards accepted.

Hotel Haberstock, Schillerstr. 4, 80336 München (tel. 55 78 55; fax 55 03 6 34), next to Hotel Helvetia, provides quiet and privacy on a noisy central block. Hazy windows, musky carpets, expansive pillows. Like Grandpa's den converted into a hotel room. Reception open 24hr. Singles DM66-75, with shower DM85, and toilet DM105. Doubles DM116, with shower DM136, and toilet DM176. Large breakfast included. Prices 10% higher during *Oktoberfest*. AmEx, Eurocard, MC, Visa.

Pension Locarno, Bahnhofplatz 5 (tel. 55 51 64; fax 59 50 45), under the AGFA sign outside the train station. Plain rooms, all with TVs and phones. Helpful, homey owners. Reception open 7am-midnight, but your key opens the outside door 24hr. Singles DM55-75. Doubles DM90. Triples DM135. Quads DM140. Discounts for Eurobus riders. Hallway showers and breakfast included. DM5 less if you arrange for no breakfast. Prices drop in off-season. AmEx, Eurocard, MC, Visa.

Pension Schillerhof, Schillerstr. 21, 80336 München (tel. 59 42 70; fax 550 18 35). From the "Bahnhofsplatz" train station exit, turn right and walk two blocks. Boring rooms surrounded by the hustle of neighborhood sex shops and kinos. In-room TVs. Singles DM55-65, with shower DM65-75. Doubles 80-95, with shower DM95-110. Extra bed DM20. *Oktoberfest* surcharge DM20-30 per person. Showers and breakfast included. AmEx, Eurocard, MC, Visa.

Hotel Helvetia, Schillerstr. 6, 80336 München (tel. 55 47 45; fax 55 02 381), at the corner of Bahnhofsplatz, next to the Vereinsbank. Though extensively renovated, it still exudes a late-70s feel. Some rooms have phones; all are neat. Singles DM68. Doubles DM100, with shower DM115. Triples, quads, and quints DM42 per person. *Oktoberfest* surcharge DM5 per person. Showers and breakfast included. In summer call ahead for singles and doubles. AmEx, Eurocard, MC, Visa.

Pension Hungaria, Briennerstr. 42, 80333 München (tel. 52 15 58). From *Hauptbahnhof*, go left onto Dachauerstr., right on Augustenstr., and right onto Briennerstr. (10min.). Or take U-Bahn #1 to "Stiglmaierplatz," and take the Briennerstr./Volkstheater exit; it's on next corner at Augustenstr. Reception (2 floors up) open 8am-10pm. Oriental rugs, comfortable furnishings, and small travel library. Singles DM50-55. Doubles DM80-85. Triples DM105. Showers DM3. Lovely breakfasts included. *Oktoberfest* surcharge DM10-20 per room.

Pension Utzelmann, Pettenkoferstr. 6, 80336 München (tel. 59 48 89; fax 59 62 28). From the *Bahnhof* walk 4 blocks down Schillerstr. and go left on Pettenkofer; it's at the end on the left (10min.). Teddy bears lounge on sofas lit by chandeliers. Rooms clean, some quite elegant. Reception open 8am-10pm. Singles DM52-78, with shower and toilet DM125. Doubles DM90, with shower and toilet DM110, and toilet DM145. DM5 for hall showers. Breakfast included. No credit cards.

Schwabing/University/City Center:

Pension Frank, Schellingstr. 24, 80799 München (tel. 28 14 51; fax 280 09 10). From the *Hauptbahnhof*, take the U-Bahn #4 or 5 to "Odeonsplatz," then switch to U-Bahn #3 or 6 to "Universität." Take the Schellingstr. exit, then the first right onto Schellingstr.; it's 2 blocks down on the right. Curious combination of scruffy backpackers, student groups, and dolled-up fashion models. Campy, casual atmosphere and big communal breakfasts. Reception open 7:30am-10pm. Singles DM55-65. Doubles DM78-85. 3-to-6-bed rooms DM35 per person. *Oktoberfest* prices slightly higher. Shower, breakfast, and use of kitchen included. Single beds in shared rooms almost always available. No credit cards.

Pension am Kaiserplatz, Kaiserplatz 12, 80803 München (tel. 34 91 90), is located a few blocks from nightlife central. Take U-Bahn #3 or 6 to "Münchener Freiheit." Take the escalator to Herzogstr., then left onto Viktoriastr. Walk down Viktoriastr. past the church; it's at the end of the street on right (10min.). Sweet owner offers elegantly decorated, high-ceilinged rooms. Reception open daily 7am-9pm. Singles DM49-59. Doubles DM75, with shower DM89. Triples DM105. Quads DM120-130. Quints DM150. 6-person room DM160-170. Breakfast (room service) and showers included. DM3 extra to shower more than once per day.

Hotel-Pension am Markt, Heiliggeiststr. 6, 80331 München (tel. 22 50 14; fax 22 40 17), is as central as it gets. Take S-Bahn #1-8 to "Marienplatz," walk through the *Altes Rathaus,* and turn right behind the *Heiliggeist* Church. Aging photographs recall the celebrities who graced the hotel's thoroughly clean rooms—recognize anyone? Singles DM58-62, with shower DM100. Doubles DM106-112, with shower DM145-155. Triples DM158, with shower DM195. Breakfast and showers included. Reserve rooms 3-4 weeks in advance, if not more. No credit cards.

Pension Theresia, Luisenstr. 51, 80333 München (tel. 52 12 50; fax 542 06 33). Take U-Bahn #2 to "Theresienstr.," take the Augustenstr./Technische Univ. exit, head straight down Theresienstr., and take the second right onto Luisenstr.; the entrance in the passageway left of the DAHLKE store. Reception (2nd floor) open 6:30am-10pm. Cheery red carpets and sweet dining room. Well-maintained rooms. Singles DM49-55, with shower DM59. Doubles DM82, with shower DM89-93. Triples DM114. Quads DM132. Breakfast included. Showers off hall DM3. DM3 surcharge for one-night stands. Reservations by phone or fax. Visa, AmEx.

Pension Geiger, Steinheilstr. 1, 80333 München (tel. 52 15 56). Take U-Bahn #2 to "Theresienstr." From Theresienstr., take a right onto Enhuberstr. and a left onto Steinheilstr.; enter through the double doors on the right. Reception (2 floors up) open 8am-10pm. Family-run pension decorated like a comfy family room. Singles DM45-55, with shower DM65. Doubles DM86, with shower DM88-96. Showers off the hall DM2. Reservations by phone only before 6pm. Closed Dec. 24-Jan.

FOOD

Munich's gastronomic center is the vibrant **Viktualienmarkt,** two minutes south of Marienplatz, with an endless open-air feast of bread, fruit, meat, pastry, cheese, honey, wine, vegetable, sausage, and sandwich shops (open Mon.-Fri. 9am-6:30pm, Sat. 9am-2pm). Located everywhere you turn, most **beergardens** (see Beer, Beer Halls, and Beer Gardens, p. 223) sell tasty, inexpensive snacks along with the brew, or you can bring your own food to the self-service areas. Grab a *Brez'n* (pretzel; pronounced "Braaayzin" by the *Müncheners*) and spread it with *Leberwurst* or cheese for a cheap (DM4-5) and authentic German lunch. One of the cheapest meals in town is also a Munich specialty: two *Weißwürste* (white veal sausages) served in a pot of hot water with sweet mustard and a soft pretzel on the side. Don't eat the skin off the sausage: slice it open to gulp down the tender meat. Traditionally, *Weißwürste* is supposed to be consumed before noon (*Frühschoppen,* when you eat, drink, and be merry before noon), but you can find it any time. Another *Münchener* lunch is a slice of *Leberkäs,* a pinkish, meatloaf-like compound of ground beef and bacon which, despite its name and dubious appearance, contains neither liver nor cheese. The **Brotzeitschänke** snack place, in the middle of the market, pours beer for DM4.50 (0.5L) and specializes in oven-fresh *Leberkäs.* Vegetarians may want to head for Italian, Indian, Chinese, or other ethnic specialties.

Tengelmann, Schützenstr. 7, straight ahead from the main station, is most convenient for grocery needs (open Mon.-Wed. and Fri. 8:30am-6:30pm, Thurs. 8:30am-8:30pm, Sat. 9am-2pm). **Käfer-Markthallen,** in the basement of the Hertie department store across from the station, serves the *Schicki-Micki* shopper with more gourmet and international options at slightly higher prices; numerous delis and cafés are

BAVARIA (BAYERN)

squeezed in the corners of this upper-class food haven (same hours as Tengelmann). *Munich Found* (DM4.20) lists a few restaurants (editors' choice of course). *Prinz* (DM5) proffers a fairly complete listing of restaurant/cafés/bars in Münich. Countless fruit and vegetable **markets** are held throughout the city.

> **University Mensas: Arcisstr. 17,** to the left of the Pinakothek Museums, just below Gabelsbregstr on Arcisstr. Open Mon.-Fri. 8:30am-3:45pm. Vacations 8am-4pm. **Leopoldstr. 13,** behind the large pink building. Open Mon.-Fri. 9am-4:45pm, Fri. 9am-3:30pm; Aug.-Nov. Mon.-Thurs. 9am-4:45pm, Fri. 9am-3:15pm. **Dachauer Str. 98b** and **Helene-Mayer-Ring,** in the former Olympic village. Open Mon.-Fri. 11am-1:45pm. Large portions of cheap food DM3-5.50. Student ID required. Buy your token from booths in the lobby *before* getting your meal. The Dachauer Str. and Helen-Mayer locations close Aug.-Sept.; the others are open year round.

Near the University

The university district off Ludwigstr. is by far the best place in Munich to look for filling meals in a lively, unpretentious (but hip) atmosphere. Many restaurants and cafés cluster on Schellingstr., Amalienstr., and Türkenstr.; the nightlife scene trickles away from the city center down Leopoldstr. Unless otherwise noted, take U-Bahn #3 or 6 to "Universität" to reach these restaurants.

> **Türkenhof,** Türkenstr. 78, has a menu that's pseudo-Turkish, but the low-key crowd isn't pseudo-anything. Smoky and buzzing at night. Variable daily menu. Creative entrees (*Schnitzel,* omelettes, soups) DM8-17. Open Sun.-Thurs. 11am-1am, Fri.-Sat. 11am-3am.
>
> **Café Puck,** Türkenstr. 33 (tel. 280 22 80). Spacious, handsome café bar that exudes a hip young, energetic attitude. The *Milchkaffees* (DM4.50) are as smooth and rich as mother's milk. Many students enjoying breakfasts (DM4.50-15) or soup (DM5-7). Open daily 9am-1am.
>
> **La Bohème,** Türkenstr. 79 (tel. 272 08 33), just across from Türkenhof. Waiter, there's an antique knick-knack in my Italian food. Pastas DM11. Pizzas DM7-11. Salads DM5-10. At dinner add DM1 to all dishes. Beer DM3.90 (0.5L).
>
> **Schelling Salon,** Schellingstr. 54 (tel. 272 07 88). Bavarian *Knödel* and billiard balls. Founded in 1872 on the philosophy that billiards is the game *"der schweigenden Männer"* (of silent men), this pool joint has racked the balls of Lenin, Rilke, and Hitler; Franz Josef Strauss used to drop by for a snack. A **billiard museum** displays a 200-year-old Polish noble's table and the history of pool back to the Pharaohs. Restaurant/museum open Thurs.-Mon. 6:30am-midnight.
>
> **Atzinger,** Schellingstr. 9 (tel. 28 28 80). Shiny light wood furniture and an abundance of late 80s tunes—YMCA rec-room, anyone? Varied menu includes pastas (DM9-11) and veggie options (DM7.80-10). Open Mon.-Tues. 10am-1am, Wed.-Thurs. 10am-2am, Fri.-Sat. 10am-3am, and Sun. 5pm-1am. Hot meals until 1am.
>
> **Gaststätte Engelsburg,** on Türkenstr. at Schellingstr. Low-key mix of students and locals. Old School Bavarian specialties including *Weißwürste, Nürnberger Rostbratwürste,* and *Spätzle.* Daily 3-course specials DM10-13. Take-out window with its own menu, including pizza (DM8.50-12). Open daily 9:30am-1am.

In the Center

Munich's touristy interior suffers from an overabundance of high-priced eateries, but some good options exist.

> **Münch'ner Suppenküche,** at the Viktualienmarkt. A Munich institution. Warm, hearty supper soup meals (DM5.80-9). *Krustis* (sandwiches) DM3.60-5. Open Mon.-Fri. 8am-6:30pm, Sat. 10am-5pm. Also at Schellingstr. 24 near the university.
>
> **Schmalznudel Café Frischhut,** Prälat-Zistl-Str. 8, just off the southwest corner of the Viktualienmarkt. For those who won't let the night end *and* for those whose nights must have ended rather early. *Krapfen* (donuts; DM2.50) and other pastries. Open Mon.-Fri. 5am-5pm, Sat. 5am-1pm.
>
> **Shoya,** Orlandostr. 5 (tel. 29 27 72), across from the Hofbräuhaus. The most reasonable Japanese restaurant/take-out joint in town. Fill up on rice dishes (DM13-19),

teriyaki (DM8-16), sushi (DM5-30), and meat and veggie dishes (DM4-16) before blowing your wad at the Hofbräuhaus. Open daily 10:30am-midnight.

Beim Sendlmayr, Westenriederstr. 6 (tel. 22 62 19), off the Viktualienmarkt. Anyone craving a *Weißwurst* will crave this slice of Little Bavaria. Specials DM7-22.50. Beer DM5.30 for 0.5L. Open daily 11am-11pm.

Elsewhere in Munich

Café Ruffini, Orffstr. 22 (tel. 16 11 60). Take U-Bahn #1 to "Rotkreuzplatz." Organic fare, homemade bread and cakes, and cheap wine (DM3.60-5.40) put that warm glow in your tummy. Veggie dishes DM6-15. Warm food served noon-6pm and 6:30-11pm. Open Tues.-Sat. 10am-midnight, Sun. 10am-6pm.

Internetcafé, Nymphenburgerstr. 145 (tel. 129 47 44). Take U-Bahn #1 to "Rotkreuzplatz." With the addition of 12 terminals, this is an average Italian joint *cum* hopping, glowing electronic haunt. Unlimited and free Internet access as long as you order pasta (DM9.50), pizza (DM8.50-10), or at least a beer (DM4.50 for 0.5L). Amaze your friends with an e-mail from abroad. Addicted? Open daily 11am-4am.

Schwimmkrabbe, Ickstattstr. 13 (tel. 201 00 80). Take U-Bahn #1 or 2 to "Fraunhoferstr.," then walk 1 block down Baaderstr. to Ickstattstr. Locals flock to this family-run Turkish restaurant. Try the delicious *Etli Pide* (lamb and veggies wrapped in a foot-long bread with salad; DM16). Hearty dishes DM15-20. Belly-dancing on Fri. and Sat. nights. Open daily 5pm-1am. Reserve on weekends.

Gollier, Gollierstr. 83 (tel. 50 16 73). Take U-Bahn #4 or 5 or S-Bahn #7 or 27 to "Heimeranplatz." A vegetarian café serving delicious homemade pizzas, crêpes, and stews for DM6-19. Lunch buffet Mon.-Fri. noon-2:30pm, Sat.-Sun. noon-3pm. Dinner Sun.-Wed. 5pm-midnight, Thurs.-Sat. 5pm-1am.

SIGHTS

The Catholic Church was long the preeminent institution in Munich; the name of the city itself is derived from the word *Mönch* (monk), referring to the small Benedictine order that the village sprouted in the 9th century. Over the centuries, the relationship proved to be architecturally fruitful, and the city has turned its stone into impressive sacred edifices, most within blocks of the **Marienplatz.** This square, an interchange for the major S-Bahn and U-Bahn lines as well as the social nexus of the city, takes its name from the **Mariensäule,** an ornate 17th-century monument dedicated to the Virgin Mary. The onion-domed towers of the 15th-century **Frauenkirche** have long been one of Munich's most notable landmarks (towers open April-Oct. Mon.-Sat. 10am-5pm; admission DM4, students DM2, under 6 free). At the neo-Gothic **Neues Rathaus,** the **Glockenspiel** makes its booty boom with jousting knights and dancing coopers daily at 11am, noon, 5 and 9pm. At 9pm (bedtime), a mechanical watchman marches out and the Guardian Angel escorts the *Münchner Kindl* ("Munich Child," the town's symbol) to bed. (Tower open Mon.-Fri. 9am-7pm, Sat.-Sun. 10am-7pm. Admission DM3, under 15 DM1.50).

Munich's ritual past is represented by the 11th-century **Peterskirche,** at Rindermarkt and Petersplatz; its interior was baroquified in the 18th century. 294 steps scale the tower, christened *Alter Peter* (Old Peter) by locals (open Mon.-Sat. 9am-6pm, Sun. 10am-6pm; admission DM2.50, students DM1.50, children DM0.50). Ludwig II of Bavaria (of crazy castle fame) rests in peace in a crypt of the 16th-century Jesuit **Michaelskirche,** on Neuhauserstr. The church's construction, designed to emphasize the city's Catholic loyalty during the Reformation, almost bankrupted the state treasury. Father Rupert Mayer, one of the few German clerics to speak out against Hitler, preached here (admission to crypt DM0.50). A Bavarian Rococo masterpiece, the **Asamkirche,** at Sendlinger Str. 32, is named after its creators; Cosmas Damian Asam painted the frescoes while Egid Quirin Asam carved the sculptures.

Continuing the tour of Munich's Most Gilded, the richly decorated rooms built from the 14th to the 19th centuries in the magnificent **Residenz,** Max-Joseph-Platz 3 (tel. 29 06 71), form the material vestiges of the Wittelsbach dynasty. The grounds now house several museums (see Museums, p. 220). To get there, take U-Bahn #3, 4, 5, or 6 "Odeonsplatz." The **Schatzkammer** (treasury) contains jeweled baubles,

BAVARIA (BAYERN)

crowns, swords, china, ivorywork, and other trinkets from the 10th century on (open Tues.-Sun. 10am-4:30pm; admission DM5, students and group members DM2.50, children under 15 with adult free). The **Residenzmuseum** comprises the former Wittelsbach apartments and State Rooms, a collection of European porcelain, and a 17th-century court chapel. The walls of the **Ahnengalerie** (Gallery of Ancestors), hung with 120 "family portraits," portray an utter loss of perspective. Charlemagne would be surprised to find himself here, held accountable for the genesis of the Wittelsbach family (hours and admission same as *Schatzkammer*).

After 10 years of trying for an heir, Ludwig I celebrated the birth of his son Maximilian in 1662 by erecting an elaborate summer playroom; **Schloß Nymphenburg,** in the northwest of town, was another desperate (albeit beautiful) attempt to copy King Louis XIV of France. To get there, take U-Bahn #1 to "Rotkreuzplatz" and then streetcar #12 (direction: Amalienburgstr.). A Baroque wonder set in a winsome park, the palace hides a number of treasures, including a two-story granite marble hall seasoned with stucco, frescoes, and a Chinese lacquer cabinet. Check out King Ludwig's "Gallery of Beauties"—whenever a woman caught his fancy, he would have her portrait painted (a scandalous hobby, considering that many of the women were commoners; a touching one, given that Ludwig grappled with an affection for men throughout his life). The palace contains a wonderful collection of antique porcelain and a modern porcelain manufacturing studio's gallery *(Schönheitgalerie)*, as well as the strange **Marstallmuseum** (Carriage Museum). This gets complicated: **Schloß** open Tues.-Sun. 9am-noon and 1-5pm; Oct.-March 10am-12:30pm and 1:30-4pm; **Amalienburg** open daily 9am-12:30pm and 1:30-5pm; **Badenburg, Pagoda,** and **Magdalenen hermitage** open Tues.-Sun. 10am-12:30pm and 1:30-5pm. (Admission to main palace DM6, students DM4; to the entire complex DM8, students DM5, children under 15 with adult free. Wander the grounds for free.)

Just next door is the immense **Botanischer Garten,** whose greenhouses shelter rare and wonderful growths from around the world (tel. 17 86 13 10). Check out the water lily room and the unassuming moss room, with an exquisitely **romantic alcove** in the back. (Open daily 9am-7pm. Greenhouses open 9am-11:45am and 1-6:30pm. Admission DM3, students DM1.50, under 15 DM0.50). Abutting the city center is the vast **Englischer Garten,** one of Europe's oldest landscaped public parks. On sunny days, all of Munich turns out to bike, play badminton, ride horseback, or sunbathe. Nude sunbathing areas are designated "FKK" *(Freikörperkultur)* on signs and park maps. *Müncheners* with aquatic daring-do (and a surfboard) ride the *Eisbach,* which flows through the park. The force of the water springing out of the ground causes a mighty swell, and swarms of wetsuited daredevils ply the waters to catch the wave just under the bridge between the Haus der Kunst and the Bayerisches Nationalmuseum (see Museums, below).

MUSEUMS

Munich is a supreme museum city, and many of the city's offerings would independently require days for exhaustive perusal. Several museums inhabit the gilded grounds of the *Residenz* and Schloß Nymphenburg (see Sights, p. 219). The city's patronage of fine arts and artists has always been remarkable, but not remarkable enough to deter rising admission costs; stick to *kostenlos* (free) Sundays, if possible (see History, p. 204). The *Münchner Volkschule* (tel. 48 00 63 30) offers tours of many city museums for DM8 per person.

Museumsinsel-Isartor

Deutsches Museum, on the *Museumsinsel* (Museum Island) in the Isar River (tel. 217 91 or 217 94 33 for recording in German; fax 217 93 24). Take S-Bahn #1-8 to "Isartor." One of the world's largest and best museums of science and technology. Particularly well-conceived are the displays on aerospace, photography, and astronomy. Don't miss the mining exhibit, which winds through a labyrinth of recreated subterranean mining tunnels. The hall of keyboard instruments ain't shabby either. Pick up an English guide to the exhibits (DM10). The planetarium (DM3) and daily electrical show will warm the cockles of any physicist's heart. Admission DM10, students DM4. Open daily 9am-5pm.

Königsplatz

Alte Pinakothek, Barer Str. 27 (tel. 23 80 50), contains Munich's most precious artistic jewels. Take U-Bahn #2 to "Theresienstr." 13th-17th century Wittelsbacher family storage covers works by Giotto, Titian, da Vinci, Raphael, Dürer, Rembrandt, and Rubens. **Closed** until 1997-98 for renovations, but its main works are shown in rooms 1-12 of the Neue Pinakothek.

Neue Pinakothek, Barer Str. 29 (tel. 23 80 51 95; fax 23 80 52 21), next to Alte Pinakothek. Sleek space for the 18th-20th centuries: Van Gogh, Gauguin, Gustav Klimt. Go crazy. Admission DM7, students DM4. Free on Sun. Open Tues. and Thurs. 10am-8pm, Wed. and Fri.-Sun. 10am-5pm.

Lenbachhaus, Luisenstr. 33 (tel. 23 33 20 00; recorded German info tel. 23 33 20 02; fax 23 33 20 03). Take U-Bahn #2 to "Königsplatz." Munich cityscapes (useful if it's raining your whole visit), along with the works of Kandinsky, Klee, and the *Blaue Reiter* school (Münter, Marc, Macke, and more), which disdained perfumed Impressionism and forged the aesthetic of abstraction.Admission DM8, students DM4. Free on Sun. Open Tues.-Sun. 10am-6pm.

Glyptohek, Königsplatz 3 (tel. 28 61 00; fax 550 38 51), around the corner from the Lenbachhaus. Take U-Bahn #2 to "Königsplatz." Assembled by Ludwig I, the collection features Greek, Etruscan, and Roman sculptures. Admission DM6, students DM3.50. Joint admission with *Antikensammlung* (below) DM10, students DM5. Free on Sun. Open Tues.-Wed. and Fri.-Sun. 10am-5pm, Thurs. 10am-8pm.

Antikensammlung, Königsplatz 1 (tel. 59 83 59, fax 550 38 51), across Königsplatz from Glyptothek. Take U-Bahn #2 to "Königsplatz." Flaunts a first-rate flock of vases and the other half of Munich's finest collection of ancient art. Admission DM6, students DM3.50. Joint admission with Glyptothek DM10, students DM5. Free on Sun. Open Tues. and Thurs.-Sun. 10am-5pm, Wed. 10am-8pm.

Elsewhere in Munich

Staatsgalerie moderner Kunst, Prinz-Regenten-Str. 1 (tel. 21 12 71 37; fax 23 80 52 21), in the **Haus der Kunst,** at the southern tip of the Englischer Garten. Take U-Bahn #4 or 5 to "Lehel," then streetcar #20. A sterling 20th-century collection showcases Beckmann, Kandinsky, Klee, Picasso, and Dalí, and others. Constructed by the Nazis as the Museum of German Art, it opened with the famous exhibit of *Entartete Kunst* (degenerate art) that included works of the Expressionists and Dadaists. Admission DM6, students DM3.50. Free on Sun. Visiting exhibitions extra. Open Tues.-Wed. and Fri.-Sun. 10am-5pm, Thurs. 10am-8pm.

Münchener Stadtmuseum, St.-Jakobs-Platz 1 (tel. 23 32 23 70 or 233 55 86 for exhibition announcements; fax 233 50 33). Take U-Bahn #3 or 6 or S-Bahn #1-8 to "Marienplatz." A collection of museums, all with a Bavarian touch: photography, film, musical instruments, weapons, and more. The Puppet and Marionette museum offers the opportunity to build your own sweet thing; the **Deutsches Brauereimuseum** (Brewery Museum), however, does not provide any hands-on activity. **Classic films** (DM8) roll every evening at 8pm. Foreign films are shown with subtitles; call 233 55 86 for a program. Museum admission DM5, students, seniors, and children DM2.50, under 6 free. Open Tues. and Thurs.-Sun. 10am-5pm, Wed. 10am-8:30pm. Open Mon. 5pm-midnight, Tues.-Sun. 11am-midnight.

ZAM: Zentrum für Außergewöhnliche Museen (Center for Unusual Museums), Westenriederstr. 26 (tel. 290 41 21). Take S-Bahn #1-8 to "Isartor" or streetcar #17 or 18. A brilliant place: brazenly corrals under one roof such treasures as the Corkscrew Museum, the Museum of Easter Rabbits, and the Chamberpot Museum. Fan of Empress Elizabeth of Austria? Your paradise is the Sissy Museum. Admission DM8, students, seniors, and children DM5. Open daily 10am-6pm.

Museum für erotische Kunst (Museum of Erotic Art), Odeonsplatz 8 (tel. 228 35 44), in same building as the Filmcasino. Take U-Bahn #3-6 to "Odeonsplatz" or bus #53. For those lonely days when you're 5000km away from your beloved (or those uninspired days when you're right next to your beloved), this museum covers all 4 bases around the world and through time. Features a French book of sex gags entitled The Circus, hot and heavy chess pieces, and a set of juicy Japanese illustrations. Admission DM8, students DM6. Open Tues.-Sun. 11am-7pm.

BMW Museum, Petuelring 130 (tel. 38 22 36 22; fax 38 22 36 22). Take U-Bahn #3 to "Olympiazentrum." The ultimate driving museum features a fetching display of Bavaria's second-favorite export. Baby, you can drive my car. Admission DM5.50, students DM4. Open daily 9am-5pm. Last entry 4pm.

Valentin Musäum, Isartorturm (tel. 22 32 66). Take S-Bahn #1-8 or streetcar #18 or 20 to "Isartor." Decidedly esoteric peek at the comical life of Karl Valentin and his partner Liesl Karlstadt; Valentin was one of Bavaria's most absurd funny men. Curiosities include sham skeletons encased in the stone wall and a photograph of a Karl Valentin snowman. Admission 299pf, students 149pf. Open Mon.-Tues. and Fri.-Sat. 11:01am-5:29pm, Sun. 10:01am-5:29pm. Those wacky Bavarians.

Spielzeugmuseum, Altes Rathaus, Marienplatz (tel 29 40 01). 2 centuries of European and American toys—compare the World War I "futuristic" wood figurines to the slick, slim Barbie. Admission DM5, children DM1, families DM10. Open daily 10am-5:30pm.

ENTERTAINMENT

Munich's cultural cachet rivals the world's best. Eleven large theaters and countless smaller stages are sprinkled throughout the city. Styles range from dramatic classics at the **Residenztheater** and **Volkstheater** to comic opera at the **Staatstheater am Gärtnerplatz** to experimental works at the **Theater im Marstall** in Nymphenburg. Leftovers tickets run around DM10. Munich's **Opera Festival** (in July) is held in the Bayerische Staatsoper (see p. 222) accompanied by a concert series in the Nymphenburg and Schleissheim palaces. Write for tickets, or call early that night (tel. 26 46 20) for leftover tickets (around DM15).

The *Monatsprogramm* (DM2.50) lists schedules for all of Munich's stages, museums, and festivals; newspapers and posters in the subway stops list **movie** showings. English films are often dubbed; search for the initials "OF" (original language) or "OmU" (subtitled) on the poster before buying your popcorn. **Cinema Programmkino,** Nymphenburger Str. 31 (tel. 55 52 55; U-Bahn #1: Stiglmaierplatz), and **Hollywood and Rick's,** Schwanthalerstr. 2-6 (tel. 55 56 70), screen non-dubbed, English-language films daily. Smack in the middle of the student district, **Türkenclolch,** Türkenstr. 74, (tel. 271 88 44) has mini-film festivals dedicated to a particular director or theme. Max out on **IMAX** flicks at the cinema in the **Forum der Technik,** Museumsinsel 1 (tel. 29 12 51 80), next to the Deutsches Museum (DM11.90, students DM8.90). Foreign films are subtitled (admission DM9). Munich's **film festival** generally runs for a week at the end of June. For schedules and information, contact **Internationale Filmwoche,** Türkenstr. 93, 80799 Munich (tel. 381 90 40).

Gasteig Kulturzentrum, Rosenheimer Str. 5 (tel. 48 09 80). Take S-Bahn #1-8 to "Rosenheimer Platz" or streetcar #18. A cultural center with quite a history, it hosts musical performances ranging from classical to non-Western in its 3 concert halls and visual arts center. The hall rests on the former site of the *Bürgerbräukeller* where Adolf Hitler launched his abortive "Beer Hall *Putsch.*" Features the **Munich Philharmonic** and a wide range of events such as public readings and ballet. Box office in the Glashalle (tel. 54 89 89) open Mon.-Fri. 10:30am-2pm and 3-6pm, Sat. 10:30am-2pm, and 1hr. before the beginning of a program.

Bayerische Staatsoper (Bavarian State Opera), Max-Joseph-Platz (tickets tel. 21 85 19 20; recorded info tel. 21 85 19 19). Take U-Bahn #3-6 to "Odeonsplatz" or streetcar #19 to "Max-Joseph-Platz." Standing-room and reduced-rate student tickets (DM15-20) to the numerous operas and ballets are sold at Maximilianstr. 11 (tel. 21 85 19 20), behind the Opera House, or 1hr. before the performance at the side entrance on Maximilianstr. Box office open Mon.-Fri. 10am-6pm, Sat. 10am-1pm. No performances Aug.-mid-Sept.

Staatstheater, Gärtnerplatz 3 (tel. 32 01 67 67). Take U-Bahn #1 or 2 to "Fraunhoferstr." and then follow Reichenbachstr. to Gärtnerplatz; or bus #52 or 56 to "Gärtnerplatz." Stages comic opera and musicals. Tickets available 4 weeks before each performance at the Staatstheater box office (tel. 20 24 11). Open Mon.-Fri. 10am-

6pm, Sat. 10am-1pm, and 1hr. before performance at the night counter; or at the Bavarian State Opera counter (see above). Standing room tickets start at DM14.

Drehleier, Balanstr. 23 (tel. 48 43 37). Take S-Bahn #1-8 or bus #51 to "Rosenheimer Platz." A mixture of theater, cabaret, and performance art romps across this offbeat stage. One of the best cabaret scenes in Munich. Kitchen serves inexpensive salads and noodle dishes (DM6-15) until 10pm. Tickets DM20-30. Reservations required. Open Tues.-Sat. 6:30pm-1am. Performances Tues.-Sat. 10:30pm.

Münchner Kammerspiele, Maximilianstr. 26-28 (tickets tel. 23 72 13 28; recorded info tel. 23 72 13 26). Take Streetcar #19 to "Maxmonument." Exceptional modern theater and classics grace its 2 stages. **Schauspielhaus,** Maximilianstr. 26, shows Goethe and Shakespeare (DM9-46). Buy advance tickets at Münchner Kammerspiele. The **Werkraum,** at Hildegardstr. 1, features avant-garde and left-critical pieces. Standing room tickets DM1. Tickets available 1 week in advance. Box office open Mon.-Fri. 10am-6pm, Sat. 10am-1pm.

BEER, BEER HALLS AND BEER GARDENS

The official coat-of-arms of Munich depicts a monk holding a bible in his right hand; unofficially, he's got a large, frothy brewski in his left. Sacrilege? Not at all. It was the Augustiner monks who first introduced beer to unsuspecting *Müncheners* in 1328, and based on the fact that Bavaria doesn't have a challenger for the title of largest producer and consumer of beer in Germany, it seems the trend caught on—in a big, big way. Local breweries produce 123 million gallons of "liquid bread" per annum; 150,000 seats in Munich beer gardens beckon the thirsty; and every year, the average local imbibes over 190 liters of this amber dew of gods. Honoring proudly the Beer Purity Law *(Reinheitsgebot)* of 1516 (see p. 79), Bavarians reaffirm their exalted and earned reputation as the ultimate, tried-and-true beer connoisseurs. The six great Munich labels are *Augustiner, Hacker-Pschorr, Hofbräu, Löwenbräu, Paulaner,* and *Spaten-Franziskaner,* but small, independent breweries abound and provide the underground (or at least backyard) beer counter-culture. "Ein bier, bitte" will get you a liter, known to those in the know as a *Maß* (DM8-11). If you want a half-*Maß* (DM4-6), you must specify it. *Frühschoppen* is drinking beer (and wolfing down *Weißwurst*) before mid-day. *Prost*—think of us when you imbibe, and good luck fitting that souvenir *Maß* in your backpack (see Beer, p. 78).

The biggest keg party in the world, Munich's **Oktoberfest,** finishes on the first Sunday of October and starts 16 days before (Sept. 20-Oct. 5 in 1997). The site of this uncontrolled revelry is known as **Theresienwiese** (Therese's meadow)—or *"Wies'n"* (shortened perhaps after one too many *Maß*). Take U-Bahn #4 or 5 to "Theresienwiese." The festivities began in 1810 when Prince Ludwig married Princess Therese von Sachsen-Hildburghausen; ironically, no alcohol was served at the original reception. But the party was so much fun that *Müncheners* decided to repeat the revelry the next year, and every year, since they couldn't resist a revival. The party kicks off with speeches, a parade of horse-drawn beer wagons, and the mayor's tapping of the first ceremonial barrel. The Hofbräu tent is the rowdiest and the most touristy; fights break out more often here than in other tents. Arrive early (by 4:30pm) to get a table—you must be seated to be served at *Oktoberfest.*

Within Munich:

Hofbräuhaus, Am Platzl 9 (tel. 22 16 76), 2 blocks from Marienplatz. Established in 1589, Munich's world-famous beer hall was originally reserved for royalty and its invited guests (the name means "court brewery house"). The Hofbräuhaus has been tapping barrels for the commoners since 1897 and now seems reserved for drunken tourists. 15,000-30,000L of beer are sold per day. Our best to all the Alpha Delts. It was in the *Festsaal* that Hitler was proclaimed the first Nazi party chair. *Maß* DM9.90. Small beer garden out back under chestnut trees. 2 original *Weißwurst* sausages DM7.60. *Leberkäs* with spinach and potatoes DM10. Open daily 10am-midnight. Remember that the Hofbräu police can carry 10L at once.

Augustiner, Arnulfstr. 52 (tel. 59 43 93), at Zirkus-Krone-Str. Take S-Bahn #1-8 to "Hackerbrücke." Founded in 1824, Augustiner is held by most *Müncheners* to be the finest beer garden in town. The lush grounds with 100-year-old chestnut trees overhead and the tasty, enormous *Brez'n* (pretzels; DM4.90), argue the case powerfully. But the real attraction is the delicious, sharp Augustiner beer (DM9-10 per *Maß*). Locals, smart tourists, scads of students. Food DM7-15. Open daily 10am-1am; warm food until 10pm. Beer garden open daily 10:30am-midnight.

Augustiner Bräustuben, Landsberger Str. 19 (tel. 50 70 47). Take S-Bahn #1-8 to "Hackerbrücke." Brand new beer hall in the Augustiner Brewery's former horse stalls. Shh, it's a local secret. Beer DM3.90 for 0.5L. For the hungry horse, try the *Bräustüberl* (duck, two types of pork, kraut, and two types of dumplings) for DM14.60. Other delicious heaps of Bavarian food at excellent prices (DM6-20). Especially popular in winter. Open daily until 11pm.

Parkrestaurant Tarock, Sophienstr. 7, in the Alter Botanischer Garten, 1 block to the left from the train station (part of the Park Café nighttime club). This peaceful outdoor beer garden, secluded from the cars and trains by oodles of greenery, is good for a train layover. *Löwenbrau* DM4.90 for 0.4L. Most meals DM6-18.

Chinesischer Turm, in the *Englischer Garten* next to the pagoda (tel. 39 50 28). Take U-Bahn #3 or 6 to "Giselastr." or bus #54 from *Südbahnhof* to "Chinesischer Turm." A fair-weather tourist favorite; lots of kids. *Maß* (*Weißbier*) DM9.50. Salads DM9.50-11.50. Pretzels DM5. Open daily in balmy weather 10:30am-11pm.

Am Seehaus, Kleinhesselohe 3 (tel. 381 61 30). Take U-Bahn #6 to "Dietlindenstr.," then bus #44 to "Osterwaldgarten." Directly on the lovely Kleinhesseloher See in the *Englischer Garten,* and beloved by locals for the lack of tourists. So don't go. *Maß* DM9. Open daily 10am-1am. Beer garden closes at 11pm.

Taxisgarten, Taxisstr. 12 (tel. 15 68 27). Take U-Bahn #1 to "Rotkreuzplatz," then bus #83 or 177 to "Klugstr." This beer garden is a gem—its small size has hidden it from tourists and kept it a favorite of locals and students. Almost always full. Saucy spare ribs, jumbo pretzels DM4.50. *Maß* DM8.60. Open daily 10am-10pm.

Augustiner, Neuhauserstr. 16 (tel. 55 19 92 57). Smaller manifestation of the main *Biergarten,* 7 entries above. Beer hall and sidewalk tables on the pedestrian zone. The restaurant (on the right) is pricier than the beer hall. Bavarian meals in the beer hall DM9-17; in the restaurant DM15-26. A beer hall *Maß* is DM9.50; a restaurant *Maß* DM10.40. Both have pleasant sidewalk seating. Beer hall open Mon.-Sat. 9am-1am; restaurant open daily 9am-1am. Hot meals until 10:30pm.

Löwenbräukeller, Nymphenburger Str. 2 (tel. 52 60 21). Take U-Bahn #1 to "Stiglmaierplatz." Castle-like entrance, festive and loud cellar. Come here to taste the real *Löwenbräu,* if you dare: the bitter taste has a loyal core of local followers, despite general disapproval—it's considered by some to be the Budweiser of Munich beers, but remember, everything's relative. *Maß* DM8.60. Hot meals 11am-midnight. Open daily 9am-1am.

Hofbräukeller, Innere Wiener Str. 19 (tel. 448 73 76). U-Bahn #4 or 5: Max-Weber-Platz. Pours the same brew as the Hofbräuhaus, only this time with Germans. It also has a beer garden. *Maß* DM9.20. Open daily 9am-midnight.

Pschorr-Keller, Theresienhöhe 7 (tel. 50 10 88). Take U-Bahn #4 or 5 to "Theresienwiese." Along with the Hackerkeller down the street, an outpost of the Hacker-Pschorr brewery. Good stuff. Come here for your breakfast beer, mostly with locals. *Maß* DM9.90. All meals under DM12.50. Open daily 8am-midnight.

Just Outside Munich:

Waldwirtschaft Großhesselohe, Georg-Kalb-Str. 3 (tel. 79 50 88). Take S-Bahn #7 to "Großhesselohe." Follow the signs; a 15-min. walk from the station. Relaxed beer garden with live music (daily from noon) and the site of Munich's recent "Beer Garden Revolution." Classic and international jazz starts on Sun. at noon. On a sunny day, it's worth the schlepp; schedule a *Frühschoppen* session for 11am or so. *Maß* DM9.80. Open daily 11am-1am; beer garden open until 10pm.

Hirschgarten, Hirschgartenallee 1 (tel. 17 25 91). Take U-Bahn #1 to "Rotkreuzplatz," then streetcar #12 to "Romanplatz." Walk straight to the end of Guntherstr. and enter the Hirschgarten—literally, "deer garden." The largest beer garden in Europe is boisterous and verdant, but somewhat remote (in the vicinity of Schloß Nymphenburg). Families head here for the grassy park and carousel. *Maß* DM9.20. Open daily 9am-midnight. Restaurant open Nov.-Feb. only Tues.-Sun.

Paulaner Keller, Hochstr. 77 (tel. 459 91 30). Also known as Salvator Keller and Nockherberg. It's big, old, and has strong beer. Take U-Bahn #1 or 2 to "Silberhornstr.," then bus #51 to "Ostfriedhof." Walk back down Bonifaziusstr. over the bridge and to the right. Famous for its March *Starkbierzeit,* when extra strong brew gets consumed in vast quantities; as you swill, thank founding Monk Pater Barnabas. Rather far out on Nockherberg Hill, which is part of its charm. *Starkbier* DM5.40 for 0.5L. *Brez'n* and *Knödel* DM11.80. Open daily 10am-11pm.

Forschungsbräuerei, Unterhachingerstr. 76 (tel. 670 11 69). Serves up some very strange brew—the name means "research brewery." Pleasant atmosphere and varieties of beer you can't find anywhere else. *Maß* DM9-9.80. Open Tues.-Sat. 11am-11pm, Sun. 10am-10pm.

NIGHTLIFE

Munich's nightlife is a curious collusion of Bavarian *Gemütlichkeit* and trendy cliquishness. The latter is often referred to as "Schicki-Micki" and loosely defined as a clubgoing German yuppie (expensively dressed, coiffed and sprayed, beautiful, shapely, blonde specimens of both sexes). With a healthy mix of students and other less-pretentious, bopping locals, the streets bustle with raucous beer halls, loud discos, and exclusive cafés every night of the week; some places are as likely to be packed on a weeknight as on a Saturday. The locals tend to tackle their nightlife as an epic voyage. The odyssey begins at one of Munich's beer gardens or beer halls (see Beer, above), which generally close before midnight and are most crowded in the early evening. The alcohol keeps flowing at cafés and bars, which, except for Friday and Saturday nights, shut off their taps at 1am. Then the discos and dance clubs, soporific before midnight, suddenly spark and throb relentlessly until 4am. The trendy bars, cafés, cabarets, and discos plugged into Leopoldstr. in **Schwabing** attract tourists from all over Europe. Notorious are **"door standers"**—neurotic bouncers with orders to protect the clientele from un-chic *personae non gratae.* Single men will have a harder time than single women. The best strategy is feigned ennui—look bored, avoid eye contact with the bouncer, and try to walk in. Dig the jaded hipster-wear out of your pack, or at least leave the white baseball hat and college t-shirt at home. If all else fails in the fashion department, return to the trusty standby: black. Early in the evening (before 9-11pm), bouncers aren't as picky.

The **Muffathalle,** at Zellerstr. 4 (tel. 29 45 00), in Haidhausen, is a former power plant that generates hip student energy with ethno, hip-hop, jazz, and dance performances (cover up to DM30; open Mon.-Sat. 6pm-4am, Sun. 4pm-1am). Take S-Bahn #1-8 to "Rosenheimer Platz" or streetcar #18 to the Deutsches Museum. Munich's alternative concert scene goes on at **Feierwerk,** Hansastr. 39-41 (tel. 769 36 00; fax 769 60 32), which has 7 stages and huge tents. Take S-Bahn #7 or U-Bahn #4 or 5 to "Heimeranplatz," then walk left down Hansastr. (10min.). In summer, there's lots of independent music, comedy, beer gardens, *Imbiß* stands, blues, and rock. Beer gardens open at 6pm; Feierwerk opens around 9pm until the music's over. **Münchener Freiheit** is the most famous (and the most touristy) bar/café district; more low-key is the southwestern section of Schwabing, directly behind the university on Amalienstr. and Türkenstr.; this area drowns in student cafés, cheap restaurants, and mellow bars (see Food, p. 217). When they close, hangers-on head for the late-night/early-morning cafés to nurse a last beer or first cup of coffee.

Scads of culture and nightlife guides are available to help you sort out Munich's scene. Pick up *Munich Found* (DM4), or get the *Münchner Stadtmagazin* (biweekly), the *Münchner Stadtzeitung* (weekly), the *Abendzeitung* (DM1; has complete listings in German), *in München* (free), or *Prinz* (monthly for DM5; the hippest) at any newsstand to find out what's up. For smaller rock clubs, scope bulletin boards around the university. Big-name pop artists often perform at the **Olympia Halle,** while the **Olympia Stadion** on the northern edge of town hosts mega-concerts. Check listings for dates and ticket information or call 30 67 24 24.

Bars

Many of the charming cafés (see Food, p. 217) double as hip nightly haunts of *Müncheners*. A few stalwarts only open the doors for drink after 5pm, and by 1am many places squeeze revelers out into more late-nite joints.

Master's Home, Frauenstr. 11 (tel. 22 99 09). Take U-Bahn #3 or 6 or S-Bahn #1-8 to "Marienplatz." A tremendous stuffed peacock greets visitors descending the gold wall-papered staircase to the subterranean bar/*faux* private house. Lounge in the elegant living room with books and dusty velvet furniture, relax in the bedroom, or chill in the tub with a beer in hand. Eat gourmet Italian with the *Schicki Micki*. Weekdays comfortable; weekends mobbed. Open daily 6pm-3am.

Günther Murphy's, Nikolaistr. 9a (tel. 39 89 11). Take U-Bahn #3 or 6 to "Giselastr." Cozy yourself up in the bathtub, bed, or "snuggle-box" with a Guinness (DM6). Good ol' Irish cheer accompanies each serving of scrumptious UK/American food (DM8-15). You won't be able to find a seat, but it's more fun to mingle with the English-speaking crowd. Open Mon.-Fri. 5pm-1am, Sat.-Sun. 11am-1am.

Wunderbar, Hochbrückenstr. 3 (tel. 29 51 18). Take S-Bahn #1-8, U-Bahn #3 or 6, or bus #52 to "Marienplatz." Oh-so-underground—diverse crowd, especially singles who flock here for telephone night on Wed. There's a phone on every table. Dark and smoky enough for mystery and suspense. Wed. only cover DM10. Disco Fri. and Sat. Open Tues.-Thurs. and Sun. 8pm-3am; Mon. and Fri.-Sat. 8pm-4am.

Treznjewski, Theresienstr. 72 (tel. 22 23 49). Take U-Bahn #2 to "Theresienstr." Handsome dark-wooded bar with stylish frescoes. Good cocktails and chatty crowds until way late. Near the university. Breakfast DM7.50-13.50. Entrees DM11-14.50. Beer DM5. Open Sun.-Thurs. 8pm-3am, Fri.-Sat. 8pm-4am.

Music Bars

Mister B's, Herzog-Heinrich-Str. 38 (tel. 53 49 01). Take U-Bahn #3 or 6 to "Goetheplatz." Live blues, jazz, and rhythm in a tiny dark room with a beautiful dark bar; this place ain't nothing if not intimate. Low-key, slightly older, local crowd rambles on about the blues days in Chicago and Paris as the suave bartender pours his cocktails. Jazz/blues performances Thurs.-Sat. DM8. Free *klavier* performances on Tues. and Sun. nights. Open Tues.-Sun. 8pm-3am.

Schwabinger Podium, Wagnerstr. 1 (tel. 39 94 82), in Old Schwabing. Take U-Bahn #3 to "Münchener Freiheit." Live jazz and "Bluesrock" for a young crowd. Sat. excellent rhythm and blues. Beer DM5.40. Cover DM5-10. Music starts at 9pm; show up then to get a table. Open 8pm-1am.

Nachtcafé, Maximiliansplatz 5 (tel. 59 59 00). Take U-Bahn #4 or 5 or S-Bahn #1-8 to "Karlsplatz." Live jazz, funk, soul, and blues until the wee hours; beware of the occasional Chorus-Line-meets-the-Patridge-Family musical atrocities. The *chic* and the wannabees rub shoulders in this modern jet-black bar. Things don't get rolling until 2am. Very *Schicki-Micki*. Breakfast served after 2am. No cover, just a bouncer. Karaoke on Sun. Beer DM7.50. Coffee DM5. Open daily 9pm-6am.

Unterfahrt, Kirchenstr. 96 (tel. 448 27 94). Take S-Bahn #1-8 or U-Bahn #5 to "Ostbahnhof." For the serious jazz lover. Excellent *avant garde*, traditional, and modern rhythms (DM5). Jam session starts every Sun. at 9pm; arrive early for a table. Professional performances DM10 and up…and up. Open Tues.-Sun. 8pm-1am.

Dance Clubs

Park Café, Sophienstr. 7 (tel. 59 83 13), is located at the fringe of the small *Alter Botanischer Garten*. Take U-Bahn #2 to "Königsplatz" or walk north from the *Hauptbahnhof*. A pleasant beer garden by day (open daily 10am-1am; *Maß* DM9.50), Park Café becomes a *Schicki-Micki* bumping disco come nightfall. Baroque, dance floor with red curtains, chandeliers, and a stocked bar with expensive drinks—we're talking DM8.50 for a small beer. Tues. and Wed.: funk, rap, soul; Thurs.: rock; Fri.: trance and house; Sat.: House; Sun.: DJ choice. Cover DM5-15. Open Tues.-Thurs. and Sun. 10:30pm-4am, Fri.-Sat. 10:30pm-5am.

Nachtwerk and Club, Landesberger Str. 185 (tel. 578 38 00). Take streetcar #18 or 19 or bus #83 to "Lautensackstr." The older, larger **Nachtwerk** spins mainstream dance tunes for sweaty mainstream crowds in a packed warehouse. Sat. is the beloved "Best of the 50s to the 90s" night. Its little sister **Club** offers a bi-level dance floor, just as tight and swinging as its next-door neighbor. Mixtures of rock, hip hop, acid rap, and house. Avoid Sun. night rehashing of German oldies-but-goodies. Beer DM6 at both places. Cover DM10 for both. Open daily 10pm-4am.

Pulverturm, Harthof-Schleißheimer-Str. 393 (tel. 351 99 99). Take U-Bahn #2 to "Harthof." A bit far out, this dance club *avec* beer garden lacks the pretension of Munich's other joints. Anything from psychedelic to grunge; Fri. is indy-rock and Sun. kicks back with reggae. Cover DM10. Open daily 10pm-4am.

Strom LInieclub, Lindwurmstr. 88 (tel. 746 02 43). Take U-Bahn #3 or 6 to "Poccistr." Watch for the omnipresent Strom-postering around town to find out themes; usually grunge, indy-rock, or house. Cover varies. Open daily 10pm-4am.

Tilt, Helmholtzstr. 12 (tel. 129 79 69). Take S-Bahn #1-8 or 27 to "Donnersberger-brücke." One of the newest warehouse discos in Munich. Sat. good, fun acid jazz (cover DM7); Mondays are "spicy sounds from the swamps." Open Mon.-Thurs. 9pm-1am, Fri.-Sat. 10pm-3am.

Oly, Helene-Mayer-Ring 9 (tel. 351 77 33), in the Olympic village. Take U-Bahn #3 to "Olympiazentrum," then walk past the bus depot to the tall high-rise buildings to your left. A renovated, slick student disco. Cheap beer (DM4.90). Student ID required. Cover Fri.-Sat. DM5. Open Sun.-Thurs. 9pm-1am, Fri.-Sat. 9pm-3am.

GAY AND LESBIAN MUNICH

Although Bavaria is said to be the region in Germany least tolerant of homosexuality, Munich sustains a respectably vibrant gay nightlife. The centers of Munich's homo-sexual scene are the streets between Viktualienmarkt and Gärtnerplatz and the side-streets between U-Bahn stations Sendlinger Tor and Fraunhoferstr. (especially Müllerstr., Hans-Sachs-Str., and heavily gay Ickstattstr.). Bars, cafés, and clubs of all atmospheres abound. Pick up the free, extensive booklet *Rosa Seiten* (pink pages) at **Max und Milian Bookstore,** Ickstattstr. 2 (tel. 260 33 20; fax 26 30 59; open Mon.-Fri. 10am-6:30pm, Sat. 10am-2pm) and at loads of other gay locales. The **Zentrum schwuler Männer** (gay men's center) offers a number of telephone services (tel. 260 30 56 or fax 260 87 90 for general information; tel. 192 28 for violence hotline; tel. 194 46 for counseling); some English spoken, depending on the staff (open Sun.-Thurs. 7-11pm, Fri.-Sat. 7pm-midnight). For lesbian information, call **Lesbentelefon** (tel. 725 42 72; open Tues.-Wed. 10am-noon, Thurs.-Fri. 5-7pm). **Sapphovision,** a les-bian film center at the **Frauenzentrum Treibhaus,** Güllstr. 3 (tel. 77 40 41), shows films every second Friday of the month. **Lillemor's Frauenbuchladen** (see Book-stores, p. 212) provides information for lesbians.

Club Morizz, Klenzestr. 43 (tel. 201 67 76). Take U-Bahn #1 or 2 to "Fraunhoferstr." Reminiscent of select Casablanca scenes, this relaxed café and bar is frequented by gays and lesbians. European and Thai dishes available until 12:30am. Open Sun.-Thurs. 7pm-2am, Fri.-Sat. 7pm-3am.

Café Nil, Hans-Sach-Str. 2 (tel. 26 55 45). Take U-Bahn #1 or 2 to "Fraunhoferstr." Large, airy café that's day- and nighttime meeting place for gay men of all ages.

Fortuna Musikbar, Maximiliansplatz 5, Reginahaus (tel. 55 40 70). Take U-Bahn #4 or 5 or S-Bahn #1-8 to "Karlsplatz." A hip and popular disco for lesbians. *The* place on Thursday evenings: salsa parties and all. Open Thurs. 10pm-4am.

New York, Sonnenstr. 25 (tel. 59 10 56). Take U-Bahn #1-3 or 6 to "Sendlinger Tor." Fashionable gay men dance this disco into the ground. Laser shows at 11:30pm and 7am. Fri.-Sun. DM10 cover (includes drinks); beer DM6.50 other nights. Open daily 11pm-4am.

Villanis Café-Bistro, Kreuzstr. 3b (tel. 260 79 72), in the passage *(Asamhof)* between Sendlinger Str. and Kreuzstr. Take U-Bahn #1, 2, 3 or 6 to "Sendlinger Tor." Raucous revelers of all orientations every night, though Sun. is unofficially "gay night." Beer DM5. Open Mon.-Sat. 10am-1am, Sun. and holidays 11am-1am.

FLEA MARKETS AND ANTIQUES

Fleamarket: Arnulfstr., to the left of the Hackerbrücke, in a former train station. Take S-Bahn #1-8 to "Hackerbrücke." Knick knacks, clothing, stuff you'll never use, but have been searching for forever. Open Fri.-Sat. 7am-6pm.

Antique and Collector's Market: Hochstr. 77 (tel. 613 15 77), right in the *Salvator Paulaner* beer garden on the Nockherberg. Take streetcar #15, 25, or 27, or bus #51 to "Ostfriedhof." If these professional antiquers prove too esoteric or expensive, have a beer. Open twice per month Sat.-Sun. 11am-6pm.

Auer Dult: Mariahilfplatz. Take U-Bahn #1 or 2 to "Fraunhoferstr.," then streetcar #27 to "Mariahilfplatz." Munich's most famous fleamarket. Since 1799, all the pots, pans, china, second-hand clothes, and antiques you can mail home. Three times per year for 9 days (April 26-May 4, July 26-Aug. 3, and Oct. 18-26 in 1997).

Christkindlmarkt: Christmas comes to Munich 4 weeks before Christmas Eve for this annual market. Open Mon.-Wed. and Fri. 9am-7:30pm, Thurs. 9am-8:30pm, Sat. 10am-7:30pm (Nov. 29-Dec 24 in 1997). Ho, ho, ho.

■ Near Munich: Dachau

"Once they burn books, they will end up burning people," wrote the 19th-century German poet Heinrich Heine. This eerie statement is posted at the **Konzentrations-lager-Gedenkstätte,** the Dachau concentration camp, next to a photograph of a Nazi book burning. The walls, gates, and crematorium have been restored since 1962 in a chillingly sparse memorial. Included in the horror and utter confusion evoked by passing row after identical row of tightly-packed barracks (now merely foundations) is the idea that the Nazis chose this average residential suburb for the site of the first concentration camp in Germany.

Dachau has, to a jarring extent, become a major sight on the routes of packaged tours. It is important for visitors to realize that while the *KZ Gedenkstätte* is treated as a tourist attraction by many, it is first and foremost a memorial; Jews and gentiles alike come here for personal reasons, to grieve over the horrors of the former Nazi concentration camp. Take a moment to read the sign-in log at the end of the exhibit; you'll find that visitors from all over the world come here to remember lost relatives or to pay respects to those who perished. Interwoven with the multitude of names and addresses from different countries are statements of resilience and hope. Respectful behavior by those with only a historical interest is in order.

The museum, located in the former administrative buildings, examines pre-1930 anti-Semitism and reconstructs the rise of Nazism, the establishment of the concentration camp system, and the lives of prisoners through photographs, documents, and artifacts. The thick guide (DM25; available in English) translates the propaganda posters, SS files, documents, and letters, though many exhibits are accompanied by short captions in English. (A display copy of the English guide is available for perusal in the center of the exhibit; proceeds from sales benefit the Dachau Survivors Association.) Also on display are the texts of the letters from prisoners to their families as well as internal SS memos. A small, annotated map is available for DM0.30. A short film (22min.) is screened in English at 11:30am and 3:30pm (and on some days at 2pm). The two reconstructed barracks and the crematoria can also be viewed. The wrought-iron gate at the *Jourhaus,* formerly the only entrance to the camp, reads *"Arbeit Macht Frei"* ("Work Makes One Free"). It was the first sight as prisoners entered the camp. There is also a Jewish memorial, a Protestant commemorative chapel, and the Catholic *Todesangst Christ-Kapelle* (Christ in Agony Church) on the grounds. Behind the back wall is a Carmelite convent, which was the subject of controversy when the Church located it on the grounds. (For more discussion about the issues surrounding concentration camps, see History: The Holocaust, p. 62.) To get there from Munich, take S-Bahn #2 (direction: Petershausen) to "Dachau" (20min.), then board bus #720 or 722 (DM2) from in front of the station to *KZ Gedenkstätte* (20min.; grounds open Tues.-Sun. 9am-5pm). Thoughtful guided **tours** in English are available from **EurAide** (see Practical Information: Tourist Offices, p. 209) in the Munich train station. (Tours leave June-mid-Aug. Tues. and Thurs. at 9:15am. Meet at the EurAide office. DM30, with railpass DM23. Reserve at least a day in advance.) Free English tours are given Saturday and Sunday at 12:30pm; meet in front of the museum or call (08131) 17 41 for more information.

In the mid-19th century, painters such as Carl Spitzweg and Max Liebermann traveled to Dachau. A 16th-century castle tops the *Altstadt.* The **tourist office,** Konrad-Adenauer-Str. 3 (tel. 845 66), has plenty of information on the city of Dachau and sells maps for DM1. The **telephone code** is 08131.

■ Near Munich: Lake Region & Andechs

Müncheners frequently get away to the nearby glacial lakes, particularly the beloved **Starnbergersee** and the **Ammersee.** Called the **Five Seas** *(Fünf Seen),* this region comprises an aquatic complex of Starnbergersee, Ammersee, Pilsensee, Wörthsee, and Wesslingersee. Take S-Bahn #6 (last stop) out to the beautiful lakeside promenade of **Starnberg,** an old resort town. The castle where mad Ludwig II was confined after he was deposed is just around the tip of the lake in **Berg.** His body was found shortly thereafter, mysteriously drowned in the Starnbergersee—a cross in the water now marks the spot. For more information inquire at the main **"Five Sea" tourist office** in Starnberg, Wittelsbacherstr. 9 (tel. (08151) 130 07; fax 132 89), at Am Kirchplatz. The **Starnberg tourist office** (tel. 130 08) offers a central room finding service (open June-Sept. Mon.-Fri. 8am-6pm, Sat. 9am-1pm).

HERRSCHING AND AMMERSEE

Take Munich S-Bahn #5 to **Herrsching** on the Ammersee (every 20min.; 40min.). Herrsching is the start of one of the many *Wanderwege* (hiking paths) established by the transit system in connection with the S-Bahn. To get to the Ammersee from the Herrsching train station, follow Zum Landungssteg right and make a right at the end; continue until you come to the touristy beach area. If you don't mind pebbly beaches, the Ammersee is for you; ducks, kids, and sailboats seem not to.

Down the path along the sea on the right is a whimsical red-tiled villa with pagoda toppings. It's the **Kurpark Schlößchen** built by Ludwig Scheuermann in 1888 as a summer escape from a Munich infested with beer-drinking tourists (even then!). Bear right through the Kurpark to cross a tiny bridge. Here you'll find **Strandbad See-winkel** (tel. 405 71), Herrsching's crowded public beach (lacking sand, but offering grass). In its pleasant terrace beer garden, a brew is DM4.30 and a meal is around DM10. Hop off the dock for a swim, but wait at least an hour after packing away that food (beach area open May-Sept. daily 9am-10pm). The restaurant inside the See-winkel is separate from the self-service beer garden (open Wed.-Mon. 5-10pm). You can catch the **Bayerische Schiffahrt,** a steamship-like tug boat that travels the northern Ammersee route to Holzhausen and Stegen for DM17 one way. Southward, chug by Riederau and Diessen for DM15. Round-trips cost DM22, under 15 get 50% off, under 6 free (boats leave almost once per hour 9am-6pm). Play **miniature golf** (DM6, under 14 DM5) back up Zum Landungssteg. (Open Mon.-Fri. 11am-9:30pm, Sat.-Sun. 10am-9:30pm. Last entrance 9pm.)

The **tourist office,** Bahnhofplatz 2 (tel. 52 27; fax 405 19), across from the train station, can help you find a room in Herrsching. They provide information on the 11 paths that leave town for the forest and sea areas, and can also find rooms in the region (open Mon.-Fri. 8:30am-noon and 2-5pm, Sat. 10am-noon). Most hotel singles run DM45-60, private rooms DM30-45, plus a DM1 surtax for everyone over 18 (because Herrsching is a *Kurort,* see (p. 388).) The nearest **Campingplatz** (tel 12 06) is in Herrsching-Mühlfeld. (DM6, under 6 DM3. Tent DM4-8. Car DM3. Caravan DM7. DM1 surtax if over 18. Open April-Sept.) Five other camping sites serve the area: one on the Wörthsee, one on Pilsensee, and three on the Starnberger See. Pick up groceries for a promenade picnic at **Norma,** 11 Zum Landungssteg (open Mon.-Fri. 8am-6pm, Sat. 8am-1pm). The **telephone code** is 08152.

ANDECHS

The monastery at **Andechs** fuses Bavaria's two most acclaimed attributes—Catholicism and beer—on a gorgeous mountaintop. The monks here brew up a pale beer and a rocking **Bockbier** that is piously not served on Sundays or Saturdays from Easter to October—young firebrands used to come up the mountain for weekend debauchery, swilling *Bock* and causing too much ruckus for the monk-waiters. The beer garden, **Klosterbrauerei** (tel. (08152) 37 60; fax 37 62 60), now serves *Bockbier* on weekdays, and other beers every day, even holy ones. The secular brewing industry is currently up in arms over what they consider an unfair competitive advantage: as a religious institution, the monastery is exempt from the beer tax. (A *Maß* of their *Bockbier* only DM11.40. *Maß* light DM9. Dark *Maß* DM10. Beer garden open 9:45am-8pm. Restaurant open 11am-11pm. Meals DM9-18.)

Pagan thoughts aside, you can tour the monastery and church to admire its ornate gold altar. The mortal remains of composer **Carl Orff** rest in the building (see Music, p. 76). To reach the monastery, take S-Bahn #5 to "Herrsching," then switch to the private bus line **Omnibusverkehr Rauner** (Mon.-Sat.; 6-11 per day) or to a public **MVV** bus (Sun.; 11 per day) for the 10-minute trip to Andechs. Bus schedules are erratic; check with the tourist office in Herrsching for departure times. The last departure and return times are around 5:30 or 6:30pm daily. Alternatively, huff and puff for a slowly sloping 3km and earn your *Bockbier*. Follow the signs marked *Fußweg nach Andechs* and stick to the trail; 11 people have recently died short-cutting down the precipitous slope.

■ Bavarian Alps (Bayerische Alpen)

South of Munich, the land buckles into a series of dramatic peaks and valleys stretching across Austria and into Italy. Throughout this magical terrain Ludwig II of Bavaria, the assertively batty "Fairy-tale King," chose to build his theatrical palaces. Mountain villages, glacial lakes, icy waterfalls, and world-class ski resorts fill the forested slopes. The rhythmic beat of cowbells ceases only at dusk, and, after a few days, cowdung no longer smells pungent and foul, but rather, fresh and springy (well, almost). This is also the region where people authentically, even nonchalantly, wear *Lederhosen*. Rail lines are sparse; buses cover the gaps. For regional information, contact the *Fremdenverkehrsverband Oberbayern*, Bodenseestr. 113 (tel. (089) 829 21 80), in Munich (open Mon.-Fri. 9am-4:30pm, Sat. 9am-noon).

GARMISCH-PARTENKIRCHEN

Once upon a time, the 1100-year-old Garmisch and Partenkirchen were beautiful but rather unassuming Bavarian villages whose location at the foot of the **Zugspitze**—Germany's highest peak—kept them in tranquil isolation. But as the 19th century back-to-nature movement discovered the mountains, the two towns quickly became Germany's most famous mountain resort area. In 1935, it took Hitler only 48 hours to persuade the mayors of the two villages to unite them in anticipation of the 1936 Winter Olympics. To this day, however, Garmischers and Partenkircheners assert their individuality; both sides of the 30,000-person town staunchly maintain that they even speak in different dialects.

Practical Information Garmisch-Partenkirchen can easily be reached from Füssen by **bus** (2hrs.; DM13; no railpasses valid), or from Innsbruck in Austria by train (90min.; DM15.40). Pick up maps of hiking trails (DM8) and city maps (free) at the **tourist office** (*Verkehrsamt der Kurverwaltung*), on Richard-Strauss-Platz (tel. 18 06; fax 180 55). From the station, turn left on Bahnhofstr. and after 200m turn left again onto Von-Brug-Str.; it's the modern building on the square (open Mon.-Sat. 8am-6pm, Sun. 10am-noon). Try the automat in front or call 194 12, if the office is closed. **Public transportation** costs DM2.50, but is free with a *Kurkarte* (see p. 232). Rent **bikes** at **Werdenfelser Sportagentur,** Marienplatz 18 (tel. 14 25;

open Mon.-Fri. 9am-noon and 1-5pm), or **Mountain-Bike Center Stefan Leiner,** Ludwigstr. 42 (tel. 795 28; fax 548 44; open Mon.-Fri. 8am-6pm, Sat. 8am-1:30pm and 4-6pm, Sun. 9-11am and 4-6pm). For a **snow** and **weather report** for the *Zugspitze,* call 79 79 79; for the *Wank* area, call 75 33 33. The **post office,** 82467 Garmisch-Partenkirchen, is across the street from the station (open Mon.-Fri. 8am-6:30pm, Sat. 8am-1pm, Sun. 10-11am). The **telephone code** is 08821.

Accommodations Reasonable rooms do exist in Garmisch-Partenkirchen, but you'll have to do a bit of detective work to find one. The tourist office will help you find *Gasthäuser* and *Pensionen* (DM35-40). Alternatively, request a list of private rooms and start making calls yourself; most rooms require a three-night minimum stay (DM30 per night). No matter where you wind up, there's a DM3 **Kurtax** levied on tourists. The compensation for paying is a green card entitling you to free rides on the bus system and one free admission to the *Alpspitz-Wellenbad,* the casino, the *Kurpark,* and concerts (see below). At the **Jugendherberge (HI),** Jochstr. 10 (tel. 29 80; fax 585 36), you awake to the tolling of church bells. Cross the street from the train station and walk 25m to your left to take bus #3, 4 or 5 (direction: Farchant) to "Burgrain." Cross the street, walk down the block perpendicular to the bus route, and turn left after the second block. Clean, somewhat institutional six- to 10-bed rooms. (Reception open 6:30-9am and 5-11:30pm. Lockout 9am-3:30pm. Curfew 11pm. Ages 18-27 only. DM17.50. Sheets DM5.50. Open Jan.-Oct.) The **Naturfreundehaus,** Schalmeiweg 21 (tel 43 22), is a friendly, independent hostel, more intimate than the *Jugendherberge,* on the edge of the forest at the east end of Partenkirchen, 20 minutes from the train station. Walk straight on Bahnhofstr., stay on it as it becomes Ludwigstr., follow the rightward bend in Ludwigstr., and turn left on Sonnenbergstr. Continue straight as this first becomes Prof.-Michael-Sachs-Str. and then Schalmeiweg. (Quiet after 10pm, but no curfew. Small, so call ahead. DM14, optional breakfast DM8.) **Camping Zugspitze,** Griesenerstr. 4 in the village of Grainau (tel. 31 80), is on highway B24 at the base of the *Zugspitze;* take the blue-and-white bus from the station to "Schmölzabzweigung." (DM8 per person, DM10 per site, DM6 per tent. Add DM1.70 Grainau *Kurtax.*)

Food Garmisch's restaurants cater to a range of tastes and wallet thicknesses. The best value in town is probably the friendly Italian **La Baita,** at Zugspitzstr. 16 (tel. 787 77), 100m from Marienplatz. Delightful pasta dishes (DM8-16), omelettes (DM9), and pizza (DM8-14; open Thurs.-Tues. 11:30am-2:30pm and 5:30pm-11:30pm). In the heart of Partenkirchen, grab a giant *Schnitzel* (DM9-11) at **Gasthof Fraudorfer,** Ludwigstr. 24 (tel. 21 76; fax 710 73), where traditional Bavarian dishes are supplemented with traditional Bavarian folk dances and songs. For those willing to explore the wonders of the American base in Garmisch, take bus #1, 2, 3, or 4 to Breitenau, cross the bridge and have a decent lunch (noodles with ham and eggs, or *Jägerschnitzel* with fries) for DM5-7 at the **US-Kantine** (open 7am-7pm). The cheapest **supermarket** is **Aldi,** at the corner of Enzianstr. and Bahnhofstr. (open Mon.-Fri. 8:30am-6:30pm, Sat. 8am-1pm).

Sights Garmisch is less a place with things to see than with things to do. Unfortunately, this doesn't make it a very wallet-friendly place. Ride up to the *Zugspitze* only if it's sunny. There are three ways up the peak. **Option 1:** Take the cog railway from the *Zugspitzbahnhof* (50m behind the Garmisch main station) via Grainau to Hotel Schneefernerhaus, then a cable car, the *Gipfelseilbahn,* to the outlook, the *Zugspitzplatt* (75min.; 60min. to the ski area; round-trip DM72 in summer, DM60 in winter). Continue with the *Gletscherbahn* cable car. **Option 2:** Get off the cog railway at Eibsee and take the *Eibseeseilbahn,* one of the steepest cable car runs in the world, all the way to the top. (80min.; 10min. to Zugspitze; round-trip in summer DM72, in winter DM60.) A **combo ticket** including the train from Munich/Augsburg and the *Zugspitze* tour costs DM87. **Option 3:** Hike it—the cheapest way to get atop the 2964m monster is to climb for about 10hrs., usually as part of a two-day trip. Get a good map from the tourist office and triple-check the weather report.

For other Alpine views at lower prices, take the **Alpspitzbahn** to Oster-felderkopf peak (2050m; 10min.; round-trip DM35), the **Kreuzeck** cable car to Kreuzeck (1650m; 8 min.; round-trip DM26), or the **Wankbahn** (1780m; 15min.; round-trip DM28). A neat day trip includes biking to the **Eibsee,** about 10km from Garmisch. The calm, crystal waters of a mountain lake against the soaring, snow-capped monumentality of the *Zugspitze* will remind you of a movie backdrop. To avoid the 14% uphill of the last 300m, take the blue and white Eibsee bus from Garmisch (round-trip DM5). One of the most popular trails leads to the dramatic, 100m deep **Partnachklamm** gorge (admission DM3). Walk up to the gorge from behind the Olympic ski stadium (35min.) and then meander for another 35min. in the narrow darkish tunnels dug in the rocks, dangerously close to the foaming water. The ski season runs from October to mid-May in all its Alpine glory. Of the six area ski schools, the cheapest **equipment rental** is at **Ski-Schule,** Am Hausberg 8, next to the *Hausbergbahn* (tel. 49 31 or 742 60). **Ski passes** in the *Zugspitzgebiet* cost DM58 per day, DM44 with railpass. More advanced leg-breakers ski in the **Ver-bundgebiet,** home of the World Cup Kandehar run, for DM47 per day. A week pass costs DM277, two weeks DM439. If the weather is not inclement, soak your weary feet in hot water or display your athletic prowess from the 5m high jumpboard at the **Alpspitz-Wellenbad,** Klammstr. 47, next to the Olympic stadium (tel. 75 33 13). The six-pool complex features artificial waves, saunas, restaurants, and paraglid-ers hovering overhead. (Open Mon.-Tues and Thurs.-Fri. 9am-9pm, Wed. 6am-9pm, Sat.-Sun. 9am-7pm. Admission DM7 for 3hr., DM9 for unlimited time; first entry free with *Kurkarte,* then DM4 and DM5.50.)

BERCHTESGADEN

Poised at the easternmost point of the Bavarian Alps, Berchtesgaden profits from a sinister and overtouristed attraction: Hitler's **Kehlsteinhaus**—a mountaintop retreat christened "Eagle's Nest" by occupying American troops. A disconcerting horde of tourists, many of them American soldiers, besieges this Bavarian town every year to catch a glimpse of this small slice of World War II history. Historically and geographi-cally, Berchtesgaden belongs more properly to Austria and the Archbishophric of Salzburg than to Germany, but Bavaria snatched it up in 1809 for its salt deposits. Just over those mountaintops in the northeast, *The Sound of Music's* Julie Andrews, her arms outstreched, turned round and round in alpine ecstasy—you could too.

Orientation and Practical Information Crouching in the south-eastern corner of Germany, Berchtesgaden is a German peninsula in a sea of Austrian moun-tains. The Berchtesgaden **tourist office,** at Königsseerstr. 2 (*Kurdirektion;* tel. 96 70; fax 633 00), is opposite the train station in an off-white building with blue shutters. Ask the *Lederhosen*-wearing staff for the *Berchtesgadener Land: General Informa-tion* pamphlet, which lists sights, concerts, and other activities. Most materials avail-able in English. Their hiking pass (DM5) includes tips on walking trails and climbs and comes free with the *Kurkarte,* a tourist card given to overnighters who pay the obligatory *Kurtax* of approximately DM3. There's no room-finding service, but they have extensive lists of rooms and an automatic hotel finder in front of the office (open June-Oct. Mon.-Fri. 8am-6pm, Sat. 8am-5pm, Sun. 9am-3pm; Nov.-May Mon.-Fri. 8am-5pm, Sat. 9am-noon.). Call 194 12 for a recording on **hotels.**

For **train**-related questions call the *Bahnhof* (tel. 50 74; open Mon.-Sat. 6:05am-7:35pm, Sun. 7am-7:35pm). Hourly trains run to Munich (2½hr.; change at Freilass-ing), Salzburg (1hr.; change at Freilassing), and Bad Reichenhall (30min.). The fare for a **bus** ride ranges from DM2 for **public transportation** in Berchtesgaden proper to DM46 for trips in the region (e.g., Bad Reichenhall DM5.50, Königsee DM3.30, Salzburg DM6.30). For bus-related questions call the bus office (tel. 54 73) in the train station (open Mon-Fri. 8am-noon and 2-4pm). Rent **bikes** at the train station (DM12-

17) or **motorbikes** from **Horst Wagner,** Am Zellerbach 6 (tel. 621 01). You can also grab a **rowboat** at the Königsee dock or a **heart-rate tester** (for hiking) at the tourist office. For the daily **pollen report** call 50 11. The **post office,** Bahnhofsplatz 4, 83471 Berchtesgaden (tel. 95 60 23), is adjacent to the train station (open Mon.-Fri. 8am-noon and 2-5:30pm, Sat. 8am-noon). Most establishments also accept Austrian *Schillings;* you can **exchange currency** at the Salzburg train station post office before departing. The **telephone code** is 08652.

Accommodations and Food The **Jugendherberge (HI),** Gebirgsjägerstr. 52, 83489 Strub (tel. 21 90; fax 663 28), is an uphill 25- to 30-minute walk from the station. Turn right from the station and follow the highly-trafficked Ransauer Str. for 15 minutes, then take the first right, and follow the signs up the steep (unnamed) gravel path on the left. Or take bus #9539 (direction: Strub Kaserne) to "Jugendherberge" (the last stop) for DM2.40. (Reception open 7-9am and 5-7pm.Curfew midnight. Under 27 only. DM18, plus DM3 *Kurtax.* Breakfast included. Sheets DM5.50. Open Dec. 27-Oct.) Most private rooms and *Pensionen* cost DM28-35, with shower DM35-50; hotels run DM80-100. **Haus Alpina,** Ramsauerstr. Str. 6 (tel. 25 17), 5 minutes to the right on the same street as the station, lures guests with clean rooms and down comforters. (DM45, DM38 per additional night. Breakfast included. Closed Nov.-mid-Dec.). **Gästehaus Hansererhäusl,** Hansererweg 8 (tel. 25 23), is just behind the tourist office. Follow Rossötzweg and bear left onto Hansererweg. (DM30 per person. Breakfast included). The campsite **Campingplatz Allweglehen,** at Untersalzberg (tel. 23 96), is more than an hour's walk downstream from the station. (DM7.20. Children 6-16 years DM6.50. Camper DM11.50.) Berchtesgaden is rife with restaurants for wealthy tourists. Pick up a *Wurst* sandwich from a vendor or groceries at the **Edeka Markt,** on Dr.-Imhof-Str., in town near Griesstätterstr. (open Mon.-Fri. 8am-12:30pm and 1:30-6pm, Sat. 8am-2pm). The relaxed **Martinklause,** Ludwig-Ganghoferstr. 20 1/3, offers inexpensive soups (DM5-7), *Wurst* sandwiches (DM8-9), beer, and pinball (open daily 10am-2pm and 5pm-midnight).

Sights The **Kehlsteinhaus** (also called "Eagle's Nest") was built for the *Führer's* 50th birthday as a place to entertain the boss. Hitler only visited the mountaintop retreat a few times, but that doesn't deter the parade of tourists. The stone resort house is now just a pricey restaurant (tel. 29 69) with no museum in sight. In fact, the best reason to visit the Kehlsteinhaus is for the trip up to the spectacular 360° view from the 1834-m-high mountain peak. The road is something of an engineering marvel, hewn into solid rock by an army of 3000 men excused from conscription for health reasons. Loosen your grip on the seat to witness 100m drops right under your window. On the way back down, inspect what little remains of another Nazi retreat: bombed by the Allies on April 25, 1945, the **Berghof** in Obersalzberg was used by Hitler to entertain foreign dignitaries. On February 12, 1938, it was here that he browbeat Austrian Chancellor Kurt von Schuschnigg into relinquishing control of the Austrian police to the Nazis, paving the way for the *Anschluß.* Seven months later, British Prime Minister Neville Chamberlain visited Hitler to hammer out the "Munich Agreement" that Chamberlain claimed would guarantee "peace in our time."

To get to the Kehlsteinhaus first take the "Obersalzburg, Kehlstein" bus from the covered platform to the right as you exit the station to "Obersalzburg, Hintereck" (round-trip DM6.50; leaves June-Oct. every 20-40min. 8:45am-3:45pm, off-season *much* less regularly, if at all; check with the tourist office for schedules). At Hintereck, buy your ticket for the bus ride to "Kehlstein Parkplatz, Eagle's Nest" (round-trip DM20; every 30min. 9:30am-4pm). At Kehlstein, reserve your spot on a return bus (we mean it) at the booth when you get off. Reserving a place on a bus leaving one hour after the time of your Kehlstein arrival will give you enough time to explore the mountaintop if you don't plan to stop for lunch at the top (buses return every 30min. until 5pm). From Kehlstein Parkplatz, go through the tunnel and up with the elevator to the Kehlsteinhaus (fare included in the second bus ticket); the elevator's mirrors are original, installed to quell Hitler's claustrophobia. Alternatively, climb 20 minutes up the winding footpath on the right as you face the mountain. Pack a light jacket for the cool weather on the peak. A short English-language **tour** of the Eagle's Nest is available daily at 10:30 and 11:30am (35min.; DM5, children free; meet at the tunnel entrance to the elevator). A 3½-hour English-language tour must be reserved one day in advance from **Berchtesgaden Mini Bus Tours** (tel. 649 71 or 648 63) in the tourist office (DM47, under 13 DM25, under 6 free; includes second bus and elevator; Mon.-Sat. at 1:30pm, meet at the tourist office).

The Berchtesgaden Royal **Schloß** (tel. 20 85) was a monastic priory until Bavarian rulers usurped the area and appropriated the property. It now houses a collection of art and weaponry (open Sun.-Fri. 10am-1pm and 2-5pm; Oct.-Easter Mon.-Fri. 10am-1pm and 2-5pm; last entry 4pm; admission DM7, students DM3.50, under 16 DM3). To reach the castle and the rest of the *Altstadt,* cross over the train tracks on the footbridge (follow the *"zum Markt"* signs) behind the station and continue to Bahnhofweg until you hit Maximillianstr.; then continue straight ahead.

Wedged into extraordinary Alpine cliffs, the **Königssee** calmly mirrors the landscape on its blue-green surface. Ships glide across the lake irregularly (round-trip to St. Bartholomä DM17.50, to Obersee DM21.50; children 50% off). In summer, boats leave around every 10 to 20 minutes starting at 7:15am; no boats go to Obersee in the winter. Call **Schiffahrt Königsee** at 96 36 13. The best lake view is at the **Malerwinkel** (Painter's Outlook), around to the left of the lake, and the best aerial view is serviced by the Jenner cable car—1170m above sea-level. Take bus #9541 (direction; Königssee) from the main train station to the end of the line (1 per hr.; DM3.30). At the **Salzbergwerke** (salt mines) near town (tel. 600 20), you can dress up in an old salt miner's outfit, slide down snaking passages in the dark, and go on a raft ride on a salt lake. From the station, take bus #9548 to "Salzbergwerke" (1-2 per hour 8:37am-7:40pm; DM2) or a 30-minute walk. (Open daily 8:30am-5pm; mid-Oct. to April Mon.-Sat. 12:30-3:30pm. Admission DM17, children 10 and under DM8.50.) For a 90-minute tour in English, call **Berchtesgaden Mini Bus Tours** (tel. 649 71). To go **moonlight-rafting,** call the Outdoor Club (tel. 50 01, fax 664 54).

OBERAMMERGAU AND ETTAL ABBEY

Since 1634, the tiny Alpine town of Oberammergau has been the site of the world-famous **Passion Plays.** After the town was spared from a plague that swept through Europe, the inhabitants promised to re-enact the crucifixion and resurrection of Christ every 10 years. The cast is composed of about 1000 locals who begin rehearsing long in advance, often growing long hair and beards. The plays last all day, with a short break for lunch. The next Passion Plays will be presented in 2000. Reserve tickets and accommodations for the plays a good two years in advance. While the plays are not being performed, the most exciting things to do in Oberammergau are watch the beards grow and visit nearby Ettal Abbey (see below).

Information and tickets can be obtained from the **tourist office,** Eugen-Papst-Str. 9a (tel. 10 21; fax 73 25), which finds rooms for a DM1 fee (rooms DM20-30 per person, DM30-40 with bath) and provides maps (open Mon.-Fri. 8:30am-4pm, Sat. 8:30am-noon, mid-June-mid-Sept. also open Sat.-Sun. 2-6pm). Turn left from the station and take a right at the town center onto Eugen-Papststr. For Oberammergau's **Jugendherberge (HI),** Malensteinweg 10 (tel. 41 14; fax 16 95), follow the right bank of the Ammer upstream from the station (7min.). It's a bit loud and unpredictable. (Reception open 7-11:30am, 4-10pm. Curfew 10pm. Under 27 only. DM17.50. Sheets DM5.50. Closed Nov.12-Dec.25.) The **telephone code** is 08822.

In 1330, Ludwig I of Bavaria—not to be confused with *the* Ludwig, of Walt Disney castle fame—founded the enormous, domed **Abbey Church** in the tiny village of **Ettal,** about 4km south of Oberammergau. Since then, the abbey has conducted a brisk business in house-fermented beer and spirits. Buy a four-bottle sampler for DM12.80 or cross the street to swig a *Kloster Ettal Dunkles* for DM4.20. Beautifully stuccoed and gilded in typical Baroque over-ornateness, this rectangular sanctuary assumed its present shape after 18th-century renovations. Be careful not to drown in the human flood of visitors (open 7:45am-7:45pm; winter 7:45am-noon). Buses to Ettal from Oberammergau leave from the train station once per hour (round-trip DM4.40; railpasses not valid).

FÜSSEN

Where the Lech River leaves the mountains on its way to the Danube, Füssen stands at the crossway of an old imperial Roman road. Curled up at the toes of the Alpine foothills and at the southern end of the Romantic Road, the sedate town has been known for 200 years as a small resort for ordinary Germans—as well as the former resort of Mad King Ludwig. The town's proximity to Ludwig's famed *Königsschlösser* (Royal Castles; see p. 236) lures legions here each year, but don't battle tourists all day; Füssen's meandering paths, mountain lakes, and jolly cows deserve a few hours of aimless wandering. Under Henry VII, this town found itself a reluctant player in the game of European intrigue and politics. To help finance his Italian campaign, Henry put up the town as collateral against a loan of 400 silver *Marks* from the prince-bishop of Augsburg. Henry died indebted, so the town was forfeited to the prince-bishop from 1313 until the great German Secularization of 1802.

Reminders of the prince-bishop's medieval reign linger in architectural astonishments. The inner walls of the **Hohes Schloß** (High Castle) courtyard scream royalty with their arresting *trompe l'oeil* windows and towers. Along with a bevy of bureaucratic offices, the **Gemäldegalerie's** (tel. 50 53 64) collection of regional late-Gothic and Renaissance art resides in what were once the work- and love-dens of late-medieval bishops and knights (open Tues.-Sun. 11am-4pm; Nov.-March Tues.-Sun. 2-4pm; admission DM4, students and seniors DM2). Just below the castle rests the eighth-century Baroque basilica **St. Mangkirche** (Church of St. Magnus) and its abbey. An ancient fresco discovered during 1950 renovations lights up the church's 10th-century subterranean crypt (tours Tues. at 4:30pm). Also in the abbey is the 18th-century, overdone Baroque library. The **Museum of Füssen,** in the monastery (tel. 90 31 45; fax 90 32 01), details the history, art, and culture of the Füssen region in four Jeopardy category installments. "Baroque Rooms" for US$500 please. Inside the **Chapel of St. Anne,** macabre skeleton-decked panels depict the *Totentanz* (death dance), a public frenzy of despair which overtook Europe during the plague (open Tues.-Sun. 11am-4pm; Nov.-March Tues.-Sun. 2-4pm; chapel free, library DM3, students DM2). Not only can you send the folks back home a postcard of the most photographed castles in Germany, but you can also bike across the Austrian border 3km away to drop them a line from Tirol.

The **tourist office** (*Kurverwaltung;* tel. 70 77 or 70 78; fax 391 81) is at Kaiser-Maximilian-Platz 1. From the *Bahnhof* walk the length of Bahnhofstr., then straight on Luitpold-Str. to the big yellow building. The staff finds rooms for free, and proffers up bike maps (DM5), hiking maps (DM7.80), and city maps (free). They organize guided hikes of the area (DM4 per person; ask about departure times) as well as expeditions to the *Königsschlösser* (open Mon.-Fri. 8am-noon and 2-6pm, Sat. 9-12:30pm, Sun. 10am-noon; Oct.-May Mon.-Fri. 8am-noon and 2-6pm, Sat. 10am-noon). **Rent bikes** at the *Bahnhof* (tel. 63 13), or at **Radsport Zacherl,** Rupprechtstr. 8½ (tel. 32 92) for DM12 per day for a 7-gear bike, DM20 for a mountain bike. From the station, turn left on Rupprechtstr.; it's 100m down on the right (open Mon.-Fri. 9am-noon and 2-6pm, Sat. 9am-noon). The **telephone code** is 08362.

Budget singles in *Gasthäuser* run DM35-40; in *Pensionen,* DM45 and up. During high season, don't expect to find a cheap room. If worse comes to worst, head to the information pavilion in front of the *Kurverwaltung,* where you can buy an information pamphlet (DM1) or peruse a computerized database of hotels (free; open 7am-12:30am). Keep your eyes open for *"Zimmer frei"* signs in private homes; prices fall dramatically as you walk away from the pedestrian zones. Füssen's **Jugendherberge (HI),** Mariahilferstr. 5 (tel. 77 54; fax 27 70), is blessed by a lovely location and a lovely staff. Turn right from the station and follow the railroad tracks (10min.). It's often packed, so double-check *before* you arrive to insure you'll have a bed; if you've made a reservation, they're obligated to find a spot for you—even if it's in a cot in a damp basement room ironically labelled "Disco." Remember to show up before 6pm, or your precious reservation will suddenly turn into a pumpkin. (Reception open 7-9am and 5-10pm. Curfew 11pm, Oct. and Dec.-March 10pm; but ask quietly about the back kitchen door. Under 27 only. DM20.50, plus DM1.40 resort tax. Sheets DM5.50. Meals DM8.50. Wash DM3, dry DM3, soap DM1. Lockers in basement DM1. Open Dec.-Oct. Call at least 1 day before you arrive.) Eleven kilometers away in Hopfensee is **Campingplatz Bauernhof J. Guggemos,** Uferstr. 42 (tel. 33 34). For food for less than DM10, grab a bottle of red wine (last year's premium vintage), fresh baguettes, a large block of cheese, and some strawberries at the grocery store, **Plus,** on the corner of Bahnhofstr. and Luitpoldstr. (open Mon.-Fri. 8:30am-6:30pm, Sat. 8am-1pm.)

Near Füssen: Wieskirche (Church of the Meadow)

Any daytrip from Füssen or Oberammergau to the Ammergau Alps ought to include the **Weiskirche** (Church of the Meadows; tel. (08861) 81 73), a splendid Rococo pilgrimage church surrounded by forests, farmland, camera-clicking tourists, and fast-food stands. The church sports two characteristic quirks; most striking at first glance is the light pastel color scheme (quite uncommon in religious architecture) which dominates the rich stucco interior. The church's windows let in torrents of light that bathe the church in astonishing brightness, and the effect is particularly riveting in the morning and evening when the sun shines directly through the arching windows. The second wonder in is the central dome's fresco, a glowing "Gate to Paradise." To fully appreciate the painter's exploitation of the dome's concavity to trick the eye, stand directly beneath the dome, then observe it again from the gallery next to the choir. The best way there is to take the 11:15am **bus** from the Füssen station (Mon.-Sat.; on Sun. there's a bus at 1:05pm); return on the 3:50pm bus from the church (1hr. each way; round-trip DM13; railpasses not valid).

■ The Royal Castles (Königsschlösser)

When Ludwig II inherited the Kingdom of Bavaria in 1864, he was young and shockingly handsome; rumor has it that he was also a bit bonkers. Unlike other "visionaries," however, Ludwig had the cash to craft his visions into realities. He spent his private fortune forging fantastic castles that soar into the Alpine skies. In 1886, a band of upstart nobles and bureaucrats deposed of Ludwig in a *coup d'état* and imprisoned him in Schloß Berg on the Starnbergersee. Three days later, the King and a loyal doc-

---

Insults for Sale

The concept of free speech in Germany does not imply *kostenlos* (cost-free) speech. While doling out compliments requires no budget, dropping insults will unload your wallet in no time. Public humiliation in Germany carries such destructive and belittling force that officials have created an insult price list. Angry, offended, or drunk budget travelers should beware. The heaviest fines will be incurred by obnoxious mouth-flappers who put down a female police officer's respectability: belting out *Trottel in Uniform* (slut in uniform) will cost you DM3000, while the lesser insult *Dumme Kuh* (dumb cow) requires a mere DM1200 payoff. Call any uniformed official *Idioten* (idiot), and you'll be out a whopping DM3000. The budget traveler's insult, *Holzkopf* (wood-headed), goes for a selling price of DM1500. If you give another driver the *Stinkefinger* (middle finger)—deservedly, of course—and he or she can round up witnesses, you'll be DM2200 poorer. Equivalent insults in English are not exempt; stories abound of policemen who've doled out thousands of *Marks* in fines to tourists who think that Germans don't understand what "asshole" means. We tell you this merely as a warning—and prices are, of course, subject to change, you idiot.

tor/adviser were discovered dead in the lake under mysterious circumstances—possibly a failed escape attempt, some hypothesize, even though Ludwig was a damn good swimmer. According to Bavarians, Ludwig gets a bad rap. The king was a bit eccentric, they concede, but only because he was bored and indifferent to politics, not because he was mentally ill. They claim that his enemies fabricated the madness story as an excuse to usurp his power.

HOHENSCHWANGAU & NEUSCHWANSTEIN

These *Königsschlösser* lie 5km across the Lech River in the village of Hohenschwangau. Ludwig II grew up in **Schloß Hohenschwangau,** the buttercup-yellow neo-Gothic castle rebuilt by his father Maximilian II. It was here no doubt that he acquired his taste for the romantic German mythologies of the Middle Ages. Atop a humble hill and forest, this palace is a bit less touristed than its cousin, but also more opulent and authentic—the rooms actually appear to be lived-in. Come here to see Wagner's maple-wood piano and a loaf of bread 106 years old. Tours in German run frequently; English-speakers will need to round up a herd of 15-20 people for a tour in their native tongue.

Ludwig's desperate building spree across Upper Bavaria peaked with the construction of the glitzy **Schloß Neuschwanstein,** now Germany's most clichéd tourist attraction, and the inspiration for Disney World's "Fantasyland" castle. The first sketches of the castle were reportedly drawn by a set designer, not an architect, which explains a lot. The young Ludwig II lived a mere 173 days within the extravagant edifice, which includes a Byzantine throne-room, a small artificial grotto, and an immense *Sängersaal* (Singer's Hall)—an acoustic masterpiece, built expressly for Wagner opera performances, but never used. The king's bed is topped by a wood carving of a familiar but unidentifiable city skyline; it depicts most of the famous towers of the world. The lines for the brisk **tours** (30min.) may seem endless, but they are the only way to get in; the best time to arrive is early in the morning. Tourists, yes—more tourists than you can possibly imagine. (Both castles open daily 9am-5:30pm; Oct.-March 10am-4pm. Admission (for each castle) DM10, students and persons with disabilities DM7. Tour included.)

Consider spending the rest of the day hiking around the spectacular environs. For the godfather of all views, hike up to the **Marienbrücke,** spanning the **Pöllat Gorge** behind the castle (10min.). Push and shove your way onto the bridge; perhaps feign a Ludwig-inspired suicide attempt to clear your way through. Those with stout hearts and legs can continue uphill from here (about 2½hr.) for a knockout overlook of the castle and nearby lake. Sane people and insane hang-gliders ride the **Tegelbergbahn** cable car (tel. 810 18) for a glimpse of—or a dive into—the same panorama. (One-way DM15, students and disabled persons DM14.50; round-trip DM25 and DM24, respectively. Open daily 8:30am-5pm; in winter 8:45am-4:30pm.)

From Füssen, hop the bus marked "Königsschlösser," which departs from the train station more or less hourly (DM2.30; railpasses not valid). The quickest way to Hohenschwangau is the *Waldweg* which runs just near the information office (about 10min.; many steps). To Neuschwanstein, take path #32, beginning at Car Park D (a.k.a. *Parkplatz Königsschlösser,* across the street from the bus stop); it's the shortest but steepest trail to the top (25min.). Alternately, clip-clop your way to the near-tippy-top in a horse-drawn carriage (uphill DM7, downhill DM3.50; daily 9am-5pm) from Car Park D or Hotel Müller. Consider trekking path #33 from Neuschwanstein (20min.; open only in summer). Virtually untouristed, this route winds its way down through the dramatic **Pöllat Gorge.** Private buses run from Hotel Lisl to a beautiful vantage point 650 steep meters uphill from Neuschwanstein (DM3.50 uphill, DM2 downhill). For maps or more information on trails, check out the **information booth** (*Schlossverwaltung Hohenschwangau;* tel. 811 27) where the bus to the castles (direction: Hohenschwangau Village) stops. **Buses** depart from the Garmisch-Partenkirchen train station and stop directly in the Hohenschwangau village (daily at 8:05am, 1:05pm, 4:15pm, 5:05pm and Mon.-Fri. at 9:35am and 11:15am; return daily at 8:50am, 9:51am, 2:35pm, 4:40pm, and 6:41pm; round-trip with *Tagesticket* DM13;

railpasses not valid; 2hrs.). From Munich, take a **train** to Buchloe and transfer for the regional train to Füssen (2hr.; DM30).

SCHLOß LINDERHOF

Halfway between Garmisch-Partenkirchen and Oberammergau lies the exquisite **Schloß Linderhof,** Ludwig II's compact hunting palace, surrounded by a meticulously manicured park. With this edifice Ludwig paid homage to the French Bourbon kings, in particular Louis XIV (the Sun King), just as he did with his *Herrenchiemsee* palace. The royal bedchamber, the largest room in the castle, is unbelievably lush, with gold leaf and a colossal crystal chandelier weighing half a ton. Dark blue velvet (the king's favorite color) encases the king-size bed; though he topped 6'5", Ludwig had no trouble fitting in between the headcarved head and foot boards—and perhaps a few mistresses fit in there as well. Across the ceiling stretches the affirmation *"Nec pluribus impar,"* which roughly translates as "I am the greatest; I am the best." Note the two malachite tables given by Russian Czarina Marie Alexandrovna, whose goal it was to match Ludwig (a bachelor to his death) with one of her daughters. Ludwig decided just to keep the tables.

More impressive than the palace itself is the magnificent **park.** The sheer force of water cascading down steps behind the palace powers the fountain in front. Every hour on the hour, the dam is opened and water shoots higher than the top of the palace. Paths weave through the ornately landscaped grounds. To the right of the palace and up the slope is an enormous, campy artificial **grotto,** complete with a "subterranean" lake and floating shell-boat as in Wagner's *Tannhäuser.* The tour overdramatically stages two different lightings of the grotto: red and blue. Tacky, tacky, tacky. But at least it's refreshingly cool inside. Farther along, brilliant red- and blue- stained-glass windows richly illuminate the **Maurischer Kiosk** (Moorish Pavilion), an elaborate, mosque-shaped building—the only building on the grounds not built expressly for Ludwig. He saw it at the 1867 World Exposition in Paris and liked it so much that he brought it home with him. Within these walls, Ludwig would smoke his water pipe and implore his servants to dress up in period costumes and read him tales from *1001 Nights.* Following the path down the hill to the left (20min.) is the newly reconstructed **Hunding-Hütte,** another of Ludwig's flights of fancy, modeled after a scene in Wagner's *Die Walküre* from *The Ring of the Nibelung.* Bearskin-covered log benches surround an artificial tree. (Linderhof open daily 9am-12:15pm and 12:45-5:30pm; Oct.-March 10am-12:15pm and 12:45-4pm. Admission DM9, students and seniors DM6; Oct.-March DM7 and DM4 respectively.)

Buses run between Oberammergau and the park somewhat hourly (9:55am-4:55pm, last bus leaves Linderhof at 5:35pm; 20min; DM7.60 round-trip). Reach Oberammergau by bus from Schongau (50min.), Füssen (90min.), or Garmisch-Partenkirchen (40min.). A *Tagesticket* (DM13) entitles castle-hoppers to unlimited bus travel on the regional Alps buses (including the ride to Linderhof); purchase it from the bus driver. **Trains** run from Munich to Oberammergau, switching at Murnau (1¾hrs.; 10 per day; DM24).

HYPERTRAVEL TO THE CASTLES

Seeing all three of the **royal castles** *(Königsschlösser)* during a daytrip from Munich requires some fancy footwork and luck with connections (and can only be done Mon.-Fri.). Take the 6:50am train from Munich to Buchloe, and transfer here onto the 7:46am to Füssen. Arriving in Füssen at 8:57am, hop on the 9:35am bus to the *Königsschlösser.* Arriving at 9:43am, you'll have three and a half hours to fight through the lines at Hohenschwangau and Neuschwanstein before you catch bus #9651 at 1:13pm to Schloß Linderhof (changing in Steingaden and Oberammergau). Until 5:35pm you can be enthralled by the surrounding opulence, but then it'll be time to mount bus #9606 to Oberammergau Post/Bahnhof (direction: Füssen). At 5:55pm you'll get to the Oberammergau train station with time to catch the 6:07pm train to Murnau, where you'll change trains at 6:58pm and hopefully grab a *Löwen-*

bräu at 7:54pm back in Munich. Double-check your schedule with a timetable before departing. A simpler and more advisable option, particularly if you don't have a railpass, is to sign on with **EurAide, Inc.** for a charter bus ride to Neuschwanstein, Linderhof, and Weiskirche. Tours leave on Wednesdays at 7:30am from early-June to late-July. Round-trip bus trip not including castle entrance fees DM70, with railpass DM55. Reserve a day ahead at the EurAide office (see Munich: Practical Information, p. 209).

▨ Allgäu Alps

MEMMINGEN

A former imperial town and the gateway to the Allgäu region, Memmingen is generally stolid. But every four years in late July and early August, Memmingen's citizens take to the streets in a 10-day celebration of the summer of 1630, when Commander-General Albrecht von Wallenstein brought his camp to Memmingen and with it a respite from the ravages of the Thirty Years War. The next "Wallenstein-Sommer" will take place in 2000. For more information and advance tickets, contact *Sonderbüro Zollergarten* (tel. 495 065 or 495 067; fax 495 015). On the off years, the town packs 'em in—on a much smaller scale—for the smiley *Kinderfest* (children's festival; July 24 in 1997) and the jolly *Fischertag* (fisher's day; July 26 in 1997). In between these frenzies, few visitors disturb Memmingen.

Memmingen's magnificent *Marktplatz* and pedestrian zone sparkle with painted and molded façades. From the station, cross Bahnhofstr. and walk down Maximilianstr. After two blocks, take a right on the pedestrian Kramerstr. and follow it to the Marktplatz. The Rococo **Rathaus,** topped by three onion domes, overlooks the market. On the other end of the pedestrian zone at Gerberplatz stands the half-timbered **Siebendächerhaus** (Seven-Gabled House), a 17th-century tannery. To the extent that *Fachwerk* is ever magnificent, this building is. Two blocks south of the *Marktplatz,* **St. Martinskirche** (St. Martin's church; the symbol of Memmingen) rises in Gothic grandeur. Of particular interest are the carved 16th-century choir stalls (open May-Sept. daily 2:30-5pm; Oct. Sun.-Fri. 2-4pm, Sat. 10am-noon; closed Nov.-April; German tours of the tower leave Mar.-Oct. daily at 3pm; DM2). South on Frauenkirchplatz stands the eponymous **Frauenkirche** (Church of Our Lady), a 14th- and 15th-century church with an exquisite fresco cycle and dramatic vaulting over the apse. Call 22 53 for info on how to get in.

Memmingen's **tourist office,** Marktplatz 3 (tel. 85 01 72; fax 85 01 78), is across from the *Rathaus.* They have information on accommodations (DM35-65) and book rooms for free (open Mon.-Fri. 8am-noon and 2-5pm, Sat. 9:30am-12:30pm). Memmingen is connected by **train** to Augsburg (1hr.; DM20.60) and Ulm (45min.; DM14.60). The **Jugendherberge (HI),** Kempter Str. 42 (tel. 49 40 87), is easily reached from the train station (10min.). Follow Bahnhofstr. left from the station until you reach the park. Turn right into the park to walk the length of it, then cross the street; the building is next to the gate with the tower, recessed from the street. Plain six- to 10-bed rooms in a quasi-medieval building. (Reception open 8-10am and 5-10pm. Curfew 10pm. Lockout 9am-5pm. Under 27 only. DM17.50. Breakfast included. Sheets DM5.50. Open March-Nov.) **Gasthaus Lindenbad,** Lindenbadstr. 18 (tel. 32 78), offers clean, spacious rooms, but can be noisy. (Singles with sink DM35, with shower DM50. Doubles with shower and toilet DM90.) **Camping am See International,** Am Weiherhaus 7 (tel. 718 00), is quite close in Buxheim. Take the bus (direction: Buxheim) to Oben am Weiher (DM7 per person, DM6 per tent, DM11 per car). The **Familien-Ferien-Campingplatz Iller,** Illerstr. 57 (tel. (07565) 54 19), is farther out. (DM7 per person, DM9.50 per car. Open April to mid-Oct.) The **telephone code** is 08331.

OTTOBEUREN

A little town with a big church, Ottobeuren lolls lazily in the rolling alpine foothills of the Allgäu. The **Benedictine Abbey Church,** on a grassy rise in the middle of town, is about as inconspicuous as an American tourist. The largest Baroque church in Germany, its towers are 82m high, the nave 90m long, and the transept 60m wide. The façade is phenomenal—from afar. As you approach, the marvelous stonework flattens out into what turns out to be only a moderately skillful painting job. The interior, however, is dazzling even up close. Intricately molded relief-work, gilded scrolling, creamy pastel marbles, and a line of frescoed domes lead mere mortals to a high altar that takes Baroque fantasy to its insanely gaudy pinnacle. If Bad Boy Ludwig's architectural fancies disturb you, Ottobeuren's church will leave you in a muttering stupor: money, church … money … tact … worship? The four altars under the central dome each contain the complete skeleton of a saint associated with the abbey; every one is neatly dressed in ecclesiastical garments (including embroidered slippers) and artfully arranged atop velvet pillows. (Open March-Nov. daily 10am-noon and 2-5pm; Dec.-Feb. daily 2-5pm; admission to library DM3.) Organ performances are Saturdays at 4pm. Contact the tourist office for an up-to-date schedule of **concerts** taking place in the church from late-May to September—Herbert von Karajan and Leonard Bernstein conducted here.

The **tourist office** *(Kurverwaltung;* tel. 68 17; fax 68 38), on the *Marktplatz* across from the abbey, provides free maps, finds rooms (DM20-30) for no fee, and sells tickets for abbey concerts (open Mon.-Thurs. 8am-noon and 3-5pm, Fri. 9am-noon and 2-4pm; May-Sept. also open Sat. 10am-noon). To reach Ottobeuren's **Jugendherberge (HI),** Faichtmayrstr. 38 (tel. 368), from the end of the *Marktplatz* opposite the church, walk down Silachweg along the church, turn right onto Luitpoldstr. and left onto Faichtmayrstr. The hostel is four blocks down to the right (20min.). Clean, comfy eight-bed rooms. The hostel would be cramped if full, but it rarely is. (Reception open 8am-noon, 5-7pm. Under 27 only. DM15.50, DM 10.50 without breakfast. Sheets DM5.50. Open March-Oct.) Private **buses** (DM6.70 round-trip; railpasses not valid) run the 11km between Ottobeuren and Memmingen's train station. Ask at the tourist office for a map of **hiking** trails (DM6) to nearby sights and resorts. The **telephone code** is 08332.

KEMPTEN

First a Celtic settlement, then a Roman military post, the nearly 2000-year-old Kempten centers around a well-preserved *Altstadt* over-shadowed by the forested hills of the Alps. Across the street from the *Altstadt* looms the large **St. Lorenz Basilika,** built shortly after the Thirty Years War. The elegant baroque **Fürstäbtliche Residenz** (Prince Abbot's Residence) is a sizable former Benedictine cloister with colorful portals. The building has served the town as everything from barracks to law courts. Behind the Residenz stretches the terraced **Hofgarten,** webbed by paths leading to the 18th-century **Orangerie** that houses a library. (Guided tours Tues.-Sun. at 10, 11am, 2, and 3pm; Oct.-April Sat. at 2pm). To reach the town center from the distant train station, take the bus #4, 6, 8, or 9 to the "Residenz" stop (DM1.80). Klostersteige leads from the *Residenz* to the cobbled pedestrian zone.

Across from the basilica on Residenzplatz, the **Römische Sammlung Cambodunum** (Roman Museum of Kempten) and the **Naturkunde Museum** (Museum of Natural History of the Allgäu) dwell in the elegant patrician **Zumsteinhaus,** Residenzplatz 31 (tel. 450; both open Tues.-Sun. 10am-4pm; admission DM4, students and seniors DM2). Along Burgstr., a forested park contains the **Burghalde;** this, the oldest part of the city, boasts a late Roman fortification with a Gothic tower, as well as an amphitheater that features German disco stars in the summer months.

Kempten's **tourist office** (tel. 252 52 37), Rathausplatz 24 in the city center, a few blocks from Residenzplatz, provides city and hiking maps (DM3-11), accommodation listings, and 1½- to two-hour city **tours** for free. (Open May-Oct. Mon.-Fri. 8:30am-noon and 1:30-5pm, Sat. 10am-1pm; Nov.-April Mon.-Fri. 8:30am-noon and 1:30-5pm.

Tours in German every Sat. at 11am.) The **Mitfahrzentrale**, Bodmanstr. 16 (tel. 230 72 or 194 40), matches riders and drivers. Built at a bend in the Iller River, Kempten can be reached by train from Lindau and Ulm, and from Munich (70min,; 3 per hr.). The noisy **Jugendherberge (HI)**, Saarlandstr. 1 (tel. 736 63), is usually packed with school groups, but opens out onto a sweeping view of the Alps beyond the Allgäu. You'll have plenty of time to enjoy the scenery on your way there, by choosing from a number of unattractive options. From the station take bus #4, 6, 8, or 9 to "Parktheater," and then switch to bus #32 (which runs only once per hr.), getting off at "Unzfriederstr./Altersheim." Take a left at the intersection; the gray structure surrounded by a wire fence on top of the hill is the hostel. Alternatively, tighten your backpack for the hour-long trek. Take Bahnhofstr. to Schumacherring, then turn right and follow this never-ending street until you see signs for the *Jugendherberge* on the right. Or split a cab ride (DM15-20). (Reception open 5-7pm. Curfew 11pm. Under 27 only. DM17.50. Breakfast included. Sheets DM5.50. Open mid-Dec. to Oct.) To reach **Camping Oeschlesee** (tel. (08376) 621 or 82 62), take the bus from the *Altbahnhof* at Sulzberg (about 20min.; DM6) and walk to the lake (DM5 per person, DM4-7 per tent). The **telephone code** is 0831.

IMMENSTADT AND BÜHL AM ALPSEE

The small town of **Immenstadt** and the even smaller hamlet of **Bühl am Alpsee** huddle deep in the Allgäu near Kempten, a world away from the resorts to the south. Streams flowing down from the Alps feed two lakes, the **Großer Alpsee** and the **Kleiner Alpsee** (Greater and Lesser Alpine Lakes), whose cool, clear waters are unspeakably refreshing after a hike into the surrounding hilly countryside.

The Kleiner Alpsee, a 15-minute walk down Badeweg towards Bühl, offers an extensive park speckled with small, unofficial swimming holes. The Großer Alpsee has *großer* wet and wild opportunities, but certain stretches are off-limits to swimmers. Boat and windsurf-board rental on the Großer Alpsee is possible but rather expensive. Go for a dip at the **Freibad Kleiner Alpsee**, Am Kleiner Alpsee, on the other side of the lake (open daily 9am-7pm; admission DM5, students DM2.80). Immenstadt is also close to two huge skiing areas: **Alpsee Skizirkus** and **Mittag Ski-Center.** The season runs roughly from December to March. Day passes cost about DM25 in each area, while week-long passes are DM130. Chairlifts and cable cars run summer-long for the dedicated wanderers.

The friendly Immenstadt **tourist office**, Marienplatz 3 (tel. 91 41 77; fax 91 41 95; mascot: Immi), has loads of hiking maps (DM6.80-9.90) and suggested routes, many of which will land you happily at a mountain *Gaststätte* around lunchtime (open Mon.-Fri. 8:30am-noon and 2-5:30pm, Sat. 10am-noon; Nov.-May Mon.-Fri. 8:30am-noon and 2-5:30pm). From the train/bus station, turn right on Bahnhofstr. and follow it to the town square. Immenstadt can be reached by **train** from Kempten along the Munich-Zürich route, or from Ulm along the Stuttgart-Oberstdorf route.

From Immenstadt, either grab a bus or just walk (30-40min.) next door to Bühl. Bühl's **tourist office**, Seestr. 5 (tel. 914 78), has many of the same maps and brochures as its counterpart in Immenstadt, but no cute "Immi loves you all!" stickers (open Mon.-Fri. 8:30am-noon and 2-5pm, Sat. 10am-noon; Nov.-May Mon.-Fri. 8:30am-noon and 2-5:30pm). Both tourist offices find accommodations. (In Immenstadt DM25-45 per person. In Bühl DM20-30 per person. Breakfast included.) Camp directly on the Großer Alpsee at **Bucher's Camping**, Seestr. 25 (tel. 77 26 or 48 28), in Bühl. (DM5.50 per person, DM4-5 per tent, DM2 per car. Add DM1.60 *Kurtax* per person. Open Easter-early Oct.) The **telephone code** for both towns is 08323.

■ Wasserburg am Inn

On a bent bank in the Inn River between Munich and Salzburg floats Wasserburg. Medieval cobblestoned paths curl around the ancient half-island starting at the **Innbrücke** (bridge). From the train station, make a left up Im Hag and then a right on

Hoffstatt down Salzsenderzeile to penetrate the *Altstadt*. Turn right down Herren-gasse to reach the **Heimat Museum,** Herrengasse 15 (tel. 105 42). This late Gothic *Bürgerhaus* shows off Wasserburg rarities, including one of the oldest postal sleds in Bavaria (open May-Sept. Tues.-Fri. 10am-noon and 1-4pm, Sat.-Sun. 11am-3pm; Oct.-mid-Dec. and Feb.-April Tues.-Fri. 1-4pm, Sat.-Sun. 10am-noon; admission DM4, students DM3, children DM1). The late-Gothic **Rathaus,** built in 1250, is back at Salzsenderzeile; inside the **Kleiner Rathaussaal** and the **Tanzhaus** host many Wasser-burg weddings (tours Tues.-Fri. at 10, 11am, 2, 3, and 4pm, Sat.-Sun. 10 and 11am; DM1.50, children DM0.50). The **Erstes Imaginäres Museum,** on Marienplatz, around the corner from the *Rathaus* at the foot of the bridge, is a private and eclectic collec-tion of German Old Masters, French Impressionists, and primitive and pop art. Recog-nize them? Every single one of these famous works is a painstakingly produced copy. (Open May-Sept. Tues.-Sun. 11am-5pm; Oct.-April Tues.-Sun. 1-5pm. Admission DM3, students and seniors DM2, under 16 DM1. A combined ticket for the Heimat Museum, the *Rathaus* rooms, and the Erstes Imaginäres Museum is available for DM5, students DM4, children DM2.)

Wasserburg can be reached by **train** from Munich (8 per day; 2hr.). The **tourist office** in the *Rathaus* (tel. 105 22) offers free maps and lists of rooms (DM20-30 per person) for rent (open May-Sept. 9am-12:30pm and 3:30-5:30pm; Oct.-April 9am-12:30pm). Daily **boat** trips paddle around starting at the Innbrücke. (40min. trip at 2pm, DM10; 90min. trip at 11am and 3pm, DM16; 2-hr. trip Tues. and Fri. at 7pm, DM20; children under 15 50% off, under 6 free.) Rent a **bike** from the tourist office or a **boat** to navigate to Soyen. **Badria,** Wasserburg's amazing recreation center, comes complete with outdoor and indoor swimming pools, the largest water slide in Ger-many, miniature golf, saunas, solariums, and bowling. To get there from the train sta-tion, take the Wasserburg city bus to "Badria." (Open Mon.-Fri. 10am-9pm, Sat.-Sun. 8:30am-7pm. Admission DM12, students and under 17 DM7.50, under 7 free.) The **telephone code** is 08071.

The nearest **Jugendherberge,** at Schillinger Str. 1 in Ebersberg (tel. (08092) 225 23), is 30 to 40 minutes away by train or bus. (Under 27 only. DM15.50. Breakfast included. Sheets DM5.50). The closest **camping** is 6km away in Soyen at **Werner Huthm,** Soyen am See (tel. 38 60), a manageable walk (open April-mid-Oct.). **Gasthof Huber am Kellerberg,** Salzburger Str. 25 (tel. 74 33), across the Innbrücke, is a sim-ple but affordable motel on the hill overlooking the town. Cross the Innbrücke from Marienplatz and take the steps up to Kellerbergweg on the left just before the gas sta-tion. Follow this footpath up the hill to the motel. (Singles DM37. Doubles DM63, with shower DM90. Breakfast included.) The **Brasserie im Stechl Keller,** Marienplatz 6 (tel. 56 53), serves a delicious *gulasch* soup (DM5) as well as beer (DM4.20 for 0.5L) and other tasty meals (DM9-18; open daily 10am-11pm).

▨ Bad Reichenhall

In Bad Reichenhall, it is considered normal to sit in front of a salt water fountain daily, cover oneself in mud, and then inhale oxygen from an intimidating apparatus. Whether or not you're here for a massage and some mud, Bad Reichenhall ("rich in salt"), famous for its "White Gold" salt deposits, is a sight. Because of its proximity to Austria, the Viennese and Salzburgian influences are strong in the architecture, dia-lect, and gastronomy. The **Salz Museum,** Alte Saline (tel. 70 02 51), travels into the 16th-century salty underworld, peppered (sorry) with exhibits of the history and pro-cess of salt-making in the area. The obligatory tour in German winds through the damp underground passageways where brine (salt water) is pumped out of the mountain (tours April-Oct. daily 10am-11:30am and 2-4pm; Nov.-March Tues. and Thurs. 2-4pm; last tour at 3pm; admission DM7.50, students DM3.50, families DM18.50). At the associated **Glashütte** (tel. 697 38), you can experience the beauty of glass-making and glass-buying (tours Mon.-Fri. 9:30am-6pm, Sat. 9am-1pm). The **Glasofenwirtshaus** hosts a musical *Weißwurstfrühschoppen* (a Bavarian practice of getting plastered in the morning) every Saturday 9am-1pm (restaurant open Mon.-Fri. 9:30am-6pm, Sat. 9am-1pm).

Walk right from the Alte Saline on Salinenstr. until it becomes Ludwigstr. On the left, in the palatial 1870 **Kurgarten** (spa garden), the *Altes Kurhaus* offers a therapeutic blue theater, restful music pavilion, and rejuvenating chess set. At the salt spring fountain, buy a *Becher* (cup) to drink from the *Trinksole* fountain (DM0.30; open Mon.-Sat. 8am-12:30pm and 3-5pm, Sun. 10am-12:30pm). The **Gradierwerk** out front is a bizarre wall known as an "open air inhalatorium." Built in 1912, it's covered with *"Dornbündel"* (branches, briars, and thorns) through which mist trickles from April to October. For best results, sit and inhale for 30 minutes. (Garden open April-Oct. 7am-10pm; Nov.-March 7am-6pm. Free except for 1-1½hr. long concerts. Concerts April-Oct. Tues. at 4 and 8pm, Wed. at 4pm, Thurs. at 8pm, Fri. and Sat. at 4pm, Sun. at 10:45am and 4pm.)

The **Predigstuhl** is the oldest cable car of its kind in the world (1928), running up 1583m of skier's paradise. In the summer you can hike the *Höhenkurweg* trail to the *Almhütte* resthouse. (Cable car runs 1 per hour May-Sept. 9am-9pm; Sept.-April 9am-5pm. Round-trip DM24, under 16 DM16, under 6 free; one-way DM15, under 16 DM10. Dogs DM8-10. Family cards available. For info call 21 27 or fax 43 84; weather info tel. 17 19). The **tourist office** *(Kurgastzentrum)*, Wittelsbacherstr. 15 (tel. 30 03; fax 24 27), is uphill to the right on the same road as the station. They provide maps, hiking advice (mountain tours and up to 500km hikes), guest information, and tips on discounts with the *Kurkarte* (open Mon.-Fri. 8am-5:30pm, Sat. 9am-noon). From the tourist office, cross Wittelsbacherstr. over to Kurstr. to the main pedestrian zone (leading up on the right) or to the lush *Kurgarten* and *Kurhaus* on the left. **Trains** run hourly to Munich (2hr.) and Salzburg (40min.) with a change in Freilassing. Rent a **bike** at **Sport Müller,** Spitalgasse 3 (tel. 37 76; fax 69 511), for DM12 for half a day, DM15 for a whole day (open Mon.-Fri. 9am-1pm, 2:30-6pm; Sat. 9am-12:30pm). Call **Club Aktiv** (tel. 67 238) to go **rafting** or **canyoning**. The **post office**, 83435 Bad Reichenhall, is on Rathausplatz (open Mon.-Fri. 8am-noon and 2-6pm, Sat. 8am-noon). The **telephone code** is 08651.

There is no *Jugendherberge* in Bad Reichenhall and hotels are expensive (DM40-150). **Private rooms** usually go for DM20-40 per person (breakfast included). Along the pedestrian zones of Salzburger and Ludwigstr. you'll find endless cafés, where you can try delectable *Mozart Kugeln* (marzipan/chocolate balls) and *Torte mit Sahne.* At **Gasthof Bürgerbräu**, on Rathausplatz (tel. 60 89), traditionally dressed waiters serve the local beer direct from the in-house brewery (DM4.50 for 0.5L). Bavarian dishes run DM11-17 (open daily 11am-11pm, Fri.-Sun. dancing after 7pm). **Restaurant Fuchsbau,** Innsbrucker Str. 19, serves pizza and Bavarian meals (DM12-20) to a hip crowd (open Tues.-Sun. 7pm-3am). For basics, head to **HL Markt,** Bahnhofstr. 20, to the right of the station (open Mon.-Fri. 8am-6pm, Sat. 7:30am-1pm).

■ The Chiemsee

For almost 2000 years, artists, architects, and musicians have chosen the Chiemsee (KEEM-zay, or Lake Chiem) as the setting for their artistic masterpieces. With its picturesque islands, meadows, pastures, forests, marshland, and dramatic crescent of mountains, the region first lured the 9th-century builders of the cloisters on **Frauen-insel,** and later the wobbly King Ludwig II, who built **Herrenchiemsee,** his third and last "fairy-tale castle," on the Herreninsel. The poet Maximilian Haushofer lived and died on the Chiemsee shores in **Prien** (see p. 245), and 11-year-old Mozart composed a mass in Seeon while on holiday. Most modern visitors to "The Bavarian Ocean" (approximately 32sq.mi.) are artists of leisure; the area has been overrun by resorts and prices have risen. But don't expect to find very many foreigners: Chiemsee is where the *nouveaux riches* of Munich and Northern Germany vacation. Summer weekends are sheer madness. Prien, the largest lake town, offers easy access to ski areas in the **Kampenwand,** the surrounding curtain of mountains, and resort paradises in **Aschau** and **Sachrang.** For information on white-water **rafting**, call (08649)

243. The **Trachtenfest,** with parades, folklore, and pilgrimages, takes place each year in a different town on the last Sunday in July.

HERRENINSEL AND FRAUENINSEL

The Chiemsee's three islands claim the majority of the regions tourist bustle. Ferries wade the waters of the Chiemsee from the port in Prien to the **Herreninsel** (Gentlemen's Island), the **Fraueninsel** (Ladies' Island), and towns on the other side of the lake. Both islands are co-ed, although this wasn't always the case: there was once a monastery on Herreninsel complementing the still-extant nunnery on Fraueninsel. Supposedly, mischievous members of the cloth (of both sexes) met up on *Krautinsel* (Vegetable Island) and practiced the eyebrow raising act of gardening; nowadays, the island remains uninhabited and unferried. (Round-trip to Herreninsel DM9, to Fraueninsel or to both islands DM11.) To get to the dock, hang a right from the Prien train station's main entrance and follow Seestr. (the major thoroughfare on the right) for about 20 minutes. Alternatively, a slow 19th-century **green steam train** takes visitors from the train station to the dock every 20 minutes. "I think I can, I think I can." To get there, take the underpass from platform 1 to the other side, or look for the huge *Chiemseebahn* sign. (One-way DM3; round-trip DM5. Total package, including train shuttle and ship passage, DM16.) The train station **information booth,** though central, has very limited hours (open July-mid-Sept. Mon.-Fri.12:45-5pm). Be sure to read the schedules to avoid getting stranded.

Schloß Herrenchiemsee

"Never can as unsuitable a location have been chosen for something as tasteless as this unfortunate copy of the palace at Versailles," Bavarian poet Ludwig Thomas pouted. Once on Herreninsel, either walk along the paved footpath to the palace (20min.) or take one of the horse-drawn carriages that run every 15 minutes (DM4, children DM3). The architecture of **Königsschloß Herrenchiemsee** (Herrenchiemsee Royal Palace; tel. 30 69) is fabulously overwrought as only King Ludwig II could manage. The entire U-shaped palace (70 rooms, less than one-fifth of which were ever completed) is a shameless attempt to be larger, better, and more expensive than Versailles, the abode of France's Louis XIV. Ludwig II was so obsessed with the "Sun King" that he commissioned exact replicas of French originals to grace the walls of his palace. Surprisingly, not a single image of Ludwig is to be found inside, though a tiny bust of him cowers in the far back of the grounds. There's even a **Hall of Mirrors,** only Ludwig's is longer than Louis'. Candle-lit concerts are hosted here throughout the summer. To build the palace, Ludwig bankrupted Bavaria, was declared insane, deposed, and promptly drowned—having spent only 10 days in the humble abode. (Open April-Sept. daily 9am-5pm; Oct.-March 10am-4pm. Admission and required guided tour DM7, seniors, students, and disabled persons DM4, under 16 free with adult. German tours every 10min.; English tours at 10:30, 11:30am, 2, and 3pm.) For Herrenchiemsee **tourist information,** call (08051) 30 69.

Fraueninsel

Fraueninsel offers subtler pleasures. It's a small world with no room for cars; only footpaths wander this village of fishermen and nuns. From the boat dock, a marked path meanders toward the island cloister, passing its medicinal herb garden. The nuns also make their own *Marzipan* and liqueurs, for sale in the convent shop. The abbey dates back to at least 866. St. Irmengard, the great-granddaughter of Charlemagne and earliest known abbess of the cloister, has a **memorial chapel** in her honor behind the main altar of the cloister church. Her sarcophagus was exhumed in the 17th century, and her remains have been encased in glass within the altar since 1928. They're not very interesting, but that's what 1000 years will do to you. The **Torhalle** (gate) is the oldest surviving part of the cloister. Various artifacts, including the 8th-century Merovingian **Cross of Bischofhofen,** are displayed in the room above the gate (open Mon.-Sat. 11am-6pm; mid-June-Sept. daily 11am-6pm; admission DM3, students

DM1.50.). The entire island can be circumnavigated on foot in 35 to 45 minutes. For **tourist information** call (08054) 511 or 603; fax 12 72.

PRIEN AM CHIEMSEE

Without question, the best thing about Prien is its idyllic Chiemsee coast and its frequented train station; use the town as a base for the real sights elsewhere on the lake. If lugging around heavy packs is getting you down, wade in the cold water of Prien's *Kneipp Water Cure* and then jump into a 90°F thermal bath—it works wonders for some famous German soccer players.

The train station is a few blocks from the city center and a 20-minute walk north of the lake. To reach the *Altstadt,* walk northeast to Seestr. (the station exit faces north) past the four-way intersection; Seestr. will become Alte Rathausstr. The large, modern **tourist office,** Alte Rathausstr. 11 (tel. 690 50 or 69 05 55; fax 69 05 40), 5 minutes up Alte Rathausstr. on the left, is full of free maps and English brochures. The tourist office finds rooms (DM20-40 with breakfast) in private houses for free (open Mon.-Fri. 8:30am-6pm, Sat. 9am-noon). If the **information booth** (tel. 690 50) at the train station is closed (open July-Sept. Mon.-Fri. 12:45-5pm), head out the main exit to find a city map 10 paces to your right. Located on the northwestern corner of the Chiemsee, Prien has a convenient and direct **train** link to Munich (1 per hr.; 1hr.) and Salzburg, Austria (1-2 per hr.; 1hr.). Call 28 74 for train information. You can rent a **bike** (tel. 28 74) at the train station for DM13-17; otherwise, try **Radsport Reischonböck,** Hochriesstr. 17 (tel. 46 31). To paddle the Chiemsee, rent a **boat** from **Schaber,** Harrasser Str. 143 (tel. 45 75 or 18 95). Phone 10 37 to find out which **pharmacy** is open on any single night. The **telephone code** is 08051.

The cheapest bed in town is at the raucous **Jugendherberge (HI),** Carl-Braun-Str. 66 (tel. 29 72; fax 634 85), a 15-minute walk from the station and 10 minutes from the lake. From the station, go right on Seestr. and under the train overpass. After two blocks, take a left on Staudenstr., which curves right and turns into Carl-Braun-Str. (Reception open 8-9am, 5-7pm, and 9:30-10pm. Outside these hours, reserve a bed through the box at the entrance. 6-bed rooms. Lockout 9am-1pm. Curfew 10pm. Under 27 only. DM19 plus DM0.80 resort tax. Showers, lockers, and breakfast included. Sheets DM5.50. Open Jan.-Oct.) There is a campground, **Campingplatz Hofbauer,** at Bernauer Str. 110 (tel. 41 36; fax 626 57), just outside of town. Walk right from the station, turn left at Seestr., and left again at the next intersection, and follow Bernauer Str. out of town (DM8.20 per person, DM9 per tent and car). Most of the restaurants in Prien cater to the vacationing bourgeoisie. Try **Scherer SB Restaurant,** Alte Rathausstr. 1 (tel. 45 91), on the corner of Alte Rathausstr. and Bernauer Str. This self-serve restaurant cooks up hearty meals and filling salads (DM5-15; open Mon.-Fri. 8am-8pm, Sat. 8am-3pm). Gather groceries from **HL Markt,** Seestr. 11, to the right and under the tracks from the station (open Mon.-Fri. 8am-6pm, Sat. 7:30am-1pm).

ELSEWHERE NEAR THE CHIEMSEE

While Prien is considered the "metropolis of the Bavarian sea," endless idyllic towns melt into the landscape, offering resort luxuries, nature rambles, and historical attractions galore. **Grabenstätt** basks in a nature reserve and bird sanctuary, proffering walking and cycling paths. Call **Verkehrsamt Grabenstätt** for info (tel. (08661) 98 87 31; fax 98 87 40). Little villages curl up at the foothills of the mountains: **Grassau Verkehrsamt** (tel. (08641) 23 40; fax 40 08 41), **Rimsting Verkehrsamt** (tel. (08051) 44 61; fax 616 94), and **Riedering Verkehrsamt** (tel. (08036) 34 48; fax 37 58) can supply more info. **Rottau,** just south of the Chiemsee, nestles in a mountain ridge; call its **Verkehrsamt,** at Grassauer Str. 9 (tel. (08641) 27 73; fax 14 19).

Sachrang is an exquisite Alpine village on the Tyrolean border. For excellent skiing, mountain climbing, and walking tours, call **Sachrang Verkehrsamt,** Dorfstr. 20 (tel. (08057) 378; fax 10 51; open Mon.-Tues., and Thurs.-Fri. 8am-noon and 2-5pm, Wed. 8am-noon, Sat. 9am-noon). **Aschau** lies near Sachrang, with skiing and hiking trails connecting the two. The panorama is perfect, and the town touts solariums, tobogganing, sailing, and skiing. The **tourist office** is located at Kampenwandstr. 38 (tel. (08052) 90 49 37; fax 47 17; open Mon.-Fri. 8am-noon and 2-6pm, Sat. 9am-noon; Oct.-Dec. Mon.-Fri. 8am-noon and 2-5pm; Jan.-April Mon.-Fri. 8am-noon and 2-5pm, Sat. 9am-noon). Aschau and Sachrang are easily reached by **train** from the Munich-Salzburg route; at Prien, switch to trains headed for your destination (2hr.). **Buses** link Aschau to Munich. Affordable **accommodations,** like bungalows and vacation homes, run DM20-40 per person.

■ Burghausen

Separated from Austria only by the Salzach River, the town of Burghausen is domi-nated by the proverbial castle-on-the-hill—in this case, the longest medieval fortress in Europe. Built in the 13th century, the 1034-m **Schloß** was considered impregna-ble—and indeed, it was only breached once. In 1742, the Habsburg Empire, eager to extend its borders into Bavaria, fell upon the border town of Burghausen. Cowed by the Austrian show of arms and lacking outside reinforcements, Burghausen opened its gates without a fight. Days later, on October 16, 1742, came Burghausen's moment of glory: the brash 26-year-old *Hofkaminkehrermeister* (Master Chimney Sweep) Karl Franz Cura recruited 40 grenadiers for the seemingly impossible task of breaking through the castle walls. In one fell swoop, Cura brilliantly freed the castle and the city. Until the Habsburgs return, Burghausen will remain a medieval gem akin to Heidelberg and Rothenburg but much less trafficked.

Stepping off the train, you'll find yourself smack in the middle of suburbia. Don't panic. Walk directly to your left through the parking lot (100m) to reach the street Marktler Str. Follow it to the right (taking the left fork 400m from the station to remain on Marktler Str.); it's a 30-minute hike to the *Altstadt* at Stadtplatz. Or you can opt to take the bus on Marktlerstr. around the corner of the train station (every 30min. 8:12am-7:12pm; fewer on weekends). It's four stops to "Stadtplatz" (DM2).

These days, the **castle** ramparts can be walked without violent reprisals, and the upper halls contain the town's **historical museum** (tel. 651 98). For the price of a punishing climb up the steep footpath, the castle also offers a ravishing view of the *Altstadt*'s roofs of red tiles and colorful gables. The footpath starts near the 1140 **St. Jakob's Kirche** across from the *Rathaus.* (Castle open Mon.-Fri. 9am-noon and 1-5pm; Oct.-March 9am-noon and 1-4pm. Museum open daily May-Sept. 9am-6:30pm; mid-March-April and Oct.-Nov. daily 10am-4:30pm. Admission DM4, students DM2.) The *Burg* also houses the town's **Photo Museum** (tel. 47 34), tracing the historical development of the camera (open April-Oct. Wed.-Sun. 10am-6pm). The castle's old **torture chamber** (tel. 615 34) was used until 1918 (open mid-March-Oct. daily 9am-6pm; Nov.-mid-March Sat.-Sun. 9am-6pm). The **Hexenturm** across the way impris-oned many accused witches until the last trial in 1751. Below the castle, the **Stadt-platz** shimmers with such glossy medieval splendor you half expect a film crew to emerge from the rows of pastel façades. At the far end of the Stadtplatz is the magnif-icent Baroque **Studienkirche St. Joseph,** a 1630 Jesuit convent.

The **tourist office** *(Fremdenverkehrsamt),* Stadtplatz 112-114 (tel. 24 35; fax 88 71 55), is located in the peppermint green façaded **Rathaus** at the far end of the Stadt-platz. On the ground floor are free maps, brochures, and information on tours of the town area (open Mon.-Wed. 7:30am-noon and 1:30-5pm, Thurs. 7:30am-noon and 1:30-6pm, Fri. 7:30am-noon). Burghausen is most easily reached by **train** from Munich (1 per hr. until 7:30pm; 2hr.; change at Mühldorf), though **buses** run from Mühldorf, the transportation hub for eastern Bavaria. For a **taxi** call 22 33. To rent a **bike,** try either **Werner Radauer,** Robert-Koch-Str. 75 (tel. 73 34), or **Bikeworld Hit-zler,** Pettenkoferstr. 37 (tel. 91 13 42). To your left as you exit the *Rathaus* is an arch-way that opens onto a narrow cobblestone street called In den Grüben; the **post office,** 162 In den Grüben, 84489 Burghausen (tel. 45 80), is one block down on the left (open Mon.-Fri. 10-11:45am and 2:30-5pm). To **exchange currency,** try the other post office on R.-Koch-Str. (same hours), which also houses the one international **telephone.** The **telephone code** is 08677.

The **Jugendherberge Burghausen (HI)**, Kapuzinergasse 235 (tel. 41 87; fax 91 13 18) is a schlepp from the train station but close to the heavily café-ed In den Grüben. From the station, take the city bus at Marktler Str. through Stadtplatz to the "Hl.-Geist-Spital" stop, walk ahead, and take a left onto Kapuzinergasse. Or follow the above directions to Stadtplatz and continue through the arch at the far side of the square onto In den Grüben. At the end, cross the intersection to the left of the church onto Spitalgasse and turn right onto Kapuzinergasse. (45min. from the station. Reception open Mon.-Fri. 8-10am and 5-7pm, Sat.-Sun. 8-9am and 5-7pm. Under 27 only. DM18, Breakfast included. Sheets DM5.50.) The tourist office can help find quieter accommodations for no fee; *Pensionen* and *Gasthöfe* in Burghausen start at DM30, breakfast included. If you're after Bavarian dishes, try **Hotel Post,** Stadtplatz 39 (tel. 30 43). After 450 years, it knows its *Würstchen* (most meals DM13.50-18, beer DM4). Ask the manager about Franz Cura's scuffle with the Austrians in the very same inn. Head to Austria for a *Mozart Kugel* and *Torte.* Follow Bruckgasse from the middle of Stadtplatz over the Alte Brücke spanning the Salzach River (2min.). Buy supplies at the **Edeka Markt,** In den Grüben, across from the post office (open Mon.-Fri. 8:15am-12:30pm and 2-6pm, Sat. 7am-noon).

▓ Passau

Strategic location is the key phrase of Passau's 2000-year history; poised on the two peninsulas forged by the confluence of the Danube, Inn, and Ilz Rivers, the *"Drei-flüssestadt"* (3-river city) embodies the ideal Old World city. As early as 80AD Roman generals fancied the powerful bluff overlooking the modern Austrian-German border, and the church followed suit in 739 by establishing Passau as the seat of a diocese. A few centuries later local merchants monopolized the central European salt trade—an impressive feat, considering Passau lacked any natural resourses. The castle, palaces, and monasteries all bear witness to Passau's past as a center of administrative, commercial, and religious power. Its Baroque cathedral, the *Stephansdom,* was the mother church that founded the *Stephansdom* in Vienna. In the 12th century, Wolfger, the bishop of Passau, supervised the recording of the epic *Nibelungenlied* on parchment, thus establishing Passau in the minds of once and future tourism boards as the *Nibelungenstadt.* Today the great hall of Passau's *Rathaus* contains extravagant frescoes depicting scenes from the epic.

ORIENTATION AND PRACTICAL INFORMATION

Close to the Austrian border, Passau is directly accessible by rail from both Munich and Vienna. Buses duplicate most rail routes and are often less expensive, but they can nearly double the travel time. Passau proper is located almost entirely on the peninsula formed by the Danube (*Donau* in German) and the Inn. The adjacent peninsula between the Danube and the Ilz is home to the local *Schloß.* Together they contain most places of interest to the *Altstadt*-minded traveler. For the scenic route to the *Altstadt* from the train station, turn right and follow the *Jugendherberge* signs; they will take you right past the *Rathaus* along the banks of the Danube. More directly, follow Bahnhofstr. to the right until you reach Ludwigsplatz. Walk downhill across Ludwigsplatz to Ludwigstr., the beginning of the pedestrian zone, which becomes Rindermarkt, Steinweg, and finally Große Messergasse. After the fountain-bedecked *Residenzplatz,* turn left down Schrottgass, and the tourist office will be on your left on the riverbank. For the *Altstadt,* continue straight on Schustergasse from Große Messergasse. Or catch a little blue **City-Bus** to the right of the station; for DM0.50 it will take you around Passau.

Tourist Office: Tourist Information, Rathausplatz 3 (tel. 572 98 or 95 59 80; fax 351 07). On the banks of the Danube next to the *Rathaus* (see directions above). Healthy assortment of free maps, brochures, schedules, and tour information.

Room-finding service DM2.50 per person; also provides information on cheaper hotels and *Pensionen* in the surrounding area. Ask for *Aktuell,* a free monthly guide to everything going down in Passau. An **automat** in front of the tourist office gives maps and a brochure for DM1. Open April-Oct. Mon.-Fri. 8:30am-6pm, Sat.-Sun. 10am-2pm; Nov.-March Mon.-Thurs. 8:30am-5pm, Fri. 8:30am-4pm. There's also a branch to the left of the train station called **Infostelle Passau/ Oberösterreich,** Bahnhofstr. 36 (tel. 955 80; fax 572 98). Open mid-Oct.-Easter Mon.-Thurs. 9am-5pm, Fri. 9am-4pm. Sat.-Sun. 10am-2pm.

Tours: German-language walking tours of the city meet at the *Königsdenkmal* (monument) in front of the church at *Domplatz.* April-Oct. Mon.-Fri. at 10:30am and 2:30pm, Sat.-Sun. at 2:30pm (1hr.; DM3.50, children DM2).

Budget Travel: ITO Reise, Bahnhofstr. 28 (tel. 540 48), across the street from the train station in the *Donau Passage,* a mall-type establishment. Open Mon.-Fri. 8am-6pm, Sat. 9am-noon.

Currency Exchange: At the **post office** next door to the train station (see hours below). Or try **Deutsche Bank,** on Ludwigsplatz. Open Mon. and Wed. 8:30am-noon and 1:30-3:30pm, Tues. and Fri. 8:30am-noon and 1:30-4pm, Thurs. 8:30am-noon and 1:30-6pm.

Telephones: In the post office, in front of the *Rathaus,* and next to the youth hostel. All are international phone booths. Beware the outrageous credit card bill.

Trains: Station located west of downtown on Bahnhofstr. (tel. 194 19). Trains to Regensburg (1 per hr.; 1hr.), Nuremberg (every 2hr.; 2hr.), Munich (1 per hr.; 2-3hr.) and Vienna (6 per day; 3¼hr.).

Buses: To various towns on the outskirts of Passau and a number of stops within the city (DM4-7). For schedules call 56 02 72. The little **City-Bus** runs from the train station to the *Rathaus* every 15min., Mon.-Fri. 6:30am-6:30pm (DM0.50).

Ferries: Danube steamers cruise to **Linz,** Austria, from late-April-mid-Oct. daily at 9am (5hrs). To get there and back in one day, take the morning steamer to Linz and return to Passau by bus or train in the afternoon (round-trip DM42 if by bus; DM44 if by train). Or stay overnight in Linz and return with the steamer the next day at 2:15pm (round-trip DM36). The "Three Rivers" Tour of the city runs daily from March to early Nov. about every 20-30min. 10am-5pm (45min.; DM10, under 15 DM5). All ships depart from the docks along the Fritz-Schäffer-Promenade in front of the *Rathaus.* Call 92 92 92 or fax 355 18 for more info.

Bike Rental: Fahrrad König, Lindental 5 (tel. 343 88). DM20 per day with ID. Repairs bikes too. Open 24 hr. The stunning **Donau Radweg** (bike path) begins in Donaueschingen and continues into Austria, passing through Passau; ask at the tourist office for information.

Laundromat: Rent-Wash, Neuburger Str. 19. From Ludwigsplatz, walk up Dr.-Hans-Kapfinger-Str. and bear left on Neuburger Str. Wash DM6. Dry DM2. Detergent DM1. Fabric softener DM0.30. Open daily 7am-midnight.

Pharmacy: 24-hr. service rotates among the city's pharmacies; check the listings in the notices section of the daily newspapers, either the *Tagespresse* or the *Passauer Neue Presse,* or in the window of **Bahnhof Apotheke,** on Bahnhofstr., just to the right of the station across from Woolworth's. Open Mon.-Fri. 8am-6pm, Sat. 8am-noon (the pharmacy, not the Woolworth's).

Hospital: Klinikum Passau, Bischof-Pilgrim-Str. 1 (tel. 530 00).

Emergency: tel. 110. **Police:** Nibelungenstr. 17 (tel. 112).

Post Office: on Bahnhofstr., 94032 Passau (tel. 50 50), to the right of the train station. Also offers **banking** services: changes money and cashes traveler's checks for DM6 per check. Open Mon.-Fri. 8am-6pm, Sat. 8am-noon. Extra window open Mon.-Fri. 7am-6:30pm.

Telephone Code: 0851.

ACCOMMODATIONS AND CAMPING

Passau's numerous *Pensionen* and cheaper hotels fill up during the summer thanks to travelers from both East and West. Most pensions run DM30-60, while vacation houses (2-6 beds) run DM30-75. The only youth hostel in town is often full of German schoolchildren (especially during June and July).

Jugendherberge (HI), Veste Oberhaus 125, 94034 Passau (tel. 413 51; fax 437 09), in the castle on the mountain across the Danube (but no view of the city), 35-45min. from the train station and 20-30min. from the *Rathaus*. Cross the suspension bridge downstream from the *Rathaus* and climb up the steps to the castle trail. The uphill trek is definitely not fun with (or without) a heavy backpack, and the trail is not lit at night. Try to catch the shuttle ("Pendelverkehr") from Rathausplatz to the front door (Easter-mid-Oct. Tues.-Sun. every 30 min. 11:30am-5pm; DM3). Cramped rooms. Reception open 7-11:30am and 4-11:30pm. New arrivals after 6pm only. Curfew 11:30pm. DM15.50. Sheets DM5.50. Breakfast included. Reservations recommended.

Rotel Inn, 94012 Passau (tel. 951 60; fax 951 61 00). Go through the tunnel in front of the train station toward the blue head of this bizarrely bright hotel. Built in 1993 in the shape of a sleeping man and bedecked in primary-colored plastics, this self-proclaimed "Hotel of the Future" packs travelers into tight accommodations reminiscent of a cruise ship from the late 80s. For these prices, it's hard to complain, and besides, everyone gets a porthole view of a rather bland section of the Danube. Reception open 24hr. Singles DM30. Doubles DM60. Separate but private bathrooms off the hall. Breakfast DM8.

Gasthof Zum Hirschen, Im Ort 6 (tel. 362 38). From the *Rathaus*, walk downstream along the banks of the Danube as far as possible, then turn right. Threadbare, clean rooms with comfortable beds. Lovely and quiet location on a cobblestone street on the *Donau*. Check-out 11am. Singles DM30. Doubles DM60, with shower DM70. Breakfast included. Reservations recommended.

Pension Rößner, Bräugasse 19 (tel. 93 13 50, fax 931 35 55). Right on the Danube, these homey rooms are some of the cheapest accomodations in the *Altstadt*. From the *Rathaus,* walk downstream along the Danube. Singles DM60-85, doubles DM80-100. All rooms come with shower and toilet. Breakfast included too.

Gasthof Pension Zur Brücke, Hans-Landrichter-Str. 13 (tel. 434 75). 1hr. north of town, but a nice hike. Best for bikers. Follow directions for camping (below) but *don't* bear right at the "Kahn/Camping" sign; instead, take the left fork and follow it until you come to a small square. Turn right, walk/pedal across the bridge (hence the pension's name), head right and up the hill, and it's on your right. Singles DM30, with shower and toilet DM35. Doubles DM54, with shower and toilet DM64. Add DM5 for 1-night stays. Booking in advance by phone is a must.

Camping: Zeltplatz der Faltbootabteilung, Halser Str. 34, 94034 Passau (tel. 414 57). Downhill from the youth hostel, 10min. from the *Rathaus*. Cross the Luitpold bridge to the castle side, follow Angerstr. to the right, walk left through the tunnel onto F.-Wagner-Str., veer left up the hill, and take the right fork at the "Kahn/Camping" sign. Or take bus #1-4 from Exerzierplatz. Reception open 8-10am and 3-10pm. DM9. Under 17 DM7. Under 6 free. Shower included. No camping vehicles. Open May-Oct.

FOOD AND NIGHTLIFE

If you're searching out the student scene, you should head to **Innstraße** near the university. From Ludwigsplatz, head down Nikolastraße and turn right on Innstr., which runs parallel to the Inn River. The street is lined with good, cheap places to eat and, more importantly, drink—the night-time action kicks off as early as 7pm.

Mensa, Innstr. 29, is complete with cafeteria meals (DM3.50-7). Most student IDs will do. From Ludwigsplatz, follow Nikolastr., turn right onto Innstr., head under the bridge, and at #29 take the stairs up alongside and turn right. The *Mensa* is the farthest entrance on the left (15min.). Or take bus #3 to "Universität" (every 20min. from Exerzierplatz). Open Mon.-Thurs. 11:15am-2pm and 5:15-6:30pm, Fri. 11:15am-2pm and 5-6pm. When school's not in session (July-Aug.) open Mon.-Thurs. 11:30am-1:30pm and 5-6pm, Fri. 11:15am-3pm. A smaller **cafeteria** with snacks is open Mon.-Thurs. 8:30am-4pm, Fri. 8:30am-3pm.

Innsteg, on Innstr (tel. 355 03), is 1 block from Nikolastr. and popular with students from morning 'til nite. Nurse a beer (DM4-8) on the balcony over the riverbank. Daily menu DM10.80-16.80. Salads DM6. Open daily 10am-1am.

BAVARIA (BAYERN)

Café Duft, Theresienstr. 22. Folky indoor and outdoor café with little lighted trees and an aquatic theme. Yummy fruit-topped muselix DM3; other breakfast items DM4-18. Soups DM5. Salads DM10. Entrees DM9-12.50. Open Mon.-Fri. 9am-1am, Sat.-Sun. and holidays 10am-1am. Kitchen open until 11pm.

Café Kowalski, Gottfried-Schäffer-Str. (tel. 350 96, fax 353 02), near the Innbrücke. Good-lookers chow down on the 2nd-floor balcony or in the dark café. Mega-burger with fries DM8.50. Tomato soup (DM4), salads (DM7.40-11), and steaks (DM12-16). Thurs. is grill night. Beer DM3.80-4. Open daily 10am-1am.

Gasthof Bayer Löwe, Dr. Hans Kapfinger Str 3 (tel. 512 74). Authentic—or at least that's what the waves of tourists seem to think. For big German food and appetites, try *Schwein Bratwurstl auf Sauerkraut* (sausages and kraut; DM6) and *Leberknödel auf Sauerkraut und Salzkartoffeln* (dumplings, spuds, and yes, kraut; DM13). Lighter dishes range DM6-9. Beer DM3.70. Open daily 9am-midnight.

Camera, on Frauengasse, around the corner from the McDonald's on Ludwigsplatz, is the city center's grooviest student dance lair. Open 10pm-2am.

SIGHTS

Passau's beautiful Baroque architecture strikes its zenith in the sublime **Stephansdom** (St. Stephen's Cathedral). Hundreds of cherubs are sprawled across the ceiling, and the **world's largest church organ** looms above the choir. Its 17,774 pipes can accommodate five organists at once (Cathedral open Mon.-Sat. 8-11am and 12:30-6pm. Free. Organ concerts May-Oct. Mon.-Sat. at noon: DM4, students and seniors DM2; Thurs. at 7:30pm: DM10, students and seniors DM5; no concerts on holidays.) Behind the cathedral is the **Residenzplatz,** lined with former patrician dwellings, as well as the **Residenz,** erstwhile home of Passau's bishops. The **Domschatz** (cathedral treasury) within the *Residenz* houses an extravagant collection of gold and tapestries purchased by the bishops with the wealth they tithed from their flocks. (Open May-Oct., Christmas-early Jan., and the week after Easter Mon.-Sat. 10am-4pm. Admission DM2, children DM1.)

Nearby stands the Baroque church of **St. Michael,** built and gilded by the Jesuits (open Tues.-Sun. 9am-5pm; Nov.-Jan. and March 10am-4pm; admission DM3, students DM1.50). The less opulent, 13th-century Gothic **Rathaus** was appropriated from a wealthy merchant in 1298 to house the city government. (Great Hall of *Rathaus* open Easter-May 15 10am-4pm; May 16-Sept. 30 10am-5pm; Oct. Mon.-Fri. 10am-4pm. Admission DM2.) The renowned **Passauer Glasmuseum** (tel. 350 71; fax 317 12), next to the *Rathaus,* houses 30,000 examples of glasswork documenting the last 300 years of glass-making (open in summer daily 10am-4pm; in winter 2-4pm; admission DM5, students DM3, children under 16 accompanied by parents free). Over the *Luitpoldbrücke,* across the river and up the footpath, is the **Veste Oberhaus,** former palace of the bishopric (open early April-Oct. Tues.-Sun. 11:30am-5pm). Once a place of refuge for the bishop and a prison for various enemies of the cloth, the stronghold now contains the magnificently placed and proud-looking **Cultural History Museum** (tel. 39 63 12), in which 54 rooms of art and artifacts span the last 2000 years; the museum's second-floor restrooms offer an incredible city-wide lookout point. (Open March-Jan. Tues.-Thurs. and Sat.-Sun. 9am-5pm, Fri. 9am-7pm. Admission DM6, students DM3). The same bus that goes to the hostel also stops in front of the Veste Oberhaus (every 30min. from the *Rathausplatz;* last bus leaves the Oberhaus at 5:15pm). In the heart of the *Altstadt,* bright arched skylights shelter the **Museum Moderner Kunst,** Braugasse 17 (tel. 340 91). The rotating art exhibitions are excellent, but decide if it suits your taste before you shell out your dough (DM8, students and children DM5; open Tues.-Sun. 10am-6pm).

■ Landshut

Landshut ("Lands-hoot"), just half an hour by train from Munich, frolics with style during the **Landshuter Hochzeit,** a three-week medieval orgy with authentic (read: excessive) feasting, armored jousting, dancing, knife juggling, slapstick comedy, and period plays to accompany the ageless *Biergarten.* First celebrated in 1475 and resurrected in 1903, the festival still brings Landshuters together every four years to re-create the magnificent *Hochzeit* (wedding) that Duke Ludwig arranged for his son Georg and his bride Hedwig, daughter of the Polish King Kasimir IV. Modern-day knights and ladies appear again from June 28 to July 20 in 1997; information and tickets are available from the tourist office.

The Landshut *Altstadt* features rows of colorful gabled Gothic and Baroque houses filled with glitzy shops and cafés. The proud, light greenish-beige **Rathaus** (tel. 88 12 16) stands at the center bearing Renaissance and neo-Gothic architectural façades. Mural paintings inside the *Prunksaal* (main hall) capture the original wedding (open Mon.-Fri. 2-3pm; free). Across from the *Rathaus* is the **Stadtmuseum,** the first Renaissance-style palace to be built in Germany (1533-37). Its gleaming white classical façade conceals a spacious courtyard with arcades of distinct Italian influence. The **Stadtresidenz Museum** (tel. 226 38) upstairs grants peeks at gloriously decadent palace rooms. (Tours April-Sept. daily 9am-noon and 1-5pm, last tour 4:30pm; Oct.-March daily 10am-noon and 1-4pm, last tour 3:30pm; 45min; DM3, students DM2.) Geometrically intriguing bricks zig-zag the 130-m spire of **St. Martin's Kirche.** Inside you can see the tasteful non-Baroque features, including 16th-century choir stalls and the late Gothic **Madonna and Child** elaborately carved by Hans Leinberger in 1518 (open April-Sept. daily 7am-6:30pm; Oct.-March 7am-5pm). Further up the main street a sign points to **Burg Trausnitz** (tel. 226 38). To the left and up the crooked brick stairway (5-10min.) sits a hefty brick and red-tiled fortress built in 1204. The castle was the luxurious abode of the Wittelsbacher Princes of Bavaria-Landshut until 1503. The highly amusing "Narrentreppe" (Fool's staircase) inside displays frescoed scenes from the famous Italian folk plays called **Commedia dell'Arte.** The castle interior can only be seen with a German-language tour, but you can borrow an English translation of the guide's words. (Same times and tours as Stadtresidenz Museum. Admission DM4, students and seniors DM3.)

Landshut is best reached by **train** from Munich (1-2 per hr.; 30-60min.) or Regensburg (1 per hr.; 40min.). From the station, it's a 20-30-minute walk into town. Walk straight on Luitpoldstr. until you come to the town gates. Continue straight ahead on Theaterstr. to Altstadt Str. and turn left toward the *Rathaus* ahead on the right. Or use **public transportation;** all buses that stop at the station run to the center of town (one-way DM2; day card DM2.70). The **tourist office,** Altstadt Str. 315 (tel. 92 20 50; fax 892 75), has primitive city maps for free or better ones for DM2. There's no private room finding service, but they will provide a list of available rooms, which become increasingly affordable outside of a 20-minute radius from the center. Pick up a pamphlet on the history of the wedding procession (open Mon.-Fri. 9am-noon and 1:30-5pm, Sat. 9am-noon). The **post office,** 84028 Landshut, is just to the left of the train station (open Mon.-Sat. 8am-noon and 1-6pm, Sun. 10:30-11:30am). The **telephone code** is 0871.

The **Jugendherberge (HI)** is at Richard-Schirrmann-Weg 6 (tel. 234 49; fax 27 49 47). From the tourist office, go up Altstadt Str. and follow the signs starting to the left of the *Burg* Trausnitz sign. Pass the stairs leading to the *Burg,* and a few steps further on your right follow Richard-Schirrmann-Weg to the end. The elegant modern villa sits on quiet, green grounds overlooking town. (Reception open Mon.-Fri. 9am-noon and 5-8pm, Sat.-Sun. 5-8pm. DM18. Breakfast included. Sheets DM5.50. Closed Dec. 23-Jan. 7.) One of the more affordable places in town is the **Pfälzer Weinstube Heigl,** Herrngasse 385 (tel. 891 32; fax 67 01 56), in a conspicuous building in the city center. Walk right from the *Rathaus* and take the fourth right onto Herrngasse. (16 clean rooms. Singles DM58-63. Doubles DM88-98.) Halfway between the *Hauptbahnhof* and the *Altstadt,* **Hotel Park Café,** Papierstr. 36 (tel. 693 39, fax 63 03 07), offers the bare necessities of a room. From the station, walk straight on Luitpold Str., take a left on Stethaimerstr., and a right onto Papierstr. (15min.). (Singles DM55-95. Doubles DM95-160. Breakfast included.) For new-wave dining in the *Altstadt,* try **Café Cappuccino,** Altstadtstr. 337 (tel. 270 92). They've got big daily specials (DM8-10), salads (DM7-15), pasta (DM9-16), and the eponymous cappuccino (DM3.90; open Mon.-

Thurs. 9am-midnight, Fri.-Sat. 9am-1am, Sun. 2-11pm). A fruit and vegetable **market** appears Monday thru Thursday and Saturday (7am-noon) in the *Altstadt*, and Friday on Am alten Viehmarkt (6am-1pm).

■ Straubing

Perched on the fringe of the Bavarian forest near the Danube, Straubing lets down its medieval hair for the 10-day **Gäubodenvolksfest,** introduced in 1812 by King Max as an agricultural fair which sprouted into a modern day drinking festival second in size only to *Oktoberfest* (Aug. 8-18 in 1997). Seven enormous beer tents welcome over a million revelers, who, after imbibing a few liters of the local brews, blow their wad on a bevy of amusement park rides. Adjoining the Volksfest is **Ostbayernschau** (East Bavarian Show), a regional trade and industry exhibition (read: more beer; Aug. 9-17 in 1997). Both are held in "Am Hagen," the *Fest* area 10 minutes north of the *Markt*. During the rest of the year, Straubing serves as a convenient entrance to the Bavarian Forest.

Orientation and Practical Information Straubing is easily reached from Regensburg or Passau. The *Altstadt* lies northwest of the train station, five minutes away on foot. To get there, cross the street in front of the station, and follow it left past the post office as it curves into Bahnhofstr. Cross the foot bridge and continue down Steinergasse to the pastel green turreted tower. Through the arch on the left is the **tourist office,** Theresienplatz 20 (tel. 94 43 07; fax 94 41 03), which has free maps and extensive brochures on Straubing and neighboring towns and tracks down rooms (DM25-30 per person) for DM3 (open Mon.-Wed. 9am-noon and 1:30-5pm, Thurs. 9am-noon and 1:30-6pm; May-Sept. also Sat. 9am-noon). German **tours** of the town leave from the tourist office (June-mid-Sept. Wed. at 2pm and Sat. at 10:30am; DM3, students and seniors DM1, under 6 free; English tours by appointment DM60). For **train** info, call 194 19. **Rent bikes** at **Bund Naturschutz,** Ludwigsplatz 14, first floor (tel. 25 12), for DM15-20 (open Mon.-Fri. 9am-noon and 1-5pm). For the **weather,** call 011 64. Lists of available **pharmacies** are posted at **Agnes Bernauer Apotheke,** Bahnhofstr. 16 (tel. 806 75). The **post office,** Bahnhofsplatz 1, 94315 Straubing (tel. 86 10), sits right across from the train station. Head here to cash traveler's checks, **exchange currency,** or call home (open Mon.-Fri. 7:30am-12:30pm and 2-7pm, Sat. 9am-12:30pm). The **telephone code** is 09421.

Accommodations The **Jugendherberge (HI),** Friedhofstr. 12 (tel. 804 36; fax 120 94), is 10 minutes from the train station (within earshot). Turn right from the front entrance of the station and follow the curve of the main road. Turn right onto Schildhauerstr. at the sign pointing to "Passau," as it curves into Äußere-Passauer-Str.; you'll spot a crosswalk and a *Jugendherberge* sign pointing left up Friedhofstr.; the hostel is on your right. Though the building is old and some rooms are cramped, this is a family place where cleanliness is king. Doubles are available if you're lucky. (Reception open 7-9am and 5-9pm. Lockout 9am-5pm. Ask for a key to circumvent the 10pm curfew (DM10 deposit). Under 27 only. DM15.50. Breakfast included. Sheets DM5.50. Showers between 6am-8am and 5-10pm. Open April-Oct.)

The cheapest and most convenient beds can be found at **Pension Fürst,** Theresienplatz 32 (tel. 107 92). Follow the above directions to the *Altstadt* and turn left at the tourist office; it's on the left. (Singles DM30. Doubles DM60. No breakfast. Showers on floor.) On a busy intersection behind the train station, **Landshuter Hof,** Landshuter Str. 36 (tel. 303 66; fax 516 24), has simple clean rooms. From the train station, take a left and follow the street under the tunnel and directly up Landshuter Str. (10min.). Shady beer garden out back. (Singles DM35. Doubles DM70. Breakfast included.) A bit further down is the **Weißes Rößl,** Landshuter Str. 65. (tel. 325 81). It's quieter—with a sweet staff. (Singles DM35. Doubles DM70. Breakfast included.)

Food Buy fresh fruits and vegetables at the **market** on Ludwigsplatz (open Mon.-Thurs. and Sat. 7am-noon, Fri. 7am-5pm). A **farmer's market** is also held on Saturdays at Theresienplatz. Don't miss **Michelangelo,** Am Platzel 3 (tel. 216 86), for tasty pizzas (DM10-14) and hefty noodle dishes (DM8.50-16) accompanied by beer (DM3.90; open Mon. and Wed.-Sat. 11:30am-2pm and 6pm-midnight, Sun. 6-11pm). **Metzgerei Königsbauer,** Ludwigsplatz 6 (tel. 815 94), serves up a hefty lunch crowd at its *Steh-café* (standing café); every entree is also available *zum mitnehmen* (take-out), including *Wienerschnitzel, Wurst, Knödel,* and every other German meat specialty (DM6-10; open Mon.-Fri. 7:30am-6pm, Sat. 7:30am-1pm).

Sights The five-turreted gothic **watchtower** in the middle of the market square is the symbol of the city. Erected in the 14th century, the teal-green structure with an inset gold figure of Mary splits the *Marktplatz* in two. (Tours in German Apr.-Oct. Thurs. at 2pm, Sat.-Sun. at 10:30am; DM3, students DM1). To the right, Ludwigsplatz hosts the daily fruit and vegetable market (see above). The **Gäubodenmuseum,** Fraunhoferstr. 9 (tel. 818 11), off the main square, sports a pink-and-grey façade adorned with carved faces and regal birds; inside is a collection of Roman treasures, and art and folklore of the region (open Tues.-Sun. 10am-4pm; admission DM4, under 19 DM3). At the end of the street, turn right and around to the late Gothic **Karmelitenkirche,** Albrechtsgasse 21, with a stunning Baroque interior. Angels and disciples peer down from the lavish gold altar and stolid white columns. A recording of the organ's greatest hits costs DM28; a bottle of genuine Karmelite spirit promises to cure the meanest case of constipation (DM7).

One block down Burggasse, the **Ursulinenkirche** suffers behind an off-putting white stone facade. Built from 1736-1741 by the renowned Asam Brothers, the interior exhibits all the opulent, overbearing kitsch of Rococo. Huge marble columns snake up to the ceiling covered in flashy gold and lavishly fanatic frescoes. Back down across Fürstenstr. on the banks of the Donau, parts of the **Herzogsschloß** (ducal palace) date from 1356. Most of the palace interior is closed to the public, its innards clogged with bureaucracy. A few renovated floors house a new state museum with a permanent, rather bland exhibition of images of worship from the 17th-20th centuries (open Tues.-Sun. 10am-4pm; admission DM4, under 19 DM3).

Entertainment and Nightlife For complete concert, live music, and club information, pick up the free magazine *in'said* at the tourist office and local bars. Nocturnal activity oscillates between bad and better disco. Steer clear of the island themes; instead go to **Max,** Hebbelstr. 14 (tel. 34 31). Hidden in the shopping complex called Gläuboden Park, this is the Friday night place to trot to techno, trance, rap, and funk. (Cover DM10, beer DM4.50. Open Wed., Fri.-Sat. 10pm-3am.)

Straubing recently opened an enormous outdoor swimming pool complex, **AQUA-therm,** Wittelbacherhöhe 50-52 (tel. 86 41 78), with an 80-m waterslide, massage parlors, an indoor pool, steam sauna, and warm salt-water pool. Follow the tunnel to the left of the Bahnhof down Landshuter Str. and turn right onto Dr. Otto Höchtl Str., which becomes Wittelsbacherhöhe Str.; it's on the right. Or take bus #2 from Ludwigsplatz to "Aquatherm." (Open May and Aug.-mid-Sept. daily 8am-8pm; June-Aug. 8am-9pm. Closes 1hr. earlier Sat.-Sun. DM4 (after 5:30pm DM2), students, seniors, and under 16 DM2, under 6 free. Open mid-Sept.-mid-May.) You can go **bowling** at **Keglerhalle am Sportzentrum Peterswöhrd** (tel. 802 48), 20 minutes from the center of town (open daily 10am-midnight).

Every four years in July, Straubing commemorates the 1435 death of Agnes Bernauer, the daughter of an Augsburg barber and wife of Duke Albrecht III of Straubing. Albrecht's father, Duke Ernst of Bavaria, was furious when he learned of his son's secret marriage to Agnes, a mere commoner, and had Agnes condemned as a witch and sentenced to drown in the Danube while his son was away. The people of Straubing re-enact the tragic love story during the **Agnes Bernauer Festspiele** (next performance July 1999).

■ Regensburg

Located at the northernmost point of the Danube's (long) passage to the Black Sea, Regensburg's *Altstadt* spills onto the numerous islands dodged by this sinuous river as it converges with the Regen. An enchanting city of patrician homes and Imperial administrative houses, Regensburg lies close to two extraordinary sights: **Walhalla,** King Ludwig I of Bavaria's tribute to German heroes, and the **Donaudurchbruch,** where the Danube has carved a deep gorge between the high, church-dotted grassy banks. What began as a fortress built by Marcus Aurelius in 179AD became the first capital of Bavaria, then the seat of the Perpetual Imperial Diet, the parliament of the Holy Roman Empire, and finally the site of the first German parliament. But when the government opened the fourth Bavarian university here in 1967, the steady flow of students through town saturated the *Altstadt* with cafés, bars, and shops and created a hipness that mixes well with Regensburg's Old World aura.

ORIENTATION AND PRACTICAL INFORMATION

Regensburg has easy train and bus connections to both Nurmberg and Passau. The historic *Altstadt* sprawls over a square-shaped cobblestone mecca; the Danube is to the north, the *Hauptbahnhof* and Bahnhofstr. to the south, Kumpfmühler Str. is to the west, and Maximilianstr. to the east. Maximilianstr. leads straight from the train station into the heart of the city.

Tourist Office: Altes Rathaus, on Rathausplatz (tel. 507 44 10; fax 507 44 19). From the train station, walk down Maximilianstr. to Grasgasse and take a left. Follow it as it turns into Obermünsterstr., then turn right onto Obere Bachgasse and follow it five blocks down Untere Bachgasse to Rathausplatz. The tourist office, to your left across the square, provides a free map, finds rooms (DM1.50), and sells tickets to local sights and events. They also have a 24-hr. **private room** information number (tel. 194 14). Open April-Oct. Mon.-Fri. 8:30am-6pm, Sat. 9am-4pm, Sun. 9:30am-4pm; Nov.-March Mon.-Fri. 8:30am-6pm, Sat. 9am-4pm, Sun. 9:30am-2:30pm. Pick up info on the Bavarian Forest at the **Fremdenverkehrsverband Ostbayern,** Landshuter Str. 13, off Dr.-Martin-Luther-Str. (tel. 58 53 90; fax 585 39 39). Open Mon.-Thurs. 7:30am-noon and 1-5pm, Fri. 7:30am-12:30pm.

Telephones: In front of the train station and the post office.

Trains: Station at Bahnhofsplatz (tel. 194 19). To Munich (via Landshut; 1 per hr.; 1½hr.), Nuremberg (1-3 per hr.; 1hr.), and Passau (1 per hr.; 1-1½hr.). Ticket office open Mon.-Fri. 7:30am-8pm, Sat. 7:30am-6:10pm, Sun. 8am-7pm.

Public Transportation: Routes and schedules of Regensburg's new bus system are available at the information desk in the train station. The transport hub is "Albertstraße," 1 short block straight ahead from the station on the right. Single rides cost DM2.50. No night buses. Ask the driver for a **Tages-Ticket** (all-day ticket), which costs DM6 (Mon.-Fri.) or DM4 (Sat.-Sun.). On weekends, groups can buy one **Tages-Ticket** for 2 people (DM4). Groups of 2 or more traveling Mon.-Fri. make out best by getting a **12-Streifenkarte** from the kiosk in the station *before* heading for the bus (DM10; punch 3 stripes each way per person). RVV bus #5 leaves from the train station to Walhalla ("Donaustauf Walhalla Str."; 25min.) Mon.-Fri. every 20min. 5:40am-11:20pm; buses return from Walhalla every 20min. 5:25am-10:53pm. On Sat. buses leave every 20-40min. 6:20am-11:20pm and return 5:40am-10:53pm; on Sun. every hr. 6:20am-11:20pm and return 6:53am-10:53pm (one way DM3.30, children under 15 DM1.70).

Ferries: Boats leave daily from the banks of the Danube between the Eiserne and Steinerne bridges for **Straubing** at 10am (4½hr.; DM22, round-trip DM28, with same-day bus return DM30). There is also a boat to **Walhalla** daily April.-Oct. at 10:30am and 2pm (45min; one way DM10, children DM5, families DM27; round-trip DM15, children DM7, families DM40). Call 521 04 for more information.

Bike Rental: Fahrradverleih PARK and BIKE, am Donaumarktplatz (tel. 700 03 65), right on the Danube by the *Altstadt.* Open daily 10am-8pm.

Lockers: Next to the train tracks (DM2, larger lockers DM4).

Lost and Found: At the *Altes Rathaus* (tel. 507 21 05).

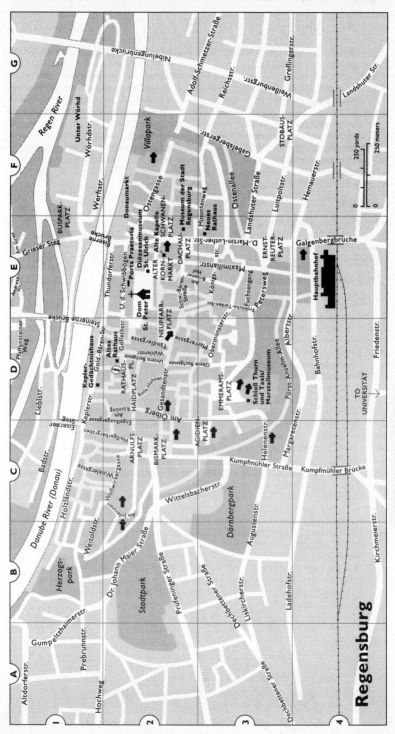

Regensburg

BAVARIA (BAYERN)

Women's Center: Badstr. 6 (back building). Information on women's rights and health. Lesbian café (tel. 816 44). Open Tues.-Wed. 10am-1pm, 2-5pm. In case of any women's emergency, call 242 59 or 240 00.

Crisis Hotline: In case of rape or other trauma, contact **Caritas** (tel. 78 20).

Pharmacy: 24-hr. service rotates among the city's pharmacies. To find out which pharmacy is on duty, visit **Maximilian Apotheke,** Maximilianstr. 29, two blocks straight ahead from the train station. Open Mon.-Thurs. 8am-5:15pm, Fri. 8am-6pm, Sat. 8am-12:30pm.

Hospital: Evangelische Krankenhaus, Obere Bachgasse (tel. 504 00), near the Thurn and Taxis *Schloß*, is the most centrally located.

Emergency: tel. 110. **Police:** Minoritenweg (tel. 192 22).

Post Office: on Bahnhofstr., 93047 Regensburg, next door to the train station. The best place to **exchange money** in Regensburg. Open Mon.-Wed. and Fri. 8am-6pm, Thurs. 8am-7:30pm, Sat. 8am-noon, Sun. 11am-noon.

Telephone Code: 0941.

ACCOMMODATIONS AND CAMPING

Most of Regensburg's cheap lodgings are centrally located, but they fill up in the summer. Reserve, reserve, reserve. If the hotels and *Pensionen* are full, the tourist office might find you a room in a private home. Otherwise, try the hotels in outlying parts of town—all are linked to the center by reliable bus service.

Jugendherberge (HI), Wöhrdstr. 60, 93059 Regensburg (tel. 574 02; fax 524 11), on an island in the Danube. From the station, walk straight ahead on Maximilianstr. all the way to the end. Then turn right at the Apotheke onto Pfluggasse and immediately left at the Optik sign into the tiny Erhardigasse. At the end, take the steps down and walk left over the Eiserne Brücke (iron bridge), which becomes Wöhrdstr. on the other side. The hostel is 5min. away on the right (25min. total). Or take bus #3, 8, or 9 from Albertstr. to "Eisstadion" (1 block in front of the station on the right). The hostel is a step ahead on the right. Renovated into pleasant though sterile modernity. Reception open 7am-11:30pm. Curfew 1pm. Under 27 only. DM20. Breakfast included. Dinner DM8.50. Sheets DM5.50. Reservations encouraged. Partial wheelchair access. Closed mid-Nov.-mid-Jan.

Spitalgarten, St.-Katharinen-Platz 1 (tel. 847 74), inside the walls of the old hospital built by Bishop Konrad IV in the 13th century. Cross the Danube at the Steinerne Bridge and go inside the gate to St. Katherine's. Pass through another gate and go past the left side of the church. On the left you'll see the entrance to the popular and lively *Biergarten*. Inquire about the *Pension* with the people behind the counter. Bus #12 from the station stops at "Stadtamhof" around the corner. Reception open until midnight. Singles DM35-40. Doubles DM70-75. Breakfast included. Call or write well ahead.

Schildbräu, Stadtamhof 24 (tel. 857 24), is over the Steinerne Brücke; follow the street for about 5min. and it's on the right. Or take bus #12 from the station to "Stadtamhof." Clean and orderly rooms with geraniums spilling out every window. Reception open 7:30am-midnight. Singles DM58, with shower and toilet DM85. Doubles with shower and toilet DM120. Breakfast included. Call ahead.

Hotel Peterhof, Fröhliche-Türken-Str. 12 (tel. 575 14), 5min. from the train station. Walk straight ahead on Maximilian Str. and take the second left onto St.-Peters-Weg, which becomes Fröhliche-Türken-Str. around the corner. Though the exterior appears somewhat iffy, the rooms are neat, simple, and definitively wallpapered. The opulent dining hall is covered in butterflies, ribbons, and artificial roses. Singles DM48, with shower DM60, with shower and toilet DM80. Doubles DM86, with shower DM96, with shower and toilet DM114. Triples with shower DM135, with shower and toilet DM145. Breakfast included.

Hotel Apollo, Neuprüll 17 (tel. 910 50; fax 91 05 70). From Albertstr. (1 block in front of the station), take bus #6 (direction: Klinikum) to "Neuprüll" (15min.; DM2.50) or walk 45min. Proximity to the university and modern furnishings make it worth the trip. Rooms have TVs and telephones. Hostel has a pool, sauna, steam bath, and solarium. Singles DM55, with shower DM65, with shower and toilet DM75. Doubles DM99, with shower DM110, and toilet DM125. Breakfast included.

Camping: Campingplatz, Am Weinweg 40 (tel. 27 00 25). From Albertstr. (one block in front of the station) take bus #11 (direction: West Bad) to "Westheim." DM8.80 per adult. DM6.40 per under-12 child. DM6.80 per tent, with car DM11.60. Prices lower in the off-season (mid-Jan.-March and Sept.-mid-Dec.).

FOOD

The 17th-century English dramatist and diplomat Sir George Etherege commented that Regensburg's "noble, serene air makes us hungry as hawks"—a laudable attempt to blame his swelling belly on the atmosphere rather than the heavy Bavarian fare and beer typical of Regensburg. A tantalizing number of cafés, bars, and beer gardens await to tempt the Imperial Diet. The supermarket **Tengelmann,** Ernst-Reuter-Platz, up Maximilianstr. from the train station on the right, is a good starting point for the makings of a lazy picnic (open Mon.-Fri. 8:30am-6:30pm, Sat. 7:30am-2pm). To stock up on fruit, vegetables, and other basics, head to the **market** on Domplatz (open March-Oct. Mon.-Sat. 7am-6pm, Sun. 10:30am-6pm). Otherwise, join the rest of Regensburg at a beer garden for a meal of *Würstchen,* pretzels, and of course, *Pils vom Faß* (*Pils* on tap).

University Mensa, on Albertus-Magnus-Str., in the park, on the university campus. Turn right from the train station and take the bridge over the tracks onto Galgenbergstr. Follow this street for about 15min. and take a right onto Albertus-Magnus-Str.; it's at the far end. The stairs on the left will lead you up to the rectangular *Mensa.* Or take bus #6 or #11 (directions: Klinikum or Burgweinting) to "Universität Mensa" from the *Altes Rathaus* or Albertstr. (DM2.50). The cheapest meal in Regensburg, with a lively student crowd. Any student ID will do. Meals DM3.50-6. Open Mon.-Fri. 11:30am-1:30pm and 5:30-7pm, Sat. 4:30-6:30pm; Aug.-Sept. open Mon.-Fri. for lunch only.

Ambrosius, Brückstr. 5 (tel. 545 40), on the *Altstadt* end of the Steinerne Brucke (stone bridge). Closely knit tables in an odd yellow setting draw Regensburger diversity. Baguettes and sandwiches (DM6-10), salads (DM5-14), beer (DM3.50-5). Good breakfast DM4-11. Open Mon.-Sat. 9am-1am, Sun.10am-1am.

Bistro Rosarium, Hoppestr. 3a (tel. 268 85). At the edge of the superbly landscaped Dörnbergpark. A Bavarian wood-framed restaurant with rose garden, umbrella-covered tables around a fountain, students, beer, red roses, and green trees. Pasta dishes (DM11-12), *Schnitzel* (DM13), fresh salads (DM7-13), and beer (DM4.30). Breakfasts start at DM6.80. Open daily 11am-1am.

Café Orphée, Untere Bechgasse 8 (tel. 529 77), off Rathausplatz. A Parisian salon with dark wooden walls, mirrors, candle-lit tables, and alabaster busts. I'm sorry, but are you going to order *that* wine with your entree? Chocolate crêpes DM7.80. Baguettes DM7.80. Salads DM8.50-16. Open daily 9am-1am.

Hinterhaus, Rote-Hahnen-Gasse 2 (tel. 546 61), off Haidplatz, just down from Rathausplatz. A politically grooving grove of left-leaning wooden tables. Excellent vegetarian dishes (DM8-14) and salads (DM5-13). Outdoor seating as well. Open Mon.-Fri. 11am-1am, Sat.-Sun. 6pm-1am.

Café Lila, Pfarrergasse 6 (tel. 555 52), off Neupfarrplatz. Light music, large open windows, black chairs, soothing plants, and little purple lilies make for a calm newspaper read. Extensive breakfast menu. Open daily 9am-1am.

Beer Gardens

Goldene Ente, Badstr. 32 (tel. 854 55). Under magnificent chestnut trees on the banks of the Danube just across the Eiserner Steg footbridge upstream from the Steinerne Brücke. The oldest inn in Regensburg; during the summer the beer garden is packed with pleasantly pilsnered students. More complex menu inside. Steaks, *Würstchen,* and *Schnitzel* grill for student-friendly prices (DM7-13). Bavarian vegetarians have the *Getreidereistaler mit Käse, Salat, und Zaziki* (DM9). Beer starts at DM3.60. Open Mon.-Sat. 11am-2pm and 5pm-1am, Sun. 10am-1am.

Kneitinger Keller, Galgenbergstr. 18. (tel. 766 80), to the right from the station and over the tracks. Regensburg's largest and most democratic beer garden (1200 seats). Devoted locals, large thirsty tourists, and angst-ridden students alike can fol-

low their noses: the smell of beer extends for blocks. Beer starts at DM4.40. 6
Würstchen with bread DM8.20. Big pretzels DM3. Open daily 9am-midnight.

Einhorn, Wöhrdstr. 31 (tel. 527 90), down the street from the hostel. A small outdoor garden surrounded by an old graying fence with relaxed folk discussing daily
odds and ends. Pasta DM10-13. Meats DM12-16. Salads DM7-11. Beer starts at
DM3.40, as does coffee: don't get them confused. Open daily 6pm-1am.

Wurstküche, Thundorferstr. (tel. 590 98), next to the Steinerne bridge with views
of the river. The oldest operating fast food joint in Europe—the 12th-century workers who built the bridge broke for lunch here. Very busy and touristy, even though
it's just a wood shack with tables. 6 small, delicious *Würstle* from the smoky
kitchen come with sauerkraut and bread (DM7.80). Open daily 8am-7pm; Nov.-
April Sun. daily 8am-2pm.

SIGHTS

A tour of Regensburg will take you through time from monuments built during the
last centuries of the Roman Empire to the Gothic, Baroque, and Rococo legacies of a
later empire. The **Porta Praetoria** (a Roman gateway) and parts of its accompanying
wall sketch a hazy outline of the city's original fortifications. They have been incorporated into a house located on Unter-den-Schwibbögen between the *Dom* and the
Donau. One block away from the river on Niedermünstergasse lies the *Domplatz,*
which hosts the soaring high-Gothic **St. Peter's Cathedral** and, inside the church,
the **Diocese Museum** (tel. 516 88; open April-Nov. Tues.-Sun. 10am-5pm; admission
DM3, students DM1.50). Begun in 1276, the cathedral was finished in 1486, not
counting the delicately carved twin 159-m spires, which King Ludwig II added in typical grandiose style between 1859 and 1869. Inside the cathedral is the **Domschatz**
(cathedral treasury; tel. 576 45), a priceless collection of gold and jewels purchased
by the Regensburg bishops back in the good old days of indulgences and economic
exploitation by the clergy. (Cathedral open April-Oct. 6:30am-6pm; Nov.-March
6:30am-4pm. Tours lasting 75min. May-Oct. Mon.-Sat. at 10, 11am, and 2pm, Sun. at
noon and 2pm; Nov.-April Mon.-Sat. at 11am, Sun. at noon. Admission DM3, students
DM2. *Domschatz* open April-Nov. Tues.-Sat. 10am-5pm, Sun. noon-5pm; Dec.-March
Fri.-Sat. 10am-4pm, Sun. noon-4pm. Admission DM3, students DM1.50.) The **Alte
Kapelle,** on Alter Kornmarkt behind the *Dom,* has an exceptionally frothy and gilded
Rococo interior (open daily 7am-5pm, Dec.-March 7am-4pm).

A few blocks away from the cathedral, the Gothic **Altes Rathaus** served as capital
of the Holy Roman Empire until 1803. The sycophantic and impotent Imperial Parliament (the first of many similar bodies in German history) lives on in the **Reichstag
Museum,** housed in the *Altes Rathaus.* The differing heights of the chairs reflect the
political hierarchy of the legislators. (Tours in German April-Oct. daily every 30min.;
Nov.-March 1 per hr.; English tour May-Sept. Mon.-Sat. at 3:15pm. Admission DM5,
students and seniors DM2.50, families DM10.)

Resting sedately in the western portion of the park across from the *Hauptbahnhof,*
the **Fürstliches Thurn und Taxissches Schloß** (tel. 504 81 33), originally a Benedictine cloister, was the residence of the Duke of Thurn und Taxis after 1812. Little
remains of the Gothic cloister beneath later Baroque additions. The Thurn und Taxis
family built a franchise, granted by Kaiser Maximilian in 1490, into a feudal postal
empire that had a tight grip over much of Central Europe until the Prussian Post,
backed by Bismarck's armies, cancelled it in 1867. The old Duke is now dead, but his
five-year-old son, and his young and *trés chic* widow have been the darlings of German tabloids for years. (Tours Apr.-Oct. daily at 11am, 2, 3, and 4pm; Sat.-Sun. an
additional tour at 10am; Nov.-March Sat.-Sun. at 10 and 11am, 2 and 3pm.) The
Dukes' beer-brewing namesake, the **Fürstliches Brauerei Thurn und Taxis,** next
door to the Kneitinger Keller at Galgenbergstr. 14 (tel. 134), guides visitors through a
demonstration of the brewer's art and hands out free samples at the end (reservations
requested several weeks in advance; free).

The iconoclastic astronomer and physicist Johannes Kepler died of meningitis in
1630 at the site of the **Kepler Memorial House,** Keplerstr. 5 (tel. 507 34 42). Period

furniture, portraits, and facsimiles of Kepler's work are on display (tours Tues.-Sat. at 10am, 11am, 2pm, and 3pm, Sun. at 10 and 11am; admission DM4, students and seniors DM2, families DM8). Up the street at Keplerstr. 2 is **Kepler's Wohnhaus,** a colorful house, where he hung his hat and spent time with his family. **All-day museum cards** (DM10, students and seniors DM5, families DM20) entitle bearers to admission to the Reichstag Museum, Kepler Memorial House, Regensburg Stadt Museum, and the town's modern art gallery; purchase them at the tourist office.

Down the river from Regensburg is **Walhalla,** an imitation Greek temple poised dramatically on the steep northern bank of the Danube. Ludwig I of Bavaria built the monument between 1830 and 1842 to honor Germans past and present whom he admired. Modeled after the Parthenon in Athens and named after the legendary resting place of Norse heroes, Walhalla stares imposingly down on the river as the boat from Regensburg approaches the dock (see Practical Information, p. 254, for ferry information). Ludwig called Walhalla "the child of my love." What a nut. The climb up the steep steps to the monument itself is tough going, but the view of the river and the opposite bank is a golden photo opportunity. In the summer, these hallowed steps provide a lively evening hangout for students who venture here by bikes and car; probably not what poor Ludwig envisioned. Inside the monument are a series of busts of German leaders and military heroes, most of whom you've thankfully never heard of (open April-Sept. daily 9am-5:45pm; Oct. daily 9am-4:45pm; Nov.-March 10-11:45am and 1-3:45pm; admission DM2, students DM1). RVV bus #5 leaves from the train station to "Donaustauf Walhallastr." in Walhalla (Mon-Sat. every 20min. and 1 per hr. on Sun.; 25min.; tickets DM3.30 one way, under 16 DM1.70). See Public Transportation, p. 254, for info on special passes.

NIGHTLIFE

Many of the cafés and beer gardens listed above (see Food, p. 257) double as local nighttime haunts. But good bars raise inebriation to Walhallian heights. Pick up the free *Logo*—it lists all events and addresses of more worthwhile bars and cafés.

Alte Mälzerei, Galgenberger Str. 20 (tel. 757 49). Regensburg's official cultural center in an old malt factory that is home not only to theater and musical events, but a ramshackle bar with pop, jazz, funk, soul, reggae, and blues. Student crowd opts for the outdoor beer garden on summer days; there's an awesome aerial view of the massive Kneitinger Keller. Cheap beer DM2.50-4. Open daily 6pm-1am. The Mälzerei is also home to a new little bar, **Cartoon,** just around the corner in the back entrance on Bischof-Werner-Str. Postered with funny old illustrations, it serves pasta, chili, and *Schnitzel* (DM8-12). Open daily 7pm-1am. For concert info call 757 38.

Wunderbar, Keplerstr. 11 (tel. 531 30).Young late-nighters pack into one of the only bars open after 1am; just a few staggers from the *Steinerne* Bridge. Beer starts at DM4, but the specialty is extravagant mixed drinks like "Flying Kangaroo" (DM12). Open Mon.-Thurs. and Sun. 10pm-3am, Fri.-Sat. 9pm-3am.

Alte Filmbühne, Hinter der Grieb 18 (tel. 520 51). Regensburg's funkiest scene attracts a diverse and bizarre crowd. Old film posters, old fans, light bulbs, and strange art scattered everywhere. Open daily 8pm-1am.

Südhaus, Untere Bachgasse 8 (tel. 519 33). One of Regensburg's best discos. Just behind Café Orphee, past a gargoyled fountain and a huge stone angel with the *Südhaus* sign. Tuesday is the night of glory. Thursday is gay night. Open Tues.-Thurs. and Sun. and 11pm-3am, Fri.-Sat. 11pm-4am.

Scala, gesandtenstr. 6 (522 93), located in the Pustet Passage between Rote-Hahnen-Gasse and Gesandtenstr. Sandwiched by three bars, hipsters bump and grind in this disco club. Open Wed.-Thurs. and Sun. 11pm-3am, Fri.-Sat. 11pm-4am.

BAVARIA (BAYERN)

■ Near Regensburg: Donaudurchbruch and Kloster Weltenburg

About 35km south of Regensburg, the **Donaudurchbruch** (Danube Passage) winds 5km through magnificent stretch of nature to *Kloster Weltenburg* (Weltenburg Monastery). The lush green slopes lining this sheltered length of the Danube River are dramatically interrupted every few hundred meters by gargantuan white cliffs, which have all been given names by the river captains of the past. (The phallic, free-standing rock has been paradoxically named *Jungfrau*—the virgin.) Gurgling ferries shuttle the oohs and aahs of visitors through the *Donaudurchbruch* from the docks at Kelheim to Europe's oldest Benedictine monastery, **Kloster Weltenburg** (founded A.D. 620). Squatting on a jut of land at a sharp bend in the Danube, the simple, red-roofed monastery encloses a surprisingly ornate church featuring a powerful, back-lit statue of St. George spearing the last life out of a screeching dragon. A huge fresco on the right shows Christopher Columbus (and the Virgin Mary) discovering America, while high above a playful statue of the church's builder, Cosma Damian Asam (in the red coat), smiles down on all good tourists. The first 400 years of daily prayers in the monastery must have been a little, well, dull, for it wasn't until in 1050AD that the good brothers decided to found the world's first monastery brewery. Taste the product of their labor in the monastery's own beer garden—by far the most popular attraction for visitors (DM4.90 for 0.5L of the holy brew).

A visit to *Kloster Weltenburg* makes an excellent daytrip from Regensburg, but plan ahead. To do the trip in a day, take the daily RBO bus to Kelheim from platform 11 in front of the Regensburg train station at 11:45am; get off at the last stop 40 minutes later. Walk across the parking lot to the Danube riverbank, and buy a round-trip ticket for the ferry (DM10, under 17 DM8, under 13 DM6, under 5 free, families DM25) which runs about every 45 minutes daily from mid-March to October. The boat trip to the *Kloster* takes about 50 minutes; allow 35 to 40 minutes for the return. (RBO buses return to Regensburg Mon.-Fri. at 4:20 and 5:30pm, Sat. at 6pm, and Sun. at 6:25 and 8:30pm. Round-trip DM14.20; Eurailpass, Interail, German Railpass and Bahncards all valid for the bus trip.) Pack a picnic lunch, and be sure to check schedules at the tourist office before you hop on the bus.

▓ Bavarian Forest (Bayerischer Wald)

A coddled national treasure, the Bavarian Forest is the largest range of wooded mountains in Central Europe. These 6000km-sq. of peaks (60 of which are over 1000m high) and countless rivers and creeks stretch from the Danube and the Austrian and Czech borders to form a vast hook that lures hikers, campers, and cross-country skiers all through the year. The **Bavarian Forest National Park,** the first national park in Germany, strictly prohibits any activities that might alter the forest ecosystem. Clearly marked trails lace 8000 hectares (20,000 acres) of forest. You can trek it alone or sign up for guided hiking tours, botanical tours, natural history tours, or tours of virgin woodlands. For information and schedules, contact either the **Nationalparkverwaltung Bayerischer Wald,** Freyunstr., 94481 Grafenau (tel. (08552) 427 43, fax 46 90); the **Dr. Hans Eisenmann Haus,** Böhmstr., 94556 Neuschönau (tel. (08558) 13 00); or the **Landratsamt,** Wolfkerstr., 94078 Freyung (tel. (08551) 571 22, fax 572 44). For news of the rest of the forest, contact the **Fremdenverkehrsverband Ostbayern,** Landshuter Str. 13, 93047 Regensburg (tel. (0941) 585 39 11; fax 585 39 39), off Maximilianstr., a 10-minute walk from the train station in Regensburg (open Mon.-Thurs. 7:30am-noon and 1-5pm, Fri. 7:30am-12:30pm). Pick up a free **encyclopedia** of the Bayerischer Wald at any tourist office in the forest—it's filled to the brim with phone numbers, maps, and listings.

The Bavarian Forest is much more than just a verdant paradise; palaces, churches, and castle ruins are tucked away in tiny villages throughout the region. **Burgruine Hals,** an extensive castle ruin high on a woody cliff north of Passau, dates from the 12th century. The 18th-century **Wiesenfelden** (lush gardens) surround the ruins. For information contact **Herr Hubert Weinzierl** (tel. (09966) 777) or the **tourist office,** 94344 Wiesenfelden (tel. (09966) 94 00 17). **Frauenzell's** 15th-century Benedictine church was lavishly *barockisert* (Baroquified), while parts of the **Annunciation Church** in **Chammünster** date from the 12th century.

The Bavarian region is famous for its crafts, particularly **glass-blowing,** which has been associated with the forest for 700 years. The glass produced here is prized throughout the world, particularly the dark green *Waldglas* (forest glass). Every little forest village seems to have its own *Glashütte* or ten. For more information, contact the **Bergglashütte Weinfurter,** Ferienpark Geyersberg (tel. (08551) 60 66), in Freyung; the **Freiherr von Poschinger Kristallglasfabrik,** Moosauhütte (tel. (09926) 940 10), in Frauenau; or **Joska Waldglashütte** (tel. (09924) 77 90) in Bodenmais.

The remoteness and hospitality—a bit mellower than typical Bavarian *Gemütlich-keit*—of Bavarian forest towns attract few English-speaking visitors, but the park maintains a heavy flow of Germans seeking healthy, sedate vacations. Use the towns below as springboards from which to explore the nooks and crannies of this mountain region. An impressive 17 **HI youth hostels** dot the forest; Regensburg's tourist office *(Fremdenverkehrsverband)* has a helpful brochure as well as current addresses and phone numbers of hostels. The towns of **Cham** and **Regen** can be reached by **train** (Cham from Regensburg or Nuremberg via Schwanndorf; Regen from Regensburg, Munich, or Passau via Platting). **Buses** run from Regensburg and Straubing to Cham and from Passau and Straubing to Regen.

ZWIESEL

Zwiesel's a great hub for scouting out the heart of the Bavarian Forest. A skier's haven in the winter, in summer its focus flips to producing postmodern wine glasses. Zwiesel (TSVEE-zel) prides itself on an 800-year-history of glass-making. Just north of town lies **Glas Park,** a village of glass-blowing houses that demonstrate for awed tourists how delicate fancies are created. Infrequent buses shuttle to the Glas Park from the *Stadtplatz* (Mon.-Fri. beginning at 9:20am; last return at 5:39pm; check the tourist office for schedules). The **Waldmuseum** (forest museum), Am Stadtplatz 29 (tel. 608 88), behind the *Rathaus,* tells the tinkly tale of glass-making in the region. (Open May 15-Oct. 15 Mon.-Fri. 9am-5pm, Sat.-Sun. 10am-noon and 2-4pm.; Oct. 16-May 14 Mon.-Fri. 10am-noon and 2-5pm, Sat.-Sun. 10am-noon; admission DM3, students DM1.) The **tourist office** *(Kurverwaltung),* Stadtplatz 27 (tel. 13 08; fax 56 55), provides maps and finds **private accommodations** for free (DM20-30). From the station, turn right and walk downhill on Dr.-Schott-Str. After a few blocks, veer left and cross the bridge, and then take your second left onto Stadtplatz; the tourist office is in the *Rathaus* on the left. Watch out: the *Rathaus* signs after crossing the bridge point to the *Rathaus* parking lot, not the building itself (open Mon.-Fri. 8:30am-5:30pm, Sat. 10am-noon, Nov.-Dec. 8:30am-5:30pm). **Trains** run hourly from Plattling on the Nuremberg-Passau line (1hr.). The **post office,** on Dr.-Schott-Str., 94227 Zwiesel, **changes money** and has telephones (open Mon.-Fri. 8am-noon and 2-5:30pm, Sat. 8-11am). The **telephone code** is 09922. The **Jugendherberge,** Hindenburgstr. 26 (tel. 10 61; fax 601 91), is a 25-30-minute walk from the station. Follow the above directions to Stadtplatz, continue past the *Rathaus,* and turn right onto Frauenauer Str. Continue straight for 10 minutes and turn left on Hindenburgstr. (1 block after the "AOK" sign); the hostel is just over the hill. Or take bus #1 from the train station to "Jugendherberge." (DM2; 1 per hr.). This clean hostel is the choicest accommodation in the Bavarian forest. "*Klein aber fein*" (small but fine), repeats the proud hostel mother. (Reception open 5-7pm. Under 27 only. Curfew 10pm, but they'll give you a key. DM17.50. Sheets DM5.50. Breakfast included.)

BODENMAIS

If ever there was a friendly, little Bavarian *Dorf,* Bodenmais ("Boden-mice") is it. Its dreamy location at the heart of the forest, amidst hills of velvet moss, is reachable by a miniature train ride from Zwiesel past cows, trees, and tiny red-tile roofed houses.

The tourist-luring **Austen Glashütte,** on Bahnhofstr. (tel. 70 06), across from the *Rathaus* hawks the glass miniature 1988 Honda World Championship-winning race car (DM495), pink and gold chandeliers (DM479), and cheaper fragile trinkets. You can view the glass being blown (Mon.-Fri. 11am-noon and 2-6pm, Sat. 9am-1pm), then enjoy a local brew in a personally-monogrammed souvenir *Stein* (DM3.90). **Hans und Hans'l,** two endearing Bavarians (complete with *Lederhosen*), sing and play the accordion on Fridays (1-5pm). (*Glashütte* open Mon.-Fri. 9am-6pm, Sat. 9am-1pm.) Wood-carving is the second-largest industry here; down Bahnhofstr. and up Bergknappenstr. is the oldest **Holzschnitzerei** (wood-carving shop; tel. 276; fax 17 15) in Bodenmais (open Mon.-Fri. 8am-noon and 1:30-6pm, Sat. 9am-noon).

The **tourist office** *(Kurverwaltung),* Bahnhof Str. 56 (tel. 778 35; fax 778 50), is in the modern *Rathaus.* They'll give you a free book (literally) of accommodations and hiking trails (open Mon.-Fri. 8am-5pm, Sat. 8am-noon, Sun. 10am-noon). **Trains** make the 20-minute journey between Zwiesel and Bodenmais 11 times per day (Mon.-Fri.; last train from Zwiesel at 8:15pm). On weekends, take an RBO train from the Zwiesel train station to the Bodenmais *Rathaus* (6 per day; 25min.; last train from Zwiesel at 6:55pm; from Bodenmais at 7:20pm). Check schedules for daily times. For a **taxi** call 484. Rent mountain **bikes** (DM20 per day) or **skis** (from DM15 per day) at **Sport Weinberger,** Jahnstr. 20 (tel. 397), 10 minutes from the station down Bahnhofstr. The **telephone code** is 09924.

Bodenmais has 3600 inhabitants and almost twice that many hotel beds. Even so, this spa town fills quickly in summer and winter, so call ahead. The **Jugendherberge,** Am Kleinen Arber (tel. 281; fax 850), is 8km from town in the mountains, a whopping 1½-hour hike (DM18.50; breakfast included). A right on Bahnhofstr. and then a right up Scharebenstr. will lead you to the trail. Unless you intend to visit every *Jugendherberge* in Germany, the trek to the hostel is probably not worth it; many of the private rooms and *Pensionen* are inexpensive. The central **Haus Marianne,** Bahnhofstr. 34 (tel. 381), has balconies and a garden in front (DM25 per person; definitely call ahead). **Haus Anne,** Bergknappenstr. 22 (tel. 76 55 or 892), cozies up with big wooden beds and a tiny fitness room and solarium (DM27-32 per person). The **Schmanterl Metzgerei Grillstube,** Bahnhofstr. 21, serves *Curry-Wurst* and fries (DM6.80; open Mon.-Fri. 8:30am-8pm). Grab a string of sausage, hop into the bakery next door for *Brötchen,* and disappear into the forest (bakery open Mon.-Fri. 7:30am-6:30pm; forest open 24hr.).

FRAUENAU

The "glassy heart of the Bavarian Forest," fragile Frauenau lies 20 minutes east of Zwiesel via toy train. Majestic wooded mountains rise around the town, and it's not only the glass-making industry that sparkles here: north of town lies an idyllic lake reflecting the rising hills on its mirror-like surface. Near the borders of the Czech Republic and away from the busier regions of Bavaria, Frauenau remains untouched by tourists, with plenty of space for private exploration. To reach the **lake** *(Trinkwasser Talsperre),* take Hauptstr. up as it curves left, then turn right on Wasserhäuslweg (30-45min.) A hiking trail on the left of Wasserhäuslweg leads to Zwiesel.

The **Glasmuseum,** at Am Museumspark 1 (tel. 718), sprawled across a beautiful green landscape, holds 2500 years of glass treasures (open May 15-Oct. 31 daily 9am-5pm; Dec.20-May 14 10am-4pm; admission DM3, students DM2.50, under 15 DM1, under 6 free). The friendly **tourist office,** Hauptstr. 12, 94258 Frauenau (tel. 710; fax 17 99), provides information on hiking trails, hotels, holiday farms, and *Pensionen.* Turn left from the station and then right up Hauptstr. For DM1 they will help find **private rooms** (DM20-25), but go for a farm holiday, a bargain at DM15-19 (open Mon.-Fri. 8am-noon and 1:30-5pm; May 15-Oct. 15 also Sat. 9:30-11:30am). You can reach Frauenau by regular **train** from Zwiesel (Mon.-Fri. 7 per day; 15min.; last train at 7:15pm). On weekends, take the bus from the Zwiesel train station to the Frauenau **post office** (4 on Sat., the last at 7:05pm; 2 on Sun., the last at 6:40pm). To reach the lake, rent a **bike** at **Electra Weiss,** Badstr. 1 (tel. 15 26), an electric-goods shop uphill and to the right from the tourist office. (Bikes DM15-20 per day with ID. Open Mon.

and Wed.-Fri. 9-11:30am and 2-5pm, Tues. 9-11:30am.) The **Jugendherberge,** Hauptstr. 29a (tel. 543), is in the same building as the post office, just uphill from the tourist office. The green hospital-like building is not so hospitable—stay in Zwiesel instead (DM15.50; breakfast included; sheets DM5.50). Every Thursday there's a farmer's **market** from 7am to noon at the foot of the *Rathaus* on Hauptstr. The **telephone code** is 09926.

SLEEPING ELSEWHERE IN THE BAVARIAN FOREST

Jugendherberge Neuschönau (HI), Herbergsweg 2, 94556 Neuschönau (tel. (08553) 60 00; fax 829), nestles in the heart of the forest, a 17-km bus ride from the train station at Grafenau; take the bus from Spiegelau or Neuschönau. (Under 27 only. DM19. Sheets DM5.50.) **Jugendherberge Mauth (HI),** Jugendherbergesstr. 11, 94151 Mauth (tel. (08557) 289; fax 15 81), is accessible from Passau. (Under 27 only. DM19. Breakfast included. Sheets DM5.50.) Most towns within the Bavarian Forest offer several *Pensionen* and *Gasthöfe* that cost DM18-30 per person (breakfast included; prices are slightly higher in summer and around Christmas). The **Nationalparkverwaltung Bayerischer Wald** offers a big brochure on **camping** in the Bavarian Forest. Drop by their offices in Regensburg or write for it. For further info, contact the **Verkehrsamt Cham,** Propsteistr. 46 (tel. (09971) 49 33), or the **Haus des Gastes** in Regen (tel. (09921) 29 29).

■ Eichstätt

Sheltered in the valley of the Altmühl river and surrounded by the **Naturpark Altmühltal** (the largest nature preserve in Germany), the small university and episcopal town of Eichstätt flaunts its moments of lavish architecture with a self-proclaimed Mediterranean flair.

Orientation and Practical Information The Eichstätt **train station** is a 25-minute ride from Ingolstadt. Perhaps in anticipation of a growth spurt, Eichstätt's train station is 5km from the edge of town. A little train shuttles back and forth between Eichstätt *Bahnhof* and Eichstätt *Stadt* (town), leaving from track 1 (every ½-1hr. 6am-11pm). The **tourist office,** Kardinal-Preysing-Platz 14 (tel. 98 800; fax 98 08 30), has free maps and helps find private rooms (DM25-30) for free. From the train station, walk right and follow the information sign across the bridge (*Spitalbrücke*). Turn right on Residenzplatz to Leonrodplatz and then go past the church to Kardinal-Preysing-Platz on the left (open April-Oct. Mon.-Sat. 9am-5pm, Nov.-March Mon.-Thurs. 9am-noon and 2-4 pm, Fri. 9am-noon). When they're closed, go next door to the tourist information office for **Naturpark Altmühtal,** Notre Dame 1 (tel. 987 60; fax 98 76 54). Cloistered in a former monastery, they provide information on trails and paths in the nature reserve (open Easter-Oct. Mon.-Sat. 9am-5pm, Sun. 10am-5pm). **Exchange money** at **Volksbank,** on the *Marktplatz* (open Mon.-Wed. 8am-4:30pm, Thurs. 8am-5:30pm, Fri. 8am-4pm). Rent **bikes** at the **Fahrradgarage,** at Herzoggasse 3 (tel. 21 10 or 899 87), the tiny alley that leads from *Marktplatz* to the footbridge (DM15 per day). **Heinz Glas,** Industrie 18 (tel. 30 55), will rent you a **canoe** for a cruise down the Altmühl River (DM20 per day Mon.-Fri., DM25 Sat.-Sun.; under 12 50% off). A convenient **pharmacy** is **Dom Apotheke,** Domplatz 6 (open Mon.-Fri. 8am-12:30pm and 2-6pm, Sun. 8am-noon). The **post office,** 85072 Eichstätt, is located at Domplatz 8 (open Mon.-Fri. 8:30am-noon and 2-5:30pm, Sat. 9am-noon). The **telephone code** is 08421.

Accommodations and Food Eichstätt's **Jugendherberge (HI),** Reichenaustr. 15 (tel. 44 27; fax 90 21 62), is clean, modern, spacious, and comfortable. Follow directions to Willibaldsburg, except turn right halfway up Burgstr. onto Reichenaustr at the *Jugendherberge* sign. (Reception open 8-9am, 5-7pm, and 9:45-10pm. Lockout 10am. Curfew 10pm. DM20. Under 27 only. Breakfast included. Sheets DM5.50.

Closed in Dec. and Jan.) The Catholic University **Mensa** is down toward the end of Ostenstr. Buy a card (DM3) from the cashier on the first floor. (Cashier open noon-1:30pm. Student ID required. Meals DM3.80-5.70. *Mensa* open Mon.-Fri. 11:30am-2pm during term; summer 11:30am-1:30pm; open mid-Sept.-Aug. 5) A relaxed **cafeteria** on the first floor has outdoor garden seating (open Mon.-Thurs. 8:15am-7pm, Fri. 8:15am-3pm; Aug. daily 8:15am-3pm). In town there's **Backstube,** Luitpoldstr. 19 (tel. 897 60), a small student hangout with beer (DM3-5) and baguettes (DM8.50-13) day and night. **La Grotta,** Marktplatz 13 (tel. 72 80), is an oasis of red-checkered tablecloths with affordable pizzas and pasta (DM10-15), set just off the *Marktplatz* (open Wed.-Mon. 10:30am-2:30pm and 5:15-11pm).

Sights Conspicuously watching over the town from its high perch across the river is the **Willibaldsburg.** To reach the castle from the train station, take a right; at the main intersection, turn right and follow the main street one block to turn left onto Burgstr. The 14th-century castle now houses the **Jura-Museum** (Jurassic Museum; tel. 29 56), filled with fossils from that geological period found in the Altmühltal Valley, once covered by the vast Jurassic Sea. Dinosaur movies are screened daily at 10am and 3pm (Oct.-March daily at 11am and 2:30pm). The **Historisches Museum** (tel. 60 01 74), also in the Willibaldsburg, picks up the story at the debut of *Homo sapiens* and continues it through the Roman presence in the area. (Both museums open Tues.-Sun. 9am-noon and 1-5pm; Oct.-March Tues.-Sun. 10am-noon and 1-4pm. Admission to each DM5, students DM4, children under 15 free.)

Across the river, Eichstätt proper is built around the extravagant **Residenzplatz,** surrounded by the Rococo episcopal palaces. The west wing has a particularly magnificent portal, and the interior is just as richly decorated. Tours of the **Residenz** (tel. 702 20) begin here if there are at least five people (Easter-Oct. Mon.-Thurs. at 11am and 3pm, Fri at 11am; Sat.-Sun every 30min. 10-11:30am and 2-3:30pm). In a corner of the *Residenzplatz*, in the middle of a fountain, stands the **Mariensäule** (Madonna Column). Behind the *Residenz* is the 14th-century **Hohe Dom** (High Cathedral): part Romanesque, part Gothic, and part Baroque. The east apse features richly colored stained glass, and the north aisle shelters the intricate 15th-century stone **Pappenheim Altar.** On the other side of the high altar is the entrance to the **Mortuarium** (Mortuary), resting place of Eichstätt's bishops, in which the carved Gothic **Schöne Säule** (Beautiful Column) rises to meet the vault.

Also in the cathedral complex is the **Diözesan-Museum,** Residenzplatz 7 (tel. 502 79), an examination of the history of the diocese since its founding in 741 by St. Willibald (open April-Oct. Tues.-Sat. 9:30am-1pm and 2-5pm, Sun. 11am-5pm; admission DM2.50, children DM1.50). Two blocks further on Leonrodplatz is the Baroque **Schutzengelkirche** (Church of the Guardian Angel), built during the Thirty Years War, containing richly carved wooden altars and a striking golden sunburst above the high altar. Five-hundred sixty-seven sculpted angels—including two black angels—fly about the church's interior. Start counting.

■ Ingolstadt

Site of the first Bavarian university from 1472 to 1800, the old Danube city of Ingolstadt is now best known as the home of the Audi. The name of this luxury car company was originally *Horch,* German for "eavesdrop," and the last name of auto innovator and entrepreneur August Horch. After World War II it was changed to *Audi,* Latin for "listen," to help exports in an international market resistant to German-sounding products. It would take more than a name change, however, to shake the traditional look of this old town. Ingolstadt possesses all the elements of a good Bavarian *Altstadt*—half-timbered houses and Renaissance façades—with half the number of tourists.

Orientation and Practical Information Ingolstadt's **tourist office,** in the *Altes Rathaus,* Rathausplatz 4, 85049 Ingolstadt (tel. 30 10 98; fax 30 10 99), hands out free maps, English-language brochures, and a list of hotels and pensions in the area but does not provide a room-finding service (open Mon.-Fri. 8am-5pm, Sat. 9am-noon.). They offer free German-language city tour on Saturdays at 2pm. To reach the tourist office and the rest of the old city from the distant train station, take bus #10, 15, 16, or 44 (DM2.30), going to the right from the station, five stops to "Rathaus-platz" (buses every 10-20min.). You can also trek down Bahnhof Str. to Münchener Str. and head left over the bridge down Donau Str. to the *Rathausplatz* (20min.). **Exchange money** at **Volksbank,** Theresien Str. 32 (open Mon.-Wed. 8am-4:30pm, Thurs. 8am-5:30pm).**Trains** roll between Ingolstadt and Munich (2-3 per hour.; 1 hr.). **Public transportation bus** routes center around the **Omnibusbahnhof,** located in the middle of the city (single fare DM2.30; day tickets DM7). For a **taxi,** call 12 66. Rent a **bike** at **Radverleih Fahrradinsel,** Krenz Str. 2 (tel. 322 11). Arrange to share a ride at the local **Mitfahrzentrale,** Münchenerstr. 25 (tel. 678 96; open Mon.-Fri. 10am-noon and 2-7pm, Sat. 10am-2pm; Berlin DM50, Munich DM10). In an **emergency,** call 192 22. The **telephone code** is 0841.

Accommodations Ingolstadt's superb **Jugendherberge (HI),** Friedhofstr. 4½ (tel. 341 77; fax 91 01 78), is located in a renovated section of the old town fortifications. From the tourist office, take Moritzstr. and make a left on Theresienstr. Follow it all the way to Kreuztor, then walk through the Kreuztor and cross Auf-der-Schanz (10min.). Or take bus #10 to "Omnibusbahnhof" and change to bus #50, 53, or 60 to "Jugendherberge/Kreuztor." Then follow Herderstr. one block to Unterer Graben, turn right, and follow Oberer Graben in a left-curving stretch all the way to the Kreuztor. Large echoing rooms and cavernous hallways. (Reception open 3-9pm. Curfew 11:15pm, but visitors have been known to climb through the large ground-floor windows. Under 27 only. DM19. Sheets DM5.50. Open Feb.-mid-Dec., but closed every 2nd and 4th weekend from Nov. 11-Dec. 15 and Feb. 1-March 15.) **Pension Lipp,** on Feldkirchenerstr. (tel. 587 36), down Schloßländestr. along the Donau and left up Frühlingstr., is pleasant if out-of-the-way. But it's the closest remotely affordable *Pension.* (Singles DM40, with bath DM45. Doubles DM75, with shower DM85.) Campers can head out to **Campingplatz Auwaldsee** (tel. 68 911), but *a car is a must.* The site is off the E45/Autobahn A9, five minutes by car from the town center. (DM7.10 per person, under 12 DM4.90. DM5.10 per tent. DM9.90 per car. Open April-Sept.) Ingolstadt's other *Pensionen* and *Gasthöfe* tend to cost dearly.

Food and Nightlife Ingolstadt's budget eats and buzzing student nightlife are both conveniently found on Theresienstraße, which becomes Kreuz Straße closer to the **Kreuztor,** the epicenter of the nighttime scene.

Glock'n, Oberer Graben 1 (tel.349 90), is the really loud café abutting the Kreuztor. Especially popular in the summer when the benches and the kegs move outside. Daily dishes form pasta to pork DM5-15. Beer starts at DM4.50 (0.5L), but save 50 *Pfennig* and buy a *Maß* (DM8.50 for 1L). You'll end up drinking that much anyway. Open daily 6pm-2am.

Sigi's Café, Kreuz Str. 6 (tel. 329 52), a few steps down from Glock'n, is small, chic, and light green. Nice outdoor seating. *Wieners,* mozzarella sandwiches, and salads for DM6.50-10.50. Open Mon.-Sat. 9am-2am, Sun. 2pm-2am.

Englwirt, Kreuz Str. 11 (tel. 324 12), is popular with the alternative set. Hip and spartan—a few trophies decorate the walls. Pinball. During the week, bring a pack of cards and join in on the games. All beers DM4 (0.5L). Open daily 8pm-2am.

Neue Welt, Griesbadgasse 7 (tel. 324 70). Right off Kreuz Str., this bar is home to the local artistic and musical crowd, with its own stage, the **Kleinkunstbühne.** Musical cabarets and concerts premier regularly on Thurs. Try the chili, a *Tsatsiki* (DM5), or a Greek salad (DM7). Open daily 7pm-2am.

Goldener Stern, Griesbadgasse 2 (tel. 354 19). Just down a step from Neue Welt, in a light yellow house with big wooden tables. Beer starts at DM3. Show up for the smoky crowds or sit outside in the beer garden. Open daily 7pm-1am.

BAVARIA (BAYERN)

Sights and Entertainment The old city wall is magnificently represented by the turreted **Kreuztor,** topped by dainty caps and stone ornamentation. Other remnants of the city's medieval fortifications (including numerous ponds as moat relics) are scattered around the city. Two blocks east of the Kreuztor stands the late Gothic **Liebfrauenmünster** (Minster of our Dear Lady), full of ornate altars and dramatic, even inspiring, vaulting. A few blocks south on Anatomiestr. is the **Alte Anatomie,** an 18th-century university building which now houses the **Deutsches Medizinhistorisches Museum** (German Museum of Medical History), Anatomie Str. 18/20 (tel. 305 18 60). It features an 18th-century "do-it-yourself" enema stool complete with a hand-operated water pump and a padded seat with a small protruding 3-inch-long pipe. The "skeleton room" displays skinned human corpses with some of the dried-up muscles still attached, and an eerie collection of shrivelled guts and limbs. The fun never ends. A very detailed English brochure describing Ingolstadt's six main museums is available for free at all museum entrances, and the Medicine History museum keeps will cheerfully lend you an even thicker English guidebook to interpret the German-only exhibits. (Open Tues.-Sun. 10am-noon and 2-5pm. Admission DM3, students and seniors DM1.50. Free on Sun.) North of the *Münster* at the corner of Jesuiten and Neubaustr. is the "Rococo jewel," the **Maria-de-Victoria-Kirche** (Church of Our Lady of Victories; tel. 175 18). This once spare chapel for students of the nearby Catholic school was rococoed with a vengeance in 1732, and an awe-inspiring frescoco now adorns the ceiling. (Open Tues.-Sun. 9am-noon and 1-5pm. Ring for the caretaker. Admission DM1.) Across town on Paradeplatz is the 15th-century **Neues Schloß,** Paradeplatz 4, a red-tiled castle which now houses the **Bayerisches Armee-Museum** (Bavarian Military Museum; tel. 350 67), collected under King Ludwig "If-I-weren't-crazy-I'd-be-dangerous" II. The display of old firearms and suits of armor is notable for its size rather than its particular interest (open Tues.-Sun. 8:45am-4:30pm; admission DM3.50, students DM1, seniors DM2, children DM0.50; free on Sun.). Right off of Donaustr. near the Konrad-Adenauer-Brücke is the brand new **Museum für Konkrete Kunst** (Museum for Concrete Art), Tränktorstr. 6-8 (tel. 305 18 06). Stare at bold geometric designs in primary colors until your eyes get screwy (open Tues.-Wed. and Fri.-Sun. 10am-1pm and 2-6pm, Thurs. 10am-1pm and 2-8pm; admission DM3, students DM1.50).

Those fascinated by automobiles can call **Audi** for information on tours (tel. 89 12 41). Ingolstadt has a fabulous outdoor **swimming pool,** just to the right beyond the *Kreuztor* (open May-Sept. Mon.-Sun. 8am-8pm). There's also a **flea market** in Ingolstadt every first and fourth Sunday of the month at Manchinger Str. 125, every second Sunday in the Donauhalle, and every third Sunday in the Herrenschwaige.

■ Augsburg

Founded by Caesar Augustus in 15BC, Augsburg was the financial center of the Holy Roman Empire and a major commercial city by the end of the 15th century. The town owed its success and prestige mainly to the Fuggers, an Augsburger family that virtually monopolized the banking industry; Jakob Fugger "the Rich" was personal financier to the Habsburg Emperors. The third largest Bavarian city was also the birthplace of Bertolt Brecht. In 1945, after years in exile, Brecht addressed the angry, haunting poem "Epistle to the Augsburgers" to the residents of the town. With a somewhat large university, a somewhat intact town wall, and a somewhat interesting set of museums, Augsburg may provide a somewhat enjoyable stopover on your way somewhere else.

Orientation and Practical Information The resourceful **tourist office,** Bahnhofstr. 7 (tel. 50 20 70; fax 502 07 45), off Königsplatz about 300m from the train station down Bahnhofstr., finds rooms for DM3 (open Mon.-Fri. 9am-6pm). There's also an office at Rathausplatz (tel. 502 07 24) with longer hours. Free brochures and maps in English (open Mon.-Fri. 9am-6pm, Sat. 10am-4pm, Sun. 10am-1pm). Walk straight from the station to the end of Bahnhofstr. and take a left at

McDonald's onto Annastr. Take the third right and you'll see Rathausplatz on the left; the tourist office is on the right. The **Mitfahrzentrale,** Barthof 3 (tel. 15 70 19), arranges ride-shares for a small fee (open Mon.-Sat. noon-9pm). **Rent bikes** at **Travel Enquires,** at the *Hauptbahnhof* (tel. 32 64 93), counter 6 (open daily 6am-8pm). Augsburg is connected by **train** to Munich (3-4 per hour.; 40-60min.), Nuremberg (1-2 per hour.; 1-1½hr.), Würzburg (change at Treuchtlingen; 1-2 per hour.; 2½hr.), and Stuttgart (2-3 per hour.; 1½-2hr.). The infamous **Europabus** line, which canvasses the Romantic Road route, stops at the Augsburg train station (northbound at 10:10am; southbound at 6:20pm). For medicinal wares, check out the **Rathaus Apotheke,** on Rathausplatz, to your left as you face the *Rathaus* (open Mon.-Fri. 8:30am-6pm, Sat. 8:30am-noon). Augsburg's **post office,** 86150 Augsburg, is on Viktoriastr. to the left of the station (open Mon.-Fri. 8am-10pm, Sat.-Sun. 8am-8pm). The **telephone code** is 0821.

Accommodations To reach Augsburg's **Jugendherberge (HI),** Beim Pfaffen-keller 3 (tel. 339 09; fax 15 11 49), take streetcar #2 (DM 1.70) from the *Bahnhof* (direction: Kriegshaber) to "Stadtwerke." Continue on foot in the same direction up Hoher Weg, then right onto Inneres Pfaffengäßchen behind the church; follow the left side of this small alley along the wall until you the reach the marked hostel drive-way. The alley is not well-lit; try to walk it during the day. Alternatively, walk straight up Bahnhofstr. from the station to Königsplatz, bear left on Annastr., then right on Karlstr. and straight on to Hoher Weg; turn left and follow the above directions from there. Bland, worn rooms feel like converted second-grade classrooms, but the hostel is central and the price is right. (Reception open 8-9am, 2-4pm, and 8-10pm. Curfew 1am. Under 27 only. DM18. Sheets DM5.50. Key deposit DM20 or an ID. Excellent breakfast included. Call ahead. Open late-Jan.-early-Dec.) Augsburg has a dearth of inexpensive, centrally located rooms. Try **Gasthof Lenzhalde,** Theolottstr. 2 (tel. 52 07 45; fax 52 87 61). From the *Bahnhof,* bear right onto Halderstr., take a sharp right onto Hermannstr., and cross the Gögginger bridge. Take the first right onto Rosenaustr. and follow it for several blocks directly to the hotel, located 0.75km from the station. (Singles DM42, with shower DM50. Doubles DM78.) Or have the tourist office find you a room in the suburbs (DM30-40 per person). To camp at **Camping-platz Augusta,** ABA Augsburg Ost, am Autobahnsee (tel. 70 75 75), take the bus (direction: Neuburg) to "Autobahnsee" and follow the signs; the camp is about 400m away (DM6 per person, DM5 per tent).

Food Don't miss the **Stadtmarkt** (farmer's market) between Fuggerstr. and Annastr., right past the St. Anna Kirche on Fuggerstr. (open Mon.-Fri. 7am-6pm, Sat. 7am-1pm). For hot and meaty items, check the **Fleischmarkt** in the middle of the Stadtmarkt. Most corner joints sell the local beer, *Riegele Augsburg.* To stock up on basics, visit the **Penny Markt** at Maximilianstr. 71, to the right from the *Rathaus* (open Mon.-Fri. 8:30am-6pm, Sat. 8am-12:30pm). The vegetarian option in town is **Bräustüble Goldene Gans,** Weite Gasse 11 (tel. 51 22 66). Facing the *Rathaus,* walk right to the end of Maximilianstr. and take a right. Filling and slightly pricey vegetar-ian dishes like *Pfannkuchen mit Sommergemüse* (pancakes with summer vegeta-bles; DM16) and a beer garden to boot (open Mon.-Sat. 11am-2pm and 6-10pm). Dine with your shades and smokes at **Café Max,** Maximilianstr. 67 (tel. 15 47 00). This side-walk hangout serves student food (including hearty breakfasts all day long) at student prices (open Mon.-Sat. 7am-11pm., Sun. noon-11pm).

Sights Old, rich Jakob Fugger founded the **Fuggerei** quarter in 1519 as the first wel-fare housing project in the world. The narrow cobblestone streets and little gabled houses are a haven for the elderly, who earn their keep by praying for the departed souls of the Fuggers and pay only DM1.72 (the equivalent of a "Rhein Guilder") rent annually. Budget travelers need not apply, but good Catholic families and widows with total yearly earnings of less than DM250 have the chance at simple, three-room accommodations with kitchens. To reach the Fuggerei from the *Rathaus,* walk behind the Perlachturm tower on Perlachberg, which becomes Barfüßerstr. and finally Jakobstr, and turn right under the archway. The gates close at 10pm. The **Fuggerei Museum** documents this classic piece of urban planning, as well as the financial adventures of its patrons (open March-Oct. daily 9am-6pm; admission DM1, students and seniors DM0.70).

Augsburg's medieval past unfolds at the brightly frescoed **Guildhaus,** down Burgermeister-Fischer-Str., now part of the marketplace area; it lies down Bahnhofstr. from the train station along the edge of the park, past the streetcars. From the Guildhaus, a left down Maximilianstr. leads to the huge Renaissance **Rathaus** (open daily 10am-6pm; free). The brightly painted ceiling of the **Goldener Saal** depicts tradesmen and women recalling the importance of commerce in Augsburg's history (admission DM2). Down Hoher Weg to the left is the **Hoher Dom** (cathedral), the regional bishop's seat. The cathedral was built in the 9th century, renovated in the Gothic style in the 14th century, and damaged in World War II. The chancel and high altar are intelligent examples of *Bauhaus*-inspired design, prevalent in German churches since the war (open Mon.-Sat. 6am-5pm; closed holidays). If you go to the left of the Perlachturm, down Perlachberg and left onto Auf dem Rain, you'll arrive at the **Bertolt Brecht Haus.** The birthplace of one of the most influential 20th-century playwrights and poets, it chronicles his life through photographs, letters, and his own poetry. (Open Tues.-Sun. 10am-5pm; Oct.-April Tues.-Sun. 10am-4pm. Admission DM2.50, students and children DM1.50.)

▓ Romantic Road (Romantische Straße)

Between Würzburg and Füssen, in the Lechtal at the foothills of the Alps, lies a beautiful countryside of walled cities, castles, elaborate churches, and dense forest. Sensing opportunity, the German tourist industry in 1950 christened these ancient, bucolic, and chivalrous backwaters the Romantic Road and set about exploiting them. Be warned—this is the most heavily touristed area in Germany; although the region is beautiful, it will be a group experience. Deutsche Bahn's **Europabus** transports lots of 50-year-old tourists on daily buses from Frankfurt to Munich (12hr., change at Dinkelsbühl for Füssen) and back from April 1 to October 31. Though this is one of the most popular ways to travel the Romantic Road, it is also one of the slowest—there is only one bus in each direction per day. Buses on the Frankfurt-Munich route stop at Frankfurt (southbound 8am/northbound 8:30pm), Würzburg (9:45am/6:35pm), Rothenburg (arrives 12:45pm, leaves at 2:45pm/arrives 2:40pm, leaves at 4:15pm), Dinkelsbühl (arrives 3:25pm, leaves at 4:15pm/arrives 12:45pm, leaves at 2pm), Nördlingen (4:55pm/12:05pm), Augsburg (6:20pm/10:25am), and Munich (7:50pm/9am). On the Dinkelsbühl-Füssen route buses stop at Dinkelsbühl (southbound 4:15pm/northbound 1:05pm), Augsburg (6pm/10:50am), Wieskirche (northbound only, 8:35am—with a 20-min. stop for sightseeing, leaves at 8:55), Hohenschwangau (Neuschwanstein Castle; 8:33pm/8:07am), and Füssen (8:40pm/8am)—this last bus does not stop in Munich. Check schedules with a tourist office before heading to the bus. The Europabus is also relatively expensive (Frankfurt to Rothenburg DM58; to Dinkelsbühl DM69; to Munich DM113. Dinkelsbühl to Hohenschwangau or Füssen, DM60. Students and under 26, 10% off; under 12 and over 60, 50% off; under 4 free. Eurail or German Rail Pass holders ride free, but each backpack must pay a ridiculous one-time "registration" fee of DM10). A more economical way to see the Romantic Road for those without railpasses is to use the faster and much more frequent **trains**, which run to every town except Dinkelsbühl (take a tourist-free bus from Nördlingen or Dombühl). Those traveling the Romantic Road by **car** may find themselves parking in large, specially-built lots outside the old city walls of some towns, but will have easy access to many suburban budget hotels, *Privatzimmer,* and campgrounds that lie outside the reach of foot travelers. Tourist offices can provide maps and information to the many travelers who **bike** the route. The Road makes a satisfying bike journey, but if you go with this option, plan carefully—most campgrounds are 10-20km apart. Some travelers reportedly hitch the route successfully; *Let's Go* does not recommend hitchhiking as a safe mode of transportation. For information or (optional) reservations call **Deutsche Touring** in Frankfurt, Am Römerhof 17 (tel. (069) 790 32 81; fax 790 32 19). For general information, contact the **Romantische Straße Arbeitsgemeinschaft,** Marktplatz, 91550 Dinkelsbühl (tel. (09851) 902 71; fax 902 79). Almost all of their brochures are available in English.

ROTHENBURG OB DER TAUBER

Rothenburg ob der Tauber is *the* Romantic Roadstop. Easily accessible from everywhere, Rothenburg is touched by everyone. Expect a camera-clicking family of four from Livingston, New Jersey or Kyoto, Japan on every corner, and watch closely as they clear out of town on the afternoon bus, headed south with bagfuls of Christmas ornaments, stomachs full of Christmas pastries, and heads reeling with happy Christmas thoughts. While Rothenburg (ROTE-en-boorg) is busy enjoying the same commercialized fate as its favorite December holiday, don't knock all the touristic pomp; this small Bavarian town is probably your only chance to see a nearly intact medieval walled city that doesn't contain a single modern building within.

Rothenburg became a first-class tourist mecca by making a virtue out of a necessity. Though it withstood plagues, earthquakes, and plundering hordes, major commercial routes shifted after the Thirty Years War, leaving poor Rothenburg, which lacked the money to finance new building projects, to stagnate. At the end of the 19th century, locals blessed with kitschy foresight set up strict preservation laws in order to preserve their 16th century town; if only they could see it now. Rothenburg narrowly escaped complete devastation in World War II, when 40% of the town was reduced to rubble by bombs. Amazingly, the 14th-century fortified walls and towers endured and today can be toured in their entirety. To see the main sights, however, you'll have do battle with the competition; these days they don't happen to be legions of plundering hordes, but throngs of camera-clicking tourists.

Orientation and Practical Information Rothenburg's **tourist office,** Marktplatz 1 (tel. 404 92), generously supplies handy maps in English and books rooms (DM40-60), usually for free (DM2 during peak times). Walk left from the station, bear right on Ansbacher Str., and follow this street straight into the city to the *Marktplatz* (10-15min.). The tourist office is on your right, across the square (open Mon.-Fri. 9am-12:30pm and 2-6pm, Sat. 9am-noon and 2-4pm). **Tours in German** depart from the steps of the *Rathaus* (April-Oct. daily at 11am and 2pm; DM5). **English-language tours** meet at the Riemenschneider Hotel, Georgengasse 11, to the left of the tourist office (daily at 1:30pm; DM5). An old tour guide with a spark in his hobble leads the special "night watchman tour," leaving from the town hall steps in the *Marktplatz* (English at 8pm; German at 9:30pm; DM4). **Trains** run every hour from major cities to Steinach, where you can transfer for a quick trip to Rothenburg (15min.). **Buses** also serve the route, sometimes in place of the train in the evening (see Europabus info, p. 274). The last bus leaves the train station for Steinach at 8:05pm. For a **taxi** call 20 00 or 72 27.

You can **exchange money** at the travel agency (tel. 46 11; fax 868 07) in the same space as the tourist office, or at **Volksbank,** on Ansbacher Str. (tel. 405 50; open Mon. 8:15am-noon and 2-6pm, Tues.-Fri. 8:15am-noon and 2-4:30pm). Rent **bikes** at the train station for DM10 per day with a train ticket, DM15 without (open Mon.-Fri. 4:30-11am and 11:45am-7pm, Sat. 7:30-9am and 9:45am-2:15pm, Sun. 7:30-10:45am and 11:45am-3:45pm), or at **Rad und Tat,** Bensenstr. 17 (tel. 879 84; DM20 per day; ID required; open daily 9am-6pm). The **Wäscherei Klaus Theu,** a **laundromat** located at Johannitergasse 9 (tel. 27 75), charges DM6.50 to wash and DM3 for 25 minutes of drying (open daily 8am-8pm). If you're feeling particularly dirty and are in a pinch, give 'em a call; the laundromat and Pension Then (see below) are owned by a father-son tandem; they absolutely *love* tourists. **Toppler-Apotheke,** Ansbacher Str. 15 (tel. 36 56), has a list in its window of opening times and addresses of all other **pharmacies** (open Mon.-Tues. and Thurs.-Fri. 8am-12:30pm and 1:30-6pm, Sat. 8am-12:30pm). The main **post office** is at Bahnhofstr. 7 (tel. 20 61), 91541 (open Mon.-Fri.

8:15am-noon and 2-5:30pm, Sat. 8:15am-noon); a smaller branch, at Milchmarkt Str. 5 (tel. 30 61), is open similar hours (open Mon.-Fri. 8:30am-12:30pm and 2-5pm, Sat. 9:30am-12:30pm). Both will exchange money and traveler's checks. The **telephone code** is 09861.

Accommodations An incredible number of **private rooms** (DM20-45) not registered with the tourist office are available—they're marked by *"Zimmer frei"* signs. Just knock on the doors with the signs to inquire. Housed in medieval buildings, Rothenburg's two youth hostels share common management. "Wonder Twin powers...activate!" Check in at the **Jugendherberge Rossmühle (HI),** on Mühlacker 1 (tel. 45 10; fax 57 62), at Rossmühleweg, a former horse-powered mill that shelters a modern set of carpeted rooms and a groovy staff. Amenities include ping-pong tables, a TV room where you can borrow movies, free storage lockers (DM5 deposit required), train schedules, and a weather board—this is what all hostels should be like. Follow the directions to the tourist office, take a left down Obere Schmiedgasse, and go straight until you see the *Jugendherberge* sign to the right—it's a good 20-minute walk from the station. (Reception open 7-9am, 5-7pm, and 8-10pm. Curfew 11:30pm, but they'll give you an access code to the door so you can come back any ol' time. DM19. Sheets DM5.50. Under 27 only. Showers and a tasty breakfast included.) The **Jugendherberge Spitalhof (HI)** exists as additional housing for Rossmühle, and is only a stone's throw down the street (same reception, curfew, and hours as Rossmühle).

Rothenburg has an unbelievable number of *Pensionen* for a town of its size, but most of them are expensive. For an exception, definitely check out **Pension Raidel,** Wenggasse 3 (tel. 31 15), on the way to the hostel. Head down Obere Schmiedgasse and make a left on Wenggasse. Bright rooms and fluffy featherbeds, each one built, carved, painted, and restored by the mellow, do-it-yourself owner, make this the most charming and authentic of the affordable *Pensionen* in the *Altstadt*. (Singles DM35. Doubles DM69, with shower DM89. Breakfast included. Call ahead.) Included in the price of a room or apartment at **Pension Then,** Johannitergasse 8a (tel. 51 77; fax 860 14), is an insider's advice on the ins and outs of Rothenburg, an optional trip to the Wednesday night meeting of the local English conversation club (of which the owner Willy Then is vice president), and the chance to go fishing on the Tauber, à la Willy aussi. (Singles DM40. Doubles DM70. Apartment with kitchen DM22.50 per person with a 3-day minimum stay.) From train station, turn left and then right on Ansbacherstr., then right on Johannitergasse. **Gasthof zum Ochsen,** Galgengasse 26 (tel. 67 60; fax 876 57), is reached by taking a left from the station, bearing right on Ansbacher Str., taking the second right after the stone archway onto Rosengasse, and then making a left at Galgengasse. These comfortable, newly remodeled rooms at staggeringly good prices are close to the town center. (Singles DM28-32, with shower DM48. Doubles DM50-55, with shower DM90. Excellent breakfast included.) A few hundred meters from the city walls but eons away from the cameras, the **Unter den Linden Gästhaus** (tel. 27 34) can hold up to eight people in its bright white, newly redone abode, next door to the Unter den Linden Café. Eat in their kitchen or outdoors in the forest on the banks of the Tauber (here merely a 5m-wide stream). Definitely call ahead. Follow same directions as to the café (see below). Camping is available at **Tauber-Romantik** (tel. 61 91), in the valley "where nobody goes." Follow the steep path toward "Detwang" for 20 minutes. (Open Easter-late-Oct. DM6.50 per person, DM6 per tent. 90 places.)

Food With a cozy Christmas theme all year-round, it's not surprising that Rothenburg is famed for its delicious *Schneeballen* (snowballs), large balls of sweet dough with a sweet center (often marzipan) that are twisted and then dipped in dark chocolate, light chocolate, nuts, or powdered sugar. **Dillers,** Hofbronner Gasse 16 or Hafengasse 4 (tel. 866 23), offers these doughy concoctions at industrially-produced rates (DM2.40-5); you can also watch the bizarre snowball-making process there as well (open Mon.-Fri. 10am-6pm, Sat. 10am-2pm, Sun. 10am-6pm). Reasonable meals can be found at **Zum Schmölzer,** Stollengasse 29 (tel. 33 71). Try the *Schweine-braten* (two scrumptious pork medallions with dumplings on the side) for DM11.60. The dumplings make up for the slightly austere atmosphere (open Thurs.-Tues. 11:30am-1:30pm and 6-8pm). If you're looking for a cheap meal, Italian food is always a good bet. **Pizzeria Roma,** Galgengasse 19 (tel. 45 40), serves hefty pasta dishes (DM8-13) and pizzas (DM4-12) long after the rest of town has gone to bed (open daily 11:30am-midnight). **Unter den Linden** (tel. 27 34), in a grove on the Tauber River, is a café-bar far off the beaten (tourist) track. Snacks are DM3-9. Head under the archway at St.-Jakobs-Kirche and follow Klingengasse through the town gate, then make a left to the sloping path into the valley to "Detwang." At the bottom (5min.), make a left; the café is down the short hill (open April-Oct. daily 10am-10pm; shorter hours in winter—call ahead). **Milchmarkt,** Milchmarkt 6 (tel. 60 68), has little pizzas for DM7.50 and pricier Franconian dishes for DM10-20 (open daily 11:30am-9pm). Pick up fresh goods at the **Markt** (open Wed. and Sat. 7am-noon).

Sights The main attraction in Rothenburg is, of course, the town itself. On *Marktplatz* stands the Renaissance **Rathaus** (open daily 8am-6pm; free). Scope out the town from the tower (open daily 9:30am-12:30pm and 1-5pm; Nov.-March Mon.-Fri. 9:30am-12:30pm, Sat.-Sun. noon-3pm; admission DM1, children DM0.50). On this site in 1631, the conquering Catholic general Johann Tilly offered to spare the town from devastation if any local resident could chug a wine keg containing almost a gallon of wine. *Bürgermeister* Georg Nusch successfully met the challenge—then passed out for several days. His saving **Meistertrunk** (master drink) is reenacted with great fanfare several times each year. Inside the courtyard behind the *Rathaus* are the **Historiengewölbe** (Historical Archways), which articulate the history of the Thirty Years War from a Rothenburg perspective. Three gloomy stone cells lurk in the dungeon, where Mayor Heinrich Toppler and his son were once imprisoned by King Ruprecht; his wife tried to dig them out (open daily 9am-6pm; Oct.-Nov. and Jan.-Apr. 10am-5pm, Dec. 1-4pm; admission DM3, students DM2, children DM1). The **Reichsstadtmuseum,** Klosterhof 5 (tel. 404 58), housed in a former 13th-century Dominican convent, displays a number of rooms whose contents are preserved from the Middle Ages. See the famous 15th-century twelve-panel painting of Christ's passion and the original wine *Krug* from the *Meistertrunk* (open daily 9:30am-5:30pm; Nov.-March 1-4pm; admission DM4, students DM3, children DM2).

The town's cool **Medieval Crime Museum,** Burggasse 3 (tel. 53 59), is definitely worth the entrance fee for anyone who can stomach the thought of iron-maiden justice. Take a picture of yourself in the stocks outside before heading into the dim, creepy basement for the **torture exhibits.** *Feel* the pain. The large rooms upstairs continue the fun, with exhibits on "eye for an eye" jurisprudence and the special punishments once reserved for bad musicians, dishonest bakers, and frivolous gossips. All displays are labeled in English (open daily 9:30am-5:30pm; Dec. and March daily 10am-3:30pm; Nov. and Jan.-Feb. daily 2-3:30pm; admission DM5, students DM4, children DM3). The **Doll and Toy Museum,** Hofbronnengasse 13, off the *Marktplatz* (tel. 73 30), offers lots of old toys displayed in neat little rows and glass cases (open daily 9:30am-6pm; Jan.-Feb. daily 11am-5pm; admission DM5, students DM3.50, families DM12).

Camp holds brazen sway at Käthe Wohlfahrt's **Christkindlmarkt** (Christ Child Market), Herrngasse 2, and the more extensive **Weihnachtsdorf** (Christmas Village), Herrngasse 1 (tel. 40 90; fax 40 94 10). They're a must-see even if you *aren't* looking for a 4-m-long nutcracker or a pea-sized porcupine. As your eyes glaze over like *Schneeballen,* head to the second floor of the *Weihnachtsdorf* for damaged items at 20-50% off; the cash registers never stop jingling, as more nutcrackers get sold than there are nuts on the planet to crack (stores open Mon.-Fri. 9am-6:30pm, Sat. 8am-2pm; also Easter-Nov. Sun. 10am-6pm). If your sanity hasn't been depleted, stop in the brand new **Teddyland,** Herrngasse 10 (tel. 89 04; fax 89 44), Germany's largest teddy bear shop. Don't be a cynic—it's cuddly and adorable (open Mon.-Fri. 9am-6:30pm, Sat. 9am-4pm).

Entertainment The **Figurentheater,** am Burgtor at Herrngasse 38 (tel. 73 54 or 33 33), is Rothenburg's fantastically nonsensical puppet theatre—better than the Von Trapp kid show. The guest book proudly displays Pablo Picasso's simple but elegant word of applause, *"Merveilleux"* (shows June-Sept. Mon.-Sat. at 3pm and 8:30pm; Nov.-May Mon.-Sat. at 8:30pm; evening shows DM15, students DM10; matinees DM10, students DM8). To go **fishing** in the Tauber River, call Herr Schmidt (the town tour guide and grave digger) at tel. 58 39.

Rothenburg prides itself on a tourist-friendly array of annual festivals. On Easter Sunday, the famed **Hans-Sachs-Spiele** (Hans Sachs play) and the **Schäfertanz** (Shepherd's Dance) are performed on the *Marktplatz*. The two displays celebrate, respectively, the shoemaker-cum-*Meistersinger* Hans Sachs, who wrote 208 plays, and the banishment of the plague from Rothenburg by dancing shepherds. On the Friday before Pentecost (Whitsun), the historic **Meistertrunk** is re-enacted. The **Reichsstadt-Festtage** (City Festival) is held in the second week of September with marches and festivals, as cattle traders, knights, and mutinous peasants all gather. Tickets for all events can be purchased at the *Reisebüro* (DM12-25). At Christmas, Rothenburg becomes a giant gingerbread house filled with mulled wine, Franconian *Bratwürst,* organ and brass band concerts, and nightly torchlight processions through the snow. A ski jump has been incorporated as part of the re-enactment of the *Meistertrunk*. But remember, the Rothenburgers are professionals who've been doing this for centuries; *Let's Go* does not recommend that you drink and ski.

DINKELSBÜHL

Forty kilometers to the south of Rothenburg, Dinkelsbühl boasts an impressive bevy of medieval half-timbered houses, a climbable 16th-century churchtower, and a navigable town wall. Sound familiar? It is, though locals claim their town's superiority lies with Dinkelsbühl's authenticity; it houses the largest collection of original, unrestored structures on the Romantic Road (repainting, of course, doesn't count.) The Gothic **St. Georgskirche** sprouts a Romanesque tower and striking fan vaulting. A tale for tourists explains why the houses along **Nördlinger Str.** are oddly-shaped—medieval superstition held that homes with right angles housed demons. Since every little town needs a cute little festival, Dinkelsbühl's got **Kinderzeche** (children's weeping), which celebrates the town's salvation during the Thirty Years War, and the **100 Years Children's festival,** an even larger bash that occurs in the summer (July 18-27 in 1997) commemorating a century of this infantile partying. The town tots' tears reputedly persuaded the invading field commander of Swedish King Gustavus Adolphus to spare Dinkelsbühl. A recreation of the event accompanies parades, fireworks, dances, and, of course, crying kids (DM3 for the required "festival badge"; seats at the various performances DM3-12). The **Park Ring** around the *Altstadt* separates the old and newer parts of town. New to the old town is the spiffy **3-Dimensional Museum** (tel. 63 36), housed in the Nördlinger Tor of the town wall (entrance through the gate and to the left). The only such museum in the world, it encompasses all the different ways (since the Middle Ages) that people have represented thick stuff in thin ways (open daily 10am-6pm; Nov.-March Sat.-Sun. 11am-4pm; admission DM10, DM9 with a coupon from the tourist office).

The **tourist office** (tel. 902 40; fax 902 79), on the *Marktplatz*, finds rooms for DM3 and distributes free maps and schedules to the *Kinderzeche* festival. The office also **rents bikes** (DM7 per day). To get there, walk right from the *Bahnhof* and take the first left. Follow the footpath over tow bridges and into the city, then take the first right onto Nördlingerstr., which empties into the *Marktplatz;* the tourist office is in the rust-colored building on your right (open Mon.-Fri. 9am-noon and 2-6pm, Sat. 10am-noon and 2-5pm, Sun. 10am-1pm; Nov.-March Mon.-Fri. 9am-1pm and 2-6pm, Sat. 10am-1pm.) The town's defunct **train station** now serves as a **bus station.** Buses go to Rothenburg (3-5 per day; DM22.50; no railpasses) and Nördlingen (5-6 per day; fewer on weekends; DM7.60; no railpasses). Schedules are posted at the tourist office and at the station. As in any Romantic Road town, be wary of the **Europabus** tour

LET'S GO® TRAVEL

DISCOUNTED AIRFARES

EURAIL PASSES

1997

CATALOG

WE GIVE YOU THE WORLD...AT A DISCOUNT

1-800-5-LETSGO

TRAVEL GEAR

Let's Go carries a full line of Eagle Creek packs, accessories, and security items.

A. World Journey

Equipped with Eagle Creek Comfort Zone Carry System which includes Hydrofil nylon knit on backpanel and shoulder straps, molded torso adjustments, and spinal and lumbar pads. Parallel internal frame. Easy packing panel load design with internal cinch straps. Lockable zippers. Black, Evergreen, or Blue. The perfect Eurailing pack. $20 off with rail pass. $195

B. Continental Journey

Carry-on sized pack with internal frame suspension. Detachable front pack. Comfort zone padded shoulder straps and hip belt. Leather hand grip. Easy packing panel load design with internal cinch straps. Lockable zippers. Black, Evergreen, or Blue. Perfect for backpacking through Europe. $10 off with rail pass. $150

ACCESSORIES

C. Padded Toiletry Kit

Large padded main compartment to protect contents. Mesh lid pocket with metal hook to hang kit on a towel rod or bathroom hook. Features two separate small outside pockets and detachable mirror. 9" x 4¾" x 4¼". Black, Evergreen, or Blue. *As seen on cover in Blue.* $20

D. Padded Travel Pouch

Main zipper compartment is padded to protect a compact camera or mini binoculars. Carries as a belt pouch, or use 1" strap to convert into waist or shoulder pack. Front flap is secured by a quick release closure. 6" x 9" x 3". Black, Evergreen, or Blue. *As seen on cover in Evergreen.* $26

E. Departure Pouch

Great for travel or everyday use. Features a multitude of inside pockets to store passport, tickets, and monies. Includes see-thru mesh pocket, pen slots, and gusseted compartment. Can be worn over shoulder, around neck, or cinched around waist. 6" x 12". Black, Evergreen, or Blue. *As seen on cover in Black.* $16

SECURITY ITEMS

F. Undercover Neckpouch

Ripstop nylon with a soft Cambrelle back. Three pockets. 5¼" x 6½". Lifetime guarantee. Black or Tan. $9.95

G. Undercover Waistpouch

Ripstop nylon with a soft Cambrelle back. Two pockets. 4¾" x 12" with adjustable waistband. Lifetime guarantee. Black or Tan. $9.95

H. Travel Lock

Great for locking up your Continental or World Journey. Anondized copper two-key lock. $5

CLEARANCE

Call for clearance specials on a limited stock of travel packs, gear, and accessories from the 1996 season.

Prices and availability of products are subject to change.

1-800-5-LETS GO

EURAIL PASSES

Let's Go is one of the largest Eurail pass distributors in the nation.
Benefit from our extensive knowledge of the European rail network.
Free UPS standard shipping.

Eurail Pass (First Class)
Unlimited train travel in 17 European nations.

15 days	$522
21 days	$678
1 month	$838
2 months	$1148
3 months	$1468

Eurail Flexipass (First Class)
Individual travel days to be used at your convenience during a two month period.

10 days in 2 months	$616
15 days in 2 months	$812

Eurail Youthpass (Second Class)
All the benefits of a Eurail pass for passengers under 26 on their first day of travel.

15 days	$418
1 month	$598
2 months	$798

Eurail Youthpass Flexipass (Second Class)
All the benefits of a Flexipass for passengers under 26 on their first day of travel.

10 days in 2 months	$438
15 days in 2 months	$588

Europass
Purchase anywhere from 5 to 15 train days within a two month period for train travel in 3, 4, or 5 of the following countries: France, Germany, Italy, Spain, and Switzerland. Associate countries can be added. Call for details.

Pass Protection
For an additional $10, insure any railpass against theft or loss.

Call for details on Europasses, individual country passes, and reservations for the Chunnel train linking London to Paris, Brussels, and Calais. Rail prices are subject to change. Please call to verify price before ordering.

DISCOUNTED AIRFARES
Discounted international and domestic fares for students, teachers, and travelers under 26.
Purchase your 1997 International ID card and call 1-800-5-LETSGO for price quotes and reservations.

1997 INTERNATIONAL ID CARDS
Provides discounts on airfares, tourist attractions and more. Includes basic accident and medical insurance.

International Student ID Card (ISIC)	$19
International Teacher ID Card (ITIC)	$20
International Youth ID Card (GO25)	$19

See order form for details.

HOSTELLING ESSENTIALS

1997-8 Hostelling Membership
Cardholders receive priority and discounts at most international hostels.

Adult (ages 18-55)	$25.00
Youth (under 18)	$10.00

Call for details on Senior and Family memberships.

Sleepsack
Required at many hostels. Washable polyester/cotton.
Durable and compact. $13.95

International Youth Hostel Guide
IYHG offers essential information concerning over 4000 European hostels............................... $10.95

TRAVEL GUIDES
Let's Go Travel Guides
The Bible of the Budget Traveler
Regional & Country Guides (please specify)

USA...$19.99
Eastern Europe, Europe, India & Nepal,
Southeast Asia......................................$16.99
Alaska & The Pacific Northwest, Britain & Ireland, California, France, Germany, Greece & Turkey, Israel & Egypt, Italy, Mexico, Spain & Portugal, Switzerland & Austria...$17.99
Central America, Ecuador & The Galapagos Islands, Ireland..$16.99
City Guides (please specify).......................$11.99
London, New York, Paris, Rome, Washington, D.C.

Let's Go Map Guides
Fold out maps and up to 40 pages of text
Map Guides (please specify) $7.95
Berlin, Boston, Chicago, London, Los Angeles, Madrid, New Orleans, New York, Paris, Rome, San Francisco, Washington, D.C.

1-800-5-LETS GO

ORDER FORM

International Student/Teacher Identity Card (ISIC/ITIC) (ages 12 and up) enclose:
1. Proof of student/teacher status (letter from registrar or administrator, proof of tuition payment, or copy of student/faculty ID card. FULL-TIME only.)
2. One picture (1 ½" x 2") signed on the reverse side.
3. Proof of birthdate (copy of passport, birth certificate, or driver's license).

GO25 card (ages 12-25) enclose:
1. Proof of birthdate (copy of passport, birth certificate, or driver's license).
2. One picture (1 ½" x 2") signed on the reverse side.

Last Name   First Name   Date of Birth

Street   *We do not ship to P.O. Boxes.*

City   State   Zip Code

Phone (very important!)   Citizenship (Country)

School/College   Date of Travel

Description, Size	Color	Quantity	Unit Price	Total Price

SHIPPING & HANDLING Eurail pass does not factor into merchandise value **Domestic 2-3 Weeks** Merchandise value under $30 .... $4 Merchandise value $30-100 .... $6 Merchandise value over $100 .... $8 **Domestic 2-3 Days** Merchandise value under $30 .... $14 Merchandise value $30-100 .... $16 Merchandise value over $100 .... $18 **Domestic Overnight** Merchandise value under $30 .... $24 Merchandise value $30-100 .... $26 Merchandise value over $100 .... $28 All International Shipping $30	Total Purchase Price	
	Shipping and Handling (See box at left)	
	MA Residents (Add 5% sales tax on gear & books)	
	TOTAL	
	From which Let's Go Guide are you ordering? ☐ Europe ☐ USA	
	MASTERCARD ☐ **VISA** ☐ ☐ Other_____	
	Cardholder Name:	
	Card Number:	
	Expiration Date:	

Make check or money order payable to:

Let's Go Travel
http://hsa.net/travel
67 Mt. Auburn Street • Cambridge, MA 02138 • USA • (617) 495-9649

1-800-5-LETS GO

groups flooding into the town around 1pm and 4pm. **St. Paul's Apotheke,** Nördlinger Str. 7 (tel. 34 35), is the most convenient **pharmacy** (open Mon.-Fri. 8am-12:30pm and 2-6pm, Sat. 8am-noon). For the **police,** call 888. The **post office,** 91550 Dinkelsbühl, is 100m to the right of the station (open Mon.-Fri. 9am-noon and 2-5pm, Sat. 9am-noon). The **telephone code** is 09851.

Built in 1508 as a grain store, the **Jugendherberge (HI),** Koppengasse 10 (tel. 95 09; fax 48 74), is a huge, half-timbered house three blocks from the town center. (Reception open daily 5-10pm. Under 27 only. DM17.50. Sheets DM5.50. Breakfast included. Open March-Oct.) **Pension Gerda,** Nestleinsberggasse 22 (tel. 18 60), is a 10-minute walk away from the *Marktplatz* (DM34 per person; breakfast included). Following the directions to the tourist office, take a left onto Turmgasse, and then a right onto Nestleinberggasse by the city wall. Another option that's closer to the hustle and bustle of the *Markt,* **Gasthof Sonne,** Weinmarkt 11 (tel. 57 670; fax 75 48), has airy rooms to which you can stumble up after visiting their *Biergarten.* (Singles DM40. Doubles DM70. Triples DM102. Breakfast included. Showers off the hall.) Check the tourist office for possibly cheaper **private accommodations** (doubles start at DM45). Over the river, north of the city on Dürrwanger-Str., is the **DCC Camping-park Romantische Straße** (tel. 78 17; DM6.50 per person, DM15 per tent and car; reservations accepted).

Budget food is hard to come by in touristy Dinkelsbühl. Head to **City Grill,** Nördlinger Str. 8, for burgers, *Döner Kebap,* and *Würst* (DM3.50-8; open daily 10am-11pm). **Café Lechler,** Nördlinger Str. 17 (tel. 73 70), is a favorite of locals and tourists alike, serving beer (DM3.40), elaborate ice cream confections (DM8-12), and portions of local cuisine (open Mon.-Sat. 9am-midnight, Sun. 1pm-midnight).

■ Würzburg

Surrounded by vineyard slopes and bisected by the Main River, Würzburg is the bustling center of the Franconian wine region and home to one of Germany's greatest palaces, the magnificent Baroque "Residenz." The splendor of the palace is all but overshadowed, however, by the imposing 13th-century Marienburg Fortress across the river that overlooks the town. The fortress is a testament to the immense secular power of Würzburg's *Fürstbischöfe* (prince-bishops), whose forerunners first established themselves when Würzburg became a bishopric in 742. Despite its origins as a religious center, Würzburg is now largely a university town. It was at Würzburg's university that Wilhelm Conrad Röntgen discovered X-rays and their medical uses in 1895, for which he was awarded the first-ever Nobel Prize six years later. Though wartime bombing destroyed much of the town's 18th-century magnificence, its older giants remain unchanged, making Würzburg a scenic portal for Germany's great tourist trail, the Romantic Road.

ORIENTATION AND PRACTICAL INFORMATION

With its three separate tourist information offices (one situated right outside the train station), Würzburg is a traveler's dream come true. To get to the city's center at the *Markt,* follow Kaiserstr. straight ahead from the station, then take a right on Juliuspromenade, and hang a left onto Schönbornstr., the main pedestrian and streetcar road; the *Markt* is a few blocks down and to your right. The Main River separates the rest of the city from the green, steep hills on which the fortress stands.

Tourist Office: Main Office, in front of the train station (tel. 374 36). Provides a packet with a free map and a hotel list for DM0.50; they also help find rooms for DM5. Open Mon.-Sat. 10am-6pm. If it's past hours, grab a hotel list from the machine outside (DM0.50). Another tourist office is in the **Haus zum Falken** (tel. 373 98), an ornamental yellow building on the *Marktplatz* that's reminiscent of a wedding cake. Open Mon.-Fri. 10am-6pm, Sat. 10am-2pm. Yet a 3rd office is located in the **Palais am Congress Centrum** (tel. 373 35), near the Friedens-brücke, where Röntgenring intersects the Main River. Open Mon.-Thurs. 8:30am-

4pm, Fri. 8:30am-noon. If you're desperate for a room, call the **24-hr. accommodations hotline** at 194 14.

Trains: Bahnhofplatz (tel 344 25). Trains run to Frankfurt (1 per hr.; 1hr.), Nuremberg (2 per hr.; 1-1½hr.), Munich (1 per hr.; 2½hr.), Hamburg (1 per hr.; 3½hr.), and Rothenburg (13 per day; 1hr.; change at Steinach).

American Express: Haugerpfarrgasse 1 (tel. 35 56 90; fax 355 69 69), right off of Kaisertr., a block from station. The usual array of services for those who don't leave home without it; commission-free money exchange even for those who did. Open Mon.-Fri. 9:15am-6pm, Sat. 10am-1pm.

Telephones: At the post office.

Buses: Europabuses head down the Romantic Road to Rothenburg (DM26) and Munich (DM82) daily at 10am, departing from bus platform #13 to the right of the station. Eurail and German Rail Passes valid (except the *BahnCard*); if you don't want to use up a precious day, buy a ticket with a railpass for 50% off. Students without a railpass get 10% off. The return bus to Frankfurt stops at Würzburg daily at 6:45pm. Reservations can be made 3 days in advance with the **Deutsche Touring Büro,** Am Römerhof 17 (tel. (069) 790 32 56), in Frankfurt.

Public Transportation: For information, call 363 52. **Streetcars** are the fastest and most convenient way around, but large sections of the city are not covered. The **bus** network is comprehensive, though most routes do not run nights and weekends. Ask for **night bus** schedules at the WSB kiosk in front of the train station. Single fare DM2, 24-hr. ticket DM6.50.

Ferries: Schiffstouristik Kurth & Schiebe (tel. 46 29 82; dock kiosk tel. 585 73) or **Veitshöchheimer Personenschiffahrt GMBH** (tel. 915 53; dock kiosk tel. 556 33) depart from the Alter Kranen wharf near the Congress Centrum to the Veitschöchheim Castle (40min.; one-way DM8, round-trip DM13).

Bike Rental: Max und Moritz, Pleicher Kirchplatz 11 (tel. 576 00; fax 576 10). DM17 per day. From the station, turn right on Röntgenring, left on Koellikerstr., right on Bohnesmühlgasse, and left on Pleicher Kurchplatz (10-15min.). Open Mon.-Sat. 8am-12:30pm, Sun. 10am-noon.

Mitfahrzentrale: Kiosk in front of train station (tel. 194 48 or 140 85). Arranges ride shares. Open Mon.-Fri. 9am-6pm, Sat. 9am-1pm, Sun. 11am-1pm.

Bookstore: Buchladung Neuer Weg, Sanderstr. 23/25 (tel. 355 91). Has an adequate selection of modern and classic novels in the back around the corner. Open Mon.-Wed., Thurs. 9am-7pm, Fri. 9am-6pm, Sat. 9am-1:30pm.

24-Hour Pharmacy: Engel-Apotheke, Marktplatz 36 (tel. 525 43), lists night-service pharmacies on the door. Open Mon.-Fri. 8:30am-6pm, Sat. 8:30am-1pm.

Rape Crisis Line: Contact **Frauenhaus** (tel. 45 00 70).

Emergency: Medical Aid: tel. 192 22. **Police:** tel. 110. **Fire:** tel. 112.

Post Office: Bahnhofplatz 2, 97070 Würzburg (tel. 330). Exchange money, cash traveler's checks, or call the folks back home. Open Mon.-Fri. 6am-9pm, Sat. 6am-8pm, Sun. 9am-8pm.

Telephone Code: 0931.

ACCOMMODATIONS AND CAMPING

The one drawback to this otherwise excellent city is the lack of budget accommodations. Aside from the youth hostel, rooms for under DM45 are a rarity—they're about as hard to find as Waldo. Würzburg's least expensive beds are around the train station, on (or just off) Kaiserstr. and Bahnnhofstr.

Jugendgästehaus (HI), Bukarderstr. 44 (tel. 425 90; fax 41 68 62), near St. Burkard's Basilica, across the river from downtown. Take streetcar #3 (direction: Heidingsfeld) or 5 (direction: Heuchelhof) to "Löwenbrücke," then backtrack, go down the stairs marked by the "Jugendherberge/Kappele" sign, turn right, walk all the way past 2 streets and a Sparkasse on the left, go through the tunnel, and it's immediately on your left. Watch out for loiterers when walking back at night. A modern, enormous villa, with views of the fortress from the carpeted, spacious (for a youth hostel) rooms. Reception open 8am-10pm. Check-in 2-5:15pm and 6:30-10pm. Curfew 1am. Top-floor beds (20 people in 1 huge room) DM23, others DM27. Under 27 only. Breakfast and sheets included.

Pension Spehnkuch, Röntgenring 7 (tel. 547 52; fax 547 60), to the right of the *Bahnhof* down Röntgenring Str. Newly redone, very white, and very bright. Laid-back, kind owner. Singles DM50. Doubles DM85, high season (April-June and Sept.-Nov.) DM90. Shower and toilet on floor. Breakfast included.

Pension Siegel, Reisgrubengasse 7 (tel. 529 41), a block down Kaiserstr. from the train station, on your left. Amateur murals of tropical isles lead up cramped stairs to small but comfortable-and-clean rooms. Reception open 2-10:30pm. Nice singles DM46. Doubles DM89. Breakfast included. Reservations recommended.

Gasthof Goldener Hahn, Marktgasse 7 (tel. 519 41; fax 519 61), in a little golden building with green-checkered stained glass windows directly off the northwest corner of the *Markt.* Clean rooms have telephones and TVs; some have partial views of the *Markt.* Singles DM40-50, with shower and toilet DM80. Doubles with shower and toilet DM140.

Pension Groene, Scheffelstr. 2, 97072 Würzburg (tel. 744 49). Streetcar #1 or 4 (direction: Randersacker) to "Ehehaltenhaus," then take a left onto Sonnenstr. and a right onto Scheffelstr. A bit cheaper, but a lot farther away. Rooms are comfort-able and clean. 11 beds. Singles DM36-38. Doubles DM63-66. Phone reservations accepted. No single-night stays. No breakfast.

Camping Kanu-Club, Mergentheimerstr. 13b (tel. 725 36). Streetcar #3 or 5 (direc-tion: Heidingsfeld) to "Judenbühlweg." Right on the river. Reception open noon-10pm. DM4 per person, DM3 per tent, DM1.50 per shower.

FOOD AND ENTERTAINMENT

For run-of-the-mill *Imbiß* fare, the area around the train station is serviceable, but you can do much better in Würzburg. To sample some of the region's distinctive wines, try **Haus des Frankenweins Fränkischer Weinverband,** Krankenkai 1 (tel. 120 93). Würzburg's answer to Munich's *Oktoberfest,* the city-wide **Kiliani Festival,** is held during first two weeks in July. The huge annual **Wine Festival** takes place in early June and late September to early October. Adventurous souls should snoop around the bohemian back alleys of the city's south side, especially on Sander Str., the heart of the university subculture, where idiosyncratic people, curious food, and low prices abound in smoky dens and grottoes. There is a farmer's market on the *Markt* (open Tues. 6am-6pm, Wed. 6am-4pm, Fri. 6am-6pm, Sat. 6am-2pm).

University Mensa, in the *Studentenhaus* on Am Exerzierplatz, at Münzstr.; through the doors to your left. Assembly-line eating. Würzburg University ID technically required, but even without it, it's cheap. Buy meal tickets at the machines outside of the dining room. Meals run DM2.25 (with ID) to DM4.50 (without ID). Open mid-Oct.-mid-July Mon.-Fri. 11am-1:30pm, Sat. 11:30am-1:30pm; evening meals Mon.-Thurs. 5:30-7:30pm. Closed on Saturdays Feb.-March. Look for job offers, roommates, and musical/cultural happenings.

Kult, Landwehrstr. 10 (tel. 531 43), right off Sanderstr., is one of the more visible bar-café-*Kneipen* for hip local alternatives. Off-beat decor, friendly staff, and revo-lutions brewing in the corner. Mexican peanuts and corn kernels in hot chili oil, with bread (DM5.80). Mellow, but crowded at night. Open Mon.-Fri. 9am-1am (if too hot outside, open 9am-2pm and 6pm-1am), Sat. 6pm-1am, Sun. 11am-1am.

Uni Café, Neubaustr. 2 (tel. 156 72), on the corner of Sanderstr. Relaxed student atmosphere and outdoor sidewalk seating. *Very* popular. Cakes, baguettes, salads, breakfasts (DM3.50-9.50). Open Mon.-Sat. 8am-1am, Sun. 9am-1pm.

Café Brückenbäck, An der Alten Mainbrücke (tel. 41 45 45). From the hostel, turn left on Saalgasse and walk 2 blocks. A view of Marienburg fortress, a view of the Main, a view of all the interesting folks crossing the main pedestrian bridge too. Tasty sandwiches (DM5-14), salads (DM 6-13), and an unending list of liquid refreshments. Open Mon.-Fri. 8am-1am, Sat.-Sun. 9am-1am.

La Clochard, Neubaustr. 20 (tel. 129 07). Crêpes (DM5-12), sandwiches (DM7-11), and vegetarian dishes like *Jogurt-Kartoffeln* (potatoes topped with yogurt, cucum-bers, and tomatoes; DM9.90) by a cozy corner fireplace. Old-World decor clashes with alternative music in this student hang-out.

Café Journal, Juliuspromenade 56. Close to the train station. International newspapers on tables and walls. Outdoor sidewalk seating. Mixed crowd of young, old, and older. Baguettes, pretzels (DM3-8), and cocktails.

Till Eulenspiegel, Sanderstr. 1a (tel. 134 73). Ivy-covered building with a beer garden out back. Big Würzburger bar scene, named after medieval Germany's merry jester. Beer and cocktails (DM3.50 and up). Entrees served after 5pm (DM4-12). Open daily.

SIGHTS

Marienburg Fortress, the striking symbol of the city, keeps its vigil high on a hillside over the Main. The footpath to the fortress starts a short distance from the **Alte Mainbrücke.** German paintings, furniture, and *objets d'art* cluster in the **Fürstenbau Museum** (tel. 438 38; open Tues.-Sun. 9am-5pm, Oct.-March Tues.-Sun. 10am-4pm; admission DM4, students DM3, under 15 free, if accompanied by an adult). The fortress also houses the **Mainfränkisches Museum** (tel. 430 16), with statues by Würzburg's native son, Tilman Riemenschneider, the **Master of Würzburg.** A genius of Gothic styling, Riemenschneider sided with the peasants in their 16th-century revolts against Luther and the powers-that-were. When the insurrection was suppressed, the sculptor's fingers were broken as punishment, and he was never able to work again (open April-Oct. Tues.-Sun. 10am-5pm, Nov.-March Tues.-Sun. 10am-4pm; admission DM3.50, students DM2; pass to both museums DM6). Masochists can make the climb to the fortress in under an hour. Or take bus #9 from the "Spitäle" bus stop at the western end of the bridge (May to mid-Oct. every 30min. 9:43am-5:43pm; DM2). On the next hill stands the **Käppele,** a graceful 18th-century church designed by the Würzburg architect Balthasar Neumann.

In 1168, 12 years after he married Beatrix of Burgundy in Würzburg, Friedrich Barbarossa raised the local bishop to the rank of "Prince." The **Residenz** palace (tel. 355 17 12), Neumann's masterpiece, was the base camp for Würzburg's prince-bishops during the Enlightenment. It stands over the sweeping Residenzplatz (a 15-min. walk down Kaiserstr. and Theaterstr. from the station). The vibrant ceiling fresco by Johannes Zick in the first-floor garden room has never been restored; in fact his use of extravagant colors got Zick fired. The Italian painter Giovanni Tiepolo was hired to finish the job in a more sedate style. His ceiling fresco in the grand staircase is the largest in the world, and certainly among the most ostentatious. (Open Tues.-Sun. 9am-5pm; Nov.-March Tues.-Sun. 10am-4pm. Admission DM5, students and seniors DM3.50. Last admission 30min. before closing.) The **Residenzhofkirche** is astounding: the gilded moldings, pink marble, and frescoes make this little church the apex of Baroque fantasy (open Tues.-Sun. 9am-noon and 1-5pm, Nov.-March Tues.-Sun. 10am-noon and 1-4pm; free).

Behind the *Residenz* complex is the **Hofgarten,** a studiously laid-out park with a large rose garden (open dawn-dusk; free). In front of the *Residenz* down Hofstr. stands the 900-year-old **Dom of St. Killian,** on Domstr. (tel. 536 91). It was rebuilt in the mid-1960s after being obliterated in 1945. Smell the paint; the cathedral appears almost toyishly new. St. Killian, an Irish missionary bishop who became the city's patron saint, was killed with two other missionaries in the ducal court in the year 689. The cathedral is supposed to hold his remains. Tilman Riemenschneider (see above) is responsible for the Gothic highlights of this large Romanesque cathedral. (Open Mon.-Fri. 10am-5pm, Sun. 1-6pm, Nov.-Easter Mon.-Fri. 10am-noon and 2-5pm, Sun. 12:30-1:30pm and 2:30-6pm. Tours April-Oct. Mon.-Sat. at noon, Sun. at 12:30pm. DM3, children DM2.) The **Stift Haus,** at the end of Bahnhofstr., is a great find with its moving altarpiece, Tintoretto's *Crucifixion.* Two different operators run **cruises** (see Ferries, p. 274) to the **Veitshöchheim Castle** (tel. 915 82). The palace grounds are a public park (open April-Sept. Tues.-Sun. 9am-noon and 1-5pm; admission DM3, students DM2). Two-hour **English tours** around the city are given mid-April to October, Tues.-Sun. at 11am. Tour fees (DM13, students DM10) includes entrance to the *Residenz;* meet at the *Haus zum Falken* tourist office. A German-language city tour without the Residenz (1½hr.) is given all year daily at 10:30 am (DM6,

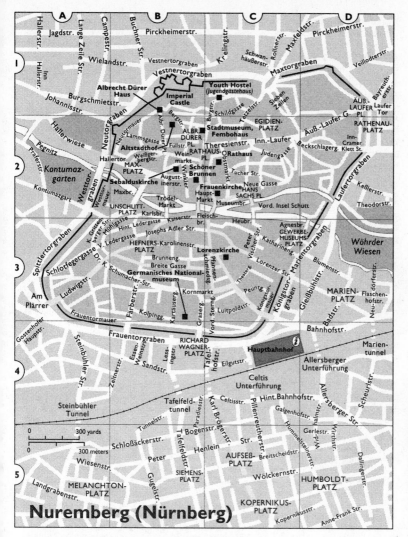

Nuremberg (Nürnberg)

students DM4). Free **Rathaus tours** (1½hr.) in German are given every Saturday at 10am and 4:30pm (Nov.-Dec. and Feb.-April at 10am only).

■ Nuremberg (Nürnberg)

Although the city's official tourist pamphlet cites *Bratwurst*, Albrecht Dürer, and the local soccer team as its most memorable cultural possessions, Nuremberg is a city inextricably bound to a darker past. The very mention of the city that provided the backdrop for massive annual Nazi party rallies from 1927 to 1935 and lent its name to the 1935 racial purity laws that paved the way for the Holocaust still conjures up totalitarian imagery of the sort immortalized in Leni Riefenstahl's film *Triumph des Willens (Triumph of the Will)*. Because of Nuremberg's close ties to Nazi power, the Allies chose this city as the site for the war-crime trials.

It was Nuremberg's long association with the imperial traditions of the Holy Roman Empire that originally attracted Hitler to the city. After Nuremberg was declared a "free city" by Kaiser Ludwig the Bavarian in 1332, its local government answered to no authority lower than the Emperor. The imperial *Reichstag* met here until 1543, the imperial jewels were locked in a tower over the *Spital*, and each of the more than 30 Holy Roman Emperors paid an obligatory visit to the town's *Kaiserschloß* (imperial castle) at some point during his reign.

Its checkered past aside, contemporary Nuremberg is a model of post-war Teutonic prosperity. The second-largest city in Bavaria after Munich, Nuremberg is home to industries which employ over 265,000 people, and the city is equipped with a bustling regional airport and a dizzyingly extensive (but efficient) public transportation system. Its wide variety of attractions (they really do have a good soccer team here) beckons visitors of every stripe.

ORIENTATION AND PRACTICAL INFORMATION

Nuremberg's thriving central district is neatly encircled by the old city wall. From the train station, cross the street onto Königstr. to find yourself in the middle of the main shopping district. Both Lorenzerplatz and the Hauptmarktplatz lie directly ahead; most of this part of the *Altstadt* is a pedestrian zone. The far end of the old city is marked by the *Burg*.

Tourist Offices: Verkehrsverein, in the central hall of the *Hauptbahnhof* (tel. 233 61 32; fax 233 61 66). Mailing address: Congress und Tourismus Zentrale, Frauentorgraben 3, 90443 Nürnberg. They will provide you with English-language city maps (DM0.50), free brochures, schedules of events, and guides for young people. They also find rooms for a DM5 fee. Open Mon.-Sat. 9am-7pm. The branch office on the northern side of the *Hauptmarkt*. Open Mon.-Sat. 9am-6pm; Dec (during *Christkindlmarkt*) Mon.-Sat. 9am-7pm, Sun. 10:30am-7pm.

Budget Travel: ABR Reisebüro, across from the tourist office in the train station (tel. 201 00), deciphers train schedules. Open Mon.-Fri. 9am-6pm, Sat. 10am-1pm.

Currency Exchange: The **AmEx** office is the cheapest opportunity for those with or without The Card; the post office is another good bet (see below). Beware of the often absurd fees and rates at *Wechsel* stands.

American Express: Adlerstr. 2 (tel. 23 23 97; fax 22 49 26), off Königstr., near Lorenzerplatz. Great rates and no service charges for changing cash and traveler's checks. Members may cash personal checks, and anyone carrying AmEx checks may receive held mail. Open Mon.-Fri. 9:30am-5:30pm (cashier closed noon-2pm), Sat. 9:30am-12:30pm.

Telephones: At the post office.

Flights: Located north of the city on Flughafenstr. (tel. 350 62 00). **City-Airport-Express** runs shuttles every 20-30min. 5:30am-11:30pm from the train station (20min.; DM6). Follow signs at the train station to the traffic island in front.

Trains: Hauptbahnhof, Bahnhofplatz 9 (tel. 194 19). To Munich (2 per hr.; 1½-2hr.), Berlin (13 per day; 5½-6hr.), Regensburg (1-2 per hr.; 1hr.), Würzburg (1-3 per hr.; 1hr.).

Public Transportation: A variety of possibilities: subway, streetcar, bus, regional train (known as *R-Bahn*), or S-Bahn. Single-ride tickets DM2.50-DM15.20, depending on distance. Day or weekend card DM7.20. Pick up a map at the tourist office.

Bike rental: Fahrradkiste, Knauerstr. 9 (tel. 287 90 64; fax 287 90 65), outside the south west corner of the walled *Altstadt*. Basic wheels DM7 per day (DM200 deposit required). Mountain bikes DM15 per day (DM400 deposit). Foreign currency accepted as deposit. Open Mon.-Fri. 11am-6pm, Sat. 10am-1pm.

Mitfahrzentrale: Strauchstr. 1 (tel. 194 44). A safer alternative to hitching. Open Mon.-Fri. 9am-6pm, Sat. 8:30am-1pm, and Sun. 11am-2pm.

Hitchhiking: *Let's Go* does not recommend hitchhiking as a safe means of transportation. Hitchers headed to Munich and Austria take U-Bahn #1 or 11 to "Bauernfeindstr.," then bus #59 to "Am Zollhaus" and the *Autobahn* interchange. Those going to Würzburg and Frankfurt take U-Bahn #1 to "Stadtgrenze" and walk to the A-3 interchange.

Lost and Found: Rothenburgerstr. 10 (tel. 26 10 70).
Laundromat: SB Waschsalon, Spitzenbergstr. 2, near the University Mensa. Take a load off for DM6, suds run DM1. Open daily 6am-11pm.
Rape Crisis: tel. 28 44 00. Counseling offered Mon. 10am-noon, Tues. 7-8pm, and Thurs. 4-6pm.
Pharmacy: City Apotheke, Königstr. 29. Open Mon.-Fri. 8:30am-6:15pm, Sat. 8:30am-2pm. Check the notices in *Nürnberger Zeitung* for 24-hr. pharmacies.
Hospital: Städtisches Klinikum, Flurstr. 17 (tel. 39 80). **Medical Assistance:** tel. 53 32 11 or 53 37 71.
Emergency: tel. 110 or 192 22. **Police:** Jakobsplatz 5, Nuremberg Mitte 1.
Post Office: Bahnhofplatz 1, 90402 Nürnberg. Cashes traveler's checks, exchanges money, and offers *Poste Restante.* Open Mon.-Fri. 8am-6pm, Sat. 8am-1pm, Sun. 11am-noon.
Telephone Code: 0911.

ACCOMMODATIONS AND CAMPING

You don't have to trek outside the *Altstadt* walls to hang your hat in an inexpensive *Pension,* but during the warmer months, you'd best phone first. If all else fails, the tourist office places dazed travelers into dazzling accommodations for a DM5 fee, or use the pocket change to hop a train to nearby Erlangen and storm the walls of the town's infrequently filled hostel/guest house.

Jugendgästehaus (HI), Burg 2, 90403 Nürnberg (tel. 22 10 24; fax 220 40). From the main hall of the train station, take the escalator down into the tunnel passage and walk straight ahead; bear right past the "U" mosaic, then left up to the sloping exit. Follow this main shopping street (Königstr.) over the bridge to the main marketplace (10min.). Head in the direction of the golden fountain on the far left and bear right on Burgstr. up to the top of the hill (in the direction of the sign pointing to the *Schulmuseum;* 20min.). Once a stable and grain storage house for the imperial castle, it's now a summer *Treffpunkt* (meeting place) for the town's high school hipsters. The hostel's Romanesque arches, wooden beams, unearthly starched sheets, fans, and friendly desk staff (prone to playing with the loudspeakers) make for good traveler storage. Reception open 7am-1am. Checkout 9am. Curfew 1am. Theoretical quiet time 10pm-7am. Under 27 only. DM27 for a room with a view, an excellent breakfast, and sheets that give "starch" new meaning. Frequently booked solid; reservations are strongly recommended.
Jugend-Hotel Nürnberg, Rathsbergstr. 300, 90411 Nürnberg (tel. 521 60 92; fax 521 69 54). Take streetcar #3 to "Ziegelstein" or bus #41 to "Felsenkeller." 25 min. north of town. Rustic and cheerful, but far out. Nice surrounding grounds complement the dorm rooms. Dorms DM24.50-28.50 per person, with shower and toilet DM26.50-30.50. Singles DM38.50, with bath DM43.50. Doubles DM62, with bath DM72. Breakfast included. Call ahead.
Bahnhofsmission, Bahnhofsplatz 9 (tel. 22 99). Located in the basement of the train station. If you're really out of luck, money, or energy to go anywhere else, you can sleep in one of their rooms, separated by curtains into primitive singles, doubles, and triples. If you're looking for comfort, this is not the place. 24-hr. guards. DM18 per person, breakfast included. You must arrive after 8pm.
Hotel Garni Probst, Luitpoldstr. 9 (tel. 20 34 33; fax 205 93 36), is 5min. from the train station. Follow the underground passage from the train station to Königsplatz, past Burger King on the left. Though the block is slightly seedy, the location is central. It's a jolly family establishment, and the rooms are neat and pink. Lucky singles in the attic run at DM37. Otherwise singles DM62, with shower DM70, and toilet DM75-85. Doubles DM90, with shower DM100, and toilet DM110-125.
Zum Schwänlein, Hintere Sterngasse 11 (tel. 22 51 62; fax 241 90 08), rests 5min. from the train station. Take the underground passage from the main hall of the train station up to Königstr. Back on your left is Frauentor Mauer Str., which runs into Hintere Sterngasse. The hotel is up on the left. Because the *Pension* borders the red light district, lone travelers may feel more comfortable passing the rather sketchy looking Frauentor Mauerstr. to take the left at Luipoldstr. 2 more lefts onto

Vordere Sterngasse and Hintere Sterngasse will bring you to the door. The *Pension* is quiet, its hallways soothing; small garden out back. Singles DM35-40, with shower DM50. Doubles DM60-70, with shower DM80. Reservations by mail only.

Haus Vosteen, Lindenaststr. 12, 90409 Nürnberg (tel. 53 33 25), is 20min. from the train station on a serene block. Follow Königstorgraben along the *Altstadt* walls until you meet Rathenauplatz. Take Maxtorgraben, then turn left onto Veillodterstr., and left at Lindenaststr. The 15 rooms are tastefully decorated with plush rugs and sunny spaces for reading. Singles DM38-55. Doubles DM80-95.

Pension Vater Jahn, Jahnstr. 13 (tel./fax 44 45 07). Take the west exit from the train station and head straight on Eilgutstr. for 3 blocks; turn left under the busy-trafficked Tafelfeld Tunnel. When you emerge you'll see *"Vater Jahn"* written on the side of the tall *Pension.* Comfortable, tidy rooms. Singles DM43, with shower and toilet DM63. Doubles DM75, with shower DM85, with shower and toilet DM95. Breakfast included.

Camping: Campingplatz am Stadion, Hans-Kalb-Str. 56 (tel. 81 11 22), in Volkspark Dutzendteich (see Sights, p. 292) behind the soccer stadium. Take U-Bahn South to "Messe Zentrum." DM8 per person. DM7 per tent. DM6.50 per car. Call ahead. Open May-Sept.

Camping: Campingplatz Am Kreuzweiher, in a neighboring town west of Nuremberg (tel. 56 79 75). From the train station take the bus to "Kalereuth Röckenhof." DM5.50 per person. DM4.50 per tent or car.

FOOD

Nuremberg is famous for its specialty foods—particularly for *Rostbratwurst* (mmm—grilled sausage), boiled *Sauerwurst,* and *Lebkuchen,* a candied variant of gingerbread (traditionally eaten at Christmas time but always available at an *Imbiß* stand near you; DM1-3).

Cince Citta, Gewerbemuseumsplatz 3 (tel. 20 66 67). Pronounced "Chinnay-Cheeta," this place packs 7 cafés, 12 movie theaters, and 1 disco into its 8-story, river-view, eating-out-and-getting-drunk multimedia mega-complex. The Italian joint, cappuccino bar, hearty Tex-Mex place, and crêperie all offer never-ending options for the budget traveler. All are open daily until 3am, and sometimes until 7am. Pick up their weekly magazine for movie schedules and opening times.

Al Castello, Burg Str. 12, sits just below the youth hostel. This rather dingy-looking building conceals some excellent pizza (DM10) and pasta dishes (DM9-14) as well as an extensive CD collection and amusing wall decoration. Don't be fooled— *Pizza Brot* means garlic bread (DM5.80). Open daily 6pm-1am.

Cafe Mohr, Färberstr. 3 (tel. 24 31 39). With an Art Deco-ish atmosphere overlooking a lively square, it's a fun place to meet and eat. Crêpes (DM4.50-8.50), healthy salads (DM6.50-11.50), and cappuccino lovelies. Open Mon.-Thurs. 9am-midnight, Fri.-Sat. 9am-1pm, and Sun. 2pm-midnight.

Bratwurst Häusle, Rathausplatz 1, next to St. Sebald's Church. This is the most famous and crowded *Bratwurst* spot in Nuremberg for a reason; as one local put it, "No one from Nürnberg comes here without his tourist." 6 *Rostbratwürste* with sauerkraut or spiced potato salad DM9-15.50. Open Mon.-Sat. 9:30am-10pm.

Salvatore, Innerer Laufer Platz 2-4 (tel. 35 56 20). Take a right on Theresienstr. (which becomes Innere-Laufer-Gasse) just uphill from the *Rathaus.* in the northeast corner of the *Altstadt* off Theresienstr. They serve 165 different dishes. Try the great spaghetti *carbonara* (DM10). Open daily 11am-2:30pm, 5pm-midnight.

SIGHTS

Allied bombing left little of old Nuremberg for posterity. A single air raid on January 2, 1945 wiped out 90% of the *Altstadt.* The churches, castle, and buildings were all reconstructed from the original stone between 1945 and 1966; most churches show empty pedestals where the exterior statues were lost in the bombing. From the train station, the closest part of the *Altstadt* is a walled-in area filled with cottages and shops; this is the **Handwerkhof,** a tourist trap masquerading as an historical attraction. The real sights lie farther up **Königstraße.**

Around the Altstadt and Castle

Nuremberg flaunts its opulence best in the *Altstadt*'s three churches. The **Lorenz-kirche** on St. Lorenzplatz was originally Catholic; like the town's other churches, it later converted to Protestantism. In World War II, all the transportable artwork was stashed to the cellar; the church itself was completely destroyed except for the towers. The beautiful Gothic structure has been completely restored and once again displays its priceless works of art. Of particular interest is the 20m-high **tabernacle,** with delicate stone tendrils curling up into the roof vaulting. The large wooden carving hanging in front of the altar is Veit Stoß's 1517 masterpiece *Engelsgruß* (Angel's Greeting; open Mon.-Sat. 9am-5pm, Sun. 1-4pm).

Across the river on Hauptmarktplatz stands the **Frauenkirche** (Church of Our Lady), a Catholic church again since 1916 (open Mon.-Sat. 8am-6pm, Sun. and holidays 12:30-6pm). The clock in the center of the façade is the site of the *Männlein-laufen* every day at noon: seven little **Kurfürsten** (nobles) circle three times around the seated figure of Kaiser Charles IV, the emperor who had the *Frauenkirche* built in 1350. Also on the Hauptmarktplatz is the **Schöner Brunnen** (Beautiful Well), which resembles nothing so much as the steeple of a Gothic church. Check out the 40 imaginatively carved figures, with Moses and the prophets way up top. On the side of the fountain facing the market, a golden ring has been incorporated into the wrought-iron railing. The trick is that there is no seam or joint in either ring or rail. Legend has it that a young metal-worker fell in love with the king's daughter and fashioned the seamless ring-rail in tribute; her father was so impressed that he allowed them to marry. The real **wish ring,** made of wrought iron, is hidden somewhere in the bannister; we'll let you find it yourself. Nuremberg superstition says that if you turn it three times, your wish will come true. It can't hurt to try.

Walk uphill from the Schöner Brunnen to find the **Rathaus** on your right. Built between 1616 and 1622 in early Baroque style with a little Renaissance classicism thrown in, Nuremberg's *Rathaus* once held the largest council chamber in central Europe, until it was destroyed by fire in 1945. Beneath the building are the **Loch-gefängnisse** (dungeons; tel. 231 26 90), containing an exhibit of medieval torture instruments. (Obligatory 25min. German tour every 30min.; English translation sheet available upon request. Open April-Sept. Mon.-Fri. 10am-4:30pm, Sat.-Sun. 10am-1pm. Admission DM4, students and children DM2.) To continue your tour of the Nuremberg Underground and rat playground, meet at the nearby Albrecht-Dürer-Platz for a one-hour guided walk through the **Felsengänge** (tel. 22 70 66), a web of passageways and cellars four to 25m below *Altstadt* street-level dating back over 100 years. Bring a jacket; it's cold enough down there to store large barrels of beer (tours descend daily from the Dürer statue at 11am, 1, 3, and 5pm; admission DM7, students DM5, children 10 and under free.) Across from the *Rathaus* is the **Sebalduskirche,** also a Protestant church. Annually the Catholic congregation celebrates the feast-day of St. Sebaldus by parading through town with his relics (that is, his corpse). During the other 364 days, he rests in his gilded cast bronze tomb in front of the altar (open daily 9:30am-6pm; Jan.-Feb and Nov. 9:30am-4pm; June-Aug. 9:30am-8pm). Up Burgstr. from the church is the fabulous **Fembo-Haus,** Burgstr. 15 (tel. 231 22 71), a lavishly ornamented patrician house which now contains the **Stadtmuseum.** (Open March-Oct. and during *Christkindlmarkt* Dec. 1-24. Tues.-Sun. 10am-5pm; Nov.-Feb. except *Christkindlmarkt* Tues.-Fri. 1-5pm, Sat.-Sun. 10am-5pm. Admission DM4, students and children DM2.)

Up the hill is the three-part castle: the **Kaiserburg** (Emperor's castle), the **Burg-grafenburg** (the castle count's castle), and the **Stadtburg** (the city castle; tel. 22 57 26). Kaiser Konrad III in the 13th century originally erected the *Kaiserburg* and the next emperor, Frederick Barbarossa, expanded it significantly. The spartan chambers of the *Kaiserburg* housed every Holy Roman Emperor after Konrad III: it was law that every German Kaiser spend at least his first day in office here. However, since the castle had no heating, the Kaisers usually spent their nights in the warm patrician homes of the *Altstadt*. Inside lurk the Romanesque **Emperor's Chapel** and the imperial living quarters. A 45-minute tour in German covers all parts of the Kaiserburg.

Maps in English cost DM2.50. (Open April-Sept. daily 9am-noon and 12:45-5pm; Oct.-March 9:30am-noon and 12:45-4pm. Last entrance at 11am in the morning and 3pm in the afternoon. Admission DM5, children DM3.50.)

Ruins of the Third Reich

The ruins of **Dutzendteich Park,** site of the Nazi *Parteitage* (Party Convention) rallies in the 1930s, ring with a deserted disquiet and an unsettling non-presence, reminding visitors of a darker time in German history. To get there, take R-Bahn #5 (direction: Neumarkt) to "Dutzendteich Bahnhof." From the train station, follow Bayernstr. to Herzogstr. until it meets Zeppelinstr. Keep walking down and you'll see the ruins on your right. Or take streetcar #9 (direction: Luitpoldhain) to the last stop, continue walking to your left until you reach the artificial lake; this is Dutzendteich (many areas are fenced off using electrified barbed wire, so be careful). **Zeppelin Field** sits on the far side of the lake near the massive marble platform from which Hitler addressed the throngs. The faint remains of a swastika, stained into the marble, is visible on the central promontory despite attempts to efface it.

The poles spaced intermittently along the desolate field once waved enormous banners, in the scenes made infamous in Leni Riefenstahl's film **Triumph des Willens** *(Triumph of the Will),* which immortalized the 1935 Party rally in one of the most terrifying, enduring documents of the "Fascist aesthetic." The overwhelming emotional power of Nazi events—which injected elements of Wagnerian theater and Catholic ritual into Fascist grandiosity—can be seen in the exhibit *"Faszination und Gewalt"* ("Fascination and Violence") located inside the **Zeppelin Tribüne** in the **Golden Hall** (entrance in rear; tel. 23 12 51). Even if you can't read German, the photographs of columns of Nazi troopers marching next to columns of concentration camp prisoners are moving. Inside the tribune, one looks up with a start and a shudder to find that the gold mosaic swastika on the ceiling of the tribune is still intact (open July-Oct. Tues.-Sun. 10am-6pm; free). The rest of the park envelops the Nazi-era **New Congress Hall** and the broad, untrafficked **Great Road.** The predominant building style represents the apogee of Nazi architecture: massive and harsh, mixing modernist straight lines with Neoclassical pretention. The litter strewn about and the overgrowth along the paths and buildings define the mood today.

On the other side of town, at Fürtherstr. 22, Nazi leaders faced Allied military judges during the infamous war-crime trials held in room 600 of the **Justizgebäude.** Take U-Bahn #1 to "Bärenschanze," and continue on Fürtherstr., walking away from the old town. Soon after the trials, in October 1946, 12 men were hanged for their crimes against humanity. The building still serves as a courthouse.

MUSEUMS

The **Albrecht Dürer Haus,** Albrecht-Dürer Str. 9 (tel. 21 32 56), uphill from the Sebalduskirche entrance, was the last residence of Nuremberg's favorite son during his final years (1509-1528). The *Fachwerk* house contains period furniture along with Dürer's etchings and copies of his paintings (most of which are in Stuttgart, Munich, and Cologne), as well as an exhibit of Dürer-derived works by modern artists alongside the originals (open Tues.-Sun. 10am-5pm; admission DM4, students DM2).

Back down Bergstr. at #19, the **Altstadthof** features an historical brewery. No free samples, but tempting liter bottles of house brew cost only DM6, including a DM2 deposit. (Tours once per hour Mon.-Fri. 2-7pm, Sat.-Sun. 11am-5pm; during *Christkindlmarkt* (Dec.1-24) daily 11am-7pm. Admission DM4.50, children DM2.50.) Across the river is the **Germanisches Nationalmuseum,** Kartäusergasse 1 (tel. 133 10). From the Königstr. exit of the tunnel from the station, turn left through the archway onto Frauentormauer and take a right on Kartäusergasse. This huge, gleaming, modern building chronicles the last millennium of German art, with huge displays of medieval sculpture and painting and scientific instruments from Baroque and Renaissance Germany, as well as a wholesome offering of rural farm costumes and furnishings. There is also a small floor devoted to toys and dollhouses (open Tues.-Sun. 10am-5pm, Wed. 10am-9pm; admission DM6, students DM3, seniors DM3).

NIGHTLIFE

The nightspots of Nuremberg run the gamut from ultra-traditional to hyper-modern. The *Altstadt* is packed with bars and clubs, or you can grab an outdoor patch of cobblestone at **Albrecht-Dürer-Platz** (uphill from Sebalduskirche), a favorite summer hangout of the teeny-bopper crowd. On weekends they're like swarms of well-scrubbed locusts. Pick up the weekly *Plärrer* (DM4), the region's best magazine, listing musical events, cultural happenings, and addresses of bars, discos, and cafés.

Bars

Starclub, Maxtorgraben 33 (tel. 55 16 82), entrance is in the back. No papparazzi, but a relaxed ramshackle garden house with rooms bathed in cool blue lights. Classy, diverse young crew. Pinball, foosball, TVs, and packed tables. Beer starts at DM3.90. Baguette DM5. Open Mon.-Fri. 9:30am-1am, Sat.-Sun. 2:30pm-1am.

Treibhaus, Karl-Grillenberger-Str. 28 (tel. 22 30 41), in the west part of the *Altstadt,* a bit south of Westtor. Metal tables and dim lighting draw a slightly older crowd (i.e. no high-schoolers) to this bistro-bar. As the candlelight softens the look of your tablemate's skin, so do the killer cocktails soften your choosiness. Snacks, salads, pastas (DM5-16). Open Mon.-Wed 8:30am-1am, Thurs.-Fri. 8:30am-2am, Sat. 9am-2am, Sun. 9:30am-1am. Kitchen open daily until 10:30 pm.

Ruhestörung, Tetzelgasse 21 (tel. 22 19 21), is 5min. from the Lorenzkirche. Relaxed atmosphere, though something of a scene; people watch with a vengeance. Outdoor seating with overgrown ivy encircling. Breakfast, sandwiches, (DM7-8.50) and hamburgers (DM9.50). Beer on tap starts at DM4.50. Open Mon.-Fri. 7:30am-1am, Sat.-Sun. 9:30am-1am.

Cartoon, An der Sparkasse 6 (tel. 22 71 70), is a central, popular gay bar just off Theatergasse, which itself is off Königstr. between the *Lorenzkirche* and the station. Open Sun.-Mon. and Wed.-Thurs. 11am-midnight, Fri.-Sat. 11am-1am.

Flohmarkt, Obere Wörthstr. 19 (tel. 22 53 17), a chaotically cluttered, endearing bar near the river where everything—the furniture, the cacti, the knick-knacks, the dishes—is for sale (the name means "flea market" in German). Beer DM3.80-5.30. Live blues or folk after 8pm; it's free, but add DM1 to your first 3 beers. From Königstr. take Kaiserstr. to Obere Wörth Str. Open Tues.-Sun. 5pm-1am.

Dance Clubs

Mach I, Kaiserstr. 1-9 (tel. 20 30 30), smack in the center of the *Altstadt* near Karlsbrücke. Grooving patrons change size, shape, and drapery depending on the day. Thurs. attracts the mellower "Best of the 70s to 90s" crowd; Fri. swings with soul and hip-hop; Sat. signifies house. Cover DM10. Open Thurs.-Sat. 10pm-4am.

Forum, Regensburgerstr. 334. Take S-bahn #2 to "Frankenstadion." 2 dance floors assuage the musical needs of hip youngsters. Fri. choose between grunge, indy rock, and house; Sat. offers techno parties and live performances. Cover DM10-15. Open Fri.-Sat. 11pm-4am.

■ Near Nuremberg: Erlangen

Once huge with the Huguenots, today Nuremberg's little neighborhood buddy is an academic and industrial powerhouse. It's here that the elegant **Friedrich-Alexander-University** (founded 1743) boasts eleven distinguished faculties educating 28,000 students. Here, too, the German electronics giant **Siemens AG** conducts its most secretive research. Walk one block straight ahead from the train station to reach the city's center, **Hugenottenplatz,** and its pedestrian artery (called **Hauptstraße** to your left and **Nürnberger Straße** to your right).

One block up Hauptstr. from Hugenottenplatz is a large square whose left part is called Marktplatz while the right part, confusingly, is named Schloßplatz. To your left on Marktplatz is the **Palais Stutterheim** (tel. 86 27 35), built in 1728. Once the town hall, it now shelves the town's books as an official library and art gallery (open Tues.-Fri. 10am-6pm, Sat.-Sun. 10am-5pm).

Across the square is the huge **Schloß.** Built in 1700 by Ludwig I, king of Bavaria, it's now home to the university administration. In front of the *Schloß* is a statue of the

Margrave Friedrich, a former occupant of the *Schloß* and founder of the university. Years of rough weather have bleached his face, leaving the eye-sockets black, which gives the eerie impression that the poor man has had his eyes gouged out. The *Schloß*'s gray façade hides the vast 18th-century **Schloßgarten,** which begins in back of the building. Jazz and classical concerts are given in the garden during the summer (open daily 9am-9pm; free). Around the left of the *Schloß* and past the semi-circular *Orangerie* lies the exotic **Botanical Garden,** cared for by the scholars of the Institute of Botany (open Mon.-Sat. 8am-4pm; Oct.-March Mon.-Fri. 8am-4pm, Sat. 8am-noon; greenhouse open Tues.-Sun. 9:30-11:30am and 1:30-3pm; free).

Erlangen's **tourist office** *(Verkehrsverein),* Rathausplatz 1, (tel. 895 10; fax 89 51 51), can cheerfully sink you under a mass of free brochures. They also find private rooms (DM20-45) for free. Walk one block straight ahead from the station, turn right at McDonald's and continue until you see the ugly, ugly *Rathaus* high-rise on the left; the tourist office is just up the open-air stairs. (Open Mon. 8am-6pm, Tues.-Thurs. 8am-4:30pm, Fri. 8am-12:30pm. 24-hr. computer information screen outside of office.) To rent a **bike,** try **Fahrradkiste** at the corner of Werner-von-Siemens Str. and Henke Str. (tel. 20 99 40), which charges DM8 per day for a tour bike or DM16 for a mountain bike. (ID and DM200 deposit required. Open Mon.-Fri. 11am-6pm, Sat. 10am-1pm.) Erlangen's **Mitfahrzentrale,** at Neue Str. 10 (tel. 290 88), will hook you up with a ride; it's DM40 to Berlin, DM25 to Munich (open Mon.-Fri. 10am-6pm, Sat. 10am-1pm). For a **pharmacy,** try **Kaiser Drogerie,** on Hauptstr. (open Mon.-Fri. 8:30am-6pm, Sat. 8am-2pm). The **post office,** Güterhallen Str. 1, 91058 Erlangen, sits two blocks to the right of the station (open 8am-6pm, Sat. 8am-1pm, Sun. 11am-noon). The **telephone code** is 09131.

The **Jugendherberge,** Südliche Stadtmauer Str. 35 (tel. 86 25 55; fax 86 21 19), is centrally convenient. Walk one block straight ahead from the station, turn right at the McDonald's, and take the second left onto Südl.-Stadtmauer-Str. The hostel is 10 minutes away in a stolid, square building. The sign reads *"Freizeitzentrum Frankenhof,"* and it's a central site for Erlangen's *Kinderkultur*—clubs, playing rooms, etc. (Reception open Mon.-Fri. 7-9am and 5-10pm, Sat.-Sun. 7-11am and 4-10pm. Curfew 10pm, but they'll give you a door key. DM17.50. Under 27 only.) The best breakfast in Bavaria is included. Inside the *Freizeitzentrum* you'll also find the **Gästehaus** (address and tel. as above) for those 18 and over. (36 beds. Singles DM36.50. Doubles DM49. Triples DM73.50.) Also try **Schwarzer Bär,** Innere-Brucker-Str. 19, 91054 Erlangen (tel. 228 72; fax 20 64 94), one block to the right from the station. The Old-World restaurant downstairs is complete with dark paneling and stuffed pheasants (on the walls, not your plate). (Clean, comfortable singles DM45, with shower DM55. Doubles DM70, with shower DM80. Great breakfast included.) Camp at **Naturfreunde Erlangen,** Wohrmühle 6 (tel. 284 99), on an island in the Regnitz river behind the station. To get there, walk under the tracks from the station, turn right onto Münchener Str., get on Gerberei Str., and left again just after the overpass onto Wohrmühlsteg. (DM6.50 per person. DM5 per tent.)

In such a lively student town, you can expect good cafés and good restaurants with affordable prices; one source of listings is Nuremberg's weekly magazine *Plärrer.* The cheapest meal in town is the usual **University Mensa,** directly on Langemarck Platz, up Henkestr. from Nürnberger Str. In this large, caramel-colored building, you can purchase a *Mensa*-card for DM3 from the cashier and eat for DM3.10-4.30. Student ID required, or try flashing your pearly whites. (*Mensa* open during the school year Mon.-Fri. 11:30am-2pm. Cashier open Mon.-Fri. 11:15am-1:30pm.) It's also a good place to find roomies and information on musical events. **Alles Paletti,** Stubenlohstr. 25 (tel. 244 18), offers campy funk—the place is decorated with Christmas lights and old postcards; a tinseled tree perches in the middle. The luscious beer garden keeps things intimate with well-watered-Chia-pet greenery. Continue on Henkestr. past the *Mensa* and take the third right onto Stubenlohstr. (open daily 11:30am-3:30pm and 5:30pm-1am, Sat. 7pm-1am). A fresh produce **market** takes over the *Marktplatz* (Mon.-Fri. 7am-6pm, Sat. 7am-2pm).

Groove, and we mean groove, at **E-Werk,** Fuchsenwiese 1 (tel. 800 50), a funked-up industrial building. Walk up Hauptstr. and turn left at Engelstr.—the building is straight ahead. Erlangen's *Kommunikationszentrum* leans left with musically and artistically hip folk. In the **Tanz-Werk** (the dance factory; tel. 80 050), Tuesday cranks out independent music, Wednesday features either *Frauendisco* or *Männerdisco,* and Thursday challenges you to "all you can groove" (open Tues-Thurs. 9pm-1:30am). Friday is "Test the Best," which translates into techno, and Saturdays is straight rock (open Fri.-Sat. 10pm-4am). On Sundays, oldies play from 9pm to 1:30am. They also have films and jazz as well as gallery exhibits weekly. The eclectic bulletin board walls may help you find a place to live (ticket office open Tues.-Fri. noon-6pm; open Tues.-Sat. noon-1am).

▓ Bayreuth

Once you've turned off of Tristan(ne)str. onto Isoldenstr., walked past Walküregasse, and finally headed into the Parsifal Pharmacy, there will be little doubt that you're in Bayreuth, the adopted home of Richard Wagner and the site of the annual *Festspiele*—an *en masse* pilgrimage of BMW-driving devotees coming to bask in his operatic masterpieces. Full of himself in all respects (not only musical), Wagner retreated to Bayreuth in 1872 to escape his creditors and other assorted folks he had pissed off. King Ludwig II conveniently paid off all his debts and kept him out of jail. The remote town promised privacy, an 18th-century opera house he fancied for his productions, and an enchanting ego-fluffing concept—fans would now have to journey long distances to experience a titillating Wagner performance. As with most "sacred" cities, the grandiosity has left Bayreuth a treasure trove of gorgeous buildings. An affection for pomp (or a need to mock Wagner groupies) makes Bayreuth worthwhile even for those less-than-enthralled with the man and his music.

Orientation and Practical Information Bayreuth is pronounced "Buy Roit," *not* "Bay Ruth"; prepare for sour looks if you speak otherwise. The *Altstadt* lies five minutes south of the train station, to the left and down Bahnhofstr. as you exit. The **tourist office,** Luitpoldplatz 9 (tel. 885 88; fax 885 38), to the left and about four blocks from the train station, provides city maps, hotel listings, a monthly calendar of events, and walking **tours** of the city (DM8, students DM5; tours offered May-Oct. Tues.-Sat. at 10am; Nov.-April Sat. at 10am only). Private rooms are only available during the *Festspiele* (DM3 fee); at other times, they will help you find a room in a hotel or pension for the same fee (open Mon.-Fri. 9am-6pm, Sat. 9am-noon). A **branch office** is located at Jean-Paul Platz 1 (same telephone number and hours). They charge DM3 for finding accommodations and sell tickets to Bayreuth's lively year-round theater, opera, and musical performances. It should be no surprise that banks ubiquitously dot the wealthy Bayreuth landscape. One place to **exchange money** is **Citibank,** Opernstr. 2, beneath Hotel Anker; it offers 24-hr. bankcard service (open Mon. and Thurs. 8:45am-1pm and 2-4pm, Wed. 8:45am-1pm and 1:30-4pm). The town is an easy day trip by hourly **trains** from Nuremberg (1hr.). The **post office,** Bürgerreuther Str. 1, 95444 Bayreuth (tel. 78 00), is across from the train station and to the right (open Mon.-Wed. and Fri. 8am-6pm, Thurs. 8am-7pm, Sat. 8am-2pm, Sun. 11am-noon). The **telephone code** is 0921.

Accommodations If you visit during the *Festspiele* and forgot to book your room last year, don't even try to stay in Bayreuth. Almost any other time, though, prices are reasonable and beds available. Bayreuth's brand–new but strangely spacious **Jugendherberge (HI),** Universitätsstr. 28, 95447 Bayreuth (tel. 252 62; fax 51 28 05), lies a bit out in the boonies next to the vast university. Take bus #4 (DM2.30) from the *Marktplatz* to the "Mensa" stop. Walk past the buildings straight ahead; the *Mensa* should be to your right up the step. Past its entrance, go down the stairs, pass the first left, and take the left fork in the stone road leading under the bridge. Make a right; after a few twists and turns you'll spot a wild yellow building with clashing green windows. Follow the path to the front, and you're there. From the large Maximilian Str. bus station (Markt), take bus #11 (direction: Wolfsbach) or bus #18 (direction: Bodenseering-Markt-Universität) to "Kreuzsteinbad" (Mon.-Fri. bus #11 leaves once per hour at 5min. after the hour; bus #18 leaves every 20min.). Follow the sidewalk up ahead (5min.) to the large square *Jugendherberge* on your right. Friendly but a tad regimented: at 10pm, *everything* locks up. (Reception open 7am-1pm and 5-10pm. Lockout 9-11:30am. Curfew 10pm. Under 27 only. DM19. Breakfast included. Sheets DM5.50. Wash DM3. Open March to mid-Dec.)

Gasthof Hirsch, St. Georgen 26 (tel. 267 14), is a 10-minute walk behind the train station, on a corner with pink geraniums spilling out of the windows. Walk left from the station to Tunnelstr., follow it until it becomes Brandenburger Str., and turn left onto St. Georgen. Clean and crisp with 18 beds in all. (Singles DM37-47. Doubles DM73-93.) At **Gasthof zum Brandenburger,** St. Georgen 9 (tel. 205 70; fax 85 23 96), the rooms are nice and sunny, as is the beer garden. Spiffy ivy wallpaper on the third floor with red geraniums this time (just as happy, though). (40 beds. Singles DM38, with shower DM50. Doubles DM70, with shower DM95. AmEx and MC accepted.) **Gasthof Kropf,** Tristanstr. 8 (tel. 262 98), lies between the train tracks and the lush Festspielhaus Park in a brick building. Though it's out of town, the rooms are clean and it's near the train station. (Singles DM47, with shower DM72. Doubles DM74, with shower DM104.)

Food Fill 'er up at the **University Mensa** (tel. 60 81) for DM3-6; any student ID should do. Take bus #4 (DM2.30) from the bus stations at the end of Luitpoldplatz on the right. Get off at the "Mensa" stop and walk past the buildings straight ahead. The *Mensa* is to the right up the steps. It's an enormous, low-roofed building (open Mon.-Thurs. 8am-6pm, Fri. 8am-2pm, Aug.-Sept. open Mon.-Thurs. 11:15am-1:30pm, Fri. 11:15am-1:15pm). **Gastätte Porsch,** Maximilian Str. 56 (tel. 649 19), serves pilecicious portions at the best prices in town. Try Bayreuth's own *Bratwürtschen*, cabbage, and fresh bread (DM8.10). *Schnitzels* and steak meals run DM11-17 (open Mon.-Sat. 7am-8:30pm). **Künstlerkneipe Eule,** Kirchgasse 8 (tel. 575 54), is tucked in a small alley to the left off Maximilan Str. *Wiener Schnitzel* with fries and salad is DM12.80 (open Mon.-Sat. 11:30am-10pm). **Braunbierhaus,** Kanzleistr. 15 (tel. 696 77), beyond Bayreuth's *Stadtkirche*, is an authentic delight nearly 900 years old; share the authenticity with other authentic tourists. Try *Holzfällersteak* (woodchopper's steak) with *Bratkartoffeln* (hash browns) for DM18, or the affordable *Paprika Schnitzel* at DM14. (open daily 11:30am-2pm and 5:30-10:30pm; Sun. 11:30am-2pm).

The **Schützenhaus,** Am Schießhaus 2 (tel. 221 90), features authentic Franconian delights, lovely candles, and a sprawling beer garden where you can jump-start your middle-aged beer belly paunch (DM15-20 for steaks and filets). Unfortunately, it's off the beaten path unless you're exploring the Wagnerian territory behind the *Festspielhaus* (open Fri.-Wed. 11:30am-10pm). **Café Wundertüte,** Richard-Wagner-Str. 33 (tel. 51 47 48), has a cup of coffee and a slice of raspberry torte with your name on it (DM4.70), or two slices of apple pie with ice cream (DM4) in a wood-paneled atmosphere. Small salads, noodles, *Wieners,* and cheeses DM5-9.50 (open Mon.-Tues., Thurs.-Fri. 8am-6pm, Wed. 1-6pm, Sat. 8am-1pm). Fill up your basket at the **market** in the Rotmainhal near Hindenburgstr. (Wed. and Sat. from 7am-5pm). **Norma,** Richard-Wagner-Str. 11, is the local supermarket with the fixings for a perfect picnic (open Mon.-Wed., Fri. 8:30am-6pm, Thurs. 8:30am-8pm, Sat. 8am-2pm).

The Wagner Fest (Festspiele) For Wagnerians, a devotional visit to Bayreuth is like a pious pilgrimage to Mecca. Every summer from July 25 to August 28 (the dates are the same every year), thousands of visitors pour in for the **Bayreuth Festspiele,** a vast and bombastic—in a word, Wagnerian—celebration of the composer's works. The music fills the **Festspielhaus** theater that Wagner built for his "music of the future." The world's operatic darlings, directors, and conductors have been taking on *The Ring of the Niebelungen, Tannhäuser, Parsifal,* and *Tristan and Isolde* here since 1876. Judging by the number of German Wagner Societies and

Clubs, the spectacle will probably continue for as long as the Holy Grail is old. Tickets (DM80-300, obstructed view DM40-50) for the festival go on sale several years in advance and sell out almost immediately. Write to Bayreuther Festspiele, 95402 Bayreuth, preferably well before the September *three years* before you wish to attend. Your request will be processed when it is received and you'll be notified some time after mid-November. Reserve a room in town as soon as you get tickets (most Wagnerophiles just write **every year** and hope for the best).

Sights If you're not a Wagner fan, you'd do well to become one for a day in this devoted opera-town. Wagner devotees without tickets to the *Festspiele* can console themselves with a **Festspielhaus** tour (tel. 202 21); go right at the train station and up at the end of Siegfried-Wagner-Allee. In order to fund the 1872 construction, the composer once again hit up Uncle Ludwig II, who was currently in the midst of his own egocentric building spree. Ludwig responded with only modest amounts of cash, and combined with Wagner's desire for ideal acoustics, the resulting structure is a bit spartan; Wagner fans must endure cushionless seats and precious little leg room to catch a show. (Tours April-Sept. Tues.-Sun. at 10 and 10:45am, 2:15 and 3pm, Oct. and Dec.-March Tues.-Sun. at 10am and 10:45am. No tours during rehearsal and performances. Admission DM3, students DM2.)

The composer's house, *Haus Wahnfried,* is now the **Richard Wagner Museum,** Richard-Wagner-Str. 48 (tel. 757 28 16, fax 757 28 22). It houses an inexhaustible collection of scores, costumes, stage sets, and personal effects in a panoply of curiously *kitsch* valuables. See Wagner playing cards, stamps, and coins as well as his spoons, mirror, and little *Wotan* and *Sieglinde* dolls (the Wagnerian Barbie and Ken). Three death masks also provided for your morbid pleasure: Wagner's, composer Carl Maria von Weber's, and that of his friend and patsy, Ludwig II. The museum's thousands of exhibits are in German only—it might be worth your while to pick up the extensive, melodramatic English guide-booklet (DM3). Wagner's compositions played in the drawing room daily at 10am, noon, and 2pm; videos shown at 11am and 3pm. Those who fail to appreciate his "Total Works of Art" (as he so modestly referred to them) should recall Mark Twain's fiendishly accurate assessment of Wagner's music: "It's better than it sounds." (Open daily 9am-5pm. Admission July-Aug. DM5, students DM2; Sept.-June DM4, students DM2. 3-day passes for the Wagner Museum, the Jean Paul Museum, and Franz Liszt Museum available for DM6.) Behind the house lie the graves of Wagner, his wife Cosima, and Russ, his big black dog.

Even farther behind the house is the **Hofgarten,** an English-style park. Turn right as you enter and be led to the **Freemason's Museum,** Hofgarten 1 (tel. 698 24; fax 512 850; ring the bell). If you've wondered what's inside those windowless temples or what those strange symbols mean (and particularly if you've ever read *Foucault's Pendulum*), this is the place for you; complete with floor plans and pink roses. The bizarre rituals have been going on in Bayreuth for 225 years (open Tues.-Fri. 10am-noon and 2-4pm, Sat. 10am-noon; admission DM2). In the shadow of the self-satisfied Wagner Museum, the **Franz Liszt Museum,** Wahnfriedstr. 9 (tel. 757 28 18) exhibits the composer's pianos and music sheets and morbidly displays the room where he died (again complete with death mask). In Bayreuth, Liszt is probably best known for fathering Wagner's wife. (Open daily 9am-noon and 2-5pm; admission DM3, students and seniors DM1.) The **Jean Paul Museum,** Wahnfriedstr. 1 (tel. 757 28 17), celebrates the life of Bayreuth's greatest poet with an endless collection of notebooks and chairs (open July-Sept. daily 9am-noon, 2-5pm; Oct.-June Mon.-Fri. 9am-noon and 2-5pm, Sat. 10am-1pm; admission DM3, students DM1).

Just down Wahnfried Str., enter the lovely gardens once again to wander down the primrose path to the 18th-century Baroque **Neues Schloß,** former residence of Friedrich the Great's sister, Margravine Wilhelmine. Considered one of Europe's most brilliant and cultured women, she married the Margrave of Bayreuth and ended up stuck in what must have seemed a provincial cowtown. After a mysterious castle fire, she redecorated and rococoed like mad King Ludwig, and when she finished gilding the home furnishings, she swept her eyes across Bayreuth and strove to cosmopolitanize it. (Castle open Tues.-Sun. 10-11:20am and 1:30-4:10pm; Oct.-March Tues.-Sun. 10-11:20am and 1:30-3pm; admission DM3, students DM1). The lavishly ornate **1748 Margravian Opera House** is the tangible result of such frustration combined with more money than is good for a person. Wagner originally thought this theater's pomp appropriate for his production, but its 500 seats and stage proved way too small for his lofty needs. (Tours every 30min. in German only, but you can borrow an English text. Open Tues.-Sun. 9-11:30am and 1:30-4:30pm; Oct.-March Tues.-Sun. 10-11:30am and 1:30-2pm. Admission DM3, students DM2).If you're sweating from all this palatial magnificence, make a splash in Bayreuth's fabulous outdoor pool, **Kreuzsteinbad** (tel. 661 07) to see that grand Wagnerian style is not limited to 18th-century opera houses. (Open June-Aug. daily 7am-8pm; Sept.-May daily 7am-7:30pm. Entrance closes 30min. before closing. DM4, students DM2. Massage DM15.)

■ Coburg

Coburg only joined Bavaria in 1920, after years spent as a member of Saxony. By making the move, the city fortuitously avoided inclusion in the GDR after WWII. The division of Germany shifted the town's geographical location from the heartland to the margins. Today, wealthy Coburg sits at the center again; but a brief trip north across the old GDR border reveals the vast incongruities the past 45 years have created. This 11th-century town has been beautifully preserved, with only an arbitrary line in the woods to thank for it.

From the train station, turn right on Lossaustr. then left at the light onto Mohrenstr., go around the large, central *Stadtcafe,* and take a final right on Spitalgasse to reach the Renaissance **Altstadt.** The huge 16th-century structure on the *Marktplatz* is the frescoed **Rathaus.** The old **Stadthaus** across the square was once the abode of the Coburg *Herzöge* (Dukes). The proud central statue is of **Prince Albert,** the Coburger husband of Queen Victoria. To the right down Herrngasse is the part Renaissance, part neo-Gothic **Schloß Ehrenburg** (Castle of Honor; tel. 808 80). When the *Herzog* built the palace, he did so without borrowing a gross amount of money and without grossly oppressing his peasantry. When the Kaiser toured the site, he remarked that it stood as a monument to the *Herzog*'s honor, and the name stuck. The palace later fell to the Saxe-Coburg-Gothas, and Albert spent his childhood within its walls. Victoria's private visitation quarters can be toured. (Mandatory tours Tues.-Sun. at 10, 11am, 1:30, 2:30, 3:30, and 4:30pm; Nov.-March Tues.-Sun. at 10, 11am, 1:30, 2:30, and 3:30pm. Admission DM4, students and DM3.)

Paved footpaths wind through the **Hofgarten,** a shaded, grassy expanse stretching from Schloß Ehrenburg to the 11th-century **Veste** (fortress). Allow 30 to 45 minutes to hoof it up the deceptively steep hill. Otherwise, take bus #8 from in front of the *Rathaus* to the "Veste" stop (DM2) and walk up about 50m. The 16th-century fortress, encircled by a double set of fortified walls, was inhabited until 1918, when Karl Eduard abdicated the dukedom. The main buildings are the **Fürstenbau** (prince's palace; tel. 920 88; open Tues.-Sun. 10am-noon and 2-4pm with tours every 30min.; Nov.-March tours at 2 and 3pm; admission DM4, students DM3, under 14 DM2, under 6 free) and the **Coburg Art Museum** (tel. 87 90 or 741 80; open Tues.-Sun. 9:30am-1pm and 2-5pm, Nov.-March Tues.-Sun. 2-5pm; admission DM4, students DM2, under 6 free). The half-timbered *Fürstenbau* contains a chapel commemorating Martin Luther's 1530 stay, as well as the beautifully furnished ducal living quarters. (Tours of the Veste, including the art museum, April-Oct. Sun. at 10am; DM7 including art museum admission.) Back in town to the right of Herrngasse is the minty-green **Coburger Puppen-Museum** (Doll Museum), Rückertstr. 2-3 (tel. 740 47). In one of its 33 fun-infested rooms, spot Lilli, a curvy German doll from the 1950s intended for adults; the then-unknown American toy company Mattel bought the rights to her in 1958, and one year later as young girls went Barbie-crazy, someone at Mattel went home with a big holiday bonus. Contemplate the corporate toy world at the adjoining Café Hello Dolly. (Open April-Oct. daily 9am-5pm; Nov.-March Tues.-Sun. 10am-5pm; admission DM3.50, students DM3, under 14 DM2.)

Most **train** travelers will need to change at Lichtenfels on the Nuremberg-Berlin line to reach Coburg. One to two trains per hour go to Bamberg (40min.) and Nuremberg (1hr. 20min.). Hourly trains go to Würzburg (2hrs.), and eight trains per day reach Berlin (5hr. 40min.). **Buses** travel once per hour to the Thuringian Forest (2hr.). Coburg's **tourist office,** Herrngasse 4 (tel. 741 80; fax 741 829), off the *Marktplatz,* offers free city maps and city tours (DM30-60) for no fee (open Mon.-Fri. 9am-6:30pm, Sat. 9am-1pm; Nov.-March Mon.-Fri. 9am-5pm, Sat. 9am-1pm). **Exchange money** at **Deutsche Bank,** on Spitalgasse (tel. 16 62 or 16 68), once a hotel patronized by Goethe, Liszt, Johann Strauss, Emperor Pedro II of Brazil, and Queen Christina of Sweden (open Mon.-Wed. and Fri. 8:30am-1pm and 2-4pm, Thurs. 8:30am-1pm and 2-5:30pm). The **post office** is at Hindenburgstr. 6, 96450 Coburg (tel. 910), to the left off Mohrenstr. on the way to the *Altstadt;* it's got lots of telephones and good exchange rates (open Mon.-Fri. 8:30am-6pm, Sat. 8:30am-1pm). The **telephone code** is 09561.

Jugendherberge Schloß Ketschendorf (HI), Parkstr. 2 (tel. 153 30; fax 286 53), rests in a sublime converted palace. The sight of play-school *Jugendherberge* furniture in the grand castle is a funny sight, but the modern rooms make spotless sense. Take bus #1 (from *Markt*) to "DJH." Park Str. is up on the left. Or walk on Ketschengasse to Ketschendorfer Str., then all the way to Park Str. to make a left (25min.). Ketschendorf proudly displays plaques proclaiming itself the "Best Bavarian Youth Hostel." Billiard tables and a disco back up the claim. (Reception open 8-9am, 5-6pm, and 8-9pm. Lockout 10am-noon. Curfew 10pm or by prior arrangement. Hot showers available 7-9am and 3-10pm. Under 27 only. DM20. Breakfast included. Sheets DM5.50.) The **Gasthof Goldenes Kreuz,** Herrngasse 1 (tel. 904 73; fax 905 02), is on the *Marktplatz.* (DM45, with shower DM50) and doubles (DM90, with shower DM100) are centrally located. Try the bargain prices at **Zum Hohenfels,** Geleitstr. 12 (tel. 385 79). Follow Lossaustr. left from the train station under the underpass, turn right, cross the intersection, and turn left onto Geleitstr. at the far side of the park (15min.). (Singles DM30. Doubles DM60. Call ahead.) The **Münchner Hofbräu,** Kleine Johannisgasse 8 (tel. 750 49; fax 904 34) is both a hopping restaurant and *Pension,* two blocks from *Marktplatz* off the Spitalgasse. (Singles with shower and toilet DM55. Doubles with shower and toilet DM105.) The restaurant serves just what you would expect, given the name—beer (DM4-6), but also plates of *Klößer* and *Rostbratwürstchen* (grilled sausages; DM8-14). Old clocks and stained glass windows add to the fun atmosphere (open daily 10am-midnight).

Two specialty foods in Coburg are the *Thüringer Klößer* (dumplings) and *Coburger Bratwurst.* Billowing clouds of smoke and the smell of grilled *Coburger Bratwürste* (sausages) hang thick in the air over the market square. There's a **farmer's market** every Wednesday and Saturday 7am-5pm and a **fruit market** on Tuesday 7am-noon. Café **Prinz Albert,** at the corner of Albertsplatz down Ketschengasse from *Marktplatz* (tel. 954 20), offers ice cream (DM4-7.80) and scrumptious cake (DM4) as well as small snacks (open Mon.-Fri. 7:45am-7pm, Sun. 10am-7pm).

For nightlife, **Café Filou,** Bahnhof Str. 11, offers a relaxed atmosphere with funky round chairs and sepia-toned photographs. (Pizza and noodle dishes DM5-15. Open Mon.-Thurs. 9am-1am, Fri. 9am-2am, Sat. 9:30am-2am.) **Café-Floh,** Herrngasse 12, off the *Marktplatz,* attracts students with its dark-wooded environment, conducive to late-night philosophizing over a beer (DM3.70). Fresh baguettes come with everything from cheese (DM4) to bananas and cheese (DM5), to ham, bananas, and cheese (DM6.60), to … sorry, no Spam. There's always pizza (DM6.40; open daily 8pm-3am).

■ Near Coburg: Vierzehnheiligen

About 20 minutes south of Coburg by car is the resplendent Rococo masterpiece, **Vierzehnheiligen Church** (FEER-tsayn-HIGH-lih-gen; Fourteen Saints' Church; tel. (09571) 950 80), that stands on a broad grassy rise above the Main River. It was on this site in 1445-46 that local villagers saw visions of the Christ Child and the "Fourteen Saints of Intercession." The spot became an important pilgrimage destination, and the present church was erected in the 18th century. The façade is a sumptuous example of detailing, with golden, glowing stone and unusually high towers for a church of its age. The Rococo interior is dominated by the *Nothelfer Altar,* which protects the square meter of holy ground on which the Christ Child vision appeared. The Christ Child sits at the top of the altar surrounded by statues of all fourteen saints, each interceding for a particular cause. Pray to the decapitated St. Dionysus if you have a headache, or to St. Christopher for budget travel tips (open daily 9am-6pm; Free). To reach Vierzehnheiligen from Coburg, take the **train** to Lichtenfels (15min.; DM5.70). The church is about 6km outside of town. An infrequent **bus** runs from the Lichtenfels station to the church (Tues.-Thurs. at 8:15am and 2pm; returns at 10:40am and 5:40pm). A **taxi** costs about DM20 from the stand outside the Lichtenfels train station and the **walk** takes 1½-2 hours. The return, at least, is downhill.

▓ Bamberg

Packed with sights, but largely overlooked by travelers, this little city on the Regnitz boasts a history spanning a thousand years. Emperor Henry II liked Bamberg so much that he made it the center of his empire and crowned it with a colossal cathedral. The magnificent building is but one shining example of the city's beauty—take time to behold the city's imperial palace, frescoes, and widely varied architecture. Bamberg's architectural treasures owe a great deal to the city's sheer luck; unlike most of its German counterparts, Bamberg escaped two virulent wars relatively unscathed. In the Thirty Years War, Bamberg survived two sieges by the formidable Swedish King Gustavus Adolphus; three centuries later, the city emerged from World War II with minor bruises. Incidentally, the residents of Bamberg drink an astounding amount of beer—330 liters per capita every year, the highest consumption rate in the world. Maybe they're celebrating.

ORIENTATION AND PRACTICAL INFORMATION

The heart of Bamberg lies on an island between the Rhine-Main-Danube Canal and the Regnitz river (named for its location at the confluence of the Regen and the Pegnitz Rivers). Across the Regnitz from the island lie the winding streets of the *Altstadt.* To reach the *Altstadt* from the *Bahnhof,* walk straight ahead on Luitpoldstr., cross the canal, and continue straight on Willy-Lessing-Str. until it empties into Schönleinsplatz. Turn right onto Lange Str. and left up Obere Brücke Str., which leads through the archway of the *Rathaus* and across the Regnitz (25-30min.). Or grab one of the city buses in front of the *Hauptbahnhof* for a quick, cheap ride into town (DM1.50).

Tourist Office: Fremdenverkehrsamt, Geyerwörthstr. 3, 96047 Bamberg (tel. 87 11 61; fax 87 19 60), on an island in the Regnitz. To get there, follow the above directions to the *Altstadt.* Once through the *Rathaus,* take 2 lefts and re-cross the Regnitz on the wooden footbridge; the tourist office is on your right under the arches. You can avoid paying DM0.50 for their map by picking up a hotel list or the *Bamberger Notizen* booklet, which has the best map (both free). A vending machine outside dispenses hotel lists and city maps for DM0.50. They also find rooms in hotels or pensions by mail or in person (DM5 per person). Open Mon.-Fri. 9am-6pm, Sat. 9am-3pm. **Walking tours** of the city meet in front of the tourist office Mon.-Sat. at 10:30am and 2pm (Nov.-March 2pm only), Sun. at 11am. DM8, students DM5. Tour of the cathedral and the *Neue Residenz* meets at the *Neue Residenz* and leaves when there are "enough people" (available daily 9am-noon and 1:30-5pm; Oct.-March daily 9am-noon and 1:30-4pm; DM8, students DM6).

Currency Exchange: Citibank, on Schönleinsplatz, accepts nearly any card. Open Mon. and Thurs. 8:45am-1pm and 2-6pm, Tues. and Fri. 8:45am-1pm and 2-4pm, Wed. 8:45am-1pm and 1:30-4pm.

Trains: The main station is on Ludwigstr. (tel. 194 19). **Lockers** DM2-4. Trains to Nuremberg (2-4 per hr.; ½-1hr.), Würzburg (1-2 per hour; 1¼hr.), Frankfurt (1 per hour; 2hrs. 40min.), and Munich (1-2 per hr.; 2½hr.).

Public Transportation: An excellent transportation net centers around the **ZOB (Zentral Omnibus Bahnhof)** on Promenadestr. off Schönleinsplatz. For schedules, ask at the tourist office. One-way bus fare DM1.50. 4-ride ticket DM5.

Bike Rental: Fahrradhaus Griesmann, Kleberstr. 25 (tel. 229 67). Walk straight ahead on Luitpoldstr. from the train station, take a right on Heinrichsdamm after the bridge, turn left at the next bridge, and take the first right onto Kleberstr. DM15-20 per day. ID required.

Bookstore: Görres Bücher, Lange Str. 24, stocks a moderate selection of contemporary novels on the top floor. Open Mon.-Fri. 8:30am-6pm, Sat. 8:30am-1pm.

Laundromat: SB Waschsalon, in the Atrium mall left of the train station, 2nd floor (tel. 20 29 40). Wash DM6. Dry DM1 for 10min. Open Mon.-Fri. 8am-7:30pm, Sat. 8am-8pm, Sun. 8am-7pm.

Women's Resources: Every Tues. evening in **Café Jenseits,** at Promenadestr. 5 (tel. 210 94), off Schönleinsplatz, a *Frauencafé* pops up with discussions of contemporary issues, films, and readings.

Crisis Rape Line: tel. 582 80.

Pharmacy: Einhorn Apotheke, Grüner Markt 3, off Lange Str., has a list of 24-hr. pharmacies in the window. Open Mon.-Fri. 8:15am-6pm, Sat. 8:30am-12:30pm.

Hospital: Klinikum Bamberg, Bugerstr. 80 (tel. 50 30).

Emergency: tel. 110. **Police:** Schildstr. 81 (tel. 18 50).

Post Office: Hauptpostamt, Ludwigstr. 25, 96052 Bamberg (tel. 83 62 81), across from the train station. International calls, telegrams, and currency exchange. Also cashes traveler's checks (DM6). Open Mon.-Fri. 8am-6pm, Sat. 8am-noon.

Telephone Code: 0951.

ACCOMMODATIONS AND CAMPING

Because, for no discernible reason, it is *verboten* to rent rooms in private Bamberg homes, its accommodations tend to be very expensive. Fortunately, a hostel sits a bit out of town, on a direct bus route from the *Zentral Omnibus Bahnhof (ZOB)*.

Jugendherberge Wolfsschlucht (HI), Oberer Leinritt 70, 96049 Bamberg (tel. 560 02 or 563 44; fax 552 11). Take bus #18 (from *ZOB*) to "Am Regnitzufer" (every 20min.; DM1.50). Pretty far from the city center, but the rooms are tidy. Reception open 3-5pm and 6-10pm. Curfew 10pm. Under 27 only. DM18. Breakfast included. Sheets DM5.50. 84 beds. Because it's the only hostel in Bamberg, it fills up snap-crackle-pop quick; call very early for summer reservations. If full, try the hostels in Erlangen or Coburg. Open Feb.-mid-Dec.

Hospiz, Promenadestr. 3, 96047 Bamberg (tel. 98 12 60; fax 981 26 66). Large doubles, balconies, great breakfast—all in a central location, off Schönleinsplatz. Reception open 7am-10pm. Check-out 11am. Singles DM45, with shower DM66. Doubles with shower DM80, and toilet DM98. Triples with shower and toilet DM128. Reservations by phone, fax, or mail accepted. Always call ahead.

Maisel-Bräu-Stübl, Obere Königstr. 38 (tel./fax 255 03), is 10min. from station. Take a left off Luitpoldstr. Large rooms with balconies overlook a pleasant courtyard. Big fluffy pillows. Reception open 9am-midnight. Singles DM37-41. Doubles DM73, with shower DM83. Breakfast included. Delectable dinners start at DM13.

Fässla, Obere Königstr. 19-21, (tel. 265 16 or 229 98; fax 20 19 89). Go right off Luitpoldstr. Also 10min. from the station. Cozy and comfortable with TVs and telephones. Fässla ("little keg" in Bavarian dialect) keeps its own brewery downstairs that's very popular with the locals. Singles DM63. Doubles DM98. Triples DM130. Parking DM5. Luggage storage available. Closed after 1pm on Sundays.

Camping: Campingplatz Insel, Am Campingplatz 1 (tel. 563 20). Take bus #18 (direction: Klinikum) to "Bug." Prime riverside locale. Showers, toilets, washing machines. DM6.50 per adult. DM4.50 per child. DM4.50 per tent. DM11 per car.

FOOD

Bamberg boasts several small breweries, but its most unusual specialty is **Rauchbier** ("smoke beer"). The daring can try its sharp, smoky taste (DM3.20 for 0.5L) at **Schlenkerla,** Dominikanerstr. 6 (tel. 560 60), *Rauchbier's* traditional home. The smoke brewery lies at the foot of the steps leading up to *Domplatz.* **Der Beck,** at Hauptwacheck, Hauptwachstr. 16, offers scrumptious stand-up food and delicious pastries from the bakery (open Mon.-Fri. 7:30am-7:30pm, Sat. 7:30am-1pm). The supermarket **Norma,** Promenadestr. 12, can provide any groceries you want (open Mon.-Wed. and Fri. 8:30am-6pm, Thurs. 8:30am-7pm, Sat. 7:45am-2pm).

   University Mensa, Austr. 37, off Grüner Markt. Serves the cheapest edible meals in town for under DM5. Dine on yellow plastic trays. Menu changes daily. Any student ID will do. Open daily 11:30am-2pm. **Snack hall** open until 7pm. Check here for info on jobs, rooms, and nightlife happenings.

   Polarbär, Judenstr. 7 (tel. 536 01). In the *Altstadt,* across the walking bridge and left a block or two. Groovy beer garden with aromatic atmosphere. Baguettes and cheese DM4.30. Salads DM4.50-11. Vegetarian dishes DM11-12. Beer (DM4.20 for 0.5L). Hip student scene. Open daily 11am-midnight. Kitchen open noon-3pm and 5-10pm. Check the walls for funky cultural events not elsewhere.

   Hofcafé, Austr. 14 (tel. 254 47), across from the *Mensa.* Sit upstairs on the balcony or inside the light rooms of this student aerie in the trees. Relax. Soups DM5.50, salads DM6.50-12.50, ice cream DM4.50-7, and of course fine spirits. They'll deliver breakfast to your door. Open Mon.-Fri. 8am-8pm, Sat. 9am-6pm, Sun. 10am-6pm. Check here for nightlife happenings.

SIGHTS

The **Altes Rathaus** guards the middle of the Regnitz River like an anchored ship. Built in the 15th century, its strategic location belied no preference for the church nor for the civic powers, both of which held seats on opposite banks of the river. Stand on one of the two bridges to gaze at this half-*Fachwerk* (-timber), half-Baroque façade with a Rococo tower in between. You'll notice a number of visual oddities in the frescoes—painted cherubs have three-dimensional limbs and bodies that jut from the wall where sculpted stone has been attached.

   Across the river and up the hill are the **Dom** (tel. 50 23 30) and the **Neue Residenz,** the former episcopal palace. Cathedral construction began in 1004, and the transition from Romanesque to Gothic can be traced in the architecture of the building. The most famous object within the *Dom* is the equestrian statue called the **Bamberger Reiter** (the Bamberg Knight), which dates from the 13th century and depicts the chivalric ideal of the medieval warrior-king. Many stories have grown up around the statue over the years, including one that the statue was a prophecy of Hitler's rise to power. People like to tell stories. The tomb of Henry II and Queen Kunigunde of the Holy Roman Empire lies near the east apse; Henry sponsored the construction of the cathedral and was later canonized. The west apse can claim the grave of the only pope buried in Germany—Clement II, who died in 1047. Henry and Kunigunde's crowns are also on display, each in a glass box on its own altar. (Cathedral open daily 9am-6pm except during services. Also 30-min. organ concerts Sat. at noon; free. For info on tours see Practical Information, p. 290, or call 50 23 30.) Across the square, the **Neue Residenz,** Domplatz 8 (tel. 563 51), strikes baroque poses amongst roses; from its prim rose garden, the town stretches out like a sea of roofs and the air smells rosy from 40 paces (open daily 9am-noon and 1:30-5pm; Oct.-March daily 9am-noon and 1:30-4pm; last entry 30min. before closing in both the morning and afternoon; admission DM4, students and seniors DM3).

   In town, the streets between the *Rathaus* and *Dom* are lined with 18th-century Baroque houses, many of them not yet renovated. At **Pfahlplätzchen,** at the head of Judenstr., you can see the bay window that G. W. F. Hegel used to peer out of while editing the proofs of the *Phenomenology of Spirit.* At the time, unable to find a university teaching position, the philosopher was serving as editor of the Bamberg newspaper (1807-08)—it's the pink house on the corner.

   Böttinger Palace, on Judenstr., displays a 1713 façade inspired by a Venetian palace and a similarly exotic courtyard. Farther down the street, the lovely **Concordiahaus** is now the local Institute for Geochemical Research. Across the river at

Schillerplatz 26 is the **E.T.A. Hoffmann House.** Author of the nightmarish "Sand-mann," Hoffmann wrote his uncanny stories in this rickety three-story house for five years. He and his wife rented two little rooms directly over one another, and they often chatted through a small opening in the floor (open May-Oct. Tues.-Fri. 4-6pm, Sat.-Sun. and holidays 10am-noon; admission DM2, students DM1).

ENTERTAINMENT AND NIGHTLIFE

Hitch Hiker Internet Café, Obere Sandstr. 18 (tel. 521 27), is an extremely hip, wood-panelled joint populated with a young crowd of students training to be chimneys and hackers—doesn't smoke affect the motherboard? Beer DM3-6. Walk down the steps from Domplatz, turn left onto Obere-Sandstr., and look for the "Keine Panik, 42" lamp over the door. Douglas Adams would be proud. Must be 18 years old to get in—it's a big, scary, electronic world out there. Open Sun.-Fri. 8pm-1am, Sat. 8pm-2am.

Jazzclub, Obere Sandstr. 18 (tel. 537 40). In the same building as Hitch Hiker. Open on Tues. and Thurs. 9pm-1am for a funky mix of gothic, alternative, punk, grunge, and mystic. Fri.-Sat. hosts the local jazz scene from 9pm-1am. Crowded, diverse student joint. Cover hovers at DM10, students DM8. DM4 on Tues.

Live Club, Obere Sandstr. 7 (tel. 536 03). Varied disco. Scenes change with the days: Mon. is oldies night; Tues., Thurs., and Fri. are "Bar and Dance club" nights; Sat. is DJ choice night; and Sun. boasts the "Music of your Dreams." Open Sun.-Tues. and Thurs.-Fri. 8pm-1am, Sat. 7pm-2am.

■ Aschaffenburg

The Bavarian king Ludwig I affectionately referred to Aschaffenburg as his "Bavarian Nizza." Today the city that served as a second residence for the Electors of Mainz still retains much of its past charm. Not even the near-total destruction of this Frankfurt suburb during World War II and its subsequent military occupation have changed the *Freundlichkeit* and hospitality of the locals. "Aschaffenburg Likes You!" proclaims a glossy brochure—and they're not kidding. After a cold spell in Frankfurt, don't be surprised if you're *Guten Tag*-ed frequently during your stay in this city, which the 8000 U.S. soldiers once stationed here used to call "A-burg."

Just past Aschaffenburg's tightly packed *Altstadt* lie the famous **Schönbusch Gardens** and the newly reopened **Schloß Schönbusch,** a country house built between 1778 and 1780 for the archbishop of Mainz. The view from the second-floor **Chamber of Mirrors** (all preserved from the original house and hence a bit distorted) reveals the surrounding city basking in the rich backdrop of the Spessart forests. The archbishop allowed no vegetation between his summer home and Schloß-Johannisburg (3km away), and the two castles remain in that aristocratic see-you-see-me stance even today. (Castle open mid-Mar.-mid.-Oct. Tues.-Sun. 10am-12:30pm and 1:30-4:30pm. Admission and tour DM4, students DM3.) The park itself was built by Elector Friedrich Karl Joseph in 1775 as an experiment in the then-new English style of landscape architecture that involved "naturalized" tree-scaping. Embellished with artificial ponds, islands, and bridges, as well as tiny buildings like the **Freundschafts tempel** (friendship temple) and the **Philosophenhaus,** the park reeks a bit too much of fairy-tale falsity. At the **Unterer Schönbuschsee,** near the entrance, **rent a boat** (DM6 for 30min.) to navigate to the *Schloß* (boat rental open daily 10am-7pm). The **Irrgarten,** close to the restaurant at the park's entrance, is a labyrinth formed by trimmed bushes, planted in 1829. To hedge the fate of the minotaur, climb the wooden tower-thing to gain an overhead view before tackling the maze (open daily 9am-dusk). Watch out for David Bowie in tight, tight pants. Reach the Schönbusch Gardens by bus #4 or 52 from the main station (DM1.50 one way).

Schloß-Johannisburg, the former domain of the Mainz bishops, is now an extensive museum of valuable art by old Dutch and German masters. A set of 48 chromatically tuned bronze bells rings across the landscape daily at 9:05am, 12:05 and 5:05pm. The annual **Carillion-Fest,** held the first weekend in August, brings renowned ringers from around the globe and tintinnabulating tourists who come to swim in the musical swell. (Castle open Tues.-Sun. 9am-noon and 1:30-5pm; Oct.-March Tues.-Sun. 10am-noon and 1:30-4pm. Museum open Tues.-Sun. 9-11:30am and 1-4:30pm; Nov.-March Tues.-Sun. 11am-4pm.) The **Schloßgarten** possesses intricate pathways, ivy-canopied benches, and old town walls that form a secluded haven for romance (open daily until 9pm). Walking south on Schloßgasse, turn left at Dalbergstr. to find the famous **Stiftskirche St. Peter and Alexander.** The repository of a millennium of cultural history, the collection includes a 10th-century crucifix, Mathias Grünewald's painting *Beweinung Christi,* and Vischer's *Magdalenenaltar* (open Wed.-Mon. 10am-1pm and 2pm-5pm). Continuing down Dalbergstr. as it becomes Sandgasse, beautiful *Fachwerkhäuser* (half-timbered houses) pepper the path to the **Sandkirche,** a carefully preserved 1756 Rococo church; it was the only Aschaffenburg church to survive World War II intact and it seems they've been adding more and more religious knick-knacks every year since then. For acute cases of cutesy church nausea, the **Rosso Bianco Automuseum** specializes in two-seater cars; the collection includes over 200 rare and unique automobiles from all over the world, including Alfa Romeos, Porsches, and Ferraris (open April-Oct. Tues.-Sun. 10am-6pm, Nov.-March Sun. 10am-6pm; admission DM10, students DM6). Motor over on bus #1 (a Mercedes-Benz bus!) from the train station.

Built on a high bank at a bend in the Main, Aschaffenburg is accessible by hourly **trains** from Frankfurt or Würzburg. To reach the *Schloß* and the **tourist office,** Schloßplatz 1 (tel. 39 58 00; fax 39 58 02), bear right on Ludwigstr. in front of the station and walk down Duccastr.; cross the street to take a left down Friedrichstr., then the next right down Erthalstr., and a final left onto Strickergstr. Stuck in an ultra-modern library, the office has free maps and a free room-finding service (open Mon.-Fri. 9am-5pm, Sat. 10am-1pm). For a 1½-hour **tour** of the town in German (DM4, children under 12 free), meet in front of the tourist office on Sunday at 2pm. **Rent bikes** at **Bazoom Bikes 'n Boards,** Ohmbachsgasse 6 (tel. 13 551; fax 13 755). From the station, veer left onto Frohsinnstr., left again on Weißenburgerstr., and then a sharp right onto Roßmarket; Bazoom will be on your right across from the Heylands brewery (DM20 per day; ID required; Visa accepted). A **laundromat, SB Waschsalon,** Beckerstr. 26, is on the corner of Kneippstr. and close to the youth hostel. (Open Mon.-Sat. 9am-9pm. Wash DM6, dry DM6; they don't accept laundered money.) The **post office,** 63739 Aschaffenburg (tel. 36 90), to the left of the train station, exchanges currency (open Mon.-Fri. 8am-noon and 1:30-5:30pm, Sat. 8am-noon, Sun. 11am-noon). The **telephone code** is 06021.

Aschaffenburg's **Jugendherberge (HI),** Beckerstr. 47 (tel. 93 07 63; fax 97 06 94), is reachable from the station by bus #40 or 41 to "Schroberstr." Head left up Kneippstr. and right onto Beckerstr.; the hostel is on the left. Try your luck at a little b-ball with the kids. (Reception open 8-9am, noon-1pm, and 5-7pm. Curfew 11:30pm. DM17.50. Under 27 only. Breakfast included. Sheets DM5.50.) Just outside the *Fußgängerzone* (pedestrian zone), the cheerful owner of **Hotel Pape Garni,** Würzburgerstr. 16 (tel. 226 73; fax 226 22), provides a home-cooked breakfast with his rooms. From the Schlopplatz, follow Schloßgasse or Pfaffengasse and turn left onto Dalbergstr., which turns into Sandgasse and then into Würzburgerstr. (singles DM45, doubles DM85; shower in the hall). Rooms at **Hotel Central,** Steingasse 5 (tel. 233 92), are lovely, but few: call ahead (singles DM60, doubles DM120). Hidden just inside the city wall, **Zum Rotenkopf** has mastered its hearty food—strong enough for a Bavarian, but made for a tourist: daily specials include soup (DM12.50). From the Schloßplatz, walk down Schloßberg to the right of the tourist office and turn left on Suicardusstr. (open Wed.-Mon. 10am-midnight). Another convenient option is the **Stadtschänke,** on your left as you exit the station. Daily menu options (DM7-15) include an entree and salad (open Mon.-Sat. 9am-midnight).

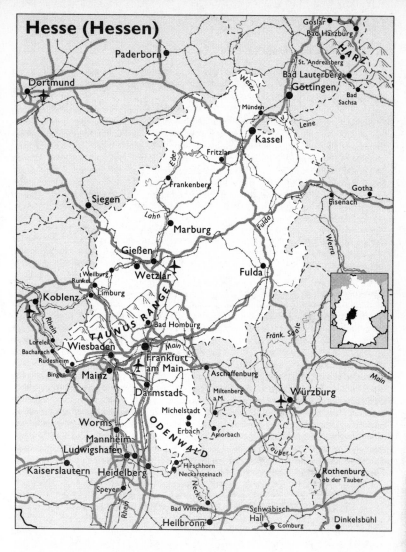

Hesse (Hessen)

Prior to the 20th century, Hesse was most commonly known for the mercenary soldiers that its various potentates farmed out to rulers such as King George III, who then sent them to America to put down an unruly gang of colonial hicks in 1776. Absorbed by Bismarck's Prussia in 1866, Hesse ceased to exist as a political entity until the Allies resurrected it in 1945. Somewhere along the line, the Hessians apparently made a collective decision to exchange their guns for briefcases; today, Hesse is the busiest commercial center in the country, led by the banking metropolis of Frankfurt. Overshadowed by Frankfurt, the rest of Hesse attracts little attention from tourists. But the *Land* is also home to the medieval university town of Marburg, the Baroque city of Fulda, and the villages of the Lahn Valley.

■ Frankfurt am Main

A city of skyscrapers and investment bankers, Frankfurt belongs more properly to the Germany of tomorrow than the Germany of yesterday. Although the city only recently acquired the derisive nicknames "Bankfurt" and "Mainhattan," its reputation as a financial and commercial center reaches back for centuries. It was here that the Rothschild family's mammoth banking empire began as a fledgling lending house. Intellectuals Max Horkheimer, Theodor Adorno, and Walter Benjamin chose Frankfurt as the home of their *Institut für Sozialforschung,* better known as the Frankfurt School, whose members started out trying to explain the failure of Germany's socialist revolution and ended up revolutionizing modern social theory. Frankfurt has the reputation among Germans and non-Germans alike of being the most Americanized city in Europe. However, despite its notoriety as the crime capital of Germany, it's still *Kindergarten* compared to New York City. Although very little of historic Frankfurt survived the carpet bombing of World War II, there's a fairly wide range of offerings—a compact section of the *Altstadt* remains intact, the zoo is among the best in the world, and the city's liberal expenditures on culture and the arts are reflected in an extraordinary variety of museums. If that isn't enough to make you come to Frankfurt, the immense likelihood of your arriving in Germany at Rhein-Main Airport probably is.

ORIENTATION AND PRACTICAL INFORMATION

A sprawling conglomeration of steel, concrete, glass, and scaffolding, Germany's fifth-largest city bridges the **Main River** 35km east of its confluence with the Rhine, in the heart of central Germany. Frankfurt's airport and *Hauptbahnhof* are among the busiest in Europe. The train station lies at the end of Frankfurt's red-light district, which in typical Frankfurt fashion brings together sex bars, foreign airline offices, and banks. From the station, the town center is a 20-minute walk down Kaiserstr. or Münchener Str. The commercial heart of the city—which itself becomes somewhat seedy after dark—is centered around **Hauptwache.** Take S-Bahn #1-6 or 8 (2 stops from the main station). The historical center revolves around the **Römerberg.** Take U-Bahn #4 (direction: Seckbacher Landstr.) to "Römer." Students, student cafés, stores, and services cluster in **Bockenheim,** as does the student graffiti demanding *Aktion, Solidarität,* and *Freiheit.* Take U-Bahn #6 or 7 to "Bockenheimer Warte." Across the Main, **Sachsenhausen** draws the *Äpfelwein*-lovers, the pub-crawlers, the Irish, and the museum-goers. Take U-Bahn #1, 2, or 3 to "Schweizer Platz."

Tourist Office: In the *Hauptbahnhof,* across from track 23 (tel. 21 23 88 49; room reservations 21 23 08 08). Maps, brochures, souvenirs, tours, and lots more. Rooms booked for a DM5 fee. Open Mon.-Fri. 8am-9pm, Sat.-Sun. and holidays 9am-6pm. The other branch borders *Römerplatz* at Römerberg 27 (tel. 21 23 87 08). Same publications and services as *Hauptbahnhof* office, except no room reservations. Open daily 9am-6pm.

Consulate: U.S. Siesmayerstr. 21 (tel. 753 50 or 75 35 24 41). Open to the public Mon.-Fri. 8am-11am; phone hours Mon.-Fri. 8am-4:30pm. Reacquaint yourself with good ol' American inefficiency. **U.K.** Bockenheimer Landstr. 42 (tel. 170 00 20; fax 72 95 53). Open Mon.-Fri. 9am-noon and 2-4pm. Phone hours Mon.-Thurs. 8:30am-1pm and 2-5pm, Fri. 8:30am-1pm and 2-4:30pm. **Australia,** Gutleutstr. 85 (tel. 273 90 90; fax 23 26 31). Public hours Mon.-Thurs. 9am-1pm and 2-4:30pm, Fri. 9am-1pm and 2-4pm.

Currency Exchange: In Airport Hall B (open daily 7:30am-9pm) or in the main train station across from track 1 (open daily 6:30am-10pm), but you're probably better off exchanging money at a post office.

American Express: Kaiserstr. 8 (tel. 210 50; fax 28 33 98). For 24-hr. hotline, call (0130) 85 31 00. Holds mail for 4 weeks. Services are free but available only to members. Open Mon.-Fri. 9:30am-5:30pm, Sat. 9am-noon.

Telephones: In the *Hauptbahnhof,* the airport, and the taxi-yellow phonebooths on every city corner. Open 24hr.

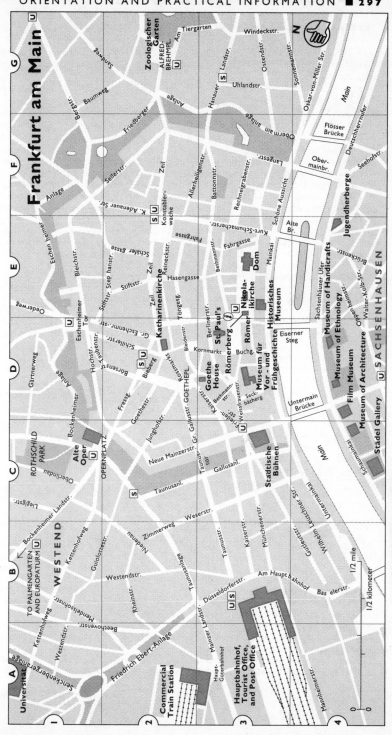

Frankfurt am Main

N

WESTEND

ROTHSCHILD PARK

TO PALMENGARTEN AND EUROPATURM

Universität

Senckenberganlage

Mendelssohnstr.
Kettenhofweg
Beethovenstr.
Westendstr.
Guiollettstr.
Rheinstr.
Westendstr.
Niederau
Zimmerweg
Kettenhofweg

Liebigstr.
Oberlindau
Bockenheimer Landstr.
Bockenheimer Landstr.
Bockenheimer
Gärtnerweg
Anlage
Hochstr.
Taubenstr.
Schillerstr.
Eschenheimer Tor
Anlage
Eschenheimer
Oederweg
Bleichstr.
Seilerstr.
Anlage
Bergerstr.
Baumweg
Sandweg
Friedberger
Anlage
K. Adenauer Str.
Zeil
Seilerstr.

Alte Oper
OPERNPLATZ

Goethestr.
Fress.
Fressg.
Junghofstr.
Neue Mainzerstr.
Gallusanl.
Taunusanl.
Taunusanl.
Weserstr.
Gutleutstr.

Bockenheimer Landstr.

Mainzer Landstr.
Düsseldorferstr.
Am Hauptbahnhof
Baselerstr.

Commercial Train Station
Haupt-Güterbahnhof

Hauptbahnhof, Tourist Office, and Post Office
Haupt-Güterbahnhof

Friedrich Ebert-Anlage

Eschenheimer
Hochstr.
Borsenstr.
Bieberg.
Schillerstr.
Gr. Eschenm.-str.
Stiftstr.
Zeil
Zeil
Zeil
Reineckstr.
Rossmarkt
Schäfer gasse
Bleidenstr.
Tongesg.
Hasengasse
Fahrgasse
Katharinenkirche
Kornmarkt
Berlinerstr.
Bethmannstr.
Kaiserstr.
Gr. Gallusstr. GOETHEPL.
Bethmann-str.
Seckbacherg.
Weissfrauenstr.
Friedensstr.
Taunus-tor
Neue Mainzerstr.
Münchenerstr.
Kaiserstr.
Taunusstr.
Weserstr.
Wilhelm-Leuschner-Str.
Gutleutstr.
Untermainkai
Schaumainkai
Mannheimerstr.

Goethe House
St. Paul's
Römerberg
Römer
Nikolaikirche
Dom
Historisches Museum
Museum für Vor- und Frühgeschichte
Buchg.
Städtische Bühnen

Konstabler-wache

Fahrgasse
Battonnstr.
Allerheiligenstr.
Rechneigrabenstr.
Kurt-Schumacherstr.
Schöne Aussicht
Bethmannstr.
Mainkai
Schöne Aussicht
Alte Br.
Eiserner Steg
Untermain Brücke

Oberm. anlage
Langestr.
Hanauer
Uhlandstr.
Windeckstr.
Ostendstr.
Sonnemannstr.
Oskar-von-Miller Str.
Landstr.

Zoologischer Garten
ALFRED BREHMPL.
Am Tiergarten
Am Tiergarten

Main

Flösser Brücke
Ober-mainbr.
Deutschherrnufer
Seehofstr.
Brückenstr.

Jugendherberge
Museum of Handicrafts
Museum of Ethnology
Film Museum
Museum of Architecture
Städel Gallery

Sachsenhäuser Ufer
Oppenheimer
Oppenheimer
Walter-Kolb-Str.

SACHSENHAUSEN

Main

1/2 mile
1/2 kilometer

0
0

Flights: Flughafen Rhein-Main is a major hub for destinations in Europe, across the Atlantic, and around the world. Call 69 01 for information. From the airport, S-Bahn #8 and 5 travel every 15min. to the *Hauptbahnhof*. Buy tickets (DM5.70) from a green automat; Eurailpass valid.

Trains: 1600 trains roll in and out of Frankfurt's *Hauptbahnhof* daily; connections to both major and minor European cities leave frequently. Munich (3½-4½hr.; at least 1 per hr.), Berlin (5-6hrs.; 1 per hr.), Paris (6-7hr.; every 2hr.). Call 194 19 for schedules, reservations, and information.

Public Transportation: For unlimited access to S-Bahn, U-Bahn, and buses, 24-hr. passes (DM8.80) are available from machines in every station. A *Frankfurt Card* (available at tourist offices and in most travel agencies; DM13) allows 2 days of travel on all trains and buses, including the airport line; it also gets you reduced admission to 14 museums, the *Palmengarten*, the zoo, and—a veritable carnival funhouse—the airport visitors' terrace. Eurailpasses valid on all S-Bahn trains.

Bike Rental: Holger's Rad-Laden, Eschersheimer Landstr. 470 (tel. 52 20 04). U-Bahn #1, 2, or 3 to "Lindenbaum." DM20 per day. Bikes are allowed on the subway, if you're too lazy to pedal back to town. Open Mon.-Tues. and Thurs.-Fri. 9am-1pm and 3-6:30pm, Wed. and Sat. 9am-1pm.

Hitchhiking: *Let's Go* does not recommend hitchhiking as a safe mode of transportation. Those headed to Munich take buses #36 or #960 from Konstablerwache south to the *Autobahn* interchange. Those bound for Cologne or Düsseldorf take S-Bahn #1 or 8 to the Wiesbaden *Hauptbahnhof* and then a local train to Auringen-Medenbach; from there they turn right, walk 800m, proceed under the *Autobahn*, and take the access road to the *Autobahn* rest stop. Hitching on the highway itself is strictly forbidden. Hitchers headed in all other directions take streetcar #19 or bus #61, and continue along Mörfelder-Landstr.

Mitfahrzentrale: Baselerstr. 7 (tel. 23 64 44 or 23 61 27). From the side exit of the *Hauptbahnhof* (track 1), take a right on Baselerstr., and it's 2 blocks down on the right. Connects riders with drivers for a fee. Call ahead. Open Mon.-Fri. 8am-6:30pm, Sat. 8am-2pm.

Bookstores: Süssman's Presse und Buch, Zeil 127 (tel. 131 07 51; fax 131 01 49). Open Mon.-Wed. and Fri. 9am-6:30pm, Thurs. 9am-8:30pm, Sat. 9am-2pm. For those who can't live without Grisham's latest novel. **British Book Shop,** Börsenstr. 17 (tel. 28 04 92). Open Mon.-Fri. 9am-6:30pm, Sat. 9am-2pm.

Laundromat: Wasch Center, Wallstr. 8, in Sachsenhausen near the youth hostel. Wash DM7, dry DM1 per 15min. Soap included. Change machine. Open daily 6am-10pm. **SB Wasch Center,** Große Seestr. 46 (tel. 77 35 80). U-Bahn #6 or 7 to "Bockenheimer Warte." From the station, head down Adalbertstr. and right on Große Seestr. Wash (with soap) DM8. Dry DM1 per 10min. Open 6:30am-10pm.

Rape/Battered Women's Hotline: tel. 70 94 94.

Pharmacy: In the basement of the train station by the subway entrances (tel. 23 30 47). Open Mon.-Fri. 6:30am-9pm, Sat. 8am-9pm, Sun. and holidays 8am-8pm. If pharmacies are closed, call 192 92 for emergency prescriptions.

Emergency: Police: tel. 110. **Fire** and **ambulance:** tel. 112.

Post Office: Main branch, Zeil 110, 60313 Frankfurt (tel. 21 11; fax 29 68 84). U- or S-Bahn: "Hauptwache." Send and be sent. Fax and be faxed. Open Mon.-Fri. 9am-6pm, Sat. 9am-1pm. **Branch office** also on the upper level of the *Hauptbahnhof*. Open Mon.-Fri. 6am-10pm, Sat.-Sun. 8am-9pm.

Telephone code: 069.

ACCOMMODATIONS

Hotel prices in Frankfurt can rise as high as the skyscrapers. The cheapest options are near the main train station (in a decidedly seedy part of town), or in the Westend/University area (a slightly longer walk, but you will avoid the slimy atmosphere around Baselstr.). If all else fails, there are four other hostels less than 45 minutes away: Bad Homburg (S-Bahn #5, direction: Friedrichsdorf), Darmstadt (S-Bahn #12), Mainz (S-Bahn #14, direction: Wiesbaden), and Wiesbaden (S-Bahn #1 or 14).

Jugendherberge (HI), Deutschherrnufer 12, 60594 Frankfurt am Main (tel. 61 90 58; fax 61 82 57). Take Bus #46 from main station (DM2.80, DM3.30 during morning and evening rush hours) to "Frankensteinerplatz." The hostel is 50m west in the large yellow building. After 7:30pm, take S-Bahn #2-6 or tram #16 to "Lokalbahnhof," then walk north on Darmstädter Landstr., which becomes Dreieichstr, and turn left on Deutschherrnufer. Newly renovated; near the Sachsenhausen pubs and museum district. Neighborhood and hostel alike tend to be lively and loud. Breakfast on the glassed-in veranda is free (7-8:30am), while lunch and dinner (DM 8.70) come in big portions for big *Schulkinder* (12:15-1pm and 6-7:30pm, respectively). Vegetarian meals available. 3-day max. stay during the summer. Reception open 24hr. Lockout 9am-1pm. Official curfew is midnight—try bargaining for later. DM23, over 20 DM28. Doubles DM40.50 per person (additional nights DM38.50), but they are *very rarely* available. Required sheet deposit of DM10. Key deposit for smaller rooms DM10. Written reservations accepted.

Pension Bruns, Mendelssohnstr. 42 (tel. 74 88 96, fax 74 88 46). From the *Hauptbahnhof,* take a left onto Düsseldorferstr., and after 2 blocks veer right on Beethovenstr. At the small circle, go right on Mendelssohnstr. (10-15-min.). Located in the Westend near *Palmengarten* and the university. Ring the bell; it's on the 2nd floor. Homey, with spacious, sunny rooms. The lone single is DM59. Doubles DM79. Triples DM99. Showers (off the hall) DM2; towels included. Home-cooked breakfast also included and served in your room! Call ahead.

Pension Backer, Mendelssohnstr. 92 (tel. 74 79 92), up the street from Pension Burns. U-Bahn: "Westend." Dark, smallish rooms, but they're adequately clean and certainly cheap enough. Singles DM50. Doubles DM70. Showers available 7am-10pm; DM3 per 8 min. Breakfast included. No credit cards accepted. Reservations taken with deposit. Call early—the 30 rooms may often be rented in bulk.

Hotel Wiesbaden, Baseler Str. 52 (tel. 23 23 47 or 23 23 48; fax 25 28 45). Turn right as you leave the *Hauptbahnhof* and follow Baseler Str. towards the river. Upscale place that offers spacious, neat rooms, with a minimalist motif. All rooms have TV and phone. Reception open until 10pm. Singles DM65, with shower DM95. Doubles DM90, with shower DM125. Triples with shower DM150.

Hotel Atlas, Zimmerweg 1 (tel. 72 39 46; fax 72 39 46). Exit the *Hauptbahnhof* and take either Kaiserstr. or Taunusstr. straight ahead. After 2 blocks, go left on Weserstr., which turns into Zimmerweg after crossing Mainzer Landstr. It's on the 4th floor. Intimate and softly-lit just like grandma's house. Sweet staff. Showers in the hall. Singles DM66. Doubles DM96. Triples DM138. Breakfast included.

FOOD

While cheap eats in Frankfurt are not nearly as rare as cheap beds, light eats may prove harder to come by, especially if you stick to the local culinary gems. Large mugs of *Äpfelwein* (apple wine, a.k.a. *Äppelwei* or *Ebbelwei*) should never top DM3, though don't expect anything akin to the sharp sweetness of cider or the dryness of chardonnay; this ain't no sippin' wine. Slow the onset of your drunken *Äpfelwein* stupor with two *Frankfurter Würtschen, gegrillte Rippchen* (grilled ribs), or *Handkäse mit Musik,* a kind of curd cheese with raw onions (the *Musik,* one discovers, comes after the meal). When it's in season (May-June), restaurants add a *Spargel* (asparagus) section to the menu: spargel pasta, spargel soup, spargel salad. Beware *Spargel*'s own *Musik.* The most reasonably priced kitchens surround the university in Bockenheim and nearby parts of Westend (U-Bahn: #6 or 7 to "Bockenheimer Warte"; the subway stop looks like a train busting through the sidewalk). Many of the pubs and taverns in both the Sachsenhausen and Alt Sachsenhausen districts serve food (U-Bahn #1,2, or 3: "Schweizer Platz"). In the warmer months, Bockenheim, the Zeil, and Römerplatz frequently attract carts and stands.

Zum Gemalten Haus, Schweizerstr. 67 (tel. 61 45 59; fax 603 14 57). One of the 2 most famous joints in Sachsenhausen, it skirts the *gemütlich* line very close. Serves up copious amounts of *Äpfelwein* home-brewed (DM2.40 for 0.3L) as well as cold cuts, hot meals, *Würste,* and *Handkäse mit Musik* (DM5-25). Open Wed.-Sun. 10am-midnight.

HESSE (HESSEN)

Adolf Wagner, Schweizerstr. 71 (tel. 61 25 65, fax 61 14 45). Another famous Sachsenhausen haunt, 4 doors down from Zum Gemalten Haus. Owned and operated by the same family since 1931. Proffers *Äpfelwein* (DM2.40 for 0.3L), hot meals, *Würste,* and all the Frankfurt specialties in heart-rending portions (DM5-25). Open daily 11am-midnight.

Römer-Bembel, Römerplatz 20/22 (tel. 28 83 83; fax 55 76 44). At the center of what little is left of Frankfurt's *Altstadt,* across the square from the Rösser. Pretend to be a local and raise your *Pilsner* (DM4.50) each time a tour group passes by. The popular restaurant also serves Frankfurt specialties at decent prices: *Rippchen* (ribs; DM12.50) and *Oschenbrust* (boiled beef brisket) with green sauce (DM17.50). Open daily 11:30am-11pm.

Historix' Ebbelwoi-Wirtschaft, Saalgasse 19 (tel. 29 44 00; fax 55 76 44), adjoining the Historisches Museum, provides a more intimate setting in an indoor beer garden with the neighborly feel of *Cheers.* In addition to the customary beverages and dishes, they also serve fresh *Eintöpfe* (stews; DM6.85). Open Tues.-Fri. 11am-10:30pm, Sat. 11am-5pm, Sun. noon-5pm.

The Kleinmarkthalle, on Hasengasse between Berlinerstr. and Töngesgasse, is a 3-story warehouse housing many countershops: bakeries, butchers, fruit and vegetable stands, and more. Buy some fresh *Spargel,* a steaming *Würst,* or a skinned rabbit (not yet decapitated), and eat on the Zeil or in the nearby *Historisches Garten.* Open Mon.-Thurs. 8am-6pm, Fri. 7:30am-6pm, Sun. 7:30am-2pm.

University Mensa, Bockenheimer Landstr. 133. U-Bahn #6 or 7 to "Brockenheimer Warte." Just outside the subway. Offers 3 standard dishes (1 of which is vegetarian) priced DM2.50-7. Mediocre, cost-effective food. Technically, a Hessian student ID is required; you may have to pay a DM2 surcharge. Open 7:30am-6:30pm.

SIGHTS

"Everywhere one looks," wrote the 18th-century author Johann Kaspar Riesbeck, "one sees the signs of a high standard of living. The furnishings of the houses, the yards, the carriages, the clothes, the jewelry of the women—in short, everything exceeds the bourgeois and borders on the most unimaginable splendor." During World War II, Allied forces leveled all of Frankfurt's showiness in a sweep of equalizer bombings. Industrious Frankfurters, however, rebuilt and restored many of the city's original structures within a few years.

The logical starting point for a tour of this city of conspicuous consumption is the **Römerberg,** the cluster of partially surviving historical buildings in the city center. The eastern end of the *Römerberg* is dominated by the **Dom,** a huge red sandstone Gothic cathedral with several splendidly elaborate altarpieces. It served as the site of coronation ceremonies for German emperors between 1562 and 1792 (open June-Aug. daily 9am-noon and 2:30-6pm; Sept.-May 9am-noon and 2:30-5:30pm). The view of the Main valley and the city's bustling vitality is well worth the punishing climb (round and round and round and round) to the top (tower admission DM3, students and children DM1; closed in winter). The **Dom Museum** inside the main entrance contains some venerated robes of the imperial electors and a recently found Merovingian girl's tomb (open Tues.-Fri. 10am-5pm, Sat.-Sun. 11am-5pm; admission DM2, students DM1). Directly in front of the *Dom* is the **Historischer Garten,** with ruins from Roman to medieval times, all discovered by chance when workers happened upon them while digging up a sewer line.

The **Römer,** a distinctively gabled red sandstone structure at the west end of the *Römerberg,* has been Frankfurt's city hall since 1405. The upper floors contain the **Kaisersaal,** a former imperial banquet hall whose walls are adorned with portraits of the 52 German emperors from Charlemagne to Franz II, 13 of which were coronated here (open Tues.-Sun. 11am-3pm; obligatory tour on the hour DM3). Next to the *Römer* on Paulsplatz stands the **Paulskirche** (St. Paul's Church; open daily 10am-5pm). In the wake of the waves of revolution that swept through Europe in 1848-49, Germany's first democratic National Assembly convened in the church to draw up a constitution for a German republic. Recognizing that Germany could not be unified without the assent of powerful Prussia, the liberal assembly attempted to flatter Prussia's Frederick William IV into accepting the crown of a constitutional monarchy. The king replied that he ruled by the grace of God, and the whole episode ended in the streets with a bloody repression of the democracy movement.

Although it dates back to the 11th century and is thus the oldest church used by Protestants in Frankfurt, **Die Alte Nikolaikirche** (The Old Nicholas Church), Römerberg 9 (tel. 28 42 35), has long been overshadowed by its more imposing neighbors, the *Dom* and the *Paulskirche*—in fact, after the Reformation, the church was used as a warehouse until finally being restored to dignity in 1721. (Open April-Sept. daily 10am-8pm, Oct.-March 10am-6pm. Advent 10am-9pm. Daily tours at noon. Organ concerts in summer Wed. at 5:30pm, followed by worship service at 6pm in English and German, and then by cake and conversation with the preacher, an American.)

Of the half-dozen or so German cities that claim to be the home of Goethe, Frankfurt legitimately claims the early years. The master was born in Frankfurt in 1749, he found his first love here (a girl named Gretchen, said to be the inspiration for Marguerite in *Faust*), and he penned some of his best-known works here as well, including *The Sorrows of Young Werther*. A few blocks northwest of the *Römer* stands his birthplace and family home, the aptly-named **Goethe Haus,** Großer Hirschgraben 23-25 (tel. 28 28 24 or 29 18 84; fax 29 38 22). Due to renovations, the museum is closed (scheduled to reopen in late 1997 or early 1998), but the house is still open to the public. Enter through the *Volkstheater*. The sumptuous interior is evidence that you don't have to suffer to produce great art. (Open April-Sept. Mon.-Sat. 9am-6pm, Sun 10am-1pm; Oct.-March Mon.-Sat. 9am-4pm, Sun. 10am-1pm. Tours Mon.-Sat. 10:30am and 2pm, Sun. 10:30am. Admission DM4, students DM3.)

The **Museumsufer** is home to a number of high-powered museums (see Museums, below), Frankfurt's weekly **flea market** (open Sat. 9am-2pm during the warm months), and the **Museumsuferfest,** a huge cultural jamboree which draws more than a million visitors over three during days in late August. For animal lovers, over 650 species from the banal to the exotic are represented at the **Zoo** (tel. 212 337 35), on the eastern side of town. Take U-Bahn #6 or 7. The feeding of the apes (daily at 4:30pm; winter 4pm) and of the piranhas (Sun. and Wed. at 11am) excites a certain visceral pleasure. (Open mid-March-Sept. Mon.-Fri. 9am-7pm, Sat.-Sun. 8am-7pm; Oct.-mid-March daily 9am-5pm. Admission DM11, under 18 and students DM5; DM9 and DM4, respectively, if you take the U-Bahn—save your ticket.) In the northwest part of town, tourists, children, businesspeople, and an extensive variety of German birds take refuge in the sprawling, lush **Palmengarten** (U-Bahn #6 or 7: "Bockenheimer Warte"). If you bring a few pieces of bread, you can lure the winged ones off the rentable wooden boats (DM4 per 30min.). The garden's greenhouses contain seven different "worlds," from the tropics to the plains. In summer, the grounds host a number of performances and exhibitions. (Open March-Sept. daily 9am-6pm; Feb. and Oct. 9am-5pm; Nov.-Jan. 9am-4pm. Admission DM7, students DM3.)

MUSEUMS

On the south bank of the Main, between the *Eiserner Stag* and the *Friedensbrücke*, sits one of the most eclectic collections of museums in Germany: the **Museumsufer** on the *Schaumainkai*. Unified by geography, if not by content, these seven culturally stocked museums offer an extensive range of media—sculpture, film, plants, old German postal trucks—at least one of which even the most casual museum surfer will find interesting.

Museumsufer

Museum für Kunsthandwerk, Schaumainkai 17 (tel. 21 23 40 37 or 21 23 85 30). Crafts and arts from Europe (the Middle Ages to the present), the Near East (9th to 19th centuries), and the Far East (Neolithic to the present). One division is devoted entirely to icons. Admission DM6, students DM3. Open Tues. and Thurs.-Sun. 10am-5pm, Wed. 10am-8pm.

Museum für Völkerkunde, Schaumainkai 29, in the courtyard of the *Museum für Kunsthandwerk.* Features a multi-cultural feast of objects liberated from several African and South American countries. Admission DM4, students DM2. Free on Wed. Open Tues. and Thurs.-Sun. 10am-5pm, Wed. 10am-8pm.

Deutsches Filmmuseum, Schaumainkai 41 (tel. 21 23 88 30). Exhibits on the development of filmmaking. Old movies shown on the 3rd floor. The only place in Frankfurt to film friends in Sam Spade's office or see yourself flying on a carpet high above the Frankfurt sky-line. Swanky **Café Kino** adjoins museum. Admission DM5, students DM2.50. Films DM8, students DM6. Free on Wed. Open Tues., Thurs.-Fri., and Sun. 10am-5pm, Wed. 10am-8pm, Sat. 2-8pm.

Architektur Museum, Schaumainkai 43 (tel. 21 23 88 44). A 3-floor survey of the last 10 years in European architecture in a beautifully designed space, all white surface and right angles. Admission DM8, students DM4. Open Tues., Thurs., and Sat.-Sun. 11am-6pm, Wed. and Fri. noon-8pm.

Bundespostmuseum, Schaumainkai 53 (tel. 606 01). A history of German travel and communication in a bright and spacious but somewhat haphazardly designed building. Interactive and video displays in German only. Open Tues. and Thurs.-Sun. 10am-5pm, Wed. 10am-8pm. An amateur radio booth on the top floor is open Wed. 3-8pm, Thurs. 10am-1pm, and the 1st Sun. of each month 2-5pm.

Städel, Schaumainkai 63 (tel. 605 09 80; fax 61 01 63), between Dürerstr. and Holbeinstr. An excellent collection of Old Masters, housed in a beautiful, stately mansion. One of Germany's leading art museums. Galleries include early Italian and old German and Dutch works, painting from the 16th century to the present, and sculpture since the 19th century. Admission DM8, students DM4. Free on Wed. Open Tues. and Thurs.-Sun. 10am-5pm, Wed. 10am-8pm.

Liebieghaus, Schaumainkai 71 (tel. 21 23 86 17). Asian and Egyptian art, and sculpture from Middle Ages. Renaissance, Baroque, and Rococo. Sit in the outdoor café and ponder the heavy architecture and landscaping. Is it a castle? A Greek temple? A shrine embedded in a dense tropical forest? Admission DM5, students DM2.50. Free on Wed. Open Tues. and Thurs.-Sun. 10am-5pm, Wed. 10am-8pm.

Elsewhere in Frankfurt

Museum für Moderne Kunst, Domstr. 10 (tel. 21 23 04 47; fax 21 23 78 82). Not to be missed. The triangular building's interior (nicknamed the "slice of cake") is an architectural wonder. It provides an ideal setting for the stunning modern art housed within, including impressive works by Claes Oldenburg, Roy Liechtenstein, and Jasper Johns. Art in every medium imaginable. The theater in the basement screens films and slide installations. Admission DM7, students DM3.50. Open Tues., Thurs.-Fri., and Sun. 10am-5pm, Wed. 10am-8pm, Sat. noon-7pm.

Schirn Kunsthalle, located next to the *Dom,* its entrance tucked in a narrow alley (tel. 299 88 20). A postmodern art gallery hosting visiting exhibits with intriguing titles like "The Occult and the Avant-garde." Admission DM12, students DM8. DM8 on Sundays. Open Tues. and Fri.-Sun. 10am-7pm, Wed.-Thurs. 10am-10pm.

Historisches Museum, Saalgasse 19 (tel. 21 23 55 99), back toward the river from the *Römer.* Presents a first-rate series of exhibitons on the history of Frankfurt, including a permanent "Äpfelwein Museum" and a comparative display of the city before and after the bombing of WWII. Admission DM5, students DM2.50. Open Tues. and Thurs.-Sun. 10am-5pm, Wed. 10am-8pm.

Naturmuseum, Senckenberganlage 25 (tel. 754 20). U-Bahn #6 or 7: "Bockenheimer Warte." Features a fully-mounted dinosaur skeleton, dinosaur bones, and some big whales thrown in. The largest natural museum in Germany attracts the largest school groups in Frankfurt. Admission DM7, students DM3. Open Mon.-Tues. and Thurs.-Fri. 9am-5pm, Wed. 9am-8pm, Sat.-Sun. 9am-6pm.

ENTERTAINMENT AND NIGHTLIFE

Frankfurt wields a nightlife commensurate with its size. There are two major theaters, the **Alte Oper** (by no means limited to opera) and the **Städtisches Theater,** as well as several smaller ones. Shows and schedules of the city's stages are detailed in a number of publications, including the *Journal Frankfurt* (DM2.80), *Fritz* (free), and *Strandgut* (free), all available at the tourist office. Students can often purchase leftover tickets at reduced prices one hour before the beginning of a performance.

Frankfurt has a renowned **jazz** scene (indeed, it was once the jazz capital of Europe) that centers around Kleine Bockenheimer Str., also known as **Jazzgasse** (Jazz Alley).

If you're looking for a drinking night, the **Alt Sachsenhausen** district, between Brückenstr. and Dreieichstr., is home to a huge number of rowdy pubs and taverns specializing in *Äpfelwein* (apple wine), the local drink of choice. The complex of narrow cobblestone streets centering on **Kleiner Rittergasse** teems with canopied cafés, bars, and restaurants, and buzzes with natives and tourists alike, especially during the summer. Irish pubs with gregarious Irish lads also abound.

Frankfurt also has a number of thriving discos and a lively techno scene. Wear something dressier than jeans—unless they're *really* hip jeans—if you plan to try your luck with the neurotic bouncers. Don't think you'll escape cover charges, either; most clubs make you pay upon exiting. A recent, revolutionary offering of nightclub organizers Schüler and Pestinger increases partying options while lowering costs dramatically; pay the cover at one of their five popular discos—including **Europaturm,** located on the 200th floor of Frankfurt's TV tower, and **Dorian Gray,** an expansive club whose three dance floors encompass the basement of a wing at the airport—and gain not only free entrance to all of their other clubs but also free transportation between them (Fri. DM10, Sat. DM15). Gay nightlife in Frankfurt is mainly centered around the area between Zeil and Bleichstr.

Der Jazzkeller, Kleine Bockenheimerstr. 18a (tel. 28 85 37). Hidden at the end of the blues alley lies Frankfurt's most renowned jazz club. Cover usually DM15-30. Call for a schedule. Wed. and Fri. nights boast a "cool music mix"; cover DM10. Open Tues.-Sun. 9pm-3am.

Die Jazzkneipe, Berlinerstr. 70 (tel. 28 71 73). U-Bahn: #1, 2, 3, or 4 to "Willy-Brandt Platz." Offers a more intimate, funky bar with less highbrow jazz (live) and blues every night 10pm-2am. Cover DM4-12. Open daily 8pm-4am.

Jazz Life Podium, Kleine Rittergasse 22-26. Where Sachsenhausen claims its roots in blues. Usually no cover, but sometimes DM5. Lotsa beer (DM4.50) and *Äpfelwein* (DM3.50). Open daily 7:30pm-whenever.

Irish Pub, Kleine Rittergasse 11-13 (tel. 61 59 86), in Sachsenhausen. Guinness on tap (DM6.50) and live music every night at 9pm. Screens every major Irish and English sporting event. Open Mon.-Thurs. 2pm-1am, Fri. 2pm-2am, Sat. noon-2am, Sun. noon-1am.

Shamrock Pub, Kleine Rittergasse 4-8 (tel. 62 39 12). A mixture of Irish folk music and disco accompany traditional Irish cuisine (DM4-15) and Guinness (DM6). Friendly, merry staff. Open daily noon-2am; 6pm-1am in the winter.

Cooky's, Am Salzhaus 4 (Tel. 28 76 62), off Goetheplatz. For the alternative crowd, there is no alternative. Live music Mon. Soul, acid jazz, and reggae tracks on other days. Cover varies. Open Sun.-Thurs. 10pm-4am, Fri.-Sat. 10pm-6am.

I Wish I Was a Frankfurter Frankfurter

Oscar Mayer may make *Wieners,* but they certainly can't claim to make *Frankfurters*—local sausage companies put a copyright on the name in a 1955 German Supreme Court ruling, and only those who use the official recipe and manufacture the sausages within a certain distance of Frankfurt's city center may legally slap the time-honored title of *Frankfurter* across their plastic packaging. What, you ask, is so hot about these Hessian dogs? Real *Frankfurter*-makers, following an official recipe from 1749, extract their meat solely from the front legs of the pig's body (the tenderest part). They then add fatty bacon, mixing it with thyme, nutmeg, salt and pepper, and more spices, before hand-stuffing the yummy concoction into the traditional *Frankfurter* wrapper: sheep intestines. Imported from Iran, these are the hardiest intestines in the world and must be 17-24mm in diameter. Ironically enough, locals refer to the sausages as *Wieners,* while in Vienna, they're called *Frankfurters*—go figure. After two hours of smoking (no added preservatives) and a vacuum-packing, these *Wieners*—oops—these *Frankfurters,* protected by their Middle-Eastern skins, enjoy a shelf-life of over three years.

HESSE (HESSEN)

Omen, Junghofstr. 14 (tel. 28 22 33). With a techno line-up, Omen is *the* place to disco. Cover varies. Open Fri.-Sat. 10pm-6am.

Cyber's: the Inter-n-Active Café, Zeil 112-114 (tel. 91 93 99 84; e-mail cybers@internet.de), on the 6th floor of the Zeil Galerie. For those of you who get that sudden (and perhaps addictive) urge to check your e-mail while dancing the night away. Where else in Frankfurt can you get this virtual? DM8 per 30min. connection. Open daily 9am-1am.

Zum Schwejk, Schäfergasse 20 (tel. 29 31 66). A relaxed, albeit popular, gay men's bar named after the good Czech soldier. Open Mon. 4pm-1am, Tues.-Thurs. 11am-1am, Fri.-Sat. 11am-2am, Sun. 3pm-1am.

La Gata, Seehofstr. 3 (tel. 61 45 85). Located near the Alt Sachsenhausen district, this dance club is for women only. Opens daily at 10pm.

■ Near Frankfurt: Wiesbaden

Wiesbaden is a city Edith Wharton would have understood. From its tiny designer boutiques to the ritzy casino which consititutes its center of gravity, the city speaks of the heady years of the 19th century when the aristocracy of Europe came to frolic away its time and money in brainless consumption and amusement. When the royalty fell from grace, so did Wiesbaden; today it is remarkable mostly for its U.S. military base, from which the Berlin airlift was launched. Though it is still possible to find less costly amusements, a bit of the old Wiesbaden is here for the taking. You can still test the curative waters of the thermal baths and, provided that you're formally attired, you can still gamble away your life's savings at the casino.

The original **Kurhaus,** now used for events ranging from business conventions to fashion shows and old-timer parades, is situated off of Wilhelmstr. and bordered on two sides by the expansive and serene **Kurpark,** where locals sprawl under century-old willow trees during the summer. Take bus #1 or 8 from the station to "Kurhaus/Theater." The **casino** *(Spielbank)* is inside the *Kurhaus* (tel. 53 61 00); compulsive gambler Fyodor Dostoevsky squandered the last 30 rubles that stood between him and destitution while visiting Wiesbaden, and so can you (coat and tie rental DM10; open daily 3pm-3am). To the right of the *Kurhaus* is the stately **Staatstheater** (tel. 12 33 25) inscribed with the ominous instruction *"Der Menscheit Würde ist in Eure Hand gegeben, bewahret sie"* (the dignity of mankind is in your hands, preserve it). The Staatstheater and the neighboring **Kleines Haus** present traditional and modern ballets, operas, and plays; tickets go for as little as DM9-15 (Staatstheater box office open Tues.-Fri. 11am-2pm and 4-6pm, Sat.-Sun. 11am-12:30pm; Kleines Haus *Abonnernentskasse* open Tues.-Fri. 11am-2pm and 5:30-7pm, Sat. 11am-12:30pm; tickets can be purchased 1hr. before show). Since Roman times, bathing in viciously hot, sulfurous water that spurts from the depths of the earth has been considered delightfully curative. Wiesbaden certainly owes much to the water that now boils and steams out of the **Kochbrunnen.** Follow Sonnenstr. left as you leave the *Kurpark* and turn left on Kranzpl. West of the Staatstheater on Burgstr., you can admire the **world's biggest cuckoo clock** as it calls every half-hour between 8am and 8pm.

The **Neroberg,** a low hill at the north end of town, provides an alternative to Wiesbaden's hustle and bustle. Take bus #1 to "Nerotal," and from there take the **hydraulic funicular** (DM2; round-trip DM3) or walk to the summit of the 254-m hill. Take a dip in the *Bauhaus*-style **swimming pool** (open 9am-8pm; DM8). 100m beyond the pool stands the **Russische-Griechische Kapelle,** easily the most impressive monument in the city. This painstakingly decorated Greek Orthodox chapel was built in 1855 as a mausoleum for Princess Elizabeth of Nassau, the niece of a Russian Czar who was married off to a local duke and died in childbirth at age 19. Her tear-jerking tomb dominates the chapel's inspiring interior (open daily April-Oct. 11am-4pm; admission DM1). Back in town, the **Museum Wiesbaden,** whose architecture would be more appropriate for a train station, houses art, many wonders of taxidermy, early machinery, and a mineral collection (open Tues.-Sun. 10am-4pm; admission DM5, students, seniors, and children DM2.50). Due to renovations, the museum will be partially closed until early 1997; for information, call 36 82 170.

Wiesbaden's **tourist office** *(Verkehrsbüro)*, Rheinstr. 15 (tel. 172 97 80; fax 172 97 99), awaits at the corner of Rheinstr. and Wilhelmstr. and books rooms (singles DM60) for a DM6 fee (open Mon.-Fri. 8:30am-7pm, Sat.-Sun. 9am-3pm). At the train station, the **DB Service Desk** dispenses terrific city and hotel maps and glossy propaganda about Wiesbaden. They also offer a telephone line to the tourist office. **American Express,** Webergasse 8 (tel. 391 44), does its thing for its members (open Mon.-Fri. 8:45am-5:30pm and first Sat. of every month 10am-2pm; financial services closed 1-2pm). The same **public transportation** tickets can be used in both Wiesbaden and Mainz. The **Mitfahrzentrale,** located in a camper on Bahnhofstr. 9 (tel. 33 35 55 or 194 40), halfway between the pedestrian zone and the train station, connects riders with drivers (open Mon.-Fri. 7:30am-6pm, Sat. 7:30am-noon). The girls' **crisis hotline** (13-17 years) is anonymous, unbureaucratic, and there to help (tel. (0611) 80 80 88). The **post office,** Kaiser-Friedrich-Ring 81, to the left as you come out of the *Bahnhof,* changes money and sells traveler's checks (Mon.-Fri. 8am-6pm, Sat. 8am-noon, Sun. 10:30am-1pm). The **telephone code** is 0611.

The **Jugendherberge (HI),** Blucherstr. 66 (tel. 486 57; fax 44 11 19), has laid-back management and a downstairs bar. From the station, take bus #14 to "Gneisenau-str." or "Elsasser Platz." (Reception open 'til midnight. Lockout midnight-6:30am. Lockers DM10 deposit. DM24, over 26 DM29. Sheets DM6. Breakfast included.) The **Ring Hotel,** Bleichstr. 29 (tel. 40 30 21; fax 45 15 73), is reached either by taking bus #4 from the train station to "Bleichstr." or by walking (15-20min.). Go straight on Bahnhofstr. and then left on Friedrichstr., which becomes Bleichstr. after crossing Schwabacher-Str. Look for the roaringly politically incorrect statue in the reception. The rooms are simple, with rather hard beds. (Reception open 24hr. Singles DM52, with breakfast DM62, with shower, toilet, TV, phone, and breakfast DM92. Doubles DM140.) The *Fußgängerzone* (pedestrian zone) west of the *Kurhaus* is brimming with pubs and restaurants. **Schänke zur Hauptwache,** Faulbrunnenstr. 8 (tel. 37 36 93), near the Platz der Deutschen Einheit, serves traditional German food (DM10-17) at untraditional prices (open Mon.-Fri. 10am-9pm, Sat. 10am-4pm). **The Irish Pub,** Michelsbergstr. 17, has live music every night and serves beer, wine, and coffee (DM3.50-7), and an enormous Irish breakfast (DM14) on Sundays (11am-3pm).

■ Darmstadt

Situated at the northwest edge of the Odenwald, Darmstadt takes pride in its title **"Großstadt im Walde"** (city in the woods), and for reasons that are not fully clear, local patriots see it as the "German Chicago." For the record, the city has no skyline, a relatively small population (144,000), a low crime rate, and no Lake Michigan. While it may not be Chicago, Darmstadt nevertheless radiates a youthful charm, primarily because of the well-preserved **Jugendstil** (Art Nouveau) architecture which is obscured only by the matchbox-style buildings that sprang up after the bombings of World War II. The city is also home to the German Academy of Language and Literature, which annually awards the Georg Büchner Prize, the most prestigious award in German letters. Named after the brilliant author of *Woyzeck* and *Danton's Death,* Büchner has always been one of Darmstadt's favorite native sons.

It's difficult to move an inch without running into some legacy of the dukes *(Herzöge)* who inhabited Darmstadt, beginning with Kaiser Ludwig's bequest to the Duke of Katzenelnbogen in 1330; they dwelt ducally in the Baroque **Schloß,** built between 1716 and 1727 by a French architect who modeled it after Versailles. Since World War II, the *Schloß* has served as a public university library. A small **Schloßmuseum** holds 17th- to 19th-century ducal clothing and furniture. To get there, walk one block east of Luisenplatz, the transit center of the city, to Ernst-Ludwig Platz. (Open Mon.-Thurs. 10am-1pm and 2-5pm, Sat.-Sun. 10am-1pm. Entrance only by 1hr.-long guided tour; last tour 1hr. before closing. Admission DM3.50, students DM2.50.) And what's a *Schloß* without a *Garten?* Across Alexanderstraße, behind the columned, yellow *Stadtarchive,* lies the **Herrngarten,** home to luscious grass and trees, procrastinating students, gamboling dogs, and ducks (which you can't feed). Even more exquisite is the **Prinz Georg Garten,** arranged in Rococo style and maintained by a brigade of six gardeners (open daily 7am-8pm). Next to it, the **Porzellanschlößchen** (little porcelain castle) houses, yes, an extensive collection of porcelain. Those with a geological, paleontological, or zoological bent will appreciate the **Landesmuseum,** at the other end of the Herrngarten (open Tues.-Sat. 10am-5pm, Sun. 11am-5pm; admission DM5, students DM2.50).

At the turn of the century, the Grand Duke Ernst Ludwig founded the **Mathildenhöhe,** an artists' colony on a hill in Darmstadt, 800m west of the city center. The Duke had fallen in love with the *Jugendstil* style during his travels, and paid for a lavish complex to demonstrate how *Judendstil* could transform the urban landscape. The seven original artists of the colony were members of the movement, as reflected by everything from the grumpy-looking statues in the garden to the five-fingered **Hochzeitsturm** (wedding tower). The 48-m tower was the city's wedding present to Grand Duke Ernst Ludwig in 1908. From the top, gaze down on the civic spread. To reach Mathildenhöhe, walk east from the Luisenplatz along Erich-Ollenhauer-Promenade or take bus F to "Lucas," and walk south on Lucasweg (open March-Oct. Tues.-Sun. 10am-6pm; elevator DM3, students DM1). The Mathildenhöhe also hosts two art museums, the **Austellungsgebäude,** Sabaispl. 1 (tel. 13 27 78), which houses rotating exhibits of modern European art and sculpture (open Tues.-Sun. 11am-6pm; admission DM6, students DM2), and the **Museum der Künstlerkolonie** (tel. 13 27 78), which features collections of *Jugendstil* works (open Tues.-Sun. 10am-5pm, tours Sun. 10:30am; admission DM5, students DM2). On the south side of the tower, a zodiac-encircled sun clock keeps the time. Also on the Matildenhöhe rests the **Russische Kapelle** (Russian Chapel), Nikolai Weg 18 (tel. 42 42 35), is a gilded, three-domed Russian Orthodox Church. It was imported stone by stone from Russia at the bequest of Czar Nicholas II upon his marriage to Darmstadt's Princess Alexandra (open summer daily 9am-6pm; admission DM1, students DM0.80).

Just south of the Mathildenhöhe, the **Institut für Neue Technische Form,** Eugen-Bracht-Weg 6 (tel. 480 08), contains the Braun Design collection, which documents the evolution of the company's many products, including razors, toasters, and stereos, since 1955 (open Tues.-Sat. 10am-6pm, Sun. 10am-1pm; free). In 1810, at the bidding of Grand Duchess Wilhelmine, who wanted a garden that "breathed the free, noble Spirit of Nature," **Rosenhöhe** was planted. Exceedingly large, it contains private houses, a mausoleum, tombs of the ducal houses, and a rose garden.

Darmstadt is accessible from Frankfurt by frequent **trains** (25min.) or by S-Bahn #12 (DM5.90). **S-Bahn** and **bus** tickets cost DM2, DM7 for 24 hours, or DM17 for a 7-day ticket (students DM13). The **tourist office,** in front of the main train station (tel. 13 27 82), provides good city maps and hotel guides, and finds rooms (open Mon.-Fri. 9am-6pm, Sat. 9am-noon); a **branch office,** at Luisenplatz 5 (tel. 13 27 80 or 13 27 81), is located in the Luisencenter (open Mon.-Fri. 9am-6pm, Sat. 9am-noon). For a taxi, you can call **Funk** (tel. 194 10) any time of the day or night, baby. **Bike rental** *(Fahrradverleih)* is available at **Prinz-Emil-Garten,** Heidelberger-Str. 56 (tel. 6 32 78). Rent before noon at the *Nachtbarschaftsheim,* up the hill, and after noon at the *Minigolfplatz,* up the hill and to the left (DM7 per day; ID needed; open 8am-8pm). To get there, take S-Bahn #1 to "Prinz-Emil-Garten." **AIDS-hilfe Darmstadt,** Saalbraustr. 27 (tel. 280 73), in addition to providing an array of AIDS-related services, also deals with gay and lesbian concerns. The **post office,** 64293 Darmstadt, **exchanges currency** and sells traveler's checks. There are two branches: Postamt 1, to your left as you exit the main train station; and Postamt 11, at Louisenplatz 3 (both open Mon.-Fri. 8am-6pm, Sat. 8am-noon). The **telephone code** is 06151.

The **Jugendherberge (HI),** Landgraf-Georg-Str. 119 (tel. 452 93; fax 42 25 35), maintains spotless facilities and bright but cramped rooms. Take bus D to "Grosser Woog." (Reception open until 1am. Lockout 1-7am. Members only. DM23.50, over 26 DM28.50. Breakfast included.) **Zentral Hotel,** Schuchardstr. 6 (tel. 264 11; fax 268 58), behind the *Neues Rathaus* at Luisenplatz, offers small but cozy rooms. (Singles DM60, with shower DM90. Doubles DM110, with shower DM150.) The *Jugendherberge* overlooks **Großer Woog** (tel. 13 23 93), an artificial lake that doubles as a *Frei-*

bad (outdoor pool; open mid-May-mid-Sept. Mon. and Sat.-Sun. 9am-7pm, Tues.-Fri. 8am-7pm; admission DM3.50, students DM2; boats DM6 per hr.).

Eating in Darmstadt can be pricey. Try **Plus,** the grocery store across from the *Schloß* (open Mon.-Thurs. 8:30am-6:30pm, Fri. 8:30am-8pm, Sat. 8:30am-2pm). Most of the city's inexpensive dining can be found in the two student areas: the *Cohannesviertel,* north and west of the city center, and the *Martinsviertel,* north and east of the city center. The university cafeteria, **Studentenwerk Stadtmensa,** Alexanderstr. 4, has cheap meals. With your back to the *Schloß,* cross the street, walk right past the five-story building, take a left, then go down the stairs straight ahead, and turn right. You need to buy stamps downstairs for the main dishes (it's rather complicated, so find a a friendly student), but at the Bistro upstairs you can pay cash and still eat for a fraction of what you would pay in a restaurant (open Mon.-Thurs. 9am-5pm, Fri. 9am-3:45pm; kitchen open 11:45am-2pm). Efendi's, 13 Landgrof-Georg Str. (tel. 29 38 09), has generous, spicy portions, occasional vegetarian options, and large salads (DM6-8; open 10am-1am daily). A favorite meeting place for students is the **Student Innenkeller,** Hochschulstr. 1 (tel. 16 31 17), a hopping and eclectic joint tucked inside the *Schloß* that hosts piano and jazz concerts and has a disco. (Cover for concerts DM5-10, for discos DM3; open daily after 9pm.)

ERBACH IM ODENWALD

As locals are quick to point out, Erbach is not just another pretty little tourist town; rather, it's a touristy little *Elfenbeinstadt* (ivory town) in a beautiful natural setting. Erbach's reputation does not derive from roaming hordes of elephants in the **Odenwald** (Oden Forest), but, rather, from an ivory-carving tradition that dates back to 1783, when Graf Franz of Erbach-Erbach introduced the unlikely craft to the region.

Next door to the town's old *Rathaus* lies the **Erbacher Schloß** (tel. 37 00), which holds the antique art and medieval weapons and armor collection of Franz I, Count of Erbach-Erbach (1754-1823), and the **African Hunting Museum** (open daily 8:30-11am and 1:30-4pm; Nov.-Feb. by appointment only). The spectacular **Elfenbeinmuseum,** Otto-Glenstr. 1 (tel. 64 64; fax 64 13), boasts over 1000 **ivory works.** Walk uphill on Hauptstr. and continue straight on Obere Markstr. (15min.); the museum appears on your left (open daily 10am-5pm; admission DM8, students DM5). The ivory exhibits range from a 30,000-year-old carving of a girl's head made from mammoth ivory to complex Asian masterpieces. Demonstrations feature masters breathing life into new works. The ethical and ecological problems of ivory carving were legally recognized in 1989 with a ban on hunted ivory; since then, only mammoth ivory, discovered in large quantities in Siberia, has been used in the workshops.

Erbach is linked by train to Darmstadt in the north and Heidelberg in the south (1 per hour; 1hr.). From the train station, turn right on Bahnhofstr., then left on (careful!) Bahnstr. to reach the *Marktplatz.* The **tourist office,** Im Städtel 13 (tel. 64 39; fax 64 66), doles out free city maps. From the *Marktplatz,* go through the old *Rathaus* tunnel. Bring your German phrasebook—not much English spoken here (open Mon.-Thurs. 9am-6pm, Fri. 9am-4pm, Sat.-Sun. 10am-noon and 2pm-4pm). The **post office,** 64711 Erbach, across from the *Sportplatz* on Michelstädter Str., has **currency exchange** and sells traveler's checks (open Mon.-Fri. 8am-noon, 2:30-6pm, Sat. 9am-noon). The **telephone code** is 06062.

If you intend to spend several days in the region, the tourist office can help find very cheap lodging on local **Bauernhöfe** (farms). E-I-E-I-O your way through a menu of fabulous farmwork and friendly families while you milk cows, brush down horses, or bake bread. No experience required; language skills are preferred, though hand-waving sometimes works. If waving isn't your thing, try the local **Jugendherberge (HI),** Eulbacher Str. 3 (tel. 35 15; fax 628 48), located next to the sports park. From the *Marktplatz,* take a left after the bridge and follow Hauptstr. uphill to the right; take a left onto Michelstädterstr., and about 300m later Eulbacher Str. will be on your right. (DM15.50, over 27 DM20.50. Reservations recommended.) Another alternative is the central **Hotel Gebhardt,** at Jahnstr. 32 (tel. 32 86), over the bridge and 1-2 blocks to the right. (Singles DM39, with shower DM43. Doubles with shower DM78.

Breakfast included.) For a cheap meal, try the **Schmucker Stube** just off the *Marktplatz,* on Bahnstr. 7-9 (tel 74 23). For historic dining, cross the bridge from *Marktplatz* to **Restaurant Erbacher Brauhaus,** Jahnstr. 1 (tel 57 32), with its own *Biergarten.* Regional specials for DM9.50-16 (open daily 10am-midnight; closed on Tues. Oct.-March).

MICHELSTADT

Within walking distance of Erbach (45min.), the town of Michelstadt joins in on the ivory-carving tradition. More so than even Erbach, Michelstadt fits the picture-book description of a pretty medieval *Städtchen* (tiny town)—heaven knows it's secluded enough. The town is accessible by bus from Erbach and by train from Darmstadt or Heidelberg. Walk right from the train station, turn left on Bahnhofstr., and take a right on Große Gasse to reach the *Marktplatz.* The layout of the city is rather labyrinthine; orient yourself by the *Marktplatz's* most striking feature—the old half-timbered *Rathaus,* built in 1484. The **Elfenbeinmuseum** (tel 31 57), behind the *Rathaus,* was opened by the ivory-carving master Ulrich Seidenberg in the creatively titled "house of ivory." It contains European, Asian, African, and Indonesian masterpieces such as the delicate *Michelstädter Rose* that first brought fame to the *Odenwälder* ivory-carving school in 1873. Look for the unusual "Erotic Art" exhibit, which displays certain—ahem—unique forms (open Mon.-Sat. 10am-noon and 2:30-5pm, Sun. 10:30am-noon and 2:30-4pm; admission DM3, children DM2).

Pick up a free map at the **tourist office,** Marktplatz 1 (tel. 741 46, fax 741 30; open Mon.-Fri. 9am-noon and 2-4pm.) Cheap rooms are available at **Zur Frischen Quelle,** Hammerweg 4-6 (tel. 23 64). (Singles DM40. Doubles DM80, with shower and toilet DM88. Breakfast included.) Another nearby option is the **Hotel-Garni Am Kellereiberg,** Am Kirchenfeld 12 (tel. 48 80; fax 716 45). (Singles with shower and toilet start at DM55, doubles at DM80; DM20 for every extra bed. Breakfast included.) For eats, try the **Grüner Baum,** Große Gasse 17 (tel. 24 09), about 2 minutes from the *Marktplatz;* they've been cooking succulent dishes since 1685 (open daily 7am-midnight). For those seeking something on the lighter side of budgetary and culinary life, try the ornamental **Elefantenhaus** (tel. 723 55), at Kirchplatz 5. From the Elfenbeinmuseum go through the narrow Elefantenpassage. They've got soups and vegetarian dishes (DM5.50-9) and a fine selection of teas, coffee, ice cream, and cocktails—something to write about to the foodstand at your zoo back home (open Mon. and Wed.-Thurs. noon-midnight, Fri.-Sat. noon-1am, Sun. 2pm-midnight). The **telephone code** is 06061.

■ The Lahn Valley

Although it falls short of the towering majesty of the Rhine Gorge, the Lahn Valley's lovely hills and quiet villages compensate with a refreshing absence of tourists, offering an unadulterated peek at life in Germany's smaller towns. Here, locals regularly greet one another on the street or on the bus with hugs and kisses. Rail service runs regularly between Koblenz and Wetzlar at the eastern extremity of the valley, as well as between Frankfurt and Limburg.

LIMBURG

Limburg an der Lahn flourished during the Middle Ages as a big kiosk for travelers schlepping down from Cologne to Frankfurt. Today, it serves much the same function, but for a different region; as the most important train station between Koblenz and Gießen, Limburg is an excellent base from which to explore the Upper Lahn Valley. Often confused with a cheesy Dutch city of the same name, Limburg an der Lahn, or "L.L." (no Cool J here—he's in Brooklyn), is known for the **St. Georg-Dom,** a majestic cathedral sporting a unique dark-orange paint job. In addition to serving as the seat for the bishop of the Limburg diocese, this architectural mingling of Romanesque and Gothic styles shelters a series of galleries and carefully restored frescoes. Next to the *Dom,* in a beautifully renovated building from 1544, the **Diözesan-museum,** Domstr. 12 (tel. 29 53 27), sports a small but significant collection of medieval religious artifacts dating back to the 12th century; in particular, the *Stau-rothek,* a Byzantine reliquary cross that a local knight spirited away from Constantinople during the Crusades (open mid-March-mid-Nov. Tues.-Sat. 10am-1pm and 2-5pm, Sun. 11am-5pm; admission DM2, students DM1). Limburg also prides itself on a complete ensemble of medieval structures.

The **tourist office** *(Verkehrsverein),* Hospitalstr. 2 (tel. 61 66; fax 32 93), finds rooms (starting at DM25) for a DM10 fee. Turn left on the street in front of the station, then make a quick right between the red- and green-trimmed buildings. Ask for details about the **Altstadt Festival** in late June and the **Wine Festival** in late July (open April-Oct. Mon.-Fri. 8am-12:30pm and 2-6pm, Sat. 10am-12pm; Nov.-March Mon.-Thurs. 8am-12:30pm and 2-5pm, Fri. 8am-1pm). The newly renovated **Jugendherberge (HI),** auf dem Guckucksberg (tel. 414 93; fax 438 73), in Eduard-Horn Park, has fuzzy green beds. By foot, walk through the tunnel, which is just off to the right of the exit of the station. When you come out of the tunnel, walk 10m, and turn right down Gartenstr.; then turn right on Wiesbadenerstr. and go left down the first paved walkway into the park—it's 10m past Goethestr. Trek down the trail to Frankfurterstr. and then follow the signs to the hostel (30min.). Or take Line #3 from the "Hospitalstr." bus stop (direction: Am Hammerberg) to "Jugendherberge." (Reception open 5-10pm. Curfew 11:30pm. DM23.50, over 26 DM28.50. Sheets DM6.) There's a **Campingplatz** (tel. 226 10) in a riverside location on the far side of the Lahn. From the station, take Bahnhofstr. into the city. When it ends in the *Alts-tadt,* turn left on Salzgasse, and take the first right over the Alte Lahnbrücke; then turn right and follow the Lahn up to the *Campingplatz.* Or take bus #4 from the train station to "Alte Lahnbrücke." (Reception open 8am-7pm. DM5 per person. DM3.50-5 per tent. Open May-mid-Oct.) The **telephone code** is 06431.

WEILBURG

As the Lahn crosses through the Taunus hills and the Wester Forest, the river bends itself into a shape not unlike that of Gumby's head. Sprawled across a high ridge, Weilburg's 14th-century **Schloß** and its terraced surroundings dominate the valley below. The residence of the Counts and Dukes of Nassau from 1355 to 1816, the castle now houses the **Schloßmuseum** (tel. 22 36), which flaunts sophisticated architecture. (Open Tues.-Sun. 10am-4pm; Nov.-Feb. Tues.-Sun. 10am-3pm. Admission DM4, children DM2, includes a 1-hr. guided tour. Free access to courtyard 10am-5pm.) In case you're feeling old and lethargic, your heart will skip a beat when you see the thousands of glittering crystals at the **Kubacher Kristallhöhle,** Germany's highest and only crystal cave. You will also feel refreshingly youthful when you learn that many of the limestone chunks are 350 million years old (open April-Oct. Mon.-Fri. 2-4pm, Sat.-Sun. 10am-5pm; admission DM4.50, students and children DM3). The **Weilburger Schloßkonzert** brings a dizzying array of international musicians to Weilburg every June and July. On a more regular basis, weekend visitors are treated to "Romantic Summer Delights" performances in the **Markt.**

The **tourist office,** Mauerstr. 10 (tel. 76 71; fax 76 75), rents **bikes** (DM12 per day) and reserves rooms (starting at DM30) for free. From the *Busbahnhof* in front of the train station, take the City Bus Weilburg to "Landtor," and then walk uphill along Vorstadtstr., which becomes Mauerstr. By foot from the train station, walk left along the tracks and over the bridge and veer right at the yellow restaurant. When you reach the 18th-century Landtor straddling the street, turn right and walk up Vorstadt-str. The newly-renovated **Jugendherberge Weilburg-Odersbach (HI),** Am Steinbühl (tel. 71 16; fax 15 42), is comfortable. From the *Busbahnhof,* take the City Bus Weil-burg to "Steinbuhl," and then walk up the path. (Reception open 5-10pm. DM 23.50, over 26 DM 28.50. Sheets DM6.) Inexpensive restaurants are rare within the city walls, but locals flock to **Bürgerhof,** Bogengasse 8 (tel. 79 97), a reasonably-priced *Biergarten,* which serves *Schnitzel* (DM15.50; open Wed.-Mon. 11:30am-2:30pm and from 6pm until the taps run dry). The **telephone code** is 06471.

WETZLAR

Wetzlar's heyday came at the end of the 17th century when the imperial legal court of the Holy Roman Empire established itself here. This, in turn, led to the city's even bigger claim to fame, when, in 1772, Goethe came to study at the court. But Germany's Shakespeare found the court's pretentiousness dull and decided instead to pursue a more exciting interest—namely, a young woman named Charlotte Buff. Though she was already engaged to a local diplomat named Kestner—a friend of the poet's—Goethe endeared himself to the happy couple for many years. Finally, unable to continue the fruitless *Spiel*, he left for Frankfurt, where he learned that his good friend Jerusalem had just killed himself. Goethe assimilated this and his own tale of woe into the enormously popular novel *The Sorrows of Young Werther*—soon dissolving the real Lotte Buff into literary legend. A number of first editions of *Werther* are enshrined today in the **Lottehaus**, Lottestr. 8-10, a museum housed in the brown-trimmed home where Lotte lived with her parents just up Pfaffengasse from the top of the *Domplatz*. Literary die-hards might also find interesting the **Jerusalemhaus**, Schillerplatz 5 (tel. 992 69), where Goethe's unlucky friend took his life (open Tues.-Sun. 2-5pm; free; access to library Fri. 3-4:30pm). The Wetzlar **Dom** serves as town mascot. Begun in 897 and repeatedly altered and enlarged over the centuries (by Frederick Barbarossa, among others), the dome was never actually finished; it remains a perpetual architectural history lesson (open until dusk).

Wetzlar's **tourist office** *(Verkehrsamt)*, situated at Domplatz 8 (tel. 993 38; fax 993 39), in the pre-1350 *Rathaus*, is itself an aesthetic and historical attraction. Take bus #18 from the station to "Domplatz," or schlepp uphill for half of the steep 25-minute walk: exit the station, walk through the passageway, and continue on Bahnhofstr. to Buderusplatz. Turn left on Brückenstr., cross the bridge, and take the first right, the first left, and then the first right again. The *Domplatz* is just over the crest of the hill. Signs lead you all the way from the bridge. The tourist office is behind the left face of the *Dom* (open Mon.-Wed. and Fri. 8am-noon and 2-4:30pm, Thurs. 8am-noon and 2-5pm, Sat. 9:30-11:30am). The **Jugendgästehaus (HI)**, Richard-Schirmann-Str. 3 (tel. 710 68; fax 758 26), offers an incredible view of the valley and private bathrooms to boot. From the train station, take bus #12 (direction: Kranken-haus) to the *second* Sturzkopf stop—there are two and the correct one is a 25-minute ride away. Then walk in the same direction following the curve around. (Reception open 8am-1pm and 2pm-12:30am. Curfew 12:30am. DM26.50, over 26 DM31.50. Breakfast included. Sheets DM6.) The **telephone code** is 06441.

■ Marburg

The Brothers Grimm spun their tales around these rolling hills, and from a distance, Marburg an der Lahn seems more of their world than ours. The city's isolation in the Lahn Valley allowed Landgrave Philipp to found the first Protestant university here in 1527. Its alumni list now reads like a syllabus for an intellectual history course: Martin Heidegger, Boris Pasternak, T.S. Eliot, Richard Bunsen (of burner fame), and the Spanish philosopher José Ortega y Gasset, to name but a few. Those less familiar with Nobel Prize winners will recognize alumni **Jakob and Wilhelm Grimm,** who briefly attended the university from 1802 to 1805; their studies inspired them to collect the fairy tales that now make their names a household term. Today, 15,000 students pore over books, conversation, and each other on the banks of the Lahn River. The rest of the Marburgers enjoy a slightly less academic but no less invigorating activity—beer. Things get hopping on the first Sunday in July, when costumed citizens parade onto the *Markt* for the rowdy **Frühschoppenfest** (Early Beer Festival). Drinking officially kicks off at 11am when the brass rooster on top of the 1851 **Rathaus** flaps its wings. Unofficially, however, the kegs of *Alt Marburger Pils* are tapped at 10am when the ribald old Marburger *Trinklieder* (drinking ballads) ensue.

ORIENTATION AND PRACTICAL INFORMATION

Built around a bend in the river, Marburg is served by frequent **trains** from Frankfurt (1hr.) and Kassel (1hr.); it also serves as the starting point for trips to Frankenberg, and from there to the Waldecker *Land*. The heart of the city is the *Oberstadt*. All buses run through Rudolphsplatz, the base of the wishbone formed by Pilgrimsteinstr. and Biegenstr. To reach Rudolphsplatz from the train station, take buses #1-6.

Tourist Office: Neue Kasseler Str. 1 (tel. 20 12 49 or 20 12 62; fax 68 15 26), to your right as you leave the station. Pick up a map (DM0.50) or have them book you a room (DM35 and up) for free. A map and hotel list is posted outside the office; call 194 14 for 24-hr. hotel information. A helpful machine outside vends information packets containing maps and a hotel list (DM1) when the office is closed. Open Mon.-Fri. 8am-12:30pm and 2-5pm, Sat. 9:30am-noon; Nov.-March Mon.-Fri. 8am-12:30pm and 2-5pm.

Trains: Information office across from the ticket counters. Open Mon. and Wed.-Fri. 10:25am-6:40pm. Frequent trains to Frankfurt (24 per day; 1hr.), Kassel (2 per hr.; 1-1½hrs.), and Gießen (2 per hr.; 30min.).

Public Transportation: Single tickets (DM2) get you anywhere in the *Oberstadt*.

Taxi: Funkzentrale (tel. 477 77). Funk is long, life is short.

Bike Rental: Velicoped, Auf dem Wehr 3 (tel. 245 11), just over the bridge from Rudolphsplatz, on a small street off the riverside path. DM15 per day. Open Mon.-Fri. 10am-4:30pm.

Bookstore: N.G. Elwert, Pilgrimstein (tel. 17 09 34), 1 block from Rudolphsplatz. An annex of the store above it at Reitgasse 7. Good selection of classics. Open Mon.-Wed. and Fri. 9:30am-6pm, Thurs. 9:30am-7pm, Sat. 9:30am-1:30pm.

Laundromat: Wasch Center, at the corner of Gutenbergerstr. and Jägerstr. Sip a beer (DM2.50-5) in its adjacent **Bistro Waschbrett** during the rinse cycle. Wash DM6. Dry DM1 for 15min. Open Mon.-Sat. 8am-10pm, Sun. 1-8pm.

Women's Concerns: Frauenhaus, Schloßsteig 1 (tel 214 38). Open Mon. 5-8pm. At other times, leave a message.

Emergency: Police: tel. 110. **Fire:** tel. 112. **Ambulance:** tel. 192 22.

Post Office: Hauptpostamt, Bahnofstr. 6, 35037 Marburg, a 5-min. walk down from the train station and on the right. Open 9am-6pm, Sat. 9am-noon.

Telephone Code: 06421.

ACCOMMODATIONS AND CAMPING

Although tiny, Marburg boasts more than 30 hotels and *Pensionen;* competition hasn't done too much to keep prices down. Most reasonably-priced accommodations range DM70-85; plan ahead if you intend to spend under DM60.

Jugendherberge (HI), Jahnstr. 1 (tel. 234 61; fax 121 91). From Rudolphsplatz, cross the bridge and turn immediately right onto the path along the river. Follow this until you reach the small wooden bridge across the Lahn (5min.). Beautiful, newly-remodeled rooms, some with private shower and toilet. The *Jugendherberge* catches the nighttime music of the *Altstadt* from across the Lahn. Reception open 9am-noon and 1:30-11:30pm, but house keys can be checked out by leaving an ID or a DM50 deposit. DM28, over 26 DM33. Breakfast buffet included.

Tusculum-Gästehaus, Gutenbergerstr. 25 (tel. 227 78; fax 153 04). Blazing colors and cool stripes decorate this artsy, well-kept hotel, renovated to embody the fanciful aesthetic of Joan Miró. Follow Universitätstr. from Rudolphsplatz and take the first left onto Gutenbergstr. Singles DM60, with shower DM100. Doubles DM75-80, with shower DM125. No breakfast, but kitchen available.

Hotel Garni im Quelle-Haus, Bahnhofstr. 14 (tel. 656 44), a 3-min. walk from the station. Tastefully furnished and fastidiously kept rooms in a homey atmosphere, though the rooms overlooking Bahnhofstr. can be noisy. Reception open 7am-9pm. Singles DM60, with shower and toilet DM85. Doubles DM125, with shower and toilet DM150. Closed for Christmas. AmEx, MC, Visa.

Camping: Camping Lahnaue, on the Lahn River (tel. 213 31). Follow directions to the *Jugendherberge* and continue down river for another 2min. DM6 per person. DM5-6 per tent. DM3 per car. Closed periodically in winter, when the Lahn overflows its banks. Call ahead.

FOOD

Marburg's cuisine caters to its large student population. Most establishments offer *Würste* or hefty pots of pasta. See Nightlife, on p. 313, for cafés with food as sidelights to drinks. The **Markt** gets crowded with vendors every Saturday (8am-1pm). *Wurst* stands, along with junk and gems, can be found past the Wettergasse pedestrian zone at the Steinweg **flea market,** held on the first Saturday of every month.

Mensa, Erleuring 5, directly across the pedestrian bridge from Wolffstr., will satisfy your hearty appetite. 3-part meals DM3.60-4.90. Open Mon.-Thurs. 11:30am-8pm, Fri. 11:30am-2:15pm and 5:45-8pm, Sat. 11:30am-2:15pm. Most lunches require a *Schlußel* (key). Get one with a DM10 deposit.

Café Local, Steinweg 1 (tel. 68 12 12). Relaxed café with outdoor terrace in the pedestrian zone. Nice views of the city. Pizza, pasta, and salads under DM10. Excellent broccoli *Auflauf* (deep-dish, baked cheese stew with ham and potatoes) DM9. Walloping cocktail list. Beer from DM3.50. Open daily 11am-1am.

Cafe Barfuß, Barfüßerstr. 33 (tel. 253 49), gets packed every day with locals. Big breakfast menu (under DM12) served until 3pm. Amusing menu with very funny cartoons helps digest any of the 5 beers on tap (DM2-5.50). Open daily 10am-1am.

Café Vetter, Reitgasse 4 (tel. 258 88), is a traditional café, quite proud of its terrace overlooking Pilgrimstein. *Kaffee und Kuchen* (coffee and cake)—Germany's 4pm sugar rush—around DM7. A town favorite for 80 years. Open Mon. and Wed.-Sat. 8:30am-6:30pm, Sun. 9:30am-6:30pm.

SIGHTS

When Jakob Grimm ordered visitors to Marburg to "move your legs and walk the stairs up and down," he really meant: "this is the ultimate fitness machine that will build endurance in every major muscle group and expand cardiovascular potential." Climbing the hillside **Oberstadt's** dizzying maze of narrow staircases and alleys would make even Jane Fonda pop out of the VCR. You can save yourself part of the climb by taking the **Oberstadt-Aufzug** (elevator to the upper city) from Pilgrimstein (less than a block from Rudolphsplatz) to Reitgasse (open daily 7am-11:30pm, free). **Enge Gasse,** an old sewer, is now as suitably scenic and half-timbered as the rest of town. Climb more than 250 steps or take bus #16 from Rudolfsplatz (every 45min.) to the exalted **Landgrafenschloß,** former haunt of the infamous Teutonic knights. Count Philip brought rival Protestant reformers Martin Luther and Ulrich Zwingli to his court in 1529 to convince them to kiss and make up, and was on the verge of succeeding when an epidemic made everyone grumpy and uncooperative. Towering over Marburg, the castle is illuminated until 11pm. It houses the university's **Museum für Kulturgeschichte** (Cultural Museum), which exhibits Hessian history and religious art, as well as the recently unearthed wall remnants in the *Westflügel* (West Wing) that move the castle's construction date back to the 9th century (open Tues.-Sun. 10am-6pm; Nov.-March Tues.-Sun. 11am-5pm; admission DM3, students DM2). Occasional performances are given in the open-air theater of the **Schloßpark,** the gardens stretching to the west of the fortress (tickets DM20); check for schedules at the tourist office.

Past a strikingly ugly boar's head, down the 140 steps of the "Ludwig-Bickell-Treppe" stairway, rests the 13th-century **Marienkirche** (tel. 252 43), with amber-colored stained glass and an elaborate organ (open daily 9am-5pm; free organ concerts Oct.-July Sat. at 6:30pm). Down Kugelgasse the 15th-century **Kugelkirche** (sphere church) owes its peculiar name not to its shape but to the hats *(cuculla)* worn by the religious order that founded it. Save some ecclesiastical awe for the oldest Gothic church in Germany (c. 1285), the **Elisabethkirche** (tel. 55 73), named for the town patroness, a widowed child-bride (engaged at 4, married at 14) who took refuge in Marburg, founded a hospital, and snagged sainthood four years after she died. The **reliquary** for her bones is so overdone, it's glorious (in the *Kunstschätze*). To get there, cross the bridge opposite the train station and take a left at Elisabethstr. (Church open April-Sept. daily 9am-6pm; Oct.-March 10am-4pm, Sun. after 11am. Church free; reliquary admission DM3, students DM2.) The church is the starting point for the free guided tour of the town (April-Oct. Sat. at 3pm). Walk up the stairs across from the Elisabethkirche to get to the 13th-century **St. Michaelskapelle** surrounded by a medieval pilgrim cemetery that looks like a time-forsaken oasis.

Today's university building was erected in 1871, but the original **Alte Universität** on Rudolfsplatz was built on the rubble of a monastery conveniently vacated when Reformation-minded Marburgers ejected the resident monks. The nearby houses flying technicolor flags are **fraternities,** now home to aristocratic pretensions and a few fine collections of old fencing equipment. Riled by nascent nationalism, these Prussian frat boys fought regular "duels" to defend their sections of sidewalk well into the 19th century. The idea of the duels was to get sliced in the face, leaving a scar that was considered a badge of aristocratic honor. Student members still strut around town in dubious, overdone suits and colorful ribbons to match their house colors. Modern *Verbindungen* (lifetime fraternities) are formed around sports, religion, or political conservatism in *Burschenschaften*. Across the Lahn is the **Universitätsmuseum für Bildende Kunst** (University Museum for Fine Art), Biegenstr. 11 (tel. 28 23 55), with a wide variety of paintings including masterpieces by Cranach, Picasso, and Kandinsky. Explore the section on Expressive Realism, the lost generation of talented artists that matured during the Nazi period (open Tues.-Sun. 11am-1pm, 2-5pm; free). Up in the *Markt,* the **Rathaus** boasts some unusual curiosities that are worth the short hike. Greeting you is a horseman slaying a figure that tragically resembles Puff the Magic Dragon.

ENTERTAINMENT AND NIGHTLIFE

Because of the student population, bars and pubs in Marburg breed faster than bunny rabbits. In the **Oberstadt** there are over 60 such establishments, giving Marburg the proud distinction of having the densest concentration of *Kneipen* in Germany. Live music and concert, theater, and movie options are listed in the weekly *Marburger Express* (free at hotels and the hostel); also be sure to ask at the tourist office about the bi-monthly program of live music and theater in the *Schloßpark.*

Kult Lager, Temmlerstr. 7 (tel. 941 85). Take bus A1 (direction: Pommernweg) or A2 (direction: Cappeler Gleiche) to "Frauenbergstr." The only disco in town, this place gets 'em all—the good, the bad, the beautiful, and, unfortunately, the ugly. Brings in some of the hottest DJs from England and the U.S. Cover a measly DM3 on weekdays, DM5 on weekends. Open Tues.-Wed. 9pm-3am. Fri.-Sat. 9pm-4am.

KFZ (Kommunication Freizeit Zentrum), Schulstr. 6 (tel. 138 98), hosts an impressive schedule of multicultural events, including concerts, theater, cabaret, and parties. Cover varies from *kostlos* (free) to DM15. Call for a schedule.

Bolschoi Café, Ketzerbach-Str. 25 (tel. 644 42). From Rudolfsplatz, walk up Pilgrimstein and turn left onto Ketzerbach-Str. You'll find it on the left side of the street. Then prepare for the *real* Left—the Communist kitsch here will warm the cockles of any Cold Warrior's heart with its red candles, red walls, a red foil ceiling, and 19 brands of domestic and imported vodka (DM3.50-5.80). Lenin's bust is stenciled on the wall. The *Rollmops* (raw pickled herring) may boost your tolerance (DM1). Open daily 8pm-1am.

■ Near Marburg: Fritzlar

The birth of the town of Fritzlar as *Frideslar* (Place of Peace) dates to a not-so-peaceful act of St. Bonitatius, who in 723 chopped down the huge **Donar's Oak,** the pagan religious symbol of the tribal Chats, and used the timber to build his own wooden church, which today is the beautiful St. Peter *Dom*. It was also here that Henry I was proclaimed king in 915, inaugurating the medieval incarnation of the Holy Roman Empire. Since then this little medieval town has grown progressively isolated from the main routes of buzzing commerce and affluence. Nevertheless, Fritzlar is content with its role as a cute, well-preserved *Fachwerkstadt* (a town of half-timbered houses) sitting on the *Märchenstraße,* the German fairy tale road.

The gem of Fritzlar is the 12th-century **St. Peter Dom,** with its two massive red sandstone towers and the sizeable *Domschatz* (dome treasure) that includes the diamond- and pearl-covered **Heinrich Cross** (created around 1020), as well as numerous precious robes and relics (open May-Oct. Mon.-Sat. 10am-noon and 2-5pm, Sun. 2-4pm; Nov.-April Mon.-Sat. 10am-noon and 2-4pm, Sun. 2-4pm; admission to *Domschatz* and *Dombibliothek* DM4, students DM2). Just around the corner lies the *Marktplatz,* with a **Rolandbrunnen** (Roland fountain) symbolically standing watch. This graceful fountain represents such noble concepts as justice, religious freedom, and the laws governing fruit-selling. The angel on the pedestal faces the *Kaufhäuschen,* the guild and merchants' house occupied by the brotherhood of St. Michael. On the western extremity of the still-standing medieval city wall, the 35-m **Grauer Turm** (grey tower) seems fully aware of its majestic distinction as the tallest defense tower in Germany. If your lungs and legs cooperate, you can climb it and enjoy the unique view from the top (get the keys from the tourist office; ID required). The **Hochzeitshaus,** on Burggraben Str., used for weddings and festivals since the 16th century, now hosts the **Regional Museum** (tel. 98 86 28), which does its best to reflect all aspects and stages of Fritzlar's bumpy history (open Sun.-Fri. 10am-noon and 3-5pm, Sat. 10am-noon; admission DM3, children DM1).

Fritzlar's is an ideal daytrip. The town is best reached by train from Wabern on the Frankfurt-Kassel line (10 per day; 15min.). The **tourist office** (tel. 98 86 43; fax 98 86 38), located in the *Rathaus,* is the oldest official building in Germany. From the station, walk out to the main road (creatively named B450) and take a right up the hill. Take the second left onto Gießenerstr, walk through the *Marktplatz,* and bear left onto the Zwischen den Kuamenstr. The office has lists of rooms (starting at DM26), but makes no reservations (open Mon.-Thurs. 10am-1pm and 2-4:30pm, Fri. 10-11:30am). City **tours** are also available (May-Sept. Tues.-Sat. at 11am and 3pm, Sun. at 3pm; DM5). **Dom-Grill,** Gießener Str. 2 (tel. 26 55), just off the *Marktplatz* on the way to town, is the place to catch up on the local gossip (if you can decipher the thick Hessian accents) and fill up on greasy *kebabs,* burgers, *Wurst,* and fries (DM3-7; open Mon.-Fri. 10am-8pm, Sat. 10am-1:30pm). Little towns seem to like big festivals, and Fritzlar is no exception. The **Pferdemarkt** (2nd weekend in July) and the **Altstadtfest** (mid-August) draw out *Lederhosen,* traditional folk music, and beer goggles. The **telephone code** is 05622.

▪ Near Marburg: Frankenberg

Frankenberg an der Eden (pop. 16,200) offers travelers a surprisingly big bag of goodies for a town of its tiny size. Dominating the skyline is the 13th-century **Liebfrauenkirche** ("Church of Our Lady"). To get there from the train station, follow Bahnhofstr. as it leads into the pedestrian zone to Neustadterstr. and continue trudging uphill as Neustadter becomes Ritterstr. Take the first right onto Neue Gasse, then the first right, and then a left onto Kirchberg. The church is graced by 14th-century glass panels depicting the life of Christ and a 6.5m-high stone statue of the Virgin Mary. Upon exiting, head directly onto *Obermarkt* to the 1509 **Rathaus;** with its whopping 10 towers, it ranks as one of the most stunningly attractive townhouses in all of Germany. Despite the entrancing exterior, the inside is disappointingly empty except for a sobering plaque dedicated to the Jews of Frankenberg. **Free city tours** depart here (Wed. at 2:30pm, Sat. at 10:30am). The bright red **Steinhaus** ("Stone House"), Pferdemarkt 20 (tel. 99 69), was built in 1270 and restored in 1976; as the oldest house in Frankenberg, it now shelters an Italian restaurant with surprisingly reasonable prices (open Wed.-Mon. noon-2:30pm and 6pm-midnight). The ominous 13th-century **Hexenturm** (Witches' Tower), the sole survivor of an original 20 towers and five gates, stands out sharply against the residential houses and blossoming flowers. Peek inside at the walls to see where *very* unlucky crooks did their time. To get there, disconnect yourself from *Oberstadt* and take a left on Auf der Heide; then take a right and then another right onto Gadengasse.

The **tourist office,** Obermarkt 13 (tel. 50 51 13; fax 50 52 03), passes out nifty maps and brochures (open Mon.-Thurs. 8:30am-noon and 2-4pm; Fri. 8:30am-12:30pm). There is no hostel in Frankenberg, but Marburg is only 40 minutes away (the last train leaves at 6:30pm during the week, at 5:30pm on weekends). Admire your bulging quadriceps as you gobble down ice cream (DM 0.70) at **Eis Café San Marco,** Neustadterstr. 32 (tel. 16 55), with its outstanding view down the entire pedestrian zone (open daily 9am-midnight). The **telephone code** is 06451.

■ Fulda

In the grim old days of east and west, Fulda earned a dubious distinction as the most likely target for a Warsaw Pact invasion and the subsequent nickname of the "Fulda Gap." Today Fulda is a graceful Baroque city and former university town offering an unusual number of large parks and public gardens for a locale its size. Its compact Baroque quarter was built by a gang of Germany's most famous 18th-century architects at the behest of the local Prince-Abbots. The extravagant **Schloß** was built between 1700 and 1737 as the residence for the Prince-Abbots, who held a monopoly on both secular and spiritual authority for nearly 700 years. Inside, the white **Kaisersaal** displays the portraits of 16 Habsburg emperors and is topped by a Baroque ceiling in typical gilded glory. To reach this sprawling yellow behemoth from the main train station, head down Bahnhofstr. and turn right in front of the church onto Friedrichstr. (Open Sat.-Thurs. 10am-6pm, Fri. 2-6pm. Admission DM5, students DM4; DM0.50 extra for a guided tour. Tours Sat.-Thurs. at 10:30am and 2:30pm, Fri. at 2:30pm; Nov.-March Mon.-Fri. at 2:30pm, Sat.-Sun. at 10:30am and 2:30pm.) Climb the **Schloßturm** (tower) to admire the lush greenery carpeting Fulda (DM2, students DM1). Behind the palace lies a luxurious **park** lined with terraces and home to the 18th-century **Orangerie** (built 1722 to 1725); its stately rooms embody the restrained possibilities of Baroque beauty.

Across the street from the **Schloß** stands the magnificent 18th-century **Dom** housing the tomb of St. Boniface. An 8th-century English monk, he came to Germany to spread the gospel and founded the abbey in Fulda. An alabaster Baroque memorial edged with black marble supposedly depicts St. Boniface surrounded by angels lifting his coffin lid on Judgment Day, though it looks more like the cherubs are trying to stuff him back in. The cathedral, built in the late 18th century as the largest church in central Europe, endured centuries of German pilgrimaging to the grave of "the apostle of Germany." (Open Mon.-Fri. 10am-6pm, Sat. 10am-3pm, Sun. 3-6pm; Nov.-March Mon.-Fri. 10am-5pm, Sat. 10am-3pm, Sun. 3-5pm. Free.) The **Dommuseum,** accessible through the crypt, displays the dagger by which St. Boniface died in 754 and his head, as well as Lucas Cranach's *Christ and the Adulteress.* (Open Mon.-Fri. 10am-5pm, Sat. 10am-2pm, Sun. 12:30-5:30pm; Nov.-March Mon.-Fri. 10am-12:30pm and 1:30-4pm, Sat. 10am-2pm, Sun. 12:30-4pm. Closed in January. Admission DM3, students DM1.50. Oddly reminiscent of the afterlife, however, in that you get in free if you can answer the doorkeeper's query.)

Trains go from Fulda to Hamburg (1 per hr.; 3hr.), Nuremburg (1 per hr.; 1hr.), and Frankfurt (2-3 per hr.; 1hr.). Due to its strategic position and post-war past, Fulda offers good rail connections. However, many departing trains are ICE—super-fast but expensive. The main **tourist office** *(Verkehrsbüro),* 36037 Fulda, is in the *Schloß* (tel. 10 23 45; fax 10 27 75). From the station, head straight down Bahnhof Str., and turn right in front of the orange and white church. The office is through the courtyard of the huge butter-colored palace. They have free maps and book rooms (free in person, DM5 by mail; open Mon.-Fri. 9am-noon, 2-4:30pm, Sat. 9:30am-noon). There's one hitch: they don't speak *any* English. There's a smaller office at the train station (tel. 230 30) that has free maps but doesn't book rooms (open Mon.-Fri. 9am-5pm, Sat.-

Sun. 10am-4pm). Rent **bikes** (tel. 183 77) at the station (DM13 per day). The **telephone code** is 0661.

To find Fulda's **Jugendherberge (HI),** Schirmannstr. 31 (tel. 733 89; fax 748 11), take bus #1B or 1A (direction: Niederrode) from the bus station at the side of the *Schloß* to the "Stadion" stop (DM1.50) and walk five minutes to the other side of the stadium. It's got standard hostel rooms. (Curfew 11:30pm. DM24.50, over 26 DM27. Breakfast included.) Frau Kremer runs a tight ship a the **Gasthaus Zum Kronhof,** Am Kronhof 2 (tel. 741 47), behind the *Dom* just outside the old city walls. From the *Schloß,* cross the street and walk downhill on Kastanian-Allee, which becomes Wilhelm-Str. to the left of the *Dom.* Take a right along the city wall and look for a bright, raspberry-pink building three blocks down. (Singles DM35. Doubles DM69, with shower DM94. Breakfast included.)

▓ Kassel

After Napolean III and his soldiers were trounced by Prussian troops at the Battle of Sedan in 1870, the unlucky French emperor managed to get himself captured. While crossing the Franco-German border on his way to the Schloß Wilhelmshöhe prison, Aacheners jeered *"Ab nach Kassel"* ("off to Kassel") at the crestfallen Frog. The slogan echoed throughout Germany. Today, hordes of travelers still answer the call, coming to see the many treasures the ultra-sophisticated metropolis of Kassel has to offer. Take the castles of Wilhelmshohe, the largest hillside parks in Europe, and the 18,000 jamming students at Kassel's university (the newest in Hesse), throw in **documenta x,** the premiere exhibition of modern art in the world, mix it in with an atmosphere that led the Grimm Brothers to create their famous **Kinder und Hausmärchen** here, and Kassel will put on a show you'll never forget.

ORIENTATION AND PRACTICAL INFORMATION

Kassel is a diffuse city, the product of a nightmarish building boom which followed the postwar housing shortage. Somehow the boom never stopped. The *Deutsche Bahn* powers-that-be have chosen Kassel to be an InterCity Express connection, and have rebuilt the **Bahnhof Wilhelmshöhe-Kassel** with streamlined contemporary specs. The Wilhelmshöhe station is the point of entry to Kassel's ancient castles and immense parklands on the west side; the older **Hauptbahnhof** is the gateway to the tightly-packed and entirely modernized *Altstadt.* The new train station is just a bit too cool for its own good, especially in comparison to the town's pit of a *Hauptbahnhof.* IC, ICE, and most IR trains only stop at Wilhelmshöhe. Frequent trains and the RKH buses shuttle between the stations; you can catch most other bus and streetcar lines at either "Rathaus" or "Am Stern." Kassel is in northern Hesse on the banks of the Fulda River, accessible by trains from Hanover (1hr.) and Frankfurt (1½-2hrs.). The underground walkway in front of the *Hauptbahnhof* is often full of shady-looking folks; don't walk there alone after dark. Instead, explore around **Treppenstraße,** Kassel's original pedestrian zone and the first in all of Germany, or around **Königsstr.,** the current pedestrian zone—both attract brighter crowds.

Tourist Office: Kassel-Service, Königsplatz 53, 2nd floor (tel. 707 71 62; fax 707 71 69), gives out free maps, a hotel list (DM0.50; rooms start at DM45), and brochures in English. Open Mon.-Thurs. 9:15am-6pm, Fri. 9:15am-4:30pm. **Branch Office,** in the Wilhelmshöhe *Bahnhof* (tel. 340 54; fax 31 52 16). As super-modern as the rest of the station. Doles out slick catalogs and maps and finds rooms for a DM5 fee. Open Mon.-Fri. 9am-1pm and 2-6pm, Sat. 9am-1pm.

Public Transportation: Kassel's ultra-sophisticated system is integrated into the **NVV** (Nordhessischer Verkehrsverbund). Tickets are priced by distance with **one-ride cards** ranging DM2.30-4.20. The **Multiticket** (DM8) is valid for 2 adults and 3 kids for a weekday or a weekend. Questions can be directed to the NVV counter in the train station or to their service number (tel. (0180) 234 01 80).

Ferries: Personenschiffahrt Söllner, Die Schlagd/Rondell (tel. 77 46 70; fax 77 77 76), just across the Leipziger Str. from the *Altstadt*, offers Fulda Valley tours (3hrs.) mid-June-Aug. daily at 2pm, May-mid-June and Sept. Wed. and Sat.-Sun. at 2pm. One-way DM10, round-trip DM16, children half-price. You can also sail to the junction of the Fulda and Werra rivers (May-mid-Sept. Sun. and Wed. at 9:30am). One-way DM20, round-trip DM30, children half-price.

Mitfahrzentrale: City Netz Kassel, Friedrichstr. 18 (tel. 194 40). Open Mon.-Fri. 9am-6pm, Sat.-Sun. noon-3pm.

Car Rental: Avis, 77 Leipziger Str. (tel. 57 10 06), on the other side of the Fulda from the *Altstadt*. Open Mon.-Fri. 7am-6pm, Sat. 8am-noon.

Bike Rental: In the futuristic train station Kassel-Wilhelmshöhe (tel. 31 30 83). Bikes start at DM20 for 24hrs., DM80 for 5 days. Open Mon.-Fri. 9am-1pm and 2-6pm, Sat. 9am-1pm.

Bookstore: Buchladung Vaternahm, Königstr. 7 (tel. 78 98 40). Broad selection of paperbacks in English from Hobbes to *Calvin and Hobbes*. Open Mon.-Wed. and Fri. 9:30am-6:30pm, Thurs. 9:30am-8pm, Sat. 9am-2pm.

Laundromat: Schnell & Sauber, at Friedrich-Ebert-Str. 83, near the hostel, is ecologically friendly and computerized. The future is *now*. Wash DM6. Dry DM1 per 15min. Open Mon.-Sat. 5am-midnight.

Rape Crisis Hotline: tel. 77 22 44.

Emergency: Fire and Ambulance: tel. 112. **Police:** tel. 110.

Post Office: Hauptpostamt, Untere Königsstr. 95, 34117 Kassel, between Königsplatz and the University. Open Mon.-Fri. 8am-6pm, Sat. 8am-noon.

Telephone Code: 0561.

ACCOMMODATIONS AND CAMPING

Hotels in Kassel actively seek conventioneers and the ICE-riding business crowd, but because of the 1997 *documenta*, no bait and hook will be necessary; guests will fill Kassel's rooms to the brim and even overflow into nearby cities. If you're planning to stay in Kassel between June 21 and September 28 in 1997, call ahead as soon as you read this section. Another option is the **Mitzwohnzentrale,** LaSallestr. 10 (tel. 194 45), which matches apartment needs with apartment offerings for stays ranging from several days to several months.

Jugendherberge am Tannenwäldchen, Schenkendorfstr. 18 (tel. 77 64 55; fax 77 68 32). From platform 2 of Bahnhof Wilhelmshöhe take streetcar #4 (direction: Ottostr. or Lindenberg) to "Annastr.," walk back 1 block, and turn right on the tree-lined Querallee; the hostel is at the top of the hill. From the *Hauptbahnhof*, it's closer to walk: go out the *Südausgang* (south exit), turn right on Kölnische Str., and turn right again onto Schenkendorfstr. Huge common areas, breakfast buffet with tasty cakes and orange juice, and a great curfew policy—there is none, except for Sun. nights and during the winter (12:30am). Reception open until 11pm. DM24, over 26 DM29. Sheets DM6. No phone reservations.

Hotel-Restaurant Palmenbad, Kurhausstr. 27 (tel./fax 326 91). Take streetcar #3 or 4 to "Wiganstr." and walk 5min. uphill. Or walk from Bahnhof Wilhelmshöhe up Wilhelmshöher Allee (towards Herkules), turn left on Baunsbergstr., and right on Kurhausstr. Flower, flower, on the wall, who's got cute lights, soft beds, and tasteful but limited furnishing near the Odenwald? Reception open Mon. 5:30-11pm, Tues.-Sat. 9am-11pm, Sun. 9am-2pm. Singles DM45, with shower and toilet DM58. Doubles DM86, with shower and toilet DM99.

Hotel-Restaurant Lenz, Frankfurter Str. 176 (tel. 433 73; fax 411 88), is too far to walk from either main station, but the Bahnhof Niederzwehren station and bus stop right around the corner is serviced by DB trains or bus #24 (from Wilhelmshöhe) and streetcar #7 (from the *Hauptbahnhof*). Sharp-looking rooms and bathrooms big enough for Herkules. Reception open daily 4-10pm. Singles DM45, with shower and toilet DM85. Doubles DM85, with shower and toilet DM150.

Hotel Am Rathaus, Wilhelmsstr. 29 (tel. 97 88 50; fax 978 85 30). Take bus #1 or 3 to "Rathaus" on Fünfenstr., turn left down Obere Karlstr., and hang a left where the statue of Landgraf Karl is striking a pose. Alternatively, take bus #2 or 4 to

"Rathaus," walk uphill to Fünfenstr., take a left, and follow the above directions. Stained-glass windows and snug rooms. Reception open until 9pm. Singles DM56, with shower DM65. Doubles with shower DM102.

Camping: Kurhessen-Kassel, Giesenallee 7 (tel. 224 33), has a stunning spot right on the Fulda and is pleasantly close to the "Island of Flowers" in the Karlsaue park. Reception open daily 7am-noon and 3-10pm. DM5 per person, under 15 DM3. DM5 per car. DM6.50 and up per tent. Open March-Oct.

FOOD

Like most things in Kassel, food doesn't come cheap. Friedrich-Ebert-Str. and the upper part of Wilhelmshöher Allee have supermarkets and cafés sprinkled among department stores and fashion boutiques. To go easy on your wallet, shop in the **Markthalle,** on Wildemangasse off of Steinweg (open Thurs.-Fri. 7am-6pm, Sat. 7am-1pm). Or pick through goodies at the humongous **Markt,** on Königsplatz (Tues.-Wed. 10am-5pm). Inexpensive meals can be found up in the university complex. From Wilhelmshöhe train station, take streetcar #1 to "Holländischer Platz," cross through the underground passage, and continue in the same direction; walk along the left side of the university to the back and hang a right onto Arnold-Bode-Str.

Student Mensa, on Arnold-Bode-Str., in the back left corner of the University, 100m across a gorge from the big red brick tower. Look for the "Mensa" sign—it's the only way to tell this brick building from the 50-odd others. Students with ID DM2.60-3.30; others tack on DM2.20. Lunch Mon.-Fri. noon-2pm. The **Moritz-Restaurant** in the same building serves a slightly more elaborate lunch with much shorter lines. Students DM4.70, others DM6.90. Open Mon.-Fri. 11am-2:30pm. Just around the corner the **Studentwerke-Pavillion,** Diagonale 13, slaps together meals later in the day for the same prices (open 5-9pm). The café downstairs sells the cheapest ice cream around (DM0.60 per *Kugel,* or scoop).

Ristorante-Pizzeria Pinocchio, Friedrich-Ebert-Str. 96 (tel. 165 65), about 3min. downhill from the youth hostel. Pizza! Pasta! *Mamma mia!* Under the eye of our long-nosed guardian, feast on fish, wine, salads, and desserts on the outdoor terrace. Entrees DM6-16. Open Wed.-Mon. 11:30am-2:45pm and 5pm-midnight.

Wok, Kölnische Str. 124 (tel. 71 11 44), on the way to the youth hostel. Surprisingly good and spicy Thai food in a cozy atmosphere awaits those who have had their fill of *Schnitzel* and *Wurst*. Entrees DM9.50-13.50. Beer DM3.80-4.90. Open Tues.-Sun. noon-2:30pm and 5:30-11pm.

SIGHTS

Kassel's sights fall into three categories: those associated with *documenta x,* those at Wilhelmshöhe, and those near the *Rathaus.* The museums and galleries of the *documenta* are scattered downhill of Königsstraße between the *Rathaus* and Königsplatz, towards the Fulda River. The sights at Wilhelmshöhe Park lie at one end of the long Wilhelmshöher Allee. At the other end stands the *Rathaus,* just after Wilhelmshöher Allee becomes (Oberer) Königstr. This latter road runs through Königsplatz (at the city's heart) to the University. Most of the big museums—Schloß Wilhelmshöhe, Ballhaus, Hessisches Landesmuseum, Neue Galerie, and Orangerie—belong to **Staatliche Museen Kassel** and are covered a good package deal: the *Tageskarte* (day pass) is good for all of these attractions and available at any one of the museums (DM5, students DM3, families DM15); the *Verbundkarte* (combination ticket) lets you visit the museums on different days (DM10, students DM7). Admission to all the Staatliche Museen Kassel is **free** on Saturdays.

documenta x

The concept behind the *documenta* is to confront and address the controversies behind expression. The city is hosting the exhibition for the 10th straight time since 1955, when local art professor Arnold Bode first conceived of the idea. The leftovers from past *documentas* like "Pickaxe" near the Orangerie and "Man Walking to the Sky" in front of Fridericianum, mere skeletons of the original exhibits, still draw the attention of art critics and continue to captivate the entire art world. In 1997 the exhibit will run daily 10am-8pm from June 21 to September 27. (Day ticket DM25, students DM15. 2-day ticket DM38, students DM22. Season ticket for the hard-core DM120, students DM70.)

The sites for the exhibition are sprawled all across the city center; even the humble *Hauptbahnhof* gets to spite its ICE brother by getting a piece of the action. From there, *documenta x* cuts a wide swath to the Fulda River, where it showcases the best works. The **Fridericianum** (tel. 707 27 20) is the heart of the exhibition, but the **Ottoneum** (tel. 787 40 14), the **Orangerie** (tel. 715 43), and **documenta Hall** (tel. 10 75 22) will also pack in art like sardines. Basic information is available at the tourist office.

Wilhelmshöhe

Wilhelmshöhe is a hillside park with one giant Greek hero, two castles, three museums, and five waterfalls, punctuated with rock gardens, mountain streams, and innumerable hiking trails. The whole park experience—a cross between the halls of Montezuma and a Baroque theme park—takes up half a day in itself; approach it with humor, or cynicism if that is your wont (love of castles is also acceptable), but do approach. Bring a picnic, bring your lover, and bring a bottle of wine. Streetcar #1 stops at the foot of the park near **Schloß Wilhelmshöhe,** the mammoth main attraction and former home of the rulers of Kassel. Napoleon III was imprisoned here once after being captured in the Battle of Sedan. The **Schloß Museum** (tel. 330 86), located in the right wing, records the extravagant royal lifestyle. (Open March-Oct. Tues.-Sun. 10am-5pm; Nov.-Feb. Tues.-Sun. 10am-4pm. Tours of private suites DM4, students DM2; they leave when there are "enough" people.) One of the main attractions at the Schloß, **The Gallery of Old Masters** (tel. 937 77), displays the works of Dürer, Rubens, Jerdaeus, Rembrandt, and other artistic big-wigs. Alas, the gallery be closed for roof repairs until September 1997, but some of the works can be seen at the Museum Fredericianum (see below).

All paths lead up to the monumental **Riesenschloß** (giant's castle, but not really one at all—except for the giant), a massive octagonal amphitheater topped by the figure of **Herkules,** the Greek hero who has become Kassel's emblem, jeering at his conquered foe, the giant Encelades, whose head is poking out of the rocks at the top of the cascades. An English author traveling in the 18th century described it as "one of the most splendid structures in all of Europe, not excluding those in Versailles, Frascati, or Tivoli." Climb the scores of steps to the feet of the statue past the spectacular steps of the water **Cascades.** The less robust can take streetcar #3 to "Druseltal" and then bus #43 to the rear of the monument. Either way, climb up onto Herkules' pedestal, and if you're brave enough, into his club (access to the base of the statue free; extra altitude available March-Nov. Tues.-Sun. 10am-5pm; DM2, students DM1). If you arrive at the top of Herkules just after 2pm on a Sunday or Wednesday, you'll see the **fountain displays** *(Wasserspiele)* that start at 2:30pm; they're timed so that a walk down the clearly designated path will land you at the next waterfall as the show begins. The grand finale comes at 3:45pm in the backyard of the *Schloß* when the *Wasserspiele* end in a 52-m-high geyser. Anyone willing to brave the crowds is welcome—stake out a vantage point early (Easter-Sept. only).

The more subtle **Schloß Löwenburg** is an amazing piece of architectural fantasy. It was built by Wilhelm in the 18th century with stones deliberately missing, in order to achieve the effect of a crumbling medieval castle; to add to the ancient look, the material used was a rapidly deteriorating basalt. For some reason he was obsessed with the year 1495 and fancied himself as a time-displaced knight. In order to supplement the credibility of this pretense, he even built a Catholic chapel on the *Schloß* to date it before the Reformation, even though he himself was Protestant. But despite his aspirations to chivalry, the castle was built as a love cottage for his favorite concubine, who bore him 15 children—13 more than his wife.

Near the Rathaus

The English Garden of **Karlsaue Park** sprawls along the Fulda. At its north end, the bright yellow **Orangerie** manor house, built 1701, is home to the **Museum of Astronomy and Technological History** (tel. 715 43), crammed full of mechanical and optical marvels along with a cool planetarium. (Open Tues.-Sun. 10am-5pm. Museum only DM3, students DM2. Free on Sat. Shows Tues., Thurs., and Sat. at 2pm; Wed., Fri., and Sun. at 3pm. Museum and planetarium shows DM5, students DM3.) Lavishly illustrated, the **Brüder Grimm Museum** is in Palais Bellevue, Schöne Aussicht 2 (tel. 787 20 33), near the Orangerie. Exhibits include the Brothers' handwritten copy of *Kinder- und Haus-Märchen,* their great collection of fairy tales, as well as translations into dozens of languages (open daily 10am-5pm; admission DM3, students DM2). But nothing quite matches the **Deutsches Tapeten Museum** (German Wallpaper Museum), Brüder Grimm Platz 5 (tel. 784 60), in the yellow **Hessiches Landesmuseum** building two minutes east from the *Rathaus.* No joke, this place is *great;* it's an unabashed celebration of everything that's ever covered a wall. Surprises include 16th-century embossed leather-and-gold Spanish hangings, a rare depiction of the battle of Austerlitz, a six-color wallpaper printer, and a letter from Goethe to Schiller mentioning an order of wallpaper. An array of shadow box scenes displays the fascinating development of styles from the Middle Ages to the 1930s. Not surprisingly, this is the only museum of its kind in the world (open Tues.-Fri. 10am-5pm, Sat.-Sun. 10am-1pm; admission DM3, students DM2).

ENTERTAINMENT AND NIGHTLIFE

The hottest night spots in Kassel change faster than the colors of Dennis Rodman's hair, but the *Kneipen* along Friedrich-Ebert-Str. between Annastr. and Bürgermeister-Brünner-Str. are usually a good bet. The city also boasts an impressive 14 *Discotheken* that hit every frequency on the music spectrum. The *Mensa* even gets it jammin' every Thursday night at 9pm. For the latest scoop on what's hot and what's not, check *INFOTIP* (available at hostel).

Alex Brasserie, Neue Fahrt 12 (tel. 739 00 60), in the Kö-Gallerie off Treppenstr. A sharp, stylish café attracting sophisticated clients of every age. Knock-out ice cream desserts DM2.20-8.50. Open Sun.-Thurs. 9am-1am, Fri.-Sat. 9am-3am.

Salzmanns Factory, Sandershäuserstr. 36 (tel. 57 17 73), pumps it up with the phattest house and techno tracks. Friday nights in **Aufschwung Ost** are famous throughout Germany for their thumping techno beat. Open Fri.-Sat. 10pm-4am.

Club 21, Friedrich-Ebert-Str. 61 (tel. 77 17 40). After admiring the 70s pictures on the walls, step into Germany's oldest *Diskothek.* Moderately smooth older crowd (ages 20-30) boogies to hip-hop, house, reggae, and billboards. Cover DM5 on Fri.-Sat.; DM2 on other nights. Opens Mon. and Fri.-Sat. at 11pm.

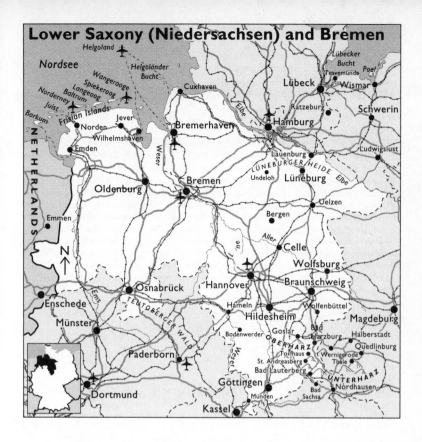

Lower Saxony (Niedersachsen) and Bremen

Lower Saxony (Niedersachsen)

Extending from the Ems River to the Harz Mountains and from the North Sea to the hills of central Germany, Lower Saxony has two distinct flavors. Along the northern coast, descendants of the Frisians run their fishing boats from ports built on a foggy marshland terrain that is unique to Germany. The vast remainder of the *Land*, however, is a broad plain which supports agricultural communities. Since the Middle Ages, the region has been the seat of intense individualism and unbridled innovation. Christianity found a foothold here in the wake of Charlemagne's march through the fringe of the deep-purple Lüneburg Heath. Lower Saxony still treasures its autonomy, harkening back to the Hanseatic traders who made the region's fortune. A pocket of its area belongs to Bremen and Bremerhaven, two seafaring cities united in a unique case of state federalism to form Germany's two smallest *Länder*.

◼ Hanover (Hannover)

Despite its relatively small size (13th largest in Germany), Hanover puts on a magical display of culture and cosmopolitan charm, rivaling that of cities twice as large. As the most important railway center in northwest Germany, the city, with its myriad attractions, easily lures in travelers moving through the Berlin-Hamburg-Cologne triangle. But Hanover has seen darker times. Because of an unusual marriage that bound the Hanoverian royalty to the United Kingdom, the city found itself being repeatedly attacked by foreign powers striking at the British throne. Later, under Prussian domination, Hanover thrived under the prosperity of a unified empire. World War II saw the end of that, as 60% of the city was flattened. Yet resonant Hanover, accustomed to severe poundings in the past, emerged like a jack-in-the-box, leaping joyfully from the ashes. Today, with great economic vigor, a wealth of museums, a matchless opera hall, and a tradition of outdoor festivals, Hanover reigns proudly as the political and cultural capital of Lower Saxony.

ORIENTATION AND PRACTICAL INFORMATION

In the heart of Hanover lies the *Hauptbahnhof,* where a statue of Ernst August, first king of Hanover, beams from the saddle of his horse, surveying the city he founded. **Bahnhofstraße** extends from the hooves of his horse, leading to the landmark **Kröpcke café.** Below the statue's feet sprawls the underground **Passerelle,** a bizarre conglomeration of cheap diners doing the tango with souvenir shops. Behind the station is the **Raschplatz,** which contains a disco and club scene. A pedestrian zone connects most of the middle city, including the major shopping districts along **Georgstraße** and the *Altstadt.*

Tourist Office: Hannover Information, Ernst-August-Platz 2 (tel. 30 14 22; fax 30 14 14). Outside the main entrance of the train station, facing the large rear of the king's splendid steed, turn right. In the same building as the post office. The superb staff finds rooms for any budget for a steep DM10 fee, provides maps and information on cultural events, sells tickets to concerts and exhibits, and has a full travel agency. Open Mon.-Fri. 8:30am-6pm, Sat. 9:30am-2pm.

Student Travel Office: RDS, Limmerstr. (tel. 44 60 37), or at Asternstr. 34 (tel. 70 24 54). Basic bargains for the budget traveler, including flights and train packages. Both open Mon.-Fri. 9am-6pm.

Consulate: U.K., Berliner Allee 5 (tel. 388 38 08). Behind the train station, across Raschplatz, inside the DG-Bank building.

Currency Exchange: DVB, in the train station, is the most convenient with the longest hours and decent commissions. Open Mon.-Fri. 7:30am-7pm, Sat. 7:30am-5pm, Sun. 9am-12:45pm and 1:30-4:30pm. No fees on traveler's checks at AmEx.

American Express: Georgstr. 54, 30159 Hanover (tel. 36 34 28), across from the Opera House. Travel agency and full cardmember services. Mail held for a maximum of 4 weeks for cardmembers, traveler's check clients, and travel agency customers. Open Mon.-Fri. 9am-5:30pm, Sat. 10am-1pm.

Telephones: In the post office and train station.

Flights: The Hanover airport is about 15-20min. from the city center. By car, take highway B522 from the *Innenstadt. Schnellbuslinie* (express bus line) #60 runs from the *Hauptbahnhof* to the airport (Mon.-Fri. every 20min. 5am-10pm, Sat.-Sun. every 30min.; DM8.80). Flights depart to Berlin, Dresden, Frankfurt, Leipzig, Munich, Nuremberg, and Stuttgart, as well as to other European centers. Call for flight information (tel. 977 12 23).

Public Transportation: ÜSTRA, Hanover's mass-transit system, is extremely thorough and fast. As soon as you arrive, walk to the lime green stand in front of the king or at the Raschplatz bus stop behind the station and pick up the free map of the U-Bahn and bus lines. Single-ride tickets DM3.10, children 4-11 DM1.50. Blocks of 6 tickets can be purchased at discount rates, but the best deal for travelers is a **24-hr. Pass** (DM7). The **Hanover Card** (DM14), available at youth hostels and **ÜSTRA** offices, permits transit on all lines and to the airport, as well as free admission or discounts for several museums. All other tickets can be purchased on board from drivers or in vending machines at stations. For more info and maps, call the **ÜSTRA Customer Service Office** in the Kröpike station (tel. 166 82 38). Open Mon.-Wed., Fri. 8am-6pm, Thurs. 8am-7pm, Sat. 9am-2pm.

Bike Rental: Prorad, Friesenstr. 48 (tel. 31 39 67), a 10min. walk behind the train station, sends you zipping past ÜSTRA for DM10 per day. Open Mon.-Tues., Wed. 2-6pm, Thurs.-Fri. 10am-1pm and 2-6pm, Sat. 10am-1pm.

Mitfahrzentrale: Citynetz, Weißekreuzerstr. 18 (tel. 194 44), matches drivers with riders. Open Mon.-Fri. 9am-6pm, Sat. 9am-1pm, Sun. 11am-2pm.

Bookstores: Georgsbuchhandlung, Georgstr. 52 (tel. 32 16 12), has English-language novels downstairs. Open Mon.-Wed. and Fri. 9am-6:30pm, Thurs. 9am-8:30pm, Sat. 9am-2pm.

Rape Crisis Line: tel. 33 21 12.

Women's Shelter: tel. 66 44 77.

Pharmacy: Europa Apotheke, Georgstr. 16 (tel. 32 66 18; fax 363 24 63), near the train station. 14 languages spoken, including English. Open Mon.-Wed. and Fri. 8am-6:30pm, Thurs. 8am-8:30pm, Sat. 8am-2pm. Information about emergency duty *(Notdienst)* during closed hours posted at the doorway.

Emergency: Police: tel. 110. **Medical Information:** tel. 31 40 44.

Post Office: In same building as the tourist office, 30159 Hannover. Open Mon.-Fri. 7am-8pm, Sat. 8am-6pm, Sun. 10am-3pm. Mail held, currency exchanged.

Telephone Code: 0511.

ACCOMMODATIONS

Finding budget accommodations in Hanover is difficult but not impossible. The youth hostel and two *Naturfreundehäuser* (similar to hostels, but not part of HI) provide affordable respite, and private accommodations through the tourist office are also worth a try. Should all else fail, traveling to the hostels in nearby Braunschweig or Celle may be cheaper than bedding down in one of Hanover's royally-priced hotels. As always, calling ahead to ensure a bed is recommended.

Jugendherberge Hannover (HI), Ferdinand-Wilhelm-Fricke-Weg 1 (tel. 131 76 74; fax 185 55). U-Bahn #3 or 7 (direction: Mühlenberg) to "Fischerhof/Fachhochschule." Cross the tracks and walk to the left of the school; follow the bike path as it veers left and over a bridge. Turn right; the hostel is 50m down on the right (15min.). Or take bus #24 (direction: Stadionbrücke) to the front door. Within walking distance of the Maschsee and the Schützenfestplatz. The walk at night is poorly lit—take care. Rooms of 6 with showers and toilets down the hall, but a scenic location and bunnies outside (Wile E. Coyote would have a field day) make for a pleasant stay. Small lockers. Reception open 7:30-9am and 2-11:30pm. Checkout 9am. Curfew 11:30pm. When there's night service, door is opened every hour from midnight to 7am. DM20.50, over 26 DM25. Sheets 5.70. **Camping sites** available for DM13.25, over 26 DM15.50. Breakfast included.

Naturfreundehaus Misburg, Am Fahrhorstfelde 50 (tel. 58 05 37, fax 958 58 36). U-Bahn #4 (direction: Roderbruch) to "Misburger Straße," then bus #31 to the "Misburg Waltfriedhof" stop. Stroll up am Fahrhorstfelde to the very end. Go 10m straight ahead on the trail and follow the sign. On a beautiful lake brimming with ducks. Rooms of 4 and 6 decked out in a homey brown. Reception open Tues.-Fri. 3-10pm, Sat.-Sun. 10am-10pm. No curfew. DM14, nonmembers DM24. Breakfast DM8. Sheets DM7.50 The *Häus*'s 30 beds fill quickly—reservations are necessary.

Naturfreundehaus Stadtheim, Hermann-Bahlsen-Allee 8 (tel. 69 14 93; fax 69 06). U-Bahn #3 or 7 (direction: Lahe or Fasanenkrug) to "Spannhagengarten." Walk 15m back to the intersection and follow Hermann-Bahlsen-Allee to the left for about 5min.; follow the sign to your right down the paved road 200m to the hostel. Tiny rooms, with a superior breakfast. Reception open 8am-noon and 3-10pm. No curfew. DM25, nonmembers DM28.50. Add DM19.50 for full *Pension.*

Hospiz am Bahnhof, Joachimstr. 2, 30159 Hannover (tel. 32 42 97 or 32 46 97). Go left out of the train station and walk 5min. New carpets, comfy sofas, and bright rooms. Reception open 24hr. but reservations recommended. Singles DM60, with shower and toilet DM90-98. Doubles DM115, with shower DM135.

Hotel am Thielenplatz, Thielenplatz 2, 30159 Hannover (tel. 32 76 91; fax 32 51 88). Luxurious furnishings in the lobby and well-maintained rooms, all with TV.

185 beds. Check-out 11:30am. Singles with shower DM85-115. Doubles with shower DM140-185. Breakfast included.

FOOD

Kröpcke, the world-renowned café at the center of the pedestrian zone, can hook you up with small snacks (from DM2.50) or nice sit-down meals (from DM12). The *Imbiß* stands around the adjacent subway stop are surprisingly good. For a more international flavor, ride on down to the **Markthalle,** where a wild variety of snacks, meals, and booze awaits (open Mon.-Fri. 7am-6pm, Sat. 7am-1pm).

Nudel Holz, Köther Holzweg 25 (tel. 21 21 22). U-Bahn #10 to "Leinaustr." Award-winning Italian restaurant offers huge pasta dishes (DM8.50) and 11 potato dishes (DM10.90). 28 wines available, from French to Californian. Open daily 11am-1am.

Mensa, on Schneiderbergstr. U-Bahn #4 or 5 to "Schneiderberg." Take a right up Schneiderbergstr., just past the small pedestrian bridge in the green-trimmed building. DM3 gets you the non-refundable card on which you can deposit however much you wanna spend. Meals DM2.10-3.50. Open Mon.-Sat. noon-2:10pm.

Pizza Piuo, Limmerstr. 4c (tel. 458 35 16). U-Bahn #10 to "Linaustr." For the Scrooge McDucks of this world—this place is dirt cheap. Hefty 20cm pizzas DM3. Spaghetti and pasta DM6. Open Mon.-Sat. 7am-9pm, Sun. noon-9pm.

Uwe's Hannen Faß Hannover, 36 Knochenhauerstr. (tel. 326 16). Located in the center of the *Altstadt,* in the timber-framed house where the master brewer of Hanover lived. The steaming *Niedersachsenschmaus* (DM7.50), a potato casserole, steadies the stomach while a *Bowle* of the house-brewed *Hannen Alt* lightens the head. Foot-long sandwiches DM9.50. Salad bar DM5.50. Daily specials served noon-3:30pm. Open Mon.-Sat. noon-2am, Sun. 3pm-2am.

SIGHTS

In 1714, the son of Electoral Princess Sophie ascended the throne of the United Kingdom as George I, and his descendents continued as the rulers of Hanover, Britain, and Ireland until 1837 when the Hanoverians refused to accept a queen, Sophie's great-great-great-great-granddaughter Victoria. The city owes much to Sophie, who furnished the three paradisiacal **Herrenhausen Gardens.** The Baroque landscaping is wild and ambitious. Take U-Bahn #4 or 5 (direction: Stöcken) to "Herrenhausengarten." The centerpiece is the **Großegarten** (Great Garden). Its **Herrenhausen Palace,** built in the 18th century, hosts frequent concerts and ballets (snap up advance tickets (starting at DM16) at the tourist office, or buy tickets at the door on the evening of the performance). During the "illuminations," geyser-like fountains shoot from the ground to glow in the warm backlighting; gushing in their midst is Europe's highest garden fountain, the **Große Fontäne** (Great Fountain). Originally 32m high, it was gradually built up to 80m. Adjacent to the Großgarten, the smaller **Georgengarten** and **Berggarten** offer equally bewitching vegetation. Various *Feuerwerkswettbewerbe* (fireworks contests), held during the summer, provide dazzling displays with musical accompaniment sponsored by different countries. (Georgengarten always open and free. Großegarten and Berggarten open April-Oct. Mon.-Tues. 8am-8pm, Wed.-Sun. 8am-11pm. Illuminations Wed.-Sun. 10-11pm. Fountains Mon.-Fri. 11am-noon and 2-4pm; Sat.-Sun. 11am-noon and 2-5pm. General admission DM3, 2½hr. before illuminations DM4, students DM2. Großegarten and Berggarten open Nov.-Mar. daily 8am-dusk. General admission DM3.) The 14th-century **Marktkirche,** Hans-Lilje-Platz, presides over the almost totally reconstructed *Altstadt.* From the station, follow Bahnhofstr. to the *Markt* (open daily 10am-4pm; check for concerts). City government outgrew the **Altes Rathaus** (Old Town Hall), just off the *Markt* in 1913, but its trellised façade and mosaic work are kept bright. Walking back towards Knochenhauerstr. and a making a quick left down Krämerstr. brings you to Holzmarkt and the **Leibnizhaus,** a beautifully restored Baroque mansion, home to brilliant mathematician, philosopher, man of letters, and royal advisor Gottfried Wilhelm Leibniz until his death in 1716 (Open Sun. 10am-1pm and 1:30-6pm. Tread carefully—this site alone cost DM22 million to restore.) A jog down Leinstr. brings you past the magnificent **Leineschloß,** seat of the Diet of Lower Saxony, to the ivy-covered shell of the crumbling **St. Aegidienkirche**. The massive damage suffered during WWII was intentionally left untouched as a grim reminder of the folly of war—step inside for the full effect.

Against the ruined remains of Hanover's medieval fortifications (the **Friedrichswall**), down Marktstr. from the *Altstadt,* rises the more modern, spectacular **Neues Rathaus**. Hanoverians painstakingly recreated this palatial turn-of-the-century complex after World War II. Step inside to see models of the city in 1689, 1939, 1945, and today. Take the slanted elevator up the tower for a miniaturized view of the real thing. (Elevator open April-Oct. daily 10am-12:15pm and 1:30-4:15pm. DM3, students DM2.) From up high, you can scout out Hanover's many parks, including the woods around the **Maschsee**. This artificial 2-km-long lake just south of the *Rathaus* is covered with sailboats and rowboats during the summer and ice skaters in winter. Hanover's links with Britain are espoused in the **Waterloo Monument** (from the Neues Rathaus, cross the Leine River bridge or walk through the tunnel near the subway), a high column commemorating the Lower Saxon citizens who fought with the British against Napoleon. To fully experience Hanover, follow the **Red Thread,** a 2½-mi. walking tour guided by a painted red line connecting all the major sites. The accompanying *Red Thread Guide* (DM3) details the tour and is available from the tourist office. Your very own Freedom Trail in Germany!

MUSEUMS

Wilhelm-Busch Museum, Georgengarten 1 (tel. 71 40 76). Take U-Bahn #4 or 5 (direction: Stöcken) to "Schneiderberg." See wit and sarcasm channeled onto paper in vivid color. Just as fun as the art books and postcards from past exhibitions—don't miss the Sebastian Krüger pieces or the history of Max and Moritz. Admission DM4, students and kiddies DM2. Open Tues.-Sun. 10am-5pm.

Landesmuseum, Willy Brandt Allee 5 (formerly Am Maschseeplatz; tel. 980 75), near the *Neues Rathaus.* This place is the jack of all trades—alas, the suit is hearts, not spades. Still, the variety is amusing. Stare down ugly fish in the aquarium and feel the pelt of the luxurious hamster. Admission DM3, students and children DM1.50. Open Tues.-Wed. and Fri.-Sat. 10am-5pm, Thurs. 10am-7pm.

Sprengel Museum, Kurt-Schwitters-Platz (tel. 168 38 75), next door to the Landesmuseum. A modern art lover's dream: James Turrell, Henry Moore, Salvador Dalí, Pablo Picasso, René Magritte, and Horst Antes. Make sure to check out the light experiments by James Turrell. Be patient—the results will amaze you. Admission DM6, students and children DM3. Permanent collection and the special exhibit DM11 and DM6.50, respectively. Open Tues. 10am-3pm, Wed.-Sun. 10am-6pm.

Historisches Museum am Hohen Ufer, Pferdestr. 6 (tel. 168 30 52), next to the Leibnizhaus, is housed in a 1960s replica of a 10th-century fortress. A very thorough exposition on Hanoverian history and the cultural links with Britain. Also houses a huge collection of dioramas depicting scenes from battlefields, as well as one from "Dances With Wolves." Admission DM5, students and children DM3. Open Tues. 10am-8pm, Wed.-Fri. 10am-4pm, Sat.-Sun. 10am-6pm.

Kestner-Museum, Trammplatz 3 (tel. 168 21 20). Through the park behind the *Rathaus.* Numismatics will go dizzy over the ancient coin collection. The centerpiece is the Greco-Roman and Egyptian art. Admission DM3. Free on Wed. Open Tues. and Thurs.-Fri. 10am-4pm, Wed. 10am-8pm, Sat.-Sun. 10am-6pm.

Kubus Museum, an der Aegidienkirche, Theodor-Lessing-Platz 2 (tel. 168 57 90). A museum organized around the alphabet. T**E**x**T** aS I**M**Ag**E**. Syntagm? We don't need no stinking syntagm. Free. Open Tues.-Fri. 10am-6pm, Sat.-Sun. 10am-4pm.

ENTERTAINMENT

If you're within a 100-km radius of Hanover between July 4 and July 13, detour to its **Schützenfest** (marksmanship festival), the largest such fête in the world. Every summer since 1539, Hanoverians have congregated—weapons in hand—to test their marksmanship and retreat to the beer gardens to get *Schützen*-faced. In that order.

The 10-day festival comes complete with parade, fireworks, chintzy stuffed animals, and rickety amusement park rides. But its main attraction is the *Lüttje Lage*, a feisty traditional drink. Without spilling, you must down the contents of two shot glasses simultaneously, holding them side by side in one hand; one glass contains *Weißbier*, the other *Schnapps*. And if this isn't enough fun for you, Hanover delivers a nifty one-two punch. After giving the liver a brief respite, the **Maschseefest** (July 30-Aug. 17, 1997) hits you with another wild combination of concerts, masked balls, and street performances. For anyone left standing and capable of walking a straight line, the knockout blow falls with the **Altstadtfest** in the first or second weekend in August. All the big *Kneipen* and cafés convene for one last hurrah until next year.

Over 20 theaters make their homes in Hanover, supplying ballet, opera, dramas, and Broadway musicals. The **Opera House**, Opernplatz 1, the **Ballhof**, Ballhofstr. 5, the **Schauspielhaus**, and the **Theater am Aegi**, on Aegienterplatz, are the four largest. Tickets for most of the theaters (starting around DM12) may be purchased at the tourist office. (Advance tickets for the Opera house and the *Schauspielhaus* may be purchased at the Opera House Mon.-Fri. 11am-5:30pm, Sat. 11am-1pm, or by calling 368 17 11 for the opera or 32 11 33 for the *Schauspielhaus* 1 hour after the box office opens.) Most theaters offer student tickets half an hour before each show. For the official line on theater listings, festival dates, and other items of interest, pick up the monthly *Hannover Vorschau* from the tourist office (DM3). The **Flohmarkt** (flea market) on the **Leibnizufer** hits town every Saturday from 7am to 4pm.

NIGHTLIFE

When the sun goes down, Hanover lets 'em rip with an impressive array of packed cafés and pumping discos. Kröpcke buzzes with an alternative scene in the small plazas. The happening university crowds swarm the area of Linden North, between Goetheplatz and Leinsustr., filling the cafés and **Kneipen**. For parties, snoop around the **Mensa** for signs or check the **Schädelspalter** (DM5), an outstanding guide to nightlife in the city, listing more concerts, performances, and get-togethers than you'll know what to do with. Each university **Fach** (department) throws monthly parties, and the best ones, believe it or not, are held by the *chemistry* students.

The Capitol, Schwarzer Bär 2 (tel. 92 98 80), sets the floor thumping with dance hits. Loosen up in a sea of bumping bodies. Next to the bar, a separate, smaller floor for hard rock gets heads banging. Opens Fri.-Sat. at 10pm. DM8. Other times, find live music, movies, or a locked door. Call for a schedule.

Osho Disco, Raschplatz 7L (tel. 34 22 17), caters to the same crowd as The Capitol. A lounge area surrounding the dance floor is the perfect place to meet people. Cover Wed.-Thurs. and Sun. DM5, Fri.-Sat. DM8. Open Wed.-Sun. at 10pm.

Boomerang, Engelbosteler Damm 45 (tel. 138 18). Take U-Bahn #6 or 11 (direction: Haltenhoffstr. or Nordhafen) to "Kopernikusstr." Step out of the subway and look for the sawed-off tail of an airplane hanging above the door. Inside, find the rest of the plane along with a huge student crowd. A kitchen whips up fine Australian treats (DM4.50). Open Mon.-Fri. 9am-2am, Sat. 9am-late, Sun. 2pm-2am.

Palo Palo, Raschplatz 8a (tel. 33 10 73), gets further away from the mainstream with acid jazz and old school 70s and 80s. Live music on Wed. Cover Thurs.-Tues. DM7, Wed. depends on who's playing (up to DM35). Open daily 10pm-6am.

Waterloo Biergarten, Waterlooplatz 1 (tel. 156 43). Walk under the highway toward the Waterloo monument. Fun, beer-drinking-song atmosphere. Stands around the *Garten* sell pretzels and hot dogs. Open daily 11am-whenever.

Schwul Sau, Schaufeldstr.29 (tel. 700 05 25). U-Bahn #6 or 11 to "Kopernikusstr." One of the most popular gay and lesbian bars in Hanover, located in the university district. On good nights, the 3-person sofa in the corner seats 15. Tues. ladies only. Wed. Men only. Sat. night parties start at 9pm (DM6).

■ Göttingen

A college town to the bone, Göttingen is home to Europe's first free university. The Georg-August-Universität boasts Otto von Bismarck as an alumnus and the Brothers Grimm as faculty members, but its real fame comes from its spectacular track record in Big Science. No less than 12 Nobel laureates have been faculty members, including Max Planck (the father of quantum mechanics) and Werner Heisenberg (the brilliant but eccentric head of the German A-bomb project). Some claim that Heisenberg was one of World War II's most unsung heroes. Reputedly he passed information on to Allied scientists and deliberately led his research teams down fruitless paths to keep the Bomb out of the Hitler's hands. Such anti-authoritarianism is a Göttingen tradition: in the years after its founding by England's King (and Elector of Hanover) George II in 1737, the university was one of the most liberal in the German lands. By the 1920s, however, it had degenerated into a hotbed of reactionary nationalism. The major exception were the physics and chemistry faculties, the members of which mostly emigrated when the Nazis took power. After World War II, the pendulum swung the other way and Göttingen earned a reputation as a "*rote Uni*" (red university). Now it has comfortably settled into moderate liberalism.

ORIENTATION AND PRACTICAL INFORMATION

Tourist Office: Fremdenverkehrsverein Göttingen, at Markt 9 (tel. 540 00; fax 400 29 98), is located in the *Rathaus*. From the station, cross busy Berliner Str. to pick up the perpendicular Goetheallee; follow it for several blocks as it becomes Prinzenstr., turn right onto Weender Str., and follow that to the market square. There the *Rathaus* will be visible. The office has maps and hotel and restaurant lists. They will also book a private room (DM35) for free. Open April-Oct. Mon.-Fri. 9am-6pm, Sat.-Sun. 10am-4pm; Nov.-March Mon.-Fri. 9am-6pm, Sat. 10am-1pm. A smaller **branch office,** Berliner Str. 11 (tel. 560 00), is located across from the train station. Open Mon.-Fri. 10am-1pm and 2-6pm, Sat. 10am-1pm.

Tours: Leave from the main hall of the *Rathaus* daily at 2:30pm. DM5, students DM3. Tours in English available for large groups only.

Currency Exchange: Commerzbank, Prinzenstr. 2 (tel. 40 80), has the best rates in town. Open Mon.-Wed. 8:30am-4pm, Thurs. 8:30am-6pm, Fri. 8:30am-3:30pm.

American Express: Goethealle 4a (tel. 52 20 70). Open Mon.-Fri. 9am-6pm, Sat. 9:30am-12:30pm.

Car Rental: Sixt-Budget, Groner Landstr. 27 (tel. 54 75 70). Open Mon.-Fri. 7:30am-6pm, Sat. 8am-1pm.

Bike Rental: The youth hostel (see below) rents bikes to guests for DM9 per day. DM30 deposit or ID required.

Mitfahrzentrale: Mitfahrbüro Cheltenham House, Friedrichstr. 1 (tel. 48 59 88), hooks up riders and drivers, and includes a **budget travel office** (tel. 575 08). English spoken. Open Mon.-Fri. 10am-6pm, Sat.-Sun. 10am-2pm.

Bookstore: Deuerlich, with the main store at Weenderstr. 33 (tel. 49 50 00), but smaller specialized branches at Weender Landstr. 6 and Theaterstr. 25. If you're feeling down, the amazing wit and humor of the *Let's Go* series is available! Open Mon.-Wed. and Fri. 9am-6:30pm, Thurs. 9am-8pm, Sat. 9am-6pm.

Laundromat: Wasch-O-Center, Ritterplan 4, opposite the Städtisches Museum. Wash DM5. Dry DM1 per 12min. Soap included. Open Mon.-Sat. 7am-10pm. There are also washers, but no driers, at the hostel (see below).

Post Office: Heinrich-von-Stephan-Str. 7, to the left of the train station. Street named after the brilliant organizer of the German postal service.

Telephone Code: 0551.

ACCOMMODATIONS

The abundance of students and visitors in Göttingen makes the long-term housing market tight. Hotels tend to be expensive. There are, however, ways to get around this: the hostel is excellent, and those wishing to stay a few days or even a few months can check the **Mitwohnzentrale,** Judenstr. 10 (tel. 194 45), which matches up potential roomies (open Mon., Wed., Fri. 10am-4pm; Tues., Thurs. 10am-1pm).

Jugendherberge (HI), Habichtsweg 2 (tel. 576 22; fax 438 87). From the station, turn left onto Berlinerstr., which becomes Nikolausberger Weg, and follow the signs (30min.). Or, take Bus #8, 10, 11, 15, or 18 to "Kornmarkt;" and then catch either Bus #6 to "Jugendherberge" or Bus #9 to "Hermann-Föge-Weg." This place puts most *hotels* to shame. Immaculate rooms with new sinks and furnishings. Reception open 6:30am-11:30pm. Curfew at midnight, but get a key with a DM30 deposit. Washers DM4.50 (no driers available). Bikes for rent. DM21, over 26 DM25.50. Room keys require DM20 deposit. Breakfast included. Sheets DM5.70).

Hotel "Zum Schwan," Weender Landstr. 23 (tel. 448 63). Walk left from the station and turn left onto Weender Landstr. (10min.). Cool tie-like patterns cover the walls of some pretty darned big rooms. Hallways bright and furnished. Reception open Mon.-Fri. 7am-10pm, Sat.-Sun. 7am-2pm. Singles DM46, with shower DM56. Doubles DM73, with shower DM87. Breakfast included.

Hotel-Gaststätte Berliner Hof, Weender Landstr. 43 (tel. 38 33 20, fax 383 32 32). Down the street from the above and neatly tucked up next to the university. Floral comforters make your dreams cozy. Reception open 7am-1pm and 3-11pm. Singles DM58, with shower and toilet DM70. Doubles with the works DM98.

FOOD

Göttingen is blessed with museum-quality specimens of the **Mensa** and the vegetable **Markt,** Germany's two great budget-food institutions. An impressive array of farm-fresh peddlers haggle in the area between Lange and Kurze Geismar Str., including in a fruit market adjacent to the Deutsches Junges Theater (Tues., Thurs., and Sat. 7am-1pm and in the square in front of the *Rathaus* Thurs. 3-8:30pm). The most central **supermarket** is **Plus,** Prinzen Str. 13, across from the library (open Mon.-Fri. 8am-6:30pm, Sat. 8am-2pm). **Goetheallee,** running from the station to the city center, has late-night Greek, Italian, and Turkish restaurants.

Zentral Mensa, follow Weenderlandstr. onto Platzder Göttinger Sieben, then turn right into the university complex, and walk to the dusty central plain to the cavernous *Studentenwerk* building off to the left. Swarming with people and plastered with listings of local events, the plain, dependable cafeteria serves meals for DM2.20-5.50. Meal tickets are sold downstairs—buy one or you can't eat. Select one of the 4 menus hung on the wall opposite the ticket booth; e.g., Stammessen 1 or Wahlessen 2. Food served Mon.-Fri. 9am-2:15pm, Sat. 10am-2pm.

Alte Mensa, in the old campus on Wilhelmsplatz, back in the *Altstadt,* is cozier than Zentral (above), with the same prices and NO schoolchildren. Tickets are interchangeable between the two. An adjacent tavern serves *Wurst.* Both open Mon.-Fri. 11:30am-2:15pm and 5:30-8:30pm, but only when school's in session (mid-April to mid-July and mid-Oct. to mid-Feb.).

Cron & Lanz, under a conspicuous sign at Weenderstr. 25 (tel. 560 22), is one of Germany's sweetest pastry shops and a real diet buster since 1876. The window displays of gorgeous dark tortes and *petits fours* will make you drool. The white-glazed, cherry-laced *Baumkuchentorte* ("tree-cake"; DM3) is their speciality. Open Mon.-Fri. 8:45am-6:30pm, Sat. 8:30am-6:30pm, Sun. 1-6:30pm.

Gro Mo-Crepes, Papendiek 10 (tel. 17 72 44 67 31), offers some drop-dead killer snacks for a low price—waffles from DM1.50; crêpes DM2. The banana and chocolate combos will melt your heart. Open Mon.-Fri. 11am-6pm, Sat. 11am-2pm.

Pfannkuchen Haus, Speckstr. 10 (tel. 418 70). Tasty, dense German griddle cakes provide with an immense variety of fillings and toppings; plain butter and sugar (DM4), roasted pork shreds with cherry-pepper sauce (DM14). Do they serve wine at your local IHOP? Open daily noon-1am; kitchen closes at midnight.

SIGHTS

The courtyard of the **Altes Rathaus** serves as meeting place for the whole town: punker, professor, and panhandler alike. Radical students and evangelists preach to the converted, with tracts to hand to passers-by. The little 1-m-high **Gänseliesel** (goose-girl) on the fountain in front of the *Rathaus* is Göttingen's symbol; graduating students, particularly budding doctors, line up to kiss the bronze beauty after receiving their diplomas. The repressed city council imposed a "kissing ban" in 1926, prompting one incensed (or perhaps just frustrated) student to sue. He lost, but town officials now turn a blind eye to extracurricular fountain activities. The bronze lion-head doorknob on the south portal of the **Rathaus** was crafted in 1300, making it the oldest town hall door knob in Germany. Step inside where elaborate murals depict 19th-century work-a-day life in Göttingen. Tours of the city depart from the *Gänseliesel* (see Practical Information, p. 327). The renowned **university** is outside the Ernst-Honig-Wall (not really much of a wall at all). The campus fills an area bounded by Weender Landstr. and Nikolausberger Weg. Far from picturesque, it is dominated by a dusty gravel plain at the center of the complex, but offers wonderful people-watching opportunities. Göttingen's students represent every possible style, appearance, outlook, and nationality: there are even some German preppies here. Further north lies the sleeker but less exciting **Universität-Nord** complex, consisting mostly of lab buildings populated by clinical researchers.

The **Bismarckhäuschen** (tel. 48 58 44) is a tiny stone cottage, also outside the city wall, where 17-year-old law student Otto von Bismarck took up residence after authorities expelled him from the inner city for boozing it up (open Tues. 10am-1pm, Thurs. and Sat. 3-5pm; free). A **Bismarckturm**, in Kleperberg (tel. 742 13), along the Stadtforest, commemorates the larger-scale trouble making of his later career. From the top of the old stone tower, there's a Göttingen-wide view. Take bus A to "Bismarckstraße/Reitsall" (open Sat.-Sun. 10am-5pm; also free). Göttingen also flaunts a few notable medieval churches. At the corner of Prinzenstr. and Weenderstr., next to the stone lambada sculpture called "Der Tanz," stands **St. Jacobi's** 72m tower. Inside, a miniature model of the impressive 1402 altar triptych is fun to play with (open daily 10am-noon; free organ concerts Fri. at 6pm). Down Weenderstr., behind the *Altes Rathaus,* stands the fortress-like **St. Johanniskirche.** The fairly typical interior is open daily 10:30am-12:30pm (the more interesting tower, where students have lived since 1921, is open Sat. 2-4pm). On Untere Maschstr. is a twisting, spiraling pyramid erected as a **memorial** to the Göttingen synagogue that was razed in 1938. Viewed from above, the structure spirals into a monumental Star of David. Elsewhere, venerable houses mark the town's zenith, constructed when Göttingen was a member of the **Hanseatic League** (1351-1572).

The **Städtisches Museum,** at Ritterplan 7 (tel. 400 28 45), one block north on Jüdenstr. from the Jacobikirche, gives a detailed, extensive examination of the city over the last several millennia or so. It starts off a bit weak, with an exhibit of bizarre **Göttinger religious art** from the 16th to 18th centuries. Much more interesting is the third floor **Göttingen History** wing; the limited scope here in fact tells the story well. After a sharp display of medieval town artifacts, the museum features the Nazi years of Göttingen. Hostel-sleepers will get a strange chill from a display of *Hitlerjugend* memorabilia which includes a number of *Deutsche Jugendherbergswerk* pins complete with swastikas on them. There's also a display of dozens of cover pages from Göttingen's Nazi-run local newspaper that offer a rather distorted view of history. The propagandists' allusions to the Pearl Harbor attack as "American war-mongering" must be read to be believed. A Nazi shadow also falls over the **university history** room. Much is made of Göttingen's intellectual distinction and liberal sentiments: in 1837, on the 100th anniversary of the university's founding, a group of professors known as the **Göttingen Seven** made German history by sending a public letter of protest to King Ernst August, who had revoked the liberal constitution established four years previously by his predecessor. Courageous signers included the Brothers Grimm, then well-known professors of literature; as expected, the Seven were all removed from office. Several were exiled. The museum does not miss the irony of comparing Göttingen's heroic first centennial with the ignominy of its bicentennial: 1937 saw the streets covered with swastikas while Goebbels and other intellectual "luminaries" renamed Theaterplatz "Adolf-Hitler-Platz." The extravaganza was held at a university devoid of Jewish faculty or students; most had emigrated or been imprisoned. A special side room exhibit commemorates the loss (open Tues.-Fri. 10am-5pm, Sat.-Sun. 10am-1pm; admission DM3, students DM2).

ENTERTAINMENT AND NIGHTLIFE

Göttingen offers travelers the unique opportunity to experience the whole spectrum of theatre. For world-class performances, the renowned **Deutsches Theater** (tel. 49 69 11; fax 53 097) puts on the classics with tickets as low as DM11. Check out the slick **DT** catalog for the schedule; it's available at the box office (open Mon.-Fri. 10am-1pm and 5-6:30pm, Sat. 10am-noon, and 1hr. before showtime, summer pause from July to mid-September). To flavor the youthful perspective, head down to the **Junges Theater** (tel. 551 23, fax 530 64), presenting both the classic and the innovative. (Adults DM19, students DM13; on Wed. DM14 and DM10, respectively.) All theaters break for the summer from July to mid-September. Otherwise shows are on daily Wednesday to Sunday (box office open Mon.-Sat. 11am-1pm and 2hr. before showtime). Tickets for theater and just about everything else going on in Göttingen or Germany can be bought at **Peukaut,** Weenderstr. 75 (tel. 54 88 80; open Mon.-Wed. and Fri. 9am-6:30pm, Thurs. 9am-8:30pm, Sat. 9am-2pm). Naturally, Göttingen's nightlife gains sophistication and variety from its legions of students. The Junges Theater's 1830 mansion positively oozes creativity. Göttingen's **KAZ** (*Kommunikations Aktions-Zentrum;* Communication Action Center) operates under the same roof. KAZ brings together more than 50 associations all with socio-cultural arms—their motto is "from everybody for everybody." They do everything from hosting hardcore concerts to offering free lessons in African drumming.

The best place to hear music and hang with students is the **Blue Note** (tel. 469 07), under the **Alte Mensa** in Wilhelmsplatz. There's a new musical theme every day, and live bands at least once a week. Jazz, reggae, and African pop are all well represented (open Mon.-Sat. 8pm-3am; when big-name DJs hop into the fray, cover DM12, students DM8). **Schroeder's Kneipe,** at the corner of Jüdenstr. and Speckstr. (tel. 556 47), across from the *Jakobskirche,* is the afternoon hangout for Göttingen's alternative types. The black clothing and smoke reach critical mass around 3-5pm (open Mon.-Thurs. 11am-2am, Fri.-Sat. 11am-3am, Sun. after 2pm). As a last resort, check out *Charakter,* a thorough listing of music, movies, and parties.

■ Goslar

Easy come, easy go. Goslar held all the aces at the beginning of its 1000-year history: during the 11th century, the Saltan and Hohenstaufen dukes ran the Holy Roman Empire from the city's solemn **Kaiserpfalz** (Imperial Palace). But when the Saxons disposed of Emperor Henry IV in 1077 with a brisk royal flush, Goslar's good fortune went with him. In the 13th century, the town hit the jackpot again: the **Rammelsberg,** a tall hill at the southern edge of town, turned out to be loaded with high-quality silver ore. Soon, prosperity hit Goslar broadside, and a powerful guild class took control of the city council. By 1340, Goslar had more money than it knew what to do with, and it was declared a Free Imperial City. The mines sustained the boom until the 16th century, when Free Goslar began to spend all of its time and money fighting off the covetous dukes of Braunschweig. Finally, in 1552, Goslar crapped out again: it was occupied and forced to cede its mine-mountain to Braunschweig.

This loss 450 years ago has proven to be an extraordinary windfall for tourists: all building halted after the occupation, and Goslar's immense 16th-century *Altstadt* section was effectively frozen in time. The town was lucky enough to escape World War II bombing, and today Goslar exudes a warm quality of anachronism, with delightfully and absurdly ornate statues scattered throughout the city. Hundreds of immaculate slate-roofed, half-timbered houses line the twisty cobblestone streets without architectural intrusions from the past four centuries. UNESCO recognized Goslar's unique character by declaring virtually the entire town a historic site, beckoning the tourists and welcoming Diva Fortuna back.

Orientation and Practical Information The **tourist office,** Markt 7 (tel. 28 46 or 28 47; fax 230 05), across from the *Rathaus,* finds rooms (from DM30) for no fee. They offer information in English, and some of the employees even speak it. From the station, turn left and walk to the end of Rosentorstr.; it becomes Hokenstr. (Open March-Oct. Mon.-Fri. 9am-6pm, Sat. 9am-2:30pm; Nov.-April Mon.-Fri. 9am-5pm, Sat. 9am-1pm.) **Trains** from Hanover (16 per day) and Göttingen (14 per day) stop at Goslar. Perched near the defunct border with the East, Goslar is a good base for a bus or hiking tour of the lush Harz Mountains. **Harzbike Goslar-Baßgeige,** Bornhardtstr. 3-5 (tel. 820 11), rents **bikes** for DM35 per day (open Mon.-Fri. 9:30am-6pm; Sat. 9am-2pm). The **Frauenzentrum Goslar,** Breite Str. 15a (tel. 422 55), provides counseling for women. The entrance is on Bolzenstr. The **post office** is at Klubgartenstr. 10, 38640 Goslar (open Mon.-Fri. 8am-5:30pm, Sat. 9am-noon). The **telephone code** is 05321. Goslar gets funky every year from August 30 to September 1 with its **Altstadtfest**—a kind of watered-down *Oktoberfest.*

Accommodations and Camping The half-timbered Goslar **Jugendherberge (HI),** Rammelsbergerstr. 25, 38644 Goslar (tel. 222 40), wins the prize for being the most confusingly located hostel in the book. Non-locals and patsies try to reach the hostel via the streets; they suffer for it. But there's a **shortcut:** from the *Marktplatz,* take twisty Bergstr. southwest until it ends at the large east-west Clausthaler Str. Directly across the street, between the trees, a stairway marked with a "Wanderweg" sign awaits. Take this pleasant path through the pines, head right at the fork at the path's midpoint, and you'll find yourself in the hostel's backyard (10min.). The hostel features crowded six-bed rooms with slightly dilapidated facilities that won't give you the most satisfying of showers; however, the dining hall is elegant and spacious. (Reception open 8:30am-10pm. Curfew 11:30pm. HI members only. DM20, over 26 DM24.50. Breakfast included. Vegetarian meals available.) **Campingplatz Sennhütte,** Clausthalerstr. 28 (tel. 224 98), 3km from town along the B241, has a restaurant and sauna (DM6 per person, DM5 per tent, showers DM1).

If you've a bit more money to spare, Goslar proffers several excellent *Pensionen.* **Gästehaus Elisabeth Möller,** Schieferweg 6 (tel. 230 98), has been a family affair for 24 years. An immense, shady garden (3000m.sq.), with a complete patio, invites afternoon lounging. Take Klubgartenstr. and Am Heiligen Grabe west from the train station, cross Von-Garssen-Str., and turn right on Schieferweg (singles DM35, with shower and toilet DM45; doubles with shower and toilet DM85-100). Next to the *Markt* in is the equally impressive **Gästehaus Schmitz,** Korustr. 1 (tel. 234 45). Despite the age of the edifice, there's a surprisingly light feel to the interior. The owner speaks a little English. From the *Markt,* turn left on Korustr. (Reception open 9am-7pm. Singles DM50. Doubles DM65. Apartment-style rooms DM60 per person.)

Food The town's mountain **Markt** yodels every Tuesday and Friday (open 8am-1pm). The beautiful market square is ringed with cafés and restaurants; unfortunately, most are of the DM5-per-beer variety. Cheaper bistros and cafés can be found along Hokenstr., where *Imbiß* stands provide meals for DM4-8. **Don Camillo Pizza-Bistro,** Bergstr. 60 (tel. 462 62), will meet the needs of the cheaper than cheap: pizzas run DM2.50-DM10, while pasta dishes consume DM6-10 (open Mon.-Fri. 11am-midnight, Sat.-Sun. 4pm-midnight). To explore Goslar's sordid underbelly, across the street from Don Camillo's, but also on Bergstr., is **Himmel Blaue Trichter Winde,** identifiable only by the sign above the door which says, "Café Theater Livemusik Café." This place has all the feel of an S&M dungeon, complete with hanging skulls and hard-core Goth music. (*Einbecker* only DM3. Open Tues.-Sat. after 8pm.)

Sights Guarded by a pair of stone Braunschweig lions, the austere **Kaiserpfalz,** Kaiserbleek 6, is a massive Romanesque palace that served as the ruling seat for 11th- and 12th-century emperors. The palace had fallen into sad decay by the 19th century but was extensively restored by nationalistic 1870s aristocrats. The interior of the **great hall** is plastered with pompous 19th-century murals; the huge paintings display carefully selected historical incidents in the mythic-pompous manner that only 19th-century Germans could properly pull off. Their unsubtle purpose is to draw a direct historical connection running from Frederick I (1050) to Bismarck and Kaiser Wilhelm I, who stare out from the central mural. In the palace's **Ulrichskapelle,** Henry III's heart lies tucked away inside a massive sarcophagus (museum and tomb open April-Oct. daily 10am-5pm; Nov.-March 10am-4pm; last entry 30min. before closing; admission DM3.50, students DM2). Below the palace at Kaiserbleek 10 is the **Domvorhalle** (Cathedral Foyer), the sad remains of a 12th-century imperial cathedral destroyed 170 years ago. The plaque on the wall is the engraved equivalent of a scrawled "Heinrich Heine wuz here."

The central **Marktplatz** is delightful: as far as the eye can peer, it finds a rush of ornate woodwork and trellises. The **Hotel Kaiserworth,** a former guild house, was for many years an eccentric but striking addition to the square, with its superb tapering gable spires and the copious wooden statues of emperors gracing the façade. Recently, though, its elegant white front has been repainted a vulgar red. The hotel's statues have been painted up, too; in full comic-book color, it's now easier to see the coarsely humorous smaller figures on the corners. Each day in the market square, small **Glocken- und Figurenspiel** figures of court nobles and the miners whose work made the region prosperous dance to the chime on the treasury roof (9am, noon, 3, and 6pm). The **Rathaus** has a wonderfully preserved **Huldigungssaal** (Hall of Homage). A 15th-century city council chamber where secret documents were stashed, it swims with depictions of town elders and pre-Renaissance biblical scenes. The **Bergkanne,** an unbelievably ornate silver and gold-encrusted tankard, and the similarly bejeweled **Goslarer Evangeliar,** an illuminated manuscript from 1230, are safe inside. An ornate facsimile of the book is on display. The hall's **imperial eagle,** circa 1220, is real, but the one atop the *Markt* fountain is faux. While the tourist office gushes about the "majesty" of the gilded bird, there's an inescapable something about it that's—chicken-like. (Tours June-Sept. every 30min. 10am-5pm; Oct.-May every 30min. 10am-4pm. DM3, students DM1.50.)

The twin towers of the reconstructed 12th-century **Marktkirche** poke up from right behind the *Rathaus.* Inside, see the stained-glass saga of St. Cosmas and St. Damian, 3rd-century twin doctors and martyrs (no relation to *Dead Ringers).* In a classic instance of the Roman empire's overkill, the saints were disciplined and punished by drowning, burning at the stake, stoning, crucifixion, and transfixion (open Tues.-Thurs. and Sat. 10:30am-3:30pm, Fri. 10:30am-2pm, Sun. noon-3:30pm). The **Mönchehaus,** Mönchestr. 3, is an outstanding modern art museum inside a small house with a sculpture garden (open Tues.-Sat. 10am-1pm and 3-5pm, Sun. 10am-

Always Fear for the Wurst!

In Germany you will undoubtedly be confronted with the dilemma of whether or not to indulge in the high culture of German cuisine by trying a *Wurst.* They're tasty, they're cheap, and dammit—they're German! There can be a severe downside, however, to leading the life of a German gourmet. Nietzsche, in *Ecce Homo,* described how the German character necessarily inflicted him with bad digestion and a few years later went completely nuts—one can only hope that it wasn't because of the *Wurst.* In Bavaria, the native *Weißwurst* is often referred to as *Scheißwurst* (Shit Wurst), because it's supposedly composed of the grotesque parts of meat remaining on a butcher's table. Yuck! But go ahead and make you leap of faith into the unknown world of *Würste.* Just remember to proclaim beforehand, *"Das ist mir Wurst!"* (I don't give a damn!).

1pm; admission DM3.50, students and children DM2). On the way back from the Kaiserpfalz, don't miss the fantastic **Puppen-und-Musikinstrumente Museum** (Puppet and Musical Instrument Museum), Hoherweg 5. Truly a labor of love: the owner has spent more than 40 years assembling the largest private instrument collection in Germany, including one of the **world's first accordions,** and a 50s Wurlitzer jukebox. Also visit the meta-museum tucked inside, billed as the "smallest musical instrument museum in the world," with a small box featuring models of miniature models of instruments (open daily from 11am-5pm; admission DM4, children DM2).

▓ Western Harz Mountains

Germany's 45-year political division allowed the **Harz Mountains** to flourish in an artificial time warp. Since the region straddled the Iron Curtain, both East and West declared much of it off-limits, sparing its natural gifts from development. Now that the armed border guards have gone, visitors have taken their places and multiplied like mosquitoes; hikers and spa-tourists alike incline to these misty, rugged hills in the heart of the restored nation. The range stretches from the northwestern **Oberharz** to the wind-sheltered, mineral-rich valleys of the south and Wernigerode in the east. The historic villages are clustered in the Eastern Harz; the attraction on the western side of the mountains is mainly outdoors. With the first snows, the terrain becomes a splendid winter playground for skiing, skating, and tobogganing. For information on the eastern towns, see the Eastern Harz, Sachsen-Anhalt (p. 517).

If possible, try to be deep into the Harz during the last week of April to join in the immense region-wide celebration of **Walpurgisnacht.** The April 30th hedonistic festivities, immortalized by Goethe, center around legendary **witches** who sweep through the sky on broomsticks to land on **Brocken,** the Harz's highest peak. Little felt **Harzhexen** (Harz witches) perched on wooden brooms are a local souvenir staple. The legendary witches dance with the devil until midnight, at which point the May King arrives to clean house. This was also a major Norse festival; the chief god Odin married Freya on the last night of April. The Christian clergy sought to usurp the ritual merrymaking by calling the party "Walpurgisnacht" after St. Walpurga (born May 1), but the pagan pleasures endured. The Harz explodes during this time with festivals, demonic skits, wilderness spook treks, and witch paraphernalia.

There is a **regional tourist office** in Goslar: the **Harzer Verkehrsverband,** Markstr. 45 (tel. (05321) 340 40), inside the **Industrie und Handels Kammer** building (open Mon.-Fri. 8am-4pm). Their indispensable *Grüner Faden fur den Harz-Gast* pamphlet (DM3) lists attractions and everything from ski schools, rentals, and lifts to tours on horseback. *Jugend und Freizeitheime im Harz und im Harzvorland* is a complete guide to youth hostels and student centers in the area. The *Museumsführer: Harz und Umgebung* booklet will tell you about every museum in every village. Also pick up the *Auto und Wanderkarte der ganzen Harz,* the map to hiking, biking, or driving through the region (DM10).

From train stations at Braunlage and **Bad Harzburg,** buses run to many towns and hamlets deep within the Harz. In addition to the towns listed below, consider expeditions to: **Hahnenklee,** a ski-area village known for its unusual **Stavekirke** (Norwegian Church), built without nails; **Lauterberg,** with tours of the abandoned Grube Samson mining works; and **St. Andreasberg** and **Bad Sachsa,** for more hiking and skiing. The easiest way to head east is by the bus line between Bad Harzburg and Wernigerode. A major drawback, however, is the fact that mountain-going motoring can be rather slow. When in the Harz, always be prepared for bad weather, especially sudden and violent rainstorms. Travelers should call the **Braunlage Wetterdienst** at (05520) 13 20 for summertime (April-Oct.) weather conditions. During the winter months (Nov.-Mar.), contact the **Goslar Wetterdienst** at (05321) 200 24.

BAD HARZBURG

The train from Hanover to the mountains ends at the Bad Harzburg *Bahnhof,* about 10 minutes past Goslar. The ruins of the imperial castle of Harzburg loom from the hills above, but there isn't much left—just flat piles of stones. Bad Harzburg may be a good place to stock up before hitting the Harz interior; otherwise, it offers little except mudbaths in costly spas. The other attraction is the **Märchenwald** (Fairy-Tale Forest), Nordhauser Str., a little play-park of mechanical houses relating 25 of the Brothers Grimm's finest tales (open daily 9am-6pm; admission DM4, children DM3).

The **tourist office** (tel. 29 27) to the left of the station will find rooms (DM30-50) for a DM5 fee (open Mon.-Fri. 9am-1pm and 3-6pm, Sat. 10am-1pm). Another branch is located at Herzog-Wilhelm-Str. 86 (tel. 753 30; fax 753 33; open Mon.-Fri. 9am-5pm, Sat. 9am-1pm). **Deutsche Bank,** at the start of pedestrian zone, provides **currency exchange** (open Mon. 8:30am-12:45pm and 2-4:30pm, Tues. and Thurs. 8:30am-12:45pm and 2-6pm, Wed. 8:30am-12:45pm, Fri. 8:30am-12:45pm and 2-3:30pm). The **post office** and **telephones** are next door in the **pedestrian zone** where Bummel Allee meets Herzog-Wilhelm-Str. (open Mon.-Fri. 8am-12:30pm and 3-5:30pm, Sat. 8am-noon). Take in some spectacular treetop scenery with the **Bergbahn,** located at the end of the pedestrian zone. Hauling skiers in the winter and snap-shooting tourists in the summer, this cable car runs up the Burgberg to 482m above sea level (DM4 to go up, DM3 to come down, DM6 round-trip; open mid-Dec. to mid-Nov.). Once on top, you can scope out the defunct castle and the stern black 1877 obelisk (dedicated to Bismarck) at the main viewpoint. For **ski rentals** and courses, see Torfhaus, p. 334. The **telephone code** is 05322.

A retreat owned by the "Naturfreunde" society, **Braunschweiger Haus,** Waldstr. 5 (tel. 45 82; fax 18 76), doubles as Bad Harzburg's **Jugendherberge.** From the station, take bus #73 and ask the driver for the "Lärchenweg" stop (the bus drives in two rings around the town and may not hit Lärchenweg until the second go-around), then take Im Bleichental to Waldstr. and go up the stone steps at the "Naturfreunde" sign. On foot, head right from the station to Silberbornstr. and follow its curves uphill to Im Bleichental (about 35min.); follow the above directions to the mountainside complex. A quintessential "cabin camp" feel. (Reception open 9-9:30am, 12:30-1pm and 6:30-7pm. DM 27, ages 12-18 DM24. Nonmembers DM35, ages 12-18 DM30. Sheets DM7. Breakfast included. Reservations recommended.) The bus to Goslar only stops at **Campingplatz Göttingerode** (tel. 812 15) if you ask the driver ahead of time. At the stop, head left. All the modern amenities: pool, sauna, hot showers, solarium, restaurant. (DM9 per tent, DM7 per person. Call ahead.)

There is a cheap, well-stocked **supermarket** to the right of the train station (open Mon.-Fri. 8:30am-6:30pm, Sat. 8am-1pm); people heading to Torfhaus and trails beyond should pick up food and camping supplies here or in the pedestrian zone, because none can be found in Torfhaus. A mountain-produce **market** appears in the park at Herzog-Julius-Str. and Schmiedstr. (open Thurs. 7am-1pm). Vegephobic Germans arrive later at the **Bad Harzburg Biergarten,** also in the market (tel. 62 30), to watch the vendors over a *Reichelbräu* (DM2.80) and a pair of Bavarian *Weißwürstchen* with sweet mustard and potato salad (DM5).

TORFHAUS

When Goethe began his first hike to the peak of the **Brocken mountain** in 1777, **Torfhaus** was nothing more than his launching point; nothing much has changed since then. The town, a humble crossroads 3km from the former inter-German border, offers worldly sophisticates little more than an airy mountain hostel, near-perfect hiking trails, and, at 1142m, the Harz's highest mountain. The Bad Harzburg-Braunlage bus (DM4.50) pauses here about every 90 minutes (Mon.-Fri. 7:45am-9pm). A left turn at the "Altenau-8km" sign will take you to the **Goetheweg;** the 16-km path to Brocken's peak hops the stream that used to divide Germany and occasionally follows the old patrol road along the Iron Curtain. About two hours from Torfhaus along the trail, you can stop and check out the **Brocken Museum** inside the **electronic war-**

fare post of the former East German state security service. The **Brockenbahn,** a narrow-gauge train, runs from the peak of the mountain to the Eastern Harz; scramble up and slide down the other side.

The **Nationalparkhaus Torfhaus,** Torfhaus 21 (tel. 263), provides maps of Brocken's trails (open daily 9am-5pm). **Ski-Verlieh,** adjacent to the tourist office and right by the bus stop, rents skis for DM5 per day. **Skizentrum Torfhaus,** Birkenweg 11 (tel. 22 75) offers weekend courses in Alpine and cross-country skiing (DM160 per 20hr., children DM140). The affiliated **Skischulbüro Stuhlpfarrer** (tel. 201), rents equipment next door (cross-country skis DM15 per day). Turn right at the "Altenau-8km" sign for the **Jugendherberge (HI),** Torfhaus 3 (tel. 242). The rooms here are designated by species of avian rather than by number. Proprietors will guide non-ornithologists to their rooms. (Reception open 8:15-9am, 12:15-1pm, and 6:15-7pm. Curfew 10pm. DM20.50, over 26 DM25. HI members only. Various levels of breakfast available; the top one, the strapping *"Harzer Oberländer,"* will add a couple of marks to your bill.) The **telephone code** is 05320.

▓ Hamelin (Hameln)

In the 700 years since the Pied Piper first strolled out of town, Hamelin has transformed from a rat trap to a tourist trap. The original story was sordid enough: after Hamelin failed to pay the piper his rat-removal fee, he walked off with 130 children in thrall. But today the legend of the *Rattenfänger,* as he is known in Germany, draws tourists as mysteriously as his flute drew rodents in 1284. What do people find so attractive about this legend? Its allegorical link to the settlement of the eastern regions, to which many of medieval Hamelin's citizens were lured? The cynical delight of comparing children to rabid rodents? In any case, the appeal of the dancing rats is a certainty upon which Hamelin has built a good deal of prosperity. Along the souvenir-choked streets today, you can almost hear the town mayor consoling grieving parents, "You haven't lost a child, you've gained a tourist industry."

Orientation and Practical Information The **tourist office,** on the Bürgergarten at Deisterallee (tel. 20 26 17 or 20 26 18; fax 20 25 00), tracks down rooms for a DM2 fee. From the station, cross Bahnhofplatz, go up Bahnhofstr., and turn left onto Deisterstr., which becomes Deisterallee (open Mon.-Fri. 9am-1pm and 2-6pm, Sat. 9:30am-12:30pm and 3-5pm, Sun. 9:30am-12:30pm; Oct.-April Mon.-Fri. 9am-1pm and 2-5pm). A smaller booth in the **Hochzeithaus** has **summertime information** (open mid-April to mid-Oct. Tues.-Fri. 11am-2pm and 2:30-4:30pm, Sat.-Sun. 10am-2pm). City **tours** take off from the Bürgergarten (Mon.-Sat. at 3pm, Sun. at 10am and 3pm). Hamelin bridges the Weser River, 45 minutes from Hanover by frequent **trains** (26 per day 4am-midnight). When riding **buses** in Hamelin, check the schedule carefully. If there is a "T" next to the time, a bus does not come. Instead, you must call 194 19 and tell the operator at least 45 minutes prior to departure that you would like a taxi; a Mercedes will then roll up and takes you along the bus route (DM2-4). **Oberweser-Dampfschiffahrt,** Inselstr. 3 (tel. 220 16; fax 230 40), runs **ferries** up and down the Weser River (April.-Sept.), offering a complete package of tours (1-hr. expeditions DM7.50, students DM5; call for a schedule and prices). **Rent a bike** (DM15 per 24hr.) from the **Troche Fahrräder repair shop,** Kreuzstr. 7 (tel. 136 70; open Mon.-Fri. 9:30am-1pm and 2:30-6pm, Sat. 9:30am-12:30pm). The hostel (see below) also rents bikes to guests (DM8 per day). For the **police** call 110. The **post office** is at Am Posthof 1, 31785 Hamelin (open Mon.-Fri. 8am-1pm and 2-5:30pm, Sat. 8am-1pm). The **telephone code** is 05151.

Accommodations and Camping The beautifully located but regrettably Piper-festooned **Jugendherberge (HI),** Fischbeckerstr. 33 (tel. 34 25; fax 423 16), sits on a dreamy bend in the *Weser.* From the station, take bus #2 to "Wehler Weg," and turn right onto Fischbeckerstr. By foot (35min.), cross Bahnhof Platz to Bahnhofstr., turn left on Deisterallee, right around 164-er Ring (along the Hamel rivulet) to Erich-str., as it bends into Fischbeckerstr. German school children *love* dreamy bends in rivers, so call ahead. Crowded rooms, but laid-back staff make a stay enjoyable. (Reception open 5-10pm. Curfew 10pm. Get a house key with a DM30 deposit. DM20, over 26 DM24.50. Breakfast included; magic flute to lure away the schoolkids is not. Sheets DM5.20. Laundry. Wash and dry DM6.)

Hamelin's tourist boom has resulted in a remarkably large number of *Pensionen*. The **Pension Grölling** (tel. 671 53), at Fuchsbau 11, is 40 minutes from the train station by foot; save yourself time by taking bus #31 to "Fuchsbau," right at the door. (DM35 per person.) Closer to the center is **Pension Wiese,** Alte Marktstr. 44 (tel. 39 72), directly across the street from the *Redenhof*. If you tire of watching that piper in tight pants prance around, ask Wiese to tell you how he escaped from the Russians in 1942 by faking nature's call—the visual accompaniment is very entertaining. (Reception open until 10pm. DM40 per person. Reservations highly recommended.) Southeast of the city center, on the Tönebön Lake, lies **Campground Jugendzeltplatz,** Tönebönweg 8 (tel. 262 23). From the *Bahnhof* or the *Altstadt*, take bus #51 to "Säd-bad." (Reception open Mon.-Fri. until 10pm, Sat.-Sun. until 11pm. DM5 per person. Open May-Sept.)

Food The streets of the *Altstadt* around the Ostenstr. and Pferdemarkt are lined by restaurants and cafés, but chances of finding a bargain are slim and none, and slim just left town. A few good deals can be found on the Bäckerstr. near the Münster. Duck into **Julia's Restaurant,** Bäckerstr. 57 (tel. 444 32). Spaghetti for DM6.40 and eight scrumptious potato dishes from DM8.50-9.90 (open mid-May to mid-Sept. Mon.-Fri. 10am-6:30pm. Sat. 10am-2pm, Sun. 11:30am-5pm; mid-Sept. to mid-May Mon.-Fri. 10am-6:30pm, Sat. 10am-2pm). *Hamelners* flock for fruit, vegetables, and other treats to the open-air **market** on the *Bürgergarten* (open Wed. and Sat. 8am-1pm). Hamelin boasts an impressive array of edible rodents. To catch these rats, pay to the tune of DM0.35 for tiny marzipan critters and up to DM6 for a jumbo pastry rat. Little crusty bread-rats cost DM3 at **Schnelz Reformhaus,** Osterstr. 18 in the *Altstadt*. The *Haus* also sells all-natural foodstuffs of every sort, a delight for the vegetarian with some cooking equipment (open Mon.-Fri. 8:30am-6pm, Sat. 8am-1pm).

Sights If you cringe at the thought of small rodents or little flute players in motley capes, Hamelin is probably not the best vacation spot; the Piper motif is inescapable. One of the few buildings unadorned by Pied Piper paraphernalia is the modern **Rat-haus.** In the courtyard out front, however, several elfin children hang suspended in mid-air, following a piper statue to the **Rattenfänger-Brunnen.** The **Bürgergarten,** right down the street, is a small but soothing relief from the tourist rat race. Chess players will enjoy the massive game board and 3-ft.-high pieces. (Garden open daily 7am-6:30pm; fountains run mid-May-mid-Sept. daily 11am-noon, 3-4pm, and 7:30-8pm.) Walk back down Kastanienwall and turn right into the massive auti-free zone that is the *Altstadt*. Off to the left, the **Rattenfängerhaus** (built in 1602) is decked out with dozens of startled-looking figureheads recalling the sudden surge in the average age of townsfolk. Trek down another 100m and find the 1589 **Leiesthaus,** Osterstr. 9 (tel. 20 22 15), where the **Museum Hameln** exhibits the Piper in 20 poses and 20,000 books (open Tues.-Sun. 10am-4:30pm; DM2, students and children DM1). The grim Rättenfänger tale is re-enacted each Sunday at noon (May-Sept., weather permitting) in a **Freilichtspiel** (open-air show) at the 1610 **Hochzeithaus** (wedding house). Small children dressed as rats chase a man in a multicolored suit and tight pants. At 10:05am the **Glockenspiel** on the *Hochzeithaus* plays the *Rattenfängerlied* (Pied Piper Song); at 11:05am you're serenaded by the *Weserlied*; and at 1:05, 3:35, and 5:35pm, a tiny stage emerges from the *Hochzeithaus* and "rats" circle around a peculiar wooden flautist.

■ Hann. Münden

Hann. Münden is embedded between forested hills where "the Fulda and the Werra kiss one another" (the newborn Weser popping out as a result of the consummation). Alexander von Humboldt called it "one of the seven most beautifully located cities in the world." With over 700 preserved *Fachwerkhäuser*, this is about the prettiest of Germany's six zillion half-timbered towns. The impeccable *Altstadt* remains refreshingly free of tourists despite its picture-book setting at the foot of the *Deutsche Märchenstraße* (German fairy-tale route). To taste the flavor of the town, strolling around aimlessly through the *Altstadt* (you can't go wrong) may work better than dragging yourself from sight to sight. If you do, however, rest assured that the town's polished façade has plenty to offer however you tackle it.

Orientation and Practical Information Get hiking maps *(Wanderkarten)* and the *Weg & Fähre*, a free and complete guide with information for the town and its environs, from the **tourist office** (tel. 753 13; fax 754 04), in the *Rathaus*. The staff will book you a room (DM30 and up) for no fee (open Mon.-Fri. 8:30am-1pm and 2-5pm, Sat. 8:30am-12:30pm; Oct.-April Mon.-Thurs. 8:30am-12:20pm and 2-4pm, Fri. 8:30am-12:30pm). Help is also on hand from the *Auskunftschalter* (information counter; tel. 750), in the same building, after the office closes (open May-Sept. daily until 9pm; Oct.-April daily until 8pm). Hann. Münden is easily accessible by **train** from Göttingen (35min.) or Kassel (20min.). **Ferries** navigate the Fulda, Weser, and Werra rivers with water tours of Hann. Münden (DM10 per adult). A confusing web of boat companies run the ferries, but the tourist office has a special department (tel. 75 31 33 15) to do all the work for you for free. Walking city **tours** of the *Altstadt* are given mid-May to October (Wed. and Sat. at 10am, Sun. at 9:30am; DM4). Rent **bikes** at **Campingplatz Münden** (see below; open 8am-10pm; DM10 per day). Paths along the Weser River lead to the *Tillyschanze* and continue on toward the **Reinhardswald Forest** area. **Hiking maps** are available at the hostel and the tourist office (DM10). The **telephone code** is 05541.

Accommodations, Camping, and Food Lodging in Hann. Münden in 1997 will be pretty tricky because of *documenta x* in Kassel (see documenta x, p. 318). Plan ahead and call early. The lace-curtained **Jugendherberge (HI),** Prof.-Oelkers-Str. 8 (tel. 88 53; fax 734 39), is just outside the town limits on the banks of the Weser. From the station (25min.), walk down Beethovenstr., turn left at Wallstr., cross the Pionierbrücke, turn right along Veckerhägerstr. (B3); or from the *Bahnhof* bus stop, take bus #135 (direction: Veckerhäger/Kasselerstr.) to "Jugendherberge." Bus #135 runs on the weekdays once per hour until 7pm, on Saturday until 2pm. On Sundays from June to September, catch bus #134 at 10:15am, 1:15 and 5:15pm only. A Bahn Card gets you a 40% discounts on all travel in the *Altstadt*. (Reception open 5-7pm and 9:45-10pm. Curfew 10pm. DM20, over 26 DM24.50. Breakfast included. Sheets DM6.) Close by the Mühlenbrücke, **Gasthaus "Im Anker,"** Bremer Schlagd 18 (tel. 49 23), offers comfortable rooms with fantastic views of the Werra. (Reception open until 10pm. DM45 per person. Breakfast included.) **Gabreiele Hansmann's Pension,** Speckstr. 4 (tel. 88 80), has four beds with a great location in the *Altstadt*. (Reception open until 10pm. DM40 per person. Breakfast included.) Pitch your tent in view of the city walls at **Campingplatz Münden,** Oberer Tanzwerder (tel. 122 57), 10 minutes from the train station on an island in the Fulda River off Pionierbrücke. There is a small **restaurant** on the premises, **canoe and bike rentals** are available, and hot showers are on tap. (Reception open daily 8am-1pm and 3-10pm. DM8.50 per person, DM3.50 per tent. DM3.50 per auto. DM2 for man's best friend. Open April to mid-Sept.) Eat out at bakeries (Langestr. is flooded with them) or catch the **Markt** behind the *Rathaus* (Wed. and Sat. 7am-1pm). For a little bit of historic action, dine at the **Tillyhaus,** Marktstr. 15 (tel. 42 48), where the infamous general lived for 5 years during the town's occupation. Beer starts at a low DM1.90 (open Mon.-Sat. 10am-2am, Sun. 2pm-2am).

Sights Weave through the angled sidestreets to admire the 14th-century *Fachwerkhäuser* (half-timbered houses); some of the oldest and most impressive are tucked away on **Ziegelstraße.** The 16th-century **Hinter der Stadtmauer 23,** a Jewish School since 1796, was gutted in 1938. A plaque stands outside in memoriam. Recent owners restored it and uncovered a ritual bath *(Mikwe)* in the basement. The ornate **Rathaus** is a prime example of the Weser-Renaissance style that originated in the area around 1550. To reach the **Rathaus** from the train station, walk straight down Bahnhofstr., take a right at Burgstr., and continue on until you reach Markstr.; take a left here, and the *Rathaus* is on your left. Centuries-old markings of Weser flood heights mark the *Rathaus* corner walls, but more artistic coloring-book scenes out of the city's past line the **Rathaushalle** walls inside. Outside, figurines appear from the upper windows of the *Rathaus* to dance to the merry melodies played on the bells hanging from the façade daily at noon, 3, and 5pm. Also outside is the wagon of Hann. Münden's former resident and favorite tourist gimmick, **Doctor Eisenbart,** an 18th-century traveling physician whose ability to treat many illnesses was overshadowed by his reputation as a quack and a swindler. The comic story of his life is played out every Sunday from June to August on the stage in front of the *Rathaus* (at 11:15am; admission DM4). The striking **St. Blasiuskirche,** opposite the *Rathaus,* is decked out in periwinkle and emerald, with ornate Solomonic columns surrounding the altar, a somber *Rittergrabmal,* and a 15th-century crucifix (open Mon.-Fri. 11am-12:30pm and 2-5pm, Sat. 11am-12:30pm, Sun. 2-6pm).

Hann. Münden's three islands, **Doktorwerder, Unterer Tanzwerder,** and **Oberer Tanzwerder** are all easily accessible by small, historic bridges on the outskirts of the *Altstadt.* The U.K.'s hired guns, the famed Hessian mercenaries, took off from the islet's former pier to face off against the upstart American colonists. The best view of the valley is from across the Fulda, atop the 1882 **Tillyschanze** tower, built to commemorate May 30, 1626. On this day during the Thirty Years War, General Tilly stormed through Hann. Münden, slaughtering over 2000 citizens. The path is unmarked; follow the occasional concrete-slab steps and wire fences. Ask at the adjacent Gasthaus kiosk to magically open the door (tower open 7am-dusk; DM1). On the banks of the Werra, the austere **Welfenschloß** proves that not all Weser Renaissance buildings look like over-iced birthday cakes. The gray parts of the building are remnants of the original Gothic structure that burned down in 1560. The sumptuous interior can only be admired on a guided tour (Sat. at 2:30pm; meet in front of the *Rathaus;* DM4). It also houses the **Städtisches Museum** that boasts a sizeable fayence collection (18-19th centuries) and several neo-Baroque sculptures of Gustav Eberlein (open Wed.-Fri. 10am-noon and 2:30-5pm, Sat. 10am-noon and 2:30-4pm, Sun. 10am-12:30pm; admission DM2, students DM1). Wander along the city walls that still show seven of the original defense towers, as well as the 1329 **Alte Werrabrücke** and the **St. Aegiden Kirche,** built in the 12th century but another victim of Tilly—a nearby *Pulverturm* (gun powder tower) exploded and ignited the church.

■ Hildesheim

The **Tausend Jähriger Rosenstock** (The Thousand-Year-Old Bush), symbolizing the prosperity of the town of Hildesheim, is known throughout the world. According to legend, Emperor Ludwig der Fromme (the Pious) lost his way after a hunt and hanged his Marian relic on the branch of a conspicuous rose bush. He managed to find his way home, and the next day, remembering his relic, returned only to find it fastened to the branch. He interpreted this as a divine sign and erected a chapel on the site, around which grew the majestic **Dom** and the town of Hildesheim. As long as the bush flourishes, so will Hildesheim. On March 22, 1945, Allied bombers flattened the town. Amazingly, the bush survived. The collapsed ruins of the *Dom* sheltered the roots from the flames. Eight weeks later, 25 buds were growing strong.

Today the chapel, called the **Annenkapelle,** and the bush, the *Tausend-Jährige Rosenstock,* are featured in the *Dom*'s courtyard (open Mon.-Sat. 9:30am-5pm, Sun. noon-5pm; admission DM0.50, children DM0.30). The **Diözesan Museum,** around to your left as you exit the *Dom*, showcases the Marian relic of old Ludwig—it's #8 on the "Schlacht bei Dinklar" exhibit—and other ecclesiastical goodies. (*Dom* open Mon.-Fri. 9:30am-5pm, Sat. 9am-2pm, Sun. noon-5pm. Museum open Tues.-Sat. 10am-5pm, Sun. noon-5pm. Cool admission ticket DM4, students DM1.50.) The **Marktplatz** is a plaza of reconstructed half-timber buildings and archways featuring the majestic **Knochenhauer-Amtshaus.** (Butcher's Guild House), reputed to be the "most beautiful wooden structure in the world." The façade is lavishly decorated with colorful paintings and German proverbs (e.g. *arm oder reich, der Tod macht alles gleich*—poor or rich, death treats all the same). South of the city center at the intersection of Gelber Stern (Yellow Star) and Lappenberg, lie the remains of Hildesheim's **synagogue.** The temple itself was torched on *Kristallnacht* in 1938, and a memorial has been erected on the site, bearing witness to scars which can't be erased by restoration. The warped façade of the 1606 **Wernerhaus** (down from Gelber Stern to Brühl) rests untouched by bombs or modernization.

Looping back around the western tip, drop in at the **Römer-und Pelizaeus-Museum,** Am Steine 1 (tel. 936 90), featuring a colorful collection of Egyptian art, as well as frequent and extensive special exhibits, ranging from "The World of the Whale" (presented by Greenpeace) to displays documenting the history of ancient Persia (open Tues.-Sun. 9am-4:30pm; admission DM12, students DM9).

The **tourist office,** at Am Ratsbauhof 1c (tel. 179 80; fax 17 98 88), two blocks from the *Rathaus,* offers brochures and also books rooms for a DM5 fee. From the *Hauptbahnhof,* walk straight up Bernwardstr. which becomes Almsstr., turn left onto Rathausstr., and turn right down Ratsbauhof (open Mon.-Fri. 9am-6pm, Sat. 9am-1pm). There is also a **branch office** in the **Kirchturm** of St. Andreas Church that passes out maps and city guides (open Sat. 10am-5pm, Sun. noon-6pm). Two-hour city **tours** start April-Nov. Sun.-Fri. at 2pm and Sat. at 10am (DM5 per person). **Telephones** are left of the train station. Hildesheim is 45km southeast of Hanover, with good *Autobahn* connections and almost hourly **trains. Bus** tickets cost DM2.20 and are good for one hour of unlimited rides. The **post office** is open Monday to Friday 8am-6pm, Saturday 8am-1pm. The **telephone code** is 05121.

To reach Hildesheim's pastoral **Jugendherberge (HI),** Schirr-manweg 4 (tel. 427 17; fax 478 47), take bus #1 (direction: Himmelstür) to "Am Dammtor" and switch onto bus #4 (direction: Bockfeld) to "Triftstr." Cross the street and climb up the hill to the hostel (25min.). Rooms have 4 to 6 beds and colors of blue. (Reception open Mon.-Sat. 8-9:30am, 5-7pm, and 9:45-10pm; Sun. 6-7pm and 9:45-10pm. Curfew 10pm, but a housekey is available for a DM50 deposit. DM20, over 26 DM24.50. Breakfast included. Sheets DM5.70.) A little further out, but well worth the extra trouble, head to **Maria Schröder's Pensione,** Bleckenstedterstr. 2 (tel. 434 21). From the train station, hop on bus #1 (direction: Hammelstür) to "Am Dammtor." Backtrack and turn left down Schützenweisestr. and turn right down Bleckenstedterstr. Frau Schroeder has got to be one of the nicest ladies in Germany, and amazingly enough, her rooms are almost as big as her heart. Plush sofas will have you feeling like a million *Marks* (DM30 per person). Another good pick is **Hotel Marheineke,** Peiner Landstr 189 (tel, 526 67). Take line 10 (direction: Bauenstedt) to "Alt Drispenstedt," backtrack 10m, make a right onto Peiner Landstr., and then a quick left through the pedestrian tunnel. Or take bus #1 (direction: Bavenstedt) to "Ehrlicherstr.," walk back 50m, hang a right on Peiner Landstr., and follow the above. (Reception open until 10pm. Singles DM50. Doubles DM80. Toss in a shower and it's DM90.) Pick up fresh fruits in the **Markt** on front of the *Rathaus* (Wed. and Sat. 7am-1pm). **Aldente,** an der Lilie 17 (tel. 13 11 20), on the street parallel to Rathausstr., features a diverse crowd and beer from DM3.80 (open Mon.-Thurs. 11am-1am, Fri. 11am-2pm, Sat. 10am-2am, Sun. 10am-1am. Kitchen open daily noon-9pm and 6-11pm).

▓ Bodenwerder

In the land of **Baron von Münchhausen,** the King of Liars, you might not be sure what to believe. Here on the banks of the Weser, the Baron first told his hunting buddies his fabulous adventure stories of flying to the Moon and sailing through a sea of milk to an island of cheese. But is the pathological genius himself a fabrication of Bodenwerder's tourist industry, an attempt to out-fable Hamelin? Verily not: the little town's church ledgers have birth and death listings for Baron Hieronymus Carolus Friedericus von Münchhausen. More useful truths can be found on the carved wooden signs which point out the various sights of Bodenwerder.

On Münchhausplatz, the Baron's mansion-turned-**Rathaus** holds the **Münchhausenzimmer Museum** (tel. 405 47), where he was born. Inside, you'll find color illustrations of his exploits along with the legendary pistol with which he shot his horse off a steeple (admission DM2, students DM1.50, children DM0.50). The same ticket gets you into the **Heimat Museum,** on the other side of the *Rathaus,* where you can see pictures of Bodenwerder as an island in the Weser before it was dammed up (both open April-Oct. daily 10am-noon and 2-5pm). The landmark **fountain** outside shows the Baron watering his horse, whose hindquarters were sliced off in battle, and later retrieved. As the story goes, the Baron's farrier sewed the poor animal's booty together with twigs and laurels, which sprouted into a tree, providing the rider shade for the rest of his expeditions. The streets lining the **Fußgängerzone** (pedestrian zone) are riddled with 114 half-timbered houses; the oldest dot Königstr, Homburgstr., and Grossestr. Further up the pedestrian zone is a beautiful fountain depicting three of the Baron's most outrageous adventures.

For a list of events in Bodenwerder, pick up a copy of *Weg und Fähre* at the **tourist office,** Weserstr. 3 (tel. 405 41; fax 405 40; open Mon.-Fri. 9am-12:30pm and 2:30-6pm, Sat. 9am-12:30pm). City **tours** start at 3pm every Wednesday out front (DM3). Bodenwerder is 24km northeast of Hamelin. Take **bus** #48/520 or #48/523 (Bahn Card valid). Rent **bikes** from **Karl-Heinz-Greif,** Danzigerstr. 20 (tel. 33 34; fax 931 45), for DM10 per day (open Mon.-Fri. 8:30am-12:30pm and 2:30-6pm, Sat. 8:30am-1pm, Sun. 9-10:30am).The **post office,** 37619 Bodenwerder, is located across the street from the *Rathaus* (open Mon.-Fri. 8:30am-noon and 2:30-5pm, Sat. 8:30-11:30am). The **telephone code** is 05533.

The **Zimmernachweis,** on the corner of Weserstr. and Münchhausen Platz, lists updated information on room addresses and vacancies. As always check the room before agreeing; after all, the town hero is a con artist. Bodenwerder's **Jugendherberge (HI),** Richard-Schirmann-Weg (tel. 26 85; fax 62 03), is a 10-minute walk from the *Fußgängerzone,* but the last 100m is steep, steep, steep. See if you can get a local to shoot you up there via cannonball, or walk across the Weser River (via bridge, that is) and turn left, then right on Siemenstr., and follow the signs up Unter dem Berge. The institutional exterior conceals a fun-filled interior brimming with *Fußball* and ping-pong. (Reception open 3-10pm. Curfew 10pm. DM19.50, over 26 DM23.50. Breakfast included. Lunch DM6.70. Sheets DM5.70.) In the *Altstadt,* **Pension Mistral** (tel. 55 70), at Mittelweg 1, is the best pick. Light, clean rooms cost DM30-40 per person. Across the street, **Pension Haus Becker,** Homburgstr. 47, offers only a handful of rooms (DM25 per person). Reception conducted through the Strand Hotel, Homburgstr 53 (tel. 20 63; fax 50 26).

Cheap meals in Bodenwerder are hard to come by, so even the locals take advantage of the food service in the youth hostel's dining hall (DM6.50-8.50; lunch at noon, dinner at 6pm). The restaurant **Andreas-Das Pils** has Italian specialties from DM9 and Balkan dishes from DM14.50. On the first Sunday of each month, from May to October, a **free play** in the Spa Gardens reenacts Münchhausen's exploits. On the second Saturday of August, Bodenwerder sets the Weser ablaze with its pyrotechnic **Festival of Lights.** When the Weser isn't scintillating, the fledgling ferry company **Personenschiffahrt Mahr** (tel. 16 19; fax 63 58) sends its flagship, the Baron von Münchhausen, on hour-long cruises of the Weser (offices directly under the Weserbrücke bridge; cruises daily starting at 11am; DM7, children 6-14 DM4).

■ Braunschweig

Now that Braunschweig's Cold War border town duties are over, this middleweight city is pumping up its cultural attractions. The history of Braunschweig (sometimes called "Brunswick" in English) began in 1166, when Heinrich der Löwe (Henry the Lion) settled here. After hanging up his hat, Henry set about building a kingdom: he erected the famous Braunschweig lion statue (now the city's most legible symbol) and inaugurated Braunschweig's ascent into a thriving center of medieval religion and commerce. The town is saturated with gargantuan cathedrals and other religious monuments that once marked the free city's economic importance to the Holy Roman Empire. An alumnus of the Hanseatic League, Braunschweig's robust economy and brash bids for tourism make it one of Lower Saxony's most vital cities.

ORIENTATION AND PRACTICAL INFORMATION

Braunschweig crouches between the Lüneburger Heide and the Harz Mountains. It serves as the crossing point for high-speed trains connecting Frankfurt and Hanover to Berlin and other lines. The *Hauptbahnhof* lies southeast of the city center, essentially an island ringed by the Oker River. Walking straight from the *Bahnhof* brings you across Berliner Platz to the wide Kurt-Schumacher-Str. This curves to the left to meet John-F.-Kennedy Platz, a major crossroad at the southeast corner of the central city. Following Auguststr. northwest from Kennedy Platz leads to the center city. Braunschweig's downtown attractions are mostly within the great circle formed by the branching Oker. Streetcars and buses criss-cross the city; most lines pass through either the "Rathaus"/"Bohlweg" stops (downtown) or "JFK Platz"/"K. Schumacher-Str." stops (a 10-min. walk from the *Bahnhof*).

Tourist Offices: There are two tourist offices in town; one is immediately in front of the train station (open Mon.-Fri. 8am-6pm, Sat. 9am-noon) and the other a block from the *Rathaus*, Pavilion Bohlweg (tel. 27 35 50 or 273 55 30; fax 273 55 19 or 273 55 39; open Mon.-Fri. 9am-6pm, Sat. 9:30am-12:30pm). An excellent free map is available from the bus-and-tram ticket booth outside the station. The Bohlweg branch is more full-featured, offers **tours** (Sun. 10:30am) and helps find rooms in pensions (DM39 and up) for a DM3 fee; they also speak English.

Mitwohnzentrale: Heinrichstr. 37 (tel. 194 45), in the suburbs of town. From the *Hauptbahnhof,* take bus #19 (direction: Europlatz) to "Jasperallee." Walk up Hagenring 2 blocks and make a right on Heinrichstr.—the office is on the right. Friendly and effective for long-term arrangements as well as overnight stays. They ask a commission of 15% of the first-night price for stays of less than a week, and the percentages go down from there. Open Mon.-Tues. 10am-1pm and 3-6pm, Wed. 10am-1pm, Thurs. 1-6pm, Fri. 11am-4pm

Currency Exchange: The **post office** offers decent rates and cashes traveler's checks for a charge of DM3 per check.

American Express: Casparistr. 1 (tel. 242 83 10; fax 428 39), located in the center of town near the "Hagenmarkt" stop. Cashes traveler's checks at no charge. Also sells traveler's checks and exchanges money. Open Mon.-Wed. and Fri. 9am-6pm, Thurs. 9am-7pm, Sat. 9am-1pm.

Telephones: Outside the post office.

Public Transportation: A thorough system of **streetcars** and **buses** laces Braunschweig and its environs. 90-min. tickets, valid for any number of line changes, are sold as single cards (DM2.80), double cards (DM4.60), or in packs of 10 (DM22); 24-hr. cards (DM7) or 48-hr. (DM12); week and month passes are also available. Pick up a network **map** *(Liniennetzplan)* at the tourist office.

Taxis: call 555 55 or 621 21. Call 444 44 for **Frauennacht-Taxi** (women's taxi).

Car Rental: Hertz, Berliner Platz 1D (tel. 710 55), near the station. Turn left from Lathe Bahnhof, and you'll see the office. Open Mon.-Fri. 7am-6pm, Sat. 8am-noon.

Bike Rental: Deutsche Bahn's **Fahrrad am Bahnhof** at the train station is a nice deal for rail travelers. Bike rental is just DM9 per day with a valid railpass or same-day DB ticket of at least DM16. Otherwise, it costs DM13 per day.

Mitfahrzentrale: ADM, Wollmarkt 3 (tel. 194 40), is the local ride-share place. Open Mon.-Fri. 10am-6pm, Sat.-Sun. 10am-2pm.

Bookstores: Pressezentrum Salzman, in the Burgpassage Galerie mall, sells paperback pulp novels as well as English and American magazines and newspapers. Open Mon.-Fri. 8:30am-6:30pm, Sat. 9am-2pm.

Library: Öffentliche Bücherei, Hintern Brüdern 23 (tel. 470 68 36), right off Langestr. Main building open Mon.-Fri. 11am-7pm, but the **foreign language library** is only open Tues. noon-6pm and Fri. 11am-4pm.

Student Agency: ASTA (tel. 391 45 55), to the right of the cafeteria on Katharinenstr. This university-sponsored office finds summer housing and has information on women's and gay and lesbian activities. Open Mon.-Fri. 10am-2pm.

Laundromat: Göttingstr. 1, near the university. Wash DM6. Open Mon.-Sat. 6am-11pm.

Pharmacy: Apotheke am Kennedy Platz, corner of Auguststr. and Kurt-Schumacher-Str., right on the Kennedy Platz. Open Mon.-Fri. 8am-6:30pm, Sat. 9am-1pm. **Notdienst** (emergency service) information posted on the door.

Emergency: Police: tel. 110. **Ambulance:** tel. 440 33.

Post Office: The main office, 38106 Braunschweig (tel. 70 90), is in the enormous 16-story building to the right of the train station. Open Mon.-Fri. 8am-4pm and 6-7pm, Sat. 8am-1pm, Sun. 9am-noon.

Telephone Code: 0531.

ACCOMMODATIONS

Considering its size, Braunschweig's budget accommodation cupboard is pretty bare. Little that is inexpensive can be found within walking distance; most affordable pensions and private rooms require a 10- to 15-minute bus or streetcar ride. Pick up a free copy of *Hotels und Gaststätten* at the tourist office. It includes a listing of accommodations and some cafés with prices, phone numbers, and city maps.

Jugendgästehaus (HI), Salzdahlumerstr. 170 (tel. 622 68 or 622 69; fax 636 54). Bus #11 (from the main station, direction: Welfenplatz): "Klinikum" (according to the map)/Krankenhaus-Salzdahlumer (according to the bus). By foot, walk left from the station on Berliner Platz to H.-Büssing-Ring, turn left on Salzdahlumerstr.; it's under the overpass, then 20min. down the road. Far from town, these antiseptic buildings contain bright, spacious rooms. Members only. Reception open 7am-10pm. No curfew. DM18-36, depending on number of roommies, over 26 DM22-36. Breakfast DM7. Kitchen facilities (DM2). Sheets included. Key deposit DM30.

Hotel-Pension Wienecke, Kuhstr. 14 (tel. 464 76; fax 464 64). From the station, walk up Kurt-Schumacher-Str. to J.-F.-Kennedy Platz, bear right onto Auguststr. and then Kuhstr. (15min.). Quiet, comfortable rooms with big windows and TVs. Singles DM65-88. Doubles DM120-130. Reservations strongly recommended.

FOOD

A plethora of *Kneipen* (bars) and *Imbiß* kiosks along **Bohlweg,** the eastern boundary of the *Innenstadt,* proffer pizzas, salads, soups, and small sandwiches at reasonable prices. There's a produce market in the *Altstadt* every Wednesday and Saturday 8am-1:30pm. The **Kohlmarkt** area, southeast of the *Altstadt Markt* in the city center, is a bustling, breezy open space with many pleasant (though not terribly cheap) cafés and restaurants.

Student-Mensa, Katharinenstr. Hardly gourmet, but five selections are offered (DM1.50-4.20). Ask a student to buy you a meal ticket, technically only available to university affiliates. Open for lunch Mon.-Fri. 11:15am-2:25pm, Sat. 11:15am-1:55pm; dinner Mon.-Thurs. 4:30-8pm.

Delicato, Münzstr. 9, straight down 3 blocks from Burgplatz, protruding from the corner of Münzstr. and Kattreppeln. A top-notch Turkish specialty deli with salads and fresh-baked lasagna. Specials like fat, warm eggplant half with spiced lamb and tomatoes, plus potato salad (DM7.90). Have them cater your next party in Lower Saxony. Open Mon.-Wed. and Fri. 9am-6:30pm, Thurs. 9am-8:30pm.

Café L'Emigré, Hinter Liebfrauen, near St. Ägidienkirche. A *papier-mâché* centaur is the centerpiece of this Turkish bistro, which features a fully stocked vegetarian menu that includes falafels and Greek salads, in addition to a large selection of kebabs. Meals DM5-15. Open Mon.-Thurs. and Sun. 3pm-2am, Fri.-Sun. 3pm-3am.

Cafe MM, Kuhstr. 6 (tel. 422 44), near Hotel-Pension Wienecke, offers omelettes, salads, and pastas (DM5.50-13.80). The ritzy sidewalk café has antipasto specials and many other tasty morsels (DM6-10.50) from noon-2pm and after 5pm. Open Mon.-Thurs. 8am-midnight, Fri.-Sat. 8am-2am, Sun. 8am-midnight.

Atlantik's Früchtchen, in the Burgpassage Galerie mall, is a fruit stand with frequent sales and unbelievably low prices. An impressive assortment of fresh fruits and veggies with a sprinkler-mist system simulating sparkling morning dew.

SIGHTS

All of Braunschweig was once crowded on a small island surrounded by offshoots of the Oker River; the streams now form a moat-like line around the *Altstadt*. Braunschweig's medieval sights encircle the cobbled **Burgplatz**, over which the city's (and Heinrich's) emblem, a **bronze lion**, stands guard. First cast in 1166 as a symbol of Heinrich's regional dominance, the lion is challenged by the **St. Blasius Cathedral,** which towers over the city center. The 12th-century **Dom** shows an endearing touch of the occult: twisting Gothic columns, deeply colored stained-glass windows, an original 12th-century wooden crucifix, and a dragon-supported candelabra. The **crypt** below holds the sarcophagi of Heinrich the Löwe, his consort, and his fan club—its eerie grounds seem like a meeting ground for vampires (open daily 10am-5pm; admission free; crypt DM2, students DM1). The original Braunschweiger lion has retreated to the confines of the **Dankwarderode Castle,** also on the Burgplatz. Originally Heinrich's 12th-century den, it now keeps a modest trove of saints' relics (open Tues.-Sun. 10am-5pm; admission to castles and museums DM6, students DM3; combined ticket for castle and Braunschweig's other museums DM11, students DM6). To reach the historic center, take streetcar #1 from the train station; or walk (15min.) along Kurt-Schumacher-Str., then bear right at J.-F.-Kennedy Platz through Ägidienmarkt onto Bohlweg. **St. Martin's Cathedral,** in the *Altmarkt*, was built concurrently with the St. Blasius Cathedral. Its magnificently ornamented interior includes sculptures of the Wise and Foolish Virgins (open Tues.-Fri. 10am-1pm and 3-5pm, Sat. 10am-1pm, Sun. 10am-noon; free).

The **Braunschweig Landesmuseum** (tel. 484 26 02), across from the castle, also has a copy of the bronze lion; more copies can be found at the *Rathaus* in the *Altstadt*, in squares of neighboring villages, and, *ad infinitum*, at the tourist office. If the sight of the cat grows tiresome, direct your cat-eyes elsewhere: like at a 200,000,000,000 Reichsmark bill (issued in the hyper-inflationary 1920s) and the Trabant and Volkswagen parked upstairs (open Tues.-Wed. and Fri.-Sun. 10am-5pm, Thurs. 10am-8pm; DM5, students DM3.50). The Landesmuseum also has a branch at Hinter Ägidien devoted to **Jewish culture** (tel. 484 26 25). A reconstruction of the main room of the old synagogue hauntingly complements memorials to victims of the Holocaust. The furniture is all authentic, rescued from the deteriorating synagogue (open Tues.-Wed. and Fri.-Sun. 10am-5pm, Thurs. 10am-8pm; DM5, students DM3.50). The **Herzog Anton Ulrich Museum,** on Museumstr. (tel. 484 24 00 00) in the eastern part of town, was the first European museum to open its doors to the general public. Its galleries are papered with Dutch masterpieces, including works by van Dyck, Vermeer, and Rubens. A special room is set aside a group of five Rembrandts, charting the artist's stylistic development over the decades (open Tues. and Fri.-Sun. 10am-5pm, Wed. 10am-8pm; DM5, students DM3.50). Down the street, the world's first motorcycle is poised at the entry to the **Städtisches Museum** on Am Löwenwall (tel. 470 45 40). It's a specialized "domestic museum;" holdings include historical originals of furniture, appliances, and things in your living room (open Tues.-Wed. and Fri.-Sun. 10am-5pm, Thurs. 10am-8pm; DM5, students DM3.50).

The **Neues Rathaus,** at the "Rathaus" bus stop on Bohlweg near the Burgplatz, is a textbook example of the turn-of-the-century neo-Gothic style. The 1900 edifice boasts jutting spires, golden sandstone walls, russet roof tiles—the works. Possibly the most relaxing place in Braunschweig, the **Löwenwall** is an oval-shaped park in the eastern part of the Innenstadt Island, near the Städtisches Museum. The obelisk flanked by lions between two splashing fountains is a monument to the city nobles who died in the Napoleonic Wars. The **Staatstheater,** built in 1861 to replace the Court Theater on Haymarkt where Lessing's *Emilia Galotti* and Goethe's *Faust* premiered, offers an extensive, inexpensive repertoire. Decent seats for good shows run DM15-46, but students get all tickets at half-price. The program for 1997 includes *Waiting for Godot, Three Penny Opera,* and *The Magic Flute.* Write or call (tel. 484 27 38) one month prior to the show, or get leftover seats one hour before the performance (box office open Mon.-Fri. 10am-1pm and 4-6pm, Sat. 10am-1pm).

NIGHTLIFE

Braunschweig has several free monthly magazines that can fill you in on local events: *Subway, Da Capo,* and *Extra Dry.* It's telling that these magazines sometimes direct readers to cities as far away as Hamburg. Still, the Braunschweig scene heats up to a steady simmer on the weekend. The most lively area is the square formed by the intersection of Sack, Vor der Burg, and Schuhstraße, as well as the nearby Neue Straße. **Movie,** Neue Straße 2, is a happy bar that has a vague thematic association with movies (open daily 10am-2am). **The Jolly Joker,** Broitzemarstr. 220 (tel. 838 90), contains everything desirable in a night club. Its titanic premises have a large dance floor, six bars, a beer garden, a cheap restaurant (fast-food meals DM5), and a Brechtian movie theater that offers a bar and pop-culture flicks. Buses #19, 5, and 6 stop at "Broitzemerstr." (open Mon. 9pm-2am, Tues. 9pm-3am, Thurs. 9pm-2:30am, Fri.-Sat. 9pm-4:30am; cover DM3; movies free).

■ Wolfenbüttel

Just a few km from Braunschweig lies Wolfenbüttel, its pretty little sister city. Most of the area suburbs are in Braunschweig, as well as the bus depots and many civil services, so the outlines of Wolfenbüttel's meticulous Baroque-era urban planning remain largely intact. Though a few of the city's old half-timbers show their age, the dominant aura is one of well-kept prosperity; the good vibes swell from the **Schloßplatz,** the riverside enclave within the city that features shady lawns and a bevy of brightly colored historical attractions.

Once a stately, pure-white vision, the ducal **Schloß** (tel. 57 13) has been repainted in crimson with white trim. The cheery castle has its roots in a 13th-century fortress of the Guelphs, but its current appearance is pure Baroque with a beautifully-proportioned 17th-century clock tower. A small **Schloßmuseum** displays restored rooms from the ducal living quarters (be sure to indulge in a view of the ceilings!). In good weather, the **Braunschweig Staatstheater** puts on open-air performances in the castle enclosure. There's only room for a few hundred seats, so call the Wolfenbüttel tourist office for dates and ticket reservations (museum and castle interior open Tues.-Sat. 10am-5pm, Sun. 10am-1pm; admission to museum DM3).

Across the street from the *Schloß* is the C-shaped **Lessinghaus** (tel. 80 80), a compact mansion that was the local duke's gift to big-time *litérateur* Gotthold Ephraim Lessing, the court librarian of the nearby Augusta-Bibliothek. The museum inside recalls Lessing's life and work through manuscripts, letters, and paintings (open Tues.-Sun. 10am-5pm). Across a tree-dotted lawn from the Lessinghaus, the stern **Herzog-August-Bibliothek** guards a priceless collection of medieval and Renaissance books. Under the loving care of bookworm Duke August (who reigned 1634-1666), the library became the largest in Europe. A series of illuminated medieval manuscripts culminates with a facsimile of the famous **Braunschweiger Evangelier,** a kaleidoscopically-illuminated gospel drawn up in the late 12th century at the request of

Heinrich der Löwe; Lower Saxony shelled out millions of *Marks* for the manuscript in 1983. The original is locked safely away. Across from the castle is the 17th-century **Zeughaus;** the festive high-gabled façade belies its former role as an armory. It now serves as a library annex holding the other half of the Herzog-August collection. (Open Tues.-Sun. 10am-5pm. The two libraries and the Lessinghaus each sell admission tickets for DM6, students DM3, but a ticket from one attraction is good for the other two. The **Schloßmuseum,** unfortunately, is separate.)

The city's other major sight, the **Hauptkirche BMV** (that's short for "Blessed Virgin Mary," not a Bavarian auto company), throws up its spires across town in the Heinrichstadt section. An aggressive stone-gray edifice, a jutting four-faced clock tower and full-sized statues of saints grace the church's exterior. (Open April-Oct. Tues.-Fri. 10am-12:30pm and 2-5pm, Sat. 10am-12:30pm and 2-4pm; Nov.-Mar. Tues.-Sat. 10am-12:30pm and 2-4pm. Free, but they encourage a donation of DM1 for the pamphlet.) The sights of Wolfenbüttel capture the atmosphere of Candyland—the pink **Trinitatiskirche** (in the Holzmarkt), the houses of Kanzlertstr. bespeckled with polka-dots, and the **Kanzlei** (Royal Chancellery), on Kanzlerstr., look like the results of architects fighting over the gingerbread man. The *Kanzlei* can only be described as an absurdist mini-castle, with red walls and a bizarre metal statue perched outside, defying architectural jargon (it looks like a wascally wabbit).

The Wolfenbüttel **tourist office,** Stadtmarkt 9 (tel. 864 87; fax 864 42), faces the half-timbered square. From the station, head left on Bahnhofstr. across the Oker River, continuing to the intersection where Kommißstr. bears slightly left. The street turns sharply right and opens onto Kornmarkt Platz; turn left and head two blocks north to reach the *Stadtmarkt.* They lack a room finding service but book rooms in hotels for no fee and lead **tours** from the *Schloßplatz* for DM3 (April-Sept. Wed. 3pm and Sun. 11am; Oct.-March Sun 11am. Office open Jan.-March Mon.-Fri. 9am-12:30pm and 2-4pm, Sat. 9am-1pm, April-Dec. Mon.-Fri. 8am-12:30pm and 2-4pm). Wolfenbüttel's **postal code** is 38300. The **telephone code** is 05331.

Wolfenbüttel has a first-class **Jugendgästehaus,** Jägerstr. 17 (tel. 271 89). Take Bahnhofstr. to Schulwall and turn left; now keep going until the Schloßplatz. From here, walk east across the river on the long Dr.-Heinrich-Jasper-Str., and take little Glockengaße left until it stops at Jägerstr. Turn right, and look for the *Fachwerk* on the far side of the street. Everything is new; you get free access to **laundry machines.** (No curfew. DM22, over 25 DM28. Breakfast included. Sheets DM2.50. Call ahead.) The **market** displays its bounty every Wed. and Sat. with fresh fruit stands (open daily 8am-1pm). Krambudenstr., just off the center of the *Stadtmarkt,* has many a bistro and bakery. **Casablanca Billard Bistro,** Okerstr. 17a, profers up sandwiches (DM4.50-7.50) and soups (DM4.50) under the shade of artificial palms and a Bogey poster (open Mon.-Fri. 10am-2am, Sat. 10am-3am, Sun. 4pm-2am).

▓ Lüneburg Heath (Lüneburger Heide)

Between the Elbe and Aller rivers stretches the shrub-covered Lüneburg Heath. The Heath clearly had strong symbolic power for German literary greats: the delicate *Heideröslein* (wild rose) found a role in one of Goethe's *Lieder* while Heine charmingly compared one lady's bosom to the "flat and bleakly desolate" landscape of the Heath. Journeying by bicycle or horseback from one mist-shrouded town to the next in the morning is a tranquil escape from the worries of backpacking. The undulating countryside moves quickly back and forth from farm to forest; green gives way to purple from July to September, when the bushes flower. The area around the town of Wilsede is reputed to be the most charming stretch in the entire Heath.

If you want to see the grassy Heath during the flowering season, but would prefer not to sleep on it, put down the book and make reservations now. All of Germany comes here to bike, hike, motor, and otherwise frolic in the late summer. Tourist offices typically recommend making reservations up to six months in advance. The most important regional towns are Lüneburg and Celle. In Lüneburg, the **Fremdenverkehrsverband Lüneburger Heide,** Barckhausenstr. 35 (tel. (04131) 737 30; fax

426 06), finds rooms in remote hamlets barely on the map, including overnight stays at barnyard bed-and-breakfasts and horse farms. Their list even tells you which animals you can expect to encounter. Biking and hiking maps as well as calendars of Heath events are also available (office open Mon.-Thurs. 8am-4pm, Fri. 8am-1pm). For those without a bike, rentals abound. Trains along the Hanover-Hamburg line run frequently but provide access to only a handful of towns. Most other towns are serviced by occasional buses. Check the threadbare schedules carefully.

■ Near Lüneburger Heide: Lüneburg

Perhaps because there is no salt-god, or perhaps because the name Salzburg was already taken, Lüneburg derives its name from the moon-goddess Luna. Regardless, this is a city built, literally and figuratively, on salt. The city made a 13th-century fortune with its natural stores of "white gold." The *Bürgers'* salt monopoly held Northern Europe in an iron grip until plague and war struck in the 1620s. Although "salt shocks" no longer pose a threat to the world economy, and Lüneburg's wealth and power have faded, neither the salt not the town have become obsolete. The former is channeled into the city's famed rejuvenating baths, and the latter, with its Gothic brick *Altstadt* and elegant half-timbered houses, retains its ancient grace. It was in Lüneburg that native poet Heinrich Heine penned Germany's greatest, most longing Romantic *Lied* (epic song), the *Lorelei*.

Orientation and Practical Information Lüneburg serves as the main transportation axis for the Heath. The 60,000-strong city lies between Hamburg (30min.) and Hanover (1hr.). The **tourist office**, Am Markt in the *Rathaus* (tel. 30 95 93 or 322 00; fax 30 95 98), will search for a room for a DM5 fee. From the **train** station, head downhill, away from the post office, take a left onto Lünertorstr., and then turn left onto Bardowicker Str. at the end (open Mon.-Fri. 9am-6pm, Sat.-Sun. 9am-1pm; Oct.-April Mon.-Fri. 9am-1pm and 2-6pm, Sat. 9am-1pm). Daily **tours** of the *Altstadt* start at 11am in front of the tourist office (DM5). A separate **regional tourist office** serves the entire Heath area (see above). Rents **cars** at **Sixt Budget**, Bardowicker Tore 21 (tel. 350 75; fax 367 95; open Mon.-Fri. 7:30am-6pm, Sat. 8am-noon). For a **bike**, try **Laden 25**, Am Weder 25 (tel. 379 60; DM12 per day, DM60 per week, DM50 deposit and ID required; open Mon.-Fri. 9am-noon and 1-5:30pm, Sat. 9am-12:30pm). The hostel has **laundry** machines (soap, wash, and dry DM5). The main **post office** is on the corner of Soltauerstr. and Saltztorstr., 21332 Lüneburg (open Mon.-Fri. 8am-6pm, Sat. 8am-noon). The **telephone code** is 04131.

Accommodations Hotels fill up with alarming speed as the Heath blooms in July, August, and September. At other times, cheap and charming go hand in hand. **Jugendherberge Lüneburg (HI),** Soltauerstr. 133 (tel. 418 64; fax 457 47), serves a great breakfast. During the week and Saturday morning until 1pm, bus #11 (direction: Rettmer/Hecklingen) runs from the train station to the hostel stop: "Scharnhorststr./DJH." During off hours, brace yourself for a long haul: turn left on the street in front of the station (Bahnhofstr.), turn right at the bottom onto Altenbrückerstr, and then left onto the very long Berlinerstr. Follow the street as it turns into Uelzenarstr., make a right at Scharnhorststr., and continue until you meet Soltauerstr. (Reception open daily until 10pm. Curfew 10pm, but pocket a housekey with a DM10 deposit. Laundry available, DM5. DM19.50, over 26 DM23.50. Breakfast included. Sheets DM5.70. Call ahead.) For accommodations in the *Altstadt*, **Hotel "Stadt Hamburg,"** Am Sande 25 (tel. 444 38), will put a grin on your face. Portraits of famous Lüneburgers line the stairway. (Singles DM40, with shower DM45. Doubles DM80, with shower DM90. Call ahead.)

Food and Nightlife Although salt is plentiful in restaurants here, the real staple in town is another of mankind's ancient preservatives: beer. At **Kronen-Brauerei**, Heiligengeiststr. 39-41 (tel. 71 32 00), you can imbibe freshly-brewed beer (from

DM3.50) in an early 15th-century beer hall (open daily noon-10pm). In the **Kartoffeln Keller,** Auf dem Kauf 13 (tel. 39 14 64), dim candlelight allows you to eat your potatoes naked (DM4.30), in a pizza (DM9.50), or in a fondue (DM24.50). (Includes salt. Open daily 11:30am-2:30pm and from 6pm). For cheap food visit the local college **cafeteria** and the **Café Vamos.** The cafeteria, Building 9, is different from the school's *Mensa.* It serves the Pizza Diablo (*Dio Mia!* DM8.50; open Mon.-Thurs. 10am-6pm, Fri. 10am-3pm). The **café,** Building 26, features live music. From #9, walk away from the street and turn left. It's in the building with the funky windows (open Mon.-Thurs. 10am-7pm, Fri. 10am-7pm and from 8pm, Sat. only if there's a party, Sun. 11am-3pm.) During the week, nightlife piles up around the Lüner Bridge. In sight of the 14th-century swinging craze, locals pack the cafés along am Stintmarkt. The patios offer cheap food and beer.

Sights Legend has it that Lüneburg's salt stores were discovered when a wild boar fell into a pit and, clawing his way out, shook salt loose from his bristles. At the **Deutsches Salz Museum** (German Salt Museum), Sülfmeisterstr. 1 (tel. 450 65), you can see, touch, taste, smell, mine, melt, and generally be one with salt. From the *Rathaus,* take Neue Sülze to Salzstr.; at Lambertiplatz, take the path behind the supermarket. The piquant museum features exhibits on salt production, ancient salt ships, salt use, and a medieval salt mill. (Open May-Sept. Mon-Fri. 9am-5pm, Sat.-Sun. 10am-5pm; Oct.-April daily 10am-5pm. Hour-long tours Mon.-Fri. at 11am, 12:30pm, 3pm; Sat.-Sun. at 11:30am and 3pm. Admission DM6, students DM4, children DM3.50. With the tour, tack on DM1.50 for adults and kiddies, DM1 for students.)

The **Kloster Lüne** (cloister; tel. 523 18), on Domänehof, just over the Lünetor bridge, proudly displays its 15th-century face (open April-Oct. Mon.-Sat. 9-11:30am and 2:30-5pm, Sun. 11:30am-12:30pm and 2-5pm; admission DM5). Side streets with old, ivy-covered houses and boutiques lead to the Gothic **Michaeliskirche** (tel. 314 00), on Johann-Sebastian-Bach-Platz in the *Altstadt.* This imposing brick, wood, and ceramic church was built in 1418 on a foundation of salt; the massive pillars have warped since then (open Mon.-Sat. 10am-noon and 2-5pm). Over the gables of the streets soars the spire of the **Johanniskirche,** Am Sande (tel. 445 42). Late 13th-century walls protect a Gothic altar and Baroque organ (open daily 10am-5pm).

The **Brauereimuseum** (Brewery Museum), Heilgengeistr. 39-41 (tel. 410 21), was a working brewery for 500 years until its copper vats became museum pieces in 1985. The museum shows you exactly how hops, malt barley, and a few extras make the magic potion that keeps Germany going, going, and going (going daily 10am-noon and 3-5pm; free). The **Ostpreußiches Landesmuseum,** Ritterstr. 10 (tel. 418 55), celebrates the sometimes troubling history and culture of East Prussia, with everything from bear hunting equipment to the philosopher Kant. Lüneberg's two other offbeat museums should be taken with a grain of...well, you know (open Tues.-Sun. 10am-5pm; admission DM3, students and children DM2).

CELLE

The powerful prince electors of Lüneberg moved to Celle in 1398 after the Lüneberger War of Succession and remained here until 1705 when the last duke croaked. During those 327 years, the royalty spent lavishly on their residence. building a massive castle and promoting the city's growth. Celle celebrates this rich cultural past with its cobblestone streets lined with half-timbered houses. In the heyday of *Fachwerk,* residents were taxed by the number of crossed diagonal beams on their houses; they quickly became coveted status symbols.

Some of the finest *Fachwerk* houses are tucked away on side streets; to find them wander down any street in the *Altstadt.* The **oldest house** in the area is at Am Heiligen Kreuz 26. The **Stadtkirche** stands just outside the massive pedestrian zone that dominates the *Altstadt.* The climb up the church tower rewards with a view of red and brown-shingled roofs fading into the countryside (church open Tues.-Sat. 9am-12:30pm and 3-6pm; tower open April-Oct. Tues.-Sat. 3-4pm; admission DM2, students and children DM1). In the *Altstadt,* the **Rathaus** is richly wrought in the *Weser-*

renaissance style. Directly across the road, fine figures out of Celle's colorful history mark the hour on the **Glockenspiel** (at 10, 11am, noon, 3, 4, and 5pm).

The **Herzogschloß** (Duke's Castle; tel. 123 73), at Schloßplatz 13 just west of the *Altstadt*, flaunts foundations that date back to 1292. One of the most renowned residents of the castle was Caroline-Mathilde; she was granted asylum here in 1772 after her politically expedient marriage to the King of Denmark collapsed and her affair with the King's minister was exposed. (Caroline-Mathilde's personal rooms open Tues.-Sun. 10am-4:30pm. Tours of the ducal staterooms Tues.-Sun. hourly from 10am; last tour starts at 4pm; Oct.-April tours at 11am and 3pm. Admission DM4, students and children DM2. Castle open Mon.-Fri. 10am-1pm, Sat.-Sun. 10am-noon, with phone service Mon.-Fri. 9am-2pm and Sat.-Sun. 9am-noon). Caroline-Mathilde's weeping likeness is found in the **Französischer Garten**, south of the *Altstadt*, but it's hard to figure out why she's crying. Right next door, the state-of-the-art **Niedersächsisches Landesinstitut für Bienenforschung** (Lower Saxony Bee Research Institute; tel. 60 54) buzzes with contentment (open Mon.-Thurs. 9am-noon and 2-4pm, Fri. 9am-noon; free).

The **tourist office,** Markt 6 (tel. 12 12; fax 124 59), reserves rooms (DM2 fee) and distributes the *Jahresveranstaltungen,* a list of concerts and musical productions, and "The Wonderful Nine," a huge, full-color English description of Lower Saxony's historical highlights. From the train station, walk up Bahnhofstr. as it becomes Westcellertorstr., turn left onto Schloßplatz, then take the second right onto Stechbahn, and finally take the second left onto Markt. Or ride bus #2 or 3 to "Schloßplatz" and follow the signs (open May to mid-Oct. Mon.-Fri. 9am-6pm, Sat. 9am-1pm and 2-5pm; mid.-Oct. to April Mon.-Fri. 9am-5pm, Sat. 10am-noon). City **tours** start from the bridge in front of the *Schloß* (April-Oct. Wed. and Sat. at 2:30pm, Sun. at 11am; DM3). Celle, a self-proclaimed "Romantic Half-Timbered City," is 40km northeast of Hanover, 20 minutes by frequent **trains** (DM11.20). **Rent cars** from **AutoHansa,** Braunschweiger-Heerstr. 43 (tel. 290 44). Or rent a **bike** from **2-Rad-Meier GmbH,** Neustadt 42a (tel. 413 69; fax 48 10 18). Follow Neustadt behind the train station for 10 minutes (7-gear bikes DM15 per day, 3-gear DM12; ID required; open Mon.-Fri. 8am-1pm and 2:30-6pm, Sat. 8am-1pm). The **post office,** 03100 Celle, is on Schloßplatz (open Mon.-Fri. 6am-7pm, Sat. 6am-1pm). The **telephone code** is 05141.

The *Herbergeltern* at the **Jugendherberge (HI),** Weghausstr. (tel. 532 08; fax 530 05), may have an obsession with plants, but you can use this to your advantage. To hide from the roving mob of ferocious schoolchildren, wear jungle camouflage clothing or simply stand amidst the greenery, and they may just leave you alone. From the train station, catch bus #3 (direction: Boye) to "Jugendherberge." Turn left out of the station, walk up the pedestrian/bike path as it becomes Biermannstr, turn left on Bremer Weg, and turn up the first right onto Petersburgstr. (Reception open until 10pm, but best time for check-in is 5-7pm. Curfew 10pm; housekeys available with a DM50 deposit. DM20, over 26 DM24.50. Breakfast included. Sheets DM5.70.) At **Pension Luhmanns Hof,** Dorfstr. 8 (tel. 530 94), a little chocolate on each bed adds the touch of elegance. From Petersburgstr, it's the first building on the right after you pass Weghausstr. (Reception open until 9pm, reservations recommended. Singles DM75. Doubles DM110. Breakfast included.) **Hotel Blühende Schiffahrt,** Fritzenwiese 39 (tel. 227 61), is considerably closer to the *Altstadt.* (DM55 per person. Breakfast included. Call ahead.) **Campingplatz Silbersee** (tel. 312 23) lies 7km northeast of the town proper; take the bus #6 (direction: Vorwerk) to "Silbersee" (DM5.50 per person. Showers included.)

Café Fricke, Neuestr. 14 (tel. 21 49 18), at the intersection with Brandplatz, sets a merry table with artsy decorations, where you can enjoy crepes from DM4.80 (open daily 10:30am-6pm). The Disenfranchised Youth, Celle Chapter, breaks bread at the chic **Alex's Antik Cafe,** Schuhstr. 6 (tel. 21 75 40), and it's easy to see why: cheap, simple food (soup and sandwich combo DM10), a spectrum of alcohol and coffee drinks, and smoky surroundings render even the most of disinterested interested. The café is too cool to post hours. During Celle's **market** (Wed. and Sat. 7am-1pm) the *Altstadt* fills with people carrying cloth-lined baskets in search of bargains on meats, fruits, vegetables, socks, and flowers.

BERGEN-BELSEN

Near the town of Bergen, 20km north of Celle, lies the site of the **Bergen-Belsen concentration camp.** Fear of a typhus epidemic led British military authorities to raze the camp buildings in May 1945, but memories of what they had witnessed inspired the construction of a monument in November of that year. The German government agreed to care for and expand it in 1952. A somber stone obelisk commemorates the 30,000 Jewish victims; mass graves flank the memorial erected in memory of the 50,000 Soviet prisoners of war who perished here; Bergen-Belsen claimed more than 100,000 lives. Most inmates of the concentration camp were Western political insurgents, European Jews, and women. The document room details the camp's history; the photographs taken by liberating British troops are powerful, moving reminders of what must not be forgotten. One of the camp's victims was young Anne Frank, immortalized by her diary of her terrifying experiences as a Jew in hiding. In it she wrote, "in spite of everything I still believe that people are really good at heart." The camp is difficult to reach, and the regional authorities do not publicize it well. The **Bergen-Belsen Memorial** (tel. (05051) 60 11) is open daily 9am to 6pm, but you must take two buses to get there: #2 to stop "Bergen-Celler Straße" and then #9 from there to the "Belsen-Gedenkstätte." Schedules change regularly and buses run infrequently; for schedule information contact **Kraftverkehr Celle** at (05141) 27 60. By car take the B3 toward Hamburg to Hinweisschild (about 20km from Celle), then turn left and continue straight to Bergen-Belsen by following the *Gedenkstätte* (memorial) signs. See Life and Times: History, p. 62, for more discussion of the Holocaust.

■ Bremen

> *Happy is the man who has reached the harbor and left the sea and storm behind and now sits warm and peaceful in the good Ratskeller of Bremen.*
> —Heinrich Heine, "Im Hafen"

In this region of Germany, "*bremisch*" (lit., from Bremen) colloquially describes something unusual, and it is a highly suitable adjective. Perhaps it's the city's cultural flair—Bremen's appeal to artists is fabled. The donkey, dog, cat, and rooster of the Brothers Grimm's fairy tale *Die Bremer Stadtmusikanten* (The Musicians of Bremen) were en route to Bremen when they terrified a band of robbers with their singing. Even the transients at the city's train station sing for attention. Closer to the *Altstadt*, more talented artists ply their crafts, creating beautiful murals with charcoal and spray paint as musicians provide accompaniment on a mind-boggling array of instruments. Or maybe it's something in the beer—Beck's, the mass-bottled beer that put Bremen on the map, is based just across the river from the town center.

One *bremisch* trait is a strong desire for independence: despite continuing struggles, Bremen and its daughter city Bremerhaven remain their own tiny, autonomous *Land* in the middle of Lower Saxony. This activism creates a strongly liberal political climate which erupted in 1980 into violent battles between police and demonstrators. People here flaunt high-flying, don't-tread-on-me attitudes—Bremen is one of the only places in Germany where jaywalkers won't feel out of place.

ORIENTATION AND PRACTICAL INFORMATION

Bremen lies south of the portal of the Weser River at the North Sea, a little over an hour from both Hamburg and Hanover by frequent trains. The city is perfect for meandering, but beware of the blocks surrounding Ostertorsteinweg and Am Dobben; as you move out of the Altstadt, bong shops replace bakeries for several blocks, and sirens drown out singers on the streets.

LOWER SAXONY

Tourist Office: The souvenir-jammed central office (tel. 308 00 51; fax 308 00 30), across from the *Hauptbahnhof,* books rooms for DM3 plus a DM10-20 deposit credited to your bill. It also offers guides to museum exhibits, theater schedules, and sells tickets for concerts and festivals. Open Mon.-Wed. and Fri. 9:30am-6:30pm, Thurs. 9:30am-8:30pm, Sat. 9:30am-2pm.

Consulate: U.K., Herrlichkeit 6 (tel. 590 90). Open Mon.-Thurs. 8:30am-12:30pm and 2:30-3:30pm, Fri. 8:30am-12:30pm.

Currency Exchange: DVB, in the train station, exchanges currency and cashes traveler's checks for a 1% commission, minimum DM10. Open Mon.-Fri. 7:30am-7pm, Sat. 8am-12:15pm and 1-4pm.

American Express: Am Wall 138, 28195 Bremen (tel. 17 46 00). Get off at Schüssel Korb and walk away from the Deutsche Bank. Follow the curve to the right and then go left onto Am Wall; it's 30m to the left. Open Mon.-Fri. 9am-5:30pm, Sat. 9am-noon.

Telephones: In the main post office and the branch office.

Flights: Bremen's international airport (tel. 559 51) is only 3.5km from the city center; take S-Bahn #5 (20min.) or drive south on Oldenburger Str. and follow the signs (15min.). Frequent flights to major German cities, the East Frisian Islands, and other countries.

Public Transportation: An integrated system of streetcars and buses covers city and suburbs. Information and connections in front of the train station. The best deal by far is the **Bremer Kärtchen** (Little Bremen Card), with unlimited rides for 2 adults for 1 calendar day *(not* 24hr. from time of purchase). DM7 per card. Single rides DM3.20, children under 16 DM1.60. Four-ride ticket DM9.60.

Ferries: Ferries from **Schreiber Reederei** (tel. 32 12 29; fax 32 61 36) shuttle to the suburbs and towns along the Weser, ending up at Bremerhaven. (May 16-Sept. 14, Wed.-Thurs. and Sat. at 8:30am. One-way to Bremerhaven DM21, round-trip DM34.) More info is available at the tourist office. From Bremerhaven, ferries are available to scenic Helgoland.

Car Rental: Avis, Kirchbachstr. 200 (tel. 21 10 77). Open Mon.-Fri. 7am-6pm, Sat. 8am-1pm.

Bike Rental: Leave a DM50 security deposit and a photo ID, and pedal away from the **Fahrrad Station** (tel. 30 21 14), a bright red stand with bright yellow bikes, situated on your left as you exit the station. DM15 per day, children DM9; DM60 per week, children DM45. Bicyclist's city map DM9.80. Open June-Sept. Mon. and Wed.-Fri. 10am-5pm, Sat.-Sun. 10am-noon and 5-5:30pm; March-May and Oct.-Dec. Mon.-Fri. 10am-5pm.

Bookstores: Storm, Langestr. 10 (tel. 32 15 23). Substantial selection of English books, dictionaries, and travel guides. Open Mon.-Fri. 9am-6:30pm, Sat. 9am-2pm. **Frauenbuchladen Hagazussa,** Friesenstr. 12 (tel. 741 40), stocks over 3000 titles of particular interest to women. Only women admitted. Open Mon. 10am-2pm, Tues.-Fri. 10am-6pm, Sat. 10am-2pm.

Gay Information Line: (tel. 70 41 70), provides information about gay events and services. Open Mon.-Wed. and Fri. 10am-1pm, Thurs. 4-5pm.

Women's Center: The offices at Am Hulsberg 11 (Streetcar stop: Am Hulsberg) provide a wide range of career services to women. Info more pertinent to travelers is available in the lobby. **Frauen Taxi** runs a women's taxi service daily 7pm-6am. Call 144 33.

Laundromat: Wasch Center, Vor dem Steintor, 30m in the direction opposite the *Hauptbahnhof.* Take S-Bahn #2, 3, or 10: Brunnenstr. DM6 for wash, soap, and spin dry; another DM1 to dry in a standard machine. Open daily 6am-11pm. Another **Wasch Center,** same S-Bahn stop, equal distance from stop but in the opposite direction. Same prices, 9 more machines. Open daily 7am-9pm.

Pharmacy: Päs Apotheke, Bahnhofplatz 5-7 (tel. 144 15). Pick up a map of the city's pharmacies with their rotating schedule of late and emergency openings. Open Mon.-Fri. 8am-6:30pm, Sat. 8am-2pm.

Emergency: Police tel. 110. **Fire** tel. 112.

Post Office: Main office at Domsheide 15, 28195 Bremen (tel. 367 33 66), near the *Markt*. Open Mon.-Fri. 8am-6pm, Sat. 9am-1pm. There is also an office on Bahnhof-platz 5, to the left of the train station. Open Mon.-Fri. 8am-2pm, Sat.-Sun. 9am-2pm.
Telephone Code: 0421.

ACCOMMODATIONS AND CAMPING

The key phrase for Bremen is "call ahead." Inexpensive hotels exist, but they fill fast. The tourist office's *Hotel-Liste* (free) lists a number of rooms in the DM40-50 range, but prices quickly rocket into the DM100 range. New bus connections have made direct links with a somewhat distant campsite possible.

Jugendgästehaus Bremen (HI), Kalkstr. 6 (tel. 17 13 69; fax 17 11 02). Bus #26 or streetcar #6: Am Brill, then walk along Bürgermeister-Smidt-Str. to the river, turn right, and walk 2 blocks. To walk from the train station, take Bahnhofstr. to Herdentorsteinweg, go right at Am Wall, then turn left on to Bürgermeister-Smidt-Str. and right along the water to the 160-bed hostel. The linen is clean, the ping-pong is fun, and the glowing Beck's brewery sign across the Weser lulls you to sleep with visions of malt dancing in your head. Reception open 24hr. Check-out 10am. No curfew. DM26, over 26 DM30. Breakfast and sheets included.

Jugendherberge Bremen-Blumenthal (HI), Bürgermeister-Dehnkamp-Str. 22 (tel. 60 10 05), in Blumenthal. Bus #10 from the *Hauptbahnhof* (direction "Gropelin-gen") to the end of the line, then change for the #70 or 71 (direction "Farge/Neu-enkirchen" or "Blumenthal"): Kreinsloger (45-50min.). Bürgermeister-Dehnkamp-Str. is down the stone steps through the trees. An oasis on the busy wharf, the hostel's small park overlooks the river. Call ahead to make sure it isn't filled with schoolchildren. Reception open 7am-10pm. Check-out 9am. Curfew 10pm. DM18.50, over 26 DM22.50. Breakfast included. Sheets DM5.

Hotel Enzensperger, Brautstr. 9 (tel. 50 32 24). Take bus #24 to stop "Am Neuen-mark," then right on Brautstr. Or, from the *Markt*, cross the Wilhelm-Keisen Bridge over the Weser, turn right on Osterstr., and right on Brautstr. Lots of space and lots of plaid. Singles DM48, with shower DM49. Doubles DM72, with shower DM82. Breakfast included. Call a few days ahead.

Pension garni Weidmann, Am Schwarzen Meer 35 (tel. 498 44 55). If Elizabeth Taylor were as young as she tries to look, she would have no qualms about living in this *pension*. The plush comforters and feet-tickling bathroom rugs are just her style. Such pampering accommodations at such bargain prices (singles start at DM40, doubles start at DM80) are in demand. Two-week advance reservations are recommended.

Hotel Weltevreden, Am Dobben 62 (tel. 78 015; fax 70 40 91), just off Ostertor-steinweg. Comfortable rooms, good prices, close to Bremen nightlife. Reception open Mon.-Sat. 7am-10pm, Sun. 7:30am-1pm and 5-10pm. Singles DM60. Doubles DM100, with shower DM115. Breakfast included. Call a few days ahead.

Camping: Am Stadtwaldsee 1 (tel. 21 20 02). Bus #26 to Hemmstr., then #28 to the door. DM7.50 per person, DM4.50 per child. Two-person tent DM5, bigger tent DM9.50. Washers and dryers DM4 each. Free showers and electrical hookup. Open from one week before Easter 'til Nov. 1.

FOOD

In the *Rathaus* itself, visit Bremen's renowned **Ratskeller** (tel. 32 16 76). Dating back to 1408, it's one of the oldest wine bars in Germany. Settle in a cozy leather-and-wood booth or among huge barrels to enjoy one of 600 German wines; most are reasonably priced (from DM4.40 per 0.2L glass), but the elegant beef and fish meals run around DM40 (open daily 11am-midnight, kitchen open noon-2:30pm and 6-11pm). A cheaper way to eat well is in the open-air **market** daily from 8am to 2pm. On the last Wednesday of May, celebration of the **Matjes Festival** (Herring Festival) replaces the market with throngs of beer-burping and fish-chowing revelers. The restaurants that pack the **Schnoorviertel** are silly, charming, and exceedingly pricey, so shop around. Bronze pigs herd pedestrians into shops and take-out cafés on **Sögerstraße,** where they sell everything from chocolate truffles to *FischBrötchen*. Student pubs proliferate farther east, on and around **Ostertorsteinweg** (see Nightlife, p. 353). Bremen is the coffee capital of Germany; over half the nation's java is roasted here.

Schnaare Schnoor Bäckerei, Landherrnamt 7 (tel. 337 93 02). Was JFK a Berliner? Nein. Taste the real *Berliner* (a yummy donut, DM1.60), or indulge yourself with a drop-dead gorgeous *Sahne Desserttörtchen* (DM2.50). A good deal since 1890. Open Mon.-Fri. 7am-6:30pm, Sat. 7am-2pm.

Ada, Ostertorsteinweg 99 (tel. 783 57). "Ardor" is this joint's subtitle. Try a *tzatuki* pizza (DM4) and chase it down with a Turkish mocha (DM3). Always open.

Café Torno, Am Dobben 71 (tel. 70 06 11). Relax nerves to Western showdown music. Their hefty gyros (DM5-9) will scare hunger from your stomach. Pasta dinners DM9-12. Open Mon.-Thurs. noon-2am, Fri.-Sat. noon-4am, Sun. noon-1am.

Kreta, Gastfeldstr. 20 (tel. 55 42 00). Leave the congested *Altstadt* and come to what locals call Little Greece. Athena benevolently gazes on patrons as they wolf down the tasty *Samos Platte* (complete meal DM13). Other delectable platters DM13-18. Open Tues.-Sun. noon-3pm and 6pm-midnight, Mon. 6pm-midnight.

Harlekin Bookshop/Café, Lahnstr. 65b (tel. 50 19 11). Bus #5: Theater am Leibnizplatz. Walk in the direction away from the *Hauptbahnhof,* past the centaur; take the second right and cross the street. Bremen's best breakfast selection (served all day) is spread out by an alternative bookstore. The generous *Türkisches Frühstück* ("Turkish Breakfast"; *Fladenbrot,* feta, olives, and cucumbers for DM7.50) makes and invigorating lunch. Café open 10am-6:30pm.

Engel, Ostertorsteinweg 31/33 (tel. 766 15). Simple, elegant dining, and prime people-watching facilities provided by the terrace's *Ostertor* location. Lunch specials (DM10.50) even include dessert. Other artful entrees cost DM10-15. Concerts on the terrace on summer weekends. Open daily 7am-2am.

SIGHTS

The best way to see Bremen is to drift down one historic street after another. The *Altstadt* revolves around the **Rathaus**, its 15th-century base decorated by an startlingly ornate Renaissance façade. It survived World War II only because the English pilot who bombed the area deliberately missed this target. (Tours, the only access to the interior of the building, are occassionally available Mon.-Fri. at 10, 11am, and noon; Sat.-Sun. at 11am and noon. Ask at the tourist office for more details.) Just left of the town hall is the 1951 sculpture by Gerhard Marcks, *Die Musikanten,* which shows the Grimms' donkey, dog, cat, and rooster in their model-mugging, robber-foiling stance. Also a war survivor, the **St. Petri Dom,** Sandstr. 10-12, next to the *Rathaus* (tel. 36 50 40), has a mosaic interior of orange, gold, and gray stone arches. The foundation dates to 798, when Charlemagne (north Germany's missionary man) had the first stone placed there. If gilded chandeliers and artwork are too overwhelming, descend into the subterranean crypts at the front and rear of the church. (Cathedral open Mon.-Fri. 10am-5pm, Sat. 10am-1:45pm, Sun. 2-5pm. Free. Tower, all 265 steps, open May-Oct. Mon.-Fri. 10am-11:20am and 12:20-4:20pm, Sat. 10am-noon, Sun. 2-5pm. Admission DM1.) In a corner of the cathedral is the **Dom Museum** (tel. 365 04 75), housed in part of the original foundation with frescoes dating back 500 years (open Mon.-Fri. 10am-5pm, Sat. 10am-noon, Sun. 2-5pm; Nov.-April Mon.-Fri. 1-5:30pm, Sat. 10am-noon, Sun. 2-5pm; admission DM3, children DM2). Your ticket from the museum is good for DM1 discount on the ticket for the **Bleikeller,** in the basement of the **Dom.** The mummified corpses of workers who had fallen from the roof of the cathedral were discovered here in 1695 and have been on exhibit for three centuries. (Open May-Oct. Mon.-Fri. 10am-5pm, Sat. 10am-2pm, Sun. 2-5pm; Nov.-April daily 1-5pm. Admission DM2, children DM1; admission ticket likewise good for DM1 discount at museum above.)

Just past the *Domshof,* turn left on Domsheide for the medieval **Schnoorviertel,** a district of red-roofed gingerbread houses, dainty shops, and dog salons. Between the *Marktplatz* and the Weser lies the narrow red brick and cobblestone **Böttcherstraße,** a winding labyrinth of gilded archways, stained-glass windows, boutiques, and craft shops. It's worth standing with all the tourists at noon, 3, or 6pm for the magic of the Böttcherstr. **Glockenspiel.** Bells ring and part of the building swings open to deliver a performance by mechanical figures, re-enacting wild sea and air exploits from the building's early memory. Come early—the prime gawking spots fill up fast. Modern offices are now housed in some of the city's beautiful Renaissance structures; look for the **Gerichtsgebäude** (municipal court), Domsheide 16. As you work the streets, stop by the **Bremer Nachrichten** building on the corner of Martin-istr. and Langenstr. to join the locals reading the daily paper page by page on a window display. The smell of brewing beer lures the helpless lush across the Weser to the **Beck's Brewery.** After a two-year hiatus from tour giving, the mysterious brewery complex will again offer group and individual tours in 1997. Call Beck's (tel. 50 94) for more details.

MUSEUMS

Neues Museum Weserburg Bremen, Teerhof 20 (tel. 59 83 90), across the Wilhelm Kaiser Bridge, then right on Herrlichkeit. on the small island that splits the Weser River. The initiated savor the irony of works by Assig and Darboven as they expose the hollowness of modernity. The novices wonder why the heck the paintings aren't finished. Either way, good stuff. Bring a black turtleneck. Open Tues.-Fri. 10am-6pm, Sat.-Sun. 11am-6pm. Admission DM6, students DM3.

Übersee Museum, next to the train station at Bahnhofsplatz 13 (tel. 361 91 76). Your fifth-grade social studies textbook comes to life. Exhibits ranging from a Shinto garden to a South Seas fishing village attempt to show young minds the wonders of the world outside Germany's borders. Open Tues.-Sun. 10am-6pm. Admission DM4, students and children DM2.

Gerhard Marcks Haus, Am Wall 208 (tel. 32 72 00), next to the Kunsthalle. An indoor and outdoor sculpture garden of works by the sculptor of *Die Musikanten*, found next to the *Rathaus*. Check the main building and adjoining shed for special exhibits from other sculptors. Open Tues.-Sun. 10am-6pm, Thurs. 10am-5pm. Admission DM4, students and children DM2.

Rundfunkmuseum, Findorffstr. 85 (tel. 35 74 06 or 35 37 97). A large-scale center that chronicles the development of telecommunications with exhibits that light up and whirl when touched. Open Mon.-Tues. and Thurs.-Fri. 9:30am-5pm.

Kunsthalle, Am Wall 207 (tel. 32 90 80), between the *Marktplatz* and the Ostertor-steinweg. A collection of artwork ranging from the Renaissance to present; the ensemble of bright, *angsty* German Expressionist pieces is very strong. Unfortunately, the museum is **closed for restoration** through 1997 and early 1998.

ENTERTAINMENT AND NIGHTLIFE

You want singing barnyard animals? Bremen delivers. Plus there's opera in the **Theater am Goetherplatz,** Am Goetheplatz 1-3 (tel. 365 33 33), new drama in the **Schauspielhaus,** Ostertorsteinweg 57a (tel. 365 33 33), and the **Bremer Shakespeare Company,** Theater am Leipnizplatz (tel. 50 03 33). The **Theater im Schoor,** Wüste Stätte 11 (tel. 32 60 54), does cabarets and revues. Summertime brings performances to parks around the city. Discount tickets are usually held for students. Check the tourist office, the theaters, or *Bremer Umschau* (DM3) for schedules and prices, as well as information on free performances. *Belladonna* lists cultural events of special interest to women. During the last two weeks of October, Bremen drinks beer and eats lard cakes in honor of its trading heritage and freedom as a *Land* with the colorful **Freimarkt** fair, an annual event since 1095. In 1997, the Freimarkt fair will be held from October 19 to November 3. The **Weserflohmarkt** (flea market), an organized cacophony of vendors, convenes every Saturday at Schlactel and Weser-promenade on the banks of the river from 8am-2pm.

Bremen rocks—big concerts are often held in the **Weserstadion** (tel. 43 45 00) behind the train station. Tickets and information for small- and large-scale events are available at the tourist office. Many clubs host live music nights that feature American bands making their European debut. **Modernes Complex,** Neustadtswall 28 (tel 50

55 53) hosts cinema, theater, concerts, and dancing (times and cover charges vary). If you want to sample Bremen's pub culture, wander carefully along the **Ostertorstein-weg** at night; it houses both the students' favorite haunts and the substantial Bremen gay scene.

Litfass, Ostertorsteinweg 22 (tel. 70 32 92). An all-day, all-night bastion of alternative chic which poses as a bar. As the eyes of the supermodel on the wall cast flirting glances, coolly take down one of their piping hot coffees. The extensive outdoor terrace and open façade make it the place to see and be seen. Open Sun.-Thurs. 10am-2am, Fri.-Sat. 10am-4am.

Aladin, Hannoverschestr. 11 (tel. 41 23 04). Bar that hosts live music. Open Wed. 9pm-2am, Fri.-Sat. 9pm-7am, sporadically for other performances. Cover DM7.

Café Homolulu, Theodor-Körnerstr. 1 (tel. 70 00 07). Gay scene usually crowded with students. Open Tues.-Wed. and Fri. from 8pm, Sun. from 3pm.

TheaLit, Im Krummen Arm 1 (tel. 70 16 32). Evening club and center for women's and lesbian events. Also contains a bar. Women only. Information office open Tues. 10am-noon, Wed.-Fri. 4-6pm. Bar opens Mon.-Fri. and Sun. at 5pm, and closes when everybody goes home.

■ Bremerhaven

ARRR, matey! Founded in 1827 as a port for land-locked Bremen, Bremerhaven is still very much a younger and saltier version of its sister city. The harbor which was the city's commercial *raison d'être* now serves as a hub for tourism. Ferries sail daily for Helgoland, Germany's own Fantasy Island, at 9:45am (see Helgoland, p. 357). The harbor also houses the **Deutsches Schiffahrts-Museum** (German Maritime Museum; tel. 48 20 78), which pays tribute to boats, boats, and more boats, with models and relics inside the building and real *Museumschiffe* (museum ships) outside. (Open Tues.-Sun. 10am-6pm. Ships open April-Sept. Tues.-Sun. 10am-6pm. Admission DM6, students, seniors, children, and soldiers DM3.50.) Docked nearby, but with separate admission, is the **U-Boot Wilhelm Bauer,** the only German submarine (U-Boat) from World War II that was neither sunk nor scrapped (open April-Oct. daily 10am-6pm; admission DM3, under 18 DM1.50). At the **Zoo am Meer,** further up the harbor; German schoolchildren hoot and dash about frantically, while animals on the other side of the bars (polar bears, sea lions, monkeys) sit calmly and watch (open April-Sept. Mon.-Sat. 8am-7pm; Oct.-March Mon.-Sat. 8am-4:30pm; admission DM4, students and children DM2; free tours available with prior reservation). Should you lose your way, info centers abound. Each year the city celebrates numerous festivals. In 1997, the Bremerhaven **Fest Woche** (Festival Week) will be held July 23-27. The *Bürger* will also be unusually drunk this year as the city celebrates the 150th anniversary of the German marines (call tourist office for details).

The **tourist office**, in the Columbus Center (tel. 430 00), finds rooms with no fee (open Mon.-Wed. and Fri. 10am-6pm, Thurs. 10am-8:30pm, Sat. 10am-1pm). Take bus # 2, 5, 9, or 12: "Große Kirche," to get there. The **Verkehrsamt**, Van-Ronzelenstr. 2 (tel. 94 64 60; fax 460 65) does the same with different hours (open Mon.-Fri. 8am-4pm). Bremerhaven is 30min. from Bremen by **train**; a **ferry** leaves Bremen each morning at 8:30am (see Bremen, p. 349). To **rent a bike,** visit the **BBU** (tel. 475 31), housed in a train car at the entrance to the harbor, near the zoo. DM10 per day, DM42 per week; children DM6 per day, DM30 per week. Free cute brochures about the zoo (open Apr.-Sept. Tues.-Sun. 10am-6pm). The **post office,** 27570 Bremerhaven, directly to the left as you leave the *Hauptbahnhof,* offers a currency exchange and cashes traveler's checks for a DM6 fee and does the usual letter-sending business (open Mon.-Fri. 8am-6pm, Sat. 8am-1pm). The **telephone code** is 0471.

Bremen's combination **Jugendgästehaus/Jugendherberge (HI),** at Gaußstr. 54-56 (tel. 856 52; fax 874 26), bus #2 or #9: Gesundheitsamt, offers a dazzling array of conveniences. As your clothes whirl in the washer and dryer (DM2.50 each), you can borrow one of the management's TVs or clock-radios for free. For a few *Marks* extra, work out in the mini-gym followed by a trip to the sun lamp and a Volkswagen-sized spa (for *Jungendgästehaus* guests only). Incidentally, the hostel also offers beds to sleep in. (Reception open 7am-6am. *Jugendherberge* DM26, over 26 DM30.50. *Jugendgästehaus* DM29.90. Breakfast and sheets included. Curfew 4:30am—yeah, we know, draconian.)

■ Cuxhaven

Just like the old rock song by Boston, the brochures for nearby Cuxhaven boast that the town is "more than a feeling." Actually, it's a play on words: in German, that would be "*mehr als ein Gefühl*," but salty Cuxhaven emphasizes "*Meer* (the German word for 'sea') *als ein Gefühl.*" Clever. Unlike the supergroup or its fellow cities to the South however, Cuxhaven innocuously and quietly follows the beat of a different drummer—that of a senile old man. While the group Boston showcased melodic vocals and soaring guitar solos, Cuxhaven offers the sinking ground of the **Watt**, Northern Germany's unusual sand-marsh landscape. While Boston was influenced by Zeppelin and the Stones, the Watt is influenced only by the contesting gravitational forces of the Earth and Moon. When the tide is out, *Wattwanderers* have the unique opportunity to walk across the semi-permanent landbridge to **Neuwerk Island**. Guides start at DM3, and can be contacted through the tourist office or found on the beach—they are highly recommended (crossing alone is *dangerous*). For those too unmotivated to make the 11-km trek by foot, the horse-drawn **Wattwagen** cart allows easy access to all that wet sand (DM25, ages 10 and under DM12.50). If you find yourself hindered by several tons of water during high tide, the **MS Flipper** makes several daily trips to the island (DM20, round-trip DM28; ages 4-17 DM21, round-trip DM 15.) Once on the island, it's possible to tour with a guide (DM3, children DM2). For more info on transportation and schedules, contact the tourist office or **Reederei Cassen Eils**, on the pier, at Alte Liebe 12 (tel. 322 11).

Pick up your schedule of high and low tide times at the **tourist office** (tel. 360 46; fax 525 64), at Lichtenbergplatz (bus #1, 4, or 21, direction "Duhnen"; open July-Aug. Mon.-Fri. 10am-5pm, Sat. 9am-noon and 2-4pm, Sun. 9am-noon; Sept.-June Mon.-Fri. 10am-5pm). While Boston (the city or the supergroup) is difficult to reach from anywhere in Germany, trains run frequently from Cuxhaven to Bremerhaven (50min.). Ferries run to Helgoland (see p. 357). For intra-Cuxhaven cruising, try a **bike**. Take the bus to Kasernenstr. (#1, 5, or 21) and walk away from Kasernenstr. on Marienstr., then veer right onto Schillerplatz, left on Schillerstr. There you'll find **Zweirad-Paulsen,** Schillerstr. 47 (tel. 362 66), where bikes may be rented for DM9 per day with ID (open Mon.-Fri. 10am-5pm). The **post office** lies at Rohdestr., 27472 Cuxhaven; travelers' checks cashed here. The **telephone code** is 04721.

Cuxhaven's **Jugendherberge (HI)** (tel. 485 52; fax 457 94) is 1½ blocks from the deep blue sea. From the station take bus #1, 2, or 4 (direction "Döse-Duhnen") to Seelust, and backtrack to the *Jugendherberge* sign (reception open 12:30-1pm and after 7pm). As you come in, avoid trampling the swarms of German schoolchildren in their rubber boots clustered around the water pump. The rooms are clean and cheery. Save your room receipt to get onto the beach for free; otherwise you'll pay DM5. Wash your laundry (DM5 with soap) and hang it to dry in the drying room. Curfew 11:30pm. DM19.20, over 26 DM23.70. Sheets DM6. Breakfast included. Partial wheelchair access. **Camping** is available just down the street at **Nordsee Campingplatz,** Cuxhavenstr. 17 (tel. 489 51; DM13 per tent, DM6 per person).

■ Lauenburg

Eight-hundred-year-old Lauenburg an der Elbe was one of the minor lights of the Hanseatic League. It still shines quietly, with picturebook ferry docks, half-timbered houses painted with posies, and winding cobblestone streets. Easy transport to Lauenburg is one of many remnants of the town's past; the town earned its bread as a stop on the great medieval canals connecting the mines of Lüneburg Heath to the perversely salt-starved towns of the Baltic coast (strange but true: Baltic waters do not yield usable table salt). Lauenburg is still on the train route from Lüneburg to Lübeck, with connections to Hamburg and Berlin at either end (2 per hour). The duck-decked **Elbe** river once formed the border between East and West Germany.

The Lauenburg *Altstadt* consists of two halves: the **Unterstadt** (lower city) down by the river, and the **Oberstadt** up above, joined by pathways of narrow steps. The apartment complexes of modern Lauenberg loom above. Most of the sites are located in the *Unterstadt*, an uninterrupted half-timbered strip, built over a stone embankment (the *Sperrmauer*) with a path called the **Uferpromenade** along the river's edge for walking or biking. Lauenberg's houses, many of which date back to the 16th century, are distinctive for their elaborately painted wood-and-brick framework. The **Mensingchehaus,** Elbstr. 49, off the Kirchplatz, is one of very few survivors of a catastrophic 1616 fire that charred the Duke, his young wife, and most of the posher houses in town. The former **Rathaus** (town hall) stands at Elbstr. 59; it now houses the **Elbschiffahrts museum,** which documents the town's shipping industry (open March-Oct. daily 10am-1pm and 2-5pm; Nov.-Feb. Wed. and Fri.-Sun. same hours). The house at Elbstr. 97, only about 6ft. wide, is one of the smallest in Germany; if you've ever wondered about what a house would look like in a fun-house mirror, look no further. Up the cobblestone hills of the *Altstadt,* the **Maria-Magdalena Kirche,** Kircheplatz 1, stands tall and solid over the city; the church tower was a signal to returning sailors that they were at long last home. The 13th-century building was commandeered by the French for a celebration in May 1804 on the day Napoleon crowned himself Emperor (open Thurs.-Tues. 9am-5pm; services Sat. at 5pm and Sun. at 10am). Just beyond the church at the *Amtsplatz* is the **Schloßturm,** built 1457-77. From the top you can see Lauenberg's last remaining windmill, now a museum (open Thurs.-Tues. 10am-5pm). Though lookouts tried to spot fires (as well as invaders) from the tower, the town suffered six town-wide fires in the Middle Ages (open daily March-Oct. 9am-5pm). Nothing remains from the **Schloß** except one wing, now used to house government offices; the building originally dated from 1616.

The **tourist office** (tel. 59 09 81) sits across from the *Schloßturm* on Amtsplatz. The fastest way there from the train station is across the bridge, then left down Hafenstr., which turns into Bahnhofstr. and then Elbstr. Then right up the *Fahrtreppe* (stairstreet), and finally left onto the Amtsplatz (open Mon.-Tues. and Thurs.-Fri. 8:30am-12:30pm and 1:30-6pm, Wed. 8:30am-12:30pm and 1:30-3pm. Closed Wed. afternoons Nov.-March). The **Jugendherberge Lauenburg (HI),** Am Sportplatz 7 (tel. 25 98), is a pleasant hike—if a long one (40min.) from the *Hauptbahnhof.* Cross the bridge and take Hafenstr. left; keep following it as it turns into Bahnhofstr. and Elbstr. At the fork in the road at Elbstr. 20, follow the "Radweg zur Jugendherberge" sign left to the *Uferpromenade* (river path). After about 10min. the paved promenade will end; make a right here onto Kuhgrund (unmarked). Turn left at the *Jugendherberge* sign and take the dirt path through the woods (5min.). The hostel is the big brick building at the top of the hill. The brightly-colored hostel offers game rooms with

---

Matjes

Matjes (MAH-ches), the Scandinavian word for herring, is all the rage in northern Germany during the first few weeks of June, which are officially dubbed the *"Matjes-Wochen"* (Herring Weeks). Several varieties exist: *nederlandisch* (Dutch), with cream sauce and vegetables; *hausfrau* (housewife), in sour cream with onion and apple; and sweet and sour, doused in sugared vinegar—but any restaurant worth its salt has its own secret recipe. Look for *Matjes* advertised everywhere, from the dives in the train station to the hip Schanzenstr. cafés in Hamburg. The fish has a very strong, sweetish taste that is not acquired—you'll either love it or hate it. Wash it down with a glass of *Alsterwasser*—literally "water from the Alster" (one of Hamburg's lakes), but actually a gentle mix of beer and lemonade which tastes a lot better than it sounds.

ping pong and a TV. (DM19, over 26 DM23.50. Breakfast included. Sheets DM6. Closed Dec. 15-Jan. 15. The hostel also plays host to a summer cooking school; DM7 to test the budding talents of young chefs.) In the *Altstadt*, right off Bahnhofstr., try the **Freidank Gästezimmer,** Große Sandberg 5 (tel. 38 36). This traditional house has big, bright singles and doubles (DM29-33 per person; breakfast included). Similar private *Pensionen* abound in the Altstadt, mostly closer to the train station; look for "Fremdezimmer" or "Zimmer frei" signs. A persistent reminder of Lauenburg's shipping life is the local consumption of *Eierspunch,* an old sailor's drink made according to an ancient alchemical recipe; ask for it by name. For food, try one of the outdoor cafés on the waterfront, such as the **Schifferbörte Café and Restaurant,** Elbstr. 82 (tel. 27 73). Enjoy Elvis-esque German music while sitting by the large windows in your blue suede shoes, surveying the open seas. Fish dishes DM15-25. The excellent **Hotel-Restaurant zum alten Schifferhaus,** Elbstr. 112 (tel. 24 08), has a wide variety of herring dishes for DM15-20. The **telephone code** is 04153.

■ Helgoland

Helgoland is less a resort island than a game show—"The Duty-Free Dash." The contestants (hordes of German tourists) must pile onto ferries, ride small skiffs to the island, and dash frantically from store to store snatching up all of the cigarettes, cheeses, and meter-tall bottles of liquor that they can legally carry before the skiffs head back to the ferry at 4pm.

But there are attractions for nature-lovers as well as bargain-hunters on Helgoland. If you have only a day to see it, don't go. "Getting there is half the fun" is a cliché, not an axiom, and three hours on this admittedly lovely island can't justify the four-to-six-hour round-trip ferry ride. An open-ended ticket (DM13 more than a day trip) will give you time to push through the throngs and enjoy the phenomenal view. The extra time will also allow you to find tiny trails and quiet corners to admire the red cliffs that give Helgoland poetic cachet equal to that of its pale English cousin Dover. *Rot ist die Wand, weiß ist der Sand, Grün ist das Land; Das sind die Farben von Helgoland* (Red are the cliffs, white is the sand, green is the land; these are the colors of...). The island itself has at various times been controlled by pirates, Frisians, the Hanseatic League, Danes, and Britons; the Germans traded Zanzibar to the U.K. for Helgoland in 1890 (there are *no* direct ferry connections to Zanzibar, and *Let's Go* does *not* recommend swimming to Britain).

The cheapest and most reliable way to get to Helgoland is through Cuxhaven, Norddeich, Bremerhaven, or Wilhelmshaven; ferries also leave from some of the Frisian Islands (including Norderney and Langeoog), but their schedules are erratic. From May to September, the **MS Wappen von Hamburg,** which sails from Cuxhaven's *Fährhafen* harbor, is probably your best bet. The ride is relatively short (2 hrs.) and the price is competitive. (Departs daily at 10:30am. Open-ended round-trip DM 68, ages 12-18 DM40. Day excursions DM 55, ages 12-18 DM36.) The **MS Frisia III,** operating from Norddeich, offers a lower fare but a longer ride (4hr.) and a skimpier schedule. (Departs May-June every Tues. at 8am, July-Aug. Tues. and Fri. at 8am. Day-trips only DM43, 12 and under DM27.) If you want to ride one momma of a ship, the **MS Helgoland** leaves from the *Seebäderkaje* in Bremerhaven for a 4-hr. sprint to the shopper's paradise. (Departs April-Oct. daily at 9:45am. Open-ended round-trip DM68, ages 12-17 DM38. Day excursions DM55, ages 12-17 DM36.) Finally, the **MS Wilhelmshaven** sets sail from its namesake; prices are the same as those for its much heftier sister, the MS Helgoland, but the ride takes a little longer. (Departs March-Oct. daily at 9am.)

With thousands of visitors coming each year, Helgoland's **tourist office** (tel. (04725) 814 30) greets travelers as they step off the skiff. Their free prospectus offers a wealth of info (and pretty color pictures), including a list of hotels and other accommodations (open Mon.-Fri. 9am-4pm, Sat. 11am-3pm). Helgoland's **Jugendherberge "Haus der Jugend" (HI),** Postfach 580 (tel./fax (04725) 341), sits right on the beach, a short 15-minute walk from the ferry dock following the signs. (Reception open

10am-2pm and 5-7pm. Curfew 10pm. DM42, over 26 DM37. Three meals included. Sheets DM10. Open April-Oct.) Call weeks ahead.

■ Oldenburg

The city of Oldenburg was spared the destruction of the Thirty Years War largely because its head honcho at the time, Count Anton Günther, raised the most beautiful horses in all of Germany. Today, if you look at a map of the city's 150,000-m-sq. pedestrian zone—the largest in the country—you'll see a striking resemblance to a two-headed, five-legged horse. Coicindence? We think not. Interest in equestrian activity has been passed even to this generation of Oldenburgers. Every morning, the city's residents jockey for positions with hundreds of tourists as daily markets bustle in two different squares: one on the **Pferdmarkt,** an erstwhile horse-showing arena near the yellow and brick state library; the other on the main square surrounding the 1888 **Rathaus.** The 13th-century **Lambertikirche,** next door, has a Neoclassical version of the Pantheon in its belly (open Tues.-Fri. 11am-12:30pm and 2:30-5pm, Sat. 11am-12:30pm; free). The center of the Weser and Ems River region, little Oldenburg was a Danish foothold from 1667 to 1773, when it blossomed in independence. The **Landesmuseum,** Schloßplatz 26, housed in the yellow-and-white *Schloß* with gingerbread trim exhibits an extensive painting collection, with special emphasis on Goethe's friend and fan, Johann Tischbein (open Tues.-Fri. 9am-5pm, Sat.-Sun. 10am-5pm; admission DM4, students, children and seniors DM2). The **Augusteum,** Elisabethstr. 1 (tel. 220 26 00), is an extension of the *Landesmuseum* with two floors of groggy surrealist dreamscapes and Kirchner's Expressionist street scenes (open Tues.-Fri. 9am-5pm, Sat.- Sun. 10am-5pm; admission DM4; students, children, and seniors DM2). For a little less esoteric action, walk another 300m to the **Naturkunde and Vorgeschichte Musuem** (Natural and Prehistory Museum), Damm 40-44 (tel. 924 43 00), and give yourself the hee-bee-jeebies with the gruesome 2400-year-old swamp bodies (open Tues.-Thurs. 9am-5pm, Sat.-Sun. 10am-5pm; admission DM3, students and children DM1.5).

If you want to go where everybody knows your name, take a hike up around Wallstr.—where almost every restaurant boasts "American-style" cuisine with Harley Davidson decor to match. Sip a Miller or a Bud (sheepishly, we hope—you're in Germany, for goodness' sake) as your eyes ogle NFL paraphernalia at **Taking it Easy,** Wallstr. 12 (tel. 158 27), down the street from the tourist office (open daily after 6pm). Where Wallstr. turns into Lappan, you can find **Alte Schmiede am Lappan,** an old-style blacksmith shop where you can watch the craftspeople at work (open Mon.-Fri. 9:30am-6pm, Sat. 10am-1:30pm). Cool your sweltered head with a beer (German, this time) at **Marvin's Biergarten,** on Rosenstr. Head up Bahnhofstr. and go left on Rosenstr. (open Mon.-Thurs. and Sun. 7pm-2am, Fri.-Sat. 8pm-3am).

Bremen is not far from Oldenburg (35min.). The old, moated city lies along an offshoot of the Weser River, opening the way to East Frisia and serves as the take-off point for most excursions. The **tourist office,** Wallstr. 14 (tel. 157 44), finds rooms (from DM35) for a DM4 fee and plies visitors with numerous North Sea brochures (open Mon.-Fri. 9am-6pm, Sat. 9am-noon). You can also visit the **Fremdenverkehrsverband Nordsee-Niedersachsen-Bremen,** Bahnhofstr. 19-20 (tel. 92 17 10), for invaluable information on the East Frisian islands as well as regional information for the area between Holland and Hamburg (open Mon.-Thurs. 8am-5pm, Fri. 8am-4pm). **Rent bikes** at the **Fahrradstation,** on Neues-Str. (tel. 163 45), right across the street from the tourist office on Wallstr. (Bikes DM12 per day, DM42 per week. Passport or other personal ID required.) The city's modern **Jugendherberge (HI),** Alexanderstr. 65 (tel. 871 35), is 1.5km from the the station. Go down Moslestr. and turn right on Am Stadtmuseum; as Am Stadtmuseum disintegrates into an impossible jumble of intersecting streets, head in the general direction in which you were previously moving until you reach the greens of the Gertruden-Friedhof cemetery, with Alexanderstr. veering to your left. Or take bus #7, 9, or 12 to "Lappen," and then #2 or 3 to "Von Finckstr." (Reception open 5-10pm. Curfew 10pm. DM20, over 26 DM24. Breakfast included. The hostel fills quickly, so call several days ahead.) The **Hotel Hegeler,** Donnerschweerstr. 27 (tel./fax 875 61), has clean rooms and a bowling alley (DM20 per hr.). From the station, cross the pedestrian bridge over the tracks (near the post office) and follow the road to Donnerschweerstr.; then turn left and walk 150m. (Singles DM45, with shower and toilet DM75. Doubles DM90, with shower DM130. Call a few days ahead.) Oldenburg's **postal code** is 26123. The **telephone code** is 0441.

■ Wilhelmshaven

The personality of Kaiser William the Great certainly doesn't match that of the city that bears his name. If you walk up to his statue on **Friedrich Wilhelm Platz,** you'll see that he certainly isn't smiling about it. Instead of the solemn authoritarianism he preferred, Wilhelmshaven is a place where people make liberal merry—and where the boats may well outnumber the people. The city's location on the **Jadebusen** and its excellent harbor enable the town to pursue its three passions—eating, drinking, and boating—in close proximity. Right by the **Kaiser-Wilhelm Brücke** floats the bright red **Feuerschiff,** used until 1981 to fight boat fires (open daily 11am-midnight, free).The boat also houses a bar and grill serving food and drinks (open daily 11:30am-3pm and 6-10pm). For more active *Schiffvergnügen* (ship pleasure), rent a sail, paddle, or rowboat at the **Boatverleih** (tel. 20 26 22), and pick up a *Bockwurst* and beer from the adjacent *Gaststätte* (DM6.50; open May-Sept. daily 11:30am-9pm, boats DM18 per hour). From the Pumpwerk stop, go south on Jadestr. then right onto Ems for 10 min., follow the signs left onto Henschelstr., then walk 200m.

For something completely different, and *extremely* disturbing to the Kaiser, visit the **Pumpwerk Kulturzentrum,** An der Deichbrücke (tel. 438 77). Witness the decline of Western civilization daily with some of Germany's most egregious pop bands, or revel in the death of theater with productions like "Stories from the Belly of the Moon," in which the comical Frau Mond (Mrs. Moon) tells tales of her observations of the Earth. Times, prices, and quality of taste vary. A few rungs higher on the hipness ladder stands the **Hotel Kling Klang,** Böxsenstr. 73 (tel. 133 22), just up the street from the tourist center. By day, it's a pleasant, unassuming café with spray-painted stools. By night, the small, dark stage showcases musical acts ranging from a KISS revival to original hip hop and DJs (open Mon.-Sat. 10am-late, Sun. 11am-late). Not even Gene Simmons can rock all night on an empty stomach; that's why there's *Auflauf* at **Pumpwerk I** (not to be confused with the Kulturzentrum), Ahrstr. 24 (tel. 445 90). Take line 3 (or line A after hours) to the Kaiser-Wilhelm-Brücke stop. Choose ingredients from broccoli to salami to add to the starchy mash that is *Auflauf* (DM11.80). Open daily from 6pm.

Walk straight out of the station along Virchowstr. and make a left on Börsenstr. to the **tourist office,** Börsenstr. 55b (tel. 92 79 30), which can find you a private room (open Mon.-Fri. 9am-6pm, Sat. 9am-1pm). Conveniently located down Gökerstr. from the hostel is Oeltermann's, Holtermanstr. 2 (tel. 321 54), where you can rent a **bicycle** for DM9 per day (open Mon.-Fri. 8am-1pm and 3-6pm, Sat. 8am-1pm). Wilhelmshaven's **postal code** is 26382. The **telephone code** is 04421.

The **Wilhelmshaven Jugendherberge (HI),** Freiligrathstr. 131 (tel. 600 48; fax 647 16), sits on the city outskirts by the botanical gardens. Take bus #1 (or bus A after hours) to Friedenstr. and follow the sign 200m. (Reception open 24hr. Curfew 11:30pm, but you get a house key. DM20, over 26 DM24. Breakfast included. Sheets DM5. Closed in Nov.). Closer to the *Hauptbahnhof,* the city, and the beach is **Privat-Pension Heine Lübben,** Rheinstr. 25 (tel. 431 69). From the station, walk along Virchowstr. toward the water and turn left on Rheinstr. Go down three blocks and look to your left. If you find yourself standing in the Jadebusen, you've gone too far. (Reception open daily 10am-10pm. Singles DM40, doubles DM80.) From Wilhelmshaven you can sail away to the sun and surf of the German vacation paradise **Helgoland** (see p. 357).

■ Jever

Jever is the small town equivalent of a happy drunk—often charming, occasionally vulgar, and wholly kept afloat by beer. The astute observer can't help but notice, next to the town water pump in the city center, a sculpture of a dog answering nature's call on the pump. Jever's charm is much easier to find. From the train station go right on Anton-Gunther Str. and left on Mühlenstr., and the town's little 15th- century onion-domed **Schloß** will appear on your left. The castle's museum is pure charm (open March-Jan. Tues.-Sun. 10am-6pm; admission DM4, students DM2, children under 6 DM1). The 16th-century **Rathaus** in the main square (open Mon.-Wed., Fri. 8am-noon, Thurs. 2-5pm) borders the **Weinhausgang.** On Kirchplatz, the old **Stadtkirche** (city church) is now thoroughly modern inside, after being burned down and reconstructed nine times in its 900-year history.

To uncover the town's frothy foundations, follow your nose to the **Jever Brewery** (tel. 137 11) for a **tour** of the complex that puts Jever on the map, and on tap, in *Kneipen* all over northern Germany. A trifling DM10 gets you the tour, a souvenir mug, a tasty *Langenbrezel* (big soft pretzel), and 0.6L of sharp *Jever* lager. (Tours April-Oct. Mon.-Fri. 9:30am-12:30pm, every half hour; Nov.-March Tues.-Thurs. at 10:30am only; DM10. Call several weeks ahead to reserve a place—you're not the only beer drinker who knows a good thing when you see it.)

The **tourist office,** Alter Markt 18 (tel. 710 10; fax 93 92 99), across from the *Schloß,* books rooms for free and directs the smell-impaired to the brewery (open May-Sept. Mon.-Fri. 10am-6pm, Sat. 10am-2pm, Sun. 10am-noon; Oct.-April. Mon.-Thurs. 10am-5pm, Fri. 9am-1pm). The **Jugendherberge Jever (HI),** Mooshütterweg 12 (tel. 35 90), idles on a small street behind the *Schloß.* The rooms, holding up to 10 beds, are a bit cramped, but plaid quilts and colored curtains brighten the atmosphere. (Reception open 5–9:45pm. Curfew 10pm. DM17, over 26 DM22. Breakfast included. No lockable doors or lockers. Sheets DM5. Open April-Oct.) The **telephone code** is 04461.

■ East Frisian Islands

Seven sandy islands bracelet the East Frisian (*Ostfriesische*) North Sea coast. Control of the dunes has shuffled between Russia, Prussia, Holland, and various Scandinavian countries for several centuries, but today their value is more therapeutic than strategic: flash floods of Germans come here to be healed by the purifying air. And trust us, you'll get plenty of it as you pedal around, furiously obeying the car ban (enforced on all islands except Norderney and Baltrum). For those seeking a less strenuous route, follow your nose to the nearest horse carriage—your olfactory sense can tell you that they're everywhere. Whether by huffing it or hoofing it, once you leave the city, you're sure to discover the serene landscape and refreshing air that beckoned the royalty of old. As you ride the ferries, keep a sharp eye out for the *Seehünde* (seals) flapping their tails at you. If you fail to wave back to the seals, the natives will think you're rude. Instead try hollering back, "Moin! Moin!" (the North German phrase for hello), to impress them (the natives, that is).

When the tide is out, the marshy landscape of the *Watt* appears, connecting the mainland to Baltrum, Norderney, Spiekeroog and Langeoog. *Never* venture out onto these *Watts* without a guide: the tide's quick return can be *extremely* dangerous. Do, however, make the trek (8-10km) with a certified guide to witness the vast and splendid desolation of the ocean floor. The tourist offices where there is *Watt* terrain have information about guides (*Wattführer*) in their area. (Tours cost about DM5 for 2hr.) If it is cold and wet outside, don't despair; try some hot **East Frisian tea,** or listen as a local tells a fish story in the incomprehensible (even to most Germans) *Plattdeutsch* dialect. Also be sure you sample the area's seafood. The region's specialty is *Matja* (baby herring); it's cheap and it's everywhere (see Matjes, p. 356).

Six of the islands—Borkum, Juist, Norderney (two hostels), Langeoog, Spiekeroog, and Wangerooge—have **HI youth hostels,** and there are several more on the mainland coast. Don't expect to show up at the hostel and get a bed, because swarms of German schoolchildren will have already beat you to it. Call weeks, even months, in advance. Most of the hostels require you to purchase *Vollpension* (full board; 3 meals per day); a resort tax also slithers its way onto the accommodation bills. The most vexing problem of East Frisian tourism is getting there: a variety of small companies run **ferries** to individual islands from separate mainland ports (railpasses not valid). However, there is no inter-island transport. An unadulterated atmosphere is ensured by **car bans** on all islands except Borkum and Norderney.

NORDERNEY

Before the beautiful people vacationed in Aspen and Acapulco, they came to **Norderney.** Germany's oldest North Sea spa, the island has served as a retreat for such illustrious guests as the Hanoverian monarchs, Otto von Bismarck, and Heinrich Heine. An endless stream of ferries from Norddeich dumps loads of luggage-toting tourists at the port (July-Aug. 14 daily departures, Sept.-June at least 9 daily; open-ended round-trip DM28.50, ages 11 and under DM14.25; call (04931) 987 24 for information.) To dodge the hordes, head east to the Norderney's desolate dunes and endless beaches. The **Fahrradverleih am Hafen** (tel. 13 26; 300m down Hafenstr. as you step off the ferry) rents **bikes** at an unbeatable location (open daily 9am-6:30pm; DM7 for 4 hrs., DM10 for the day, children DM5 and DM8 respectively).

If you want to spent the night, the friendly folks at the **tourist office,** Bülowallee 5 (tel. 918 50; fax 824 94), sniff out rooms in *Pensionen* (DM40) or private homes (longer stays only, DM30) for a DM7.50 fee (open March-Oct. Mon.-Fri. 9am-12:30pm and 2-6pm, Sat. 10am-12:30pm and 2-4pm, Sun. 10am-12:30pm; Nov.-Feb. Mon.-Fri. 9am-12:30pm and 2:30-6pm). The **telephone code** is 04932.

Norderney's two **Jugendherbergen (HI)** are both extremely crowded and expensive; they require you to pay for full pension (3 meals) for the duration of your stay. The owner of the hostel at **Südstraße** (tel. 24 51; fax 836 00) will take pains to provide a haven for stranded travelers. Follow Zum Fähranleger to Deichstr., then onto Südstr. (Reception open 8:30-9am, 5:15-6pm, and 9:45-10pm. DM37.40, including both the local tourist tax and full board. Members only. Sheets DM5. Open March-Oct.) Closer to the nude beach, but not much else, is the hostel **Am Dünensender 3** (tel. 25 74; fax 832 66); if you miss the bus (destination: "Leuchtturm"; 1 per hr.), you'll have to rent a **bike** in town or suffer the1½-2-hour walk. Follow Deichstr. to its end, and head left on Karl Reger Weg, where signs point you to the hostel, the dunes, and the nude beach. Choose your destiny. (Reception open 8:30am-10am. DM33, over 26 DM42. Full board included. Open March-Oct.) **Camping** is available in summer for HI members only. (DM11 per person with breakfast.) **Camping Booken,**Waldweg 2 (tel. 448), is expensive, but the next best thing to the hostels. Call ahead. (Reception open 10am-noon. DM12 per person, DM12 per tent. DM10 per mobile home. Warm showers included. Washer DM6, dryer DM5.)

BORKUM, JUIST, AND BALTRUM

The largest and western-most of the islands, Borkum is a perfect choice for idle perambulation. The island offers a spectrum of seaside pleasures from beacon (the 1576 **lighthouse** on Richthofenstr.) to bakin' (the **nude beach,** or "FKK Strand"— *FreiKörperKultur*). For the latter, take the bus to "FKK-Strand." In winter, Borkum locals go crazy during the **Klaasohm folk festival** every year on December 6.

Make reservations for **private rooms** and pick up a bus map at the **tourist office,** Goethestr. 1 (*Kurverwaltung*; tel. 30 33 10; for rooms call 841). Hours fluctuate wildly. The **ferry** ride leaves from the dock in Emden, the first port on the train from Oldenburg. (Ride lasts 2 hr. Departures March-Oct. and last week in Dec. 22-31 daily at 8, 11am, and 2, 5pm; Jan.-March and Oct.-Dec. Mon.-Thurs. and Sat. 8am and 3:30pm, Fri. and Sun. 8am and 4:30pm. Day excursion DM25, children 4-11 DM12.5; round-trip DM46, children DM23. Weekend ticket (depart Fri., return Sun.) DM35, children DM17.50.) Double-hulled **catamarans** also skim across to the island. (Trip lasts 1hr. Departures irregular. DM15 surcharge on regular prices.) A second ferry runs from Borkum to **Eemshaven** in the Netherlands (day-excursion DM21, children DM10.50; round-trip DM38, children DM19). Seasonal schedule varies from year to year. For more information and specific dates, call **Reederei Aktien-Gesellschaft** (tel. (04921) 89 07 22). The **telephone code** is 04922. Borkum's **Jugendherberge (HI)**, Jann-Berghaus-Str. 63 (tel. 579; fax 71 24), a five-minute walk from the dock, fills up quickly. To get a room, a prior request in writing is required. (Curfew 10:30pm, but house keys are available. With *Vollpension* DM33, over 26 DM37.) **Insel-Camping**, at Hindenburgstr. 114 (tel. 10 88), is 15 minutes from the train station by foot. (DM20 per person, tent included. Open mid-March to Oct.)

Juist (yoo-IST) is just 17km long, 500m wide, and famous for its birds. First settled in 1398, it's a bit tough to settle there now. Ferries leave from the port at Norddeich at odd times, depending on tides and season; call (04931) 98 70 for details. (Ferries June-Oct. roughly 2 per day. Day excursion DM28.50, round-trip DM40, children ages 4-11 half-price.) The **tourist office** (*Kurverwaltung*; tel. 80 90; fax 80 92 23), Friesen-str. 18, has maps and a free room-finding service (rooms DM30-40 per person; open May-Sept. Mon.-Fri. 8:30am-noon and 3-5pm, Sat. 10am-noon; Oct.-April Mon.-Fri. 3-6pm). The rental shop **Germania**, Wilhelmstr. 17 (tel. 297), right on Wilhelmstr. as you disembark on the island (300m away), has over 600 **bikes** to lease (DM10 per day and up, ID required; open daily 9am-6pm). The tiny island also has its own **Jugendherberge**, Loogster Pad 20. (tel. 929 10; fax 82 94. Reception open daily 8-10pm or whenever a boat arrives. DM28.30 with breakfast and dinner, over 26 DM32.30. Open Mar.-Dec.) The **telephone code** is 04935.

The smallest of the Frisian Islands, with a population of 500, **Baltrum** is the ideal escape from civilization. A total ban on automobiles and electric cars, combined with the lack of a bicycle rental, creates an atmosphere of unusual peace. To reach **Baltrum** take the bus from the Norden train station (one short stop from Norddeich) to **Neßmersiel** to meet the ferry (open-ended round-trip DM36; day excursion DM22; children half-price). Train, bus, and boat are all timed for a convenient rendezvous (June-Nov. 2-3 per day; last ferry to the island does not have a corresponding ferry back). For more information, check the schedule, call the ferry company at 235, or visit the **tourist office**, Rathausstr. 130 (tel. 800; fax 80 27; for rooms call 80 48) in the *Rathaus*. The office also offers hotel information and books private accommodations for a 5% commission (open March-Oct. Mon.-Fri. 8:30am-noon and 2-5pm; Nov.-Feb. Mon.-Fri. 9am-noon). The **telephone code** is 04939.

LANGEOOG, SPIEKEROOG, AND WANGEROOGE

The bus from Norden (DM7.50) or from **Esens** (DM3.50) takes you to Bensersiel, the departure point for ferries to "Long Island"—not the one in New York, but **Langeoog,** which once served as a base for 18th-century pirates. (May-Sept. 6 daily departures, Oct.-April 3 departures. Open-ended round-trip DM34, children half-price; day excursion DM28.) For more info or to book a room (DM30), visit the **tourist office** in front of the *Bahnhof*, at Hauptstr. 28 (tel. 693 201; fax 65 28; open Mon.-Sat. 9am-7pm, Sun. 10am-2pm; in winter, Mon.-Fri. 9am-5pm). Rent a bike next door at **Fahrrad Verlein** (tel. 64 74; open daily 9am-12:30pm and 1:30-6pm).

Langeoog's **Jugendherberge Domäne Melkhörn (HI)** is smack-dab in the middle of the island (tel. 276; fax 66 94). Direct bus service from the port spares you the 4km walk. (DM34.55, over 26 DM38.55. Members only. Full board included.) The hostel also runs a **campground**. (Curfew at 10pm, but if you're 18 or older, you can get a key. DM29.55. Members only. Full board included. Reservation required. Open April-Sept.) The **telephone code** is 04972.

The **Bäderbus** also goes to Neuharlingersiel, the departure point for **Spiekeroog,** the island that takes pride in its historic shipwrecks and its natural silence—"No festivals celebrated here," brags the official brochure. Its **tourist office**, Noorderpad 25 (tel. 919 30; for rooms call 919 25), has information on ferries, rooms, and dune paths (open March-Oct. Mon.-Fri. 9am-noon and 2-4pm, Sat. 9am-noon). Spiekeroog's **Jugendherberge,** Bid Utkiek 1 (tel. 329), is a trifling 10-min. walk from either the port or the beach. (DM35 per person. Full board included. Written reservations are required 1 year in advance! Open April-Oct.). The **telephone code** is 04976.

The journey to **Wangerooge** is a Herculean labor, but worth it for the island's lack of crowds; enjoy the beach and the sea of solitude (no pun intended). From Norden take a 90-minute bus ride on the *Bäderbus* to the sea town of **Harlesiel**. Boats leave the dock two to five times daily from April to October and once or twice daily the rest of the year; exact times vary widely with the season. (Open-ended round-trip DM44, children 4-11 half-price; day excursion DM29). Wangerooge's own **tourist office** on the Strandpromenade (tel. 990; fax 991 14; for room-finding service, call 948 80) has ferry information (open Mon.-Fri. 9am-noon and 2-5pm, Sat.-Sun. whenever a ferry arrives.) They can also direct you to the haunting **Westturm**, a landmark that's been converted into a striking **Jugendherberge (HI)**, a 20-min. walk from the station (tel. 439). Look for the old stone tower. (Reception open daily 7-9am, 1-3pm, and 5-7pm. Curfew 10pm. DM31.90 with full board, over 26 is DM35.90. Open May-Sept.) The **telephone code** is 04469.

EMDEN

If you end up stuck in **Emden** while waiting for the ferry to Borkum, don't despair. After picking up a map at the *Hauptbahnhof*, head on to the *Innenstadt* (bus #3001: Rathaus or take the 15-min. walk along Grosse Straße). The **tourist office,** on Am Stadtgarten near the *Rathaus* (tel. 974 00; fax 974 09), gives out brochures for free and sells a bargain ticket that'll let you into four of the city's different museums (DM9, under 18 D4.50; open May-Sept. Mon.-Fri. 9am-6pm, Sat. 10am-1pm, Sun. 11am-1pm; Jan.-April Mon.-Fri. 9am-1pm and 3-5:30pm, Sat. 10am-1pm). The **Kunsthalle,** Hinter dem Rahmen 13 (tel. 209 95), is a perfect afternoon outing; the permanent collection includes Picasso and Franz Marc, and excellent special exhibits abound in the summer. For the clueless, but Germanophonic, rooms atop the museum's spiral staircases offer crash courses in 20th-century art (open Tues. 10am-8pm, Wed.-Fri. 10am-5pm, Sat.-Sun. 11am-5pm; admission DM7, students, seniors, and children DM4).

The newest museum in town is the highly-acclaimed **Bunker Museum** (tel. 271 06; open May-Oct. Tues.-Fri. 11am-1pm and 3-5pm, Sat.-Sun. 1-2pm). For only DM3 (students DM1) you can explore six floors of an old air-raid shelter stocked with memorabilia which traces the sad fate of Emden's population from 1933 to 1944, when the city was firebombed, and 85% of its buildings destroyed. For a more light-hearted experience, a visit to **Das Otto Haus** is in order. The three-story edifice is a shrine to comedian, children's entertainer, and **living legend** Otto Waalkes, a native Emdener. The first floor is free; see kissing elephants (Otto's symbol) and buy images of Otto on everything from rubber to silicon. (Does Benny Hill have his own Sega video game? We think not.) To see the second and third floors, featuring photos of Otto clowning with Boris Becker and Steffi Graf, and other madcap antics, pilgrims must pay (admission DM4, children DM1.50; open April-Oct. Mon.-Fri. 9:30am-6pm, Sat. 9:30am-1pm and 3-6pm, Sun. 10am-4pm; Nov.-Mar. Mon.-Fri. 9:30am-1pm and 3-6pm). Call 862 390 to get on a tour of the town's mammoth **Volkswagen plant** (open Mon.-Thurs. 9:30am-1:30pm). The **telephone code** is 04921.

Jugendherberge Emden (HI), An der Kesselschleuse 5 (tel. 237 97; fax 321 61), overlooks a small stream and offers bikes and canoes for rent. If you miss Bus Linie 3003 to Herrentor (1 per hr.), it's a 20-minute walk from the *Rathaus*. The hostel caters to the kiddies with comical paintings of cartoon animals. (DM19.50, over 26 DM23.50. Breakfast included. Sheets DM6. Reception open 5-10pm).

NORDEN AND NORDDEICH

Norden is the transportation polestar for any excursion around Frisia. By train, it connects to Emden and Norddeich (DM3; every hr.), and as the anchor of the **Bäderbus** and the only public link to Neßmersiel, it provides easy access to every other port town. Call or visit the **tourist office** (*Kurverwaltung;* tel. 986 02; fax 98 62 90) in the marketplace, next to the *Rathaus* (open Mon.-Fri. 8am-3pm, Sat. 9am-1pm) for specific transportation info, or to book rooms (from DM20) for no fee.

From the *Rathaus*, not even a Gomer Pyle could miss the gigantic steeple across the market. The spire belongs to the 15th-century Ludgerkirche, famed for its exquisite organ. (Church open April-Sept. Mon. 10am-12:30pm, Tues.-Sat. 10am-12:30pm and 3-5pm.) One of the peculiarities of the North Sea coast is its natives' great love of **tea,** even more than beer; perhaps this is because of the region's proximity to Britain, or the sobriety required for sound nautical exploits. You can revel in the gift of the leaves at the one and only **East Frisian Tea Museum,** am Markt (tel. 121 00), in the town square. For DM1 on Wednesdays (May-Aug. only), you can participate in an East Frisian **tea ceremony,** which resembles its Japanese counterpart only in its placid atmosphere. The ceremony takes place at tea time (2 and 3pm), of course (open March-Oct. Tues.-Sat. 10am-4pm; admission DM4, children DM1.50). In the same building is the **Heimat Museum,** which shows the early culture of *Ostfriesland*, including dike construction and shoemaking. You can visit the distant ancestors of Nike here, but remember that Neon Deion ain't gonna dance in these blocks of carved wood for nuthin'.

Ten minutes away by bus or rail, the port of **Norddeich** provides an outstanding **Jugendherberge (HI),** Strandstr. 1 (tel. 80 64; fax 818 28), for the dune-weary traveler. From the train station, facing the sea, follow the road behind the dike, walk 30m past the Hotel Regina Maris, and turn left on Strandstr. (Reception open 5-8pm. DM20.10, over 26 DM24.10. Breakfast included.) The hostel's backyard tent sleeps eight (DM15.50 per person); they'll also let you pitch your own (DM14.75 per person). Staff here is unparalled in youthful cheer and hospitality. **Nordsee-Camp,** Deichstr. 21 (tel. 80 73; fax 80 74), is 20 minutes further down Badestr., which turns into Deichstr. Impressive views, but dike-side camping gets chilly at night. (Camping DM5 per day, DM8.25 per person, plus DM3 tourist tax. Open mid-Mar. to Oct.)

The Norddeich **tourist office,** Dörperweg 22 (tel. 98 62 00), accepts donations to the Save-the-Seals Fund and finds rooms in *Pensionen* (DM23-35). From the train station, head down Badestr. and turn left on Dörperweg (open Mon.-Thurs. 8:30am-1pm and 2-4:30pm, Fri. 8:30am-4pm, Sat. 10am-4pm). The **postal code** is 26506; the **telephone code** for both cities is 04931.

■ Osnabrück

In 1648, the Peace of Westphalia, ending the Thirty Years War, was negotiated in Osnabrück. The peaceful vibes haven't stopped flowing since—the town is perhaps the feel-good capital of Germany, complete with syrupy tourist brochures that say "Have a Nice Day." While walking through the old city square, take time out from spreading sunshine to visit the **Rathaus.** Here Osnabrückers have preserved the **Friedenssaal** (Hall of Peace) for three and a half centuries in memory of their 15 minutes of historical fame as the site of the negotiations (*Rathaus* open Mon.-Fri. 6am-7pm, Sat. 9am-1pm, Sun. 10am-1pm. Free tour of the Friedenssaal Sun. at 10:30am. Call 323 44 13 for more info.) When the long-awaited reconciliation finally took place in 1648, children flocked to the streets of Osnabrück in celebration. Every 25th of October in remembrance, regiments of children ride hobby horses to the mayor to demand their reward of a pretzel. Next to the *Rathaus* stands the **Marienkirche,** completely destroyed during the war, but now fully rebuilt (open Mon.-Sat. 10am-noon and 3-5pm). The **tower** can be toured Sundays from 11:30am to 1pm (admission DM2, children DM1).

A reminder of a less warm and fuzzy Germany is the permanent **Felix Nussbaum** (1904-1944) exhibit at the **Museum of Cultural History;** Nussbaum's paintings depict the tragedy of the Holocaust with heart-wrenching symbolism (open Mon.-Fri. 8:30am-6pm, Sat.-Sun. 10am-1pm; admission DM3, students and children DM1.5). Perhaps the most famous son of Osnabrück is Erich Maria Remarque, the acclaimed author of *Im Westen, nicht Neues (All Quiet on the Western Front).* Though Allied bombing completely destroyed his house on Hafenstr., which was never rebuilt, literary diehards are welcome to see the new **Erich Maria Remarque-Archive,** Alte Münze 16 (tel. 969 45 11), which documents his life and times (open Mon. and Wed.-Thurs. 9am-noon, Tues. 9am-noon and 2-4pm).

The **tourist office,** Krahnstr. 58 (tel. 323 22 02; fax 323 42 13), stands between the *Dom* and the *Marienkirche* (open Mon.-Fri. 10am-6pm, Sat. 10am-2pm, Sun. 11am-1pm). From the station, walk up Möserstr. as it turns into Herrenteichsstr., follow the curve around, and turn onto Krahnstr. The office will peacefully book you a room (DM30 and up per person) for free. The **Fahrradverleih,** in the train station (tel. 25 91 31), leases the *Rikscha-Fahrrad* (rickshaw cycle), the Euro-Asiatic equivalent of a go-cart (DM70 per day, DM299 per week), as well as rents simpler, more modest **bikes.** (DM8 per day, DM35 per week. Open Mon.-Fri. 6am-8pm, Sat. 7am-2pm. ID and DM20 deposit required.) The other transportation option is to take the bus around the city center (DM2) or to the outer zones (DM2.50). Launder your dirty duds at **Wasch Center,** on the corner of Kommenderiestr. and Petersburger-Wall (open 6am-11pm). While waiting for your clothes to dry, whip out a calendar and count down the days to May Week, a 10-day celebration characterized by huge open air markets (May 9-19, 1997). The **telephone code** is 0541.

South of the city center is the newly outfitted **Jugendgästehaus Osnabrück,** Iurger Str. 183a (tel. 542 84; fax 542 94). From in front of the station, take bus #13, 15, 62, or 83 and change at "Neumarkt" for the #23, 25 or 27 to "Kinderhospital," then turn left and follow the signs up a tree-lined path. (Reception open 5-10pm. DM25, over 26 DM29.50. Breakfast and sheets included. Bathrooms wheelchair accessible.) Clean rooms fill the **Hotel Jägerheim,** Johannistor-Wall 19a (tel. 216 35). From the station, turn left on Konrad-Adenauer-Ring, which becomes Petersberger-Wall and then Johannistor-Wall. (Reception closes at 9pm, so call ahead. DM39 per person, with shower DM44, with shower and toilet DM61.) For **camping,** try **Freizeitpark Attersee,** Zum Attersee 50 (tel. 12 41 47). Take bus #22 from the train station to "Attersee." (DM5.50 per person, DM6 per tent. Showers included).

Droves of students attending the local university and conservatory stimulate the nightlife in Osnabrück. The glazed walls of **Grüner Jäger,** Cinder Katharinenkirche 1 (tel. 273 60), reveal throngs of bodies. Go down Neumarktstr. away from the train station and turn right at the 200-ft-tall candy striper (Lederhof Music Library); then walk behind the small wall and follow the footpath as it veers left (open Mon.-Sat. at 11am, Sun. at 7pm). For some great live music and some even better *tsatsiki,* join students at **Unicum,** Neue Graben 40 (tel. 224 92), where they serve lots of homemade treats, including *Auflauf* (open Mon.-Sat. 7pm-3am).

LOWER SAXONY

Schleswig-Holstein

Between Schleswig-Holstein's twin coastlines lies a flat, green countryside of small towns populated primarily by cows. Scenic cycling paths wind from the North Sea beaches across the cobblestone hills of Lübeck, and on to the vivaciously gritty port of Kiel. Schleswig-Holstein became a Prussian province in 1867 following Bismarck's defeat of Denmark and chose to remain part of Germany at the end of World War I. However, the state retains close ties with Scandinavia; numerous Danish libraries and schools (and plenty of tourists) are scattered within its borders. The state's major ports are connected by ferries to Danish, Swedish, and Norwegian docks. Hamburg, the sultry, progressive metropolis on the region's southern border, is a politically autonomous *Land*, but looms influentially over the region.

■ Hamburg

The largest port city in Germany, Hamburg radiates an inimitable recklessness. Calling its atmosphere "liberal" or "alternative" does not do the place justice: with a licentious sex industry comparable only to Amsterdam's and a fierce activist population that recently convinced the *Land* government to plant 6000 new trees every year, Hamburg is a crazy coupling of the progressive and the perverse. Welcoming in and shipping off goods and passengers from all over the world for centuries, Hamburg has gracefully grown into a seaside industrial center of nearly two million. Having gained the right to navigate the Elbe in 1189, Hamburg held off pirates and trading rivals to emerge by the 13th century as a leading power of the Hanseatic League. Straddling several rivers, it was an early hub for overland trade from the Baltic Sea, and the growing profits of the lucrative shipping trade led to dabbling in other financial concerns. The first German stock exchange convened here in 1558, and the Bank of Hamburg dates back to the early 1600s. In 1618 the status of Free Imperial City was granted to Hamburg, and a proud tradition of autonomy endures to this day. The commercial city's jealously-guarded neutrality thankfully protected it through the Thirty Years War, when the rest of northern Germany was ravaged.

Poised on the crest of Germany's break-neck industrialization and naval construction drive, Hamburg had become one of Europe's wealthiest metropolises by World War I. The *Hamburg-Amerika Linie* ruled the oceans of industry as the largest shipping firm in the world. The city suffered severe pummeling at the outset of World War II, when it became the first stop for the Royal Air Force's wrath. Thousands of dockworkers lived in crowded tenements right up against the port; that being the primary Allied target, a single air raid killed 50,000 civilians. The conflagration in the streets reached temperatures of 1800°F (1000°C), leaving nearly half the city's buildings charred rubble. Fortunately, Germany's richest city could afford the reconstruction of much of its copper-roofed brick architecture. Since the late 1960s, an active conservation movement has steadily lobbied for the restoration of historic buildings, including museums, hotels, and houses. In the early 80s, violent riots erupted when police attempted to evacuate warehouses occupied by anarchists and left-wing intellectuals protesting property speculators' acquisition of the real estate. Today, Hamburg actively restores and renovates all historic sites, even if privately owned.

ORIENTATION AND PRACTICAL INFORMATION

Hamburg's fame as a North Sea port actually relies upon its harbor 100km inland, on the north bank of the **Elbe River.** The city is squeezed between the river and the two city lakes (**Außenalster** and **Binnenalster**) formed by the confluence of the Alster and Bille Rivers with the Elbe. Most major sights lie between the **St. Pauli Landungsbrücken** ferry terminal in the west and *Hauptbahnhof* in the east. Much of the city around the docks is part of the *Freihafen* (duty-free zone), so be prepared for cus-

Schleswig-Holstein and Hamburg

toms stops when leaving this area. Both the **Nordbahnhof** and **Südbahnhof** S-Bahn stations exit onto the *Hauptbahnhof.*

The **Hanse Viertel** is a mall thick with shops, art galleries, and auction houses; the glamour makes window-shopping a study in popular aesthetics. The area around **Sternschanze** is dominated by students and quirky shops selling everything from junk jewelry to exotic spices, with a flea market on Saturdays. The **Altona** district, with its own major train station, was once an independent city ruled by Denmark; as Hamburg grew, the Danes were ousted. At the south end of town, an entirely different atmosphere reigns in the **Fischmarkt** along the Elbe at **St. Pauli**—near the houses that the anarchists covered with murals, a different kind of anarchy reigns as the day's North Sea catch is hauled in, and vendors hawk endless varieties of fish, produce, CDs, and more. The Fischmarkt is fascinating in the morning, as early risers mix with revelers from St. Pauli who are rallying to keep the night going. Listen for cries of "*Ohne Geld!*" ("No Money!") and look sharp—to grab attention, the fruit vendors toss free pineapples into the crowd (market open Sun. 5-10am, off-season 7-10am; U- or S-Bahn: "Landungsbrücken" or S-Bahn: "Königstraße").

Tourist Offices: Hamburg's two main tourist offices supply free maps and other pamphlets. The **Hauptbahnhof office,** Kirchenallee exit (tel. 30 05 12 01; fax 30 05 13 33), will book rooms for a fee of DM7-8. Open daily 7am-11pm. Information is also available at the much less crowded **St. Pauli Landungsbrücken office,** between piers 4 and 5 (tel. 30 05 12 00). Open daily 10am-7pm, Nov.-Mar. 9:30am-5:30pm. A third office is in the **Hanse Viertel** mall. Open daily 9am-6pm.

Consulates: U.S.: Alsterufer 27 (tel. 41 17 13 51), on the west side of the Außenalster. Open Mon.-Fri. 9am-noon. **U.K.:** Harvestehuder 8a (tel./fax 448 03 20), near the Hallestr. U-Bahn station. Open 9am-noon and 2-4pm. **Ireland:** Feldbrunnenstr. 43 (tel. 44 18 62 13). U-Bahn: Hallerstr. Open 9am-noon.

American Express: Ballindamm 39, 20095 Hamburg (tel. 30 90 80, refund service tel. (0130) 85 31 00). Mail held for cardmembers for up to four weeks (no charge). All banking services. Open Mon.-Fri. 9am-5:30pm, Sat. 10am-1pm.

Currency Exchange: The **bank** at the Kirchenallee exit of the train station boasts long hours but bad exchange rates and high commissions (DM5 on transactions of DM100 and less; DM10 on transactions above DM100, only DM7.50 for American Express). Open daily 7:30am-10pm. Better rates are available at downtown banks (usually open 9am-1pm and 2:30-4pm; Thurs. 9am-1pm and 2:30-6pm).

Telephones: Make international calls (with German telephone card) at post office in the *Hauptbahnhof*. Phone cards come in DM12 and DM50 denominations.

Flights: For information call 50 75 25 57 or contact individual carriers: **Lufthansa** (tel 35 92 55) and **Air France** (tel. (01805) 36 03 70) are the two heavy-hitters that fly to Hamburg. Buses zoom off to **Fuhlsbüttel Airport** (serving most major European and German cities) from the Kirchenallee exit of the *Hauptbahnhof* (every 20min. 5am-9:20pm (30min.); adults DM8, ages 12 and under DM4, family DM18; round-trip DM12). The bus leaves for the *Hauptbahnhof* from terminal 4 in the airport (every 20min. 6:30am-11pm). Or take the U-Bahn to "Ohlsdorf" and catch a bus to the airport from there (every 10min., daily 5:30am-11pm, DM3.90).

Trains: The **Hauptbahnhof** (main train station) handles most traffic with connections to Berlin (3½hr.; IC), Bremen (1hr.), Munich (5½hr.; ICE), Copenhagen (6hr.) and Zurich (9½hr.; ICE). For **train information** call 194 19. **Dammtor** station is across the Kennedy/Lombards bridge, and **Altona** station is in the west of the city. Most trains to and from Kiel, Schleswig, Flensburg, and Westerland stop only at **Altona.** Frequent trains and the S-Bahn connect the 3 stations.

Buses: The long-distance bus station is located on Adenauerallee, around the corner from the *Hauptbahnhof.* Buses go to Berlin several times daily (3½hr.; one way DM39, round-trip DM62). Prices vary slightly by carrier. **Eurolines** (tel. 24 71 06; fax 280 21 27) will take you to Amsterdam (6½hr.; DM63 one way, DM95 round-trip), Paris (28hr.; DM 90 one way, DM155 round-trip), or London (15hr.; DM90 one way, DM155 round-trip). **Becker Reisen** (tel. 31 43 41; fax 317 45 07) sends buses as far away as Krakow, Poland (16hr.; 3 per week; DM100 one way, DM170 round-trip; students under 26 DM90 one-way, DM155 round-trip).

Public Transportation: The efficient public transportation system (buses, U-Bahn, and S-Bahn) charges DM2.50-6.40, depending on distance. The U- and S-Bahn sleep from 12:30-4:30am, when only a few **night buses** shuttle off from the *Rathaus Markt.* Get **day tickets** *(Ganztageskarte)* for the U-Bahn and S-Bahn from orange automat machines or at the tourist office (DM9.20-13.90; includes up to 3 children). The new **9-Uhr-Tageskarte,** a 9-hr. ticket, costs DM7.70-12.40. A_**family day ticket** (DM13.20-17.70) is good for up to 4 adults and 3 children under 12. A **3-day ticket** sells for DM22.30. The **Hamburg Card** provides free travel on all public transportation and free or reduced admission to most of the city's museums (1-day card DM12.50 for 1 adult and 3 children, DM24 for 4 adults and 3 children; 3-day card DM24.50 and DM39 respectively). All cards may be purchased at tourist offices; 1-day cards can also be bought at *Automaten.*

Ferries: Scandinavian Seaways, Van-der-Smissenstr 4 (tel. 38 90 30, fax 389 03 71), about 1km west of the Fishmarkt (U-Bahn: "Königstr."), sets sail daily for destinations in England and Ireland. Overnight ferries run to Harwich, England (20hr.) every other day. The cheapest tickets (during the high season) are DM163 weekdays, DM183 Fri. and Sat.; 20% for students under 26. They also sail to Copenhagen, Oslo, and Amsterdam; call for details.

Tours: Sight-seeing tours *(Stadtrundfahrt)* leave several times daily from Pier 4-5. Tours last 2hr., include all major sights, and are conducted in English (adults DM24, children under 14 DM10; reduction for *Hamburg Card* holders). For an additional DM5-10, they'll throw in a tour of the port. Call 10 24 43 39 or ask at the tourist office for times. **Alster-Touristik** (tel. 34 11 41), across from the Hotel Atlantic on

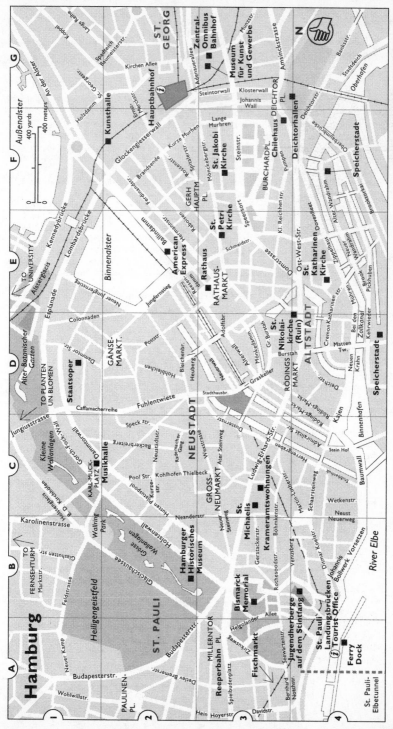

Hamburg

ST. GEORG

Zentral-Omnibus Bahnhof

Museum für Kunst und Gewerbe

Kunsthalle

Hauptbahnhof

DEICHTOR

Chilehaus

Deichtorhallen

Speicherstadt

St. Jakobi Kirche

BURCHARDPL.

St. Petri Kirche

American Express

Rathaus

RATHAUS-MARKT

St. Katharinen Kirche

St. Nikolai-kirche (Ruin)

ALTSTADT

Staatsoper

GÄNSE-MARKT.

Alter Botanischer Garten

TO PLANTEN UN BLOMEN

Binnenalster

Außenalster

TO UNIVERSITY

RÖDINGS-MARKT

Speicherstadt

Kleine Wallanlagen

Musikhalle

KARL-MUCK-PLATZ

NEUSTADT

GROSS NEUMARKT

St. Michaelis

Krameramtswohnungen

Karolinenstrasse

TO FERNSEHTURM

Hamburger Historisches Museum

ST. PAULI

Heiligengeistfeld

Bismarck Memorial

River Elbe

Budapesterstr.

MILLERNTOR PL.

Reeperbahn PL.

PAULINEN-PL.

Fischmarkt

Jugendherberge auf dem Stintfang

St. Pauli Landungsbrücken

St. Pauli Tourist Office

Ferry Dock

St. Pauli-Elbetunnel

the Außenalster (S-Bahn: "Dammtor"), will give you a 1-hr.-long jaunt around the lakes (daily every hr. from 10am-5pm; DM12, children DM6).

Boat Rental: You can rent sailboats, paddleboats and rowboats on the Außenalster from **Kpt. Pieper,** on An der Alster (tel. 24 75 78), directly in across from the Hotel Atlantic at the foot of the Kennedy bridge. S-Bahn to "Dammtor," then east along Alsterglacis. Sailboats DM25-28 per hour for 1-2 people (additional DM3-4 apiece), paddleboats and rowboats DM17 per hour. Sailing license required to rent sailboats.

Car Rental: Hertz, Kirchenallee 34-36 (tel. 280 12 03), is opposite the train station. Open Mon.-Fri. 7am-6pm, Sat. 8am-4pm, Sun. 10am-4pm.

Bike Rental: Fahrrad-Scholz-Verleih, Ludolfstr. 7 (tel. 480 77 38), U-Bahn: "Eppendorfer Baum," rents touring bikes, mountain bikes, and tandems for DM10 per day. DM100 deposit and photo ID required. Open Tues.-Fri. 10am-6pm, Sat. 10am-1pm. **O'Niel Bikes,** Beethovenstr. 37 (tel. 22 12 16; fax 22 14 78), offers German-language bike tours of the city and environs. Prices range from DM49 for 3-hr. to DM129 for an all-day extravaganza. They also rent bikes (DM25 per day).

Hitchhiking: *Let's Go* does not recommend hitchhiking as a safe mode of transportation. Those headed to Berlin, Copenhagen, or Lübeck take S-Bahn #1 to "Wandsbeker Chaussee," then walk up Hammerstr. to Hamburg Horn (a treacherous traffic rotary at the base of the *Autobahn).* Hitchers aiming for points south take S-Bahn #3 (direction: Harburg) to "Veddel," and walk 5min. to the *Autobahn.*

Mitfahrzentrale: City Netz Mitfahrzentrale, Gotenstr. 19 (tel. 194 44), near U-Bahn #3: "Berliner Tor," offers hi-tech computerized matching. Open daily 9am-7pm. Prices (fee for information/fee paid to driver): Berlin DM12/17, Munich DM24/47, Amsterdam DM 18/27.

Bookstores: English Books Second Hand, Stresemannstr. 169 (tel. 851 44 78), a few blocks to the left of the Holstenstr. S-Bahn stop. A bit disorganized but cheap. Open Mon.-Fri. 12-6:30pm, Sat. 10am-2:30pm. If you can read German, don't miss the block-long **Heinrich-Heine-Buchhandlung,** Grindelalle 24-28 (tel. 441 13 30; fax 44 11 33 22), in the university district. Open Mon.-Fri. 9:30am-6:30pm, Sat. 10am-1pm. Or visit them on-line at http://www.buchkatalog.de.

Library: Staats- und Universitätsbibliothek, Von Melle Park 3 (tel. 41 23 22 33), near the university. Fine English-language section. To acquire a borrowing card, come between 10am and 4pm. Photo ID required. Open Mon.-Fri. 9am-9pm.

Lesbian and Gay Center: Magnus Hirschfeld Centrum, Borgweg 8 (tel. 279 00 60). U-Bahn #3 or bus #108 to "Borgweg." Daily films and counseling sessions. A good source of info on gay and lesbian community information. Evening café, open daily 5pm-midnight, mostly for men. Women only on Wed. and Thurs. 3-6pm. Center open Mon.-Fri. 9:30am-1pm.

Laundromat: Schnell und Sauber, Grindelallee 158. S-Bahn #21 or 31: "Dammtor." In the university district. Wash 6kg for DM6, dry 15min. for DM1. Soap included. Open daily 6am-11pm. There are also several laundromats on Simon-von-Utrecht-Str., heading towards the Altona station from St. Pauli.

Rape Crisis Line: tel. 25 55 66, Mon. and Thurs. 9:30am-1pm and 3-7pm; Tues.-Wed. 9:30am-1pm and 3-4pm; Fri. 9:30am-1pm. **Opferhilfe Beratungstelle,** Paul-Nevermann-Platz 2-4 (tel. 38 19 93), offers advice to male and female victims of sexually-related crimes. Phone line open Mon. and Fri. 10am-1pm, Tues.-Thurs. 10am-1pm and 2-5pm. Appointments can be arranged.

Pharmacy: Central Apotheke, Rödingsmarkt 1 (tel. 378 67 30), is open Mon.-Wed. and Fri. 8am-6:30pm, Thurs. 8am-9pm, Sat. 8am-2pm. Check the list in the window for the rotating 24-hr. schedule. This one's open 24hr. on Tues.

Emergency: Police: Kirchenallee 46, opposite the train station (tel. 110). **Ambulance:** tel. 112. Headquarters at the Berliner Tor U-Bahn station.

Post Office: Branch at the Kirchenallee exit of the *Hauptbahnhof,* 20099 Hamburg (open Mon.-Fri. 8am-8pm, Sat. 8am-6pm, Sun. 10am-4pm). **Poste Restante** *(Postlagernde Briefe),* 20097 Hamburg, is at the main branch on Alter Wall, about a block south of the *Rathaus.* Open Mon.-Fri. 8am-6pm, Sat. 8am-12pm.

Telephone Code: 040.

ACCOMMODATIONS AND CAMPING

Hamburg is not a cheap place to stay: single rooms start at around DM60, doubles rising from DM75. Many of these are tawdry establishments with few creature comforts. A slew of small, inexpensive *Pensionen* line **Steindamm, Bremer Weg,** and **Bremer Reihe** to the north of the *Hauptbahnhof.* Check out your hotel before you accept a room; Herbertstraße isn't the only place in Hamburg where you can pay and get screwed. Let the tourist office's *Hotelführer* (DM1) help steer you clear. For longer stays, try the **Mitwohnzentrale** at Lobuschstr. 22 (tel. 39 13 73, open Mon.-Fri. 9am-5:30pm, Sat.9am-1:30pm). A passport is required, as well as a deposit of either DM100 cash or DM50 and a bank account number.

Hostels and Camping

Jugendgästehaus-und-Gästehaus Horner-Rennbahn (HI), Rennbahnstr. 100 (tel. 651 16 71; fax 655 65 16), U-Bahn #3: "Horner-Rennbahn." From the main exit of the station, turn right—the hostel is about 10min. by foot, at the corner of Tribünenweg. Or take bus #160 or #231 (DM3.50) 1 stop (direction: Wandsbek). A bit farther from the sights than Auf Dem Stintfang (below) but about the same distance from the *Hauptbahnhof.* Extremely clean and secure. Soundproof walls ensure that you won't hear a peep from the disco downstairs. Reception open 7:30-9am and 1pm-1am. Curfew 1am, but stragglers admitted at 2am. 1 or 2 nights DM29, over 26 DM34.50. 3 nights or more DM26.50, over 26 DM32. Sheets and excellent buffet breakfast included. Open Mar.-Dec.

Jugendherberge auf dem Stintfang (HI), Alfred-Wegener-Weg 5 (tel. 31 34 88; fax 31 54 07). S-Bahn #1, 2, or 3, or U-Bahn #3 (from the main station): "Landungsbrücke." Follow the signs in the U-Bahn and hike up the steps to the hill above. A great location near the Reeperbahn and the subway, a beautiful view of the harbor, and kitchen facilities, but what really draws travelers to this hostel is the **Fantasy Island chessboard,** with 3ft. high pieces!—"Checkmate, Mr. Rourke." Use the storage lockers. Call ahead, since not even clout with Tattoo can get you a bed during busy weekends. Reception open noon-1am. Curfew 1am. Check-out 9am. DM21.50, over 26 DM26. Sheets DM6. Breakfast included.

Camping: Campingplatz Buchholz, Kielerstr. 374 (tel. 540 45 32). S-Bahn #3 (direction: Pinneberg) or S-Bahn #21 (direction: Elbgaustr.) to "Stellingen." Walk straight on Volksparkstr. and turn right on Kielstr. Reception open daily 3-10pm. DM8 per person, DM14 per tent. Showers DM2.50. Call ahead.

Hotels

Hotel Annerhof, Lange Reihe 23 (tel. 24 34 26). From the station's Kirchenallee exit, take the second street on your left. High, corniced ceilings in spacious rooms. Call ahead. Singles DM48. Doubles DM82. Breakfast DM8.

Pension Sarah Peterson, Lange Reihe 50 (tel./fax 24 98 26). This small, artsy *Pension* occupies an historic building with bohemian flair. Musically-inclined guests occasionally perform for other patrons. Singles DM69. Doubles DM98. Triples DM140. Quads (with private bathroom) DM180. TV and breakfast included. Call ahead in summer. They plan to close for renovation in the winter of 1996-97 and operate out of another location in the same neighborhood; call for the address.

Schanzenstern Übernachtungs-und-Gasthaus, Bartelsstraße 12 (tel. 203 57). U-and S-Bahn: "Sternschanze," south on Schanzestr., right on Susannenstr., left to Bartelsstr. Location, location, location. In the middle of the student district. Singles DM60. Doubles DM90. Breakfast in ecologically-minded restaurant DM10.

Hotel Terminus, Steindamm 5 (tel. 280 31 44; fax 24 15 18). Near train station, around corner from the Kunst-und-Gewerbe Museum. Sprightly service and fetching rooms. Call ahead. Reception open 24hr. Singles DM65. Doubles DM100. Triples DM150. Quads DM180. Breakfast included. Major credit cards accepted.

Hotel-Pension Kieler Hof, Bremer Reihe 15 (tel. 24 30 24; fax 24 60 14), on the corner. From the *Hauptbahnhof's* Kieler Allee exit, turn right, then left on Bremer Reihe. A welcoming spot, but be aware of shady bars nearby. Kitchen facilities available. Tastefully designed rooms. Singles DM60, with shower DM70. Doubles DM100, with shower DM110. Triples DM165, with shower. Breakfast included.

Hotel Alt Nürnberg, Steintorweg 15 (tel. 24 60 23; fax 280 46 34). From the station, go straight ahead from Kirchenallee, veering off toward Steintorplatz on the right; then look for Steintorweg on the left. Classy, dimly-lit lobby and colorful rooms help you forget that you're only minutes from the parade of grime that is the Hamburg *Hauptbahnhof.* Singles DM60, with shower DM90. Doubles DM130, all with bath. Some rooms have telephones.

Pension Helga Schmidt, Holzdam 14 (tel. 280 21 19; fax 24 37 05), off An der Alster, a few blocks north of the *Hauptbahnhof.* Beautifully-outfitted, large rooms in a classic building. Worth the money. Reception 8am-11pm. Singles w/ shower DM65-70. Doubles DM105-125. Triples DM155. Breakfast DM12-14. Call ahead.

Hotel Kochler Garni, Bremer Reihe 19 (tel. 24 95 11; fax 280 24 35), 2min. from the *Hauptbahnhof.* Clean, well-run, respectable complex with quite spacious rooms. Call ahead. Singles DM70. Doubles DM110. Breakfast included.

FOOD

Walk along St. Pauli's Quai, **Landungsbrücke,** for small fish restaurants and fry stands. Smack in the middle of the Rathausmarkt, the aptly named **Rathausmarkt** serves up all things edible at honest prices. A generous portion of *Swäbische Spätzle* (noodles with onions, ham, and cheese) runs about DM7. Cheap dives dot **Kirchenallee,** serving dishes from *Schnitzel* to *kepabs.* Better deals are to be had at the inexpensive cafés and restaurants of the university area around **Renteelstraße, Grindelhof, Grindelallee,** and **Schanzenstraße.** In **Altona,** the *Fußgangerzone* (pedestrian mall) leading up to the train station is packed with ethnic food stands and produce shops. No one has visited Hamburg until they've downed a plate of the city's specialty stew, *Labskaus.* An affront to the eyes and arteries, it consists of a mash of fried potatoes, pickled beets, pickled cucumbers, and pickled herring topped with a fried egg. As appalling as this sounds, it's delicious— proof of the culinary truth Germans have known for ages: grease is the soul of flavor.

Geo Pizza aus dem Holzbackofen, Beim Schlump 27 (tel. 45 79 29). Walk 400m down Beim Schlump from the Schlump U-Bahn station; on your left. Possibly the best pizza in Germany (DM7.70-14.50). Formidable vegetarian offerings. Crammed with students. Open Sun.-Thurs. 11am-1am, Fri.-Sat. 11am-2am.

Gorki Park, Grindelallee 1 (tel. 45 70 17), near the university at Bundesstr. The new face of socialism serves up a *Proletarier* feast (DM8-20) amidst red velvet drapes, antique furniture, communist *Kitsch,* and Russian folk music. The Sunday brunch buffet nearly is as big as the former USSR (DM16). Open Mon.-Thurs. 6pm-2am, Fri. 6pm-3am, Sat. 7pm-3am, Sun. 11am-3pm.

Fischerhaus, St. Pauli Fischmarkt 14 (tel. 31 40 53). S-Bahn #21 or 31: "Dammtor." Fresh fish and superb service explain this restaurant's appeal. Wolf down a delicious plate of *Labskaus* (DM14.50) and horrify tourists. Open daily 11am-11pm.

Mensa, Schlüterstr. 7. University cafeteria. Head north on Rothenbaumchaussee, left on Moorweidenstr., then right onto Schlüterstr. A place to catch up with students and check bulletin boards for special events. Student ID required. Meals DM1.70-6. Serves lunch 11am- 2pm and dinner 4pm-7pm Mon.-Fri.

Brauhaus Hanseat, Zippelhaus 4 (tel. 32 25 52), near the St. Katherinenkirche. Go out of the back of the church and head left. Cook your own pair of *Weißwürste* (white veal sausages; DM8.50) on a little grill in the middle of your table while sipping a home-brew and munching pretzels. Open Mon-Fri. 11am-until you've had enough, Sat. 5pm-until you burst.

Grill Gijnaydin, Kleiner Schäferkamp 14 (tel. 410 29 56). U-Bahn: "Schlump." This Turkish restaurant has a wide variety of both Middle Eastern and German dishes— integration at last. The menu has a vegetarian section. Sandwiches, salads, and entrees (DM5-12). Daily lunch special (DM9). Open daily 11am-10pm.

Café Backwahn, Grindallee 148 (tel. 410 61 41). U-Bahn #1: "Hallestr.," then west on Hallerstr. and left on Grindallee. Light food and a large assortment of breakfast items served daily. Big windows look out on busy Grindallee. Special *Mittagstisch* (lunch platter; DM9). Open daily 10am-7pm.

Piceno, Hein-Hoyer-str. 8 (tel. 31 04 77). If you're longing for the simpler times of old Sicily, step into this Italian restaurant just off Reeperbahn. Classics like *macaroni arabbiata*, an indulgence in spicy tomato sauce with peppers and basil that you won't regret the morning after. Meals DM8-15. Open daily 5pm-midnight.

Libresso Antiquariat, Binderstr. 24 (tel. 45 16 63). U-Bahn: "Hallerstr.," south on Rothenbaumchaussee, then right onto Binderstr. Bookstore-café mixes up its dark espresso with a high grade of used printed matter, served up for students at the nearby university. Open Mon.-Fri. 9am-6pm.

Frauenbuchladen und Café, Bismarckstr. 98 (tel. 420 47 48). U-Bahn: "Hoheluftbr." Pick up the *Hamburger Frauenzeitung* (DM6) if you can read German. Good cooks go with good books. Women only. Open Mon.-Fri. 10am-6:30pm, Sat. 10am-2pm.

SIGHTS

The **Hamburg Hafen,** the largest port in Germany, lights up at night with ships from all over the world. More than 100,000 dockers and sailors work the ports, and their presence permeates Hamburg. After sailing the East Indies, the 19th-century **Windjammer Rickmer Rickmers** (tel. 319 59 59) was docked at Pier 1 and restored as a museum ship. Come for the old navigation equipment, all brass and polish, alongside newer technology (open daily 10am-5:30pm; admission DM4, students DM3, children ages 4-12 DM2). At Pier 4, the **Old Elbe Tunnel** connects St. Pauli to Steinwerder. Take an elevator down to the lower level, then walk the 426.5m tunnel (also open to motor vehicles; beware of fumes). East of the docks near the copper dome of the **St. Katherinenkirche,** across the river from Zippelhaus, lies the historic warehouse district known as the **Speicherstadt.** These elegant late 19th-century brick warehouses are filled with cargo, spices, and swarms of stevedores.

The copper spire of the **Rathaus,** a richly ornamented, neo-Renaissance monstrosity, rises above the city center. From the train station, head down Mönckebergstr. Across the foyer from the main entrance is a small stone courtyard in which a burbling fountain flows. Shields representing each continent ornament the front of the building, symbolizing Hamburg's distinction as an international city. (Tours in German are conducted every half hour Mon.-Thurs. 10am-3pm, Fri.-Sun. 10am-1pm. Tours in English and French leave hourly Mon.-Thurs. 10:15am-3:15pm. Fri.-Sun. 10:15am-1:15pm. Call 36 81 24 70 for details.) Built in 1932, the **column** to the left of the *Rathaus* stands in memorial to the 40,000 Hamburg men who died in World War I. In the square, the extraordinarily sad statue of poet **Heinrich Heine** gives Rodin's "The Thinker" a run for his money.

To the north of the *Rathaus* are the two **Alster lakes** bordered by tree-lined paths. The **Binnenalster** is a quiet lake surrounded by elegant promenades and commercial façades, while the larger **Außenalster** is dominated by windsurfers, sailboats, and paddleboats. Ferries, more personal than the bigger Hamburg boats, sail from the Außenalster. To the west of the lakes is the **Planten un Blomen,** a park that extends almost down to the harbor and provides a home for flowers, ponds, ducks, fountains, and water games. Near the Karolinenstr. entrance is a medicinal herb garden with explanations of the particular therapeutic value of each plant. *Let's Go* does not recommend stealing herbs to ease your aches and pains. Free concerts shake the nearby outdoor **Musikpavillon** nearly every day throughout the summer. Check the *Oxmox* (available free in hostels and many cafés) for listings.

After much of the old city was destroyed by fire in 1842, Hamburg's city government launched an ambitious reconstruction project that created the current urban landscape, including its familiar six green copper spires. Just south of the *Rathaus,* off Ost-West-Str., stand the somber ruins of the old **St. Nikolaikirche.** An early example of neo-Gothic architecture, it was flattened by Allied bombing in 1943. City officials have left the ruins unrestored as a memorial to the horrors of war. Just east of the *Rathaus* are the 12th-century **St. Petrikirche** (tel. 32 44 38; open Mon.-Fri. 9am-6pm, Sat. 9am-5pm, Sun. 9am-noon and 1-5pm; English services first Sun. of every month at 5pm) and **St. Jacobikirche** (tel. 536 60 79), known for its 14th-century **Arp-Schnit-**

tger organ (open daily 10am-5pm). On the other side of the busy Ost-West-Str., on a breezy side street, stands a fourth copper tower; it rises up from the medieval **St. Katharinenkirche,** built by three generations of townspeople from 1350 to 1420 (U-Bahn: "Meßberg"; open daily 9am-6pm; Oct.-April 9am-4pm). Way up north by the Hallserstr. U-Bahn stands the (new) **St. Nikolaikirche;** its mosaic altar is based on a design by Expressionist Oskar Kokoschka (open daily 9am-5pm).

But the granddaddy of all Hamburg's churches is the gargantuan 18th-century **Große Michaelskirche** (tel. 31 10 26 24), affectionately (if somewhat fearfully) referred to as *"der Michael."* While the exterior is a bit imposing—the statue of St. Michael above the doorway looks as if he is about to hurl down his cross on the unsuspecting hordes of tourists below—the inside looks like a wedding cake with its scalloped walls. The *Michael*'s bulbous Baroque tower is the official emblem of Hamburg, as well as the only one of the city's six spires that can be ascended; it even has an elevator. (Tower and church open May-Oct. daily 9am-6pm; Nov.-April 10am-5pm. Church entrance DM1; elevator DM4, students and children DM2; crypt (for the living) DM2.50. Organ music April-Aug. daily at noon and 5pm.)

For architecture of a different generation, head farther east along Ost-West-Str. to the **Chilehaus.** This striking *trompe l'oeil* office building is the work of Expressionist architect Fritz Höger, also responsible for the **Sprinkenhof** building across the street. The Great Fire of 1842 broke out several blocks away on Deichstraße, where 17th-19th-century merchants' offices have been carefully restored. Locals gather in the quiet sidewalk cafés on summer afternoons. The last block of **Peterstraße,** up Neanderstr. from the Michaelskirche and then left, is a pedestrian zone for the ages, a quiet cobblestone street lined with 17th- and 18th-century High Baroque houses.

Outside of the city center are reminders of Hamburg at war in the 1940s. In 1923, Communist labor leader Ernst Thälmann led a march on the police headquarters that ended in a riot that left 61 protestors and 17 police officers dead and resulted in nearly 1000 arrests. Thälmann was later murdered by the Nazis at Buchenwald. His life and times are chronicled at the **Ernst-Thälmann Gedenkstätte,** on Ernst-Thälmann-Platz (tel. 47 41 84; open Tues.-Fri. 10am-5pm, Sat.-Sun. 10am-1pm; free).

In the midst of warehouses stands the **Gedenkstätte Janusz-Korczak-Schule,** Bullenhuser Damm 92 (tel. 78 32 95), S-Bahn: "Rothenburgsort." Walk north from the station and make a right onto Bullenhuser Damm; the school is 200m down on the right. It serves as a memorial to 20 Jewish children brought here from Auschwitz for "testing" and murdered by the SS hours before Allied troops arrived. Visitors are invited to plant a rose for the children in the flower garden behind the school (open Mon.-Thurs. 9am-5pm, Fri. 9am-3pm, Sun. 10am-5pm; free).

The site of the **KZ** (concentration camp) **Neuengamme,** Jean-Doldier-Weg (tel. 723 10 31), is located in an idyllic agricultural village east of Hamburg. Take S-Bahn #21: "Bergdorff," then bus #227 (about 50min. from Hamburg). The bus stops at the base of the road on its way there, so watch for the sign; it makes several stops along Jean-Doldier-Weg on its return trip. Here the Nazis murdered approximately 50,000 prisoners through slave labor. In 1948 Hamburg prison authorities took over the camp and demolished all of the buildings to construct a prison on the site; the mayor at the time believed that a prison would cleanse Neuengamme's sullied reputation. But in 1989 the Hamburg Senate decided to have the prison be moved in order to build a more appropriate memorial. Banners inscribed with the names and dates of death of each of the victims hang in the **Haus des Gedenkens** (House of Memory), located on the road to the camp. Pick up a map of the camp here.

Blankensee (S-Bahn: "Blankensee"; 30min.) was once a small fishing village. The **Kirche Am Markt** in the center of town is still decorated with model ships. Boutiques and craft shops line the streets of the city center. The hillside town then sweeps down to a strand at the banks of the Elbe. Narrow, crooked steps lead from the top of the hill to the river through a collection of summer houses and thatched-roofed homes. From the top of Süllberg, there is a view of the mile-wide Elbe.

MUSEUMS

The dozens of museums in Hamburg include everything from erotica and high *Kunst* to history and folk art. The one- or three-day **Hamburg card** (see p. 368) allows access to most of these museums, with the exception of the Deichtorhallen and the Erotic Art Museum. Hamburg also has a thriving contemporary art scene; pick up a list of the city's galleries and their current exhibits at the **Hamburg Kunstverein,** directly across from the Deichtorhallen.

Hamburger Kunsthalle, Glockengiesserwall 1 (tel. 24 86 26 12), 1 block north of the *Hauptbahnhof.* This first-rate art museum has a split personality: the first half of the collection contains one of the world's best exhibitions of German and Dutch art, from the medieval period up through the 19th century; the rest of the museum contains works by major 19th-century French painters, including Millet, Courbet, Manet, and Monet. Norwegian Painter Edvard Munch is well-represented, as is Swiss-born artist Henri Fuseli, whose "Creation of Eve" should not be missed. In February 1997 a new building will be opened; a Max Liebermann exhibition is slated for fall. Open Tues.-Wed. and Fri.-Sun. 10am-6pm, Thurs. 10am-9pm. Admission DM12, students DM8; extra charge for special exhibitions.

Museum für Kunst und Gewerbe (tel. 24 86 26 30), Steintorplatz 1, 1 block south of the *Hauptbahnhof.* A fantastic, rich collection of handicrafts, china, and furnishings ranging from ancient Egyptian and Roman to Asian and *Jugendstil;* sure to inspire you to new heights of interior decoration. Check for special events like Japanese tea ceremonies. Open Tues.-Wed. and Fri.-Sun. 10am-6pm, Thurs. 10am-9pm. Admission DM8, students and children DM1.

Deichtorhallen Hamburg, Deichtorstr. 1-2 (tel. 32 37 35). U-Bahn: Steinstr. Follow signs from the subway station; look for 2 entwined iron circles in front of the museum. Hamburg's contemporary art scene cuts loose here: every season sees a new exhibit of international art, showcasing artists such as Andy Warhol, Roy Lichtenstein, and Keith Haring. Open Tues.-Wed. and Fri.-Sun. 11am-6pm, Thurs. 11am-9pm. Prices vary by exhibit, with discounts for students and children.

Museum of Hamburger History, Holstenwall 24 (tel. 35 04 23 80), at the end of Peterstr. U-Bahn: "St. Pauli." Not a shrine to McDonald's, but a museum that recalls the city's history. The 3rd floor is a large maze of model railroad tracks that reproduce Hamburg's own rail connections. Open Tues.-Sat. 10am-5pm, Sun. 10am-6pm. Admission DM6, students and children DM1. The museum is parent to the **Historic Emigration Office,** Beiden St. Pauli Landungsbrücken 3, D-20359 Hamburg (tel. 30 05 12 50), a meticulous archive that maintains the names, hometowns, and vital statistics of the 5 million Germans and East Europeans who emigrated through Hamburg 1850-1914. Write or drop by to track your roots. Open Tues.-Sat. 10am-1pm and 2-5pm.

Erotic Art Museum, Bernhard-Nocht-Str. 60 (tel. 31 34 29). S-Bahn, U-Bahn west along St. Pauli Hafenstr., curve right onto Davidtreppe, turn left onto Bernhard-Nocht-Str. Art or just classy porn? Hamburg's newest museum delightfully toes the fine line. Whatever your verdict, the exhibits, boasting some Picassos, prove stimulating. Open Tues.-Sun. 10am-midnight. Admission DM15, students DM10.

Krameramtswohnungen, Krayenkamp 10 (tel. 31 10 26 24), left of the main entrance to the Große Michaelskirche. The slanted-roof almshouses on this narrow 17th-century cobblestone street provided shelter for Hamburg's widows. Open Tues.-Sat. 10am-5pm. Admission DM1.

Hamburgisches Museum für Völkerkunde, Rothenbaumchausee 64 (tel. 44 19 55 24). U-Bahn: "Hallerstr." Experience world culture through puppets, coins, and re-created villages. Check for concerts and demonstrations. Open Tues.- Wed. and Fri.-Sun. 10am-6pm, Thurs. 10am-9pm. Admission DM8, students DM4.

ENTERTAINMENT

The cultural capital of the North, Hamburg patronizes the arts generously with money and attention. Since high culture in Germany is so heavily subsidized, tickets are much more affordable than one might think, and most tickets and concert halls offer generous student discounts. The **Staatsoper,** Dammtorstr. 28, houses one of the best opera companies in Germany (vying with Munich). In February and March 1997, they will stage Wagner's entire "Ring cycle"—a rare and *echt Deutsch* event. For **tickets,** call 35 17 21. To get there, take S-Bahn #28: "Dammtor." John Neumeier has directed the associated **ballet company** for the last decade, building it up to be the acknowledged dance powerhouse of the nation. The **Hamburger Ballet-Tage,** a special six-week dance festival, will debut there in 1997 (May 4-June 19). **Orchestras** abound—the **Philharmonie,** the **Nord-Deutscher-Rundfunk Symphony Orchestra,** and **Hamburg Symphonia,** the big three, all perform at the **Musikhalle** on Karl-Muck-Platz (tel. 24 20 25), U-Bahn: "Gänsemarkt" or "Messehallen." **Chamber music** concerts frequently take place here too. Hamburg's churches also offer a wide variety of classical concerts (most free); pick up a schedule at any of the major churches. The German **cabaret** tradition is still alive and kicking its legs high at a number of venues, including **Das Schiff,** on Holzbrückestr. (tel. 36 47 65), U-Bahn: "Rödeingsmarkt," and at the drag theater **Pulverfass,** Pulverkich 12 (tel. 24 97 91), U-Bahn: "Hauptbahnhof." Call the tourist office for information.

The **Deutsches Schauspielhaus,** Kirchenallee 39 (tel. 24 87 13), U-Bahn: "Haupt-bahnhof," refuses to be overshadowed by the musicians of the city. Peter Zadek is one of a group of virtuoso directors who have emerged as the main German drama figures in the 1980s; he produces both new and old plays with a distinctly personal, sometimes shocking, stamp. The **Thalia,** Alstertor 1 (tel. 32 26 66), S-Bahn: "Jungfern-steig," offers slightly more avant-garde musicals, plays, and staged readings. Most the-aters sell **half-price tickets** to students both at the regular box office and at the **Abendkasse** (evening box office), which generally opens one hour before perfor-mance times. In July and August, many theaters close down, but only to make way for the **Hamburger Sommer** festival of the arts. The **Theaterkarten Last-Minute** kiosk in the Hanse-Viertel tourist office (see p. 367) sells tickets for regular and special events. The **English Theater,** Lerchenfeld 14 (tel. 22 55 43), U-Bahn: "Mundsburg," has English-language productions, naturally. Check with the tourist office for all per-formance schedules and dates.

Happily, the movie scene in Hamburg is not limited to American blockbusters dubbed in German. The **Kommunades Kino Metropolis,** Dammtorstr. 30a (tel. 34 23 53), a non-profit cinema, features new independent films and revivals from all over the world, including the US, France, Germany, and Italy. **Kino 3001,** Schanzenstr. 75 (tel. 43 76 79), U-Bahn: "Sternschanze," also shows alternative flicks.

Hamburg has an extensive live music scene that can satisfy all tastes. Traditional jazz at its best can be found at the **Cotton Club** (see Nightlife, below) and on Sunday mornings at the Fish Auction Hall of the **Fischmarkt.** International rock groups play at **Große Freiheit,** Große Freiheit 36 (tel. 31 42 63), and at **Docks,** Spielbudenplatz 19 (tel. 319 43 78). The renowned **Fabrik,** Barnerstr. 36 in Altona (tel. 39 10 70), fea-tures everything from funk to punk. For more info, check the 'zines *Szene, Oxmox,* or *Prinz* (available at newsstands for DM5; hostels keep free copies).

The city's biggest party is the **Hafengeburtstag,** or "Harbor Birthday." Hamburg owes its prosperity to May 7, 1189, when Frederick Barbarossa granted the town the right to open a port. The city still celebrates the anniversary for a weekend in early May featuring music and other events. In 1997, the party will run May 9-11.

Three separate months each year, the **Heiligengeistfeld Square,** just north of the Reeperbahn, is transformed for a month into the **Dom,** a huge amusement park, with booths, kiosks, and fun rides. In 1997, the *Frühlingsdom* (Spring Fair) will be held from the end of April until the end of May; the *Sommerdom* (Summer Fair), through-out August; and the *Winterdom* (take a guess), throughout December. Allegedly, the festival commemorates an earlier festival that took place in the church, but it's prima-rily another excuse for Hamburgers to party like rock stars.

NIGHTLIFE

The heart of Hamburg's nightlife lies in St. Pauli, and the heart of St. Pauli is the **Reep-erbahn,** home to the St. Pauli girls (and the eponymous beer). The best way to describe the atmosphere here is "Mardi Gras with a hard-on;" this isn't summer camp, folks. The sex clubs, sex shops, porn theaters, prostitutes, and other sleaze peddlers on the streets accommodate any fantasy or fetish one might imagine, and a few one might rather not. **Herbertstr.**, south of the Reeperbahn off Davidstr., is Hamburg's only remaining legalized prostitution strip, open only to men over 18. Women cannot realistically expect to walk unaccosted in the Reeperbahn district; it is one of the limitations of Hamburg life. Many men on the street will address women as merchandise; if you're female and out late, take a cab. For those on foot, a simple, barked *"kein Deutsch"* ("No German") is a surprisingly effective way to ward off most of the pimps, pushers, and prostitutes. Note that the street-walkers are not subject to health inspections, as are the licensed prostitutes who pose behind windows. Men and women flock to this district to revel all night long, and the area simmers with sultry energy. Packed U- and S-Bahn cars deliver hordes of pleasure-seekers at around midnight, and the action rages until dawn. Police patrol extensively; the **Davidwache police station** is on the corner of Davidstr. and the Reeperbahn. Despite all the vulgarity, or even partly because of it, St. Pauli houses many of Hamburg's best bars and clubs, even for those not seeking sex for sale.

Clubs and **bars** are scattered throughout the city. Clusters of popular student bars can be found along Grindelallee and Schanzenstr., and swarms of street-side cafés line the three squares **Gänsemarkt** (U-Bahn #2), **Rödingsmarkt** (U-Bahn #3), and **Großneumarkt** (S-Bahn #1 or 2: "Stadthausbrücke"). Much of the Hamburg gay scene is located in the **St. Georg** area of the city, near the *Hauptbahnhof.* Whether or not you are gay, some of the bars in this area are more welcoming and classsier than those in the Reeperbahn. In general, clubs open late and close late, with some techno and trance clubs remaining open until noon the following day. *Szene, Oxmox,* and *Prinz* list events and parties. Lesbians and gays alike are clued in on special events by the *Dorn Rosa* journal (available at newsstands; DM5).

Mojo Club, Reeperbahn 1 (tel. 319 19 99), has more attitude than it knows what to do with. Called the best club in Germany by MTV. Go Mojo. The attached **Jazz Café** attracts the trendy. Features jazz, dance-floor jazz, and acid-jazz. Open Fri.-Sat. from 11pm; cover usually DM10. Café open Wed.-Sat. from 10pm; no cover.

Frank und Frei, Schanzenstr. 93 (tel. 43 48 03). Drink beer and shoot stick by candlelight with the local students while listening to German alternative music. Sidewalk tables in summer. Open Mon.-Sat. 11am-3am, Sun. 10am-3am.

Molotow, Spielbudenplatz 5 (tel. 31 08 45), parallel to the Reeperbahn. Mention *Funk* in most of Germany, and people think you're a ham-radio nut. This place knows better. The "Motor-Booty Club," Sunday night's program, offers rump-shaking funk and homemade snacks past the wee hours. Cover DM5-10. Opens Wed. at 10pm, Thurs.-Sat. at 11pm, Sun. at 9pm. Stays open late.

Logo, Grindelallee 5 (tel. 410 56 58). If you can play it live, you can play it at Logo. Nightly live music at this smoky club near the University gives locals a chance to be rock stars. Call far enough ahead, and you can probably book yourself a gig. Open nightly from 9:30pm. Cover varies.

La Paloma, Gerhardstr. 2 (tel. 31 46 41), on the corner of Friedrichstr. At the heart of St. Pauli but not sordid. A local painter opened this bar-club-café to fill with friends' work. Despite the pretension, the mood is open-minded. Some say the beer is better than the art. You decide. Open daily 7pm-until everyone leaves.

Gröninger Braukeller, Ost-West-Str. 47 (tel. 33 13 81), has been serving its own brew since 1750. Sit on a keg, eat off a keg, drink out of a keg. Marry a keg and raise little keglings. Open Mon.-Fri. 11am-1am, Sat. 5pm-1am.

Entrée, Juliusstr. 13-15 (tel. 430 40 42). A beatnik's dream, man—live jazz mingled with international poetry nights. Bring your own bongoes, dig? Concerts at 8pm. Call for listings.

Cotton Club, Alter Steinweg 10 (tel. 34 38 78). Gives a different traditional jazz band a chance every night at 8:30pm. Smoky atmosphere, mostly older crowd. The jazz is great. Open Mon.-Sat. 8pm-midnight. Cover varies, usually DM5-10.

Front, Heidencampsweg 1 (tel. 23 25 23), plays house music to the hip. Substantial gay scene. Open Fri.-Sat. 11pm. Cover varies, usually DM10-15.

Café Schöne Aussichten, Gorch-Frock-Wall 2 (tel. 34 01 13). Young lushes congregate under the lush foliage of the *Planten un Blomen* park to gear up for the evening. Very popular with students.

Frauenkneipe, Stresemannstr. 60 (tel. 36 12 29), is a bar and meeting place for women. Visitors who are disconcerted by the Reeperbahn and drunken-sailor-scene will discover here that red-lighters do not represent the whole of Hamburg. Men are distinctly unwelcome here, but women, gay or straight, will feel comfortable. Open Mon.-Fri. 8pm-1am, Sat. 9pm-3am, Sun. 8pm-1am.

■ Lübeck

Once the robust capital of the Hanseatic League, Schleswig-Holstein's most engaging city, Lübeck, flourished in the Middle Ages as a link in the prosperous Baltic salt trade. The famous literary brothers, Thomas and Heinrich Mann, drew the inspiration for their masterful portrayals of the German bourgeoisie from observing the unchecked mercantilism and hypocrisy of this city. Its merchants devoted their profits to red-brick architecture and interior decoration, a pastime unrewarded until 1987, when UNESCO declared Lübeck's *Altstadt* a World Heritage Site. Lübeck still thrives as a harbor and as a vital link between Germany and Scandinavia, witnessed by the abundance of Scandinavian restaurants and the bank machines which dispense Swedish and Danish currencies.

ORIENTATION AND PRACTICAL INFORMATION

Lübeck lies on the Baltic Sea approximately 60km northeast of Hamburg. The elliptical *Altstadt* is an island completely surrounded by rivers and canals, making it impossible to wander too far afield from the city without falling into water.

Tourist Office: In the train station (tel. 86 46 75; fax 86 30 24). Open Mon.-Sat. 9am-6pm. Grab a free map here, then make for the larger **main office,** Breitestr. 62 (tel. 100 22 or 180 06), which books rooms for a DM3 fee and is located in back of the *Marienkirche.* Open Mon.-Fri. 9:30am-6pm, Sat.-Sun. 10am-2pm.

Trains: Lübeck is a main transfer point for crossing the former West/East border. Departures frequent for Schwerin (1½hr.), Rostock (2hr.), Hamburg (40min.), Berlin (4hr.), Munich (9hr.), Copenhagen (5½hr.), and Amsterdam (6½hr.).

Public Transportation: Although the *Altstadt* is easily seen by foot, Lübeck has an excellent bus network. The **ZOB** (central bus station) is across from the train station. A single ride costs DM2-2.80, children DM1.50. **Mehrfahrkarten,** books of 6 tickets, cost DM10-14. The best value is the **Lübeck-karte**—it's valid for 24hr. on all local buses, including those going to Travemünde (DM8, children DM4.50).

Ferries: Cruises around the *Altstadt* and harbor depart several times per day from the bridge in front of the *Holstentor* (DM10, students DM8). For ships to Scandinavia, the best deals are from Travemünde.

Taxi: tel. 811 22. Available 24hr., but best to call at least 30min. ahead.

Car Rental: Hertz, Willy-Brandt-Allee 1, around corner from the train station, next to Mövenpick hotel. Open Mon.-Fri. 7am-6pm, Sat. 7am-1pm, Sun. 9-10am.

Bike Rental: Buycycle, Schwartauer Allee 97 (tel. 479 17 44), *rents* bikes, despite the name. DM8 per day. ID required. Open Mon.-Fri. 9am-5pm, Sat. 10am-1pm.

Bookstore: Buchhandlung Weiland, Königstr. 67a (tel. 16 00 60), has a great stock of English-language paperbacks in the basement. Open Mon.-Wed. and Fri. 9am-6pm, Thurs. 9am-8:30pm, Sat. 9am-2pm.

Laundromat: McWash, on corner of An der Mauer and Hüxterdamm. McWash 7kg for DM7. McDry 10kg for DM1/15min. McOpen McMon.-McSat. 6am-11pm.

Rape Crisis Line: tel. 70 46 40. Pick up a copy of **Zimtzicke,** a women's events calendar containing other important numbers and addresses, at the tourist office.

Pharmacies: Apotheke am Lindenplatz, Moislinger Allee 2c (tel. 830 61), off Konrad-Adenauer-Str. on your way towards the *Altstadt* from the train station. Open Mon.-Fri. 8am-6pm, Sat. 8am-1pm. **Adler Apotheke,** Breitestr. 71 (tel. 798 85 15), is located across from the *Marienkirche.* Open Mon.-Fri. 9am-6pm, Sat. 9am-1pm. Late-night pharmacies are listed in the windows of all *Apotheken.*

Emergency: Fire/Ambulance: tel. 112. **Police: tel.** 110.
Post Office: Königstr. 44-46, 23552 Lübeck, 1 block north of the *Marktplatz.* Currency exchange and a 24-hr. ATM. Open Mon.-Fri. 8am-6pm, Sat. 8am-12:30pm.
Telephone Code: 0451.

ACCOMMODATIONS AND CAMPING

Sleep-In (CVJM), Große Petersgrube 11 (tel. 789 82), near the *Petrikirche.* Walk past the *Holstentor,* turn right on An der Obertrave, left on Große Petersgrube, look to the right for the sign. Germany's answer to the YMCA comes complete with pub and foosball. In the old town, 10min. from the station. Whip up food in the guest kitchen. Reception open July-Aug. daily 8am-noon and 5-10pm; Sept.-June Mon.-Fri. 9am-noon and 5-10pm, Sat.-Sun. 9-10am and 5-10pm. 10-bed dorms DM15 per person. Doubles DM20 per person. Sheets DM6.50. Breakfast DM5.

Jugendgästehaus Lübeck (HI), Mengstr. 33 (tel. 702 03 99; fax 770 12). From the train station head for the *Holstentor,* cross the river and make a left on An der Untertrave, and then right on Mengstr. Though slightly more expensive, this superb hostel is ideally located. The historic-building-turned-hostel has singles, doubles, triples and quads. Reception open 7:30am-midnight. Curfew midnight. Single or double DM29.50 first night, DM27 additional nights, over 26 DM35 and DM32.50, respectively. 3- or 4-bed room DM27.50 and DM25, over 26 DM32.50 and 30. Breakfast and friendly resident cat included. Call ahead.

Jugendherberge Lübeck (HI), Am Gertrudenkirchhof 4 (tel. 384 33; fax 345 40), northeast of the historic center. From the *ZOB,* take bus #34 or 39 (direction: Roter Hahn), 31 (direction: Travemünde), or 3 (direction: Brandenbaum) to "Gustav-Rad-bruch-Platz." Walk approximately 100m along Travemünder-Allee and turn left, then right. In a calm neighborhood just outside the *Altstadt,* the hostel's cheerful staff makes up for its slightly cramped rooms. Reception open 7:35-9am and 12:05-11:30pm. Lockout 9-11:30am. Curfew midnight. DM20.20, over 26 DM24. Sheets DM6. Breakfast included. Closed Dec.10 to Jan. 10.

Rucksack Hotel, Kanalstr. 70 (tel. 70 68 92), on the north side of the *Altstadt* by the canal. From the station walk past the *Holstentor,* turn left on An der Untertrave, right on Beckergrube which becomes Glockengießerstr. On the corner of Glockengießerstr. and Kanalstr. (20min.). Peter and Kalli welcome you to their friendly ski-chaletish accommodation. Reception open daily 9am-10pm. Doubles with bath DM75. Quads with bath DM136. Dorm-style rooms available: 6-bed room DM25 per person, 8-bed room DM20 per person. Self-serve kitchen. Breakfast DM7.50, served in Café Affenbrot (see Food, below). Wheelchair-accessible.

Camping: Campingplatz Lübeck-Schönböcken, Steinraderdamm 12 (tel. 89 30 90 or 89 22 87), on a grassy site northwest of the city, is somewhat distant. Showers, washing machines, and cooking facilities available. From the ZOB, take bus #8 (direction: Bauernweg) to the end; then walk 300m along Steinraderdamm toward the city. DM7 per tent, DM8 per person.

FOOD

You'll find yourself surrounded by plenty of oh-so-cute cafés with not-so-cute prices in Lübeck. During the summer, the **market** offers an amazing array of exotic fruit and vegetables. A local specialty is *Lübecker Marzipan,* a gratifying candy made from sugar and almonds. The confectionery **I.G. Niederegger,** Breitestr. 89 (tel. 530 11 26), across from the *Rathaus,* is renowned for its beautifully-shaped marzipan. The **Mädchen und Frauencafé,** located on the second floor at An der Untertrave 97 (tel. 122 57 46), is a friendly women-only café that serves coffee, tea, and cake, and hosts a daily "Women's breakfast" from 10am to 1pm (open Sun. 3-8pm). Check out listings in **Zimtzicke** (see p. 378).

Café Affenbrot, Kandstr. 70 (tel. 721 93), on the corner of Glockengießerstr., is a popular vegetarian café. Dine on *Salattasche* (salad in pita bread; DM6) at tables made from old-fashioned sewing machines. Vegetarian meals DM4.50-10. Open daily 9am-midnight, but the kitchen closes at 11:30pm.

Café Amadeus, Königstr. 26 (tel. 70 53 57). If the name conjured up images of a sophisticated café in Vienna, think again—the decor is as cheesy as the pizza. Good Italian meals can be had for DM6-14. Open Sun.-Thurs. 8am-12:30am, Fri.-Sat. 8am-2am.

"Bei Ulla," Mühlenstr. 19 (tel. 764 41). Ulla serves hearty German fillers such as *Bratkartoffeln mit Spiegeleier* (fried potatoes with fried eggs; DM8). Open daily 11am-12:30am.

SIGHTS

On the eve of Palm Sunday, 1942, most of Lübeck was flattened by Allied bombers. Since then, the city has been renovating its beautiful historic *Altstadt*. The core of the *Altstadt* is the **Rathaus**, a striking 13th-century structure of glazed black-and-red bricks (admission DM4, students DM2; *Rathaus* tours leave Mon.-Fri. at 11am, noon, and 3pm). Behind the *Marktplatz* towers the schizophrenic **Marienkirche**, begun in the Romanesque style c. 1200 but finished as a Gothic cathedral in 1350. Inside, the bent and broken pieces of the multi-ton church bells still rest where they fell during the big 1942 raid. The church's music comes from the largest **mechanical organ** in the world. Free 10-minute soundbites of world-famous organ concerts are played daily at noon. The saints literally come marching in, also at noon, on the church's newly-restored **astronomical clock**. The famous medieval **Totentanzbild** (death-dance mural) used to encircle the chapel opposite the astronomical clock, but it was also destroyed in 1942; all that remains is a reproduction, including one of the *Kaiser* holding hands with skeletons, a representation of the plague. (Church open daily 10am-6pm, winter 10am-4pm. Services Sun. at 10am and 6pm.)

Opposite the *Marienkirche* is the **Buddenbrooks House**, Mengstr. 4 (tel. 777 88), where literary giants Thomas and Heinrich Mann lived as children, and where Thomas Mann's later 1911 novel took its name. The house is now a museum dedicated to the life and works of both brothers, and to their dear friend Michael Knittel. While Thomas, who received the Nobel Prize for Literature in 1929, is one of this century's most important writers, his brother also wrote a number of important works, including *Professor Unrat*, on which the famous Marlene Dietrich film *Der Blaue Engel* (The Blue Angel) is based. Thomas's post-war works, most notably *The Magic Mountain*, a tale of life in a Swiss sanitorium, were built on his deep ambivalence about German culture; he wrote: "Such musicality of the soul must be paid for dearly in other spheres—in the political, the sphere of the common life of human beings." Much of the exhibit is textual and includes original manuscripts and letters (open daily 10am-5pm; admission DM6, students DM3). The house holds special summer events, including a "literary walk" through Lübeck every Sunday from June to September (DM10, students DM8); pick up a schedule of events at the museum.

The medieval **Jacobikirche**, farther north on Breitestr., traditionally a church for seafarers, contains one of the oldest and most beautifully ornamented organs in Germany. (Open daily 10am-6pm, services Sun. at 9:40am. Organ recitals Sat. at 5pm. DM3, students DM2.) Behind the Jacobikirche stands the **Heiligen-Geist-Hospital**, Am Koberg 9. The long corridor of tiny cabins was built as a hospital in 1280 and served as an old-age home from 1518 to 1970. The neighboring **cloister** contains a small medieval murals (open Tues.-Sun. 10am-5pm, Oct.-April Tues.-Sun. 10am-4pm; free). Heading south on Königstr., the **Katharinenkirche** (tel. 122 41 80), which served as a Franciscan monastery from 1225 to 1531, now houses modern art exhibitions (open April-Sept. Tues.-Sun. 10am-1pm and 2-5pm). Next door at Königstr. 11, the **Museum Behnhaus/Drägerhaus** (tel. 122 41 48) consists of two townhouses presenting the Expressionist works of Max Liebermann, Edvard Munch, and Ernst Barlach (open Tues.-Sun. 10am-5pm; admission DM4, students DM2).

Between the inner city and the train station is the massive **Holstentor**, one of the four gates built in the 15th century to guard the entrance to Lübeck. Until 1991 it appeared on the back of the 50-*Mark* bill. Inside, the **Museum Holstentor** (tel. 122 41 29) displays exhibits on ship construction, trade, and quaint local implements of torture (open Tues.-Sun. 10am-5pm; Oct.-March 10am-4pm; admission DM3, students DM1.50, under 18 free). The **Petrikirche,** east on Schmiederstr., is about 750 years old. An elevator climbs to the top of the steeple for a sweeping view. (Church open Tues.-Sun. 11am-4pm. Tower open April-Oct. 9am-6pm. Admission DM3, students DM1.50.) At the southern end of the inner island lies the **Dom,** on Domkirchhof (tel. 747 04), founded by Henry the Lion in 1173; the **lion statue** is his insignia— "Roar, Lion, Roar!" (Open 10am-6pm, March and Oct. 10am-5pm, Nov. 10am-4pm, Dec.-Feb. 10am-3pm; services Sat. at 6pm and Sun. at 10:40am; free).

The **Lübeck Marionette Theater** (tel. 700 60) and **Puppet Museum,** Kleine Petersgrube 4-6 (tel. 786 26), just below the Petrikirche, has 13 rooms filled with more than 700 puppets (oopen daily 10am-6pm; admission DM6, students DM5, children DM3). The **St. Annen-Museum,** St.-Annen-Str. 15 (tel. 122 41 37), off of Mühlenstr., displays a collection of bejeweled religious artifacts, and recounts the cultural history of Lübeck in ceramic, wood, and bronze (open Tues.-Sun. 10am-5pm; admission DM4, students and children DM2, free on Fri.).

ENTERTAINMENT AND NIGHTLIFE

Lübeck is world-famous for its **organ concerts.** At least two per week are held in various churches throughout the summer; schedules are available in churches or at the tourist office. For entertainment listings, pick up *Piste, Zentrum,* or (for women) *Zimtzicke* from the tourist office. Lübeck's two major theaters, the huge **Theater Lübeck,** which puts on operas and symphony concerts as well as mainstream German and imported American plays, and the smaller, more avant-garde **Theater Combinale,** Hüxstr. 115 (tel. 788 17), both offer generous student discounts. **Finnegan,** an Irish pub at Mengstr. 42 (tel 711 10), has Guinness on tap and is frequented by a surprising number of locals (open weekdays 4pm-1am, weekends 4pm-4am). **Brauberger,** Alfstr. 36 (tel. 714 44), is located in a dark, romantic cellar, and brews its own beer (open daily 6pm-2am).

■ Near Lübeck

TRAVEMÜNDE

The attractive town of Travemünde (15km north of Lübeck) is a land of beaches, sun, casinos, and spas. Boutiques line the town streets and wicker chairs *(Strandkorben)* clutter the stretch of beach near the north pier. The **Aqua-Top,** Strandpromenade 1b (tel. 804 42), a fun-filled glass complex of spas and swimming pools, will pamper you with saunas, massages, and waterslides (open daily 10am-9pm; day pass DM16, children DM8; including saunas DM22, children DM16). Cross the harbor to the nearby island of **Priwall** (ferries depart every 10min. near the Aqua-Top, DM0.60). Also across the inlet, the four-mast trade ship **Passat** is moored (open May to Sept. 18 daily 10am-5pm; admission DM4, students and children DM2). From the deck, look back on the 16th-century **lighthouse** situated on Trelleborg Allee (tours March-Sept. Wed. at 5pm; admission DM2). **Travemündewoche** takes place every year in the last week of July and includes outdoor concerts and sailing activities.

Travemünde is easily accessible from Lübeck by **train** (hourly; 20min.) or by **bus** #30 or 31 from the *ZOB* (45min.; day pass valid); trains also run from Hamburg (one per hour; 1¼hr.). There are three main train/bus stops: **Skandinavienkai** accesses the Scandinavia-bound ferries, **Travemünde-Hafen** is close to the town center, and **Travemünde-Strand** leads directly to the beach. The overworked but friendly **tourist office,** Strandpromenade 1b (tel. 804 30; fax 804 60), is located in the Aqua-Top building that faces the beach. Walk from the Travemünde-Strand station down Bertlingstr. and turn left on Strandpromenade. They'll find rooms for a 10% fee or give you a list (open Mon.-Sat. 10am-6pm, Sun. 10am-2pm). **Boat tours** of Travemünde run every hour from various spots along the pier (DM5, children DM3). **TT-Line** runs daily to Trelleburg, Sweden (DM60, students DM45; round-trip DM120, students DM90). For more information, contact **TT-Line** in Hamburg (tel. (040) 36 01 442), or

Nordische Touristik Information in Travemünde (tel. 66 88) Mon.- Fri. 9am-5pm. Travemünde's **telephone code** is 04502.

The **Jugend-Freizeitstätte Priwall,** Mecklenberger Landstr. 69 (tel. 25 76; fax 46 20), is right across the inlet. Take the ferry to Priwall, walk along the beach path for 200m; it's on your right. Surrounded by a standing army of green tents, the camp-like hostel will make you feel like you've enlisted in the *Bundeswehr.* Decent 6-bed rooms. (Reception open 2-10pm. DM18.70, over 26 DM21.70. Sheets DM5. June-Sept. *Kurtax* DM5, other times DM2. Curfew 10pm. Breakfast included. Open April-mid-Oct. Call ahead.) Pitch your tent next door at **Strandcamping-Priwall,** Dünen-weg 3 (tel. 28 35; DM9 per tent, DM7 per person; open April-Sept.; reception open 9am-noon, 3-7pm). Decent fast food and bakeries can be found on the beach path, or if you're on Priwall, similar fare can be located down Düneweg.

RATZEBURG

The island town of Ratzeburg, founded in the early Middle Ages by Henry the Lion, lies about 15km from Lübeck near the top of the former Lübeck-Lüneburg salt trail. The natural beauty of the town and the surrounding area hypnotically draws bicy-clists and hikers. The German Olympic crew team trains daily on the huge lake sur-rounding the island. Other than the scenery, Ratzeburg's main attraction is its art; two small but significant museums offer unique collections of works by 20th-century art-ists A. Paul Weber and Ernst Barlach, both of whom lived in the town.

Weber's astounding, satirical lithographs and watercolors are on permanent dis-play at the **A.-Paul-Weber-Haus,** Domhof 5 (tel. 88 83 26). Weber is perhaps best remembered for his depictions of Hitler, as in the pamphlet *Hitler—ein deutsches Verhägnis* (a German disaster; open Tues.-Sun. 10am-1pm and 2-5pm; admission DM2, students DM1). Ratzeburg's **Dom,** built by Henry the Lion soon after he colo-nized Schleswig-Holstein, houses galleries containing religious works (open April-Sept. daily 10am-noon and 2-6pm; Oct.-Mar. Tue.-Sun. 10am-noon and 2-4pm; ser-vices Sun. at 10:15am). Between the Weber-Haus and the Dom lies the **Kreismuseum** (regional museum; tel. 123 25), housing an assortment of Biedermeier furniture and graphic art by Weber, Günther Grass, and Barlach (open Tues.-Sun. 10am-1pm and 2-5pm; admission DM2, students DM1). A larger collection of Barlach's work sits across the *Marktplatz* in the **Ernst-Barlach-Museum,** Barlachplatz 3 (tel. 37 89); haunting, meditative bronzes and manuscripts are on display (open Tue.-Sun. 10am-noon and 3-6pm; admission DM3, students DM1.50; closed Dec.-Feb.).

The **tourist office,** Schloßwiese 7 (tel. 800 080, fax 53 27), is between the train sta-tion and the *Marktplatz.* From the station, head down Bahnhofsallee until it becomes Lüneburger Damm (15min.); it's in a huge parking lot on the left. They book **private rooms** (DM30-40) for free (open Mon.-Wed. and Fri. 9am-5pm, Thurs. 9am-6pm, Sat.-Sun. 10am-4pm). Hourly **trains** connect Ratzeburg with Lübeck (15min.) and, via Lüneburg, with Hamburg (1hr.). Join the hordes of nature-lovers by renting a **bike** from the **Fahrrad Verleih Schloßweise,** on the lake, just past the tourist office (DM8 per 3hr., DM15 per day). A combined bike rental and ferry ticket (DM12) will take you to the other side of the lake, where there are additional bike paths. For food, the **Burgtheater café,** on Theaterplatz, around the corner from the hostel, has the best prices in town (open daily 2pm-midnight). The **post office,** Herrenstr. 12 (tel. 239 09), is around the corner from the *Marktplatz* (open Mon.-Fri. 8am-noon and 3-6pm, Sat. 10am-noon). The **telephone code** is 04541.

To reach Ratzeburg's **Jugendherberge (HI),** Fischerstr. 20 (tel. 37 07; fax 847 80), take any bus from the train station to the *Marktplatz,* or just follow Bahnhofsallee as it becomes Lüneburger Damm, Unter den Linden, Herrenstr. and finally empties out into the main square. Continuing straight, turn right onto Große Wallstr. and follow it until it becomes Fischerstr.; it's at the end of the street. (Reception open 7am-10pm; if desk closed, go into the kitchen. Curfew 10pm, but you can ring the bell 'til 11:30pm. DM19.20, over 26 DM23.70. Sheets DM6. Laundry DM6, including soap.)

■ Kiel

Site of the 1936 and 1972 **Olympic sailing events,** the waters around Kiel swim cease-lessly with brightly-colored sails. The last full week of June sees the annual **Kieler Woche,** an internationally renowned regatta that enlivens the harbor and floods the town with music, food, and beer, particularly around the Olympia Zentrum (bus #44 north). Kiel's mainstay shipping industry thrives on the traffic through the world's busiest artificial waterway, the **Nord-Ost-See-Kanal** (North- Baltic Sea Canal). A 700-year-old port, Kiel's history is bonded to the sea. Kiel's most heroic moment came in 1918, when a mutiny of sailors touched off the revolution that sent the *Kaiser* pack-ing. The city was also home to Germany's first submarine, built in 1850, as well as the base of Germany's deadly **U-Boot** (submarine) warfare in World War II. Thus, Allied bombings were ruthless, destroying 80% of the city.

The sight and sounds of the harbor, the city's focal point, are ever-present in stolid, modern Kiel, the capital of Schleswig-Holstein. The highlight is the largest team of **canal locks** in the world. The view of the canal and the harbor alone are worth the trip. Take bus #4 north to its end (at "Kanal"), and then the free ferry that runs across every 15 minutes. Walk right, along Kanalstr. from the ferry dock to the *Schleusen-insel* (Lock Island; 10min.). Alternatively, land-lubbers can take bus #1 or #41 (30min.) directly to the "Schleuse" stop. (Tours daily at 9, 11am, 1, and 3pm; admission to the locks only by guided tour. Tours DM2, 50% off with *Kieler Karte,* students DM1.) Hugging the west coast of the **Kieler Förde** (Kiel Harbor), the **Schiffahrtsmuseum** (Navigation Museum; tel. 98 10) displays model ships (open daily 10am-6pm, mid-Oct. to mid-April Tues.-Sun. 10am-5pm; free). North of the ship museum is the **aquar-ium** (tel. 597 38 57), home to the greatest collection of Baltic Sea creatures known to civilization (open daily 9am-7pm, Oct.-March 9am-5pm; admission DM2, students DM1, children DM0.50).

To the left of the **St. Nikolaikirche** (tel. 950 88; open Mon.-Fri. 10am-1pm and 2-6pm, Sat. 10am-1pm; services Sun. at 10am and 7:30pm; free) stands Barlach's haunt-ing statue, *Der Geistkämpfer* (ghost-fighter; see Güstrow, in Mecklenburg-Vorpom-mern, p. 529, for more on the controversial artist). Every February, Kielers celebrate the *"Umschlag,"* when a flag, *"Der Bürgermeister sin Büx"* (that's *Plattdeutsch* for "the mayor's pants"), is hung outside of the Nikolaikirche. Tours of the nearby **Rathaus** include a trip up into the steeple during the summer. (Sat. only at 3:40pm; DM15, students DM7.50; buy tickets at the tourist office.)

Kiel's **tourist booth** (tel. 67 91 00) is located in the *Sophienhof* mall across from the train station. Its finds rooms for DM3.50; maps are a stingy DM1 (open Mon.-Sat. 9am-6:30pm, Sun. 9am-1pm; Oct-April Mon.-Fri. 9am-6:30pm, Sat. 9am-1pm). The **Mitfahrzentrale,** Sophienblattstr. 54 (tel. 194 40; fax 67 67 42), two blocks south of the train station, matches riders and drivers; they also sell discount train tickets (open Mon.-Wed. and Fri. 9am-7pm, Thurs. 9am-8pm, Sat. 10am-3pm, Sun. 11am-3pm). If you plan on using **public transportation,** invest in a **Kieler Karte** (one-day DM12, three-day DM17): it allows unlimited use of the buses and ferries that circulate through the harbor, and gets you a nifty little book of coupons good for a free map at the tourist office and many discounts. Otherwise each bus trip costs DM2.90. One-day cards may be bought aboard the bus; three-day cards must be purchased at a **Kieler-Verkehrs-AG** (Kiel Transit Authority) office or from the tourist office. Most of Kiel's buses pass through the rows of stops outside of the train station; the ones on the train station side of the street *generally* head north, while the ones on the *Sophienhof* side go south. Every two hours, a **bus** leaves from the *ZOB*, around the corner from the train station, for the Hamburg **airport** (1½hr.; DM20); buses also go to the Hamburg train station, 100km to the south. **Ferries** leave from the piers on the west side of the harbor. Don't worry about not being able to find the right one: **Baltic Line** (tel. 98 20 00) will take you to St. Petersburg, Russia, via Nynäshamn, Sweden (weekly; 60hr.; DM430); **Color Line** (tel. 97 40 90) sails to Oslo (daily; 18hr.; DM150, students 50% off on selected sailings); and **Langeland-Kiel** (tel. 97 41 50; fax 945 15) will transport you to Bagenkop, Denmark (2½hr.; DM7, in July DM9). The **post office,**

Stresemannplatz 1-3, 24103 Kiel, is a long block to the right of the train station (open Mon.-Fri. 6am-6pm, Sat. 6:30am-1pm). The **telephone code** is 0431.

To reach Kiel's **Jugendherberge (HI),** Johannesstr. 1 (tel. 73 14 88; fax 73 57 23), take bus #4 from the train station on the *Sophienhof* side. Get off at "Kielerstr." and backtrack one block, then turn right on Johannesstr. (Reception open 7am-11:30pm. Curfew 1am. DM21, over 26 DM25.50. Sheets DM7). Camping is distant at **Camping-platz Falckenstein,** Palisadenweg 171 (tel. 39 20 78), about 10km north of the city center. From the train station, take bus #44 (direction: Strand) to "Seekamp." Back-track to Scheidekoppel and hike for 20 minutes through wheat fields until Palisaden-weg. Turn left. The runs down to the beach (DM6 per tent, DM7 per person). Holstenstr. and the *Marktplatz* are the best places in town for a meal. **Fahrenheit 13,** Alter Markt 13 (tel. 67 91 00), serves temperate German fare. Get groceries at **Kai-ser's,** a supermarket on the ground floor of the *Sophienhof.*

■ Near Kiel: Laboe and Molfsee

While swimming is possible in the **Kieler Förde,** alluring clear water and quieter beaches await in nearby **Laboe.** Bus #4 or #54 from the *Sophienhof* side of the bus stop (direction: Laboe) will take you on a tour through the 'burbs to the beach (45min.; DM2.90, *Kieler Karte* valid). Laboe's primary attractions aside from the sand, however, cast a figurative as well as a literal shadow on this beach fun. **U-Boat 995,** washed up on the beach about 1km from the bus stop, is a submarine used by the Nazis during World War II. If you think the beds beat hostel-life, then check out the cramped micro-kitchen that cooked for 52 people (open daily 9am-6pm, until 5pm in winter; admission DM3, with the *Kieler Karte* DM2.50, children DM2.) Across the street, the **Marine-Ehrenmal** (tel. (04343) 87 55) claims to commemorate "the sailors of all nations who died on the seas," but the exhibits have a distinctly Ger-man slant (open daily 9:30am-6pm; admission DM4, with *Kieler Karte* DM2.50, chil-dren DM2). If you're too lazy to knock on one of the doors with "Zimmer frei" signs posted on them, Laboe's **tourist office,** on the boardwalk at Strandstr. 25, will hook you a room (DM30-50). The sands along the boardwalk have food vendors; fish sand-wiches (surprise!) of all varieties go for DM3-4.

Molfsee's main attraction is the **Schleswig-Holsteinisches Freilichtmuseum** (tel. 655 55), a miniature ghost town of transplanted cottages from all over northern Ger-many, some more than 200 years old, filled with original furniture, farming tools, and other artifacts. In keeping with the farmhouse theme, there are lots of barnyard (*not* Barnard) animals running around. (Take bus #1680, 1669, or 1670 from the *Sophien-hof* bus stop (direction: Flintbek) and get off at "Rammsee-Freilicht- museum." Open daily 9am-6pm; Nov.-Mar. on Sundays and holidays *only* 11am-4pm. Admission DM7, with the *Kieler Karte* DM3, students DM5.)

■ Flensburg

Flensburg is Germany's northernmost city, with the Danish border lying only a hop, skip, and a stumble away. The presence of a large and international student popula-tion from the university and lots of locally-brewed alcohol combine to make it north-ern Germany's liveliest town as well. You can't go anywhere in northern Germany without seeing **Flensburger Pilsner** on tap; the town itself is swimming in it. Flens-burg is located around the perfect harbor that forms the tip of the **Flensburger Förde;** the streets run along the water to wind into the hills above. If all of a sudden you can't understand what the people around you are saying, don't blame it on that extra glass of *Pils*—they're either locals speaking *Plattdeutsch,* a North German dia-lect, or Danes on a serious beer run. The local greeting, *Moin, Moin,* is a *Plattdeutsch* variation of *"Guten morgen,"* but you'll hear it all times of day.

Heading straight down Bahnhofstr. from the station and zig-zagging across Friedrich-Ebert-Str. will lead you to the lively *Altstadt* and Flensburg's huge pedes-trian zone along **Holmstraße** and **Großestraße.** Along the way you'll pass the **Deut-**

sches Haus, a *Bauhaus*-style concert hall donated to Flensburg in recognition of the city's loyalty in the 1920 referendum, quite contrary to the Kieler rebellion (see p. 383). In the **Südermarkt,** the beautiful 14th-century **Nikolaikirche** boasts the largest organ in Schleswig, the *Organ Maximus* (open Tues.-Fri. 9am-5pm, Sat. 10am-1pm; free). Just beyond the **Nordermarkt** stands the **Marienkirche,** with its superb stained-glass windows (open Tues. and Thurs.-Fri. 10am-4pm, Wed. and Sat. 10am-1pm; free). Continuing along Norderstr., climb the 144 steps of the **Marientreppe** to ogle at the mass of orange-roofed houses. And to your left, dear passengers, Denmark. Along the pier, several retired ships have been turned into museums along the **Museumshafen.** At Schiffbrücke 39, a 150-year-old customs house has become the **Schiffahrtsmuseum** (Navigation Museum; tel 85 29 70), documenting Flensburg's nautical history and role in Denmark's once-thriving Caribbean trade. The **rum** exhibit is impressive. Yo ho, yo ho, it's a pirate's life for me (open Tues.-Sat. 10am-5pm, Sun. 10am-1pm; admission DM2, students DM1). The last weekend of May sees the **Rum Regatta,** an event for traditional boats and sober sailors only.

The **tourist office,** Speicherlinie 40 (tel. 230 90; fax 173 52) lies off Großestr.; follow the signs through the courtyard (open Mon.-Fri. 9am-6pm). They'll help you find a private room (DM15-35) without a fee and can arrange tours of the brewery. Flensburg's high-tech bus system saves a lot of uphill walking; practically all buses circulate through the *ZOB* (central bus station), close to the city center (one-way fare DM2.30, 24-hr. *Tageskarte* DM6.50). **Trains** link the city to Hamburg (2hr.) and Kiel (1½hr.) at least every other hour, while others head north to Copenhagen (5hr.) and many other Danish cities. **Buses** from the *ZOB* bus station also cross the border to the Danish towns of Sønderborg (1¼hr.) and Aabenraa (50min.). From the west bank of the harbor, ferries country-hop between Flensburg and Glücksburg in Germany and Gravenstein and Kollund in Denmark (DM3). **Ferries** also leave for Sønderberg from the nearby town of **Kappeln** (reachable by bus). You can rent a **bike** from the train station for DM8 per day. The main **post office,** near the train station at Bahnhofstr. 40, 24939, **exchanges currency** (open Mon.-Fri. 8am-6pm, Sat. 8am-1pm). The **telephone code** is 0461.

Flensburg's **Jugendherberge (HI),** Fichtestr. 16 (tel. 377 42; fax 31 29 52), rests in a nature reserve. A buffet breakfast and a super-friendly atmosphere compensate for eight-bed rooms. From the train station, take bus #1 (direction: Lachsbach) or #4 (direction: Klueshof) to the *ZOB* and change to #3 or #7 (direction: Twedter Plack) to "Stadion," then follow the signs. (Reception open 8-8:45am, 5-6pm, and 9:30-10pm. DM18.70, over 26 DM22.70. Sheets DM6.) The **Nordermarkt** simmers with a slew of cafés and bars. **Hansen's Brauerei,** Großestr. 83 (tel. 222 10), brews its own beer and has reasonably priced German dishes.

Just 10km away from Flensburg, **Glücksburg** boasts beautiful beaches (DM4) and a fairy-tale **Schloß** (tel. (04631) 22 13) surrounded by a looking-glass lake. Glücksburg can be reached by bus from Flensburg (35min.; DM3.30) or by ferry via Kollund, Denmark (6 per day; 50min.; DM3; passport necessary.) From the Glücksburg *ZOB*, walk down towards the post office and follow the signs left to the *Schloß*, or get off at the beach (one stop earlier) and follow the signs around the lake (2.5km). Skate around the waxed floor in the provided slippers while discovering just how inbred—and from looking at the beds, short—19th-century royals were. On the third floor, Gobelin tapestries depicting scenes from Ovid's *Metamorphoses* are displayed. Don't miss the "corpses" in the dungeon (open April-Oct. 10am-5pm, Nov.-March 10am-4:30pm; admission DM7, students DM4.50).

■ Husum

Although home-town hero and 19th-century novelist Theodor Storm called Husum "the grey town by the sea," this little town of 20,000 now shines as the economic and cultural capital of wind-swept North Frisia. Germans may also think of North Sea shrimp when you mention Husum—the town's fishing boats venture into the *Wattenmeer* daily from the *Hafen;* catch them returning with the day's catch.

Husum is centered around its **Marktplatz.** From the train station, head up Herzog-Adolf-Str. and turn left on Ludwig-Nissen-Str.; head right through the shopping center (5min.). At one end of the square stands the solemn and plain **Marienkirche,** built between 1827 and 1832 from the designs of Danish master Christian Frederik Hansen. Across the square is the 17th-century **Rathaus.** Everywhere in Husum, statues, paintings, and restaurants are dedicated to Theodor Storm. He cried and wet his diaper for the first time on September 14, 1817 at Marktplatz 9, next to the *Rathaus.* The building is now a bank. The **Theodor-Storm-Haus,** Wasserreihe 31 (tel. 66 62 70), was the writer's residence from 1866 to 1880 and is now a museum with original furnishings and manuscripts (open April-Oct. Tues.-Fri. 10am-noon and 2-5pm; Mon., Sat., and Sun. 2-5pm; Nov.-March Tues., Thurs., and Sat. 2-5pm; admission DM2, students and children DM1). Completing our tour of the three ages of Man, Storm is buried in the *Klosterkirchhof* in Osterendestr., east of the *Marktplatz.*

The **Schloß vor Husum** (tel. 897 30), two blocks in the opposite direction from the *Marktplatz,* was built by the Gottdorfer dukes at the end of the 16th century but was later remodeled into a Baroque castle. Didn't they know?: if it ain't Baroque, don't fix it. The *Schloß* is only worth visiting for the special art exhibitions featuring works by both German and international artists and for the free flower garden in back. The *Schloß* also hosts concerts on summer evenings (open April-Oct. Tues.-Sun. 11am-7pm; admission DM5, students DM2.50, special exhibitions DM1 extra). The **Nissenhaus,** Herzog-Adolf-Str. 25, was donated by a wealthy German-American and houses the **North Frisian Museum** (tel. 25 45). It has a collection on the art of dike-building and an exhibit on migratory birds (open daily 10am-5pm, Nov.-March Mon.-Fri. 10am-4pm; admission DM5, students DM2, children under 14 DM1). For a glimpse of capitalism in action, visit the **Tabak-Museum** and **Kinder-Museum** (Tobacco Museum and Children's Museum), Wasserreihe 52 (tel. 612 76). An enterprising man decided to display those sorts of antiques you always find languishing in the attic (open daily 10am-6pm; admission DM3, students DM2.50, children DM1.50). The **Ostenfelder Haus,** Nordhusumstr. 13 (tel. 897 30), built in 1600, was Germany's first *Freilichtsmuseum* (open-air museum), containing ancient articles of farmhouse life (open April-Oct. Tues.-Sun. 10am-noon and 2-5pm; admission DM2, students DM1.)

Husum has hourly rail connections to Hamburg (1¾hr.) and Kiel (1½hr.). The **tourist office** (tel. 898 70; fax 47 28) in the *Rathaus* books rooms in private homes for a 15% down payment: call ahead, they're often booked solid. They also arrange daytrips to the Halligen Islands (open Mon.-Thurs. 9am-noon and 2-4:30pm, Fri. 9am-noon and 2-3pm). Rent **bikes** from **Fahrradhandel Cornils,** Ludwig-Nissen-Str. 31 (tel. 21 19, fax 23 85) for DM10 per day. A bike is particularly useful if you want to visit Husum's gorgeous **swimming pool** (the center of the town's weekday nightlife) at Flensburger Chaussee 28 (tel. 899 71 55). It has two heated pools, a waterslide, and a sauna (open Tues.-Fri. 2-10pm, Sat. 8am-5pm, Sun. 8am-6pm; admission DM6). The **post office** is at Marktplatz 5 (open 9am-6pm); Husum's **postal code** is 25813. The **telephone code** is 04841.

To reach the **Jugendherberge Theodor Storm (HI)** (tel. 27 14; fax 815 68), head left from the tourist office and make a right onto Neustadtstr., which turns into Marktstr. Make a left at Adolf-Brütte-Str. and continue as it turns into Schobüller Str. until #34. Or take bus #51 from the *ZOB* (central station) just down the street from the train station (*Westercampweg,* DM1). If ever a hostel could be called romantic, it would be this one. German school groups, however, are the albatross. (Reception open intermittently from 4:30-10pm. Lockout 9-11:30am. Curfew 10pm. DM19.60, over 26 DM24.10. Breakfast included. Closed Jan.15-Feb.15. Call ahead.) The area around the harbor is filled with restaurants and *Imbiß* stands. Sustain yourself with a crab sandwich, the local specialty. **Seiers Gasthof,** Schiffbrücke 1 (tel. 29 63), on the harbor, serves traditional German dishes for under DM12 (open Mon.-Fri.10am-2pm and 5pm-1am, Sat. 10am-noon, 5pm-2am, Sun. 10am-noon and 5pm-2am). Thursday is **farmer's market** day—from 8am until the afternoon, stands selling everything from pickles to cheap clothing, line the *Marktplatz.*

■ Schleswig

At the southernmost point of the **Schlei inlet,** Schleswig is a quiet town bordered by fields and the bluest of waters. Once a major Viking settlement, Schleswig became an important fishing and trade center in the Middle Ages. The city subsequently became the seat of the Gottorfs, lesser German nobles who, despite their social status, built a grandiose castle on the Schlei banks. When Bismarck annexed Schleswig-Holstein from Denmark in 1867, he made Schleswig the region's capital, a post it retained until 1945. Today, Schleswig is a relaxed, tranquil town boasting a rich history and a fine heritage of fishing. At the end of August, Schleswig celebrates its sailing tradition with the colorful **Twiebakken-Regatta.**

The large, Baroque **Schloß Gottorf** is on a tiny island off the Schlei, a pleasant 20-minute walk along the harbor from the *Altstadt;* it now houses a complex of museums. The *Schloß* itself contains a collection of 19th-century Realist and Impressionist German art, and artifacts dating back to the mad, mad world of medieval Schleswig-Holstein. To the left of the *Schloß,* the **Nydamhalle** museum (scheduled to re-open spring 1997) boasts a hoard of unusual archaeological finds dating back to the last Ice Age, including a complete Viking ship and, for those drawn to the macabre, the remains of four big Vikings who were preserved in the sea for more than 1200 years. The **Kreuzstall Museum** (tel. 81 30), on the right, houses an extensive collection of works by artists from the *Brücke* School, including Ernst Ludwig Kirchner, Emil Nolde, and Max Pechstein. The other building includes samples of every major 20th-century German artist, including Oskar Kokoschka, Käthe Kollwitz, and the haunting sculptures of Ernst Barlach and Hans Wimmer. (All museums open March-Oct. 9am-5pm, Nov.-Feb. daily 9:30am-4pm, except Monday. Normally Nydamhalle is open on Monday. Admission DM7, students DM3).

If you find yourself longing for more breast plates and horned helmets, ferries travel from the Stadthafen port near the *Dom* to the **Wikinger Museum Haithabu** (tel. 81 33 00). The museum, next to an archeological excavation of a former **Viking settlement,** covers all aspects of Viking life. (Open daily 9am-6pm, Nov.-March Tues.-Fri. 9am-5pm, Sat.-Sun. 10am-6pm. Admission DM2, students DM1. Ferries DM3.50, round-trip DM6.) About five minutes south of the *Schloß,* the **Städtisches Museum,** Friedrichstr. 9-11 (tel. 81 42 80), houses documents and *objets trouvés* from Schleswig's history, including an unbearably cute collection of teddy bears. On a darker note, it also documents the 1920 *Schleswiger Putsch,* during which soldiers occupied the *Schloß* and government buildings and all of Schleswig's workers, including the doctors, went on strike. The tension came to a climax when the workers encircled the *Schloß* and demanded that the soldiers surrender. The castle was eventually returned to the people. Heading back towards the harbor, the copper steeple of the 12th-century **St. Petri Dom** towers above Schleswig's *Altstadt.* It houses an intricately carved altar by Brüggeman (open Mon.-Thurs. 9am-5pm, Fri. 9am-3pm, Sat. and Sun. 1-5pm; Oct.-April Mon.-Thurs., Sat. 10am-4pm, Fri. 10am-3pm, Sun. 1-4pm; organ concerts DM5-8). Continuing east of the *Altstadt,* you'll reach the **Holm** district, a postcard-perfect fishing village.

The **tourist office,** Plessenstr. 7 (tel. 248 78 or 207 03), is up the street from the harbor; from the *ZOB,* walk two blocks right. They book private rooms and hotels (DM40-60) for a DM8 fee, or you can hunt by yourself on the computer (open May-Sept. Mon.-Fri. 9:30am-12:30pm and 1:30-5pm, Sat. 9am-12:30pm; closed Fri. afternoon and Sat. Oct.-April). Schleswig's **train station** is located, strangely, quite a distance from the city center; take any bus from the stop outside to the *ZOB,* which is close to the *Altstadt* (single ride DM1.70, 6-ride card DM8.50). The **post office,** at Poststr. 1, 24837, will allow you to **exchange money** at counter 5 (open Mon.-Fri. 9am-12:30pm and 2:30-6pm, Sat. 9am-noon). The **telephone code** is 04621.

The **Jugendherberge (HI),** Spielkoppel 1 (tel. 238 93), lies closer to the center of town than the circuitous bus ride would make you think. To get there, take bus #2 (direction: Hühnhauser-Schwimhalle) from either the train station or the *ZOB* to the "Schwimmhalle" stop, on Suadicanistr.; the hostel is across the street. Or it's a 10-

minute walk from the *Altstadt*: from the *ZOB*, go up Plessenstr. to Stadtweg and head left. Turn right on the entrance to the pedestrian path, next to the church at Stadweg 86, and follow the path up and to the left, all the way up the hill, to the park. It's on the right across from the school. It has a view of the Schlei inlet, but the eight-bed rooms are *extremely* cramped (reception open 7:30-8:30am, 12:30-1pm, 4:30-5pm, and 6-10pm. Curfew 10pm. DM19.20, over 26 DM23.70. Sheets DM6. Breakfast included.) For a night in a former *Fischerhaus* overlooking the water, try **Pension Schleiblick,** Hafengang 4 (tel. 234 68), around the corner from the tourist office. (Singles with showers DM55. Doubles with showers DM90-115. Breakfast included. TV in all rooms.) **Da Paolo,** Stadtweg 65 (tel. 298 97), serves up traditional pizza and pasta on red-checkered tablecloths (DM8-15; open Mon.-Sat. noon-7pm, Sun. 1-7pm). For German food, **Panorama,** up the street from the *ZOB,* at Plessenstr. 15 (tel. 239 46), has lunch specials for DM8.50.

■ North Frisian Islands

SYLT

The sandy, windswept island of **Sylt** ("Zullt") stretches far into the North Sea to culminate in Germany's northernmost point. Connected to the mainland by a 7½-mile railtrack built in the 1920s, Sylt—Germany's Martha's Vineyard—has become a favorite spot for government luminaries and other wealthy vacationers. The areas around the island's three main towns—**List, Hörnum,** and **Westerland** (the largest)—have all sprouted pseudo-thatched-roof houses and condos, but most of Sylt consists of sand dunes and fields. The best way to explore is by bicycle. The main **bike path,** which follows the highway (a 2-lane road), is useful for inter-town travel, but the smaller dirt and gravel paths lead to white beaches, clear water, and dunes carpeted with purple flowers. The streets of **Westerland,** the main tourist town, are stuffed with designer shops and spa-hotels. The town's signature statue, which looks like a female Buddha, bathes placidly in the main square.

The **tourist office** (tel. 99 88; fax 99 81 00) to the left of the train station will reserve rooms for an 8% fee (DM30 and up) and give you a super-beachin' island map for DM4.90 (open summer Mon.-Sat. 9am-6pm, Sun. 9am-1pm). The beaches, euphemistically designated "FKK" (*Freie Körper Kultur,* or "free body culture") are strictly nude; the others are bathing-suit-optional. Trains from Hamburg **Altona** travel to Westerland via Niebüll (about 18 per day; 3hr.). **Public transportation** on the island is quite expensive (DM6 to reach either hostel from Westerland, day card DM20). Buses leave from the *ZOB* terminal to the left of the Westerland station. **Rent a bike** at the Westerland train station, across from gate 1 (DM9 per day, DM49 per week; open daily 8:30am-6:30pm). To use any of the beaches (including *Bühne 16,* a famous nude beach), or to spend a night in Westerland, you must pay a levy called a *Kurtaxe* (May-Oct. DM6; Nov.-April DM3; under 18 free). The **post office** is at Kjeirstr. 5, around the corner from the train station (open Mon.-Sat. 9am-6pm, Sun. 9am-1pm). The **postal code** is 25992. The **telephone code** is 04651.

Die Kur

In Germany, "The Cure" is not a British rock band, but a venerated excuse for going to the beach. The well-funded German healthcare system subsidizes trips to spa towns for those over 50, which might explain why more than six million Germans take spa vacations each year. Yet German doctors are divided about the value of the *Kur.* Some believe it to be mostly psychological therapy, while others lend it more credence. The *Kurschatten* (spa romance)—which has become such a tradition that now it's not always admissible as grounds for divorce in Germany—probably helps vacationers stay healthy more than anything else. This might explain why so many spa towns have at least one *"FKK"* ("Freie Körper Kultur"), better known to English speakers as a nude beach.

Ferries run hourly from the List harbor to **Havneby** on the Danish island of **Rømø** (less frequently in winter; round-trip DM8, seniors and children DM6). Call **Rømø-Sylt Linie** (tel. 87 04 75) in List for reservations and information. **Adler-Schiffe** (Boysenstr. 13; tel. 987 00), also runs daytrips to the Halligen Islands (see below) from Hörnum, as well as excursions to Denmark's **Legoland** theme park (every Thursday at 7:15am; DM70, children DM60). Passport required, or you'll have to deal with the Legoland border guards, who tote menacing Lego Uzis.

Sylt's two youth hostels are located in **List** and **Hörnum**, 16km to the north and south of Westerland, respectively. List's **Jugendherberge Mövenberg** (tel. 87 03 97; fax 87 10 39) is close to the beach but very little else. Catch the bus (direction: List) from the Westerland *ZOB* to List-Schule. If you're lucky you can change for the infrequent List-Strand bus to Mövenberg; otherwise, return to the intersection, turn right and follow the *Jugendherberge* sign about a mile, past the sheep and dunes. (Reception open 7-9am, noon-2:30pm and 4-10pm. Curfew 11pm. DM19.60, over 26 DM24.10. Breakfast included. Written reservations strongly advised: write to Jugendherberge Mövenberg, 25992 List/Sylt. Definitely call ahead. Closed Nov. to mid-March.) On the other end of the island, **Jugendherberge Hörnum (HI)**, Friesenplatz 2 (tel. 88 02 94; fax 88 13 92), is more accessible to a bus stop and life in general. From the *ZOB* take the bus (direction: Hörnum) to "Hörnum-Nord" and continue along Rantumerstr., turning left at the *Jugendherberge* sign. Behind the hostel, a sheltered, secluded beach stretches for miles. (Reception open noon-1pm and 5-10pm. Curfew 11pm. DM19.60, over 26 DM24.10. Reservations strongly recommended. Closed Dec. 12- Jan. 13.)

As far as food goes, Westerland's **McDonald's,** at the corner of Friedrichstr. and Elisabethstr., may be the only place in town where you can get a meal for under DM10. There are also the ubiquitous fish stands, but beware of the paltry portions.

HALLIGEN ISLANDS

To the south of Sylt stretch the clean beaches and marshy, green plains of the **Halligen Islands.** A mini-archipelago surrounded by the *Wattenmeer* (cotton sea), the Halligens' flood problems and many dike breaches result in rare forms of amphibious vegetation. All of the islands are part of the **Schleswig-Holstein Wattenmeer National Park,** where wildlife is vigilantly protected. The islands are equally well-known for their popularity as a spa-cure destination for wealthy, elderly Germans, who flock there to be revitalized by the sea air.

Föhr, the largest island and the closest to the mainland, features numerous spas, as well as tiny boutiques lining the streets of **Wyk,** the island's biggest town. **Amrum** (the closest to Sylt), while still somewhat commercialized, manages to preserve a bit more of the natural atmosphere. The other Halligens—**Hooge, Pellworm, Langeneß,** and **Gröde**—are nearly uninhabited and shelter unique flora and fauna, as well as beaches populated by sea lions, the symbol of the region. **Adler-Schiffe** (tel. 987 00; fax 263 00) runs daytrips to the Halligens (Hooge, Amrum, and Föhr) from **Hörnum** and **List,** on Sylt. (DM32-34, under 14 DM16-17. The ferries usually leave about 10am, returning by 6pm and allowing 5hr. on the islands; call for schedules and reservations). To reach the islands from **Husum,** ask the tourist office about daytrips leaving directly from Husum's harbor, or take the train to **Niebüll** (1 per hour; 40min.; DM10) and transfer to the NVAG train to Dagebüll, which connects with the ferries to Föhr and Amrum. Buy a combined train-ferry ticket in the NVAG office directly across from the Niebüll train station (ferries leave several times daily during the summer; combined ticket DM 23-35, depending on whether you want to see just one island or many).

Föhr's **tourist information** (tel. 30 40) is in the *Rathaus,* right across from the port (open daily 9am-12:30pm and 1:30-5pm). They book rooms in private homes (DM30-80 per person), or you can surf for the info yourself on the nifty little computer. Rent a **bike** for DM9 per day from **Fahrrad Verleih Petra,** Königstr. 3 (tel. (04681) 89 89), around the corner from the main square. Föhr's Jugendherberge, **Haus-Atlantis (HI),** has risen from the sea at Fehrstieg 41 (tel. (04681) 23 55). It's a long walk from the port—take bus #1 from pier 3 to "Schullandheim" (2 per hr.; DM1.50). The hostel is about a block straight ahead. (Reception open 7am-10pm. Curfew 10pm. DM19.60, over 26 DM24.10. Sheets DM7. *Kurtaxe* DM0.80. Laundry DM5, including soap.) Amrum's **Jugendherberge Wittdün,** Wandelbahn 9 (tel. (04682) 20 10), is filled to the gills with stuffed island wildlife and clean rooms. Follow the signs from the ferry dock. (Reception open 11:30am-1pm and 4:30-9:30pm. DM19.60, over 26 DM24.10, *Kurtaxe* DM0.80. Sheets DM7.) Even the fast food on Föhr is overpriced—the **grocery store** across from the bike rental is your best bet.

Greater Berlin and Environs

N ↑

TO ROSTOCK
Oranienburg
Wandlitz
Bernau
E26
E55
E26
E55
TO HAMBURG
Tegeler See
PANKOW
Tegel
B E R L I N
SPANDAU
CHARLOTTEN-BURG
Spree
PRENZLAUER BERG
FRIEDRICHSHAIN
MITTE
Hauptbahnhof
TO HANOVER
E51
WILMERS-DORF
Berlin Zoo
KREUZBERG
Bahnhof Lichtenberg
Grunewald
SCHÖNE-BERG
Tempelhof
Berliner Stadtforst
Havel
STEGLITZ
ZEHLEN-DORF
NEUKÖLLN
Großer Müggelsee
Wannsee
Potsdam
BABELS-BERG
E51
Templiner-see
Schönefeld
0   5 miles
0   5 kms
TO DRESDEN/ PRAGUE
TO LEIPZIG

Berlin

"Als das Kind Kind war, wüßte es nicht, daß es Kind war."
—*Wings of Desire*

"When the child was a child, it didn't know it was a child." The opening words of Wim Wenders's *Wings of Desire* still piercingly reflect contemporary Berlin, an inchoate tangle of experiences that are unknowingly in search of an identity. One of the most fascinating cities on Earth, Berlin has been the showpiece and mouthpiece, hothouse and charnel-house, fracture point and rallying point for Western civilization. It is Berlin's role as a crucible of opposing forces that yields its excitement. Any attempts to use the city to define a new Germany are tainted with a hint of absurdity amid the cacophony of languages that echo throughout the city's subways and indicate the eminently international flavor of its populace.

It has been said that Berliners have experienced more history than any other people in Europe. For 40 years, the divided city personified the undeclared Cold War. Raised in the shadow of global conflict, Berliners responded with a glorious storm of cultural activity and the sort of nightlife you might expect from a population that has its back against the wall. With the collapse of the Berlin Wall in 1989, Berlin suddenly gained the opportunity to reinvent itself. When Communist governments fell across Eastern Europe, Berlin found itself it in a unique position, straddling the border of two distinct but no longer separate worlds. Almost overnight, it became a gateway— *the* gateway—between East and West.

Now, as Eastern and Western Europe stitch themselves together, the result will be a new city for a new millennium, redefining Berlin as Germany's cultural capital. Berlin's appeal is thus not only how different it will be in 10 years, but simply *that* it will be different in 10 years. Even so, this self-fashioning must occur without the benefit of an historical umbilical chord, as the pre-division days of the Third Reich cannot absolve Berlin of its role as the symbolic fault line of Western Civilization. The brash assumption on the part of proponents of reunification, that Berlin would be able to fall back upon its striking cosmopolitan history of the 18th to early-20th centuries, turned out to be false. Today all efforts to recreate Berlin as it "had been" are illusory—the issue at hand is what it will become.

The period since reunification has brought dizzying change, and Berlin is both better and worse off as a result. As vigorous students protest over contemporary social problems—and there's no lack these days—tempers flare up frequently. While the post-war West underwent an enormous period of growth fostered by the Marshall Plan and the ensuing *Wirschaftswunder,* the East stood still. The cascade of money flowing eastward since 1991 has turned much of eastern Berlin into rubble-strewn construction sites; indeed, the giant cranes towering over the horizon at Potsdamer Platz have come to symbolize reunited Berlin as much as the ruined Kaiser-Wilhelm-Gedächtniskirche or the Alexanderplatz television tower. But despite the current plethora of construction jobs, eastern Berlin suffers from massive unemployment as the transition from communism to capitalism proves more painful than the German government predicted. The economic hopelessness and social alienation have encouraged many young Berliners towards xenophobic neo-Nazi movements. Berlin's disorganized police force has been largely ineffective against these groups and their often brutal attacks on immigrants and nonconformists.

It will continue to be social chasms and contradictions that represent Berlin in the coming decade, as the radically liberal artist communes continue to coexist with the disaffected, unemployed masses. In this sense, Berlin suffers from a disheartening historical continuity, spawning a battleground of social forces that is reminiscent of the later years of the Weimar Republic. Today, this often discordant clash of various elements of Berlin's past and present can easily be heard in the city's restless air. Yet it has always been this way in Berlin. After all, this is the home of Christopher Isherwood and the cast of characters he immortalized in *Goodbye to Berlin* (better known as the musical *Cabaret*), of eminent philosopher Moses Mendelssohn, of revolutionary playwright Bertolt Brecht, and of Adolf Hitler and his Gestapo. Ironically, the parliament that once tried to seal the destiny of the world let itself be packaged in 1995, when the *Reichstag* was wrapped by the artist Christo.

Despite its art and history, Berlin is a bundle of contradictions that have never been pretty to look at or easy to figure out. Physically it has neither the architectural glory of Paris nor the towering hardiness of New York. But, to use a phrase once applied to the Rolling Stones, "it's so ugly, it's beautiful." For now, Berlin is a kaleidoscope of GDR apartment blocks and designer boutiques, decaying buildings pockmarked with bullet holes and gleaming modern office complexes. But the occasional melancholy of the city's tumultuous past is more than made up for by the exhilaration of being on the cutting edge. As Weimar decadent Karl Zuckmayer wrote, "Berlin tasted of the future, and for that one happily accepted the dirt and the coldness as part of the bargain."

■ History

PRUSSIAN KINGDOM TO WORLD WAR I

Berlin took its time attaining international importance. Although populated since the Stone Age, the first mention of a town called "Berlin" appeared first in 1237; despite political and economic links, it was not until 1709 that the five towns by the river

Spree united into the city of Berlin, capital of the Prussian kingdom. In the 18th century, Berlin flourished under the progressive rule of Frederick II (the Great), and intellectuals such as Gotthold Ephraim Lessing and Moses Mendelssohn turned the growing city into a center of the Enlightenment. Voltaire, who fled the stifling atmosphere of French absolutism to enjoy Frederick's patronage, marveled at the transformation of Berlin: "Things have changed visibly: Sparta has become Athens." Berlin suffered a decline in the 19th century as it was conquered by Napoleon and later beset by revolution in 1848. As it grew, it remained a hotbed of political and economic discontent. In 1871, Berlin became the capital of the German Empire established after Bismarck's wars. Its new position as national capital ushered in a period of prosperity, stability, and hypocrisy documented in the novels of Theodor Fontane. Hundreds of years of political fragmentation left its mark on Germany, however, and imperial Berlin never became the center of the new nation in the same way that Paris was for France or London for Britain. Munich and Frankfurt remained cultural and commercial rivals, and many Germans felt little affection for the Prussian capital. It was not until the end of World War I and the establishment of the first German Republic that Berlin became the undisputed center of national life.

REVOLUTION AND WEIMAR CULTURE

World War I and the Allied blockade brought about near-starvation conditions in Berlin. A popular uprising led to the Kaiser's abdication and Karl Liebknecht's declaration of a socialist republic, with Berlin as capital. Locally, the revolt—led by Liebknecht and Rosa Luxemburg—turned into a full-fledged workers' revolution which wrested control of the city for several days. The Social Democratic government enlisted the aid of radical right-wing mercenaries, the *Freikorps,* who brutally supressed the rebellion and murdered Liebknecht and Luxemburg. But when the *Freikorps* chose the new government as its next target, the workers demonstrated their commitment to democracy and staged a massive strike to defeat the coup. Political and economic instability continued until 1923, when Chancellor Gustav Stresemann's economic plan and generous loans from the United States improved the situation. Meanwhile, Berlin had become one of the major cultural centers of Europe. The Expressionist painters flourished, Bertolt Brecht developed revolutionary new theater techniques, Alexander Döblin applied Joycean method in his novels about Berlin, and artists and writers from all over the world flocked to the city. It was an era of decadence and tolerance. Christopher Isherwood and W. H. Auden were among the prominent openly gay men who found acceptance in Berlin with other refugees from rigid mores elsewhere in Europe, as did Ernst Röhm, the gay future leader of Hitler's *Sturmabteilung* (storm troopers). The city's "Golden Twenties" ended abruptly with the 1929 economic collapse. Mass unemployment preceded bloody riots, radicalization, political chaos, and the ascent of the Nazis.

CAPITAL OF THE THIRD REICH

When Hitler took power on January 30, 1933, traditionally left-wing "Red Berlin" was not one of his strongholds. He consolidated his control over the city through economic improvements and totalitarian measures, and found plenty of supporters for the savage anti-Semitic pogrom of November 9, 1938, known as the *Kristallnacht* (Night of Shattered Glass). Berlin was hit extremely hard during World War II; Allied bombing and the Battle of Berlin leveled a fifth of the city. With almost all of the healthy men dead or gone, it was Berlin's women, known as the *Trümmerfrauen* (rubble women) who picked up the broken pieces of the city. The pre-war population of 4.3 million sank to 2.8 million. Only 7000 members of Berlin's once-thriving Jewish community of 160,000 survived the Nazi genocide.

After the war, the Allies took over control of the city, dividing it into French, British, American, and Soviet sectors under a joint Allied Command. On June 16, 1948, the Soviets withdrew from the joint Command and demanded full control of Berlin. On June 26 they began an 11-month blockade of most land and water routes into the western sectors. The population would have starved were it not for a massive Allied airlift of supplies known as the *Luftbrücke* (air bridge). On May 12, 1949, the Soviets ceded control of the western half of Berlin to the Western Allies.

A DIVIDED CITY

On October 5, 1949, the Soviet-controlled German Democratic Republic *(Deutsche Demokratische Republik)* was formally established, with East Berlin as its capital. The city was thus officially divided. Dissatisfaction was great in East Berlin, and it manifested itself in the workers' uprising of June 17, 1953, when widespread popular demonstrations were crushed bloodily under Soviet tanks. One result of the repression was an increase in the number of refugees who fled from East to West Berlin—200,000 in 1960 alone. On the morning of August 13, 1961, the government of the East responded to this exodus of many of its most talented citizens with the almost instantaneous construction of the Berlin Wall, which stopped virtually all interaction between the two halves of the city. A commercial center around Breitscheid Platz and the renowned Kurfürstendamm was created and nurtured to become *das Schaufenster des Westens* (the shopping window of the West).

West Berlin remained under joint French, British, and American control. Although there was an elected mayor, final say rested with the Allied commander-in-chief. The city was not officially a part of the Federal Republic of Germany, but had a "special status." Although Berlin adopted the resolutions of the Federal Parliament, the municipal Senate still had to approve them, and the Allies retained ultimate authority over the city right up until German reunification in 1990. One perk of this special status was the exemption of West Berliners from military conscription. Thousands of German artists, punks, and left-wing activists moved to Berlin to escape the draft and formed an alternative political and artistic scene without parallel anywhere in the world. The West German government, determined to make a showcase of the city, subsidized its economic and cultural life, further enhancing its vitality.

THE WALL OPENS

On November 9, 1989—the 71st anniversary of the proclamation of the Weimar Republic, the 66th anniversary of Hitler's Beer Hall *Putsch,* and the 51st anniversary of *Kristallnacht*—a series of popular demonstrations throughout East Germany, riding on a decade of discontent and a year of rapid change in Eastern Europe, culminated in the opening of the Berlin Wall. The image of jubilant Berliners embracing atop the Brandenburg Gate that night provided one of the most memorable images of the century. Berlin was officially reunited (and Allied authority ended) along with the rest of Germany on October 3, 1990, to widespread celebration. Since then, the euphoria has evaporated. East and West Berliners have discovered that they don't really like each other as much as they once envisioned. Resignation to reconstruction has taken the place of the biting criticism and tasteless jokes that were standard in the early 90s. Eastern Berlin remains politically volatile and economically disadvantaged, and Western Berliners have responded with their own form of xenophobia; in 1995, voters in the western Wedding district voted a handful of far-right nationalists onto the town council. The city is slowly restitching itself, but it may take a long time before its residents truly consider themselves neighbors.

Although the first united, freely-elected Bundestag symbolically convened in Berlin on December of 1990, the June 1991 vote to move the parliament back here bodes no immediate action; Bonn remains the seat of government, and the transfer is not expected to be complete until 1999. November 1996 saw a referendum on uniting Berlin and Brandenburg into one *Land,* with Berlin as its capital. If and when this happens, perhaps the "post-war" era in Berlin will have a definitive endpoint, more than 50 years after World War II; and on the doorstep of the 21st century.

■ Orientation and Practical Information

Berlin surveys the Prussian plain from the northeastern corner of a reunited Germany and is again becoming the hub of the national rail network. About 4 hours southeast of Hamburg by rail and 8 hours north of Munich (though ICE trains cut down on travel time), Berlin has a web of rail and air connections to other European capitals. Berlin is well-connected to Eastern European countries: Prague is five hours by rail; Warsaw six hours. Almost all European airlines, Western or Eastern, have frequent service to one of Berlin's three airports. For the time being, West Berlin's **Bahnhof Zoologischer Garten** (almost always called **Bahnhof Zoo**) remains Berlin's major train station and a central focus of Berlin's subway and surface rail systems. The situation is changing, however, as reconstruction is allowing the eastern **Hauptbahnhof** station to supercede the space-constricted Zoo station. Within the next few years, the *Hauptbahnhof*—a 20-minute S-Bahn ride from the Zoo station—should once again become the main station. At the moment trains from the new federal states and from eastern Europe are evenly split between this station and **Berlin-Lichtenberg**, significantly farther east (about 45min. by S-Bahn from the Zoo). Trains coming from the west and south arrive either at the Zoo or the *Hauptbahnhof*. **Friedrichstraße** and **Alexanderplatz** are other important eastern stations.

Berlin is an *immense* agglomeration of what were once two separate and unique cities: the former East, which contains the lion's share of Berlin's architectural landmarks and historic sites, and the former West, which functioned for decades as a small, isolated democratic state and is still the commercial heart of united Berlin. As businesses and embassies are starting to move their headquarters back to the east, however, this situation is changing.

The commercial district of West Berlin lies at one end of the huge **Tiergarten** park, and is focused around Bahnhof Zoo and **Breitscheidplatz.** It is marked by the bombed-out **Kaiser-Wilhelm-Gedächtniskirche,** the boxy tower of **Europa Center.** A star of streets radiates from Breitscheidplatz: toward the west run **Hardenbergstraße, Kantstraße,** and the great commercial boulevard of modern Berlin, the renowned and reviled **Kurfürstendamm,** or **Ku'damm.** Down Hardenbergstr. 700m is Steinplatz and the enormous Berlin **Technical University (TU).** Down Kantstr. 800m is **Savignyplatz,** home to cafés, restaurants, and *Pensionen.*

The grand tree-lined **Straße des 17. Juni** runs west-east through the Tiergarten to end at the triumphant **Brandenburg Gate,** which opens out onto **Pariser Platz,** a site of landmark public addresses. Heading south from the Brandenburg Gate and the nearby **Reichstag,** newly-asphalted **Ebertstraße** runs uncomfortably along the path of the demolished Berlin Wall to **Potsdamer Platz.** Toward the east, the gate opens onto **Unter den Linden,** Berlin's most famous boulevard and the site of many historic buildings, particularly around the **Lustgarten** plaza. Continuing east, one arrives at teeming **Alexanderplatz,** the center of the East's growing commercial district and the home of Berlin's most visible landmark, the **Fernsehturm.** The alternative **Kreuzberg** and **Mitte,** for 45 years the fringe, back-against-the-wall neighborhoods of the West and East respectively, are once again at the city's heart. Distinctions between east and west are withering away as communication networks—transportation, telecommunication, and utilities—are synthesized and built from scratch to serve the sprawling metropolis that was reborn with unification.

The ferry-laden **Spree River** snakes its way from west to east through the center of Berlin; it forms the northern border of the Tiergarten and splits just east of Unter den Linden to close off the **Museumsinsel** (Museum Island), East Berlin's cultural epicenter. The windswept waters of the **Wannsee, Tegelersee,** Niederneuendorfer See, and Heiligensee lap the city from all sides, and are connected by narrow canals.

If you're planning to stay more than a few days in Berlin, the blue-and-yellow **Falk Plan** (available at most kiosks and bookstores) is an indispensable and convenient city map that includes a street index and folds open like a book (DM11). Dozens of streets and transit stations in Eastern Berlin once took their names from Communist heroes and heroines. Many, but not all, have been renamed in a process completed only

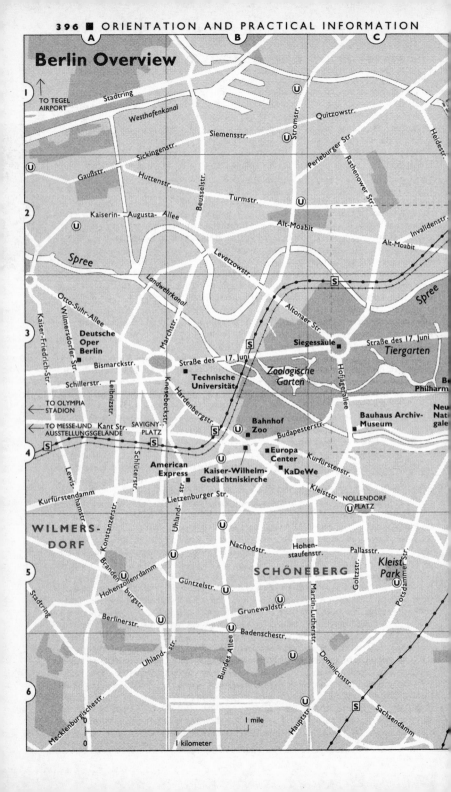

Berlin Overview

D
E
F

U

Dimitroffstr.

Bernauerstr.

Schönhauser Allee

Kastanien Allee

Chorinerstr.

Käthe-Kollwitzstr.

Immanuelkirchstr.

PRENZLAUER
BERG

Greifswalderstr.

U

Chausseestr.

S

Invalidenstr.

U

Wilhelm-

Pieck-

Str.

Rosenthalerstr.

Prenzlauer Allee

(former)
Berlin Wall

ROSA-
LUXEMBURG
PLATZ

H.-Beimler-Str.

Mollstr.

Luisenstr.

U

Oranienburger

Str.

S

Alte
Synagogue

ALEXANDER
PLATZ

S

Bodemuseum

K.-Marx-Allee

U

S

S

MUSEUMS-
INSEL

Liebknechte-Str.

S

Reichstag

Entlastungsstr.

MITTE

Pergamon-
museum

Karl-

Fernsehturm
(TV Tower)

FRIEDRICHS-
HAIN

Altes
Museum

Alte
National
galerie

Brandenburger
Tor

Unter den Linden

Wilhelmstr.

Friedrichstr.

Französische Str.

U

S

Berlin
Haupt-
bahnhof

TIER-
GARTEN

Ebertstr.

Spree

Berlin
honic

U

POTSDAMER
PLATZ

Leipziger Str.

Brücken
str.

U

Köpenicker Str.

Site of
Checkpoint
Charlie

Staatsbibliothek

Henrich-Heine-Str.

TO
TREPTOWER
PARK

nale
ionalerie

U

Kochstr.

Lindenstr.

Oranienstr.

Mariannenstr.

S

Transport and
Technology
Museum

Stresemannstr.

KREUZBERG

Prinzenstr.

Skalitzer Str.

U

Kort-

busser Damm

Landwehrkanal

U

Möckernstr.

Wilhelmstr.

U

Urbanstr.

Sonnenallee

Yorckstr.

Gneisenaustr.

U

Mehringdamm

Bergmannstr.

Hasenheide

U

Victoria
Park

U

Dudenstr.

U

Hermannstr.

Columbiadamm

Tempelhofer Damm

TEMPELHOF

N

S

Zentralflughafen
Tempelhof

recently; be sure that your map is up-to-date. In newly united Berlin, many **municipal services** are gradually being joined and coordinated. Novelist Peter Schneider called the East and West Siamese twin cities, with, for instance, two matching television towers as navels. When services are duplicated in both parts of the city, *Let's Go* lists those in Western Berlin first, then their Eastern counterparts.

> **Safety Warning!** Although neo-Nazis represent a tiny minority of Berliners, Africans, Asians, and other conspicuously non-German individuals should be on guard in the less-touristed areas of Eastern Berlin. These extreme-right groups have also been known to target gay and lesbian couples. The violent skinhead groups tend to identify themselves by wearing white-laced boots. Left-wing, anti-Nazi "alternative" skinheads also exist; they favor red laces. The neo-Nazis have been linked to late-night attacks on foreigners on the S-Bahn.

Tourist Offices:
Main Office: Berlin-Touristen-Information, Europa Center, Budapesterstr. 45 (tel. 262 60 31). From Bahnhof Zoo, walk along Budapesterstr. past the Kaiser-Wilhelm-Gedächtniskirche; the office is on the right (5min.). Helpful staff speaks fluent English. Open Mon.-Sat. 8am-10:30pm, Sun. 9am-9pm.

Branch offices: In the main hall of **Tegel Airport,** at the Lufthansa Airport Center (tel. 41 01 31 45). Open daily 5:15am-10pm; also inside the **Brandenburger Tor,** south wing (tel. 25 00 25). Open daily 9:30am-6pm.

Services: Thanks to recent privatization, the tourist offices no longer provide the plethora of free services and information they used to. However, they all sell a useful city map (DM1) on which sights and transit stations are more clearly marked than on the *Falk Plan.* They book same-day hotel rooms for DM5—though room prices start at DM50 and rise to stratospheric heights. The offices don't have many entertainment listings; you're better off buying *Tip* or *Zitty* (2 German-language bi-weeklies) at any newsstand (DM4 each) or the English-language *Metropolis* (DM3), which has sparser listings but is designed for tourists.

Tours: Berlin Walks (tel. 301 91 94) offers a range of English-language walking tours, including their famous Discover Berlin tour, as well as tours of Infamous Third Reich Sites, Jewish Life in Berlin, and Prenzlauer Berg. Tours last about 2½hr. and meet at 10am and 2:30pm in front of the Zoo station. DM14, under 26 DM10.

Rad Zeit, a monthly pamphlet (available in bike shops and in some cafés), lists bike tours of Berlin (in German only) and the surrounding countryside—a great way to meet people. **Bus tours** are offered by various companies in English and German (they're rather touristy), leaving nearly every hr. from the Ku'damm near Europa Center and the Kaiser-Wilhelm-Gedächtniskirche.

Budget Travel:
Kilroy Travels, Hardenbergstr. 9 (tel. 313 04 66; fax 312 69 75), across from the Technical University. The friendly staff will cheerfully help you navigate through the intricacies of European planes, trains, and buses. **Branch offices** at: **Takustr. 47** (tel. 831 10 25; fax 832 53 76). U-Bahn #1: "Dahlem-Dorf." **Nollendorfplatz 7** (tel. 216 30 91; fax 215 92 21). U-Bahn #1, 2, or 4: "Nollendorfplatz." **Mariannenstr. 7** (tel. 614 68 22; fax 614 99 83), in Kreuzberg. U-Bahn #1 or 8: "Kotbusser Tor." **Georgenstr.,** Stadtbahnbogen 184, in Mitte. S-Bahn or U-Bahn #6: "Friedrichstr." All open Mon.-Fri. 9am-6pm, Sat. 9am-1pm.

SRS, Marienstr. 25 (tel. 281 67 61; fax 281 51 33). U-Bahn #6: "Friedrichstr." Books student flights and has a useful binder of last-minute specials. Open Mon.-Fri. 9am-6pm, Sat. 9am-2pm.

Embassies and Consulates: U.S. Embassy, Neustädtische Kirchstr. 4-5 (tel. 238 51 74). S-Bahn: "Unter den Linden." Just recently opened, though at the moment they're not open for business; maybe by 1997. If not, contact **U.S. Citizens Service,** 170 Clayallee (tel. 832 92 33; fax 832 12 65). U-Bahn #1: "Dahlem-Dorf." Open Mon.-Fri. 9am-noon. Telephone advice available Mon.-Fri. 9am-5pm; after hours, a machine will give you emergency instructions. **Canadian Embassy,** Friedrichstr. 95 (tel. 261 11 61; fax 262 92 06) S-Bahn or U-Bahn #6: "Friedrichstr." Open Mon.-Fri. 8:30am-12:30pm and 1:30-5pm. **U.K. Embassy,** Unter den Linden 32 (tel. 20 18 40). S-Bahn #1 or 2: "Unter den Linden." Open Mon.-Fri. 9am-noon and 2-4pm.

Irish Consulate, Ernst-Reuter-Platz 10 (tel. 34 80 08 22; fax 34 80 08 63). U-Bahn #2: "Ernst-Reuter-Pl." Open Mon.-Fri. 10am-1pm. **Australian Consulate,** Uhlandstr. 181-183 (tel. 880 08 80). U-Bahn #15: "Uhlandstr." Open Mon.-Fri. 9am-noon. **South African Consulate,** Douglasstr. 9 (tel. 82 50 11; fax 826 65 43). Open Mon.-Fri. 9am-noon. **New Zealand** citizens should contact their embassy in Bonn.

Currency Exchange: Deutsche Verkehrs-Kredit Bank, on Hardenbergstr. at Bahnhof Zoo (tel. 881 71 17). Long hours, terrible rates—1% commission on traveler's checks (DM7.50 min. fee). Open Mon.-Sat. 7:30am-10pm, Sun. 8am-7pm. Branch office at **Hauptbahnhof** (tel. 426 70 29). Open Mon.-Fri. 7am-7:30pm, Sat.-Sun. 8am-4pm. **Berliner Bank,** in Tegel Airport. Open daily 8am-10pm. You can also change money at most **post offices,** which cash traveler's checks for DM6 per check. **Sparkasse** and **Deutsche Bank** have branches everywhere; their ATMs usually accept Visa and MC, though only a few still take EuroCard. Sparkasse changes cash free, but charges 1% commission on traveler's checks (with a DM7.50 min.). **Citibank** has branches with 24-hr. ATMs at Kurfürstendamm 72. S-Bahn or U-Bahn #2 or 9: "Zoo"; at Wittenbergpl. 1. U-Bahn 1, 2, or 15: "Wittenbergpl."; at Wilmersdorferstr. 133. U-Bahn #2 or 7: "Bismarckstr."; and at Karl-Marx-Allee 153. U-Bahn #5: "Strausbergerpl." There's also a Citibank ATM at Tegel Airport. ATMs are the best (and cheapest) way to get money.

American Express: Main Office, Uhlandstr. 173, 10719 (tel. 884 58 80). Mail held, all banking services rendered. No commission for cashing AmEx traveler's checks. On Fri. and Sat., expect out-the-door lines of U.S. students carrying *Let's Go* books. Open Mon.-Fri. 9am-5:30pm, Sat. 9am-noon. **Branch offices:** Bayreuther Str. 37 (tel. 21 49 83 63). U-Bahn #1, 2, 12, or 15: "Wittenbergplatz." Traveler's checks cashed and sold, but no mail held. Also at Friedrichstr. 172, 10117 (tel. 238 41 02). S-Bahn or U-Bahn #6: "Friedrichstr." Full services. Both branch offices open Mon.-Fri. 9am-6pm.

Telephones: At any post office. Also, an especially large number in and around Bahnhof Zoo. Note that public phones are slightly less common in the eastern part of the city. When calling Eastern Berlin from overseas, if dialing (30) doesn't work, you'll probably need operator assistance. With the shortage of new phone lines, many homes and businesses in Eastern Berlin use mobile phones. Apartments with telephones are still exceptional in the eastern part of the city.

Flights: Flughafen Tegel (tel. 410 11) is Berlin's main airport. Take express bus X9 (from Bahnhof Zoo) or bus #109 (from Bahnhof Zoo or the Jakob-Kaiser-Platz U-Bahn station: "Tegel"). **Flughafen Tempelhof** (tel. 690 91), the smallest of Berlin's airports, is mostly used for intra-Germany travel and flights to the former Soviet Union. Bus #119: "Kurfürstendamm." **Flughafen Schönefeld** (tel. 678 70), in Eastern Berlin, is for charters, although El-Al flies here too. Take S-Bahn #3.

Trains:

Stations: For now, **Bahnhof Zoo** is Berlin's principal station for trains to the west, while the **Hauptbahnhof** is the main source of eastern and southern-bound trains. The stations are connected by S-Bahn. Trains to and from the east also use **Berlin-Lichtenberg.** Exceptions do exist, so check before you set off.

Connections: Zoo: Hamburg (IC; 4hr.), Düsseldorf (IC; 5½hr.), Cologne (IC; 5½hr.), Munich (ICE; 8hr.), Frankfurt (ICE; 5hr.), Amsterdam (IR; 7hr.), Paris (IC; 12hr.), Zürich (IC; 12hr.). **Hauptbahnhof:** Munich, Hamburg, Leipzig (2½hr.), Warsaw (6½hr.), Krakow (8hr.), and Malmö, Sweden (9hr.). **Lichtenberg:** Hamburg, Dresden, Prague (5hr.), Krakow (9hr.), Rostock (2½hr.), Vienna (10hr.), Budapest (13hr.), Moscow (36hr.), and St. Petersberg (36hr.).

Information: Deutsche Bahn Information (tel. 194 19). Be prepared for a long wait. Also long lines at offices in **Bahnhof Zoo** (open daily 5:30am-10:30pm) and **Hauptbahnhof.** Both stations have recently installed computers to help you figure out your own itinerary but there are lines for these, too—*arrive early.* For **recorded information** about departures and arrivals (in German) there are several lines depending on your destination: Hamburg, Kiel, Rostock, and Scandinavia (tel. 01 15 31); Hanover, Cologne, the Netherlands, France (tel. 01 15 32); Halle, Erfurt, Frankfurt, Switzerland (tel. 01 15 33); Leipzig, Munich, Austria, Italy (tel. 01 15 34); Dresden, Czech Republic, Hungary, Romania, Bulgaria (tel. 01 15

35); Poland, Lithuania, Latvia, Russia (tel. 01 15 36). Some timetables confusingly include all stations; make sure you're at the right one.

Buses: ZOB, the central bus station (tel. 301 80 28), is by the Funkturm near Kaiserdamm. U-Bahn #1: "Kaiserdamm." Check *Zitty* and *Tip* for deals on long-distance buses—they aren't comfortable but they are often much cheaper than the train. To: Paris (10hr.; DM109 one-way); Vienna (10½hr.; DM85 one-way).

Public Transportation: The **BVG** (*Berliner Verkehrsbetriebe*, or transit service) is in the midst of a massive spate of construction and renovation which will affect S- and U-Bahn service for the next few years. Under the slogan *"Freie Bahn für Berlin,"* the construction will bring service in Eastern Berlin up to snuff with the West, adding new lines and stops as well as increasing the frequency of trains to existing stops, not to mention removing unexploded World War II bombs from below the streets. To cushion the blow, the BVG has put up posters everywhere introducing Berliners to **Max,** a bespectacled cartoon mole who will appear on announcements of disruptions to service. In most cases, the worst inconvenience is that you'll wait an extra 30min.

Orientation and Basic Fares: It is impossible to tour Berlin on foot—the public transit system is fortunately quite efficient (but expensive). The extensive **bus, U-Bahn** (subway), and **S-Bahn** (surface rail) systems of Berlin operate as 1 network, the **BVG.** A single ticket for the combined network (*Einzelfahrschein Normaltarif;* DM3.90) is good for 2hr. after validation. An *Einzelfahrschein Kurzstreckentarif* (short-trip fare; DM2.50) allows travel up to 6 bus stations (with no transfers; not valid on airport bus lines) or 3 U- or S-Bahn stops (with unlimited transfers). A 4-trip *Sammelkarte* (Multiple Ticket) costs DM13; each "click" is good for 2hr. A short-trip 4-ride *Kurzstreckensammelkarte* is available for DM8.50. You can buy tickets from machines, bus drivers, or ticket windows in the U- and S-Bahn stations. Inspections are not as frequent here as in some other German cities; but the cost of cheating is steep (DM60 and tremendous humiliation). Children under 6 accompanied by an adult travel free; children under 14 pay a reduced fare. *All tickets must be canceled in the red validation box before boarding to be valid.* Tickets bought on the bus are automatically valid.

Special Passes and Maps: Information, maps, and tickets are available at the **BVG Pavillon,** Bahnhof Zoo (24hr. tel. 25 62 25 62). Open daily 8am-8pm. The **Berlin Tagesticket** (DM13, ages 6-14 DM6.50) is a 24-hr. pass for the bus, U- and S-Bahn. A **7-Day Ticket** (DM40) is a good value for moderate-length stays. A monthly **Umweltkarte** costs DM93, and is good for longer stays. After 8pm on weekdays and all-day Sat. and Sun., this ticket allows you to bring 1 other adult and 3 children with you for free. A discount version of this pass is also available, but it's only for Berlin students. The **Kombi-Ticket** is valid for 1 day of unlimited travel on all BVG services as well as the ferry services of **Stern und Kreisschiffahrt** (DM25; also see Ferries, below). The extensive **Liniennetz** map can be picked up free at any ticket office and clearly depicts all U- and S-Bahn routes. The *Falk Plan* also demarcates all routes, including buses.

Note: Most of the BVG tickets and passes actually come in 2 versions—"Tariff A," which can be used to travel between both Western and Eastern stops, and "Tariff B," which can be used only in West Berlin by permanent residents of East Berlin, but can be used by anyone to travel on routes solely within East Berlin. "B" tickets are about 15% cheaper than "A" tickets; all prices in *Let's Go* are for "A" tickets. BVG maps show the ragged boundary between Western and Eastern stops, but these can be difficult to interpret—when in doubt, buy an "A" ticket.

Night Transport: U- and S-Bahn do not run 1-4am, except for the **U12** and **U9,** which run all night Fri.-Sat. (The U12 line, which only runs at night, combines the routes of the U1 and U2 and runs east-west; the U9 line runs north-south.) Most regular lines start their final runs by 12:15am. There is an extensive system of **night buses** centered on Bahnhof Zoo that run about every 15min.; you can pick up the free *Nachtliniennetz* map at the BVG pavilion. All night bus numbers are preceded by **N.**

Ferries: Stern und Kreis Schiffahrt, Puschkinallee 16-17 (tel. 536 36 00; fax 53 63 60 99), operates ferry services along the Spree from April-Oct. Ferries leave from locations throughout the city, including Friedrichstr., Museum Island, the *Dom,* and the Nikolaiviertel. Fares depend on distance traveled (DM3.50-22). Pleasure cruises also available. *Berlin Kombi-Tageskarte* is valid on all regularly scheduled services. For further information contact tourist office or BVG Pavilion.

Taxis: tel. 21 02 02, 26 10 26, or 690 22. Call at least 15min. in advance. Women can request a female driver.

Car Rental: Avis, Budapesterstr. 43 (tel. 793 19 80), is closest to Bahnhof Zoo. Open Mon.-Fri. 7:30am-6pm, Sat. 8am-noon. Former O.J. Simpson endorsee **Hertz** has an office at the corner of Spandauerstr. and Karl-Liebknecht-Str. (tel. 242 44 40), near Alexanderplatz. Open Mon.-Fri. 8:30am-6:30pm, Sat. 8am-noon. Both companies also have offices at Tegel airport.

Automobile Clubs: ADAC (tel. 018 02 or 22 22 22). 24-hr. breakdown service.

Bike Rental: The best deal is at the **Hauptbahnhof** (tel. 65 76 22 86). DM1.50-2.50 per hr. DM10-20 per day. ID required. Open daily 9am-7pm. **Bahnhof Zoo,** next to the baggage check, prices are steeper. DM25 per day. DM60 for 3 days. DM120 per week. Open daily 6am-11pm. **Herr Beck,** at Goethestr. 7 (tel. 312 19 25), near Ernst-Reuter-Platz. DM12 per day. Mountain bikes DM20 per day. Call for selection and deposit information. Bring passport. No English spoken.

Mitfahrzentrale: City Netz, Kurfürstendamm 227, in the Ku'damm Eck mall, 3rd floor (tel. 194 44 or 882 76 04; fax 882 44 20), has a computerized **ride-share** database. U-Bahn #7: "Südstern." Prices: Hamburg (DM11 fee for info; DM18 paid to driver); and Vienna (DM18/DM39). Driver fee is less if more than 1 person shares the ride. Open daily 8am-9pm. **Branch offices** at: Südstern 2, in Kreuzberg (tel. 693 60 95). U-Bahn #7: "Südstern." And Bahnhof Zoo, on the U2 platform (tel. 31 03 31). Both open daily 9am-8pm. **Mitzfahrzentrale Alex,** in the Alexanderplatz U-Bahn station (tel. 242 36 42), specializes in the East. Open Mon.-Fri. 8am-8pm, Sat. 8am-6pm, Sun. 10am-6pm. The **Mitfahrtelephon für Schwule and Lesben,** Yorckstr. 52 (tel. 194 20 or 216 60 21), matches gay and lesbian drivers and passengers. U-Bahn #7: "Yorckstr." Open Mon.-Fri. 9am-8pm, Sat.-Sun. 10am-6pm. Berlin has many other small *Mitzfahrzentralen;* check *Zitty, Tip,* or *Metropolis* magazines for addresses and phone numbers.

Hitchhiking: *Let's Go* does not recommend hitchhiking as a safe mode of transportation. No, no, no. Those who hitch west and south (Hanover, Munich, Weimar, Leipzig) take S-Bahn #1 or 3: "Wannsee," then bus #211: *Autobahn* entrance ramp. Those headed north (Hamburg, Rostock) take U-Bahn #6: "Tegel," then bus #224 and ask the driver to be let out at the *Trampenplatz.* Both have huge crowds, but someone gets picked up every few minutes.

Luggage Storage: In the **Bahnhof Zoo** train station (lockers DM2; larger lockers DM4; 72hr. max.). If all the lockers at Bahnhof Zoo are full, you can check your luggage at the center near the post office for DM4 per piece per day. Open daily 6am-11pm. At the **Hauptbahnhof** (lockers DM2; larger DM4; 72hr. max.). At Bahnhof **Lichtenberg** and S-Bahnhof **Alexanderplatz** (lockers DM2, 24hr. max.).

Lost Property: BVG Fündbüro, Lorenzweg 5 (tel. 751 80 21). U-Bahn #6: "Ullsteinstr." For items lost on the bus or U-Bahn. Many, many umbrellas. Open Mon.-Tues. and Thurs. 9am-3pm, Wed. 9am-6pm, Fri. 9am-2pm. **Fundbüro Deutsche Reichsbahn,** in the Hackescher Markt S-Bahn station (tel. 29 72 16 71), is for items lost on trains or S-Bahn. Open Mon. and Wed.-Thurs. 10am-4pm, Tues. 10am-6pm, Fri. 8am-noon. **Fundbüro der Polizei,** Platz der Luftbrücke 6 (tel. 69 90), is the police headquarters for anything (mostly valuables) lost anywhere else.

Bookstores: Marga Schoeler Bücherstube, Knesebeckstr. 34 (tel. 881 11 12), at Mommsenstr., betweeen Savignyplatz and the Ku'damm. Large selection of books in English includes politics, history, poetry, lit crit, and fiction. Open Mon.-Wed. and Fri. 9am-6:30pm, Thurs. 9am-8:30pm, Sat. 9am-2pm. The **British Bookshop,** Mauerstr. 83-84 (tel. 238 46 80), around the corner from Checkpoint Charlie. An artfully-stocked addition to Berlin's English book club, with well-chosen literature and history sections and English-language newspapers and mags. Open Mon.-Fri. 10am-6pm, Sat. 10am-2pm. **Literaturhaus Berlin,** at Fasanenstr. 23, in Mitte (tel. 882 65 52), is in a wonderful old mansion complete with garden café and frequent readings of German and international literature. Their resident bookstore, **Kohlhaas & Co.** (tel. 882 50 44), has many second-hand German books, as well as Berlin's best Judaica *and* Nazi history sections, right next to each other.

Libraries: Staatsbibliothek Preußischer Kulturbesitz, Potsdamerstr. 33 (tel. 26 61), and Unter den Linden 8 (tel. 210 50). 3.5 million books—one for every Berliner—but not all are stored on site. Some can take 2 days to retrieve. Lots of English-language newspapers. The Potsdamerstr. library was built for West Berlin in the 1960s, after the Iron Curtain went down on the original *"Staabi"* on Unter den Linden, next to the Humboldt University. Now Berliners can choose between them—and so can you. Both open Mon.-Fri. 9am-9pm, Sat. 9am-5pm.

Cultural Centers: Amerika Haus, Hardenbergstr. 22-24 (tel. 310 00 10). The library includes English-language books and day-old editions of *The New York Times,* and presents readings by visiting American authors. Offices open Mon.-Fri. 8:30am-5:30pm. Library open Tues. and Thurs. 2-8pm, Wed. and Fri. 2-5:30pm. **British Council,** Hardenbergstr. 22, is next door. Enter through the Informationszentrum Berlin, 2nd floor. Office open Mon.-Fri. 9am-12:30pm and 2-5pm. Library open Mon., Wed., and Fri. 2-6pm; Tues. and Thurs. 2-7pm.

Language Instruction: Goethe Institut, Friedrichstr. 209, 10969 (tel. 25 90 63; fax 25 90 64 00), is the best known and the most expensive. U-Bahn #6: "Kochstr." All levels of German available. DM1510 for 4 weeks, 25hr. of instruction per week. **Fokus** *(Forum für Kultur und Sprachen),* Haubachstr. 23, 10585 (tel. 341 47 37), also has a good reputation. U-Bahn #7: "Richard-Wagner-Platz." DM360 for 4-weeks, 15hr. per week. *Tip* and *Zitty* are filled with ads for other schools and private tutors—check the classifieds under "Unterricht" and shop around.

Laundromat: Wasch Centers (tel. 852 37 96) are at various locations. **Leibnizstr. 72,** in Charlottenbur. U-Bahn #7: "Wilmersdorferstr." **Wexstr. 34,** in Schöneberg, U-Bahn #9: "Bundesplatz." **Bergmannstr. 61,** in Kreuzberg. U-Bahn #7: "Gniesenaustr." **Behmstr. 12,** in Mitte. S-Bahn #1 or 2, or U-Bahn #8: "Gesundbrunnen." And **Jablonskistr. 21,** in Prenzlauer Berg. U-Bahn #2: "Eberswalderstr." Wash DM6 per 6kg. Dry DM2 for 30min. Soap included. All open daily 6am-10pm. **Waschcenter Schnell und Sauber,** 61 Uhlandstr. U-Bahn #15: "Uhlandstr." Wash DM6 per 6kg. Open daily 6am-11pm.

Crisis Lines: Sexual Assault Hotline: (tel. 251 28 28). Open Tues. and Thurs. 6-9pm, Sun. noon-2pm. **Schwules Überfall** (gay bashing) hotline and legal help: (tel. 216 33 36). Open daily 6-9pm. **Drug Crisis:** (tel. 192 37). Open Mon.-Fri. 8:30am-9pm, Sat.-Sun. 2-9:30pm. **Frauenkrisentelefon** (women's crisis line; tel. 615 42 43). Open Mon. and Thurs. 10am-noon; Tues., Wed., and Fri. 7-9pm; Sat.-Sun. 5-7pm. English speakers at all crisis lines.

Pharmacies: Europa-Apotheke, Tauentzienstr. 9-12 (tel. 261 41 42), by Europa Center (close to Bahnhof Zoo). Open daily 9am-9pm. **Münz-Apotheke,** Münzstr. 5, just off Alexanderplatz. Open Mon.-Fri. 8am-6:30pm, Sat. 9am-1pm. Closed *Apotheken* post signs directing you to the nearest open one. For information about late-night pharmacies call 011 41.

Emergency Computer Help: (tel. 78 78 50). For PCs only. Open Mon.-Fri. 8:30am-4:30pm.

Medical Assistance: The American and British embassies have a list of English-speaking doctors. **Emergency Doctor:** (tel. 31 00 31). **Emergency Dentist:** (tel. 841 91 00). English-speaking dentists available.

Emergency: Police: Platz der Luftbrücke 6 (tel.110 or 69 90). **Ambulance** and **Fire:** tel. 112.

Post Offices: In the **Bahnhof Zoo** (tel. 313 97 99). Interminable lines, but the best hours. Open Mon.-Fri. 6am-midnight, Sat.-Sun. 8am-midnight. **Poste Restante** (held at window 7) should be addressed: Poste Restante/Hauptpostlagernd, Postamt Bahnhof Zoo, 10612 Berlin. Branch office at **Tegel Airport** (tel. 430 85 23). Open daily 6:30am-9pm. In Eastern Berlin, around the corner from the **Hauptbahnhof,** Postamt Berlin 17, Str. der Pariser Kommune 8-10, 10243 Berlin. Open Mon.-Fri. 7am-9pm, Sat. 8am-8pm. Neighborhood branches are everywhere (usually open 9am-6pm, Sat. 9am-noon); look for the little yellow "POST" signs.

Telephone Code: 030.

■ Accommodations and Camping

Even though tourists mob Berlin during the summer, thanks to the ever-growing hosteling and hotel industry, same-day accommodations aren't impossible to find, but, as always, it's best to call ahead. If you plan on visiting during the Love Parade, however you'd better book ahead or plan on dancing all night (see p. 429).

For a DM5 fee, **tourist offices** will find you a room in a hostel, *Pension*, or hotel. Be prepared to pay at least DM70 for a single and DM100 for a double. There are also over 4000 private rooms (*Privatzimmer*) available in the city; the overwhelming majority are controlled by the tourist offices. Expect to pay DM80 for singles, DM100 for doubles, plus a single-night surcharge of DM5. For that price, there's an wide spectrum of locations, comfort levels, and amenities. Press for details, and be sure that they know your language abilities (if any). They often prefer to fill up the *Pensionen* first, so you may have to ask for private rooms.

Although most accommodations are in Western Berlin, the office does have some listings for private rooms in the eastern part of the city. The tourist offices have the pamphlet *Accommodations, Youth, Hostel, and Camping Places in Berlin,* which lists hostels and inexpensive guest houses and hotels in English and German (DM2). See the introductions to Hostels and Hotels (p. 42) for specifics.

For longer visits (more than 4 days) the various **Mitwohnzentralen** can arrange for you to housesit or sublet someone's apartment. Prices start at DM40 per night, plus a percentage fee, and go down the longer you stay. The **Mitwohnzentrale,** Kurfürstendamm 227/228, in the Ku'damm Eck mall, 2nd (tel. 88 30 51; fax 882 66 94), is the biggest (open Mon.-Fri. 9am-7pm, Sat. 11am-3pm). **Erste,** Sybelstr. 53 (tel. 324 30 31, fax 324 99 77), tends to be less chaotic (open Mon.-Fri. 9am-8pm, Sat. 10am-6pm). To get there, take U-Bahn #7: "Adenauer Platz." Usually the **Mitwohnzentralen** require you to pay your fee up front unless you have, or can find a friend who has, a German bank account. Keep their fees in mind—for short stays (less than a month) the standard commission is 20% of the final sum while for longer stays the rate is usually 25%, although the monthly prices are lower. Leases in Berlin start at any time—you don't need to wait for the beginning of a calendar month. Women tend to have an easier time than men finding long-term accommodations.

HOSTELS AND DORMITORY ACCOMMODATIONS

Hostels fill quickly with German school groups (especially in summer and on weekends)—always call ahead. All HI-affiliated hostels are for members only; they tend to attract school groups, and are liable to be overbooked. For an extra DM4, some hostels will give nonmembers a stamp and let you spend the night. To buy an **HI card,** head to Tempelhofer Ufer 32, 10963 Berlin (tel. 264 95 20; fax 262 04 37; open Mon., Wed., and Fri. 10am-4pm, Tues.-Thurs. 1-6pm). For non-Germans, membership cards cost DM36. HI-hostels also have curfews which hinder night-ragers and tend to have strict regulations. Many hostels accept written or faxed reservations.

Kreuzberg

The Backpacker, Köthener Str. 44, 10963 Berlin (tel. 262 51 40). U-Bahn #2: "Potsdamer Platz," turn right on Stresemannstr., then right on Köthener Str. As long as you don't mind the worn interior, it's one of the best budget options in Berlin. Amenities include a kitchen, free city map, and a supremely hip staff that can fully update you on nightlife. 4-6-bed rooms in a friendly Anglophile atmosphere, close to Mitte's action. Reception open all day, but check-in easiest from 9-11am. No curfew. DM25, sheets DM3. Laundry facilities (DM5). Rooms generally available if you call in the morning. Closed until April 1997 for renovations.

Die Fabrik, Schlesische Str. 18, 10997 Berlin (tel. 611 71 16; fax 618 29 74). U-Bahn #1: "Schlesisches Tor." *Pension qua* hostel in a beautifully converted factory with lush green interior within walking distance of Kreuzberg's mad nightlife. Breakfast not included, but the café run by the hostel and restaurants on Schlesische Str. serve gourmet tastes at low cost. Singles DM61. Doubles DM90 (one stunning oak double DM105). Triples DM115; surprisingly comfortable *Mehrbettzimmer* sleep-in deal puts you up in a 16-bed room for DM30. Reception open 24hr. Reserve or call ahead. Curfew? Rage all night, little pumpkin.

Schöneberg—Wilmersdorf

Jugendgästehaus (HI), Kluckstr. 3, 10785 Berlin (tel. 261 10 97; fax 262 95 29). From Kurfürstendamm, take bus #129 (direction: Hermannplatz): "Jugendgäste-haus," or U-Bahn #1: "Kurfürstenstr.," then walk up Potsdamerstr., go left on Pohl-str., and right on Kluckstr. A highly abstract 8-m conceptual "DJH" archway stands in front. The chaos in the lobby feels like a riot, but the 4-6-bed rooms are clean and modern. From Easter until fall 1997 the hostel will close for renovations. Reception open 1-1:45pm, 2:35-9:45pm, and 10:15pm-midnight. Lockout 9am-noon. Curfew midnight; stragglers admitted at 12:30 and 1am. DM32, over 26 DM45. Sheets and breakfast included. Key deposit DM10. Lockers and laundry facilities available. Call more than 2 weeks in advance.

Studentenhotel Berlin, Meininger Str. 10, 10823 Berlin (tel. 784 67 20; fax 788 15 23). Take U-Bahn #4: "Rathaus Schöneberg" or U-Bahn #7: "Eisenacherstr.," or by bus #146 (from Zoo): "Rathaus Schöneberg," walk right on Freiherr von Stein, then cross Martin Luther Str. to Meininger Str. Barren interior feels like a sanitarium, but same day rooms often available if you call from the station. Within walking distance of Schöneberg action. Reception open 24hr. English spoken. Singles DM58. Dou-bles DM42 per person. Quads DM38 per person. Breakfast included.

CVJM-Haus, Einemstr. 10, 10787 Berlin (tel. 264 91 00; fax 261 43 08). U-Bahn #1, 2, or 4: "Nollendorfplatz." Young men: it's fun to stay at the German YMCA, despite the institutional exterior. Palpably wholesome interior, all in tranquil blue. Act like a macho, macho man in the billiard and casino rooms or recede to the solace of the tea room. Reception open 8-11am and 4-9pm. DM40 per person for singles, doubles and dormitory rooms. Quiet time 10pm-7am and 1-3pm. You can get a key for curfew-free revelry. Breakfast included. Book ahead.

Jugendgästehaus Feurigstraße, Feurigstr. 63, 10827 Berlin (tel. 781 52 11; fax 788 30 51). U-Bahn #7: "Kleistpark," or bus #146 or 148. An unadorned brown stucco building in a busy district. 4- and 6-bed rooms that won't cramp your style. 200 beds. Good location for the bars and clubs of Schöneberg. Reception open 24hr. Dorms DM38. Singles DM55. Doubles with shower DM90. Breakfast included. Sheets DM5 if staying less than 3 nights. Call ahead from the station.

Steinplatz-Tiergarten

Jugendgästehaus am Zoo, Hardenbergstr. 9a, 10623 Berlin (tel. 312 94 10; fax 401 52 83), opposite the Technical University *Mensa*. Take bus #145 or the short walk from Bahnhof Zoo: go out the back exit and straight down Hardenbergstr. Advan-tage: it's within spitting distance of the Bahnhof Zoo. Disadvantage: the rooms are spartan and poorly lit. Macintosh stayed here his first time in Berlin. It's on the 5th floor; ride up in the elevator with graffiti by frat boys from all over. Reception open 24hr. Check-in 10am; check-out 9am. No curfew. Singles DM47, over 26 DM52. Doubles DM85, over 26 DM90. Small dorms (4-8 beds) DM35, over 26 DM40. No reservations, but tends to have room if you call in the morning.

Haus Wichern, Waldenserstr. 31, 10551 Berlin (tel. 396 50 91, fax 396 50 92). The hostel's attractive stone exterior is a mere façade for the plain interior filled by lots of school groups. 4-bed rooms with thin mattresses are often available, however. Reception open 24hr. No lockout. DM40. Breakfast included.

Tegel

Jugendherberge Ernst Reuter (HI), Hermsdorfer Damm 48, 13467 Berlin (tel. 404 16 10; fax 404 59 72). U-Bahn #6: "Tegel," then bus #125 (direction: Frohnau/Invalidensiedlung): "Jugendherberge." Distant from the center in a placid suburb, on the edge of the forest. Lots of school groups necessitate reservations. 6-bed rooms. Curfew midnight. Stragglers admitted until 1am. DM26, over 26 DM33. Breakfast and sheets included. DM8 for laundry facilities. Fluent English spoken. Key deposit DM10. Closed Oct.-Dec.

Jugendgästehaus Tegel, Ziekowstr. 161, 13509 Berlin (tel. 433 30 46; fax 434 50 63). U-Bahn #6: "Tegel," then bus #222 or night bus N22: "Titusweg." Old brick outside, new and bright inside, with linoleum halls. On the north end of town by the Tegel parks. For a more communal experience, check out neighboring Internationales Jugendcamp Tegel (see Camping, p. 407). No curfew. Under 27 only. DM38. Breakfast and sheets included. Same-day rooms sometimes available.

Elsewhere in Berlin

Jugendgästehaus Nordufer, Nordufer 28, 13351 Berlin (tel. 451 70 30; fax 452 41 00). U-Bahn #9: "Westhafen," left over the bridge and left onto Nordufer for about 15min. Away from the center, but on the pretty, blue, swimmable Plötzensee Lake. Some singles, but more 4-bed rooms. Reception open 7am-midnight. No curfew. DM38. Buffet breakfast and sheets included. Swim in the adjacent *Freibad* (swimming pool) for DM5, students DM3.

Jugendgästehaus am Wannsee (HI), Badeweg 1, 14129 Berlin (tel. 803 20 34; fax 803 59 08). S-Bahn #1 or 3: "Nikolassee," turn left at the main exit, cross the bridge, and head left for 5min. Far from the center, but Wannsee has its own charm. The tan tile floors, open spaces, white plaster walls, and bright red trim are reminiscent of a municipal swimming pool. 62 rooms, all with 4 beds. Toilets shared between 2 rooms, showers between 6. Large groups of jolly kids make it impossible to get a room without booking 2 weeks in advance. DM31, over 26 DM40. Sheets and breakfast included. Key deposit DM20.

HOTELS AND PENSIONEN

Many small *Pensionen* and hotels are within the means of budget travelers, particularly since most establishments listed in *Let's Go* are amenable to *Mehrbettzimmer,* where extra beds are moved into a large double or triple. However, these benefits are really only for groups of three or more; hotels will not usually allow random individuals to crash together (lest an orgy spontaneously erupts). Most affordable hotels are in Western Berlin; the hotels in Mitte are ridiculously expensive, and other areas in the east still do not have the facilities to support many visitors. The best places to find cheap hotel rooms are around Savignyplatz and down along Wilmersdorfstr. and its sidestreets.

Steinplatz

Hotelpension Bialas, Carmerstr. 16, 10623 Berlin (tel. 312 50 25; fax 312 43 96). Bus #149: "Steinplatz," or a walk down Harderbergstr. from the Zoo (10min.). Unusually convenient for Berlin if you don't mind the somewhat run-down furniture and facilities. Reception open 7am-10pm. Singles DM65, with shower and toilet DM95. Doubles DM95, with shower and toilet DM150. Breakfast included.

Savignyplatz

Hotelpension Cortina, Kantstr. 140, 10623 Berlin (tel. 313 90 59; fax 31 73 96). S-Bahn #3, 5, 7, or 9 or bus #149: "Savignyplatz." High-ceilings, bright, convenient, and hospitable. Reception open 24hr. Extra beds in rooms upon agreement. Dinky singles DM75. Doubles DM120, with shower DM130. *Mehrbettzimmer* DM45-50 per person. Breakfast included.

Pension Knesebeck, Knesebeckstr. 86, 10623 Berlin (tel. 312 72 55; fax 313 34 86). S-Bahn #3, 5, 7, or 9: "Savignyplatz." Just north of the park. Friendly, large *Alt-Berliner* rooms, with faux Baroque stylings come with offerings for voluptuaries like couches and sinks. Hearty buffet-style breakfast served in a rather flyly decorated dining room. Reception open 24hr. Singles with showers DM95. Doubles DM120, with showers DM140. Big *Mehrbettzimmer* DM55-60 per person. Phone reservations must be confirmed by fax or letter. Laundry machines DM2.

Wilmersdorf-Schöneberg

Hotel-Pension München, Güntzelstr. 62 (tel. 857 91 20; fax 853 27 44). U-Bahn #9: "Güntzelstr." *Pension cum* gallery saturated with art by contemporary Berlin artists and sculptures by the owner. White-walled rooms with TVs and telephones. Singles DM60, with shower DM110. Doubles DM80, with shower and toilet DM125. Breakfast DM9. Written reservations are best, but try calling before 2pm.

Hotel Sachsenhof, Motzstr. 7, 10777 Berlin (tel. 216 20 74; fax 215 82 20). Small and plainly decorated rooms that are clean and well-furnished in the middle of the Schöneberg café scene. Reception open 24hr. Singles DM57, with shower DM65. Doubles DM106, with shower DM116, with cute bathtub with feet and a bathroom DM126-156. DM30 per extra bed. Breakfast DM10 per person.

Frauenhotel Artemesia, Brandenburgischestr. 18, 10707 Berlin (tel. 873 89 05; fax 861 86 53). U-Bahn #7: "Konstanzer Str." Pricey, but a rare bird—an immaculate, elegant hotel for women only. Rooms celebrate famous women in Berlin's history, while an outdoor terrace provides a damn nice view of contemporary Berlin. The Artemesia Café serves breakfast (Mon.-Fri. 7:30-10:30am, Sat.-Sun. 8-11:30am) and evening drinks (5-10pm) to an all-female, largely lesbian crowd that really digs Tracy Chapman. Reception open 7am-10pm. Singles DM99, with shower DM149. Doubles DM169, with shower and bath DM200. Breakfast included. Extra beds DM45 per person. Alternatively, try to get the "last-minute, same-day" specials, with singles from DM79 and doubles from DM139 (without breakfast).

Kreuzberg

Hotel Transit, Hagelbergerstr. 53-54, 10965 Berlin (tel. 785 50 51; fax 785 96 19). U-Bahn #6 or 7: "Mehringdamm," or bus #119 or night bus N19 (every 10-15min.). Party hard and crash gently in this tragically hip *Pension*. Reception area jams to techno. Big-screen MTV lounge open 24hr. Bar open until 2-3am. Rooms adorned with sleek, fake Bauhaus furnishings and showers. Reception seems to know its coolness quotient. If you anticipate a hangover, you can request breakfast at noon or later. Curfew? Lockout? Pshaw. Singles DM85. Doubles DM102. Triples DM135. Quads DM170. Their "Sleep-In" deal allows you to share a *Mehrbettzimmer* with any other traveler (DM34). Breakfast included.

Pension Kreuzberg, Grossbeerenstr. 64, 10963 Berlin (tel. 251 13 62; fax 251 06 38). U-Bahn #6 or 7: "Mehringdamm" or bus #119. Decently-priced rooms, small but well-decorated with things abstract in an old but grand building close to the Kreuzberg scene. Watch your head in the doorway to the bathroom lest you suffer the fate of Dennis Hopper in *Speed*. Reception open 8am-10pm. Singles DM75. Doubles DM95. *Mehrbettzimmer* DM42 per person. Breakfast included.

Charlottenburg

Charlottenburger Hof, Stuttgarterpl. 14, 10627 Berlin (tel. 32 90 70; fax 323 37 23). S-Bahn #3, 5, 7, or 9: "Charlottenburg" (across the street) or U-Bahn #7: "Wilmersdorferstr." Slick but expensive *Pension* with wall-art: Miró, Klee, and Dalí in the rooms. Spotless modern rooms with phones and TVs, plus a peaceful guest lounge with funky black chairs. Singles DM110 (Dow!). Doubles DM150. Prices for triples (DM180) and quads (DM200) return from orbit. Shower and bathroom in all rooms. Winter discounts Nov.-Dec. Breakfast in the adjoining Café Voltaire (see Food, p. 409) DM5. Sometimes has same-day space.

Elsewhere in Berlin

Hotel-Pension Hansablick, Flotowstr. 6 (tel. 390 48 00; fax 392 69 37). Near Tiergarten. Somewhat pricey, but it's an absolute *Jugendstil* pearl, from the decorative ceilings to the marble entrance and lamps gracing the cobblestone streets in front. Breakfast room like a salon. All rooms have shower, toilet, hair dryer, phone, and cable TV. Some have patios from which you can watch ferries on the Spree. Few places like this survived WWII bombing, so call, write, or fax ahead for reservations. Reception open 24hr. Singles DM150. Doubles DM175-215. In the low season (mid-July-Aug. and mid.-Nov.-Feb.) singles DM125, doubles DM150-170. Extra bed in the big doubles DM55. 5% discount if you mention *Let's Go*. July-Aug., sameday specials are available but without the *Let's Go* discount.

Hamburger Hof, Kinkelstr. 6 (tel. 333 46 02), in the old quarter of Spandau. U-Bahn #7: "Altstadt Spandau" (second-to-last stop). Easily accessible. A tiny, comfortable hotel with only 18 beds, but so far from the action that they usually have room.

Small-town charm, but no English spoken. Diminutive singles DM50. More spacious doubles DM100. Breakfast and showers included.

CAMPING

Deutscher Camping-Club runs 2 of the major campgrounds in Berlin; both are adjacent to the imaginary line tracing the site of the Berlin Wall. Written reservations can be made by writing the Deutscher Camping-Club Berlin, Geisbergstr. 11, 10777 Berlin. Otherwise, call in advance. All sites charge DM8.50 per person, DM5.50 for a tent, and DM3.50 for children.

Dreilinden (tel. 805 12 01). Take U-Bahn #1: "Oskar-Helene-Heim," then bus #118: "Kätchenweg"; follow Kremnitzufer to Albrechts-Teergfen (about 20min.). A city campsite, surrounded on 3 sides by the vestiges of the Berlin Wall. The remains of a stretch of the *Autobahn* which fell into disuse after 1949 can be seen through the trees. The site's bar is an old border checkpoint. Open March-Oct.

Kladow, Krampnitzer Weg 111/117 (tel. 365 27 97). U-Bahn #7: "Rathaus Spandau," then take bus #135 to "Alt-Kladow" (the last stop). Switch to bus #234 to the "Krampnitzer Weg/Selbitzer Str." stop, follow Krampnitzer Weg 200m. A store and restaurant complement the relaxed atmosphere by a swimmable lake.

Internationales Jugendcamp Fließtal, Ziekowstr. 161 (tel. 433 86 40). U-Bahn #6: "Tegel," then bus #222 or night bus N22: "Titusweg." Next to Jugendgästehaus Tegel (see Hostels, p. 405). Far away, but it's the next best thing to rolling a groovy doobie in your VW van, man. Blanket and mattress under a big te t with free showers DM10. Officially under 27 only, but rules are made for conformists, and they aren't into that sort of thing here. Lockout 9am-5pm. No reservations accepted—just show up and dig the far-out experience. Open July-Aug.

■ Food

Berlin's cuisine has joined the melting pot, with many delectable international culinary options saving you from the ubiquitous *Würste* and *Schnitzels* of other German cities. While many offerings from the German cuisine are palatable, Berlin's most notable home-grown option is the tasty, sweet **Berliner Weiße mit Schuß,** a concoction of local wheat beer with a shot of syrup. *Rotes* (red) is the most popular variety, made with fruity *crème de cassis* (blackberry) or *kirsch* (cherry) syrup; be careful when ordering a *Grünes* (green), which sometimes entails lemon-lime syrup, but may also mean a stomach-turning depth charge of *Jägermeister* liqueur.

Unfortunately, Berlin's **beer** offerings are like water compared to other national brews; the ubiquitous locally-brewed *Schultheiss* and *Berliner Kindl* brands are among Germany's more lackluster brands. The breweries east of the former Wall offer little consolation, with the **Berliner Bürgerbrau** providing little for the refined palate. If you must try a Berlin brand, sample **Bären Pils** for a slightly bitter, flavorful experience. Fortunately the city's *Kneipen* offer typical Berlin cosmopolitanism: you'll be too busy sampling *Kölsch,* Guinness, and Munich beers to feel deprived.

Much typical Berlin food is Turkish: almost every street has its own Turkish **Imbiß** (snack bar) or restaurant. The *Imbiß* stands are a vital lifeline for the late-night partier; most are open ridiculously late, some 24 hours. The *Döner Kepab,* a sandwich of lamb and salad, has cornered the fast-food market, with *Falafel* running a close second. For DM3-5, either makes a small meal. The second wave of immigration has brought quality Indian restaurants to Berlin, and Italian is also a good choice.

There is no clear distinction between *Kneipen,* cafés, and restaurants; indeed cafés often have better food and a livelier atmosphere than restaurants for much more reasonable prices. A gloriously civilized tradition in Berlin cafés is **Frühstück,** breakfast served well into the afternoon, sometimes 24 hours a day. Leisurely natives read the paper and linger over their fruit and cheese breakfasts; join them and relax with *Milchkaffee.* New cafés in Mitte and Prenzlauer Berg are rapidly providing stiff competition for their western counterparts; prices tend to be somewhat lower and portions larger, attracting a crowd of starving artists looking for a respite from their ascetic regime. In addition, street vendors with all shapes, sizes, and flavors of cheap eats fill **Alexanderplatz** every day, and the sprawling grocery department on the first floor of the nearby **Kaufhof am Alex** comes with a salad bar.

Aldi, Bolle, and **Penny Markt** are the cheapest supermarket chains, along with **Plus** stores which are omnipresent in Wilmersdorf, Schöneberg, and Kreuzberg. Supermarkets are usually open Monday to Friday 9am-6pm, Saturday 9am-1pm, although the ridiculously strict laws that regulate their opening hours are starting to relax in the face of competition from smaller neighborhood stores which stay open later. The best **open-air market** fires up Saturday mornings in Winterfeldtplatz, though almost every neighborhood has one; there's a kaleidoscopic **Turkish market** in Kreuzberg on the banks of the Landwehrkanal every Friday. Take U-Bahn #1 to "Kottbusser Tor." In eastern Berlin, markets often set up under S-Bahn platforms.

WESTERN BERLIN

Mensen (University Cafeterias)

Mensa der Freie Universität, in the huge complex at Habelschwerdter Allee 45. U-Bahn #2: "Thielplatz" or "Dahlem-Dorf." Conveniently located near the Dahlem museum. Meals from DM2 (ISIC required). Open Mon.-Fri. 11:15am-2:30pm. The **cafeteria** on the first floor has less hot food, more sandwiches, and is somewhat more expensive. Open Mon.-Fri. 8:15am-4pm.

Mensa TU, Hardenbergstr. 34. Bus #145: "Steinplatz," or walk 10-min. from Bahnhof Zoo. The place is hard to miss; it says "MENSA" in big letters on the building. Conveniently located, with passable food. Meals from DM3. Open Mon.-Fri. 11am-2:30pm. There's also a cafeteria to the right of the main doors with better hours and slightly higher prices (meals DM4-5). Open Mon.-Fri. 8am-4pm and 4:30-8pm. The building also houses a small and friendly *Mitfahrzentrale*.

Bahnhof Zoo-Ku'damm area

Café Hardenberg, Hardenbergstr. 10. Big *belle époque* spot, opposite the TU *Mensa,* but with a bit more atmosphere. Funky music, artsy interior, and lots of students. Breakfast served 9am-5pm (a good value at DM4-8). Most entrees well under DM13. Also good for a few drinks (grog DM4). Open daily 9am-1am.

Restaurant Marché, Kurfürstendamm 15, just a couple of blocks down from Bahnhof Zoo and the *Gedächtniskirche*. Run by the ubiquitous Mövenpick restaurant company, this place themes itself around a French marketplace. Probably the most affordable lunch on the Ku'damm. The colorful, very *Euro* cafeteria area is full of fresh produce, salads, grilled meats, pour-it-yourself wines, and hot pastries (DM12-25). Free ice water! Open daily 8am-midnight. AmEx and Visa accepted.

KaDeWe, Tauentzienstr. 21 (tel. 212 10). U-Bahn #1, 3, or 4: "Wittenbergplatz." Satiate every desire in the 6th-floor food emporium of this tremendous department store. Bright, beautiful stands happily heaped with cabbage and caviar. An entire wing devoted just to tinned fish. The prices? Ah, but such a joy! Open Mon.-Wed. and Fri. 9:30am-6:30pm, Thurs. 9:30am-8:30pm, Sat. 9am-2pm.

Savignyplatz

Schwarzes Café, Kantstr. 148 (tel. 313 80 38), near Savignyplatz. Knotty interior full of hip young folks. Dark walls, big-band music, and dapper waiters. It's not so cool to pay DM4.20 for 0.2L of apple juice—but hey, they have breakfast at all hours (DM7-13). Open Wed.-Mon. 24hr., Tues. from 6pm on.

Mexico Lindo, Kantstr. 134 (tel. 312 82 18), on the corner of Wielandstr. S-Bahn: "Savignyplatz." One of the cheaper Mexican restaurants that've been popping up all over Berlin. Lunch specials (including vegetarian dishes) DM9-13. Quesadillas from the *Imbiß* stand (open Mon.-Fri. noon-7pm) DM3.50. Open Mon.-Fri. noon-1am, Sat. 6pm-1am, Sun. 5pm-midnight.

Schöneberg-Wilmersdorf

Baharat Falafel, Winterfeldtstr. 37. U-Bahn #1 or 4: "Nollendorfplatz." Perhaps the best falafel in Berlin. 5 plump chick-pea balls in a fluffy pita, covered with veggies and heavenly sesame, mango, or chili sauce, for an absolute pittance (DM5). Bright shop with world music and watercolors depicting falafel balls leaping into waiting pita. Open Mon.-Sat. noon-2am, Sun. 1pm-2am. Closed last week in July.

Café Belmundo, Winterfeldtstr. 36 (tel. 215 20 70), on a street loaded with bohemians. U-Bahn #1 or 4: "Nollendorfplatz." Young crowd, with outdoor tables and breakfast until 3pm. Salads DM4.50-10. Open Mon.-Sat. 9am-1am, Sun. 10am-1am.

Rani, Goltzstr. 32 (tel. 215 26 73), behind the church on Winterfeldtplatz. U-Bahn #1 or 4: "Nollendorfplatz." Very casual and cheap Indian restaurant popular with students. Most dishes DM6-10. Generous portions. Open daily 11am-midnight.

Kurdistan, Uhlandstr. 161 (tel. 883 96 92). U-Bahn #15: "Uhlandstr." One of Berlin's most exotic and most appetizing offerings. Fabulously spiced *Yekawe* (meat with rice, raisins, and cinnamon) DM15. Most entrees DM15-20. Brush up on your Kurdish with one of the grammar books lying around, or challenge the owner to a game of backgammon. Open Mon.-Fri. noon-midnight, Sat.-Sun. 5pm-late.

Charlottenburg-Tiergarten

Café Voltaire, Stuttgarterplatz 14 (tel. 324 50 28). S-Bahn #3, 5, 7, or 9: "Charlottenburg," or U-Bahn #7: "Wilmersdorferstr." Café-bistro-gallery with a talkative crowd. Close to a whole array of cafés and the *Kino Klick,* farther down the street at Winterscheidstr. An extensive menu with great breakfasts 5am-3pm (DM6-8) and warm meals (noon-5am). Open Tues.-Sun. 24hr., Mon. 7am on.

Rogacki, Wilmersdorferstr. 145. A gargantuan delicatessen, with everything from stuffed grape leaves to caviar. A nice selection of meats and cheeses for do-it-yourself sandwiches. The fish stands inside are very popular at lunchtime. Soups DM5. Herring with potatoes DM6. Open Mon.-Fri. 9am-6pm, Sat. 9am-1pm.

Ashoka, Alt-Moabit 49 (tel. 313 20 66). U-Bahn #9: "Turmstr." A friendly, entirely vegetarian, neighborhood Indian place. Huge portions DM6-10, including the exotic and delicious banana curry. Open daily 11:30-midnight.

Kreuzberg

Morena, Wiener Str. 60 (tel. 611 47 16). U-Bahn #1 or 12: Görlitzer Bahnhof. A gracious, roomy café with some of Kreuzberg's best *Frühstück* (breakfast; DM5-8.50, served until 5pm), as well as a selection of international magazines and newspapers. Spend a leisurely morning or afternoon here, enjoying breakfast and people-watching. Great blue-tiled interior. Open Sun.-Thurs. 9am-4am, Fri.-Sat. 9am-5am.

Die Rote Harfe, Oranienstr. 13 (tel. 618 44 46), in Heinrichplatz, the center of Kreuzberg. U-Bahn #8: "Moritzpl" or U-Bahn #1: "Kottbusser Tor." Leftists and grizzled types eating solid German food. The *Schweizer Schnitzel* (DM15.90) and the *Algäuer Käsespätzle* (DM9.90) are bound to spark the radical in even stodgy you. Daily 3-course lunch menu (DM15). Open Tues.-Sun. 10am-2am.

Café Abendmahl, Muskauer Str. 9 (tel. 612 51 70). U-Bahn #1: "Görlitzer Bahnhof." While some of the *Ecce Homo* decorative motifs are a touch overbearing, the restaurant is a favorite for gay and lesbian (and even hetero) Berlin with delicious vegetarian and fish dishes. Substantial salads and artichoke dishes run DM9.50-15.50. Open daily 6pm-1am; best to reserve on weekends.

Max und Moritz, Oranienstr. 163 (tel. 614 10 45), in Kreuzberg. U-Bahn #8: "Mortizplatz." Old German atmosphere taken to the height of campiness. Big hot plates of traditional food. *Wiener Schnitzel* with all the trimmins (DM15.80). The faded painted-wood faces of Max and Moritz themselves—local Katzenjammer kids—grin down at you. Fun fact: because the restaurant is located beneath a theater, you must be vewwy vewwy quiet during performances (Kiww the wabbit!). Open daily 6pm-1am; kitchen open until 12:30am. Closed in July.

Restaurant V, Lausitzer Platz 12 (tel. 612 45 05). U-Bahn #1: "Görlitzer Bahnhof." Not an 80s flick, but Berlin's oldest vegetarian restaurant. Try the *Tofu-Würstchen* with scrambled eggs and tomato sauce (DM10.50). Open daily 10am-2am.

PowWow, Dieffenbachstr. 11. U-Bahn #8: "Schönleinstr." Large satisfying helpings of "American Indian" food. Yes, many Germans *are* obsessed with the American West. Ours is not to question why. Dishes have names like "General Custer's Disaster" (steak with herb butter and french fries; DM19). Among the Teutonic cowboys are a number of Kreuzberg artists, who revel in the campiness of it all. Open summer Sun.-Thurs. 10am-3am, Fri.-Sat. 10am-4am; kitchen open until 1am. In winter open Mon.-Fri. 5pm-5am, Sat.-Sun. 11am-5pm.

Sieben-Leben Vollkornbäckerei, Manfred von Richthofenstr. 13 (tel. 784 14 47). U-Bahn #6: "Platz der Luftbrücke." An alternative breadbasket, this whole-grain bakery grinds every seed imaginable into 30 different *Brot* and 20 *Brötchen* varieties. Very granola. Salads at lunch. Open Mon.-Fri. 10am-6pm, Sat. 7am-1pm.

Pagode, Bergmannstr. 88 (tel. 691 24 40). U-Bahn #6: "Mehringdamm" or U-Bahn #7: "Gniesenaustr." Thai noodles, salads, and spring rolls prepared to order in a tiny green bamboo-decked room. Kreuzberg youth fill the outdoor tables in summer. *Pad thai* DM16. Open daily noon-midnight.

Austria, Bergmannstr. 30 (tel. 694 44 90). U-Bahn #7: "Gniesenaustr." One of the best and most romantic places to get "German" food in Berlin. A classy interior and friendly sidewalk seating make up for slightly higher prices. Gulash DM21.50. Austrian *Kaiserschwarm* (a type of pancake) DM9.50. Open Tues.-Sun. 6pm-1am.

EASTERN BERLIN

University Mensa

Humboldt University Mensa, Unter den Linden 6, in the back of the University's main building. The cheapest of Berlin's *Mensen,* and conveniently located for sightseeing in eastern Berlin. Full meals from DM1.50. Student ID required. Open Mon.-Fri. 11:30am-2:30pm.

Oranienburger Straße-Mitte

Taba, Chausseestr. 106 (tel. 282 67 95). U-Bahn #6: "Zinnowitzerstr." Big portions of delicious, spicy Mexican and Brazilian food gets even spicier with occasional live salsa music. While most of the entrees are DM15-20, you can indulge in great quesadillas for DM13.50 or *empanadas* for DM11.50. On Wed., all entrees are DM10, all cocktails DM8. Eat until you yell, with smug satisfaction, "I am the great Cornholio!" Open Mon.-Thurs. 6pm-midnight, Fri.-Sun. 6pm-1am.

Beth Café, Tucholskystr. 40 (tel. 281 31 35), just off Auguststr. S-Bahn #1 or 2: "Oranienburgerstr." Located in Mitte's small Orthodox Jewish neighborhood, it's a genuine kosher restaurant. Serves inexpensive Israeli specialties and a generous selection of kosher wines. Bagel with lox and cream cheese DM4. Other dishes DM5-15. "Kibbutz-style" breakfast buffet every Sunday. Open Sun.-Thurs. 11am-10pm, Fri. 9am-5pm (in winter 9am-3pm), Sat. after Shabbatt-midnight.

Buffalo Argentinisches Steakhaus, Niederkirchner Str. 3-5 (tel. 23 25 19 45). U-Bahn #2 or S-Bahn #1 or 2: "Potsdamer Platz." The name is a misnomer—the place offers a changing daily menu that includes vegetarian dishes. Why is it so cool? Because the restaurant is located in the *Preußischen Landtag,* which means that you can eat the cheap entrees (DM4-9) while sitting next to German ministers. Open Mon.-Fri. 1:30-3:30pm, in Aug. Mon.-Fri. 8am-3:30pm.

The Oscar Wilde, Friedrichstr. 122a (tel. 282 81 66). U-Bahn #6: "Oranienburger Tor." The home-away-from-home for Berlin's expatriate Irish. Irish Stew, fried eggs, chips (i.e. fries), and Guinness for reasonable prices. Live music, usually of the Irish persuasion (Thurs.-Sat). Open Sun.-Thurs. 11am-2am, Fri.-Sat. 11am-3am.

What's a Döner?

When this question was posed to Germany's *Döner* dealers, the response was astonishment. After all, everyone knows what a *Döner Kebab* is—chunks of lamb stuffed in a Turkish *Fladenbrot* topped with vegetables and a mysterious sauce. Yet where does the name come from? Vendors in northern Germany unanimously insisted that it comes from Berlin and told us not to get any ideas about this being authentic Turkish food. But we learned that the German "Dön" comes from the Turkish word meaning "to turn," and that the meat is thus named a *Döner* because it revolves as it cooks. The origin of *"Imbiß"* is also intriguing. Today it's used to refer to a snack bar, but the term actually comes from the Middle High German *entbeißen,* which means, literally, "to bite something out of something else"—kind of like picking the lamb out of the *Döner.*

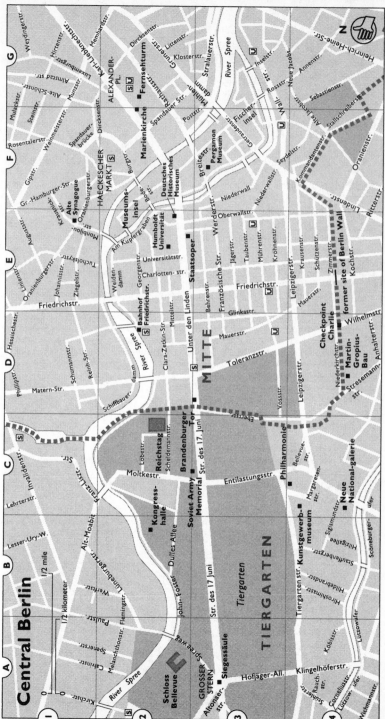

Central Berlin

1/2 mile

1/2 kilometer

N

Schloss Bellevue

River Spree

Spreeweg

Pauli-str.

Spenerstr.

Kirchstr.

Calvinstr.

Melanchthonstr.

Flemingstr.

Alt-Moabit

Lüneburgerstr.

Werftstr.

Lesser-Ury-W.

Lehrterstr.

Invalidenstr.

Franz-Liszt-Str.

John-Foster-Dulles-Allee

Matern-Str.

Phillipstr.

Schumannstr.

Reinh.-Str.

Hessischestr.

Kongress-halle

Moltkestr.

Reichstag

Löbestr.

Scheidemannstr.

Brandenburger Tor

Soviet Army Memorial

Str. des 17 Juni

Str. 17 Juni

GROSSER STERN

Siegessäule

Altonaer-str.

Hofjäger-All.

Klingelhöferstr.

Stülerstr.

Rauch-str.

Lützow-Ufer

Cornelius-str.

Wichmannstr.

Hiroshimastr.

Stauffenbergstr.

Hildebrandstr.

Tiergartenstr.

Tiergartenstr.

Sigismundstr.

Hitzigallee

Schöneburger-str.

Margareten-str.

Bellevue-str.

Entlastungsstr.

Kunstgewerb-museum

Philharmonie

Neue National-galerie

Kobisstr.

TIERGARTEN

Tiergarten

Schiffbauer-damm

River Spree

Clara-Zetkin-Str.

Bahnhof Friedrichstr.

Weiden-damm

Mittelstr.

Georgenstr.

Am Kupfergraben

Unter den Linden

Friedrichstr.

MITTE

Toleranzstr.

Mauerstr.

Eberstr.

Voßstr.

Leipzigerstr.

Mauerstr.

Behrenstr.

Französische Str.

Glinkastr.

Friedrichstr.

Jägerstr.

Taubenstr.

Mohrenstr.

Kronenstr.

Leipzigerstr.

Krausenstr.

Schützenstr.

Zimmerstr.

Checkpoint Charlie

former site of Berlin Wall

Wilhelmstr.

Niederkirchstr.

Martin-Gropius-Bau

Stresemann-str.

Anhalterstr.

Kochstr.

Lindenstr.

Oranienstr.

Ritterstr.

Alte Jacobstr.

Kommandantenstr.

Seydelstr.

Niederwallstr.

Niederwallstr.

Oberwallstr.

Werderstr.

Staatsoper

Humboldt Universität

Museums-insel

Bode-Str.

Deutsches Historische Museum

Pergamon Museum

Breitestr.

Fischer-Insel

Gertraudenstr.

Poststr.

Wall-str.

Rossstr.

Neue Jacobs-str.

Annenstr.

Sebastianstr.

Stallschreiberstr.

HAECKESCHER MARKT

Alte Synagoge

Oranienburger-str.

Monbijou-str.

Gr.-Hamburger-Str.

Oranienburgerstr.

Linienstr.

Augustr.

Johannistr.

Ziegelstr.

Tuchołskystr.

Universitätstr.

Charlotten-str.

Friedrichstr.

Marienkirche

Spandauer Str.

Burgstr.

Rathausstr.

Mühlendamm

Mühlen-str.

Posstr.

Spandauer Brücke

Weinmeisterstr.

Rosenthalerstr.

Gipstr.

Steinstr.

Mulackstr.

Alte-Schönhauser

Almstad str.

Alte-Schönhauser-str.

Nürtzstr.

ALEXANDER-PL.

Fernsehturm

Dircksenstr.

Grunerstr.

Karl-Liebknechtstr.

Hirtenstr.

Luxemburgstr.

Memhardstr.

Weydingerstr.

Dircksenstr.

Littenstr.

Klosterstr.

Stralauerstr.

River Spree

Inselstr.

Heinrich-Heine-Str.

Nikolaiviertel

Zur Letzten Instanz, Waisenstr. 14 (tel. 212 55 28). U-Bahn #2: "Klosterstr." A wonderfully preserved old Berlin restaurant, established in 1621. A light-gray row-house with top-notch *Deutsche Küche* (German cooking) served in small, wood-panelled rooms. Attracts an older, tweedy crowd. Many excellent entrees under DM20. The restaurant lies in the shadow of the Supreme Court—its name means "the last appeal." Open Mon. 4pm-midnight, Tues.-Sat. 11am-midnight.

Prenzlauer Berg

Die Krähe, Kollwitzstr. 84 (tel. 442 82 91), off Kollwitzplatz. U-Bahn #2: "Senefelder Platz." Check out the psychedelic "crow" tapestry. Bright crowd orders from changing weekly menu; mighty satisfyin' breakfasts under DM10, big-ass salads DM11. The popular Sunday buffet lets you load up until you burst for DM13.50. Open Mon.-Thurs. 5:30pm-1am, Fri.-Sat. 5:30pm-2am, 10:30am-1am.

Ostwind, Husemannstr. 13 (tel. 441 59 51). U-Bahn #2: "Senefelder Platz." Chinese food that seeks to bridge the cultural divide between East and West. Prenzlauer hipsters indulge in the dim sum or *Shao-Lin Min* (noodles with tofu, lotus, broccoli and carrots) for DM12.50. Open daily 11am-midnight.

Café Restauration 1900, Husemannstr. 1 (tel. 442 24 94), at Kollwitzplatz. U-Bahn #2: "Eberswalderstr." Alternative interior on a street decorated in Potemkin-village-esque 19th-century style. Decent food at reasonable prices. German, French, and Italian wines. Open Mon.-Fri. noon-1am, Sat.-Sun. 11am-1am.

Daye, Danziger Str. 24. U-Bahn #2: "Eberswalder Str." Turkish *Imbiß* option with hours to get you through a Prenzlauer Berg night and delectable *Döners* that are spicy enough to send unprepared Germans reeling. The hearty chicken *Döner* is a good meal (DM4.50). Open daily 9am-5am.

Village Voice, Ackerstr. 1a (tel. 282 45 50). U-Bahn #8: "Rosenthaler Platz." Café and bar cum bookstore trying hard for NYC hipness. Multi-lingual literature and inex-pensive fare. Beavis and Butthead come here for the nachos and tacos, not the campy books. Open Mon.-Sat. 3pm-2am, Sun. 11am-2am. On Thurs. at 9pm, they show high-brow films, some in English (DM2).

▦ Sights

Berlin can be just as disconcerting in its complexity as it is stunning. For a guide to the city's major neighborhoods, see page 395. Below, the sights are organized into five major sections: **central** sights, **western** Berlin, **eastern** Berlin, **museums**, and the **outer boroughs.** Most of central Berlin's major sights lie along the route of **bus #100,** which travels from Bahnhof Zoo to Prenzlauer Berg, passing the Siegessäule, Bran-denburger Tor, Unter den Linden, the Berliner Dom, and Alexanderplatz along the way. A typical way to sight-see is to purchase a four-trip *Sammelkarte* public trans-port ticket (DM12) and use it to follow the route of the bus, getting off periodically to view sights of interest. Remember that each "click" is good for two hours after valida-tion. This method is cheaper than a package tour, and there's usually an amateur tour guide on the #100 bus trying to impress his friends.

BETWEEN EAST AND WEST BERLIN

For decades a barricaded gateway to nowhere, today the **Brandenburger Tor** (Bran-denburg Gate) is perhaps the one structure that most symbolizes reunited Berlin. Standing directly in the center of the city, it opens east onto Unter den Linden and west onto the Tiergarten park and Straße des 17. Juni. Built during the reign of Fred-erick Wilhelm II as an image of peace, in recent years the gate has become a symbol of east-west division. This locked door embedded in the Berlin Wall did not actually open until December 22, 1989, more than a month after the Wall fell. The images broadcast around the world of east and west Berliners dancing together atop the Wall were all filmed at the Brandenburg Gate, since this section of the wall was the only part with a flat top—everywhere else, the top was curved in order to prevent world-be escapers from getting a good grip.

The **Berlin Wall** itself is a dinosaur, with only fossil remains still visible. Erected overnight on August 13, 1961 (initially as a fence), the 140km-long wall separated families and friends, sometimes even running through people's homes. In the early 1970s, a second wall was erected parallel to the first; the space in between them (about the width of a street) became known as the "death strip." The 1989 wave of liberalization in other Communist countries and mass demonstrations of East Germans demanding the right to travel freely finally drove the government to open its borders and dismantle the Wall (and itself). Portions of the reinforced concrete structure of the Wall are preserved near the *Hauptbahnhof* and by Potsdamer Platz. The longest remaining bit is the brightly painted **East Side Gallery,** a 1.3km stretch of cement slabs that also passes as one of the world's largest open-air art galleries. To get there, take the S-Bahn: "Hauptbahnhof." The murals are not the remnants of Cold War graffiti, but rather the efforts of an international group of artists who gathered here in 1989 to celebrate the city's openness. The scrawlings of later tourists have been added to their work. Occasionally, late-coming *Mauerspecher* (wall-peckers) nibble at the edges of the Gallery, trying to knock off a chunk for posterity, but most of the pieces you'll see for sale at the tourist stands are fake.

The demolished wall has left an incompletely healed scar across the city center. From the western side, newly-planted trees extend the Tiergarten park a few more meters. But the numerous cranes jutting up into the sky on the eastern side have become as much a symbol of Berlin as the TV tower on Alexanderplatz. **Potsdamer Platz,** cut off by the wall, was once a major Berlin transportation hub designed under Frederick Wilhelm I to approximate Parisian boulevards, with the same primary purpose of moving troops quickly. The land surrounding the *Platz* is now a chaotic mess of construction machinery and half-dug foundations. The shiny new **"InfoBox,"** a temporary bright-red structure near the Potsdamerplatz U- and S-Bahn station, contains an exhibit describing in exhaustive and enthusiastic detail the future Daimler-Benz-sponsored office complex on the site, as well as various railway improvements that will supposedly make Berlin the transport hub of Europe. The construction was supposed to be finished by 2000, but now the date has been pushed up to 2004 (InfoBox open daily 9am-7pm; free). Near Potsdamer Platz, unmarked and inconspicuous, lies the site of the **Führerbunker,** where Hitler married Eva Braun and then ended his life. In macabre irony, the actual bunker site is now a playground (behind the record store at Wilhelmstr. 92); tourists looking for it often mistakenly head for the visible bunker at the southern edge of Potsdamer Platz. Plans to restore the bunker were shelved amid fears that the site would become a shrine for the radical right. As with the re-opening of *Geisterbahnhöfe* ("ghost stations" under East Berlin, once guarded by troops and bypassed by the U-Bahn), reunification has let all sorts of forgotten underground ghosts loose in Berlin.

Just south of Potsdamer Platz, between the center of Schöneberg and the former no-man's-land surrounding the wall, stands the **Martin-Gropius-Bau,** at Stresemanstraße 110. The decorous edifice was designed by Martin Gropius, a pupil of Schinkel and uncle of *Bauhausmeister* Walter Gropius. There's nothing Bauhaus-like about the red-and-white Neoclassical building, though it's more graceful than most Prussian turn-of-the-century fare. Today the building holds a museum of applied and fine arts as well as a dynamic **Jewish Museum** (see Museums, p. 424). Nearby at Potsdamerstr. 33, funkadelic Modernism rules the exterior of the huge **Staatsbibliothek Preußischer Kulturbesitz** (tel. 26 61), the library that starred in Wim Wenders's *Wings of Desire*—the angels found its main reading room a perfect spot to observe humanity. Good thing they didn't come at exam time, or even they would have had trouble finding a table (open Mon.-Fri. 9am-9pm, Sat. 9am-5pm).

A blood-red Soviet flag hangs over the door of the **Haus am Checkpoint Charlie,** Friedrichstr. 44 (tel. 251 10 31). Take the U-Bahn to "Kochstr." or bus #129. A strange, fascinating museum on the site of the famous border crossing point, with an uneasy mixture of blatant Western tourist kitsch and didactic Eastern earnestness, is still one of Berlin's most popular tourist attractions. On the ground floor, flashiness is the order of the day; an expensive snack bar is crammed against a ticket desk covered with postcards, mugs, posters, books, and "Communist" baubles. Right by the door stands the car in which Johannes Ehret smuggled his girlfriend across the border in 1988. Upstairs you can find out everything you've ever wanted to know about the Wall or various ways of escaping over it, as well as learn about the history of human rights struggles throughout the world. The exhibits are in German, English, French, and Russian. Documentaries in German are shown daily from 9am to 5:30pm (open daily 9am-10pm; admission DM7.50, students DM4.50).

WESTERN BERLIN

The Reichstag

Just to the north of the Brandenburg Gate sits the imposing, stone-gray **Reichstag** building, former seat of the parliaments of the German Empire and the Weimar Republic, and future home of Germany's governing body, the *Bundestag*. In 1918 Philipp Scheidemann proclaimed a German republic from one of its balconies with the words *"es lebe die deutsche Republik"* ("the German Republic lives"). His move turned out to be wise, since two hours later Karl Liebknecht, in the Imperial Palace a few kilometers away on Unter den Linden, announced a German Socialist Republic, ironically on the site that later supported the parliament of the GDR. (For more on the Imperial Palace, see Eastern Berlin, p. 417.) Civil war followed in Berlin, and in much of the rest of Germany. The government fled to Weimar to draw up a new constitution, but over the course of the next decade the Reichstag became the fractured center of the economically troubled Republic. As the Republic declined, Nazi members showed up to sessions in uniform, and on February 28, 1933, a month after Hitler became Chancellor, fire mysteriously broke out in the building. The fire provided a pretext for Hitler to declare a state of emergency, giving the Nazis broad powers to arrest and intimidate opponents before the upcoming elections. The infamous end result was the Enabling Act, which established Hitler as legal dictator and abolished democracy. A conceptual monument outside recalls the 96 members of the Reichstag executed by the Nazis. In the summer of 1995, the Reichstag was the center of a major "art event," when husband-and-wife team **Christo** and **Jeanne-Claude** wrapped the dignified building in 120,000 yards of shimmery metallic fabric. Tourists and residents alike marvelled at the effect, but after 3 weeks, the cloth came down and less picturesque scaffolding went up. The building's entire interior must be restored before it is usable; the plans call for a huge, striking glass dome to be erected in the center. The government is scheduled to move in 1999, but construction work may well push this deadline back as well.

Tiergarten and Kurfürstendamm

The lush **Tiergarten** in the center of old Berlin is a relief from the neon lights of the Ku'damm in the west and the din and dust of construction work in the east. Spreading over the northeast corner of western Berlin, the vast landscaped park was formerly used by Prussian monarchs as a hunting ground. As you walk along its canals, notice the old streetlamps; each Prussian city sent one to the capital. In the heart of the Tiergarten, the slender 70m **Siegessäule** (victory column), topped by a gilded statue of winged victory (where Bruno Ganz hung out in *Wings of Desire*), commemorates Prussia's humiliating defeat of France in 1870. In 1938, the Nazis moved the monument from its former spot in front of the *Reichstag* to increase its height and make it more impressive. Despite the bad taste their militarism leaves in the mouth, they did improve the view. Climb the 285 steps to the top for a panorama of the city (open April-Nov. Mon. 1-5:30pm, Tues.-Sun. 9am-5:30pm; admission DM1.50, students DM1). Radiating out from the column, the **Straße des 17. Juni** bisects the park from the west to east. At the eastern ends stands the **Soviet Army Memorial** (but yes, you're still in Western Berlin!) flanked by a pair of giant toy tanks. South of the memorial, Entlastungstr. leads to the highly modern, bright yellow buildings of the **Tiergarten complex,** which includes the Philharmonic, the *"Staabi"* library (see above), and a host of museums (see Museums, page 422).

After the city's division, West Berlin centered around **Bahnhof Zoo,** the only train station in the world to inspire a rock album (the U2 subway line runs through the station, but this is just a coincidence). At the nearby Breitscheidplatz, the shattered **Kaiser-Wilhelm-Gedächtniskirche** stands as a sobering reminder of the destruction caused during World War II. The shattered tower, its jagged edges silhouetted against the sky, serves as one of Berlin's most striking sights. The ruins house an exhibit showing what the church looked like whole, as well as shocking photos of the entire city in ruins just after the war (exhibit open Tues.-Sun. 10am-4pm). The ruins have unfortunately been submitted to the eternal torture of juxtaposition with a hideous "modern" church, built in 1960s concrete-and-stained-glass chic (church open daily 9am-7pm). In the summer, Berlin's many leftists, foreigners, young people and others often gather in front of the church to speak out, converse, sell watches, play bagpipes and sitars (not at the same time), breakdance, perform crude imitations of Chancellor Kohl, and act up in general. Stretching several kilometers to the west from Breitscheidplatz, the **Kurfürstendamm** (always called **Ku'damm,** or Koo-dahm) is Berlin's biggest and fanciest shopping strip, lined with designer boutiques and pricey hotels. The renowned **Zoo** (not the station, but the menagerie) is one of the best in the world, with many animals displayed in open-air habitats instead of cages (main entrance is directly across from the train station). The second entrance at Budapesterstr. 34 (across from Europa Center) is the famous **Elephant Gate,** a delightfully-decorated pagoda of pachyderms (open daily 9am-6:30pm; Oct.-Feb. 9am-5pm; March-April 9am-5:30pm; admission DM11, students DM9, children ages 3-15 DM5.50). Next door at Budapesterstr. 32 is the excellent **Aquarium,** which houses broad collections of insects and reptiles as well as endless tanks of wide-eyed, rainbow-colored fish. Its pride and joy is its 1000-lb. **Komodo dragon,** the world's largest reptile, a gift to Germany from Indonesia. Also check out the psychedelic jellyfish tanks, filled with dozens of translucent sea nettles. (Open daily 9am-6pm. Admission to aquarium DM8, students and kids DM5. Combination card to aquarium and zoo DM17, students DM14, children ages 3-15 DM8.50.)

Schöneberg

Further south in the district of Schöneberg stands the **Rathaus Schöneberg,** where West Berlin's city government used to convene during the 1960s. Take U-Bahn #4 to "Rathaus Schöneberg." On June 26, 1963, 1.5 million Berliners swarmed the streets beneath the sleek tower to hear John F. Kennedy reassure them of the Allies' commitment to the city. Kennedy's speech ended with the now-famous words, "All free men, wherever they may live, are citizens of Berlin. And therefore, as a free man, I take pride in the words *Ich bin ein Berliner."* For the record: this is a grammatically correct expression, and it means what Kennedy wanted to say, although a native might say *"Ich bin Berliner."* In 1993, a conceptual art exhibit was set up on the streets near the *Rathaus.* If you look closely, you'll notice some of the street signs have black-and-white placards above them—they state some of the Nazi edicts against Berlin's Jews. A number of these signs can be seen on Grunewaldstr. Not too far away is **Fehrbelliner Platz,** a standard example of Nazi architecture. These gruesomely regular prison-like blocks were meant to be model apartment houses; try to imagine a city full of them. Take U-Bahn #2 or 7 to "Fehrbelliner Platz."

Charlottenburg

The borough of Charlottenburg, one of wealthiest areas in Berlin, includes the area between the Ku'damm and the Spree river; like many of Berlin's neighborhoods, it was once a separate town. **Schloß Charlottenburg,** the vast, bright Baroque palace built by Frederick I for his second wife, Sophie-Charlotte, presides over a carefully landscaped park on the western edge of the region. Take U-Bahn #2 to "Sophie-Charlotte-Platz" or bus #145 from Bahnhof Zoo. The *Schloß's* many buildings include **Neringbau,** the palace proper, which contains many rooms filled with historical furnishings; the **Schinkel-Pavillion,** a museum dedicated to the Prussian architect; **Belvedere,** a small building housing the royal family's porcelain collection; and the

Mausoleum, the final resting spot for most of the family. The **Galerie Der Romantik,** a state museum housing Berlin's first-rate collection of German romantic painting, is located in a side wing (see Museums, p. 422). (Castle open Tues.-Fri. 9am-5pm, Sat.-Sun. 10am-5pm. Mausoleum open March-Nov. Admission to the individual sections of the castle DM2.50-4, students DM1.50, under 14 free. Entire palace complex *Tagekarte* DM8, students DM3, under 14 free.) Seek out the **Palace Gardens** behind the main buildings, with their small lakes, footbridges, fountains, and carefully planted rows of trees (open Tues.-Sun. 6am-9pm; free).

At the western edge of Charlottenburg is the **Olympia Stadion** (Olympic Stadium), one of the more restrained architectural remnants of the Nazi Party. It was erected for the 1936 Olympic Games, in which Jesse Owens, an African-American, triumphed against the Nazis' racial theories by winning four gold medals. Hitler refused to congratulate Owens because of his skin color, but there's now a Jesse-Owens-Allee to the south of the stadium. Take U-Bahn #1 to "Olympia Stadion."

Kreuzberg

Indispensable for a sense of Berlin's famous *alternative Szene,* or counter-culture, is a visit to **Kreuzberg,** an area loaded with cafés and bars. Kreuzberg has long been proud of its diverse population and liberal leanings: this is the place to see anti-Nazi graffiti and left-wing revolutionary slogans (in English, Turkish, Russian, Spanish, and German). During President Reagan's 1985 visit to Berlin, authorities so feared protests from this quarter that they cordoned the whole Kreuzberg district off without warning—an utterly unconstitutional measure. Much of the area was occupied by *Hausbesetzer* (squatters) during the 60s and 70s. A conservative city government decided to forcibly evict the illegal residents in the early 1980s, provoking riots and throwing the city into total consternation.

For a look at the district's more respectable face, take U-Bahn #6 or 7 to "Mehringdamm" and wander around. Particularly interesting is the area around **Chamissoplatz,** bordered by Bergmannstr. and Fidicinstr. Bergmannstr. features an especially large number of old buildings and second-hand shops. At night, many bohemian cafés and punk clubs overflow onto **Gneisenaustraße,** which heads west from the intersection with Mehringdamm. The cafés and bars on Oranienstr. boast a more radical element; the May Day parades always start on Oranienplatz. Take U-Bahn #1 to "Kottbusser Tor."

The **Landwehrkanal,** a channel bisecting Kreuzberg, is where Rosa Luxemburg's body was thrown after her murder in 1919. The tree-dotted strip of the canal near Hallesches Tor, **Paul-Linke Ufer,** may be the most beautiful street in Berlin, with its shady terraces and old facades. The east end of Kreuzberg, near the old Wall, is home to Turkish and Balkan neighborhoods and has a correspondingly wealth of ethnic restaurants, popular with radicals and students. From the Schlesisches Tor U-Bahn station, a three-minute walk takes you across the **Oberbaumbrücke,** through a fragment of the wall and into the Friedrichshain district of the former East.

Spandau

Spandau is one of the oldest parts of Berlin. To get there, take U-Bahn #7 to "Altstadt Spandau." Many of the old buildings have been restored, including the massive 16th-century **Zitadelle** (citadel). Take U-Bahn #7 to "Zitadelle." Surrounded on all sides by water so as to be nearly impregnable, the star-shaped enclosure was the anchor of the medieval town. In 1945, the fort was pressed into service as a prison to hold accused war criminals in preparation for the Nuremberg Trials. Despite its grim name and past, the citadel is now a wistful place filled with old field cannons and statues and a **medieval history museum.** The thickly-fortified *Juliusturm* tower, dating to c. 1200, is Spandau's unofficial symbol. (Open Tues.-Fri. 9am-5pm, Sat.-Sun. 10am-5pm. Admission DM1.50. Complete tour Sat.-Sun. at 10am. DM3.) You can catch a boat from near the fort, or take bus #145 to "Johannestift" (the last stop) into the **Spandau Forest.** Also notable is the exceptionally fine **Rathaus,** which Spandauers defiantly constructed from 1911 to 1913 (at a cost of 3.5 million Marks) in a futile effort to stave off absorption into Berlin. Take U-Bahn #7 to "Rathaus Spandau." **Spandau Prison** was demolished after its last inmate, Hitler's deputy Rudolf Hess, hanged himself in 1987 at age 93. Hess, a devoted party member from the beginning (he participated in the Beer Hall *Putsch* and took dictation for Hitler's *Mein Kampf*) was an unrepentant Nazi until his death. Lately this unsavory character has made a controversial comeback as a latter-day idol for neo-fascist groups; but, to Berlin's credit, the local anti-Hess response has been even stronger.

To the South: Dahlem, Zehlendorf and the Grünewald

In the southern suburb of **Dahlem,** Berlin's **Botanischer Garten,** on Königin-Luise-Str., is a delight, especially the tropical greenhouses. Nearby, a sprawling cultural complex holds several important museums (see Museums, p. 422). The even more sprawling *Freie Universität* complex is next door. Take U-Bahn #1 to "Dahlem-Dorf." Dahlem was the center of the former American Sector, home to many American military personnel stationed in Berlin. Although the Allied forces have almost entirely pulled out of Berlin, there is still a strong American presence in the area.

West of Dahlem lies **Zehlendorf,** Berlin's ritziest residential district. At the southwestern corner of the district, the **Glienecker Bridge** crosses the Havel into Potsdam and what was once the GDR. Closed to traffic in Cold War days, it is famed as the spot where East and West once exchanged captured spies. The most famous such incident traded American U-2 pilot Gary Powers for Soviet spy Ivanovich Abel. To get there, take bus #116 from the Wannsee bus station to the end of the line.

In summer, clear your head in the nearby **Grünewald,** a 745-acre birch forest. While there, visit the **Jagdschloß** (tel. 813 35 47), a restored royal hunting lodge housing a worthwhile collection of European paintings, including works by Rubens, van Dyck, and Cranach (open Tues.-Sun. 10am-6pm; admission DM2.50, students DM1.50). On summer evenings, concerts sound in the **Schloßgarten,** around 8pm (call for schedule information). To reach the Jagdschloß and the Grünewald, take bus #115 to the Brücke Museum and follow Pücklerstr. into the forest.

EASTERN BERLIN

Unter den Linden

The Brandenburg Gate opens eastward onto **Unter den Linden,** once one of Europe's best-known boulevards and the spine of old Berlin. All but a few of the venerable buildings near the gate have been destroyed, but farther down, by the statue of Frederick the Great atop his horse, many 18th-century structures have been restored to their original splendor. The pompous architecture can only hint at the Prussian conception of a capital and kingdom, with Unter den Linden as its axis. Past Friedrichstr., the first massive building on your left is the eastern branch of the **Deutsche Staatsbibliothek** (library), with a pleasant café inside. Beyond the library is the statue-crested, H-shaped main building of the **Humboldt Universität,** which boasts an imposing history as one of the finest universities in the world. The university's past faculty includes Hegel, Fichte, and Einstein, and the Brothers Grimm and Karl Marx are among its alumni. In the wake of a recent ideological *Blitzkrieg,* in which "tainted" departments were radically revamped or simply shut down, many younger scholars from the West have found Humboldt an exciting place to work.

Next door, the **Neue Wache** (new guard house) was designed by Prussian architect Friedrich Schinkel in unrepentant Neoclassical style. During the GDR era, it was known as the **"Monument to the Victims of Fascism and Militarism,"** and, ironically, was guarded by a goose-stepping East German soldier. After reunification, the building closed briefly but was reopened in 1993 as a war memorial. Buried inside are urns filled with earth from the Nazi concentration camps of Buchenwald and Mauthausen as well as from the battlefields of Stalingrad, El Alamein, and Normandy. Inside the dark enclosure, a statue by Käthe Kollwitz (Mother with Dead Child) broods alone on the stone floor. The statue is not a Kollwitz original but a replica, enlarged by a factor of 30 thanks to a laser-guided lathe and the will of Chancellor

Kohl. The replica has caused protests from the Kollwitz estate and other artists, as well as endless academic discourse about the nature of a copy vs. an "authentic original." The inscription reads: "To the victims of war and tyranny."

Across the way is **Bebelplatz,** where on May 10, 1933 the Nazis (aided by local students and faculty) burned nearly 20,000 books by "subversive" authors such as Heinrich Heine and Sigmund Freud, both Jews. The square is now the site of an excellent commemorative piece of art entitled "Bibliothek" (Library), by Israeli artist Micha Ullman; it consists of a hollowed-out chamber lined with illuminated empty white bookshelves. A plaque nearby is engraved with Heine's shockingly prescient 1820 quote: *"Nur dort wo man Bücher verbrennt, verbrennt man am Ende auch Menschen"* ("Wherever books are burned, ultimately people are also burned").

The building with the curved façade is the **Alte Bibliothek.** Once the royal library, it is now used by Humboldt University. On the other side of the square is the handsome **Deutsche Staatsoper,** fully rebuilt from original sketches by Knobelsdorf, the same architect who designed Schloß Sanssouci in Potsdam. The most striking of the monumental buildings is the **Zeughaus,** an old armory across the street near the bridge, which served before the war as the Prussian Army Hall of Fame and military museum; it has calmed down a bit as is now the **Museum of German History** (see Museums, p. 425). From the museum you can enter the enclosed courtyard and see the tormented faces of Andreas Schlüter's "Dying Warriors."

Gendarmenmarkt

Berlin's most impressive ensemble of 19th-century buildings is a few blocks south of Unter den Linden at **Gendarmenmarkt,** also known as the French Quarter, since it was the main settlement for Protestant Huguenots. The twin cathedral **Deutscher Dom** and **Französischer Dom** grace opposite ends of the square. In the middle, the Neoclassical **Schauspielhaus,** designed by Schinkel, is Berlin's most elegant concert space and hosts many international orchestras and classical performers. When it was first built, the hall was described as "music made solid." Destroyed by an air attack in 1945, it was painstakingly reconstructed and reopened in 1984.

Lustgarten and the Museumsinsel

Unter den Linden, after crossing over a small bridge, passes by the **Museumsinsel** (Museum Island), the home of four major museums and the **Berliner Dom** (BerlinCathedral). Immediately to the left stands the pillared **Altes Museum,** created by Schinkel, who envisioned Berlin as the "Athens on the Spree." The huge granite bowl in front was supposed to adorn the main hall, but it didn't fit through the door. Next door, the beautifully bulky, multiple-domed Berliner Dom proves that Protestants can go overboard just as well as Catholics. Severely damaged by an air raid in 1944, the cathedral, built during the reign of Kaiser Wilhelm II, recently emerged from 20 years of restoration. The ornate gold-and-jewel-encrusted interior, with its distinctively Protestant idols (Calvin, Zwingli, and Luther), is stunning if tacky. (Open daily 9am-7:30pm. Admission DM3, students DM1.50. Free organ recitals daily at 3pm. Frequent concerts in summer; buy tickets in the church.) There's also a **Kaiserliches Treppenhaus** upstairs, with exhibits of period art and imperial stuff (open Mon.-Sat. 10am-6pm, Sun. 11:30am-7pm; admission DM3, students DM1.50).

Behind the Altes Museum lie the complex's three other enormous museums: the **Pergamon,** the **Bodesmuseum,** and the **Alte Nationalgalerie** (see Museums, p. 422). The current **Altes Museum** was once the **Neues Museum,** but when the old museum was bombed, the Neues Museum became the Altes Museum by default. Now the old museum is being restored and is known as the Alte Nationalgalerie, since the Neue Nationalgalerie is in the Tiergarten complex. Got it? The cobblestone square in front of the Altes Museum is known as the **Lustgarten.** Once a small park, it became a military parade ground under the Nazis; there are tentative plans to turn it back into a park, but for now it hosts occasional open-art concerts and art exhibits. Across the street, the Lustgarten turns into Marx-Engels-Platz under the glaring, amber-colored **Palast der Republik,** where the GDR parliament once met. In 1990, city authorities discovered that the building was full of asbestos and shut it down, and it has remained closed ever since; Berliners argue about whether it ought to be demolished. The problems associated with the building itself are further complicated by the fact that the entire square used to be the site of the **Berliner Schloß,** the Hohenzollern family palace. Remarkably, the palace survived the war, although Soviet authorities demolished it in the 1950s in censure of its royal excess. The **Staatsrat** (Councils of the State) currently resides on the site—look for the modern building with a slice of the palace façade embedded in the middle. This section was preserved because in 1918 Karl Liebknecht supposedly proclaimed the German socialist republic from the balcony. The newest plans for the site aim to demolish the Palast der Republik and rebuild the façade of the palace, with a modern entertainment center behind it, but whether this plan will change is anybody's guess.

Crossing the Liebknecht Brücke leads you to a small park in the right-hand side of the street; in the middle of the park stands a "conceptual memorial" consisting of steel tablets engraved with images of worker struggle and protest surrounding a huge statue of a seated Marx and a standing Engels. In 1990, a graffito appeared on the base of the statue: *"Wir sind unschuldig!"* ("We're innocent!"). The park and the street behind it used to be collectively known as the Marx-Engels Forum; the park has not been renamed, while the street is now called Rathausstr.

Alexanderplatz and Nikolaiviertel

On the other side of the *Museumsinsel,* Unter den Linden becomes Karl-Liebknecht-str., and leads into the teeming, concrete **Alexanderplatz.** Formerly the frantic heart of Weimar Berlin, the plaza—known somewhat affectionately to Berliners as "Alex"—was the setting for Alexander Döblin's montage-novel of the modern metropolis, *Berlin-Alexanderplatz.* Friends from all over Berlin often meet at the plaza's **Weltzeituhr,** the international clock, but the undisputed landmark of the district is the **Fernsehturm** (television tower). The tower, the tallest structure in Berlin, is a truly awkward piece of design: picture the Death Star impaled on a long, thin, candy cane-striped spike. *Fernsehturm* is the German word for television tower, but the literal translation of "see far tower" is just as appropriate in this case—the view from the top (the spherical node 203m up the spike) is magnificent. A crowded express elevator whisks tourists to the top. The Fernsehturm is the universal point of reference. No matter where you are in the city, you can always pinpoint your location in relation to Alexanderplatz. In a city with few tall buildings, it can be seen from almost every part of Berlin, as far west as Charlottenburg and as far east as Pankow and Weissensee. (Open May-Oct. 9am-1am; Nov.-April 10am-midnight. DM8, children DM3).

The buildings surrounding the square include some GDR concrete-block classics, including the **Hotel Forum.** In the 1970s, the East German government made a concession to the people's implacable craving for bright lights by erecting some enormous neon signs, thus giving the area around Alexanderplatz the superficial trappings of a Western metropolis: "Chemical Products from Bitterfeld!" and "Medical Instruments of the GDR—Distributed in All the World!" Now nearly all of the buildings are covered with scaffolding, as the government tries to disguise the blatant GDR-era look of the façades. The constant demolition (or reconstruction) of GDR buildings has annoyed some *Ossies,* who are offended by what they view as an attempt to wipe out their history. In the first post-Communist months, Alexanderplatz was a rough place, the natural meeting ground for antagonistic gangs. But the pedestrians, working Berliners, and tourists prevailed. During the day, the square hums with con artists and vendors selling everything from Turkish *Fladenbrot* to black-market cigarettes smuggled from Russia. Around the U- and S-Bahn stations, the picture becomes seedier. Crowds congregate after dusk; watch your pockets.

The **Marienkirche,** a graceful 15th-century church, stands on the wide open plaza in front of the *Fernsehturm.* Nearby is the ornately gabled **Rotes Rathaus,** Old Berlin's famous 1869 red-brick town hall. Between 1949 and *die Wende,* it was home to East Berlin's city government; since 1990, the *Oberbürgermeister* and senate of the unified city have had their seat here. Behind the *Rathaus,* the twin spires of the **Nikolaikirche** mark Berlin's oldest building. Inside the 13th-century structure, a small museum documents the early history of the city (open Tues.-Sun. 10am-6pm). The church gives the surrounding **Nikolaiviertel,** a carefully reconstructed *Altstadt,* its name. The Nikolaiviertel's narrow winding streets are popular and crowded; among the two dozen historic buildings are the **Knoblauchhaus,** at Poststr. 23, which houses a small museum documenting the history of medieval Berlin (Tues.-Sun. 10am-6pm; admission DM2, students DM1) and the **Ephraim-Palais,** at the corner of Poststr. and Muhlendamm. The Nazis used this Rococo building as a sports museum; since 1970, the more laid-back **Sportmuseum Berlin** has found its home here (open Tues.-Sun. 10am-6pm; admission DM3, students DM1.50).

Scheunenviertel—Oranienburgerstraße

Northwest of Alexanderplatz lies the **Scheunenviertel,** once the center of Berlin's Orthodox Jewish community. Take the U- or S-Bahn to "Alexanderplatz" or S-Bahn #1or 2 to "Oranienbergerstr." Berlin never had a ghetto; rather, Jews lived all throughout the city, although during World War II they were deported to ghettos in Poland. Wealthier and more assimilated Jews tended to live in western Berlin (Wilmersdorf was once 12% Jewish), while more Orthodox Jews from Eastern Europe settled in the Scheunenviertel (literally, "barn district," because in medieval times barns were placed here, just outside the city walls). Though evidence of Jewish life in Berlin dates back to the 13th century, the community was expelled in 1573 and not invited back for 100 years. Berlin's first synagogue opened in 1714 on the tiny **Heidereutegasse,** near the corner of Rochstr. and Rosenstr Remarkably, this synagogue was not destroyed during the *Kristallnacht,* because of the presence of a post office which had been renting space in the building—however, it was later bombed during the war, never to be reconstructed. The spot is marked by a huge construction site. The former **Jewish welfare office** was located at Rosenstr. 2-4. In the adjacent park, a terracotta memorial was put up in October 1995—on the 54th anniversary of the first deportation of the Berlin Jews.

The shell of the **Neues Synagoge** (New Synagoge) stands at Oranienburgerstr. 30. This huge, "oriental-style" building was designed by the famous Berlin architect Knoblanch; its in-your-face quality reflects the community's heightened status. The synagogue, which seated 3200, was used for worship until 1940, when the Nazis occupied it and used it for storage. This synagogue, amazingly, also survived *Kristallnacht*—the SS torched it, but a local police chief, realizing that the building was an historical monument, ordered the Nazis to extinguish the fire. The synagogue was destroyed by bombing, however; its restoration, largely financed by international Jewish organizations, began in 1988. The temple's beautiful gold-laced domes and some of the sumptuous interior have been reconstructed, and finally were opened to the public in May 7, 1995—the anniversary of Germany's surrender. Two first-class exhibits (tel. 280 13 16) are housed here: **The New Synagogue 1866-1995,** chronicling the synagogue's history, and **Jewish History in Berlin,** documenting the history of Jews in Berlin since the 1660s (open Sun.-Thurs. 10am-6pm, Fri. 10am-2pm). But it is a somber sign of the times that the synagogue has been placed under 24-hour protection by machine gun-equipped Berlin police; to enter, you must pass through a metal detector and, if you have a camera, demonstrate that it is not a weapon. A simple sign on the side of the building reads "Never forget this."

At the end of Große Hamburgerstr. near the intersection with Monbijoustr. are the remains of the **Alter Jüdische Friedhof** (Old Jewish Cemetery). Destroyed by the Nazis, the site now contains only the restored gravestone of the Enlightenment philosopher and scholar Moses Mendelssohn; the rest is a quiet park. In front, a plaque marks the site of the **Jüdische Altersheim,** the Jewish old-age home which after 1942 served as a holding place for Jews before their transportation to concentration camps. Next door, yet another plaque marks the location of Berlin's oldest **Jewish school,** where Moses Mendelssohn taught. Mendelssohn, who was known as "the German Socrates," translated the Hebrew Bible into German, and supported interaction between Berlin's Jewish and non-Jewish communities. Corresponding with his humanist outlook, the school's pupils were half-gentile, half Jewish. The building was reopened as a school in 1992; in accordance with Mendelssohn's vision, its student body is still half-and-half.

The area around the Berlin Synagogue served as a showpiece for the East German government; many of the old buildings have been restored, and many of the new constructions have a flair unusual for Berlin. In particular, **Oranienburgerstr.** has become a center of a community of artists and squatters, including many from the West, with a correspondingly rich quality of cultural and café life.

North Mitte

If any single man personifies the maelstrom of political and aesthetic contradictions that is Berlin, it is **Bertolt Brecht,** who called the city home. "There is a reason to prefer Berlin to other cities," the playwright once declared, "because it is constantly changing. What is bad today can be improved tomorrow." The **Brecht-Haus Berlin,** Chausseestr. 125 (tel. 282 99 16), near the intersection with Schlegelstr., is where Brecht lived and worked from 1953 to 1956. Take U-Bahn #6 to "Zinnowitzerstr." If you understand German, you should take the guided tour, given in a flamboyant Brechtian style. The **Brechtforum** on the second floor sponsors exhibits and lectures on artistic and metropolitan subjects; pick up a schedule. (Open Tues.-Wed. and Fri. 10-11:30am, Thurs. 10-11:30am and 5-6:30pm, Sat. 9:30am-1:30pm. Admission DM4, students DM2. Tours every 30min.) Directly adjacent to Brecht's house, the **Dorotheenstädtischer Friedhof** (cemetery) contains the graves of a host of German luminaries, including Brecht and his wife Helene Wegel. Fichte and Hegel are buried side by side a few yards away; both graves are often festooned with flowers by admirers. At the end of the entrance path, next to the chapel on the right, is a map to the locations of the departed (open May-Aug. daily 8am-8pm; Feb.-April and Sept.-Nov. 8am-6pm; Dec.-Jan. 8am-4pm).

Prenzlauer Berg

Northwest of Oranienburgerstr. and Alexanderplatz lies **Prenzlauer Berg,** a former working-class district largely neglected by East Germany's reconstruction efforts. Many of its old buildings are falling apart; others still have shell holes and embedded bullets from World War II. The result is the charm of age and graceful decay, slightly less charming for phoneless local residents with bad plumbing. Don't be surprised, however, at the mind-blowing rate of gentrification underway here; Prenzlauer Berg is one of the most sought-out locales for Berlin's wealthy jetset. Fancy shops and restaurants are popping up left and right, disturbing this neighborhood's reputation as a mellow, low-key retreat for artists and students. Unlike the loud, raucous scene in Kreuzberg and Mitte, Prenzlauer Berg is still more sedate and cerebral—which is not to say that it isn't lively. The streets here are studded with hip but casual cafés, bars, and squats, frequented by an ever-burgeoning crowd.

Restored **Husemannstraße** is especially worthy of a stroll, home to the **Museum Berliner Arbeiterleben um 1900,** Husemannstr. 12, with a meticulously accurate reproduction of a Berlin working-class family apartment at the turn of the century (open Tues.-Thurs. and Sat. 10am-6pm, Fri. 10am-3pm; admission DM2, students DM1). The street also contains the **Friseurmuseum** (see Museums, p. 425). The city government's anti-commune policy, heavily supported by the mainstream press, is in danger of destroying this counter-cultural renaissance. Meanwhile, the scene around green **Kollwitzplatz** is especially vibrant—a number of cafés have popped up within the past year. The statue of artist Käthe Kollwitz has been painted over a number of times in the past few years, in acts of affectionate rather than angry vandalism, most notably with big pink polka-dots.

Prenzlauer Berg's slightly remote location made it a perfect place for Berlin's Jews during the 19th and early 20th centuries. The well-preserved **Jewish cemetery** on Schonhauser Allee contains the graves of composer Giacomo Meyerbeer and painter Max Liebermann (open Mon.-Thurs. 8am-4pm, Fri. 8am-1pm). To get there, take U-

Bahn #2 to "Senefelderpl." Just off Kollwitzpl. at Rykestr. 53, stands one of Berlin's loveliest **synagogues,** miraculously unharmed during *Kristallnacht* due to its inconspicuous location in a courtyard. It's generally not open to the public, but you can call 448 52 98 and arrange to be let in.

▦ Museums

Berlin is one of the world's great museum cities, with collections of art and artifacts encompassing all subjects and eras. The **National Prussian Cultural Foundation** *(Staatliche Museen Preußischer Kulturbesitz)* runs the four major complexes—Charlottenburg, Dahlem, Museumsinsel, and Tiergarten—that form the hub of the city's museum culture. Since these museums are all government-run, their prices are standardized: admission DM4, students DM2. A *Tageskarte* (good for all of the national museums, including the 4 above) is a real bargain: DM8, students DM4. All of the national museums and most of the private ones are closed on Monday; on the first Sunday of each month admission to the national museums is free. Smaller museums deal with every subject imaginable, from hairstyles to sugar.

MUSEUMSINSEL

Museum Island, Bodestr. 1-3 (tel. 20 35 54 44). S-Bahn #3, 5, 6, or 9: "Haeckescher Markt." The island holds the astoundingly broad treasure hoard of the former GDR in three separate museums. Unfortunately, a *Tageskarte* doesn't get you entrance to the Altes Museum. Admission (usually) DM6-10, students DM3-5.

Pergamonmuseum, Kupfergraben (tel. 20 35 54 44). One of the world's great ancient history museums from the grand old days when archaeology was king and Heinrich Schliemann traversed the world, uncovering the debris of ancient civilizations. The scale of its exhibits is mind-boggling: huge rooms can barely contain the entire Babylonian Ishtar Gate (575 BC), the Roman Market Gate of Miletus, and the majestic Pergamon Altar of Zeus (180 BC). The altar's great frieze (125m long and 2.5m high) depicting the victory of the gods over the giants symbolizes the triumphs of Attalus I. The museum also houses extensive collections of Greek, Assyrian, Islamic, and Far Eastern art. Tours of Pergamon Altar at 11am and 3pm. Open Tues.-Sun. 9am-5pm. Islamic art section open Wed.-Sun. 10am-6pm. On Tues., only the architectural exhibits are open. Last entry 30min. before closing. Entrance includes a free and nifty audio.

Alte Nationalgalerie, Bodestr. (tel. 220 03 81). 19th-century art in a beautiful historic building. The collection is mostly German but also includes a sizable number of works by French Impressionist painters. Open Tues.-Sun. 9am-5pm.

Bodemuseum, Monbijoubrücke (tel. 20 35 55 03; fax 200 46 31). A world-class exhibit of Egyptian art, as well as late-Gothic wood sculptures, early Christian art, 15th- to 18th-century paintings, and an exhibit on ancient history. The *Kindergalerie* holds interactive educational exhibits designed for kids. Open Tues.-Sun. 9am-5pm. Egyptian and papyrus collections open Tues.-Sun. 10am-6pm.

Altes Museum, Lustgarten. Converted into a special-exhibit museum, it has recently showcased powerhouse exhibitions of 20th-century avant-garde and political art. Regrettably, a *Tageskarte* for the other museums is not valid here. Exhibits run up to DM10, students DM5. Open Tues.-Sun. 10am-5pm, except during major exhibitions when Thurs. hours extend to 8pm.

DAHLEM

Staatliche Museen Preußischer Kulturbesitz, Dahlem, Arnimallee 23-27 and Lansstr. 8 (tel. 830 14 65), near the *Freie Universität.* U-Bahn #2: "Dahlem-Dorf." 7 globe-spanning museums in one enormous building, plus another across the street. Pick up a map at the entrance; the museums are laid out very strangely. Various connections among the wings make it impossible for them to charge admission to any of the museum except the Gemäldegalerie and the Museum für Volkskunde. Admission DM4, students DM2. The complex is open Tues.-Fri. 9am-5pm, Sat.-Sun. 10am-5pm.

Gemäldegalerie (Painting Gallery). One of Germany's most famous museums, and rightly so. It houses a stunning collection of Italian, German, Dutch, and Flemish masters. The world-class collection includes 26 Rembrandts (and *The Man with the Golden Helmet*, once incorrectly attributed to him), Bruegel (including *Netherlandish Proverbs*), Vermeer, Raphael, Titian, and Botticelli.

Skulpturen-Galerie (Sculpture Gallery), adjacent to the Painting Gallery. Mostly German statuary, with many gnarled, distraught-looking Gothic pieces, and others intended for churches. Worth a walk through.

Museum für Ostasiatische Kunst (East Asian Art). Mercifully empty of the blue-and-white porcelain you usually see in east Asian museums, this museum possesses a fabulous 17th-century Chinese throne with a representation of the Taoist paradise, as well as some exquisite Japanese screen-printing.

Museum für Islamische Kunst (Islamic Art). Probably the most international of the museums, it follows the culture of Islam around the world. Captivating tapestries hang from the ceiling to floor, but the illuminated manuscripts are probably most interesting.

Museum für Indische Kunst (Indian Art). One of the most extensive collections around, with art and artifacts from all of India and Southeast Asia.

Museum für Völkerkunde (Ethnography). Fascinating collections of tools, artifacts, musical instruments, weapons, and clothing from Africa, Polynesia, Central and South America, and Southeast Asia. The Polynesian exhibit climaxes with a giant display of ornately decorated boats, many of which you can climb into. In the African section, you can play the *baláfon* (xylophone).

Museum für Volkskünde (Folklore), Im Winkel 6/8 (tel. 839 01 01). A hop away from the main Dahlem complex, this museum is dedicated to artifacts of lower- and middle-class life over the past 400 years, from all over the world. The exhibit on 50s-80s pop culture is charming—never thought you'd see "Garbage Pail Kids" in a museum, did you? Same prices and opening hours as for Dahlem.

CHARLOTTENBURG

Schloß Charlottenburg, Spandauer Damm (tel. 32 09 11). U-Bahn #2: "Sophie-Charlotte-Platz" or bus #145. The castle's wide-flung wings hold several museums, set against the romantic *Schloßgarten*. The **Kleiner Orangerie** sports special exhibitions. Admission to the historic rooms of the *Schloß* costs DM8, students DM3 (see Sights, p. 415, for more on the *Schloß* and its grounds).

Ägyptisches Museum (Egyptian Museum), across Spandauer Damm from the castle. This stern Neoclassical building, a former barracks for the castle guard, houses a fascinating collection of ancient Egyptian art. The most popular item on display is the stunning 3300-year-old bust of **Queen Nefertiti** (1350 BC), thought to be the most beautiful representation of a woman in the world. Open Tues.-Fri. 9am-5pm, Sat.-Sun. 10am-5pm.

Sammlung Berggruen, on Schloßstr. (tel. 311 16 14), in an identical building across the building across the street from the Egyptian museum. An incredible collection of Picasso and other modernists, this newly-opened museum replaces the Antiquity Collection that was housed here until 1996. Open Tues.-Fri. 9am-5pm, Sat.-Sun. 10am-5pm.

Galerie der Romantik, in the palace's Neuer Flügel, holds the Prussian crown's dynamic collection of 19th-century art. The unquestioned show-stealers are works by early 19th-century Prussian artist Caspar David Friedrich, whose specialty was hypnotically beautiful, bleak landscapes: infinite, looming skies and seas with tiny human figures precariously placed in their midst. Admission DM4, students DM2. Open Tues.-Fri. 9am-5pm, Sat.-Sun. 10am-5pm.

TIERGARTEN

Tiergarten-Kulturforum, is a complex of museums at the eastern end of the Tiergarten park, near the Staatsbibliothek (see Sights, p. 417) and Potsdamer Platz. Bus #129 from the Ku'damm or S-Bahn #1 or 2 or U-Bahn #2: "Potsdamer Platz." All are open Tues.-Fri. 9am-5pm, Sat.-Sun. 10am-5pm. Admission same as other national museums except for the Musical Instrument museum (which is free).

Neue Nationalgalerie, Potsdamerstr. 50 (tel. 266 26 51). This sleek building, designed by Mies van der Rohe, now houses the entire 20th-century painting collection of the *Preußischer Kulturbesitz.* Brilliant works by Kokoschka, Kirchner, Beckmann, de Chirico, and more, plus a roomful of American abstractionists. The paintings are all on the underground level; upstairs, a sunlit exhibition floor hosts varied exhibits of design artifacts (a recent show traced various motifs in Calvin Klein's advertisements). Sometimes the permanent collection is stored away to make room for special exhibits, so you might want to call ahead.

Kunstgewerbemuseum (Museum of Applied Arts), Matthäikirchplatz 10 (tel. 26 66 29 02). Displays ceramics, porcelain, and various handicrafts in wood, silver, and gold from the Middle Ages to the present.

Musikinstrumenten Museum (Museum of Musical Instruments), Tiergartenstr. 1 (tel. 25 48 10). Fittingly next door to the Philharmonic, this museum is a must for anyone even remotely interested in classical music. Musical instruments from every period, from 16th-century virginals to player pianos. You can hear recordings of the period instruments being played. Tours Sat. at 11am (DM3).

Kunstbibliothek/Kupferstichkabinett, on Matthaikirchplatz (tel. 266 20 02). A stellar collection of lithographs and drawings by Renaissance masters, including many Dürers and Botticelli's fantastic illustrations for the *Divine Comedy.*

ELSEWHERE IN WESTERN BERLIN

Martin-Gropius Bau, Stresemannstr. 110 (tel. 25 48 60). S- or U-Bahn: "Anhalter Bahnhof." Walter Gropius' uncle Martin designed this neo-Renaissance wedding cake as a museum for and tribute to the industrial arts. The building alone is worth the price of admission (DM6, students DM3). Open Tues.-Sun. 10am-8pm.

Berlinische Galerie, on the second floor, is devoted to rotating exhibits of contemporary German art, much of it focused on the city and its inhabitants. Lots of photography and architecture.

Jüdisches Museum, on the third floor, hosts extremely varied exhibits of painting, sculpture, and design; the only common thread is that the art has something to do with Jews in Germany.

Topographie des Terrors, in back of the Martin-Gropius-Bau, is built on top of the ruins of a Gestapo kitchen; the area used to be the site of the notorious Gestapo headquarters at Prinz-Albrecht-Str. (now Nieder-kirchnerstr.). Very comprehensive exhibit (in German) details the Nazi party's rise to power and the atrocities that occurred during the war. English guides are available (DM2), but you don't need to understand the captions to be moved by the photographs. Free. Open Tues.-Sun. 10am-6pm. The adjacent **Prinz-Albrecht-Gelände,** a deserted wasteland near the site of the Wall, contains the ruins of most of the Gestapo buildings. Signs describe what once took place. Free. Open during daylight hours.

Bauhaus Archiv-Museum für Gestaltung, Klingenhöferstr. 13-14 (tel. 254 00 20). Bus #129 (from Ku'damm): "Lützowplatz" or U-Bahn #1, 2, or 4: "Nollendorfpl." A building designed by Bauhaus founder Walter Gropius that houses a permanent exhibit devoted to the development of Bauhaus. The temporary exhibits are based around questions of art theory. *The* place in Berlin to pick up design students. Admission DM4, students DM2. Free on Mon. Open Wed.-Mon. 10am-5pm.

Käthe-Kollwitz-Museum, Fasanenstr. 24 (tel. 882 52 10). U-Bahn 15: "Uhlandstr." A marvelous collection of works by one of Germany's most prominent modern artists, much of it focusing on the themes of war and poverty. Admission DM6, students DM3. Free on Mon. Open Wed.-Mon. 11am-6pm.

Brücke Museum, Bussardsteig 9 (tel. 831 20 29). From Bahnhof Zoo take bus #249 a few stops to "Güntzelstr.," then pick up bus #115 to "Clayallee/Pücklerstr." (13 stops; 30min.). Along with the *Neue Nationalgalerie,* this is *the* Expressionist museum in Berlin, with wildly colorful works by the German Expressionist school *die Brücke,* a group of young artists who exploded on the Berlin/Dresden art scene (1909-1913). Admission DM4, students DM2. Open Wed.-Mon.11am-5pm.

Museum für Verkehr und Technik (Transport and Technology), Trebbinerstr. 9 (tel. 25 48 40). U-Bahn #1: "Gleisdreieck" or "Möckernbrücke." Souvenirs from *Autobahn* speed-devils, medieval printing presses, and trains that run on time. World War I fighting planes hang from the ceiling. Combined admission to a yard of antique locomotives down the street. Admission DM4, students DM2. Open Tues.-Fri. 9am-5:30pm, Sat.-Sun. 10am-6pm.

Postmuseum Berlin, An der Urania 15 (tel. 21 71 17 17). Bus #109 or 219 from Bahnhof Zoo or a short walk from U-Bahn #1 or 4: "Nollendorfplatz." Exposes the Post's growth with lots of historic video and techno-fun—play with the toy mail train, light up a historic mail-route map. Also check out the competing Postal Museum in Eastern Berlin. Free. Open Mon.-Thurs. 9am-5pm, Sat.-Sun. 10am-5pm.

Zucker-Museum, Amrumerstr. 32 (tel. 31 42 75 74), U-Bahn #9: "Amrumerstr." A cultural history of sugar and the political implications of the development of the sugar industry. Yum. Admission DM4, students DM2. Open Mon.-Wed. 11am-5pm, Sun. 11am-6pm.

ELSEWHERE IN EASTERN BERLIN

Otto Nagel Haus, Märkisches Ufer 16-18 (tel. 279 14 24). U-Bahn: "Märkisches Museum." A collection of art exploring social themes, taken from the *Preußischer Kulturbesitz* collection. Includes works by Käthe Kollwitz and an exciting collection of photomontage by the famous anti-Nazi satirist John Heartfield. Admission DM4, students and seniors DM2. Open Tues.-Sun. 9am-5pm.

Deutsches Historisches Museum (Museum of German History), Unter den Linden 2, in the former arsenal (tel. 21 50 20; fax 21 50 24 02). Across from the *Museum-sinsel.* Once a paean to the advent of socialism, now the site of provocative multimedia exhibitions on recent German history. The *Zeughaus-Kino* on the side shows documentaries and films Thurs.-Sun. at 4, 6:15, and 8:30pm. The café (open daily at 10am) sports a nice view of the river. Open Thurs.-Tues. 10am-6pm. Free. Tours Sat.-Mon. at 3pm and by appointment (tel. 21 50 23 78). English- language tours can be arranged, but all exhibits are in German.

Friedrichswerdersche Kirche, Werderstr. (tel. 208 13 23), south of Unter den Linden. U-Bahn #2: "Hausvogteiplatz." 19th-century French and German sculpture in a unique church built by Schinkel. Admission DM4, students DM2. Free with SMPK *Tageskarte.* Open Tues.-Sun. 9am-5pm.

Postmuseum, Leipziger Str. 16 (tel. 22 85 47 00). U-Bahn #2 or 6: "Stadtmitte." Like the Western Postmuseum (see above), it looks backward in mail history, though with less glitz. A fascinating look at how the GDR and other regimes have stamped their image into a corner of everyday life. Admission DM1, students DM0.50. Open Tues.-Sat. 10am-6pm.

Friseurmuseum, Husemannstr. 8 (tel. 442 25 81). U-Bahn #2: "Eberswalder Str." One of the city's strangest and most appealing museums. Contains exhibits on the history of shaving, wigs, and hairstyles. This is the dawning of the age … Admission DM2, students and seniors DM1. Open Tues.-Thurs. and Sat.-Sun. 10am-5pm.

■ Entertainment

Berlin has one of the most vibrant cultural scenes in the world. Exhibitions, concerts, plays, and dance abound, although cutbacks in government subsidies have recently resulted in slightly fewer offerings and higher prices. Nonetheless, Germany still has one of the most generously subsidized art scenes, and tickets are usually reasonable, especially with student discounts. Varied festivals celebrating everything from Chinese film to West African music spice up the regular offerings.

You can reserve tickets by calling the box office directly. Always ask about student discounts; most theaters and concert halls offer them up to 50%, but only if you buy at the *Abendkasse* (night box office), which generally opens one hour before a performance begins. There are numerous other ticket outlets which will charge you a commission and do not offer student discounts. Remember that while most theaters do accept credit cards, most other ticket outlets don't. The main box offices are **Theaterkasse Centrum,** Meinekestr. 25 (tel. 882 76 11; fax 881 33 32), with branches in all Karstadt department stores and in KaDeWe, Tauentzienstr. 21 (tel. 218 10 28; all charge a small commission and are open Sept.-June Mon.-Fri. 9am-noon and 3-5:30pm, Sat. 9am-3:30pm; Oct.-May Mon.-Fri. 9am-3pm). **Theaterkasse Zehlendorf,**

Teltower Damm 22 (tel. 801 16 52 or 801 30 56), also sells Berlin tickets (open Mon.-Fri. 7:30am-6pm, Sat. 8am-1pm). For last-minute 50%-off tickets contact **Hekticket,** Rathausstr. 1 (tel. 242 67 09), by the Alexanderplatz S-Bahn station. Shows to which tickets are available are posted in the window (open Mon.-Sat. 4-8pm). Unfortunately, major theaters and operas close from mid-July to late August.

CONCERTS, OPERA, AND DANCE

Berlin reaches its musical zenith during the fabulous **Berliner Festwochen,** lasting almost the entire month of September and drawing the world's best orchestras and soloists, and the **Berliner Jazztage** in November. For more information on these events (and tickets, which sell out months in advance), write to Berliner Festspiele, Budapesterstr. 48-50, 10787 Berlin (tel. 25 48 92 50; open daily noon-6pm). In mid-July, **Bachtage** (Bach Days) offer an intense week of classical music; every Saturday night in August, **Sommer Festspiele** turns the Ku'damm into a multi-faceted concert hall with punk, steel-drum and folk groups competing for attention.

In the monthly pamphlets *Kultur in Berlin, Berliner Programm,* and *Metropolis,* as well as in the biweekly magazines *Tip* and *Zitty,* you'll find notices of concerts in the courtyard of the old Arsenal, on the **Schloßinsel Köpenick** (castle island), or in the parks. The programs for many theaters and opera houses are additionally listed on huge posters in U-Bahn stations. Tickets for the *Philharmonie* and the *Oper* are often impossible to acquire through conventional channels, unless you write months in advance. Try standing out in front before performances with a small sign saying, *"Suche Karte"* (I seek a ticket); invariably a few people will try to unload tickets at the last moment. Remember that concert halls and operas close for a few weeks during the summer months.

Berliner Philharmonisches Orchester, Matthäikirchstr. 1 (tel. 261 43 83 or 25 48 81 32). Take us #129 from Ku'damm: "Potsdamer Str." and walk 3 blocks north or S-Bahn #2: "Potsdamer Platz." The big yellow building, designed by Scharoun in 1963, is as acoustically perfect within as it is unconventional without. The *Berliner Philharmoniker,* led for decades by the late Herbert von Karajan and currently under the baton of Claudio Abbados, is perhaps the finest orchestra in the world. It is well-nigh impossible to get a seat; check an hour before concert time or write far in advance. The *Philharmonie* is often closed during the summer months. Tickets around DM30. Box office open Mon.-Fri. 3:30-6pm, Sat.-Sun. and holidays 11am-2pm. Tickets cannot be ordered by phone. Write to: Kartenbüro, Berliner Philharmonisches Orchester, Matthäikirchstr.1, 10785 Berlin.

Konzerthaus (Schauspielhaus Gendarmenmarkt), Gendarmenmarkt (tel. 20 90 21 57). *Großer Konzertsaal* and *Kammermusiksaal.* U-Bahn #2 or 6: "Stadtmitte."

The Love Parade

Berlin's annual Love Parade is a three-day fest of crazy clothes, multi-colored hair, general chaos, and, of course, techno. What began in 1989 as a techno Woodstock with 150 participants has expanded exponentially; every year, people from the entire continent descend upon Berlin and overwhelm the city's accommodations to dance the entire weekend. The "parade" takes place on Saturday afternoon in the second weekend in July and involves a snail-paced procession of tractor-trailers loaded with blasting speakers and people dancing on top. In past years, the trucks have crept down the Ku'damm. But because of mounting attendance, the 1996 parade was moved to the more spacious Str. des 17. Juni, where it extended from the Siegessäule all the way to the Brandenburg Gate. The gala is thinly disguised as a political event—the motto for 1996 was "We are one family"—but it's really an excuse for Germans to celebrate their love affair with techno. As *Zitty* explains, "Anyone who thinks about the Love Parade too much is not in the right spirit." Attendance at this year's Love Parade reached 750,000, as people from all over the world flocked to the mecca of techno.

The opulent home of the Berlin Symphony Orchestra, *if* it continues to survive cuts in subsidies. Call for performance info. Last-minute tickets are somewhat easier to come by. Box office open Mon.-Fri. 10am-6pm. Chamber music throughout the summer, but the orchestra goes on vacation late July-mid-Aug.

Deutsche Oper Berlin, Bismarckstr. 34-37 (tel. 341 02 49 for info, 343 84 01 for tickets). U-Bahn #2 or 12: "Deutsche Oper." Berlin's best opera, featuring newly-commissioned works as well as all the German and Italian classics. Student discounts of up to 50% (depending on the price of the ticket) 1 week or less before performance. Tickets DM15-140. Main box office open Mon.-Sat. 11am-1hr. before performance, Sun. 10am-2pm. Evening tickets available starting 1hr. before performance. For tickets, write to Deutsche Oper Berlin, Richard-Wagner-Str. 10, 10585 Berlin or fax 343 84 55. For program info, write to Deutsche Oper Berlin, Bismarckstr. 35, 10627 Berlin. Closed July-mid-Aug.

Deutsche Staatsoper, Unter den Linden 7 (tel. 20 35 44 94; fax 20 35 44 83). U-Bahn #6: "Friedrichstr." or bus #157. East Berlin's leading opera company led by Daniel Barenboim (also the conductor of the Chicago Symphony Orchestra). Ballet and classical music, too, although the orchestra fluctuates between good and mediocre. Tickets DM18-35. Box office open Mon.-Sat. noon-6pm, Sun. 2-6pm.

Komische Oper, Behrenstr. 55-57, 10117 (tel. 20 26 03 60, fax 20 26 02 60). U-Bahn #6: "Französischestr." Its reputation was built by famous post-war director Felsenstein, but in recent years zany artistic director Harry Kupfer has revitalized the opera with clever stagings of the classics. Program ranges from Mozart to Gilbert and Sullivan. Tickets DM10-20. 50% student discounts almost always available. Box office open Mon.-Sat. 11am-7pm, Sun. 1pm-1½hr. before performances.

Tanzfabrik, Möckernstr. 68 (tel. 786 58 61). U-Bahn #6: "Mehringdamm." Down the alley to your left, up 3 flights of stairs. Modern dance performances and a center for dance workshops. Box office open Mon.-Thurs. 10am-1pm and 5-8pm. Tickets DM15. Occasional weekend performances start at 8 or 8:30pm. Often when the main theaters close down for the summer, dance companies take up residence inside. Check posters at the *Komische Oper* and the *Staatsoper.*

THEATER

Theater listings are available in the monthly pamphlets *Kultur in Berlin, Berlin Programm,* as well as *Ti,* and *Zitty.* They are also posted in most U-Bahn stations; look for the yellow posters. In addition to the best German-language theater in the country (or in the world), Berlin also has a lively English-language theater scene. *Metropolis* lists English-language theater separately from German, or look for theater listings in *Tip* or *Zitty* that say *"in englischer Sprache"* ("in English") next to them. There are a number of privately-run theater companies called "off-theaters," which feature occasional English-language plays. As with concert halls, look out for summer closings *(Theaterferien);* see the introduction to Entertainment, p. 425, for box office information. There is an international **Theater Festival** in May.

Deutsches Theater, Schumannstr. 13a (tel. 287 12 25). U-Bahn #6 or S-Bahn #1-3, 5, 6, or 9: "Friedrichstr." The word has finally spread to Western Berlin: this is the best theater in the country. Max Reinhardt made it great 100 years ago, and it now has innovative productions of the classics and newer works (especially strong on Heiner Müller). Latter-day director Dieter Mann, a virtual deity to theater-lovers in the GDR, stepped down in 1991. The repertory runs from Büchner to Mamet to Ibsen. The **Kammerspiel des Deutschen Theaters** (tel. 287 12 26) has smaller and often controversial productions. Tickets DM15-40, but 50% student discount often available. Box office open Mon.-Sat. noon-6pm, Sun. 3-6pm.

Hebbel Theater, Stresemannstr. 29 (tel. 251 01 44). U-Bahn #1 or 6: "Hallesches Tor." The most *avant* of the *avant-garde* theaters in Berlin, drawing cutting-edge talent from all over the world. Watch out for tomato-throwers in the audience.

Freie Volksbühne/Musical Theater Berlin, Schaperstr. 24 (tel. 88 42 08 84). U-Bahn #2 or 9: "Spichernstr." *Avant-garde* musical theater, with many English-language productions imported from Britain. You won't find *Katzen* or *Der Phantom* *der Oper* here. Tickets DM45-135, students 50% off. Box office open Mon. noon-6:30pm, Tues.-Fri. noon-8pm, Sat. noon-8:30pm, Sun. noon-6:30pm.

Friends of Italian Opera, Fidicinstr. 40 (tel. 691 12 11). U-Bahn #6: "Platz der Luft-brücke." First of all, this ain't no opera; the moniker is a joking reference to the great flick *Some Like It Hot.* What it is, is Berlin's leading English-language theater, home to the renowned Berliner Grundtheater company as well as a grab-bag of English-language performances. The locale is neat too—the theater is hidden in a *Hinterhof* (courtyard) in Kreuzberg.

Berliner Ensemble, Bertolt-Brecht-Platz 1 (tel. 238 31 60). U-Bahn #6 or S-Bahn #2, 3, 5, 6 or 9: "Friedrichstr." The famous theater established by Brecht has recently been undergoing a renaissance. Hip repertoire, including Heiner Müller, and some young American playwrights, as well as Brecht's own plays. Also some premieres. Tickets DM12-40. Box office open Mon.-Sat. 11am-6pm, Sun. 3-6pm.

Maxim Gorki Theater, Unter Den Linden 2 (tel. 2 22 10 or 20 22 11 15). U-Bahn #6 or S-Bahn #2, 3, 5, 6 or 9: "Friedrichstr." Excellent contemporary theater with wonderfully varied repertoire—everything from Molière to Beckett. Tickets DM5-25. Box office open Mon.-Sat. 1-6:30pm, Sun. 3-6:30pm.

Die Distel ("The Thistle"), Friedrichstr. 101 (tel. 200 47 04). U-Bahn #6 or S-Bahn #2, 3, 5, 6 or 9: "Friedrichstr." During GDR days, this was a renowned cabaret for political satire—but reunification has taken the bite out of some of the jokes. Box office open Mon.-Fri. noon-2pm and 3-6pm, Sat.-Sun. 2hr. before performance.

FILM

Berlin is a movie-lovin' town; it hosts an international **Film Festival** (late Feb.-March), and on any night in Berlin, you can choose from 100 different films, many in the original languages. (*"O.F."* next to a movie listing means original version. *"O.m.U."* means original version with German subtitles. Everything else is dubbed.) Check *Tip, Zitty, Metropolis,* or subway posters. Numerous city cineplexes offer the chance to see dubbed Hollywood blockbusters. **Zoo-Palast,** at Hardenbergstr. 29a (tel. 25 41 47 89), near Bahnhof Zoo, is one of the biggest and most popular, with upwards of a dozen screens. Tuesdays and Wednesdays are *"Kinotage"* at most movie theaters, with prices reduced a few marks. Bring a student ID.

Freiluftkino. In summer, Berliners take to open-air film festivals with screenings in parks. 2 venues show films in English: **Freiluftkino Hasenheide** at the Sputnik in Hasenheide Park shows anything from silent films to *Get Shorty.* Take U-Bahn #7 or 8: "Hermannplatz." **Freiluftkino Kreuzberg,** Mariannenplatz 2 (tel. 238 64 88), gets avant-garde contemporary with films like *Smoke* and *Pulp Fiction.* Take U-Bahn #1 or 8: "Kottbusser Tor." Admission DM10 for both theatres.

Eiszeit, Zeughofstr. 20 (tel. 611 60 16). U-Bahn #1: "Görlitzer Bahnhof." Shows Hollywood's slightly alternative products (e.g. *Crumb*) in English, as well as more independent films and documentaries.

fsk am Oraienplatz, segitzdamm 2 (tel. 614 24 64). u-bahn #1 or 8: "kottbuser tor." this wacky lower-case moviehouse with a flair for self-approbating concretism seeks to void films of meaning by awkwardly juxtaposing incongruous films in double features. watch primarily original-language screenings of *I Know the Way to the Hofbrauhaus* followed by *From Dusk Till Dawn.*

Filmtheater Babylon-Mitte, Rosa-Luxemburgstr. 30 (tel. 242 50 76). U-Bahn #2: "Rosa-Luxemburg Platz." Shows classics and art films often in their original language. Admission DM8, students DM7. The Kreuzberg **Babylon,** Dresdener Str. 126 (tel. 614 63 16). U-Bahn #1 or 8: "Kottbuser Tor." Plays off-beat comedies (such as *Flirting with Disaster*) and, yes, Tarantino.

Blow Up, Immanuelkirchstr. 14 (tel. 442 86 62). S-Bahn #8 or 10: "Greifswalder Str." Always has something entertaining going on—see *Unzipped* followed by a fashion show or catch them when they're showing the eternally cool Bogey flicks. They always screen something in English.

■ Nightlife

Berlin's nightlife is absolute madness, a teeming cauldron of debauchery that runs around the clock and threatens to inflict coronaries upon the faint of heart. Bars, clubs, and cafés typically jam until at least 3am and often stay open until daylight; during the weekends, you can literally dance non-stop from Friday night until Monday morning. Take advantage of the night buses from the U-Bahn stations and **U-Bahn 12,** which runs all night on Fridays and Saturdays. The best sources of information about bands and dance venues are the bi-weekly magazines *Tip* (DM4) and the superior *Zitty* (DM3.60), available at all kiosks and newsagents, and the free *030* that's distributed in many bars.

In western Berlin, the best places to look are the **Savignyplatz, Schöneberg, Wilmersdorf,** and particularly **Kreuzberg.** The Ku'damm is best avoided at night, unless you enjoy fraternizing with drunken businessmen, middle aged, unenlightened tourists, and dirty old men who drool to the sight of strip shows. The north is a bit more inviting to the youthful: the middle point is Savignyplatz and it includes Café Hardenberg and the Schwarzes Café (see Food, p. 407), both excellent for a drink at night. South of the Ku'damm, the area between Uhlandstr. and Olivaer Platz is littered with crowded late-night cafés. The main focus of Schöneberg nightlife is around **Nollendorfplatz,** encompassing café-*Kneipen* on Winterfeldplatz and Goltzstr., and more bars on Kleiststr. Pushing up against the remains of the Wall in the western section of the city is the center of the **Kreuzberg** *Szene.* The scene in East Kreuzberg is wild; in the midst of the heavily-Turkish neighborhoods, along Oranienstr. between U-Bahn #1: "Kottbusser Tor" and U-Bahn #1: "Görlitzer Bahnhof," roost a menagerie of radically alternative clubs that range from laid-back to breathtakingly salacious. The area is not well-lit at night and can be somewhat unsafe for those traveling alone.

Despite Kreuzberg's funky appeal, the center of gravity of the *Szene* is shifting inexorably eastward. The east, in a word, is hot: low rents and a fascinating new "alternative" population give it an edge in nurturing new spots that the expensive west can't match. Its cafés and bars have a grittier, more vital (albeit transient) feel and attract an exciting mixture of people in makeshift clubs located in squatter houses, many of which are here today, gone tomorrow—just wander along the streets with friends and listen for the music. Some of the more interesting bars abound in the **Scheunenviertel,** especially along Oranienburgerstr. (not to be confused with Kreuzberg's Oranienstr.) near the old synagogue. The **Prenzlauer Berg** area boasts some fun, interesting places along Schönhauser Allee, Kastanienallee, and especially by the gritty, seedy, bombed-out clubs around the Water Tower. Streetlights are sparse on many of the residential streets of the east, making a midnight club crawl a little creepy. East Berlin is still safer than most American cities, but it's wise to avoid empty alleys and parks and to travel in groups when possible.

If at all possible, try to hit Berlin during the **Love Parade,** usually held in the second weekend of July (see The Love Parade, p. 426). It's an experience that you'll never forget unless you ingest or consume something that makes you. In that vein, it's also worth mentioning that Berlin has de-criminalized marijuana possession of up to eight grams. Smoking in public, however, has not been officially legalized. *Let's Go* does not recommend puffing clouds of hash smoke into the face of police officers.

BARS AND CLUBS

This is the section of *Let's Go: Germany* where we dance.

Savigny- and Steinplatz Area

Quasimodo, Kantstr. 12a (tel. 312 80 86). S-Bahn #3, 5, 7, or 9: "Savignyplatz." This unassuming basement pub with attached *Biergarten* is one of Berlin's most crucial jazz venues, drawing in big names and lively crowds. Superfly swingers John Abercrombie, Defunkt, and Betty Carter jammed here recently. It's totally dead until 10pm when the shows begin. (An extraordinary fact: the men's bathroom here is lit by fluorescent "black light" bulbs. Why is this extraordinary? Because **human**

urine glows under fluorescent light.) Cover depends on performance, ranging from free to DM30. Concert tickets available from 5pm or at Kant Kasse ticket service (tel. 313 45 54; fax 312 64 40). Open daily from 8pm.

Big Eden, Kurfürstendamm 202 (tel. 882 61 20). U-Bahn #15 to "Uhlandstr." It's no paradise, but the magnitude of its neon and mirrors will leave you dizzy. Funked-out post-Saturday Night Fever crowd shakes to disco, house, and techno. Open Sun.-Thurs. 8pm-4am, Fri.-Sat. 8pm-6am. Cover can run as much as DM15, but if you show up before 10pm (Sun.-Thurs.), they won't charge a *Pfennig*.

Schöneberg

Metropol, Nollendorfplatz 5 (tel. 216 41 22). U-Bahn #1 or 4: "Nollendorfplatz," or night buses N19, N29, or N85. The architecture of Metropol, long one of Berlin's most famous discos, is stunningly reminiscent of The Tower of Babel in Fritz Lang's *Metropolis* (absent are the 50,000 baldies Lang hired for the scene); fractile lights illuminate the dance floor in the loft, where lots of 16-25-year-olds groove. Sometimes big-time concerts take place in between dances. Cover DM15, DM10 if you show up 9-10pm. Open Fri. 9pm-6am, Sat. 9pm-8am. Concert ticket prices vary; call 216 27 87 for info. and prices (Mon.-Fri. 11am-3pm and 3:30-6pm).

M, Goltzstr. 33 (tel. 216 70 92). U-Bahn #7: "Eisenacherstr." One of the more interesting Schöneberg bars, stark and neon-lit, and slightly wild late at night. Black is eternally in. "Karlheinz, you are beautiful and angular." Open daily 8am-2am.

Makao, Goltzstr., just down the street from M. U-Bahn #7: "Eisenacherstr." An unassuming and peaceful little café that serves its customers as well as any joint in Amsterdam.

Kreuzberg

SO 36, Oranienstr. 190 (tel. 615 65 81). U-Bahn #1: "Görlitzer Bahnhof." A mishmash of wild oeuvres: Mon. serves up the funky techno Electric Ballroom, Wed. is gay and lesbian disco night, Thurs. provides ska, hardcore, and metal, Fri. and Sat. are parties that get wild. The Toasters grooved here. The name celebrates the prewar postal code for what is now the funkiest part of Kreuzberg; this venue sends 90210 through the looking glass. Open Sun. after 7pm, Mon. after 11pm, Wed.-Thurs. after 10pm, Fri.-Sat. 'til whenever they damn well feel like it.

Schnabel Bar, Oranienstr. 31 (tel. 615 85 34). U-Bahn #1 or 8: "Kottbuser Tor." Raucously upbeat swingers shake dat booty non-stop to jungle music. Open 24hr., but the most heated dance scene runs midnight-6am. A *Let's Go* favorite, if only because it features *The Voodoo Lounge* on Thurs.

KitKat Club, Glogauer Str. 2 (tel. 611 38 33). Lascivious? The word loses its meaning here. Erotic? This implies innuendo, a quality which has no place on this dance floor. Sex. SEXSEXSEX. People with varying degrees of clothing, some copulating, some just digging the cool trance music in the jaw-dropping, fluorescent interior, leave their inhibitions outside. Open Tues.-Sun. after 11pm. Cover DM10. The Sun. after-hours party (8am-7pm) is popular, free, and more fully clothed. On Thurs., the club cross-dresses as the **Crisco Club** for some serious homoerotics (men only!). Not for the faint of heart.

Ex, Mehringhof, Gneisenaustr. 2a (tel. 693 58 00). U-Bahn #6 or 7: "Mehringdamm" or night bus N19. A *Kneipe* in an old Berliner courtyard run by a famed collective and hangout for the people from the alternative scene. Anarcho-communists who hate hierarchies proffer up cheap drinks and Indian food amid a funk and jazz backdrop well-suited for chillin'. Nascent bands rattle the little stage on weekends. Punk/hip-hop disco on Sat. Open daily noon-3am, in winter noon-2am.

Flammende Herzen, Oranienstr. 170 (tel. 615 71 02). U-Bahn #1 or 8: "Kottbusser Tor." Angry. Very angry. Compare nose, ear, and body rings, or listen to English-language punk inside. The decor's a trip: hot orange-and-black walls with huge mirrors and surreal constructions over the bar. Open daily from 11am.

Wild at Heart, Wienerstr. 20 (tel. 611 70 10). U-Bahn #1: "Görlitzer Bahnhof." Hard-core and punk with savvy decor smattered with tweaked little witches, gnomes, angels, and kitsch in spades. Local live bands tear it up on Wed., Fri., and Sat. nights. Open daily after 8pm.

Milchbar, Manteuffelstr. 40-41 (tel. 611 70 06). U-Bahn #1 or 12: "Görlitzer Bahnhof." For years a staple of the punky crowd, the Milchbar has a raucous, loud, smoky, aggressively anti-techno atmosphere. The interior is strikingly aquatic, more evocative of your Junior Prom than of the hardcore scene that unfolds here. Open daily 8pm-4am, Fri.-Sat. 8pm-6am.

Oranienburgerstraße-Mitte

Tacheles, Oranienburgerstr. 53-56 (tel. 282 61 85). U-Bahn #6: "Oranienburger Tor." This bombed-out ex-department store which serves as a copacetic congregating point for alternative-type folks is likely to be the greatest source of artistic pretense in all of Berlin. The art commune that operates Tacheles has decorated the interior from top to bottom with graffiti, collages, and exhibits. Don't even think about taking pictures unless you don't mind being assaulted by some tortured genius yelling about art for art's sake. Bands, films, raves, and three bars serve up nightly entertainment. The sculpture garden in the back is like a playground for the *Exorcist.* If you're unimpressed by the art, sit in the garden, where you may be able to expand your mind and reconsider. Open 24hr.

Tresor, Leipziger Str. 8 (tel. 229 23 46). U-Bahn #2: "Mohrenstr." One of the most rocking techno venues in Berlin, packed from wall to wall with enthusiastic, screaming ravers. 2 dance floors and an outdoor garden get hot and sweaty. Open Wed., Fri., and Sat. after 11pm. Cover DM5 on Wed., DM12 on weekends. The garden stays open all day Sat. with free entry after 7am.

E-Werk, Wilhelmstr. 43 (tel. 252 20 12). U-Bahn #1: "Mohrenstr." The renowned center of all things techno in Berlin. Psychedelic interior sports industrial machinery and blue-and-red strobe lights that throw you into the world of 3-D. They search those trying to artificially enhance the experience before entry. Techno and British house all night long on weekends. Cover DM16 on Fri., DM20 on Sat. Open Fri.-Sat. from midnight.

Café Silberstein, Oranienburger Str. 27 (tel. 281 20 95). S-Bahn #1 or 2: "Oranienburger Str." Post-everything art decor offers sushi, ambient music, and a hipper than hip clientele. Dieter, his Sprockets, and even his little pet ("touch my monkey! love him!") come here. Open daily 4pm-4am.

Delicious Doughnuts Research, Rosenthaler Str. 9 (tel. 283 30 21). U-Bahn #8: "Weinmeisterstr." A contemplative Homer Simpson muttering something about "Hu-uh-uh-uh…delicious doughnuts" sticks to the café in front, bypassing the enthusiastic acid jazz scene in the back room. Café open daily, from noon.

Prenzlauer Berg

Franz-Klub, Schönhauser Allee 36-39 (tel. 442 82 03). U-Bahn #2: "Eberswalder Str". The east's most reliable rock venue—a favorite among Prenzlauer Bergers and *Wessies* in the know. Cover varies. Live music every damn night of the year under the gaze of a big sphinx, including world music acts, local ska bands, blues, and rock. Bands usually start around 10pm, followed by dance and a DJ until late.

Knaack-Klub, Greifswalderstr. 224 (tel. 442 70 60). S-Bahn #8 or 10: "Ernst-Thälmann Park." Smaller and more grungy than Franz. In a perpetual state of musical identity crisis, this club waffles between indy rock, disco, techno, and karaoke. Frequent live shows. Cover around DM4.

Café-Kunstfabrik Schlot, Kastanienallee 29 (tel. 448 21 60). This respite from the "in-your-face" Berlin night scene serves up jazz Fri.-Mon. and cabaret Tues.-Thurs. Free for Mon. jam session; DM5 all other days. Open 7pm-4am.

Elsewhere in Eastern Berlin

Insel der Jugend, Alt Treptow 6 (tel. 534 88 51). S-Bahn #8,9. or 10: "Treptower Park," then bus 265 or N65: "Alt-Treptow." The name means "island of youth," and is indicative of the club's location on an island in the middle of the park. 3 fiercely decorated floors of dancing have the feel of a fishbowl with fluorescent silver foil, and netting all over the place. Very cool. Top 2 floors spin reggae, hip-hop, ska, and house (sometimes all at once), while the frantic techno scene in the basement claims the casualties of the upper floors. Hipsters chill in the café during the day and indulge in occasional John Woo and Cheech and Chong classics. An outdoor patio overlooking the trees and river serves as a peaceful venue for the locals to roll mad joints. Café open daily 2-9pm. Club open after 9pm on Thurs., after 10pm on Fri., after 11pm on Sat. Cover for club DM5-15.

Die Halle, An der Industriebahn 12-16 (tel. 467 42 91). S-Bahn #8 or 10: "Prenzlauer Allee," then bus #156 to "Gehringstr./An der Industriebahn." Berlin's hard core punk scene moshes it up in this somewhat spooky former tractor factory *way* out in the Eastern suburb of Weissensee (but not far from Prenzlauer Berg).

■ Gay and Lesbian Berlin

Gay and lesbian life in Berlin is out, integrated, and in a word, FABulous. Traditionally, the social nexus of gay and lesbian life has centered around the **Nollendorfplatz,** the so-called "Pink Village." Christopher Isherwood lived at Nollendorfstr. 17 while writing his collection of stories *Goodbye to Berlin,* later adapted as the Broadway musical *Cabaret.* A marble pink triangle plaque outside the Nollendorfplatz U-Bahn station reads: "Beaten to death; abandoned to death," and remembers the thousands of gays and lesbians deported to concentration camps from the station.

The both demure and wild history of homosexuality comes out at the **Schwules Museum,** Mehringdamm 61 (tel. 693 11 72; open Wed.-Sun. 2-6pm; admission DM7, students DM4). **Spinnobden-Lesbenarchiv,** Anklamer Str. 38 (tel. 448 58 48), tends towards culturally hip lesbian offerings, with exhibits, films, and all kinds of information about current lesbian life (open Wed. and Fri. 1-8pm). Take U-Bahn #8: "Bernauer Str." **Lesbenberatung,** Kulmer Str. 20a (tel. 215 20 00), offers a library, movie viewings, and counseling on lesbian issues (open Mon.-Wed. 4-8pm). Take U-Bahn #7: "Kleistpark" The gay info center **Mann-o-Meter,** Motzstr. 5 (tel 216 80 08), off Nollendorfplatz, dispenses everything from K-Y jelly to posters for political activities. They have pamphlets and a notice board with listings of apartments and other accommodations and a café in back (open Mon.-Sat. 3-11pm, Sun. 3-9pm).

The **Prinz Eisenherz** bookstore, Bleibtreustr. 52 (tel. 313 99 36), has lots of information and books, many in English (open Mon.-Wed. and Fri. 10am-6:30pm, Thurs. 10am-8:30pm, Sat. 10am-2pm). The travel guide *Berlin von Hinten* (Berlin from Behind) costs DM19.80, but details gay life in Berlin extensively in English and German. The free magazine *Siegessäule* details gay events for the month and is available in gay bars and bookstores. **Lilith Frauenbuchladen,** Knesebeckstr. 86 (tel. 312 31 02), is a women's bookstore with a focus on lesbian issues (open Mon.-Fri. 10am-6:30pm, Sat. 10am-2pm). **Marga Schoeller Bücherstube,** Knesebeckstr. 33 (tel. 881 11 22), offers women's issue books in English. *Blatt Gold* (DM5 from women's bookstores and some natural food stores) has information and dates for women on a monthly basis. Many of the *Frauencafés* listed are not exclusively lesbian, but offer an all-woman setting. Some do have "mixed" nights or days. Berlin's queer population ecstatically celebrates its **Christopher Street Day** Parade in the last weekend of June with parades, floats, and wild parties. Have fun. Berlin is an open city.

Rose's, Oranienstr. 182, U-Bahn #1 or 8: "Kottbusser Tor." One of the most popular gay and lesbian bars in Berlin, and deservedly so. The atmosphere celebrates kitsch, glitter, and Madonna, while the drinks are a delight to order from the bartenders, who are more flamboyant than RuPaul. Open daily from 9:30pm.

Café Anal, Muskauerstr. 15 (tel. 618 70 64). U-Bahn #1: "Görlitzer Bahnhof." Spirited alternative gay and lesbian bar in east Kreuzberg. The decor hovers between Salvador Dalí and Pee-Wee's Playhouse: shiny gold ceiling, stuffed-pumpkin light fixtures, plump multi-colored cushions in corner nooks, seashell-shaped canopy. Mondays women only. Open Mon.-Sat. from 5pm, Sun. from 3pm.

Drama, Oranienstr. 169 (tel. 614 53 56). U-Bahn #1 or 8: "Kottbusser Tor." Sensual interior of red and black drapes attracts a gay/lesbian/mixed 20-something crowd that delights in dancing to house and funkadelic. Open Sun.-Thurs. 9pm-3am, Fri.-Sat. 9pm-5am.

90°, Dennewitzstr. 37 (tel. 262 89 94). U-Bahn #1: "Kurfürstenstr." Exceptionally popular gay and lesbian techno dance scene for the sartorially splendiferous (dress sleekly!) on Thurs. and Sun. "Dance! Dance, I say. Now prance! Prance girl." Open Thurs.-Sun. after 11pm.

Hafen, Motzstr. 19. U-Bahn #1,2, or 4: "Nollendorfplatz." Less raucous than the other clubs listed, but the eminently friendly atmosphere doesn't send out the fashion police if you don't feel like dressing up. Gay/lesbian/mixed crowd. Open daily after 9pm.

Schocko-Café, Mariannenstr. 6 (tel. 615 15 61). U-Bahn #1 or 8: "Kottbusser Tor." Lesbian women's central; a café with a cultural center upstairs, billiards, and dancing every second Sat. of the month. Open Sun.-Thurs. 2pm-1am, Fri.-Sat. 2pm until whenever.

Jane Bond, in SO36, see (p. 430). This lesbian disco of discos knocks the roof off Oranienstr. every 3rd Fri. of the month after 10pm. Best lesbian joint in town.

Connection, Fuggerstr. 33 (tel. 218 14 32). U-Bahn #1 or 2: "Wittenbergplatz." Exceedingly intense gay techno dance scene. An aptly named bar in the basement, The Twilight Zone, has a labyrinthine dungeon that tops all charts of prurience. "Bring out the gimp." Boys and girls the first Fri. of every month, only (bad) boys every other night. Cover DM3-5. Open Fri.-Sat. after 11pm.

Andreas Kneipe, Ansbacher Str. 29 (tel. 218 32 57). U-Bahn #1 or 2: "Wittenbergplatz." Exceptionally popular gay bar, decorated with bizarre murals of men with tank tops, moustaches, and mohawks, all vaguely emblematic of the clientele. Open daily 11am-4am.

■ Shopping

When Berlin was a lonely outpost in the Eastern Bloc consumer wilderness, Berliners had no choice but to buy native. Thanks to the captive market, the city accrued a mind-boggling array of things for sale: if a price tag can be put on it, you can buy it in Berlin. The high temple of the consumerist religion is the seven-story **KaDeWe department store** on Wittenbergplatz, the largest department store in Europe. The name, pronounced "kah day vay," is a German abbreviation of "Department Store of the West" *(Kaufhaus des Westens);* for the tens of thousands of product-starved Easterners who flooded Berlin in the days following the Wall-opening, KaDeWe *was* the West—prompting warnings such as, "OK now, we're going in. Just act normal," as intrepid children stood on the threshold of consumerism. Even Westerners would do well to follow the advice, with the materialism on display alternatively proving awe-inspiring and sickening. (No photography allowed!) The store's food department, sixth floor, has to be seen to be believed (see Food, p. 407).

The entire **Kurfürstendamm** is one big shopping district, but the **Ku'damm Eck,** (the corner of Joachimstalerstr.) and **Ku'damm Block** (around Uhlandstr.) are the most notable areas. Bleibtreustr. has stores closer to the budget traveler's reach, while the hagglers around **Brandenburger Tor** will sell you cheap GDR memorabilia—don't accept their stated prices and don't fool yourself into thinking the relics are authentic; there just aren't *that* many "real" pieces of the Berlin Wall.

Theodore Sturgeon astutely observed that "90% of everything is crap," and the **flea markets** that regularly sprout up in Berlin are no exception. Nevertheless, you can occasionally find the fantastic bargain that makes all the sorting and sifting worthwhile. The market on **Straße des 17. Juni** probably has the best selection of stuff, but the prices are higher than those at a lot of other markets (open Sat.-Sun. 8am-3pm). **Winterfeldmarkt,** by Nollendorfplatz, overflows with food, flowers, and people crooning Dylan tunes over their acoustic guitars (open Wed. and Sat. mornings). The market on **Oranienburger Str.** by Tacheles generally offers works by starving artists and a variety of other non-sensical things in which Dadaists delight (open Sat.-Sun. 8am-3pm).

Zweite Hand (second-hand), an aptly named newspaper appearing at news stands for DM3.50 on Tuesdays, Thursdays, and Saturdays, consists of ads for anything anyone wants to resell, from apartment shares and plane tickets to silk dresses and cats; it also has good deals on **bikes** (DM3). **Bergmannstraße,** in Kreuzberg, is a used clothes and cheap antique shop strip. **Made in Berlin,** Potsdamerstr. 63, generally has funky second-hand stuff, all priced reasonably cheap. Get your leather jacket here. To get there, take the U-Bahn #1 to "Kurfürstenstr."

■ The Outer Boroughs

The suburbs of Berlin lie within the *Berliner Außenring,* a massive roundabout of highways and train lines which circles the greater metropolitan area. The towns and city districts listed below are generally accessible by public transportation, and make good afternoon or daytrips. See Brandenburg, p. 438, for other excursions.

WANNSEE

Most Berliners think of the town of Wannsee, on the lake of the same name, as the beach. Wannsee has long stretches of sand along Havelufer Promenade. To reach the lake, take the triangle bus from the Wannsee or Nikolassee S-Bahn stations to "Strand-bad Wannsee" (for the beach) or the end of Nikolskoer Weg (for the boats).

Unfortunately, the reputation of the charming village of Wannsee is indelibly tarnished by the memory of the notorious Wannsee Conference of January 20, 1942. It was here that and leading officials of the SS completed the details for the implementation of the "Final Solution." The conference took place in the **Wannsee Villa,** Großer Wannsee 56, formerly a Gestapo Intelligence Center. In January 1992, the 50th anniversary of the Nazi death-pact, the villa reopened as the **Haus der Wannsee-Konferenz** (tel. 805 00 10), an excellent documentary museum with permanent Holocaust exhibits and historic film series, as well as a look at the strange history of the villa itself. In fact, until recently, its association with the conference was not generally known. The villa is discomfitingly lovely, and its grounds offer a dazzling view of the Wannsee. (Open Tues.-Fri. 10am-6pm, Sat.-Sun. 2-6pm. Free. Tours and info in English.) To get there, take bus #114 from the S-Bahn station to the "Haus der Wannsee-Konferenz" stop. Along the shores of the **Kleiner Wannsee,** the brilliant young author **Heinrich von Kleist** and a terminally-ill companion committed suicide in 1811. Kleist's works gained acclamation only after his death.

From Wannsee, ferries also run to the **Pfaueninsel** (Peacock Island; DM10.50), where Frederick the Great's successor Frederick William II built a *trompe l'oeil* "ruined" castle as a private pleasure house in which he and his mistress could play alone. A flock of the island's namesake fowl roams about the gardens surrounding the castle. From Wannsee, ferries also sail to Tegel, Charlottenburg's Schloßbrücke, Spandau, Potsdam, Werder, and Kladow. Contact **Stern und Kreisschiffahrt** (tel. 536 36 00) or visit them at the Wannsee waterfront near the S-Bahn station.

TEGEL AND PLÖTZENSEE

The forest and lake in Tegel are among the most serene in Berlin. You can swim, water-ski, or go boating on the lake (head down Alt Tegelstr.). The forest has been left mostly untouched, and you can follow *Wanderwege* (walking paths) to deserted parts of the woods. Take U-Bahn #6 to "Tegel." From the U-Bahn, walk up Karolinen-str. or take buses #133 or 222 two stops to get into the heart of the forest.

An understated yet haunting monument to the victims of Nazism, the **Gedenk-stätte Plötzensee** (Plötzensee Memorial; tel. 344 32 26), housed in the former execution chambers of the Third Reich, exhibits documents recording death sentences of "enemies of the people," including the officers who attempted to assassinate Hitler in 1944. More than 2500 people were murdered within these walls.Still visible are the hooks from which victims were hanged. The stone urn in front of the memorial contains soil from Nazi concentration camps. English Literature available is at the office (open daily 8am-6pm, Feb. and Oct. 8:30am-5:30pm; Nov. and Jan. 8:30am-4:30pm; Dec. 8:30am-4pm; free). To get there, take the U-Bahn #9 to "Türmerstr.," then bus #123 (direction: Saatwinkler Damm) to "Gedenkstätte Plötzengee."

DENMARK

Lolland

Puttgarden

Fehmarn

Baltic
Sea

Rügen
Islands

Saßnitz

**Eastern Germany:
The New
Federal States**

Stralsund

Bergen

Wismar

Rostock

Greifswald

Lübeck

Ratzeburg

Güstrow

MECKLENBURG-VORPOMMERN

Mecklenburg Lake Plain

Waren

Neu-
brandenburg

Hamburg

Schwerin

Plauersee

Lauenburg

Müritzee

Szczecin

Lüneburg

Elbe

Pritzwalk

POLAND

BRANDENBURG

Oder

Stendal

Havel

Oranienburg

Berlin

Tanger-münde

Frankfurt
an der Oder

Hanover

Brandenburg

Oder

Braunschweig

Magdeburg

Potsdam

Spree

Spreewald

SAXONY-
ANHALT

Dessau

Lübben

Halberstadt

Wittenberg

Lübbenau

Wernigerode

Saale

Cottbus

Goslar

Halle

Niesse

Harz Mountains

Nordhausen

Leipzig

Göttingen

Bautzen

Görlitz

THÜRINGIA

Naumburg

Meißen

Dresden

Weimar

SAXONY

Upper Lusati

Eisenach

Gera

Bad Schandau

Zittau

Gotha

Erfurt

Jena

THURINGIAN FOREST

Rudolstadt

Chemnitz

Suhl

Zwickau

Erz Mountain

Plauen

CZECH REPUBLIC

BAVARIA

Prague ✪

TREPTOW

The powerful **Sowjetische Ehrenmal** (Soviet War Memorial), is a mammoth promenade built with marble taken from Hitler's Chancellery. Take the S-Bahn to "Treptower Park." The Soviets dedicated the site in 1948, honoring the millions of soldiers
of the Red Army who fell in what Soviets, and Russians today, know as the "Great
Patriotic War." Massive granite slabs along the walk are festooned with quotations
from Stalin, leading up to colossal bronze figures in the Socialist Realist style, symbolically crushing Nazism underfoot. It's quite moving, despite the pomp. Buried
beneath the trees surrounding the monument are the bodies of 5000 unknown Soviet
soldiers who were killed during the Battle of Berlin in 1945. The memorial sits in the
middle of **Treptower Park,** a spacious wood ideal for morbid picnics. The neighborhood adjoining the park is known for its pleasant waterside cafés.

LICHTENBERG

In the suburb of Lichtenberg on Normannenstr. stands perhaps the most hated and feared building of the GDR regime—the headquarters of the East German secret police, the **Staatsicherheit** or **Stasi.** On January 15, 1990, a crowd of 100,000 Berliners stormed and vandalized the building to protest the continued existence of the police state. The building once contained six million individual dossiers on citizens of the GDR, a country of only 16 million. Since a 1991 law returned the records to their subjects, the "Horror-Files" have rocked Germany, exposing informants—and wrecking careers, marriages, and friendships—at all levels of the political and cultural world. The exhibit displays the offices of Erich Mielke (the loathed Minister for State Security from 1957-1989), surveillance equipment employed by the *Stasi,* and loads of *Stasi* kitsch (including innumerable Lenin busts). The **Forschungs-und-Gedenk-stätte Normannenstr.,** Ruschestr. 59 (tel. 553 68 54), is close to the U-Bahn station. Take U-Bahn #5 to "Magdalenenstr." Lichtenberg suffers from severe unemployment and has become a somewhat dangerous haven for squatters. When visiting the memorial (open Tues.-Sat. 11am-6pm, Sat.-Sun. 2-6pm; admission DM5) be cautious among the remaining emblems of GDR misery. This warning goes for all the eastern outer boroughs, where right-wing and other disaffected youths sometimes roam. Visible non-Germans should be very careful in these areas, if not avoid them entirely.

■ Near Berlin

BERNAU AND WANDLITZ

The eastern satellite town of Berlin, **Bernau** is surprisingly provincial considering its proximity to The Big City, but does provide a soothing respite from the noise. It offers a well-preserved, 600-year-old city wall and precious little else. Its saving grace is the nearby forest, accessible by bike or bus. If **biking** is your thing, rent a bike in Berlin and bring it with you on the S-Bahn—bike rental shops do not seem to have made it here yet. Beautiful rides through the woods end at stunning lakes, including **Wandlitz,** the former retreat of East German government bigwigs. To get there from Bernau (6km), follow the bike trail or take bus #94 (DM3). When the GDR regime fell, Wandlitz became one of the more notorious symbols of its corruption. Few things angered ordinary East Germans more than the aristocratic **hunting lodges,** complete with stables and stocked with game. Grim, garden-variety totalitarians were bad enough, but hypocritical ones were just a bit too much to bear.

To get to Bernau from Berlin, take S-Bahn #8 from Ostkreuz (1hr.; Berlin rapid transit ticket valid; you may have to change in Pankow). From the train station, go straight until the first corner, turn left, zigzag right and left until you reach the *Marktplatz.* The **tourist office** *(Fremdenverkehrsamt),* Am Marktplatz 2 (tel. (03338) 36 53 88; fax 87 36), books private rooms (DM20-35 per person) and provides brochures (open April-Sept. Mon.-Fri. 9am-6pm, Sat. 9am-1pm; Oct.-March Mon., Wed., and Fri. 9am-5pm, Tues. and Thurs. 9am-6pm). The local **Jugendherberge (HI),** Prenzlauer Chaussee 146 (tel.(033397) 221 09), 300m to the left of the bus stop, is in Wandlitz. (Reception open 4-10pm. DM18.50, over 26 DM22. Sheets DM6.)

ORANIENBURG AND SACHSENHAUSEN

The small town of Oranienburg, just north of Berlin, was home to **KZ Sachsenhausen,** a Nazi concentration camp in which more than 100,000 Jews, communists, intellectuals, gypsies, and homosexuals were killed between 1936 and 1945. In 1961, the GDR opened the site as the **Gedenkstätte Sachsenhausen,** Str. der Nationen 222, 16151 Oranienburg (tel. 80 37 15). Parts of the camp have been preserved in their original form, including the cell block, where particularly "dangerous" prisoners were kept in solitary confinement and tortured daily, and a pathology department where Nazis performed medical experiments on inmates both dead and alive. Only the foundations of Station Z (where prisoners were methodically exterminated) remain, but the windswept grounds convey the horrors which were committed here. A GDR slant is still apparent; the main museum building features Socialist Realist stained-glass windows memorializing "German Anti-Fascist Martyrs." The museums themselves, however, have been totally overhauled recently. The main one hosts special shows of Holocaust-related art, as well as a fascinating permanent textual exhibit (in English and German) on the history of anti-Semitic practices throughout the world. To get to Sachsenhausen, take S-Bahn #1 (direction: Oranienburg) to the end of the line (40min.). From the station, walk along Stralsunder Str., turn right on Bernauer Str., left on Str. der Einheit, and right on Str. der Nationen (15min.). (Open April-Sept. Tues.-Sun. 8am-6pm; Oct.-March Tues.-Sun. 8:30am-4:30pm. Museum closed on Mon. Free). The **telephone code** is 03301.

Brandenburg

Surrounding Berlin on all sides, the province of Brandenburg is overshadowed by the sprawling metropolis within it. The Hohenzollern family, which eventually ruled the German Empire, came out of the forest here and onto the political stage. The stunning palaces in Potsdam are what remains of that moment in Brandenburg's past. Many believe that Brandenburg, now an agrarian hinterland, will unite with Berlin in the future, to form a single federal state, Berlin-Brandenburg. Potsdam, essentially a suburb of Berlin has served as the seat of the state government since 1990. Brandenburg's lakes and forests are all easily accessible from Berlin, and provide a soul-saving break from the overloaded circuits of the capital.

■ Potsdam

Visitors disappointed by Berlin's distinctly unroyal demeanor can get their fix by taking the S-Bahn to nearby Potsdam, the glittering city of Frederick II (the Great). While his father Friedrich Wilhelm I (a.k.a., "the Soldier King") wanted to turn Potsdam into a huge garrison, the more eccentric Friedrich II made it his goal to beautify the city. Although most of downtown Potsdam was destroyed in a single 20-minute air raid in April 1945, the castle-studded **Sanssouci Park** still stands as a monument to Fred II's (sometimes dubious) aesthetic taste. Potsdam was Germany's "Little Hollywood" from 1921 until World War II, as the suburb of Babelsberg became one of the capitals of the European film industry. As the site of the 1945 conference where the Allies divied up Germany, Potsdam's name became synonymous with Germany's defeat. After serving for 45 years as the home of Communist Party fat cats, the 1000-year-old city finally recovered a sense of dignity in 1991, when Brandenburg voters restored its status as the *Land*'s capital.

Orientation and Practical Information The **tourist office**, Friedrich-Ebert-Str. 5 (tel. 27 55 80), is between the streetcar stops "Alter Markt" and "Platz der Einheit"—all trains from the Potsdam Stadt bus/train station go to one of the two stops. To get to the tourist office, go across the *Lange Brücke* (bridge) and head straight on Friedrich-Ebert-Str. The office provides a usable city map (Potsdam is also on the more expensive Berlin "Extra" *Falk Plan*) and info on private accommodations, which they'll book for DM5. (Rooms DM20-40 per person. Private bungalows DM35-50 per person. For accommodations info, call 275 58 16. Open April-Oct. Mon.-Fri. 9am-8pm, Sat. 10am-6pm, Sun. 10am-4pm; Nov.-March Mon.-Fri. 10am-6pm, Sat.-Sun. 10am-2pm). You can buy the **Berlin-Potsdam Welcome Card** (DM29)—it gets you 48 hours on the Berlin-Brandenburg public transport network and reduced or free admission to museums in Berlin and Potsdam.

The tourist office offers three-hour **bus tours** from the **Filmmuseum**, at Schloßstr. 1. (Tours leave Tues.-Sun. at 12:45pm, Fri.-Sun. at 10:45am; available in English. DM35 with admission to Castle Sanssouci, DM27 without, students DM30.) **City Rad,** 100m from the Potsdam-Stadt station (tel. 61 09 52), offers three- to four-hour **bike tours** every Saturday at 11:30am. (Tours DM15 (not including bike rental) and can be conducted in English if you ask. **Bike** rental (not permitted in Sanssouci Park) open April-Oct. Mon.-Fri. 9am-7pm, Sat.-Sun. 9am-8pm.) S-Bahn #3 runs directly from Berlin to Potsdam-Stadt (30min. from Bahnhof Zoo); Potsdam is connected by **rail** to most of Brandenburg. Berlin rapid-transit tickets are valid on the S-Bahn for regular public transportation but are *not* valid for the bus lines to Sanssouci and Neues Palais (another DM3). However, bus #695 stops directly at the *Schloß* and is included in the regular ticket; Sanssouci is within walking distance of the city center. The **post office,** 14476 Potsdam, is at Platz der Einheit (open Mon.-Fri. 9am-6pm, Sat. 9am-noon). The **telephone code** is 0331.

Brandenburg and Berlin

BRANDENBURG

Accommodations and Camping Potsdam has no hostel—the closest is the one in Wannsee (see Berlin, p. 434), 10 minutes away by S-Bahn. Hotels are scarce and expensive; see Practical Information, above, for information on private rooms. The main campground, **Intercamping-platz Riegelspitze am Glindower See** (tel. (03327) 23 97), lies 13km away, on the other side of Lake Havel. Catch bus #631 (direction: Werder) either from the main bus station or from Bassinplatz. (Reception open daily 8am-1pm and 3-10pm. DM5 per person. DM4-7 per tent.)

Food Bright, renovated Brandenburger Str., the local pedestrian zone, encompasses most of the city's restaurants, fast-food stands, and grocery shops—including two bakeries that are open on Sunday. One of the street's better cafes, **Märkischer Landmann,** Brandenburger Str. 46 (tel. 236 26), is a sunny place that whips up big salads for DM11-12 and big German meals for DM14-17 (open Mon.-Sat. 9am-9pm, Sun. 11am-9pm). The **Hollandisches Viertel** (see Sights, below) is lined with chic little cafés where you can have a civilized afternoon glass of wine or coffee. The merchants at the **flea market,** on Bassinplatz, include a number of farmers with fresh produce and fake Levi's (open Mon.-Fri. 9am-6pm).

Sights and Entertainment Frederick the Great's bizarre and authoritarian personality is on display in every manicured square meter of the 600-acre **Sanssouci Park.** Countless fountains and nudes line the intersecting footpaths that convey tourists between the park's Baroque castles and exotic pavilions. The largest of the four royal castles, the 200-room **Neues Palais** (tel. 97 31 43), was built by Frederick to demonstrate Prussia's power and, incidentally, to house his guests. Inside is the 19th-century **Grottensaal,** a reception room whose ribbed walls glitter with seashells. The palace also houses a luxurious café (open daily 11am-7pm; closed 2nd and 4th Sat. of the month) and a **Sommertheater** (tel. (030) 210 02 10) with occasional classical-music performances (open most of the summer). In a macabre reunification gesture, Fred's remains, spirited away in 1945 to a Hohenzollern estate near Tübingen to save them from the Red Army, were brought back to rest on the grounds of Schloß Sanssouci in 1991. (Open April-Oct. daily 9am-5pm; Feb.-March and Oct. 9am-4pm; Nov.-Jan. 9am-3pm; closed 1st and 3rd Mon. of each month.)

At the other end of the park's long, long **Hauptallee** (central path) stands the main attraction, the Versailles-esque **Schloß Sanssouci** (tel. 239 31), atop an incredible landscaped hill stair-stepped with garden terraces. The orange-tinted palace is small and airy, but richly decorated with figures of Bacchus and other Greek gods; Fred used to go here to escape his wife and drown his sorrows (*sans souci* is French for "without cares," and, incidentally, the alma mater of Columbia University). Unfortunately, visits are not always carefree; reunification has made this truly beautiful site accessible, and thousands of Western tourists and Hohenzollern groupies are making up for lost time. Tours of the castle in German (strictly limited to 40 people) leave every 20 minutes, but the final tour (5pm) usually sells out by 2pm during the high season—come early. If you want an English-language tour, go on the one led by the tourist office, but note that it includes only the main *Schloß* (you're free to wander around afterwards, though). Inside, the style is cloudlike French Rococo (Fred was an unrepentant Francophone until his dying day)—all pinks and greens with startlingly gaudy gold trim. A high point is the **Voltairezimmer,** a chartreuse languor of a room decorated with colorful carved reliefs of parrots and tropical fruit. Voltaire never stayed at the palace, though—the room was only built in his honor. The library reveals another of Fred's eccentricities: whenever he wanted to read a book, he had five copies printed, one for each of his palaces—and in French, of course. By the way, the **"ruins"** the castle overlooks are fake: Fred liked the look of ancient ruins, so he had these built in the style of what's left of the Roman Forum. (Schloß Sanssouci open April-May and July-Sept. daily 9am-12:30pm and 1-5pm; Feb.-March and Oct. 9am-12:30pm and 1-4pm; Nov. and June 9am-12:30pm and 1-3pm. Closed 1st and 3rd Mon. of each month.)

Next door is the **Bildergalerie,** whose brilliant collection of Caravaggio, van Dyck, and Rubens recently opened after extensive restoration, with gorgeous results (open mid-May-mid-Oct. 9am-noon and 12:45-5pm; closed 4th Wed. of each month). Romantic **Schloß Charlottenhof,** whose park surroundings were a Christmas gift from Frederick William III to Frederick William IV, melts into landscaped gardens and grape arbors at the south of the park. Nearby lie the **Römische Bäder** (Roman baths). Overlooking the park from the north, the pseudo-Italian **Orangerie-Schloß** is famous for its 67 dubious Raphael imitations: they serve to replace originals swiped by Napoleon (open mid-May-mid-Oct. 9am-noon and 1-5pm; closed 4th Thurs. of each month). Next door are the **Neue Kammern** (royal guest chambers), which also served as a recital hall for the dilettante king. The former ball and festival rooms are lavishly decorated; check out the Hohenzollern porcelain collection in a huge gold-trimmed closet room (open April-Sept. daily 9am-noon and 12:30-5pm; Feb.-March and Oct. 9am-noon and 12:30-4pm; Nov.-Jan. 9am-noon and 12:30-3pm). The most bizarre of the park's pavilions is the **Chinesisches Teehaus,** a gold-plated fantasy, complete with a rooftop Buddha toting a parasol. (Admission to each palace DM8, students DM4, except Neue Kammern DM5, students DM3. Pavilions each around DM4, students DM2. Compulsory German tours of Sanssouci, Neue Kammern, and Schloß Charlottenhof; in others you can wander on your own.)

Back in town, the **Brandenburger Tor,** a smaller, vanilla cousin of Berlin's Brandenburg Gate, sits amid traffic flowing through Luisenplatz. From here, Brandenburgerstr. leads down to the 19th-century **Kirche St. Peter und Paul,** Potsdam's only Catholic church. One block before the church, Friedrich-Ebert-Str. heads left to the **Hollandisches Viertel** (Dutch quarter), streets lined with red-brick Dutch-style houses. Now the most sought-after real estate in the city, Mittelstr. offers many quiet cafés. Towards the waterfront on Friedrich-Ebert-Str., the impressive dome of the **Nikolaikirche** rises above its neighbors. On closer inspection, the dome and the granite cube it sits on don't seem to match. The interior was renovated à la GDR with glass and sound-tiles that somehow lessen the aesthetic impact (open Mon. 2-5pm, Tues.-Sat. 10am-5pm, Sun. 11:30am-5pm). Down Friedrich-Ebert-Str. towards the bridge, the **Filmmuseum** (tel. 29 36 75), housed in the old Orangerie (which also served as Fred I's stables), documents Potsdam/Babelsberg's glory days as a film mecca with artifacts like Marlene Dietrich's costumes and a huge silent film archive (open Tues.-Fri. 10am-5pm, Sat.-Sun. 10am-6pm; admission DM6, students DM3).

Potsdam's second park, the **Neuer Garten,** nuzzling the Heiligersee, contains several royal residences. The most worthwhile is **Schloß Cecilienhof** (tel. 239 31), built to look like an English country manor. Exhibits document the **Potsdam Treaty,** signed at the Palace in 1945. Visitors can see the tacky rooms in which the Allied delegates stayed (open daily 9am-5pm; closed 2nd and 4th Mon. of each month; admission DM3, students and seniors DM2, under 6 free). Take bus #695 to "Cecilienhof" or tram #96 to "Platz der Einheit," then change to tram 95 to "Alleestr."

In the beginning of the 19th century, General Yorck brought 500 Russian soldiers to Prussia, and Frederick Wilhelm III, a great fan of Russian culture, discovered that many of them had singing talent. Unfortunately, by the 1820s, only 12 of the original group were left—the rest died of homesickness. To make up for the depressing atmosphere, Fred III built each soldier an ornate wooden house. The nearby onion-domed **Kapelle Alexander Newski,** designed by Schinkel, was also intended as compensation. To the northeast, the crumbling villas of the Berliner Vorstadt were luxury homes for politicos during the heyday of the GDR. Berlinerstr. leads through here to the **Glienicker Brücke** (a.k.a. "The James Bond Bridge"), which used to be swallowed up by the "no man's land" between the GDR and West Berlin. Until 1989, it was used for the exchange of spies. Take tram #93-95 to "Burgstr."

■ Near Potsdam: Werder and Babelsberg

On the other side of Lake Havel lies Werder, an idyllic town with almost as many orchards and vineyards as people. To get there, take bus #631 from Bassinplatz or RB3 from the Potsdam Stadt station. Bring out the farmer in yourself at the **Obstbau Museum** (fruit cultivation museum), Karl-Marx-Platz 2 (tel. (03327) 446 88), which displays closely-argued comparative histories of apples, cherries and grapes (open Wed. 11am-5pm, Sun. 1-5pm; admission DM2.50, students DM1).

Back in the Golden Age of European cinema, Potsdam was Germany's Hollywood. Fritz Lang made *Metropolis* and Marlene Dietrich and Leni Riefenstahl got their first breaks in the Disneylandish **Filmstadt Babelsberg,** August-Bebel-Str. 26-52 (tel. (0331) 721 27 55). Take S-Bahn #3 to "Greiebnitzsee," then bus #696 to "Bahnhof Drewitz." Film buffs will enjoy old film sets and costume and cutting rooms (open April-Oct. daily 10am-6pm; admission DM11, students DM8).

▓ Brandenburg

One-thousand-year-old Brandenburg has long been a reluctant wielder of power; even when it was capital of the province to which it lends its name, it allowed Berlin civic freedom. When Albrecht the Bear built the town's cathedral in 1165, the surrounding *Neustadt* and *Altstadt* became the region's political epicenter. The city's industry took off during the 19th century, when the Brennabor bicycle factory and the Lehmann toy factory first began churning out their wares. Today Potsdam has officially usurped Brandenburg's political limelight, leaving the town to fade gently into obscurity. Reconstruction of the decaying buildings is proceeding slowly, and the winding cobblestone streets are wistfully quiet.

Brandenburg is surrounded by lush greenery and water. The river Havel, dotted with rowboats, flows gently by the **Dom St. Peter und Paul,** begun in Romanesque style in 1165 and completed in Gothic. Architect Friedrich Schinkel couldn't resist adding a few touches: the "Schinkel-Rosette" and the window over the entrance. The cathedral's many wings fold off from the center into darkness, ending in little rooms like the 1235 **Bunte Kapelle** (the name means "colorful chapel"). The **Dommuseum** inside displays an array of relics and local-history treasures. (Cathedral open daily 10am-6pm, except Wed. 10am-noon and Sun. 11am-6pm. Museum open daily 10am-4pm except Wed. 10am-noon and Sun. noon-4pm. Admission free.) The **St. Katharinen Church,** built at the end of the 14th century, is a beautiful example of *Backstein* (glazed brick) Gothic. The carved altar dates back to 1474 (open daily 10am-6pm). Both churches are the focus of cultural events: both regularly schedule organ concerts and the *Dom* hosts theater in the *Petrikloster* during the summer months. For 500 years a 6-m statue of the legendary hero Roland has stood in front of the **Rathaus**—the socialist GDR-era was just a ripple in time to this medieval symbol of free commerce. Several remaining towers from the 12th-century city walls add historic flavor to the *Altstadt* and the streets around **Neustädter Markt.** Incidentally, *Neustadt* (new town) is a relative term—it was founded in 1196.

Two routes run to Brandenburg from Berlin: you can either hop on trains heading towards Magdeburg and Hanover or take S-Bahn #3 or 7 to "Potsdam-Stadt," and change to the RB33 (40min.; DM14 round-trip). The **tourist office,** Hauptstr. 51 (tel. 194 33), is just off Neustädter Markt. To get there from the train station, walk along Große Gartenstr., follow it until it turns into Steinstr., and head left on Hauptstr. Or take tram #1, 2, or 9 from the train station to "Neustädter Markt." The immensely helpful staff will answer questions and book rooms free of charge. Brandenburg does not yet have a strong hotel culture, but private rooms run DM30 for singles, DM40 for doubles. The tourist office also supplies cultural and historical information and distributes free maps and brochures in English (open Mon.-Fri. 9am-7pm, Thurs. 9am-8pm, Sat. 10am-2pm). The **telephone code** is 03381.

The **Jugendherberge "Walter Husemann" (HI),** Hevellerstr. 7 (tel./fax 52 10 40), sits on a tiny island right across from the *Dom.* From Domlinden, make a right on Hevellerstr. and when you get to #7, head through the courtyard and cross the bridge to the hostel. Bus B also stops near here—get off at "Domlinden," and keep walking for a few blocks. The rustic lakeside locale and old volleyball nets in back transcend backwaterhood; this is charm, East German style. (Reception open 7-9am and 5-7pm. No English spoken. Curfew 10pm, but you can get a key. Members only. DM18, over 26 DM22. Breakfast included.) When the hostel is booked up, they've been known to provide overflow housing in tents outside for DM12 per night. **Campingplatz Malge** is in the middle of the woods, but only 20 minutes away from the city center. Take bus B from Neustädter Markt, and ask the driver to let you off at the campground. You can rent boats to fish in the nearby lake. (DM4 per person. DM3-5 per tent. Showers included. Fishing permits from campground reception or tourist office. Open April-Oct.) The campground also has a few two-person bungalows for DM30 per night. To make reservations, call **Amt für Tourismus** (tel. 51 21 34) or the tourist office. Inexpensive **restaurants** line the pedestrian area of Hauptstr., which also features a **supermarket** and an open-air **farmers' market** (open daily 8am-6pm) behind the St. Katharinen Church. **Zum Kaffeekannchen,** Hauptstr. 16, serves coffee and ice

McDonald's Straße please?

If ever proof was needed that capitalism has taken over the new *Bundesländer,* the formerly sleepy little town of Blumberg, in Brandenburg, provides it. In an attempt to balance its budget, Blumberg cast its civic pride aside, and decided to sell its street names to companies. One of the first takers was none other than the indomitable McDonald's, and other companies are due to follow. "We have debts and would have had to close the day care center and the school without financial support," the town's mayor was quoted as saying. It hasn't yet been reported whether the renowned burger joint has put in a bid for that rather large arch in the center of Berlin—Brandenburger Tor—but we'll keep you posted.

cream on a balcony. (Namesake coffee pot DM4. Ice cream DM6-8. Open Mon.-Sat. 10am-7pm, Sat.-Sun. 1:30-6:30pm.)

■ Frankfurt an der Oder

When writer **Heinrich von Kleist** was born here in 1777, Frankfurt an der Oder was a sleepy locale—even Kleist couldn't wait to skip town for the greater excitement of Dresden, Paris, and ultimately Berlin. Founded in 1226 by merchants who found the location on the Oder ideal for trade with Poland and Northern Germany, Frankfurt remained a trading post until the **Universität Viadrina** was established in 1506. The university moved to Wroclaw (Breslau), Poland in 1811, the same year that Kleist committed suicide on the banks of the Kleiner Wannsee in Berlin (for entirely unrelated reasons). Frankfurt became a garrison town in the 19th century, and consequently was flattened in World War II. After the big sleep of the Communist era, the feeling here is not as much of a town *re*-building as of one building for the first time. In 1991, the Viadrina University returned, and quickly came to represent the youthful energy now surrounding "Frankfurt/O." This energy is attributable to the constant traffic of Germans and Poles crossing the border to transact business; though Polish town Slubice is only 10 minutes by foot across the Oder bridge, the lines of BMWs and Polski Fiats waiting on either side sometimes extend for kilometers. As Poland becomes an increasingly important trading partner for Germany and the West, Frankfurt an der Oder promises to be a vibrant city in years to come.

Orientation and Practical Information Frankfurt an der Oder is less than an hour from Berlin by regular **trains.** The **tourist office,** on the main drag at Karl-Marx-Str. 8a (tel. 32 52 16; fax 225 65), provides maps and information about various sights within Frankfurt and the surrounding countryside. From the train station, head down the curving Bahnhof Str. and go right at the next major intersection onto Heilbronner Str. A block later, turn left on Karl-Marx-Str. and the office is on the right (15min.).They find private rooms (DM30-50 with breakfast) for a fee of DM5 per person (open Mon.-Fri. 10am-noon and 12:30-5:30pm, Sat. 10am-12:30pm and 1:30-3pm, Sun. 10am-noon). There is a 24-hour **ATM** in the train station. The main **post office,** on the far right side of Heilbronner Str., at the intersection of Lindenstr. and Logenstr, is in a beautiful red brick building (open Mon.-Fri. 8am-6pm, Sat. 8am-noon). The **postal code** is 15230. The **telephone city code** is 0335.

Accommodations Budget accommodations in Frankfurt an der Oder are sparse and in a state of flux. A *Privatzimmer,* booked through the tourist office, is probably the best option (DM25-45). Otherwise, stay at an authentic remnant of the GDR, the **Gästehaus des Bildungszentrums,** at Heinrich-Hildebrand Str. 20a (tel. 556 32 27). From the station, walk 15 minutes through the tunnel on the left up Dresdener Str., then go left at Fürstenbürger Str. as it becomes Johann-Eichorn-Str. Another 10 minutes of walking awaits; at the streetcar overpass, turn right on Friedensweg, and left on Heinrich-Hildebrand-Str. Or take tram #1, 5, 6, or 7 to "Friedenseck" (DM1.80; tickets available at machines at tram stops, but *not* from the driver). The rather run-down-looking guest house conceals 20 clean and comfortable rooms. (Open 24hr., but the office closes on weekends and takes no reservations. Singles DM35. Doubles DM78. Breakfast included. Call ahead.)

Food Aside from the many outdoor food markets and stands in town, the **Studentenpassage** in the Schmalzgasse, one block down from the tourist office on Karl-Marx-Str., serves cheap and good meals for under DM6 (open Mon.-Fri. 8am-6:30pm, Sat. 8am-1pm). Try **Café Calliope,** Lindenstr. 4 (tel. 32 52 59), for Italian fare (DM6-14) in an outdoor sculpture garden (open Mon.-Fri. 9am-11pm, Sat. 5-11pm). Afterwards stroll in the cool galleries of the **Haus der Künste,** a Neoclassical building erected in 1787. For coffee and ice cream, the delightful **Café im Museum,** on Heilbronner Straße 19 (tel. 227 63), is located inside the **Museum Junge Kunst** (open Tues.-Sat. 1-

5:30pm, Sun. 11am-4:30pm). Pack for a picnic on the Oder at **Rewe** supermarket (tel. 404 21), at Johann Eichorn Str. and Spartakusring (open Mon.-Fri. 8am-6:30pm, Sat. 8am-1pm). Another alternative is crossing the bridge from Rosa-Luxemburg-Str. to Slubice and eating cheaply in **Poland** (passport required). It's possible to pay in German currency, but for better prices convert your *Marks* to Polish *zloty* at exchange stands *(kantor)* on the Polish side. Or skip the restaurants in town and head to the **market** (following the "Targowisko" signs from the bridge), where the ubiquitous cigarettes are available for low Polish prices.

Sights Most historical sights in Frankfurt an der Oder are conveniently located within a few blocks of the main *Marktplatz*. From Karl-Marx-Str. one can easily see the beautiful but scarred **Marienkirche.** Built in the early Gothic style of the 13th century, it was once one of Frankfurt an der Oder's grandest sights. Unfortunately, the deteriorated cathedral is now closed indefinitely while undergoing renovations.

Brilliant author **Heinrich von Kleist** is the town's claim to fame. Born to a noble but impoverished Prussian military family, young Heinrich enlisted in military school at 14. From 1793 to 1795 he participated in campaigns against the French, but, influenced by Enlightenment ideals, he quit the army in 1799, citing the inequality of conditions between officers and enlisted men. Rejecting his birthright, he lived as a pauper, attempting to start journals in Dresden and Berlin. Meanwhile, he wrote plays—among them his comedy *Der Zerbrochne Krug* (The Shattered Jug) and the intense, imagistic tragedy *Penthesilea*—and short stories (the most famous being his novellas *Michael Kohlhaas* and *Die Marquise von O*). Kleist wrote famously complex prose describing bourgeois society with irony and sympathy. Although his works did not find an audience during his lifetime—his scathing eye may have been too much for contemporaries to take—they are now considered classics of German literature. Penniless and dissatisfied, Kleist and a terminally-ill friend committed suicide on the shore of the Kleiner Wannsee in Berlin in 1811.

Kleist's birthplace was destroyed during World War II—all that remains is a plaque on an ugly GDR-era apartment block on Große Oderstr., opposite the *Marienkirche*. The **Kleistmuseum,** on Faberstr. 7 (tel. 231 85), at the end of Bischof Str., is housed in a small blue building in which the young Kleist attended school. The musuem is a little disappointing—its three floors feature facts and documents about the Kleist family as well as manuscripts, but very little about Kleist himself. It's understandable that the museum should be so spare in personal information—when Kleist died, his only possession was a black leather *Rucksack* which was sold to pay his debts (open Tues.-Sun. 11am-5pm; admission DM2.50, children and students DM1; audio tours in English DM2).

Two blocks down is the **Museum Viadrina,** Carl-Phillipp-Emanuel-Bach Str. 11 (tel. 22 23 15; this younger Bach studied at the Viadrina 1734-38), on the Oder promenade. Built in 1675 and once a house for the **Junkers** and **Kurfürst** princes, the museum contains exhibitions on regional history and a collection of Baroque-era musical instruments (open Tues.-Sun. 11am-5pm; admission DM1, students DM0.50). The **Museum Junge Kunst,** Heilbronner Str. 19 (tel. 227 63), is the place to see contemporary paintings and sculpture in Brandenburg. Housed in a beautiful villa, the exhibits are a worthy attempt to bring modern East German art to light (open Tues.-Sun. 11am-5pm; admission DM1, students DM0.50).

■ Spree Forest (Spreewald)

The Spree River splits apart about 100km southeast of Berlin and branches out over the countryside in an intricate maze of streams, canals, meadows, lakes, and primeval forests stretching over 1000km-sq. This is the home of the legendary **Irrlichter,** a sort of Saxon leprechaun who lights the waterways (for a price) for travelers who lose their way, and leads to their deaths those who refuse to pay. Folklore, tradition, and wildlife have survived here with remarkable harmony in tiny villages and towns first settled in the Middle Ages. Hire a barge, rent a paddle boat, or take to the trails by foot or bicycle to see why locals insist that the Spreewald—not Amsterdam, Stockholm, or St. Petersburg—is the true "Venice of the North."

But this is an agrarian Venice, where farmers row to their fields and noisy children paddle home from school. It's a green Venice as well—the fields and forests teem with owls, storks, kingfishers, otters, and foxes, animals known to most Europeans only through textbooks or television documentaries. In a country infamous for pollution and its *kaputt* environment, the Spreewald is idyllic.

Until the 17th century, these waterways wound through one of Europe's densest forests. The Prussian kings, however, directed a clearing of the trees—they wanted to use the wood for furniture and to sow the newly-created fields with pumpkins. Though heavily bombed in World War II, the forest recovered quickly and the rich diversity of flora and fauna flourished once more. But socialist industry was not so kind: until 1990, coal-power stations towering outside of Lübbenau drew their cooling water from these streams as their smoke choked the sky.

Reunification brought the mixed blessing of greater environmental protection and hordes of forest-trampling tourists. But the power plants should all be closed by the end of 1996, and the Spreewald is now recognized as a *Biosphärreservat* (a biosphere nature reserve) by the U.N. Some sections of the forest are closed to the public at all times; other sections are closed during mating and breeding seasons, but not tourist season. **Guided tours** are offered by reservation, camping spots abound, bicycles can be rented everywhere, and excellent hiking trails and footpaths weave their way through the peaceful forest. Each local tourist office has information on these leisure activities. They won't let you forget, however, that the forest is protected by the government, and tourists are urged to be environmentally responsible.

Lübben and **Lübbenau,** two tiny towns that open up into the labyrinths of canals that snake through the forest, are the most popular tourist destinations and lie within day-trip range of Berlin. **Cottbus,** close to the Polish border, is a bit farther east, but is the only place to witness **Sorb** culture.The Sorbs, Germany's native Slavic minority, originally settled the Spreewald region; see the introduction to Upper Lusatia (Oberlausitz), p. 466, for more. Although the traditional Sorbian culture survives in several Lusatian towns, it is (with a few exceptions) otherwise encountered mostly in museums, Sorbian souvenirs, and in the occasional use of Sorbian place names alongside their German counterparts. If your German is shaky, the **Spreewaldbüro,** Zwinglistr. 5a, Berlin 21 (tel. 392 30 22), is your best source of regional information. They speak English and will reserve private rooms in the Spreewald (open Mon.-Fri. 9am-6pm). It's best to make reservations ahead, particularly for June-August, when a mass of tourists invades. Take U-Bahn #9 to "Turmstr."

LÜBBEN

A good base for Spreewald excursions, Lübben is about an hour southeast of Berlin by train or by the Berlin-Cottbus *Autobahn*. The **harbor** is watched over by the ancient **Schloßturm** (castle tower), built in the 15th century by the Brandenburg Prince Frederick II as an imposing defense against invaders. Even World War II, which destroyed 80% of the **Altstadt,** could not topple the tower.

The *Altstadt*'s architectural pride is the newly-restored **Paul Gerhardt Kirche,** named for the most famous German hymn writer since Martin Luther. Gerhardt is buried inside (open Wed. and Sun. 10am-5pm). If you wish to wander or picnic in Lübben's lush green park, **Der Hain,** the entrance is at the end of Breite Str. Near Lübben stands **Straupitz,** an otherwise forgotten village where Neoclassical architect Karl Friedrich Schinkel erected a strikingly unusual church. Saved from obscurity by ample transportation, Straupitz is accessible by barge or bus.

Lübben's **tourist office,** Lindenstr. 14 (tel. 30 90; fax 25 43), directly on the harbor, provides trail maps and finds rooms (primarily doubles for DM25-35 per person) for a DM5 fee. From the train station, head right on Bahnhofstr., left on Logenstr., right on Friedenstr., and left on Spreenferstr., then head down to the intersection; it's on the right. They charge DM2.50 for a highly helpful city map; it's worth avoiding a mapless meander through town. They also rent **bikes** for DM2.50 per hour or DM10 per day with ID (open April-mid-Sept. 9am-6pm, Sat. 10am-4pm, Sun. 10am-noon). During winter months and after hours, the tourist office posts a list of private rooms just outside the entrance. You can also rent a **bike** at the train station for DM10 per day (open daily 7am-9pm). For a **taxi**, call 37 16. The **post office** is located at Poststr. 4, 15907 Lübben. The **telephone code** is 03546.

The **Fährmannsverein Lübben/Spreewald**, Ernst-von-Houwald-Damm 16 (tel. 71 22 or 80 05), offers many different **boat trips** exploring different regions of the Spreewald (open daily 9am-4pm; 1½-8hr., DM4-5 per hour). Trips depart from Strandcafé-Kahnanlegestelle after 9am; the boats leave when full. Go straight from the tourist office down Ernst-von-Houwald-Damm, cross the bridge, and go right. The **Kahnfährhafen "Flottes Rudel,"** Eisenbahnstr. 3 (tel. 35 45), also straight ahead from the tourist office (bear right through the lot before the bridge), offers boat and barge trips with picnics for the same prices as the Fährmannsverein, starting daily at 10am. You can do it yourself by renting a **boat** at **Bootsverleih Gebauer,** on Lindenstr. (tel. 71 94). From the tourist office, go straight and take a right just before you reach the bridge. (One-seat paddle boat Mon.-Fri. DM24 per day, Sat.-Sun. DM28. Rowboats for up to 4 people Mon.-Fri. DM45, Sat.-Sun. DM49. Canoes for 2 adults and 2 children under 7 Mon.-Fri. DM40, Sat.-Sun. DM45. You can also rent by the hour (DM5-10). Everyone must know how to swim. Lifejackets are provided for kids; those under 10 must be accompanied by an adult. ID required. Open April-Sept. daily from 9am, Oct.-March daily from 10am.)

The **Jugendherberge Lübben (HI)**, Zum Wendenfürsten 8 (tel. 30 46), is a 20-minute hike from the train station. Turn right down Bahnhofstr. until you hit the end of Luckauer Str., then turn right and take the first left onto Eisenbahnstr., cross Pushkinstr., and follow Dorfstr. until it curves back toward three gray buildings along the water; the hostel is as rustic as the surrounding landscape, but the staff is friendly. (Reception open after 3pm. Curfew 10pm. 84 beds. DM18.50, over 26 DM22. Breakfast included. Book several days in advance or call ahead. Open April-Oct.) It takes an even longer hike (30min.) to **camp** at **Am Burglehn.** From the station, turn right on Bahnhofstr., left on Luckauer Str., right on Burgtehnstr., and continue along the footpath to the campground. (Reception open 7am-10pm. DM6 per person. Tents DM5-8. 4-person cabins DM30.) While you're in Lübben, sample the Spreewald's particular pickled delicacies, famous throughout Germany. The **Gurken Paule**, Ernst-von-Houwald-Damm-Str. (tel. 89 81), is an outdoor stand offering the freshest of the *Spreewald*'s unique *Gurken* (cucumber) assortment (*Salzdillgurken*—salty, *Senfgurken*—mustard, *Gewürzgurken*—spicy). Pay DM0.50 per pickle, DM5 for a hefty jar (open daily 9am-6pm).

LÜBBENAU

Tiny Lübbenau is actually the largest and most famous of Spreewald towns. For many tourists (and there are tons), the village serves as a springboard for trips into the **Oberspreewald.** Winding streets of the town center open directly onto the wooded paths and villages of the upper forest. The landscape here is much denser than that above Lübben, as well as more intricately interwoven with canals.

The *Altstadt* is a 10-minute trot from the station. Go straight on Poststr. until you come to the marketplace dominated by the Baroque **Church of St. Nikolai.** The carved stone pillar in front served as an 18th-century crossroads post marking the distance in *Stunden,* an antique measurement equalling one hour's walk (approximately 4.5km). The interior can be visited only as part of a guided tour of the town on Tuesdays (DM4, children DM3), or by attending services on Sundays at 10am. The town's aristocracy came to an end in 1944 when the local Duke was executed after being implicated in an attempt on Hitler's life. After the *Wende,* his three sons returned from the West to restore the familial **Schloß,** now a handsome (but terrifically expensive) hotel and restaurant. The lush castle grounds *(Schloßbezirk)* are open to the public and shelter the **Spreewaldmuseum Lübbenau,** offering a fascinating overview of Spreewald development and its unique customs. This is the place to see traditional

Spreewald costumes (open April-mid-Sept. Tues.-Sun. 10am-6pm; mid.-Sept.-Oct. 10am-5pm; admission DM3).

There are two main departure points for **gondola tours** of the forest: the **Großer Hafen** (big harbor) and the **Kleiner Hafen** (little harbor). Follow the signs to either from the town center. The Großer Hafen offers a larger variety of tours, including two- and three-hour trips to Lehde (DM8.50-10, children half-price). Longer trips (4-8hr.) cost around DM5 per hour; for the same price, you can design your own tour. The boats take on customers starting at 9 or 10am and depart when full, continuing throughtout the day (2-7hr.; DM8-14; no English tours, but hilarious if you speak German and can decipher Saxon dialect). The gondolas are a great way to see the scenery. From the *Kleiner Hafen*, at the end of Spreewaldstr., tours leave daily from 9am on and last 1½ to 10 hours. From the *Kleiner Hafen* a beautiful leafy path begins just over the wooden bridge. Stroll or bike down it. If a float with drunken elderly Germans isn't your thing, rent a **paddle boat** at **Manfred Franke,** Dammstr. 72 (tel. 27 22; DM29 per day for a 2-person boat). To get there from the station, turn right down Bahnhofstr. and left at the next intersection (open 8am-7pm).

Lübbenau lies only 13km past Lübben on the Berlin-Cottbus line. The **tourist office,** at Ehm-Welk-Str. 15 (tel. 36 68, fax. 467 70), just left of the church, provides maps, information on bike trails, and finds rooms for DM25-45 (open Mon.-Fri. 9am-6pm, Sat.-Sun. and holidays 10am-6pm). **Kowalski,** on Poststr. 6 (tel. 28 35), near the train station, rents **bikes** for DM10 per day (open Mon.-Sat. 9am-6pm). For a **taxi,** call 31 43. In an **emergency,** call 81 91 or 22 22. The **telephone code** is 03542.

Even though the closest youth hostel is the Lübben (10min. by train), finding a room shouldn't be a problem in friendly Lübbenau. Many houses post *Zimmer frei* signs, or you can knock on the door of **Zimmervermietung-Haus Jerkel,** Max Plessner-Str. 22 (tel. 436 96), which is just 10 minutes from the station. Take Poststr. straight, and then turn right on Max Plessner Str. **The Jerkels** offer 14 comfortable beds in their white stone house. They often have same-day rooms, but call ahead. (Doubles DM62, with full bath DM72. Breakfast included). Lots of restaurants also have cheap rooms hidden above; check for signs. There are two camping options: directly on the road to Lehde, **Campingplatz "Am Schloßpark"** (tel. 35 33; emergency 28 11) offers 300 plots for tents (DM5-8 per night) with cooking and shower installations on site (DM1-3). There are also 55 bungalows (DM25 for up to 6 people) and 21 trailer spots (DM11-13), as well as a small store with soap, soup, pickles, and other daily necessities. (Reception open daily 7am-10pm. Open May-Oct.).

For cheap food and Spree pickles, beets, and beans by the barrel, check out the snack bars and stands along the harbor. On the way to the campgrounds, the **Café-Garten,** on the Lehder stream (tel. 36 22), offers a self-service outdoor café that serves Munich potato salad (DM2.50) or filet of pike (DM9.80; open daily 9am-10pm). In town, try **Spreewald Idyll,** Spreestr. 13 (tel. 22 51), for game specialties like *Wildschweinbraten in Sahnesoße mit Wildpreiselbeeren und Salzkartoffeln* (DM13; open Mon.-Thurs. 11am-11pm, Fri.-Sat. 11am-midnight, Sun. 10am-9pm).

LEHDE

It's only a hop and a paddle from Lübbenau to **Lehde,** a UNESCO-protected landmark and the most romantic village of the Spreewald, accessible only by foot, bike, or boat. You can drive to the Lehde outskirts, but cars (except those owned by residents) are banned in the village. By foot, it's just a 15-minute trek; follow the signs from the *Großerhafen.* If you're partial to water, take a boat from the harbor. Most farmers here still depend on the canals for access to the rest of the world. Check out the **Freilandmuseum Lehde,** where things remain as they were when an entire Spreewalder family slept in the same room and newlyweds spent their honeymoons heaving in the hay. The museum displays three restored farm houses, and local artists also show their work (open April-mid-Sept. daily 10am-6pm; mid-Sept.-Oct. 10am-5pm; admission DM3, students and seniors DM2, children DM1).

Because Lehde is extremely protective of its landmark status, few guest beds are offered, but a few *Pensionen* cower on the outskirts. Don't expect to stay in Lehde overnight, but if you really want to, talk to the Lübbenau tourist office. Just before you reach the bridge to the museum, you'll see **Zum Fröhlichen Hecht,** Dorfstr. 1 (tel. 27 82), a large café, restaurant, and *Biergarten.* Sit upstairs on the wooden benches for a view of the languidly passing boats. Try *Kartoffeln mit Quark* (potatoes with cream cheese) in a special Spreewald sauce (DM7) or pickles with a side order of *Schmalz* (lard; DM3), another Spreewald specialty. Say a prayer for your heart, and dig in (open daily 10am-5pm). The **telephone code** is 03542.

BURG

Farther east and accessible by bus, bike, or (if you're lucky) car, Burg is an amazingly expansive village—over 600 farms and 200 private homes sprawl across 52 square km. From Lübben, take bus #700 (direction: Cottbus) to "Burg Bleske." From Cottbus, take bus #700 (direction: Lübben) or 46 (direction: Burg) to "Burg Bleske" (one-way DM4.10). The ride itself is stunning; you'll see a tremendous landscape of fields, forests, and farmers oblivious to the industrial towns 30 minutes away. The most impressive view of Burg is from the 27-m high 1914 **Bismarckturm** (Bismarck tower) overlooking the surrounding forests and the 300 streams and bridges that thread through them. From the bus, head right on Hauptstr. toward the main harbor. Cross the bridge and follow the trail signs ahead for 1km (open April-Oct. Tues.-Sun. 10am-6pm; admission DM2, children DM1). Tower closes in bad weather.

The **tourist office,** Am Hafen 1 (tel. 417), is to the left just before the bridge. They find rooms for DM5 (private rooms DM25-35; *Pension* rooms DM50-70) and provide information on Burg and Sorb festivals (open Mon.-Fri. 9am-noon and 1-6pm).To rent any kind of **boat**—canoe, paddle boat, or kayak—try **Bootsverleih Lukas,** Willisaschzaweg 42 (tel. 867). For a **taxi** call 603 65. **Zweiradhaus Schmidt** at Bahnhofstr. 17 (tel. 376) rents **bikes** for DM8-10 per day with ID (open Mon.-Fri. 8am-6pm, Sat. 8-11:30am). The **pharmacy** Spreewald-Drogerie, Bahnhofstr. 1 (tel. 232), has a condomat outside (DM5 per pack). Who knows: in this romantic village, it may come in handy. The **telephone code** is 035603.

The local **Jugendherberge (HI)** Dorf #220 (tel. 225), is just a few steps away from the bus stop; follow the signs. This pastoral hostel has comfortable rooms right on the river. (Reception opens at 7pm. Curfew 10pm. DM18.50, over 26 DM22. Breakfast included. Dinner DM5. Sheets DM6). **Edeka supermarket** on Hauptstr. offers basic groceries (open Mon.-Fri. 8am-6pm, Sat. 7:30-11am). On a sweeter note: the delicious bakery **Werner Mieth** at Bahnhofstr. 39 (tel. 348) serves pretzels and pastries (DM2-3; open Tues.-Fri. 6:30am-6pm, Sat. 6:30am-11am).

COTTBUS (CHOSEBUZ)

The second-largest *Burg* in Brandenburg, Cottbus dwells in **Niederlausitz** (Lower Lusatia) on the southernmost edge of the Spree Forest. Founded by Sorbs in the 8th century, Cottbus's distinguishing quality is its substantial Sorb population. All street signs are printed in both Sorbian and German, several local Sorbian newspapers and radio stations flourish, and the study of Sorbian is growing popular in local schools. Cottbus's other claim to fame is the tongue-twister every German child knows: *"Der Cottbuser Postkutscher putzt den Cottbuser Postkutschkasten"* (regardless of your language skills you're probably stumped; it means something like "the stagecoach driver from Cottbus cleans the interior of his Cottbus stagecoach"). The stagecoach is the town symbol, which at least partially explains the above nonsense.

Orientation and Practical Information With a direct rail link to Berlin (2hr.) and bus lines to Burg and other hamlets, Cottbus is the nexus for Spreewald tours. The bus station is a 15-minute walk from the train station. Head straight on Bahnhofstr. and take a right on Marienstr. Or take the streetcar #1 from the train station (DM2) to "Marienstr." (two stops); the bus station is on the right. The **tourist office,** Berlinerstr. 1a (tel. 242 55 or 242 54; fax 79 19 31), at the corner of Bahnhofstr., finds rooms for a DM5 fee (singles DM40-60, doubles DM70-105). They give out a free but nearly illegible map (open Mon.-Fri. 10am-6pm, Sat. 10am-noon). **Schenker, Friedrich-Ebert Str. 15** (tel. 330 95), rents **bikes** for DM5 and up (open Mon.-Fri. 9am-6pm, Sat. 9am-noon). The **telephone code** is 0355.

Accommodations Cottbus's two **Jugendherbergen** sit kitty-corner to each other on the quiet square behind the *Klosterkirche*. From the "Stadtholle" train stop, head up Berlinerstr. toward the *Altstadt*, take a left on Wendestr., and go around the church. The **Bettenhaus (HI)**, Klosterplatz 2-3 (tel. 225 58), is clean and modern and offers 54 beds in three- to 10-bed rooms. (Reception open Mon.-Fri. 8am-1pm and 7-9pm. Curfew 10pm. DM18.50, over 26 DM22. Nonmembers DM26.50. Breakfast included.) **Pension Schiemenz,** Karlstr. 22a (tel. 79 12 29), is a sweet deal. It's got six rooms luxuriously furnished with TV and telephone. (Reception open until 10pm or by arrangement. Singles DM50, with private bath and cable TV DM60. Doubles DM90, with private bath and cable TV DM110. Breakfast included.) It's about a 15-minute walk north of the city center. From Berlinerplatz, head straight on Friedrich-Ebert-Str. and follow it as it turns into Karlstr. Or take tram #1 or #4 to "Bon-maskenpl." The **Pension** at Klosterplatz 4 (tel. 225 58) is in a historic building embedded in the town wall. (Singles DM45, with shower DM60. Doubles DM80, with shower DM100. Triples DM140. Breakfast included.)

Food and Nightlife The restaurant **Buffalo,** Spremburgerstr 27. (tel.228 38), specializes in German food and potato concoctions such as potatoes with tomatoes and mozzarella for DM9 (open daily 11am-9pm). For a more romantic atmosphere, try **Café Altmarkt,** Altmarkt 10 (tel. 310 36), where you can have a beer and a view of the *Altmarkt* from beneath the 16th-century arch (café open daily 8am-1am; basement open 11am-1am). On the other side of town, **Café Baum,** Marienstr. 6 (tel. 311 20), to the right of the bus station, serves all four food groups: coffee, wine, beer, and ice cream (open Mon.-Fri., Sun. 9am-midnight, Sat. noon-2pm).

Sights and Entertainment Cottbus, like most East German cities, was severely scarred by World War II. But the city's post-war *Neue Sachlichkeit* (New Objectivity) architecture has not penetrated the *Altstadt,* which is liberally sprinkled with historic buildings. Heading down Berlinerstr., the church on the left is the **Klosterkirche** (tel. 248 25), also known as *Wendische Kirche* (*"Wendish"* is German for Sorbian). Built in 1300 by Franciscan monks, it is the oldest church still standing in Cottbus (open Tues.-Sat. 10am-5pm). The **Altmarkt** lies a bit further down Berlin-erstr. The **Niederlausitzer Apotheke,** at Berlinerstr. 21 (tel. 239 97), first started dealing drugs in 1573. The shop still sells herbal teas and other potions, but the back has been turned into a museum with a poison chamber (tours Tues.-Fri. at 11am and 2pm, Sat.-Sun. at 2 and 3pm or by appointment; store open Tues.-Fri. 10am-5pm). At the eastern end of the *Altmarkt*, Sandower Str. leads to the 1400 **Oberkirche St. Nikolai,** the largest church in the Niederlausitz and home to frequent concerts by regional orchestras (open Mon.-Sat. 10am-5pm, Sun. 1-5pm; tickets DM12, students DM6). Sorbian culture buffs can head to the **Wendisches Museum** (Sorbish museum), at Mühlenstr. 12 (tel. 79 49 30), down Spremburgerstr., which houses unique Sorbian folk art and costumes, particularly the distinctive headdress (open Tues.-Fri. 8:30am-6pm, Sat.-Sun. 2-6pm, admission DM2, students DM1).

Farther down Sprembergerstr. lies the strangely-named **Schloßkirche**—it's tiny. The Huguenots who rebuilt it had no delusions of grandeur. At the end of the street, you've left the *Altstadt* and entered the *Neustadt*. The 1908 cherub-sprinkled **Staatstheater Cottbus,** Schillerplatz 1 (tel. 222 73 or 222 75), is Europe's only extant example of the late *Jugendstil* architectural style. The 1997 program includes works by Verdi, Goethe, and Brecht; call 237 61 for tickets. While the inner city is somewhat congested, Cottbus is surrounded by a beautiful landscape. The riverside panorama leads to **Schloß Branitz** (tel. 751 50), a Baroque castle built in 1772 by Prince Hermann von Pückler-Muskau, a globetrotter with a love of larger-than-life architecture. From the *Altstadt,* follow Spremberger Str. to Str.-der-Jugend, and bear left at

Bautzener Str., turn left at Stadtring, and right at Gustav-Hermann-Str., which leads you to the park (open Tues.-Sun., 10am-6pm; Nov.-March Tues.-Sun. 10am-5pm). **Branitzer Park,** which surrounds the castle, is peppered with oddities. The landscape in the western park includes several pyramids which will forever bear witness to Pückler-Muskau's Egyptophilia. One appears to float in the center of the lake.

Saxony (Sachsen)

Saxony (Sachsen)

Saxony is known to foreigners primarily for Leipzig and Dresden, the most fabled cities of eastern Germany after Berlin, but the entire region provides a fascinating historical stratification that reveals a great deal about life in the former east. The castles around Dresden attest to the bombastic history of Saxony's electors, while the socialist monuments of Chemnitz and the formless architecture of other major cities depict the colorless world of the GDR. On the eastern edge of Saxony, Saxon Switzerland and the Zittauer Gebirge provide a respite from the aesthetic violence done by East Germany's city planners with hiking trails that march through a land of escape to the borders of the Czech Republic and Poland.

▇ Dresden

Dresden pulses with a historical intensity that is both sublime and vicious, an emblem of everything that was and is East Germany. No matter where you go, you will not be able to forget the fact that the "Florence on the Elbe," a city of minimal military importance but formidable cultural value, was incinerated by Allied bombs in February 1945, claiming more than 50,000 lives and destroying 75% of the *Altstadt*. The city offers spectacular ruins, an array of world-class museums, and unparalleled history as the cultural capital of pre-war Germany. As partially reconstructed palaces and churches burst forth from the surrounding rubble that remained during the "deep freeze" of the GDR years, Dresden finds itself a focal point for the efforts of reunification; a skyline of over 200 cranes steadily assists the reconstruction, which is scheduled to be completed for the city's 800-year anniversary in 2006. While you'll hear tourists everywhere waxing pretentious about a "phoenix-from-the-ashes" and "the hope of tomorrow," the raw Dresden of today offers a unique vitality that simply goes beyond the process of reincarnation.

ORIENTATION

The capital of the *Land* (federal state) of Saxony, Dresden stands magnificently on the Elbe River 80km northwest of the Czech border and 180km south of Berlin. This city of half a million people is a major transportation hub between Eastern and Western Europe—during the mass emigrations from Germany in 1989, Dresden was the most frequented point of departure into Czechoslovakia. From the **Dresden Hauptbahnhof** (main train station), travelers shoot off to Warsaw, Paris, Prague, Kraków, Berlin, Budapest, Copenhagen, Munich, and Frankfurt. Another station, **Bahnhof Dresden Neustadt,** sits on the other bank of the Elbe and bears a striking physical resemblance to its mate; trains leave from here to Leipzig and other eastern cities.

Dresden is bisected by the Elbe. The *Altstadt* lies on the same side as the *Hauptbahnhof;* the *Neustadt* to the north, having escaped most of the bombing, is now paradoxically one of the oldest parts of the city. South of the *Altstadt* are the contrasting suburbs of Plauen and Strehlen. Dresden has finished removing socialist-era names from streets and squares; pick up a map at the tourist office, or at a postcard stand (if you pay less than DM5, ask how old it is). Many of Dresden's major tourist attractions are centered between the *Altmarkt* and the Elbe. From there it's a five-minute scenic stroll to the banks of the *Neustadt.* Four immense bridges (Marienbrücke, Augustbrücke, Carolabrücke, and Albertbrücke) connect the city halves.

> **Safety Warning!** Visitors should exercise caution if traveling in the Dresden-Neustadt region to the north of the Altstadt, in the industrial suburbs of Strehlen, and farther south. Neo-Nazi and skinhead activities, although sporadic, do pose a threat to non-white and conspicuous non-Germans in the economically depressed regions outside the center of the city. The well-travelled *Altstadt* area remains fairly safe despite an increase in crime in Dresden since reunification.

PRACTICAL INFORMATION

Tourist Offices: Dresden Information, Pragerstr. 10 (tel. 49 19 20; fax 295 12 76). Exiting the *Hauptbahnhof* from the side exit on Wiener Platz, cross the *Straßenbahn* tracks and head toward the main square straight ahead. Walk straight on Pragerstr. until you see a Burger King (2min.). The office is on the right, behind the McDonald's. Decent English. They help find **private rooms** (DM35 and up) or hotel rooms for a DM5 fee, sell theater tickets, and offer guided **tours.** Their free maps cover the major sights in a panoply of languages. Open Mon.-Fri. 10am-6pm, Sat.-Sun. 10am-2pm. If closed, try the ultra-funky automated "Info-Tour" in the window. The **Tourist Information Neustädter Markt** (tel./fax 804 35 39), in the tunnel to the right when you walk off the Augustusbrücke, provides the same services. Open Mon.-Fri.10am-6pm, Sat.10am-2pm.

Discount Card: The **Dresden Card,** available at the tourist office, provides 48hr. of free rides on buses and trains and entry into many major museums (DM29).

Currency Exchange: Deutsche Verkehrsbank AG Hauptbahnhof, in the main hall of the train station. Open Mon.-Fri. 7:30am-7:30pm, Sat. 8am-noon, 12:30-4pm, Sun. 9am-1pm. DM3 charge for cash currency exchange; DM7.50 for traveler's checks. There are also a number of banks on Pragerstr. After hours, the self-service exchange machine in the *Hauptbahnhof* will do, but the rates are poor.

American Express: Müntzgasse 10 (tel. 494 81 17), in front of the Frauenkirche in a booth a bit larger than a shoe box. Money sent, mail held, and other standard AmEx offerings. Open Mon.-Fri. 10am-1pm and 2-5:30pm.

Telephones: At the post offices.

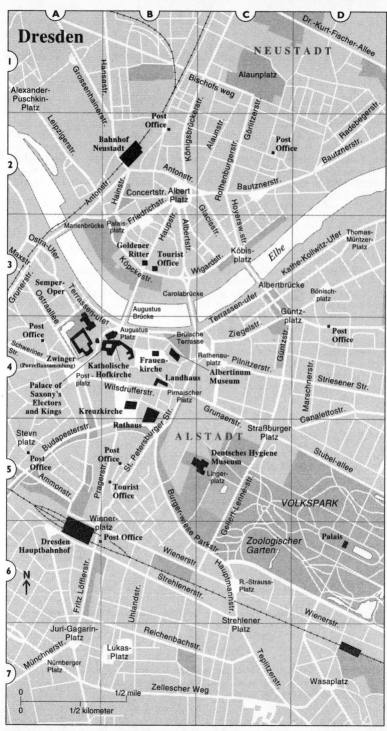

Dresden

NEUSTADT

Alexander-
Puschkin-
Platz

Alaunplatz

Bahnhof
Neustadt

Post
Office

Post
Office

Concertstr. Albert
Platz

Marienbrücke

Palais-
platz

Goldener
Ritter

Tourist
Office

Elbe

Köbis-
platz

Thomas-
Müntzer-
Platz

Semper-
Oper

Carolabrücke

Albertbrücke

Bönisch-
platz

Augustus
Brücke

Güntz-
platz

Post
Office

Augustus
Platz

Brülsche
Terrasse

Post
Office

Zwinger
(Porzellansammlung)

Katholische
Hofkirche

Frauen-
kirche

Rathenau-
platz

Landhaus

Albertinum
Museum

Striesener Str.

Palace of
Saxony's
Electors
and Kings

Post-
platz

Wilsdrufferstr.

Pirnaischer
Platz

Kreuzkirche

Stevn
platz

Rathaus

ALSTADT

Straßburger
Platz

Post
Office

Post
Office

Deutsches Hygiene
Museum

Stubel-allee

Tourist
Office

Linger-
platz

VOLKSPARK

Wiener-
platz

Post Office

Zoologischer
Garten

Palais

Dresden
Hauptbahnhof

Juri-Gagarin-
Platz

Nürnberger
Platz

Lukas-
Platz

R.-Strauss-
Platz

Strehlener
Platz

Wasaplatz

Zellescher Weg

N

0   1/2 mile

0   1/2 kilometer

Flights: Dresden's airport (tel. 88 10) is about 15km from town. The **Airport City Liners** bus (one-way DM6-8) leaves both stations for the airport every hr.; call 416 15 81 for schedules and information.

Trains: For information, call 471 06 00 or use the computerized schedule center in the main hall of the *Hauptbahnhof.*

Public Transportation: Dresden is sprawling—even if you'll only spend a few days, familiarize yourself with the major bus and streetcar lines. Most bus lines are a mess due to reconstruction—get the bus map to prepare for necessary route changes. **Punch your ticket as you board.** DM1.20 for one ride. DM2.40 for 1hr. DM7 for a 24-hr. day pass. Weekly pass DM18, students DM10. Tickets and maps are available from friendly *Fahrkarten* dispensers at major stops and from the **Verkehrs-Info** stand outside the *Hauptbahnhof* (open Mon.-Fri. 6am-7pm, Sat.-Sun. 7am-7pm). Most major lines run every hr. after midnight. Dresden's **S-Bahn** network reaches from Meißen (DM4.40) to the Czech border (DM6); buy tickets from automats in the *Hauptbahnhof* and validate them in the red contraptions; insert the ticket and press *hard.* Harder.

Ferries: The **Sächsische Dampfschiffahrt** (tel. 86 60 90) grooves with a restaurant, band, and dancing on board; it travels to Pillnitz (90min.), Meißen (1hr.), and the entire Sächsische Schweiz (day pass DM26, children under 14 DM15).

Taxis: tel. 459 81 12.

Car Rental: Budget Rent-a-Car, in the Hilton by the Frauenkirche (tel. 864 29 72). Open Mon.-Fri. 7am-6pm, Sat.-Sun. 8am-noon.

Bike Rental: Pacher und Partner, on Wallstr., 2 blocks left of the intersection of Pragerstr. and the *Altmarkt.* DM15 per day. Open Mon.-Wed. and Fri. 9:30am-6pm, Thurs. 9:30am-8pm, Sat. 9:30am-1pm.

Mitfahrzentrale: SMZ, Bishofsweg 66 (tel. 801 05 48). Prices are DM0.03 per km. Berlin: DM18. Frankfurt an der Main: DM44. Munich: DM46. Hamburg: DM46. Call one day in advance. Rides to Prague are easy to come by on weekends. Open Mon.-Fri. 10am-7pm, Sat. noon-2pm.

Hitchhiking: *Let's Go* does not recommend hitchhiking as a safe mode of transportation. Hitchers stand in front of the *"Autobahn"* signs at on-ramps; otherwise they are heavily fined or smacked by oncoming traffic. Those headed to Berlin take streetcar #3 or 6 to "Liststr.," then bus #81 to "Olter," and walk back to the Autobahn interchange. Those headed to Prague take bus #76 to "Südhöhe," then hitch southbound on Innsbruckerstr. Those headed to Eisenach and Frankfurt am Main take streetcar #1 to "Zschonergrundstr." (4 stops past "Dresden Cotta"—hitchers tell the driver they want to get off at the *Autobahn* to make sure the bus stops), then walk left (away from the river) to the interchange.

Luggage Storage and Lockers: At both train stations. Lockers DM2-4. Storage DM4 per piece per day, DM10 per checked bicycle. Open Mon.-Fri. 6am-10pm, Sat. 6am-9pm.

Bookstore: Das Internationale Buch, on Kreuzstr., directly behind the Kreuzkirche, puts the State Dept. to shame with its bevy of flags. English books on the 2nd floor. Open Mon.-Wed. and Fri. 9am-6pm, Thurs. 9am-7:30pm, Sat. 9am-2pm (first Sat. of the month 9am-4pm).

Laundromat: Groove Station, Katharinenstr. 11/13. A laundromat and much, much more. Wash your clothes (DM5-6 per load) while getting tattoos, piercings, drinks, or *"Erektionsbekleidung"* (condoms). Open Sun.-Fri. 11am-2am, Sat. 10am-late. Also at **Jugendherberge Rudi Arndt,** in the cellar. DM3-4 per load.

Crisis and Counseling Lines: Frauenbildungszentrum, Dornblüthstr. 18 (tel. 33 77 09), focuses on women's issues, with a special phone line (tel. 352 75) for confidential crisis counseling. Open Tues. and Thurs. 8am-6pm, Wed. 9am-4pm; crisis line Tues. 10am-6pm, Thurs. 10am-noon. **Beratungsstelle für Ausländer und Aussiedler,** Wiener Str. 41 (tel. 464 02 60), counsels victims of xenophobia.

Gay and Lesbian Organizations: Gerede-Dresdner Lesben, Schwule und alle Anderen, in Haus der Jugend, Wienerstr. 41 (tel. 464 02 20), near the station. Also **LAMBDA,** *Junge Lesben und Schwule,* Louisenstr. J6 (tel. 801 10 45).

Pharmacy: Call 011 50 00 to find out which pharmacy is on 24-hr. duty. Closed pharmacies usually post signs indicating open ones.

Medical Assistance: For life-endangering sickness call 522 51.

Emergency: Ambulance: tel. 115. **Fire:** tel. 112. **Police:** tel. 110.
Post Office: The **Hauptpostamt,** Königbrückerstr. 21/29, 01099 Dresden (tel. 444 10), is in Dresden-Neustadt. Open Mon.-Fri. 8am-6pm, Sat. 8am-noon. **Postamt 72,** Pragerstr., 01069 Dresden (tel. 495 41 65), is near the tourist office.
Telephone Code: 0351.

ACCOMMODATIONS AND CAMPING

Dresden is prepared for a convergence of all the citizens of the world, if need be. The excess of available rooms means that you can often find same-day deals at some of the hotels on Prager Str., if you don't want to stay in one of the hostels. The tourist offices can also facilitate stays in private rooms (see p. 452).

Jugendgästehaus Dresden (HI), Maternistr. 22 (tel 49 26 20; fax 492 62 99), formerly the Hotel-kongress-business-center. Head left on Wiener Platz from the station and zig-zag onto Ammonstr. Turn right onto Rosenstr, then left on Maternistr; it's on your right. Over 400 beds virtually ensures open spaces; the 2-3 bed rooms have a posh feel, and the breakfast buffet will leave you happier than Wilber. Singles, family rooms, and apartment-style rooms available. Reception open 4-10pm. No lockout. DM30.50, over 26 DM35.50; non-members pay DM5 extra.

Jugendherberge Dresden Rudi Arndt (HI), Hübnerstr. 11 (tel. 471 06 67; fax 472 89 59). Take streetcar #5 (direction: Südvorstadt) or #3 (direction: Plauen) to "Nürnberger Platz," continue down Nürnberger Str., turn right onto Hübnerstr.; the hostel is at the first corner on right. Or, from the *Hauptbahnhof*, walk down Fritz-Löffler-Str., bear right onto Münchener Str., turn right onto Nürnberger Str. Walk 1 block, turn left onto Hübnerstr. Central and pacific. Crowded 8-bed rooms don't detract from the convenience. Book 1-2 days ahead. Reception open Mon.-Sun. 10am-3pm, 1am-6am. Check-in 3-10pm; lockout 10am-3pm and 1am-6am. DM21.50, over 26 DM26. HI members only. Mandatory one-time linen fee (DM5).

Jugendherberge Oberloschwitz (HI), Sierksstr. 33 (tel./fax 366 72). From the train station take S-Bahn #3 or 5 to "Pirnaischer Platz" (7min.) and change to S-Bahn #1 to "Schillerplatz." After 8pm, take S-Bahn #3 to "Albertplatz" across the Elbe, then S-Bahn #6 to "Schillerplatz." Once at Schillerplatz, there are 2 options. **Option 1:** Chill out in the *Biergarten*, indulging in libations. Then stumble across the Elbe on the Loschwitzer bridge to Körnerplatz and take the intoxicatingly scenic *Schwebebahn* (hill train, not the *Standseilbahn*) to "Siekstr." (DM2.50, covered by bus passes and Dresden Card). **Option 2:** Forget the beer and take bus #61 (direction: Weißeg, Buhlau) to "Steglicherstr." (4 stops), then switch to bus #84 to "Malerstr." The friendly-looking hostel will be up on your right. Big rooms in a lovely setting, but remote location. Reception open 7-10am and 4-8pm. Get a key to escape curfew. DM21, over 26 DM25. Members only. Breakfast included.

Jugendherberge Radebeul, Weintraubenstr. 12 (tel./fax 830 52 07). From either train station, take the S-Bahn (direction: Meißen) to "Radebeul-Weintraube." Turn right as you leave the station and follow the street that curves left; the hostel is at the first gate. It lacks the aesthetic grace of the other hostels, but same-day beds are sometimes available. DM22, over 26 DM27; non-members pay DM5 extra.

Ibis Hotel, Prager Str. (tel. 485 66 66). Three huge hotel skyscrapers on Prager Str. just across the street from the train station offer summer same-day specials that are a pretty good bargain for people traveling in pairs. Suites for two (DM98) come with a TV, phone, and shower or bathroom, but no breakfast.

Camping: Campingplatz Altfranken, Altfranken (tel. 649 12 15). Only 7km outside of Dresden and 1km from the nearest bus stop. Take S-Bahn #7 to "Betriebshof Naußlitz" and change there to bus #70. Take it to the end. Reception open Mon.-Fri. 7am-9pm, Sat. 11am-3pm, Sun. 9am-1pm. DM8 per tent. 25 bungalows available. Singles DM50, doubles DM90.

FOOD

Unfortunately, the surge in Dresden tourism has also meant a surge in prices, particularly in the *Altstadt*. The cheapest eats are at supermarkets or *Imbiß* stands on Pragerstr. and at the daily **Markt** on the *Altmarkt* (open Mon.-Sat. 7am-2pm). The *Altmarkt* also features good Italian and Turkish restaurants. The *Neustadt* area has many exotic and less-expensive offerings.

> **Neue Mensa,** Bergstr. 47 (tel. 463 64 95). From Nürnberger Platz, go down Nürnbergstr. away from the youth hostel, turn right on Bergstr., and walk uphill a few minutes. From the *Hauptbahnhof,* take Fritz-Löffler-Str. to Fritz-Löffler-Platz and bear left at the next main intersection, Fritz-Foerster-Platz. The institutionally dismal university *Mensa* on the 2nd floor serves meals for DM5-10. Open Oct.-Aug. Mon.-Fri. 11am-2pm. A **cafeteria** occupies the 1st floor offering baguettes and light fare for under DM2.50. Open Mon.-Thurs. 8am-6pm, Fri. 8am-2pm.
>
> **Raskolnikov,** Böhmische Str. 34 (tel. 931 72 22). A Dostoevskian haunt in a ramshackle pre-war brownstone. Hidden beneath a sign for *Galerie Erhard.* Russian and Afghan fare DM8-15. Open daily 7pm-2am.
>
> **Café Aha,** Kreuzstr. 7, across the street from the church. More crunchy than Rice Krispies. The upbeat atmosphere celebrates things indigenous and detests meat. Spinach and mushroom dishes as well as the *Nudelauflauf* (noodle and cheese stew) DM6.50-DM14. Open Tues.-Sat. 11am-midnight, Sun.-Mon. 11am-10pm.
>
> **Planwirtschaft,** Louisenstr. 20. Refined punk graced with Lenin memorabilia in the *Neustadt.* Steaks, *soljanka* (hearty soup), and mozzarella sandwiches (DM8-14). Open daily 10am until after 3am.

SIGHTS

From the banks of the Elbe, the **Electors of Saxony** once ruled nearly the whole of central Europe. The extravagant collection of Emperor August the Strong and the magnificent palace he built to house it, the **Zwinger,** once rivalled the Louvre. Today hordes of tourists flock to its array of decadent Baroque ornaments. The statues that line the museum grounds are still charred, although workers are quickly making an effort to restore everything back to aesthetic perfection. The northern wing of the palace, a later addition, was designed by Gottfried Semper, revolutionary activist and master architect. Semper's famed Opera House, the **Semper-Oper,** reverberates with the same robust style as the palace wing. Its painstaking restoration has made it one of Dresden's major attractions. The interior is open for tours between shows every few weeks. (DM8, DM5 for students. Believe us, it's worth it.) Check the main entrance for tour times or call 491 14 96. Many guided city tours take off from *Theaterplatz* for better rates than those offered by the tourist office.

Across from the Zwinger lies the nearly restored **Residenzschloß** (Residential Palace of Saxony's Electors and Kings). Once the proud home of August the Strong, its restoration has proceeded piecemeal since it was firebombed on February 13, 1945. It features a display on the Renaissance and Baroque eras of the palace and the history of its reconstruction. (Open Tues.-Sun. 10am-6pm. Admission DM3, students and seniors DM1.50. *Tageskarte* valid.) Across the street, the Kempinski Hotel once served as the **Taschenbergpalais,** the home of August the Strong's mistresses. After poor Countess Cosel was banished to Stolpen (see p. 462) it became a residence for princes. A private walkway once connected the *Residenzschloß* to the **Katholische Hofkirche** (Catholic Royal chapel). The church was built to hide the family's Catholic pageantry from their Protestant subjects. (Tours Mon.-Fri. at 2pm, Sat. at 1pm and 2pm, Sun. at 1pm. Open during the day for unguided perusal.) Adorning the **Fürstenzug** (Procession of Kings), the alley leading to the cathedral entrance, is a 105-m mosaic in Meißner porcelain tiles tracing Saxon history since the Middle Ages. If you've been mistaking Frederick the Earnest for Frederick the Pugnacious, you may want to double back here for a quick history lesson.

From the Catholic Cathedral, the 16th-century **Brühlische Terrasse** offers a prime photo opportunity of the Elbe. Within its casements, Johann Friedrich Böttger was imprisoned by August the Strong until he finally solved the secret recipe for porcelain (interestingly, Böttger had originally promised he could produce gold). Turn right at the end of the terrace to reach the **Albertinum,** another of Dresden's fabulous museum complexes (see Museums, p. 457) that now hosts a courtyard collection of

Greek and Roman sculptures. From the Albertinum, a walk to the *Neumarkt* leads to the ruined shell of the **Frauenkirche,** once Germany's most splendid Protestant church. The first Protestant celebration of communion in Dresden took place at the **Protestant Kreuzkirche** on the *Altmarkt.* Now the fourth church to be erected on the site, its interior remains in rough plaster as a reminder of the war's devastation. Some tourists are fortunate enough to catch a performance by the world-famous **Kreuzchor,** a boys choir with a tradition dating back to the 13th century. Climb to the top for a bird's-eye view of the colossal jigsaw puzzle known as downtown Dresden. (Church open Mon.-Sat. 10am-4:30pm, Sun. noon-4:30pm. Sun. services at 9:30am. Tower open Mon.-Tues. and Thurs.-Fri. 10am-6pm, Wed. 10am-5pm, Sat. 10am-4:30pm. Admission to tower DM2, kids DM1.)

The main promenade of the **Neustadt,** once *Straße der Befreiung* (Street of Liberation), has been renamed **Hauptstraße** (Main Street) in a surge of nomenclatorial genius. The cobblestone pedestrian avenue stretches from the magnificent **Augustus Brücke** over the Elbe past the **Goldener Reiter,** a gold-plated vision of Frederick August II (a.k.a. August the Strong). The nickname was reputedly a homage to his remarkable (some might say unseemly) virility—legend has it that he fathered over 300 kids, although the official tally sits at 15. Still, the gilded August sports a legendary visage which almost seems to pronounce, *"Ich bin der Mac-Daddy des Daddy-Macs!"* At the other end of Hauptstr., **Albertplatz** (formerly Platz der Einheit) is surrounded by handsome 19th-century mansions. Also see the **Dreikönigskirche** (Church of the Three Kings), one of the oldest original structures in the city, farther down Hauptstr. (open daily 9am-6pm; free organ concerts Mon.-Fri. 5:30-6pm).

In the direction of Blasewitz, Loschwitz, and Striesen, you'll find the old haunts of the author Friedrich Schiller; really, really committed fans (fans who should be committed?) can check out the **Schillerhaus,** Schillerstr. 19 (tel. 49 86 60; open May-Sept. Sat.-Sun. 10am-5pm or by appointment; admission DM1, students and seniors DM0.50). For a taste of Dresden's pre-war atmosphere, venture just a bit farther out to Blasewitz and Loschwitz: the **Blaues Wunder,** Dresden's favorite bridge, connects them. A 19th-century suspension bridge, it is a true visual wonder—also the only bridge not destroyed by the SS when the Soviets invaded the city.

In a particularly dismal section of town, the **Schlachthofringe** (Slaughterhouse Circle) is an original 1910 housing complex. In World War II, the buildings were commandeered as a camp for prisoners of war. Novelist Kurt Vonnegut was imprisoned here during the bombing of Dresden, inspiring his masterpiece *Slaughterhouse Five.* The box-like buildings are chilling, even without any exhibits. To get there, take streetcar #9 (direction: Friedrichstadt) to the last stop and walk up (don't do this at night). On the way, you'll pass one of Dresden's architectural oddities, the former **Zigarretenfabrik** (cigarette factory). Keep an eye out for its brown, stained glass dome. Built in 1907, it was modeled on a tobacco factory in Turkey.

MUSEUMS

As reconstruction of the *Zwinger* and the *Residenzschloß* nears its end, Dresden's museum exhibits are gradually moving back to their pre-war homes. If you're going to visit the *Albertinum,* the *Alte Meister* collections, or the *Zwinger,* a worthwhile investment may be the *Tageskarte* (DM10, students and seniors DM5). It covers one-day admission to the Albertinum museums, the *Residenzschloß,* most of the *Zwinger* and a melange of other sights. Purchase it at any of the major museums.

Zwinger

Gemäldegalerie Alte Meister, Zwinger Palace, Semper Wing (tel. 491 46 19). From the front portal, walk through the main courtyard to the building across the way; the museum is on the left. Certainly one of the world's premier collections of paintings from 1500 to 1800. A myriad of works by Rembrandt, Raphael, Vermeer, Dürer, Lucas Cranach, El Greco, and Rubens, among others. The Canaletto collections commemorate the magnificent Dresden of the 18th century. The 3rd floor

SAXONY (SACHSEN)

displays the pomposity of the august Augusts. Admission DM7, students and seniors DM3.50. Free tours Sun. at 4pm. Open Tues.-Sun. 10am-6pm.

Rüstkammer (tel. 491 46 19). Across from the *Alte Meister* in the Semper Wing. An exhibit of the royal court's toys, including the knightly apparel that the Saxon electors donned for jousting tournaments. What appears to be a collection of midget armor is, in fact, that of the Wettin (Windsor) family's toddlers. Admission DM3, students and seniors DM1.50, covered by admission to Old Masters gallery.

Porzellansammlung (tel. 491 46 19). Entry across from the *Residenzschloß*. The "show-and-tell" centerpiece of Dresden, it traces Saxony's porcelain industry through a procession of outlandishly delicate knick-knacks. Enough to make anyone feel like a bull in a china shop. Admission DM3, students and seniors DM1.50. Open Mon.-Wed., Fri.-Sun. 10am-6pm.

Mathematisch-Physikalischer Salon (tel. 495 13 64). To the left of the main gate, a fascinating collection of historical scientific instruments (globes, clocks, atlases, etc.). Not included in the *Tageskarte*. Admission DM3, students DM1.50. Open Fri.-Wed. 9:30am-5pm.

Albertinum

Gemäldegalerie der Neuen Meister (tel. 491 46 19). A solid ensemble of German and French Impressionists, including many Renoirs and Gauguins, leads into a sublime assembly of Expressionists, with particularly moving works by Otto Dix. Admission DM7, students and seniors DM3.50. Open Fri.-Wed. 10am-6pm.

Grünes Gewölbe, on the second floor of the *Albertinum*. Provides a dazzling collection of the completely gratuitous refinements possessed by the House of Saxony. A carved cherry pit with 185 tiny heads proves to be one of the most decadent miniatures you'll ever see. Open Fri.-Wed. 10am-6pm.

Elsewhere in Dresden

Museum Für Sächsische Volkskunst (Museum of Folk Art), Köpckestr. 1 (tel. 491 46 19). Displays a litany of folksy artifacts from Saxony's past. Admission DM2, students DM1. Open Tues.-Sun. 10am-6pm.

Verkehrsmuseum (Transport Museum), Neumarkt (tel. 495 30 02), rolls through the history of German transport, from carriages to bullet trains and BMWs. Admission DM4, students and seniors DM2. 50% discount on Fri. Open Tues.-Sun. 10am-5pm; last entry at 4:30pm.

Museum für Geschichte der Stadt Dresden, Wilsdrufferstr. 2 (tel. 49 86 60), in the 18th-century Neoclassical **Landhaus,** provides an exhaustive history of Dresden from the Middle Ages to the present. The 2nd floor poignantly documents the destruction of February 13-14, 1945, as well as a history of the tumult in 1989, when Dresden's train station served as the primary means of escape into Prague; upon the closure of the German border on Oct. 3, violence erupted. Organized resistance quickly sprang up in Dresden, as evidenced by the numerous marching posters from *Montagsdemos* on display in the museum. Admission DM3, students DM1.50. Open Sat.-Thurs. 10am-6pm, Wed. to 8pm from May-Sept.

Deutsches Hygienemuseum, Lingnerplatz 1 (tel. 484 60). Opened in 1930, this ill-named museum long celebrated the health and cleanliness of GDR Germans. Now that the party's over, it exhibits models of our guts. Admission DM5, students and seniors D3. Open Tues.-Sun. 9am-5pm.

Richard-Wagner-Museum, Richard-Wagner-Str. 6 (tel. 482 29). Houses an array of colorful displays on the bombastic and brilliant composer's life during his Dresden years (1842-49). Frequent concerts. Admission DM3. Open Tues.-Sun. 9am-noon and 1-4pm.

ENTERTAINMENT AND NIGHTLIFE

While not yet up to par with Berlin and Leipzig, Dresden's sprawling nightlife still provides ample entertainment. Much of the hustle and bustle takes place around Albertplatz in the *Neustadt*, with the big time bar and hard-core scene on Alaunstr. The local magazine *Blitz* (free at the tourist office) runs down the city's cultural calendar, but *SAX* (DM2.50 at the tourist office or any newsstand) is more complete and the best source for the *Szene*. For centuries, Dresden has been a focal point of theater, opera, and music. The superb **Semper-Oper** has premiered many of Strauss and Wagner's greatest, but tickets are hard to come by. Dresden also offers summer film festivals in July and a cabaret festival in the first week of October.

Bars and Clubs

Scheune, Alaunstr. 36-40 (tel. 804 55 32). The heart of the *Neustadt* bar scene (Dresden's *Kulturzentrum*), in a former youth center. A Pee Wee's Playhouse that serves Indian food cooked by the German Shiva Team. Open Tues.-Fri. 7pm-2am, Sat. 10am-2pm and 7pm-2am, Sun. 10am-2pm. The culturally eclectic dance floor invites you to disco to West African roots and Baltic and Yiddish piano songs (not at the same time). Club opens at 8pm. Call for schedule of events.

DownTown, Katharinenstr. 11-13 (tel. 801 18 59). *The* place to shake your booty and indulge in Dresden's fluorescent-and-neon techno scene. One of the few night venues capable of convincing skeptical foreigners that some Germans *can* dance. Open Thurs.-Mon. 9pm-5am with hot and heavy dancin' on all these days except Sun.; Thurs.-Sat. cover DM5, Sun.-Mon. DM3).

Studentenklub Bärenzwinger, Brühlischer Garten 1 (tel. 495 14 09), not far from the Albertinum. Students congregate in this bizarre tunnel under the Brühlische Terrasse to nurse cheap drinks and partake in the disco action. Some hard-core interspersed with canonical American "alternative" music. Over 18 only. Bring student ID for discounts. Open Tues.-Thurs. and Sun. 8pm-midnight, Fri.-Sat. 9pm-3am for live shows and dancing.

Fritz-Löffler-Str. 10-12. It's not a name, it's a student apartment complex that has a few clubs with eminently romantic titles—**M14,** on the 8th floor of building C/D, and **Club 10,** in building A, among others. Show up after 9pm and see where the twentysomethings are heading. Student ID saves money on the cover charges.

Die Tonne, Tzschirnerplatz 3 (tel. 495 13 54), boasts an offering of "cool drinks and hot jazz" in the cellar of one of Dresden's skeletal ruins by the Albertinum. Performances most nights at 9pm. Cover DM6.50-18. Free on Wed. and Thurs.

Theater and Cabaret

projekttheater dresden, Louisenstr. 47 (tel. 804 30 41). Experimental theater with an international twist in the heart of the *Neustadt.* So cool they don't use capital letters. Tickets DM6-12. Box office opens 30min. before performances.

Der Herkuleskeule, Sternplatz 1 (tel. 492 55 55). Cabaret with an angry political outlook revels in blasting U.S. culture. Tickets DM15-25.

Schauspielhaus, Postplatz (tel. 491 35 67; box office tel. 491 35 55), produces classics from Kleist to Shakespeare. Tickets DM7-60. Box office open Mon. and Wed.-Fri. 10am-6pm, Tues. 10am-6:30pm, Sat.10am-3pm. The Schauspielhaus also runs the Kleines Haus (see below).

Kleines Haus, Glacisstr. 28 (tel. 491 35 67). Performances of the macabre 20th-century variety, including Kafka, Franz Werfel, and avant-garde contemporaries. Tickets available at Schauspielhaus (see above) 15 days in advance (DM15-25).

Theater Junge Generation, Meißner Landstr. 4 (tel. 421 45 67). Shakespeare, opera, fairy tales, and more. DM15, students DM10. Tickets available 1hr. before performance or Mon.-Sat. 10am-noon, Wed. also 2-6pm, Fri. also 2-7:30pm.

Puppentheater der Stadt Dresden, Leipziger Str. 220 (tel. 849 04 18; fax 849 06 68). Children's performances during the day for young and older folk. DM5, children DM3, family ticket (up to five people) DM13. Box office opens 30min. before performances on weekdays, 45min. before performances on weekends.

Concerts, Opera, and Dance

Sächsische Staatsoper-Semper Oper, Theaterplatz 2 (tel. 491 17 16). See opera's finest in the most majestic of surroundings. The box office unloads tickets 1hr. before performances for DM5-10, but you have to get lucky; otherwise, call ahead for tickets from DM10-85. 50% student and senior discounts. Box office at Schinkel-wache, by the opera, open Mon.-Wed. and Fri. 10am-noon and 1-5pm, Thurs. 10am-noon and 1-6pm, Sat.10am-1pm, and 1hr. before performances.

Kulturpalast, Am Altmarkt (tel. 486 60). Home to the **Dresdner Philharmonie** (tel. 486 63 69) as well as other small music groups and dance ensembles. Box office at

Schloßstr. 2. Main entrance open Mon.-Fri. 9am-6pm, Sat. 10am-2pm. Leftovers go on sale 1hr. before curtain rises.

Staats Operette, Pirnaer Landstr. 131 (tel. 223 87 63). Performs musical theater from Lerner and Loewe to Sondheim. Ticket office open Mon. 11am-4pm, Tues.-Fri. 11am-7pm, Sat. 4-7pm, Sun. 1 hr. before performances.

■ Near Dresden

MEIßEN

Just 30km from Dresden, Meißen sits on the banks of the Elbe as yet another testament to the frivolity of August the Strong. In 1710, the Saxon emperor developed a severe case of *Porzellankrankheit* (the porcelain "bug"—an affliction that continues to manifest itself in tourists today) and turned the city's defunct *Schloß* into a porcelain-manufacturing base. Those visitors who would otherwise feel little affinity for the craft now indulge in a couple of glasses of Meißen's fine wines and soon find themselves toasting the beauty of "white gold" (china, not cocaine). Meißen has a distinct aesthetic advantage over its comrade Dresden: its medieval nooks and crannies were barely scathed by the World War II bombs. Meißen is an easy daytrip from Dresden by S-Bahn (45min.) or via a scenic cruise (round-trip from Dresden DM23).

Wander the narrow, romantic alleyways of the *Altstadt* and climb up to the **Albrechtsburg** (tel 47 07 10), a castle and cathedral overlooking the city. From Bahnhof Meißen, walk straight onto Bahnhofstr. and follow the banks of the Elbe to the aptly-named Elbbrücke (Elbe bridge). Cross the bridge and continue straight to the *Markt* and turn right onto Burgstr.; at the end of Burgstr., on Schloßstr., you'll find the stairs that lead up to Albrechtsburg. The castle foundations were first built in 929AD as fortifications for the protection of the area Sorb population. The interior was lavishly redecorated in the 15th century; sliding through the gilded vaults to see the porcelain products and royal memorabilia becomes truly sensual in the felt slippers provided to protect the floor. (Open Mar.-Nov. daily 10am-6pm; Feb.-Dec. 10am-5pm; last entry 30min. before closing. Admission DM6, students DM3.) Next door dwells the **Meißener Dom,** an early Gothic cathedral. Four priceless 13th-century **statues** by the Naumburg Master (see Naumburg, p. 482) stand behind the altars built in the workshop of Lucas Cranach the Elder. (Open April-Oct. 9am-6pm; Nov.-Mar. 9am-4pm. Last entry 40min. before closing. Admission DM3.50, students DM2.50. Organ music daily at noon May-Oct. for DM3, students DM2.)

Meißen's porcelain factory was once more tightly guarded than KGB headquarters for fear that competitors would discover its intricate techniques. But today anyone can tour the **Staatliche Porzellan Manufaktur,** at Talstr. 9. (tel 46 87 00). The **Schauhalle** serves as a museum where you can peruse finished products (open daily 9am-5pm; admission DM7, students DM5). The **Schauwerkstatt** shows the process from clay to painted porcelain (English tapes available; open daily 9am-noon and 1-4:45pm; admission DM7, students DM5). Meißen's Gothic **Rathaus** stands alongside the **Frauenkirche,** whose porcelain bells chatter every 15 minutes over the main market square (open daily May-Oct. 10am-noon and 1-4pm).

The **tourist office,** An der Frauenkirche 3 (tel. 45 44 70), is tucked neatly to the left behind the church. Pick up maps or find a room in a private home (DM25-50 per bed with breakfast) for a DM4 fee (open Mon.-Fri. 10am-6pm, Sat.-Sun. 10am-3pm; Nov.-Mar. Mon.-Fri. 9am-5pm). Meißen's **Jugendherberge (HI),** Wilsdruffer Str. 28 (tel. 45 30 65), is a crap shoot—its 45 beds are often fully booked; should they have space, they'll put you up in a crowded 4- to 6-bed room with showers in the adjacent outhouse. From the station, cross the Elbe footbridge and take Obergasse to the end where it meets Plosenweg. Turn left and continue up the hill until you see the small EDEKA market; the hostel is across the street. An infrequent bus (line D) also leaves from the train station up the steep hill. (Reception open 7am-noon and 4-8pm. No lockout, no curfew. DM18, over 26 DM22. Breakfast included.) In a pinch, Meißen is also close to the Radabeul hostel and the other hostels of Dresden (see p. 455). The **telephone code** is 03521.

A very puffed, almost hollow pastry, the *Meißener Fummel* owes its origin to August the Strong. One of his couriers was a spirited sort whose penchant for Meißen wine became known to the king. To keep tabs on his bacchanalian behavior, August commanded the Meißen bakers' guild to create an extremely delicate, fragile biscuit. The courier was to carry the *Fummel* with him when he delivered messages without any sign of damage. Many *Altstadt* bakeries vend this puffery. For less fluff, try **Zum Kellermeister**, Neugasse 10 (tel. 45 40 88). Most *Schnitzels* run DM5-10 (open Mon.-Fri. 11am-9pm). The farmer's **market** is in the Platz der Berufsschule, just off the main market (open Tues.-Fri. 8am-5pm). In the last weekend of September, Meißen frolics in merriment during its annual **wine festival.**

PILLNITZ

August the Strong must have led a happy life. Among his many castles (almost as numerous as his mistresses), **Schloß Pillnitz** produces a singularly fantastic effect. Built in 1720 as a summer residence, the turrets of the **Bergpalais** and **Wasserpalais**—modeled on Chinese architectural forms—seem to float above the adjacent Elbe. The residences now house Dresden's **Kunstgewerbmuseum** (arts and crafts museum), some modern art displays, and lots of porcelain amidst the sumptuously sensual and suggestively salacious deep greens and reds of the courtly rooms. Outside, brilliantly-colored flowers heighten the mystical effect of the architecture. Summer **concerts** take place every Sunday in the garden. (Museum open May-Oct. 9:30am-5:30pm. *Bergpalais* closed Mon. (with the *Kunstgewerbmuseum*) and *Wasserpalais* closed Tues. Admission DM3, students and seniors DM1.50. Permission to take photos DM2. Grounds open 5am-8pm.) To reach Pillnitz from Dresden (30min.), take *Straßenbahn* #14 from Pirnaischer Platz (direction: Kleinzschachwitz). Get off the *Straßenbahn* and walk toward the banks of the Elbe, where you'll see the *Fähre* (ferry) that shuttles passengers back and forth every 15 minutes (DM1.20, children DM0.80; surcharge DM1 for bicycles, DM7 for cars). Bus #85 also runs from Schillerplatz. The **Weiße Flotte** will also carry you safely there.

MORITZBURG

Never one to be bashful about leaving his mark on the Saxon landscape, August the Strong tore down a little palace in 1723 and replaced it with **Schloß Moritzburg** (tel. 814 39; fax 814 58), his titanic hunting lodge of ribaldry. For his princely comfort, a vast and splendid array of paintings, porcelain, tapestries, and hunting trophies were lugged from Dresden every summer. The immense *Schloß* lounges arrogantly at the end of *Schloßallee* on an island created by an artificial lake. Inside, lavish rooms, leather wallpaper, and leering deer skulls commemorate the courtly hunting penchant. (Open May-Oct. daily 10am-5:30pm; March and Nov. Tues.-Sun. 10am-4:30pm; April Tues.-Sun. 10am-5:30pm; Dec. Tues.-Sun. 10am-3pm. Admission DM6, students and seniors DM4.) To get to the *Schloß* from the *Schmalspurbahn* train station, join the pilgrimage out to the left then right onto *Schloßallee*. Near the *Schloß*, the smaller **Fasanenschlößchen** was built by the great-grandson of August the Strong, Frederick August III, as a more delicate summer residence. Its ornithological exhibition is unexciting unless you're really pining to see the dinky head of a stuffed ostrich. Outside, sculptures of moose in tremendous pain remind you that this, too, is a hunting lodge (open daily 9:30am-4pm; admission DM1, children DM0.50). From Schloß Moritzburg, follow Meißner Str. to the right until Große Fasanenstr.; the Fasanenschlößchen appears on the left. Farther down Große Fasanenstr., the curious structure peeking out of the forest is the **Leuchtturm** (lighthouse), which once served as a backdrop to the mock sea battles of the decadent princes. Moritzburg is also surrounded by extensive parks in addition to a huge gaming reserve and the **Sächsisches Langestüt** ("Saxon Stud-Farm"), where animals procreate almost as frequently as did August the Strong (see p. 457).

In addition to its monuments of Wettin flight and fancy, Moritzburg also has a rich art tradition, having served as a point of inspiration for *Die Brücke* art school. Another prominent artist, **Käthe Kollwitz**, resided in the region for a time. After Kollwitz's home in Berlin was bombed near the end of World War II, Prince Ernst Heinrich von Sachsen offered her a place of retreat here. Though Kollwitz passed away in 1945, only one year after her arrival, her house now holds the **Käthe Kollwitz Gedenkstätte**, Meißner Str. 7. Inside, the museum depicts some of her artwork while providing biographical insight into Köllwitz's Moritzburg days. (Open April-Oct. Tues.-Fri. 11am-5pm, Sat.-Sun. 10am-5pm; Nov.-March Tues.-Fri. noon-3pm, Sat.-Sun. 11am-4pm. Admission DM3.50, students and seniors DM2.)

The fastest way to Moritzburg from Dresden is by **bus.** Take #326 (direction: Radeburg) from the *Hauptbahnhof.* The most scenic route (but also slowest, bumpiest, and noisiest) is the 110-year old *Schmalspurbahn* (narrow-gauge railway; four stops; 30min.). **Trains** also run round-trip (daily 6am-11pm). Moritzburg's **tourist office,** at Schloßallee 3b (tel. 854 10; fax 854 20), provides info on guided **tours** of the *Schloßpark,* concerts in the *Schloß*, love and marriage, horse-and-carriage rentals, and for DM2 they will book rooms (DM25-30 per person, breakfast included) and honeymoon suites (open Easter-Oct. Mon.-Fri. 9am-6pm; Sat.-Sun. noon-4pm; Nov.-Easter Mon.-Fri. 10am-4pm). For a meaty Saxon meal, go to **Zum Dreispitz**, Schloßallee 5 (tel. 822 00), which offers Saxon meat and mushroom dishes for DM10-20 (open daily 11am-midnight). The hunting-tradition-laden **Hengstparade** (equestrian parade) takes place every year on three consecutive Sundays in September. The **telephone code** is 035207.

STOLPEN

The Saxon King August the Strong entertained an extensive array of mistresses, but perhaps the most well-known was the Countess Cosel. As a result of a lovers' quarrel about the king's new mistress and his anti-Protestant stance, she was imprisoned without official sentence in the old castle of Stolpen from 1716 to 1765. Her 49 years of confinement were perhaps made bearable, however, by the spectacular views of Bohemia and Saxon Switzerland from every window of her lonesome look-out. The 13th-century **Burg Stolpen**, Schloßstr. 10 (tel. 63 87), can be reached by bus #261 (direction: Sebnitz) from Dresden (50min.). Disembark, walk right around the building and up the street into the *Markt;* turn left in the *Markt,* then left again onto Schloßstr. where you'll find the castle entrance. The first of four courtyards houses a **torture chamber** that should delight any gothic S&M reveler with its maces and handcuffs. The next three courtyards contain the courtroom, the old castle cannons, the castle tower (which can be climbed), and the castle **chapel and tomb** where Countess Cosel is buried. The **castle well** in the fourth courtyard is the deepest basalt well in the world; it took the castle miners 22 years to find water. (Open daily April-Oct. 9am-5pm; Nov.-March 9am-4pm, weather permitting. Last entrance 30min. before closing. Admission DM5, students and seniors DM3.)

The Stolpen **Tourist Information Center,** Schloßstr. 14a, just relocated and currently lacks a phone number; despite their Luddite spirit, they're still nice and offer maps and a list of accommodations (private rooms DM25-30; open daily 10am-4:30pm; Nov.-March 10am-4pm, weather permitting). **Gar Küche,** on Dresdener Str., right between the *Markt* and the Nieder Tor, is Stolpen's oldest *Gaststätte,* founded in 1659. They serve *Schnitzels* with veggies and potatoes for DM9 (open Mon.-Thurs. 10am-2pm and 3:30-10pm, Fri. 10am-2pm and 3-11pm, Sat. 11am-11pm, Sun. 11am-9pm). Alternatively, load up on delicious fruity goodness at the **Obst und Gemüse** grocery store, Schulstr. 21 (open Mon.-Fri. 8am-6pm, Sat. 8-10:30am). Stoplen's **postal code** is 01833. The **telephone code** is 035973.

■ Saxon Switzerland (Sächsische Schweiz)

Saxon Switzerland gives you the full Swiss nature experience without the funny Swiss German. One of eastern Germany's most beloved holiday destinations, Saxon Switzerland has become Germany's newest national park since reunification. The region is "Swiss" because of the stunning landscape—sandstone cliffs emerge from dense vegetation, sumptuous summits and excellent hiking beckon adventurous tourists. If you do plan to do some hiking, a handy trail map of the region is available from all tourist offices in the area for DM9.50. Less than an hour from Dresden on the Dresden-Prague rail line, this uniquely beautiful yet inexpensive region is a must-see for those convinced that eastern Germany comes only in shades of gray.

PIRNA

Pirna gloats in the fame it gleaned from Canaletto's picturesque depiction of its marketplace. Once a 16th-century trading town that overshadowed its golden neighbor, Dresden, today Pirna is something of a toadstool compared to the more prominent towns higher on the mountains. The *Markt*'s beauty is still evident, although the city's greatest significance now lies in its role as "the door to Saxon Switzerland."

Pirna is a mere 30 minutes from Dresden by S-Bahn. To see the *Markt* that fills the natives with so much pride, walk straight down Gartenstr. from the train station, turn left on Grohmannstr., and right on Jacobäerstr. which turns into Schuhgasse and leads into the **Markt**. The **Rathaus** once served as a mall for merchants purveying the latest in silk tunics. The 16th-century **Marienkirche** on the right of the market place is graced by a huge baptismal fountain once admired by Goethe. At Obere Burgstr. 1, you can see the 16th-century **Teufelserker** (devil's bay window), named for its three evil overhanging figures. At Barbiergasse 10, its Manichaen counterpart, the **Engelserker** (angel's bay window) is adorned with a heavenly gold figure. The **Stadtmuseum Pirna,** Klosterhof 2-3 (tel. 31 30; fax 842 66), provides a thorough explanation of these architectural oddities, as well as its own collection of tricks and trinkets that vaguely represent the city's history. You can also see the **Schützenröcklein,** one of the oldest military dresses left in the region (open May-Oct. Tues.-Sun. 10am-6pm, Nov.-April Tues.-Sun. 10am-5pm; admission DM2, students and seniors DM1). The **Schloß Sonnenstein** overlooks the city and was its often unsuccessful defender against invading Swedes, militant Prussians, and Napoleonic looters; it now houses bureaucratic offices.

Pirna's **tourist office,** Dohnaische Str. 31 (tel. 52 84 97; fax 55 63 31), provides free maps and books rooms (DM20-40) for a DM5 fee (open Mon.-Fri. 9am-6pm, Sat. 9:30am-1pm). The **post office** is located at Garten Str. 29/30, 01784 Pirna. To bypass the pricey hotel scene, try the **Jugendherberge-Pirna-Copitz Weltfrieden** (world peace), Birkwitzer Str. 51 (tel. 52 73 16). This socialist box holds 160 beds and rents **bikes.** Take bus Line F from the *Busbahnhof* across the Elbe. It will drop you off right in front *("vor der Jugendherberge")* if you ask nicely. (DM22, over 26 DM26. Breakfast included.) For a meal in Pirna, scale the 150 steps up to the **Biergarten** in Schloß Sonnenstein, Schloßhof 4. Treat yourself to some grill fare (DM3.50-6) and a beer (open May-Oct. Mon.-Thurs. 5pm-midnight, Fri.-Sat. 3pm-2am, Sun. noon-midnight). If you have no interest in hiking up to the castle, grab a quick bit at **Bier-Pub,** Am Markt 16, where burgers and *Würste* run DM3.50-7 (open Mon.-Fri. 9am-6pm, Sat.-Sun. 11am-6pm). The **telephone code** is 03501.

You can also get to **Liebstadt** by bus to visit the exceptionally curious **Schloß Kuckucksstein,** Am Schloßberg 1 (tel. (035027) 426). Once a robber baron's castle, the *Schloß* was taken over by a family devoted to Freemasonry. The museum inside details the history of the lodges, but let it be known: Freemasons rule the world.

RATHEN

The jagged sandstone cliffs that are often referred to as "those jagged sandstone cliffs" but officially called **Die Bastei** loom over the dinky town of **Rathen,** connected only by a sandstone bridge that prevents their visitors from plummeting into the abyss below. You can ascend the cliffs either from **Wehlen** or Rathen itself; the path from Wehlen, starting across the Elbe from the S-Bahn station by the Ratskeller, provides a gentle incline that August the Strong used to ascend with his carnivorous pals (look for the **Höllengrund am Steinernen Tisch,** his big-ass dining table, at the top). The climb from Rathen is steeper but will get up quicker. Because of Rathen's prime location at the edge of **Sächsische Schweiz National Park,** hiking trails of varying difficulty abound in the region. One leads to Rathen's **Felsenbühne,** one of the most beautiful open air theaters in Europe: 2000 seats face a stage carved into the cliff. Tickets and schedules are available from Theaterkasse der Felsenbühne (tel. 704 97). Beautifully-wooded trails connect Rathen to Hohnstein (see below).

There's no tourist office in Rathen; look to the **Gemeindeamt Kurort Rathen,** on the first floor of the *Gästeamt* (tel. 704 22) for maps, stacks of information on hiking trails, and a list of private rooms or area hotels. To get there from the S-Bahn station, take the ferry across the Elbe (DM1, children and bikes DM0.50) and walk down the main street in Niederrathen for 10 minutes until you see the office on the left by the fire station (open Mon.-Fri. 9am-noon and 2-6pm, Sat. 9am-2pm; in winter closed Sat.). Panoramic boat trips on the **Motorschiff "Bastei"** (300 seats) or the more personal **Dampschiff "Sachsenwald"** (80 seats) leave every two hours from Rathen's shores (one way to Wehlen DM7; round-trip to Bad Schandau DM23). Stash all your heavy packs and burdens at the **lockers** in the station (DM4). The **Jugendherberge Carl Stein,** Auf den Halden 33 (tel. (035024) 704 25), in the nature park above Rathen near the *Bastei* stones, isn't aesthetic delight, but it's cheap. To get there, turn left once you've crossed the Elbe and walk down the path for 20 minutes until you see the "JH" sign on the right. (Reception open 7am-8pm. DM9.50 (yee-haw!), over 26 DM12. Breakfast DM6. Sheets DM6.) The **telephone city code** is 035024.

HOHNSTEIN

The small village of **Hohnstein** ("high stone" in old Saxon), with its grand forest vistas on all sides, is a mere hop, skip, and hike from Rathen. The hefty trek (1hr. 15min.) traverses the inner valleys of the *Sächsische Schweiz.* To get there from Rathen, follow the **path of the red stripe** (a hiking trail, not a Maoist paramilitary clan) which starts behind the *Gästeamt.* It's 20km from Königstein or Pirna by rail and then a half-hour bus ride (direction: Hohnstein). The town encircles the **Hohnstein Jugendburg** (tel. (035975) 202; fax 203) which holds a *Jugendherberge,* a history and nature museum, *Aussichtsturm* (lookout tower), café-restaurant, and an outdoor garden. The **Museum der Geschichte des Burg Hohnstein** covers the history of the *Burg* with medieval armor, weapons, and a powerful exhibit on anti-fascist resistance in Dresden and *Sächsische Schweiz.* The museum commemorates Konrad Hahnewald (the beloved father of Hohnstein's *Jugendherberge* and later the first political refugee of the Hohnstein Concentration Camp). (Open March-Oct. 9am-5pm; by appointment only at other times. Admission DM2.) The main office of the **Jugendherberge** is in building #5. Campfires, grills, and special disco and fondue nights spice up the hostel's scene free of charge; you can rent guitars, skis, and alarm clocks. Dull but clean rooms with one to four beds (DM21, over 26 DM26) and titanic six- to 18-bed rooms that often house school groups (DM16, over 26 DM19; reception open 7am-noon and 2-10pm; breakfast included). The **tourist office** in the *Rathaus* (tel. 250) doles out information on trails and historical sights of the *Burg,* and finds rooms (open Mon.-Wed. 9am-noon, 1:30-5pm, Tues., Thurs., and Fri. 9am-noon and 2-6pm, Sat. 10am-1pm). The **telephone code** is 035975.

KÖNIGSTEIN

The next stop on the Dresden S-Bahn's journey into the hills and dales of the Sächsische Schweiz is **Königstein.** The *Weiße Flotte* boat also alights on these shores south toward **Schöna** (one-way from Dresden DM23, children DM12). The **fortress** is incredible—drawbridges, impenetrable stone walls, and a huge complex put this mammoth on the list of legendary medieval royal abodes. Once an oft-exploited retreat for the kings of Saxony during times of civil unrest and marital discord (the Saxon electors tended to flee faster than the French), it was later converted into a feared state prison; Nikolai Bakunin and August Bebel were imprisoned here. During the Third Reich, it was used by the Nazis to stash stolen art, and between 1949 and 1955 it served as a juvenile correctional center. Recently, skeletons were found in the fortress's torture chamber; no one yet knows which of its incarnations produced them. The complex now houses museums on everything from weapons to porcelain. The view from the fortress is worth sweating for—from the city, it's a half-hour struggle straight up from Hain Str. to Kirchgasse then to Goethe Str. Around the left side of the rickety movie theater are the stairs, and then the stairs, and then the stairs up to the fortress. If you're a limping sissy tourist and too tired for the trek, the cheeky **Festungs Express** will drag your lazy ass uphill while touring Königstein (DM2.50, kids DM1; round-trip DM4, kids DM1.50). Rides leave from the square regularly, just to the right down Bahnhofstr. (Festungs Express runs May-Sept. daily 8am-8pm; Oct.-April 9am-5pm. Fortress open Easter-Sept. 9am-8pm, Oct. 9am-6pm, Nov.-Easter 9am-5pm. Admission DM6, students DM4. Tours in English available.) Paths also lead from the town up to the challenging 415-m **Lilienstein,** hiked by August the Strong in 1708 (the 2km hike takes a steep half-hour).

The **tourist office,** Schreiberberg 2 (tel. 261), on the *Marktplatz* close to the "Festungs Express" stop, books rooms for DM20-30, but in summer it's wise to call ahead. They have a list of available rooms, vacation houses, and *Pensionen;* prices are in the window when they're closed (open Mon.-Tues. and Thurs.-Fri. 9am-5:30pm, Wed. 1-5:30pm, Sat. 9am-noon; Nov.-March may be open shorter hours). Königstein's **Naturfreunde Jugendherberge,** Halbestadt 13 (tel. (035022) 424 32), is a lot nicer than most hostels but also a helluva lot more expensive—the stunning one- to four-bed rooms have showers in them. To get there, cross the river by ferry and turn right. The hostel will emerge on your right in about 10 minutes. (Reception open 7-10am, 3-5:30pm, and 7-8pm. DM42, over 26 DM50; non-members DM6 extra. Breakfast included.) The **campground** (tel. 682 24) is on the banks of the Elbe about 10 minutes upstream from the station in the shadow of the fortress. It's got washing facilities, a small supply shop, and a playground (DM12 per person with tent; open April-Oct.). The **telephone code** is 035021.

BAD SCHANDAU

One stop farther upstream from Königstein lies Bad Schandau, a miniature village sitting daintily between the Elbe and the mountains. Though it's not perfect in its looks, the town feels sweetly quiet and surprisingly untouristed. Yet another small-town **Heimat Museum,** Badallee 10 (tel. 421 73), sets you straight on Saxon geology, geography, shipping, and Bad Schandauer history (open Tues., Thurs., and Fri. 2-5pm; Sun. 9:30am-12:30pm; admission DM2, children DM0.50). From the train station, take the **ferry** (DM1) and follow the signs to the **tourist office,** Markt 8 (tel. 424 12), for hiking maps and a list of rooms. One office wall is plastered with transport schedules. Take the solar-powered, environmentally friendly *Kirnitzschtalbahn* train (May-Oct. 31 every 30min.) to the **Lichtenhainer Waterfall,** a favorite starting point for full-day hikes on the **Schrammsteine.** The office can provide suggestions for shorter or longer hikes, but daytrippers beware: the ferry back to the train station stops running as early as 6pm on some days. The office also capitalizes on its proximity to the Czech Republic. Bus **tours** to **Prague** are offered on some Wednesdays (DM49 round-trip); the Czech towns Decin, Hreusko, and Prebischtor are nearby (office open Mon.-Fri. 9am-noon and 1-6pm, Sat. 9am-noon). To rent a **bike,** try **Fahrradverleih,**

Post Str. 14 (tel. 428 83; DM15 per day with ID). Overnighters should head up to the **Jugendherberge** in Ostrau, Dorfstr. 14 (tel./fax 424 08), poised on a plateau above the town. (Reception open 7-10am and 4:30-10pm. DM21, over 26 DM25. Breakfast included.) The **telephone code** is 035022.

SEBNITZ

If ever you've sat in a restaurant idly staring at artificial flower displays on the table and wondered, "who the hell thought of these?" a visit to Sebnitz is in order. Sebnitz has been producing the **fleurs du mal** for the past 150 years and offers its perplexed tourists a chance to see that their manufacturing requires some skill and craft. You can check out the creation of flamboyant faux flowers at the **Schauwerkstatt der Seidenblummenmannfaktur** (display factory of plastic flower production), on Schillerstr. 3 (open Tues.-Sun. 10am-5pm; admission DM2.50, kids DM1.50).

"Quatsch!" you exclaim. "Who cares about plastic flowers? You can't do anything with 'em!" But *au contraire*, campers—the **Kunstblumen and Heimatmuseum** (plastic flower and city museum), at Hertigswalder Str. 12, displays a history of the (gasp!) social functions of plastic flowers and other things germane to little Sebnitz (open Tues.-Sun. 10am-5pm; DM3, children DM2). Sebnitz is on the outer boundaries of the *Sächsische Schweiz,* with hiking trails that will make you feel like a rugged international badass, taking you into the Czech Republic in a mere 25 minutes.

You can arrive in Sebnitz from Bad Schandau via bus from Bad Schandau's train station (40min.). The **tourist office,** Schillerstr. 3 (tel. (035971) 530 79), can set you up in a *Pension* for as little as DM12-15 with breakfast (open Mon.-Fri. 10am-6pm, Sat. 9am-noon). Enjoy a meal (no plastic contents) at the **café** in the Heimatsmuseum. (Daily special (Mon.-Fri.) DM4.50. Open daily 8am-10pm).

■ Upper Lusatia (Oberlausitz)

Between Dresden and the Polish border stretch the rolling green hills of Upper Lusatia (Oberlausitz). Dotted with cows, farmers, and little cheery-looking villages, this expanse of land is bordered by two former Warsaw Pact neighbors, Poland and the Czech Republic. As a result, throughout the GDR's reign, Upper Lusatia remained largely untouched by Western tourism and the Politburo *apparatchiks* left much of the region's magnificent medieval, Renaissance, and Baroque architecture to decay. But today, as in much of eastern Germany, Upper Lusatia is now undergoing extensive restoration and renewal, in pursuit of its former shine.

As the homeland of Germany's only national minority, the **Sorbs** *(die Wenden* in German), the area around Bautzen is rich in customs long abandoned elsewhere. The Sorbs are a Slav minority stemming from Serbian tribes who streamed into the Lower and Upper Lusatian areas between the Spreewald and Lusatian mountains during the 6th century. Sorbish is similar to Czech and Polish but spoken with two different pronunciation patterns (Lower and Upper). *Niedersorbisch* is spoken in and around Cottbus and *Obersorbisch* in the Bautzen region. Since the crystallization of the Sorb nationalist movement in 1848, small Sorbian-speaking communities totaling about 75,000 members have maintained their regional identities. Under Hitler's *Reich,* Sorbish was ruthlessly suppressed as a program of liquidation commenced in 1937; after the war, the *Sorbengesetz* (Sorbs Law) was established to assure the protection and promotion of the culture and language. However, the Sorbs still encountered many barriers as they tried to preserve their unique culture. They were pressured to leave villages, channeled to the coal mines, and Sorbian schools were kept under particularly harsh state supervision.

Though the pressures to integrate and Westernize still exist, today, Sorbish literature and arts are flourishing once again. After reunification, a special bureau was created to guarantee Sorbian civil rights in the German constitution. The Sorbs are particularly renowned for their ornamental Easter eggs, the Easter rides organized throughout various towns, and their traditional love of marriage and weddings.

Zapust is a merry Sorbian festival when dance and music are celebrated from the end of January to the beginning of March. The Sorbs have their own fairy tales and musical instruments—the fiddle-type *Dudelsack* as well as a wind instrument called the *Tarakawa.* Foreign tourists are increasingly gaining the opportunity to take part in the merriment and pageantry, as foreign-language brochures and improved travel infrastructure provide access for visitors in search of the Sorbish experience.

BAUTZEN (BUDYSIN)

Where else in the world can you find a witch's house, a church where Protestants and Catholics can attend church hand-in-hand, and a binational theater that puts on puppet shows in Sorbish and German? Nowhere but Bautzen. A millennium-old cultural capital, with ancient towers on a hill high above the Spree River, Bautzen is the seat of several Sorb institutions and was the home of the first Sorb tribe centuries ago. Bautzen has survived pillage, war, and fire; today its romantic cobblestone streets wind among medieval, Baroque, and Art Nouveau residences. The GDR locked political prisoners away here, but today you can wander without care through the Sorb treasures. You can also see the unique "Easter Riding Event," when lavishly-decorated Sorb horses parade through town. Bilingual street signs are a clear sign that Bautzen (Budysin) is indeed the Sorbian capital of the world.

Orientation, Practical Information, and Accommodations The **tourist office,** Hauptmarkt 1 (tel. 420 16; fax 53 43 09), offers listings of accommodations in hotels, *Pensionen,* and private homes (open Mon.-Fri. 9am-6pm, Sat.-Sun. 10am-noon; Oct.-April closed on Sun.). At the ancient defense-tower-turned-**Jugendherberge (HI),** Am Zwinger 1 (tel. 440 45), just to the right through Nikolaiturm, you can get packed into a 22-bed room if the more habitable doubles upstairs are not available. While the 20-minute walk to the tower from the train station is unthreatening, reconstruction around the tower might necessitate flexibility and conversations with some locals to find alternate routes. (Reception open daily 6:30-8am and 6-8pm. No lockout. Curfew 10pm. DM16, over 26 DM18.50. Breakfast included.) The **post office,** 02607 Bautzen, is located on Postplatz (open Mon.-Fri. 7am-6pm, Sat. 8am-noon). The **telephone code** is 03591.

Food For a lick of local cuisine, **Zum Karasek,** Kornstr. 8, will weigh you down with its *Oberlausitzer Bauernfrühstück* (DM9) or an indulgently tasty *Soljanka* soup (DM3.90; open Mon.-Sat. 11am-1am, Sun. 11:30am-11pm). For excellent Italian food and an entertaining decor heavy on gangsta motifs, **Al Capone's,** Schülerstr. 4, dishes out pizzas (DM6.50) and pastas (DM7.50; open Mon. 5pm-midnight, Tues.-Sun. 11:30am-2pm and 5pm-midnight). **Bistro Adria,** Reichenstr. 16, will serve you a quick bite in a central location. *Schnitzel* and *Wurst* (DM2-8.50).

Sights and Entertainment To reach the **Altstadt** from the station, walk straight through Rathenauplatz and bear left onto Bahnhofstr., then left at the post office onto Karl-Marx-Str. Follow the Marxist path to the intersection up ahead, and on your left will be the **Stadt Museum,** Kornmarktstr. 1 (tel. 49 85 00), specializing in the regional history of Bautzen, its customs and traditions. The museum also displays a collection of wood carvings and copper engravings from the 15th to 17th centuries (open Wed.-Sun. 10am-5pm; admission DM3, children and students DM2). Up Kornmarktstr. from the museum is the leaning tower of Bautzen, the **Reichen Turm,** on Reichenstr. It was built in 1490, with a Baroque top added in 1715. It deviates exactly 1.44m from the perpendicular. Climb up to take in the marvelous view. (Open daily April-Oct. 10am-5pm. Last entrance at 4:30pm. Admission DM1, students and children DM0.50.) A block away, at the intersection of Wendische Gasse and Wendische Str. is the **Alte Caserne** (old barracks), an elegant building designed by Dresden master Gottfried Semper that housed unappreciative 19th-century troops and currently provides business offices.

Left from the Reichen Turm down Reichenstr. is the **Hauptmarkt.** The grand yellow building is the **Rathaus** (built in 1213), with the *Fleischmarkt* behind it alongside the Gothic **Dom St. Petri** (tel. 441 02). Built in 1213, it has been eastern Germany's only *Simultankirche* (simultaneously Catholic and Protestant) since 1524. The division of the church was a remarkably peaceful 16th-century compromise (open June-Sept. Mon.-Sat. 10am-noon and 1-5pm; May and Oct. Mon.-Sat. 10am-noon and 1-3pm). Farther along sits the abode and clerical administrative in an ornate Baroque red-and-gold building. Within it dwells the **Domschatz** (cathedral treasury), a phenomenal collection of jewel-studded gowns, icons, and gold stuff (open Mon.-Fri. 10am-noon and 1-4pm; free). Follow the narrow street An der Petrikirche downhill from the cathedral until you see the **Nikolaiturm** down the hill on your right. Crossing under the gate, note the face carved above the entrance. Locals claim that this is a likeness of a former mayor: he was bricked alive into the tower as retribution for opening the city to Hussite attackers in the 16th century.

If you head back through Nikolaiturm and right onto Schloßstr. you'll find the **Sorbisches Museum** in the Orlenburg complex of the *Altstadt* (tel. 424 03); it details the intriguing history and culture of the Sorbs, including samples of their writing, life-sized costumes, the area's special Sorbian Easter eggs, and those crazy *Dudelsacks* that look like psychedelic water-filtration devices (open daily 10am-12:30pm and 1-5pm, Nov.-March 10am-12:30pm and 1-4pm; admission DM3, students DM2). From the Nikolaiturm or the Sorbisches Museum, follow the **Osterweg** path around the city walls and along the Spree, taking in the views of the 1480 **Mühlbastei** (mill tower), the 1558 **Alte Wasserkunst** (old water tower), and the spire of the 1429 **Michaeliskirche.** On the way back up the hill, on the other side of the fortress, lies the brown-shingled **Hexenhäusrl** (witches' cottage). This small wooden structure, the oldest house in the area, was the only home in the area to survive two devastating fires; the villagers subsequently shunned the inhabitants as witches (though the fire was actually averted by a well inside the house). A fine, new family lives there now. If you find the Sorbs particularly absorbing, visit **Sorbische Kultur Information,** on Kurt-Pchalek-Str. 26 (tel. 421 05), directly adjacent to the Sorbische Café and around the corner from the post office. Purchase Sorb CDs, Sorb literature, and darling ornamented Easter eggs (open Mon.-Fri. 9am-4:30pm).

Near Bautzen: Panschwitz-Kuchau and Neuschwitz

Today the Sorbian language is seldom heard in the city, but buses leave regularly for villages such as **Panschwitz-Kuckau** and **Neuschwitz,** where both the mother tongue and colorful traditional costumes are alive and well. If your timing is right, you can witness one of the celebrations held on Catholic holidays. On Easter, the people of Bautzen and neighboring towns gather to ride around on horses, "proclaiming the good news." January 25 marks the **Marriage of the Birds** *(Vogelhochzeit),* when children dressed in bird costumes run through the village to represent local birds' gratefulness for the birdseed left by their human friends and to celebrate the happiness of marriage. For more information, head to the **Sorbische Kultur-Information** (p. 468). For regional bus information, go to the terminal at August-Bebel-Platz in Bautzen where the **Überlandlinien** (long-distance) boats depart, and take time to decipher the schedules.

GÖRLITZ

The easternmost town in Germany, Görlitz offers an exquisite, untouristed *Altstadt* that has changed little since Napoleon trudged through it on the way to his unsuccessful invasion of Russia. Many of the elegant pastel Renaissance and Baroque homes of former *Bürgermeister*s still stand. In fact, Görlitz was one of the only German towns to survive completely unharmed after World War II. With straightforward rail connections to Bautzen (45min.), Zittau (1hr.), Dresden (2hr.), and Breslau/Wroctaw in neighboring Poland (2½hr.), plus easy access to major bus routes, Görlitz is an excellent starting point for exploring Upper Lusatia.

Most of Görlitz's central sites are located around the **Obermarkt.** From the train station, go straight ahead and you'll find yourself strolling down **Berliner Straße,** Görlitz's main shopping mall. On the street, you'll find shops and pedestrians. Within a matter of minutes you'll reach **Postplatz** where you'll see a beautiful central fountain, the gloomy and sooted main post office, and the darkly stained **Frauenkirche** (a late Gothic cathedral built in 1431). Directly past it is the formidable **Karstadt-Haus** shopping forum; built in 1912, it was one of the last architecturally original shopping centers in Germany. Walk inside for a pleasant startle: the glass roof produces a stunning illumination that lends an aesthetic component to commercialism (the sound you hear is Adorno rolling over in his grave). From here walk down Marienplatz and Steinstr. into the Obermarkt and look for house #29; the bountifully Baroque abode served as a tourist residence for August the Strong and Napoleon, and now houses a fully egalitarian **tourist office.**

Across the *Markt,* you'll see the **Dreifaltigkeitskirche.** Originally a 13th-century Franciscan monastery, the church bears marks of frequent expansion. Walking past it down Brüderstr. you will come to the *Untermarkt.* Practically every side street and alley offers some little landmark—a gargoyle or an historical apothecary. Here you'll find the **Rathaus** (built in 1537, remodeled in 1902-1903). At its top is a clock-face in which a sculptured head's chin yawns with the passing of each minute. House #22 is the **Whisper Arch** *(Flüsterbogen)*—even if you're traveling solo, grab the nearest Görlitzer (preferably one who doesn't tattle) to stand on the stone steps; put your ear to the stone while your partner whispers his or her darkest secrets. On the corner is the **Ratsapotheke,** a Renaissance building from 1550 that still has an astrology and astronomy chart painted on its crumbling surface—the confluence of tweaked clocks is indicative of Görlitz's position on the 15-degree meridian, the center point of the Central European time zone. Don't miss the **St. Peter and Paul Church** down Peterstr. from the *Untermarkt.* Its brightly adorned interior, speckled with gilded suns and clocks, is enough to impress even the most jaded of travel guide writers (open Mon.-Fri. 10:30am-5pm, Sat. 10am-6pm, Sun. 11:30am-6pm).

Pick up information on other local sights from the **tourist office,** at Obermarkt 29 (tel. 475 70; fax 47 57 27). They sell maps and find rooms (DM30-40) in private homes for no charge (open Mon.-Fri. 10am-6pm, Sat. 10am-4pm, Sun. 10am-1pm). For a **taxi,** call 40 68 93. Görlitz has an awesome *Jugendstil* **Jugendherberge (HI),** at Goethestr. 17 (tel. 40 65 10). This historical villa, poised over beautiful shaded grounds, is one of the coolest hostels for miles around. Take the south exit *(Südausgang)* of the train station, bear left up the hill, turn right onto Zittauer Str., and continue until Goethestr. Turn left, and the hostel is ahead on the right, just before the street curves (25min.). Enter the gate up the stairs to reach the entrance on the right. The huge, stained-glass windows are almost as brilliantly colorful as the comforters (we exaggerate—*nothing* is as colorful as the comforters). Accordions and guitars are supplied for guest use; you can also rent skis, baby carriages, and grills (only the carriages are recommended for use with babies). Mostly four-bed rooms with balconies. (Reception open Mon.-Fri. 2-10pm, Sat.-Sun. 4-10pm. No lockout. Curfew 10pm. DM22, seniors DM26. Handicapped accessible. Breakfast included, but they'll jack you for DM2.50 if you need a cup of coffee that's as black as a moonless midnight to begin your day's journey.) The **telephone code** is 03581.

Choose among the many cost-effective options on Berliner Str. or check out the nooks and crannies of the *Altstadt* for Slavic culinary offerings. **Destille,** on Nikolaistr. (tel. 40 53 02), directly across from the Nikolaiturm, serves *Soljanka* soup with sour sauce, lemons, olives, and toast (DM5) to the many locals who flock to its wooden tables. Try a hefty farmer's omelette with ham and potatoes (DM10; open Tues.-Sat. 11:30am-midnight, Sun. 11am-10pm). The immaculate chain seafood restaurant **Gastmahl des Meeres,** Struve Str. 2 (tel. 40 62 29), whips up Alaskan fish for under DM10 (open Mon.-Sat. 11am-9:30pm, Sun. 11am-3pm). The **E-Markt** grocery store on Goethe Str. is an easy walk from the hostel towards Zittauer Str.; if you're really lazy, have a friend push you in the baby carriage.

■ Zittauer Gebirge

In a sliver of Germany that borders Czech Bohemia and Poland rise the rocky cliffs of the Zittauer Gebirge. These beehive-shaped mountains were a favored spot of medieval monks; today monks are out, but skiers, hikers, and landscape lovers are in. No wonder that Romantic artists like Ludwig Richter found some of their most sublime inspirations in this mystical region. But matters have not always been so picture-perfect. In 1491, the Gebirge was the scene of the vicious **Bierkrieg** (beer war), when the citizens of Görlitz protested Zittau's success as a beer-brewing town by destroying barrels of the beverage. The incensed townspeople stole a menagerie of animals from surrounding Görlitzer farms in retaliation, an example of boar-for-a-beer justice. More recently, the local forests and workers of this region have experienced a nasty socialist hangover, as inefficient factories that belched pollution into the trees are being shut down, leaving many residents unemployed.

ZITTAU

Nestled between three lands—Poland, the Czech Republic, and Germany—Zittau has served as a trading and cultural center for many years. Under the rule of the Bohemian kings in 1238, Zittau took on an dominant role in Upper Lusatia, and later within the textile industry.

The more important sites lie along the *Altstadt.* From the train station, follow Bahnhofstr. to Bautzner Str., which will lead you directly to the **Johanniskirche Platz.** There you can see the towering **Johanniskirche,** rebuilt in 1837, and climb to the tower (open Mon.-Fri. noon-6pm, Sat. and Sun. 1-6pm; Nov.-March closed on weekends; admission DM2, students and seniors DM1). From the church, walk directly down Bautzner Str. to the grand **Marktplatz.** In the center flows the 1585 **Rolandbrunnen** (fountain), directly across is the **Rathaus,** designed by Prussian architect Friedrich Schinkel in 1843 in a Renaissance style. Heading left down Johannistr., you'll see the late Gothic **Kloster Kirche,** and farther up the street, the **Stadtmuseum,** housed in a former 13th-century Franciscan monastery. A gruesome collection of standard medieval torture devices awaits in the cellar (open Tues. 10am-noon and 1-4pm, Wed. 10am-noon and 1-6pm, Thurs. 10am-noon and 1-4pm, Fri. 10am-1pm, Sat. 2-4pm, Sun. 9am-noon and 2-5pm; admission DM3, students DM2).

The **tourist office** is in the *Rathaus* (tel. 75 21 37; fax 75 21 61), on the first floor near the left side entrance. It provides hiking maps and a room-finding service (room DM20-40 per person) for a DM5 charge (open Mon.-Fri. 8am-6pm, Sat. 9am-1pm, Sun. 10am-4pm). A room-finding service is also operated at the equally friendly **Oberlausitzer Tourist Information,** Bahnhofstr. 9 (tel. 51 24 51). The **post office,** 02763 Zittau, is located on Poststr. (open Mon.-Fri. 8am-1pm, Sat. 2-6pm and 9am-noon). A pretty good deal if you're not looking for elegant drapes is the **Studentenwerk Dresden,** at Zittau's technical school, the Hochschule für Technik und Wirtschaft, Hochwaldstr. 12 (tel. 688 10; fax 68 81 30). Rooms in the high school dorms are DM12 per night (shower and toilet down the hall). There's no breakfast and the furnishings are relatively crude, but a bed and sheets are guaranteed. You must call at least one working day in advance. Head up Johannisstr. from the tourist office for the historic, hearty fare of the **Kloster Stüb'l,** Johannisstr. 4 (tel. 51 25 76). Pictures of merry monks with large glasses of beer greet your entrance into this brewery restaurant, built in 1810. Try the *Mauke mit Gewiegtebrutl und Sauerkraut* (potatoes, beefsteak, and sauerkraut) for DM12, or lighter *Soljanka* soup with toast and lemon for DM4. There's also an all-you-can-eat salad bar for DM9 (open Mon.-Tues. 11am-10pm, Fri. and Sat. 11am-midnight). A myriad of cafés and pastry shops in the *Markt* provide tasty delicacies. The **telephone code** is 03583.

OYBIN

From the Zittau train station, hop on the **Schmalspurbahn** (narrow gauge steam train; one-way DM3.60) for a 45-minute ride into scenic Oybin in its 100-year-old coach.

This little train has remained in continuous operation as a normal railway line to the present day, making it a premier attraction for locomotive buffs. Called "the pearl of the Zittauer Gebirge," Oybin is a nice half-day trip to half-timbered houses and bulbous cliffs, and will keep hikers and skiers happy and challenged. At the top of the cliffs are the ruins of a high gothic fortress and cloister built in the 14th century. In the summer, open-air concerts are held in the halls of the **cathedral.** From the trails along the top cliffs one can see far into Czech Bohemia. To get there from the station, head right onto Hauptstr. The stairs will be on the right of the church (admission DM4, students DM2.50). If it's just railroad memorabilia you're tracking, cross the tracks from the station to visit the **Schmalspurbahn Museum,** where you can see the first tickets ever sold for the adorable little train in 1890 (open Mon.-Fri. 1-4pm, Sat.-Sun. 10am-noon and 1-4pm; admission DM1, children DM0.50).

The **tourist office,** Freiligrathsstr. 8 (tel. 703 46; fax 702 78), will outfit you with hiking maps, town maps, bus schedules, and rooms in private homes or *Pensionen* (DM20-50) for free (open Mon.-Fri. 9am-5:30pm, Sat. 10am-3pm). If the office is closed, they leave a list of available rooms at **Hotel Oybiner Hof,** Saupstraße 5. The **telephone code** is 035844. The nearby town of Jonsdorf is home to the **Jugendherberge Jonsdorf (HI),** which consists of two houses about 1km apart. The office is at Hainstr. 14 (tel. 702 20); call in advance (DM18, over 26 DM22; youth hostel ID required). You can also pay for a half-pension (includes lunch; DM25, over 26 DM28). Take the *Schmalspurbahn* from Zittau to the last station (Jonsdorf) and then turn down Hainstr. For info regarding lovely little Jonsdorf, call the **tourist office,** Auf der Heide 1 (tel./fax 706 16). You can also take the *Schmalspurbahn* here to get to Jonsdorf's twin hostel in Waltersdorf. **Jugendherberge Waltersdorf** (tel. (035841) 70 26 50) is accessible only by foot from the village (5km); if you call ahead, they'll pick you up by car for DM1 (DM14, over 26 DM16. Breakfast DM6).

▓ Chemnitz

If you ever wanted visible proof of the triumph of capitalism over Communism, visit Chemnitz. Beginning in 1953, the city went by the name "Karl-Marx-Stadt" in a rather unsubtle tribute to the philosopher, who never even called it home. In 1990, however, the workers of the city united in a plebiscite to disavow the town of its Marxist associations and return it to its earlier title. While the city's name no longer serves as a monument to Communism, many of the Communist monuments remain, giving Chemnitz a strange, nostalgic value. But if you've come to see streets named Karl-Marx-Str. and signs reading "*Es lebt die machtige Sowjetische Union!*" ("Long live the mighty Soviet Union!"), you've arrived too late. Western *Marks* have begun to infiltrate Chemnitz, forcing the citizens to pit the city's promising future against its backward past.

Orientation and Practical Information Tourist Information Chemnitz, Rathausstr. 1 (tel. 450 87 50; fax 450 87 60), is located in a little booth inside the *Stadt Halle,* straight across from the glaring bust of Marx. Exit the train station and take the first right on Carolastr. The next street is Straße der Nationen. Go left and continue until you see the *Stadt Halle* on your right. For a **taxi,** call 44 62 44 or 30 22 51. **Laundry machines** can be found at the corner of Hartmannstr. and Theaterstr. The **main post office,** a Marxist architectural fantasy, is on Straße der Nationen, across from the tourist office (open Mon.-Fri. 9am-6pm, Sat. 9am-noon). The **postal code** is 09009. The **telephone code** is 0371.

Accommodations To a large degree Chemnitz defies the penny-pinching efforts of budget travelers, with hotels and *Pensionen* frequently running over DM100. The tourist office can help out with private rooms for DM25-40 per person with a DM2 finder's fee tacked on. **AIGNER** (tel./fax 451 91), a private room agency in the main hall of the train station, will find you a pad at DM35-50 per person (fee included; open Mon.-Fri. 8am-8pm, Sat.-Sun. 8am-2pm). The stunningly renovated

Jugendherberge (HI) awaits at Augustusburger Str. 369 (tel. 713 31). It's easiest to take bus T-245 from the bus station located just down the street from the train station to the "Walter-Klippel-Str." stop on Augustusburgerstr.; after 5pm, take streetcar #1 or 6 (direction: Gablenz) to "Gablenzplatz" (5 stops). Augustusbergerstr. runs parallel to the tracks on the left hand side. It's a 15-minute walk from there. Don't even think of walking from the city. Out here you'll have the opportunity to see the inviting green countryside that surrounds poor old Chemnitz. (Reception open 2-7pm with reservations, 4-7pm without. DM22, over 26 DM26.50. Breakfast included. Best to call ahead to make sure there's space—in a pinch, you can always head for the hills of Augustusburg (p. 473).)

Food The supermarket in the train station keeps amazing hours (open Mon.-Fri. 6am-9:45pm, Sat.-Sun. 7am-9:45pm). It's also remarkably easy to find cheap eats of the fast food variety along Straße der Nationen. For simple snacky fare, head to the neighborhood behind the *Stadt Halle.* To find a more satisfying meal, take a stroll down the Brühl, a pedestrian zone lined with moderately priced restaurants. **Zum Bacchus,** on the corner of Bruhlstr. and Hermanstr. (tel. 41 53 11), offers good German meals (DM9-16) as well as decent salad plates (DM5-8; open Mon.-Fri. 11am-midnight, Sat.-Sun. 3pm-midnight). **Bogart's,** Hartmannstr. 7d, serves up a healthy vegetable platter (DM12) as well as tasty blueberry shakes (DM5) amidst Bogie posters (open Mon.-Fri 8am-11pm, Sat.-Sun. 10am-3am). The intersection of Klosterstr. and Theaterstr. provides some hearty culinary options, with **Central-Eck** offering cafeteria German food sprinkled with oom-pa-pa for around DM8 (open Mon.-Fri. 9am-8pm, Sat. 9am-2pm, Sun. 11am-6pm) as well as more refined culinary dishes at **Café Oben,** on the second floor of the *Rathaus;* it's so well established, they've even got it on the city map (open Mon.-Sat. 8am-midnight, Sun. 10am-11pm).

Sights There's an interesting Communism-theme-park atmosphere to Chemnitz; its most interesting attractions are the surviving socialist-inspired public artworks, although its museums and conventional tourist attractions are showing renewed signs of life. Every street corner, particularly along **Straße der Nationen,** boasts a statue of frolicking socialist children or happily scrubbed workers. Nothing, however, can outshine the monstrously pompous **bust of Karl Marx** at the corner of Straße der Nationen and Brückenstr.; the dour Marx, however, is insulted by the adjacent McDonald's across the street.

Continuing down Straße der Nationen will take you through the diminished remnants of the city's once-sprawling **Altstadt.** Chemnitz's strategic industrial importance guaranteed heavy Allied bombing in the war. Practically all that remains is the **Roter Turm,** a 12th-century relic of the city walls, and the **old Rathaus.** Closer to the train station is the **König-Albert-Museumsbau,** with the **Städtische Kunstsammlungen Chemnitz** (City Art Exhibit) and the **Museum für Naturkunde Chemnitz** (Natural History Museum). The art exhibit features a nice sampling of 19th- and 20th-century German art, as well as a couple of Rodin sculptures (open Tues.-Sun. 11am-5pm; admission DM4, students and seniors DM2). The Naturkunde Museum showcases its animals (open Tues.-Fri. 9am-noon and 2-5pm, Sat.-Sun. 11am-5pm).

To reach the **Schloß Complex,** Schloßberg 12, continue down Straße der Nationen past the train station and turn left onto Elisenstr., which merges with Mullerstr, which in turn will then lead you to the Schloßberg, on the right. The castle that stood here was destroyed in the Thirty Years War; the **Schloßbergmuseum** occupies a reconstructed building that approximately imitates the old castle structure. While the first floor offers some medieval artwork and rotating exhibits, the genuine goods reside upstairs in the **Stadtgeschichte** (city history) display. A large room documents the history of Chemnitz from its founding in the 12th century; the 20th century exhibits provide fascinating evidence that Chemnitz was not immune from the trends that defined the Eastern German landscape. The posters advertising Hitler's *Entartete Kunst* (Degenerate Art) exhibit, on display in Chemnitz at the outside of World War II, and the collections of Communist kitsch from the Karl-Marx-Stadt days, are particularly intriguing (open Tues.-Sat. 10am-5pm, Sun. 10am-6pm; admission DM4, students and seniors DM2).

Entertainment and Nightlife Chemnitz offers a burgeoning theater and film scene. **Chemnitzer Kabarett,** An der Markthalle 1-3 (tel./fax 67 50 90), dishes out the comedy nearly every night. (Performances begin at 8pm. DM15, DM10 for seniors and students (except Fri. and Sat.). Mondays every seat is DM10.) The **Chemnitz Opern** (opera), Theaterplatz 2 (tel. 488 48 80), does it all, from *West Side Story* to Wagner. (Seats DM12-35. Open Mon.-Fri. 10am-6pm, Sat. 2-6pm.) For the scoop on Chemnitz's theater scene, check the program at the **Schauspielhaus** (tel. 488 48 15), located at Park der Opfer des Faschismus. Chemnitz city magazines **Blitz** and **Stadtstreicher** can point you in the direction of the Chemnitz jet-set. **Tanzhaus Heideschänke,** Eubaerstr. 103 (tel. 74 13 27; open Thurs.-Sun. after 8pm), and **Fuchsbau,** Carolastr. 8 (tel. 67 17 17; grooves Wed.-Sun. after 9pm), is where local cats head for disco, techno, and jazz. Feeling downright hot and sweaty from the inner-city congestion? Down Brückenstr. from Straße der Nationen, and right on Mühlenstr., is the **Stadtbad** (municipal swimming pool), built in 1929 *à la* Bauhaus. At that time it was Europe's most modern indoor swimming pool. Ah, the old days.

■ Near Chemnitz: Augustusburg

After the exhaustion of post-industrialist, post-Marxist, monochromatic Chemnitz, catch a bus from the Chemnitz *Busbahnhof* (down Georgstr. from the train station) for Augustusburg (2min.), a princely mountaintop hamlet. Bus T-244 or T-245 (DM3.70) will stop at the foot of the path to the castle. The Renaissance **hunting lodge** of the Saxon Electors is perched 1500m above town. A guided tour (required) of the royal playhouse will lead you through the **Brünnenhaus** (well house) and the intimate **Schloßkapelle** (church chapel), the only Renaissance chapel left in Saxony. The altar is graced by a Lucas Cranach painting which portrays the dour Herzog August, his wife Anna, and their 14 pious children; all those damn kids might explain why the Saxon elector was so stingy—he conscripted poachers into well-digging duties that ran around the clock. (Tours every hr. at 30min. past the hr.; admission DM3, students and seniors DM1.50.) On your own time, explore the **Motorcycle Museum,** the **Hunting and Game Museum,** or the **Carriage Museum.** A day pass for all the museums costs DM10, students and seniors DM5. Tickets for all museums can also be purchased separately. (*Schloß* open Mon.-Fri. 9am-6pm, Sat.-Sun. 9am-6:30pm. Closed Nov.-Mar. Mon.) In the first weekend of August, the *Schloß* offers an American-style **Country Fest** for absolutely no apparent reason—satisfy your lust for bull-riding here. The **Jugendherberge (HI)** in the castle (tel. (037291) 202 56) will keep you well-chilled in the former royal brewery. Each room comes in the three six-pack (18-bed) variety. (Reception open after 3pm. DM20, students DM24. Breakfast included.)

"I wish they all could be East German girls ..."

Among the many concerns of lost cultural and social identity that would result from reunification, sex was not the least of them. A professor at University of Leipzig performed a study in the wake of the Wall's shattering which found that "the rate of orgasms in the Eastern part of Germany is substantially higher" than the rate in the West, with 37% of East German women regularly achieving orgasm against an average of 26% of women in the West. The findings were greeted with such headlines as "Experts Fear Cooling of East German Sex." While this fact is entirely frivolous, it might say something about the very liberated women of the former East: the GDR's many social programs—daycare, guaranteed maternity leave, and virtually certain employment—produced an image of independence that was one of the few things West German women admired about their Eastern counterparts.

■ Zwickau

Zwickau is best known as East Germany's Motor City. For over 35 years, the city's Sachsenring-Auto-Union produced the GDR's ubiquitous consumer car, the tiny *Trabant*. An ill-engineered, two-cylinder plastic vehicle, the *"Trabi"* was Communist industry's inferior answer to the West's *Volkswagen*. Like cockroaches, the wheezing little cars persist; indeed, leftover *Trabis* are still among the most common vehicles on the streets of the east. Officially, the city would prefer to play up its more genteel distinctions, such as its active art tradition, which launched composer Robert Schumann and a couple of members of the Brücke painting school into the world. But it may be a losing battle; the tinny whine of *Trabi* laboring up a hill is never far from the ears of a visitor.

The dusky-colored, four-story **Schumann Haus** stands at Hauptmarkt 5. The museum plays up the Romantic composer's childhood in Zwickau before moving on to his Leipzig period, when the young Schumann decided to bag a career as a lawyer in order to compose music full-time. To its credit, the museum also devotes several parts of the display to Schumann's wife, Clara Wieck, one of the most accomplished pianists of her day. (Today, Clara lives on as "the woman on the 100-*Mark* bill.") No mention here of Schumann's impending insanity, although the less-than-flattering busts of the composer which look like a drunken and bloated old politician hint at the fact that all was not well with the artist. Recitals are given sporadically in the *Klavierhalle*, and they almost always include pieces by Schumann (open Tues.-Sat. 10am-5pm; admission DM5, students and seniors DM 3).

Besides a smothering of Schumann memorabilia, Zwickau has an old cathedral, a newly-renovated central *Platz*, and other goodies typical of many German cities. Zwickau's unique offering, however, resides in its **Automobilienmuseum**. To find it, make your way north from the Ring on Walther-Rathenau-Str. (about a 20-min. trip) to an out-of-the-way little building past the auto factory. Before the days of GDR mediocrity, Zwickau actually turned out very good cars—its early productions days spawned the Audi company, and auto pioneer August Horch came up with some roadsters that would've knocked your socks off. Over a dozen *Trabant* models are on display, prompting wonder at the design's invulnerability to innovation over the years. The sight of the last *Trabi* ever produced (in 1991) in all of its pink "splendor" and emblazoned with the words, "Trabant: Legend on Wheels," is enough to make even the most ardent Cold Warrior misty-eyed (open Tues. and Thurs. 9am-noon, 2-5pm, Sat.-Sun. 10am-5pm; admission DM3, students and seniors DM1.50).

Zwickau's location in the middle of the busy Saxony-Thuringia rail network makes it an easy daytrip; it's easily reached by train from Leipzig (13 trains per day), Dresden (16 per day), and Altenburg (17 per day). Its oldest attractions and most beautiful streets are conveniently confined to a circular region in the *Altstadt*, bounded by a bustling three-lane roundabout named **Dr.-Friedrichs-Ring**. Zwickau's **tourist office**, Hauptstr. 6 (tel. 29 37 13; fax 29 37 15), lies in the center of the circle; from the station, head along the left fork which becomes Bahnhofstr. until it ends at Humboldtstr. Turn right, and then quickly left on Schumannstr., which will lead you across the Ring. The street resumes as Innere Plauensche Str., a pedestrian zone, which takes you past the Marten Kirche. Hang a left onto the Markt and the first left is Hauptstr. They can provide you with maps and book rooms (DM35 per person; open Mon.-Fri. 9am-6pm, Sat. 9am-noon). Before setting out for the Ring, you can stash your pack at the station **luggage storage** for DM4 per day or DM3 if it's small. The main **post office**, Humboldtstr. 3, 08056 Zwickau, is just outside the Ring. The **telephone code** is 0375.

Due to the absence of a youth hostel, Zwickau's plate of budget accommodations is rather sparse. The least expensive option is the privately-run **Beherbergungsgewerbe** (a tongue-twister that just means "hostel service"; tel. 21 54 10 or 30 14 00), offering fairly nice rooms with satellite TV and refrigerators at two different locations. One of the buildings is in a rather aesthetically challenged neighborhood well north of the Ring at Alexanderstr. 7, off of Zwickau's major north-south artery, Leipziger Str.

Take bus route #4 (direction: Pöblitz) from the "Neumarkt" or "Zentrum" stops (DM1.40) and get off at "Schlachthofstr.," four stops north of "Neumarkt." Continue walking down Leipziger Str. when you get off; Alexanderstr. will be on your left. The other lies on Hilfegotteschachtstr. 20. From the train station, walk down Am Bahnhof and then turn right onto Reichenbacherstr. Continue down Reichenbackerstr. for about 10 minutes, until you see a billboard with the street name on your left. (Singles DM30. Doubles DM50. No breakfast. Call ahead, especially since the service tends to be particular about where they want you stay.)

The **Markt** serves up food stands every Thursday and Friday from 8am to 6pm. A number of cheap dining options can be found along the *Hauptmarkt* and Innere Schneeberger Str. during the day. Just outside of the Ring, **Bistro International,** Schumann Str. 10 (tel. 29 88 09), has Turkish pizzas (DM8-10) that should prove pleasing to the palate (open daily 10am-midnight). To imbibe some spirits and GDR nostalgia, head to **Roter Oktober,** at the corner of Leipzigerstr. and Kolpingstr. Toast the hammer and sickle if you really feel like getting crazy.

■ Leipzig

Forget about Goethe and Bach—you're in Leipzig, and it's all about today. Leipzig is full of energy and attitude; the city jumps out from the transformations of eastern Germany in a fiery Faulknerian blaze, screaming, "now, Now, NOW!" Its inhabitants have nicknamed the city *"L.E.,"* which in German sounds a lot like "L.A." But the mood here is nothing like Los Angeles, for Leipzig is not about glitz—it's about grace and style, and while the town is lively, its Saxon inhabitants are also reserved and ironic. In the face of reunification, half of the city rushed out to cash in on Westernization, while the other half decided to play it cool and catch up on movies that were banned under Communism. While the western entrepreneurs and speculators do pose a threat to Leipzig's hipster vibe, the city's *Uni*-culture, spawned by over 20,000 students, provides the counterbalance.

More recently, Leipzig has become famed as Germany's *Heldenstadt* (city of heroes) for its role as the crucible of *die Wende,* the sudden toppling of the GDR in 1989. What began as regular Monday meetings at the Nikolaikirche soon turned into massive weekly demonstrations *(Montagdemos)* in which ever-growing numbers of Leipzigers called for an end to the Communist government's policies. On October 7, 1989, the nerves of the Communist government erupted in a display of police violence against unarmed citizens. Nevertheless, despite the heightened security measures, over 70,000 people showed up for the Monday demonstration on October 9. For reasons that remain unclear and virtually inexplicable to historians, the armed forces allowed the protest to pass without a response, avoiding an East German Tiananmen Square. The following Monday demonstration drew 120,000 emboldened citizens, and on October 18 party chief Erich Honecker resigned. The city's revolutionary spirit shines in more remote history as well, as zealous Leipzig is celebrated as a cradle of German liberty. The "Wars of Liberation" that kicked Napoleon out of Germany began with the Battle of Leipzig in 1813. In the abortive revolutions of 1830 and 1848, Leipzig again convulsed to try to throw off authoritarian rule.

Like its less liberal sister Dresden, the city long epitomized the highbrow intellectualism of the German cultural tradition. Goethe loved Leipzig for its cultivated inhabitants; his *alma mater,* Leipzig University, still carries on a tradition embracing the names of Leibniz, Lessing, and Nietzsche, among others. The many bookstores and antiquariats in the *Altstadt* recall Leipzig's pre-war post as capital of the European publishing industry, and several major international book fairs convene here annually. In 1723, Johann Sebastian Bach settled in as choirmaster of Leipzig's Thomaskirche, entrancing churchgoers for 27 years. A century later, Felix Mendelssohn founded the *Leipzig Gewandhaus Orchester,* still a world-class orchestra.

ORIENTATION AND PRACTICAL INFORMATION

Leipzig is a compact city; most of the sights and the entertainment district dwell in the circular *Innenstadt*. It's a 10-minute walk from the main train station on the north edge of the *Innenstadt* to the Leipzig University tower in the southeast corner. The cavernous **Leipziger Hauptbahnhof** is a sight in itself—its curved-beam roofs enclose one of Europe's largest train stations and recall the grander days of rail travel; the station has the proud distinction of being the biggest terminus rail station in Europe. Fast inter-city trains bring you to Berlin within two hours, and Dresden in 90 minutes. Few trains run out of the **Bayerischer Bahnhof,** but it is worth seeing for its looming, Neoclassical façade. By the summer of 1994, the project of changing socialist-era political street names (Ho-Chi-Minh-Str., etc.) was completed, and all street signs bear the new names; make sure that any map you purchase is current.

Tourist Office: Leipzig Information, Sachsenplatz 1 (tel. 710 42 60; fax 710 42 76). Walk across the Platz der Republik in front of the main station and bear right past the Park Hotel (5min.). Among gorgeous brochures, there's a useful free map of the *Innenstadt* and suburbs; ask for it. They book rooms in opulent hotels and *Pensionen* for free and provide tickets to local events. They will move in Dec. 1996; be sure to check the nifty information machines in the *Bahnhof* to verify their location. Pick up free copies of the magazines *Fritz* and *Blitz* to find out about nightlife. Open Mon.-Fri. 9am-7pm, Sat.-Sun. 9:30am-2pm. Room-finding service (tel. 710 42 75) open Mon.-Fri. 9am-6pm, Sat. 9:30am-2pm. Another branch lies at the regional airport, **Flughafen Leipzig-Halle** (tel. 224 11 56). Open Mon.-Fri. 7am-9pm, Sat.-Sun. 9am-6pm.

Tours: The tourist office leads bus tours (2½hr.) daily at 10am and 1:30pm. DM28, seniors DM20, students DM16. Walking tours (2hr.) depart daily in the summer at 4pm. DM12. From Oct.-April there are no tours Sat.-Sun. There are also shorter tours available (Tues.-Thurs. at 1pm; DM8). Some guides are English-speaking.

Budget Travel: Bavaria Geschäfts-und-Studentenreisebüro, Augustusplatz 9 (tel. 30 30 90), in the university courtyard. Affiliated with STA and Kilroy travel. Open Mon.-Fri. 9am-7pm, Sat 9am-1pm.

Consulates: U.S., Wilhelm-Seyferth-Str. 4 (tel. 213 84 20). Entrance on Wächstr. behind the Museum der Bildenden Künste. Open Mon.-Fri. 9am-noon or by appointment. Also home to the **Amerika Haus Bibliothek** (tel. 213 84 25). Open Tues. and Thurs. 11am-5pm, Wed. 11am-7:30pm.

Currency Exchange: Deutsche Verkehrsbank, in the *Hauptbahnhof* (tel. 29 48 89), is convenient but has poor rates (DM2 to change cash; 1% or DM7.50 minimum for travelers checks). Open Mon.-Fri. 7am-7:30pm, Sat. 8am-6pm. There is no place in Leipzig that will change money on Sun., so plan accordingly.

American Express: Dorotheenplatz 224 (tel. 96 70 00). On the far side of the central city from the *Hauptbahnhof.* Head down Schillerstr. from Dittrichring about a block; it's on the left. Currency exchanged, money wired, mail held, English spoken. Changes currency and cashes AmEx checks absolutely free. Open Mon.-Fri. 9:30am-6pm, Sat. 9am-noon.

Telephones: At the post office, or card booths all over the city.

Flights: Flughafen Leipzig-Halle in Schkendingasse, about 20km from Leipzig. International service throughout Central Europe. Buses leave the *Hauptbahnhof* Mon.-Fri. and Sun. every 30min. 5am-9pm; Sat. every 45min. 5am-8:45pm.

Trains: (tel. 702 11). Leipzig lies on the Berlin-Munich line with regular InterCity service to Frankfurt am Main. Information counter on the platform near track 15.

Public Transportation: Streetcars and buses cover the city; the hub is on Platz der Republik, in front of the *Hauptbahnhof.* Tickets come in 2 varieties: 15min. for DM1.40 and 60min. (with line changes) for DM2. Streetcars and S-Bahn run from 5:30am-3am, although each line varies in its nightly duration. Free maps at the tourist office. Day passes available for DM7.

Taxis: tel. 48 84, 98 22 22, or 401 41 03.

Car Rental: Avis, Augustusplatz 5/6 (tel. 214 68 91). Open Mon.-Fri. 8am-6pm, Sat. 8am-noon. **Hertz,** next to the train station in the Hotel Astoria (tel. 128 47 01). Open Mon.-Fri. 7:30am-6pm, Sat. 8am-noon. **Europcar InterRent,** in the west hall

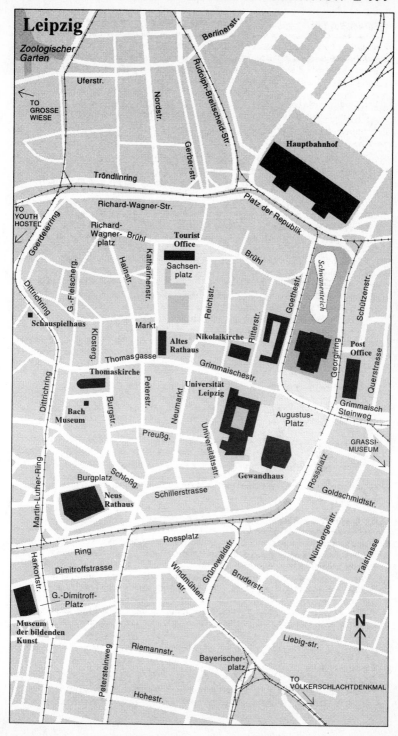

Leipzig

Zoologischer Garten

Berlinerstr.

Uferstr.

Nordstr.

Rudolph-Breitscheid-Str.

Gerber-str.

TO GROSSE WIESE

Tröndlinring

Hauptbahnhof

Platz der Republik

TO YOUTH HOSTEL

Richard-Wagner-Str.

Goerdelerring

Richard-Wagner-platz

Brühl

Katharinenstr.

Tourist Office

Sachsenplatz

Brühl

Schwanenteich

Dittrichring

G.-Fleischerg.

Hainstr.

Reichstr.

Ritterstr.

Goethestr.

Schützenstr.

Schauspielhaus

Klosterg.

Markt

Altes Rathaus

Nikolaikirche

Georgiring

Post Office

Querstrasse

Thomasgasse

Grimmaischestr.

Dittrichring

Thomaskirche

Peterstr.

Universität Leipzig

Grimmaisch Steinweg

Bach Museum

Burgstr.

Neumarkt

Augustus-Platz

GRASSI-MUSEUM

Preußg.

Universitätsstr.

Gewandhaus

Rossplatz

Martin-Luther-Ring

Burgplatz

Schloßg.

Schillerstrasse

Goldschmidtstr.

Neus Rathaus

Nürnbergerstr.

Talstrasse

Rossplatz

Ring

Harkortstr.

Dimitroffstrasse

Windmühlen-str.

Grünewaldstr.

Bruderstr.

G.-Dimitroff-Platz

N

Museum der bildenden Kunst

Riemannstr.

Peterssteinweg

Bayerischer-platz

Liebig-str.

TO VÖLKERSCHLACHTDENKMAL

Hohestr.

of the *Hauptbahnhof* (tel. 211 38 84). Open Mon.-Fri. 7am-9pm, Sat. 8am-noon. More offices at the airport. Names of smaller (and frequently cheaper) outfits are available through the tourist office.

Mitfahrzentrale: Rudolf Breitscheid-Str. 39 (tel. 211 42 22), next to the *Hauptbahnhof*, organizes ride-shares, a standard deviation from the risks of hitching. Open daily 9am-8pm. Another *Mitfahrzentrale* is located at Universität Leipzig (tel. 973 78 55), near the *Mensa*. Open Mon.-Fri. 9am-6pm.

Hitchhiking: *Let's Go* does not recommend hitchhiking as a safe mode of transportation. Those headed to Dresden and Prague take S-Bahn #2 or bus #65 to "Engelsdorf Ost," then turn left onto Bahnhofstr., right onto Leipzigerstr., and then walk to the *Autobahn* interchange. Those hitching to Berlin take streetcar #16 to "Essener Str.," switch to bus F, get out at Sachsenpark, and walk to the *Autobahn*.

Luggage Storage: Lockers at the station are located by tracks 3 and 24 and between the east and west halls of the station (DM2, big ones DM4). The luggage storage office downstairs from platform 1 charges DM4 per piece per day. Open daily 6am-9:15pm.

Lost Property: Fundstelle, at the eastern side of the station (tel. 724 32 65; fax 724 31 50). Open Mon.-Fri. 7am-3:15pm.

Bookstores: Reisefibel, Salzgäßchen 21/Handelshof (tel. 29 17 94), specializes in foreign novels and travel guides. **British Studies Information Centre,** Lumumbastr. 11-13 (tel. 564 71 53), runs an excellent **library** with an open reading room and English books a-plenty. Bus stop: "Nordplatz." Open Mon., Thurs.-Fri. 11am-5pm, Tues. 11am-7pm, Wed. 11am-6pm.

Watch Stores: Swatch, in the Mädler passage, with a plaque and pictures commemorating one Gene Mazo's purchase of an *Armbanduhr* in 1993.

Gay and Lesbian Information: AIDS-Hilfe, Ossientzkystr. 18 (tel. 232 31 36), is open daily and features a popular gay café on Tues. and Thurs. from 3-9pm. Also offers the updated **Queer Stadtplan,** a map of the gay and lesbian nightlife.

Laundromat: Maga Pon, Gottschedstr. 11 (tel. 960 79 22), takes the cake as the jazziest laundromat in Saxony—it doubles as a hep-cat student bar and restaurant, so come in your coolest dirty clothes (unless you want to wash them). Wash DM6 for 5kg. Open daily 9am-3am.

Frauenzentrum: Frauen-Notruf, B.-Göring-Str. 152 (tel. 306 52 46). Open Mon.-Fri. 6am-10pm.

Pharmacies: Löwen Apotheke, Grimmaischestr. 19 (tel. 960 50 27). Open Mon.-Wed. and Fri. 8am-6:30pm, Thurs. 8am-7:30pm, and Sat. 9am-2pm. Whenever the shop is closed, push the button by the door for emergency service.

Emergency: Ambulance: tel. 115. **Police:** tel. 110.

Post Office: Hauptpostamt 1, 04109 Leipzig (tel. 212 25 88), across from Augustusplatz on Grimmaischestr. A 5-min. walk from train station: bear left past the opera to Augustus Platz and cross to the 50s-style structure. Open Mon.-Fri. 8am-6pm, Sat. 9am-noon.

Telephone Code: 0341.

ACCOMMODATIONS AND CAMPING

Leipzig's budget accommodations are on the verge of disaster, with both of its hostels giving way to expensive real estate development in the near future. While **private rooms** are tolerable at around DM35 per person, the private *Zimmervermittlung* service, located in the tourist office, rudely sticks you with a DM10 booking fee for the first three nights, followed by a charge of DM5 for each additional night. Ouch! As a result, if you want to stay at a hostel or at a camping sight, be sure to call ahead, especially during tourist high season (June-Aug.), when everybody else is trying to get the same spots. You can save some money by asking at the tourist office desk for a copy of **Übernachten in und um Leipzig,** which can point you to some small and cheap but well-appointed *Pensionen*. The **Jugendherberge Grethen (HI)** in Grethen (tel. (03437) 76 34 49) is a tolerable distance (30min.) by bus (destination: "Groß Steinberg") from the station (DM20, over 26 DM24; breakfast included). For longer stays, the helpful **Mitwohnzentrale,** Rudolf-Breitscheider-Str. 39 (tel. 211 42 22), has

English-speaking staff willing to help you avoid the clutches of the tourist office (open daily 9am-8pm).

Jugendherberge Leipzig Am Auensee (HI), Gustav-Esche-Str. 4, 04159 Leipzig (tel. 461 11 14), in the nearby suburb of Wahren. From the main station, take streetcar #10, 28, or 30 (direction: Wahren) to "Rathaus Wahren," then turn left at the city hall and follow the signs. A restful abode with small rooms neatly packed into a pacific area. Unfortunately, it's scheduled to close sometime in 1997, intensifying the already existing imperative to call as far ahead as possible. Reception open 7am-7pm. No curfew. DM22, over 26 DM26. Nonmembers pay DM6 extra.

Jugendherberge Leipzig Centrum (HI), Käthe-Kollwitz-Str. 64 (tel. 47 05 30; fax 47 58 88). From the main station take streetcar #2 (direction: Plagwitz) or 1 (direction: Lausen) to "Marchnerstr." (4 stops). Continue down the street; the hostel is on the right. A large, well-run place with plenty of beds but numbered days—it will have closed as of Dec. 1996. Management hopes to open a new hostel in 1997; contact the tourist office for updated information. Reception open 6:30-9am, 9:30am-noon and 12:30pm-1am. Curfew 1am. DM21, over 26 DM25.

Am Auensee, Gustav-Esche-Str. 5 (tel. 461 19 77). A budgetary *deus ex machina* in the absense of hostels. To get there, follow directions to Jugendherberge Leipzig Am Auensee (above), turning left at the Rathaus Wahren, and then right at the end of the street onto Gustav-Esche-Str. Reception open 6am-10pm. **Camping** area charges DM6-10 for tents, DM12 for caravans. Small tent-huts function as 2-bed bungalows. DM50 per hut, DM55 in winter. More extravagant **motel rooms** also available. Singles DM50. Doubles DM90.

Camping: Campingplatz am Kulkwitzer See, Seestr. in Markrandstadt (tel. 941 13 15). Take streetcar #8 (direction: Lausen) to the last stop, then bear right. Reception open 7am-5pm. Open April 15-Oct. 15.

FOOD

Budget meals are not as hard to find in Leipzig as budget rooms, but it's still no cakewalk (so to speak). The **Innenstadt** is well-supplied with *Imbiß* stands, bistros, and restaurants for consumption on the go. The Brühl, running in front of the Sachsenplatz, offers a **Kaiser's Supermarket** and the veritable beacon in the night, a **McDonald's**, whose golden arches sing like so many of Heinrich Heine's sirens (open Sun.-Thurs. 6am-3am, Fri-Sat. 24hr.). Sachsenplatz also offers a **market** on Tuesdays and Fridays.

Universität Leipzig Mensa, in the university complex just off Grimmaischen Str. Less than astounding university food for DM6. A better bet is the **Eck-Café**, also in the university complex across from the mensa. The café serves daily specials for about DM3 that are more freshly prepared than the putrifax in the *Mensa*. *Mensa* open Mon.-Fri 7am-7pm. Eck-Café open Mon.-Thurs. 9am-10pm, Fri. 11am-3:30pm. Both open only Oct.-Feb. and April-mid-July.

Messehaus am Markt, a food complex on the Markt with some swank sidewalk perusing options. In particular, **Nudel Macher** offers cheap specials with an all-you-can-eat pizza and pasta buffet (DM8.90) every Mon.-Wed. 3-8pm and all day on Sun. Eat until you're comatose.

Maga Pon, Gottschedstr. 11 (tel. 960 79 22), has delicious spaghetti dishes for DM7-9.50 and an awesome breakfast buffet (9am-6pm) that includes a hangover breakfast to help ease in the next day, with coffee, water, and aspirin (DM3).

Pleißenberg, Schulstr. 2, a couple of blocks from the Thomaskirche. One of the few German meat-and-potatoes restaurants in Leipzig with good prices and even better hours. Meals DM6-9. Open Mon.-Fri. 7am-5am, Sat.-Sun. 10am-5pm.

Kultur Café Alte Nikolaischule, across the street from the Nikolaikirche. Daily specials DM10-15 come dripping in free pretense. Occasional art exhibits and jazz performances round out the atmosphere. Open daily 10am-1am.

SIGHTS

Leipzig's historic *Innenstadt* suffered less at the hands of World War II bombers than it did from the poorly planned architectural endeavors of the socialist era. The heart of the city beats on the **Marktplatz,** a colorful, cobblestone square guarded by the slanted 16th-century **Altes Rathaus** (Old Town Hall), with its elegant **clock tower** showing four bright-blue faces. Inside, a grand festival hall runs above the **Museum für Geschichte der Stadt Leipzig** (Museum of Leipzig's City History), offering a straightforward look at Leipzig's history (open Tues.-Fri. 10am-6pm, Sat.-Sun. 10am-4pm; admission DM3, students DM1.50, children DM0.50).

Behind the *Altes Rathaus,* on Nikolaistr., the 800-year-old **Nikolaikirche** served as witness to the birth of Bach's *Johannes Passion* as well as the GDR's peaceful revolution. The sandstone exterior, an unfortunate product of 19th-century *fin-de-siècle* malaise, hides a truly empyrean interior. The ceilings and columns feature a surprisingly majestic array of pinks and greens—not your usual flavor for a church, but the late-18th-century renovation was, after all, inspired by the not-so-usual *French* Baroque school, if you know what we mean. The end result is far removed from the days of fire and brimstone; instead, the attempt to make the columns resemble palms proves more evocative of the sunny tropics (open Mon.-Sat. 10am-6pm, Sun. after services; free).

Continuing away from the *Marktplatz,* take Universitätsstr. to the former Karl Marx University, now rechristened **Universität Leipzig.** Its "Sharp Tooth" tower, a steel and concrete behemoth, displaced the centuries-old Universitätskirche and other popular buildings following a wave of faculty protests in 1968. Structural renovations are planned, as the cloud-stabbing tower's design has proven increasingly unstable over the years. The university also has an **Ägyptisches Museum** (Egyptian Museum), located at Schillerstr. 6 (tel. 973 70 10; open Tues.-Sat. 1-5pm, Sun. 10am-1pm; admission DM3, students DM1.50).

Past the university and down Grimmaischer Steinweg is the **Grassimuseum,** on Johannisplatz, an Art Deco home for three small museums. The university's **Musikinstrumenten-Museum** contains more than 3500 musical instruments, some dating back to the 16th century (open Tues.-Sat. 10am-5pm, Sun. 10am-1pm; admission DM5, students DM2). Enter the courtyard to find the **Museum des Kunsthandwerk** (handicrafts; open Tues. and Thurs.-Fri. 10am-6pm, Wed. 10am-8pm, Sat.-Sun. 10am-5pm; admission DM4, students DM2). The **Ausstellungsraum Grassimuseum,** on Pragerstr. (tel. 214 21 11), on the far side of the Grassimuseum, is a well-noted magnet for international art exhibitions (open Mon. and Sat.-Sun. 10am-8pm, Tues. and Thurs.-Fri. 10am-6pm; admission DM12, students DM8).

The **Neues Rathaus** (New Town Hall) on Schillerstr. provides a vexing spectacle —the gray monster, which contains over 800 rooms, seems large enough to house its own city. The place is currently closed for repairs while the city tries to figure out what the hell they should do with it. Behind it, cross over Martin-Luther-Ring and walk south on Harkortstr. a block to the **Museum der Bildenden Künste** (Museum of Fine Arts), at Georg-Dimitroff-Platz 1. The museum provides a fairly thorough survey of German art from the late 1700s to the present day, with three rooms dedicated to some of the surprisingly creative art works which developed in spite of the stifling East German government. Expressionist works are notably absent from the collection as a result of the purging that claimed over 400 paintings for Hitler's "degenerate art" collections (open Tues., Thurs.-Sun. 9am-5pm, Wed. 1-9:30pm; admission DM5, students DM2.50, free on the second Sun. of each month).

Just north of the *Neues Rathaus* and close to the Marktplatz is the **Thomaskirche,** where Bach served as cantor. When his original burial site was destroyed in World War II, his remains were interred here in front of the altar. The memorial statue, showing Bach with empty pockets, says a lot about the genius's impoverished success. A stained-glass window commemorates Martin Luther's trip here in the early Reformation. Mozart and Mendelssohn also performed in this church, and Wagner was baptized here in 1813 (open daily 8am-6pm; in winter 9am-5pm; services Sun.

9:30am and 6pm). Across the street, the **Johann-Sebastian-Bach-Museum,** Thomaskirchhof 16, chronicles Bach's work and years in Leipzig, 1723-1750. (Open daily 10am-5pm. Last entry 4:30pm. Admission DM4, students and seniors DM2.50. Tours daily at 11am and 3pm; with tour, admission is DM8 and DM5. The museum's *Sommersaal* hosts concerts 2-3 times per week for DM10-15, students DM6-8.)

Not far north of the Thomaskirche lies Leipzig's newest, most fascinating museum. The **Museum der "Runden Ecke"** (Museum of the Round Corner), Dittrichring 24, was the former headquarters of the East German Ministry for State Security or **Stasi;** its permanent exhibition, *"Stasi-Macht und Banalität"* (Power and Banality, an echo of German philosopher Hannah Arendt's line on the "banality of evil") provides a glimpse into the eyes of the Panopticon. The sinister tools of the *Stasi* trade included mechanisms for monitoring all mail and phone calls as well as breath samples which, much like phrenology, were used to determine criminal personalities. While the surveillance equipment is enough to inflict eurythmia on any conspiracy theorist, the museum also chronicles the triumph of the resistance that overthrew the *Stasi* terror. The Monday demonstrations in the Nikolaikirche often ended at the *Stasi* headquarters; the wax from candlelight vigils on the front steps can still be seen. On the night of December 4-5, 1989, the people of Leipzig took over the *Stasi* building. Inside they found some 50,000 letters seized over the last 40 years and entire floors devoted to documentation of the actions of suspected resistors (open Wed.-Sun. 2-6pm; free).

Outside of the city, a towering stone monument commemorates Leipzig's first self-liberation. The **Völkerschlachtdenkmal** (tel. 878 04 71) on the *Süd-Friedhof* remembers the 400,000 soldiers engaged in the 1813 Battle of Nations—a struggle that turned the tide against Napoleon and determined many of Europe's present national boundaries. The monument is an absolutely massive pile of sculpted brown rock overlooking a large pool. A dizzying 500 steps spiral up in a nearly windowless one-person-wide passage to the very top of the monument. From the top on clear days, you can see the Harz mountain range. To get there (the monument), take streetcar #15 or 20 from the *Hauptbahnhof* (direction: Meusdorf or Probstheida) to "Völkerschlachtdenkmal" (20min.; open May-Oct. daily 10am-5pm; Nov.-April 9am-4pm; admission DM3.50, students DM2).

ENTERTAINMENT

You need not be dead to have heard a good concert in Leipzig. The musical offerings are top-notch, particularly at the **Gewandhaus Orchestra,** a major international orchestra since 1843, where Kurt Masur will preside until 1997. Some concerts are free, but usually only when a guest orchestra is playing; otherwise buy tickets (DM7 and up; 30% student discount) at the Gewandhaus **box office,** at Augustusplatz 8 (tel. 127 02 80; fax 127 02 22), next to the university (open Mon. 1-6pm, Tues.-Fri. 10am-6pm, Sat. 10am-2pm; no concerts in August). Leipzig's **Opera** (tel. 126 10) receives wide acclaim and gives Dresden's *Semper* company a run for its money. Tickets run DM8-50, with a 50% student discount (except for premieres). Head to the ticket counter at Augustusplatz 12 for more information (open Mon.-Fri. 10am-6pm, Sat. 10am-1pm, and from 90min. before a show). **Bach Festivals** every July and August bring the orchestra and opera to the streets with free performances (ask at the tourist office for exact dates).

The opera house is also the entry point to Leipzig's diverse **theater** scene. The opera company hosts the experimental **Kellertheater** (tel. 126 10) in its basement. Known for its theater, Leipzig has unleashed a wave of experimental plays in the wake of the revolution. The **Schauspielhaus,** Bosestr. 1 (tel. 126 81 68), just off Dittrichring, serves up established plays, including offerings from Euripides, Heiner Müller, and Brecht (open Mon.-Fri. 10am-6pm, Sat. 10am-1pm). The cabaret scene centers around the understated **academixer,** Kupgergasse 6 (tel. 960 48 48), run by the Leipzig student body (open Mon.-Fri. 10am-6:30pm, Sat. 10am-3:30pm) and the more brash **Gohglmohsch,** Markt 9 (tel. 960 40 78).

While movie theaters are easy to come by, Leipzig also offers serious avant-garde at its annual **film festival** at the end of October (call 980 39 21 for information).

NIGHTLIFE

Bars, Clubs, and Discos

Moritzbastei, Universitätsstr. 9 (tel. 960 51 91; tickets tel. 960 51 92), right next to the university tower, is itself one of the more fascinating sights in Leipzig. In the 16th century it served as a place of execution; now, it houses the largest student club in Europe with a diverse alternative crowd. Multiple bars and dance floors cater to all tastes in a supercool underground labyrinth with frequent live shows; above ground, **Café Barbakan** (open Mon.-Fri. after 10am, Sat. after 2pm) and an **open-air movie theater** (screenings June-Aug. Mon.-Tues. and Thurs.-Sat. at 10pm, weather permitting) provide a respite from the wild music scene. Things kick off after 9pm, with a particularly salacious scene for the jam-packed *"Papperlapop"* disco night every Wed. Admission DM4-10. Bring student ID for discount.

Stockartstraße. It's not a bar or club—it's a whole street, and it must be seen to be believed. In a makeshift space, open-air concerts are held here several times a week (check posters on the street or around the university), as well as running a cool bar called **LiWi,** at Stockartstr. 11. Take bus #10, 11, 22, or 24 (direction: Connewitz, Dölitz, or Markkleeberg) to "Pfeffinger Str.," then make a left.

Distillery, on the corner of Kurt-Eisner-Str. and Lößinger Str. Features a dynamite techno and rave scene on Wed. and Fri.-Sat. after 10pm. To get there, take S-Bahn #5 or 16 (direction: Lößing) to the "K.-Eisner-Str./A.-Hoffman-Str." stop. Distillery is 1 block down.

Barfußgäschen, a street just off the Markt, serves as the see-and-be-seen bar venue for everyone from students to folks carrying cellular phones. **Markt Neun** and **Spizz** start to fill up between 8-10pm, and remain packed into the wee hours.

Blauer Pudel, Katherinenstr. 17, in an alcove just off the street. Bring your pierced and punked-out self here to cast aspersions on the mainstream while throwing flippant pastries into the abyss; a bar and dance floor for disaffected students screams "alternative" every night after 8pm.

Killiwilly, Karl-Liebknecht-Str. 44 (tel. 213 13 16). Ballsy Irish pub in southern part of town packs 'em in for 60 varieties of whiskey plus great Irish beers, including the incomparable Guinness (among the only foreign beers capable of impressing the Germans). Interesting mix of locals, students, Irishmen, and other lovers of the foamy stuff. Open Mon.-Fri. after 11:30am, Sat. 6pm-2am, Sun. 11am-2am.

RosaLinde, Lindenauer Markt 21 (tel. 484 15 11). It's not exactly in the middle of the *Markt,* but it features a hellaciously cool gay scene on Fri. and Sat. nights, in addition to its daily gay bar. Tues. amply entertains with "Queer Film Night." Reputed to be the epicenter of Leipzig's gay scene. Open daily after 8pm.

Kutsche, on Brandenburger Str., by the *Hauptbahnhof.* Gay bar and disco that's not as commercial as Rosablinde. Dancing every Fri.-Sun. with a mad pick-up scene dubbed *"Kennen Lernen Party"* on Wednesdays. Open daily after 7pm.

■ Near Leipzig: Naumburg

Between Leipzig and Weimar, the phenomenal **Naumburger Dom** merits a short pilgrimage and circumambulation. Begun in the 11th century, it was glamorized two centuries later by 12 striking stone figures hewn by one of Germany's greatest sculptors. Too humble to carve his name in the cathedral's stone, the artist is remembered today simply as the *Naumburger Meister* (the Naumburg Master). The red blood splashed on the wounds of the master's life-size crucifixion, combined with the freaky winged skulls by the entrance, makes for some cool visuals. (Open April-Sept. Mon.-Sat. 9am-6pm, Sun. noon-6pm; Nov.-Feb. Mon.-Sat. 9am-4pm, Sun. noon-4pm; Mar. and Oct. Mon.-Sat. 9am-5pm, Sun. noon-5pm. Admission DM4.50, students and seniors DM3. There's a steep fee—DM10—for the right to take photos or use video cameras inside.) The helpful staff at the front desk will provide English-language pamphlets on request. Foreign-language tours are also available. To reach the *Dom,* head down Markgrafenweg from the station, bearing right until you reach the end of the street. To your left is the winding cobblestone path that leads uphill to the town proper. At the top of the path a sign points to the *Dom;* follow it until the cathedral's huge towers peep into view over the rooftops to guide you.

The rest of Naumburg has recovered amazingly well from its 45 years as a backwater Red Army post and is in better shape than most of the small towns of the former GDR. A jaunt past the *Dom* on Steinweg leads to Naumburg's bright, lively **market.** Just off the market square is the **Wenzelskirche,** the *Dom*'s earnest runner-up. It features a couple of Cranach paintings and an impressive 18th-century organ that even received Bach's approval (open Mon.-Sat. 10am-4pm, Sun. and holidays noon-4pm; free). Lest you think Naumburg functions solely as a bastion of religious relics, think again. In spite of the awe-inspiring monuments, Friedrich Nietzsche spent some of his formative years here from 1850 to 1858 (before he sported the bushy mustache); he returned in 1890 to visit his mother, who wouldn't let little Friedrich leave because he was crazy. The **Nietzsche-Haus,** Weingarten 18, a couple of blocks away from the *Markt*, offers biographical snippets in addition to displaying exhibits of folks who were inspired by the erstwhile professor (open Tues.-Fri. 2-5pm, Sat.-Sun. 10am-4pm; admission DM3, students DM1.50).

Despite its intrigue, Naumburg is at best a daytrip; well-situated along the rail network, it's an excellent sidelight during a visit to Leipzig, Halle, Weimar, or Erfurt. You can get a room, however, through the **tourist office,** Markt 6 (tel./fax 20 16 14), right on the market square. The best bets here are rooms with private families (open Mon.-Fri. 9am-6pm, Sat. 10am-4pm, Sun. 10am-2pm). There are several full-service banks in town, as well as an **ATM** on Markgrafenweg, immediately to the right as you exit the train station. Cheap meals can be had by the *Markt* and the Holzmarkt area, which are within three blocks of each other. Naumburg's most interesting culinary surprise is **China-Garten,** Rosbacher Str. 4 (tel. 30 90), near the cobblestone path. An authentic American-Chinese restaurant, it flaunts lacquer trim, mirrors, and pseudo-Asian instrumental pop. The lunch specials (DM9-12) are the best deal: tons of food plus a big veggie-laden, pastry-like spring roll (open daily 11:30am-2:45pm and 5:30-11:30pm). The **telephone code** is 03445.

SAXONY (SACHSEN)

Thuringia (Thüringen)

Affectionately dubbed the "Green Heart of Germany," Thuringia is the hub of a wheel formed by Bavaria, Saxony, Saxony-Anhalt, Lower Saxony, and Hesse. Certaintly the most beautiful of the new Federal States, Thuringia might also be called Germany's Culture Belt. Echoes of Thuringia are heard throughout Europe's cultural canon: Bach, Goethe, Schiller, Luther, and Wagner all left their mark on this landscape, which in turn left its mark on their work. The Thuringian Forest *(Thüringer Wald)* is the deep green nucleus of the *Land*. One route through Thuringia is to follow the necklace of historic cities—among them Jena, Weimar, Erfurt, and Eisenach—joined by a direct east-west rail line. Extending downward from the cities is the forest itself, bisected by the historic Rennsteig hiking trail. The best way to the forest is through the state capital, Erfurt. Every summer, Thuringia celebrates its musical giants with a series of concerts; the *Musiksommer* plan of events is available at most regional tourist offices.

■ Weimar

Weimar thrives on the laurels of daring cultural achievement and spectacular political failure. Intellectual energy resonates throughout the city of Goethe and Schiller, the fathers of German humanism, and German philosopher Johann Gottfried von Herder, grandfather of the Romantics. Weimar expanded the boundaries of the avant-garde into the 20th century, spawning both the Bauhaus architectural movement and the Weimar Republic's remarkably liberal Constitution of 1919. After the collapse of these latter experiments, however, the city returned to the memory of its majestic past. With its recent selection to be crowned Europe's cultural city in 1999, a gigantic reconstruction process has commenced, and many of the monuments are being packaged in plastic or scaffolding—this time, not by Christo—in preparation for the impending hoopla. But a historical *Geist* prepossesses Weimar, evidenced by the annual art festival that takes place in June and July, the Goethe birthday celebrations at the end of August, and the Liszt festival each October.

ORIENTATION AND PRACTICAL INFORMATION

Weimar is near the center of Germany, well-situated on the Dresden-Frankfurt and Berlin-Frankfurt rail lines. It is also situated on a handy rail route running from Jena in the east to Erfurt and Eisenach in the west (call 33 30 for more information). Weimar's intelligently-designed bus system runs through two nerve centers: the train station and the central **Goetheplatz**. To get to Goetheplatz from the station, head straight down Carl-August-Allee (10min.). Walk down the pedestrian **Schillerstraße** to get to the *Markt* and major sights.

Tourist Office: The seriously modern and efficient **Weimar Information,** Marktstr. 10 (tel. 240 00 or 656 90; fax 612 40), is within view of the city's *Rathaus*. They provide maps, brochures, and all that jazz, as well as act as a ticket agent for the *Deutsches Nationaltheater*. The office also books rooms in private homes or calls ahead to hotels, *Pensionen*, or hostels for a DM5 fee. **Walking tours** depart from the office daily at 11am and 2pm (DM8, students and seniors DM4). English language tours leave on Fri. and Sat. at 2pm (DM10). Alternatively, you can be your own guide by purchasing their walking tour brochure (DM1.50), available in various languages. Open March-Oct. Mon.-Fri. 9am-6pm, Sat. 9am-4pm; Nov.-Feb. Mon.-Fri. 9am-6pm, Sat. 9am-1pm; also Sun. 10am-4pm in summer.

Currency Exchange: A number of banks line Schillerstr. and Goetheplatz, but beware—none are open between Sat. afternoon and Mon. morning.

Public Transportation: Weimar's lack of streetcars is more than compensated for by an extensive **bus network.** If you buy tickets from the driver, you'll have to pay an inflated price (DM2.50). Instead, buy your tickets at the *Hauptbahnhof* (open

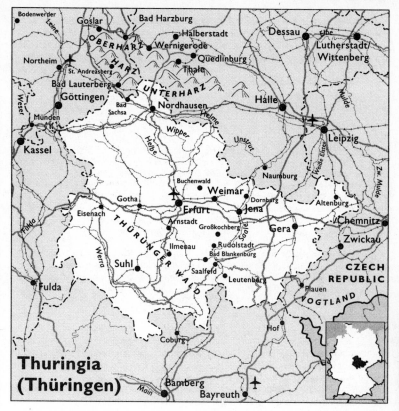

Thuringia
(Thüringen)

Mon.-Fri. 5:45am-6pm, Sat. 8am-2pm). Buses run until midnight. If you are staying 3 or 4 days and plan to use the buses or visit museums, you can save some dough by buying a 72-hr. **Weimarcard.** For DM25, you get unlimited free bus travel, free entrance to almost all of Weimar's museums, 50% off city tours, and 10% off theater tickets. What a deal!

Taxis: tel. 36 00.

Luggage Storage: At the *Hauptbahnhof.* Snazzy digital lockers DM2-4.

Pharmacy: Bahnhof Apotheke, Carl-August-Allee 14 (tel. 614 24), near the station and the *Jugendherberge* (see below). It has evening hours as well as a *Notdienst* (emergency) buzzer and a list of night pharmacies.

Women's Center: Frauenzentrum, Freiherr-von-Stein-Allee 22 (tel. 85 01 86). Open Mon. and Thurs.-Fri. 10am-6pm, Tues. 2-6pm, Wed. 10am-11pm.

Help Line: Telefonseelsorge ("Telephone Soul Care") will be of assistance (tel. (0361) 111 01 or 111 02). Open Mon.-Fri. 5pm-6am, Sat.-Sun. 24hr.

Emergency: Police: tel. 110. **Fire:** tel. 112. **Ambulance:** tel. 115.

Post Office: Mail postcards of Goethe and Schiller from the *Hauptpostamt,* Goetheplatz, 99423 Weimar (tel. 23 10). Open Mon.-Fri. 8am-6pm, Sat. 8am-noon.

Telephone Code: 03643.

ACCOMMODATIONS

Weimar is home to one of eastern Germany's most extensive tourist industries; unfortunately, that translates into ever-increasing room prices for budget travelers. Thanks to the city's three youth hostels and new "youth hotel," however, finding a cheap place to stay should now be easier than in many cities in the East. If the city's nearly

300 hostel beds are full, despair not; private accommodations are available and accessible through the tourist office. Remember that prices vary according to location, not comfort; a room near the city center may cost DM50, while many of the nicer rooms in Weimar's southern suburbs go for DM25-30. Weimar's "finest," **Hotel Elephant,** Am Markt 19 (tel. 80 20; fax 653 10), has catered to such discerning travelers as Napoleon, J.S. Bach, Richard Wagner, Leo Tolstoy, and Thomas Mann (who set his novel *Lotte in Weimar* there). In case you don't have the requisite DM155-530 per person, console yourself: Hitler stayed here, too.

Jugendherberge Germania (HI), Carl-August-Allee 13 (tel./fax 20 20 76). Friendly staff and an unbeatable location. Arriving exhausted at the train station, head straight down the hill for a mere 2min.; it's on your right. A stately foam-gray vision with newly-renovated facilities. Reception open 7-10am and 3-11pm. Lockout 10am-1pm. DM22, over 26 DM26. Breakfast included. Sheets DM7.

Jugendhotel, Geleitstr. 4 (tel. 51 50 63 or 50 29 48 or 641 71). Smack in the middle of the sights, this hostel, run by a bunch of architecture students, is the best-located place to stay in Weimar. From Goetheplatz, turn left on Geleitstr. and follow its twist to the clearing with the statue on the left. The hostel *wants* to serve backpackers and travelers, which means fewer rabid school groups and screaming kids. Reception open 24hr. DM15. No breakfast (yet).

Jugendgästehaus Maxim Gorki (HI), Zum Wilden Graben 12 (tel./fax 34 71). Take bus #8 from the station (direction: Merketal) to "Wilder Graben." A converted villa in one of Weimar's tranquil suburbs. With only 58 beds, it has a homey feel but fills quickly. Cellar bar and a volleyball court outside. Careful: buses stop running in this direction early; the walk back is poorly lit. Reception open 4-8pm, but you can call in the morning. DM24, over 26 DM28. Also has four 4-bed "family rooms" with showers for DM50. Breakfast included.

Jugendherberge Am Poseckschen Garten (HI), Humboldtstr. 17 (tel. 640 21), is situated near the city center (although fairly distant from the train station). Take bus #6 from the station (direction: Merketal) and get off at "Poseckschen Garten." Make a right onto Am Poseckschen Garten, then a left onto Humboldtstr.; the hostel is immediately on your left. A big turn-of-the-century brownstone with 8- to 10-bed rooms. The hostel tends to fill with school groups because of its proximity to cultural attractions, so come early. Reception open 6-10am and 2:30pm-12:30am. No curfew. DM22, over 26 DM26. Breakfast included. Lunch and hot dinner DM6-7 each. Closed for repairs Dec. 1996 to July or Aug. 1997.

FOOD

No town in Thuringia beats Weimar at serving up rich cooking for rich tourists. Try the daily **produce market** in the *Marktplatz* or the **Rewe grocery store,** which is at the corner of Wielandplatz and Frauenplan (open Mon.-Fri. 8:30am-6:30pm, Sat. 8:30am-12:30pm). Another option is the array of **bakeries** and **bistros** ringing the *Markt* and Karl-Liebknecht-Str., located between the *Markt* and the train station.

Bistro Donecker, Theater Platz 1. A cafeteria-style restaurant that serves German and international foods (DM5-12). Toast Goethe and Schiller (or at least their statues) while enjoying the comforts of sleek chairs that look like they were ripped off from the Bauhaus Museum. Open Mon.-Sat. 7am-6pm, Sun. 9am-6pm.

C-Keller-Galerie, Markt 21 (tel. 50 27 55), blends Expressionism and crunchiness in its café and art gallery with a small beer garden. The vegetarian dishes are tasty and cheap (DM3-6); the best breakfasts in town can be had here on Sun. noon-6pm. Open Tues.-Sun. noon-11pm.

Ristorante Pizzeria, Windsichenstr. 12 (tel. 611 80). Delicious, no-foolin' Italian food within spittin' distance of Schiller's house—so Italian they hardly understand German. Pizzas from DM5.50, pastas from DM8.50. Open daily 10am-1am.

Am Stadtpark, Amalienstr. 9/10 (tel. 418 30). Mourn the loss of Goethe and Schiller at this restaurant by the *Friedhof.* 17 asparagus dishes embrace the *Spargelgeist* with verve for DM5.50-12. Open daily 11am-11pm.

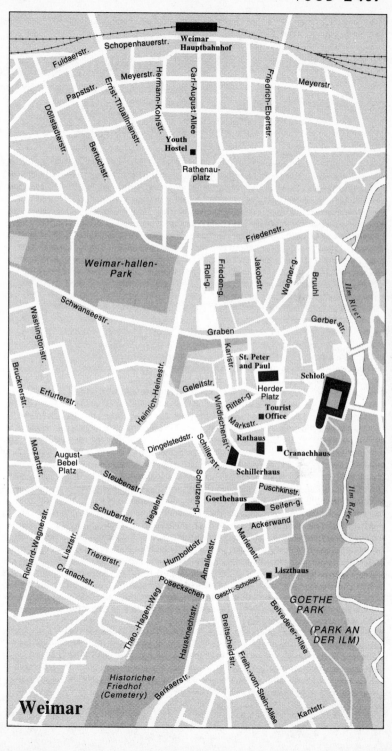

Weimar

Anatolia, Frauenplan 15. Ruminate on the immortals while nourishing yourself on a *Doner Kebeb* (DM5) with a view of a giant park statue and Goethe's house. Open Mon.-Sat. 9am-9pm, Sun 11am-9pm.

Hochschule für Architektur und Bauwesen, on Marienstr., just across the footpath in front of the Bauhaus building. Also accessible from Park an der Ilm. Flee the omnipresent Goethe and Schiller in this sanctuary of modernism. The **Mensa** (cafeteria) offers eats that aren't exactly delicious—but damn *cheap*. Meals DM2-5. Open Mon.-Fri. 6:45am-7pm.

SIGHTS AND ENTERTAINMENT

Goethe and Schiller

One hundred and fifty years after his death, the spirit of the botanist, geologist, doctor, artist, novelist, and poet Johann Wolfgang von Goethe still looms in these streets. Such immortality would not surprise the egotistical poet— nor would the numerous sights in his adopted home of Weimar, which dwell upon him and his friend, collaborator, and rival Friedrich Schiller. While countless German towns leap at any excuse to build memorial *Goethehäuser* (proclaiming Goethe slept here, Goethe went to school here, Goethe once asked for directions here), Weimar features the real thing. *The* **Goethehaus,** Frauenplan 1, is an elegant butter-colored mansion with a commanding view of the entire central pedestrian zone. The house shows off the immaculately-preserved private chambers where the poet entertained, wrote, studied, and ultimately died after 50 years in Weimar. It's jammed to the bursting point with busts, busts, and more busts, as well as paintings and sculptures from Goethe's 50,000-piece art collection (not all are on display). The master's tastes were pleasantly Bacchanalian: rampant Neoclassical images dominate the collection, including a bottle-stopper in the shape of the bust of Napoleon (apparently, Goethe felt the need to take revenge for the little general's criticisms of his works). To get the most out of the largely-unlabeled **Wohnhaus** exhibits, pick up the handy English guide "Goethe's House on the Frauenplan at Weimar" (DM3) at the desk (open Tues.-Sun. 9am-5pm; admission DM6, students DM4).

The **Schillerhaus,** Schillerstr. 17, sits a neighborly distance from Goethe's pad. This was Schiller's home during the last three years of his life, after he had resigned from his academic chair at Jena. Showcasing the backgrounds to *The Maid of Orleans* and *William Tell,* both written here, the house offers original drafts and early editions of plays, and a detailed biographical chronicle of its owner's life (open Wed.-Mon. 9am-5pm; admission DM5, students DM3). One block away on Hummelstr., Schiller and Goethe are reconciled in bronze before the **Deutsches Nationaltheater,** which first breathed life into their stage works. The theater is the epicenter of Weimar's cultural and political intensity—in addition to operating as a first-run venue for their plays, it was also the locale from which the Weimar Constitution emerged in 1919. The contemporary repertoire varies, but still includes works by Weimar's favorite sons, as well as avant-garde favorites like Robert Wilson and Schönberg. Ticket prices vary from DM9 for seating in orbit eight miles above the theater to DM44 for orchestra seats (with a bit more oxygen). There are 50% discounts for students, plus great deals on unsold seats one hour before the show (box office open Mon. and Fri. 10am-2pm, Tues.-Wed. 10am-1pm and 2-5pm, Thurs. 10am-1pm and 2-6pm). Directly across from the theater is the slick new **Bauhaus-Museum** (tel. 54 60; fax 54 61 01), featuring, in an appropriately well-designed space, historical artifacts about, and works produced by, the Bauhaus School of Design and Architecture. A 25-minute documentary (produced by the BBC, then ruthlessly dubbed into German) runs continuously (open Tues.-Sun. 10am-6pm; admission DM4, students and seniors DM2). At the **Wittumpalais,** across the square at Palais 3, Goethe, Schiller, and Herder sat at the round table of their patron, Duchess Anna Amalia. Under the same roof, the **Wieland Museum** documents the life and works of the extraordinary duchess (open March-Oct. Tues.-Sun. 9am-noon and 1-5pm, Nov.-Feb. Tues.-Sun. 9am-noon and 1-4pm; admission DM6, students DM4).

Park an der Ilm ("Goethe Park"), on the river, was landscaped by Goethe and sports numerous 18th-century pavilions and shelters for grazing sheep and goats. Of particular note are the fake ruins built by the Weimar shooting club and the eerie Soviet war memorial, complete with hammer and sickle. Perched on the park's far slopes is Goethe's **Gartenhaus,** on Corona-Schöfer-Str., the poet's first home in Weimar and later his retreat from the city. It was here that Goethe first put the moves on a certain *Fräulein* Christiane Vulpius, who later became *Frau* Goethe (open March-Oct. Wed.-Mon. 9am-noon and 1-5pm, Nov.-Feb. 9am-noon and 1-4pm; admission DM4, students and seniors DM3). South of the town center, Goethe and Schiller lie in rest together at the **Historischer Friedhof** cemetery (open March-Sept. 8am-9pm, Oct.-Feb. 8am-6pm). Goethe arranged to be sealed in an airtight steel case. Schiller, who died in an epidemic, was originally buried in a mass grave, but Goethe later combed through the remains until he identified Schiller and had him interred in the tomb. Skeptics argued for a long time that Goethe was mistaken, so a couple of "Schillers" were placed here side by side for a while. In the 1960s, a team of Russian scientists finally determined that Goethe had been right after all. (Tomb open daily 9am-1pm and 2-5pm. Admission DM4, students DM3.)

Elsewhere in Weimar

The cobblestone **Marktplatz,** straight down Frauentorstr., spreads out beneath the neo-Gothic **Rathaus** and the colorful Renaissance façade of the **Lucas Cranach Haus,** where the prolific 16th-century painter spent the last year of his life. Both are closed to the public, but the *Cranachhaus* shelters an **art gallery** of fairly hip modern paintings and photos (open Tues.-Fri. 10am-6pm, Sat. 11am-3pm). From the *Marktplatz,* wind your way left to the **Schloßmuseum,** at Burgplatz 4. The first floor is a Lucas Cranach-fest; the second floor is a minor-league collection of 19th- and 20th-century German works, as well as a Rodin sculpture and one of Monet's Rouen cathedral paintings (open Tues.-Sun. 10am-6pm; admission DM4, students DM2). Just in case you're interested, Cranach himself rests in the churchyard of the **Jakobskirche** on Am Graben (open Mon.-Fri. 10am-noon). Cross back over Vorwerkgasse to reach the **Stadtkirche St. Peter und Paul,** featuring Cranach's last triptych altarpiece (open Mon.-Sat. 10am-noon and 2-4pm, Sun. after services are over until noon and 2-3pm; free). The church is also called the **Herderkirche,** in honor of philosopher Johann Gottfried von Herder, who preached here regularly in the 1780s. Herder's works spurred two later cultural developments: the Romantics embraced his sermons about freedom, and his groundbreaking discussions of the progression of human history pointed directly to the works of a certain later German philosopher, named, well— let's just say it rhymes with "bagel." Herder was buried in the church in 1803. The church's interior is at odds with its solemn exterior: dazzlingly colorful coats of arms painted on all the balconies give the hall a festive air which came in handy in the August 1994 celebration of Herder's 250th birthday.

The **Bauhaus school,** now at the **Hochschule für Architektur und Bauwesen** (College for Architecture and Construction) on Marienstr., ironically offers no exhibits related to the iconoclastic design movement. (For Bauhaus exhibits, see the Bauhaus Museum, p. 488.) Instead, its sleek, prim yellow buildings are the 1911 creation of Henry van de Velde, a pioneer of the *Jugendstil* movement. Steps away is the **Franz Liszt Haus,** where the composer spent his last years. The instruments and furnishings are supposedly original, but given Liszt's torrid love life, the single bed seems improbable (open Tues.-Sun. 9am-1pm and 2-5pm; admission DM4, students and seniors DM3).

Down Humboldtstr. from the *Jugendherberge* is the **Nietzsche-Archiv,** Humboldtstr. 36. In this house Nietzsche spent the last three wacky years of his life (he was pretty far gone by the end, as is painfully evidenced by his cross-eyed glares that emanate from the myriad of pictures and busts). The archive was founded by Nietzsche's sister Elisabeth, a strange, jealous woman whose misunderstandings helped to set the stage for the Nazis' cynical distortion of her brother's philosophy after his death—she gave Hitler a tour of the house in 1932 (open Tues.-Sun. 1-5pm; admission DM4, students and seniors DM3).

NIGHTLIFE

Hopefully you came to Weimar to hear Mozart or Liszt and not techno. The night scene is, strangely enough, hotter during the week, since all of the students flee to Erfurt or the *Uni*-culture of Jena on the weekends; but while Weimar's nightlife is often dismissed as dead, if you listen closely enough, you'll hear a pulse. A good place to start is the design school's *Mensa* where posters and bulletin boards direct you to what's going down (see Food, p. 486). The **Studentenklub Kasserturm** (tel. 58 49 55) is in an old medieval tower on Goetheplatz opposite the main post office. With a disco up top (Mon.-Sat. nights after 8pm) and a groovy beer cellar down below, this is one of the oldest student clubs in town and currently *the* place to go in Weimar (cover varies). The **Studentenklub Schützengasse,** on Schützengassestr., has a disco on Friday nights, with a beer garden outside (open Mon.-Thurs. after 7:30pm, Fri.-Sat. after 8pm). **Gerber III,** Gerberstr. 3, offers straight-up, hardcore punk. Imagine the bus that Dr. Teeth rode around in during "The Great Muppet Caper" being hijacked by the Sex Pistols (that's Gerber III for you). Weimar also has a burgeoning gay scene. **Jugendclub Nordlich,** on Staufenbergstr., has a gay disco open every other Saturday night (10pm-3am). **AIDS-Hilfe,** Erfurterstr. 17, holds a popular gay café (open Tues.-Sat. at 8pm).

■ Near Weimar: Buchenwald

"Why?" Buchenwald lies at the edge of disbelief, its history of atrocity producing only questions. But what makes a visit to this town so difficult is not that the place is horrible, but, rather, that it is not. It is one of the most bitter ironies of the Third Reich that many *KZ Lager* (concentration camps) were situated within beautiful natural milieux. Buchenwald was built on a hill with a stunning view of Weimar (it was one of Goethe's favorite mountain retreats). It is chilling to realize how easily the woods could reclaim this site and erase all record of the crimes committed here. As Hannah Arendt observed, the most frightening thing about Nazi evil was that it was banal, ordinary, everyday. Buchenwald is just a place—nothing except the relics and monuments maintained here would tell you otherwise. There's no black cloud perpetually hanging over it, it's not surrounded by a ring of thorns, and there are no symbols scorched into the earth. If it weren't for the human labors that preserve the historical value of this place, nature would swallow it up. What makes a visit to Buchenwald so difficult is the effort each visitor must make—against so many contrary forces—to remember what could so easily be forgotten.

The best way to reach the camp is to take bus #6 from the station or from downtown Weimar. Check the bus schedule carefully: half the departures have "EB" after the departure times. They terminate in Etterburg, a full 5-km walk from the memorial site. Instead, seek out the buses with a "B" (Buchenwald) after the departure times. These buses leave every hour (every other hr. on weekends) from the train station and will take you directly to the camp's reception.

From 1937 to 1945, the concentration camp held over 250,000 Jews, political prisoners, gypsies, and gays (after 1942, there was also a large Communist contingent); most did not survive the Holocaust. What remains is the **Nationale Mahn-und Gedenkstätte Buchenwald** (National Buchenwald Memorial). At the memorial, signs will point to two destinations: the **KZ Lager** and the **Gedenkstätte.** The former refers to the remains of the camp, while the latter is a solemn monument overlooking the valley, a 20-minute walk away.

The film "O Buchenwald" is shown regularly, in German, but not even a language barrier can keep you from being moved by the film's images (daily viewings at 11am and 2pm). Expect apologies from the monument staff for the pre-1989 ideological content of the film, which emphasizes the stories of the Communist detainees over the experience of the many Jews who were murdered here (the staff assures that a new documentary film is nearing completion).

Death claimed members of many groups at Buchenwald. A plaque near the former commandant's horse stable matter-of-factly states that an estimated 8000 Soviet prisoners were executed by firing squad in the little space before the war's end. Many Jews were sent here, but after 1942, most of them were deported to Auschwitz. For the most part, Buchenwald served to detain and murder political enemies of Nazism and prisoners of war. The Soviet Union used the camp from 1945 to 1950 as an internment camp in which over 28,000 Germans, mostly Nazi war criminals and opponents of the Communist regime, were held; 10,000 died of hunger and disease. A museum exhibit detailing the Soviet abuses will open in 1997.

The central camp area, downhill from the reception, is now a vast, flat, gravel plain; gone are the ramshackle wooden *Blocks* (barracks) into which prisoners were crammed. The former crematorium building has been preserved with a wrenching suggestion of the terror wrought here; many place flowers around this exhibit. In the large storehouse building, a museum documents both the history of Buchenwald (1937-1945) and the general history of Nazism, including German anti-Semitism. The museum sets real documents (most of which are translated into or summarized in English) in wrought-iron boxes visibly riveted together. A moving installation by Polish artist Jòzef Szajna features thousands of photos of inmates pasted onto large silhouettes of human figures. Just outside the museum lies a brutally ironic symbol: the charred stump of the *"Goethe-Eiche"* (Goethe oak), left standing in the middle of the camp to commemorate Buchenwald's former role as a get-away for Germany's greatest cultural figure. The memorial stones recently embedded in the ground around the former children's barracks read, in English, German, and Hebrew: "So that the generation to come might know, that the children, yet to be born, may rise and declare to their children." Tiny candles and flowers are regularly placed near the stones (camp open May-Sept. Tues.-Sun. 9:45am-5:15pm; Oct.-April Tues.-Sun. 8:45am-4:15pm). The camp **archives** are open to anyone searching for records of family and friends between 1938 and 1945. Call ahead to schedule an appointment with the curator (tel. (036431) 430 154).

To get to the **memorial bell tower** *(Glockenturm)* from the camp, start by facing the reception at the bus stop and head right. Around the corner of the right-most building is the footpath to the **Mahnmal** (monument). After a short walk through the woods, it emerges at a two-way fork in the street. Head right, and keep walking past a parking lot and a bus stop. Keep going as the street curves left, and soon you'll come to the somber GDR-designed bell tower, with no marking other than an immense "MCMXLV" carved on each side. The plaque inside commemorates the memory of the anti-fascist "resistance fighters of the Republic of Germany." On the great stone plaza behind the tower unfolds a commanding view of the surrounding countryside, overseen by the slightly awkward **Plastikgruppe,** a sculpture of ragged, stern-jawed socialist prisoners claiming their freedom. Like the rest of the grounds outside of the buildings, the memorial can be visited until nightfall.

■ Jena

In the 19th century, Jena was home to Germany's premier university; today the name "Jena" still triggers intellectual fireworks in the German historical consciousness. Under the stewardship of literary greats Schlegel, Novalis, Tieck, and Hölderin (Hegel and Schelling's college roommate, who went insane in 1807 and is now considered Germany's greatest post-Goethe poet), Jena first transplanted the Romantic movement to German soil. It was here that philosophers Fichte and Schelling argued for a new conception of intellectual and political freedom, and where, in 1806, a then-unknown junior philosophy professor named Georg Wilhelm Friedrich Hegel wrote the epoch-making *Phenomenology of Spirit* by candlelight in his ramshackle lodgings by the centuries-old *Collegium Jenense.* Today, the university bears the name of

Friedrich Schiller, who in 1789 graced its halls with his lectures on the ideals of the French Revolution.

True to its traditions, Jena remains a campus town, and an increasingly Westernized one at that. Students keep this town youthful, left-leaning, and multicultural. Thankfully, Jena's dearth of sightseeing excitement is made up for by the fact that the town hasn't been burdened by its history—it's one of the few places in Thuringia where the present takes precedence over the past.

Orientation and Practical Information Jena lies in the Saale Valley, about 25km east of Weimar. Trains between Dresden and Erfurt stop at **Bahnhof Jena West,** while trains on the Berlin-Munich line stop at the slightly more distant **Jena Saalbahnhof,** about 15 minutes north of the center. The main transfer point for Jena's bus and streetcar system is the **Zentrum** stop, on Löbdergraben near Eichplatz and the *Markt.* From Saalbahnhof, take bus #15 three stops in the direction of Westbahnhof. From Bahnhof Jena West, head toward Westbahnhofstr. until it becomes Schillerstr. Turn left up the street to the towering university building. Constructed of black glass and a black metal frame and resembling a New Age shrine, **Jena-Information,** Löbderstr. 9 (tel. 58 63 20; fax 58 63 22), just off Teichgraben, hands out maps and schedules of special events (open May-Oct. Mon.-Fri. 9am-6pm, Sat. 9am-2pm). Rent **bikes** for DM15 per day in advance plus a valid photo ID as collateral at **Kirscht Fahrrad,** on Löbdergraben, near the Zentrum bus stop (open Mon.-Fri. 9am-6pm, Sat. 9am-noon). There's **luggage storage** at the Jena Saalbahnhof and Westbahnhof (unless it's *huge,* your pack will fit in a locker for DM2 per day). The **"Goethe-Apotheke" pharmacy** is conveniently located on Weigelstr., just north of the vast concrete Eichplatz; a sign directs you to other pharmacies that are open when it's closed (open Mon.-Fri. 8am-6:30pm, Sat. 8am-2pm). The **telephone code** is 03641.

Accommodations and Food Jena's **Jugendhaus,** Am Herrenberge 3 (tel. 68 72 30), is brand spanking new and contains all the amenities of a *Pension,* but it's a touch pricey and a bit of a trek from the city center. The best way to get there is to take bus #10 (direction: Lobeda Ost) or 11 (direction: Beutenberg) to "Mühlenstr." Follow Mühlenstr. until it turns into Am Herrenberge. (Reception open 7:30am-8pm. First night DM35.50, over 26 DM39.50; additional nights cheaper. Breakfast included. Curfew 12:30am.) Another price-competitive option is to stay in a **private room** booked by the tourist office for a DM5 fee; it's possible to get a quiet bedroom with breakfast for DM25-35. To sup with the student body, hit **Café Daneben,** on Eichplatz, right underneath the mega-tower (hence the name). On Tuesdays and Fridays, a disco graces the café's slick black and white interior. Light bites and ornate salads run DM5-13; try the spiced potato/carrot soup with sausage for DM9 (open daily 9am-1am). A crunchier clientele frequents the nuclear-free zone of **Café Immergrün** (tel. 44 73 13), tucked inside an old building at Fürstengraben 30. An unofficial recycling and environmental center, this intimate café is decorated with Green Party pamphlets. Tasty green specialties like veggie pizzas run for DM5 (open Mon.-Sat. 11am-midnight, Sun. 3-10pm). Numerous **bakeries** and **butcher shops** cluster around Eichplatz and the St. Michaelkirche—pick up a cheap breakfast or lunch here. The **Markt** on Eichplatz provides a panoply of cheap culinary options (open Tues. and Thurs.-Fri. 10am-6:30pm).

Sights The **Romantikerhaus,** Unterm Markt 12a, just off the old market square, once bubbled with the raw creative energy of the Romantic period. Owned by philosopher and fiery democrat Johann Fichte, who held his lectures here, it later hosted the poetry and philosophy parties of the Romantics. It's a curious museum: first-edition books and portraits scattered around the interior are interspersed with big stenciled quotes of great thinkers on the walls. Upstairs is the solid but unspectacular **Fine Arts Museum of Jena;** its collection reflects, perhaps, as much ingenuity as was possible given the former GDR's disdain for non-representational art (open Tues. and

Thurs.-Sat. 10am-1pm and 2-5pm, Wed. 10am-1pm and 2-6pm; admission DM5, students and seniors DM3). A few blocks to the southwest sits the **Schillergedenkstätte,** Schiller's summer home on Schillergäßchen (tel. 63 03 94), just off (you guessed it!) Schillerstr. The museum is small and has seen better days despite recent restoration attempts; the sculptured garden in back, however, is delightful (open Tues.-Fri. 10am-noon and 1-4pm, Sat. 11am-4pm; admission DM1, students and seniors DM0.50). An ironically neglected tourist site is Jena's most visible structure: the cylindrical, 24-story **new university tower.** A product of the late-GDR architectural imagination, it looks like what you thought the future would look like back when Buck Rogers was popular. The sky-high lecture halls on the top floor are used for special recitals and events. A competing, more contemporary vision of the future is the **Jenoptik** building, across Leutragraben from the university tower. This ultra-slick modern edifice underscores the high-tech corporate aspirations of Jena. The **original university building,** just up Oberlauengasse from the *Romantikerhaus,* dates from the 13th century. It housed a Dominican monastery until the Wittenberg University temporarily relocated here to dodge the plague.

The **Stadtkirche St. Michael,** just off Eichplatz, presides proudly over **Luther's tombstone.** He's not here, though the stone was intended for him; the folks at the Stadtkirche claim it was shipped here by mistake, while back at the gravesite in Wittenberg, tour guides mutter something under their breath about 17th-century plundering. The 16th-century church is unusually frightening and black outside, but the interior is graceful and light (open Mon.-Tues. and Thurs.-Fri. 10am-6pm, Wed. 1-2pm, Sat. 10am-2pm, Sun. 2:30-5:30pm). Up Weigelstr., and left onto Fürstengraben, visit the **Botanischer Garten** (open dawn-dusk), or the row of statues of the university's distinguished faculty; notice that teachers and students of **Marx** are given particularly large statues. But there's one glaring exception—Marx's intellectual godfather and Jena's most famous professor, **Hegel,** has no bust at all. In fact, the only mention of him in the entire city is a piddly plaque on the back of the *Romantikerhaus.* Oooh … busted. Maybe it's a legacy of Communist *Angst* about Hegel, whose writings inspired Marx's work but themselves propounded a spiritual, bourgeois-centered political vision (to make Hegel's theories right, Marx once wrote, you had to "stand him on his head").

The **Wagnergasse,** which extends from the Eichplatz (face the university tower, walk around the right side of the tower, walk past the small battlement (the *Pulverturm*) on your right, then bear right at the fork) is shaping up to be Jena's funkiest area. Rave culture invades the East at **Backstage** and the adjacent **Stahlwerkt m-Bossy,** clothing stores on Wagnergasse 3 and 4 (both open Mon.-Fri. 11am-6pm, Sat. 10am-1pm). At the end of the Wagnergasse lies the **Studentenhaus Wagner,** the source of the funk, as it were. This university-sponsored bar/hang-out place doubles as a performance space for plays, readings, live music, and movie showings (open Mon.-Thurs. 1pm-1am, Fri.-Sat. 7:30pm-1am). The **Zentrum** area is saturated with swinging saloons every night.

■ Near Jena: Dornburg

Among Jena's attractions is its proximity to the little *Dorf* of **Dornburg** (18km to the north), home to the **Dornburger Schlößer,** a series of three palaces perched high above the Saale River valley. First in line is the **Altes Schloß,** the oldest castle and by far the homeliest; it was built back in 937, when the Kaisers still visited Dornburg. The first German *Reichstag* met here, and the building was used as a prison by both the Nazi and Communist regimes. The interior is closed to the public. The summer residences of the Grand Duke of Sachsen-Weimar-Eisenach, the **Renaissanceschloß** and the **Rokokoschloß,** preside majestically and frivolously (respectively) over the magnificent rose gardens where Goethe practiced his horticultural skills while writing letters to his lover, Charlotte von Stein (see the section under Gloßkochberg, p. 503, for the steamy details). Inside the 16th-century Renaissance castle, the plain royal belongings are spiced up with stories about Goethe's frequent visits to the

Schlößer. Goethe actually never napped on the big ottoman in the guest bedroom; he traveled everywhere (and at great expense) with his portable bed, but one look inside the lush chambers of this 1740 Rococo pleasure palace will reveal why Goethe favored it with the most stays. Visitors can partake in the voluptuous pleasure of gliding along the slick surface of the main hall in the slippers provided to protect its surface while glancing up at 17th-century French sexual paintings. The castles are a grueling climb up a very steep hill. Fortunately for pedestrians (you can also drive the route), steps lead towards the summit. Use them; otherwise you'll face a hike up a mile of winding, steep highway. From the tiny *Bahnhof,* turn left and then take the first right onto Am Born; the stairs will be immediately on your left. (Open April-Oct. Tues.-Sun. 9am-noon and 1-5pm; Nov.-March Wed.-Sun. 9am-noon and 1-4pm. Last entry about 15min. before closing. Gardens open daily until 8pm. Admission DM6, students DM4.)

Dornburg is also known for rose cultivation. During the last weekend in June, the **Dornburg Rose Festival** marks the anniversary of King Karl August's lavish birthday parties held here a century ago; the townspeople elect a sort of homecoming queen who hands out food and candy to spectators. Locals don their party hats again during the last week in August to celebrate **Goethe's birthday.** Dornburg fills up quickly during festivals, but otherwise rooms are usually available through the **Stadtverwaltung** (tel. 209), the closest thing in town to a tourist office, located in the *Rathaus* just up the steps from the castles. To reach Dornburg from Jena, hop a **train** from either the Jena Saalbahnhof or Bahnhof Jena-Paradies, on Kahlaische-Str., a 5-minute walk from Bahnhof Jena-West (the main train station). Dornburg is also an easy and attractive **bike ride** from Jena, though you may want to save your strength for the climb to the castles. **Gaststätte am Born,** by the entrance to the stairs, will serve a tasty *Schitzel* with roasted potatoes and cucumber salad for DM8 (open Mon.-Fri. 8am-9pm, Sat. 9:30am-1pm). The **post office,** right by the castle and on the *Markt,* doubles as a grocery store. The **telephone code** is 036427.

■ Altenburg

The dominant impression derived from Altenburg is that its domineering hilltop castle is built upon a house of cards. The manufacture of playing cards provides for Altenburg's claim to fame, with the creation of the fast-paced game *Skat* topping the charts of notable historical achievements. So proud are they, in fact, that the city declares itself the *Skatstadt.* Despite all of the dealing (if not wheeling), Altenburg's political significance isn't taken very seriously; a couple of visits by Barbarossa in the 12th century and the delightful abduction of the two princes from the castle in the 15th century produce nothing more than two pairs—kings over jacks.

Orientation and Practical Information Altenburg has extensive rail connections, as most of the trains running between Leipzig and Zwickau (and there are many) stop here. To reach the **tourist office,** Moritzstr. 21 (tel. 59 41 74), turn left from the train station and walk to the end of Wettinerstr., then turn right onto Gabelentzstr., and follow it past the *Schloß* until Burgstr. emerges on your right. Turn left from Burgstr. into the *Markt;* on the opposite side of the *Markt* is Moritzstr. The tourist office books rooms for DM3 and provides free maps with information in English (open Mon.-Fri. 9:30am-6pm, Sat. 9:30am-noon). **Store luggage** at the train station for DM4 per day. The **postal code** for Altenburg is 04600. The **telephone code** is 03447.

Accommodations and Food Altenburg sadly lacks a youth hostel, but a viable alternative, to book a private room through the tourist office, may cost less than DM40 per person. A novel (and cheap) option is a stay at the **Magdalenenstift,** Stiftsgraben 20 (tel. 31 16 13). The *Stift* is a Lutheran-run home for the elderly partially converted into friendly hostel-style multiple-guest rooms. It's best to call ahead on weekends to make sure rooms are available. To get there, head straight uphill from the *Schloß* driveway on Unterm Schloßgasse, which becomes Marstallstr. Turn right at the light when you reach the top of the hill on Münsaer Str.; Stiftsgraben will be on the next right. The office is on the second floor in Building G. Heavenly peace reigns under Martin Luther's gaze. (Beds DM20 plus a one-time DM7.50 fee for a linen change. Breakfast DM3.50.) While the restaurants in the *Markt* are a touch pricey, the decent number of **food markets** can soften the budget sting (most open Mon.-Fri. 8am-6pm, Sat. 8am-noon). The less expensive restaurant scene resides close to the *Schloß* driveway. **Eiscafé Angela,** Luxemburg Str. 14, has a menu of daily Thuringian specials (DM6-8.50; open Sun.-Thurs. 10am-10pm, Fri.-Sat. 10am-11pm). The *Biergarten* and restaurant **Kulisse,** Theaterplatz 18, has cheap sandwiches (DM3.50-6.50) to prepare you for the beer they'll foist into your greedy hands (beergarden open Tues.-Sun. 2-10pm; restaurant open Tues.-Thurs. 5pm-1am, Fri.-Sat. 5pm-3am, Sun. 2pm-midnight).

Sights The wide cobblestone footpath leading up to the looming **Schloß** winds from the Theaterplatz in the heart of town. A massive enclosure the color of dark sand, the castle was begun in the 11th century and expanded over the next 700 years. The architecture ranges from a humbly squatting 11th-century guard tower called the **Flasche** (bottle) to the dazzlingly Gothic 15th-century **Schloßkirche.** The church organ, the **Trostorgel,** was given a thumbs-up by Bach after a trial performance in 1730. Unfortunately, the only way to view the inside of the church and its organ is through guided tours which leave from the second floor of the museum every hour. Adjacent to the church is a museum that cunningly combines Altenburg's two claims to fame in one neat package: the **Schloß-und-Spielkartenmuseum** (castle and playing card museum; church and museums open Tues.-Sun. 9am-5pm; admission DM5, students DM2.50). The *Schloß* amply entertains with its huge, hanging portraits of the Dukes of Sachsen-Gotha-Altenburg, the former owners. The **Waffenmuseum** (weapons museum) section sports ornately gilded muskets, jagged-edged Bavarian cavalry sabres, and those bizarre pointy helmets; the **Stadtgeschichte** (city history) displays, which have yet to recover from their socialist days, place Altenburg in the middle of all rebellious proletarian activities. You'll find a full house in the **Spielkarten** wing: it occupies gorgeous, Rococo-ceilinged rooms jammed with giant playing-card displays. The most occult element of the exhibit are the hand-enameled extra-large 15th-century Florentine *tarot* cards, each the size of a hand. The cards of the former GDR are fascinatingly comical—meant to indoctrinate the incorrigible, frenzied schoolgroups who make your life in hostels hell, they come in four suits: the October Revolution, solidarity, anti-Fascism, and the triumph of Communism. Presumably, no kings, queens, or jacks are in this set.

Altenburg's ace in the hole is a hidden cultural treasure: the **Lindenau-Museum** at Gabelentzstr. 5, visible straight down Wettinerstr. from the train station. It possesses an unexpectedly sophisticated collection of cutting-edge modern paintings and some second-stringers of past major art movements. Sadly, the museum lacks the picture of dogs playing poker (open Tues.-Sun. 10am-6pm; admission DM3, students DM1.50).

■ Erfurt

Erfurt is the point of connection between Thuringia's political and economic spheres. Hardly a cultural powerhouse like Dresden, or even Gotha or Eisenach, it has certainly attracted its fair share of politicos. Napoleon based his field camp here for over a year, Konrad Adenauer lived here before World War II, and more recently, Willy Brandt met with Erich Honecker in Erfurt in 1970, in the early stages of German-German reconciliation. For the budget traveler, Erfurt offers a stunning cathedral, a handful of museums, and a civic atmosphere fueled by three educational institutions. Because of its political importance as the capital of Thuringia and its recent 1250th birthday celebration, most of the city center has been beautifully restored, giving Erfurt a look all too rare in the cities of the east. Everything that hasn't

THURINGIA

been renovated looks eerily similar to sets from *Dr. Caligari's Cabinet.* Erfurt is also a prime gateway into the hills and forests of the Thuringian Forest.

ORIENTATION AND PRACTICAL INFORMATION

Erfurt lies in the heart of Thuringia, only 15 minutes from Weimar, 90 minutes from Leipzig, and three hours from Frankfurt. The train station stands south of the city center. Head straight down Bahnhofstr. to reach the **Anger**—the main drag—and then the *Altstadt,* which is cut through by the **Gera River.** Take Schloßerstr. across the river to the market in front of the **Rathaus.** Marktstraße then leads to the **Domhügel** hill, one of the oldest districts and site of the cathedral.

Tourist Office: Erfurt Fremdenverkehrsamt, Bahnhofstr. 37 (tel. 562 62 67; fax 562 33 55). From the station, head straight down Bahnhofstr. to the intersection with Juri-Gagarin-Ring; the office is on the left. Pick up the monthly *Erfurt Magazin* with a worthy map in the center, and get a copy of *In* magazine for nightlife tips. Maps of the Thuringian Forest are available as well. The office reserves tickets and books rooms in costly hotels (and more affordable private rooms) for a DM5 fee (singles DM30-50). Open Mon.-Fri. 10am-6pm, Sat. 10am-1pm. Another branch in a cottage on the **Krämerbrücke** (tel. 562 34 36; fax 562 11 16) has weekend hours, though they don't book rooms. **Tours** of the city leave from the *Krämerbrücke* April-Oct. daily at 1pm; Nov.-March Sat. at 1pm (DM6). *Krämerbrücke* office open Mon.-Fri. 10am-6pm, Sat. 10am-4pm, Sun. 10am-1pm.

Currency Exchange: Deutsche Verkehrs Bank is perfectly located in the train station. It offers money transfer, phonecards, and cash advances on credit cards. Nice hours, but somewhat stiff rates. Open Tues.-Fri. 8:30am-7:45pm, Sat.-Sun. 10am-4pm. Also close to the train station, and with better rates, is the **Deutsche Bank** on the corner of Bahnhofstr. and Juri-Gagarin-Ring, across from the tourist office. It has a 24-hr. ATM. Open Mon. and Wed. and Fri. 8am-4pm; Tues. and Thurs. 8am-5:30pm.

Trains: From the *Hauptbahnhof,* trains shoot off to Dresden (every 2hr.), Leipzig (every 2hrs.), Würzburg (every 3hr.), and Frankfurt (every 3hr.).

Public Transportation: An effective combination of **buses** and silent **streetcars** for pedestrian zones. DM1.60 per trip. Seniors get a 50% discount. Validate your tickets on board. For info call 642 13 22 or stop by the office at the *Hauptbahnhof.* Streetcars and buses stop at midnight.

Taxis: tel. 511 11.

Bicycle rental: Velo-Sport, on Juri-Gagarin-Ring. From the tourist office turn left. DM10-15 per day, and you must leave a passport. Open Mon.-Fri. 9am-6pm, Sat. 9am-1pm.

Luggage storage: No luggage-checking office, but small (DM2) and large (DM3) lockers in the train station do the trick.

Laundry: Jump for joy at the sight of washing machines across the street from the *Hauptbahnhof.* Open Mon.-Fri. 6am-10pm, Sat.-Sun. 9am-8pm. What hours!

Pharmacy: Bahnhof-Apotheke, on Bahnhofstr. near the Anger, has a wider selection than most and a listing of the all-night pharmacy of the week. Open Mon.-Fri. 8am-6:30pm, Sat. 9am-noon.

Women's Center: Frauenzentrum, Espechstr. 3 (tel. 562 60 68), in the southwest part of the city, has information, counseling, and a café—all open Mon. 2-6pm, Tues.-Thurs. 9:30am-9:30pm, Fri. 9:30am-2pm, Sat. 2-6pm.

Emergency: Police: tel.110. **Fire:** tel 112. **Ambulance:** tel. 115.

Post Office: The main post office, 99084 Erfurt, occupies an overadorned beast of a building probably larger than some of the punier European countries; it's the focal point of the Anger. Open Mon.-Fri. 8am-6pm, Sat. 9am-noon.

Telephone Code: 0361.

ACCOMMODATIONS

Housing options are a dice roll. The best bet is the **Jugendherberge Karl Reiman (HI),** Hochheimerstr. 12 (tel. 562 67 05), an old white-and-maroon mansion in a once-ritzy suburb a fair distance from the city center. From the station, take streetcar #5 (direction: Steigerstr.) to the last stop. Backtrack a little, turn left onto Hochheimerstr., and the pillar-fronted hostel is on the left corner at the first intersection. The renovated interior, with sparkling new showers and bathrooms, is more inviting than the dilapidated exterior. There's foosball in the lounge. Considering Erfurt's size and the hostel's lack of competition, it's a pleasant surprise that it's sometimes possible to book same-day rooms. July and August are good months to try—the bed-gobbling school groups disappear, replaced by less-trying lone travelers. (Reception open 6-9am and 3-10pm. Lockout 10am-3pm. Curfew 10pm. DM21, over 26 DM26. Breakfast included.) If the hostel is booked, the **Zimmervermittlung** at the tourist office (see p. 496) can book private rooms costing about double what you'd pay in the hostel. If they're out of rooms, head to the gracious people who run the private agency **Tourismus Agentur Otto,** Schmidstedter-Str. 28 (tel./fax 643 09 71), down the road across from the tourist office, which has rooms in private homes for DM40-50 (fee included; open Mon.-Fri. 9am-8pm. Sat. 10am-12:30pm). As always when booking private rooms, be sure to take a look around before agreeing to stay. In a pinch, Weimar's hostels are a 15-minute train ride away.

FOOD

What it lacks in accommodations, Erfurt makes up for with food. If you're traveling on the cheap, you can head to the **Rewe** supermarket on Bahnhofstr., less than 100m from the train station (open Mon.-Fri. 6:30am-7:30pm, Sat. 6:30am-2pm), or fill up at the **market** on Domplatz (open Mon.-Sat. 6am-2pm). But Erfurt does offer some of the better restaurants in the *neue Bundesländer.* Replenish necessary spices at some of the more exotic Chinese, Italian, or Argentine restaurants.

On the domestic front, the capital of Thüringen is a good place to discuss the region's wondrous specialty, *Thüringer Bratwurst.* At markets, street corners, and train stations throughout the province, you will see countless stands proffering up these succulent roasted sausages for DM2-3. The *Wurst*s begin a pale color, but brown appetizingly with a few minutes of grilling. Also known as *Roster, Thüringer Brat, or Rostbrat* (but not to be confused with *Thüringer Rostbrätl,* a pork chop), they are the direct ancestors of the American "hot dog." To bite into a spicy, juicy *Roster* flecked with mustard and cupped in a flaky *Brötchen* (which comes with the sausage) is to appreciate how far the sickly-pink American frank has degenerated from its noble roots. Many budget meals can be had from the fast- and semi-fast-food restaurants on the **Anger,** several of which have appealing, late-night hours.

Istanbul-Kebab, Johannesstr. 19. A laid-back place that is both a stand- and a sit-down restaurant, serving yummy Turkish *Kebab* (also called *Gyros*) for DM5-6.50 and delectable falafels for DM4. Play pool at the billiards table, or drop a coin in the old-style video games. Open Mon.-Sat. noon-10pm.

Schmalztopf, Domplatz 12-13. Locals who are in-the-know come here to dine on native specialties amid the owner's self-congratulatory pictures of hearty customers eating gustily. Dinner specials DM6.50-12.50, with a good view of the *Dom* at no extra charge. Open daily 11am-midnight.

Bistro-Angereck, directly on the Anger (above it, really). Serves ice cream and decent Italian food (the Germans still have a way to go before mastering Italian cooking). DM6.50-12.50. Open daily 10am-midnight.

SIGHTS

Completely dominating the view from the marketplace at its perch on Domhügel hill is the mammoth Erfurt **Dom,** one of Germany's most impressive cathedrals. This is a Gothic extravaganza—the central part of the cathedral dates back to 1154. Its spires explode against the sky with rusty, green towers. Inside, the most impressive part of the cathedral is the 15th-century **Hochchor** in the eastern wing; the **altar** is fully 17m high, embellished with miniature oil paintings and intricate carvings. The fifteen **stained glass windows** rise higher than the altar and are currently about halfway through a massive cleaning that will make them brighter than they've been in centuries. Already, the density of adornment in the clean parts is enough to make your eyes cross. Luther was invested as a priest here, and word has it that his first mass was disrupted by a visit from … *Satan.* In mid-liturgy, the doughty Luther hurled his Bible across the altar, which sent the Dark One fleeing but did not impress the Bishop. The *Dom* complex is further enriched by the adjacent **Church of St. Severi,** whose biggest draw is not so much its simple sandstone interior as the way the three great towers of its exterior combine with the bristly *Dom* to create a pleasing symmetrical whole. (Cathedral and church open Mon.-Fri. 9-11:30am and 12:30-5pm, Sat. 9-11:30am and 12:30-4:30pm, Sun. 2-4pm. Mass is celebrated on Sundays at 11am and 6pm. Free).

From *Domplatz,* Marktstr. leads down to the breezy, open **Fischmarkt,** bordered by restored guild houses with wildly decorated façades. Overlooking the space is the brazenly neo-Gothic **Rathaus,** whose bonanza of **paintings** depicting mythical sequences, including Faust and Tannhaüser portrayals, is open for public gawking. Late-19th-century Thüringians weren't into subtlety (open Mon.-Fri. 9am-4pm).

Further down Marktstr. flows the quietly babbling **Gera River,** which provides the *raison d'être* for one of Erfurt's oddest architectural attractions. The little river is spanned by the **Krämerbrücke,** a medieval bridge completely covered by small shops, some of which date back to the 12th century. In the 1400s, this bridge was part of a great trade-route running from Kiev to Paris. When you're walking on the bridge, it is impossible to see the water; it looks for all the world like a "regular," narrow Central European street. Even more fascinating is the view from underneath: glance up from the water's edge. A point worth mentioning is that anarchists used to meet here in the early 90s. On the far end (away from the *Altstadt*) is the **Brückenmuseum,** a small house that chronicles the bridge's history as well as medieval period costume (open Tues.-Sun. 10am-6pm; admission DM2, children DM1).

From the far side of the bridge, follow Gotthardtstr., and cut left through Kirchengasse to reach the **Augustinerkloster,** where Martin Luther spent 10 years as a Catholic priest and Augustine monk. He got his way; the cloister now functions as a Protestant college. (Tours leave every hr. Tues.-Sat. 10am-noon and 2-4pm; there's also a tour on Sun. after morning services, around 10:45am. From Nov.-March tours are only available by prior arrangement. The cloister won't lead a tour if fewer than five people show up for it; they're strict about this. You may get bumped back an hour or more. DM4.50, students DM3.) The **library** here has one of Germany's most priceless collections, including a number of early Bibles with personal notations by Luther himself. During World War II, the books were moved to make room for a bomb shelter. When U.S. bombers destroyed the library in February 1945, 267 people lost their lives, but the books remained unscathed.

From the Krämerbrücke, head down Futterstr. and turn right on Johannesstr. to reach the **Kaufmannskirche,** where Bach's parents tied the knot (open Mon. 11am-1pm, Tues.-Fri. 2-5pm, service Sat. 6pm and Sun. 10am). In front of the church, feet planted firmly on a pedestal decorated with scenes from his days here, a squat **Martin Luther** casts an indifferent stare over the **Anger,** Erfurt's wide pedestrian promenade. Beautified with numerous statues and fountains, the Anger is one of the most attractive shopping streets in Eastern Germany. No, it's not Milan (or even Dortmund, for that matter) but the street's collection of Benettons, mega-cafés, fast food- joints, and multiplex cinemas bring Erfurt solidly into the realm of conspicuous consumption. The architecture lining the street—most of it 19th-century Neoclassical or *Jugendstil*—is for the most part fascinating, though some GDR-era behemoths mar the effect. Across from the post office lies **House #6,** where Russian Czar Alexander I stayed when he came to Erfurt to meet with Napoleon in 1808.

The **Angermuseum,** in an immaculate yellow mansion at Anger 18, is not dedicated to chronicling the history of rage, or of fashion accessories, but rather to displaying a respectable variety of Erfurtian medieval stuff. (Open Tues.-Thurs. and Sun. 10am-5pm, Fri. 10am-1pm, Sat. 1-5pm. Admission DM3, students DM1.50. Free on Wed. The conventional part of the museum usually costs DM2, students DM1.)

Bear right at the end of the Anger and follow Regierungstr. to the **Statthalterei,** the massive Baroque building from which the Communists ruled the city. Here, in a small salon on the second floor, Napoleon had breakfast with Goethe in 1808. Goethe later wrote that Napoleon spent the entire time chastising him for his gloomy tragedies, which the French emperor seemed to know inside and out, while Goethe listened passively (both understood themselves to be immortals; Goethe also realized, however, that Napolean's immortality was backed up by an army). The building is being converted to the office of Thuringia's Minister-President; it's not open to the public, but the *Statthelterei* is still worthy of a healthy gawking.

ENTERTAINMENT AND NIGHTLIFE

Erfurt's 220,000 inhabitants manage a fairly indulgent nightlife. Take in opera or drama at the **Opernhaus** (Opera House) or **Schauspielhaus** whose combined ticket agency (tel. 223 31 58) is in the Opera House at Dalbergsweg 2 (open Tues.-Fri. 10am-1pm and 2-5:30pm, Sat. 10am-1pm, Sun. 10am-noon, and 1hr. before performances, when prices drop 60% on unsold seats). Just off the Domplatz is the **Theater Waidspeicher** (tel. 562 38 28), with an intricate wooden marionette and puppet theater (DM10, children DM2.50) and a cabaret on weekend nights (box office open Tues.-Fri. 10am-2pm and 3-5:30pm). The **Double ß,** Marbacher Gasse 10, near the Domplatz, functions as a hybrid Irish pub, German beer garden, and Amsterdam café; all the cool kids in Erfurt show up there to indulge in things fast and decadent (open Mon.-Fri. 8am-1am, Sat.-Sun. 9am-1am).

The **Studentenclub Engelsburg,** Allerheiligenstr. 20/21 (tel. 290 36), just off Marktstr., is down with the disco and moderate punk scene of Erfurt's student population, especially at the frat-like musical grotto within (open Wed.-Sat. 9pm-1am; cover charge DM8, DM4 for students). Erfurt also has a nascent rave and hip-hop scene—find out about impending events at **Planet House,** Neuwerkstr. 38/9, a clothing store for the jilted generation whose staff is as cool as they are pierced (open Mon.-Wed. and Fri. 10am-6pm, Thurs. 10am-7pm, Sat. 10am-1pm).

■ Thuringian Forest (Thüringer Wald)

"The area is magnificent, quite magnificent…I am basking in God's world," wrote Goethe from the Thuringian Forest in a letter more than 200 years ago. Today, Goethe's exuberant exclamation has lost none of its accuracy. The time-worn mountains make for perfect skiing during the winter and excellent hiking, camping, and walking in the summer; the peaceful pine woods of the Thuringian Forest have attracted Germans for generations. Cradled within these mighty but gentle hills, the small towns and villages of Thuringia have cultivated and inspired many of Germany's composers, philosophers, and poets from the Classical period and beyond. Most famous among them were Goethe and Schiller, who scribbled some of their most brilliant poetry on these slopes (and on the walls of huts). The unspoiled forests stretch south of Eisenach, Weimar, and Erfurt to the border with Bavaria. Trains and buses trek regularly from larger cities to the smaller, wood-framed villages.

The **Rennsteig,** a famous scenic hiking trail, snakes through this forest. Before the war, the Rennsteig was one of Germany's favorite wilderness trails. History books date the trail at 1330, but locals claim that it was first trodden by prehistoric hunter-gatherers. During the years of division, much of the route was closed because of its potential as an escape route. But now hikers can wander all 168km from Hörschel near Eisenach right into Bavaria. Veterans of the five-day hike can't shut up about the route's delights. **Erfurt,** the new state capital, is without question the door to the Thuringian Forest. The **tourist office** (see Erfurt, p. 495) can equip you with guides and maps for an extended jaunt. Keep in mind that foreign tourists and the conveniences they expect are rare here. English is only understood in larger tourist offices, although increasing numbers offer brochures and other literature in English.

ARNSTADT

The oldest town in Thuringia, the stately **Arnstadt** (founded in 704) lies at the fringe of the forest just beyond Erfurt. As construction occurs all over the place, the city's age is definitely beginning to show. Johann Sebastian Bach began his career here as an organist in today's **Bachkirche** (open March-Sept. Tues.-Sat. 10:30am-12:30pm and 2-4pm, Sun. 2-4pm). Before they were naming holy edifices after him, however, the local authorities found Bach's license with musical forms as well as local women "shocking to community standards." They politely but firmly asked him to leave town for good. Nevertheless, a statue on the *Marktplatz*—the young Bach slumped on an organ stool, looking mildly displeased—commemorates the life of the trumpeted composer. The Renaissance-era **Haus Zum Palmbaum,** Markt 3 (tel. 60 29 78), serves as a **town museum** and **Bachmuseum** (open Mon.-Fri. 8:30am-12:30pm and 1-5pm, Sat.-Sun. 9:30am-5pm; admission DM4, students DM2).

The **Neues Schloß** (New Palace), Schloßplatz 1 (tel. 60 29 32), houses one of Germany's more fascinating doll museums, **"Mon Plaisir."** In the mid-18th century, the local princess whimsically demanded that court employees and craftsmen fashion a miniature panorama of the community. More than 400 wax and wooden dolls are displayed in 24 dollhouses, with a total of 82 furnished rooms decorated with thousands of miniature props from spinning wheels to musical instruments (open May-Oct. Tues.-Sun. 8:30am-12:30pm and 1-5pm; Nov.-April Tues.-Sun. 9:30am-4pm; admission DM3.50, students and seniors DM2.50). The old medieval town walls still stand in glorious decrepitude throughout the **Schloßgarten.** The magnificent ruins of **Schloß Niedeck** are undergoing restoration until 2004; you can still visit its gardens and theater, with cabaret and Shakespeare productions in the works for 1997 (call 61 86 33 for info; ticket sales open Tues. and Thurs. 10am-noon and 4-6pm; tickets DM9-20, students and seniors DM3). With a less gossipy history than the nearby Bachkirche, the **Liebfrauenkirche** (tel. 74 09 65) is still one of the most beautiful churches of the Romanesque Gothic period (open March-Sept. Tues.-Sat. 10:30am-12:30pm and 2-4pm, Sun. 2-4pm; otherwise, call the tourist office for opening hours and tours). At the end of Marktstr., the **Jakobsturm** stands with all the glory it possessed in 1484. A historical tidbit has it that in the top golden orb, the secret documents of Arnstadt are stowed away to be opened in the 21st century, when *Let's Go* researchers will all be computer-programmed robots from Mars.

Near Arnstadt, the ruined monastery of **Paulinzella** lies along the line to Saalfeld and Rudolstadt. It remains one of the most striking monuments of the Romanesque period in Thuringia. The **Zinnsboden museum** nearby has a model of the monastery and information about its history (open May-Sept. daily 9am-noon and 2-5pm).

The **tourist office,** Arnstadt Information, Markt 3 (tel. 60 20 49), finds rooms for DM3 (room DM25-40). From the station, turn left and then right on Bahnhofstr., continue down on Erfurter Str., and then walk up Ledermarkt to the *Markt.* They can tell you about bus connections to the **Drei Gleichen** (three matching castles), near Arnstadt, and will provide you with information on hiking trails (open Mon.-Fri. 9am-noon and 12:30-6pm, Sat. 9am-noon). Arnstadt is best reached by **train** from Erfurt or Ilmenau (1-4 per hour, 20-40min.). **Exchange money** at the **post office,** Ritterstr., 99310 Arnstadt, on the edge of the park off Bahnhofstr. (open Mon.-Fri. 8:30am-6pm, Sat. 8:30am-noon). The **telephone code** is 03628.

The streets of Arnstadt lead to some Thuringian culinary treasure troves. **Feinbäckerei und Cafe am Jakobsturm,** Ried 18, bakes the freshest cakes, breads, and pastries (DM5) for miles around (open Mon.-Fri. 6:30am-6pm, Sat. 7-11am and 2-5pm, Sun. 2-5pm). At the hearty **Hotel-Restaurant Goldene Sonne,** Ried 3 (tel. 60 27 76), you can dine on *Bratwürstchen* (DM7.80) or the forest's special meatballs (DM7.80). Most meals run DM7.50-14 (open Mon.-Thurs. 10am-3pm and 6-10pm, Fri. 10am-3pm, Sun. 11am-3pm). For typical Thuringian meals (read: hot sausages) hovering around DM10, try the **Ratsklause,** Ledermarkt 3 (tel. 480 73; open Mon.-Thurs. 7:30am-4pm, Sat. 7:30am-2pm). At night, check out the **Kulisse Cafe,** Kohlenmarkt 8

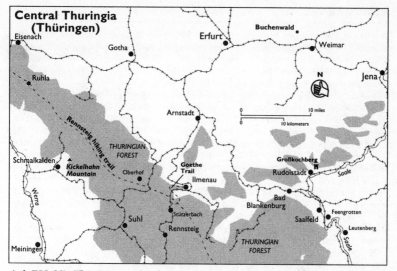

Central Thuringia (Thüringen)

(tel. 782 88). This joint used to be a brew house; now it teems with locals (open Mon.-Fri. 10am-midnight, Sat.-Sun. 2pm-midnight).

ILMENAU AND GOETHE TRAIL (GOETHEWANDERWEG)

Thuringia claims several geniuses, but its favorite offspring by far is Johann Wolfgang Goethe. Johann's beginnings in the region were tediously bureaucratic. Goethe first worked in Ilmenau reorganizing the Thuringian mining industry while he was a government minister under the Duke of Weimar. Only later did he come back to the area as a poet looking for a place of his own. "Ilmenau cost me much time, effort, and money," he wrote, "but I learned something as well and developed a way of looking at nature which I would not give up at any price." Today, in turn, the main attractions on the way to the market square are the stunning scenery and a number of his old haunts. South of the city center, parallel to Waldstr., stretches the 18.5-km **Goethe Trail (Goethewanderweg)**, marked by Goethe's over-flourished "g" monogram, that leads through the forest to **Stützerbach.**

From the delightful market area, with its ubiquitous classical statues, pedestrian-friendly fountains, and sidewalk cafés, the trail begins at Ilmenau's **Amtshaus,** Am Markt 1 (tel. 20 26 67; open May-Oct daily 9am-noon and 1-4:30 pm; Nov.-April 10am-noon and 1-4pm; admission DM2, students and seniors DM1). Follow the "g" signs to the **Grab Corona Scröters,** the grave of the first actress to portray Goethe's renowned *Iphigenia.* Next along the trail is the **Schwabenstein,** the rock upon which Goethe wrote Act IV of *Iphigenia.* At this point, practically every rock, stone, and pebble seems to be significant: Goethe observed this tree in 1779; Goethe enjoyed reclining on this rocky ledge in 1782; etc. About 4km into the trail (much of which is uphill) is the **Goethehäuschen** on the **Kickelhahn,** where you can read the poetry he scratched on the walls as a young man. A year before his death at age 83, Goethe himself returned to the hut on a tour of his past, to trace his own handwriting and remember it all. Farther along lies the **Jagdhaus Gabelbach** (tel. 20 26 26), often visited by Goethe in summer and now a display of his scientific experiments. (Open May-Oct. Tues.-Sun. 9am-noon and 1-5pm; Nov.-March Wed.-Sun. 9am-noon and 1-4pm. Admission DM4, students DM2.) The hike ends in **Stützerbach,** where the local glass-works magnate often hosted the poet. The house is now a **Goethe memorial,** but as a nod to the patron there are demonstrations of traditional **glass-blowing** (open

May-Oct. Tues.-Sun. 9am-noon and 1-5pm, Nov.-April Wed.-Sun. 9am-noon and 1-4pm; admission DM3, students DM2).

Ilmenau also makes a good starting point for a hike along the **Rennsteig** (take the train to Schmiedefeld). Other destinations easily accessible by train include **Lauscha** and its glass-blowing museum; **Sonnenberg** and its toy and doll museum, the weapon museum in **Suhl, Schmalkalden** and the late-Renaissance castle, **Oberhof** with its *Rennsteiggarten* (botanical garden), and the theater-town of **Meiningen.**

The **tourist office** awaits at Lindenstr. 12 (tel. 20 23 58; fax 20 25 02). From the *Hauptbahnhof,* walk straight ahead on Wetzlarer Platz and follow the pedestrian zone until it becomes Lindenstr. (15min.). From the Ilmenau-Bad station, turn left on Waldstr. across the river and continue straight on Lindenstr. (5min.). They provide maps and hiking brochures (DM5) and book private rooms (DM20-35) for a DM2 fee per person (open Mon.-Fri. 9am-6pm, Sat. 9am-noon). You can obtain a map of the trail from the tourist office, or head for the **Amtshaus** (see above). Ilmenau can be reached by **train** from Erfurt and Arnstadt (1 per hr., 1hr.). Rent **bikes** at **Mountain Sport,** Lindenstr. 38 (tel. 84 12 45), for DM25 per day with ID. The academic clientele post ride-share notices at the **Mitfahrzentrale** (tel. 67 10 27) in the same building (open Mon.-Thurs. 3-7pm, Fri. 8am-7pm, Sat.-Sun. 9am-noon). The **post office** on Poststr., 98693 Ilmenau, is located just uphill from Wetzlarer Platz (open Mon.-Fri. 8am-12:30pm and 2-5:30pm, Sat. 9am-noon). The **telephone code** is 03677.

The **Jugendherberge,** Waldstr. 22 (tel. 20 24 13), lives in a beautiful building at the start of the trail. From Bahnhof Ilmenau-Bad, turn right over the tracks and walk uphill to the end of the street (10min.). From the *Hauptbahnhof,* follow the directions to tourist information; continue straight over the river and across the railroad tracks onto Waldstr., and straight up the hill. The hostel is very attractive, complete with stained-glass windows, high ceilings, and spacious rooms. (Reception open 7am-8pm. Curfew 10pm. DM12, over 26 DM14. Breakfast DM5, lunch DM8, dinner DM6. Sheets DM7.) In 1997, the hostel will be moving closer to the *Hauptbahnhof;* call the hostel or the tourist office to find its new location.

Die Arche, Str. des Friedens 28 (tel. 89 41 11), is half a café featuring international cuisine (*paella*—rice with mixed-in vegetables, DM8.20) and half a shop for African and Indian jewelry and trinkets; it's popular with students (open Mon.-Sat. 10am-6pm). **Zur Post,** on Wetzlarer Platz at Mühltor 6 (tel. 20 48), offers Thuringian specialties at excellent prices (DM9-15). Try *Thüringer Rostbrätel* (roasted sausage) with fresh peasant bread for DM7 (open Mon.-Fri. 8:30am-midnight, Sat.-Sun. 11am-midnight). Behind the Raiffeisenbank on the right side of Bahnhofstr., a **market** offers fresh fruits and vegetables (open Mon.-Fri. 8am-5pm, Sat. 8am-11am).

RUDOLSTADT

Below Jena, the Saale Valley meanders down to Rudolstadt. A litany of rich and famous persons have wandered the cobblestone streets of this small city. Richard Wagner got his big break here while working as a local choir director. **Schillerstraße 25** marks the spot where Goethe and Schiller first met in an otherwise ugly and trivial building. For decades after this initial acquaintance, the two authors worked in close concert, editing each other's work. Arthur Schopenhauer also wrote his dissertation here, and Paganini and Liszt reserved a special place for Rudolstadt in their musical hearts. Embraced by miles of incurably romantic forest with plenty of secret woodsy groves and grottos, Rudolstadt is also a route to the scene of one of Goethe's torrid affairs (see Großkochberg, p. 503).

During the 18th century, social life in Rudolstadt centered on the princes of Schwarzburg-Rudolstadt and the Baroque-towered **Heidecksburg palace,** accessible by Vorwerkgasse (an uphill path behind the *Rathaus*). The **museum** in Heidecksburg (tel. 429 00) features furnishings and paintings as well as a light-wood sunlit library for guests to use by prior appointment. Rare pieces of porcelain are on view (Rudolstadt's stock-in-trade through the 19th century). Local craftworkers still deal in hand-painted china dolls (open May-Sept. Tues.-Sun. 10am-6pm; Oct.-April Tues.-Sun. 1-5pm, last entrance 30min. before closing; admission DM6, students and children

DM3). The **Volkskundemuseum Thüringer Bauernhäuser** (Thuringian Farmhouse Museum; tel. 42 24 65), is an open-air display of several regional farmhouses, completely restored and furnished. Go right from the station and cross the bridge into the park (open May-Aug. Wed.-Sun. 9am-noon and 1-5pm; Sept.-April Wed.-Sun. 9am-noon and 1-4pm; admission DM2, children DM1).

Trains and **buses** from Weimar (bus #14) and Erfurt (bus #13) take about an hour to reach Rudolstadt. To reach the **tourist office,** Marktstr. 57 (tel. 41 47 43; fax 42 45 43), from the *Rudolstadt Thür* station walk straight ahead to the right of the park *(Platz der Opfer des Faschismus),* walk down Bahnhofsgasse to Marktstr., and turn left. Look through the free brochures on the information rack to find Rudolstadt maps and hotel lists—the ones they try to sell you from the counter cost DM1 and up. They find rooms (DM30 and up) for a DM3 fee (open Mon.-Fri. 9am-6pm, Sat. 9am-noon). **Exchange money** at **Deutsche Bank,** Marktstr. 45 (tel. 223 51; open Mon. 8:15am-4pm, Tues. 8:15am-5pm, Wed. and Fri. 8:15am-3pm, Thurs. 8:15am-6pm). To explore town, rent a **bike** from **Kern,** Markt 32 (tel. 42 73 71), for DM20 plus a DM20 deposit. The **telephone code** is 03672.

Zum Brummochsen, Alte Str. 12 (tel. 243 55), serves heavy food of the Thuringian forest for DM6-7.50 or small *Wurst* meals for DM4-6; their mascot is a big, smiling cow (open Sun.-Thurs. 11am-10:30pm, Sat. 6-10:30pm). For lighter fare, **Café Brömel,** Bahnhofsgasse 1 (tel. 220 76), serves pastries, pies, and other meals that won't immobilize you (stuffed chicken DM9.30; open Mon.-Sat. 8am-6pm, Sun. 1-6pm). Stock up on basics at the **Lebensmittel** supermarket on Marktstr. 56 (open Mon.-Wed. 8am-6:30pm, Thurs. 8am-7:30pm, Fri. 8am-6:30pm, Sat. 8am-12:30pm). On Wednesdays (6am-6pm) and Saturdays (6am-noon), buy fresh vegetables and fruits at the **farmer's market** on the Marktplatz.

GROßKOCHBERG

From Rudolstadt, big, comfortable buses and bumpy, serpentine foot trails run the 8km north to **Großkochberg.** Here lies the moated **Schloß Kochberg,** once the summer home of **Charlotte von Stein.** Von Stein was the inspiration for many of Goethe's powerful love poems, the proximate source for his sentimental hit novel *The Sorrows of Young Werther,* and in general the *ewig Weibliche* (eternal feminine) of his life—or so he thought. Goethe and Frau von Stein frolicked here in the beautiful English gardens while her husband stayed in Weimar with the kids. For 10 years, they lived this charged lifestyle until Goethe fled to Italy to find himself. When he returned two years later, he took up with a simple factory girl twenty years his junior. Understandably a mite bitter, Frau von Stein promptly returned everything Goethe had ever given her. When he did likewise, she publicly burnt her letters to him and composed the nasty tragedy *Dido,* a fictive act of retaliation and character assassination against the poet. The castle lost nothing in the nasty breakup; it did, however, get custody of the children. Just kidding. Today you can wander its 11 furnished rooms to see the first letter Schiller wrote Goethe (June 13, 1794) and the first letter Goethe wrote Schiller (June 24, 1794). When you get tired of trying to read the handwriting, check out the odd sketch of Schiller riding a donkey. In the adjoining room, peruse a marble statue of Charlotte's left hand and the hand warmer she used to fire up her love letters. Move on to see the table that supported Goethe's 1700 love letters to her. Behind the castle, the landscaped gardens are soggy with ponds and paths (castle open May-Aug. Tues.-Sun. 9am-noon and 1-5pm, Sept.-April Wed.-Sun. 9am-noon and 1-5pm; admission DM6, students DM4). If you have a moment before the bus comes, visit the church just down the hill with a touching **memorial** to the victims of the Franco-Prussian and World Wars. To make the trip in a day, take the 10:50am bus from platform 5 of Rudolstadt's bus station (direction: Engerda); last return is at 4:30pm. As always, double-check these schedules with the Rudolstadt tourist office before you go, or call 42 26 12 for updated schedules. **Rosas Bauernstübel,** down the street on the left, is a quaint white farm house where you can have the *Bauernfrühstück* (farmer's breakfast) at dinnertime (DM7.40; open Tues.-Sun. 11am-9pm). At **Goetheplatz,** on Goetheplatz (surprise), meals range from DM4.50-12 for

Schnitzels, roasted potatoes, and jellied meats—just the way Goethe liked 'em (open Thurs.- Mon. 11:30am-9pm).

LEUTENBERG

Leutenberg proper remains a scarred city; it was razed and plundered during the Thirty Years War, 200 years before a fire raised hell in the town once again. While the diminuitive city is itself nothing spectacular, its location in the middle of bunches of foothills (Leutenberg's nickname is "the city of the seven hills"), makes it a magnificent point of departure for hiking excursions.

For an in-town excursion, a walk up Schloßstr. and up the path of the Schloßberg will, not surprisingly, bring you to Leutenberg's 9th-century **castle** in about 15 minutes. **Schloß Friedensburg** is mostly unspectacular—an old-school type of domain that lacks the jaw-dropping punch of the later German castles. In point of fact, the *Schloß* is now a hospital clinic that proffers up little more than a sweet view of the city and a commentary on the sickness of decadence and the decay of lying (what a line!). A network of **ten hiking trails** offers to transport you to, well, ten really grand hiking trails; most trails start at either Leninstr. (yes, that's Lenin!) or **Bayrische Bierstube,** where you can nurse one of the local brews before your journey.

Leutenberg's **tourist office,** Herrngarten 7 (*Kur und Fremdenverkehrsamt*; tel. 222 62), can give you trail maps of the region and offers room booking services at no charge (private rooms DM15-20, *pensionen* DM20-40). To get there from the **train station** after arriving on one of the hourly **trains** from Rudolstadt (40min.), take a right at the station down Bahnhofstr., turn left at the post office onto Am Ilmbach, then make a right onto Hauptstr. The office will be on your right (open Mon.-Thurs. 8am-noon and 1-5pm, Fri. 8am-2pm). Leutenberg's **telephone code** is 036734.

For tasty eats of the sit-down variety, **Gute Quelle,** Am Ilmbach 17, will provide you with a *Stammer Max* chicken meal for DM7.50; for those who resist the pull towards poultry, they also serve a *Reispfanne* (rice and veggies in a creamy mushroom sauce) for DM9.80 (open Tues.-Fri. 11:30am-2pm and 5-11pm, Sat.-Mon. 11:30am-11pm). Grab grub at **E Aktiv** supermarket at the end of Bahnhofstr. (open Mon.-Wed. and Fri. 8am-6pm, Thurs. 8am-8pm, Sat. 8am-1pm).

■ Gotha

Literally and figuratively, the city of Gotha (that's GO-ta, not Goethe, like the poet) centers around its beautifully landscaped hilltop castle, former home of the Dukes of Saxony-Coburg-Gotha. Perhaps the most prominent of the hyphenated dukes was Prince Albert, who married Queen Victoria of England. Queen Elizabeth and Prince Charles are direct descendants of this house; the royal family's name of "Windsor" is the product of a World War I-era name change, effected because suddenly no one liked being German. Charlemagne didn't have to worry about such banalities when he slept here only for only one night—apparently that was enough time for him to scope out the whole city.

Orientation and Practical Information From the far side of the palace, you'll see the *Hauptmarkt,* a collection of 17th-century homes and businesses set on a 45-degree incline. A wave of renovation is currently unearthing a number of streets; since reconstruction of the *Altstadt* started, the **tourist office,** Blumenbachstr. 1-3 (tel. 540 36; fax 22 21 34), has left the Marktplatz for the low-rent district. Facing the *Rathaus* entrance, go left down the narrow Hützelsgasse past the Socialist-era apartment block until you see it. Get information on the *Schloß* and the nearby Thuringian Forest, or book a room in private quarters (DM35-40 per bed) for a DM3 fee. Weekly **tours** of the city leave on Wednesday at 11am from the steps of Gotha's *Rathaus,* overlooking the market. The tourist office also sells the Gotha *Touristenticket* (DM8) which knocks a mark or two off the price of most attractions and is good for one free trip each on Gotha's bus system and the *Thüringer Waldbahn,* which leads from the train station into hiking country. Unless you're going to use the *Waldbahn,* don't bother; Gotha is small enough to see on foot, and there just isn't much besides the castle (open Mon.-Fri. 9am-5pm, Sat. 9am-noon). Gotha is connected by frequent **trains** to Erfurt and Eisenach, both 20 minutes away. Clean your stinky clothes at the **laundromat** on Mohrenstr., just down the street from the *Busbahnhof.* The city **postal code** is 99867. The **telephone code** is 03621.

Accommodations and Food Gotha's **Jugendherberge (HI)** is sweetly located at Mozartstr. (tel. 540 08), right on the corner of the Schloßpark. From the train station, walk an easy two blocks straight ahead; the light beige hostel is on the right. They'll rent you an accordion (DM5) or an acoustic guitar (DM3). It features ancient video games (which delight the many school groups). (Reception open 3-8pm. Curfew 10pm, but guests over 18 can ask for a night key. DM16, over 26 DM19. HI members only. Breakfast DM5, lunch DM5, dinner DM6. Call ahead.)

The number of well-located sit-down restaurants in Gotha can be counted on the fingers of one hand, and none astounds; load up at the *Markt* (daily food bonanza Mon.-Fri. 8am-6pm, Sat. 8am-1pm) and picnic in the palace gardens. **Bella Italia Eis-café/Ristorante,** Erfurter Str. 11/13, provides decent Italian food (pizzas and pastas DM6.50-10) at a sidewalk café with a great view of the ice cream monstrosities that Germans are crazy enough to consume here (open Mon.-Fri. 8:30am-midnight, Sat. 10am-midnight, Sun. 11am-midnight). Another solid option is **Kuhn and Kuhn,** a few blocks down from the castle at Hühnersdorfstr. 14, adjacent to the Buttermarkt. They offer café fare as well as German standards (DM7.50-14). At night, Kuhn's upstairs club, **Tanzbar Coconut** (tel. 567 14), sells drinks and gives off as much heat as Gotha's nightlife is likely to generate; it fancies itself somewhat highbrow, so no sneakers allowed. (Restaurant open Mon. 9am-1am, Tues.-Sat. 9am-3am, Sun. 2pm-1am. Dance bar open Wed.-Sat. 8pm-4am.)

Sights Gotha is saved from being just another castle town by its political history; the Social Democratic Workers' Party (a radical forerunner of Germany's moderate-left SPD party) was founded in a Gotha guest house in 1875. Still, the big draw is definitely the white-and-gray **Schloß Friedenstein,** whose three wings and entrance wall square off an immense gravel courtyard. For sightseers used to the Gothic intricacy or Rococo fantasy of other German castles, the 17th-century *Schloß's* exterior may be a bit of a let-down; the crisp, unadorned rectangular windows and doors were intended to be built in the early Baroque style, then at the cutting edge of architecture. The lack of glitz, however, is made up for by the castle's sheer size. Duke Ernst I, the ruler who made the decision to build it in contemporary style, was a visionary in other ways as well: his peace initiatives and healthy support for the arts earned him the title *Ernst der Fromme* (the pious). A *Sammelkarte* (DM10, students and seniors DM5) allows entry to the *Schloß* and surrounding museums.

A nice portrait of the duke hangs in the **Schloßmuseum,** which includes the royal family's art collection—a respectable lot of 16th- and 17th-century works highlighted by a series of Cranachs and the serene *Gothaer Liebespaar* (Lovers of Gotha), a late 15th-century work by a German artist known only as "The Master of the Housebook." The collection of ancient and classical artifacts is superb; check out the sepulcher filled with Egyptian sarcophagi and mummies.

Upstairs are the royal apartments, whose splendor contrasts strikingly with the castle's spartan exterior. It's a treat to follow the red carpets that lead through the 16 fully restored, lavishly furnished ducal rooms. The Rococo *Festsaal* (feast hall), decorated with colorful crests from each of the duchy's provinces and cities, houses the original royal silver service. Other highlights include beautifully inlaid walls in the smaller rooms and the royals' bedroom cabinets. It must have been good to be the duke (open daily 9am-5pm; admission DM8, students and seniors DM4). Also in the palace buildings are the **Museum für Regionalgeschichte,** a small *Waffensammlung* (arms collection) of guns and knives, and the world's first museum of maps, the **Kartographisches Museum.** The Renaissance and early Mercator maps (named for a

THURINGIA

Flemish cartographer) are especially fascinating: watch the Americas slowly, awkwardly take their correct shape. At the castle corner, clever architectural tricks and optical illusions broaden the tiny stage of the 1683 **Eckhof Theater** (call the tourist office for tickets and information), one of the oldest indoor theaters still in use (open Tues.-Sun. 9am-5pm; admission DM2.50, students and seniors DM1.25). Gotha's Baroque **palace garden** is the largest in Europe. Much of it is densely grown, like a city park, which is how the *Gothaer* use it.

The **Haus am Tivoli,** at the intersection of Cosmartstr., was where August Bebel and others got the Social Democratic Party (SPD) together. The modern SPD is still one of the largest political parties in Germany. A GDR-era **plaque** outside the house commemorates the founding as a "glorious moment in the history of the German working class," even though Marx himself had accused the Social Democrats of selling the proletariat short in his scathing *Critique of the Gotha Programme.* Now that Gotha's residents are sorting out their history, they don't know exactly what to do with the Socialist past of the place, and Am Tivoli is closed indefinitely. The SPD does, however, maintain an office in the purple house next door to the Tivoli, but don't go with any big expectations.

■ Eisenach

Birthplace of Johann Sebastian Bach and home-in-exile to Martin Luther, Eisenach boasts impressive humanist credentials. Yet inside the walls of the town's Wartburg Castle, student fraternities convened in 1817 to promote a bizarre agenda of democracy and xenophobic nationalism; they celebrated their dedication to liberal tolerance by burning conservative books. The writings of Marx and Engels were so well received in Eisenach that the duo called the local communist faction "our party." Adolf Hitler is said to have called the idyllic Wartburg "the most German of German castles," and fought a pitched (and unsuccessful) battle with the local church to replace its tower's cross with a swastika. More recently, the East German regime tapped into old associations by dubbing its "luxury" automobile the *Wartburg.* It's fitting that Eisenach—this romantic, rationalist, conservative, radical, democratic, despotic bundle of contradictions—should be home to one of the new Germany's most treasured national symbols.

Orientation and Practical Information Eisenach's **tourist office** (tel. 672 60), a short walk from the station at Bahnhofstr. 3-5, has plenty of information on the *Wartburg* and books rooms in private homes (DM30-40) for no fee (open Mon. 10am-6pm, Tues.-Fri. 9am-6pm, Sat. 10am-2pm). The best **train** connections to Eisenach are from Erfurt or Weimar in the east, and through Bebra on the IC or IR from the west. Eisenach's *Bahnhof* provides a world of services for budget travelers; there's **luggage storage** (DM4 per day), an **ATM, a grocery store** with late hours, a bakery, a flower shop, and basically everything short of a hot tub. For a **taxi,** call 220 220. The **Ost-Apotheke,** Bahnhofstr. 29 (tel. 20 32 42), has a list of **pharmacies** open in the evening (open Mon.-Fri. 8am-6pm, Sat. 8am-noon). The **Frauenzentrum** at Marienstr. 57 (tel. 62 51 78) has walk-in consultation for women's issues Tues. 10am-6pm and Fri. 9am-1pm. Send your Wartburg postcard from the **post office** on the *Markt,* 99817 Eisenach (open Mon.-Fri. 8am-6pm, Sat. 8am-noon). The **telephone code** is 03691.

Accommodations and Food Jugendherberge **Artur Becker (HI),** Mariental 24 (tel. 20 36 13), fills a comfortable old villa located fairly far from the center, a bit beyond the castle. From the station, take Bahnhofstr. to Wartburger Allee, which runs into Mariental. Here you can walk down the street until the hostel comes up on your right, past the pond (35min.). Alternatively, grab the #3 bus (direction: Mariental) and get off at Lilienstr. A sign points out the uphill path to the hostel; next comes a stairway on your right. The hostel is a touch worn—lots of wood trim and nice sunny terrace outside, while the showers are less than fully operational. (Reception open 9am-

8pm. Curfew 10pm. DM20, over 26 DM24. Breakfast included. If you don't have a sleepsack, you'll have to pay DM7 (once) for sheets.) You probably can't afford to stay at the **Hotel Wartburg,** just below the castle (DM150-280), but breakfast is included; marvel at its pseudo-castle styling and its parking lot full of BMWs and Mercedes-Benzes. The nearest **camping** is at **Am Altenberger See** (tel./fax 21 56 37), offering showers, a sauna, and a view of the lake in the hamlet of Eckartshausen. From the Eisenach station, take the **bus** toward Bad Liebenstein (4 departures daily 7:35am-5:35pm) and tell the driver your destination. About 10km from town. 13 cabins are available, with four rooms each. (Reception open until 8pm. DM5-25 per person.) Take in the well-priced local food specialties at the **Gastätte Zum Schwan,** Bahnhofstr. 12, with lunch deals starting around DM8 (open Mon.-Fri. 8am-7pm). **Olympia,** on Goldschmiedenstr. just past Querstr. on the way from the *Bahnhof* to *Markt,* serves a daily Greek lunch menu from noon-5:30pm for a sweet DM6.90.

Sights High above Eisenach's half-timbered houses, the **Wartburg Schloß** lords over the northwestern slope of the rolling Thuringian Forest. In 1521, the deservedly-hyped castle sheltered Martin Luther after his excommunication. To thwart the search, Luther grew a beard and spent his 10-month stay disguised as a nondescript noble named "Junker Jörg." He spent his time working on his landmark German translation of the Bible; word has it that after working a bit too late one night, the reformer was visited by the devil (the perceptive traveler can't help but marvel at how often the Prince of Darkness and Luther's paths crossed during his (Luther's) travels). By Luther's account, it only took a toss of an ink pot to dispel the Beast. Later pilgrims took the fable literally and mistook a smudge of stove grease for the blessed ink spot, gutting the wall (now a big hole) in their search for a souvenir.

Petty vandalism aside, the Romanesque Wartburg is notable for the peaceful character of its history—besides sheltering Luther, it was a haven for the 12th-century *Minnesänger,* the originators of German choral music. In one of the castle's restored chambers, a wall-sized copy of lyrics from Wagner's *Tannhäuser* is illustrated with ornate murals of the 12th-century battle of musicians that inspired the opera. Like many of the more dazzling chambers in the Wartburg, the mural room is a product of 19th-century imagination, not medieval reality. The Romantics' obsession with Wartburg began in 1777 when Goethe visited, fell in love with the place, and convinced some backers in the nobility to restore the interior and set up a museum. As a general rule, anything you see that's frayed and restrained-looking is old; anything shiny and ornate is the product of the 19th-century fan club. The castle's **Festsaal** preserves the memory of the 1817 meeting of 500 representatives of university fraternities who threw a party, got inspired, and formed Germany's first bourgeois opposition (ruthlessly crushed 2 years later); the flag they toasted still hangs in this room. From the walls of Wartburg's courtyard, trace the line of your path through the countryside below. The view is spectacular—if you turn to the side opposite Eisenach, you can see the Thuringian Forest and all the way to Hesse. The first floor of the tower is a deep dungeon dating from darker days.

Wartburg sits on the south side of Eisenach; the foot of the hill can be reached by a stroll down **Wartburger Allee** from the train station. A multitude of city-sponsored **tourist buses** run between the city center, the castle, and the foot of the hill every 15min. (roundtrip DM2.50, one-way DM1.50). For the more adventurous, however, there are a number of well-cleared **footpaths** up the incline. Arriving at the medieval stronghold after a 30-minute hike through rich-smelling pines and lilacs, you'll wipe your sweat and feel like a pilgrim. If you weigh 60kg (132 lbs.) or less, you can opt for a donkey ride for the last stretch (DM5). When eastern Germany was East Germany, West Germans were issued special visas that allowed them to visit the castle and nothing else, and even these visas were hard to come by. Now, legions of sightseers are making up for lost time. On weekday mornings, expect crowds of schoolchildren; on weekday afternoons, crowds of German pensioners; on weekends, just be prepared for crowds. The interior of the castle can be visited only with a tour, and you may have to wait an hour to enter. (Open April-Oct. daily 8:30am-4:30pm; Nov.-

THURINGIA

March 9am-3:30pm. Admission to the whole complex DM11, students and children DM6, seniors and people with disabilities DM8. Admission to museum and Luther study only DM6, DM4, and DM5 respectively.)

Back at the base of the mountain, the **Bachhaus,** Frauenplan 21 (tel. 20 37 14; fax 764 37), where Johann Sebastian stormed into the world in 1685, recreates the family's living quarters. Downstairs are period instruments such as a harpsichord, a spinet, and a beautifully preserved "house organ" from 1750, about the size of a telephone booth, with a little stool for the player. Many guides perform snippets on the instruments, and if you understand German, you can follow the guides' hilarious anecdotes about Bach's progressively more tortuous pedagogical techniques. Turn off Wartburger Allee down Grimmelgasse to reach the house (open Oct.-March Mon. 1-4:45pm, Tues.-Sun. 9am-4:45pm; April-Sept. Mon. noon-5:45pm, Tues.-Sun. 9am-5:45pm; admission DM5, students and seniors DM4). The **Reuter-Wagner-Museum,** Reuterweg 2, below the Wartburg, is dedicated to the joint memory of writer Fritz and composer Richard (open daily 10am-8pm, Oct.-April 10am-5pm; admission DM4, students and seniors DM2). Town life centers on the pastel **Markt,** bounded by the tilting dollhouse of a **Rathaus** and the latticed **Lutherhaus,** Lutherplatz 8 (tel. 298 30), home of young Martin's school days from 1498 to 1501 (open May-Sept. daily 9am-5pm; Oct.-April Mon.-Sat. 9am-5pm, Sun. 2-5pm; admission DM5, students DM2). If you want to see the showcase of Eisenach's recent past in the form of its *Wartburg* cars, the **Autobilbaumuseum,** Wartburgallee 54, displays the grandest of East German performance cars (open Tues.-Sun. 9am-5pm; admission DM4, students, seniors, and kids DM2).

THURINGIA

Sachsen-Anhalt

Saxony-Anhalt (Sachsen-Anhalt)

Sachsen-Anhalt's endless grass plains offer the most tranquil of Eastern German land-scapes. The region once served as the stronghold of the Holy Roman Empire; today, unfortunately, it is not only home to the highest unemployment rates in eastern Germany but is also the most polluted province of the former GDR. Cities here once belched enough toxic filth into the air to make a smoggy day in Los Angeles seem healthy. But with the help of Western tourist dollars, Sachsen-Anhalt is rapidly clean-ing up its act and gradually creating a stable work force; in the meantime it contains a number of worthwhile destinations that include Wittenberg, the city of Martin Luther and crucible of the Protestant Reformation, and Magdeburg, home to a splendid gothic *Dom* where the first Holy Roman Emperor is buried. The many cathedrals fill-ing the skyline attest to the region's former importance.

■ Wittenberg

Wittenberg does everything in its power to milk Martin Luther for what he's worth; in 1938, the town even went so far as to rename itself **"Lutherstadt Wittenberg."**

Luther claimed that Wittenberg was the source and font of his life's work: he preached, taught, married (a scandal to the Catholic clergy), raised children, and led the Protestant Reformation in this picturesque town. The city's fondest memories are of Luther nailing the 95 Theses to the **Schloßkirche** (castle church) in 1517, and of his scandalous (and exceptionally contrived) wedding, an almost made-for-TV event that is re-enacted in the town every June. 1996 witnessed the 450th anniversary of Martin Luther's death. If you missed it, don't worry. Martin's remains still remain; when he died in Eisleben in 1546, his body was returned here and buried directly beneath the pulpit of the *Schloßkirche*.

Luther managed to hang onto his celebrity status even in the officially atheistic GDR; after all, he was a harsh critic of Catholic wealth, inciting early bourgeois revolutions. He also had a presence in the civil sphere—for many East Germans the image of Luther risking his life to nail up his 95 Theses became an emblem of courageous resistance. A successor of Luther at the *Schloßkirche* pulpit, Pastor Friedrich Schorlemmer, was a key player in a more recent revolution: the largely peaceful upheaval in the GDR in 1989. Since that time, religious pilgrims have returned in full force to Luther's city. The slow shuffle of Scandinavian church groups has pushed up *Schnitzel* prices and given a fresh gleam to the town's architectural remnants.

Orientation and Practical Information When you arrive in Wittenberg, walk alongside the tracks down the street from the train station. Hook a right under the overpass and keep going until you reach **Collegienstr.,** Wittenberg's main tourist artery. **Wittenberg Information** is at Collegienstr. 29 (tel. 40 22 39 or 41 48 48), between the Lutherhalle and the market. They have helpful maps and lovely postcards for sale (open Mon.-Fri. 9am-6pm, Sat. 10am-2pm, Sun. 11am-3pm). German Romanticism persists at the **regional tourist office,** on Mittelstr. 33 (tel. 40 26 10), by Lutherhalle, where they'll tell you that an "ideal" daytrip is different for all individuals (open April-Oct. daily 9:30am-5:30pm; Nov.-March Mon.-Sat. 9:30am-5:30pm). Wittenberg is a mere hour and a half by **train** from Berlin, Halle, or Leipzig, making it an excellent daytrip from any of these hubs. **Store luggage** at the station for DM4 (open Mon.-Fri. 6am-6pm, Sat.-Sun. 8am-6pm). The **pharmacy** on the Marktplatz, where painter Lucas Cranach pushed drugs to support his art habit, posts a rotating schedule of all-night pharmacies (open Mon.-Fri. 8am-1pm and 2-6pm). The **post office,** 06886 Wittenberg, is near Lutherhalle (open Mon.-Fri. 8am-6pm, Sat. 9am-noon). The **telephone code** is 03491.

Accommodations Hotels in the *Altstadt* are overpriced, but a feasible option is to locate a **private room.** The Wittenberg information center will find rooms for a DM3 fee. Expect to pay DM25-75 for a single with breakfast in the city. Alternatively, you can pick up a list of accommodations at the information center and find bargains on your own. The **Jugendherberge (HI),** located in the castle (tel. 40 32 55), is simultaneously haunted by the ghosts of the Reformation and by the rabid kids who tear through the place in summer. The hostel is a 10-minute walk down Colliegenstr. and Schloßstr. Take a left into the castle's enclosure, walk by the Bart Simpson graffiti, and then up the spiraling stairs to the right. There are a few rooms with habitable two- to four-bed rooms, and a bunch of fairly spacious 10- to18-bed rooms. Showers are somewhat dry. (Reception open Mon.-Fri. 7am-10am, Sat.-Sun. 7am-9pm. Lockout 10pm, but hostel keys are available. DM19.50, over 26 DM25.50. Sheets DM6 extra. Breakfast included. Reservations recommended.)

For a sociable atmosphere with private rooms, there's the eminently friendly *Gaststätte-Pension* **"Zum Tender,"** Bahnstr. 5 (tel. 41 39 36). It's tricky to find. From the Lutherhalle, head north on Friedrichstr. and stick with it as it kinks right at the intersection with Sternstr. Turn right onto Bahnhofstr. and follow it all the way to a lot in the rail yard overlooking the train station. A building with conspicuous beer signs in the front houses a friendly little *Kneipe* (one of the few drinking places in Wittenberg open late). Call a few days ahead. (Reception open 10am-1pm and 6-11pm, although it often remains open as long as the bar does. Singles DM35. Doubles DM70. Breakfast included.) A little further down from the beaten path, a touch far from the center of town, is the **L und K Bauunternehmen** pension, at Sternstr. 58 (tel. 40 40 50 or 810 06). To reach it, follow Sternstr. for about one mile; it'll be on your right, just past Theodor-Fontane-Str. The rooms are superfly, featuring TVs, closets, and sinks. (Reception open 6am-4pm. Singles DM25. Doubles DM60.)

Food A number of delectable delights at low-cost lie along the Colliegenstr.-Schloßstr. strip, including a **supermarket** and a store that sells all of its wares (including many snacks) for just DM1. **Bosphorus,** a Turkish restaurant at Collegienstr. 64, cooks up a filling, spicy *Döner Kebab* platter with a cucumber-tomato salad (DM10); tasty vegetarian entrees, like falafel (DM4), provide a cheap respite from the tyranny of *Schnitzel* (open Mon.-Fri. 9am-10pm, Sat.-Sun. 11am-10pm). Get Guinness on tap and eat pub grub at the **Irish Harp Pub,** Collegienstr. 71, where live English and Irish folk and rock music debuts on Saturdays (open daily 3pm-3am; cover DM5). For a cup of coffee, there's no place more ideal than the **Judenhaus** at Neuestr. 10. Turn from Mittelstr. onto Neuestr. and look for it in a clearing on the left, past Mauerstr. The young attendants are more than happy to answer questions about what's going on in Wittenberg that doesn't involve dead people. The place simultaneously functions as coffee shop, hang-out joint, youth singles bar, and game room. Find angst-ridden German youth here (open 10am-8pm).

Sights Luckily the town's name does not function as a performative contradiction; the sights provide unending adulation of the eminently historical Luther. Plan your sight-seeing around **Collegienstr.;** the street is less than 1.5km long and encompasses all of the major sights. On your right stands the sickly **elm tree** under which Luther defiantly burned a papal bull (a decree of excommunication, not a Catholic horned beast). At Collegienstr. 54 lies Luther's home, the (ingeniously named) **Lutherhaus,** to which he moved in 1508. Inside the minister's rather posh digs is a museum that features lots of paintings analogizing Luther to geese; while the metaphor may seem strained (Luther was indeed portly, but certainly not a goose), the representation is supposed to symbolize Luther's triumph in the face of the adversity he encountered in the fallout over his 95 Theses. Nonetheless, you can see Luther's ground-breaking translation of the Bible, considered a model of the German language in the same manner that the King James translation is for English, as well as an original **Gutenberg Bible,** and many angry responses to the feisty minister's theses. An obnoxious tourist's graffito has also been preserved: Russian Czar Peter the Great scribbled his name above the door when he stopped by in 1702. (Open Tues.-Sun. 9am-6pm. Last entry 5:30pm. Admission DM6, students and seniors DM3.)

　　St. Marienkirche (St. Mary's Church), known for its dazzling altar painted by pharmacist-*cum*-artistic genius **Lucas Cranach the Elder,** lies at the end of Mittelstr., near Collegienstr., at the *Marktplatz*. The interior is a blend of Protestant severity and Catholic adornments; the massive organ holds dominion in a Gothic interior (open Mon.-Sat. 9am-noon and 2-5pm, Sun. 11am-noon and 2-5pm). Near the church Wittenberg's **Rathaus** (city hall) towers with an imposing façade. Matching statues of Luther and Melanchthon share the square with the **Jungfernröhrwasser** (fountain of virginity), a 16th-century well whose refreshing (and potable) waters still flow through original wooden pipes. The tourist office sells small bottles of this "water of innocence," actually filled with good German *Schnapps*.

　　Further down Collegienstr., the **Schloßkirche,** crowned by a sumptuous Baroque cupola, holds a copy of the complaints that Luther nailed to its doors. At the front of the church, the man who fought to translate the scriptures into the common man's tongue is interred, ironically, under a Latin plaque. Also featured are the graves of Wittenberg's other important dead folks: Prince Electors Friedrich the Wise, Johann the Steadfast, and Reformation hero Philip Melanchthon the non-adjectivally monikered. In the 1840s, it was arranged that 15 people would check and make sure that old Luther was really buried here. The crypt was opened in secret for fear that failure to find Luther would discredit the church (sort of like Geraldo and Al Capone's vaults).

SACHSEN-ANHALT

They found the remains—or so they said. (Open May-Oct. Mon. 2-5pm, Tues.-Sat. 10am–5pm, Sun. 11am-5pm; Nov.-April Mon. 2-4pm, Tues.-Sat. 10am-4pm, Sun. 11am-4pm. Services Sun. at 9am.) At the top of the castle's enormous tower, you can digest the surrounding lands with pleasure (open Mon.-Fri. 2-4pm, Sat.-Sun. 10am-noon; admission DM1, students DM0.50). Should the view excite your appetite for nature, take a bus from Mauerstr. (5 per day) to the **Wörlitzer Park,** built by a local prince who wanted his quaint palace and Gothic house to be surrounded by exotic flora and fauna (open dawn to dusk).

■ Dessau

The postmodern philosopher par excellence Homer Simpson one dismissed idealism by saying: "In theory communism works—*in theory*." About 30km west of Witten-berg, Dessau, which houses the sleek Gropius-designed **Bauhaus art school,** suffers from the divide between theory and practice. For a brief period from 1925 to 1932, *Bauhaus* instructors Walter Gropius, Hannes Meyer, Lazlo Moholy-Nagy, and their students struggled with aesthetic representations of modernity and attempted to rec-oncile human living space with 20th-century industrialization. Ironically, today Des-sau is home to some of the least successful building projects of recent memory; row upon row of soulless GDR-era apartment blocks burden the city streets, which retain the monikers of Communist heroes.

The history of Dessau stretches back into antiquity. Founded as a medieval fortress in 1341, Dessau became one of the first Renaissance settlements of Germany. With the backing of the Princess Henrietta Catharina von Oranien, Dessau flourished as a thriving center of cultural and economic importance. It quickly evolved into a factory town during the late-blooming German Industrial Revolution. When the Nazis seized power in 1933, they transformed Dessau's factory infrastructure into a center for armament production. Dessau subsequently suffered inestimable damage in World War II—nearly 80% of the inner town was destroyed by bombing. Nevertheless, Des-sau prides itself on a unique civic culture as well as its two major historical offspring. Moses Mendelssohn, one of the greatest German-Jewish philosophers and a fervent proponent of religious tolerance in the 19th century, lived in Dessau, as did the greatly admired modern composer Kurt Weill (1900-1950), whose critical theater, in theory, created artistic resistance against Nazism. In effect, Weill's *Verfremdungsef-fekt* (alienation effect) makes its listeners feel drunk and confused. In the first week of March, Dessau holds a **Kurt Weill Festival** devoting one week to performances of his theater and music.

Orientation and Practical Information For daytrippers, Dessau is easily accessible from most major cities of Germany; trains leave hourly to undertake the 35-minute journey from Wittenburg and the two-hour train ride from Berlin, while trains from Leipzig depart about every two hours for the one-hour trip. To reach the local **tourist office,** Friedrich-Naumann-Str. 12 (tel. 21 46 61), take streetcar #1 or #2 from the front of the station's main exit to the "Museum" stop. Go up the street with the McDonald's (an increasingly trustworthy landmark in eastern Germany) on the corner—this is Friedrich-Naumann-Str. The tourist office is on the right (open Mon.-Fri. 10am-6pm, Sat. 9am-noon). They find rooms for a DM5 fee (rooms DM30-75) and provide city maps that fulfill all aesthetic expectations (some are shaped like *Bau-haus* buildings!) free of charge. **Bicycle rentals** help navigate the scattered sights of the city and protect you from the perils of pedestrianism. **Fahrradverleih Dieter Becker und Sohn,** Coswigerstr. 47 (tel. 21 61 29), can make you an honorary Sprocket with rentals (open Mon. 2-6pm, Wed. 9am-noon and 2-6pm, Fri. 2-6pm, Sat. 9am-noon, Sun. 9am-noon and 2-6pm; DM5 for 4hr., DM 10 for full day). In an **emer-gency,** call 21 44 55. The **post office** is at the corner of Friedrichstr. and Kavalierstr. (open Mon.-Fri. 8am-6pm, Sat. 8am-noon). The **postal code** is 06844. The **telephone code** is 0340.

Accommodations and Food The Jugendherberge (HI), Waldkarterweg 11 (tel. 61 94 52) is a bit of a schlepp, requiring a 20-minute winding trek from the train station. Exit from the smaller back entrance of the station (through the underground tunnel), make a left onto Rathenaustr. as you emerge, and follow it to the end; at the intersection zig-zag across and follow the main street (Kühnauer Str.) for about 10 minutes until you see the signs for the *Jugendherberge*. Take Waldkarterweg straight to the woodsy entrance. The hostel is slightly sterile, but the surrounding residential area, well-lit common rooms, and nourishing breakfast more than make up for it. (Reception open daily 7am-10pm. No lockout. Checkout 9am. DM19, over 26 DM24. Sheets DM6. Breakfast included.)

Affordable restaurants are difficult to come by in Dessau. The stunningly hip **Klub im Bauhaus,** in the *Bauhaus* school basement, is a delightful place to indulge in angsty pretense over a light meal. To feel like the coolest cat ever to walk the earth, order the **anarchisten Frühstück** (anarchist's breakfast) of a pot of coffee, some bread, and a *Karo* cigarette (DM4, other light meals under DM10; open Sun.-Fri. 10am-midnight, Sat. 10am-1am). Other inexpensive meals can be procured along Kurt-Weill-Str., which features a supermarket, a bakery, and a fruit shop fittingly called **Obst und Gemüse.** Just off Kurt-Weill-Str., **K-I-E-Z Café,** on Bertolt-Brecht-Str. 29a, is a good locale for a nightcap in the company of students.

Sights The *Bauhaus* began in Weimar in 1919, but was pressured into leaving by the conservative local oligarchy. The school toted its theory of constructive and artistic unity to Dessau in 1925; in 1932 the school fled yet again to the more brash Berlin before being entirely exiled from the country by the Nazis in 1933. Despite the necessity of remaining itinerant to avoid total dissolution, the *Bauhaus* masters inspired an architectural renaissance that attained its aesthetic zenith with the sleek skyscrapers of America's metropolarum. After the war, as Dessau rebuilt, the shapely *Bauhaus* legacy perversely translated into building-block-shaped mono-tony. Since 1977, the **Bauhaus,** Gropiusallee 38 (tel. 650 82 50; fax 650 82 26), has been open as a design school for international architecture. The school currently decorates its sparsely linear walls with the works of legendary *Bauhausmeisters* Gropius, Klee, Kandinsky, Geinger, and Brandt. To get there from the station, turn left and go up the steps, then head left over the railroad tracks. Veer left at the first street onto Kleiststr., then right onto Bauhausstr. (Open Tues.-Sun. 10am-5pm. Last entry 4:30pm. Admission DM4, students and seniors DM2.) A couple of blocks from the Bauhaus, the **Kurt Weill Zentrum,** Ebertalle 63 (tel. 61 95 95), is located amidst the famous Bauhaus **Meisterhäuser.** The center has been restored to its original Bauhaus splendor, thus providing lucid insight into the school's musings. Occasional concerts celebrate the wacky Weill (open Tues. 2-4pm, Thurs. 10am-noon, Sat. 2-5pm; admission varies depending on performances).

SACHSEN-ANHALT

The PDS: Socialism with a Human Face

The West was shocked when the 1990 German elections, held immediately after reunification and the "fall of communism," resulted in a 30% vote in Eastern Berlin for the PDS—*Partei der Demokratischen Socialismus*—the successor to the East German Communist Party. The party, based on a platform of democratic anti-capitalism and left-wing social reform, has emerged as a power to be reckoned with in Eastern elections. However, attempts by the PDS to attract Western supporters and gain acceptance from other political parties have largely been a failure. With a formidable campaign treasury leftover from its Communist past, the PDS is headed by the charismatic Lothar Bisky and Gregor Gysi, a former East German lawyer and politico. Its members are a funky mixture of idealistic, twentysomething students and 60-year-old Communists. Bisky's main deputy is a 24-year-old woman from Berlin's squatter movement; the party's oldest member is East German writer Stefan Heym. The party rallies and proselytizes in eastern Berlin—pick up a free PDS button, the coolest souvenir in Berlin today.

On the other side of the intersection of Puschkinallee and Kleiststr. squats the **Schloß Georgium,** home to the **Anhaltische Gemäldegalerie** (tel. 61 38 74). Set in the midst of carefully-tended formal gardens, this 17th-century country estate displays a range of lesser-known Old Masters' paintings from the 16th-19th centuries. The Lucas Cranach works are exceptionally vivid. (Open Tues.-Sun. 10am-5pm. Admission DM5, students and seniors DM3. Gardens open to the public 24hr.) The **Rococo-Schloß Mosigkan,** on Knobelsdorfallee (tel. 52 11 81), about 20 minutes by bus from central Dessau, is an historic castle built in 1752 as a summer hangout for the Princess Anna Wilhelmine. Furnished in opulent Baroque style, the castle displays works by such masters as Rubens and van Dyck. For the botanist brewing in us all, there are 100-year-old plants in the surrounding gardens. To get to *Schloß Mosigkan,* take bus D or L (direction: Kochstedt); buses leave every 30-60 minutes from the main train station. Parking costs DM1. (Open May-Sept. Tues.-Sun. 10am-6pm, Nov.-March Tues.-Fri. 10am-4pm, Sat.-Sun. 11am-4pm, April and Oct. Tues.-Sun. 10am-5pm. Admission DM5, students and seniors DM2.50.)

If Dessau really floats your boat, then visit the **Museum für Stadtgeschichte,** Wolfgangstr. 13 (tel. 21 29 13). Opened after the *Wende,* the museum is located on the third floor of Dessau's *Volkshochschule.* A central room hosts changing exhibitions focusing on Dessau's regional history and contemporary political, historical, and cultural concerns in rather offbeat ways. On the way up to the museum, traverse the 75-year-old *Volkshochschule* building—catch a glimpse of socialist school life. Classes are still held here. (Museum open Mon., Wed., and Thurs. 9am-4pm, Tues. 9am-6pm, Fri. 9am-1pm. Admission DM3, students and seniors DM1.50.)

▓ Halle

Halle an der Salle, the fortunate town saved by Katrin's drumming in the climactic scene of Brecht's *Mother Courage,* was lucky enough to emerge from World War II relatively unscathed. Three months after the war's end, occupying Americans swapped Halle for a bit of Berlin under the terms of the Yalta agreement; in the post-war decades, it drew tens of thousands of new residents as Sachsen-Anhalt's political and industrial capital. Ironically, the historical twists and contradictions of German history are visibly apparent in the physical and social landscape of Halle today. Since reunification, tens of thousands of workers have lost their jobs, adding a grim edge to the urban outlook. However, visible efforts are being made on nearly every street corner to salvage Halle's former beauty from the cascade of gray that dominates its streets. The *Neustadt,* an immense, shoddily constructed district of housing projects built under the Communist regime of the 1960s, still stands untouched by capitalist evolution. Amidst the crumbling vestiges of socialism, stumble across sights of historic beauty in the *Altstadt.* The historic Moritzberg Fortress, with its offerings of 20th-century avant-garde art, the lively university culture, and the contemporary theater scenes all provide a glimpse into Halle's forward-looking gaze.

Orientation and Practical Information Halle is divided into several town sectors; most significant are Halle **Neustadt** (GDR era) and the historical **Altstadt,** between which flows the scenic Saale River. Come nightfall, *Neustadt* is not so secure; politically extreme groups (both right and left) reportedly roam this area. The train station and major streetcar lines run predominantly through the *Altstadt.* If you haven't come to see the dingy GDR-era housing (historic in its own right, to be fair), stick with the safer, brighter *Altstadt* areas.

Though most of Halle is walkable, the streetcar system efficiently covers the town (DM2.50 per ticket, day pass DM7) and nears the perimeter of Halle's *Neustadt.* To reach *Neustadt,* you will need to take the bus. The S-Bahn system is easy to use, and all stops are clearly marked. The main street is Große Ulrich Str.; as you move away from the *Marktplatz,* it becomes Geiststr., then Bernburger Str. With the cold war a thing of the past, Lenin and Honecker Streets and Squares have been replaced by "Freedom" and "Spirit" Boulevards. Pick up an updated map from the tourist office.

The **tourist office** is in the *Roter Turm* on the *Marktplatz* (tel. 202 33 40; fax 50 27 98 for information; tel. 202 83 71 for room-finding service). From the main station, cross beneath the underpass to the left as you exit the building; follow the pedestrian tunnel to Leipzigerstr. and past the *Leipziger Turm* to the *Marktplatz* (15min.). Or take streetcar #4 (direction: Heide/Hubertusplatz) or 7 (direction: Kröllwitz) to "Markt" (four stops). They hand out city maps and a number of informative pamphlets on cultural events around Halle, as well as find rooms (DM35-50, with shower DM50 and up; children under 10 free) for DM5 per person. (Open Mon.-Tues. and Thurs.-Fri. 9am-6pm, Wed. 10am-6pm, Sat. 9am-1pm; April-Sept. also Sun. 10am-2pm). **Tours** leave from the *Marktplatz* and vary in historical theme. They are offered Mon.-Fri. at 2pm, Sat. at 11:00am and 1:30pm, and Sun. at 11am. **Mitfahrzentrale** is at R.-Paulick-Str. 5 (tel. 690 05 91), arranges ride shares. **Women's Agency: Unabhängiger Frauenverband Dornrosa,** Große Klaus Str. 11 (tel. 202 17 65). Halle's **post office** is at the corner of Hansening and Großessteinstr., across from the opera, 5min. from the *Marktplatz*. Open Mon.-Fri. 8am-6pm, Sat. 8am-noon. The **postal code** is 06108. The **telephone code is** 0345.

Accommodations Hotels and *Pensionen* are generally far above the budgetary means of simple traveling folk (most singles are more than DM100), but the tourist office lists some reasonable rooms in private homes; these are usually the best bet in town. Halle's **Jugendherberge (HI),** August-Bebel-Str. 48a (tel. 202 47 16), rests in a newly restored mansion north of the market. Thin mattresses do little to detract from the quiet residential location and hardwood elegance of the common areas. Take streetcar #7 (direction: Kröllwitz) to "Geiststr.," 2 stops from the *Markt*. Follow Geiststr. 1 block, turn right onto Puschkinstr., and then right onto August-Bebel-Str. at the Hong Kong restaurant. Walk 2 blocks down; the hostel is on your left. 72 beds. (Reception open 7-10am and 5-11pm. Lockout 10am-5pm. Curfew 11pm. DM23, over 26 DM28.50. Sheets DM6. Breakfast included. Dinner DM6.) **Hotel Am Stadtbad,** Große Streinstr. 63-65 (tel. 50 32 70), just down the street from the post office. Its charm is in its location and prices, both of which are intended to be student-friendly. The diminutive *Pension*-style rooms (singles DM70; doubles DM90) and the more spacious apartment-style rooms with telephones (singles DM90, doubles DM150) both come with breakfast. Same-day rooms are available on occasion, but calling ahead wouldn't hurt. Over 100 beds.

Food Affordable sit-down restaurants are a difficult find in this town, but coffeehouses, ice cream parlors, and cafés line Leipziger Str. and the *Marktplatz*. Between the *Marktplatz* and Moritzburg crouch cafés which cater to a younger and livelier student crowd. Halle also boasts several outdoor markets and cheap supermarkets. **EDEKA-neukauf** is on Große Ulrichstr., about two blocks from the *Marktplatz* on the left side of the street, and on Leipzigerstr., approximately one block from the train station (both open Mon.-Fri. 8am-6:30pm, Sat. 8am-1pm.) **Cafe Nöö,** Große Klausstr. 11, at the end of the street facing Domstr., is nöö and cööl. Changing daily menu of international cuisine. Salad and spaghetti DM4-8. Find out about the latest concert blowouts in Halle. They also provide the newspaper *Queer* (open 11am-8pm). At **Café Unikum,** Universitätsring 23, there's serious hipster *Uni*-action amidst smoke and modern art. Cheap salads, sandwiches and daily specials (DM4.50-10; open Mon.-Fri. 8am-midnight, Sat 4pm-midnight, Sun. 10am-1pm). Local flavor suffers an identity crisis at **Zur Apotheke,** Mühlberg 4a, between the *Dom* and Moritzberg Fortress. Thuringian morsels (DM5.50-10) served in Sachsen-Anhalt (open Mon.-Thurs. 8:30am-1am, Fri. 8:30am-2am, Sat. 5pm-2am, Sun. 5pm-1am).

Sights Halle central revolves around the **Marktplatz,** which bustles with traffic, vegetable stands, and three-card monte con-artists. At its center stands the **Roter Turm,** a 400- year-old bell tower. A number of popular myths surround the origin of the tower's name; some credit the copper roof, while others say the architect was a Herr Rote. The most gruesome version relates that after it was built (1418-1506), the blood of the people being executed on the adjoining gallows, either by hanging or beheading, splattered onto the tower, lending it a grisly tinge (tower interior closed to the public). Across from the tower lies the **Marktkirche Unsere Lieben Frauen,** whose altar is adorned with a triptych painted by students under the direction of Lucas Cranach. Above the altar is the organ on which Händel began his musical studies, silent for over 100 years until recent renovations. (Open Mon.-Fri. 10am-noon and 3-6pm, Wed. 3-4pm, Sat. 10am-noon and 3-6pm. Sun. services at 10am. Free 30min. organ concerts Tues. and Thurs. at 4:30pm.) The 16th-century **Marktschlößchen,** a rather small castle, overlooks the *Marktplatz* with its unassuming presence. Inside, one can find the **Galerie Marktschlößchen,** Markt 13 (tel. 202 91 41). Wander these galleries free of charge to see the works of lesser-known contemporary European artists (open Mon.-Fri. 10am-7pm, Sat.-Sun. 10am-6pm). The second floor houses the **Musikinstrumentensammlung des Händel-Hauses** (musical instrument collection of Händel's House), with an impressive collection of keyboard instruments, as well as three majestic music boxes on display (open Wed.-Sun. 1:30-5:30pm; admission DM2, students DM1, free on Thurs.).

An 1859 centennial memorial to composer Georg Friedrich Händel decorates the *Marktplatz,* but the most important Händel shrine remains his familial home. The outstanding **Händelhaus,** Große Nikolaistr. 5-6 (tel. 50 09 00), is only a short walk from the market down Kleine Klausstr. They offer soundtracks with voice-overs in 19 languages to guide pilgrims through the composer's career in Germany, Italy, and England (open Mon.-Wed. and Fri.-Sun. 9:30am-5:30pm, Thurs. 9:30am-7pm; admission DM4, seniors and students DM2, Thurs. free). June 5-10, 1997 witnesses the annual **Händel-Festspiele,** a celebration of Baroque music and one of its masters. Tickets are available from the tourist office. The stroll from Händel's home to the **Dom** is a quick five minutes down Nikolaistr. This ancient complex, begun in 1250, remains a significant repository of religious relics. Today the church's most treasured offerings, renovations permitting, are 17 life-size figures by Peter Schroh from the 16th century.

To reach Halle's most impressive sight, the **Moritzburg Fortress,** go around the far side of the *Dom* and head downhill, then turn right on Schloßburgstr. and walk up the hill. Most of this 15th-century giant is dedicated to the **Staatliche Galerie Moritzburg Halle** (tel. 370 31; fax 299 90). The largest art museum in Sachsen-Anhalt, it focuses mostly on 19th- and 20th-century German painters. Halle's extensive Expressionist collection—including works by Max Beckmann, Paul Klee, Edvard Munch, and Oskar Kokoschka—was particularly offensive to Hitler, who drew heavily from this museum to furnish the infamous exhibit of "degenerate art" that toured Nazi Germany. Although much of the collection was either burnt or sold off by the Nazis, the salvaged works remain an impressive monument to artistic freedom (open Tues. 11am-8:30pm, Wed.-Fri. 10am-5:30pm, Sat.-Sun. 10am-6pm; last admission 30min. before closing; admission DM5, students DM3, free on Tues.).

Entertainment and Nightlife A swiftly growing theater scene ranging from productions of ancient playwrights to German contemporary writers calls Halle home. The cool and culturally hopping area of the **Moritzburg Turm** is where you'll find your entertainment as well as gastronomical pleasures. Halle hosts a number of organ concerts in the **Konzerthalle** (affectionately referred to as "Konzert Halle" by the locals), Kleine Brauhaus Str. 26 (tel. 202 89 36; tickets can be bought Mon.-Tues. and Thurs. 10am-1pm and 3-6pm, Wed. and Fri. 10am-1pm). Pick up a free copy of the **city magazines Fritz** and **Blitz** to remain on top of Halle's groovin' nightlife—the best in Sachsen-Anhalt.

neues theater, Große Ulrich Str. 50 (tel. 512 59 49; fax 202 62 48), was completed in 1990 and features works of a wide palate—everything from Schiller, Shakespeare, Moliere, and Brecht to Halle's own homegrown playwrights. (Orchestra tickets DM15, all others DM10-12.50. Students, seniors 50% off. Call ahead for tickets. Box office open Mon.-Fri. 8am-8:30pm, Sat. 10am-1pm, Sun. 4-8:30pm on days of performances.) Halle's satirical theater, **Die Kiebitzensteiner,** in the Moritzburg Turm,

South Tower (tel. 202 39 81 for tickets), is tucked beneath the fortress and serves as a contemporary forum for satirical criticism, holding spicy and engaging performances, often as benefits for current noble causes. The downstairs restaurant **Kiebitzkeller** offers snacks and spirits for the nightly performances. (Theater open Tues.-Sat. from 7pm on. Ticket office open Tues.-Sat. 5-8pm.) Restaurant opens at 6pm on evenings of performances. **Kleines Thalia Theater,** on Thaliapassage (tel. 20 40 50), off of Geiststr., premiers avant-garde theater productions as well as kiddy performances. (Admission DM12, children and students DM7, seniors DM6.50. Box office open Tues. and Fri. 10am-noon and 1-4pm, Wed. 10am-noon, Thurs. 10am-noon and 1-6pm.) **Turm,** in the northeast tower of the Moritzburg Turm (tel. 202 92 26), hosts the city's *Studentenklub* for the music-loving and grooving literary set in Halle. The music is a mishmash of disco, punk, funk, blues, techno, and rock performed by local bands. *Biergarten* and grill outside (open 7-10pm). Foreign students with ID (18 and over) are welcome. (Open Sun., Tues., and sometimes Thurs. from 8:30pm; Wed. and Fri.-Sat. from 9pm. Closed during university vacations.) **Pierrot,** Großer Sandberg 10, just off Leipziger Str., is a popular gay bar and disco that alternates with **Zoom,** Rudolf-Breitscheid-Str. 92, as the queer hot spot. (Bar open Tues., Thurs., and Sun. 8pm-1am. Disco open Wed. 8pm-2am, Fri.-Sat. 8pm-4am. Cover DM3 on Wed., DM6 on Fri. and Sat.)

■ Eastern Harz Mountains (Ostharz)

Heinrich Heine wrote that even Mephistopheles stopped and trembled when he approached the Harz, the devil's dearest mountains. It's easy to see why Heine—as well as Goethe, Bismarck, and a host of others—fell in love with these mist-shrouded woodlands. Harz towns find their common denominator in the ubiquitous statues of **Roland,** the mustachioed, sword-wielding nephew of Charlemagne, immortalized in the "Song of Roland" and co-opted for obscure reasons by local communities as a folk hero. Stubborn, half-abandoned castles stand over Wernigerode, Quedlinburg, and Halberstadt. The **Harzquerbahn,** an antique, narrow-gauge railway steams through gorgeous Harz scenery from Nordhausen to Wernigerode, passing through the unfortunately named towns of **Sorge** and **Elend** (Sorrow and Misery) and reaching a 540-m peak on **Drei-Annen-Hohne.** The removal of Germany's internal border has opened the mountains to ever more vacationers seeking historic villages, good skiing, and better hiking.

Nordhausen is technically in Thuringia, yet touristically relevant only as the end of the line of the Harzquerbahn. **Nordhausen Information,** Bahnhofsplatz 3a (tel. (03631) 38 25) books rooms. Some of the smaller towns in the area include **Ilsenburg,** with its open-air theater (DM2.20) and mining museum, and **Elbingerode,** home to the **Shaubergwerk "Buchenberg"** mining caverns and museum. The famed **Hermannshöhle** and **Baumannshöhle** of **Rübeland** are also just a bus ride away; learn again, and forget again, the difference between stalactites and stalagmites in these two monstrous caves. (Both caverns open daily 9:15-4:15pm. Admission DM7, students DM3.50.)

Pick up a copy of the *Fehrplan der Verkehrs und Tarifgemeinsschaft Ostharz* (DM2) to get a comprehensive list of bus and rail lines in the East Harz. From the main Wernigerode *Bahnhof,* the end of the Querbahn, it is a short trek to the regional **bus station,** which has tentacles extending throughout the Eastern Harz and provides the best means to reach small mountain towns. The Harz is a region of intersections, as the state borders of the three *Länder* meet here. This synthetic effect has been heightened by new bus lines between Wernigerode and the Western Harz, which restore the area's common identity. Buses run regularly between Bad Harzburg and Wernigerode (for information on the Western Harz Mountains, see p. 333). Every year in June, the mountains' famed cherries, *Harzkirschen,* are in season on both sides of the former political division.

WERNIGERODE

Wernigerode was one of Goethe's secret spots in the hills, and in some ways, it's still the same small town he visited on trips through the Harz—teeming with half-timbered houses and crowned with the cool stone of a magnificent hilltop castle. This *Bergstadt* (mountain city) is a well-preserved, well-worth-it destination for riders of the **Querbahn.** Wernigerode is the natural crossing-over point from Western to Eastern Harz; but more than that, it is the region's most-touristed town—for good reason. Recently, the town has employed a cosmopolitan artifice in an effort to increase tourism; the subsequent flood of visitors is constantly pushing prices up in picturesque Wernigerode.

Wernigerode's **Schloß** (tel. 233 25), on its looming perch in the wooded mountains above town, is a plush and pompous monument to the Second Reich. Though the place was maintained by the GDR as a museum of feudalism, its guiding spirit was much more recent. Graf Otto, one of Bismarck's main flunkies, hosted Kaiser William I here for wildly extravagant hunting expeditions. The perfectly-preserved **Königszimmer** guest suite, where the Kaiser stayed, oozes inbred, masculine luxury down to the deep red-and-green brocaded wallpaper in the bedroom. The dozen other regal rooms include a chapel, two drawing rooms, and the jaw-dropping main dining hall *(Festsaal),* featuring a sky-high inlaid wooden ceiling, panoramic murals of glorious Teutonic dukes, and the heaped wealth of the ducal table service. Outside on the flower-trimmed terrace, cannons are still poised in defense, and a fountain is angled to catch the sun; from here, you can see straight to the peak of the **Brocken,** the Harz's highest and supposedly most haunted mountain. (Castle open May-Oct. daily 10am-6pm; Nov. Sat. and Sun. 10am-6pm; Dec.-April Tues.-Sun. 10am-6pm. Last entry 5pm. Admission DM7, students DM6, under 14 DM3; add DM1 for a tour.) Ride up to the *Schloß* on the bumpy **Bimmelbahn,** a train-truck that leaves from the clock at the intersection of Teichdamm and Klintgasse, behind the *Rathaus.* (Departures May-Oct. Mon.-Sat. every 20min., Sun. every 40min. 9:30am-5:30pm; Nov.-April every 40min. daily 10:30am-4:30pm. One-way DM3, under 10 DM2.) To walk it, take the gravel *Christiantalweg* path or follow the white brick road marked "Burgberg," and branch off for a hike in the wooded park around the castle.

Wernigerode relishes its *Fachwerk* (half-timbered) streets and squares. The **Krummelsches Haus,** Breitestr. 72, is so completely covered with ornate wood carvings that the original *Fachwerk* is hardly visible. The **Ältestes Haus,** Hinterstr. 48, is the oldest house in the city, having survived several fires, two bomb runs, and various acts of God since its construction in the early 15th century. The **Normalstes Haus,** Witzestr. 13, has no distinguishing traits. The **Kleinstes Haus,** Kochstr. 43, is 2.95m wide, 4.2m to the eaves—and for the less-than-tall, the door is only 1.7m high. Come and coo like Goldilocks herself. Wernigerode has two museums: the **Krellsche Museum Schmiede,** Breite Str. 95, is a smithy (open Mon.-Sat.1-5pm; admission DM1, students DM0.50). The **Harz Museum,** right by the Marktplatz on Am Klint (tel. 328 56), is an all-Harz gathering of … well … mountain stuff (open Mon.-Sat. 10am-4pm).

Wernigerode's busy **tourist office,** on Breitestr. around the corner from the *Rathaus* (tel. 330 35), books rooms in private homes or hotels (DM30-40) for a 10% commission (open Mon.-Fri. 9am-6pm, Sat.-Sun. 10am-3pm). It also sells maps (DM3). **Tours** leave the tourist office Tues. and Sat. at 10:30am, Wed., Thurs., and Sun. at 2pm. To reach Wernigerode from Halle or Magdeburg, change trains at Halberstadt; a bus also runs directly to Bad Harzburg. The town has two central **train stations** that serve its 37,000 citizens. **Wernigerode-Westentor** is the next-to-last stop on the *Harzquerbahn* and close to the city center—just head up Mittelstr., and then right on Bahnhofstr. to arrive at the *Markt.* The antique steamer also stops at the main **Bahnhof Wernigerode,** next to the regional **bus terminal** (see p. 518). **H. J. Hallerman,** located in the alcove above Breitestr. 27 (tel. 325 08), offers street and mountain **bike rentals** (DM15 per day) for roughshod running over Goethe's walking paths (open Mon.-Fri. 9:30am-12:30pm and 1:30-6pm, Sat. 9:30am-noon). **Exchange currency** and

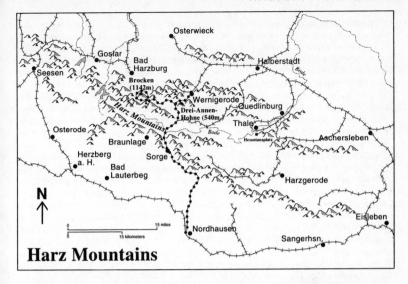

Harz Mountains

mail cards at the **post office,** Marktstr. 14, 38855 Wernigerode (open Mon.-Fri. 8am-11:30am and 2:30–6pm, Sat. 9am-noon). The **telephone code** is 03943.

To reach Wernigerode's **Jugendgästehaus,** Friedrichstr. 53 (tel. 320 61), take bus A or D to Kirchstr. or walk from the Westerntor station right on Unter den Zindeln and turn right on Friedrichstr. (25min.). The rooms have recently been refurbished and sport modern facilities and warm mountain *Gemütlichkeit* (coziness). All you can say is "quaint." (Reception open 5-7pm. DM15. Breakfast DM6. Dinner DM7. You *must* buy one meal. Sheets DM5. Reservations strongly recommended.) **Frucht-haus Lucke,** a good bit west of the city center on Westernstr. 36, has a good stock of fresh fruits and other groceries (open Mon.-Fri. 9am-6pm, Sat. 9am-noon). There is a **farmers' market** in the pedestrian zone (Tues. and Thurs. 10am-5pm). The **Big Woper,** next to the market on Westernstr., is a pseudo-fast-food restaurant, where meals range DM4-9. This ain't no Burger King, but, then again, there aren't too many deals in Wernigerode for under DM10.

The *Harzquerbahn* steam train stops at Drei-Annen-Hohne for a few minutes after it leaves Wernigerode, enough time to either look around the highest point of the route or to jump on the **Brockenbahn** that spirals up around the mountain (round-trip DM40). For more on the bewitching beauty of Brocken's peak, see Western Harz Mountains, on p. 333.

HALBERSTADT

If you plan to travel any farther east than Wernigerode, chances are good you'll have to make a connection here, so make Hans-Georg Busch—Halberstadt's mayor and Elvis impersonator—happy by visiting. Halberstadt, known before the devastation of World War II as a producer of cigars, gloves, and sausages (everything a gentleman needed), seems a grimy town from the moment you enter the train station. Reserve your final judgment until you gaze upon the remains of the *Altstadt.* Follow Bahnhofstr. and turn left on Magdeburgerstr. to reach the multi-colored bricks of **Breiter Weg;** this pedestrian lane ends at the **Fischmarkt,** where citizens gather every Tuesday, Friday, and Saturday to sell their wares in front of the **Martinikirche** (market open Tues. and Fri. 8am-5pm, Sat. 8am-noon). The opposite façade boasts a **Roland statue,** which thankfully does not depict Charlemagne's brave nephew having his brains blown out of his ears while playing the trumpet; the statue, built in 1433, is now scarred by time and bombs.

The unquestioned focus of the *Altstadt* is the **Domplatz,** framed by the awesome flying buttresses of the 13th-century **Dom St. Stephanus** and the not-so-flyly-buttressed Romanesque **Liebfraukirche.** The effect of the former's midnight-sooted spires is heightened by the sheer bulk of the edifice: it's a couple sizes too large for a city center like Halberstadt's. The only way to see the **Dommuseum** and its **treasury,** complete with gilded everything and the oldest known tapestries in the world, dating from 1150, is to take a combined tour of it and the *Dom.* (Open May-Oct. Mon.-Fri. 10-11:30am and noon-5pm, Sat. 10-11:30am and noon-4:30pm, Sun. noon-4:30pm. Tours Mon.-Fri. at 10am, 11:30am, 2pm, and 3:30pm, Sat. 10am and 2pm, Sun. 11:30am and 2:30pm; Nov.-April Mon.-Sat. 10am and 2pm, Sun. 11:30am.) The *Dom*'s enormous **organ** belches out concerts every Saturday from June until September (prices and times vary, but there are discounts for students and seniors). In the 1930s, the *Dom* was the sight of several *Hitler-Jugend* rallies. In an act of *Vergangenheitsbewältigung* (coming to terms with the past), a group of quartz-like stones placed in front of the cathedral pay tribute to Halberstadt's once-thriving Jewish community, completely wiped out in the Holocaust. On the night of the dedication in 1992, the memorial was plastered with fascist and neo-Nazi symbols; the *Denkmal* (monument) was fully cleaned the following morning. Follow the *Dom's* **rose garden** out and around to the **Städtisches Museum** (tel. 55 14 71), a scrapbook of Halberstadt history, and the **Museum Heineanum** (tel. 55 14 60), a gallery of our feathered friends. (Both open Tues.-Fri. 9am-5pm, Sat.-Sun. 10am-5pm. Admission to both museums DM5, students DM2.50.)

The newly renovated **tourist office,** Düsterngraben 3 (tel. 55 18 15; fax 55 10 89), down an alley just in front of the *Dom,* will have information on these sights and more, and will find you a room (from DM30) in one of the three hotels or myriad of guest houses for free (open Mon.-Fri. 9am-1pm and 2-6pm, Sat. 10am-1pm). There's no *Jugendherberge* here, but the juicy exoticism of the words **Campingplatz SH 200** (tel. 245 96) will surely lure you to the *Halberstädter See* (Lake) in the northeast part of town. From the station follow Bahnhofstr., go right on Magdeburger-Str., and left on Warmholzberg (30min; reception open daily 1-3pm; DM7.50 per person, DM8 per tent). Cheap food is a bit hard to come by, although there are three **food stores** on Düstergraben: **Franke** (open Mon.-Fri. 8am-6pm, Sat. 8am-noon); **Votwitzkei,** a bakery (open Mon.-Fri. 6:30am-6pm, Sat. 6:30am-noon); and **Ahrens** (open Mon.-Fri. 7am-6pm, Sat. 7am-noon). The **Museumscafé** in the *Domplatz* offers light meals for DM5-10. The **telephone code** is 03941.

QUEDLINBURG

For sheer authenticity, no other destination in the Harz can match Quedlinburg. This town gets medieval on your ass, and comes complete with spires, castles, torure chambers, and half-timbered houses that look as though they've been around since 919, when Henry I waited in the market square for the news that he'd been chosen as emperor. In 1994, the city was crowned by UNESCO as one of the world's most important cultural treasures. Quedlinburg has been a bit run-down for the past forty years, but locals are busy painting and patching. Unfortunately, navigational difficulties will no doubt survive the renovations: the tiny alleys, bends, kinks, and crazily oblique intersections are the price of Quedlinburg's historic charm. Get a free map from the tourist office as soon as you arrive, and use it. If you have to ask for directions, try to get the person to show you the route to your goal on the map: this is not the place to test your grasp of German prepositions. Recently, Quedlinburg has gained some notoriety as party to an international art-theft scandal. In 1945, ecclesiastical gems from the church were hidden in a basement to protect them from the bombing. An American G.I. came across them, threw the lot in his pack, and took it all home to Texas. The story came out only after his recent death, when his heirs tried to dispose of the goods. German government officials mounted a knock-out legal battle, and this small town got the prize, now on display in the church in the Burgberg castle above town.

Henry I died within the original walls of the **Burgberg** (tel. 27 30), an old Saxon stronghold, in 936. The current 13th-century structure has been a favorite residence-in-exile for the ruling family's widows and inconvenient relatives. The castle complex consists of three parts: the **Schloßmuseum,** the **Schloßgarten,** and the **Stiftskirche.** The museum depicts city history from the Paleolithic era until the present, all according to good old Marxist historiography (open May-Sept. Tues.-Sun. 10am-6pm; Oct.-April daily 9am-5pm; admission DM5, students DM3). The **Stiftskirche** is the castle church, where the purloined art treasures are on permanent display. (The church is only accessible by guided tour. There are tours every 30min. May-Sept. Tues.-Sat. 10am-3:30pm, Sun. noon-3:30pm; Nov.-April Tues.-Sat. 11am-3:30pm, Sun. noon-3:30pm.) Loiter in the gardens around the *Schloß,* or walk down the castle path past an impressive row of old houses, cramped together on the hillside.

Underneath the castle, the **Lyonel Feininger Museum** is tucked away in a smart, more-modern-looking white house at Finkenherd 5a (tel. 22 38). Inside is an *Angst*-heavy selection of works by the artists in the *Die Brücke* artistic circle, including Feininger's own bleak landscapes and portraits, vivisected by characteristic fracture-like lines (closed until Jan. 1997; for further information, inquire at the tourist office). The unavoidable stone statue of **Roland** guards the ivy-covered **Rathaus,** while the neighboring **Benediktikirche** graces the *Markt* with its 13th-century base; the twisting Solomonic columns of the altar are truly exceptional. The **Schreckens-Turm,** at the end of *Neuendorf,* served as Quedlinburg's 14th-century S&M torture palace; now, it is disintegrating in the midst of a couple of virtually abandoned blocks. The **Wipertikirche,** a glowing example of Romanesque architecture, can only be visited with a guided tour organized by the tourist office (tours April-Sept. daily at 11am; meet at the tourist office).

If you're looking for a hostel, or even a hotel under DM60 per person per night, you're in the wrong town. Quedlinburg's **tourist office,** Markt 22 (tel. 77 30 12; fax 28 66), will find you a private room for no fee (DM28 and up), sell you museum tickets, take you on tours, and provide everything short of a massage. (Open May-Sept. Mon.-Fri. 9am-8pm, Sat.-Sun. 9am-6pm; Oct. Mon.-Fri. 9am-6pm, Sat.-Sun. 10am-3pm; Nov.-Feb. Mon.-Fri. 9am-5pm; Mar.-Apr. Mon.-Fri. 9am-6pm, Sat.-Sun. 10am-3pm). **Exchange money** at decent rates in the ultra-modern **Deutsche Bank,** Am. Markt 3 (open Mon. and Wed. 8:30am-1pm and 2-4pm; Tues. and Thurs. 8:30am-1pm and 2-6pm; Fri. 8:30am-1:30pm). From Wernigerode, change **trains** at Halberstadt for Quedlinburg (every 2hr.). The **telephone code** is 03946.

On the way to the castle, grab some local brew at the **Brauerei Lüdde,** Blassistr. 14 (tel. 32 51). The interior is a high-ceilinged, circular wooden brewing hall with a bar and a rank of dark-wood kegs along the walls. There's also a pleasant courtyard *Biergarten,* where you can sip a glass of the brewery's excellent, nutty **Lüdde-Alt** (ale) for DM3.30. They also offer a cheap, low-alcohol *Pils* beer called *Pubarschknall* (a name which hardly merits translation; something about bad digestion) for DM1.90 per glass. Tasty snacks and meals at around DM12 may improve that rumbling down under (open Mon.-Thurs. 11am-midnight, Fri.-Sat. 11am-1am, Sun. 11am-10pm). **Pasta Mia,** Steinbrücke 23 (tel. 21 22), faces the *Marktplatz* and serves up inexpensive Italian meals. Pizzas DM5.50-12. Pastas DM8.50-13.50. On Mondays, the pizza special serves up any pizza for DM6; the Thursday pasta special also offers the DM6 deal (open Mon.-Sat. 11am-10pm). Local **farmers** sell their most treasured foods at the *Marktplatz* (Wed. 9am-5pm, Sat. 9am-noon).

THALE

Above the serene front of Thale's flowing rivers and mountainside scenery lurks a region of myths, legends, witches, and demons. Like most towns in the Harz, Thale boasts that Goethe fancied its **Bodetal** hills—hence, the *Goetheweg.* Nevertheless, Thale's primary attraction lies in the town's fetishization of its mystic past.

Legend dates Thale's cultic history back to prehistoric times, when a sorceress named **Watelinde** led pagan rituals that, like the head-banging masses of Ozzy Osborne, forced incorrigible youths down a path of destruction in the fast-lane lifestyle of witchery. A few thousand years later a Harz resident named **Hilda** got lost in the woods for a couple of years—her re-appearance was, by all accounts, a touch sketchy. Watelinde freaked out at the sight of Hilda and begged God to save her from the frightening countenance before her. Amidst explosive thunder and lightning, a whirlwind threw poor Watelinde into some rocks, which now comprise the nifty attraction **Hexentanzplatz.** Amidst the celebrated spot of splattering are statues of demonic and ghoulish creatures, adorned with parasitic animals. Adjacent to *Hexentanzplatz* is the **Walpurgishalle,** a museum commemorating the Harz history of witchcraft that boasts displays of Thale's cultic ceremonies, as well as animal heads with pentagrams attached. Definitely a wildly entertaining experience. (Open May-Sept. daily 9am-5pm, Oct.-Apr. 9am-1pm. Admission DM3, students DM1.) Also located on the Hexenplatz is the rather impressive **Harzer Bergtheater Thale** (tel. 23 24), a huge outdoor amphitheater vacillating between the sublime and the infernal, the sacred and the profane, with performances ranging from broadway musicals and operas to Goethe's *Faust* and the *Hexenkonzerts* (witches' concerts). (Shows run sporadically April 30-Sept. Starting times also vary. 30% discount for students.) One can ascend to the Hexenplatz either by following the adventure-filled **winding trail** that begins by the hostel (30min.)—on foggy days its teeming life and poor visibility are reminiscent of Yoda's cave in the Degoba system—or by means of the **Kabinenbahn,** a cable car which travels from the entrance of the Bodetals to Hexenplatz (May-Sept. daily 9:30am-6pm, Oct.-April 10am-4:30pm; DM8, students and youths DM5).

Across the street from the train station, the **tourist office,** Rathausstr. 1 (tel. 25 97 or 22 77; fax 22 47), can hook you up with a private room (DM25-40 per person) for no charge. You can also purchase spirits here in the form of the *Hexen Gesoff* alcohol sold in cute little bottles (open Oct. and Dec.-April Mon.-Fri. 9am-5pm; May-Aug. Mon.-Fri. 9am-6pm, Sat. 10am-3pm; Nov. Mon.-Fri. 9am-4pm). When he wrote for *Let's Go: Germany 1884,* Theodor Fontane described Thale as a place where "one is up-lifted, well-served, and well-nursed." The **Jugendherberge,** Bodetal Waldkater 1 (tel. 28 81), attempts to deserve this lofty laud; its cavernous eight-bed rooms look out into the mountains and the running river below. The *Jugendherberge* may or may not be haunted; check with the tourist office for more details (reception open 7am-10pm; DM21, over 26 DM26.50; sheets DM6; breakfast included). To get there from the train station, cut diagonally through the park, past the *Opfer des Fascismus* statue on the right and the cute cathedral on the left; then go straight and continue walking along the river and until you reach it (10-15min.). The hostel's cafeteria has lunch and dinner specials (DM7.50-9). Otherwise, the many food stands by the *Hexenplatz* can fill your need for cheap eats. Thale goes crazy every year on April 30 for the **Walpurgisnacht,** but only go if you dare commit yourself to an orgy of sin. **Trains** leave for Thale from Halberstadt hourly. The **telephone code** is 03947.

▓ Magdeburg

Magdeburg has three claims to fame: it has a spectacular cathedral, it's the birthplace of 18th-century composer Georg Phillipp Telemann, and it was devastated in both the Thirty Years War and World War II. On May 10, 1631, the city was decimated in one of the most gruesome battles of the Thirty Years War, after Protestant town leaders refused to cut a deal with Catholic troops outside the gates. The industrial output of the city made it a prime target for the Allied forces in World War II. After the war, Magdeburg was rebuilt GDR-style—blessed with enviably broad boulevards and parks but cursed by concrete cookie-cutter apartment blocks. Luckily, in the months before reunification, Magdeburg had the good luck to triumph over Halle to become the new capital of Sachsen-Anhalt. Now brightness and shine have invaded. Magdeburg offers its visitors a *Dom,* some excellent museums, and historical sites, all set in a cosmopolitan shopping district. Yet Magdeburg's increased popularity has brought increased trouble—skinheads have begun to congregate here, causing the city some problems.

In the old cold days of the Iron Curtain, Magdeburg was one of the few rail links between West Germany and West Berlin's centrally located Bahnhof Zoo. As a result, travelers en route to Berlin from eastern cities can often save time by routing through Magdeburg. Otherwise, you'll probably end up in either the Berlin Hauptbahnhof (a 20-min. S-Bahn ride to the city center) or Bahnhof Lichtenberg (a good 45min. away). Magdeburg is also connected to the ICE bullet trains from Hanover and Munich. The city is conveniently configured for pedestrians: most of the sights and museums are located on Otto-von-Guericke-Str. and Breiter Weg, parallel streets that lie less than 15min. away from the train station via Ernst-Reuter-Allee.

Orientation and Practical Information The **tourist office,** Alter Markt 9 (tel. 540 49 03), is on the main market square. From the train station, head straight out on Ernst-Reuter-Allee (it's a bit to the left from the front doors) then left at the second intersection onto Breiter Weg; turn right onto the market. The **Zimmervermittlung** (tel. 540 49 04), in the same building, will help find you a room (DM25-75) for a DM3 fee. (Office open Mon.-Fri. 10am-6pm, Sat. 10am-1pm.) Inquire about tours and maps in English. Tours Mon.-Fri. at 11am, DM5. The Zimmervermittlung closes for a break 1-1:45pm. Pick up a copy of Dates magazine, which has hotel and pension listings, as well as an up-to-date schedule of cultural and nightlife activities (free). If it's late and the many banks in town are closed, you can use **Deutsche Verkehrsbank** in the train station for **currency exchange,** but you'll pay a commission: DM7.50 minimum on traveler's checks, DM3 for cash exchanges. (Open Mon.-Fri. 7am-7:30pm, Sat. 8am-noon, Sun. 9am-noon.) For towns near Magdeburg, the **bus** station is to the right of the train station. For **bicycle rental, Herr Koch,** Simonstr. 2 (tel. 572 09) charges DM10 per day (cheap!). Limited stock (open Mon.-Fri. 9am-noon and 2-6pm). **Mitfahrzentrale,** Lessingstr. 64 (tel. 731 80 80) is open Mon.-Fri. 10am-6pm. The **Women's Information Center: Courage** is at Porsestr. 14. The **post office** is a great dark hulk on Breiter Weg, 39104 Magdeburg, in the direction of the Dom (open Mon.-Fri. 8am-6pm, Sat. 9am-noon). The **telephone code** is 0391.

Accommodations and Camping Because the local youth hostel has closed down, choices are somewhat limited. As in many former East German cities, hotels are not the best budget option; ask about rooms in **Pensionen** or **private homes** at the tourist office. Also, check the back page of *Dates* magazine, available everywhere, to find *Pensionen* without any service charge. In a pinch, Magdeburg is 1½ hours from the ever-accommodating Berlin. Camp at **Campingplatz Am Barleber See** (tel. 50 32 44); take streetcar #10 (direction: Barliber See) to the last stop, continue down the main street, then cross underneath the highway bridge. **Bike rental** available (reception open daily 7am-9pm). DM4 per person, DM2 per tent.

Food Many of the cheaper restaurants crowd into the street around the intersection of Breiter Weg and Einsteinstr. in Hasselbachplatz. This was also the only section of the downtown to survive wartime bombing. Buy vegetables and fruits at the **Alter Markt** (open Tues.-Fri. 9am-6pm, Sat. 9am-1pm). The **Karstadt Cafeteria** offers groceries as well as basic meals, including a large salad bar (open Mon.-Fri. 9am-6:30pm, Sat. 9am-2pm). It seems that the Magdeburgers traded in their hammer and sickle for the golden arches; two **McDonald's** grace the town: one at the *Hauptbahnhof;* another three blocks away at the corner of Ernst-Reuter Str. and Breiterweg. (Both open Mon.-Wed. 6am-midnight, Thurs. 6am-1am, Fri. 6am-2am, Sat. 7am-2am, Sun. 8am-midnight.) **Ratskeller,** Alte Markt, is a historical set-up, in the basement of the Baroque *Rathaus.* If you play your cards right, this can be the best food deal in Magdeburg: while *a la carte* dinners are prohibitively expensive, the restaurant offers two special deals. Each weekday features a different *Stamm-essen* (lunch special) from noon-2pm including an entree, starch, and dessert for a delightful DM8-10. Get there by 1pm if you can. The other sweet deal occurs every day: 3-5pm is *Ratsherrenzeit*—all entrees reduced to half price plus DM1. Late eaters can get flavorful steaks and copious seafood dishes for DM8-14 (open Mon.-Sat. 11am-11pm, Sun.

11am-9pm). **Mausefalle,** well south of center on Breiter Weg 224 (tel. 543 01 35), attracts a young crowd, particularly students. The big wall over the bathroom doors is decorated with old newspaper clippings and antique-car memorabilia. Solid spaghetti dishes for DM10; extensive liquor and mixed-drink selection (open Mon.-Fri. 8:30am-2am, Sat.-Sun. 8:30am-3am; kitchen open until 2am).

Sights Dominated by nondescript modern grays and beiges, Magdeburg's urban neutrality offers no challenge to the city's few dazzling sights. The main landmark and city symbol is the sprawling **Magdeburger Dom,** adjacent to the old square on Breite Str. The cathedral's major-league status is backed up by a display of photos and schematic plans comparing it to other gothic heavyweights like Aachen, Cologne, and Reims. In fact, the *Dom* was famed as the largest cathedral in the nation until reunification forced it to yield that honor to Cologne. But there's nothing second-rate about the spectacle of the wide **courtyard** quadrangle with the cathedral's twin dark towers spearing the skies above. At the front of the cathedral lies an inconspicuous tomb; this is the 973 grave site of Otto I, the second Holy Roman Emperor (after Charlemagne). Local ghost stories credit the Kaiser's spectral guardianship with preservation of the cathedral during the destruction of 1631 (Catholic raiders) and 1945 (B-17 bombers), though in fact the bombs did give the cathedral quite a buzz. (Open Mon.-Sat. 10am-6pm, Sun. 11:30am-6pm. Tours Mon.-Sat. 10am and 2pm, Sun. 11:30am and 2pm. Admission free; tours DM4, students DM2. A *Touristenkarte* can be purchased for DM6, providing cover charge for most of the city's sights.)

Near the *Dom,* between all the faceless apartments, lies the ancient **Kloster Unser Lieben Frauen,** Regierungstr. 4/6 (tel. 56 50 20); an 11th-century nunnery, it now serves as a museum for visiting exhibitions and a concert hall. The grounds about the cloister still shimmer in sheltered peacefulness; sit and cogitate on the benches or on the remains of stone walls (open Tues. and Thurs.-Sun. 10am-6pm, Wed. 10am-8pm; DM3, DM1.50 for students and seniors). Head through the parking lot in front of the *Dom* onto Breiter Weg and go down Danzstr. On your left will be the **Kulturhistorisches Museum,** Otto-von-Guerike-Str. 68-73 (tel. 543 26 45; fax 543 26 46), where you can view everything from creations by Magdeburg's own junior-varsity Einstein, Otto von Guerike, to the history of the city (open Tues.-Sun. 10am-6pm; admission DM1, students DM0.50). Back down Danzstr., a left on Breiter Weg will take you back to the Alter Markt. The ruins of the **Johanniskirche** are a harrowing and tremendously moving monument to the bombing of 1945; the grandiose framework of the church is just about all that's left. The statues outside juxtapose the terror of the bombings with the image of a **Trümmerfrau** (rubble woman), which serves as an emblem of the city's difficult past. Climb the **tower** for a magnificent view of the city (open daily 10am-6pm; admission DM1, students DM0.50; tower admission DM0.50). Across from the Johanniskirche rises the clock tower of the elegantly-proportioned 17th-century **Rathaus.** Directly on the *Marktplatz* in front of the *Rathaus* is the **Magdeburger Reiter** (built in 1240), the oldest free-standing equestrian figure in Germany. Behind the cathedral lies the Elbe River; follow the Remtergang just off the Domplatz and look out over the river from **Auf dem Wall,** the ramparts of the old city fortifications.

Entertainment The Magdeburger *Kabarett* (cabaret) **Die Kügelblitze,** Breiter Weg 200, was already well-known during the GDR era, and the last five years have fed its sardonic sensibility. (Performances every evening, starting at around 8pm. Tickets DM20, students and seniors DM10. Call 543 39 56 for ticket information.) There's also straight-out drama at the **Freie Kammerspiele Theater,** Otto-von-Guericke-Str. 64.

Mecklenburg-Vorpommern

Over 1700 lakes, the marshy coast of the Baltic Sea, and labyrinthine medieval towns characterize the lonely landscape of Mecklenburg-Vorpommern. Once a favored vacation spot for East Germans, this sparsely populated, northernmost province of the former GDR retains a sturdy, raw-boned natural beauty. Cyclists and hikers flock to the Mecklenburg Lake Plain and to Rügen Island, which offers some of Germany's most spectacular scenery. As restoration work in the region's main cities continues, dramatic Hanseatic architecture is starting to emerge from the rubble. Though many visitors pass ceaselessly through this region en route to the Baltic Sea beaches or to Scandinavia, Mecklenburg-Vorpommern's cities remain economically and politically troubled, and the presence of neo-Nazis is, unfortunately, noticeable.

■ Schwerin

A keepsake of Henry the Lion's 12th-century march through the East, Schwerin (shvay-REEN) is a rejuvenating stop on the way to the swarming Baltic seacoast. With reunification, the city regained the status it lost in the former GDR as capital of Mecklenburg-Vorpommern. Now Schwerin again administers this *Land* of fallen *Junkers*, rye bread, and brick churches. The Swedes burned much of it to the ground in 1616, but the Allies spared it in World War II. Today's *Altstadt* is therefore well-preserved, with an elegant look of shabby gentility. Surrounded almost completely by lakes and largely free of Communist "architectural innovations," Schwerin's *Altstadt* and *Schloß* are also thus far unmarred by tourist-trap capitalism.

Orientation and Practical Information Schwerin lies on the Magdeburg-Rostock rail line and is easily accessible from all major cities on the Baltic coast. Hourly **trains** connect Schwerin to Rostock (1¼hr.) and other major cities in the East. **Schwerin Information,** Am Markt 11 (tel. 56 09 31; fax 55 50 94), sells maps for DM1 and books private rooms (DM25-50) for free; cheap rooms go quickly, so call ahead. From the station, go right on Wismarchestr. (first Gründthalplatz), left on Arsenal, right on Bischofstr., and left on Schmiedestr. (open Mon.-Fri. 10am-noon and 1-6pm, Sat. 10am-2pm). The **Apotheke am Markt,** Puschkinstr. 61 (tel. 592 350), just off the *Marktplatz,* posts addresses of pharmacies and has an emergency bell (open Mon.-Fri. 8am-6pm, Sat. 8:30am-1pm). At the **SB Münz Wasch Center,** Werderstr. 6, to the left of the *Schloß,* you can do laundry for DM6, including detergent (open daily 6am-11pm). **Rent bikes** from the station for DM10-12 (open Mon.-Fri. 8:30am-6pm, Sat.-Sun. 8:30am-7pm). The main **post office** resides at Mecklenburgstr. 6, 19053 Schwerin. From the *Markt,* go down Schmiedestr. and turn right (open Mon.-Fri. 8am-6pm, Sat. 9am-noon). The **telephone code** is 0385.

Accommodations and Food The **Jugendherberge (HI),** Waldschulenweg 3 (tel. 21 30 05), lies south of town in a beautiful woodsy setting overlooking the lake. Catch bus #15 from the train station; get off at the end and walk towards the zoo (see p. 527). It's on the left. With Schwerin's increasing popularity, the friendly hostel frequently fills up, so call ahead. (Reception open 4-10pm. Curfew 10pm. DM19.20, over 26 DM24.10. Breakfast included. Sheets DM6.) **Kaiser's,** on Schmiedestr., is the most convenient supermarket for fresh groceries (open Mon.-Fri. 8am-6pm, Thurs. 8am-8:30pm, Sat. 8am-1pm). The fancy **Friesenhof Restaurant,** on Mecklenburgerstr. next door to the post office, offers all meals at half-price daily 3-5pm; steaks and seafood dishes miraculously become a reasonable DM9-12 (open daily 11:30am-10:30pm). For budget eats around the clock, try the friendly **fischbar** at the end of Klosterstr.; sandwiches and fish dishes (surprise!) DM3-10 (open Mon.-Fri. 8am-7pm, Sat. 8am-6pm).

Sights Schwerin's strangely Byzantine **Schloß** (tel. 525 19 20) is situated just south of the city center, over the bridge at the end of Schloß-str. This grandiose residence was the seat of the Dukes of Mecklenburg, who ruled the area until the 1918 upheaval that chased the Kaiser from power; the castle's intricately gilded Baroque cupolas runneth over with luxury. But even the red silk wallpaper and mahogany floors pale in comparison to the sumptuous throne room, with its gilt-and-marble columns (open Tues.-Sun. 10am-6pm; admission DM6, students DM3). Across from the *Schloß,* the **Alter Garten** square was the site of mass demonstrations preceding the downfall of the GDR in 1989. Atop a cascade of stairs on the right sits the **Staatliches Museum,** which houses a good collection of 15th-19th century Dutch and German art, including a few works by Rembrandt, Cranach, and Rubens (open Tues.-Sun. 10am-5pm; admission DM4, students DM2). The striking cream-pillared building next door is the **Mecklenburgisches Staatstheater Schwerin** (tel. 88 21 26), currently in the midst of a dramatic revival (box office open Tues.-Fri. 10am-1pm and 2-6pm, Sun. 10am-1pm; tickets DM15-25, students DM10). Looking uphill, the nearest spire belongs to the central **Gothic cathedral,** am Domplatz, which dates from the 13th century. For DM2 you can sweat your way up the 110m tower tacked on at the tail of the last century (open Mon. 10am-1pm and 2-4pm, Tues.-Sat. 10am-1pm and 2-5pm, Sun. noon-5pm. Services Sun. at 10am.). Schwerin's former **synagogue** sits silently at Schlachterstr. 3, off the Marktplatz; the temple was destroyed in a pogrom in 1938. The building used to house the region's memorial to its Jewish community, but closed several years ago after an interior looting by local skinheads. The town keeps its own historical house with permanent exhibits on Schwerin's checkered past in the **Heimatmuseum** (tel. 86 43 81) on the *Markt* (open Tues.-Sun. 9am-6pm).

If you're looking for something on the wilder side, the **Schweriner Zoo** (tel. 21 30 00) borders the *Jugendherberge*, which lies close to the **Fauler See.** The zoo specializes in waterfowl, but it has its share of large ferocious mammals, especially once *you* get there (open May-Sept. Mon.-Fri. 9am-5pm, Sat.-Sun. 9am-6pm, Oct.-April Mon.-Fri. 9am-4pm; admission DM6, students DM3). Another option for nature lovers is the reserve on **Kaninchenwerder Island,** set in the midst of the Schweriner See. In summer, ferries leave at least once an hour from the docks to the left of the *Schloß* to visit the rabbits on the island (one-way DM2.80, children DM1).

■ Mecklenburg Lake Plain (Mecklenburgische Seenplatte)

When things got hectic in Berlin, Otto von Bismarck often found refuge among the reserved but sincere folk of the Mecklenburg Lake Plain *(Mecklenburgische Seenplatte)*. Long derided by their Saxon neighbors as country bumpkins (the insult is tossed right back), the locals are not noted for opening their hearts to strangers. They will, however, give you the opportunity to trace the necklace of lakes in this most sparsely populated region of the country. With the exception of Neubrandenberg, the reminders of the GDR are not as painfully obvious here as in other regions of eastern Germany, perhaps because the socialist-era architects were wise enough to leave the forests and hills alone. A popular vacation area for more than a century, the Lake Plain attracts plenty of summer crowds; consider advance reservations.

WAREN

Conveniently located within an hour of Rostock and two hours of Berlin, Waren draws many German tourists to the northern edge of the **Müritz,** Germany's second-largest freshwater lake. Smaller streams weave from the lake into **Müritz National Park,** a unique preserve of rare birds and marshland. The Waren tourist office has tons of info about guided tours of this paradise for hikers or bikers, ranging from early-morning bird-watching jaunts to all-day canoeing, biking, and hiking triathlons.

Since Waren's primary attractions are nature-related, it's not suprising that restoration of the former *Altstadt* is not a top priority. The weather-beaten 14th-century **Altes Rathaus,** the crumbling **Speicher** (granary) that presides over the harbor, and the 290-year-old **Altes Schulhaus** (old schoolhouse), have all seen better days. Next door, the **Georgenkirche** lost its roof to fire in 1699 and received only a modest, flat replacement. The **Müritzmuseum Waren,** Friedenstr. 5 (tel. 37 42 or 43 67), houses a museum of natural history. More interesting for the tourist, however, is its **salt-water aquarium** and garden, on Herrenseebrücke, near the train station (open May-Sept. Tues.-Fri. 9am-6pm, Sat.-Sun. 9am-noon and 2-5pm; Oct.-April Tues.-Fri. 10am-4pm, Sat.-Sun. 10am-noon and 2-5pm; admission DM4, students DM2).

Waren Information, Neuer Markt 21 (tel. 66 43 92; fax 66 61 83), in the town square, has maps of the park, brochures, and a free room-finding service (rooms DM25-30). As well as offering tours in the park, they also lead guided tours (DM3, students DM2) through the town (Mon.-Tues., Wed., and Fri. at 10am). To get there from the **train station,** cross under the tracks to Schweriner Damm and walk left, then turn right on Friedenstr. and left on Langestr. (open Mon.-Fri. 10am-noon and 2-6pm, Sat 10am-noon and 1-4pm; winter Mon.-Fri. 10am-4pm). **Warener Schiffahrts-gesellschaft GmbH,** Kietzstr. 14a (tel./fax 47 57), and **Müritzwind Personenschif-fahrt,** Strandstr. (tel. 66 66 64, fax 66 58 79), both offer boat **tours** of the Müritz lake that vary in length from one to four hours (DM7-22, children half-price). **Bikes** can be rented at the train station (tel. 590) for DM10 to DM12 (open Mon.-Fri. 6am-10pm, Sat.-Sun. 8am-8pm). A **pharmacy** *(Löwenapotheke;* tel. 66 61 53) lives in the same building as the tourist office (open Mon.-Fri. 8am-6:30pm, Sat. 9am-noon). The **post**

office, Güstrower Str. 24, 17192 Waren, can be reached by turning right as you exit the train station and following the road along the tracks (open Mon.-Fri. 10am-noon and 2-6pm, Sat. 10am-noon and 1-4pm). The **telephone code** is 03991.

The **Jugendherberge (HI),** Auf dem Nesselberg 2 (tel. 22 61), dwells in the woods south of town. Cross under the tracks to Schweriner Damm, bear right at the fork in the road, and then walk along the harbor down the successive streets Zur Steinmole, Strandstr., Müritzstr., and Am Seeufer. When you reach the wooded hill on the left, head straight up the path (25min.). Or simply go 100m to the left as you leave the train station and take bus #3 from the Schweriner Damm (direction: Ecktannen) to "Wasserwerk." The 42 beds in barracks book quickly, but the hostel boasts a lovely location, and the friendly management will try to set up tents outside if they're full. (Reception open briefly at 9am, 3, 6, and 8pm. DM12.50, over 26 DM16. Lodgers must buy either breakfast (DM5.50) or dinner (DM6.50). Optional boxed lunches DM7. Open March-Nov.) There is regular camping at **Azur,** on Fontanestr. (tel. 26 07). Follow the directions to the youth hostel (above), but keep going on Am Seeufer until you reach Fontanestr. The **City Ristorante,** Friedenstr. 8 (tel. 66 87 03), offers big and small pizzas (DM5-12) and other dishes (open Mon.-Thurs. 10am-10pm, Fri.-Sun. 10am-11pm).

NEUBRANDENBURG

Poet Fritz Reufer referred to the city as "the pearl of the Mecklenburg realm," and maybe it once was. But after Allied bombers blew up the entire *Altstadt* in 1945, only the medieval wall around the city remained intact; now the fortified wall protects a city center crammed with socialist-style architecture. Ranked on UNESCO's list of international cultural treasures, the 2.3-km long medieval fortifications (*Wehranlage*) with four arched gates (*Tore*) are the landmarks of the town. Countless biking and hiking trails connect Neubrandenburg with the nearby lake **Tollensee,** making it a good base for exploration of the lake area.

The city center is bounded by Friedrich-Engels-Ring (old habits die hard), a huge traffic circle (on the outside), and the cobblestone Ringstr. following the wall on the inside. The best way to get a sense of the structure and its four main gates is to walk around—literally. Crossing Friedrich-Engels-Ring from the train station puts you at the foot of **Stargarderstr.,** the main north-south street; from here head in either direction around the ring. Turning right leads you to the 19m-high **Fangelturm,** a prison tower that looks like it came straight out of a Brothers Grimm tale. *Rapunzel, Rapunzel, let down your hair!* Turning left takes you to the **Friedländer Tor,** the city's oldest gate, now home to an art gallery. Keep an eye out for the 26 meticulously-maintained *Fachwerk* (half-timbered) houses built directly into the wall.

Keep heading around the wall and you'll pass the **Neues Tor** (521 years young) and the **Stargarder Tor,** whose facade is ornamented with nine female figures; nobody knows what they represent. The **Treptower Tor,** the tallest of the gates, is now home to the **Regionalmuseum Neubrandenburg** (tel. 582 29 06) and hosts exhibits on the town's archaeology (open Tues.-Fri. 9am-5pm, Sat. and Sun. 1-5pm; admission DM2, students DM1). The Gothic **Marienkirche,** in the southern part of town, has recuperated nicely from WWII damage but won't open to the public until spring 1997. Mecklenburg's oldest theater, the **Schauspielhaus,** Pfaffenstr. 22, is housed in two huge *Fachwerk* houses joined by an Art-Deco glass pavillion (call 544 26 17 for a schedule). Though the **Neubrandenburger Philharmonie** occasionally performs at the *Schauspielhaus,* its permanent home is the hideous **Haus der Kultur und Bildung,** on the *Marktplatz* (call 581 95 15 for listings). The **"Latücht" Kommunales Kino,** Gr. Krauthöfer Str. 16 (tel. 544 25 70), in the former Catholic church, puts on art-house movies.

Neubrandenburg is well-connected by **train** to Rostock (3hr.), Dresden (4½hr.), and Berlin (1½hr.). The friendly **tourist office,** Turmstr. 11, 17033 Neubrandenburg (tel. 19 43 31; fax 582 22 67), offers maps and a free room-finding service (rooms DM 25-40). To get there from Stargarderstr., take a left on Turmstr. before the *Kaufhof* department store (open April-Sept. Mon.-Fri. 9am-6pm, Sat. 9am-noon; Oct.-March

Mon.-Fri. 10am-5pm, Sat. 9am-noon). **Margaret Klimst,** Hufelandstr. 31 (tel. 737 32), runs a **Mitfahrzentrale** and offers rides to Berlin (DM15). Call ahead. You can rent a **bike** at the *Bahnhof* (DM10-12), although **Fahrradhaus Jürgen Leffin,** Friedrich-Engels-Ring 22 (tel. 36 75 30), offers slightly better deals. (Three-speed bikes DM8 per day. Mountain bikes DM10 per day. Open Mon.-Fri. 9am-6pm, Sat. 8:30am-noon.) The **Jugendzentrum,** Lindenstr. 12 (tel. 23 82), near Lake Tollensee, rents bikes starting at an unbelievable DM2 per day (open Mon.-Thurs. 8am-4pm, Fri. 8am-2pm). The **post office** is at Stargarderstr. 6, 17033 Neubrandenburg (open Mon.-Fri. 8am-6pm, Sat. 8am-noon). The **telephone code** is 0395.

The **Jugendherberge** is at Ihlenfelderstr. 73, 17034 Neubrandenburg (tel./fax 422 58 01), From the bus station that is adjacent to the train station, take bus #7 (direction: Trollenhagen or Monckeshof) to "Wolgasterstr." On weekends, take bus #5 (direction: Monckeshof) to "Ihlenfelderstr." By foot, go left on Friedrich-Engels-Ring and cross the bridge onto Demminerstr.; at the first intersection head right on Torgelowerstr. Ihlenfelderstr. will be the first left (25min.). It could use a fresh coat of paint but has clean beds and big breakfasts. (Reception open Mon.-Fri. 5-10pm, Sat.-Sun. 6-10pm. Curfew 10pm. DM18, over 26 DM21. Breakfast included. Sheets DM6.) The adorable little **Tor Café,** in front of the mighty Friedländer Tor, takes *Gemütlichkeit* to as-yet-unheard-of levels (meals DM8-15; open Mon.-Sat. 11am-midnight, Sun. 3pm-midnight). **Lake Tollensee** is only 20 minutes by foot outside the city wall, and a wonderful place to spend the afternoon tanning and swimming. To get there, walk through the Treptower Tor crossing the bridge.

GÜSTROW

Güstrow would be just like any other east German town were it not the permanent home of a huge collection of works by **Ernst Barlach,** one of Germany's most important 20th-century artists, whose figures spread their aura of eerie beauty throughout the town. Perhaps just as important as Barlach's contribution to modern sculpture was his fierce opposition to rising German nationalism and militarism. Güstrow is also the hometown of **Uwe Johnson,** the famous GDR author who was subjected to constant surveillance and eventually went into exile in 1959 for his "subversive" writings on the divisions between East and West. How this otherwise staunchly traditional outpost of the Dukes of Mecklenburg became the breeding ground of political division is a mystery —apparently when the nobles split in 1811, their influence left with them, though the *Schloß* wouldn't fit in their luggage.

The Barlach tour of Güstrow begins on the southwest side of town with the **Dom,** which houses Barlach's most famous work, *Der Schwebende Engel* (The Hovering Angel). Created as a testament to the horrors of war, it was originally designed to hang above the pews of the *Dom* but is now tucked away in a corner. The statue was originally cast in 1926, but was then publicly melted down and cast into bullets by the Nazis in 1941; the Nazis intended to show the futility of pacifism while defaming the dangerously popular artist. After World War II, a plaster cast of the statue was found buried in Western Germany, and in 1952, the angel was restored and rededicated to the war's victims. Once you've recovered from the impact of this work, check out the Renaissance sculptures by the altar: they depict Heinrich Borwin II, the *Dom* builder, and his wife, as well as to the pious-looking Herzog Ulrich (who renovated the *Dom*). All are shown with a meek, ascetic demeanor even though modesty didn't prevent them from scrawling the names of their ancestors on the wall (open Mon.-Sat. 10am-noon and 2-4pm, Sun. 1-5pm; tours Sat. at 2pm).

If you walk back to Domstr., you'll see the recently renovated **Schloß** up ahead. Hailed as the best example of Renaissance architecture in Northern Germany, it comes complete with a cute **Schloßgarten** surrounded by an ingenious shrub wall (gates and windows included). The **Schloßmuseum** (tel. 75 20) brims with Italian and Dutch paintings from the 15th to 17th centuries, which might be impressive in any other *Schloßmuseum* but are eclipsed by the brilliance of Barlach's works here (open April-Oct. Tues.-Sun. 10am-6pm; in winter 10am-5pm). What you won't see are traces of the transition camp (where anti-fascists were isolated and tortured) that was set up within the *Schloß* after 1933. On the east side of town, the **Gertrudenkapelle,** Gertrudenplatz 1 (tel. 68 30 01), houses an excellent collection of Barlachs in its lovely, octagonal white chapel and peaceful garden. From the station, walk down Eisenbahnstr. to take a right on Gertrudenstr. (open March-Oct. Tues.-Sun. 10am-5pm, Nov.-Feb. 11am-4pm; admission DM3, students DM2). The only church in town that doesn't contain any works by Barlach is the **Pfarrkirche St. Marien.** Sitting silently in the shadow of the *Dom,* the church is still one of the most artistically rich in the region. It displays an impressive, recently restored altarpiece from 1522: over 180 sculpted figures by Brussels artist Jan Borman narrate the Passion of Christ on the stage. Organ music can be heard on Wednesdays at 12:15pm (open Mon.-Sat. 10am-4pm, Sun. 2-4pm). Barlach's **Atelierhaus** (studio), Heidberg 15 (tel. 822 99), hosts the largest collection of his works in the very house in which they were created (open Tues.-Sun. 10am-5pm). It's a 50-minute walk form the *Altstadt,* so you may want to rent a bike. Head down Glevinerstr. from the *Marktplatz* and follow it as it turns into Planerstr. until you see the bike path signs for "Barlachweg"; follow this the path all the way around the lake until you reach the "Boots-Verleih," then head down to the parking lot on the left and cut up to Bükoner Chausee; the museum is 200m to the right. Bus #4a runs here very infrequently.

Güstrow Information, Domstr. 9 (tel. 68 10 23), finds rooms (DM20-30) for DM3 (open Mon.-Fri. 9am-6pm, Sat. 9:30am-1pm). The office offers guided city **tours** (DM4, students DM2) that leave from the *Rathaus* at 11am (June-Sept.). Rent a **bike** from the train station (DM10-12) to explore the eighty small lakes that lie within 20km of the town. Do laundry across the street at **SB Waschsalon,** Pferdemarkt 34. (Wash DM6 for 7kg. Dry DM2. Open 7am-10pm). The **post office,** Pferdemarkt 52-56, 18271 Güstrow, close to the *Markt,* is one of the loveliest in Germany (open Mon.-Fri. 8am-6pm, Sat. 9am-noon). The **telephone code** is 03843.

A brand-new **Jugendherberge,** at Heidberg 33, right around the corner from the Barlach Atelierhaus, was scheduled to open in Güstrow in February 1997 (that's the good news). It does not yet have a phone number, however, and it's about an hour walk from everything (that's the bad news). With the opening of the hostel, public transportation to this area of town should improve; ask at the tourist office for information when you arrive or simply enjoy the hour-long hike. **Cafe Küpper,** on Dom-str., boasts a 143-year history of serving up sweets, sandwiches, and (more recently) pizza for under DM7 (open Mon.-Fri. 8am-7pm, Sat. 11am-7pm, Sun. 1-7pm).

WISMAR

If you want to get a glimpse of what Germany looked like after World War II, go to Wismar. Unlike similar towns in other parts of the East which have been quickly spruced up for tourists, a great deal of reconstruction in Wismar has not yet begun. The *Marktplatz* and the immediately surrounding streets are fully restored, but just a few blocks away, the houses that survived the bombings stand shockingly high alongside their crumbled neighbors. Restoration is still underway at two of the town's once-grand cathedrals. Off the *Marktplatz* on Sargmeisterstr., the 80-m **Turm** (tower) of the **St. Marienkirche** is the only remaining shred of a beautiful 14th-century *Basilika* that was destroyed in World War II. The four clocks of the lovely tower still chime daily at noon, 3, and 7pm. The **St. Georgenkirche,** west of the St. Marien-turm, was the local church for craftsmen and traders. Restoration is now progressing at snail's pace. The **Nikolaikirche,** nearer the port, with its disproportionately small tower (the original was destroyed in a 1703 hurricane), gives a hint as to what Wismar's churches must have once looked like. Its interior contains one of the oldest organs in Mecklenburg (open Mon.-Sat. 1-6pm). Information available in English and just about every other language). Closer to the *Marktplatz,* the **Heilige Geist Kirche,** Wismar's other intact church, also contains medieval art (open Mon.-Sat. 10am-noon and 2-4pm, Sun. 11am-noon and 2-4pm).

The *Marktplatz* itself boasts a slightly dizzying juxtaposition of architectural styles. The fortress-like **Rathaus,** stemming from the 14th century, was rebuilt in 19th-century Neoclassical style after its roof collapsed in 1807 and destroyed most of the original building. On the east side of the Marktplatz stands the **Alter Schwede;** built around 1380, it is Wismar's oldest Bürgerhaus (citizen's house). Across the square is the elaborate 16th-century Dutch Renaissance pavillion known as the **Wasserkujst,** which regulated the town's water until the beginning of this century. Heading back towards the Nikolaikirche, the **Heimatsmuseum Schaffelhaus** psychoanalyzes the region's colorful past as well as the church tower's castration complex (open Tues.-Sun. 10am-8pm, admission DM2, students DM1).

Frequent **trains** connect Wismar to Schwerin and Rostock. From the train station, follow Bahnhofsallee right, make a left on Am Poeler Tor, and follow it up past the Nikolaikirche to reach the *Marktplatz.* The busy **tourist office,** Stadthaus am Markt 11 (tel. /fax 28 29 58) has helpful brochures and maps (some in English) and finds rooms (DM25-40) for a DM5 fee. Call ahead (open daily 9am-6pm). For a bite to eat, head to **Das Kittchen** (prison, in slang), Vor dem Fürstenhof 3 (tel. 259 43 20). It's decorated with cheerfully black humor in a jailhouse motif. Enjoy the *Sauerfleisch Knastfrüder* (prisoners' pickled meat; DM11) while waiting for your parole (open Mon.-Sat. from 5pm, Sun. from 10am. Meals DM6-12, discounts available if you have a criminal record). The **post office,** Mecklenburgerstr.18, 23966, is around the corner from the *Marktplatz.* The **telephone city code** is 03841. The nearest beach to Wismar is on the small island of **Poel.** Catch a bus from Gerberstr. (30min.; DM4).

■ Rostock

East German schoolchildren were always taught to think of Rostock, the largest and most active port of eastern Germany, as socialist Germany's "gateway to the world." This red-bricked Hanseatic trading town has always had a rocky history, but after reunification, Rostock's booming business declined as industrial ships began to shift their home harbors to Hamburg. Then, five years ago an event occurred that would change the way the world viewed the city forever. On August 24, 1992, a hostel for foreigners seeking political asylum in Germany was attacked and set ablaze by neo-Nazis and other right-wing youths. The tension caused by an immigratory flood finally caused the dam to break here in Rostock. "The chanting was filmed and syndicated abroad… There were no distractions this time, not Kabul, not Sarajevo. ROSTOCK it said in big letters wherever you looked," wrote Günter Grass.

As far as the events of 1992 are concerned, today most Rostock natives would like to place them in the past; many walls spray-painted with swastikas also carry the more comforting message, *"Nazis raus!"* ("Nazis out!"), added by a later hand. Both psychologically and physically, the people here have made an effort to move on. Reconstruction and restoration work can be seen in most quarters of the *Altstadt* and the number of tourists flocking to the beaches is once again high. Indeed, what happened in 1992 should not discourage you from a visit to Rostock, but rather leave you aware of continuing problems in the new Germany. You might come to see the old church towers, or pass through on your way to Scandinavia; whatever the case may be, recall Grass's words, "since Rostock, Germany has changed."

ORIENTATION AND PRACTICAL INFORMATION

The majority of Rostock's sights lie in the downtown area, with the exception of **Warnemünde,** a peaceful fishing village and resort town to the northwest of the city center. If you are going to spend a night in Rostock, it will be impossible to avoid the newer city suburbs, which consist of huge brick-and-concrete apartment blocks linked by long, wide roads. These areas are not well-lit, and their residents have been known to be hostile and aggressive toward foreigners. **Single travelers, particularly women, should avoid these areas at night.** Rostock is well-served by an extensive network of S-Bahn trains, buses, and trams; they run less frequently during the late hours and at night, so check schedules before you set out. Rostock is also a regional transportation hub.

Tourist Office: Schnickmannstr. 13/14, 18055 Rostock (tel. 49 79 90 or 194 33; fax 497 99 23). Take streetcar #11 or 12 (from the main station to "Langestr."), then follow the signs to the right. **Room service** finds rooms for a DM5 fee (free if you call in advance). They also lead 1½-hr. **tours** through the town (May-June and Sept. Wed. and Fri.-Sun. at 2pm). Open May-Sept. Mon.-Fri. 10am-6pm, Sat.-Sun. 10am-2:30pm; Oct.-April Mon.-Fri. 9am-6pm, Sat. 10am-4pm. There is also an office in **Warnemünde,** Heinrich-Heine-Str. 17 (tel. 511 42). Walk across the bridge from the train station, cross Kirchenplatz, and turn right on Heinrich Heine Str. Open Mon.-Fri. 10am-5pm, Sat. 10am-noon.; Sept.-June 10am-4pm.

Currency Exchange: Citibank, on Kropelinerstr. near Universitätsplatz, charges a 1% fee for exchanging cash. ATM open 24hr. Bank open Mon. and Wed. 9am-1pm and 2-4:45pm, Tues. and Thurs. 9am-1pm and 2-6pm, Fri. 9am-1pm.

Trains: Hourly connections to Schwerin (1hr.), Stralsund (1½hr.), and Wismar (1¼hr.). Daily connections to Berlin (2½hr.), Hamburg (3hr.), and Dresden (7½hr.). Call 493 44 54 for information.

Public Transportation: Streetcars #11 and 12 shuttle from the main station to the *Altstadt.* Single ticket DM2. *Tageskarte* (combined 1-day ticket) for streetcar, bus, and S-Bahn DM7.50. The **S-Bahn** leaves from the main station for Warnemünde and the newer suburbs every 15min. To get to the bus station for lines to smaller towns, exit the station through the Südstadt exit.

Ferries: Boats for **Scandinavia** leave from the **Überseehafen** docks. **TT-Linie,** Hansakai (tel. 67 07 90; fax 670 79 80) runs to Trelleborg, Sweden (2 per day, 5hr.; one-way DM50, students DM33, children DM22). **Europa-Linie GT link** (tel. 670 06 67; fax 670 06 71) sails to Gedser, Denmark (5 per day, 2hr., one-way DM8, children DM4). Ferries also leave from the **Warnemünde** docks; the Deutsche Bahn's **Fahrverkehrsgesellschaft Ostsee,** (tel. 514 06; fax 514 09) sails to Gedser, Denmark, with special trips to other Scandinavian ports (8 per day; one-way DM10-16, children DM5-8; round-trip DM20-32, children DM10-16).

Mitfahrzentrale: Mitfahrzentrale Rostock, Am Kabutzenhof 21 (tel. 493 44 38) matches riders and drivers. Open, generally 10am-4pm, but calling is advisable. Prices start at 6pf per kilometer.

Bike Rental: Fahrradverleih Strandläufer, in the Inter-City Hotel (tel. 45 28 27), next to the train station. DM10 per day, DM7.50 per day if five or more days. ID required. Open Mon.-Fri. 9am-6pm.

Women's Hotline: Frauen in Not, Kinderkrippe Lichtenhagen, E. Warnkestr. 10 (tel. 711 167).

Pharmacy: Rats-Apotheke, Neuer Markt 13 (tel. 493 47 47), posts a list of 24-hr. pharmacies. Open Mon.-Fri. 9am-6pm, Sat. 9am-1pm.

Emergency: Ambulance: tel. 115. **Police:** tel. 110. **Fire:** tel. 112.

Post Office: *Hauptpostamt,* Neuer Markt, 18055 Rostock. *Postlagernde Briefe* at counter 8. Open Mon.-Fri. 8am-6pm, Sat. 8am-noon.

Telephone Code: 0381.

ACCOMMODATIONS

Rostock currently has three youth hostels, but one of them will be closing in the near future; call ahead. Please note: the Jugendgästeschiff is located in the suburbs—women and single travelers may not feel comfortable **walking there at night** and will probably want to stay at Rostock-Warnemünde. Private rooms cost only a bit more than hostel accommodations, particularly for those over 26.

Jugendherberge Rostock-Warnemünde (HI), Parkstr. 31 and 46 (tel. 523 03). Two youth hostels with common management and telephone number. **The one on Parkstr. 31 will close sometime in 1997.** Take the S-Bahn (direction: Warnemünde) to the end, cross the bridge, and head straight on Kirchenstr. which becomes Mühlenstr. and then Parkstr. (20-25min.). To avoid the walk, take the S-Bahn to "Lichtenhagen" and then bus #36 (direction: Warnemünde-Strand) to "Haus Stoleraa"; the bus lets you off directly in front of Parkstr. 31. The Parkstr. 46 hostel is brand-new and more spacious than its older sister; the proprietor will do whatever she can to keep travelers happy. Reception open 2-9pm. DM19.50, over 26 DM23. Breakfast and resort tax included. Sheets DM5.

Jugendgästeschiff Rostock-Schmarl, a hostel that has taken over a great old ship in the harbor (tel. 71 62 24; fax 71 40 14), is reached from the main station by the S-Bahn (direction: Warnemünde) to "Lütten Klein." Head right out of the S-Bahn station, follow Warnowallee past the Kolumbusring housing complex, and go down toward the harbor and around to the left; the hostel is docked (docked!) at the end of the road. The walk takes 25min. The bus runs infrequently at night, when you need it most. Women and lone travelers may feel more comfortable at Warnemünde. DM20, over 26 DM25, including sheets. Breakfast DM6.

FOOD AND NIGHTLIFE

It's hard to find good restaurants with reasonable prices in Rostock, but there's plenty of decent food-on-the-run available at the numerous *Imbiß* booths on Kröpelinerstr. and Universitätsplatz. **Supermarket Spar,** on Kröpeliner Str., near the Kröpeliner Tor, offers a sizeable selection (open Mon.-Wed., Fri. 8am-6pm, Thurs. 8am-8pm, Sat. 8am-1pm). In Warnemünde, several restaurants along the beach proffer up the bounties of the ocean. If you're trying to stay financially afloat, try the fast food joints on Kirchplatz. Watch for the fish market on weekends.

Mensa, on the corner of Südring and Albert Einstein Str. From the train station or the *Altstadt,* take tram #11 (direction: Neuer Friedhof) to the end and change to bus #27 (direction: Biestow) or #39 (direction: Stadthalle/ZOB) to "Mensa" (one stop). Generous helpings of good food. Students with ID DM2-4, others DM4-6. Come early to avoid long lines. Open Mon.-Fri. 11:15pm-2pm. Downstairs there's a cheap **café,** and what according to students is the best **disco** in Rostock. Open Thurs.-Sun. after 10pm. Cover DM5 and up. The **Filmclub** shows movies every Tues. and Wed. at 9pm. Admission DM2. Call 459 12 48 for the program.

Studentenkeller, Universitätsplatz (tel. 45 59 28). This backyard café attracts a lively student crowd. Walk into the *Universitäts Bibliothek,* across from the fountain. Open daily 8:45am-5:30pm. After dark, hang out in the bar, where there's live music. Open daily 9pm-1 or 2am. Cover DM5, Sat.-Sun. DM6, students DM3.

Krahnstövers Kneipe, Große Wasserstr. 30 (tel. 72 52 54), just east of the *Neuer Markt.* A friendly, high-spirited bar and wood-paneled restaurant that serves alcoholic concoctions in the form of *Suppen* (soups). Waiter, there's a screwdriver in my soup. Taste wines from the adjacent cellar. Open Tues.-Sat. 5pm-2am.

In Warnemünde:
Seehund Warnemünde, Am Strom 110 (tel. 511 93), is a cheerful and relatively cheap oasis of drinks built organically into the promenade of the *Alter Strom* (you can tread its roof on the upper road). Open daily 10am-2am or later.

Café 28, Mühlenstr. 28 (tel. 524 67), on the way to the youth hostel, is a shiny, happy hangout. Soups, salads, and small but tasty dishes run DM4-20. Vodka and coffee served. Open May-Oct. Mon.-Fri. 9am-2am, Sat.-Sun. 10am-2am.

SIGHTS AND ENTERTAINMENT

In the 12th century, Rostock's Baltic harbor made it a proud Hanseatic League member, and relics of its mercantile past still stand. Although half of the city was destroyed in World War II, many of the half-timbered and glazed-brick houses and Gothic churches have been restored. **Kröpeliner Straße,** the main pedestrian mall, lined with 16th-century *Bürger* houses, runs east to the **Kröpeliner Tor,** the former town gate. The main buildings of the **Universität Rostock,** one of the oldest universities in North Central Europe, are just a bit farther down Kröpeliner Str. Next to the university, along the remains of the city wall, sits the **Kloster zum Heiligen Kreuz,** a restored cloister originally built by the Danish Queen Margaret in 1270. The museum contains medieval art, sculptures by the omnipresent Ernst Barlach, and special exhibits (open Tues.-Sun. 10am-6pm; admission DM4, students DM2).

The greatest architectural landmark in Rostock is the 13th-century **Marienkirche,** a monster of a brick basilica near the main square, at the end of Kröpliner Str. (open Tues.-Sat. 10am-5pm, Sun. 11am-noon). In the final days of the revolution of 1989, the services here overflowed with political protesters who had come to hear the inspiring sermons of Pastor Joachim Gauck. In one of the more heroic gestures of the revolution, Pastor Gauck began to publicly chastise the secret police by calling out the names of those *Stasi* members whom he could identify from the pulpit; after reunification, Gauck was entrusted with the difficult job of overseeing the fate of the *Stasi* archives. The church features a richly-ornamented Baroque organ that covers the entire west wall, a finely-sculpted Renaissance pulpit crafted by the 16th-century Antwerp master Rudolf Stockmann, and a massive bronze baptismal font consecrated in 1290. The 12-m **astronomical clock** behind the altar dates from 1472. At noon and midnight, mechanical apostles strut out in a circular procession.

Rostock's Renaissance **Rathaus,** a strawberry-pink eyesore on *Neuer Markt,* was originally composed of three separate *Bürger* houses visually united by a Gothic wall with seven towers; elaborate detailing can still be seen above some of the portals. The **Steintor, Kuhtor,** and **Lagesbuschturm** are all in close proximity to Steinstr. and are connected by remnants of the recently renovated town wall. The **Alter Markt,** Rostock's commercial center before the war, now buzzes with the sounds of machinery; the area is in the midst of extensive restoration. The **Petrikirche** hides beautifully-restored medieval art and a set of bright stained-glass windows (open Tues.-Sat. 10am-noon and 2-4pm, Sun. 11am-4pm; tower admission DM2). South on Altschriedestr., Rostock's oldest church, the **Nikolaikirche,** Rennbahnalle 21, reveals its newly uncovered murals. In a subversively secular move worthy of the GDR, the altar has been removed to make way for a café (open Wed.-Sun. 1-5pm). The church is slightly west of the *Mensa;* take streetcar #11 or bus #39. Rostock's **Zoo** deserves the adoration of the 800,000 visitors who pilgrimage here annually; animals include polar bears, elephants, and other biggies (open daily 9am-5pm, Oct.-March 9am-4pm; admission DM7, students DM5, children DM4). The **Schiffahrtmuseum der Hansestadt,** August-Bebel-Str. 1 (tel. 492 26 97), tells tales of wild seafaring along the rocky Baltic coast (open Sat.-Thurs. 9am-5pm; admission DM2).

Rostock was once home to one of northern Germany's largest Jewish communities (see below). The town's synagogue was destroyed on *Kristallnacht* and the Jewish community was annihilated soon afterwards. But the **Jewish cemetery** still stands—in a way. The cemetery was only partially damaged during the war; in the 1970s, the government decided to embed the gravestones face-down into the earth in order to create the city's **Lindenpark.** The international Jewish community put pressure on, however, and most of the stones were finally put back up in 1988 to mark the 50th anniversary of *Kristallnacht.* A memorial in the shape of a menorah was also erected. The cemetery is at the southern end of the Lindenpark. Take tram #1, 3, or 11 to "Saarplatz," then head south through the park for five minutes. The sign outside claims that Rostock began renovating the cemetery in 1945 but didn't complete the work until 1988—with no mention of the detour along the way.

The Jews of Mecklenburg-Vorpommern

Conspicuously absent from the tourist literature and state history museums, the Jews were an important part of Mecklenburg-Vorpommern's past. They arrived in the region in 1266, settling mostly in the larger cities and towns. When pogroms occurred in Güstrow and Wismar in 1325, however, and 27 Jews were burned at the stake in the small town of Sternberg in 1492, their fortunes quickly took a turn for the worse. Jews were expelled from Mecklenburg-Vorpommern for the next 200 years. After the Thirty Years War, Duke Christian Ludwig I allowed them back in, but they continued to be viciously persecuted. Ironically, Rostock, which did not allow Jews to take up residence until 1869, later had the largest Jewish community in the region—this is evidenced by the fact that many American and European Jews still carry the last name "Rostock" today.

Warnemünde, officially a part of Rostock since 1323, combines fishing village and spa resort in a way perhaps only a north German town could. Fortunately, with the beach's monumentally ugly Hotel Neptune as an exception, the village was spared both Communist and post-Communist development. The crystal-clear, swimmable water and tranquil beaches provide ample reason to stroll along the promenade or just relax in the sun after the rigors of sight-seeing. The **Alter Strom** (old harbor), across the wooden bridge from the train station, teems with small, colorful boats offering fresh fish and tours. Along the *Alter Strom* toward the sea stands a **watch tower** whose middle platform is accessible during the day (DM3). For a comprehensive survey of those tiny, colorful *Pfister* houses, visit Warnemünde's **Heimatmuseum,** at Alexandrinerstr. 31, just off the Kirchenplatz (open Wed.-Sun. 9am-12:30pm and 1-5pm; admission DM3, students DM1.50).

▓ Stralsund

Albrecht von Wallenstein, commander of the Catholic army during the Thirty Years War, lusted after Stralsund. "Even if it were chained to heaven, I'd want to have it," he panted, but Stralsund resisted his advances. The beauty that seduced Wallenstein is now unfortunately obscured somewhat by dust and rubble, and as in so many eastern German medieval towns, restoration work is far from complete. But even though it may be crumbling around the edges, the once-spectacular architecture is still a poignant testimony to Stralsund's former wealth. As a free city, Stralsund helped to found the Hanseatic League in 1293, and quickly asserted itself as a trading hub and ship building center. Sweden ruled the town for two centuries after the Thirty Years War, leaving permanent Scandinavian traces behind. Today the key to Stralsund's charm is its unique geography; the hill of the *Altstadt* is bordered to the south and west by two natural ponds and slopes gently north toward the *Strelasund,* the sound that separates the mainland from Rügen Island.

ORIENTATION AND PRACTICAL INFORMATION

Stralsund is directly connected by trains to Rostock (1 per hr.), and to Binz and Bergen on Rügen; trains also leave several times daily for Hamburg and Berlin. The major sights and attractions are concentrated in the *Altstadt,* where the distinctive spires of the city's three churches make excellent navigational beacons. **Ossenreyerstraße** is the main pedestrian zone; it runs north-south and encompasses a department store, supermarkets, and bakeries. Two of the city's former gates, the **Kutertor** and the **Kniepertor,** sit to the west and north, respectively. If you are planning on going to Rügen Island, **Der Touristen Paß** (The Tourist Pass), which covers entry fees for all local museums, ferry trips, and select stretches of railroad on Rügen (DM21, children DM10.50), is a wise investment.

Tourist Office: Ossenreyerstr. 1/2 (tel. 246 90; fax 24 69 49). From the train station, head straight on Jungfernstieg (not marked), turning right on Küterdamm to transverse Knieper Teich, continue straight through the Kütertor, and turn left on Ossenreyerstr. Or take bus #4 or 5 to "Kütertor." The office distributes free maps (in English) and finds private rooms (DM25-100) for a DM5 fee. Sells tickets for **tours** through the *Altstadt* (DM7). Open Mon-Fri. 9am-6:30pm, Sat.-Sun. 9am-1pm; Oct.-May Mon.-Fri. 10am-5pm, Sat. 10am-1pm. The office in the **train station** (tel. 29 38 94) books rooms exclusively (DM5 fee). Open daily 10am-8pm.

Currency Exchange: Volksbank, across from the *Rathaus,* has good rates as well as an automatic teller. Open Mon. 8am-1pm and 2-4pm, Tues. and Thurs. 8am-noon and 2-6pm, Wed. and Fri. 8am-1pm.

Public Transportation: Bus lines #1-6 circle the *Altstadt,* serving the outskirts of town. Single fare DM2. The central **bus station** at Frankenwall is the departure point for **intercity buses** to Rügen and other surrounding areas (although trains are usually cheaper); check the **information desk** at the train station.

Ferries: Water tours of the harbor and the Strelasund depart daily from the dock
behind the conspicuously floating hotel (1hr.; DM6, children DM5). **Reederei
Hiddensee** (tel. 28 81 16) runs 3 times per day to the ports of Kloster, Vitte, and
Neuendorf on Hiddensee (round-trip DM22-26, children DM12, bikes DM10) and
to Schaprode on Rügen's west coast (DM3, children DM1.50).

Bike Rental: In the train station. DM11-13 per day. Technically open Mon.-Fri. 6am-
9pm, Sat. 7am-2:30pm, Sun. 9am-4:30pm., but you may need to ask at the tourist
office in order to track somebody down.

Pharmacy: Bahnhofsapotheke, Tribseer Damm 6 (tel. 29 23 28), across from the
train station.

Emergency: Ambulance: tel. 115. **Police:** tel. 110. **Fire:** tel. 112.

Post Office: Main Office, Neuer Markt, 18439 Stralsund, in the red-brick building
opposite the Marienkirche. Open Mon.-Fri. 9am-6pm, Sat. 9am-noon. There's also a
branch office next to the **train station.** Open Mon.-Fri. 9am-noon and 2-4pm, Sat.
9am-noon.

Telephone Code: 03831.

ACCOMMODATIONS

Jugendherberge Stralsund (HI), Am Kütertor 1 (tel. 29 21 60; fax 29 76 76). From
the station, turn right onto Tribseer Damm and go straight to the "Hauptbahnhof"
bus stop. Take bus #4 or 5 to "Küter Tor" (the 2nd stop), then turn right and take
the first left onto Heilgeiststr.; the hostel is just before the big gate on the left. By
foot, it's a gorgeous 10-min. walk from the *Bahnhof*. Follow the directions to the
tourist office (above), but stop at Küter Tor. Located in an old town hall with a
courtyard, the hostel is convenient, but watch those strange angles and low ceilings. Many school groups in summer. Reception open 7-9am and 3-10pm. Lockout
9am-3pm. Curfew 10pm, but you can ring the bell until 1am. DM18.50, over 26
DM22.50. Sheets DM6. Buffet breakfast included. Closed Dec.15-Jan.15.

Jugendherberge Stralsund-Devin (HI), Strandstr. 21 (tel. 27 03 58). From the station, take us #4 or 5 to "Devin" (25min.; DM2.80), then walk straight into the
woods; turn right at the café and left when you hit Strandstr. (5min.). Located in
the nearby village of Devin, this place is bigger and more modern than the Stralsund hostel but harder to reach. The 20 buildings are close to the beach, and
they're sometimes generous even when "full." Reception open 3-8pm. Curfew
10pm. DM18.50, over 26 DM22.50. Breakfast included. Open March-Oct.

FOOD

Most of Stralsund's restaurants and cafés are located in the city center near the main
squares. The cheapest offerings are the numerous snack bars operating out of little
trailers all over town. Try **"Teddybär,"** in the pedestrian zone, for German fast food
(open daily 8am-6pm). Stock up on goods at the super cheap **Spar** supermarket, on
Ossenreyerstr. (open Mon.-Fri. 8am-6pm, Sat. 9am-noon).

Al Porto, Seestr. 4 (tel. 28 06 20), right on the harbor in a freshly painted white
building with bright blue trim. Serves the usual pizza, pasta, and salad plates, with
a slight seaside twist (DM8-16). Raviolifish? Open daily 11am-11pm.

Zur Kogge, Tribseerstr. 26 (tel. 29 38 46). Fish and matching maritime interior-
decor. Chairfish? Open Mon.-Sat. 11am-2:30pm and 5:30pm-midnight.

Café Lütt, Alter Markt 12 (tel. 29 23 48), serves brightly-iced little cakes (DM3-5),
including some Northern German rarities. Cakefish? Open daily 9am-6pm.

Stadtbäckerei und Café, Ossenreyerstr. 43 (tel. 29 40 82). A cheap place to
indulge in *Kaffee und Kuchen*. Fish coffee? Open Mon.- Fri. 7am-6pm, Sat. 8am-
5pm, Sun. 1-5pm.

SIGHTS

Stralsund's compact *Altstadt* island is unpolluted by GDR-era architecture. The **Alter
Markt,** to the north, is surrounded by several of the town's oldest buildings. The
spectacular 14th-century red-brick façade of the Gothic **Rathaus** displays the coats-of-

arms of the other major players in the Hanseatic League, such as Rostock and Hamburg, as well as Stralsund's trademark green and gold 12-point stars. The courtyard was designed in 1680 after a devastating fire precipitated the decision to transform this former warehouse into the town hall. The interior is closed to visitors, but you can get a glimpse of it from the outside.

Behind the *Rathaus,* the two massive red-brick towers of the **St. Nikolaikirche** recall the church's troubled history. In 1270 the church was torn down and rebuilt in French Gothic style after the model of Lübeck's *Marienkirche.* After a fire in 1662, one of the towers received a sophisticated Baroque dome. The nave and transept have been entirely restored, while the chapels and frescoes are still undergoing construction. The astronomical clock was restored for its 600th anniversary in 1994 (open Tues.-Fri. 10am-5pm, Sat. 10am-4pm, Sun. 2-4pm; services Sun. at 10am). From the *Alter Markt,* stroll along the Fährstr. with its Gothic and Baroque buildings, including the **Scheele-Haus,** home to an expensive restaurant. On the other side of the *Markt,* the "newer" **Mönchstraße, Muhlenstraße,** and **Papenstraße** feature Renaissance architecture undergoing serious restoration—most of these streets are seriously dilapidated and temporarily closed to all but construction vehicles.

From the *Alter Markt,* **Ossenreyerstraße** (turn right at the end) takes you to the lovely **Neuer Markt** (new market) and the Gothic **Marienkirche,** with its 104-m tower, where an awesome Baroque organ built in 1659 by the master Stellwagen of Hamburg orgles Fri.-Wed. at 11am. Keep an eye out for occasional concerts (usually every other Wed. at 8pm; admission DM7, students DM5). A window into the **Grabskapelle** (chapel grave) gives you a creepy glimpse at the coffins (open Mon.-Sat. 10am-5pm, Sun. 11am-5pm, services Sun. 10am). In front of the church is an odd remnant of the Communist era: an exaggerated monument lauding the **Soviet Army.** The third of Stralsund's monumental churches, the **St. Jakobi,** on Böttcherstr., was heavily damaged in 1944 and is currently being restored.

Between the *Alter* and *Neuer Markt,* Stralsund's two major museums have replaced the monks in the adjoining buildings of the **St. Katharinen Monastery.** The seaweed is green at the **Oceanographic Museum,** Katharinenberg 15 (tel. 29 51 35), which explores marine biology. Foreign and domestic fish, turtles, and corals stare out of tanks—well, not the coral. Next door at the **Kulturhistorisches Museum** (tel. 29 51 35), you can see some beautiful old photographs and paintings of Stralsund when it was in better shape. (Both museums open Mon.-Thurs. 9am-6pm, Fri.-Sun. 10am-5pm; Sept.-April daily 10am-5pm; admission DM7, students DM3.50).

A stroll along the **Sundpromenade** at sunset reveals a glowing red Rügen across the bay. Another beautiful walk runs along **Knieperwall,** alongside the **Knieperteich** (pond) and the remains of the **town wall.** The gates **Kniepertor** and **Kütertor** date back to the 13th century. An alternate route from the *Alter Markt* follows Külpstr. to Schillstr. to end at the **Johanniskloster,** a Franciscan monastery built in 1254—45 years after Francis of Assisi founded the order. Nestled down by the harbor, the monastery is a glory of Gothic hallways, 14th-century mosaics, murals (rescued from 30 layers of peeling paint), roses, and red-brick walls. The former **Johanniskirche,** ruined in 1944, now hosts occasional open-air concerts. The quiet courtyard (usually locked, but they'll open it if you ask) contains a dramatic Ernst Barlach *pietà,* as well as a **memorial** to Stralsund's lost Jewish community. The sculpture used to sit on the Apollonienmarket, near the former site of the synagogue, but was placed in the cloister for safe-keeping after it was vandalized by neo-Nazis in 1992; graffiti marks still remain. (Open Tues.-Sun. 10am-6pm. Admission DM3, students DM2, including a tour that tells you neat stuff. Free last Wed. of every month.)

■ Rügen Island (Insel Rügen)

Bathing in the Baltic Sea northeast of Stralsund, Germany's largest island wears an intricate mantle of 597km of beautiful coastline. The island's wildly varied landscape offers white beaches, rugged chalk cliffs, farmland, beech forests, heaths, and swamps. But Rügen is not all unsettled wilds; the island has a long and occasionally tumultuous history. Stone Age ruins and megalithic graves (easily identified piles of big stones) are scattered about like enormous paperweights. Teutonic tribes were pushed out by Slavs during 5th-century migrations; 500 years later, the rule of the pagan Slavs was broken by invading Danes, who bestowed the joys of Christianity upon the not-so-eager Slavs. In the 19th century, the island was discovered by the nobility and transformed into a resort stacked with expensive Neoclassical buildings that are now showing their age after decades of neglect.

The most striking architectural achievement of the island is understandably under-stated in the official tourist literature. An important part of Hitler's racial purification plan was the **Kraft durch Freude** (*KdF;* strength through joy) initiative, intended to cultivate healthy, happy Aryans for the new Germany. As part of this plan, the Nazi authorities designed a 3.5km complex of interconnected five-story buildings at **Prora** (5km north of Binz) that were intended to provide seaside lodging for 20,000 German workers at the negligible cost of three *Reichsmarks* per day. After the war, the nearly-finished complex fell into the hands of the GDR, which intended to dynamite the whole thing. But after two unsuccessful attempts at demolition (whose skeletal legacies still stand), the durability of the armored-concrete walls proved stronger than the will of East German authorities to purge the past. The buildings lodged the military until 1989. Except for a hotel, a youth hostel (see p. 540), a *Kindergärten,* and a few cafés, the mile-long hallways are now empty.

Today the tourist industry in Rügen is treading water. Once the prime vacation spot for East Germans, the island is suffering now that they are free to travel to more exotic destinations. Still, summer months are busy. We strongly recommend that you book a room in advance by phone or by writing ahead to any of the tourist offices or hostels on the island; be sure to specify how many people you need lodging for, how long you want to stay, and what you're willing to pay. If you don't speak German, write in English. For groups of three or more (sometimes even couples), a *Ferien-wohnung* (vacation apartment) can be a surprisingly practical option (DM20-30 per person). There are only two youth hostels, one in **Prora** and the other in **Binz,** and the latter is almost constantly booked by groups. Take your camping gear and you'll be safe; campgrounds pepper Rügen. A handy helper is the map *Wander und Freizeitkarte von Rügen und Hiddensee* (DM9.90) which includes hiking trails, campgrounds, and sights—you can pick it up at any bookstore. Many tourist offices provide a free brochure of the island's campgrounds as well.

Rügen is so close to Stralsund's coast that you could almost swim there; since **trains** leave hourly for Bergen, Binz, and Saßnitz, however, you can probably leave your water wings at home. It's only an hour from Stralsund to Saßnitz, which makes daytrips feasible, especially if the hostels on Rügen are booked. **Buses** connect Stralsund with Rügen's largest towns, and a **ferry** runs to Schaprode, near Hiddensee, on Rügen's west coast. Major towns on the island include **Bergen** in the center, **Patbus, Binz,** and **Göhren** in the south, and **Saßnitz** in the north.

Once on the island, public transportation gets to be little tricky—most visitors come with cars. The *Deutsche Bahn* connects Bergen with Binz and Prora, with Saßnitz, and with Putbus and Lauterbach. To get to Kap Arkona in the north or Göhren in the south, however, you'll have to take the bus (which runs somewhat infrequently); check schedules carefully, and make sure you know when the last bus leaves, or you'll be stuck. The **Rasender Roland,** a narrow-gauge rail line, runs from Putbus to Göhren with stops in many spa towns—unfortunately, the railway is more of a tourist attraction than a means of practical transportation. Although the island is large, the major points of interest generally lie no more than 20km from one another. The best way to get around is by combining the train and buses with walking, hiking, and biking. **Trails** are well-marked and cover the entire island.

BERGEN

You may be wondering why the capital of a beautiful island full of beach towns is a landlocked city. We don't know either. Bergen doesn't offer much in the way of nat-ural beauty, but it is a transportation hub that you will inevitably pass through at some point. Bergen tends to be less touristed than the rest of the island, so if every other place you try is full, chances are you might be able to find a private room here; it's only a half-hour train or bus ride to Binz or Saßnitz. Even if you're not planning on spending the night, there are still good ways to kill time before the next train.

The **Marienkirche,** a Romanesque basilica built around 1200, is Rügen's oldest building. Its interior is covered with beautifully faded frescoes of Biblical scenes and adorned with vaulted ceilings and stone floors. The church harbors a 700-year-old diamond-covered chalice *(Kelch)* which is not ordinarily on display. (Open May-Sept. daily 9am-6pm; April and Oct. daily 10-11am and 2-3pm. Closed in winter. To arrange a tour, call 231 00.). See a picture of the grail-like chalice and an exhibit documenting the history of Christianity on the island, in the tiny **Städtmuseum Bergen,** behind the church (open Mon.-Sat. 10am-12:30pm and 1-4:30pm; admission DM2, students DM1). On the hillside stands the **Ernst-Moritz-Arndt-Turm,** containing a memorial to the 19th-century writer and revolutionary (open May-Oct. daily 10am-6pm; in winter daily 10am-5pm; admission DM2, children DM1). To get there, head left from the *Marktplatz* until you reach the woods, and follow the signs (15min.).

Trains and **buses** run every hour from Bergen to Binz and Saßnitz and about every two hours to Putbus. The friendly **tourist office,** Markt 11 (tel. 81 12 06), in the *Rathaus,* finds private rooms (DM25-35) free of charge. To get there, take a left from the station to head up on Bahnhofstr., then take a left onto the *Markt* (open June-Oct. Mon.-Fri. 10am-8pm, Sat. 10am-2pm; winter Mon.-Fri. 10am-6pm). **Bike rental** at the station costs DM10-12 per day (open daily 5am-8:30pm). The **Rügard Apotheke,** Markt 26 (tel. 220 12), is a **pharmacy** with a 24-hour emergency bell outside (open Mon.-Fri. 8am-6:30pm, Sat. 8am-noon). **Rügenscher Hof,** Bahnhofstr. 5 (tel. 228 34), serves reasonably priced meals starting at DM7.80 (open Mon.-Sat. 7am-11pm). For light meals and cake, try **Café Meyer,** on the corner of Bahnhofstr. and Dammstr. (tel. 223 32; open Mon.-Fri. 9am-6pm, Sat.-Sun. 2-6pm). Slightly north of Bergen in the small town of **Ralswick,** a huge open-air theater hosts the yearly **Störtebeker Festspiele** (end of July-late-Aug.), a big theatrical production loaded with special effects that tells the tale of the *Seeräuber* Klaus Störtebeker, a local legend who was a Robin Hood-style rowdy (call 31 31 89 or fax 31 31 92 for exact dates and prices). The **post office,** 18528 Bergen, is at Markt 25 (open Mon.-Fri. 9am-6pm, Sat. 9-noon). The **telephone code** is 03838.

PUTBUS AND LAUTERBACH

Colloquially known as *"Weiße Stadt"* (White Town), **Putbus** was founded by Prince Walter von Putbus as a private residence and resort in 1810. Its most striking architectural landmark is the **Circus,** a now-empty plaza encircled by crumbling Neoclassical villas. Between the circus and the shabby *Marktplatz* lies Rügen's only **theater,** a large white building tastelessly adorned with paintings of Greek gods and goddesses. Alleestr. leads past the *Marktplatz* to the English-style **Schloßpark** (Palace Park), a more pastoral manifestation of the Prince's personal aesthetic. The statue of the prince still stands, though the palace, condemned as "decadent" by the Communists, was torn down in 1962. Walking south through the park, the glass-cupolaed **Affenhaus,** on Kastanienallee, served as a huge monkey cage for the amusement of the primates outside until the turn of the century. The **Rügener Puppen-und-Spielzeugmuseum,** on Kastanienallee (tel. 609 59), lives there today with a kitschy collection of more than 300 antique bisque dolls, 30 doll houses, and 50 teddy bears (open daily 10am-8pm, Oct.-March noon-5pm; admission DM5, students DM3). But the area's best attraction may just be Kastanienallee itself, which branches off into dozens of hiking trails that lead to fields, ponds, and wildflowers.

The very friendly **tourist office,** August-Bebel-Str.1 (tel. 431), off the *Marktplatz,* gives out free maps and has a bulletin board where people post room listings. **Room booking** is monopolized by **Rolf Kempe,** Bahnhofstr. 2 (tel. 605 13, fax 613 95), who charges a DM10 fee (rooms DM30-40) and has lots of info on recreation activities in the area (open Mon.-Fri. 9am-6pm, Sat. and Sun. 10am-4pm). **Rent bikes** for from **Albert's Fahrrad-Service,** Bahnhofstr. 5 (tel. 429), for DM8-10 per day (open 9-11am and 5:30-6pm). Putbus is also the start of the line for the **Rasender Rolad,** the narrow-gauge steam train that wheezes and lurches its way through south Rügen at the whirlwind speed of 30kph (single fare DM3-12, depending on distance, children 50% off; railpasses valid). The **post office,** on Marienstr., 18581 Putbus, is right off the Circus (open Mon.-Fri. 9am-noon and 1-5pm, Sat. 9-11am).

Three kilometers east of Putbus lies the sleepy little spa town of **Lauterbach.** The town is accessible by train, bike, or foot and offers a quiet beach, a beautiful Neoclassical spa house built by the Prince of Lauterbach, and a cute harbor. Lauterbach is the departure point for ferries to **Vilm,** a tiny island once owned by Prince Putbus which now houses a nature reserve. Cruises go around the island but aren't allowed to actually stop on it (several per day; 2 hr.; adults DM25, children DM10).

BINZ AND PRORA

Binz is the biggest of Rügen's spas and a seaside town with a long, pristine beach. Once a fashionable and luxurious resort for both German and foreign aristocrats, the town has slipped over the years and today displays a faded glory. The promenade along the beach is lined with sadly dilapidated white wooden mansions, many of which are being spiffed up for their next incarnations as luxury hotels. The **Kurhaus,** once Binz's biggest hotel and social scene, is still the center of what action there is, although the entertainment is mostly aimed at families. Just like Vegas. The advantages of being in a major tourist magnet are largely culinary; you'll be bombarded with fine food, drinks, and ice cream. Try the **Strandcafé Binz/Pizzeria Ristorante da Barbara,** Strandpromenade 29, for pasta and herring specialities (DM8-15; open daily 11am-midnight). A popular hang-out farther north along the Strandpromenade is the glassy **Vitarium,** home to several restaurants and free bathrooms.

The downside of Binz's popularity is that finding a room can be hellish; hotels are completely booked in the summer months. Try the **room-finding service,** Schillerstr. 15, 18609 Binz (tel./fax 27 82), which charges no fee and has rooms starting at DM25 (open Mon.-Fri. 9am-6pm, Sat.-Sun.9:30am-3pm). The separate **tourist office,** Heinrich-Heire-Str. 7 (tel. 20 84; fax 20 83), hands out the usual free maps and brochures. The **Rasender Roland** stops in Binz, but not at the *Hauptbahnhof* (where the trains from Bergen and Stralsund stop); there's a separate train station, **Binz-Ost,** responsible for the *Roland.* From the main station, head east on Dollahner Str., continue on Jasmunder Str., and then turn onto Bahnhofstr. (20min.). To ride along the dunes, stop at **Zweirad-Haus Deutschmann,** by the train station (tel. 324 20), where you can rent a bike (DM10-12 per day) and buy a map to get you started on your way (open daily 8am-4pm). The **post office,** 18609 Binz, is at Zeppeliastr. 3 (open Mon.-Fri. 9-noon and 2-6pm, Sat. 9am-noon). The **telephone code** is 038393.

The scarcity of rooms swells at the better-located of Rügen's two youth hostels, the **Jugendherberge Binz (HI),** Strandpromenade 35, 18609 Binz (tel. 325 97; fax 325 96), located directly on the beach. (Reception open 8am-noon and 7:45-9:30pm. Curfew 10pm. DM18, over 26 DM21.50. Resort tax. Breakfast included. Additional DM1 if you stay more than 1 night. Sheets DM6.) The **Edeka supermarket,** down the street from the post office, boasts amazingly long hours for a German supermarket (open Mon.-Fri. 8am-8pm, Sat. 8am-6pm, Sun. 3-6pm).

More dependable **accommodations** await in the **Jugendherberge Prora (HI)** (tel. 328 44), a hostel almost as huge (400 beds) as the Nazi-designed *KdF* building complex it belongs to (see p. 538). Located 5km north along the beach in **Prora,** the hostel is near the "Prora-Ost" train station; the Bergen-Binz trains stop here, as does the Binz-Saßnitz bus (but *not* the Binz-Göhren bus). From the bus/train stop, follow the signs to the hostel (5min.). The gray Orwellian exterior and endless corridors may not be the very inviting, but the hotel-like quads are comfortable. The beach is very close, but you may want to leave a trail to find your way back; all of the buildings are identical. (Reception open 7am-9am and 4-10pm. Curfew 11pm. DM18.50, over 26 DM23.50. Resort tax DM1 per day if you stay more than 1 night. Call in advance or show up by 4pm.) This hostel has an even stranger definition of the word "full" than most German hostels; even if they swear they are, keep begging. They hold mail for guests and **rent bikes** for DM8 per day—a *very good idea* if you don't want to trek the 5km to Binz every time you're hungry. The **Hotel Internat,** a few buildings down from the hostel in the same horrendous complex (tel. 343), is an old Communist-style dinosaur, but it's cheap (for Rügen) and usually has space. (Singles DM60. Doubles without shower DM40 per person. Breakfast included.)

SAßNITZ

Saßnitz was a 19th-century seaside resort on northern Rügen so popular it prompted Theodor Fontane to pen in *Effi Briest:* "To travel to Rügen means to travel to Saßnitz." In the socialist era, Saßnitz had a highly subsidized fishing industry, which is floundering (sorry!) today. Saßnitz is still a great place to go to the beach, but its real distinction is that it's an excellent base for exploration of the **Jasmund National Park,** the nature reserve which contains the *Große Stubbenkammer* (see below), as well as other gorgeous chalk cliffs. The Jasmund peninsula, which sits to the northeast of the main port of Rügen, is surrounded by the *Große und Kleine Jasmunder Bodden* and the Baltic Sea; *Bodden* are shallow salt-water lakes that are scattered over Rügen and divide it into several peninsulas. The National Park covers one-third of Jasmund peninsula and incorporates two *Bodden* and the accompanying wildlife. Several marked hiking trails run through the **Stubnitz beech forest,** also part of the park.

Saßnitz's **tourist office,** Seestr. 1, 18546 Saßnitz (tel. 320 37, fax 360 80), is in the Rügen Hotel. From the train station, head straight down to Seestr. The staff books rooms (DM30-40) for free (open Mon.-Fri. 8am-7pm; Apr.-Oct. also Sat. and Sun. 3-7pm). **Ferries** leave Saßnitz for Trelleborg, Sweden, the Danish island of **Bornholm,** and Poland. The **Arkona-Reederei,** Am Hafen (tel. 578 50; fax 578 52), has ships that leave Saßnitz at 9am, reach Bornholm 3½ hours later, and leave Bornholm at 4:30pm (May-Sept. round-trip DM30, children DM20). **DFO-Linie,** Trelleborger-Str. (tel. 641 80; fax 642 00), offers trips to Trelleborg (5 per day; 4hr.; DM30, children under 11 DM20). Other companies send boats out for **water tours** around the *Stubbenkammer* and to Kap Arkona (daily 9am-5pm; DM10-15). The station **rents bikes** for DM10-12 per day (open daily 7:30am-4pm). The **post office,** 18546 Saßnitz, is at Hauptstr. 34 (open Mon.-Fri. 8am-5pm, Sat. 9am-noon). The **telephone code** is 038392.

The closest campground is **Campground Nipmerow,** under ancient beech trees next to the National Park (tel. (038302) 92 44), near the *Königstahl.* Catch the bus to the *Stubbenkanner* from Saßnitz and ask the driver to let you out at the campground. (Reception open daily 6am-10pm. DM5 per person. DM5 per tent. Washing machines DM5, but no dryers. Open mid-April-Oct.) **Am Kai** fries fish (DM8-12) directly on the harbor (open daily 10am-midnight).

GROßE STUBBENKAMMER

The spectacular chalk cliffs rising up just north of Saßnitz and culminating in the famous **Große Stubbenkammer** (Great Chests of Drawers) were built up by massive glaciers 12,000 years ago; despite some erosion over the years, they'll still give you the chills. There are a couple of options for approaching the cliffs. The most direct (but also the least fun) way is to take the **bus** from the stop outside the Saßnitz train station (DM2.20); it runs hourly during the summer and lets you off about 500m away from the **Königstuhl** (king's chair), the most famous of the cliffs. You can also follow one of the bike trails through the forest from Saßnitz to the Königstuhl (8km), but these bypass the most dramatic scenery. For the best views, take the **Hochuferweg** (high coastal trail) all the way from Saßnitz to the *Stubbenkammer.* Despite the intimidating name, the 8.5-km trail (about a 2½-hr. hike) is fairly easy (honest) and runs from one incredible scenic lookout to the next. To pick up the trail, follow the "Stubbenkammer" signs through Saßnitz up the hill until you reach the parking lot. Here there's a detailed map of the park showing all of the trails and their corresponding blazes—follow the ones for *"Hochuferweg."*

The trail takes you first to the **Wissower Klinken** (3km away), which you might recognize from Caspar David Friedrich's paintings—these were his favorite chalk cliffs. Even though they've lost about 3m to erosion since he painted them, their beauty still seems almost supernatural. Continuing for another 5km, you'll reach the **Victoriasicht** lookout, named after a German empress, and then the famous *Königstahl*, which is an anti-climax after all of the beautiful views. Follow the mob to the lookout area—believe it or not, you have to pay for the view, which actually isn't much better than what you've already seen for free (DM2, students DM0.50).

Legend has it that the kings of Röf had to climb up to the top of the 110m *Königstuhl* to be crowned upon the stone chair. If you look up to the left, you'll notice a the small guard post once used by GDR authorities to make sure no one escaped by boat to Sweden. For a bit of solitude, walk down the steep and windy paths to the flint-covered beach; the last part of the path is a necklace of ladders set into the stone. If you're not tired yet, another trail leads from the *Königstahl* to the lovely **Herthasee**, a lake named after the German harvest goddess Hertha. According to the myth, Hertha drowned her mortal servants in this lake, and their spirits supposedly still gather on the banks each night, although we didn't stick around to find out. Nearby, the **Herthaburg,** a U-shaped earth wall built by the Slavs in the 7th century, recalls the less peaceful periods of this violently beautiful landscape.

GRANITZ, SELLIN, AND GÖHREN

The **Jagdschloß Granitz** is a sort of cheesy castle-like hunting lodge built in 1836 and designed by the Prussian architect Schinkel, whose unmistakable creations can be picked out from miles away all over the island. Built atop the *Tempelberg* hill, its 38m tower offers a breath-taking panorama of the island. Inside the "castle," the **Jagdmuseum** (hunting museum) will tell you everything you've always wanted to know about killing little deer but were afraid to ask. (Tower and museum open May-Sept. Tues.-Sun. 9am-5:30pm. Admission DM4.50, students DM3.50.) The *Roland* stops at the *Jagdschloß,* as does the (little) **Jagdschloßexpress** (that could), which makes round-trips from the *Kurhaus* in Binz (DM10, children DM6). To walk or bike the 5km from Binz, pick up the trail near the Binz *Roland* station. If you head south from the *Roland* "Jagdschloß" stop to the village of Lancken-Granitz, you'll pass by a bunch of huge prehistoric graves; one dates back to 2300BC. A few km south of Granitz, the *Roland's* next stop is **Sellin,** another small spa town that's somewhat less bombarded with tourists than Binz—you probably don't want to stay here unless you have a car, though. Sellin's claim to fame is its **tourist office for the whole island of Rügen,** August-Bebel-Str. 12, 18586 Sellin (tel. 334, fax 14 70).

The *Roland's* final stop is **Göhren,** on the easternmost tip of the forested **Münchgat peninsula,** which looks like a glove with only four fingers. The peninsula was settled in the 13th century by monks (hence the name), who believed in total self-sufficiency; the area thus developed unique customs and costumes. Things move at a noticeably slower pace than the rest of Rügen. Göhren, like every other town worth its salt on Rügen, has a nice beach; it's also the base of numerous **hiking and biking trails** leading through beautifully empty beaches, forests, and the rolling hills of the **Zickersche Alpen.** If you fall in love with the region and decide to sleep with it, one-night stands can be arranged with **Kurverwaltung Thiessow,** Hauptstr. 36 (tel. 82 80), or with **Camping Oase Thiessow,** Hauptstr. 4 (tel. 82 26; fax 82 97).

If it's raining or you're particularly interested in monk-culture, the **Münchguter Museum** (tel. 21 75), with four separate outposts in Göhren, is worth checking out. The **Heimatsmuseum,** on Theissowerstr., muses over local customs with exhibits of clothing, artifacts, and furniture (don't miss the antique loom). A few blocks down, the **Museumshof** is an old thatched-roof barn filled with strange old farming implements. The **Rookhus** is a 17th-century thatched-roof fishing cottage. The **Museumsschiff** (museum ship), a testament to traditional freight shipping, is a 1906 Dutch ship stashed behind the dunes on the southern shore outside of town. The **Schulmuseum,** in a one-room schoolhouse, recalls the days of simple education. (Each museum admission DM3, students DM2. A day card for the 4 museums, including the schoolhouse DM12, students DM8. All museums open July-Aug. daily 10am-6pm; June-Sept. Tues.-Sun. 10am-5pm; May-Oct. Tues.-Sun. 10am-4pm.)

MECK.—VORPOMMERN

Buses connect Göhren to Binz and Bergen, and to Saßnitz and Klein Zicker in the south. The **tourist office** *(Kurverwaltung)*, Schulstr. 8, 18586 Göhren (tel./fax 21 50), provides information and helps find rooms. From the train station, follow Strand-str. up and to the left, then go right on Waldstr., and right again onto Schulstr. (open Mon.-Thurs. 8am-6pm, Fri. 8am-12:30pm and 4-6pm, Sat.-Sun. 4-6pm). **Sparkasse Rügen,** on Strandstr., cashes traveler's checks for free and has an ATM (open Mon.-Tues. and Fri. 8:30am-12:30pm and 2-4pm, Wed. 8:30am-12:30pm, Thurs. 8:30am-12:30pm and 2-6pm). **Tilly Fahrräder,** Poststr. 2 (tel. 22 40), rents sturdy one-speeder bikes for DM7 and touring bikes for DM9 (open Mon.-Fri. 9am-6pm, Sat.-Sun. 9am-noon and 5-6pm). The **post office,** 18586 Göhren, is at Poststr. 9 (open Mon.-Fri. 11am-noon and 3-5pm, Sat. 11am-noon). The **telephone code** is 038308.

The **campground** (tel. 21 22) is close to the beach. From the train station, turn right, follow the signs. They have **bike rental,** a cinema, restaurants, and a **laundro-mat.** (Reception open 7am-10pm. DM6 per person. DM3.50-6 per tent.) **Haus Nor-strand,** Strandstr. 14, a big white restaurant with Christmas lights, serves hearty half-chickens for DM5 and other standard German fare (open daily 11:30am-7pm).

KAP ARKONA AND VITT

The northernmost attraction of Rügen is **Kap Arkona,** Germany's one and only cape, flanked on either side by the villages of **Putgarten** and **Vitt.** Buses run hourly (more or less) from Saßnitz to the nearby town of **Altenkirchen;** you can transfer here to the bus to Putgarten (10min.; DM2) or you can bypass Putgarten altogether and follow the bike/hiking trail from Altenkirchen directly to Vitt (6km). As you approach, only the white octagonal church will be visible, but trust us—there's a village here. A cache of thatched-roof **Häuschen** is nestled in the hill below. This tiny port was once one of the most important fishing posts on Rügen; beleaguered fishermen now prof-fer boat trips around Kap Arkona to supplement their income (departures daily 10am-6pm). Vitt is also the home to Rügen's most famous restaurant, **Zun Goldenen Anker**—if you haven't had enough of *Matjes mit Bratkartoffeln* yet, theirs is the best (meals DM10-15). From Vitt, walk along the cliffs 1km to Kap Arkona itself, and enjoy the windy view from the top across the Baltic Sea—it's only 77km to Sweden. If you walk along the beach under the cliff, you may find a piece of *Bernstein* (amber) washed up on shore.

Before reunification, the two **lighthouses** on Kap Arkona resided in a restricted area belonging to the GDR's National People's Army. The **Leuchtfener Arkona,** designed by Schinkel, has been open to the public since 1993. Built in 1826, it was used to guard the GDR's sea borders (1945-90). Nearby, the **Marinepeilturm** was built in 1927 and rigged up with a fancy electronic system that could eavesdrop on British radio communications. Now it houses archeological finds from the former **Tempelburg Arkana,** a Slavic fortification built in the 8th century and destroyed by the Danes in 1168. You can ascend in horse-drawn wagons that go from Putgarten to Kap Arkona and Vitt (DM10, children DM5) or the new *Arkona-Bahn,* another silly motorized train (DM7, children DM5). Back in the town of **Altenkirchen,** the **Dor-fkirche,** dating from 1200, is one of the oldest surviving witnesses to Rügen's Chris-tian evolution; a funeral stone displaying the image of Swantewit, the chief Slavic god, can be seen on the east wall of this beautiful red-brick church.

The new **tourist office,** in the parking lot by Kap Arkona (tel. 419; fax 419 17), about 300m down the road form the bus stop in Putgarten, finds rooms for a 10% fee (open Jan.-March daily 11am-5pm; March-May daily 10am-5pm; June-Oct. daily 10am-7pm). While there, pick up a free guide to Kap Arkona or rent a **bike** to wheel around on (DM2 per hour; DM8 per day; ID required). The **Drewoldke campground** (tel. 124 84) is just east of Altenkirchen. (Reception open 8am-9pm. DM6 per person, DM4-6 per tent. Open April-Oct.) The **telephone code** is 038391.

■ Near Rügen: Hiddensee

West of Rügen lies the slender island of Hiddensee, known in the *Plattdeutsch* dialect as *dat söte Länneken* (the sweet island). Its beauty and natural seclusion have always attracted artists and scientists—Sigmund Freud, Albert Einstein, Thomas Mann, Käthe Kollwitz, and Richard Korb all spent their vacations here. The great naturalist author and social dramatist Gerhardt Hauptmann summered on Hiddensee from 1930 to 1943 and is buried in the village of **Kloster,** where there is a memorial to him and his work (open daily 10am-5pm; admission DM3, students DM1.50). The huge wine cellar reveals that Hauptman loved alcohol nearly as much as letters. The tiny **Heimatmuseum,** also in Kloster, has some art by local painters and an exhibit of stuffed birds (open daily 10am-4pm, admission DM4, students DM1.50). From the northern tip at Hiddensee called the **Dornbusch** (thorn-bush), hike up to the **Leuchturm** (light house) and enjoy a view across the whole island to Rügen. Slightly south of Kloster, the Hiddensee flatlands, covered partly by heath, include the villages **Vitte** and **Neuendorf.** The south consists solely of sand dunes with hiking trails and sandy beaches. The greatest attraction is the natural beauty of the narrow 16km-long island itself: grassy paths bordered by wildflowers are well-marked and can take you from one end of Hiddensee to the other. What makes the island so unique, however, is the **prohibition of motor vehicles**. So wrangle two wheels, or just stroll around to connect with nature in one of the last pristine spots in the "civilized world."

The **tourist office,** Norderende 162, 18565 Vitt (tel. 642 26; fax 642 25), operates a room-finding service (rooms DM30) for which it charges a 10% fee (open Mon.-Fri. 8am-noon and 12:30-5pm). **Ferry** connections are available to Hiddensee from Stralsund on the mainland (see Stralsund, p. 535) and Schaprode on Rügen's west coast. Ferries leave Schaprode approximately four times per day (45min.; DM8, children DM6; round-trip DM12, children DM8; bikes DM10). You can **rent bikes** in the harbors at Neuendorf (tel. 406), Vitte (tel. 386), and Kloster (tel. 404) for approximately DM10 per day. The **telephone code** is 038300.

Appendices

▥ Telephone

COUNTRY CODES

U.K. (including Northern Ireland):	44	Netherlands:	31
Republic of Ireland:	353	Belgium:	32
USA:	1	Luxemburg:	352
Canada:	1	France:	33
Australia:	61	Switzerland:	41
New Zealand:	64	Austria:	43
South Africa:	27	Czech Republic:	42

▥ Area Codes

Berlin	30	**Göttingen**	551	**München**	89
Bremen	421	**Hamburg**	40	**Nürnberg**	911
Bonn	228	**Hannover**	511	**Regensburg**	941
Dresden	351	**Heidelberg**	6221	**Rostock**	381
Düsseldorf	211	**Kiel**	431	**Saarbrücken**	681
Erfurt	361	**Koblenz**	261	**Schwerin**	385
Essen	201	**Köln**	221	**Stuttgart**	711
Frankfurt	69	**Leipzig**	341	**Weimar**	3643
Freiburg	761	**Lübeck**	451	**Würzburg**	931

▥ Mileage (km)

	Berlin	Bremen	Dresden	Düsseldorf	Frankfurt	Hamburg	Hannover	München	Rostock	Stuttgart
Berlin		390	214	565	564	285	285	587	219	652
Bremen	390		488	298	467	119	133	745	297	657
Dresden	214	488		568	471	485	371	494	474	572
Düsseldorf	565	298	568		231	423	272	618	577	414
Frankfurt	564	467	471	231		497	362	399	651	216
Hamburg	285	119	485	423	497		163	775	184	679
Hannover	285	133	371	272	362	163		640	338	565
München	587	745	494	618	399	775	640		761	221
Rostock	219	297	474	577	651	184	338	761		833
Stuttgart	652	657	572	414	216	679	565	221	833	

APPENDIX

■ Business Hours

Store hours in Germany have traditionally been maddeningly brief, thanks to the *Ladenschlußgesetz* (store-closing law), which applied to most businesses. However, in June 1996, the Bundestag passed a bill allowing shops to expand their hours to 8pm on weekdays and 4pm on Saturdays. This decision has already caused a labor strike in Berlin and may not have immediate impact in the retail sphere. **Store hours** before the new allowance were typically Monday-Friday 9am-6pm, Saturday 9am-1pm. Some stores may already have expanded their hours, but don't count on it. Thankfully, bakeries are now allowed to open for three hours on Sunday. Avoid trying to buy anything from 5-6:30pm, when working wives try to cram all of their shopping in. To avoid starvation after hours and on Sunday, try shops inside train stations in larger cities, which are allowed to remain open longer. Many smaller shops take a mid-day break *(Mittagspause)*, usually noon-2pm. **Bank hours** are often extremely bizarre. In all but the biggest cities, it is unwise to put off financial chores until the weekend; many towns have no banks open between Saturday morning and Monday.

■ Climate

Climate varies across Germany, but is usually cloudy and temperate, comparable to New England in the U.S. Summers are rarely unbearably hot—32°C (90°F) is about tops, 21°C (70°F) average. Spring and fall temperatures mostly range 4-18°C (40-65°F); winter averages -10°C (14°F). The Alps are perpetually cool, and everything north of Hamburg is rainy.

■ Holidays and Festivals

Consult the German National Tourist Offices's publication *Forthcoming Events: 1997* for the dates of major trade fairs, art exhibitions, theater and music festivals, folk fairs, and sporting events. Each town's tourist office can provide specific information. Where possible, *Let's Go* lists specific 1997 dates in individual cities. Holidays in European countries are listed daily in the International Herald Tribune. Be aware of them, as banks, restaurants, stores, and museums may all close, potentially leaving you broke and hungry. These are Germany's national holidays in1997:

January 1:	*Neujahrstag*	New Year's Day
January 6:	*Heilige Drei Könige*	Epiphany
February 26:	*Aschermittwoch*	Ash Wednesday
March 28:	*Karfreitag*	Good Friday
March 30:	*Ostersonntag*	Easter Sunday
March 31:	*Ostermontag*	Easter Monday
May 1:	*Tag der Arbeit*	Labor Day
May 18:	*Pfingstsonntag*	Whit Sunday (Pentecost)
May 19:	*Pfingstmontag*	Whit Monday
May 29:	*Fronleichnam*	Corpus Christi
May 8:	*Christ Himmelfahrt*	Ascension Day
Aug 15:	*Maria Himmelfahrt*	Assumption Day
October 3:	*Tag der deutschen Einheit*	Day of German Unity
October 31:	*Reformationtag*	Reformation Day
November 1:	*Allerheiligen*	All Saint's Day
December 25-26:	*Weihnachtstag*	Christmas

■ Language

"Life," wrote Thomas Love Peacock, "is too short to learn German." But as Germany extends its commercial tentacles, German stakes a firmer claim to the status of an international language. It is most definitely the language of tourism in Central Europe. That does not change the fact that it is a difficult tongue to learn, with three genders, four cases, and five ways of saying the word "the." Fortunately, most Western Germans involved in the tourist industry speak at least a smattering of English (the situation can be considerably different in the former GDR). All schoolchildren now must take English, and most are quite anxious to practice. Don't, however, assume that all Germans speak English, especially outside the major cities; always preface your questions with a polite *"Sprechen Sie Englisch?"*

PRONUNCIATION

Although you cannot hope to speak correct German without studying it, you can make yourself understood by learning only a little German. The first step is to master the pronunciation system. Unlike English, German pronunciation is consistent with spelling; once you learn the rules, everything is easy. There are no silent letters.

Consonants are pronounced as in English with the following exceptions: **C:** exists in German only in borrowed foreign words, and is pronounced like a K. **J:** always pronounced as a Y. **K:** always pronounced, even before an N. **P:** always pronounced, even before an F. **QU:** pronounced KV. **S:** pronounced as Z at the beginning of a word. **V:** pronounced as F. **W:** pronounced as V. **Z:** pronounced as TS.

The hissing, aspirant German CH sound, appearing in such basic words as "Ich" (I), "nicht" (not), and "sprechen" (to speak), is quite tricky for untrained English-speaking vocal cords. After A, O, U, or AU, it is pronounced as in the Scottish "loch." After other vowels, CH sounds like the English H in "huge" or "hubris" if you draw out this sound before saying the U. If you can't hack it, use an SH sound in the south and a KH sound in the north.

German has one consonant which does not exist in English, **the "ß";** which is alternately referred to as the *"scharfes S"* (sharp S) or the *"Ess-tsett."* It is simply a shorthand symbol for a **double-S,** and is pronounced just like an English "ss." It appears in two of the most important German words for travelers: *die Straße,* "the street," which is pronounced "SHTRAH-ssuh" and abbreviated "Str."; and *das Schloß,* "the castle," simply pronounced "SCHLOSS." Note that the use of the "ß" is slowly being elimated from modern German in an effort to standardize spelling and create less confusion for German schoolchildren learning the language.

German vowel and dipthong sounds are also pronounced differently: **A:** as in "father." **E:** like the A in "hay." **I:** like the EE in "creep." **O:** as in "oh." **U:** as in "fondue." **Y:** like the OO in "boot." **AU:** as in "sauerkraut." **IE:** as in "thief." **EI:** like the I in "wine." **EU:** like the OI in "boil."

An **umlaut** over a letter (e.g. Ü) changes the pronunciation. An umlaut is often replaced by an E following the vowel, e.g. "schön" becomes "schoen." In the speech of most Germans, Ä is the equivalent of an American long A (as in "hay"). To make the Ö sound, round your lips to say "oh," freeze them in that position, and try to say "a" as in "hay." To make the Ü sound, round your lips to say "ooh," freeze them in that position, and try to say "ee" instead. Germans are very forgiving towards foreigners who butcher their mother tongue. There is, however, one important exception—place names. If you learn nothing else in German, learn to pronounce the names of cities properly. Berlin is "bare-LEEN," Cologne (Köln) is "KURLN," Hamburg is "HAHM-boorg," Munich (München) is "MEUWN-khen."

Once you've learned a bit of German, you can appreciate the startling differences among dialects. When both speak in the vernacular, a *Kölner* and a *Münchener* cannot understand each another. The Austrian and Swiss German dialects diverge even more strongly from the *Hochdeutsch* (High German) of the north. In general, linguistic distinctions in Germany follow the same pattern as in the U.S.; southerners speak in a more relaxed fashion, while the northern style is harsh and refined, with fully enunciated consonant sounds. For the purposes of the traveler, the crucial distinction is that southerners say *"zwo"* (TSVO) instead of *"zwei"* for the number two.

■ Glossary

BASIC EXPRESSIONS

Good morning/day/evening	Guten Morgen/Tag/Abend	(GOO-ten MOHR-gen/ tahg/AH-bend)
Good day (in Bavaria)	Grüss Gott	(grews goht)
Goodbye	Auf Wiedersehen/ Auf Wiederschauen	(Auf Veedersayen/ Auf Veedershawen)
Hello	Hallo	(hah-loh)
Please	Bitte	(BIT-tuh)
Thank you	Danke	(DAHN-kuh)
You're welcome.	Bitte	(BIT-tuh)
Excuse me.	Entschuldigung	(Ent-SHOOL-dee-gung)
Yes/No	Ja/Nein	(ya/nine)
I'm sorry.	Es tut mir leid.	(es toot meer leid)
I don't speak German.	Ich spreche kein deutsch.	(Ikh SPRAY-shuh kine doytch)
Does anyone here speak English?	Spricht jemand hier englisch?	(sprikht YAY-mant heer AYN- glish?)
Can you help me?	Können Sie mir helfen?	(KUR-nen zee meer HEL-fen?)
I don't understand.	Ich verstehe nicht.	(ikh fair-SHTAY-uh nikht)
Do you understand?	Verstehen Sie?	(fair-SHTAY-en zee?)
How do you say ... in German?	Wie sagt man ... auf deutsch?	(vee zahgt mahn...auf doytch?)
I would like	Ich möchte	(ikh MURSH-tuh)
How much does ... cost?	Wieviel kostet?	(vee-feel KOHS-tet...?)
Where is ...?	Wo ist?	(Vo ist?)
When is ...?	Wann ist?	(Vann ist?)
more/less	mehr/weniger	(mayr/VAY-nih-ger)
open	geöffnet	(geh-UHRF-net)
closed	geschlossen/zu	(geh-SCHLOSS-sen / tsoo)
left	links	(links)
right	rechts	(rechts)
straight ahead	geradeaus	(geh-RAH-duh-auws)
coming to terms with the past	Vergangenheitsbewältigung	(Fair-GAHNG-en-hights-be- VAYL-tee-gung)

TRAVEL NECESSITIES

ticket (for travel)	die Fahrkarte	(die Fahrkarte)
ticket (theater, etc.)	die Karte	(die Karte)
reservation	die Reservierung/ Vorbestellung	(Reh-zehr-FEER-oong/ FOAR-beh-SHTEL-oong)
one-way	Hinfahrt	(Hinfahrt)
round-trip	Hin- und Rückfahrt	Hin- und Rückfahrt
arrival/departure	Ankunft /Abfahrt	(AHN-kunft/AHB-fahrt)
train	der Zug	(tsoog)
train station	der Bahnhof	(BAHN-hohf)
main train station	der Hauptbahnhof	(HOWPT-bahn-hohf)
bus station	der Busbahnhof	(der Busbahnhof)
airplane	das Flugzeug	(FLOOK-tsoyg)
airport	der Flughafen	(FLOOK-half-en)
(train) track	das Gleis	(das Gleis)
train platform	der Bahnsteig	(BAHN-shteig)
airport gate	der Flugsteig	(FLOOK-shteig)
bus	der Bus	(der Bus)
(bus, subway) stop	die Haltestelle	(HAHL-tuh-shtel-luh)
entrance/exit	der Eingang /Ausgang	(der Eingang /Ausgang)
hospital	das Krankenhaus	(das Krankenhaus)

police	die Polizei	(poh-lee-TSEI)
Help!	Hilfe!	(HIHL-fuh!)
I am tipsy.	Ich bin beschwippst.	(ikh bin beh-SHVIPST)
I am drunk.	Ich bin betrunken.	(ikh bin BETROONKEN)
I am sick.	Ich bin krank.	(Ich bin krank.)
toilet	die Toilette/W.C.	(vay SAY)
shower	die Dusche	(DOO-shuh)
youth hostel	die Jugendherberge	(YOO-gend-hair-BAIR-guh)
campground	der Campingplatz	(der Campingplatz)
post office	die Post	(die Post)
tourist office	der Verkehrsamt/	(Fair-KAYR-zahmt/
	Verkehrsverein	Fair-KAYRZ-fair-ein)
cathedral	der Dom	(dohm)
palace	das Schloß	(shloss)
church	die Kirche	(KEER-shuh)
old city	die Altstadt	(AHLT-shtahtt)
museum	das Museum	(moo-ZAY-uhm)
bridge	die Brücke	(BREW-kuh)
theater	das Theater	(tay-AH-ter)
waiter/waitress	der Kellner/die Kellnerin	(der Kellner/die Kellnerin)
beer	das Bier	(das Bier)
sausage	die Wurst	(voorst)
bread	das Brot	(broht)
water/ tap water	das Wasser/Leitungswasser	(VAS-ser / LEI-toongz-vas-ser)
cheese	der Käse	(KAY-zuh)
breakfast	das Frühstück	(FREW-stewk)
lunch	das Mittagsessen	(MIT-tahg-ess-sen)
supper	das Abendessen	(AH-bend-ess-sen)

RESERVATIONS BY PHONE

Mastery of the following phrases should help you get through the process of reserving a room by telephone. Remember that many proprietors, particularly in larger cities, are used to dealing with the minimal German of callers; with a little patience and politesse you should be able to make yourself understood.

Phone greeting	Guten Tag!
Do you speak English?	Sprechen Sie Englisch?
	(SPRAY-khen zee AYN-glish?)
Do you have a room	Haben Sie ein Zimmer (Einzelzimmer, Dop-
(single room, double room) free...	pelzimmer) frei...
	(HAH-ben zee ein TSIM-mer (EIN-tsel-tsim-
	mer, DOHP-pehl-tsim-mer) frei?)
for tonight?	für heute abend?
	(fewr HOY-tuh AH-bend?)
for tomorrow?	für morgen?
For a day / for two days?	für einen Tag / zwei Tage?
	(fewr EIN-nen tahg / TSVEI tah-guh?)
from the fourth of July...	vom vierten Juli...
until the sixth of July?	bis zum sechsten Juli?
with bathroom/ shower?	mit W.C./ Dusche?
My name is...	Ich heiße... (ikh HIGH-sse)
I'm coming immediately/ at eight	Ich komme gleich/ um acht Uhr am Morgen/
o'clock in the morning/evening.	Abend.

Return phrases to watch out for:

No, we're booked/full.	Nein, es ist alles besetzt/voll/komplett.
Sorry.	Es tut mir leid.
We don't make reservations by phone.	Wir machen keine Vorbestellungen/
	Reservierungen am Telephon.
You have to arrive before two o'clock.	Sie müssen vor zwei Uhr ankommen.

■ Numbers, Dates, and Time

A space or period rather than a comma is used to indicate thousands, e.g. 10,000 is written 10 000. Instead of a decimal point, Germans use a comma, e.g. 3.1415 is written 3,1415. Months and days are written in the reverse of the American manner, e.g. 10.11.92 is November 10, not October 11. The numeral 7 is written with a slash through the vertical line, and the numeral 1 is written with an upswing, resembling an inverted "V." Note that the number in the ones place is pronounced before the number in the tens place; thus "zweihundertfünfundsiebzig" (TSVEI-hun-duhrt-fuhnf-oont-ZEEB-tsikh) is 275, *NOT* 257. This can be very hard to keep in mind.

0	null	10	zehn	20	zwanzig
1	eins	11	elf	30	dreißig
2	zwei	12	zwölf	40	vierzig
3	drei	13	dreizehn	50	fünfzig
4	vier	14	vierzehn	60	sechzig
5	fünf	15	fünfzehn	70	siebzig
6	sechs	16	sechszehn	80	achtzig
7	sieben	17	siebzehn	90	neunzig
8	acht	18	achtzehn	100	ein hundert
9	neun	19	neunzehn	1000	tausend

TELLING TIME

Germany uses West European time (abbreviated MEZ in German). Add six hours to Eastern Standard Time and one hour to Greenwich Mean Time. Subtract nine hours from Eastern Australia Time and 11 hours from New Zealand Time. Germany uses the 24-hr. clock for all official purposes: 8pm equals 20.00. Thus, *vierzehn Uhr* is 2pm, *fünfzehn Uhr* is 3pm, etc. When Germans say "half eight" (halb acht), they mean 7:30; "three quarters eight" (dreiviertel acht) means 7:45 and "quarter eight" (viertel acht) means 7:15.

At what time...?	Um wieviel Uhr...?
What time is it, please?	Wie spät (VEE SHPAYT) ist es, bitte?
yesterday	gestern
today	heute
tomorrow	morgen

THE CALENDAR

Months: *Januar, Februar, März, April, Mai, Juni, Juli, August, September, Oktober, November, Dezember.* **Days of the week:** *Montag, Dienstag, Mittwoch, Donnerstag, Freitag, Samstag/Sonnabend, Sonntag.*

WEIGHTS AND MEASURES

Germany uses the metric system. Germans also commonly use some traditional measurements, but they have been modified to match the metric system more closely. Thus, a *Pfund* is half a kilogram and a *Meil* is two kilometers. All you really need to know to get around is that a meter is a little more than a yard, a kilometer is three-fifths of a mile, a liter is a little more than a quart, a kilogram is a little more than two pounds, and 100 grams of cheese or sausage is plenty for lunch. To convert from °C to °F, multiply by 1.8 and add 32. To convert from °F to °C, subtract 32 and multiply by 5/9, or refer to this handy chart.

°C	35	30	25	20	15	10	5	0	-5	-10
°F	95	86	75	68	59	50	41	32	23	14

Index

Berlin Transit

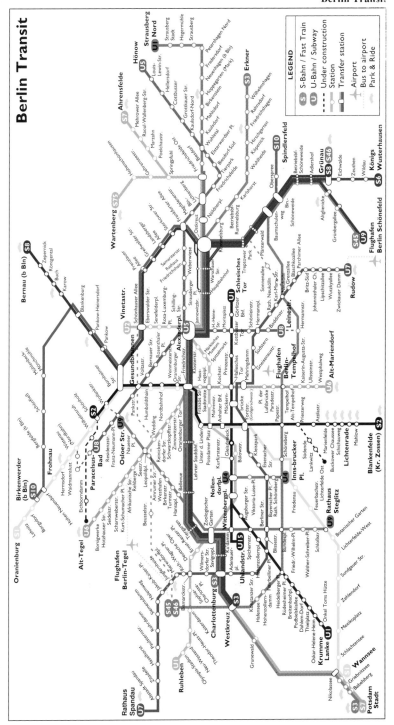

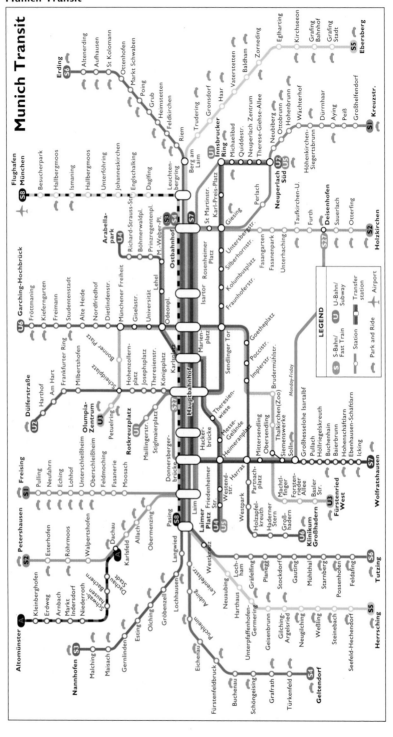

Munich Transit

Hamburg Transit

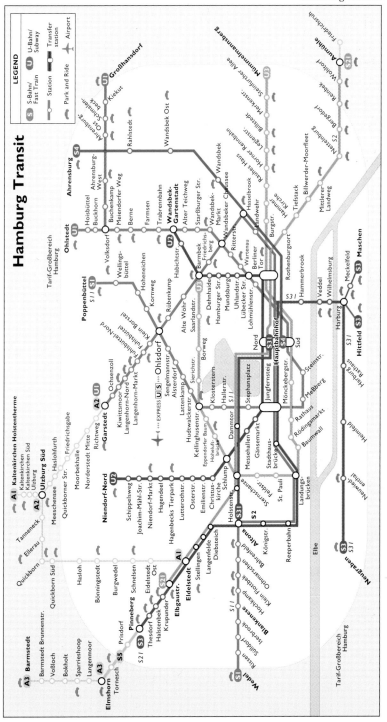

Frankfurt Transit

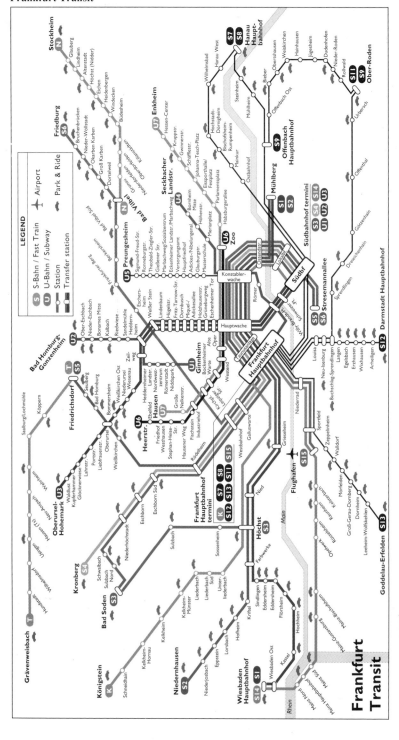

Frankfurt Transit